AN INTRODUCTION TO TAXATION

1981 EDITION

1981 EDITION

AN INTRODUCTION TO TAXATION

RAY M. SOMMERFELD
The University of Texas at Austin

HERSHEL M. ANDERSON
North Texas State University

HORACE R. BROCK
North Texas State University

HARCOURT BRACE JOVANOVICH, INC.
New York   San Diego   Chicago   San Francisco   Atlanta
London   Sydney   Toronto

Library of Congress Catalog Card Number: 76-20384

ISBN: 0-15-546313-6

preface

For the second time in our five annual editions, no major tax bill is under consideration by Congress as we go to press. Because the economic forecast is so cloudy, however, it is difficult to predict whether or not the *1981 Edition* will require a lengthy supplement before it is routinely replaced in another year. If a serious recession were to develop suddenly, some form of tax reduction would likely follow in short order. On the other hand, if rampant inflation continues, no immediate tax relief seems probable. If both occur, not an unlikely prospect, then—who knows?

The *1981 Edition* is generally similar to its immediate predecessor. We have, of course, updated the text for all changes required by the Revenue Act of 1978 and the Windfall Profits Tax Act of 1980. We have again separated those problems requiring work beyond the text from those that can be answered with no outside reference; the former are identified as "Supplemental Problems." Finally, we have added an entirely new Chapter 7 on tax rates and have divided the old Part Two into two parts. We believe that each of these changes is pedagogically sound. If you desire further modification in future editions, please write to one or all of us and offer your suggestions for continued improvement. Clearly, the best suggestions for improvements come from those instructors who have used the text.

This edition retains the conceptual approach of its predecessors. Nevertheless, we continue to include a few I.R.S. forms (fully realizing that all tax forms rapidly become obsolete) to allow instructors a convenient way to demonstrate how the very human process of taxation actually proceeds. Packets of current federal tax forms, for student use in answering return problems, are available to instructors for classroom distribution (see the Instructor's Manual for details). All discussions of reporting details have been placed at the end of the chapter so that instructors who prefer to ignore the mundane matters of reporting can readily do so.

We have also continued to put considerable emphasis on the source of most tax law—the 1954 Code—because we believe that students should get some of their knowledge (and some of their frustration) from reading the original text. This edition includes approximately one hundred partial or complete quotations of Code Sections (see the Index for specific page references to the quoted sections). At the same time, the *1981 Edition* continues our tradition of explaining the tax law in its political, social, and economic context to the maximum extent possible. As in previous editions, each chapter concludes with a number of short-answer questions that provide specific illustrations of how a general tax rule applies in the real world.

In our own classes, we cover the complete text in a one-semester course. We remind you, however, that several chapters can be covered lightly or even excluded entirely. For example, Part One (Chapters 1–4) can be reviewed quite swiftly or omitted without serious damage to the general flow of ideas. It is also possible to eliminate some or all of Chapters 11, 15, and 17.

Some instructors prefer a different sequence of chapters. A few begin with Part Eight (Chapter 27). The Instructor's Manual presents alternative course outlines for use with this text. We believe that you will find the *1981 Edition* to be an entirely self-contained unit with maximum flexibility.

This tax text, unlike many others, discusses in detail several controversial topics. We have tried, whenever possible, to state our own biases clearly. In a few instances, we do not even wholly agree with each other. Obviously, therefore, the opinions expressed here do not reflect any official position of our employers—past, present, or future!

In the very near future, a second-semester tax text will be available from Harcourt Brace Jovanovich. That text, *An Introduction to Taxation: Advanced Topics,* will provide tax instructors with maximum flexibility for a follow-up course. We hope that you will examine a review copy carefully. We believe that the new volume offers coverage not currently available in any other tax text and that these two volumes provide superior text material for undergraduate and graduate tax courses.

R.M.S.

H.M.A.

H.R.B.

contents

PART TWO
the income tax: fundamentals

taxpayers   Ease and consistency of administration   Social and economic objectives

TAX ACCOUNTING METHODS   5/9

The cash basis   The accrual basis   The "mixed" basis   Other bases and changing methods

INCOME: FINANCIAL ACCOUNTING AND TAX DIFFERENCES   5/11

Differences in timing   Permanent differences

CHAPTER **6**   deductions: general concepts   6/1

GENERAL REQUIREMENTS FOR A DEDUCTION   6/2

The basic authorization: the revenue code   The general provisions   The specific provisions

TAX ACCOUNTING METHODS—DEDUCTIONS   6/8
DEDUCTIONS: FINANCIAL ACCOUNTING AND TAX DIFFERENCES   6/9

Differences in timing   Permanent differences   Should tax rules conform to generally accepted accounting principles?

DEDUCTIONS: PERSONAL DEDUCTIONS FOR INDIVIDUALS   6/12

Large, unusual, involuntary expenses   Deductions that amount to subsidies   Taxes paid to local and state governments   Personal exemptions

ZERO BRACKET AMOUNT OF TAXABLE INCOME   6/14

CHAPTER **7**   tax rates: general concepts   7/1

FUNDAMENTAL CONCEPTS   7/1

Progressivity   Unitary system   Entity differences

MAJOR ABERRATIONS FROM FUNDAMENTAL CONCEPTS   7/4

Maximum tax   Capital gains   Income averaging   The add-on minimum tax   The alternative minimum tax   The taxation of nonresident aliens

ADMINISTRATIVE CONSIDERATIONS   7/11

Tax tables   The FICA tax

WHAT'S LEFT OF THE UNITARY SYSTEM?   7/11

PART THREE
taxable entities

PART FOUR
the general welfare

PART FIVE
full employment and national defense

PART SIX
capital gains and losses

PART SEVEN
the wherewithal-to-pay concept

CHAPTER   **26**   recognition postponed: corporate-shareholder transactions   **26**/1

PART EIGHT
taxation: a dynamic process

CHAPTER   **27**   the compliance process   **27**/1

CHAPTER   **28**   the reform process   **28**/1

AN INTRODUCTION TO TAXATION
1981 EDITION

Taxes are what we pay for civilized society. . . .

JUSTICE OLIVER WENDELL HOLMES, JR.,
Compania de Tabacos v. Collector (1927)

Has he not also another object, which is that they may be impoverished by payment of taxes, and thus compelled to devote themselves to their daily wants and therefore less likely to conspire against him?

PLATO,
Dialogues

PART

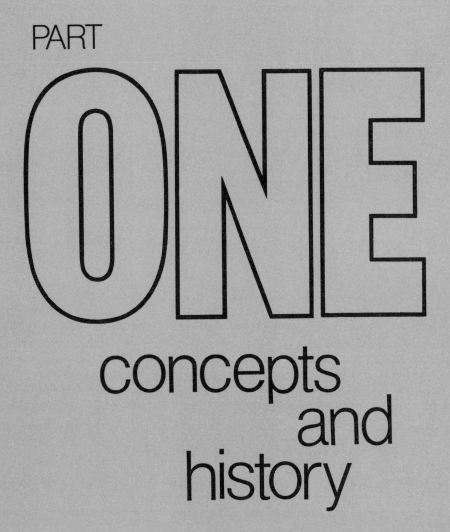

ONE

concepts
and
history

... if 200 years ago men revolted on the principle that 'Taxation without representation is tyranny,' then today men may rise in righteous wrath because taxation with representation but beyond human comprehension is even worse.

JUDGE WILKEY,
"American United" Inc. v. *Walters*, 477 F2d 1169 (CCA—D.C., 1973)

taxation defined

What is a tax? Why do governments collect taxes? If governments decide to impose taxes, what should they tax? How should they tax those things—proportionally, regressively, or progressively? Although a thorough understanding of possible answers to these questions is not mandatory to the determination of a particular tax liability, such an understanding often makes intelligible what otherwise appears to be a wholly arbitrary tax provision. Furthermore, such an understanding constitutes an important part of the hallmark of any educated person. Part One of this book is an attempt to provide tentative answers to these questions for business and accounting students. Hopefully, it also will encourage some students to enroll for further study of these important aspects of taxation.

Part One consists of four chapters. The first places taxes in perspective by comparing them to alternative means of accomplishing similar social and economic objectives. Because a government's tax policies are so closely related to its economic and social objectives, a few of the more significant of these objectives are also considered briefly. In Chapter 2 we shall discuss some of the more common tax bases. Once a government has decided to use taxation in lieu of some other method of accomplishing the same goal, it must decide what item or what events will be the tax base. Having determined the tax base, a government must settle upon an appropriate tax-rate structure. Thus, in Chapter 3, regressive, proportional, and progressive tax rates are discussed, with particular attention to the progressive rate structure that has generally been associated with income taxation in the United States. Chapter 4 completes this introduction with a brief overview of the United States income tax.

In the present chapter, the word "tax" is defined to help the student recognize both some alternatives to and some objectives of taxation. Any particular tax (or any tax provision) may be evaluated only in the light of these alternatives and objectives. The chapter is divided into three elements—namely, a discussion of our definition of the word "tax"; a brief examination of some major alternatives to taxation; and a review of some major objectives of taxation.

WHAT IS A TAX?

A tax can be defined meaningfully as *any nonpenal yet compulsory transfer of resources from the private to the public sector, levied on the basis of predetermined criteria and without receipt of a specific benefit of equal value, in order to accomplish some of a nation's economic and social objectives.* To understand this definition, we must consider several phrases in greater detail.

"Nonpenal"

A tax may be distinguished from a criminal or civil penalty (or fine) in a crude way. Nearly always, a penalty is devised solely to dissuade a person from engaging in some specific act deemed detrimental to society. For example, a government may decide to impose a fine of $10,000 on the willful failure to file a tax return, the mere possession of a specified drug, or the striking of a police officer. In these instances the government demands a relatively large exaction for a single act. Ultimately, of course, the government may have no real interest in prohibiting a specific act—for example, the act of possessing (as opposed to consuming) a drug is in and of itself of very little consequence—but it may consider the act detrimental to maintaining general order, to maintaining a stable government, or to some other broad objective deemed of primary importance.

Taxes, on the other hand, generally do not have such a specific objective, though they often are intended to influence more general behavior patterns. They typically provide for lesser exactions for more general behavior that ordinarily is not considered detrimental to society. Thus, for example, a relatively small exaction may be devised to discourage spending (or, more accurately, to decrease aggregate demand), even though spending per se certainly is not considered an undesirable activity. Alternatively, a relatively small exaction may be imposed to discourage, say, the consumption of alcohol or tobacco products. If the consumption of these items comes to be considered sufficiently dangerous, the tax may be increased to the point that it would be more accurate to label it a penalty.

In summary, the major differences between a tax and a penalty are (1) the relative size of exaction demanded and (2) the specific objective behind the exaction. The larger the exaction and the more restrictive the objective, the more likely that the exaction should be classified as a penalty rather than a tax.

But the line is not clear-cut. Certainly "penalty taxes" have been enacted and imposed in the United States. Two good examples are the tax on personal holding companies and the tax on the unreasonable accumulation of earnings in a corporation. These taxes are imposed to discourage individuals from significantly reducing their personal income-tax liabilities through the use of a corporate entity. The rates are set in such a way that the "undesirable" action becomes more expensive than the "desired" action. Penalty taxes have also been imposed in other countries. For example, the Canadian province of Ontario recently enacted tax laws intended to restrict sales of Canadian vacation land to foreigners. Ontario now imposes a 20 percent land-transfer tax on sales of vacation properties to aliens. In addition, Ontario imposes a 50 percent tax on any profit made on the sale of a vacation property to an alien. These two taxes reportedly have, for all practical purposes,

ended the rush of (especially) United States citizens' purchases of vacation homes in Ontario.

Historically the United States has preferred to influence behavior through the granting of tax privileges rather than the imposing of penalty taxes. A survey conducted by the Research Department of *Better Homes and Gardens* magazine reveals that a significant majority of 2,000 respondents preferred the penalty mechanism. For example, 38 percent of the respondents favored the granting of tax credits for companies that use air and water pollution control devices, whereas 73 percent favored the imposition of a penalty tax on companies that pollute the air or water.[1] If this attitude were adopted by our legislative bodies, the change in our tax structure could be significant.

"Yet compulsory . . . without receipt of a specific benefit of equal value"

The phrase "without receipt of a specific benefit of equal value" is typically the most difficult to understand phrase in our definition of the word "tax." By using these words we are trying merely to distinguish between (1) a *price* that must be paid before anyone may receive a private good and (2) the cost of producing a public good. Private goods and services are defined as those that can be rationed or allocated among all would-be benefactors solely by means of a price mechanism; that is, by operation of the laws of supply and demand. In a purely competitive economy, the decision on how to spend one's wealth is entirely up to the individual. If an individual elects to purchase product A and to forgo the purchase of product B, automatically he or she will receive the full benefit of product A but get no benefit whatsoever from product B. Only those who are willing and able to pay the market price can benefit from a private good or service. Public goods, on the other hand, are defined as those goods and services that *cannot* be allocated by means of a price mechanism. For example, it is impossible to allocate the benefits of a good police force or a legal system by means of a pricing mechanism. Everyone benefits from the mere existence of a public good, whether or not he or she has an immediate and direct need to consume that good or service. Stated another way, society generally considers it improper to spread the cost of, say, a good police force or a fair legal system over

---

[1] *Better Homes and Gardens Tax Questionnaire Report,* Meredith Corporation, 1971, pp. 39–40.

only those few who have direct need for that particular public service in a given year because everybody—user and nonuser alike—benefits from its mere existence.

On the other hand a government, like a private business, can and often does engage in transactions that are completely optional and involve the imposition of a user's charge, or *price,* approximately equivalent to the value of the good or service rendered by the government. For example, the charge imposed on the user of the postal services and the price paid for TVA-produced electrical energy cannot be described accurately as taxes because (1) the payer receives a good or service proximate in value to the charge imposed; (2) the decision to use the service, or receive the good, is an elective rather than a coerced decision; and (3) persons not paying the charge are unable to receive the good or service.

Public goods and services, distinguished from private goods and services, are those items for which a reasonable price and an optimum level of output cannot be determined or maintained by the market forces of supply and demand. The national defense force, the legal system, public educational institutions, and the network of highways are among those services that cannot be parceled out to a nation's populace in any *acceptable* manner by a free-market mechanism. Society has deemed it imperative that such goods and services be equally available to everyone, whether or not they are used directly and without regard for the degree of use.

Nevertheless, an occasional attempt is made to justify a particular tax on some "benefit-received" principle. That is, it is argued that a particular tax is realistically nothing more than a reasonable price paid for a given benefit received. For example, the federal and state excise taxes on gasolines, lubricants, and tires are sometimes justified as constituting a reasonable charge for the use of public highways. Any thorough study of this proposition, however, reveals innumerable loopholes in this justification. Nearly everyone benefits from the mere existence of the highways, regardless of how much he or she uses them directly and, therefore, regardless of personal gasoline, oil, and tire consumption. A motel owner conceivably might never drive on a highway; yet to deny that he or she benefits from the existence of the highway would be absurd.

The notion that certain taxes are really nothing more than a reasonable price paid for a good or service received is enhanced by the practice of channeling certain taxes into specified government

"funds" or "accounts" from which expenditures are restricted. This practice is known as *earmarking.* Thus, gasoline tax receipts are often channeled into a Road-Use Tax Fund that can be used solely for building or improving public highways. This benefit principle is reinforced further when non-highway users of gasoline—for example, a farmer who uses gasoline in a tractor or a student who uses gasoline in a water-ski rig—receive a refund of the gasoline tax. Although it has become fairly common in the past quarter century, earmarking taxes has both advantages and disadvantages worthy of separate study by anyone seriously interested in taxation. On balance, the disadvantages probably outweigh the advantages. Among the disadvantages are unnecessary confusion; Revenue Ruling 77-29 recently held that "fees" based on the assessed value of real property are not deductible as real property taxes, at least in part because the proceeds were earmarked for sanitation purposes.

Whatever may be the merits of earmarking tax revenues, the bookkeeping procedure does not in some occult manner transform what is realistically a compulsory payment (or tax) into a charge that is equal even roughly to a free-market price. In short, a compulsory transfer of resources, *unless specifically related to a definite and roughly equivalent benefit received,* is sufficiently different in purpose and result from a voluntary transfer that the one (a tax) ought to be distinguished clearly from the other (a beneficiary's charge, or market price). Ideally, the word "tax" would never be used to refer to the payment made for rationable goods and services that only incidentally were produced by the public sector.

"From the private to the public sector"

Since the definition specifies a compulsory transfer of resources, perhaps it is redundant to add "from the private to the public sector." Obviously no person or group of persons acting privately can, in the absence of a legal debt, compel any other person to transfer resources to him or her except under conditions of duress. This power of compulsion is restricted to the public sector—that is, to a sovereign government. The phrase "from the private to the public sector" serves only to exclude the possibility of labeling as a tax any intragovernmental transfer of funds. Thus, if the administrators of a Road-Use Tax Fund were ordered by a higher governmental authority to transfer funds to a General Fund, the transfer would not be a tax.

"Predetermined criteria"

A tax may be distinguished also from an outright confiscation of resources (which can be very much like a tax in both result and objective) because a tax is levied on the basis of predetermined criteria and on a recurring basis. Predetermined criteria hopefully make a tax more equitable than confiscation, but this depends, of course, on the governmental body determining the criteria. In the free-world countries, taxes must generally have a socially acceptable result, since the governmental bodies setting the tax criteria are themselves subject to expulsion without revolution. Except in times of national crisis, few countries have used outright confiscation as a primary method of achieving the nation's nonmilitary objectives, and no country has used it on a recurring basis.

"Economic and social objectives"

Today taxes are a major tool by which the federal government directs and influences the reallocation of resources necessary to achieve a nation's economic and social objectives. Whether or not taxes *should* be used in this manner has become a topic of great controversy and of great political significance, but that they *are* being so used is unquestionable. Before we examine briefly a few of the economic and social objectives that have been paramount to our federal government over the past ten to twenty years, let us look at alternative methods by which a government could accomplish these economic and social objectives and at the reasons a government has for selecting one method over another. An appreciation of the present objectives, as well as likely economic and social objectives of future administrations, may be as important to long-range tax planning as any knowledge of the present law could be, no matter how thorough that knowledge is.

TAXES IN PERSPECTIVE

The government, by taxing, has in fact diverted a substantial proportion of the national income or wealth away from the control of the private sector to the control of the public sector. The manifold reasons a government has for diverting resources will be discussed later. At this juncture it is necessary to understand only that taxes are but one of several

TABLE **1-1**

TAXES AS A PERCENTAGE OF GROSS DOMESTIC PRODUCT FOR SELECTED COUNTRIES IN 1977

Country	Percentage
Sweden	53
Norway	48
Netherlands	46
Belgium	43
Denmark	42
Finland	41
France	40
Austria	39
Germany	38
Italy	38
United Kingdom	37
Canada	32
United States	30

SOURCE: Adapted from Revenue Statistics of OECD Member Countries. 1965–1978—A Standardized Classification, Table 1, p. 82.

alternative methods by which a government can accomplish this same result. Admittedly, however, taxes are the only generally accepted method for large-scale diversion of resources in an industrial nation. Table 1-1 suggests the amazing degree to which taxes do restructure the flow of several nations' incomes. Most citizens of the United States probably would be surprised to learn that in 1977 our country was well down the list of developed nations in terms of the percentage of gross domestic product diverted by taxes.

Confiscation of wealth

The most direct method of diverting resources from the private to the public sector is the outright confiscation of wealth. This method has been used almost exclusively in times of political chaos or military crisis. The Chilean expropriation of foreign copper mines by the Allende government is illustrative of a recent confiscatory action. (Admittedly, some payment was made, but most impartial observers conclude that the payment was less than adequate to compensate the former owners of the properties confiscated.) Obviously, in this case the result is a net decrease in the wealth of the private sector and a corresponding increase in that of the public sector. In this important result, taxes are much like confiscation.

Beneficiary's charges

Although the beneficiary's charge (or "price") collected by the government may be another way to decrease the net quantity of resources in the hands of the private sector, it is more likely simply to restructure the resources that the private sector holds. That is, if the beneficiary's charge is in fact equal to the value of the good or service received by the private-sector payer, then the private sector has not decreased its net resources by incurring the charge; it has simply exchanged money for goods or services. To repeat an earlier observation, the beneficiary's charge can be distinguished from a tax because the former provides a *definite and identifiable* thing of roughly equivalent value that could not be obtained by the party incurring the charge except by payment of the charge (or price). On the other hand, in the case of taxes, no direct or proximate benefit received for the payment of the tax can be identified. In addition, the tax itself need not determine the quantity of any public benefit produced or consumed. Finally, the amount of any tax need not be determined directly by the cost of any publicly produced goods or services. In short, *at the individual, or micro, level,* there is no functional relationship between a tax and publicly produced goods or services; at some collective, or macro, level, in an equilibrium situation the aggregate social cost of taxes should equal the aggregate social value of the publicly produced goods and services. The marginal analysis of economic theory would suggest that the level of governmental activity should be determined by the point of intersection of the marginal social cost and the marginal social benefit of any government program. Unfortunately, our present measurement techniques are so imprecise that a comparison of social cost and social benefit is not likely to convince the skeptics.

Many small payments to the public sector are commonly considered to be nothing more than a price paid for a benefit received, but often an examination of the transaction does not support this belief. For example, state governments typically impose a minimal fee on persons who seek to become licensed automobile operators. Additionally, of course, the states impose relatively heavy penalties on unlicensed drivers found operating a motor vehicle. Through the earmarking of funds and numerous press releases, the state governments foster the notion that this fee is in reality the "price" the citizen must pay to be a licensed driver and is deter-

mined solely by the costs of operating the Licensing Division of the Highway Patrol. A thorough examination of this transaction would reveal that the personal economic benefit received is, for most individuals, far in excess of the cost incurred, given the fact that one may not drive without a license. Additionally the real benefit sought through the licensing arrangement never was the economic benefit that might accrue to the person granted the license but rather the social benefit of highway safety that applies equally to drivers and nondrivers by assuring everyone concerned that only qualified persons may operate vehicles on public highways. Finally, the price of the license is in no sense determined by the intersection of the pertinent supply and demand functions. In summary, therefore, the amount paid for the traditional driver's license is more aptly classified as a head tax on motor vehicle drivers only rather than as a price or beneficiary's charge for the rights received.

Government bonds

In a sense, the sale of a government bond is similar to a beneficiary's charge collected by a government. Both the incurrence of the charge and the purchase of a bond are, under normal circumstances, voluntary acts; both simply restructure the composition of the assets of the purchaser, since both provide for the receipt of an item equivalent in value to that surrendered in the purchase; and both may leave the private sector with less "money" (or "current assets").[2]

Bond sales are also somewhat comparable to taxation—that is, both taxes and bond sales tend to reduce the private sector's ability to purchase additional goods and services without increasing private debt. In that sense they are substitutes for each other. Thus, under circumstances in which a government desires simply to reduce aggregate demand, a sale of government bonds may be an acceptable alternative to an increase in taxes. On the other hand, the persons who typically purchase government bonds may have characteristics, such as high incomes or great wealth, that make the end effect or result of a bond sale differ significantly from the imposition of additional taxes. This depends too, of

[2]Whether the purchase does or does not reduce the quantity of current assets held by the private sector depends on the classification of the item received. If the item purchased is a long-term bond, which will become payable at some distant date, the current assets of the private sector have been reduced. If it is a short-term bond, it serves only to restructure the form in which the current assets are held.

course, upon the particular tax utilized—certain taxes also "demand more from those who have the most." In other words, whether or not a bond sale can or cannot be substituted for any given tax depends on the ultimate reasons the government has for selling the bond or imposing the tax in the first instance.

Inflation

Finally, since a government typically is in a net debtor position, inflation becomes another method of transferring resources from the private to the public sector. At the same time, of course, inflation redistributes the real wealth *within* the private sector. (That is, the creditors tend to lose during an inflationary period because debtors are able to satisfy debts with dollars having less purchasing power than those they borrowed.)

As noted earlier, bond sales are generally more like beneficiary's charges than like taxes. In an inflationary setting, however, this is less true since the values exchanged are less than equal; the greater the rate of inflation, the more the bond sale resembles a tax. If bond sales were made compulsory in a highly inflationary setting, the characteristics that distinguish them from a tax would rapidly disappear.

In summary, taxation is only one of several methods available to a government determined, for one reason or another, to divert resources from the private to the public sector of the economy. Taxation, confiscation, and inflation are forced or compulsory methods of achieving that end; bond sales and beneficiary's charges are voluntary ways to achieve some, though not all, of the same objectives.

Taxation seems destined, however, to be the main method of achieving numerous national objectives. The selection of a particular method should be based on tests of efficiency and equity. Obviously, a government can use many nontax incentives to assist in achieving its goals. The method that "best" accomplishes the objective should be the one selected. Here, as in all other human endeavors, the choice between alternatives should be based on a prediction of the consequences of the alternative actions. Such predictions require a marshaling of facts and an operational theory of the socioeconomic environment. Hopefully, the use of computers and the development of better economic and social models will make such predictions more accurate in the future.

OBJECTIVES OF TAXATION

To many persons the very title of this section will seem absurd because to them the sole objective of taxation is "to raise revenues." Politicians and news editors often strengthen this concept by stating that particular tax increases are necessitated "to pay for a war," "to improve education," or to do any of the many other things governments do. A closer examination of the facts will reveal that the concept is, at best, a half-truth.

Raising revenues

In one sense, taxes are to governments what incomes are to businesses and to individuals. For all nonfederal levels of government, this characterization is essentially accurate; most taxes at the state and local levels are for the purpose of raising revenues—providing the governmental unit with an income. The federal government, however, is wholly unlike state and local governments, private businesses, and individuals. Theoretically, the federal government can expend any amount of money it wishes without ever collecting any taxes because the federal government alone controls the power to create money. Most people wish that somehow, somewhere, this were not in fact the case, and, therefore, they often reject the notion as ludicrous. In order to understand federal taxation today, however, it is absolutely essential to understand what it is that governments seek to accomplish through taxation. Abba Lerner, an economist, expressed this same idea clearly when he wrote:

> First, there is never any need for the government of a well-established sovereign state to raise an amount of money by taxes just because it needs the money, if it does not wish to bring about the actual effects of the tax on the economy. If there is merely a need for money it is easier to borrow it and much easier to print it. . . . A rational taxing policy is directed at the effects from the taxpayers' having to pay the money and not at the government's gain in getting it.[3]

Even a brief review of our federal government's operations over the past fifty years supports the contention that governments, unlike persons, can continually expend more than they receive. Between

[3] Abba Lerner, *The Economics of Control* (New York: Macmillan Co., 1959), p. 233.

1926 and 1979 the federal government operated with a cash-budget deficit in 41 and a surplus in 13 years. The total of the cash deficits amounted to approximately $614 billion; the cash surpluses totaled some $38 billion. The difference—$576 billion, a truly astronomical amount—demonstrates clearly that at least one government has found it unnecessary to tax "because it needs the money." [4] In fiscal year 1980, the deficit is estimated to be in excess of $30 billion.

Until the mid-1950s, it was difficult to cite any comparable evidence to support the contention that tax policies were in fact being used to achieve any objectives other than "raising revenues." In the past 20 years, however, the changes enacted in the United States' income-tax laws increasingly support such a proposition. The acceptance of rapid depreciation; the institution, subsequent suspension, early reinstatement, later abolition, sudden reinstitution, and recent liberalization of the investment credit; the institution of various energy credits; and the targeted jobs credit are all illustrative of recent modifications of our income-tax laws that were enacted to achieve specific, nonrevenue, economic objectives. These and similar facts justify the conclusion that taxation is being used by the government partially as a non-revenue policy instrument; therefore, understanding the use of tax law as an instrument of policy is crucial. Those students who rebel at the notion that a government would use taxation for other than revenue purposes should remember that understanding a process need not be equated with advocacy of it. Furthermore, realization that the tax law has become an instrument of policy is essential to understanding and predicting the future course of the law.

Economic price stability

Perhaps the most fundamental reason a government has for taxing its citizens is to provide a reasonable degree of price stability within the nation. Whether the government does this for the benefit of its citizens or as a matter of self-preservation is a moot question. If a government purchases any substantial amount of goods and services without taxing, aggre-

gate spending by the public and private sectors will quickly generate a strong excess demand and, therefore, an inflationary bias in the economy. The closer the nation is to a full-employment equilibrium position without government spending, the greater will be the inflationary pressure created by government spending without taxation.

The subtle difference between taxing to pay for government purchases (that is, "to raise revenues") and taxing to achieve economic price stability is an important difference that goes a long way toward explaining recent and probable future changes in our federal tax laws. Certainly our federal government each year does relate aggregate revenues to aggregate expenditures when it considers a budget proposal. At the all-important margin, however, it does *not* decide to accept or to reject any single expenditure proposal on the grounds that it does or does not have the wherewithal to pay for the project. Rather, the government increasingly commits the nation to selected projects with only limited or secondary concern for the source of payment; then it *separately* sets the tax policy for the next year, giving due consideration to both the expenditures budget that has been approved and the economic milieu in which it must operate. Say the government finds, for example, that, with the present tax structure and level of economic activity, combined public and private spending is likely to create serious inflation. If price stability is to be maintained, the government must then either decrease its own spending or decrease private spending. Politicians and citizens alike harbor honest differences of opinion over what part of federal spending can and should be decreased, and ultimately the decision concerning the amount of federal spending must be made in the political arena. Once that decision is formulated, the government then is ready to set tax policy. In this way, taxation has become the residual buffer that regulates private demand to keep private plus public demand more or less in line with output. [5] In this manner taxation can become a primary method of contributing to the reasonable price stability of a nation. Obviously, tax policy is not the only weapon against inflation available to a government; monetary policy (which is faster but has more limited effects) can also be used to promote price stability.

---

[4] A text dealing with taxation is not, in the opinion of the authors, an appropriate place to discuss the significance of the national debt that necessarily accompanies a deficit. However, because a discussion of the one is likely to raise doubts about the other, those who are interested might read Chapter 7, "Fiscal Policy and the National Debt," in Ott and Ott, *Federal Budget Policy.*

[5] Of course, a change in the tax provisions also causes much controversy. No one wants his tax bite increased, and everyone thinks his should be the first to be reduced. Thus spending decisions ultimately trigger revenue decisions that can be of major political significance.

Unfortunately, inflation has more than one cause. What has been described thus far is what economists call "demand-pull inflation," a form of inflation especially susceptible to treatment by changes in tax policy. Another form, known as "cost-push inflation," is characterized by growing unemployment, retardation of economic growth, and rising prices. Because, under these conditions, unemployment already is extant in undesirable proportions, a tax increase could serve only to exacerbate the unemployment problem while achieving little additional control over inflation. Although noted economists differ on the recommended remedy for cost-push inflation, some governmental restrictions on wage and price movements generally are deemed appropriate. In any event, articulation and attempted resolution of those remedies must remain beyond the confines of this tax book.

Economic growth and full employment

The federal government has determined that, in addition to maintaining reasonable price stability, it should promote the near-full employment of all resources and ensure a satisfactory rate of economic growth. Collectively, economic growth with full employment and reasonably stable prices has become the *raison d'être* for most of the monetary and fiscal policies implemented since the early 1950s. Taxation, as part of fiscal policy, is generally accepted as one of the more potent tools available to the government for achieving these economic goals.

The reductions in personal and corporate income tax rates in 1962 were a particularly interesting experiment. At the time these reductions were enacted, aggregate demand was inadequate to maintain the desired level of economic activity. If it had followed its own precedents, the government would have increased spending without increasing taxes in order to bring aggregate demand up to the desired level. Unfortunately, there are numerous drawbacks to the initiation of such deliberate government spending programs. Among the more serious shortcomings is the length of time required to devise and implement economically sound projects; hence, the time lag between perception of the need and fruition of the desired effect on the economy is unduly long. Furthermore, once started, it is difficult to terminate a spending program successfully, even if termination is warranted by a change in economic conditions. Whether for these or other reasons, the govern-

ment decided in 1962 that, rather than increase *public* spending, it would reduce the income taxes on individuals and corporations in order to stimulate *private* demand. While proposing this alternative to the Congress, the executive branch of the government argued that the decrease in income-tax rates would actually increase total tax revenues through the increase in incomes generated by the rate reductions. History supports the thesis: Personal income tax collections increased from approximately $45.6 billion in 1962 to $48.6 billion in 1964, while corporate income tax collections for the same period increased from $20.5 billion to $23.5 billion. Based on the apparent success of this 1962 experiment, it seems reasonable to expect similar actions in the future whenever economic circumstances require them. The present economic circumstances are something of an anomaly. The problem of unemployment seems to warrant another tax reduction or, alternatively, an increase in government spending. The concurrent problem of inflation, however, argues against such an action.

Economic development

A goal closely allied with economic growth is the attainment of economic development. The governments of the lesser developed nations of the world are engaged in a quest for improvement in economic and social conditions within their countries. For the developing nations as a group, a common problem is that the portion of the nation's income devoted to investment is too small, while the portion devoted to consumption is too large. The tendency to consume nearly all the GNP is inevitable when a large and growing population is located in an economically poor country. Yet some savings and investment is essential if the country is ever to break out of the poverty cycle. Carefully selected forms of taxation can help rectify this shortcoming by reducing private consumption. Obviously, however, this is only half a solution; if there is to be any net decrease in real consumption and any corresponding increase in real investment, the government must see to it that its spending programs, whether or not they are supported by tax collections, are devoted to investment purposes. Sometimes it is even necessary for the developing nation to ensure that the investment is of the particular type—usually called social-overhead investment—that is a precondition to further private investment. For example, large public investments in roads, harbors, bridges, and education may be necessary before private investment in business enterprise can be successful.

To some degree the United States also has attempted in the recent past to alter private investment decisions. Specifically, the acceptance of rapid depreciation methods and the introduction of the investment credit were both enacted at least in part because of our government's desire to increase *investment* spending. Much more will be said about these investment-incentive devices in Part Five.

Wealth redistribution

Many of the objectives associated with tax policies are as much social as they are economic. Wealth redistribution, for example, may be sought either because of a social value judgment that excesses in the distribution of private wealth are undesirable or because of an economic judgment that wealth redistribution is required to maintain a desired level of economic health. The latter argument typically proceeds on the assumption that large concentrations of wealth and income tend to reduce aggregate demand below a satisfactory level since high-income earners spend a smaller proportion of their incomes than do persons with lower incomes. One noted student of income taxation forcefully argued that the progressive rate structure associated with our personal income tax can be rationalized satisfactorily *only* on the basis that progressive income taxation contributes to a more equal distribution of a nation's wealth.

Other objectives—the future

The intimate connection of taxation to public policy makes future modifications of the United States' federal tax laws probable. What might some of the changes be? Six of the more interesting proposals, all related to our energy-shortage problem, that have recently been seriously considered by Congress are

1. A penalty tax on gas-guzzling automobiles.
2. A tax credit for purchasers of electric cars.
3. Rapid amortization for equipment that burns waste products for fuel.
4. A tax credit for expenditures on improved insulation of homes and business buildings.
5. An excise tax on the business consumption of oil and natural gas.
6. A tax credit for taxpayers installing solar heating equipment.

Although only two of the six proposals cited have been enacted into law at the date of this writing, the mere fact that all six were seriously considered by Congress suggests how far federal tax policy has strayed from the traditional objective of simply raising revenue.

The sooner a student becomes accustomed to the idea that taxes are being used to accomplish economic and social objectives, rather than simply raising revenues for government purchases, the sooner he or she will be able to anticipate correctly many changes in the tax law. Randolph Paul, a noted tax authority and lawyer, commented on this reemphasis in taxation as follows:

> The point is that taxes, wholly apart from their revenue-producing qualities, may achieve desired effects on particular occasions. This is more than inquiring into effects when imposing taxes. It puts effects first, and taxes in the role of means to desired ends. It recognizes that the highest function of taxes is to accomplish positive social or economic objectives beyond the revenue. They then become more than exactions to defray the cost of government; they reach the higher level of operation as instruments of human welfare.[6]

The successful business manager of tomorrow—as well as the successful tax practitioner—will be able to predict many changes in the tax law with reasonable accuracy. It is interesting to observe that the more sophisticated a nation's citizens become in tax matters—that is, the more capable the citizens become of predicting tax changes accurately—the less effective the changes will be. This result is predicated on the proposition that people correctly anticipating a tax change will modify their own actions to their personal advantage before the tax change is announced. If, for example, taxpayers correctly anticipate an increase in income tax rates, they will expedite the realization of gains and delay their realization of losses and their recognition of deductions in order to minimize their own aggregate tax liabilities over some period of time. To the extent they are capable of doing this, they may minimize a government's ability to achieve its objectives in increasing the tax rates. The fumbling that has surrounded the investment tax credit (see Chapter 17) suggests that the United States—government and citizens alike—is a long way from this degree of sophistication in tax matters.

[6]Randolph E. Paul, *Taxation in the United States* (Boston: Little, Brown and Company, 1954), p. 652.

PROBLEMS

1. Citizens frequently make payments other than taxes to governmental units. Write a short essay distinguishing taxes from penalties or fines, from charges for goods or services (beneficiary's charges), and from confiscation.

2. F.I.C.A. (social security) has often been described and justified as old age insurance. Are payments made to the government under this act beneficiary's charges or taxes? Why?

3. An increase in any federal tax is often justified as "necessary to pay for a war." How adequate is this explanation? Why? If Congress refused to enact a requested tax, how would the United States pay for various government programs, including a war?

4. Which of the following payments would you classify as a tax? How would you classify the other payments?
   a. Payment for automobile registration (that is, license plates)
   b. Payment for a hunting or fishing license
   c. Payment for a "safety sticker" on an automobile
   d. Payment for parking on a "metered" street
   e. Payment for federal stamps required on transfer of a real estate deed
   f. Payment for riding a city-owned and -operated bus
   g. Payment for a bottle of liquor purchased in a state-owned store

5. In what significant way are the "fiscal resources" of a national government different from those of a state or local government?

6. Explain alternative ways a federal government might "pay for" the goods and services it purchases. What reasons are there for preferring one method over another?

7. List the objectives, other than raising revenue, for which taxes may be levied.

8. Is the price paid for postage more accurately classified as a "price" (beneficiary's charge) or a "tax"? Explain your answer.

9. Assume that a city requires that every dog be licensed and that the fee for this annual service is $5. Assume further that the money collected in this way is put into a special fund used to pay the cost of the city dog patrol operation. Is this $5 fee more accurately classified as a "price" or a "tax"? Explain your answer.

10. "The purposes of federal taxes may be significantly different from the purposes of state or local taxes." Discuss.

11. Write a short essay to support the idea that mandatory military service is a form of progressive taxation.

12. Must taxes involve the transfer of money? Under what circumstances might you expect a government to impose a nonpecuniary tax?

13. Politicians seldom increase their popularity by advocating a tax increase. Nevertheless, in spite of the fact that the United States federal government really does not "need" to collect taxes before it can spend, no federal politician has ever advocated the end of all tax collections at the federal level of government. Explain the apparent contradiction.

14. Section 164(a) of our Internal Revenue Code (the basic statutory authority for the U.S. federal income tax) authorizes a taxpayer to deduct certain taxes in the determination of taxable income. That subsection reads, in part, as follows:

> Except as otherwise provided in this section, the following taxes shall be allowed as a deduction for the taxable year within which paid or accrued:
> (1) State and local, and foreign, real property taxes.
> (2) State and local personal property taxes.

Based on the authority of Sec. 164(a)(2), taxpayers in some states can deduct the cost of their automobile license plates, whereas taxpayers in other states cannot claim that same deduction. How might you explain the apparent conundrum?

15. What good reasons might a free-world government have for imposing a tax of, say, $5 on a pack of cigarettes? If that were done, would it be correct to refer to the $5 charge to the consumer as a "tax"? Explain briefly.

16. Explain why the United States government rarely undertakes a major marketing effort for the sale of savings bonds in times of peace, whereas it routinely does so during times of war.

17. The sale of a 30-day U.S. Treasury note is in some ways significantly different from the sale of a 30-year U.S. Treasury bond. Explain briefly.

SUPPLEMENTAL PROBLEMS

18. Consider the taxes normally paid by consumers in the United States. Make a list of the ones that have some characteristics of a penalty; make a separate list of those that have some characteristics of a beneficiary's charge.

19. Imagine that you are the Minister of Finance in a small developing nation. What features might you incorporate in your tax program to encourage economic development?

20. Taxes are often defined solely in terms of their revenue-producing function. Nevertheless taxes often have other effects that are as important, or more important, than their ability to produce revenue. Historically what problem has this fact created for the courts?

    (NOTE: To answer this question correctly, remember that the Tenth Amendment states: "The powers not delegated to the United States by the Constitution, nor prohibited by it to the States, are reserved to the States, respectively, or to the people.")

The schoolboy whips his taxed top—the beardless youth manages his taxed horse, with a taxed bridle, on a taxed road;—and the dying Englishman, pouring his medicine, which has paid 7 percent., into a spoon that has paid 15 percent.—flings himself back upon his chintz bed, which has paid 22 per cent.—and expires in the arms of an apothecary who has paid a license of a hundred pounds for the privilege of putting him to death. His whole property is then immediately taxed from 2 to 10 percent.

SYDNEY SMITH,
Statistical Annals of the United States of America (1818)

the tax base

After a government has decided that it will impose a tax in lieu of or in addition to other means of achieving the same objective, it must then decide what should be the tax base. In this chapter we shall consider some of the more common tax bases and the criteria that have been used in selecting them. The chapter ends with a discussion that relates the more common tax bases to the various levels of government that, in the United States, have historically imposed them.

The list of possible tax bases—that is, the item, event, or value on which any tax is imposed—is limited only by the boundaries of human imagination. If, for example, a government elected to do so, it could impose a tax on the value of all the rings worn on all right hands. In that case, the value of any ring worn on the right hand would constitute a *tax base*. A few of the historically more important tax bases are discussed in this chapter so that the student may appreciate the multiplicity of taxes that exist today in most complex economies.

The selection of tax bases in the past has proceeded more on political than on economic grounds. As the objective of taxation shifts away from simply raising revenues and toward accomplishing specified economic objectives, the selection of a tax base becomes increasingly important. The intelligent selection of a tax base is complicated because: (1) we are unable to determine with any precision the ultimate incidence of most taxes (that is, who *really* pays the tax); (2) tax objectives often are conflicting,

and no ordinal ranking of their importance has been stipulated; and (3) the distribution of tax bases does not always coincide with the distribution of needs (many tax bases are mobile, and imposition of a high tax causes them to move to another jurisdiction; hence we have much tax sharing—of federal and state tax funds with local units—to equate needs with bases).

COMMON TAX BASES

Several years ago the Tax Foundation reported the results of research undertaken to determine the actual taxes imposed on various goods.[1] To do this it divided selected goods into component parts and then determined the tax imposed on the producer and transporter of each of the parts. For example, a loaf of bread was determined to be a mixture of flour, yeast, shortening, sugar, milk solids, malt, and salt. The research suggested that the yeast producer and the milk-solids producer each paid seven federal and six state taxes. The railroads, assumed to transport the ingredients, paid five federal and unnumbered state taxes—unnumbered because railroad beds pass through varying numbers of state and local tax jurisdictions. The study suggests that each of these taxes

---

[1]The Tax Foundation, Inc., is a private, nonprofit organization that was founded in 1937 to engage in nonpartisan research and public education on the fiscal and management aspects of government. It is supported by contributions from business entities and individuals.

is hidden in the cost of the ingredients and, therefore, in the eventual price of a loaf of bread. By algebraic summation of the number of the taxes imposed on each party responsible for the eventual production of a loaf of bread, the Tax Foundation estimated that a minimum of 151 taxes are hidden in the price of one loaf of bread. It also estimated 100 hidden taxes in the price of an egg; 116 in a man's suit; and more than 600 in a house. The majority of these taxes could be classified as some form of income, wealth, excise, or transaction tax, each of which is considered in some detail below.

Income taxes

The income tax has been imposed in various forms. The most common forms are (1) as a tax on "ordinary taxable income," (2) as a tax on "excess profits," and (3) as a tax on "value added." A decision to tax income necessitates, of course, a selection of the basic entities to be recognized as earning income. In the United States, the basic taxable entities are individuals, corporations, and fiduciaries (estates and trusts).

Ignoring for the moment the important details of income taxation, we may generalize that the "ordinary incomes" earned each year by individual persons, corporations, and fiduciaries have since 1913 become a common tax base in our country. For all levels of government in the aggregate, more revenues are generated from income taxation than from any other tax. This predominance of income taxation is perhaps the major distinguishing characteristic of U.S. taxation; other countries tend to rely relatively more on other tax bases.

The excess-profits tax has reappeared in the United States with major military crises, including World Wars I and II and the Korean conflict. The definition of "excess" profits, as a tax base, is a particularly troublesome one. The usual solution has been to define "normal" profits or income as either (1) some average of the entity's prewar profits, or (2) some arbitrary percentage of invested capital. The difference between the actual income earned in a given war year and normal income (as defined above) is then designated as an excess profit to be taxed at a higher than normal rate. The rationale used to justify the excess-profits tax is the notion that no one should be permitted to profit from the increased incomes induced by wartime production.

The value-added form of the income tax has never been widely utilized in the United States; how-ever, it has been imposed by the state of Michigan and by France. In a way, the value-added concept approximates the income concept used in national income accounting. In that branch of economics, income is defined as the sum of consumption, investment, and government spending—or, alternatively, as the market value of the goods and services produced within a nation during a given time period. As a tax base, value added may be defined alternatively as (1) a company's "sales to customers less purchases from all other companies that are themselves subject to the tax and also less any federal excise tax or state and local sales or excise taxes"[2] or (2) the algebraic sum of "wages, interest, rent, profits, and any other payments to factors of production."[3] This definition of value-added obviously departs significantly from the more traditional micro-income concepts in that companies operating at a loss could still have a substantial value-added tax base, since they too add to the value of the output of the entire economy.[4]

Early in 1979 Senator Russell Long of Louisiana, Chairman of the Senate Finance Committee, stated that the time may have come for the United States to give more serious consideration to VAT (a value-added tax). Congressman Al Ullman, of Oregon, Chairman of the House Ways and Means Committee, subsequently introduced the Tax Restructuring Act of 1979, which calls for the institution of a value-added tax in the United States. Hearings are to be held on this bill in late 1980. Although this support of VAT by two key persons in matters of tax legislation is significant, the United States is still a long way from the imposition of such a tax. The recent interest in VAT is related to the beliefs that: (1) our social security tax is in need of major revision; (2) a national (and quite expensive) health insurance program is imminent; and (3) the income tax has been extended to its limits of public tolerance in the United States. Several of those who have shown some desire to study VAT have also been quick to state that they would support it only if related changes can be guaranteed. For example, some would support VAT only if it were made a complete substitute for any social security tax *and* the maximum marginal income tax

[2]Committee for Economic Development, *A Better Balance in Federal Taxes on Business* (New York: CED, 1966), p. 25.
[3]*Ibid.*
[4]For this reason some persons undoubtedly would insist that the value-added tax be discussed with sales or excise taxes rather than with income taxes. We would not quarrel with such reclassification; we include the discussion here only to emphasize the fact that the usual definitions of income can be substantially altered if one defines income from a macro point of view.

rate were reduced to (say) 30 percent. Obviously, a major political battle lies ahead for the proponents of any such drastic changes in our present tax system.

Employment taxes

In a very limited sense, employment taxes could also be included in a discussion of income taxes. Because the employment taxes are typically imposed only on some portion of the wage or salary earned,[5] however, and because they are often viewed as a contribution to a retirement fund, they cannot be equated to the more comprehensive income taxes. Additionally, they sometimes are imposed at least in part on the employer who pays the wage or salary, rather than on the person who earns it. In that case, the employment taxes have virtually no relation to the income of the *taxpayer,* who is the employer.

For purposes of this introduction, therefore, it would be most useful to divide employment (or social insurance) taxes into two major groups: those imposed on the self-employed and the employee and those imposed on the employer. The former—which would include the contributions by both the self-employed and the employee to the F.I.C.A. program—could be classified conceptually with the income taxes. The latter—including the employer's contributions to the F.I.C.A. program as well as to various unemployment programs—could be classified conceptually with the transactions taxes. Alternatively, if we could prove that the employee ultimately pays the employer's share of these taxes, through lower wages, then the entire amount could be classified as part of the income tax.

Wealth taxes

Wealth taxation, like income taxation, appears in various forms. Selective forms of wealth taxation, such as taxes on real property or taxes on certain personal properties, are far more common than a comprehensive net wealth tax. The beginning student of taxation should understand that a tax on wealth technically does not duplicate an income tax. The former is a levy on an aggregate accumulation of net wealth at one moment in time—hence a *stock concept*—whereas the latter tax is a levy on the net increase in wealth during a given period of time—

hence a *flow concept.* The accounting student should immediately recognize the parallel between these two tax bases and the two basic financial statements—the balance sheet (or statement of financial position at one moment in time) and the income statement (or statement of profit and loss for a given period of time).

Real property is generally defined for tax purposes as land, buildings, and other assets that are permanently attached to the land. Because of the difficulty of concealing ownership, and because of the obvious ability to identify the situs, or location, of the real property, the value of real property has been a primary tax base for many, many years. The major problem in the taxation of real estate has been the difficulty of determining accurately and equitably the fair market value of real estate on any given date. The less frequent the sales of comparable realty in any geographical area, the greater the difficulty in estimating value.

One interesting aspect of the tax generally imposed on the real estate of this country is the nearly universal practice of taxing the owner of the property on the *gross* value of the realty. Thus, a taxpayer who owns outright a piece of realty valued at $100,000 would presumably pay no more real property tax than another taxpayer in the same jurisdiction who owns realty valued at $100,000 but whose property is mortgaged for $80,000, even though the second taxpayer obviously has only a $20,000 interest in the property. Thus, the tax on real estate cannot be equated even roughly to a true net-wealth tax, since it (1) considers only one form of wealth and (2) taxes it on a gross basis.

Ownership of various kinds of personal property also serves as a common tax base in the United States. Probably the most common is the tax on automobile ownership. In some jurisdictions this tax is levied on market values alone, whereas in other jurisdictions such factors as age and/or weight of the automobile are also considered in determining the tax liability. Other forms of selective personal-property taxes include taxes on boats, television sets, phonographs, stocks, bonds, and household furniture. Partially because of the ease in concealing ownership of these assets, and partially because of the administrative problems associated with valuing the assets and enforcing the law, the personal-property taxes on property other than automobiles are rapidly disappearing from the American scene.

A tax based on aggregate net wealth would be more equitable than the typical selective wealth tax-

[5] Effective January 1, 1980, the F.I.C.A. tax base for employees, employers, and the self-employed consists of only the first $25,900 of earned income per year. Amounts earned annually in excess of $25,900 generally are exempt from these taxes.

es because the former tax would apply equally to all forms of wealth and to only the net excess of the fair market value of property owned over debt. Nevertheless, net wealth never has been popular as a tax base. Its unpopularity must be attributed to the administrative difficulties of placing a value on a multiplicity of assets at frequent time intervals as well as to the ease of concealing ownership of many assets. For most persons the largest single asset they "own" is their ability to work. Thus, a truly comprehensive net-wealth tax might even necessitate the valuation of a human life—that is, assessment of the value of the personal services the individual might render—based, perhaps, on the discounted value of an estimated-earnings stream. The administrative difficulty in estimating income streams and in selecting a discount rate is apparent. Similar valuation problems apply to many more conventional forms of wealth.

Wealth-transfer taxes

In addition to the various taxes on asset ownership per se, governments frequently impose a tax on the transfer of an individual's ownership interest to anyone other than a bona fide purchaser. For example, the federal donative transfers tax and the state inheritance taxes are based on the gratuitous transfer of an ownership interest.

The Tax Reform Act of 1976 combined what previously had been two separate wealth-transfer taxes—the federal gift tax and the federal estate tax—into a single donative transfers tax. Conceptually the new tax is relatively simple. If in any year a taxable gift is made during the donor's life, that donor must pay a tax determined by applying the new tax rates to the *aggregate* value of all taxable gifts made since birth, less a tax credit (similarly determined) for all taxable gifts made in *prior* years. In this manner current gifts are taxed at progressively higher marginal tax rates. At the donor's death, a similar tax calculation is made, as follows:

Compute the value of the *taxable* estate[6]	$XXX
Add aggregate value of *taxable* gifts made during life	XXX
The sum equals the donative transfers tax base	$XXX

---

[6] A few details explaining some of the more important differences between the gross value of an estate and the taxable estate are included in Chapter 10.

Compute the gross tax on the above value using the tax rate schedule printed in Appendix C	$XXX
Subtract an aggregate gift tax based on all gifts made during life using the tax rate schedule in Appendix C	XXX
The remainder is the federal estate tax	$XXX

The estate tax is payable by the executor from the estate's assets left by the deceased person. Observe that this estate tax is equivalent to a true net-wealth tax because it is based on the excess of the fair market value of the decedent's assets over the debts owed (plus certain other special exemptions written into the law). Technically, however, it is considered a transfer tax (based on the value of the assets transferred) rather than a wealth tax. As noted above, the law contains a long list of special provisions (or exceptions), most of which were enacted either to allow smaller estates to escape taxation or to make the administration of the law feasible.

Most small estates will wholly escape the federal estate tax because of a relatively generous tax credit. The amount of this credit is scheduled to increase over a period of five years. For persons dying in 1980 the credit is $42,500; and for those dying after 1980 it will be $47,000. A $42,500 credit is equivalent to a tax exemption of $161,563; a credit of $47,000 is equal to an exemption of $175,625. This means, of course, that persons with an estate of less than $175,625 will pay no estate tax if they die after 1980. In addition, if a decedent leaves property to his or her spouse, up to the larger of one-half the decedent's adjusted gross estate or $250,000 may be claimed as a "marital deduction." Consequently, if a decedent is entitled to the maximum marital deduction, his or her estate will escape any federal estate tax after 1980 if it is equal in value to $425,625 or less. (The $425,625 is obtained by combining the $250,000 marital deduction with the $47,000 tax credit.)

The gift tax aspect of the new law is made administratively feasible by allowing every individual to make gifts of $3,000 per year to as many donees as he or she wishes without incurring a gift tax. In other words, the law provides that there is no *taxable* gift until a person gives more than $3,000 to one person in one year. In addition, gifts to charity are excluded from the gift tax base. If it were not for these exemptions and deductions, the I.R.S. would be faced with the truly Herculean task of discovering small gifts among family members and exacting a tax from the donor for each gift.

On the other hand, because of these relatively generous deductions, exemptions, and credits, little revenue is obtained from the donative transfers tax. That fact might lead one to the conclusion that the expenditure of time, effort, and money required to enforce the law is greater than the benefit received from enforcing it. Such a conclusion is doubtful for two reasons. First, and most important, the donative transfers tax has the primary objective of wealth redistribution. That is, this tax is intended to redistribute wealth from the very wealthiest segment of our society to the poorer segments. It is interesting to note that in 1972, only 6 percent of our population owned assets with a net value in excess of $60,000. The total assets of that same 6 percent, however, had an estimated value of $2.2 trillion! Second, because of the combined effects of our realization criterion and certain "basis rules," which are explained in Parts Six and Seven of this book, the appreciation in value that occurs between the time a taxpayer acquires a property and the time he or she dies is never subject to an *income* tax as long as the property is never sold or exchanged in a taxable transaction. This means, of course, that a significant amount of income—at least as that word is defined by economists—wholly escapes income taxation. And many theorists believe that the donative transfers tax at least partially makes up for this failure to impose an income tax on unrealized appreciations in value. At any event, relatively few persons will ever pay tax on gifts or estates.

Transactions taxes

Numerically, the most frequently encountered tax is that imposed upon the consummation of a retail sale. In the process of classifying the various tax bases, the retail sales tax can logically be grouped with other taxes that are levied upon the occasion of a specified transaction. Under this classification scheme, it is possible to distinguish (however hazily) between taxes imposed on specific commodities (usually called excise taxes) and taxes imposed on all commodities (inevitably subject to a list of exceptions) that enter into a specified transaction.

The sale transaction undoubtedly is the one most often singled out for tax purposes. A depth study of sales taxation, however, reveals that even it quickly becomes complicated, since not all sales are subject to the sales tax. Generally speaking, governments have tried to tax sales only at one of three levels: that is, the manufacturer's level, the wholesaler's level, or the retailer's level. Retail sales taxation is further complicated by the frequent exclusion of the sale of such items as services, food (when not consumed on the premises), work clothing, and selected medicines and drugs.

Exclusions, such as those suggested in the preceding sentence, require comprehensive definitions. What, for example, is a *retail* sale? Is the sale of one ream of 20-lb bond paper to a business, which will use the paper as stationery in routine correspondence, a retail sale? Is the sale of the same paper to a student who is writing a research paper on taxation a retail sale? Finally, if the end use of the paper is determinative of its tax status, how is the clerk who completes the sale supposed to know from whom to collect the tax? Equally troublesome questions can be raised about the definitions of "food," "work clothing," and "services." Thus, for example, under Texas law candy sold by Campfire Girls is not "food," while cookies sold by Girl Scouts *are* "food." The tendency to capricious definitions is apparent.

Other transactions or events that have been made the basis for a tax include stock transfers, severance of natural resources from the earth, and official certification of selected legal and business papers. Thus, in certain jurisdictions, the act of transferring stock ownership from one party to another, whether or not by sale, has been made a taxable occasion. In other jurisdictions, the separation of a natural resource from the earth (for example, natural gas, petroleum, and iron ore) is a taxable event. In yet other jurisdictions a stamp tax is imposed on the registration of a deed, the notarization of a document, and the filing of a business paper. As noted earlier, the payment of a wage or salary is usually made the base for one or more of the social insurance (employment) taxes. In each of these instances the amount of the tax is usually determined by application of the tax rate to the dollar values involved in the specified transactions. For example, the exchange price of the stock (assuming an arm's-length transaction) has been made the base for the stock-transfer tax. Similarly, the value of the unrefined natural gas removed from the earth has constituted the base for a severance tax. The dollar value of salaries paid is the base for the employment tax.

Excise taxes

The manufacture, sale, or consumption of various commodities has also been singled out as an appropriate base for taxation. Taxes imposed on only *selected* commodities are widely referred to as excise taxes. Historically, however, we discover that the term "excise tax" has also been used (or, rather, misconstrued) to refer to the tax on corporate incomes. In 1909, before the passage of the Sixteenth Amendment to the Constitution, a tax on corporate incomes was upheld as constitutional because, the Court found, it was an *excise* tax rather than an *income* tax.[7] Income was found to be simply the base to which the excise tax rate was applied. Classification distinctions such as this do little to facilitate the ready acquisition of any meaningful knowledge of taxation.

Currently, excise taxes are, roughly, those taxes imposed on selected commodities and/or activities. The taxes on alcoholic beverages, tobacco products, and highway fuels are perhaps the most common. They are by no means, however, the only items selected for special tax treatment. Many students may be surprised to learn that the following items (along with many others not listed) are bases for federal taxes in the United States: fishing equipment; pistols and revolvers, shells and cartridges; tires; truck parts; telephone and teletypewriter service; wagers and the occupation of accepting wagers; sugar; narcotic drugs, as well as opium for smoking; white phosphorus matches; adulterated butter; filled cheese; cotton futures; machine gun transfers; and transportation of persons by air.

Finding a common rationale for the taxation of this diverse list of commodities and services is indeed difficult. Several of the excise taxes are allegedly imposed to regulate the use of items that are or may be dangerous to society. There is considerable question, however, about precisely how the taxation of alcoholic beverages, opium, or machine gun transfers helps to control abuse of these items. Admittedly, the imposition of these taxes does make the items more expensive to the users (assuming, of course, that they purchase them through legitimate channels), but that does not necessarily support the conclusion that this reduces their use or consumption. If, in fact, the demand for these items is generally inelastic (as some sociologists and economists would have us believe), then the existence of the tax could even be the source of still greater evils—having to pay a higher price for the taxed article may cause the users to engage in activities (for example, theft, smuggling, or depriving their families of food) that thus require still more state control. This discussion, it should be noted, is not concerned with whether (or

how) such diverse objects as alcohol, tobacco, opium, and machine guns *should* be used. It merely points out that there are serious questions about the presumption made by some persons (including some legislators) that the taxation of these commodities contributes to the regulation of their abuse. Perhaps the most that can be said for taxes on these commodities is that such taxes afford yet another basis for prosecution in some criminal cases.

On *a priori* grounds, two other rationalizations for the existence of certain excise taxes seem more plausible. First, many excise taxes may exist simply because they are "good revenue producers"; second, other excise taxes undoubtedly exist because legislators consider them to be something of a beneficiary's charge.

Historically, many taxes have been considered good taxes as long as they produced substantial amounts of revenue every year without fail. *Using that criterion,* commodity taxes on those items for which there exists a relatively large and inelastic demand would produce a *good* tax. For this reason, taxes have been imposed on salt and on matches (especially prior to the days of refrigeration and in relatively underdeveloped nations).

The idea that the (immediate) highway user ought to pay for the cost of the highways was considered in some detail in Chapter 1 (see p. **1/3**). The same basic idea, with slight modification, is sometimes used to justify the excise taxes on air fares (to pay for the government's investment in air terminals), alcoholic beverages (to pay for police protection necessitated by the abuse of alcohol), and wagering (to pay for the policing of legalized gambling). Obviously, this justification presumes that the ultimate incidence of the tax rests with the person who receives the benefit from the government expenditure or with the person who makes the expenditure necessary in the first instance. As suggested earlier, however, the ultimate incidence of most taxes cannot be established with any degree of reliability.

Other miscellaneous taxes

The preceding discussion is by no means a thorough cataloging of all tax bases. Among the more important or interesting tax bases not mentioned earlier are import and export taxes (customs duties); head taxes; franchise taxes; and the expenditures tax.

Import and export taxes closely resemble commodity (excise) taxes in that they are imposed only on selected items imported into (or, occasionally,

---

[7] See *Flint v. Stone Tracy Company,* 220 U.S. 107 (1911).

exported from) a sovereign state. Sometimes these taxes become so universal that they approximate a transactions tax—that is, a tax on the *transaction* of importing and exporting, regardless of the commodity involved. Under these circumstances, customs duties resemble sales taxes more closely than they do excise taxes. On the other hand, the historical, economic, and political rationales for customs duties more often parallel the rationale for excise taxes than that for sales taxes. In both underdeveloped and developed countries, import duties are typically used to suppress the importation of only those foreign products that can, at least theoretically, be made domestically. The hope is, of course, that this protection will encourage the development of the local industry. Export duties are used fundamentally as a method of increasing government revenues, primarily by countries with little economic diversification. Thus, the developing country whose economy has been heavily dependent on the production of one product—for example, coffee, sugar, or tin—has often relied on an export tax as the primary source of government funds.

For even less developed countries, the head tax (a flat tax on each human) has produced substantial revenues. As countries develop, the head tax often evolves into a crude form of income taxation, as the amount of tax "per head" may vary with some crude measure of income. Thus, in our own early Virginia Colony, the amount of the head tax is reported to have been dependent on personal apparel worn to church. For a study of some elementary head-tax systems, the interested student should read John F. Due's "The African Personal Tax."[8]

A franchise tax is a tax on a right granted by a sovereign government. That is, when a government grants one or more persons the right to do something that they would otherwise not have the authority to do, the granting government often imposes a special yearly tax on the recipient of the right. A most common form of the franchise tax is the one imposed for the privilege of carrying on a business as a corporate entity. The actual tax base for the franchise tax has varied widely and included, among other measures, the dollar amount of sales, earnings, dividends, par or stated value of capital issues, and tangible assets owned by the corporation.

The expenditures tax is a novel idea that, to our knowledge, has not been implemented in the last 200 years. Stated very crudely, the idea is that progres-

sive income taxation imposes as great a burden on those who save and invest (and who thus make possible even greater national incomes) as on those who spend their entire incomes on consumption. The expenditures tax would turn this around; it would tax total consumption during a given time period and exempt from taxation any portion of income not spent on consumption items.[9]

The purpose of this discussion of alternative tax bases has *not* been to provide students of elementary taxation with a comprehensive discussion of the merits or shortcomings of any particular tax or even to acquaint them with all the taxes known to humanity. Rather, it has been simply to impress on them the ubiquitousness of taxation. All too frequently, even educated persons think only of those taxes that impinge directly on them. We shall dismiss any detailed consideration of the various taxes mentioned above, however, not because they are non-existent or unimportant, but because they are overshadowed in U.S. taxation by the giants: the personal and corporate income taxes. Before turning our attention to these giants, however, a few more aspects of taxation in general ought to be considered.

INTERGOVERNMENTAL FISCAL RELATIONS AND TAX BASES

One of the tax problems given a great deal of attention in the past few years is that of intergovernmental fiscal relations. Because a relatively few taxes produce the vast bulk of the total revenue collected, there has been an increasing tendency for two or more levels of government to impose and collect taxes on essentially the same tax base. For example, the federal government, most state governments, and several municipal governments are using an income-based tax. Most states and an increasing number of local governments are imposing a sales tax. This tendency raises an obvious question: Should two or more governments consolidate their taxes when they are imposed on essentially the same tax base? If the answer to that question is "yes," such subsidiary questions arise as: What level of government should collect the tax? How should the proceeds be distributed? Will the recipient become unduly dependent on the distributor? These, then,

---

[8] See the *National Tax Journal*, December 1962, pp. 385–98.

[9] For details see Nicholas Kaldor, *An Expenditure Tax* (London: Allen and Unwin, 1955).

TABLE **2-1**

FEDERAL, STATE, AND LOCAL TAX RECEIPTS[a] FOR SELECTED FISCAL YEARS, 1902-79[b]

Year	Receipt (in millions)				Percentage distribution			
	Total	Federal	State	Local	Total	Federal	State	Local
1902	$ 1,373	$ 513	$ 156	$ 704	100.0	37.4	11.4	51.3
1913	2,271	662	301	1,308	100.0	29.2	13.3	57.6
1934	8,854	2,942	1,979	3,933	100.0	33.2	22.4	44.4
1942	22,962	13,351	4,979	4,633	100.0	58.1	21.7	20.2
1950	54,799	37,853	8,958	7,988	100.0	69.1	16.3	14.6
1960	126,678	88,419	20,172	18,088	100.0	69.8	15.9	14.3
1970	274,996	185,670	50,486	38,840	100.0	67.5	18.4	14.1
1979	668,200	465,200	124,500	78,500	100.0	69.6	18.6	11.8

[a] Includes social insurance taxes.
[b] Data for 1979 estimated by the authors.
NOTE: Because of rounding, detail may not add to total.
SOURCE: Data for 1902–70 from Tax Foundation, Inc., *Facts and Figures on Government Finance,* 18th Biennial Edition, 1975, Tables 8 and 9, pp. 20–21.

are some of the problems of intergovernmental fiscal relations.

Collections by level of government

Only 50 years ago, our country's tax structure was dominated by locally collected taxes, and total tax collections were relatively small, both absolutely and as a percentage of national income. After the Great Depression of the 1930s, and especially during the Second World War, this picture changed drastically. By 1945 we had evolved a tax structure dominated by a rather sizable federal tax. Table 2-1 clearly demonstrates those changes in tax structure.

In reviewing these data, the student should note that even though state and local taxes decreased as a percentage of total tax collections between 1934 and 1960, they increased significantly in absolute amounts. In addition, state tax receipts increased rapidly and have now resumed roughly their depression position relative to total tax receipts. The increasing claims on tax funds at all levels make the issue of intergovernmental fiscal relations a most important one today.

Tax base and level of government

During the past 50 years, state and local governments in the United States depended heavily upon property and sales taxation, whereas the federal government became increasingly reliant on personal and corporate income taxes. Table 2-2 reveals the distribution of tax collections among the various tax bases, by level of government, for fiscal year 1979.

This table demonstrates clearly that the income tax is indeed the most productive tax utilized today. Of the $526 billion in tax collections, excluding social insurance taxes, in 1979, $332 billion (or about 63 percent) came from income taxes alone. At the federal level, almost 88 percent of the roughly $324 billion came from the personal and corporate income taxes combined. At the state level, about 51 percent of the roughly $125 billion came from sales, gross receipts, and motor fuel taxes. At the local level, about 78 percent of the roughly $79 billion came from

TABLE **2-2**

TAX REVENUES BY TAX BASE AND LEVEL OF GOVERNMENT, FISCAL YEAR 1979 (IN MILLIONS)

Tax base	Total	Federal	State	Local
Individual income	$254.4	$217.8	$32.5	$4.1
Corporate income	77.7	65.7	12.0	—[a]
Sales, gross receipts, and customs	100.3	26.6	63.2	10.5
Property	63.9	—	2.4	61.5
Motor vehicle and operators licenses	5.5	—	4.5	0.7
Death and gift	7.2	5.4	1.8	—
All other	17.6	8.1	7.8	1.7
Total tax revenues	$526.6[b]	$323.6[b]	$124.5	$78.5

[a] Included in individual income-tax collections.
[b] Excluding social insurance taxes.
NOTE: Because of rounding, detail may not add to total.
SOURCE: Preliminary estimates, Bureau of the Census, Washington, D.C., 1980.

property taxes. Our present national tax structure can therefore be summarized as follows:

Tax base	Level of government		
	Federal	State	Local
Income	Primary	Secondary	
Property			Primary
Sales and excise	Secondary	Primary	Secondary

Forget for the moment the distribution of tax bases by the levels of government and try to comprehend the sheer magnitude of the numbers involved. The statement that our federal and local governments collect more than $500 billion in taxes each year doesn't really mean much to most of us. We can comprehend the number 500, but we really cannot sense the meaning of one billion, let alone 500 billion. To help put these magnitudes in perspective, consider the fact that one billion *seconds* ago the first atomic bomb was just exploded. Christ was on earth about one billion *minutes* ago. And a billion *hours* ago, man lived in caves! Then recall that our governments collect more than one billion dollars in tax revenues every single day of the year! And taxes are only a part of total government revenues.

Each level of government also receives funds from nontax sources. For example, all levels of government receive substantial sums from various insurance trust funds and from miscellaneous charges. Most state and local governments receive funds from the federal government, and several of them also operate utility companies, liquor stores, and so on. For these reasons, total tax receipts are always less than total governmental revenues. If we expand the data for the federal government to include social insurance taxes and contributions, the rapid growth in social security taxes is obvious. (See Table 2-3.)

Because of the growth in social security taxes, along with a concurrent reduction in income taxes for individuals in the lower income classes, about one-half of the United States population currently pays more in social security tax than in federal income tax! The strength of the opposition to recently enacted increases in social security taxes suggests that further major changes can be anticipated.

Intergovernmental transfers

In fiscal 1980 the federal government is expected to disburse about $80 billion to state and local governments. This is equivalent to about 30 percent of the total expenditures of those governments. Twenty-

TABLE 2-3

FEDERAL BUDGET RECEIPTS BY MAJOR SOURCE, VARIOUS YEARS

(PERCENTAGE DISTRIBUTION)

Major source	Fiscal year		
	1968	1972	1979[a]
Individual income taxes	44.7	45.4	46.8
Corporation income taxes	18.7	15.4	14.1
Social insurance taxes and contributions	22.5	25.8	30.4
Excise taxes	9.2	7.4	5.7
Customs, estate, and gift taxes	3.3	4.2	1.6
Miscellaneous receipts	1.6	1.7	1.4
Total receipts, by source	100.0	100.0	100.0

[a] Data for 1979 are estimated by authors from Monthly Treasury Statement of Receipts and Outlays of the United States Government, Table I.

SOURCE: Representative Charles Vanik, "Sixth Annual Corporate Tax Study," Table III. Congressional Record, January 26, 1978.

four years ago, less than $6 billion was transferred in this manner. Thus it is apparent that a program of sharing tax revenues is already well underway. The major questions remaining are how far it should be expanded and how the disbursements should be allocated.

The question of extent is of real importance because the nonfederal levels of government are, like the federal government, constantly expending greater sums, but they have not found a source of revenue that can expand at the same rate. This means that the nonfederal governments must either decrease their rate of growth (in terms of expenditures) or find new sources of revenue. Politically, the latter alternative seems to be the only acceptable one. Urbanization and increased expenditures in the public sector seem to go hand in hand. The incredibly complex problems of the super-cities seemingly can be solved only by the collective efforts of states and municipalities. If this be true, the states can either (1) impose duplicate taxes on tax bases already heavily taxed, (2) try to find entirely new sources of revenue, or (3) attempt to get an increasing amount of intergovernmental transfers. Many nonfederal governments are currently deeply engaged in studies intended to determine a preferred mixture from among these options. Without investigating the desirability or practical limitations on each of these options, the last of the three is likely to become the dominant solution in the next decade. If history is any indication, local governments will continue to shift the onus of taxation to the state and federal levels. The willingness of a governmental unit to levy new taxes seems to be inversely related to its proximity to the voters. The experiences of New York City and Cleveland suggest that the state and federal governments may be reluctant to rescue the troubled cities, even in times of financial crisis. Whatever the solution, if the tax imposed on any tax base is to be increased significantly, the criterion for selecting a desirable tax base becomes a question of primary importance.

CRITERIA USED IN THE SELECTION OF A TAX BASE

Because the number of possible tax bases is very large, it is necessary for governmental units to choose among them. The criteria for choice have never been adequately investigated or articulated. One of the earliest attempts to identify such criteria is credited to Adam Smith who, in 1776, suggested that a "good" tax ought to be equitable, convenient, certain, and economical.[10] He called these criteria the "canons of taxation." A review of the current literature would support the statement that Smith's criteria are still being considered today.

Equity

Tax equity is commonly defined as the equal treatment of similarly situated taxpayers. The obvious problem encountered in implementing this criterion is that the definition fails to provide a method or basis for measurement to determine under what conditions two or more taxpayers are "similarly situated." As the phrase "tax equity" is used in the literature and in political discussions, it seems to imply that the appropriate measure is implicit in the tax base. That is, a tax imposed on the purchase of a given commodity is assumed to be equitable as long as all purchases of the identical commodity (with possible modification for quantity, quality, price, or intended use) have to pay an equivalent tax. By this same standard, a tax imposed on income is deemed to be equitable as long as two persons earning the same amount of income during a given time period pay the same amount of income tax.

[10]*The Wealth of Nations,* Book V, Chapter II, Part II (New York: Dutton, 1910).

The larger problem is, of course, that this standard considers only one dimension of the total taxpayer (the standard is best categorized as unidimensional *horizontal equity*), and, in many cases, the dimension given consideration is not the most significant one for purposes of taxation. The problem can be demonstrated easily as follows: Suppose that each of two taxpayers purchases, for personal consumption, a 60-cent loaf of bread on which there is imposed a sales tax or an excise tax of 4 cents. Since each purchaser paid an identical tax on an identical purchase, the tax may be said to be equitable. If we expand the number of variables considered to include incomes, wealth, marital status, physical condition, or any of hundreds of other possible factors common to these two taxpayers, then we may decide that the tax is not truly equitable in any meaningful sense. If one purchaser is married, has ten dependent children, and is spending his or her last dollar to purchase this loaf of bread and feed the children, whereas the other purchaser is single, independently wealthy, and buying the bread to feed the swan, the 4-cent tax on the loaf of bread may be said to be grossly inequitable *in a social sense*.

In an attempt to expand this simple concept of horizontal equity, a related but not necessarily equivalent tax criterion—that of *ability to pay*—has become increasingly popular. The latter criterion can be referred to as *vertical equity*. Roughly speaking, the notion of vertical equity suggests that unequally situated taxpayers should be treated differently. Specifically, it is typically used to suggest that those who have a greater taxpaying ability should pay a larger part of the total taxes so that, in the aggregate, the tax collections will be "equitably" distributed among all taxpayers.

In applying this criterion, two further problems are readily apparent. The first is that, as applied, the concept is again unidimensional. That is, in application a single measure is often used as an appropriate index of ability to pay. Unfortunately, no singular measure is really adequate. The most frequent measure being utilized in this way today is income; the next most frequent is wealth; and the vehicle used to achieve what is presumed to be vertical equity is the progressive tax-rate structure. We shall defer further examination of this aspect of tax equity until Chapter 3, when we can consider the problems of tax-rate structures in greater detail.

The second major problem is the fact that to date no one has discovered a satisfactory method of determining just how differently unequally situated taxpayers ought to be treated. Even if we could measure in some manner each person's ability to pay, we would still be faced with the problem of determining how much more the most able should pay than the least able. Once again, since this objective is typically attacked through the application of a progressive tax-rate structure, we shall postpone consideration of it until Chapter 3. Fortunately, the three other tax criteria proposed by Adam Smith are somewhat easier to explain and are therefore less subject to the wide differences of opinion that exist on the subject of tax equity.

Convenience

Both taxpayers and tax administrators place great stock in administrative simplicity. And in practice this tax criterion is often controlling. Any tax that can be easily assessed, collected, and administered seems to encounter the least opposition. Thus, for example, the retail sales tax has become popular in many jurisdictions at least partially because most taxpayers find it relatively convenient to pay two, three, or four cents per dollar of purchase. Individually these small sums seem immaterial; no formal tax return has to be completed by the purchaser; and few additional records have to be maintained by the vendor.

Even the income tax, which is generally conceded to be a most inconvenient tax, has been made more tolerable by the creation of the standard deduction, withholding, and tax tables. Some experts argue, of course, that we are willing to pay too high a price for convenience in terms of other criteria. Those experts might contend that inconvenience would be a better criterion for tax policy; in other words, a good tax is one that hurts! A majority of the taxpayers, however, would probably not agree with that conclusion.

Certainty

Certainty, like convenience, is high on most taxpayers' list of criteria for the "good" tax. Most citizens like to know, with a reasonable degree of security, just what their tax bill will be, given any set of circumstances. Obviously the existence of certainty also permits a maximum of advance planning. The major problem with using certainty as a criterion for the selection of tax policy is the fact that different economic and social conditions may demand different tax provisions. Therefore, as taxation is increasingly used to achieve nonrevenue objectives, the

criterion of certainty will necessarily diminish in importance—at least from the government point of view.

Tax administrators have attempted to increase the certainty of some aspects of income taxation by providing detailed instructions, advanced rulings, regulations, and other interpretations of the law. Property taxation often is made more palatable by widespread publication of annual tax rates, infrequent property reappraisals, and provisions for review boards. These and other efforts to increase the certainty of many taxes have added measurably to their general acceptance in America.

Historically, the term *certainty* has also meant consistency in the amount of revenue collected. For many years, taxes that produced widely fluctuating amounts of revenue were considered undesirable, whereas those providing stable amounts were favored. Government administrators solely dependent upon revenue collections in the conduct of their operations were particularly concerned about this kind of tax certainty. For the last three decades, however, the notion that tax collections should vary with the economic cycle has become increasingly accepted as the desirable alternative to certainty of collections. This change, obviously, necessitates nontax sources of revenue (including debt financing) during recession periods.

Economy

Undoubtedly, a good tax should involve a minimum cost for compliance and administration. Like many cost studies, however, attempts to quantify the cost of the various taxes have not been particularly successful because of the difficulty of measuring the pertinent data. Press releases about the "cost" of collecting a dollar of any given tax usually refer only to the efficiency of the tax collector's operation. An accurate statement of the cost of a tax would, of course, include the cost of taxpayer compliance as well as the cost of collection and enforcement. It might include even the social costs of mental and emotional strain associated with many tax decisions. The federal income tax is generally conceded to be one of the "cheapest" taxes to collect. Nearly every year the Internal Revenue Service reports that it cost the government less than 50 cents for every $100 of revenue collected. But the statistics supporting this conclusion include only the government's cost of administration, and the complexity of the tax makes compliance costs very high. The total "cost" of the income tax, or any other tax, is anyone's guess.

TABLE **2-4**

TAX OBJECTIVES ON A HISTORICAL BASIS, FEDERAL
GOVERNMENT ONLY

Tax base	Revenue	Regulation	Economic considerations	Social considerations
Income	Primary importance	—	Growing importance	Some importance
Wealth	—	—	—	Major importance
Transactions	—	Some importance	—	—
Excise	Primary importance	Some importance	—	—

Productivity

Although the ability to produce large amounts of
revenue was not included by Adam Smith as one of
the canons of taxation, it is a factor given much
consideration by present-day politicians. Generally,
taxes that cannot produce a significant amount of
revenue are not popular today even if they are equitable, convenient, certain, and economical. As a
practical matter, most taxes could not be both of
limited productivity and economical. A relatively
unproductive tax is typically as expensive to enforce
as a much more productive one. On the state and
local level, many governments are currently examining their tax structures in an attempt to delete the
less productive taxes while increasing other already
productive ones.

Social and economic effects

As noted in Chapter 1, taxation is increasingly being
used to reallocate resources for the achievement of
specified economic and social objectives. For those
persons who approve of this use of taxation, a new
tax criterion becomes immediately evident: Does the
tax (or tax provision) contribute to the rapid and
efficient attainment of the economic or social goal
stipulated for it? The opponents of this criterion
allege that deliberate intervention with free-market
forces through taxation is wholly improper. To this
latter group, the proper tax criterion becomes one of
nonintervention. The tax that disrupts the free-market mechanism the least is considered to be the most
desirable tax.[11]

From a historical perspective, only income and

wealth taxes have been deliberately utilized to any
major degree to achieve stipulated economic and
social objectives—and those experiments are of relatively recent vintage. In summary, tax objectives
(considered in Chapter 1) and tax bases (considered
in Chapter 2) can be related roughly as shown in
Table 2-4. On the state and local level, wealth and
transactions taxes are dominant and are imposed
almost exclusively for revenue reasons. The taxation
of income by state and local governments is a recent
phenomenon of growing importance. As noted earlier, the problems of taxation are complicated by the
fact that conflicting objectives and conflicting criteria
are encountered all too often in establishing tax
policy.

Unfortunately, relatively little research has been
directed toward determining the criteria of the most
desirable tax structure. Empirical measurements of
critical data are all too rare. Most taxes have historically been enacted on the basis of political expedien-
cy, with minimal attention given to the social and
economic consequences of the tax. Thus, taxes have
often been considered desirable as long as they provided adequate revenues with minimal political
discontent.

In the recent past, economists have been devot-
ing an increasing amount of attention to tax-related
problems because they have been consulted by the
many legislators who have become convinced, correctly or erroneously, that the traditional taxes are
already being utilized to their upper limits. Since the
demand for additional government goods and services appears to be increasing, these legislators are
looking for new sources of revenue. The problem is
especially acute at the state and local levels, where
the government is often legally restrained from creating additional debt to pay for the goods and services
provided. As noted in Chapter 1, the federal govern-

[11] For a detailed consideration of the problem, the interested student should
take a course in public finance. There exists a sizable body of literature on
the subject.

ment, unlike all other units in our society, is not so restricted. Nevertheless, members of Congress have also given a great deal of attention to tax considerations, and economists have been particularly active in the formulation of national tax policy.

Public opinion

If public opinion surveys can be relied on as a fair measure of taxpayer sentiment, our present tax structure might be considered in need of change. Possibly the best surveys are those conducted by the Opinion Research Corporation of Princeton, New Jersey, for the Advisory Commission on Intergovernmental Relations (ACIR) each year since 1972.[12] By asking the same question for a period of years, the ACIR can observe trends in attitudes; by asking different questions, they can serve as a sounding board for new tax ideas. A few of their many interesting findings are summarized below.

Until recently, the federal income tax was frequently deemed to be the *fairest* tax; however, both the federal income tax and the state property tax decreased in relative popularity between 1972 and 1974. Those conclusions are apparent when one compares responses to this question: "Here is a list of the major types of taxes in the country today. Which do you think is the fairest?"

Responses	Percent selecting in 1974	1972
Federal income tax	26	36
State income tax	13	11
State property tax	24	33
Local property tax	14	7
Don't know	23	13

In both 1979 and 1974, however, the federal income tax was selected as the *least fair* tax; in five other years the local property tax held that distinction. Those conclusions are suggested by the responses to the question: "Which do you think is the worst tax—that is, the least fair?"

Responses	Percent selecting in 1979	1978	1977	1975	1974	1973	1972
Federal income tax	37	30	28	28	30	30	19
State income tax	8	11	11	11	10	10	13
State sales tax	15	18	17	23	20	20	13
Local property tax	27	32	33	29	28	31	45
Don't know	13	10	11	10	14	11	11

[12]The annual reports for each year are available from the Advisory Commission on Intergovernmental Relations, Washington, D.C. 20575.

If state taxes must be raised, most people prefer an increase in the sales tax to other alternatives. That fact is apparent in the answers to the inquiry: "Suppose your state government must raise taxes substantially, which of these do you think would be the best way to do it?"

Responses	Percent selecting in 1976	1972
State sales tax	45	46
State income tax	25	25
State property tax	10	14
Other	6	5
Don't know	14	10

Prior to 1979 the federal government was generally viewed as giving the most for the money. That conclusion was established by the several answers to this question: "From which level of government do you feel you get the most for your money—federal, state, or local?"

Responses	Percent selecting in 1979	1978	1977	1976	1975	1974	1973
Federal	29	35	36	36	38	29	35
Local	33	26	26	25	25	28	25
State	22	20	20	20	20	24	18
Don't know	16	19	18	19	17	19	22

In general, the population is satisfied with the present size of government spending. However, that conclusion was less valid in 1979 than it was two years earlier, as evidenced by the responses to the question: "Considering all government services on the one hand and taxes on the other, which of the following statements comes closest to your view?"

Responses	Percent selecting in 1979	1977	1975
Keep taxes and services about where they are	46	52	45
Decrease services and taxes	39	31	38
Increase services and raise taxes	6	4	5
No opinion	9	13	12

Students interested in making further comparisons between our actual tax structure and taxpayer preferences are encouraged to consult the annual reports of the Advisory Commission on Intergovernmental Relations.

PROBLEMS

1. Early in the 1960s, a new national party, the Constitutional Party, was formed. Its principal platform was elimination of the federal income tax and substitution of a general sales tax and beneficiary's charges. On what grounds could such a movement be criticized?

2. Large cities often impose a heavy tax (for example, 10 percent) on the cost of hotel and motel rooms. What good reasons can be given in support of such a tax?

3. Two objectives of the U.N. are peaceful settlement of international disputes and encouragement of cultural and economic intercourse between nations and peoples. Under its present charter, the U.N. has no taxing power. Assume that everyone agreed that the U.N. should have the power to tax the citizens of member nations. What problems would arise in selecting a tax base?

4. Some states have recently tried lotteries as a means of raising revenue (primarily for public education). Relate the use of lotteries to the states' objectives and to the problem of selecting a tax base.

5. Governmental units in the United States depend primarily on property, income, and sales taxes to raise revenue. Rate each of these tax bases in terms of Adam Smith's canons of taxation.

6. In the recent past, personal property taxes—that is, taxes on the value of bank accounts, stocks, bonds, furniture, television sets, refrigerators, and similar personal assets—have been disappearing from the list of tax bases used by state and local governments. Why are these particular taxes disappearing despite the fact that almost every state and local government is currently looking for new sources of revenue?

7. Forty-four states now impose an income tax. What practical problem does this present for businesses engaged in interstate commerce? What comparable problem exists with the federal government?

8. The federal estate tax allows a tax credit for a limited amount of inheritance tax paid to a state government. Most states impose an inheritance tax equal to the maximum credit allowed against the federal tax, but only a few states are willing to impose additional state inheritance or estate taxes. Why should this be true?

9. Why has the widespread movement of citizens and businesses to the suburbs caused a major tax problem for large metropolitan cities?

10. What reasons can you see for the federal government to increase its tax collections if the additional tax revenues are to be remitted to the state and local governments? What reason can you see for opposing such a federal-collection–local-spending program?

11. Some tax scholars have noted that as the economy moves from the very primitive to the highly industrialized state, tax systems typically evolve from poll taxes, to property taxes, to flat-rate income taxes, to graduated income taxes. Furthermore, these scholars suggest, at the various stages of economic progress each of these taxes can be said to approximate some social measure of "ability to pay."

    a. Explain how a poll tax or a property tax might reflect an ability to pay.

    b. What sociological factors augur well for this sequence in tax systems?

12. Proposals to eliminate the federal income tax have been made. For each of the alternative bases listed below, indicate briefly the major political and economic problems that would arise in shifting to such a base at the federal level.

a. Wealth tax

b. Employment taxes

c. Excise taxes

13. In terms of revenue yield, which tax base is generally most important at the federal level of government? At the state level? At the local level?

14. Which tax base is growing most rapidly both in terms of absolute dollars collected and in relative significance at the federal level of government? Is this trend likely to continue? Why or why not?

15. Define both horizontal and vertical equity.

16. If Taxpayer X has a taxable income of $10,000 and pays an income tax of $2,000, and Taxpayer Y has a taxable income of $50,000 and pays an income tax of $8,000, what statement can you make concerning horizontal equity in that taxing jurisdiction? Concerning vertical equity?

17. What do salt, white phosphorus, motor fuels, tobacco, and alcoholic beverages have in common as far as a tax base is concerned?

18. If the retail sale of marijuana is legalized in the United States, what good reason(s) do you have for predicting that it will become a common tax base?

19. Although just less than one-half of those surveyed for the ACIR in 1979 agreed that government taxes and services were at a preferred level, this conclusion was not shared equally by everyone. Which of the following groups would you guess to be the strongest supporter of the idea that we should "increase services and raise taxes?" Give reasons for your choice.

a. Persons with less than a high school education

b. High school graduates with no college education

c. Persons with some college education, but no degree

d. College graduates

20. People who own their own homes have views that differ strongly from those who rent their homes when it comes to the best method to increase state revenues in times of need. Which group, owners or renters, would you expect to be the strongest supporter of the sales tax? Why?

21. Our educational background seems to influence the way we feel about different taxes. Which of the following groups of persons do you suppose think that the state sales tax is the *fairest* tax of all? Give reasons for your choice.

a. Those with less than a high school education

b. High school graduates with no college education

c. Those with some college education

SUPPLEMENTAL PROBLEMS

22. Congress made "buttlegging" or smuggling large quantities of cigarettes across state lines a federal crime in 1978.

a. Why do people "smuggle" cigarettes?

b. Why was buttlegging made a federal crime?

c. What broader implications do these facts portend for tax policy generally?

23. Per capita state and local tax collections vary significantly among the 50 states, from a high of $1,896 to a low of $454. What two states would you guess to have the highest per capita collections? The lowest per capita collections? Verify your guesses.

24. The maximum wage or salary subject to social security taxes, as well as the

maximum social security tax payable by an employee, has increased dramatically over the past 40 years, as demonstrated in the following table:

Year	Maximum base	Maximum tax
1937	$ 3,000	$ 30
1959	4,800	120
1972	9,000	468
1979	22,900	1,404
1980	25,900	1,588

Based on legislation passed in 1977, those maximums will increase even more dramatically in the next 10 years. In 1987 the maximum base is scheduled to be $42,600; the maximum tax, $3,046. Explain these large increases. What political response do you predict for the recent changes? (Watch your newspaper for details!)

25. Do you think that most Americans would prefer lower taxes (for themselves) to a grossly simplified tax system? Comment on the significance of the option you deem to be the more popular. Can you locate any evidence to support your own conclusions? That is, are your opinions shared by many other people?

tax rates

After a government has decided what items or events it will use as a tax base, it must determine what tax rate(s) it will apply to each tax base. Any one of three fundamentally different tax-rate structures—"proportional," "progressive," or "regressive"—could be employed. In this chapter, we shall first define the terms proportional, progressive, and regressive. Then, because progressive rates are associated with the personal income tax in this country and because progressive taxation has engendered wide debate and wider misunderstanding, we shall discuss briefly a few of the major arguments about it.

Following an initial selection of tax rates and tax bases, most governmental units seem to spend a disproportionately large amount of their time and effort discussing the advisability of modifying either the rates or the bases. While these bodies may, from time to time, increase or decrease an existing tax rate, they seldom switch from one basic rate structure to another. Similarly, though they frequently make minor modifications of existing tax bases, they only rarely delete an old tax or add an entirely new one. During their deliberations, however, legislators, their constituents, lobby groups, and the general press make frequent references to the proportional, progressive, or regressive nature of the various taxes in force and the new ones being considered. As an integral part of the emotional political dialogue, the references often confuse the issues.

DEFINITION OF TERMS

In the simplest way, a tax can be defined as the product of the tax base and the tax rate. In equation form, then,

$$T = B \times R$$

where T stands for tax, B for tax base, and R for tax rate. By elementary algebraic manipulation, this equation can, of course, be rearranged to read:

$$R = \frac{T}{B}$$

Procedural definitions

"Proportional," "progressive," and "regressive" can be defined readily in terms of the preceding equation. If the ratio T/B remains constant for all possible values of B, then the tax rate R is *proportional*. If the ratio T/B increases as B increases and decreases as B decreases, then the tax rate R is *progressive*. Finally, if the ratio T/B increases as B decreases and decreases as B increases, then the tax rate R is *regressive*.

In other words, when defined in this manner, a tax is proportional if one flat rate is equally applicable to every measure of the tax base. The largest number of our common taxes are in this category. For example, sales, real property, personal property, customs, and excise taxes are generally imposed with a proportional tax rate. If, on the other hand, a higher tax rate is applied to increasingly larger values of the tax base, then the tax is progressive. Income, estate, and gift taxes are typically imposed with a progressive tax rate structure. To the best of our knowledge, no U.S. tax has been imposed with a regressive rate structure, *defined as it is here*.

Limitations of these definitions

The preceding definitions are based on the premise that the most appropriate basis for comparison is the tax base itself. Thus, for sales taxation, only the amount involved in a *taxable sale* is deemed to be included in the denominator of the ratio *T/B*; for income taxation, only *taxable income* is included. As the terms "proportional," "progressive," and "regressive" have been used in the popular press and in political propaganda, however, they are not defined in this manner. Rather, they are defined, albeit loosely, by the following ratio:

Aggregate tax liability over some time period

Some measure of ability to pay, frequently personal income

If the ratio above is constant, even roughly so, for most values of, say, personal income, common usage of the terms would classify the tax as a proportional tax. If the ratio tends to decrease with increasing values of personal income, then the tax is alleged to be regressive. Although this alternative definition lacks the precision of the earlier one, it may be the more meaningful of the two. Without doubt, it is the one implicit in virtually all nonacademic discussions of tax matters. Unfortunately, it is a very crude measure for several reasons.

Incidence problems

The first major problem encountered in any precise application of the popular definition of tax-rate structures is our inability to determine who *finally* pays most taxes. The assumption typically postulated by the general public is that the tax is assignable to (borne by) the person who pays it. For example, the retail sales tax is assumed to be borne by the purchaser of the taxed good or service; the personal

income tax is assumed to be borne by the immediate taxpayer.

Several questions can be raised about the validity of this common assumption. Suppose, for example, that a man decides to purchase a new automobile. Because of the competitive nature of the market at this time, he is able to arrange a deal whereby the seller of the car agrees to "pay the sales tax" via a reduction in the price of the car. Thus the buyer, instead of paying, say, $5,000 plus sales tax, effectively pays $4,750 plus a $250 sales tax. If we could establish that the market price for the car in question actually was $5,000, exclusive of the tax (a very difficult question to establish in fact), the *initial* effect of the transaction would be to shift the retail sales tax from the car buyer to the car seller, even though the tax was legally and technically imposed on the purchaser. Even then we cannot safely conclude that the sales tax has simply been shifted from the purchaser to the seller of the car. To reach an accurate conclusion, we would have to determine if it was possible for the car dealer to shift the tax to: labor, via substandard wages; suppliers of capital, via reduced interest payments; other less-informed purchasers, via higher prices; or some other party, in some other manner. Obviously an accurate answer to these questions remains largely out of reach because of our necessarily limited knowledge of the real world. The complexities of measuring all the pertinent variables make such measurements practically impossible.

Given the state of relative ignorance in which we live, it is not surprising that tax experts are in less than complete accord on their assumptions about tax incidence.[1] And, unfortunately, far too many persons make decisions about taxation based on totally erroneous premises about the incidence of many, if not most, taxes. One often reads, for example, statements suggesting that middle- and upper-class property owners are about to be ambushed by unduly heavy taxes on real property. The premise behind these statements rests squarely on the assumption that the real property tax is borne entirely by the landlord. It seems more probable that the renter pays most of the landlord's property taxes, even though the form of the rent payment camouflages this fact. This is especially likely in a period of rapidly expand-

---

[1] For example, see Joseph Pechman and Benjamin Okner, *Who Bears the Tax Burden?* (Washington, D.C.: The Brookings Institution, 1974). Also compare Arnold C. Harberger, "The Incidence of the Corporation Income Tax," *The Journal of Political Economy,* 70 (June, 1962), pp. 215–40, and Marian Krzyzaniak and Richard A. Musgrave, *The Shifting of the Corporate Income Tax* (Baltimore: The Johns Hopkins Press, 1963).

ing population (and, therefore, of great demand) coupled with a limited supply of real property.

If, then, we accept the "popular" definition of proportional, progressive, and regressive as applied to taxation, we must understand that our conclusions can be no more valid than our data are accurate. One of the most complicated and unresolved issues in all of taxation is the determination of the final incidence of any tax. Observe that it is necessary to determine who finally must "bear" each tax before we can accurately determine the numerator of the ratio

$$\frac{\text{Aggregate tax liability over some time period}}{\text{Some measure of ability to pay, frequently personal income}}$$

Ability to pay

The second major problem encountered in any precise application of this popular definition of tax-rate structures lies in our failure to find a truly adequate measure of ability to pay taxes. Progressive-regressive notions have achieved their greatest application in statements related to welfare economics. For example, it is frequently argued that retail sales and (most) excise taxes are regressive because they require a greater relative contribution by the poor than by the rich. They do so, it is explained, because poorer persons are forced to spend a greater percentage of their income for consumer items (which items typically are subject to either sales or excise taxes or both) than persons with larger incomes.

If the assumptions about spending patterns are valid, then, of course, the conclusion of regressivity is also valid. Many persons unwittingly go one step further, however, and presume that regressivity necessarily fails to conform to generally accepted notions of ability to pay. This last conclusion requires a further assumption—that personal income is a meaningful measure of the ability to pay taxes.

Without a doubt, annual income is one of the major ingredients of a person's ability to do anything of a financial nature, including the payment of taxes. However, it is certainly not the only ingredient. The amount of a person's accumulated wealth and his or her prospect of earning equal or greater sums in the future are two other items of major significance. Finally, the taxpayer's age, marital status, health, and number of dependents are usually of real importance.

In short, before it is possible to determine whether a tax *is* regressive relative to the taxpayer's ability to pay, we must find some comprehensive measure of taxpaying ability. Although personal income is frequently used in this manner, it is, as we have said, a less than comprehensive measure.

Several of the considerations deemed pertinent to the ability-to-pay concept have been incorporated into our Internal Revenue Code, in its definition of *taxable income,* and will be examined in greater detail in Parts Two and Three. Unfortunately, these modifications add one final complication to the definition of the terms "proportional," "progressive," and "regressive" as applied to taxation.

This complication can be readily understood in terms of an illustration common to much of the literature that has grown up around the progressive tax controversy. Many writers take care to point out that inclusion of a provision for a personal exemption makes a progressive tax of an otherwise proportional income tax.[2] The arithmetic of their conclusion is simple. Suppose, for example, that country *A* imposes a (flat) tax of 10 percent on all income in excess of $500 per year earned by each of its citizens. The progressive nature of this otherwise proportional tax is shown in Table 3-1. In other words, this tax is a proportional (constant 10 percent) tax on *taxable*

[2]For example, see Walter J. Blum and Harry Kalven, Jr., *The Uneasy Case for Progressive Taxation* (Chicago: The University of Chicago Press, 1953), p. 4.

TABLE **3-1**
THE PROGRESSIVE EFFECT OF THE PERSONAL EXEMPTION

	Taxpayer 1	Taxpayer 2	Taxpayer 3
Income earned	$500	$1,000	$1,500
Less $500 exemption	500	500	500
Taxable income (tax base)	$ 0	$ 500	$1,000
Times tax rate	.10	.10	.10
Equals tax liability	$ 0	$ 50	$ 100
Effective tax rate (tax/income)	0/500 = 0%	50/1,000 = 5%	100/1,500 = 6⅔%

income (defined as all income over $500) but a progressive (increasing percentage) tax on total income. Whether this tax is judged to be proportional or progressive depends on which kind of income is used as the denominator of the ratio to determine the effective tax rate. The only important point of the illustration is very simple: The meanings of the terms "proportional," "progressive," and "regressive," as applied to tax-rate structures, are often elusive, and persons who use the terms to advocate a particular position frequently fail to articulate the assumptions implicit in their analysis. This failure, in turn, often results in misapplication, misstatement, and general misunderstanding.

In conclusion, the student should be aware that in most discussions about progressive and regressive taxation, the writer often assumes both (1) that the tax is not shifted—that is, the tax is presumed to be borne by the party it is legally imposed on—and (2) that the appropriate measure for determining progressivity (or regressivity) is some vaguely defined but apparently "generally accepted" notion of personal income. From this frame of reference, it is commonly believed that the U.S. personal income tax and the estate and gift tax are highly progressive, whereas most other taxes (those typically imposed at a uniform rate) are regressive.

MARGINAL, AVERAGE, AND EFFECTIVE RATES

Other distinctions in tax-rate structures are the differences among marginal, average, and effective tax rates. First we shall distinguish between marginal and average rates; next we shall consider the differences between the nominal-average and the real- or effective-average rate.

Marginal-average distinctions

The *marginal* tax rate is the rate that would be applicable to the next unit of any tax base. For any tax that is proportional, in a technical sense of that term, the marginal tax rate is (obviously) the basic tax rate. For any tax that is either progressive or regressive, in a technical sense, the marginal tax rate can be determined only if one knows both (1) the rate structure and (2) the aggregate measure of the tax base prior to considering any incremental amount. The *average* tax rate is simply an arithmetic expression of an aggregate tax liability divided by a given amount of a tax base.

To demonstrate the difference between the marginal and average tax rates, let us consider the present United States income tax on single individuals. The current tax rate structure applicable to individual taxpayers is reprinted in Appendix A. A single (unmarried) individual who reports a $12,900 taxable income has a marginal tax rate of 26 percent; this means, of course, that an increase in taxable income of, say, $100, would result in the taxpayer's paying $26 of that additional $100 to the government in personal income tax. A $100 increase in the taxable income of a single taxpayer reporting an $81,800 taxable income would result in the taxpayer's paying $68 of that additional $100 in personal income tax because he or she is in the 68 percent marginal tax bracket. On the other hand, the average tax rate of the former individual would be approximately 16 percent (that is, $2,059 tax liability divided by $12,900 taxable income), whereas the average tax rate of the latter individual would be approximately 46 percent ($37,677 divided by $81,800). Obviously, the marginal tax rate is always greater than the average tax rate for any progressive tax after the first step in that progression.

One common misunderstanding about the federal taxation of personal incomes can be clarified by this difference between marginal and average tax rates. Not infrequently one hears otherwise knowledgeable people relate the tale of someone who experienced a cut in income because of a pay raise that "threw him into the next tax bracket." The marginal tax rates always apply only to the *additional* dollars of income in each new and higher bracket, not to the aggregate income earned. Therefore, as long as the marginal tax rates do not exceed 100 percent, it is patently impossible to reap a cut in income from a pay raise.[3]

At present, the highest federal income tax rate applicable to income earned by individuals is 70 percent. Therefore, even if a taxpayer is in the highest possible tax bracket, a $1 pay increase will always yield no less than $.30 after taxes. A crude graphical presentation of the present marginal and average federal income tax rates, applicable to the separate return of a single individual, is shown in Figure 3-1.

It is important for the student to grasp the significance of the marginal tax rate early in studying taxation, because it is the marginal rate that determines

---

[3]Use of tax tables, an administrative simplification that eliminates the multiplication of rate times base by assigning a single tax to a bracket or range of income, can on rare occasions give a slightly higher tax when the pay raise is very small. Tax tables for 1979 are reproduced in Appendix B.

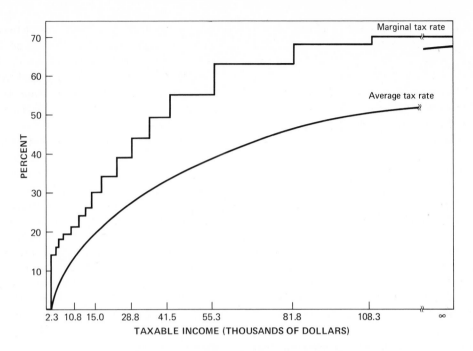

FIGURE **3-1** Current Average and Marginal Federal Personal
Income Tax Rates for Single Persons

how intelligent taxpayers act in many circumstances. In an important sense, the marginal tax rate is to business what the law of gravity is to physics: Tax bases tend to seek their lowest level just as water does! In other words, taxpayers tend to arrange their financial affairs so that any tax base will be subject to tax at the lowest possible marginal tax rate. It is this fundamental rule that causes (1) many individuals to create short-term trusts for the benefit of their children or parents (and thereby substitute the lower marginal income tax rate of their children or their parents for their own marginal rate); (2) individuals to incorporate their sole proprietorships and partnerships (and thereby substitute the lower marginal income tax rate of the corporation for the higher marginal income tax rate of the proprietor and/or partner); and (3) individuals to convert what would otherwise be ordinary income into either personal service income or capital gain (and thereby substitute the lower marginal income tax rate applicable to either personal service income or capital gain for the higher marginal income tax rate that would otherwise apply to their ordinary taxable income). Although the multitude of important details pertinent to each of the managerial actions suggested in the preceding sentence is far beyond comprehension at this juncture, it is not too early to grasp the significance of the marginal tax rate to numerous business decisions. Relative to the income tax, financial affairs should nearly always be arranged to report incremental units of taxable income at such times and/or in such ways as to allow the application of the lowest possible marginal tax rates, other things being equal, whereas incremental units of deductions and losses should be reported at such times and/or in such ways as to allow the application of the highest possible marginal tax rates, other things being equal.

Nominal-average and real-average distinctions

The preceding discussion of average tax rates is based on the premise that the pertinent comparison is that existing between the aggregate tax liability and the tax base determined in a technical way; that is, using a technical rather than a popular definition of the tax base. As explained earlier in this chapter, the popular descriptions of various tax rates are often significantly different from the technical definitions. In the same manner, average tax rates are frequently computed using a popular surrogate for a more technical tax base. The average rate determined in a technical sense, as illustrated in Figure 3-1, might better be labeled the *nominal-average* rate.

For certain purposes, such as making a social value judgment about our existing tax provisions, an average tax rate might better be determined by dividing the aggregate tax liability by an adjusted tax base.

The appropriateness of the adjustments depends on the purpose of the calculation. Thus, for example, if one wanted to know an individual's income tax based on a real or economic measure of income, rather than on a technical tax base called taxable income, it would be appropriate to divide the individual's aggregate income tax liability by his or her economic or real income.

To illustrate the notion of a real-average (some tax scholars prefer to call this an effective-average or an actual-average) tax rate, consider the calculation pertinent to a single individual who receives a $108,-300 salary and $100,000 in tax-exempt state-bond interest each year. Ignoring many additional details, and simply assuming that this individual's $108,300 salary is equal to his or her $108,300 taxable income, we could readily determine that the nominal-average tax rate was 51 percent (that is, $55,697 aggregate tax liability divided by $108,300 taxable income). On the other hand, this same individual's real- or effective-average tax rate would be closer to 27 percent (that is, $55,697 aggregate tax liability divided by $208,300 real or economic income). As a practical matter, there are many differences between income as commonly perceived by the average person and taxable income as defined in the Internal Revenue Code. We shall examine most of the important differences in a technical way in the remainder of this book; other authors have approached the same differences in more popular literature.[4]

In a well-documented study, Joseph A. Pechman prepared a chart that not only demonstrated admirably the substantial difference between the nominal-average and the real-average[5] rates in 1973 for federal income-tax purposes but also revealed the major reasons for those differences. (See Figure 3-2.) Although in 1973 the facts apparently supported the conclusion that our federal income tax was definitely not as progressive as the nominal-average rate structure made it appear, our personal income tax is frequently attacked (and sometimes supported) on the grounds that it *is* a highly progressive tax!

A Treasury Department study submitted to Congress in conjunction with the initial proposals for the Tax Reform Act of 1969 included another interesting graph, which clearly demonstrated not only that the effective tax rates of the higher income level persons were on the average relatively low, but also that a great deal of interpersonal inequity existed at the higher income levels. (See Figure 3-3.) This chart was prepared before enactment of the 1969 Act;

[4] For example, see Philip M. Stern, *The Rape of the Taxpayer* (New York: Random House, 1973).
[5] Pechman labels this the "actual effective rates." See Figure 3-2.

FIGURE **3-2**   Influence of Various Provisions on Effective Rates of
Federal Individual Income Tax, 1969 Act[a]

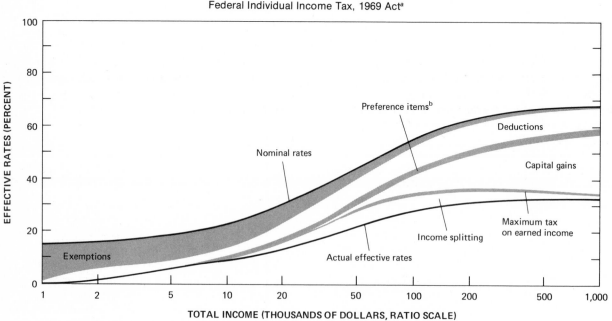

[a] Rates, exemptions, and other provisions of the Tax Reform Act of 1969 scheduled to apply to calendar year 1973 incomes.
[b] Preference items as defined by the Tax Reform Act of 1969, except excluded net long-term capital gains.
SOURCE: Joseph A. Pechman, *Federal Tax Policy* (Rev. ed.) (Washington, D.C.: The Brookings Institution, 1971), p. 69. Reprinted by permission.

FIGURE **3-3**   Tax Inequities: Illustrated by the Percent of Returns in Each Income Class Paying Various Different Rates of Tax

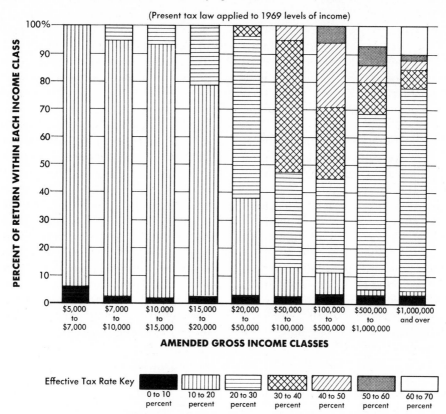

(Present tax law applied to 1969 levels of income)

Effective Tax Rate Key

| 0 to 10 percent | 10 to 20 percent | 20 to 30 percent | 30 to 40 percent | 40 to 50 percent | 50 to 60 percent | 60 to 70 percent |

SOURCE: *Tax Reform Studies and Proposals*, U.S. Treasury Department, Part 1, February 5, 1969, p. 96.

therefore, the reference to "present tax law" must be interpreted for the most part as the tax law applicable to years ending prior to January 1, 1970. The chart demonstrates, for example, that approximately 10 percent of the taxpayers earning $1 million or more a year paid an average tax of between 60 and 70 percent, approximately 70 percent of the persons in that same income class paid between 20 and 30 percent, and another 4 percent paid from 0 to 10 percent. It is hoped that a comparable chart will soon be made available for years after the 1978 Revenue Act. If we have made any progress in achieving horizontal equity, it would quickly be apparent in such a chart.

PROGRESSIVE TAXATION: PROS AND CONS

The multiple considerations that must be carefully evaluated in making sound judgments about the desirability or undesirability of nominally progres-

sive tax-rate structures cannot be examined adequately in this introductory text. Thus, we have elected simply to introduce a few of the major arguments generally debated in such an undertaking. We urge interested students to make their own studies of this fascinating aspect of taxation.[6]

Some arguments for progression

Scholars have found that the United States taxpayer typically is not deeply concerned about the distribution of the national "tax burden" and that he or she has only a hazy notion of what progressive taxation really means.[7] Our citizens do seem to agree that the rich should pay more in taxes than the poor, but this conclusion does not necessitate a progressive rate

[6] Although we do not wholly agree with their conclusions, we strongly recommend that such a study begin with a review of the Blum and Kalven work, *op. cit.*, because it in turn references most of the scholarly work on this subject.

[7] See Blum and Kalven, *op. cit.*, 1st Phoenix ed., 1963, "Introduction—1963," p. x.

schedule. Observe, for example, that a flat 15-percent (proportional) income tax would take $750 from the $5,000-a-year earner and $1,500 from the $10,000-a-year earner. What progression requires, of course, is a *relatively* greater contribution from the richer person; that is, the $10,000 earner is required to pay *more than twice* what the $5,000 earner pays in taxes. This concept has been defended on several grounds including economic ones.

ECONOMIC GROWTH AND STABILITY   In the relatively recent past, a number of economists have argued that the progressive aspect of our personal income tax has contributed to the economic growth and stability of this country. Since income tax collections and effective rates tend to vary directly with the economic cycle, the progressive rate proponents observe that this factor combined with a relatively constant level of government expenditures provides an automatic stimulus in the recession phase of the cycle and a deterrent against inflation in the recovery phase. Governmental units not forced to balance budgets on an annual basis need not be hampered by the revenue fluctuations as long as they can find alternative sources of funds (usually through increased borrowing) in the low-revenue years. Thus, the progressive personal income tax has been viewed as something of an automatic, compensatory mechanism that contributes to the maintenance of reasonable economic stability.

Because a progressive income tax, by definition, requires a relatively greater contribution from the high-income earner, and because the high-income earner is believed to have a relatively low marginal propensity to consume, the progressive tax has also been alleged to increase net consumption within a nation. That is, by redistributing income from high- to low-income earners, the progressive income tax is said to increase the average propensity to consume. Most economists have argued that this net increase in consumption is important to any nation in an economic depression. Many economists have pointed out that this same increase in consumption is necessary to maintain full employment in a mature economy, which would otherwise tend to "underconsume." Still others have contended that wealth redistribution is desirable in and of itself.

REDUCING ECONOMIC INEQUALITY   A progressive tax necessarily alters the pretax distribution of income and/or wealth within a nation. Henry Simons has argued most forcibly that this must ultimately be the basis on which the case for a progressive tax rests:

"The case for drastic progression in taxation must be rested on the case against inequality—on the ethical or aesthetic judgment that the prevailing distribution of wealth and income reveals a degree (and/or kind) of inequality which is distinctly evil or unlovely."[8] The opponents of progression generally are quick to equate the redistributive aspect of a progressive tax with the equalitarianism of the socialist and communist ideologies. The issue thus becomes one of normative judgments about the degree of inequality deemed desirable (or undesirable) within a nation.

To date it would appear that our apparently progressive income and estate and gift taxes have done relatively little in the way of actually redistributing existing fortunes. On the other hand, the mere existence of these taxes has made necessary the careful tax planning that is now common to all families of substantial means.[9] Since our progressive taxes have never been based *overtly* on any clearly specified social objectives of wealth redistribution, it is impossible to gauge the efficiency of this method of achieving such theoretically possible objectives. Suffice it to note here that a great deal of basic research must be done in this area before we can reach any meaningful conclusions.

MINIMIZING AGGREGATE SACRIFICE   Although the classical arguments have lost popular support in the recent past, many early tax scholars attempted to justify progressive tax-rate schedules on the premise that only this form of taxation could minimize the aggregate sacrifice associated with the collection of any given amount of tax revenues. The critical tenet in this argument is that increasing income yields a decreasing utility to its possessor.[10] From this observation, many persons have concluded that a minimum *aggregate* sacrifice could be achieved by taxing most heavily those who have the most.

Several variations and conditions of the minimum-aggregate-sacrifice notion have been articulated in the professional literature, and our limited knowledge of utility curves justifies the skepticism that is now generally associated with that notion. Of particular importance to this conclusion is the observation that although money (and many other things)

[8]Henry Simons, *Personal Income Taxation* (Chicago: The University of Chicago Press, 1938), pp. 18–19.

[9]For some interesting details on the real effect of the estate tax, see Gerald R. Jantscher, *Trust and Estate Taxation* (Washington, D.C.: The Brookings Institution, 1967), or Carl S. Shoup, *Federal Estate and Gift Taxes* (Washington, D.C.: The Brookings Institution, 1966).

[10]In other words, the 5,001st dollar of any person's income is presumed to yield a greater utility than the 10,001st dollar of income. That dollar, in turn, provides greater utility than the 50,001st dollar of income.

may indeed be subject to decreasing utility generally, any comparison of precise interpersonal utility curves would of necessity be wholly speculative. It is hardly likely that every person views the utility of each dollar of income or wealth in the same way. Some persons appear to be wholly content with relatively small incomes, whereas other persons are thoroughly dissatisfied with much larger ones. Validation of the minimum-sacrifice concept would require that all people have identical utility curves, among other things.[11]

PART OF A TAX SYSTEM   Disregarding the more academically refined, theoretical justifications of progressive taxes, several scholars have emphasized the fact that such taxes are best justified as one part of a greater tax system. These persons point out that many of our taxes, including retail sales taxes and most property taxes, are generally conceded to be regressive relative to income. Therefore, they say, the country also imposes some deliberately progressive taxes so that the overall tax system may be something less than predominantly regressive.

Like so many theoretical questions relating to taxation, this conclusion needs empirical support. The major problem is that of tax incidence. Since we cannot determine unequivocally who ultimately bears the cost of any particular tax, we cannot say what each person's aggregate tax burden is. Therefore, we cannot determine empirically whether or not the whole tax system is regressive, proportional, or progressive in relation to income.[12]

Recently, however, Pechman and Okner completed a very thorough study of this problem, which removes some doubts about the distribution of the tax burden in the United States.[13] This study is unique on two counts. First, their conclusions are based on economic information of 72,000 American families. Second, the authors did not rely on a single set of assumptions about the incidence of the various federal and local taxes. Instead, they used eight combinations of assumptions about the incidence of various taxes.

The results of that study are shown in Figure 3-4. Although the data are for the year 1966, the changes in our national tax structure since that date would have only a limited effect on the results. Those figures show that for about 87 percent of the population the effective rates for *all* taxes are generally proportional. The most progressive set of assumptions is that the corporate income tax is borne equally by investors and individuals with property income, that property taxes on land and land improvements are borne entirely by the property owners, and that payroll taxes are borne entirely by employers. The least progressive assumptions are that 50 percent of the corporate income tax is passed on to consumers while the remaining half falls on property income generally, that the property tax on land falls on the owner but that the tax on land improvements is passed on to the consumer or lessee, and that 50 percent of payroll taxes are passed on to consumers.

If one agrees with the least progressive assumptions, the effective total tax rate is somewhat regressive for most taxpayers. At the other extreme, the most progressive assumptions result in only a mildly progressive rate for most taxpayers. The highly regressive rates for the low income family are due in large measure to the annual nature of the tax. The temporarily unemployed and some elderly taxpayers will have very little income for a given year yet still pay a sizable tax on their savings, which are used for consumption.

This study also reached two other important conclusions. When state and local taxes are considered alone, the effective rates are slightly regressive for all taxpayers (except that the most progressive assumptions result in progressive rates for the very wealthy). If one considers only federal taxes, the effective rates are generally progressive for all taxpayers. Thus, without a federal income tax that results in progressive effective rates for most taxpayers, the tax system in the United States would be a regressive system without regard to the assumptions made about tax incidence. These findings, the authors submit, are a most persuasive argument for a progressive federal income tax.

ABILITY TO PAY   The popular support given progressive taxation in this country has rallied behind the key phrase "ability to pay." What the phrase may lack in academic precision it makes up in emotive appeal. In its most elementary usage it connotes that persons having more accessible dollars, more wherewithal to pay, ought to pay more in taxes than those with a lesser number of dollars. Whether or not those

[11] As a matter of fact, validation of this thesis would seem to require that no less than seven postulates be satisfied; on *a priori* grounds we conclude that less than half of them are in fact satisfied. See Elmer D. Fagan, "Recent and Contemporary Theories of Progressive Taxation," *Journal of Political Economy,* XLVI (August, 1937).

[12] Studies based on assumed incidence have, of course, been published. For example, see Rufus D. Tucker, "Distribution of Tax Burdens in 1948," *National Tax Journal,* IV (1951), pp. 269–86; or R. A. Musgrave, "Distribution of Tax Payments by Income Groups: A Review," *Proceedings of the Forty-Fifth Annual Conference (1952) of the National Tax Association,* pp. 179–95.

[13] Pechman and Okner, *op. cit.* (Note 1 *supra*)

FIGURE **3-4**   Effective Rates of Federal, State, and Local Taxes
under the Most and Least Progressive Incidence Variants,
by Population Percentile, 1966

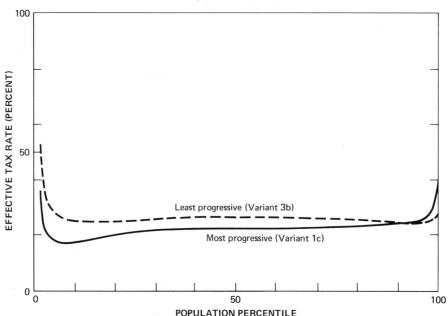

SOURCE: Pechman and Okner, *Who Bears the Tax Burden?* (The Brookings Institution
Washington, D.C., 1974), p. 5.

who frequently invoke this phrase intend that those with more dollars should pay *relatively* more in taxes is often unclear. Those who do so advocate typically defend their viewpoint by economic growth and stability arguments, income and wealth redistribution arguments, aggregate sacrifice notions (often discussed in terms of decreasing marginal utilities), or some other arguments not discussed here. Regardless of its precise meaning, the phrase "ability to pay" has become so widely accepted it is frequently cited as an authoritative justification for progressive taxation.[14]

Some arguments against progression

Not all students of taxation have argued in favor of progressive taxation. Like the arguments for it, the arguments against progression range from the academic to the highly emotive. Some of the more colorful, rhetorical attacks against progressive taxation warn against communism, observing that the *Communist Manifesto* predicted early the use of a graduated (progressive) income tax to achieve a transfer of capital from the bourgeoisie to the proletariat.[15] Other arguments against progression have been based on economic grounds.

THE QUESTION OF INCENTIVES   The assumption of profit maximization has, until quite recently, been considered central to most discussions of free-enterprise economies. Since a progressive income tax by definition takes an increasing share of larger and larger incomes, this form of taxation has been alleged to have a particularly detrimental effect on the incentives to work, to save, and to invest. The charge has been that business (or economic) decisions must be based on a marginal analysis, and the marginal profit analysis that encompasses a progressive income tax inevitably yields a decreasing profit margin. Combining this fact with a subjective judgment about "natural tendencies" against increased work, the critics conclude that the net effect of the progressive tax is to reduce the productivity of the economy. Furthermore, say these critics, the effect is particularly

[14]See, for example, Edwin Griswold, "Can We Limit Taxes to 25 Per Cent?" *Atlantic Monthly* (August, 1952). See also Louis Eisenstein, *The Ideologies of Taxation* (New York: Ronald Press, 1961).

[15]See Homer D. Crotty, "A Few Observations: The Communist Manifesto in America," *American Bar Association Journal,* 37 (January, 1951), pp. 413–16.

severe for those who are financially able to save and to invest—a select and important sector in the capital creation process.

Other scholars, however, argue that the net effect of the progressive income tax on incentives could be just the opposite of that suggested above. If the individual's goals are cast in terms of an absolute amount of after-tax income, then the progressive income tax would serve only to stimulate still greater effort to achieve the goals established.

Several researchers have attempted to study the possible *disincentive* effect of the income tax. One of the more recent studies is particularly interesting: The investigators found that the most highly paid executives (and, therefore, those subject to the highest marginal tax rates) were influenced only very slightly in their attitude toward more work by the existence of the progressive income tax. On the other hand, they discovered that lower paid executives seemed to be more directly and negatively influenced (against more work) by the tax. Obviously, this finding is not consistent with the usual assumption.[16]

Other scholars have been more concerned with the tax effect on the incentives to save and to invest. Although each of their studies discusses the apparent implication of a progressive tax, each has some problem in measuring the real effect in the everyday world. To date, while no definitive statement about the net effect can be made, it seems safe to conclude that the arguments concerned with the incentive questions have often been either overstated or based on doubtful hypotheses.

POLITICAL IRRESPONSIBILITY   During the debate over the Sixteenth Amendment to the Constitution (the amendment that made the personal income tax legal), the opponents of the progressive income tax frequently argued that approval of it would contribute significantly to political irresponsibility. Since the relatively poor majority are theoretically free, under a graduated income tax, to impose unlimited taxes on the rich minority, the early opponents of the tax forecast bitter class warfare following enactment. Now, many years later, it appears clear that these fears too were largely unfounded.

[16] See Robin Barlow, Harvey E. Brazer, and James N. Morgan, *Economic Behavior of the Affluent* (Washington, D.C.: The Brookings Institution, 1966). For other similar investigations see Lewis H. Kimmel, *Taxes and Economic Incentives* (The Brookings Institution, 1950), and J. Keith Butters, Lawrence E. Thompson, and Lynn L. Bollinger, *Investment by Individuals* (Cambridge: Harvard University, Graduate School of Business Administration, 1953).

A less catastrophic version of the same theme opined that the tax would contribute significantly to excessive government spending. The premise on which this notion is based is an interesting inversion of the minimum-sacrifice idea mentioned earlier. That is, since the income taxed away from the more wealthy is presumed to carry a relatively low utility, the chance of the government collecting (and spending) unduly large sums of money was presumed to be greater than could have occurred under a proportional (or regressive) tax, where the sacrifice (and, therefore, political resistance) would have been greater. The comments that were pertinent to the minimum-sacrifice arguments are equally applicable here. In addition, it is possible that the richer minority tend to be politicians (or to control politicians), and it seems unlikely that they would ever overtax themselves.

EXCESSIVE COMPLEXITY   Finally, progressive taxation has been opposed as being unduly complex. As noted in Chapter 2, both the taxpayer and the tax administrator tend to prefer the simple to the complex tax. The complexities arise from two primary factors.

First, a progressive tax must apply to a tax base that cannot readily be subdivided by the taxpayer in order to avoid the effective progression. For example, if the retail sales tax were made sufficiently progressive, the purchaser would find it economical to make numerous small purchases rather than a few large ones. In addition, the tax base for a progressive tax must be one that the taxpayer can calculate with a reasonable degree of accuracy and with minimal additional record keeping; at the same time, it must be subject to verification by the taxing authorities. As a consequence of these administrative requirements, progressive tax rates have seldom been applied to anything other than income and estates and gifts.

The second complexity is that a taxpayer may incur an unintended high tax if his or her tax base for a given period is inordinately large. For example, a progressive income tax may impose an unduly high tax for the taxpayer whose income is earned erratically. The tax collected in years when income is high must in some way be balanced against that collected in years when income is low if only the desired progression is to be achieved. Similarly, a progressive tax on asset-value increments, accumulated over long periods of time but recognized for tax purposes only in the year of sale, may result in an unusually large tax liability. The relief built into the

United States federal income tax for these and other special situations is considered later. Suffice it to observe here that there can be no question about the existence of such complexities. Thus, the pertinent question is whether the advantages of a progressive rate schedule equal or exceed the costs associated with it.

PROGRESSIVE INCOME TAXATION AND INFLATION

Before leaving the topic of progressive taxation, we should examine briefly the impact of inflation on a progressive income tax with a fixed-rate structure. The general impact of a fixed-rate structure during a period of substantial inflation is, of course, to force taxpayers into higher and higher tax brackets and thus to cause them to transfer a larger and larger portion of their real income to the government. To illustrate this important conclusion, consider the plight of a single taxpayer who reports a $12,900 taxable income in the base year and who receives salary increases exactly equal to the rate of inflation as reflected in the consumer price index. If we use today's rate schedule as that applicable to the base year (see Appendix A), we could determine that this taxpayer would pay a personal income tax of $2,059 per year; an amount equal to approximately 16 percent of his or her income. If the rate of inflation were one that would cause the taxpayer's monetary salary to double every 10 years, and if the same tax-rate structure were still applicable, that taxpayer would pay $6,264 in income taxes just 10 years later. Obviously this amounts to about 24 percent of his or her income, or an 8 percentage point reduction in the real income the taxpayer commands. If salary increases and inflation were to continue at that same pace for another 10 years, the same taxpayer would then pay approximately 37 percent of his or her income in tax. Observe that even with an annual rate of inflation of substantially less than 10 percent, this taxpayer would have lost control of over 20 percent of his or her real income in just 20 years, solely because of the progressive tax-rate structure currently in effect. The size of the impact is due largely to the fact that most of the progression in our income tax rates occurs at the lower end of the rate scale. In other words, the rate of progression is significantly greater on the first $50,000 in taxable income than it is on the next $50,000, and so on. This conclusion is apparent if one

will but examine the slope of the marginal tax-rate curve in Figure 3-1.

Inflation has further distorting effects when deductions are either fixed in amount or are subject to maximum limitations that are not increased to compensate for price level changes. Thus, for example, a personal exemption deduction of any fixed amount that is appropriate at a time when the consumer price index is at 100 would, in all probability, be inadequate when the price index had increased to 150 or 200. For the same reason, a zero-bracket amount of any fixed amount would no longer be reasonable if there were a substantial change in the general price level. And for identical reasons, a corporate surtax exemption of any fixed amount can hardly be appropriate during years of rapid change in the price level.

The conceptual problems created by a progressive income tax during a period of rapid inflation (or deflation) could readily be corrected in one of two ways. First, it would be possible to require each taxpayer to adjust his or her monetary measure of taxable income to a price-deflated (or price-inflated) equivalent before applying the fixed tax rate at the end of each taxable year. Although the arithmetic involved in such a calculation would not be complicated unduly, it would be beyond the comprehension of many taxpayers and it would complicate taxpayer compliance in what is already deemed to be an intolerably complex tax. Second, it would be possible for the government to adjust automatically the rate schedules as well as all fixed deductions or deduction limits annually, in order to accommodate any change in the price level experienced during the prior year. Although this would still create serious complications for fiscal year taxpayers, it would provide a relatively straightforward adjustment mechanism for the vast majority of taxpayers.

Largely because of inflation, the relative contribution in taxation required of the average- versus the high-income taxpayer has narrowed appreciably in the past 20 years. In 1953 the average family income was approximately $5,000, and 12 percent of that income was diverted to taxes. In that same year, a family with four times the average income, or $20,000, paid about 20 percent of its income in taxes. By 1975 the average family income had increased to nearly $14,000, of which 23 percent went to taxes. The family with four times that income, or $56,000, paid about 30 percent of its income in taxes. Although the percentage point spread between the tax rates of these two families remained nearly constant—that is, the spread was 8 percentage points in 1953 and 7 points in 1975—the relative proportion of income diverted to taxes by the average family had nearly doubled whereas that of the higher income family had increased by one-half.

The invidious effect of inflation on corporate (really business) income taxes is largely reflected through understated deductions based on historical cost measures, not through the tax-rate structure. For example, the determination of a depreciation deduction based on historical costs generally has a greater impact on the determination of a corporation's taxable income than does the fixed-rate schedule because the corporate income tax-rate schedule has never been highly progressive. Historically, corporations have paid a proportional tax on all corporate taxable income in excess of a relatively low but fixed amount. Consequently, the corrective mecha-

nism appropriate in the case of the corporate income tax must focus on a better measure of historical costs consumed during the year, not on an automatic adjustment of the tax rate. If the rate of inflation is not significantly reduced in the United States within the next few years, the importance of appropriate corrective mechanisms for both individuals and corporations will soon become grossly evident. It is hoped that Congress will realize that it would be preferable to make an automatic adjustment each year rather than to try to tamper with tax rates and deductions on an *ad hoc* basis. The history of our income tax, as explained in the next chapter, suggests, however, that there is reason to believe we may not get the preferred alternative.[17]

[17] For an additional discussion of the important impact of inflation on income taxation, see Henry R. Cheeseman, "How to Create an Inflation Neutral Tax System," *The Journal of Accountancy* (August 1975), p. 44–51.

PROBLEMS

1. Prepare three graphs representing tax *payments* under proportional, progressive, and regressive tax systems. Record the amount of taxes paid on the vertical scale and the tax base on the horizontal scale.

2. Prepare three graphs representing tax *rates* under proportional, progressive, and regressive tax systems. Record the tax rates on the vertical scale and the tax base on the horizontal scale.

3. a. Taxpayer Kane earned a total income of $10,000 in 19x1. Only $6,000 of his income, however, was included in the tax base for the income tax. Kane paid a tax of $1,200 during 19x1. What nominal-average tax rate is paid by Kane? What is the real- or effective-average rate paid by Kane?

   b. In 19x2, Kane had taxable income (tax base) of $8,000. That year he paid a tax of $1,700. Assuming that the tax-rate structure was not changed by the government unit imposing the tax, what was the marginal rate of tax paid by Kane on the additional income of $2,000 in 19x2? What was the nominal-average rate paid by Kane in 19x2?

4. In a technical sense, is the present F.I.C.A. (social security) tax progressive, proportional, or regressive in relation to income? Explain with a simple diagram.

5. If the federal government were suddenly to increase the amount of the personal exemption from $1,000 to $1,250, how much would the increased tax deduction save the single taxpayer in the lowest (14-percent) income tax bracket? How much would it save a single taxpayer in the highest (70-percent) bracket? Is this result consistent with generally accepted notions of tax equity? Comment.

6. Examine the current United States tax-rate schedules (see Appendix A) and explain how the amount entered in the "basic amount" column (the third column from the left) is computed. For example, how is the $630 figure determined for the taxpayer who is married, files a joint return, and earns more than $7,600 but less than $11,900?

7. Using the data contained in Figure 3-3, answer the following questions:
   a. Prior to the 1969 Act, did horizontal equity exist for most taxpayers earning $15,000 or less per year?
   b. In what income class did the least horizontal equity exist?
   c. What fact do you suppose accounts for the large percentage of upper income persons paying an average tax rate of between 20 and 30 percent?
8. Taxpayer A, a single individual, has a total income of $50,000. Taxable income for the current year, however, is only $40,000.
   a. Determine A's marginal tax rate.
   b. Determine A's nominal-average tax rate.
   c. Determine A's real- or effective-average tax rate.
9. Assume that your state legislature were to enact, and your governor were to sign, a new tax law that imposed a tax on the sale of all new and used gasoline engines at the following rates:

0 to 50 horsepower	—	$5 per horsepower
50 to 100 horsepower	$250 plus	$4 per horsepower over 50
100 to 150 horsepower	$450 plus	$3 per horsepower over 100
150 to 200 horsepower	$600 plus	$2 per horsepower over 150
over 200 horsepower	$700 plus	$1 per horsepower over 200

   a. If A were to purchase a Buick with a 175 horsepower engine and B were to purchase a Ford with a 90 horsepower engine, who would pay the greater tax, A or B?
   b. Who would be in the higher marginal tax bracket, A or B?
   c. What would A's nominal-average tax rate per horsepower be?
   d. In a technical sense, would this new tax be progressive, proportional, or regressive?
   e. If the new tax applied only to gasoline engines, what should happen to the price of diesel-powered automobiles? Explain briefly.
10. The government of Neverneverland, a small, strange, island republic in the middle of the Ancient Ocean, imposes two taxes on its citizens and resident aliens. One monthly tax is based on the size (measured in cubic feet) of the taxpayer's residence, an igloo, according to the following rates:

First 3,000 cubic feet	¢10 per cu ft
Next 3,000 cubic feet	¢18 per cu ft
Next 6,000 cubic feet	¢34 per cu ft
Next 12,000 cubic feet	¢62 per cu ft
Remainder	¢100 per cu ft

(Note: the basic monetary unit in this imaginary country is the cube, or ¢.)

The second tax is a tax of ¢5 on each ounce of wonderdrug, which is made and distributed only by a secret agency of the government. Neverneverland, you see, is a very strange country indeed: Humans can live there only if they take exactly one ounce of wonderdrug on the first day of each full moon. If they fail to take this drug at the prescribed time or in the prescribed amount, they will die within 20 hours.
   a. In a technical sense, is the tax imposed on igloos progressive, proportional, or regressive?
   b. In a technical sense, is the tax imposed on wonderdrug progressive, proportional, or regressive?

c. In a popular sense, is the tax imposed on wonderdrug progressive, proportional, or regressive?

d. Fred Jidair's home in Neverneverland contains 9,000 cubic feet of space. Is the nominal-average tax paid by Fred on his home less than, equal to, or more than ¢34 per cubic foot?

e. If Fred decided, after the birth of his seventh child, to expand the size of his igloo from 9,000 to 12,000 cubic feet, would his marginal tax rate be less than, equal to, or more than ¢34 per cubic foot?

11. Sam Sharp lives in the Empire of Konform, which is ruled by King Kon. Sam, an employee of King Kon, earns an annual salary of $20,000 (his only source of income). The income tax in Konform is determined according to the following rate schedule:

$ 0–$1,000	—	5 percent of income
$1,001–$5,000	$ 50 plus	7 percent of income in excess of $1,000
$5,001–$100,000	$330 plus	10 percent of income in excess of $5,000

In addition, however, any relative of King Kon is entitled to deduct 50 percent of his salary in the calculation of his income tax base; any employee of King Kon can deduct 10 percent.

a. Technically, should the income tax in Konform be classified as proportional, progressive, or regressive?

b. Determine Sam's nominal-average tax rate.

c. Determine Sam's real- or effective-average tax rate.

d. Determine Sam's marginal tax rate.

12. Cost-of-living adjustments are often inadequate during periods of rapidly rising prices. Explain briefly.

13. The F.I.C.A. tax rate for 1980 is a flat 6.13 percent; the income tax rates begin at 14 percent and increase to 70 percent. Nevertheless, a single-income family of four with an annual salary of $10,000 pays more in F.I.C.A. tax ($613) than in income tax ($374). Explain the apparent conundrum.

14. According to the empirical studies conducted by Messrs. Pechman and Okner, the aggregate (federal, state, and local) effective tax burden in the United States is highly regressive for most of the population. True or false? Explain briefly.

SUPPLEMENTAL PROBLEMS

15. Statistical studies have shown that the ratio of after-tax net income to total assets employed for large corporations has remained fairly constant since 1913 despite major changes in the tax rates. What does this fact indicate about the incidence of the income tax? List and discuss changes in accounting practices and procedures since 1913 that might invalidate this condition.

16. What can be done to make a sales tax (relatively) more progressive in relation to income? Explain.

17. Why might taxpayers in the higher tax brackets be less influenced by tax disincentives than other taxpayers earning lesser incomes?

18. If a government desired to decrease consumption spending and increase investment, other things being equal, you would expect it to advocate regressive rather than progressive taxes. True or false? Explain briefly.

The income tax ... must be viewed primarily as a regional victory of the South and Middle West over the Northeast, part of the same sectional movement that produced the Interstate Commerce Act in 1887, the Sherman Antitrust Act in 1890, and the unsuccessful campaign for bi-metallism.

BORIS I. BITTKER,
Federal Income, Estate, and Gift Taxation (1964)

the United States income tax: history and source

There can be no doubt today that the income tax dominates the United States tax structure. Income taxation provides approximately 63 percent of the $526 billion in taxes collected annually by all levels of government. The largest single tax is the federal tax on individual incomes; in 1979 it provided nearly $255 billion in revenue. During that same fiscal year the federal tax on corporate incomes provided $78 billion for the United States Treasury. Because of this dominance and because an income tax liability is so amenable to modification, we will hereafter restrict our concern to the federal income taxes.

Before we begin to examine the details of our present income tax provisions, however, let us consider the general development of those provisions in broad historical context. Although income taxation has conceptual roots that are over 2,000 years old, most of our present rules have evolved in the past 65 years. In this chapter, we shall divide our discussion into two major periods: that prior to the Sixteenth Amendment (1913) and the years after that Constitutional change. The latter period is further subdivided into three, possibly four, periods that can be distinguished from each other by the kind of legislation that dominated those years.

INCOME TAXATION PRIOR TO 1913

Historians suggest that elementary forms of income taxation were imposed by the Roman Empire even

before the birth of Christ. Indeed, the fact that Christ was born in the city of Bethlehem may be attributable to one form of "income" taxation. Saint Luke relates the events in this manner: "there went out a decree from Caesar Augustus, that all the world should be taxed. . . . And all went to be taxed, everyone into his own city. And Joseph also went up from Galilee, out of the city of Nazareth, into Judea, unto the city of David, which is called Bethlehem; (because he was of the house and lineage of David) to be taxed with Mary his espoused wife. . . ."[1] Although no details concerning this tax are available, the fact that the taxpayer was required to respond to the tax personally and with his family suggests that it may have been some form of the poll or head tax as well as a census mechanism. A poll tax with graduated tax rates—often called a "faculties tax"—constitutes the most elementary form of the income tax. Essentially, a faculties tax is a tax on *estimated* income. This form of income taxation is not uncommon today in preindustrial societies.[2]

Other early traces of income taxation may be seen in the Florentine Republic in Italy in the fourteenth and fifteenth centuries.[3] What had begun

---

[1] Luke 2:1–5 (King James Version).

[2] The "progressive poll tax" is still utilized today in some of the African countries. See John F. Due, "The African Personal Tax," *National Tax Journal,* XV (December, 1962), pp. 385–98.

[3] The authors owe a considerable debt to Professor Edwin R. A. Seligman for much of the early history of income taxation. Persons interested in additional details should see his book, *The Income Tax,* published by The Macmillan Company in 1911 and again in 1914 in an enlarged and revised edition.

there as a tax on property evolved into a tax on income. By 1451 much income and wealth could be attributed to established industry and commerce rather than to the more traditional forms of property. Consequently, the value base for taxation became a capitalization of the earnings stream. Because of administrative complications and political favoritism in the earnings calculations, this early income-based tax fell into disrepute and was largely replaced by indirect taxation on consumption.

The colonial faculties taxes

The earliest variant of the income tax in the United States appeared in 1643 in the colony of New Plymouth as a tax based on a "a person's faculties." Although no measurement techniques were provided in this law, the appointed assessors were supposed to base the tax on "personal faculties and abilities."[4] Three years later (1646), the Massachusetts Bay Company enacted a similar tax based on the "returns and gains" of artists and tradesmen. Early in the eighteenth century, faculties taxes based on estimated incomes were commonplace among the New England colonies, and the definitions of the tax base slowly became increasingly comprehensive definitions of income. This gradual expansion is attributed to recognition that taxation based only on selective forms of property does not give adequate recognition to every citizen's tax capacity or ability to pay. Thus, income taxation began in this part of the world as a supplement to more traditional forms of property taxation.

The colonial faculties taxes had largely disappeared by the middle of the nineteenth century, to be replaced by partial income taxes in a few of the new Southern states, including Virginia, North Carolina, and Alabama. These newer forms of income taxation can be traced to England, where, under the leadership of William Pitt, the first "modern" income tax was adopted in 1799. Generally, the Northern and Middle states avoided income taxation before the twentieth century, although during the Civil War the federal (Union) government did utilize such a tax.

The Civil War income taxes

The first United States federal income tax was enacted into law on August 5, 1861, to raise revenue in

support of the Civil War. Although this law was never enforced, the 1861 tax was extended by a law adopted on July 1, 1862, and limited collections were made under the latter act. The law imposed a tax of 3 percent on most incomes between $600 and $10,000 and a rate of 5 percent on all income in excess of $10,000. Enforcement of the law was greatly confused and evasion was widespread. The 1863 tax return form is of historic interest, and a copy appears in Figure 4-1. Perhaps the most striking thing about the return is its similarity to present-day tax returns.[5]

The 1864 Revenue Act revised the earlier income tax rates and provided a maximum tax rate of 10 percent, applicable to incomes in excess of $10,000. The rate structure was again revised in 1865 and in 1867. The latter change instituted a flat (proportional) tax of 5 percent on most incomes in excess of $1,000. All Civil War income taxes lapsed in 1872, when the need for war financing was eliminated.

Although the Civil War income taxes were not an overwhelming success, they did serve to illuminate some important aspects of income taxation. First, although the income tax never challenged the dominance of the tariff duties during this period, it did prove to be a major revenue producer. During the 10 year period that they were enforced, the Civil War income taxes provided the federal government with $376 million. The largest single year was 1866, when approximately $73 million (of a total of $490 million of federal revenue) was collected in income taxes.

A second important lesson learned during that decade was that a detailed taxpayer guidance system is essential to successful income taxation. Major problems were encountered in administration. Surprisingly, perhaps, these early laws did provide for withholding at the source on wages and salaries, interest and dividends. But other aspects of the administrative machinery were not so advanced. For example, it remained for the state of Wisconsin to demonstrate (in 1911) the importance of a central tax commission, autonomous from local officials.

Perhaps the most surprising fact of that decade of income taxation is that the tax functioned as well as it did. Richard Goode, an economist with special competence in tax matters, once suggested that there are six prerequisites to a successful income tax: (1) a money economy, (2) general literacy, (3) minimum accounting records, (4) acceptance of the idea of

---

[4]*Ibid.* (1911 edition), p. 368.

[5] The first Commissioner of Internal Revenue, George S. Bantwell, was appointed by President Lincoln in 1862.

FIGURE 4-1   Pages 2 and 3 of the Income Tax Form Used in the 1860s

DETAILED STATEMENT OF SOURCES OF INCOME AND THE AMOUNT DERIVED
FROM EACH, DURING THE YEAR 1863.

☞ *Gross Amounts must be stated.* ☜

	AMOUNTS

1. Income of a resident in the United States from profits on any trade, business, or vocation, or any interest therein, wherever carried on .
2. From rents, or the use of real estate .
3. From interest on notes, bonds, mortgages, or other personal securities, not those of the United States .
4. From interest on notes, bonds, or other securities of the United States .
5. From interest or dividends on any bonds or other evidences of indebtedness of any railroad company or corporation .
6. From interest or dividends on stock, capital, or deposits in any bank, trust company, or savings institution, insurance or railroad company, or corporation .
7. From interest on bonds or dividends on stock, shares or property in gas, bridge, canal, turnpike, express, telegraph, steamboat, ferry-boat, or manufacturing company or corporation, or from the business usually done thereby .
8. From property, securities, or stocks owned in the United States by a citizen thereof residing abroad, not in the employment of the Government of the United States .
9. From salary other than as an officer or employee of the United States .
10. From salary as an officer or employee of the United States .
11. From farms or plantations, including all products and profits .
12. From advertisements .
13. From all sources not herein enumerated .

TOTAL .

DETAILED STATEMENT OF DEDUCTIONS AUTHORIZED TO BE MADE

	AMOUNTS

1. Expenses necessarily incurred and paid in carrying on any trade, business or vocation, such as rent of store, clerk hire, insurance, fuel, freight, &c .
2. Amount actually paid by a property owner for necessary repairs, insurance, and interest on incumbrances upon his property .
3. Amount paid by a farmer or planter for—
   (a) Hired labor, including the subsistence of the laborers .
   (b) Necessary repairs upon his farm or plantation .
   (c) Insurance, and interest on incumbrances upon his farm or plantation .
4. Other national, state, and local taxes assessed and paid for the year 1863, and not elsewhere included .
5. Amount actually paid for rent of the dwelling-house or estate occupied as a residence .
6. Exempted by law (except in the case of a citizen of the United States residing abroad,) $600 . 600 00
7. Income from interest or dividends on stock, capital, or deposits in any bank, trust company, or savings institution, insurance, or railroad company, from which 3 per cent. thereon was withheld by the officers thereof .
8. Income from interest on bonds, or other evidences of indebtedness of any railroad company or corporation, from which 3 per cent. thereon was withheld by the officers thereof .
9. Salaries of officers, or payments to persons in the civil, military, naval, or other service of the United States, in excess of $600 .
10. Income from advertisements, on which 3 per cent. was paid .

TOTAL .

SOURCE: *Income Taxes 1862–1962, A History of the Internal Revenue Service*, I.R.S. Publication No. 447 (Washington, D.C.: U.S. Government Printing Office), p. 9.

voluntary compliance with tax laws, (5) political acceptance of an income tax, and (6) an efficient administrative machine.[6] Considering the situation in the United States in 1872 with regard to each of these six criteria, it is not surprising that the income tax was permitted to lapse once the pressure for war financing ended.

The constitutional question

Even many educated persons are surprised to learn that the United States government imposed and collected an income tax prior to 1913, for the common belief is that this form of taxation was unconstitutional prior to the ratification of the Sixteenth Amendment. This belief, however, is only partially accurate.

Article I, Section 9, Clause 4, of the Constitution reads as follows: "No Capitation, or other direct, Tax shall be laid, unless in Proportion to the Census or Enumeration herein before directed to be taken." Since incomes are not equally distributed between people or states, there is no way for an income tax to be divided among states in proportion to population. When the Civil War income tax was tested in the Supreme Court, the question for the Court to decide was, therefore, a straightforward one: Is an income tax a "direct tax" as that term was understood by those who drafted the Constitution?[7]

The most important early decision of the Supreme Court on this question was in the 1880 case of *Springer* v. *United States,* and the decision was unanimous and negative—that is, the income tax was deemed to be an indirect tax. The Court said, "Our conclusions are, that *direct taxes,* within the meaning of the Constitution, are only capitation taxes, as expressed in that instrument, and taxes on real estate; and that the tax of which the plaintiff in error complains is within the category of an excise or duty."[8] Fourteen years later the Court changed its mind.

Between the *Springer* decision in 1880 and the Revenue Act of 1894, income taxation became a political football. Generally, the states of the West and the South favored the income tax, whereas the Eastern states opposed it. The income tax was part of the Populist program, along with railroad regulation, expanded currency, and the direct election of senators. This was the program of an "oppressed" agrarian midland, revolting against the Eastern bankers and industrialists—in short, a program for the poor against the rich.[9] No less than 14 income tax bills were introduced into Congress between 1873 and 1879, but none of them gained the majority necessary to become law. Finally, on August 28, 1894, such an act was made law, without the signature of President Cleveland. By this date the lines were well drawn and a final political showdown was inevitable.

Once the income tax had found its way through the halls of Congress, the battle was transferred from the legislative arena to the judicial, with the executive standing by. The proceeding, *Pollock* v. *Farmers' Loan and Trust Co.,*[10] was instituted by a stockholder (Pollock) to restrain the corporate officers from paying a tax the stockholder deemed unconstitutional. The issue in the case was almost identical to that raised in the earlier *Springer* case. There were, however, slight factual differences: In *Springer,* the income in question involved income from personal property and from professional earnings; in *Pollock,* the income was derived from land. The plaintiff argued that if a tax on real estate is a direct tax, then a tax on the income from real estate must also be a direct tax. The first *Pollock* decision was a 6–2 decision holding that the 1894 act was unconstitutional to the extent that it taxed income from real estate (as well as income from municipal bonds).[11] Because so many other aspects of income taxation were unanswered by this decision, the counsel for the appellants requested a rehearing, which was granted.

On the rehearing, nine justices were on the bench and, by a scant 5–4 vote, reaffirmed the earlier decision in a second opinion. Interestingly, the reports do not reveal the name(s) of the vacillating judge(s).

---

[6]Richard Goode, "Reconstruction of Foreign Tax Systems," *Proceedings of the Forty-Fourth Annual Conference of the National Tax Association* (1951), pp. 212–22.

[7]Here we are discussing only the legal (or constitutional) meaning of the phrase "direct tax." Actually, the phrase is originally one adopted from the economics literature. For a discussion of that matter see C. J. Bullock, "Direct and Indirect Taxes in Economic Literature," *Political Science Quarterly,* XIII (1898), pp. 442–86.

[8]*Springer* v. *United States,* 102 U.S. 602 (1880).

[9]See Richard Hofstadter, *The Age of Reform* (New York: Vintage Books, 1955), for a most informative history of this politically tumultuous period. While the Populists were never successful as a party, their program was certainly successful after it was adopted by other reform groups.

[10]157 U.S. 429 (1895); 158 U.S. 601 (1895).

[11]The latter portion of the decision is not particularly germane to the immediate discussion and is, therefore, dismissed. Later statutes have taken care to exempt this income from tax, although many persons are now prepared to argue again the constitutionality question.

This second opinion extended the earlier decision to income derived from personal property and, for all practical purposes, to all income.

Today, most historians would concede that the decision was heavily influenced by the political and social tenor of the times. Although Chief Justice Fuller's words were clear, they had a hollow ring. He noted that "the distinction between direct and indirect taxation was well understood by the framers of the Constitution and those who adopted it."[12] Justice Field, in a long concurring opinion, concluded his statement with more telling words:

Here I close my opinion. I could not say less in view of questions of such gravity that go down to the very foundation of the government. . . . The present assault upon capital is but the beginning. It will be but the steppingstone to others, larger and more sweeping, till our political contests will become a war of the poor against the rich; a war constantly growing in intensity and bitterness.[13]

It is hard for us today, when the income tax is an accepted part of our economic and political life, to comprehend the political heat generated by the issue in 1895. The following quotes from editorials in the popular press at the time of the *Pollock* decision seem to come from a different world:

The St. Louis Post Dispatch: Today's decision shows that the corporations and plutocrats are as securely entrenched in the Supreme Court as in the lower courts which they take such pains to control.

The New York Tribune: The great compromises which made the Union possible still stand unshaken to prevent its overthrow by communist revolution. The fury of ignorant class hatred, which has sufficed to overthrow absolute power in many lands . . . has dashed itself in vain against the Constitution of the United States, fortified by the institutions which a free people have established for the defense of their rights.

In short, the issue of income taxation at the turn of the twentieth century was as controversial as some of the cultural and political issues of today.

Professor Seligman's analysis of the constitutional issue is both more thorough and more convincing than the analysis offered by the bench. After a lengthy study, Seligman concludes

With this general uncertainty as to the use of the older terms, it need not surprise us to find that there was no agreement at all as to the use of meaning of the newer term, "direct tax." As a matter of fact, the term was scarcely employed at all before 1787. We have found only one instance of its use in the United States before that date, namely, in a Massachusetts act of 1786.

. . .

From the above review of the origin of the direct-tax clause it is clear that it was due simply and solely to the attempt to solve the difficulty connected with the maintenance of slavery. But for that struggle Gouverneur Morris would never have introduced the term "direct tax," and there would have been no reason to introduce it anywhere else.[14]

The battle for the income tax did not end with the Supreme Court. The friends of the tax decided that a constitutional amendment would provide a surer route to acceptance than would a new statute and another judicial review. Thus, in 1909 the Congress was persuaded to pass a joint resolution that on February 25, 1913, was ratified as the Sixteenth Amendment to the United States Constitution. It states that "[T]he Congress shall have power to lay and collect taxes on incomes, from whatever source derived, without apportionment among the several States, and without regard to any census or enumeration."

The 1909 corporate income tax

Even before ratification of the Sixteenth Amendment, the income tax had reappeared in a limited form. In 1909 Congress enacted, and President Taft signed, a bill that imposed a tax of 1 percent on all corporate incomes in excess of $5,000. This tax was tried, in 1911, again on constitutional grounds, in the case of *Flint* v. *Stone Tracy Co.*[15] This time the Supreme Court found that the tax on corporate incomes was not a direct tax but rather a special form of excise tax on the privilege of doing business.

This special corporate tax was short lived, for the revenue measure for 1913 included provisions for both personal and corporate income taxes. During the next half-century, the income tax was transformed from a levy of minor importance to the position of preeminence it holds today.

[12]*Pollock* v. *Farmers' Loan and Trust Co.,* 157 U.S. 429 (1895), p. 573.
[13]*Ibid.,* p. 607.

[14]Seligman, *op. cit.,* pp. 555, 561.
[15]*Flint* v. *Stone Tracy Co.,* 220 U.S. 107 (1911).

THE UNITED STATES INCOME TAX SINCE 1913

The history of the federal income tax from 1913 to the present is a mirror reflecting the economic and social environment of the times. Like the Civil War, World War I necessitated vast changes in federal fiscal operations. Income tax collections rose from some $35 *million* in 1913 to nearly $4 *billion* in 1920. With the end of the war, tax collections decreased, but they never returned to prewar levels. In 1930 the combined individual and corporate income tax collections totaled approximately $2.5 billion, slightly more than half of total federal receipts. This pace of taxation was roughly maintained until World War II. During the years 1941–45, income tax collections averaged nearly $20 billion annually, representing approximately two-thirds of total federal receipts. The Cold War, the Korean "conflict," and the Vietnam "involvement" have all contributed significantly to the maintenance of record-level tax collections since 1945. As we have said, income tax collections today exceed $332 billion annually, which is nearly 63 percent of total government receipts. The sheer magnitude of these numbers makes any meaningful comprehension difficult. In 1913, however, the income tax was not so difficult to comprehend.

The period 1913–39

The 1913 income tax was a modest affair. The tax applicable to individual incomes began at 1 percent on taxable incomes in excess of $3,000 and increased to a maximum of 7 percent on taxable incomes in excess of $500,000. The $3,000 exemption was increased to $4,000 for a married taxpayer who lived with a spouse. The tax imposed on corporate incomes was a flat 1 percent, with no provision for any exemption. Withholding was provided at the source for interest, rents, salaries, and wages but not for domestic dividends.

The 1913 law, and particularly the progressive nature of the tax, was subject to judicial review in the case of *Brushaber* v. *Union Pacific Railroad Co.*[16] Counsel for the plaintiff argued that the progressive rate structure was tantamount to an arbitrary abuse of power and therefore violated the due process clause of the Fifth Amendment. The Supreme Court, however, disagreed, and since 1916, progressive income taxation has never been subject to any real threat from either the legislative or judicial branches of the government.

The legislative branch has, of course, frequently modified earlier statutes. In 1916, for example, the tax rates were increased to range from 2 to 12 percent (on incomes in excess of $2 million). That year also ushered in the first United States war-profits tax on munitions manufacturers, which was broadened into an excess-profits tax in 1917. The withholding provisions were eliminated in 1916.

A limited dependent's deduction ($200 for one child) was introduced in 1917 and was extended (to $200 for each dependent) in 1918. The Revenue Act of 1918 also introduced "discovery-value depletion," the predecessor of percentage depletion. Special provisions for "capital gains" were introduced in 1921—a modification that has provided more complexity than any other single provision ever enacted—and provisions for loss deductions were frequently modified during the period 1918–34. A graduated corporate income tax was introduced in 1936.

Between 1913 and 1939 some 17 income-tax-related laws had been enacted by Congress. While the language of each act tended to reflect closely the earlier provisions, a single codification, to bring together these many laws, was deemed desirable. By the joint efforts of the Justice Department and the Bureau of Internal Revenue, this desire was realized with the enactment of the Internal Revenue Code of 1939. All revenue acts passed between 1939 and 1954 were integrated into the 1939 Code.

The period 1939–54

In 1939 less than 6 percent of the United States population were required to pay a federal income tax. Just six years later (1945) more than 74 percent of an enlarged population had to pay that same tax.[17] Thus, as a mass tax the income tax is a relative newcomer to our country. Its drastically increased coverage is attributable largely to a major reduction in exemptions during a period of rapidly rising personal income and inflation. Wide coverage was facilitated by the reintroduction of withholding provisions in the Current Tax Payment Act of 1943. In order to avoid the "doubling up" of two years' tax liabilities in a single year, the federal government in 1943

[16]240 U.S. 1 (1916).

[17]For more details of this growth see Richard Goode, *The Individual Income Tax* (Washington: The Brookings Institution, 1964), pp. 2–4.

forgave 75 percent of the lower of the 1942 or 1943 tax liabilities.

During the period 1940–54, several changes were enacted to simplify the administration of the income tax laws. For example, the optional "tax table," now familiar to every taxpayer, was introduced in 1941 and extended to larger incomes in 1944, at which time the exemption and dependent rules also were simplified. The administration of the law was further improved by the reorganization of the Bureau of Internal Revenue in 1952. The old Bureau operated through 64 "collectors," who were political appointees. The new Internal Revenue Service was organized to operate through 9 regional commissioners and 64 district directors selected on a merit system.

Social and economic "equity considerations" also weighed heavily in the income tax modifications enacted between 1939 and 1954. For example, a deduction for personal medical expenses was first introduced in 1942. A special exemption for the blind was granted in 1942; another for old age was permitted in 1948. Income splitting, to equalize the federal tax treatment of incomes earned in community- and non-community-property states, was also enacted in 1948. And a "head-of-household" provision was adopted in 1951 to give single persons with family responsibilities some of the tax advantages that attach to marriage. By 1954 Congress was convinced of the necessity of rewriting the 1939 Code.

The period 1954–69

The Internal Revenue Code of 1954 constituted a comprehensive revision of the 1939 Code. It rearranged many of the old provisions in a more logical sequence; it deleted much obsolete material; it sought to make the language of the Code more understandable; and it instituted numerous substantive changes.[18] All revenue measures modifying the income tax since 1954 have been incorporated into that codification. Thus, the pertinent statute for federal income taxation today remains the Internal Revenue Code of 1954, as amended. Subtitle A of the Code is the income tax law.

The dominant objectives of the revisions between 1954 and 1969 were economic, although matters of equity and administration continued to receive con-

siderable attention. In the former category, two innovations deserve special comment. The investment credit provisions—introduced in 1962, liberalized in 1964, suspended in 1966, reinstated in 1967, deleted in 1969, reintroduced in 1971, and further liberalized in 1975 and 1978—have as their primary purpose the stimulation of *investment* spending. The second major innovation of economic significance enacted between 1954 and 1969 was the general tax reductions of 1964 and 1965, which were granted to stimulate *consumption* spending. The proponents of the tax reductions argued that the cut in taxes would even serve to reduce the budget deficit by stimulating the economy to the point that more income taxes would actually be collected at the lower rates than would have been collected at the old, higher rates. This experiment is now generally conceded to have been successful.

Income-averaging provisions were enacted in 1964 and liberalized in 1969 to reduce the tax inequity that could result from the combined forces of an annual income period and a progressive rate structure. In the absence of income averaging, the taxpayer whose income varies widely from year to year will often pay more taxes in the aggregate than will a person who earns an equivalent income at a constant rate. Whether the present income-averaging provisions adequately remedied this inequity remains an open question.

Experiments intended to improve tax administration took various forms. Perhaps the greatest advance was the computerization of much tax information by the Internal Revenue Service in Regional Service Centers. In addition, a Small Claims Division of the Tax Court was introduced to handle in an informal manner the adjudication of many small tax disputes without much cost to the taxpayer. Finally, a revised tax form was devised in an attempt to simplify the reporting process.

The period 1969–78

Historical "periods" are, of course, arbitrary classifications. Additionally, the closer in time an observer is to the events, the more difficult it is to determine whether or not a change of such magnitude has taken place that it becomes meaningful to speak in terms of a new period. We are of the opinion that the Tax Reform Act of 1969 marked the beginning of a distinctive period in U.S. tax history, which ended with the Revenue Act of 1978. That period was characterized by periodic and systematic attacks, supported

---

[18]The objectives of the 1954 revision are stated clearly in both the House Ways and Means Committee Report [H. R. Rept. No. 1337, 83d Cong., 2d Sess. 1 (1954)] and the Senate Finance Committee Report [S. Rept. No. 1622, 83d Cong., 2d Sess. 1 (1954)].

by well-documented studies, on the tax provisions that had permitted large-scale tax avoidance in prior years.

Clearly, the effectiveness of many notorious tax avoidance schemes was seriously curtailed between 1969 and 1978. The relative advantage of specified capital gains was substantially reduced; major avoidance opportunities in charitable contributions and private charitable foundations were eliminated; the ability to claim a deduction for losses from oil and gas properties, motion pictures and video tapes, vacation properties and certain farm-and-ranch operations, citrus groves, and livestock operations were sharply limited; percentage depletion allowances were drastically cut; the early deduction of prepaid interest was eliminated; the deduction of investment interest was also limited; and the minimum tax on tax preferences was significantly increased.

The Tax Reform Act of 1976 made major changes in the federal gift and estate taxes. Major revisions to those two taxes had been promised for many years, but it was not until 1976 that something was finally done to correct many well-known shortcomings of the prior law. President Carter campaigned strongly for still greater tax reforms, and shortly after taking office, Treasury Secretary W. Michael Blumenthal announced the new administration's support of a drastic simplification proposal.

The Carter administration's support for additional reforms and drastic simplification in income taxation was short-lived. By midsummer 1977 it was apparent that the president had given up on the more dramatic tax changes initially considered. Even with a large Democratic majority, there was little chance of getting further tax reform measures approved by Congress. Furthermore, public opinion surveys revealed that the general public would neither understand nor fully appreciate many of the recommended tax law changes that had great theoretical merit. In summary, President Carter quickly came to understand the political realities that had constrained many prior administrations in making tax reform proposals.

A period since 1978?

Instead of continuing the trend of tax reform started in 1969, the Revenue Act of 1978 was, in many ways, a reversal of the recent past. Most importantly, it made major cuts in the taxation of capital gains (effectively returning them to their pre-1969 preferred position); deferred the effective date on the carryover basis rules for inherited property (which

had represented a hard fought victory for reform proponents in the 1976 Act); and reduced the minimum tax on tax preference items in a couple of significant ways. Although the 1978 Act did include a few reform-type provisions, those provisions were clearly of minor significance. The reasons for this dramatic turn of events are still not entirely clear. It would appear, however, that Congress interpreted the success of the property tax revolt in California—commonly known as Proposition 13—as a harbinger of general dissatisfaction with high taxes. Coupling these political concerns with a growing interest in the need for greater capital formation, Congress clearly reversed its field and returned to political compromises that probably satisfied no one.

The originally temporary deferral of the 1976 carryover basis rules for inherited property became permanent when a provision to that effect was tacked on to the Windfall Profits Tax Bill late in 1979. President Carter previously had threatened to veto *any* bill that included a provision to modify carryover basis. The proponents of repeal knew, however, that Carter wanted the Windfall Profits Tax too badly to veto that bill to achieve a lesser administration objective. Consequently, the opponents of carryover basis in 1980 had adroitly achieved a major reversal of one tax reform that looked certain four years earlier.

The future

The various governmental units existing within the United States have, in the past forty years, continued to expand the scope of the goods and services they provide the private sector. Today it seems doubtful that this trend will be suddenly reversed, even though a growing number of politicians are arguing for that alternative. If our judgment is correct, income taxation seems destined for a position of continued prominence. For income, with all its shortcomings, still provides a tax base that can be continually recast to achieve lesser and changing objectives at the same time that it diverts an extremely large portion of the national income from the private to the public sector. In other words, the income tax can assist in the achievement of numerous lesser social and economic objectives at the same time that it can "pack a big wallop." No other tax base seems capable of this diverse service, at least within the constraints of the accepted social and political order.

Except for sales taxation and, possibly, the value-added tax, most tax bases are restrained by considerations of jurisdiction, administrative complication, or size to the extent that they are already deemed inadequate for the task required. Thus it seems probable, as we have indicated, that the next decade or two in United States taxation will see the continuation of strong income (and sales) taxation, coupled with increasing centralization of the taxing authority and redistribution of the proceeds to lower levels of government. The introduction of VAT is also a growing possibility.

The details of any tax are first determined by a legislative process and then administered by a complex government bureaucracy. Before we begin to examine the detailed rules of our current income tax law, we should stop briefly to consider in broad outline the major steps that surround the enactment of every new tax provision.

HOW A NEW TAX LAW IS MADE AND INTERPRETED

The initial major step in the complex taxing process is passage of a revenue bill by Congress and the approval of it by the president. Following this legislative action, the I.R.S. makes and releases its interpretation of the statute, primarily in the form of Treasury Regulations. The taxpayer must then accept the responsibility for knowing what the internal revenue laws require and for complying with them.

Congressional action

The Constitution provides that all revenue measures must originate in the House of Representatives.[19] Once passed by the House, revenue measures go to the Senate for consideration. The committee of the House that is concerned with revenue bills is the Committee on Ways and Means.

COMMITTEE ON WAYS AND MEANS   The formal procedures of the House of Representatives provide that all bills must be introduced by a member of the House. Technically, then, representatives initiate tax bills by placing them in the legislative "hopper." Once introduced, all revenue bills are referred to the Committee on Ways and Means; unless the chairman is willing to have his committee consider a bill, referral to the committee amounts to an unceremonious

burial. Through various stratagems, the chairman can block effectively all action on a measure, because no action by the House of Representatives is possible until the bill is reported to the floor of the House by the committee. On occasion, committee chairmen may block action on a measure that has both administrative backing and majority support in Congress. Historically, therefore, the chairman of the Committee on Ways and Means effectively initiates legislative action on revenue bills.

The idea that proposals for changes in our tax laws originate with our elected legislators placing a bill in the legislative "hopper" is a gross oversimplification of a very involved part of the tax process. Historically, most major proposals for change are presented to Congress by the Secretary of the Treasury. New proposals are often a major component of an administration's fiscal policy and reflect the economic philosophy of the president and his economic advisors. Most long-run policies, however, originate in what is best described as a "kitchen" bureau, which advises both the administration and Congress. The important characteristic of this unofficial part of the process is the fact that the influential policy makers in the bureau are not elected and generally have a long tenure.

The "kitchen" bureau is made up of economists and lawyers who serve in nonappointive posts in higher echelons of the Treasury Department, on the staff of the Joint Committee on Taxation in Congress, and as research fellows at various nonprofit organizations concerned primarily with national economic policy. Communications between members of this group are quite close, and their influence on the changes in the tax law is substantial. The chief of staff of the Joint Committee advises both the chairman of the House Ways and Means Committee and the chairman of the Senate Finance Committee on tax matters. The civil servants in the Treasury Department advise the Secretary. And the research fellows appear before congressional committees regularly to offer advice. The influences of the "kitchen" bureau will obviously vary from one administration to the next, depending on the general economic policy of the two groups. For the long run, however, the important point is that this group of unofficial policy makers will still be around after the next election.

SENATE AND CONFERENCE ACTIONS   Upon passage by the House, the bill goes to the Senate, where it is referred to the Committee on Finance. Here, as in the House, public hearings are usually held. After

[19]For a thorough explanation of legislative action on tax bills, see Roy Blough, *The Federal Taxing Process* (Englewood Cliffs, N.J.: Prentice-Hall, 1952).

those hearings, a bill may be reported out of Committee to the Senate floor. The Senate has no "closed" rule comparable to that in the House; that is, there is no limit on debate, and amendments may be offered freely from the floor. Where the party of the current administration has a strong majority in Congress (and good relations with the chairmen of the Committee on Ways and Means and the Committee on Finance), the floor of the Senate is often the first place that "outsiders" may influence directly the content of the bill.

The bill finally passed by the Senate normally will be different from that passed by the House. The House may, of course, simply accept the Senate version, but the two versions of the bill are usually referred to a conference committee for compromise of these differences. If a compromise is reached in this committee, the revised bill is reported back to both bodies for final ratification. If both houses adopt the conference bill (which must be accepted or rejected without change), it goes to the president for signature or veto.

The conference procedure is one that increases the power of the committee chairmen, particularly that of the chairman of the Senate Finance Committee. In conference he can readily dispose of any amendments added on the floor by the Senate. The chairmen of the committees effectively select the members from the full committee who will make up the conference committee, and each house votes as a unit in conference. On rare occasions, members selected by a chairman may disagree with his position. Even then the chairman is not necessarily thwarted; he may increase the membership of the conference committee until he has a majority on his committee who favor his position.

Historically, conference committees have been small and have hammered out the necessary compromises in executive session. The conference for the Tax Reform Act of 1976 broke this long precedent. The meetings were open, with the conferees exposed to an audience of about 200 spectators, many of whom took notes furiously as each decision was reached. What we do not know is how many private conversations were held before and after the official sessions. In any event, everything *appeared* to be open and aboveboard.

The "kitchen" bureau can have considerable impact on legislation during the conference procedures, especially the staff of the Joint Committee on Taxation (and through this group, indirectly by other members of the bureau). In conference, the compromises reached are reduced to writing by the staff of the Joint Committee. While this group cannot write new "law" that runs counter to decisions made by the legislative conferees, their interpretation of the agreements reached by the legislators on complex provisions do become a part of the law—the Representatives and Senators typically do not have the needed expertise to write the tax law in many complicated areas.

The president, of course, has the final power of the veto, but this veto is exercised sparingly in tax matters.

The process just described is certainly less than perfect. The committee chairmen have a great deal of power, and appointments to the key committees can result in tax legislation that is not responsive to the desires of a majority of Congress. Further, due to the complexity of the law, elected politicians must often depend on the advice of the "kitchen" bureau, which is never accountable to the electorate directly. Without passing judgment on it, we can only note that the legislative process just described is one with which we must live. It exists as described, and there exist no serious proposals for major changes in it.

Sources of law in the legislative process

The Internal Revenue Code is the end result of the legislative process, and the Code is the beginning point for all research and planning in taxation. The legislative process, nevertheless, results in many other sources that can be helpful to tax practitioners and to the taxpayer. The sources listed below are often valuable in the interpretation of what a word, clause, or sentence in the Code means; that is, of the congressional intent behind the bare words of the Code.

1. The most important sources for interpretation are the committee reports that accompany the revenue acts when they are submitted to the House or Senate. Each revenue bill from the Committee on Ways and Means is accompanied by a House Report that explains the problems as well as the changes in the law proposed in response to the problem. Reports also accompany the bills reported by the Senate Finance Committee and the conference committee.

2. Hearings before the Committee on Ways and Means and the Committee on Finance are often published. These hearings provide invaluable insights into the political, economic, and social problems the legislators must confront.

3. The *Congressional Record* contains the floor

debates in the House and Senate on revenue bills. Often the responses to questions raised shed some light on congressional intent.

Organization of the code

The organization of the Internal Revenue Code of 1954, the basic law of federal income taxation that is operative today, can be depicted as follows:

(7) SUBTITLES (designated by upper-case English letters A–G: SUBTITLE A is titled "Income Taxes").

(92) CHAPTERS (designated by Arabic numerals 1–92; Chapter 1 is titled "Normal Taxes and Surtaxes").

SUBCHAPTERS (designated by upper-case English letters as required; for example, Chapter 1 has 20 Subchapters, A–T).

PARTS (designated by Roman numerals as required; for example, Chapter 1, Subchapter A, has 6 Parts, I–VI).

SUBPARTS (designated by upper-case English letters as required).

SECTIONS (designated by Arabic numerals as required. See text below for important details of this subdivision of the Code).

SUBSECTIONS (designated by lower-case English letters in parentheses, as required).

PARAGRAPHS (designated by Arabic numerals, in parentheses, as required).

SUBPARAGRAPHS (designated by upper-case English letters, in parentheses, as required).

A student can get an excellent overview of our tax laws by examining the titles to the Subchapters and related Parts of Chapter 1 of the 1954 Code. They are as follows:

SUBTITLE A—INCOME TAXES

Chapter 1. Normal Taxes and Surtaxes.

Subchapter A.	Determination of tax liability.
Part I.	Tax on individuals.
Part II.	Tax on corporations.
Part III.	Changes in rates during a taxable year.
Part IV.	Credits against tax.
Part V.	Tax surcharge.
Part VI.	Minimum tax for tax preferences.
Subchapter B.	Computation of taxable income.
Part I.	Definition of gross income, adjustable gross income, and taxable income.
Part II.	Items specifically included in gross income.

Part III.	Items specifically excluded from gross income.
Part IV.	Standard deduction for individuals.
Part V.	Deductions for personal exemptions.
Part VI.	Itemized deductions for individuals and corporations.
Part VII.	Additional itemized deductions for individuals.
Part VIII.	Special deductions for corporations.
Part IX.	Items not deductible.
Part X.	Terminal railroad corporations and their shareholders.
Subchapter C.	Corporate distributions and adjustments.
Part I.	Distributions by corporations.
Part II.	Corporate liquidations.
Part III.	Corporate organizations and reorganizations.
Part IV.	Insolvency reorganizations.
Part V.	Carryovers.
Part VI.	Treatment of certain interests as stock or indebtedness.
Part VII.	Effective data of subchapter C.
Subchapter D.	Deferred compensation, etc.
Part I.	Pension, profit-sharing stock bonus plans, etc.
Part II.	Certain stock options.
Subchapter E.	Accounting periods and methods of accounting.
Part I.	Accounting periods.
Part II.	Methods of accounting.
Part III.	Adjustments.
Subchapter F.	Exempt organizations.
Part I.	General rule.
Part II.	Private foundations.
Part III.	Taxation of business income of certain exempt organizations.
Part IV.	Farmers' cooperatives.
Part V.	Shipowners' protection and indemnity associations.
Subchapter G.	Corporations used to avoid income tax on shareholders.
Part I.	Corporations improperly accumulating surplus.
Part II.	Personal holding companies.
Part III.	Foreign personal holding companies.
Part IV.	Deduction for dividends paid.
Subchapter H.	Banking institutions.
Part I.	Rules of general application to banking institutions.
Part II.	Mutual savings banks, etc.
Part III.	Bank affiliates.
Subchapter I.	Natural resources.
Part I.	Deductions.
Part II.	Exclusions from gross income.
Part III.	Sales and exchanges.
Part IV.	Mineral production payments.
Part V.	Continental shelf areas.

Subchapter J. Estates, trusts, beneficiaries, and decedents.
Part I. Estates, trusts, and beneficiaries.
Part II. Income in respect of decedents.
Subchapter K. Partners and partnerships.
Part I. Determination of tax liability.
Part II. Contributions, distributions, and transfers.
Part III. Definitions.
Part IV. Effective date for subchapter.
Subchapter L. Insurance companies.
Part I. Life insurance companies.
Part II. Mutual insurance companies (other than life and certain marine insurance companies and other than fire or flood insurance companies which operate on basis of perpetual policies or premium deposits).
Part III. Other insurance companies.
Part IV. Provisions of general application.
Subchapter M. Regulated investment companies and real estate investment trusts.
Part I. Regulated investment companies.
Part II. Real estate investment trusts.
Subchapter N. Tax based on income from sources within or without the United States.
Part I. Determination of sources of income.
Part II. Nonresident aliens and foreign corporations.
Part III. Income from sources without the United States.
Part IV. Domestic international sales corporations.
Subchapter O. Gain or loss on disposition of property.
Part I. Determination of amount of and recognition of gain or loss.
Part II. Basis rules of general application.
Part III. Common nontaxable exchanges.
Part IV. Special rules.
Part V. Changes to effectuate F.C.C. policy.
Part VI. Exchanges in obedience to S.E.C. orders.
Part VII. Wash sales of stock or securities.
Part VIII. Distributions pursuant to Bank Holding Company Act of 1956.
Part IX. Distributions pursuant to orders enforcing the antitrust laws.
Subchapter P. Capital gains and losses.
Part I. Treatment of capital gains.
Part II. Treatment of capital losses.
Part III. General rules for determining capital gains and losses.
Part IV. Special rules for determining capital gains and losses.
Subchapter Q. Readjustment of tax between years and special limitations.
Part I. Income averaging.
Part II. Mitigation of effect of limitations and other provisions.

Part III. Involuntary liquidation and replacement of LIFO inventories.
Part IV. War loss recoveries.
Part V. Claim of right.
Part VI. Other limitations.
Part VII. Recoveries of foreign expropriation losses.
Subchapter R. Election of certain partnerships and proprietorships as to taxable status. [Note: Subchapter R was repealed, effective January 1, 1969.]
Subchapter S. Election of certain small business corporations as to taxable status.
Subchapter T. Cooperatives and their patrons.
Part I. Tax treatment of cooperatives.
Part II. Tax treatment by patrons of patronage dividends.
Part III. Definitions; special rules.

Nearly all the ''popular'' income-tax literature makes reference only to the sections or lower subdivisions of the Code. Thus, for example, ''Section 71'' refers (without specific mention) to the 1954 Code, Subtitle A, Chapter 1, Subchapter B, Part II. This reference is workable because section designations get progressively larger, beginning with Subchapter A, Part I, although not all numbers are utilized. The omission of numbers permits Congress to insert (or to delete) changes in the law continuously without renumbering the entire Code. In a sense, then, the Code is like a chart of accounts in an accounting system. To illustrate, Subchapter A, Part I, utilizes section numbers 1 through 6—there are at present no sections numbered 7 through 10; Part II utilizes section numbers 11 and 12; Part III utilizes number 21 only, and so on.

Because most of the tax literature explicitly refers only to a section number, or an even lower subdivision of the Code, we must understand clearly what is represented in a common Code citation. To illustrate, suppose that you saw a reference to ''the limitation of Sec. 74(b)(2).'' What does that reference mean? What limitation are they talking about? To answer that question you would have to (1) have access to the 1954 Code and (2) know how to locate the requirement referenced. A few instructors require even their introductory tax students to purchase a paperback copy of the current Code.[20] Other students can locate the Code volume of almost any

---

[20]The Code is usually printed twice each year by both CCH (Commerce Clearing House) and P-H (Prentice-Hall, Inc.) in paperback editions costing approximately $12.50. Special prices may be available when ordering in large quantities.

tax reference service in a library if they will just look carefully. Still others may be satisfied with frequently reprinted exerpts from the Code, such as those included in this text.[21]

Regardless of exactly where and how you find the Code, any reference to Sec. 74(b)(2) should lead to the following words:

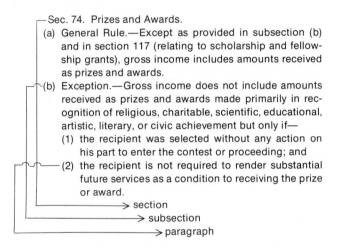

Sec. 74. Prizes and Awards.
(a) General Rule.—Except as provided in subsection (b) and in section 117 (relating to scholarship and fellowship grants), gross income includes amounts received as prizes and awards.
(b) Exception.—Gross income does not include amounts received as prizes and awards made primarily in recognition of religious, charitable, scientific, educational, artistic, literary, or civic achievement but only if—
(1) the recipient was selected without any action on his part to enter the contest or proceeding; and
(2) the recipient is not required to render substantial future services as a condition to receiving the prize or award.

→ section
→ subsection
→ paragraph

As indicated above, Section 74, Subsection b, Paragraph 2 (which is read simply as ''Section 74, b, 2'') specifically prohibits the winner of an otherwise tax-exempt prize or award from rendering any ''substantial future service'' as a condition for the award, if the award is to retain its tax-exempt status. To illustrate, if a Nobel Peace Prize winner were *required* to give four one-hour speeches in each of four designated cities as a condition for receiving that award, then the otherwise exempt award *might* be made taxable by operation of Sec. 74(b)(2). Note that we said the Nobel Peace Prize *might* become taxable by the action suggested. Whether it would or not depends on a statutory interpretation of the word ''substantial.''

Interpretation by the Treasury Department

The Internal Revenue Code authorizes and instructs the Secretary of the Treasury or his delegate to issue regulations interpreting the tax law. The I.R.S., a subdivision of the Treasury Department, also issues many pronouncements under the generic class of ''rulings'' dealing with the administration and interpretation of our tax laws.

REGULATIONS The regulations, which contain the Secretary's interpretation of the Internal Revenue Code, have the force and effect of the Code, unless they can be shown to be in conflict with congressional intent.[22] Instructions printed on and accompanying the official tax return forms also constitute part of the regulations. Regulations contain helpful amplifications of the Code and many useful examples. Before regulations are officially released on a new or amended provision, *proposed* regulations are published and circulated. The Treasury Department invites comments and suggestions on the proposed regulations from all interested parties. After a period specified in the proposed regulations, final regulations are adopted, incorporating changes necessitated by the comments received. The Secretary revises and expands the regulations when Congress amends the Code and adds new provisons to it.

When adopted, regulations for all federal taxes are printed in Title 26 of the Code of Federal Regulations. Title 26 is subdivided into parts that correspond with the subtitles in the Internal Revenue Code. Thus Part 1 of the regulations deals with Subtitle A of the Code, the income tax. In addition, the parts are subdivided into sections that correspond with sections of the Code. Thus, Part 1, Section 162, of the Regulations deals with the ordinary and necessary expenses of carrying on a trade or business. The complete citation for that section of the regulations is 26 CFR 1.162, which means Title 26, Code of Federal Regulations, Part 1, Section 162. For brevity, the citation often is reduced to Reg. 1.162.

When trying to determine how any particular transaction will be taxed, the researcher should go first to the Internal Revenue Code (and perhaps to the hearings and reports of the congressional committees). The regulations should be consulted also. Often the congressional intent is inscrutable without the help of the regulations. The experts who prepare the regulations often have firsthand information derived from participation as advisors in the legislative process. Their elaboration of the statute greatly reduces the number of conflicts between the government and taxpayers. Some tax practitioners do not turn to the regulations until after they have examined all other sources, feeling that a reading of the regulations early in the research reduces their capacity to conceive of other interpretations of congressional intent that might be more favorable to their clients. Only rarely, however, have the courts held that the regulations run counter to the intent of Congress.

---

[21]See the approximately 100 entries under ''Internal Revenue Code'' in the Index for cross-reference to the Code sections partially or completely reprinted in this text.

[22]*Maryland Casualty Co.* v. *U.S.*, 251 U.S. 342 (1920).

RULINGS   The *Internal Revenue Bulletin,* which is published weekly by the Internal Revenue Service, contains much of the information referred to in the preceding pages. For example, the *Bulletin* will include copies of the Internal Revenue Acts and committee reports on these acts. In addition, the *Bulletin* contains the following:

Treasury decisions. Regulations and amendments or revisions to regulations are first issued as Treasury Decisions (TD). These releases must have the approval of the Treasury Department, and after release they may be relied on as a precedent; that is, they are binding on the government. Formal organization of the regulation, as explained above, is in the Code of Federal Regulations.

Revenue rulings. The Commissioner's interpretation of certain provisions of the law in relation to a specific fact case is released from time to time as a revenue ruling. These rulings do not constitute a comprehensive coverage of the Internal Revenue Code. The Commissioner is not required by law to follow his interpretation in a revenue ruling in all cases, although a ruling generally is binding on the government with respect to the facts on which the ruling was requested. Revenue rulings are consecutively numbered each calendar year and are cited Rev. Rul. 1980-1, etc.[23] Any taxpayer, prior to filing his or her return, may ask the I.R.S. for a private ruling on how to treat a completed transaction. Rulings may also be requested for prospective transactions. The form used to request a ruling is specified by the Commissioner. The I.R.S., however, is not compelled to make the ruling.

Each year the I.R.S. issues a large number of rulings, but until recently, it selected only a small number for publication in the *Bulletin.* Determination of which rulings to publish historically was made by the I.R.S. based on its opinion of the usefulness of the ruling to taxpayers generally. The Tax Reform Act of 1976, however, contained a provision that requires the I.R.S. to make private rulings and certain other written determinations available to the public. Just how useful this huge mass of new information will be to tax experts remains uncertain.

Other releases. Tax information releases deal with timely topics of general interest and are released to the popular press. Revenue procedures (Rev. Proc.) explain procedures and other duties of taxpayers. There are various other forms of releases. On occasion these releases can be very important to taxpayers—for example, the depreciation guidelines were originally published as a revenue procedure.

The material in the *Bulletin* is reorganized and printed in a bound volume on a semiannual basis. The bound volumes are called *Cumulative Bulletins* and are cited C.B. Thus 1980-1 C.B. would contain Rev. Rul. 1980-1, as well as other information.

Statutory interpretation by courts

As suggested above, the Treasury Department and the Internal Revenue Service both publish "official" interpretations of the Code in such pronouncements as Treasury Regulations and Revenue Rulings, respectively. But, as you may already suspect, not everyone agrees with the government's interpretations of the Code. Hence, disputes frequently develop between I.R.S. agents and taxpayers. If these two parties cannot otherwise agree, the only way to resolve a disputed interpretation of the Code is through a court; that is, through a judicial interpretation of the statutory law. Chapter 27 includes a detailed account of the judicial proceedings available in the settlement of tax disputes. For this introduction to tax research, however, it is sufficient to know that a record of most judicial interpretations is—like an administrative interpretation by the Treasury Department or the I.R.S.—published and made available to the general public. The common form of citation for any judicial proceeding consists of two sets of numbers and one set of letters, as follows:

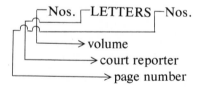

The first set of numbers refers to the volume number of a particular reporter series. The letters tell you which reporter series is being cited. Finally, the last set of numbers *usually* refers to the exact page number on which that particular judicial interpretation may be located. For example,

54 AFTR 2d 310

refers to

1. Volume 54 of
2. The American Federal Tax Reporter, second series
3. At page 310.

---

[23]Prior to 1953, citations for rulings identified the source of the ruling. There were many different series, each with its own alphabetic identification. A list of the varied citations is available in most tax services.

Immediately preceeding such a citation you will ordinarily find the ''name'' of the case being litigated. Immediately following a citation you will often find additional information, such as the court and, possibly, the year in which the opinion was rendered. Thus, for example, you might see a citation as follows:

Tax Students, Inc. v. Comm'r. of Internal Revenue,
54 AFTR 2d 310 (CCA-5, 1980).

This fictitious citation would refer to litigation between a corporation titled Tax Students and the Commissioner of the Internal Revenue Service; the decision in the case could be found at page 310 of the 54th volume of the American Federal Tax Reporter (second series). The opinion found there would be that of the Fifth Circuit Court of Appeals, an opinion rendered in 1980.

Although there are many commercially competitive court reporter series, the ones that you are most likely to encounter in researching an introductory tax problem summarized below.

A good deal of overlap exists between the various court reporters, and each has unique features too numerous to mention or explain here.[24] In general, however, you may use any one of the court reporters in doing basic tax research. Use whatever is available in your library. Rather than which reporter to use, your first big problem is more likely to be locating an appropriate citation to a pertinent administrative or judicial interpretation of the Code.

Tax services

Your instructor may ask you to try and locate additional authority on almost any tax question. If and when that happens, you are likely to have to rely on one of the major tax services to find your answer. Among the most popular tax services are the following:

Name of the tax service	Publisher
Federal Tax Service	Prentice-Hall, Inc.
Standard Federal Tax Reports	Commerce Clearing House
Tax Management	Bureau of National Affairs

Each of these tax services is prepared and updated in a unique way, which you can discover either through trial and error or through reading descriptive materials distributed by the publisher or independent evaluations published in other works (see footnote 24). Regardless of which tax service you use, and regardless of how you learn to use it, elementary tax research usually begins with a key-word index that will eventually lead you to additional references to:

1. The Code (specific sections, subsections, paragraphs, etc.)
2. Treasury regulations
3. Revenue rulings, and/or
4. Judicial decisions

Learning how to use a key-word index successfully takes a bit of practice. With experience, however, you can quickly learn how to do some elementary forms of tax research. Like any true skill, however, learning how to complete more complex tax research assignments will require long hours of practice, but it can pay handsome dividends for those who find it to be a challenge.

[24]For those interested in additional details, see Chapter 4, Ray M. Sommerfeld and G. Fred Streuling, *Tax Research Techniques* (AICPA Tax Study No. 5), New York: American Institute of Certified Public Accountants, 1976.

Citation	Court reporter series referenced	Publisher
AFTR	American Federal Tax Reporter	Prentice-Hall, Inc.
AFTR 2d	American Federal Tax Reporter, second series	Prentice-Hall, Inc.
USTC	United States Tax Cases	Commerce Clearing House
TC	Tax Court	Government Printing Office
US	United States Supreme Court	Government Printing Office
BTA	Board of Tax Appeals	Government Printing Office
S.Ct.	Supreme Court	West Publishing Company
Ct. Cl.	Court of Claims	West Publishing Company
F. 2d	Federal Reporter, second series	West Publishing Company
F. Supp.	Federal Supplement	West Publishing Company

In Part One, we have touched only the surface of some quite complex subjects. It is hoped that some students will be sufficiently stimulated by this brief introduction to make a more exhaustive examination at another time. The remainder of this book is concerned exclusively with income taxation because it is the dominant form of taxation in our economy today. Bear in mind throughout, however, that the income tax is but one part of a complex tax structure. As taxpayers and tax practitioners, we must be concerned with how much tax must be paid in a given situation. As citizens and students of taxation, we must also strive to gain an appreciation of the place of the tax laws in the social, economic, and political fabric of our time.

PROBLEMS

1. How would you characterize the major changes in the federal income tax between 1913 and 1939? Between 1939 and 1954? Between 1954 and 1969? Between 1969 and 1977? Since 1978?

2. If it is true that the income tax was unconstitutional prior to the ratification of the Sixteenth Amendment in 1913, how is it possible that the United States actually imposed and collected an income tax for approximately ten years in the 1870s and 1880s?

3. What is a direct tax? What is an indirect tax?

4. The federal income tax on individuals did not become a "mass tax" until approximately 1942. Explain what this means and what was necessitated by the transition from a "select tax" to a "mass tax."

5. Is it likely that either the personal or the corporate income taxes will be repealed in the near future? Explain briefly.

6. Between 1861 and 1872, several of the revenue acts passed by Congress included an income tax.
   a. Was the constitutionality of these acts ever tested before the U. S. Supreme Court? If so, what did the Court find?
   b. List four reasons why these early experiments in income taxation may be considered significant for subsequent income tax laws.

7. How many Internal Revenue Codes have been enacted by the Congress? Which Code is in effect today?

8. In reading a tax article, you note the two following references. Explain briefly what each means.
   a. Reg. Sec. 1.101-2(b) (2).
   b. Rev. Rul. 68-10, 1968-1 CB 18.

9. Outline the channels through which federal tax legislation normally passes before enactment.

10. What is the difference between a Treasury regulation and an I.R.S. ruling?

11. Before enacting substantial increases in social security (F.I.C.A) taxes, Congress in 1977 considered and rejected the possibility of funding anticipated shortages in the social security trust fund from general-fund revenues. Nevertheless, almost immediately after the passage of the bill that will dramatically increase social security taxes between 1979 and 1987, both the president and Congress began in 1978 to advocate major reductions in income taxes, at least partially, to offset the social security tax increases! What does this sequence of events suggest as to (1) earmarking as a federal tax concept, and (2) acceptance of the notion that "contributions" to the social security trust fund are really a

tax? Explain briefly. (If necessary, review page 1/3 for a definition of "earmarking" and page 1/1 for a definition of "tax.")

12. What two reasons do the authors suggest for restricting the remainder of your introduction to taxation to issues of federal income taxation?

SUPPLEMENTAL PROBLEMS

13. Using the daily newspapers or weekly news magazines available in your library, determine if any major changes in tax laws have been proposed or enacted within the past 6 months. If so, what reasons have been given in support of these new provisions?

14. Tax-sharing—that is, the redistribution of federal revenues to state and local governments for spending—has become a significant political issue within the past year or two. What differences of opinion are currently being expressed on this issue?

15. Your text refers to Richard Goode's six prerequisites of a successful income tax: (1) a money economy, (2) general literacy, (3) minimum accounting records, (4) acceptance of the idea of voluntary compliance with tax laws, (5) political acceptance of an income tax, and (6) an efficient administrative machine. Considering the economic and political situation in the United States during Reconstruction, what accounts for the repeal of the Civil War income tax in 1872? Explain, considering each prerequisite.

16. The income tax is a "self-assessment" tax; each taxpayer assesses himself or herself, and the government merely reviews the assessment of selected individuals. Explain briefly what would be required to change over to governmental assessment of each taxpayer.

I guess you will have to go to jail. If that is the result of not understanding the Income Tax law I shall meet you there. We will have a merry, merry time, for all of our friends will be there. It will be an intellectual center, for no one understands the Income Tax law except persons who have not sufficient intelligence to understand the questions that arise under it.

ELIHU ROOT,
quoted in Randolph E. Paul, *Taxation in the United States*

... it is probable that the income tax has come to stay. Let us be thankful that it has come in such a shape, and let us look forward with hopeful anticipation to a future in which the income tax, improved and amended, will play its important part in bringing about greater justice in American taxation.

EDWIN R. A. SELIGMAN,
The Income Tax (1914)

PART

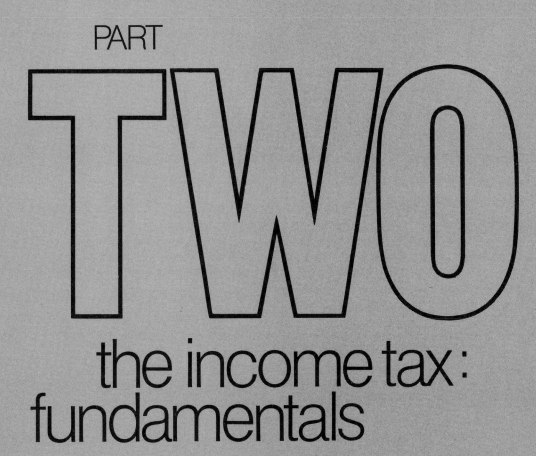

TWO

the income tax: fundamentals

The first nine pages of the Internal Revenue Code define income; the remaining 1,100 pages spin the web of exceptions and preferences. The average taxpayer rarely gets beyond the nine pages.

SENATOR WARREN MAGNUSON,
Congressional Record (1966)

gross income: general concepts

The procedure for determining an income-tax liability can be expressed as an apparently simple mathematical formula. And, indeed, the arithmetic involved in the formula is no more complicated than simple addition, subtraction, and multiplication. The simplest and most general formula to determine the income-tax liability of *any* taxable entity is as follows:

$$
\begin{array}{l}
\ \text{Income broadly conceived} \\
-\ \text{Exclusions} \\
\hline
=\ \text{Gross income} \\
-\ \text{Deductions} \\
\hline
=\ \text{Taxable income} \\
\times\ \text{Applicable tax rate} \\
\hline
=\ \text{Gross tax} \\
-\ \text{Tax credits and prepayments} \\
\hline
=\ \text{Net tax payable}
\end{array}
$$

But here simplicity ends, for the application of the formula is dependent on myriad classifications, definitions, distinctions, and exceptions contained in the Internal Revenue Code. To make matters even more complex, the Code sometimes gives common words a special meaning for tax purposes. Furthermore (and most important), to understand tax provisions, a person often must understand not only the literal wording of the Code but the social, economic, and political forces that motivated its enactment, the administrative considerations that attach to a particular interpretation of it, and the personal opinions of the individuals assigned the responsibility of interpreting it. Justice Learned Hand stated this conclusion most explicitly and colorfully when he said, " . . . as the articulation of a statute increases, the room for interpretation must contract; but the meaning of a sentence may be more than that of the separate words, as a melody is more than the notes, and no degree of particularity can ever obviate recourse to the setting in which all appear, and which all collectively create."[1]

In the remainder of this book, we shall be trying to untangle at least part of the "web of exceptions and preferences" that enter into the interpretation of this basic formula. We shall begin by examining in this chapter the first three items in the formula: "Income Broadly Conceived," "Exclusions," and "Gross Income." The other elements of the formula will be analyzed in subsequent chapters.

In reading Parts Two and Three you should be cautioned against getting too involved with the numerous details common to income taxation. The relationship between these seven chapters and the rest of the book can be compared meaningfully with the relationship between a globe and a state road map. That is, these chapters are intended only to provide the broad perspective of income taxation within the United States. To the extent that the con-

[1]*Helvering* v. *Gregory,* 69 F. 2d 809 (CCA 2nd, 1934).

fines of a single volume permit, significant details will be reconsidered in greater depth in the rest of this book. The later chapters concentrate on the tax provisions that, when applied to the process of income measurement, differ significantly from the procedures used in general financial accounting. Thus, by restricting our attention to detail to those instances of variance between income taxation and financial accounting, we may determine not only what the major differences are but also why the differences first arose and the meaning of them to our country today.

INCOME, EXCLUSIONS, AND GROSS INCOME UNDER THE REVENUE CODE

In all of economic thought, the income concept is one of the most complex and controversial. Innumerable forces have, through time, created and recast several distinct income concepts, and major differences can be observed today among the usual definitions of income proposed by economists, lawyers, and accountants.

Not only are there different concepts of the term "income," but also income must be clearly differentiated from the concepts of "gross receipts" and "revenue." Income is a *net* measure (that is, revenue less expenses), whereas revenue and gross receipts are *gross* measures. "Gross receipts" are essentially equivalent to total cash receipts collected during a given time period. Revenue, on the other hand, refers to a monetary quantity "earned" during a given time period regardless of the amount collected.

Although the details of the concept of taxable income will be further examined later in this chapter, it should be noted here that the Code begins with a presumption that all income is taxable income; it subsequently provides a relatively brief list of exceptions to that presumption. The explicit provisions are provided in Subchapter B, which is entitled "Computation of taxable income."[2] Subchapter B is subdivided into ten parts, the first three of which are pertinent to the gross income concept. They are

Part I.   Definition of gross income, adjusted gross income, and taxable income
Part II. Items specifically included in gross income
Part III. Items specifically excluded from gross income

[2]Chapter 4 contains a broad outline of Chapter 1 of the Internal Revenue Code, the chapter concerned with federal income taxation. We recommend that you review this section to get an overview of how the Code is arranged and what, in general, it contains.

The general tax definition of gross income is located in Sec. 61 (a) of Part I and reads as follows:

(a) General Definition.—Except as otherwise provided in this subtitle, gross income means all income from whatever source derived, including (but not limited to) the following items:
  (1) Compensation for services, including fees, commissions, and similar items;
  (2) Gross income derived from business;
  (3) Gains derived from dealings in property;
  (4) Interest;
  (5) Rents;
  (6) Royalties;
  (7) Dividends;
  (8) Alimony and separate maintenance payments;
  (9) Annuities;
  (10) Income from life insurance and endowment contract;
  (11) Pensions;
  (12) Income from discharge of indebtedness;
  (13) Distributive share of partnership gross income;
  (14) Income in respect of a decedent; and
  (15) Income from an interest in an estate or trust.

Note the phrase "but not limited to"; the general provisions of Sec. 61 (a) apply to *all* income, regardless of source, except for items that are specifically excluded elsewhere in the Internal Revenue Code.

The statutory exclusions detailed in Part III of Subchapter B are supposed to be equally applicable to corporate and individual taxpayers. Even a cursory review of the list proves, however, that most of the items are more relevant to the individual than to the corporate entity. The list includes

Sec. 101. Certain death benefits.
Sec. 102. Gifts and inheritances.
Sec. 103. Interest on certain governmental obligations.
Sec. 104. Compensation for injuries or sickness.
Sec. 105. Amounts received under accident and health plans.
Sec. 106. Contributions by employer to accident and health plans.
Sec. 107. Rental value of parsonages.
Sec. 108. Income from discharge of indebtedness.
Sec. 109. Improvements by lessee on lessor's property.
Sec. 110. Income taxes paid by lessee corporation.
Sec. 111. Recovery of bad debts, prior taxes, and delinquency amounts.
Sec. 112. Certain combat pay of members of the Armed Forces.
Sec. 113. Mustering-out payments for members of the Armed Forces.
Sec. 114. Sports programs conducted for the American National Red Cross.
Sec. 115. Income of States, municipalities, etc.
Sec. 116. Partial exclusion of dividends received by individuals.
Sec. 117. Scholarships and fellowship grants.
Sec. 118. Contributions to the capital of a corporation.

Sec. 119. Meals or lodging furnished for the convenience of the employer.
Sec. 120. Amounts received under qualified group legal services plans.
Sec. 121. One-time exclusion of gain from sale of principal residence by individual who has attained age 55.
Sec. 122. Certain reduced uniformed services retirement pay.
Sec. 123. Amounts received under insurance contracts for certain living expenses.
Sec. 124. Qualified transportation provided by employer.
Sec. 125. Cafeteria plans.
Sec. 126. Certain cost-sharing payments.
Sec. 127. Educational assistance programs.
Sec. 128. Cross-references to other Acts.

This seemingly clear list of *inclusions*, coupled with the long listing of specific *exclusions* in Secs. 101 through 128, may give the student who is unfamiliar with the myriad controversies surrounding the nature and measurement of "income" a false and unwarranted sense of security and assurance about his or her understanding of income. Certainly no area of tax law has been more hotly debated than the question, "What is income?" The astute reader has already realized that Sec. 61(a) does not answer this question. Unfortunately, neither the related regulations nor other interpretations of the Code contain a clear-cut definition.

INCOME CONCEPTS

In this chapter we shall examine some of the fundamental issues underlying the problem of income definition and measurement. We will be concerned with major distinctions between the concepts of income found in economics, accounting, and taxation, especially with the conflicts between the accounting and tax concepts of income.

The income of economics

A traditional starting point is to analyze the definitions of income given by Robert M. Haig and Henry C. Simons. These men were two of the early scholars of tax theory who were well versed in economics. Haig's definition of income is simple and straightforward: "Income is the *money value of the net accretion to one's economic power between two points of time*."[3] A similar definition is given by Simons: "Personal income may be defined as the algebraic

sum of (1) the market value of rights exercised in consumption and (2) the change in the value of the store of property rights between the beginning and end of the period in question."[4]

Professor Harvey Brazer has restated the concept of income held by Simons and Haig (and even before them by the German economist George Schanz and others) in easily understood terms: "Under this concept income is equal to the algebraic sum of consumption plus the change in the individual's net worth during the year or other accounting period. . . . It asks simply, how much could this individual have spent for consumption during the year while remaining as well off in terms of net worth at the end of the year as he was at the beginning of the year."[5] Perhaps the most important aspect of Simons's definition of income, at least from the viewpoint of the accountant, is his suggestion that consumption and the net change in the individual's store of claims ideally are "both evaluated at market price, with the latter [increase in store of claims] computed on an accrual rather than on a realization basis."[6]

The major difficulty in using this definition for such practical purposes as taxation is in obtaining reliable measures of net worth and consumption. Basically, the problem is one of valuation. Unfortunately, only a relatively insignificant portion of total assets will have easily ascertainable and accurate market values. The "value" of most assets is a subjective characteristic that depends on someone's estimate of the satisfaction to be derived from the object in question in comparison with the expected satisfaction that could be obtained from other objects that might be purchased as an alternative.

Another problem arising from this economic concept of income is in distinguishing between "monetary" income and "real" income. This difference refers to the familiar problem caused by changes in the value of the monetary unit—in accounting the problem is commonly called the price-level problem. The changing price level does not cause a serious problem in measuring consumption, but it may be very important in measuring the change in accumula-

---

[3] Robert M. Haig, "The Concept of Income—Economic and Legal Aspects," *The Federal Income Tax* (New York: Columbia University Press, 1921), p. 7.

[4] Henry C. Simons, *Personal Income Taxation* (Chicago: University of Chicago Press, 1921), p. 50.

[5] Harvey E. Brazer, "The Economics of Tax Reform," *Proceedings of the Fifty-Sixth Annual Conference* (1963) *of the National Tax Association*, p. 47.

[6] Melvin I. White, "Consistent Treatment of Items Excluded and Omitted from the Individual Income Tax Base," *1959 Compendium*, p. 318. (The complete reference is *Tax Revision Compendium: Compendium of Papers on Broadening the Tax Base*, submitted to the Committee on Ways and Means, beginning November 16, 1959. This three-volume collection of papers on income taxation is one of the modern classics and is quoted frequently throughout this text. To simplify the footnotes, all subsequent references will simply cite the *1959 Compendium*.)

tion in value during the year if the price level has changed markedly. Most economists stress *real* capital accumulation, measured by the increase in command over scarce resources. Presumably, "fictitious gains that are due merely to an increase in price level can be approximately eliminated by deflating by an index of consumer prices."[7]

A broad view of income would presumably include *all* receipts from *all* sources, including such gratuitous receipts as gifts, inheritances, and bequests—mainly on the basis that including such items eliminates the need "to distinguish among an individual's receipts according to the intentions of second parties" and that it makes the definition simpler, more precise, and more definite.[8]

The income of accounting

There are major discrepancies between the broad definition of income discussed in the preceding pages and the computation of income under generally accepted accounting principles. The primary difference is the complete absence of any "realization" criterion in the economic view of income.[9]

Generally accepted accounting principles suggest that income should be measured on the basis of completed transactions. Note the importance of this distinction: Economists define income in terms of *value,* depending essentially on expectations about the *future.* Accountants define income basically in terms of the *past,* expressed in money measurement. They are concerned with the flow of transactions of the enterprise because completed transactions—presumably at arm's length—provide independent judgments of "value" on which accountants can rely. The economists' concept is, in general, deemed by accountants to be too impractical and difficult to apply and too lacking in objectivity and accuracy to be used as a basis for measuring periodic income in the accounts. The recognition of unrealized gains or losses requiring detailed annual listings and subjective valuations of assets and liabilities is frightening to many accountants, who are steeped in the virtues of practicality and conservatism and who are saddled with legal liability for the accuracy of the financial statements they certify.

The student of accounting may be surprised to discover that economists frequently fail to understand the reluctance of accountants to use subjective valuations to the extent that they are used by economists. Professor Simons, for example, once charged that accountants prefer to sacrifice relevance for accuracy.[10] On the other hand, he admitted that "outright abandonment of the realization criterion would be utter folly; no workable scheme can require that taxpayers reappraise and report all their assets annually; and while this procedure is implied by the underlying definition of income, it is quite unnecessary to effective application of that definition. . . ."[11]

The contrast between economic and accounting concepts of income can be seen easily from a grossly simplified example. Suppose that on January 1, 19x1, John Glover, a young attorney fresh from law school, took inventory of his financial condition. His only assets at this time consisted of a bank account and his clothing. On that date he took a job with a law firm. He also decided to invest $1,000 of his bank account in a new highly speculative mining company, leaving him a bank balance of only $500. During the year 19x1, he earned a salary of $15,000; he also was allowed to accept a few cases outside the firm for which he received fees of $2,000 and incurred expenses of $400. Glover's mother made a gift to him of $2,000 cash in 19x1. In addition, the mining company discovered uranium and was highly profitable; he received dividends of $900 on the shares, which increased in value so that they were worth $9,800 on December 31, 19x1. Glover was not frugal, however, and on December 31 his only asset, other than the shares of stock, was a bank account of $400; the remaining $19,600 of cash that he had available during the year was spent purely for consumption items.

Using the general ideas previously described (but ignoring price-level changes) the economist would compute Glover's income as $28,300:

	Value at beginning of year	Value at end of year	Increase (or decrease)
Cash	$ 500	$ 400	($ 100)
Shares of stock	1,000	9,800	8,800
Increase in "net worth"			$ 8,700
Plus consumption expenditures			19,600
Total "economic" income			28,300

[7]Richard Goode, *The Individual Income Tax* (Washington: The Brookings Institution, 1964), p. 15.

[8]Haig, *op. cit.,* p. 37.

[9]For an interesting discussion of the legal and economic origins of the realization concept, see Lawrence H. Seltzer, *The Nature and Tax Treatment of Capital Gains and Losses* (New York: Bureau of Economic Research, 1951), pp. 25–46.

[10]See Simons, *op. cit.,* p. 80.

[11]*Ibid.,* pp. 207–08. This conclusion was reaffirmed by Professor Simons in his later book, *Federal Tax Reform* (Chicago: University of Chicago Press, 1950). Both books are excellent reading for the serious tax student.

The accountant, on the other hand, would compute Glover's income as $17,500:

Salary		$15,000
Fees from outside cases	$2,000	
Less: expenses	400	
		1,600
Dividends		900
Total "accounting" income		$17,500

Note that the accountant includes only *realized* income, deducting the applicable expenses that can be matched against that income. A gift generally is not considered by the accountant to be income. Even more important, the increase of $8,800 in the value of the stock is disregarded by the accountant because it has not been "realized" through sale or exchange.

Consumption and income

One further way of looking at income should be mentioned because it is closely related to the realization principle. Under this concept, generally associated with the name of Professor Irving Fisher, realization is ultimately represented only by *consumption,* because only when an item is consumed is there a logical stopping place among the sequence of economic relations.[12] From this viewpoint, income represents satisfaction derived from consumption and is measured in monetary terms by the amount spent on consumer goods plus the use value (imputed income) of durable goods "consumed" during the period—for example the use value derived from an owner-occupied home. The source of what the individual consumed (and only individuals can consume) is immaterial. Obviously the computation of imputed income is highly subjective; however, the failure to include imputed income in any income-tax base inevitably decreases the (theoretical) equity of the tax.

An income tax based on a consumption definition of income would, for all practical purposes, become an expenditures tax. Although the consumption-expenditures approach to taxation is interesting from an academic viewpoint, it has relatively little significance in the present tax structure of most countries. The most thorough statement of this approach to

taxation is attributed to Nicholas Kaldor, an English economist.[13]

The net-worth method of estimating taxable income

The all-inclusive approach to income measurement attributed to Simons and Haig approaches a method used, albeit infrequently, by the I.R.S. to reconstruct the income of taxpayers who are without adequate and accurate accounting records. This is the "net-worth method," which relies heavily on the basic assumption that all inflows of wealth are taxable unless specifically excluded by law. Essentially, this method of measuring income compares the taxpayer's net worth at the beginning and end of a period. The change in net worth is then combined with estimated consumption expenditures for the period to get an estimate of total income.

Although rarely used, the method is subject to strong criticism on the grounds that the taxpayer has the burden of proving that any portion of the computed income was derived from excluded sources. On the other hand, it is sometimes the only realistic alternative available to the I.R.S., and the possibility of its use certainly encourages gamblers, prostitutes, and other such people in our society to keep a set of reasonable financial records for tax purposes, if for no other reason.

The net-worth method of estimating income for tax purposes, of course, yields different results than would the economic concept of income we have been discussing. This is so largely because of the exclusion under tax law of certain types of income, the use of realization criterion for tax purposes, and the allowance of certain specified deductions in arriving at taxable income. For example, assume that a taxpayer whose tax return is audited has almost no records. The I.R.S. agent determines the taxpayer's net worth at the end of the tax year as follows:

Cash	$ 400
Stock in mining company (at fair market value)	9,800
Total assets	$10,200
Liabilities	0
Net worth	$10,200

Based on the taxpayer's living standards and cir-

---

[12] See Irving Fisher, *The Nature of Capital and Income* (New York: Macmillan, 1906); "Income in Theory and Income Taxation in Practice," *Econometrica,* 5, No. 1 (January, 1937), pp. 1–55; and (with Herbert W. Fisher), *Constructive Income Taxation* (New York: Harper, 1942).

[13] See Nicholas Kaldor, *An Expenditures Tax* (London: Allen and Unwin, 1955).

cumstances, examination of the few records available, and discussions with those familiar with the taxpayer's activities, the agent estimates the taxpayer's consumption expenditures to be approximately $19,600. Further examination leads to the conclusion that the taxpayer's net worth on January 1 was $1,500. The agent thus concludes that the taxpayer's income in the broad economic sense was approximately $28,300.

Increase in net worth during the year	$ 8,700
Consumption expenditures (estimated)	19,600
Total "income"	$28,300

To continue the illustration, suppose that the taxpayer is able to show that the shares of stock were purchased during the year for $1,000 with cash on hand at the start of the year. The increase in the stock's value is not taxable. In addition, the taxpayer can prove that during the year his mother gave him $2,000 as a gift. Also, it is shown that he received $900 in dividends; of this amount he may exclude $100 from taxable income. Based on these additional data, the taxpayer's gross income for tax purposes is estimated to be $17,400:

Total income in economic sense		$28,300
Deduct:		
Unrealized increase in stock value	$8,800	
Tax-free gift from mother	2,000	
Excludable portion of dividends	100	
		10,900
"Income" for tax purposes		$17,400

By now you should have observed that the data in this example are identical to those previously given on page 5/4 for John Glover. Observe that even though the *procedure* used under the net-worth method to reconstruct the initial measure of income is almost identical to the "economic" income computation on page 5/4, the final *result* is much nearer the accounting measure of income. The major difference between income in the tax sense and "accounting" income in this example is the exclusion of $100 of dividends for tax purposes. (After 1980, the dividend exclusion will be $200.)

It is impossible in the span of a few pages to examine all the various economic concepts of income that have been developed during the past two hundred years. But even our brief discussion has shown that the term "income" does not mean the same thing to all people and has suggested the fundamental differences between the economist's and the accountant's concepts of income. If these differences could be summarized in two words, they would be "realization" and "objectivity."

UNDERLYING TENETS IMPORTANT IN THE MEASUREMENT OF TAXABLE INCOME

Let us now turn to the more practical matter of the differences between income determined under generally accepted accounting principles and that computed for tax purposes. These differences are created by the many factors that enter into and influence the federal tax structure. Primary among these factors are the underlying body of economic, social, and legal philosophies of the people and the Congress; the (proper and improper) exercise of power by groups and lobbies with vested interests; the variation in interpretations of laws and regulations by the courts (which often conflict because of opposing values and ideologies of those handing down decisions and because of changing "public policy"); and the increasing use of tax policy as an instrument of economic planning and control. Sometimes these influences are direct and obvious; at other times they are subtle and obscure.

Our purpose is not to examine all the broad and complex forces that influence tax policy, which would be completely beyond our scope, but to develop an understanding of some basic tenets that underlie the body of tax laws and lead to major conflicts between the measurement of income for tax purposes and the computation of income for general accounting purposes. This is not to say that such differences are always logical and explicable. Nevertheless, many instances do exist in which tax regulations that at first glance appear completely untenable and improper to the student of accounting can actually be explained and justified on the basis of concepts that outweigh the correctness or logic, or both, of generally accepted accounting principles. The basic tenets that we shall discuss are:

1. Wherewithal to pay.
2. Realization and objectivity.
3. Equity and uniformity among taxpayers.
4. Ease and consistency of administration.
5. Social and economic objectives.

Wherewithal to pay

As noted in Chapter 3, philosophical discussions about taxation frequently center on the idea that each taxpayer should be taxed in accordance with ability to pay. In that context, the phrase "in accordance with ability to pay" denotes the idea that the larger a taxpayer's income (or the larger his or her wealth if we are dealing with such taxes as the property tax), the greater should be his or her share of the tax burden. For the purposes of this chapter, however, the apparently similar phrase "wherewithal to pay" has quite another meaning, which has been stated succinctly by former Commissioner of Internal Revenue Sheldon Cohen: "As a practical matter, the timing of the tax should occur when the taxpayer can most readily pay and the I.R.S. can most readily collect."[14] The concept may be expressed in less sophisticated terms as, "Get the tax when the taxpayer has the money to pay it."

The requirement that, generally, unearned revenues be reported as taxable income in the year received regardless of the year(s) in which they will actually be earned is a classic example of application of this concept.[15] This requirement, the subject of much acrimonious debate, is designed to provide maximum possible assurance that the tax will be collected, presumably because the taxpayer has the cash available for paying the tax in the year the prepayment is received, whereas he or she may not have the cash available to pay taxes in later years when the income is actually earned. Alternatively, the taxpayer may still have the cash at the later date, but may be outside the jurisdiction of the U. S. tax authorities.

Although the unearned-income rule is frequently cited as a deviation from generally accepted accounting principles that is unfair to the taxpayer, the concept of wherewithal to pay more often works to the advantage of the taxpayer. For example, often a taxpayer may elect to defer the tax recognition of gain on an installment sale until he or she receives the cash, even if financial accounting would report the entire gain in the year of the sale. A taxpayer may similarly defer the recognition of taxable gain in many barter-type transactions, in the event of an involuntary conversion of property, in the sale of a personal residence, and in many transactions between the taxpayer and a related business entity.

These and other illustrations of tax provisions that are related to the wherewithal-to-pay concept will be discussed in detail in Part Seven. Suffice it to note here that these rules often are of tremendous benefit to a taxpayer.

Realization and objectivity

Closely related to the principle of wherewithal to pay is the realization concept, which we encountered in the early part of this chapter. Fundamentally, the realization criterion states that income is recognized when, and only when, it is realized through a conversion into new assets or a liquidation of existing liabilities.

The importance of the realization concept to the taxpayer can be readily seen. A mere increase in the value of an asset—even if easily measurable and readily convertible into cash—is not taxed. For example, the taxpayer who purchases shares of stock for $1,000 and finds, at the end of the year, that the stock has a quoted market value of $1,500 has no income to report because none has been realized; that is, there has been no change in the assets held. Only when the shares are sold or exchanged for other assets will the gain be recognized.

Similarly, the taxpayer who, to his good fortune and surprise, discovers under his land valuable oil and gas reserves worth millions of dollars recognizes no income until this increase in value is realized through conversion into other assets through sale or exchange.

On the other hand, the concept may also work to the disadvantage of a taxpayer. Declines in asset values generally are not recognized until they are realized through disposition of the asset, no matter how real the decline seems to be. (There are some minor exceptions to this rule—notably in the case of accounts receivable and merchandise inventory.) Thus, the taxpayer who purchases shares of stock for $1,000 and finds that the stock is worth only $300 at the end of the year has no deductible loss until realization takes place through conversion of the shares by sale or exchange.

A major reason for the rather strict adherence to the realization concept (in addition to the notion of wherewithal to pay already discussed) is the need for a high degree of objectivity and certainty in the tax computation. Tax authorities are even more wed to the concept of objectivity than are accountants generally. This is not surprising, since there must be at least one specific point at which the amount of tax can be computed and levied with reasonable certain-

---

[14]Sheldon S. Cohen, "Accounting for Taxes, Finance and Regulatory Purposes—Are Variances Necessary?" speech before the 19th Annual Tax Conference, The University of Chicago Law School, October, 1966. Reprinted in *Taxes,* 44, No. 12 (December, 1966), p. 784.

[15]Admittedly this generalization is overstated, especially since the I.R.S. issued Revenue Procedure 70–21 on August 6, 1970. In that announcement the Service finally agreed that, in a very limited number of fact situations, a taxpayer who has received advance payments for future services may be able to defer the recognition of taxable income from that receipt until up to one year later. At the same time Regulation 1.451–5 was issued to modify the prior tax treatment of advance payments for merchandise. The precise conditions which permit deferral are detailed in most tax services.

ty and accuracy. As previously observed, abandonment of the realization criterion would result in considerable subjectivity, making the tax dependent on the whims of personal judgments. This would mean constant litigation and dispute and would become an administrative nightmare.

It is important to note that the realization concept does not dictate that assets must be converted into monetary claims in order for gain to be recognized, even though this requirement would result in greater objectivity and easier tax administration. For example, if the taxpayer exchanges shares of stock for land (or any other asset), a gain or loss must generally be recognized. The amount of the gain or loss depends on the basis of the stock given up and the fair market value of the land (or other asset) received. It is obvious that subjectivity is immediately introduced in this situation; that is, the determination of the value of the land or other asset is often not a simple or objective process. It is also apparent that unless realization is deemed to have taken place at the time of the exchange, a rather simple device for tax avoidance (the barter transaction) would have been introduced. Thus, even though the I.R.S. would prefer to use only objective data, it is nevertheless forced to establish market values in many cases even when it retains the basic realization criterion.

As has already been noted, there are a number of extremely important exceptions to the general realization concept. For example, when the taxpayer exchanges certain types of assets used in trade or business for like assets, even though he or she may actually realize a gain, the gain may not be recognized for tax purposes. Similarly, if the taxpayer's property is destroyed by involuntary conversion (for example, fire or theft), any gain resulting from insurance or other sources may not be taxable if the taxpayer reinvests in replacement property an amount at least equal to the sum of the profit and the basis of the asset converted. These exceptions to the general rule that income is to be taxed when it is realized exist primarily because of the wherewithal-to-pay concept (the taxpayer has no cash for payment of taxes after replacement of the destroyed property). The need for objectivity is a secondary but related consideration.

Equity and uniformity among taxpayers

As you saw in Chapter 3, one of the basic premises underlying our tax structure is that horizontal equity is desirable—that is, the premise that, essentially,

equal incomes should bear equal taxes. This doctrine has obviously been ignored in many instances by treating different types of incomes differently for tax purposes. For example, long-term capital gains receive beneficial treatment (see Part Six). Similarly, interest received by the taxpayer on obligations of state and local governmental units is completely tax free. As a result of these and many other special provisions, tax benefits often discriminate among taxpayers with identical dollar incomes. However, often these apparent violations of the equity concept are justified (or rationalized) on the very basis of equity. For example, the special tax treatment given long-term capital gains is frequently supported on the grounds that the long-term gain results from selling at a price in excess of its cost an asset held for a long period of time and that the increase in value, at least in part, is a result of price changes. Thus, it is argued that a portion of this excess of selling price over cost is not real income and, therefore, for the sake of equity to the taxpayer, should not be fully taxable. In spite of the many apparent aberrations of the equity concept, it is an important though illusive cornerstone of our tax structure.

Ease and consistency of administration

Closely allied to the concept of equity and uniformity among taxpayers is the "administrative need for a taxable event to be fixed with adequate certainty in order to avoid disputes as to the occurrence of the event or the amount involved."[16]

This goal often creates a distinct conflict between what is generally accepted in financial accounting and what is required for tax purposes. The conflict occurs more often in relation to expense items than in relation to income items because expenses often are estimated for financial accounting purposes even though they may not be deductible on the tax return. To quote former Commissioner Cohen:

> It is often proper or even necessary to reflect future events of a contingent nature, such as potential losses or pending lawsuits, in a financial statement. However, an attempt to reflect this type of transaction in the computation of a tax liability could result in protracted controversy between the government and the taxpayer over the likelihood of the occurrence of the event and the amount potentially involved. The tax accounting rule is easier to administer because it involves fewer subjective judgments and estimates.[17]

[16]Cohen, *op. cit.*, p. 785.
[17]*Ibid.*, p. 785.

Similarly, tax requirements stricter than generally accepted accounting rules are often justified because they are easier to administer and produce more uniform results among different taxpayers. In short, administrative convenience frequently becomes important in explaining differences between taxable income and the net income of accounting.

Social and economic objectives

Finally, tax laws often result from a desire to achieve stipulated social or economic goals. More and more frequently, tax laws are changed to secure full employment, to combat inflation, to relieve social pressures, or to attain other goals of the national administration or the Congress. As a matter of fact, many critics today complain violently that tax laws have become little more than economic tools, whereas others, of course, think that's just what they should be.

TAX ACCOUNTING METHODS

As every student of elementary accounting knows, income measurements differ significantly depending on both the general method of accounting used and the specific accounting procedures applied in any given circumstances. For example, an income statement prepared on a cash basis will often differ significantly from another income statement (for the same entity and time period) prepared on an accrual basis; an income statement prepared on a completed contract basis will differ greatly from one prepared on a percentage-of-completion basis. Additionally, even if two statements are prepared on an accrual basis, the results may differ noticeably if, say, different depreciation procedures or different inventory costing procedures are applied in each of the two statements.

Subchapter E of the Internal Revenue Code contains the ground rules for "accounting periods and methods of accounting." Section 446 provides the specific rules for tax accounting methods:

(a) General Rule.—Taxable income shall be computed under the method of accounting on the basis of which the taxpayer regularly computes his income in keeping his books.

(b) Exceptions.—If no method of accounting has been regularly used by the taxpayer, or if the method used does not clearly reflect income, the computation of taxable income shall be made under such method as,

in the opinion of the Secretary [of the Treasury], does clearly reflect income.

(c) Permissible Methods.—Subject to the provisions of subsections (a) and (b), a taxpayer may compute taxable income under any of the following methods of accounting—

(1) the cash receipts and disbursements method;

(2) an accrual method;

(3) any other method permitted by this chapter; or

(4) any combination of the foregoing methods permitted under regulations prescribed by the Secretary.

(d) Taxpayer Engaged in More Than One Business.—A taxpayer engaged in more than one trade or business may, in computing taxable income, use a different method of accounting for each trade or business.

(e) Requirement Respecting Change of Accounting Method.—Except as otherwise expressly provided in this chapter, a taxpayer who changes the method of accounting on the basis of which he regularly computes his income in keeping his books shall, before computing his taxable income under the new method, secure the consent of the Secretary.

Additional and more specific procedural requirements on detailed accounting provisions are spread throughout the Code.

The cash basis

Most individual taxpayers, especially wage earners and individuals in the professions, use the cash basis of accounting. The cash basis is not only simpler, in that it requires less record keeping than other methods, but it also gives the taxpayer limited control over the timing of expenses by accelerating or deferring cash payments. A taxpayer on the cash basis generally reports income when it is received in cash and deducts expenses when they are paid; however, there are many modifications and exceptions to these two basic rules.

Most individuals are prudent, and if taxed only on *cash* receipts, they could easily avoid the tax by arranging to receive noncash property for services rendered. To eliminate this tax-avoidance ruse, the concept of "cash equivalent" has been developed. Essentially, the cash-equivalent concept suggests that whenever a taxpayer receives a noncash asset in a transaction, the fair market value of the asset received serves as a measure of the cash equivalent realized from the transaction. Thus, income is realized on the exchange of services for a noncash asset even in the case of a cash-basis taxpayer.

Another doctrine intended to reduce the opportunity for the cash-basis taxpayer to defer income by not taking cash, even though he could do so at will, is the concept of "constructive receipt." This doctrine finds clear and explicit expression in Regulation 1.451-2(a):

> Income although not actually reduced to a taxpayer's possession is constructively received by him in the taxable year during which it is credited to his account, set apart for him, or otherwise made available so that he may draw upon it at any time, or so that he could have drawn upon it during the taxable year if notice of intention to withdraw had been given. However, income is not constructively received if the taxpayer's control of its receipt is subject to substantial limitations or restrictions.

Obviously this rule is designed to prevent cash-basis taxpayers from deferring *receipt* of cash (and thus deferring the income tax) in order to take advantage of the "present value" of money or to avail themselves of lower tax rates in later periods of lower income. The doctrine has little application to accrual-basis taxpayers since they ordinarily report income when it is earned in any event.

As noted in the above quotation from the Regulations, the doctrine of constructive receipt is applied whenever a taxpayer has control, without substantial limitations or restrictions, over the amount involved. In addition, it is often held that for an amount to be constructively received, (1) the payer must have credited or set aside that amount for the payee and (2) the payer must have been able to make payment. Two of the most common applications of the rule will suffice to show its scope and importance:

1. Amounts of interest credited to a depositor's account in banks, credit unions, and so on, are taxable when credited even though not withdrawn by the depositor until a later year.

2. Dividends on corporate stock are constructively received when unqualifiedly made subject to the demand of the shareholder. This has been interpreted to mean that if dividend checks are mailed late in the year and are not received by the shareholder until the following year, then they are not taxable until the latter year.

One additional concept needs to be mentioned at this point even though it is applicable to both cash-basis and accrual-basis taxpayers. The "claim of right doctrine"—a judicial concept—holds that an amount is includable in income when actually or constructively received even though the taxpayer might be required to repay the amount at some future time. Money received by a taxpayer and treated as his own, under a claim that it is his, will be taxable to him even though the claim is disputed. Some examples of funds held to be taxable income to the taxpayer under the claim of right doctrine are

1. Profits and gains from illegal transactions.

2. Bonus in year of receipt even though it was computed in error and had to be repaid in a later year.

3. Contingent legal fees that must be repaid in the event of reversal by an unfavorable court decision.

When amounts required to be reported as income in one year under this doctrine must be repaid in later years, a deduction is allowed in the year of repayment. A special rule is available to the taxpayer in most cases to ensure that the tax benefit in the year of deduction is as great as the increased tax liability in the prior year.

Similar to the claim of right doctrine, but still independent of it, is the rule governing tax treatment of prepaid income. As a general rule, income received in advance is wholly taxable when received rather than over future years when earned. For example, a taxpayer received $24,000 in 19x1, representing three years' rent on property he owned. The entire $24,000 will be taxed to him in 19x1 even though he is on the accrual basis of accounting. An accrual-basis taxpayer, however, may defer recognizing income for services (but not interest, rents, or services under warranty or guaranty contracts) until the next year *if* all the services will be performed within that next year; if any services are to be performed after the next year, all the advance receipts are taxable when received.

The accrual basis

A taxpayer on the accrual basis generally reports income when it is earned, even though not yet received, and deducts expenses when they are incurred, even though not yet paid. As you have already discovered, however, income received in advance is generally taxed when received, even by an accrual-basis taxpayer. Also, you have seen that under the claim of right doctrine income may be taxed although not yet entirely "earned" by the taxpayer. In general, the rules for measuring gross income for an accrual-basis taxpayer are the same as those for financial accounting. The accrual basis *must* be used to account for sales and purchases by a taxpayer with inventories of stock in trade. In addition, a few other taxpayers—for example, some corporations engaged in farming, or some partnerships engaged in farming and having a corporate partner—must use the accrual basis.

The "mixed" basis

Although Regulation 1.446-1(c)(2) generally requires that an accrual basis be used to account for sales and purchases of inventory items, a taxpayer may nevertheless use the cash basis in computing all other items of income and deduction. This procedure is quite commonly followed by owners of small businesses and is called the "mixed" basis of accounting. If a taxpayer uses the cash basis in computing gross income, however, he must also use the cash basis in computing his deductions.

Other bases and changing methods

In addition to the cash, accrual, and "mixed" methods of accounting, a taxpayer may sometimes elect to use the installment method or the long-term construction contract method. The former accounting method effectively spreads the gain (or gross income) realized on the sale of goods or property over the years during which the seller receives payment for the asset sold. The latter accounting method allows a contractor to spread the gain realized on the construction of a property over the years during which the construction takes place. Both these methods are discussed in somewhat greater detail in subsequent chapters.

A taxpayer who desires a change in tax-accounting methods must generally obtain the prior approval of the Commissioner. Such a change often necessitates an adjustment to avoid the duplication or omission of certain items of gross income or deduction. Under some circumstances these "adjustments" may be reported by a taxpayer over several years (up to 10 years). In still other circumstances the Commissioner may not approve a request for a change in accounting method unless the taxpayer agrees to use the new method for financial accounting as well as tax purposes. And in yet other circumstances, the Commissioner may insist that a taxpayer change his accounting method to more clearly reflect income. Obviously, the details of each of these "special circumstances" cannot be investigated at this point in our study of income taxation. Suffice it to observe, however, that in general, a taxpayer is relatively free in the initial selection of an accounting method but

may be more restricted on electing to change that method at a later date.

INCOME: FINANCIAL ACCOUNTING AND TAX DIFFERENCES

Differences between taxable income, as defined by the tax laws, and net income, as measured under generally accepted accounting principles, may conveniently be classified into two categories for purposes of discussion.

1. Some variations merely represent differences in the *time* (year) of reporting income or expenses on the tax return and in the financial accounts. Tax rules may require (or permit) income or expenses to be reported on the tax return in one period, while they should be recognized in a different period in accordance with generally accepted accounting principles. An excellent example of timing differences is the previously noted tax rule that income received in advance may be taxable in the year received regardless of when earned. Financial accounting principles demand that unearned revenue be recognized as income only in the period when actually earned.

2. Other variations represent *permanent* differences between income reported on the tax return and that reported in accordance with financial accounting. These variations redistribute the burden of taxation among taxpayers and may affect the total amount of taxes collected by the government. The permanent differences take various forms. For example, certain items of income are wholly or partially excluded from taxable income; specific groups of taxpayers are wholly or partially excused from paying an income tax; special deductions may be allowed other taxpayers; and selected deductions may be limited or denied to specified taxpayers.

Differences in timing

Mere timing differences do not generally have a significant effect on the total income ultimately reported, or on the aggregate tax liability eventually paid, by any taxpayer. Because of the time value of money, however, these provisions may be extremely important to the taxpayer in the short run. As a general rule, a taxpayer would much prefer to pay a $1,000 tax liability five years hence than to have to pay the same amount today.

The tax and financial accounting variations that result from differences in timing can be subdivided into four categories:[18]

1. Gross income is taxable in a period before it is accrued for financial accounting purposes.
2. Gross income is taxable in a period after it is accrued for financial accounting purposes.
3. Expenses or losses are deducted for tax purposes before they are deducted for financial accounting purposes.
4. Expenses or losses are deducted for tax purposes in a period after they are deducted for financial accounting purposes.

Several of the major differences that would be included in the first two categories have already been explained by such underlying tenets of taxation as wherewithal to pay, objectivity, and administrative convenience. The details of several of these provisions will be examined later in this text. The major differences relative to the timing of deductions will be reviewed in Chapter 6.

Permanent differences

Many of the differences between gross income as reported on a tax return and on a financial statement result from provisions in the Code that exclude from the tax base specific items of income. Collectively, these items constitute the group defined earlier in this chapter as exclusions. Although the total amount of these exclusions is not known, they are of major importance.

In the following pages, we have made an attempt to classify some of the major exclusions according to their apparent purpose. In many cases the classification must be a matter of personal opinion, either because there are multiple bases for the exclusion or because the purpose of a particular exclusion is not at all apparent. These examples by no means illustrate all exclusions authorized by the Code.

EXCLUSIONS RELATED TO ILLNESS   Sections 104, 105, and 106 provide for certain exclusions of income related to accident and illness.

Under Sec. 104, rather broad exclusion is given to:

1. amounts received under worker's compensation acts as compensation for personal injuries or sickness;
2. amounts of any damages received (whether by suit or agreement) on account of personal injuries or sickness;
3. amounts received under accident or health insurance for personal injury or sickness (whether or not specifically designated as reimbursement for medical expenses) *unless* the amounts are received by an employee and (a) are attributable to an employer's contributions to an insurance program that were not includible in the gross income of the employee or (b) are paid by the employer. (Section 105, however, provides for the exclusion of amounts received under employer-financed plans if the amounts received are to pay for, or to reimburse the employee for, actual medical costs incurred.); and
4. pensions and other allowances received for personal injuries or illness resulting from active service in the armed forces and a few other government services.

For example, if a taxpayer were to receive $200 under a health or accident insurance policy that she has purchased herself, this amount would be excluded (although it would, if it is reimbursement for medical expenses incurred, be offset against the amount of deductible medical costs). If, however, reimbursement is received in one year for medical expenses that were deducted on the tax return in a prior year, the amount of reimbursement would be included in gross income to the extent that the reimbursement is attributable to the deduction previously allowed. This problem is discussed further in Chapter 12.

Section 106 is also quite simple. It excludes from the taxable income of the employee the value of any contributions made by the employer on behalf of the employee to accident or health plans for compensation (through insurance or otherwise) for personal injuries or sickness of the taxpayer, spouse, or dependents. Note that Sec. 106 is *not* concerned with the amounts *received* by an employee from an insurance company. Rather, it excludes from income the cost of the premiums *paid* by the employer to purchase insurance or contributions made by the employer to a fund that may later provide for payments to the employee.

---

[18]This four-way subdivision of timing differences was well developed by former Commissioner Cohen, *op. cit.,* pp. 782–83.

For example, suppose that James Wilson's employer purchased a health and accident insurance policy that will reimburse Wilson and other employees for expenses related to injury or illness. During the tax year, the employer paid a total of $360 on the policy covering Wilson and his family. This $360 is *not* taxable income to Wilson.

The provisions of Sec. 106 have frequently been criticized. For example, the Carter administration's 1978 tax proposals pointed out the possibly discriminatory aspects of this provision and urged that only premiums contributed to nondiscriminatory plans should be tax free. That proposal was not adopted; however, certain payments made to reimburse officers and employees for medical costs where no insurance policy is involved were made taxable by the 1978 Act if the plan involved is discriminatory.

In 1979, both the U.S. General Accounting Office and the Congressional Budget Office issued reports critical of the exclusion of employer's contributions to health insurance programs for employees. These two groups claim that the exclusion is inflationary because it encourages employees to acquire more health insurance coverage than they otherwise would, and this encourages more frequent use and more elaborate forms of medical care. This, in turn, drives up health care costs. The reports also concluded that employees have opted for more tax-free benefits, such as improved medical insurance, instead of wage increases, which are taxed. The reports estimate that the exclusions resulted in $9.6 billion in lost revenues to the federal government in 1979. In that year, a controversial proposal was introduced in Congress to eliminate the tax-free status of employer contributions to health insurance policies. This question is certain to be debated vigorously in future sessions of Congress.

Section 105 is the most complicated of the three provisions. Under Sec. 105(b), amounts paid directly by the employer to the employee or indirectly (through insurance plans) to reimburse the employee for costs of medical care of the taxpayer, the taxpayer's spouse, and the taxpayer's dependents are generally excluded from income to the extent they do not exceed the actual costs incurred. Section 105(h) provides, however, that for tax years beginning after December 31, 1979, all or part of amounts paid to "highly compensated" employees or officers under "self-insured medical reimbursement plans" (where reimbursement is not provided under an insurance policy) will be taxed to the recipient if the plan does not meet specified nondiscrimination tests.

Section 105(c) excludes from gross income amounts received by the taxpayer from employer-financed plans where the payments are for the permanent loss or loss of use of a member or function of the body, or the permanent disfigurement of the taxpayer, spouse, or dependents, provided the payments are computed with reference to the nature of the injury without regard to the period the employee is absent from work.

Section 105(d) permits the taxpayer, under limited circumstances, to exclude a maximum of $100 per week from payments made by the taxpayer's employer (or under an insurance plan paid for by the employer) as wages, or in lieu of wages, while absent from work because of injury or illness. The "disability income" exclusion is now available only to taxpayers under 65 years of age who retire on disability and are totally and permanently disabled at the time they retire. In general, total and permanent disability means inability to perform substantial gainful activity as a result of physical or mental impairment that is expected to last for at least 12 months or to result in the taxpayer's death.

The exclusion is $100 of sick pay per week. However, the amount excludable for the year is reduced by the amount that the taxpayer's adjusted gross income (computed before the sick pay exclusion) exceeds $15,000. Thus, there is no exclusion for a taxpayer whose adjusted gross income, including sick pay, exceeds $20,200. If a taxpayer is married, the taxpayer and spouse must file a joint return (unless they lived apart throughout the taxable year) and the $15,000 ceiling applies to their combined incomes. Special rules apply to retired military personnel and other public servants and to taxpayers 65 or over who receive disability income in the form of an annuity.

EXCLUSIONS RELATED TO DEATH   Code Sec. 101 excludes from taxable income a number of income items related to the death of an individual. The tax law of 1913 provided that amounts received under a life insurance contract paid because of death of the insured are, with minor exceptions, tax free; this rule continues today. It was presumably designed to encourage individuals to provide adequate insurance for their survivors. Presumably, too, the Congress assumed that the recepient of insurance proceeds would typically face financial hardships meriting the exclusion.

A further exclusion of up to $1,000 of *interest* income per year is allowed by Sec. 101. This exclusion is available only to the surviving spouse of a decedent where life insurance proceeds (payable because of the death of the taxpayer's spouse) are left with the insurer, under an option or agreement in the insurance contract, to be paid in installments. Presumably this provision is designed to protect beneficiaries by encouraging them to leave life insurance proceeds in the "safety" of the insurance company. This exclusion will not benefit them if they elect to leave the entire principal with the company and collect only the interest payment. Note also that this exclusion is available only to the deceased taxpayer's spouse; it does not extend to his or her children, even if they are minors.

For example, suppose that an individual dies leaving an insurance policy with face value of $50,000 payable to his wife. Under an option provided for in the policy, the wife elects to receive annual payments of $12,200 per year for five years. Of the amount received each year $10,000 ($50,000 ÷ 5) is assumed to be payment of the policy's face amount. The remaining $2,200 received each year is considered to be interest. Of this amount, the widow may exclude $1,000 each year; the remaining $1,200 per year is taxable. (Had the beneficiary been someone other than the surviving spouse, the entire $2,200 interest each year would have been taxable even though the $10,000 return-of-policy proceeds would be tax free.)

An exception to the exclusion of insurance proceeds paid on account of the death of the insured is proceeds from a policy obtained "for a consideration." For example, suppose that Arner the insured, owed a debt of $4,000 to Milroy. In settlement of the debt, Arner assigned to Milroy an insurance policy on Arner's life. The policy provided for a death benefit of $14,000. After acquiring the policy, Milroy paid premiums of $2,000 on the policy. On Arner's death, Milroy was paid the full amount of $14,000. Milroy must report income of $8,000. ($14,000 − $4,000 − $2,000).

In addition to life insurance benefits, certain other proceeds to beneficiaries relating to death are nontaxable. One of these provides that beneficiaries of a decedent may exclude a total of $5,000 paid by an employer, or employers, of the decedent if the payments are made solely on account of death. Where the decedent has more than one beneficiary who receives payments, the exclusion is prorated among the beneficiaries in proportion to the amount that each receives. For example, suppose that Smith,

a long-time employee, dies. Because of his death, the employer makes payments of $8,000 to Smith's widow and $4,000 to each of his two children. The beneficiaries may exclude a total of $5,000, divided as follows:

$$\text{Wife: } \frac{\$8,000}{\$16,000} \times \$5,000 = \$2,500$$

$$\text{Each child: } \frac{\$4,000}{\$16,000} \times \$5,000 = \$1,250$$

Thus the widow would include in her taxable income $5,500 of the amount received; each child would include $2,750.

This provision was first enacted in 1951 and was intended to "eliminate the 'hardship' resulting from the fact that the exclusion for death benefits under the then existing law was limited to life insurance."[19]

The exclusions related to death benefits from life insurance, like most other exclusions have long been debated by tax scholars. As Goode points out, if all life insurance proceeds payable because of death are tax free, "no distinction is drawn between the components of death benefits, which comprise pure insurance proceeds, the return of the insured person's savings, and the interest earned of savings."[20] The question may be raised whether the three elements of proceeds should be treated differently for tax purposes. Certainly, the insured's savings element should be returned tax free, but there is less unanimity of opinion concerning taxability of the other two elements.

Another exclusion related to life insurance is provided in Sec. 79, which encourages employers to establish life insurance programs for employees. Premiums paid by an employer for group term insurance, up to $50,000 face amount of insurance for each employee, may be excluded from the employee's income, although premiums paid by the employer on whole-life insurance for either an individual or a group, as well as premiums paid on individual term policies, are taxable to the employee.

If an employee is covered by group term insurance with a face value greater that $50,000, the premium applicable to the excess is taxable. The amount includable is determined by referring to a table in Treasury Regulation 1.79-3. For example,

[19]Senate Report 781, 82d Congress, 1st Sess.
[20]Goode, *op. cit.*, p. 130. Goode presents a very thorough and interesting discussion of this topic, pp. 130–39.

the table provides that for a taxpayer 40 to 44 years of age, the premiums applicable to each $1,000 of face amount over $50,000 is $0.23 per month. Thus, if an employee who is 44 years old is covered throughout the year by a group term life insurance policy with a face amount of $80,000, and if the premiums paid by the employer are $336, the amount taxable will be $82.80 ($0.23 × 12 × 30), and the amount excluded will be $253.20. Obviously, in this example, use of the I.R.S. table results in a greater amount being excluded if the premium paid had been prorated between the $50,000 subject to exclusion and the $30,000 not subject to exclusion.

EXCLUSIONS RELATED TO AGE   In recent years our tax laws have been freely amended to reflect a growing concern about the social and economic needs of the aged. Many provisions provide special deductions, while others relate to the definition of income. For example, the taxpayer who is 65 or over is allowed an extra personal exemption deduction of $1,000 per year. Similarly, Social Security benefits, railroad retirement benefits, state-provided "old-age pensions," and similar payments are excluded from taxable income.

In addition, there are two other special provisions that merit attention. The first is the "credit for the elderly" (Sec. 37), which permits the taxpayer who is 65 or older to reduce his or her tax bill by an amount up to $375. This "tax credit" is discussed in detail in Chapter 15.

Under Code Sec. 121, which was greatly liberalized by the Revenue Act of 1978, a person who is 55 or older may exclude from gross income all or part of the gain realized on the sale of a personal residence. This provision is examined in detail in Chapter 25.

EXCLUSIONS AND INTERGOVERNMENTAL RELATIONS A traditional aspect of the tax structure of this country has been an immunity of governmental units from taxation by other units. As a result of this concept, Code Sec. 115(a) specifically excludes from the federal income tax:

(1) income derived from any public utility or the exercise of any essential governmental function and accruing to a State or Territory, or any political subdivision thereof, or the District of Columbia; or
(2) income accruing to the government of any possession of the United States, or any political subdivision thereof.

One of the most controversial provisions of the Code is Sec. 103, which provides that interest on "the obligations of a State, a Territory, or a possession of the United States, or any political subdivision" is excluded from gross income. This exclusion, which has been a part of our tax laws since 1913, has been supported on a number of different bases—most vigorously on the basis of an alleged constitutional relationship between governmental units. Under the 1894 income-tax law, which was declared unconstitutional in the Pollock case (see Chapter 4), interest on state and local bonds was specifically included in income, and this inclusion was partially responsible for the Court's decision. The Court's logic was that taxing of income from the bonds was essentially taxing the bonds themselves and was therefore an encroachment on a sovereign power of the State.

Perhaps a more pertinent argument is that removing the exclusion would substantially increase the costs of state and local governments. The traditionally low interest rates on bonds issued by these governments exist because high-income purchasers are willing to accept a low tax-free income that in the past has had a high degree of security in preference to substantially higher income subject to the federal tax. In other words, the exclusion can be viewed as an indirect means for the federal government to grant financial assistance to state and local governments. It has been estimated that the yield on newly issued state and local government securities is about 30 percent less than it would be were the interest subject to the federal income tax.[21] Some who support the exclusion predict very dire results if the exclusion is removed. For example, Cushman McGee, an investment dealer and financial adviser, states

It is my opinion that the burden would vary, issue by issue, municipality by municipality, with the lower credit ratings bearing the progressively heavier burden, and the unrated issuers being critically affected. The burdens would be so substantial that thousands of municipalities would not be able to borrow within the maximum interest rates permitted by their state and local laws.

To measure the harm of such a proposal is beyond arithmetical calculation alone.[22]

---

[21] David J. Ott and Allan H. Meltzer, *Federal Tax Treatment of State and Local Securities* (Washington: The Brookings Institution, 1963), p. 60. Although this estimate was made several years ago, it is a reasonable assessment of bond interest rates today.
[22] Cushman McGee, "Exemption of Interest on State and Municipal Bonds," *1959 Compendium*, p. 738.

McGee's analysis was substantiated by events surrounding passage of the Tax Reform Act of 1969. The original version of the Act passed by the House of Representatives substantially curtailed the tax benefits of interest on state and local bonds. In January, 1969, before the House Ways and Means Committee began public hearings on the Reform Act, the Dow Jones Municipal Bond Index stood at 4.82 percent. In late August, after the House passed its original version of the Act, the index had increased to 6.22 percent, an increase of 30 percent in the interest rates paid.[23] In October of that year, the Senate Finance Committee decided to retain the tax-free status of these securities and " prices of State and Local Bonds soared" (interest rates fell).[24] During that uncertain period, many cities, school districts, and state-supported universities simply could not find buyers for bonds at the interest rates they were legally allowed to pay.

Critics of interest exclusion base their arguments on the equity concept that equal incomes should bear equal taxes and on the supposition that tax-free governmental securities are held primarily by corporations and by individuals with high incomes. Thus, they argue, the exclusion provides tax benefits where they are least needed, especially since these securities can be freely bought and sold with little risk or expense. Robert J. Lampman estimated in 1962 that 90 percent of all state and local securities in the hands of individuals are owned by taxpayers with a gross estate of $500,000 or more.[25] Although "municipal bond investment trusts" have made it possible for those with less wealth to invest in tax-exempt securities in recent years, the vast majority of state and local bonds are still owned by taxpayers with high incomes. Critics object, not only to the inequitable distribution of tax benefits, but to the diversion of high-income investors from risky private investments to government securities. This diversion of resources is alleged to reduce risk-taking and innovation. The difficulties encountered by some American cities, however, especially New York City, in meeting their debt obligations in recent years has definitely increased the risk that an investor assumes in buying bonds of a local government. It should also be noted that a large increase in interest rates has accompanied the growth of uncertainty.

[23]*Wall Street Journal,* Vol. CLXXIV, No. 59 (September 24, 1969), p. 1.
[24]*Wall Street Journal,* Vol. CLXXIV, No. 71 (October 10, 1969), p. 26.
[25]Robert J. Lampman, *The Share of Top Wealth Holders in National Wealth* (Princeton: Princeton University Press, 1962), p. 173.

In recent years, another controversy has arisen over the tax-free status of interest on state and local securities. Many municipalities and other governmental units have issued tax-free bonds to procure funds, which are then loaned to either nonprofit or profit-seeking groups for certain purposes. In other cases, governmental units may acquire assets to lease or resell to these groups. Usually, the funds are intended to promote industrial growth of the municipality or other governmental body, or to finance other specific activities. Subsection 103(b) contains complicated rules, amended many times recently, that disallow the interest exclusion for certain "industrial development bonds"—bond issues where the proceeds are used directly or indirectly in any trade or business carried on by a person who is not exempt, or where payment of the principal or interest is either secured by property used in trade or business or is derived from revenues from property to be used in a trade or business. There are many exceptions to this prohibition, however, and there are many "industrial development" purposes for which bonds may be issued without impairing their exempt status.

One of the specifically permitted uses is for proceeds to be used "to purchase residential real property for family units." Many municipalities have issued bonds for this purpose—frequently for housing developments that might be considered luxury single-family housing. Thus, legislation was introduced in late 1979 that would eliminate the exclusion where funds are used for single-family residences, except for low-income taxpayers, on the basis that these are expensive, unnecessary, and inflationary. This prohibition will probably become law.

One final aspect of the interrelationship between governmental units should be mentioned. Before 1941, interest on bonds issued by the United States was exempt as a part of the overall philosophy of government tax immunity, and before 1939, the salaries and wages of state and local employees were exempt from the federal income tax. The tremendous pressure for tax funds during those years was largely responsible for elimination of these two exclusions.

EXCLUSIONS AND DOUBLE TAXATION   Several provisions of the law stem from the ideal that income should be taxed only once, to the persons earning it. The most important relevant sections are

Sec. 71—Alimony and Separate Maintenance Payments

Sec. 102—Gifts and Inheritances (and related Sec. 74 governing taxability of prizes and rewards)

Sec. 116—Partial Exclusion of Dividends Received by Individuals

Sec. 243—Dividends Received by Corporations

Section 71 provides that payments made as "child support" by a divorced husband to his former wife (or wife to her former husband) shall not be taxable to the former spouse or to the children, presumably on the basis that this is still a division of income within the family unit. The Code does specify, however, that *periodic alimony* payments *are* taxable to the wife (and deductible by the husband). Generally, the word *periodic* is taken to mean payable either for an indefinite period or for a definite period exceeding 10 years. Alimony payments that are *not* periodic payments are excludable by the wife. Lump sum payments are not periodic and thus are not taxable. If payments are to be made for a fixed period of more than 10 years, only those amounts up to 10 percent of the principal sum paid in any one year are considered periodic. Amounts paid in any one year in excess of 10 percent of the principal amount are not considered periodic. For example, suppose that Tim and Eloise are divorced in 19x1. The divorce decree requires Tim to pay Eloise the sum of $50,000 in 19x1 and to pay $1,000 per month for 150 months, beginning January 1, 19x2. Of the $50,000 received by Eloise in 19x1, only $20,000 (10% × $200,000) is included in her gross income. The entire amount she receives in 19x2, $12,000, will be included. (Deductibility of alimony by the payor is discussed further in Chapter 14).

Section 102 provides that "gross income does not include the value of property acquired by gift, bequest, devise or inheritance." These exclusions are usually supported on the theory that such transfers of property are a redistribution of a donor's or deceased taxpayer's income rather than the creation of a new income, especially in the case of transfers to close relatives. In addition, cumbersome administrative problems would arise if such items as small Christmas and birthday gifts were to be included in taxable income. On the other hand, the exclusion of gifts itself creates the administrative problem of separating donative transactions from nondonative ones—in many cases a difficult line to draw. The donee who renders any service to the donor will likely have a difficult time proving that what he or she received was in reality a tax-free gift rather than taxable compensation.

A special problem arises in the case of prizes and awards. Section 74 recognizes the difficulty of distinguishing between a gift and a prize:

(a) General Rule.—Except as provided in subsection (b) and in section 117 (relating to scholarships and fellowship grants), gross income includes amounts received as prizes and awards.

(b) Exception.—Gross income does not include amounts received as prizes and awards made primarily in recognition of religious, charitable, scientific, educational, artistic, literary, or civic achievement, but only if—
   (1) the recipient was selected without any action on his part to enter the contest or proceeding; and
   (2) the recipient is not required to render substantial future services as a condition to receiving the prize or award.

Thus such awards as "door prizes," "drawings," and the like are almost always taxable, while an award such as a Pulitzer Prize or Nobel Prize is tax free.

Some tax scholars favor including transfers by gift, bequest, or inheritance in gross income. Others do not support taxation of the total value of such transfers but suggest that unrealized gains on property transferred by gift or death should be taxed at the time of the transfer, arguing that present laws act as a deterrent to the transfer of assets because taxpayers are encouraged to retain assets that have increased in value. If these assets are sold, taxable gains would result. On the other hand, if they are retained until death, no income tax is paid on the gain. In addition, there is a degree of inequity involved because these provisions provide benefits primarily to those who can arrange their affairs in such a way as to avoid having to realize the gains prior to death. Transfer taxes are levied on gifts and estates by the federal government and also by most states, but they tend to be less than the income taxes that would result if unrealized gains were taxed at the time of transfer.

Section 116 of the Code permits individual stockholders to exclude from income the first $100 of dividends received each year from domestic corporations. This provision was first introduced to alleviate the "double taxation" that may result from taxing both corporation profits (to the corporation) and corporate dividends (to the individual shareholder) when the after-tax profits are distributed by the corporation. Although this provision eliminates the double taxation on the first $100 of dividends received by each shareholder in a year, it does not eliminate the

GROSS INCOME: GENERAL CONCEPTS

double tax completely, since many stockholders receive more than $100 in dividends each year. If dividends are community income, the dividends are deemed to have been received equally by the husband and wife, even though the stock is held in the name of only one spouse. Each spouse is, of course, entitled to an exemption of $100. In a noncommunity income state, however, the dividends are deemed to be income solely of the spouse who is owner of the stock. If the securities are jointly owned, each spouse is deemed to have received income. In 1979 and 1980, a number of bills were introduced in Congress to increase the dividend exclusion. These additional exclusions were proposed as incentives for taxpayers to increase their rate of savings, rather than as relief from double taxation. (The problem of "double taxation" of corporations is discussed further in Chapter 10, page **10**/12.)

Finally, in March 1980, as part of the "Windfall Profit Tax" bill, these efforts came to partial fruition. For tax years beginning in 1980 and 1981 only, the dividend exclusion is increased to $200 for a single person and $400 for a married couple. In addition, for those two years, the exclusion will apply not only to qualified dividends, but also to interest from the following domestic sources:

1. Interest from a deposit in a banking savings or thrift institution.

2. Interest from mutual funds and other financial "intermediaries."

3. Interest on obligations in registered form issued by a domestic corporation.

4. Interest from governmental units or agencies (including the U.S. government).

5. Interest on certain trusts.

One can reasonably forecast that this increased exclusion designed to encourage savings and capital formation will be extended beyond its current projected life of two years and that it may be subsequently increased.

A similar provision under Sec. 243 permits a corporation to deduct a part of the dividends received from stock in other domestic corporations. The full amount of dividends received is included in gross income, and a deduction is then allowed equal to 85 percent (or up to 100 percent in limited cases) of dividends included. Note that this provision (discussed in greater detail in Chapter 10,) although technically a deduction, operates in most situations as an exclusion.

Several other provisions in the Code are indirectly related to the concept of double taxation. The most important of these are based on the "return-of-capital" concept, which permits a taxpayer to recover tax free an investment in an asset because the original investment represents a capital base that has already been taxed.

Suppose, for example, that a taxpayer worked for a salary and each payday invested a portion of her net pay in a simple annuity. During her working life, she invested a total of $10,000 in the annuity. She has reached 60 years of age and, under the contract, will now be paid $2,000 a year for eight years. How are the $2,000 payments to be taxed? Obviously, a portion of each $2,000 represents a return of her original investment, and a portion represents income. To determine the part that is a tax-free return of investment, she simply divides the total investment of $10,000 by the number of years (eight) over which she is to receive payments and finds, in this way, that each year she is getting back $1,250 of her original cost. The remaining $750, then, is taxable income.

As a practical matter, however, it is occasionally difficult to determine what portion of an amount received is income and what portion is a return of capital as you will see in Chapter 15. Other applications of the return-of-capital idea will be examined in detail in later chapters.

EXCLUSIONS RELATED TO EDUCATION   One exclusion of special interest to students is that of scholarships and fellowships under Sec. 117. Although there are a number of special rules, generally if a college student who is a candidate for a degree receives an award that does not require him or her to perform such duties as teaching classes or grading papers, the scholarship is tax free. (If such duties are required of all candidates for the same degree, the award may still be nontaxable.) If the student is *not* working toward a degree, scholarships are tax free only if they are awarded by tax-exempt organizations, governmental units or agencies, or certain other organizations, and even then only $300 per month may be excluded for a total of not more than 36 months.

The exclusion of scholarships was originally permitted only if it could be established that the scholarship represented a gift and no service was required. Later, Congress enacted Sec. 117 to exclude scholarships and fellowships under specified conditions. The scholarship exclusion serves the dual purpose of encouraging expansion of the economic resources devoted to education and promoting scholarship on the part of students.

The I.R.S. has also ruled that athletic scholarships do not result in taxable income. Athletic scholarships are interesting from a tax point of view because they usually call for a service in return, which in other circumstances would create taxable income. Technically, however, no service is *required* in the standard athletic scholarship.

Another exclusion related to education benefits received by employees under "educational assistance plans" merits attention. In recent years, many employers have encouraged employees to receive additional education by providing assistance through such acts as paying tuition, purchasing books and supplies, and so on, for employees. Before 1979, such benefits were generally includable in the employee's income, and the employee might or might not be able to deduct the related expenses (Chapter 14). In order to reduce the administrative difficulties of determining whether such costs were deductible, Sec. 127 was introduced by the Revenue Act of 1978. Under this section, payments made by the employer on behalf of the employee for such costs as tuition and books will be tax free to the employee if made under nondiscriminatory educational assistance programs. At the same time, no deduction is allowed the employee for expenses for which he or she has been reimbursed under such tax-free plans.

EXCLUSIONS RELATING TO SERVICE IN THE ARMED FORCES   Although regular pay for members of the armed forces is taxable, certain benefits and allowances to service personnel and their dependents may be excluded. For example, the value of quarters provided a serviceman or the cash payment made to him in lieu of quarters is tax free, as is the basic allowance for quarters to the serviceman's dependents. Similarly, the value of subsistence, or allowances in lieu of subsistence, is not taxable. Uniform and equipment allowances are likewise excluded.

Enlisted personnel and warrant officers may exclude all pay received in official combat zones, and officers may exclude up to $500 per month in such areas. The intent is, of course, to provide a small measure of reward for hazardous duty.

Former service pesonnel also receive certain tax breaks. The mustering-out pay on termination of service is tax exempt. Although pensions paid to military retirees who have retired because of length of service are taxable, pensions or other allowances based on personal injury or sickness resulting from active duty are exempt. As previously pointed out, under Sec. 104, personnel entering service after September 24, 1975, may exclude disability pensions only if the benefits are based on a combat-related injury. Payments made for education and training allowances (the "GI Bill") are excluded, as are bonus payments received by veterans from state governments.

MISCELLANEOUS EXCLUSIONS RELATING TO EMPLOYMENT   It is not feasible to discuss all the wide variety of income items specifically excluded from gross income, but a few additional items relating to compensation merit a passing reference.

Generally, all forms of compensation made by an employer to an employee are taxable. This includes such things as salaries and wages, bonuses, commissions, substantial discounts on the price of property (though routine "courtesy" employee discounts are not taxable), and cash "gifts." (However, traditional gifts such as a ham or turkey during the holiday season are treated as nontaxable.)

Certain forms of compensation have been made tax free on the basis that they are "for the convenience of the employer." For example, the value of meals furnished by an employer to an employee for a "substantial noncompensatory" business reason are nontaxable, unless the employee has an option to take cash instead. Under this rule, meals provided food-service employees have generally been excluded, even though meals are consumed before or after duty hours. Cash allowances in lieu of meals are generally taxable. For example, in a recent decision involving New Jersey state troopers who were given a mid-shift meal allowance and were permitted to eat wherever they desired as long as they remained on call in their assigned duty area, the Supreme Court upheld that the meal allowances were compensation, in part at least, because the meals were not served on the employer's premises.[26] Similarly, the value of lodging provided the employee is excluded only if the employee *must* accept the lodging on the employer's premises in order to perform his duties properly.

We have already seen that certain contributions by employers to health and hospital insurance plans, premiums paid for certain group life insurance programs, and a few other items of this type are excluded by employees. Under Sec. 125, employer contributions for certain tax-free employee benefits (those

---

[26] *Kowalski*, Supreme Court of the United States, No. 76-1095 (1977).

that would not normally be included in the employee's gross income, such as premiums on health insurance or premiums on group term life insurance up to $50,000 face value) made under a "cafeteria plan" (plans in which the employee may choose between tax-exempt benefits and benefits that would be taxable, such as cash or property) will be tax free if the cafeteria plan does not discriminate in favor of highly compensated participants. In Chapter 15, the exclusion of contributions to profit-sharing and retirement plans will be examined.

The Internal Revenue Service in recent years has been studying carefully the tax status of many fringe benefits in preparation for issuing regulations on that topic. The 1978 Act, however, prohibited the I.R.S. from issuing new regulations governing fringe benefits and commuting expenses before 1980; and in December 1979, the Senate passed legislation to extend the prohibition until 1981. Nevertheless, in 1979 several proposals were made in Congress to require employees to include in income the fair value of many fringe benefits received. The S.E.C. (Securities and Exchange Commission) has also shown interest in reporting the value of fringe benefits given to corporate executives. Because of the combined interest of the I.R.S., the S.E.C., and some members of Congress, it seems safe to predict that the taxation of many fringe benefits that formerly escaped taxation is now a likely possibility.

On the other hand, some social and economic developments act to enlarge the realm of tax-free employee benefits. For example, the Energy Act of 1978 added Code Sec. 124, which specifies that the value of transportation provided by an employer under a nondiscriminatory plan that provides commuting transportation in a highway-commuter vehicle (one holding at least eight persons in addition to the driver) will be tax free provided the transportation is in addition to regular compensation, not a part of the regular compensation. Obviously, this exclusion is designed to encourage the use of multipassenger vehicles as an energy-saving device.

Another controversy relating to compensation for personal service is whether income earned abroad for "personal services" by American citizens should be subject to the U. S. income tax. Prior to 1979, if the U. S. citizen was a "bona fide resident" of a foreign country or was present in a foreign country (or countries) for at least 510 days during a period of 18 consecutive months, he or she could exclude up to $15,000 per year of such gross income ($20,000 prior to 1978).

This exclusion was apparently based on the premise that Americans living abroad do not get the same benefits from services and facilities provided by the federal government within the United States and therefore should be excused from paying a part of the cost of these services. Another factor leading to the exclusion has been the emphasis on the value and benefits of international development and business and on the need and desirability of having Americans work abroad.

The Foreign Earned Income Act of 1978 eliminated the exclusion but permits U. S. citizens abroad to deduct a portion of their living costs in specified circumstances. This is discussed in Chapter 14.

OTHER EXCLUSIONS   There are many other exclusions from income. Three of these warrant brief discussion.

Improvements constructed by tenant.   The first exclusion stipulates that a property owner generally has no income either at the time a tenant constructs improvements on the lessor's property or at the time the property, including improvements, reverts to the lessor on termination of the lease. If the improvements are constructed *in lieu of rents,* however, the lessor must report as income the fair value of the improvements when they are placed on the property.

Discharge of indebtedness.   The second exclusion worthy of mention relates to income from discharge of debt (Sec. 108). In general, the discharge of the taxpayer's debt for less than its "book" value is considered as giving rise to taxable income. If the discharge is of a debt that was incurred in connection with property used in the taxpayer's trade or business, however, the taxpayer may elect to exclude the "gain" from income and to treat it, instead, as a reduction of the property's basis.

The amount of indebtedness eliminated in bankruptcy proceedings is also excluded from income.

In cases where creditors reach a "compromise" agreement, the forgiveness of all or a part of the taxpayer's debt will result in taxable income, but not in excess of the amount by which the taxpayer is solvent after the compromise. For example, if the taxpayer has assets of $100,000 and liabilities of $120,-000 before the compromise settlement, and if the creditors reduce the debt to $87,000, the taxpayer must report $13,000 of the forgiveness as income.

Unemployment compensation.   One additional interesting exclusion should be mentioned. Prior to 1979, all amounts received as "unemployment compensation" under federal and state governmental plans were tax free. Beginning in 1979, however, under Sec. 85, all or a part of such payments may be taxable. Benefits are included in gross income to the extent of one-half the excess of (1) the sum of the taxpayer's adjusted gross income other than unemployment compensation benefits, all unemployment compensation, and all excludable disability income over (2) the taxpayer's base amount. The base amount is $25,000 in the case of a married individual filing a joint return, zero in the case of a married individual filing a separate return (unless the taxpayer lived apart from his or her spouse for the entire tax year), and $20,000 for all other individuals.

For example, assume Husband and Wife file a joint return. During the year Wife earned $20,000 and Husband earned $4,000. In addition, Husband received unemployment benefits of $3,000 for the year. Of the $3,000 unemployment benefits, $1,000 (one-half of $2,000) must be included in gross income.

Among the reasons cited by the House of Representatives for including this provision is that total exclusion of unemployment compensation benefits paid under government programs tends to decrease the incentive to work and thus increase the incentive to remain unemployed.

SUMMARY   The exclusions that have been examined here are representative of many that exist; they were selected to demonstrate some of the reasons that have been advanced for exempting specific items from federal income taxation. They also show, even to the most casual observer, that exclusions result in a computation of gross income that is far different, not only from the definition advanced by the economists quoted earlier in this chapter but even from the more limited definition of income offered in accounting theory.

PROBLEMS

1. What are the major obstacles to using the economic concept of income as a measure of income for accounting and tax purposes?
2. Listed below are a few of the ways gross income for income-tax purposes differs from gross income for financial accounting purposes. In each case, suggest a probable reason for the difference (for example, lack of wherewithal to pay, administrative convenience, double taxation of income).
   a. Interest received on bonds of a state government is tax exempt.
   b. Dividends received by a corporation (on its investment in stocks of another corporation) are included in income, but the recipient corporation is allowed a deduction equal to 85 percent of the dividends received.
   c. All proceeds collected on a casualty insurance claim are exempt from tax *if* the taxpayer reinvests that amount (or more) in similar property.
   d. Social security benefits are tax free.
   e. A taxpayer may exclude from taxable income up to $1,000 per year of interest received on life insurance proceeds payable on the death of the taxpayer's spouse if the proceeds have been left with the insurance company to be paid in installments.
   f. Unearned revenues (prepaid income) may be taxable when received, even though they may not be earned for several years.
   g. No gain or loss is recognized when a taxpayer "trades in" depreciable business property for property of a "like kind."
   h. Amounts contributed by an employer as premiums on health and hospitalization insurance policies payable to employees are not taxed as income to the employee.
3. How does "real income" differ from "monetary income"? Which of the two income concepts is used as a basis for measuring taxable income? Why?

4. Briefly describe the "consumption expenditures" approach to income measurement. Is it suitable as a basis for taxation? Explain.

5. Imagine that you are a special agent from the I.R.S. investigating the tax affairs of a notorious gambler. You have decided that the net-worth method will have to be used. Develop a list of the information you would need and the sources of such information.

6. Explain the effects of a progressive tax-rate structure on the taxpayer's disposable income during a period of inflation.

7. It has been suggested that businesses should be permitted to "deflate" their reported income by "price-level" adjustments. What would be the effects of this action on the relative tax burden of wage earners as opposed to businesses?

8. Distinguish between the "constructive receipt" doctrine and the "claim of right" doctrine.

9. What is the rationale underlying the general rule that prepaid income is taxed in the year of receipt, even for an accrual-basis taxpayer?

10. Explain the rationale that exclusion of some amount—for example, $500—of interest each year would increase the rate of savings by individuals.

11. In each of the following independent cases, indicate the amount that the taxpayer would report as "gross income" for the year.
   a. Taxpayer was involved in an accident and as a result received $5,000 personal damage judgment plus $800 reimbursement for medical costs incurred.
   b. Taxpayer inherited land from a deceased aunt. The land had a fair market value of $60,000 when inherited.
   c. Amos is injured on the job. As a result of his injury, he is paid $400 under workmen's compensation insurance and also receives $800 under health and accident insurance policies to reimburse him for medical costs. Additionally, he receives $500 under a disability income policy that he purchased and paid for himself.
   d. Peter and his wife were injured in an automobile accident during the year. Because of the accident, Peter and his wife were paid $1,300 to reimburse them for medical costs and $8,900 for personal injury and suffering.

12. In each of the following independent cases, indicate the amount that the taxpayer should report as "gross income" for the year.
   a. Mary's husband died during the current year, leaving a life insurance policy with a face value of $50,000 payable to Mary. She received the $50,000 from the insurance company, but after consultation with friends she returned the money to the insurance company and they agreed to pay her $13,000 per year for 5 years. During the year she received one of the $13,000 checks.
   b. Assume the same facts as in part a, except that the $50,000 was not withdrawn from the insurance company at time of death of the insured, but was left with the company under an option provided in the policy, with five installments of $13,000 each to be paid her. During the year she received her first installment of $13,000.
   c. Farmer's mother died during the current year, leaving an insurance policy with face value of $50,000 payable to Farmer. Under an option provided in the policy, he left the proceeds with the insurance company to be paid in five equal annual installments of $13,000 each. During the current year he received the first installment of $13,000.
   d. Jones, who had been holding two jobs, died during the current year. Because of Jones's death, the first employer paid Mrs. Jones $8,000 and the second employer paid her $6,000.
   e. Mrs. McDonald died during the current year. Her employer paid Mr.

McDonald $8,000 and each of her two children $3,500. Payments were made solely on account of death.

    f. Rufus died during the current year. His wife was paid $10,000 under a group life insurance policy that had been paid for by Rufus's employer. In addition, the employer paid Rufus's wife $4,000 on account of Rufus's death.

    g. T. Cash surrenders his life insurance policy and receives a lump sum of $8,000. He paid total premiums of $7,200 on the policy in previous years.

    h. Mr. Friendly loaned $5,000 to his neighbor, Adams. Adams ran into financial difficulty, so he agreed to assign a life insurance policy to Friendly, naming Friendly beneficiary. Face amount of the policy was $7,000. After receiving the policy, Friendly paid premiums of $420. At that point, Adams died and Friendly received a check for $7,000 from the insurance company.

    i. Teresa inherited several bonds of the State of Illinois upon the death of her uncle during the current year. The bonds had a fair value of $60,000 at date of his death. After receiving the bonds, Teresa was also paid $1,800 by the state representing interest earned on the bonds after the uncle's death.

13. In each of the following independent cases, indicate how much, if any, of the amounts involved must be reported as income by the recipient.

    a. Anthony's employer carries a substantial insurance program for his employees. During the current tax year the employer paid premiums of $960 on health and hospital insurance policies for Anthony. In addition, the employer pays life insurance premiums of $400 under a group term insurance program. This life insurance provides for a death benefit of $40,000 payable to Mrs. Anthony in the event of Anthony's death.

    b. Stewart works as an airline steward for Great Fly Airlines. One of his fringe benefits is the right to fly free of charge on the airline. On his "days off" and during vacation, Stewart takes advantage of this right. He estimates that during 19x1 the flights taken on short vacations would have cost him $1,200 if he had been required to pay for them.

    c. Taxpayer is a real estate salesperson. During the year she purchased a residential lot from her employer for $4,500. Similar lots were sold to purchasers at their advertised price of $9,000.

    d. Taxpayer is a university student. He works in the university cafeteria and receives as payment three meals each day. Total value of the meals consumed during the current year was $1,450.

    e. Taxpayer manages an apartment house throughout the year. He is required by his employer to live in one of the apartments, which is given to the taxpayer rent free. Similar apartments were rented to tenants for $3,600 per year. Taxpayer's salary as manager is $12,000 per year.

    f. Taxpayer manages an apartment house throughout the year. He is making a cash salary of $4,000 for the year. In addition, his employer offered to give him another $200 per month in cash or to let him live rent free in an apartment. Choosing the latter, taxpayer received an apartment that has a fair rental value of $4,000 per year.

    g. Maude is a waitress in a local cafe. Her income for the year consists of wages of $6,500 and tips of $3,200. In addition, she eats her noon meal while on duty at the cafe, free of charge. She estimates that the value of meals consumed during the year was $650.

    h. Guardman lived rent free in a house owned by his employer on the employer's premises during the year. The rental value of the house was $1,800 for the year. Although Guardman lived in the house for the convenience of the employer, he was not required to live there and could have lived somewhere else.

    i. Taxpayer's employer purchased an ordinary whole-life insurance policy for every employee. During the current year the employer paid premiums of $400 on the taxpayer's policy.

    j. A college student worked for Giant Corporation during the summer months. In return for her services, the student received $500 cash and 50 shares of Giant stock. The 50 shares had a par value of $500 and a fair market value of $2,000. Their book value was $1,500.

14. State the amount to be included in gross income in each of the following cases.

    a. Roger invested $20,000 in an annuity. Beginning in 19x1 and continuing through 19y0, a total of 10 years, he is to be paid $3,000 each year. How much, if any, of the $3,000 received in 19x1 must be included in gross income?

    b. John Wilkins and his wife Ann live in a community property state where one-half the income belongs to the husband and one-half to the wife. During the current year they received dividends of $800. All the stock is held in the name of Ann, as owner. They plan to file a joint return.

    c. Friedsam, single, lost his job in August of the current year. He could not secure another job; during June and July, he received unemployment benefits of $380. In October, he became old enough to receive social security retirement benefits, and during the remainder of the year he received $980 of social security. His only other income was a salary of $19,900 for January through August.

    d. Lamarque had savings accounts at a bank and a credit union. On December 31 of the current year, the two institutions credited Lamarque's accounts for a total of $185, but Lamarque did not withdraw the money during the year.

15. a. Alice, a university student working on her B.B.A. degree, received a scholarship of $2,000 from the university. The scholarship was based on grades, and she had no services to render.

    b. Assume the same facts as in part a, except that the scholarship was awarded by an industrial firm.

    c. Assume the same facts as in part a, except that Alice is working on a Ph.D. degree.

    d. Robert received his Ph.D. degree in 1978. Beginning in September 1978, and continuing to December 1981, he received a postdoctoral fellowship from a tax-free foundation to continue study and research. The fellowship paid him $500 per month. How much, if any, must he include in 1978, 1979, 1980, and 1981, assuming he received $2,000 in 1978, $6,000 in 1979, $6,000 in 1980, and $6,000 in 1981?

    e. Margaret S. is working toward a Ph.D. in chemistry. She receives a $5,000 "scholarship" from the school. In order to get the scholarship, she is required to work 10 hours each week in the laboratory. This laboratory work is required of all students working toward the Ph.D. in chemistry at that university.

    f. A graduate student at State University received a $1,000 fellowship grant, $350 for grading accounting papers, and $2,000 from her father. She used the $3,350 to finance her year at school.

In Problems 16–21, give the dollar amount that should be included in the computation of the taxpayer's gross income.

16. a. Thompson served in the U.S. Army in Southeast Asia. As a result of injury in combat in 1967, Thompson was retired from the military and awarded a

pension. During the current tax year he received total payments of $8,400 from the pension.

   b. On January 1, of the current year, Careerman retired from the U.S. Air Force after 25 years of service. During the current tax year he received retirement pension payments of $7,600.

17. a. Professor Graham was selected by the business students at State University as their "outstanding" teacher and was given a cash award of $1,000 by the student association.

   b. Sue was chosen "Miss City." She won both the bathing suit contest and the talent contest. Many speculate that she will ultimately become Miss America. As an award for being chosen Miss City, she was given cash and merchandise totaling $2,000.

   c. Kamp, a rabid baseball fan, attended every home game of the city team. He was surprised one evening when his ticket stub contained the "lucky number" and he won an automobile with a fair value of $7,000 in the ticket drawing.

   d. Professor Samples was awarded a Pulitzer Prize of $15,000 for writing a book on the history of the Apache Indians.

18. a. Bill and Jane Rollins were divorced during the current year. The divorce decree provided that Bill should pay Jane a lump sum of $42,000, which he paid this year. What part, if any, of this is taxable to Jane?

   b. Tommy and Betty Moore were divorced during the current year. The divorce decree provided that Tommy should pay alimony of $500 per month for 15 years and also should pay "child support" to her of $300 per month. During the current year Tommy made payments of $3,000 for alimony and $1,800 for child support. How much, if any, of this is taxable to Betty? How much, if any, is taxable to the children covered by the child support agreement?

   c. George and Grace Hopkins were divorced during the current year. In the divorce decree, George was directed to pay Grace a total of $18,000, with $8,000 to be paid in the year of the divorce and $1,000 per year to be paid in each of the succeeding 10 years.

   d. A woman obtained a divorce decree from her husband that provided for her to receive a $60,000 property settlement, in lieu of alimony. The settlement was payable in sums of $10,000 for the first year (the current year) and $5,000 per year for the next 10 years.

19. Several years ago Howard leased a piece of land that he owned to a local businessman. During the current year, the lease expired and the land use reverted to Howard. He discovered that the tenant had constructed a building on the property, and on the date the lease expired the building had a fair market value of $22,000.

20. A salaried worker purchased an annuity policy from an insurance company when he was 35 years old. The policy required that the worker pay the company $500 per year for the next 30 years. At that time, when the worker was 65 years old, the insurance company was to pay him either (1) a lump-sum payment of $20,000 or (2) annual payments of $1,300 for 20 years.

   a. Assume that the worker elected option (1).

   b. Assume all facts as before, except that this worker elected option (2). (Answer relative to one year's payment of $1,300.)

21. For each of the following items, indicate the amount included in the taxable income of Mr. Y, a bachelor, and the year of inclusion. Y is a cash-basis taxpayer.

   a. Mr. Y's car was struck in the rear by a speeder in September 19x1. Mr. Y suffered from whiplash and had severe pains in the neck and upper back. He filed a claim for damages against the speeder and his insurance company. Y went to the doctor with the problem but was never hospitalized because the doctor could not diagnose the ailment. To avoid a costly court fight, the speeder's insurance company settled with Y in February 19x2 for $1,000.

b. Mr. Y has two health and accident policies on which he pays all premiums. During 19x2, when he was hospitalized for hepatitis, his hospital and doctor bills amounted to $500. Y paid these bills and, before the end of 19x2, collected $300 on one policy and $350 on the other policy.

c. In 19x3, Y took a new job where the employer pays premiums for a health and accident policy for each employee. During 19x3, the employer paid $250 on behalf of Y.

d. During 19x2, Y received the following items:
  (1) Cash dividends on GMC stock, $75.
  (2) Interest on corporate bonds, $125.
  (3) Interest on City of Denton bonds, $300.
  (4) Dividends from a Canadian corporation, $90.
  (5) "Dividends" on his savings account at the credit union, $220.
  (6) "Dividends" on his life insurance policy, $300. (The insurer was a "mutual" company, and the dividend represented a return of part of the premiums paid.)

e. Y owns a small building, which he leased in January, 19x2. The lessee paid the rent for 19x2 and 19x3 in advance. The annual rental is $1,000.

f. Y was ill throughout most of 19x4. He received $300 per month for nine months from a wage-continuation insurance policy. Y paid all premiums on the policy.

g. During 19x5, Y's father died, and Y received $10,000 from an ordinary life policy on his father's life. The father's premiums on this policy had totaled only $8,500. The father's employer also paid Y $3,000 "in memory of your father, who was a good employee."

22. Horner borrowed $18,000 from his good friend, Plentee. Horner experienced financial difficulties and approached Plentee with the proposition that Horner would transfer a $25,000 face value life insurance policy on his life to Plentee in settlement of his debt to Plentee. Plentee accepted the proposal, and after receiving the policy paid an additional $3,400 in premiums before Horner died. On Horner's death, Plentee received the $25,000 face value of the policy from the life insurance company. What part, if any, of the $25,000 is taxable to Plentee?

23. Salmonson owned a small plot of land in Midcity. In 1960, he leased the land to Acme Company. Acme Company built a small building on the property. When the lease expired in the current year, the building became the property of Salmonson. At that time, the building had a fair market value of $6,000. When the building was built in 1960, it had cost Acme $24,000 to construct. This amount was also considered to be the building's fair market value at that time.

a. How much income did Salmonson have in 1960 as a result of the building's being constructed?

b. How much income did he have in the current year when the lease expired?

24. Johnson, a retired military officer, had "net assets" of $218,000 on January 19x1. During the year, he had the following receipts:
  (1) Retirement pay (retired because of combat injury), $16,200
  (2) Dividends received during year on stock investments, $400
  (3) Inheritance of $6,000 cash from deceased aunt

(4) Wages from part-time job, $6,200

Johnson's personal consumption expenditures during the year totaled $18,000. At the end of the year, Johnson's net assets had a value of $278,000. Most of the increase was due to an increase in the value of stock owned by Johnson.

   a. What is the amount of Johnson's income in the economic sense, ignoring price-level changes?

   b. What is the amount of Johnson's "gross income" for tax purposes?

   c. What is the amount of Johnson's gross income in the financial accounting sense?

   d. Assuming that the general price level increased by 10 percent during the year 19x1, what would be the effect of price-level changes on gross income for tax purposes? On his gross income in the economic sense?

25. Art had been in business for many years. Because of his illness in 19x1, Art's corporation suffered severe losses during the year. As a result, on September 1, the corporation's assets totaled only $180,000, while its liabilities were $231,000. Because Art had been a valuable customer for many years, and because he had recovered from his illness and the outlook for future profits were good if Art could solve the immediate insolvency, the creditors agreed to reduce the corporation's debt.

   Indicate the amount of taxable income that would result to Art's corporation under each of the following circumstances:

   a. The debts were reduced to $200,000.

   b. The debts were reduced to $171,000.

26. In each of the following cases, compute the amount, if any, that the taxpayer may exclude under the "disability income exclusion."

   a. Taxpayer, age 42, became ill on January 23 of the current year and was absent from work because of illness until August 12. During this period, taxpayer's employer continued to pay taxpayer's regular pay of $1,020 per month. Total adjusted gross income, including sick pay, for the year was $12,800.

   b. Taxpayer became ill on Sunday, June 5 of the current year and entered the hospital that day. Employer continued to pay the employee's regular salary of $900 per month. Taxpayer died on Saturday, August 26 without returning to work. Total A.G.I. (adjusted gross income) for the year, including sick pay, was $12,600.

   c. Taxpayer was injured on his job on Monday, October 3 of the current year. He received severe injuries and is expected to be permanently disabled. The employer continued to pay his regular weekly salary of $120 throughout the year. Taxpayer's total A.G.I., including sick pay, was $15,800.

27. a. In the current year, Taxpayer, single, was employed during the first nine months of the year, earning $20,600. He lost his job in early October, and then drew unemployment benefits under the state unemployment compensation plan during the remainder of the year. The unemployment benefits totaled $800. What amount, if any, of the unemployment compensation benefits will be included in gross income?

   b. Assume the same facts as in part a, except that the taxpayer's salary during the first nine months of the year had been $19,600. What amount, if any, of the unemployment benefits will be included in gross income?

28. Acorn Corporation adopted a plan under which the corporation would pay the costs of tuition, books, and supplies for any officer of the corporation or for any operating department head who enrolled in not more than two courses at an accredited university. Zemat Turin, the corporation's controller, enrolled in a tax course at the university. The corporation reimbursed Turin $270 for tui-

tion, $22 for books, and $6 for other supplies. What part, if any, of the reim-bursement is taxable to Turin?

SUPPLEMENTAL PROBLEMS

29. Assume that you are the tax counselor for Mary, who is in the process of agree-ing on a divorce settlement with her husband, John. Mary is unemployed, and all the couple's property is legally in John's name. John owns a large amount of property and has a high income. The couple have three children, who are to remain in Mary's custody. John's attorney is proposing the following settlement:

John is willing to pay Mary $500,000, at the rate of $4,000 per month for 125 months. In addition, John is willing to give Mary the right to live in their present home until such time as Mary should remarry, and John will make the mortgage payments of $1,000 per month on the home, pay taxes on the home (estimated to be $6,000 per year), pay utilities (estimated to average $500 per month), and pay for all necessary repairs, maintenance, and upkeep (estimated to be $200 per month).

What are the income tax implications of this proposal for Mary? What counter-offer would you advise Mary to make?

30. H. McGregor Malcolm is President and Chairman of the Board of Malcolm Industries, Inc. In preparing Malcolm's tax return for the year, you discover the following facts.

(1) The company provides Malcolm with an automobile for his business and personal use. Each year the automobile is traded in for a new one.

(2) The company also provides Malcolm's wife, who works on a part-time basis for the company, with an automobile for her exclusive use. Her car is replaced every third year.

(3) Malcolm Industries has 325 employees. It does not have a general hos-pitalization insurance plan for employees, but it has secured a medical insur-ance policy for Malcolm that covers all medical costs for Mr. and Mrs. Mal-colm. During this year, premiums on the policy totaled $1,500.

(4) Malcolm attends many "marketing" and "trade association" meetings. His wife always accompanies him because he thinks she is very helpful in mak-ing business contacts and in securing sales orders. The corporation pays all expenses for both.

(5) The company has a dining room for officers, directors, and selected higher level managers. Meals are served at a price that is roughly one-half the price charged for similar meals at public restaurants.

(6) The company frequently receives "premiums" from suppliers. These premiums are usually resold, but occasionally Malcolm and the other stock-holder-employees take premiums for their personal use. During the current year Malcolm took a color television set, a microwave oven, and a television computer game for his use.

(7) Malcolm Industries subscribes to many magazines for use in its recep-tion areas. When they are received, several of these magazines are regularly taken home by Malcolm. After the Malcolms have read them, the magazines are returned to the company's offices.

(8) During the year, as part of a promotional campaign, one of Malcolm

The passage of the bill will mark the dawn of a brighter day, with more of sunshine, more of the songs of birds, more of that sweetest music, the laughter of children well fed, well clothed, well housed. Can we doubt that, in the brighter, happier days to come, good, even-headed, wholesome democracy shall be triumphant? God hasten the era of equality in taxation and in opportunity. And God prosper the Wilson bill, the first leaf in the glorious book of reform in taxation, the promise of a brightening future for those whose genius and labor create the wealth of the land, and whose courage and patriotism are the only sure bulwark in the defense of the Republic.

CONGRESSMAN DAVID A. DE ARMOND,
Congressional Record (1894)

deductions: general concepts

As explained in Chapter 5, the income tax is levied against taxable income, a statutory and legalistic quantity determined by subtracting authorized deductions from gross income. These deductions are spawned by such diverse forces as common sense, tradition, politics, and administrative convenience, and they are as complex as the forces that created them. The advocates of new deductions inevitably forecast, as in the headnote to this chapter, the dawn of a new and better world if Congress will but grant their request.

The term "deductions," as used in federal income taxation, can be defined only procedurally—for example, as those items that collectively constitute the difference between the quantity called "gross income" and the quantity called "taxable income." A few considerations implicit in this purely procedural definition are, however, important. Note that the two quantifications, gross income and taxable income, describe purely legalistic quantities; outside the realm of federal income taxation, neither quantity has particular meaning.[1] It is a widely accepted notion in federal income taxation that *nothing is deductible unless authorized by the Code or the regulations.*[2]

At this point, a well-grounded student of accounting is apt to have misgivings. It is apparent that income is itself a net concept, generally conceded to be the difference between properly matched revenues and expenses for some arbitrary time period. Thus, it seems implicit that all "properly matched expenses" must be "deductions" for purposes of determining income. Ignoring possible differences in timing—that is, ignoring the accounting refinements common to the "matching concept"—the accounting student's intuition is only partially correct for matters of federal income taxation. As a general proposition, most of the items that would fall into the accountant's classification called "expenses" are also "deductions" for tax purposes; in addition, however, the Code provides for many other deductions in the calculation of taxable income. Thus, the term "deduction" is a much broader, more generic and legalistic term than the term "expense." This is

---

[1] Admittedly the term "gross profit" did gain acceptance in the general financial accounting literature several years ago. Recently, however, accounting has refined its terminology and now such phrases as revenue and gross profit (margin) on sales have replaced the former usage.

[2] For an argument to the contrary see Erwin N. Griswold, "An Argument Against the Doctrine that Deductions Should be Narrowly Construed as a Matter of Legislative Grace," *Harvard Law Review,* 56 (June, 1943), pp. 1142–47.

especially true for the individual taxpayer, although the comment also has limited relevance for the corporate taxpayer.

The deductions allowed a corporation are roughly comparable to the expenses that appear on its annual income statement prepared in accordance with generally accepted accounting principles. This generalization also applies to the computation of taxable income from a sole proprietorship or a partnership. There are, however, numerous and major exceptions to the general rule. Some of these exceptions relate only to differences in the timing of deductions; others involve the aggregate amount to be deducted in the long run. In this chapter, we shall examine some of the more important differences between "tax deductions" and "accounting expenses."

In addition, we shall discuss the broad outline of the deductions granted to individual taxpayers, although detailed consideration of such deductions will be deferred until Part Four.

GENERAL REQUIREMENTS FOR A DEDUCTION

Under ordinary circumstances, every taxpayer wishes to maximize deductions to arrive at the lowest possible taxable income and tax liability. In spite of the almost unlimited number of possible deductions, however, the average taxpayer is entitled to deduct only a relative few. What, then, are the basic types of allowable deductions, and what are the general concepts that underlie them?

The allowable deductions may be grouped into three broad categories:

1. Deductions applicable to a trade or business, including business-related expenses of an employee.
2. "Nonbusiness" deductions related to production of "nonbusiness" income.
3. Purely personal deductions specifically provided for individual taxpayers.

The basic authorization: the revenue code

In order to deduct any item, the taxpayer must be able to point to some provision of the Code that authorizes the deduction. It is not necessary that the statute list the specific item by name, but the item must clearly fall under one of the provisions of the

law. In this regard, a mere reading of the Code may not reveal whether or not an item is deductible, since Treasury Regulations, Revenue Service rulings, and court decisions constantly interpret the meaning of the statute. It is knowledge of these *interpretations,* therefore, that constitutes the real stock in trade of the tax practitioner.[3]

In addition to being able to prove that he or she is entitled to the deduction, the taxpayer must maintain adequate records to support any deduction claimed. Although in most situations neither the Code nor the Regulations dictate the form or content of the necessary records, taxpayers should retain reasonable records to protect their right to all tax deductions.

The Code provides for a multitude of deductions for very dissimilar items, including losses, expenses, and "special" items not necessarily involving monetary outlays. These provisions can be usefully divided into two major categories: the general (or universal) provisions and the specific deduction authorizations.

The general provisions

Two Code sections that serve as the most general basis for deductions are Sec. 162, Expenses of Carrying on a Trade or Business, and Sec. 212, Expenses for Production of Income. In addition, as discussed on page **6/5**, Sec. 165 permits a deduction for losses incurred in a trade or business or in any transaction entered into for a profit. The importance of these Sections warrants a closer examination of the three provisions.

EXPENSES OF TRADE OR BUSINESS   The broadest provision pertaining to deductions—and, incidentally, the provision that comes closest to approximating the expense concept in accounting—is located in Sec. 162(a), which reads in part as follows:

(a) In General.—There shall be allowed as a deduction all the ordinary and necessary expenses paid or incurred during the taxable year in carrying on any trade or business, including—
(1) a reasonable allowance for salaries or other compensations for personal services actually rendered;
(2) traveling expenses (including amounts expended for meals and lodging other than amounts which are lavish or extravagant under the circumstances)

---

[3]Every would-be tax advisor should become thoroughly familiar with one or more of the excellent loose-leaf tax services, which are the only way to maintain a complete and current compilation of the changing legislation and of new court interpretations.

while away from home in the pursuit of a trade or business; and

(3) rentals or other payments required to be made as a condition to the continued use or possession, for purposes of the trade or business, of property to which the taxpayer has not taken or is not taking title or in which he has no equity.

Although these general words may suggest to the unsuspecting taxpayer (or student) that virtually every "business expense" is deductible, an investigation of the interpretation given these words by tax administrators and courts would not support such a conclusion.

The definitional boundaries of a *trade or business,* although they are of particular importance to the individual taxpayer, are as elusive as the definitions of "ordinary" and "necessary." The intention to make a profit is necessary; the actuality of a profit is not. On the other hand, the intention to make a profit is not a sufficient condition. Many transactions and business ventures are profit-oriented, but they are not deemed to constitute a trade or business for tax purposes. Rather, there must be some personal effort of an entrepreneurial nature before any income-producing activity can be said to constitute a trade or business. This distinction becomes particularly difficult to draw with relatively passive investment ventures. Thus, the ownership of a single rental unit has been found not to constitute a business.[4]

A second major problem arises in determining whether a particular venture constitutes a trade or business or whether it is a hobby. Many taxpayers, particularly those of financial means, enjoy such expensive endeavors as building racing automobiles, breeding race horses, and feeding beef cattle. Obviously, such endeavors may be very sound and profitable business ventures. In those cases in which a taxpayer consistently reports losses, however, the tax administrators suspect that the real motivation is purely personal enjoyment rather than a desire to conduct a profitable business. Whenever the I.R.S. can prove its suspicions, a host of otherwise deductible expenses are lost. These cases are obviously difficult ones and are often brought to the courts for adjudication. Prior to 1970 the Code provided that when a taxpayer claimed a loss of more than $50,000 per year for at least five consecutive years, the activity was deemed a hobby. This provision was obviously very limited in its application and the 1969

Reform Act added Sec. 183, which prohibits a net loss deduction from a "hobby."[5] Further, it provides that, unless the I.R.S. establishes to the contrary, an activity is presumed to be engaged in for profit if the gross income for 2 or more out of 5 consecutive tax years exceeds the deductions attributable to the activity. If the gross income from the activity does not exceed expenses for at least 2 out of 5 consecutive years, there is not an automatic presumption that the activity is not engaged in for profit. Even for a hobby, expenses will generally be deductible to the extent of the gross income from the hobby.

A few employee expenses also are allowable as deductions under Sec. 162. Generally, the employee must be able to demonstrate that any business expenses deducted are directly related to the performance of duties or are required by an employment agreement. Nonreimbursed costs of special clothing not suitable for off-duty wear, union dues, tools of trade, and membership dues of professional employees in professional organizations are typical examples of such employee expenses. Travel, transportation, and entertainment are also frequently encountered employee business expenses. The Code and the regulations are rather precise in describing the purpose and nature of costs that may be deducted as travel, transportation, and entertainment, and the regulations specify the nature of records that must be maintained when such expenses are claimed. Entertainment expenses in particular are often held to be personal expenditures and therefore not deductible. Although the I.R.S. requirements are frequently criticized, it is obvious that when it comes to travel and entertainment there is a fine line between bona fide business costs and personal expenditures by either an employee or a self-employed individual. Here, again, the importance of the tests of reasonableness, necessity, appropriateness, and "direct business connection" become crucial in deciding whether an item is or is not deductible.[6]

Obviously, the difficulty created by allowing deductions of this type lies in the rather arbitrary distinction between what constitutes a cost of earning income and what constitutes a personal expense. It might be argued, for example, that every person employed outside the home incurs extra costs

---

[4]For an interesting discussion of the issue see "The Single Rental as a 'Trade or Business' Under the Internal Revenue Code," *University of Chicago Law Review,* 23 (Autumn 1966), pp. 111–21.

[5]Of course, some expenses such as interest and taxes would be deductible even though the activity were considered a hobby. Other expenses of a hobby are deductible only to the extent that the gross income from the activity exceeds the deductions such as interest and taxes, otherwise deductible.

[6]The "directly-related-to-business" tests are prescribed for entertainment expenses in Code Sec. 274 and Regs. 1.274-2.

because of his or her job. The cost of commuting to work, the extra expense incurred in eating restaurant meals, the additional costs of wearing appropriate clothing and of personal grooming all result from the taxpayer's employment, but they are all considered to be personal expenses.

Another situation in which it is difficult to distinguish between personal living costs and business-related expenses is created when the taxpayer uses a part of his or her home for business purposes. In past years, controversies have developed between taxpayers and the Internal Revenue Service over this issue. Consequently, the Tax Reform Act of 1976 (Sec. 280A) introduced very severe limitations on the deduction of such expenses. This new rule, discussed in some detail in Chapter 14, provides that only expenses of that part of the taxpayer's home exclusively used on a regular basis as the taxpayer's principal place of business may be deducted. (However, the Tax Reduction and Simplification Act of 1977 removed the "exclusive use" requirement for a residence used as a day-care center.) Obviously, this provision may be inequitable to many taxpayers, especially some artists, authors, and others who often use a part of their home as an office or studio.

In Chapter 14 the distinction between business-related expenses and nondeductible personal expenditures is examined in some detail.

EXPENSES FOR PRODUCTION OF INCOME   As already explained, many business-oriented activities do not qualify as a trade or business for tax purposes because no personal effort of an "entrepreneurial nature" is involved. Until the Revenue Act of 1942, taxpayers were frequently denied deductions for expenses related to these income-producing activities because they did not qualify as a "trade or business." For example, in 1941 the United States Supreme Court found that expenses incurred by a wealthy taxpayer to maintain an office for the purpose of managing his securities and real estate were not those of a trade or business and were, therefore, nondeductible personal expenses.[7] Following this decision, Congress enacted the first two paragraphs of the present Sec. 212. (The third paragraph, relating to deduction of expenses related to taxes, was incorporated later by the Revenue Act of 1954.) The present section reads as follows:

Sec. 212. Expenses for Production of Income.
In the case of an individual, there shall be allowed as a

[7]*Higgins* v. *Commissioner*, 312 U.S. 212 (1941).

deduction all the ordinary and necessary expenses paid or incurred during the taxable year—
(1) for the production or collection of income;
(2) for the management, conservation, or maintenance of property held for the production of income; or
(3) in connection with the determination, collection, or refund of any tax.

The result of this section is to make many income-related expenses deductible even though not incurred in a trade or business. For example, an expense attributable to the renting of a single property may not be deductible under Sec. 162 because such limited rental activity does not constitute a trade or business. Nevertheless, Sec. 212(2) authorizes such a deduction. The Regulations help delineate what is meant by "production of income." Regulation 1.212-1(b) states in part:

The term "income" for the purpose of section 212 includes not merely income of the taxable year but also income which the taxpayer has realized in a prior taxable year or may realize in subsequent taxable years; and is not confined to recurring income but applies as well to gains from the disposition of property. For example, if defaulted bonds, the interest from which if received would be includible in income, are purchased with the expectation of realizing capital gain on their resale, even though no current yield thereon is anticipated, ordinary and necessary expenses thereafter paid or incurred in connection with such bonds are deductible. Similarly, ordinary and necessary expenses paid or incurred in the management, conservation, or maintenance of a building devoted to rental purposes are deductible notwithstanding that there is actually no income therefrom in the taxable year, and regardless of the manner in which or the purpose for which the property in question was acquired. Expenses paid or incurred in managing, conserving, or maintaining property held for investment may be deductible under section 212 even though the property is not currently productive and there is no likelihood that the property will be sold at a profit or will otherwise be productive of income and even though the property is held merely to minimize a loss with respect thereto. . . .

Section 212 is the primary authority for the deduction of such expenses as safety deposit box rental and investment counsel fees that relate to investments in securities that produce taxable income. Many other expenses associated with property or an activity intended to produce income also become deductible under Sec. 212. In determining whether any expense is deductible, the major consideration is whether it is related to an activity entered into with the hope of making a profit or merely engaged in for pleasure or personal reasons. In a few cases, expenses associated with the production of income may be subject to special, restrictive rules. For example, the Tax Reform Act of 1969 placed a limit on the deduction permitted taxpayers other than corporations for interest paid on indebtedness incurred to purchase or carry property held for investment, and this limitation was further tightened by the Tax Reform Act of 1976. This limitation is discussed in Chapter 13, page **13/11**. Interestingly, most of the expenses incurred by a corporate taxpayer are assumed to be incurred in a trade or business.

DEDUCTIONS FOR LOSSES   The general authorization for the deduction of losses is found in Sec. 165(a), which reads as follows:

> There shall be allowed as a deduction any loss sustained during the taxable year and not compensated for by insurance or otherwise.

Subsection 165(c), however, restricts the general provision for individual taxpayers as follows:

> In the case of an individual, the deduction under subsection (a) shall be limited to—
> (1) losses incurred in a trade or business;
> (2) losses incurred in any transaction entered into for profit, though not connected with a trade or business; and
> (3) losses of property not connected with a trade or business, if such losses arise from fire, storm, shipwreck, or other casualty, or from theft.

Here again we observe the same three-way classification of losses incurred by an individual taxpayer: that is, a loss may be (1) incurred in a full-fledged trade or business, (2) incurred in a "nonbusiness" but profit-oriented transaction, or (3) incurred in a purely personal connection. In the event of losses to purely personal properties, no deduction is allowed unless the loss is attributable to a casualty or a theft.

Unfortunately, each set of facts is to some extent unique, and in order to determine whether or not any particular loss is deductible it may be necessary to determine the intent and motive of the taxpayer for entering into a particular transaction. This is a difficult, if not impossible, task in many cases. Limited application of this often troublesome Code provision will be examined in later chapters. A few special rules, however, should be noted at this early juncture. For example, the I.R.S. generally maintains that many anticipatory expenditures cannot be deducted as losses unless a taxpayer has already established himself or herself as being "in business." Thus, expenditures for travel incurred by a taxpayer to investigate the possibility of opening a *new* business may be denied. However, to confuse the issue, the I.R.S. has ruled that if a person attempts to acquire a *specific* business or investment and the attempt fails, expenses related to the attempt may be capitalized and deducted as losses. Losses of anticipated gains are similarly denied; only actual losses sustained (as measured by the adjusted "cost" of the property) can be deducted. And losses must be those of the taxpayer before a deduction can be granted. The other subsections of Sec. 165 are of less general interest, although they, too, deal with deductible losses.

One other Code Section of interest at this point is Sec. 172, dealing with a "Net Operating Loss Deduction." Under Sec. 172, a "net operating loss" (essentially the net loss from the taxpayer's trade or business) can be allowed as a deduction against income of other tax years. The "NOL" is carried back and offset against income of the third year preceding the year in which the loss occurred. Any amount not used in the third prior year is then offset against income of the second year preceding the loss year, and then against income of the first year preceding the loss year. Any amount unused in the three years preceding the loss year is then carried forward and offset against income of the year following the loss year, and any amount of loss still unused is then carried forward for six more years in order. Thus, the net operating loss can be carried back three years and forward for a total of seven years. The taxpayer, however, may elect (irrevocably) to relinquish the carryback right and only carry the loss forward for seven years.

GENERAL PROVISIONS: POSITIVE CRITERIA   In both Secs. 162 and 212 (but not in Sec. 165), the terms "ordinary" and "necessary" are used. In addition, Sec. 162 contains a "reasonableness" test. The meaning of each of these words in income taxation differs somewhat from customary usage. An expense need not recur frequently in order to be *ordinary*. In fact, an expenditure may be labeled as an ordinary expense for tax purposes if no more than, say, one in one hundred taxpayers ever incurs the expense and if he or she incurs it only once in a lifetime. The essence of the ordinary criterion seems to be that it would be commonplace among other taxpayers who find themselves in comparable circumstances. In the usual meaning of the term, the "comparable circumstances" may indeed be extraordinary. In the case of *Welch* v. *Helvering,* the Court, struggling with the meaning of the word "ordinary," said that "the decisive distinctions are those of degree and not of kind. One struggles in vain for any verbal formula that will supply a ready touchstone. The standard set up by the statute is not a rule of law; it is rather a way of life. Life in all its fullness must supply the answer to the riddle."[8]

To be *necessary* an expense must be capable of making a contribution to a trade or business. Fortunately for the taxpayer, the courts and tax administrators do not insist that necessity be determined on an *ex post* basis; it is sufficient if the expense appeared to be necessary at the time it was incurred. The courts generally do not second guess business people on the necessity of making expenditures. As a practical matter, therefore, this positive criterion is probably the least significant of those considered. When invoked, it frequently relates to illegal activities. For example, fines paid for overweight trucks were found to be unnecessary, to frustrate public policy, and therefore to be nondeductible.[9]

Finally, even an ordinary and necessary expense incurred in a trade or business or in connection with the production of income must be *reasonable in amount* before it can be deducted for tax purposes. Technically, this requirement is stated in Sec. 162(a)-(1) only in relation to compensation, but the courts have found that "the element of reasonableness was inherent in the phrase 'ordinary and necessary.'"[10] As a practical matter, the reasonableness criterion is important most frequently in the case of related taxpayers. For example, a corporation may attempt to pay its sole stockholder-executive (or his or her children) an unreasonably large salary, interest, or rental payment. If allowed, these expenses could be used to disguise payments that in reality were dividends—a result of particular importance since dividends, unlike business expenses, are not deductible to the corporation paying them. Therefore, the I.R.S. is constantly screening transactions between related parties to determine their reasonableness.

GENERAL PROVISIONS: NEGATIVE CRITERIA   In addition to the positive criteria, there exist four negative criteria that must also be satisfied before any unspecified expense may be tax deductible. Any expenditure not specifically authorized as a deduction will be disallowed if it is found to be *purely personal,* a *capital expenditure, related to tax-exempt income,* or *contrary to public policy.* The Code sections pertaining to nondeductible expenses in general include:

Sec. 262.—Personal, Living, and Family Expenses.
Sec. 263.—Capital Expenditures.

Sec. 265.—Expenses and Interest Relating to Tax-Exempt Income.
Sec. 162.—(expenses contrary to public policy.)

There are, in addition, many other Code provisions that prohibit such specific expenses as selected taxes (Sec. 275). As explained earlier, our concern at this point is limited to the provisions of more general application.

Personal living and family expenses.   Section 262 states that "except as otherwise expressly provided in this chapter, no deduction shall be allowed for personal, living, or family expenses." In light of the earlier discussion, we can suggest that all expenses must be categorized as either (1) directly related to a trade or business, (2) related to a profit-making venture that is not a trade or business, or (3) incurred without any intention of profit. Only the last category, the purely personal expenses, are categorically disallowed unless some section of the law specifically provides for their deduction. The difficulty in everyday tax practice, of course, comes in categorizing actual expenses. The problem of hobby losses is again pertinent.

Capital outlays.   Section 263(a) states that

no deduction shall be allowed for—
(1) any amount paid out for new buildings or for permanent improvements or betterments made to increase the value of any property or estate. . . . [or]
(2) any amount expended in restoring property or in making good the exhaustion thereof for which an allowance is or has been made.

(The omitted portion of Sec. 263 recognizes that other Code provisions specifically authorize the immediate deduction of a number of expenditures that could be classified as capital expenditures.) Any student acquainted with intermediate accounting is well aware of the practical difficulties in determining whether or not a particular expenditure is a "capital expenditure" or a "revenue expenditure." In general, the tax solutions to such riddles parallel the accounting solutions; therefore, no detailed consideration of them is presented here.

However, the mere fact that a capital outlay is not deductible at the time of the outlay does not prevent its recovery (deduction against income) at a later date. There are three general methods by which future deductions might be accomplished:

1. Deferral of deduction of cost until property is sold or otherwise disposed of. For example, the costs of land and securities are offset against the ulti-

[8]290 U.S. 111 (1933), pp. 114–15.
[9]*Hoover Motor Express Co., Inc.* v. *United States,* 356 U.S. 38 (1958).
[10]*Commissioner* v. *Lincoln Electric Co.,* 176 F. 2d 815 (6th Cir., 1949), p. 815.

mate selling price. (This process is discussed in Chapter 20.)

2. "Timetable" deductions of the cost may be made. The costs of buildings, machinery, furniture, and equipment are "depreciated" over an assumed useful life on a more or less arbitrary timetable (as discussed in Chapter 16).

3. A deduction based on a percentage of income from the property over its life (for example, the depletion of natural resources, discussed in Chapter 18) may be made.

Expenses related to tax-exempt income. Section 265 disallows a deduction for any interest or other expense that is paid or incurred in order to realize tax-exempt income. This provision closes a loophole that would otherwise exist for persons in the higher tax brackets. That is, if it were not for this provision, a person in a top tax bracket might, because of income taxation, actually obtain a positive cash flow by borrowing high-interest money and investing it in low-interest state or local obligations. To illustrate, let us assume that a taxpayer in the 70 percent marginal tax bracket borrowed $1 million at 14 percent and invested the proceeds in an 8 percent state bond issue. The annual interest expense would amount to $140,000, which, if it were not for Sec. 265, would reduce the borrower's tax liability by $98,000 (70 percent of $140,000). The tax-exempt interest earned on the state bonds would amount to $80,000, thus producing a net positive cash flow of $38,000 per year to the taxpayer. As stated above, Sec. 265 prevents this kind of tax legerdemain.

Expenses contrary to public policy. Prior to the 1969 Tax Reform Act, no statutory authority specifically disallowed such "expenses" as bribes, kickbacks, and fines. Nevertheless, the courts frequently disallowed such expenses on the grounds that allowing the deduction would frustrate public policy, and taxpayers were frequently required to go to court to determine whether various items were contrary to public policy. Now, Sec. 162 specifies several types of expenditures that controvert public policy and are disallowed:

1. Fines or penalties for violation of law.
2. Bribes or kickbacks paid to public officials.
3. A portion (usually ⅔) of treble damages paid under antitrust laws in criminal proceedings.
4. Payments such as kickbacks and bribes other than to government officials and employees if such payments are illegal under any generally enforced United States or state law providing for a criminal penalty or loss of license or privilege to engage in trade or business. This includes any kickback under medicare.

Kickbacks, bribes, and so on, other than those specified above, would still be deductible if ordinary and necessary. Payments to officials of foreign governments are not deductible if such payments would be a violation of U.S. laws.

However, the addition of these provisions does not solve all the questions involving public policy. The boundaries of this prohibition are especially difficult to specify because the courts have consistently held that expenses are deductible even if the income that the expense produces is illegal. For example, the expenses incurred by a gambler are deductible for tax purposes even if the gambler operates his business in a state that prohibits gambling. In a way, this is only equitable, since the illegal income has been held to be fully taxable. On the other hand, the granting of the deduction does make the activity more profitable (after taxes) and to that extent serves to controvert the laws of the state.

In sum, then, an expense is ordinarily deductible in the computation of taxable income if it either is authorized by a specific Code section or satisfies eight general criteria. An unspecified expense may be deducted if it is

1. Ordinary
2. Necessary
3. Reasonable in amount
4. Incurred in connection with a trade or business or in the production of income

and if it is *not*

5. A capital expenditure
6. A personal expenditure
7. Related to tax-exempt income
8. Contrary to public policy

The specific provisions

In addition to the general provision under Sec. 162 discussed above, Part VI of Subchapter B authorizes almost 30 specific deductions in Secs. 163–191. Some of these are of general importance; for example,

Sec. 163. Interest.
Sec. 164. Taxes.
Sec. 167. Depreciation.

On the other hand, several Sections apply to very few taxpayers; for example,

Sec. 184. Amortization of certain railroad rolling stock.
Sec. 185. Amortization of railroad grading and tunnel bores.
Sec. 186. Recoveries of damages for antitrust violations, etc.
Sec. 188. Amortization of certain expenditures for child-care facilities.

Most deductions are very much like the expenses appearing on published financial statements. On the surface, then, there would appear to be little problem in determining either the nature or the amounts of items that may be deducted as business expenses. Unfortunately for the student, this is not always true. A detailed examination of each of the Code Sections in Part VI of Subchapter B would yield the usual list of exceptions, exceptions to exceptions, limitations, and special definitions. We will explore, therefore, the main ways in which the deductions for taxation differ significantly from the expenses of general financial accounting. However, it is first necessary to understand the application of tax accounting methods to deductions.

TAX ACCOUNTING METHODS— DEDUCTIONS

The quoted portions of Secs. 162 and 212, earlier in this chapter, include the words "paid or incurred during the taxable year" in specifying which deductions are allowable. As pointed out in Chapter 5, the cash-basis taxpayer ordinarily deducts expenses only when paid, whereas the accrual-basis taxpayer is entitled to take a deduction as soon as there is a fixed and determinable liability incurred by the taxpayer.

Regulation 1.461-1(a)(1) further explains how to determine the year in which a deduction is to be taken by a cash-basis taxpayer.

Under the cash receipts and disbursements method of accounting, amounts representing allowable deductions shall, as a general rule, be taken into account for the taxable year in which paid. Further, a taxpayer using this method may also be entitled to certain deductions in the computation of taxable income which do not involve cash disbursements during the taxable year, such as the deductions for depreciation, depletion, and losses under sections 167, 611, and 165, respectively. If an expenditure results in the creation of an asset having a useful life which extends substantially beyond the close of the taxable year, such an expenditure may not be deductible, or may be deductible only in part, for the taxable year in which made. . . .

Note that payment must actually be made; there is no doctrine of constructive payment equivalent to the doctrine of "constructive receipt," which was explained in Chapter 5. (However, a deduction may be allowed for a payment made with a noncash asset.) When payments are made by mail, the usual rule is that mailing constitutes payment because the postal system is deemed to be the agent of the addressee as well as the mailer, but there are conflicting court decisions on this point.

Questions are frequently raised about prepayment of expenses. Ordinarily a prepayment, such as a purchase of supplies, can be deducted in the year of payment even if the supplies are not used until the following year. If the payment creates an asset extending substantially beyond the end of the year, however, only that part used up in the current year is deductible. There are conflicting decisions over the proper period for deduction of prepaid rent, interest, and insurance by cash-basis taxpayers. As a generalization, however, it can be said that such prepayments must be allocated over the period for which payment was made if to do otherwise would result in a material distortion of income. The I.R.S. apparently holds that prepaid insurance and prepaid rent must be allocated in almost every case, and Code Sec. 461(g) requires cash-basis taxpayers to deduct prepaid interest over the period of the loan, except for "points" on home mortgages, which generally can still be deducted currently.

Deposits made in advance on goods or services are deductible in years when the goods or services are received. Obviously, expenditures for capital assets such as equipment must be capitalized and depreciated, even by the cash-basis taxpayer. Deposits on inventory goods also become a part of the cost of the goods acquired.

Normally, an accrual-basis taxpayer is entitled to a deduction whenever there is a fixed and determinable liability incurred by the taxpayer. Thus, if there are substantial contingencies, or no reasonable estimate of the amount of expense can be made, there is no deduction. As explained below, there are many "timing differences" between deductions on the tax return and those that are generally accepted in financial accounting. Many of these exist because there is no "fixed" liability even though an expense may be estimated (with reasonable accuracy) for financial accounting purposes. A good example is the timing difference resulting from a deduction in the financial reports for estimated costs of guarantees and warranties at the time the related product or service is sold; these costs cannot be deducted on the tax return until the service under the warranty is actually rendered.

DEDUCTIONS: FINANCIAL ACCOUNTING AND TAX DIFFERENCES

In Chapter 5 we examined the significant differences between gross income items reported in the tax return and income (revenue) items reported in the published income statement. Similar differences exist between the deductions reported in a tax return and the expenses entered in a financial statement. Obviously, these differences may be either permanent or temporary. The latter are properly described as differences in timing.

Differences in timing

Timing differences are themselves divisible into two subgroups:

1. Expenses or losses deducted for tax purposes *after* being accrued for financial accounting reports.
2. Expenses or losses deducted for tax purposes *before* being accrued for financial accounting purposes.

As you may suspect, the first group is the larger of the two. The reasons for the differences are essentially the same as the reasons for differences in income items, as discussed in Chapter 5 (see pages **5/6–5/12**).

DELAYED TAX DEDUCTIONS There are several important instances in which expenses deducted currently for accounting purposes are deferred to be deducted on later years' tax returns. The following important situations are among those summarized by the Accounting Principles Board of the American Institute of C.P.A.s:

Estimated costs of guarantees and product warranty contracts are recorded in accounts at date of sale and deducted in tax returns when later paid.

Current expenses for self-insurance are recorded in accounts based on consistent computations for the plan and are deducted in tax returns when losses are later incurred.

Estimated losses on inventories and purchase commitments are recorded in accounts when reasonably anticipated and deducted in tax returns when later realized.

Provisions for major repairs and maintenance are accrued in accounts on a systematic basis and deducted in tax returns when later paid.

Depreciation recorded in accounts exceeds that deducted in tax returns in early years because of:
accelerated method of computation for accounting purposes
shorter lives for accounting purposes.

Organization costs are written off in accounts as incurred and amortized in tax returns.[11]

Many of these timing problems are created because it is frequently permissible, or even preferred, in financial accounting to estimate future costs relating to goods or services sold and to deduct these as expenses of the period in which the corresponding revenue is recognized. In fact, the estimating process is required by the matching concept of financial accounting. The estimated transaction is recorded through the so-called reserve method, under which a liability is set up for the estimated future costs. This procedure is rarely permitted for tax purposes, however; instead, most expenses are deductible only when paid or when the exact liability can be computed with mathematical accuracy and legal certainty. The only major exceptions to this rule concern the amortization of fixed asset costs and the estimation of bad debts.

Although this deviation of tax law from accounting practice is often criticized by accountants as resulting in a mismatching of revenues and expenses, the tax rule has been supported because of the uncertainty of the estimating process in regard to both quantities and prices. It is obvious that several of the basic tenets of taxation are served by postponing deductions until they can be measured with accuracy. Certainly postponement results in a higher degree of objectivity and grossly simplifies the administration of the law. It can also be argued that it increases equity and uniformity among taxpayers.

ACCELERATED TAX DEDUCTION There are also a few instances in which expenses or losses may be deducted for tax purposes before they are accrued

[11] Accounting Principles Board of the American Institute of Certified Public Accountants, *APB Opinion No. 11, Accounting for Income Taxes* (New York: American Institute of Certified Public Accountants, 1967), pp. 184–85. See also Homer A. Black, *Interperiod Allocation of Corporate Income Taxes,* Accounting Research Study No. 9 (New York: American Institute of Certified Public Accountants, 1966), pp. 8–10.

for accounting purposes. The following examples indicate the most important cases:

> Depreciation deducted for tax purposes exceeds that recorded for accounting purposes in early years because of:
> accelerated method of computation for tax purposes
> shorter guideline lives for tax purposes
> amortization of emergency facilities under certificates of necessity.

> Unamortized discount, issue cost and redemption premium on bonds refunded are deducted for tax purposes in the year of redemption or refunding and are deferred to be amortized for accounting purposes.

> Preoperating expenses are deducted for tax purposes when incurred and are deferred to be amortized to future periods for accounting purposes.[12]

Most of these tax provisions, especially those related to depreciation, research and development costs, and preoperating expenses, were enacted to achieve specific economic goals.

Permanent differences

Most permanent differences between the taxable income and the financial income of a business occur because certain business expenses are held to be nondeductible for tax purposes or because the amount deductible in the tax return is limited. In addition, a limited number of statutory tax deductions are not considered to be expenses for accounting purposes.

Various sections in Part IX of the Code are written to prohibit the deduction of specific items. Some of these are:

Sec. 264.	Certain amounts paid in connection with insurance contracts.
Sec. 265.	Expenses and interest relating to tax-exempt income.
Sec. 275.	Certain taxes.
Sec. 276.	Certain indirect contributions to political parties.
Sec. 280B.	Demolition of certain historic structures.

In other instances, within a section basically designed to allow a deduction, there may be a subsection or paragraph devoted to the disallowance of specified items. For example, Sec. 162(e)(2), which is related to lobbying expenses, states

> (2) Limitation. The provisions of paragraph (1) shall not be construed as allowing the deduction of any amount paid or incurred (whether by way of contribution, gift, or otherwise)—
> (A) for participation in, or intervention in, any political campaign on behalf of any candidate for public office, or
> (B) in connection with any attempt to influence the general public, or segments thereof, with respect to legislative matters, elections or referendums.

The law does, however, permit individual taxpayers to take a credit for limited amounts of contributions to political campaigns and parties (see Chapter 8).

Another example of a limitation placed within a section allowing a deduction is Sec. 164(c), which states

> (c) Deduction Denied in Case of Certain Taxes. No deduction shall be allowed for the following taxes:
> (1) Taxes assessed against local benefits of a kind tending to increase the value of the property assessed; but this paragraph shall not prevent the deduction of so much of such taxes as is properly allocable to maintenance or interest charges.

There are many such limiting subsections; these two are merely examples.

The Code and the regulations also place maximum limits on the amounts that may be deducted for certain expenses, even though the entire amount may be deducted on the published income statement. In effect, these restrictions specify the maximum amount considered as ordinary and reasonable. Among the more important of these are

1. Charitable contributions made by a corporation may be deducted only to the extent of 5 percent of taxable income as determined before such deduction.

2. Deductions for amounts paid to employee pension and profit-sharing plans by employers are limited to a percentage of salaries and other compensation paid to ''covered'' employees during the year.

However, in both of the above examples the ''excess'' not allowed as a deduction in the year paid may be carried forward and deducted in future years, so that in effect they may become merely ''timing'' differences.

In addition, there are literally thousands of court

---

[12] Accounting Principles Board, *op. cit.,* p. 16.

decisions that limit the amount deductible in individual cases. For example, as noted earlier in this chapter, numerous decisions disallow part of an excessive salary paid by a corporation to an officer-stockholder, permitting the corporation to deduct only that portion of the salary deemed to be "reasonable" in the circumstances.

Finally, there are the few deductions permitted for tax purposes but not considered bona fide expenses in accounting. Perhaps the most controversial and celebrated of these is the "statutory" or "percentage" depletion allowance (discussed in detail in Chapter 18) that permits some producers of natural resources to charge to expense a percentage of their gross income from production. Although the percentage depletion deduction may be limited in any one year, there is no lifetime limit related to the cost of the depletable asset. Statutory depletion, although now severely limited for oil and gas producers, has been allowed on the basis that the deduction is necessary to encourage producers of natural resources to search for and produce adequate quantities of minerals and metals.

Another particularly interesting tax deduction allowed to self-employed individuals is the deduction for contributions to certain retirement plans. (These are discussed in some detail in Chapter 15.) Basically, the law stipulates that if the owner-employee provides coverage for all full-time employees with more than three years' service, and if the pension plan meets certain other requirements, then the contributions are, within limits, deductible even though the major beneficiary at a later date will be the person making the contributions and getting the deduction. In financial accounting, of course, it would be considered proper to deduct contributions to the plan made on behalf of the employees but not those made for the benefit of the self-employed taxpayer. This provision of the law was adopted after many years of urging by self-employed business people, especially professionals such as certified public accountants, dentists, lawyers, and physicians, who until very recently were prohibited (by their rules of ethics and/or state laws) from incorporating their practices. The deduction is intended to provide greater equity between this group of self-employed taxpayers and the officer-employees of closely held corporations who may be covered under employer-financed retirement plans. The privilege to deduct contributions to retirement plans has been further extended to include taxpayers who are employed by businesses that have no pension plan and to permit limited deductions by a self-employed person to a plan that does not cover his or her employees.

Another group of deductions allowed for tax purposes but unacceptable for financial accounting has been mentioned previously—the "special corporate deductions" contained in Secs. 243 through 247. Most of these were designed to avoid the double taxation of income. The list includes:

Sec. 243. Dividends received by corporations.
Sec. 244. Dividends received on certain preferred stock.
Sec. 245. Dividends received from certain foreign corporations.
Sec. 246. Rules applying to deductions for dividends received.
Sec. 247. Dividends paid on certain preferred stock of public utilities.

Finally, there are numerous other "special-special" deductions that apply only to specific industries or special situations.

Should tax rules conform to generally accepted accounting principles?

It is often suggested that rigid tax requirements be changed so that income will be computed in accordance with generally accepted accounting principles. Section 446(a) of the Revenue Code is frequently cited as proof that this was the intent of Congress:

(a) General Rule.—Taxable income shall be computed under the method of accounting on the basis of which the taxpayer regularly computes his income in keeping his books.

The primary argument for conformity (certainly from the viewpoint of accountants) is that generally accepted accounting principles lead to a realistic, accurate, and meaningful yearly net income. There are also strong practical arguments:

From a practical standpoint, however, there are compelling reasons for substantial conformity to accounting principles in the determination of taxable income. Only through such conformity is it possible to achieve reasonable ease of computation and to avoid intolerable record-keeping cost to the taxpayer. It is suggested, therefore, that the initial tentative basis of taxable income should be business income as determined according to generally accepted principles of accounting.[13]

[13]Willard J. Graham, "An Analysis of Accounting Provisions," *1959 Compendium*, p. 1175.

On the opposite side is the opinion that such tax tenets as wherewithal to pay, objectivity, equity, ease of administration, and social and economic objectives are far more important than matching revenues earned with the costs of earning them. Horace Givens, an accounting professor, put the argument this way:

> It becomes questionable when one compares the purposes of the tax laws with those of the body of accounting principles whether there is any real justification for attempting to equate the final figures obtained from following the two different procedures. . . . The problem is that constant characterization of the income tax as a tax on income has led many to believe that there should be a relationship between taxable income and book income.[14]

In addition, it is frequently pointed out that accounting principles are in such a state of flux, and accounting rules are so flexible (with many alternative accounting methods available), that they do not offer a consistent and equitable basis for determining tax liability.[15]

The alternate suggestion sometimes advanced— that whatever accounting methods are followed for tax purposes should also be required for all other purposes—would surely be rejected by most accountants:

> Probably the most important reason for avoiding such a rule is the fact that a requirement that financial statements and accounting for all purposes be made to conform to the accounting followed for tax purposes would be tantamount to the assumption by the Congress of the responsibility for legislating accounting rules to be followed by all taxpaying business enterprises. This follows because all accounting decisions necessarily would then have to be made with a careful eye to the tax consequences.[16]

It is also likely that most accountants would reject the idea of *requiring* the taxpayer to follow generally accepted accounting principles in preparing a tax return. In recent years, however, the I.R.S. has followed the practice of giving its consent to a change

in accounting methods for tax purposes in most cases only if the taxpayer agrees to use a consistent financial accounting method. This means that all financial reports would have to agree with tax returns where such changes have been made.

Brief mention should be made of one ill-fated effort to bring tax reporting requirements into line with accounting practice. The 1954 Revenue Code originally contained two sections designed to correct the much-criticized rule that prepaid income is taxable when received, regardless of when earned, and the rule that generally prohibits the deduction of estimated future expenses under guarantees, service contracts, and so on. Section 452 of the 1954 Code provided, basically, that prepaid income would be spread over the periods to which it actually applied. Similarly, Sec. 462 permitted the deduction in the year of sale of estimated future costs relating to goods and services sold. These provisions were hailed by the accounting profession as significant steps forward. But when tax returns for 1954 began to flow into the Revenue Service, it became obvious that the reduction in revenue resulting from these provisions had been grossly underestimated when the provisions were recommended. As a consequence the two sections were repealed in 1955, retroactive to 1954. It is often suggested that the major shortcoming of these 1954 Code Sections was their failure to provide transitional rules to permit the effects of the change to be spread over several years. Instead, all the loss in revenue resulting from the change occurred in one tax year. Incidentally, a few limited provisions have been added to the Code since 1954, indicating some shift toward greater conformity.

DEDUCTIONS: PERSONAL DEDUCTIONS FOR INDIVIDUALS

Earlier in this chapter it was noted that deductions allowable under the federal income tax laws may be classified into three groups:

1. Expenses and losses incurred in a trade or business.
2. Expenses and losses related to nonbusiness production of income.
3. Personal deductions for individuals.

The general characteristics of the first two groups

---

[14] Horace R. Givens, "Redefining 'Taxable' Income," *Management Accounting* (March, 1966), p. 40.

[15] See Sheldon S. Cohen, "Accounting for Taxes, Finance and Regulatory Purposes—Are Variances Necessary?" speech before the 19th Annual Tax Conference, The University of Chicago Law School, October, 1966. Reprinted in *Taxes,* 44, No. 12 (December, 1966), pp. 786–88.

[16] Leslie Mills, *op. cit.,* p. 1170.

have been explained in the preceding discussion. In the remainder of this chapter we shall briefly review the general types of purely personal deductions allowed to individual taxpayers. You are urged to resist the temptation to become enmeshed in details at this point. The detailed provisions will be examined in much greater depth in subsequent chapters.

1. Large, unusual, involuntary personal expenditures.

2. Deductions that amount to subsidies to specific groups.

3. Taxes paid to local and state governments.

4. Personal and dependent exemption deductions.

Large, unusual, involuntary expenses

The tax laws recognize that unusually large expenditures or losses beyond the control of the taxpayer effectively reduce available income and thus wherewithal to pay a tax. Equity seems to suggest that consideration should be given to these expenditures in computing the tax liability by permitting deduction of that portion of the expense or loss deemed to be unusual or excessive. Perhaps the two most meaningful applications of this concept are the deductions for medical expenses and casualty losses.

Unreimbursed medical costs paid by the taxpayer for himself or his dependents generally are deductible only to the extent that they exceed 3 percent of "adjusted gross income." (Adjusted gross income, commonly called A.G.I., is a technical concept, which will be examined in Chapter 9.) Special rules apply to medical insurance premiums and to drugs. Medical costs include such items as physicians' charges, dental care costs, hospital charges, the cost of nursing care, a part of hospitalization insurance premiums, costs for travel necessary to obtain medical care, and the costs of drugs and medicines in excess of 1 percent of A.G.I. The 3 percent rule related to overall medical costs, and the special 1 percent rule related to medicines and drugs, give effect to the concept that a limited amount of such items constitutes normal living costs of a personal nature and that only the abnormal or unusual costs in excess of this norm should be deductible.

A similar provision applies to losses of the taxpayer's property from fire, storm, or other casualty, or from theft. Unreimbursed loss in excess of $100 from each such involuntary conversion may be

deducted. In effect, this rule requires the taxpayer to bear a portion ($100) of such personal losses without tax benefit, but recognizes that losses above this norm work an undue hardship.

Two problems encountered in allowing the deduction of such expenses and losses immediately become apparent. First, which of the many possible losses shall be made deductible? Second, what amount shall be considered "normal"? These questions are examined in Chapter 13.

Deductions that amount to subsidies

A number of deductions of a personal nature have been introduced into the Code to achieve desired economic, social, and other objectives. In effect, these deductions provide subsidies for specific groups. Two of the more important of these deductions are for charitable contributions and for interest paid.

Section 170 provides that contributions, up to 50 percent of the taxpayer's A.G.I., made to qualified organizations—primarily organizations formed for religious, charitable, scientific, or educational purposes; veterans' organizations; and governmental units—may be deducted. Obviously, this provision is intended to encourage giving to worthwhile groups, but it is also in effect a subsidy to the donee organization because a part of the gift represents an amount that would otherwise have been paid as income tax. Additionally, limited deductions can be taken for contributions to political campaigns.

Similarly, the taxpayer is allowed to deduct almost all interest paid. (The major exceptions are interest on money borrowed to purchase tax-free securities and the limit on "investment interest" mentioned earlier.) Presumably the deduction is allowed because of the difficulty in distinguishing between interest on funds borrowed to be used for income-producing activities (and thus a necessary deduction) and that related to funds used for purely personal reasons. This deduction, especially the allowance of interest on home mortgages, has been severely criticized as inequitable because it permits the homeowner to deduct a large portion of his or her monthly mortgage payments as interest but allows no deduction to the tenant, whose monthly rental payments include an interest factor. Thus, in effect, it grants the homeowner a subsidy. The more general argument is that in many cases interest is a voluntary personal expense incurred solely because the taxpayer is willing to pay interest in order to obtain present goods or services—which leaves little reason to treat it as a deductible item.

Taxes paid to local and state governments

Some state and local taxes (primarily property, sales, and income taxes) are allowable as itemized deductions, largely on the basis that they help the smooth functioning of the federal system of government by making nonfederal taxation less costly to the taxpayer. In addition, there is support for allowing the deduction of state and local income taxes because of the possibility of *combined* marginal tax rates (state rates (state and federal) in excess of 100 percent.

Personal exemptions

In addition to the "itemized" personal deductions just discussed, individual taxpayers are permitted a deduction of $1,000 for each personal and dependent *exemption*. The number of exemptions to which an individual is entitled depends on the taxpayer's age, family situation, and other factors. The deduction for exemptions is discussed in detail in Chapter 9.

ZERO BRACKET AMOUNT OF TAXABLE INCOME

Before 1977, individual taxpayers were permitted a *standard deduction,* which could be taken *in lieu of* the allowable itemized personal deductions and most of the deductions permitted under Sec. 212 related to "nonbusiness" income. Although the standard deduction was eliminated after 1976, the same result is achieved by specifying that a certain amount of taxable income, the amount being determined by the taxpayer's filing status, is subject to a tax rate of zero. Since every taxpayer is entitled to an appropriate amount of "zero bracket" taxable income, itemized deductions and most Sec. 212 deductions are deductible only to the extent that their total exceeds the zero bracket taxable income. However, deductions for personal exemptions are always allowed in full.

For example, for 1979, a single taxpayer with itemized personal deductions of $3,600 would actually deduct only $1,300 ($3,600 minus $2,300, the amount of taxable income subject to a rate of zero for a single person) in arriving at his or her "taxable income." The astute observer will quickly note that since the tax rate is zero on the first $2,300 of taxable income, the taxpayer is in effect deducting this amount in addition to the $1,300 technically deducted.

On the other hand, if the single taxpayer's itemized deductions were only $1,600, he or she could deduct no part of these costs in arriving at taxable income because they are less than $2,300. Because the first $2,300 of taxable income is subject to a tax rate of zero, however, the taxpayer is in effect getting the benefit of a $2,300 deduction.

The student who pursues a study of taxation will discover that much of the controversy in this field revolves around (1) identifying or selecting the costs that should be deductible in computing taxable income and (2) determining just when these costs should be deductible. In the remaining chapters, we shall examine several of these problems in detail.

PROBLEMS

1. Section 262 of the Internal Revenue Code of 1954 specifically disallows the deduction of "personal, living, and family" expenses. Yet many persons may deduct a purely personal contribution to a local charity. Explain the apparent contradiction.
2. It is conceivable that the cost of a taxpayer's subscription to the *Wall Street Journal* would be tax deductible, whereas the cost of a subscription to the *New York Times* would be disallowed. Explain the fact circumstances that would lead to such a situation. Explain other fact circumstances that might justify the deduction of the cost of a subscription to the *New York Times*.
3. List and explain the general criteria (positive and negative) that may be applied to determine whether many expenditures are deductible or nondeductible.
4. What advantages would accrue to taxpayers if the government would accept as

a proper tax deduction any item that could be treated as an expense for financial accounting purposes? What disadvantages to taxpayers would result from such a law?

5. One of the social costs associated with multiple deductions is the complexity of the tax laws. What social advantages accrue to offset this social cost?

6. A number of expenses—for example, estimated guarantee and warranty costs—are estimated and deducted by many businesses in measuring financial income. These items generally may not be deducted on a tax return until they are actually incurred. Accountants often criticize the tax restriction on the grounds that it results in a "mismatching" of revenues and expenses. What reasons might be given to support this tax requirement?

7. Some of the most significant (in terms of dollars deducted) "personal deductions" of individual taxpayers are criticized as inequitable subsidies to specific groups. Perhaps the most notorious of these are the deductions for state and local real estate taxes and the deductions for interest paid. Explain why each of these two deductions might be considered inequitable. Why might they be considered desirable?

8. What is meant by the terms "reasonable," "ordinary," and "necessary"?

9. In what fundamental way do the deductions allowed individual taxpayers differ generally from the deductions allowed corporate taxpayers? What forces explain this difference?

10. a. Name three items that might appear as an expense on a corporation's financial statement but would not be allowed as a deduction on the same corporation's tax return.

 b. Name three items that might be allowed as a deduction on a corporation's tax return but would not be allowed as an expense on the same corporation's financial statement.

11. Distinguish between a tax-deductible "nonbusiness expense" and a nondeductible "personal expense."

12. a. What tax treatment is given expenses of a "hobby"?

 b. How does one distinguish between a hobby and a business venture?

13. Do the "claim of right" and "constructive receipt" doctrines have their counterparts in the rules governing expense deductions? Explain.

14. Distinguish between a "trade or business expense" and a "nonbusiness expense related to income production."

15. There is a limit on the amount of interest deductible on money borrowed to purchase investment property. What is the likely reason for this restriction?

16. What is the likely reason for the existence of the zero bracket income provision?

17. A taxpayer who owns a textile manufacturing plant in New York is visited by an important customer. The taxpayer "wines and dines" this customer and his wife during their stay in New York. Total cost of this entertainment is $350. Is this a reasonable, ordinary, and necessary business expense?

18. Which of the following expenditures do you think would be deductible?

 a. Cost of entertaining customers by an outside salesperson at a private club.

 b. Fines paid by a trucker for inadvertently exceeding the state's maximum weight laws.

 c. Current research and development expenses related to business.

 d. Cost of a personnel director's meals while entertaining prospective employees.

 e. Advertising intended to help defeat specified legislation proposed to the state legislature.

 f. Estimated costs of warranty on products sold during the year.

19. a. Indicate whether or not each of the following expenditures would be deductible by a *corporate* taxpayer.
   (1) Cost of prizes given away by a television manufacturer as part of a sales contest.
   (2) Cost of uniforms and equipment for company-sponsored baseball team.
   (3) Assessment for benefits paid to union employees during periods of illness.
   (4) Fee paid to speaker to address employees about the importance of voting in an upcoming election.
   (5) Fee paid to speaker in support of a particular candidate in an upcoming election.
   (6) Estimated charge for self-insurance program in lieu of commercial insurance coverage.

   b. Indicate whether or not each of the following expenditures would be deductible by an individual taxpayer.
   (1) Contribution to purchase gift for employee's supervisor.
   (2) Cost of keeping watch in good repair. (Taxpayer is a registered nurse.)
   (3) Penalty for late payment of federal income taxes.
   (4) Interest associated with late payment of federal income taxes.
   (5) Cost of subscription to *Journal of Accountancy*. (Taxpayer is employed by local C.P.A. firm.)
   (6) Wages paid caretaker of former residence that is presently listed "for sale or rent."

20. Indicate whether each of the following items is deductible. In those cases where only part is deductible, indicate the amount to be deducted.

   a. Taxpayer operates a truck on a contract basis. While hauling gravel under a contract, he was stopped for speeding. He paid a fine of $25 for speeding and a fine of $30 for carrying an overweight load.

   b. Assume the same facts as in part a, except that the taxpayer is an employee instead of an independent contractor. He was not reimbursed by his employer for either fine.

   c. Agnew operates a contracting business. During the year he gave a member of the city council a new watch, which cost $200. Agnew hopes that the city councilman will "throw some city business my way."

   d. Stinchcomb, who is an attorney, also operates a farm. During each of the past five years he has had expenses on the farm of $9,000 and income of only $4,000. During the current year he has income of $4,800 and expenses of $9,200.

   e. Toledo owns 60 percent of Ace Corporation's outstanding stock. During the current year, Ace Corporation paid Toledo a salary of $82,000. Executives in similar situations earn about $40,000 per year.

   f. Black borrowed $50,000 from the First State Bank and used the money to buy City of Blanksville bonds. He paid interest of $4,200 on the borrowed funds. Interest received on the bonds was $3,500.

   g. White purchased a piece of land for $45,000 in order to get a location for his new office building. However, he has to tear down an old building on the property, paying $3,200 to a demolition company for clearing the building.

   h. A gambler won $45,000 during the year. In order to earn this income, however, he incurred expenses for travel and other items totaling $10,200.

   i. The taxpayer operates a department store. He uses the "Reserve for Doubtful Accounts" method of accounting for bad debts. During the current year, he made additions to the reserve, based on estimated bad debts, of $3,455. Actual worthless accounts charged against the reserve were $3,100.

j. Curry works as a staff accountant for a public accounting firm. The firm requires him to dress "appropriately," which means wear a dark suit, white shirt, and conservative tie. Curry estimates that conforming to the firm's dress requirements cost him $285 more during the current year than he would have paid if allowed to dress "casually."

k. Benson is married and has three children. Normal living costs for the home, utilities, food, and clothing total $12,000 for the current year.

21. Corona is a self-employed manufacturer of electronics equipment. During the year, he had the following expenditures that he thinks may be somewhat questionable when preparing his tax return. Indicate whether each is deductible or nondeductible.

a. Trip to Washington, D.C., to testify before Congressional committee holding hearings on proposed legislation to restrict foreign imports of electronics equipment. Corona is very interested in curtailing imports and asked to be heard. Transportation, $280; lodging, $72; meals, $43.

b. Cost of telephone calls, letters, and telegrams to Congressmen from his state urging them to vote for import restrictions bill recommended by the Congressional committee, $118.

c. Contribution to electronics manufacturing association to help pay for cost of television campaign to urge public support for anti-import bill, $1,200.

d. Gift to Congressman Doe (a new color television set costing $600). Corona expects Doe to support the anti-import bill.

e. Kickbacks to purchasing agents of companies who buy substantial amounts of Corona's products, $4,000.

f. Kickbacks to purchasing agents of four cities buying Corona's products, $2,000.

g. Cost of television ads purchased for an opponent of Congressman Doe, who after all did not support the anti-import bill, $1,000.

22. a. The president of Unlimited Aviation Corporation traveled to a foreign country to talk to a group of military officers in that country about purchasing military aircraft manufactured by Unlimited. The officers hinted that a "gift" to them might increase the likelihood that Unlimited would receive the contract sought. The president thus authorized payment, and the company paid $500,000 to each of the six officers (a total of $3,000,000). Are these payments deductible by Unlimited?

b. During a severe cold wave in 19x1, Randolph Company paid $50,000 to officers of a natural gas pipeline company to "insure" that gas supplies to the company were not curtailed. Although supplies to Randolph's competitors were greatly reduced, Randolph had no curtailment. Can Randolph deduct the $50,000 payment?

23. Samantha Wilson, an appliance dealer, included the following expenses in computing her income for financial accounting purposes in 19x1:

a. "Estimated Loss from Bad Debts," $1,200. This amount was based on assumed losses of one-fourth of 1 percent of net sales.

b. "Estimated Expenses Arising from Guaranties and Warranties," $4,000. This amount was based on experience showing that normally future service costs amount to about 2 percent of the sales price of certain products sold under guaranty and warranty. During 19x1 these sales totaled $200,000.

c. "Estimated Repair Expense," $800. In order to prevent large fluctuations in income resulting from the fact that major repairs to buildings and equipment tend to occur at irregular intervals, Wilson estimates the average annual repair expense and deducts this amount each year.

d. "Amortization of Advertising Costs," $3,000. (In 19x0 the company spent $15,000 for a large newspaper advertising campaign. Because the amount was large and expected to benefit several years, Wilson decided to defer the cost and charge it off over a 5-year period.)

Indicate whether each of the above items would also be allowed as a deduction on the tax return. If the item is not deductible for tax purposes, indicate how the amount is to be handled on the tax return. (Disregard the question of whether the procedures followed were "generally accepted" for financial accounting purposes.)

24. Wilson, a college teacher, also writes textbooks and conducts a limited public accounting practice. He has no separate office, but a portion of his bedroom is equipped with a desk, filing cabinets, calculator, typewriter, and other equipment used in his income-producing activities. Because his office at the college is noisy, he finds it almost impossible to grade papers or prepare for classes. Thus, almost all of his college-related work, in addition to his writing and accounting practice activities, are performed in the "bedroom-office." Comment on the deductibility of such expenses as depreciation of the home and equipment, heating, cooling, lighting, taxes on the home, interest on the home, insurance on the home, and other such costs.

SUPPLEMENTAL PROBLEMS

25. Toledo is sales manager of Ace Products Company. During this year he went to the national convention of sales managers held in Hawaii. He took his wife since the convention offered a good reason for taking his vacation at the same time. Although the convention ended on July 13, Toledo and his wife stayed in Honolulu for an additional four days. The following costs, none of which were reimbursed by Toledo's employer, were incurred on the trip.

a. Taxi fare from Toledo's home to airport for him and wife, $7.50.

b. Airline tickets for Toledo and wife, $600. Normal fare for one person is $400; because of special family travel plan, Toledo's wife's ticket was only $200.

c. Limousine fare from airport to hotel for Toledo and wife, $5.00 each.

d. Hotel room (double rate) for 7 days, $420. The room rates are $51 per day for a single room and $60 for two people.

e. Registration for Toledo at conference, $60. No registration fee for Mrs. Toledo.

f. Cost of official meals (at meetings) for Toledo, $50. Mrs. Toledo did not attend these.

g. Cost of registration for women's activities for Mrs. Toledo, $50.

h. Cost of seven breakfasts for Toledos, $70. This was for both persons at rate of $5.00 per meal.

i. Cost of meals taken together, other than breakfast, for Mr. and Mrs. Toledo, during convention at $15 per meal, $30.

j. Cost of meals during 4 days of vacation, $212.

Which, if any, of these costs are deductible by Toledo?

26. John Apple, an auto mechanic, lost his job in April 19x1, when his employer decided to close shop. After futilely seeking employment, Apple arranged for

potential financing to open his own shop. He concluded that his best opportunity would be in another city, so Apple spent 4 days in a town located 200 miles from his home, investigating possible locations, studying competition, and engaging in other activities to determine the likelihood of success of a new shop. Apple spent $208 on this trip, but decided against opening the new business.

    a. What are the tax effects of the $208 spent?

    b. Would your answer be different if Apple had decided to open the new business? Explain.

27. In 19x1, Alvin invested $10,000 in a ''limited partnership'' formed to purchase several acres of land. Of the $10,000, $2,000 represented a management fee to the organizers of the venture; $4,000 represented ''prepaid interest,'' and $4,000 represented Alvin's ''permanent capital.'' The organizers assure Alvin that since he is on the cash basis of accounting, the $4,000 of prepaid interest would be deductible by him in 19x1, the year paid. Comment on this advice.

28. Refer to Problem 30 in Chapter 5. For each of the items presented, discuss the effects on expense deductions of Malcolm Industries and on deductions by Mr. Malcolm.

29. Herman Melville, a self-employed businessman, operates a ''manufacturer's representative'' business. He employs eight salespersons who travel throughout the western part of the United States. Manufacturers pay Melville a commission of 10 percent on all products sold. To assist his employees in making sales, Melville owns a lodge in the Colorado mountains to which his employees can invite customers or prospective customers for periods up to 4 days. In addition, each salesperson can use the lodge a maximum of 5 days per year for his or her personal use. Melville and his family also use the lodge for 2 weeks each summer to take a family vacation. During the current year, total operating costs of the lodge, including depreciation, were $18,000.

    Are the costs of operating the lodge deductible by Melville? Explain.

30. Susan borrowed $50,000 to purchase shares of a regulated investment company. During 19x1, she paid interest of $5,000 on the loan. She received total dividends of $6,000 on the shares, of which $4,200 was tax-exempt distributions and $1800 was taxable distributions. What amount, if any, of the $5,000 interest paid is deductible?

If for any taxable year an individual has personal service taxable income which exceeds the amount of taxable income specified in paragraph (1), the tax imposed by section 1 for such year shall, unless the taxpayer chooses the benefits of part I (relating to income averaging), be the sum of . . .

Sec. 1348(a)

tax rates: general concepts

As indicated in the general formula at the beginning of Chapter 5, a gross income tax liability is determined by multiplying the applicable tax rate(s) times the difference between a taxpayer's gross income and deductions for the year. In Chapters 5 and 6, we examined the general concepts of gross income and deductions. In this chapter, we shall examine the general concept of the U.S. income tax rates.

At the outset, observe that income tax rates are applied to the *annual* income of *each* taxable entity. The concept of income has meaning only for a period of time, and the annual period has a long tradition. Thus, income tax rates are applicable each year to each taxpayer without regard to the taxpayer's previous history. In addition, the gross tax liability of each entity is determined independently, and the applicable tax rate for any one taxpayer ordinarily will be determined without regard to the tax burden of any other taxpayer. Although the two facts just stated may appear intuitively obvious, their importance to tax planning is easily overlooked. As will be explained later, major tax savings can often be achieved by the entirely legal shifting of income or deductions or both between (1) two or more tax years and (2) two or more taxable entities.

In the United States, three fundamental taxable entities are recognized: *every* individual, *every* corporation, and *every* fiduciary (that is, every estate or trust). As will be explained in Part Three, many special rules apply to the determination of the net tax liability of each of these three different taxable entities. For the moment, however, we shall ignore those differences to the maximum extent possible and focus on the more fundamental concepts related to tax rates.

FUNDAMENTAL CONCEPTS

The U.S. Internal Revenue Code implicitly accepts three fundamental concepts regarding income tax rates. First, all income tax rate schedules for all types of entities are progressive. Second, the United States purports to apply a single, or unitary, tax rate schedule to the entire income realized by each taxpayer. Third, the tax rate schedule applicable to each different taxable entity—that is, to individuals, corporations, and fiduciaries—is unique. As we shall soon discover, however, these fundamental concepts are, in reality, quite often more illusory than real.

Progressivity

The tax rates for individual taxpayers are stipulated in Sec. 1(a) through (d); those for corporate taxpayers, in Sec. 11; and those for fiduciaries, in Sec. 1(e). For reasons explained in Chapter 9, the Code actually provides not one but four different sets of tax rates for individual taxpayers. Ignoring those sometimes important differences for the moment, we may observe the general progressivity of the tax rate structure imposed on taxable income by the federal government by an examination of Table 7-1.

Conceptually, when you think of the federal income tax rates, you should think of a rate schedule that looks something like the hypothetical one depicted in Figure 7-1, which has seven tax brackets ranging from 15 to 45 percent. The gross tax payable is represented by the area under the curve for any given amount of taxable income. For example, a taxable income of Ox dollars would be subject to a gross tax liability equal to the shaded area in Figure 7-1.

TABLE **7-1**

GENERAL PROGRESSIVITY OF U.S. TAX RATES

Taxpayer	No. of Tax Brackets	Range of Marginal Rates	
		Minimum	Maximum
Individuals	15[a]	14[b]%	70%
Corporations	5	17	46
Fiduciaries	15	14	70

[a] The schedule for unmarried individuals, stipulated in Sec. 1(c), has 16 tax brackets.
[b] Ignoring the zero bracket amount, which is explained on page **9**/5.

To simplify the arithmetic, tax rate schedules are usually stated in the Code in columnar form. For example, if the distances *Oa, ab, bc,* and so on, in Figure 7-1 were each equal to $2,000, the related but imaginary Code section might read as follows:

There is hereby imposed on the taxable income of every taxpayer a tax determined in accordance with the following table:

If taxable income is		*The tax is*	*plus*	*Marginal rate*	*times*	*Amount in excess of*
Over	*But not over*					
$ 0	$ 2,000	$ 0		15%		$ 0
2,000	4,000	300		20		2,000
4,000	6,000	700		25		4,000
6,000	8,000	1,200		30		6,000
8,000	10,000	1,800		35		8,000
10,000	12,000	2,500		40		10,000
12,000		3,300		45		12,000

This form of rate schedule facilitates the actual computation of the tax because it accumulates the tax in each preceding bracket and eliminates the need for repeated application of the rates in each bracket. For example, based on this hypothetical schedule, a taxpayer with an income of $10,200 would pay a tax of $2,580 [$2,500 + 0.40 ($10,200 − $10,000)].

To abstract from reality only slightly more, it is sometimes useful to think of our income tax rates as a smooth or continuous curve, rather than as a series of tax brackets. Thus, for conceptual purposes only, let us think of our income tax rates as something approximating that depicted in Figure 7-2. In other words, we can usually think of our rate schedules as indiscrete curves, such as the imaginary one depicted, even though the schedules are in fact a series of discrete progressions, such as depicted in Figure 7-1.

Unitary system

That the United States purports to have a unitary income tax system is implicit in the fact that we have only one income tax base—that is, taxable income. Many other countries have a schedular income tax system. A schedular system is like a unitary system in that tax rates are applied to an annual tax base for each entity each year. A schedular system differs, however, in that each taxpayer may have different types of income subject to different rates each year. In other words, each taxpayer will separate total income each year into predesignated types or kinds of income and apply the stipulated tax rate(s) to each type of income, beginning with the lowest marginal tax rate for that type (year-by-year and entity-by-entity). In some of these countries, the stipulated tax rates are proportional, rather than progressive, at least for certain types of income. In Mexico and Cen-

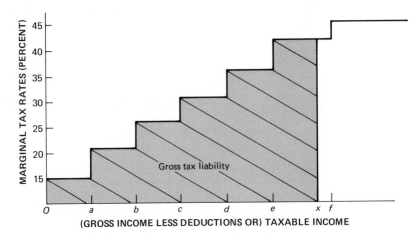

FIGURE **7-1**   A Hypothetical Progressive Tax Schedule

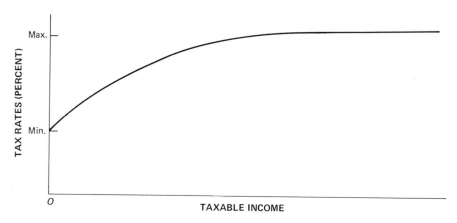

FIGURE **7-2**   A Conceptual Progressive Tax Schedule

tral and South America, the number of schedules varies from two to nine, depending on the country under consideration. A hypothetical South American schedular tax system might look something like that shown in Table 7-2.

Although a schedular income tax system at first appears to be fundamentally different from a unitary system, that disparity is often only a matter of degree. Neither system is really found in pure form. The schedular system overtly recognizes a social distinction in kinds of income, and it frequently provides different tax rates for the different kinds of income. The unitary system—either by law or by administrative caprice—usually makes similar distinctions, although they are more difficult to identify.

TABLE **7-2**
A HYPOTHETICAL SCHEDULAR TAX SCHEDULE

Schedule	Income	Marginal tax rates	
		Minimum	Maximum
A	Interest from government securities	3%	6%
B	Compensation as an employee	1	10
C	Income from agriculture	0	
D	Income from rents	5	20
E	Oil and mining profits	6	30
F	Lottery prizes and other chance winnings	0	10
G	Income from sources not reported under any other schedule	1	8

In the United States, we purport to have a unitary tax system. Nevertheless, as we have already learned in Chapter 5, by law, no federal income tax is imposed on the interest paid to creditors of state and local governments and, by administrative fiat, no federal income tax is levied on social security receipts. Considering only these two exclusions, therefore, already we could accurately argue that the United States really has at least three tax rate schedules, two of them imposing a zero tax rate. In the remainder of this chapter, we shall explain several other current federal tax provisions that have similar results and that often make our law quite difficult to comprehend.

Entity differences

Although the Code does not overtly recognize different tax rates for different kinds of income, it clearly stipulates different tax rates for the different taxable entities. As noted in Table 7-1, the marginal tax rates for individuals and fiduciaries begin at 14 percent and increase to 70 percent. The tax rates for corporations, on the other hand, begin slightly higher (at 17 percent) but increase to only 46 percent.

Because of the unique and explicit differences between the federal income tax rates applied to the taxable incomes realized by individuals and those realized by corporations, the corporate entity has become a common form of tax shelter in the United States. Figure 7-3 illustrates the potential tax savings currently available to any married couple who can arrange to have their personal taxable income *realized and retained* within a single corporate entity. In general, of course, this result is easily achieved by the mere act of incorporating any business that

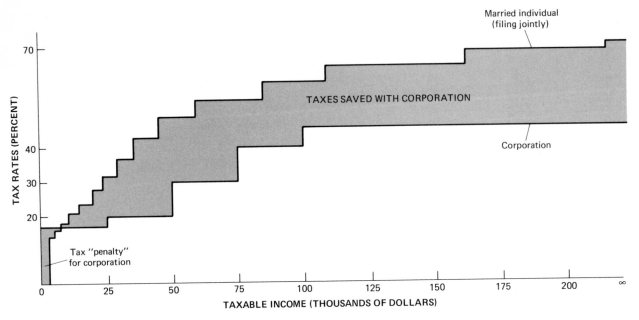

FIGURE **7-3** Current Corporate vs. Married Individuals' Tax Rates

would otherwise operate as a sole proprietorship or a partnership.

The less obvious income tax cost associated with a corporate entity stems from the additional individual income tax that is likely to occur when the corporate owner later extracts for personal use some of the income previously retained within the corporation. Unfortunately, the complex tax provisions that govern the many transactions between a corporation and its shareholders must await further explication in subsequent chapters of this (and other) books. Suffice it to observe here that the obvious differences in the marginal tax rates applied to individual and corporate taxpayers serve as a primary force in many tax-planning situations. To the extent that individuals can and do incorporate and retain within a corporation their otherwise personal incomes, the apparent tax rates applicable to individuals are, of course, effectively avoided.

Fiduciaries are also used to offset the individual tax rates, but not because the income tax rates applicable to fiduciaries are significantly different from those applicable to individuals. Indeed, the rates applicable to the taxable incomes of the two entities are approximately equal—beginning at 14 percent and rising to 70 percent. An individual who transfers income-producing property to a trust can effectively divide his or her income into two parts and then apply the lower rates on the schedules to each part each year, thereby reducing the total tax paid.

Unfortunately for the student, this is but the tip of the tax-rate iceberg. The Code explicitly recognizes several exceptions to the general federal income tax rate schedules imposed in Secs. 1 and 11. In the next several pages, we shall examine the general concepts of those major aberrations.

MAJOR ABERRATIONS FROM FUNDAMENTAL CONCEPTS

The details of the several difficult Code provisions to be briefly examined here must necessarily await a more complete treatment in later parts of this book. In the overview presented in Part Two, you need only understand the general concepts of such income tax phenomena as the maximum tax, capital gains, income averaging, and the minimum tax. As you consider each of these aberrations, keep in mind that fundamentally, we have a unitary system in which progressive rates are applied annually to each entity's taxable income. Our purpose here is to gain a general understanding of the major exceptions to the fundamentals, leaving further details until later.

Maximum tax

Although the maximum marginal rate in the rate schedules for individuals is 70 percent, Sec. 1348 limits the maximum marginal rate to 50 percent for *per-*

sonal service taxable income realized by an individual. Personal service taxable income is generally income earned in exchange for the performance of services, less the deductions applicable to that income. This special provision means that every *individual* taxpayer's taxable income may have to be divided into two distinct parts: one part that is *personal service income* (which we call Type I income) and another residual part (which we call Type II income). If the taxpayer has such a large amount of personal service taxable income (Type I income) that some portion of it ordinarily would be subject to a marginal tax rate of *more than* 50 percent, then the taxpayer will not compute his or her tax in the normal manner. Instead, he or she will tax that portion of his or her personal service taxable income in a normal way only up to the point at which a marginal rate in excess of 50 percent would ordinarily apply; from that point forward, any remaining amount of personal service taxable income would be subject to a flat or proportional tax rate of 50 percent.

The concept of the maximum tax is illustrated in Figure 7-4. In that figure, distance Ob represents total personal service taxable income. Distance Oa represents that portion of personal service taxable income that, if the normal rate schedule is applied, would be subject to a marginal tax rate of 50 percent or less; distance ab represents the remainder of the personal service taxable income, which is subject to the special 50 percent maximum marginal rate. Accordingly, the area I(a) plus I(b) represents the total tax on this imaginary taxpayer's personal service taxable income. The shaded area above area I(b) represents the income tax saved by operation of this special provision. The area labeled II represents the normal income tax on that portion of the taxpayer's taxable income that is *not* personal service taxable income—that is, on taxable income equal to distance bx. The appropriate tax on the taxable income represented by distance bx is determined residually. In other words, the taxpayer first determines (1) the normal tax on a taxable income equal to distance Ox. Then, he or she determines (2) the normal tax on a taxable income equal to distance Ob. Finally, by subtracting (2) from (1), above, the taxpayer automatically has determined the gross tax liability on a taxable income equal to distance $bx,$ beginning with the normal marginal tax rate determined by distance Ob.

Although the procedure may sound unduly complex, the actual application of Sec. 1348 is reasonably straightforward. Additional details and illustrations appear in Chapter 28. Observe, however, that this provision is of major interest to business executives, professional persons, entertainers, athletes, and others who typically have large amounts of income from the rendering of personal services.

Capital gains

A second major aberration from the apparently unitary federal income tax rate structure is the tax treatment of net capital gains. A net capital gain is generally the gain from the sale or exchange of capital assets held by the taxpayer for more than one year. Part Six is devoted to a complete explanation of the rules concerning capital gains and associated problems.

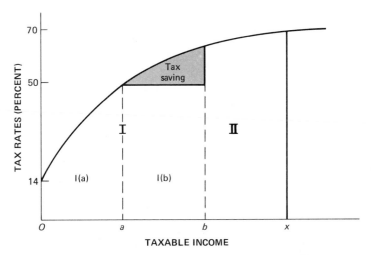

FIGURE **7-4**   Graphic Illustration of the Maximum Tax

The Code provides a special treatment for the net capital gain of both corporate and noncorporate taxpayers, but the rules differ for each entity. We shall consider the corporate rules first.

CORPORATE NET CAPITAL GAINS   Sec. 1201 imposes an alternative marginal tax rate of 28 percent on the net capital gains realized by a corporate taxpayer if that rate provides a lesser tax than the normal corporate rates would impose. Conceptually, therefore, this 28 percent alternative tax rate may be viewed in a manner somewhat comparable to the maximum tax for individual taxpayers. In this instance, a corporation's taxable income must also be divided into two parts: one portion (Type I income) is income other than net capital gain; the other portion (Type II) is the net capital gain. Observe that in this instance the portion of the corporation's taxable income receiving the special treatment is the second tier of income, not the first tier (as it was in the case of the maximum tax). The concept of the alternative tax for corporate capital gain is depicted in Figure 7-5.

In that figure, the distance Oa represents the non-capital gain income, and the distance ax the net capital gain. (The distance Ox is, of course, the corporation's total taxable income for the year.) The area labeled I represents the normal corporate income tax on the non-capital gain income; the area labeled II represents the alternative tax on the net capital gain. The shaded area above II represents the tax saving as a result of the 28 percent alternative tax rate. Observe that the special provision is of benefit only if some portion of the corporate taxable income is subject to marginal rates in excess of 28 percent.

NONCORPORATE NET CAPITAL GAINS   Sec. 1202 authorizes all noncorporate taxpayers (that is, individuals and fiduciaries) to claim a special deduction equal to 60 percent of the net capital gain realized in a year. Observe that in this instance the Code says absolutely nothing about modifying the normal tax rate structure. To conclude that the net capital gains of individuals are subject to all normal tax rates would, however, be a gross error. A special deduction equal to 60 percent of the income realized is the equivalent of a 60 percent reduction in the normal tax rates. If in one year an individual or a fiduciary reported a taxable income that consisted solely of net capital gain, the *real*, or *effective*, tax rate for that taxpayer would range not from the normal 14 to 70 percent, but from 5.6 (40 percent of 14 percent) to 28 percent (40 percent of 70 percent).

In the normal year, an individual taxpayer in the upper income groups will have some amount of personal service income, some net capital gain, and some "other" income. The latter (residual) category of income would include such passive income items as taxable dividends, interest, rents, and royalties. To illustrate this concept, let us return to Figure 7-4, but this time we shall also divide the Type II income into two separate parts, II(a) and II(b).

Figure 7-6 depicts the treatment of net capital gains for noncorporate taxpayers. Note in this figure that the Type II income really comprises two elements, which may be commingled for purposes of the calculation but not for purposes of understanding the rates applicable to the two different sources of income. Continue to think of distance bx as the total non-personal service taxable income, but consider the tax represented by the area II(a) as the tax on the net capital gain after the 60 percent deduction. In other words, the distance bx really equals 40 percent of the net capital gain plus 100 percent of the other (passive) income. Hence, the area II(a) represents the tax on the net capital gain (at 40 percent of the normal tax rates), and area II(b) represents the nor-

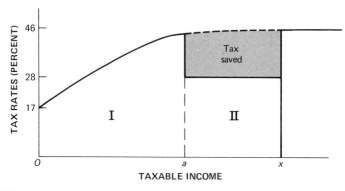

FIGURE **7-5**   Graphic Illustration of Corporate Alternative Tax on Capital Gains

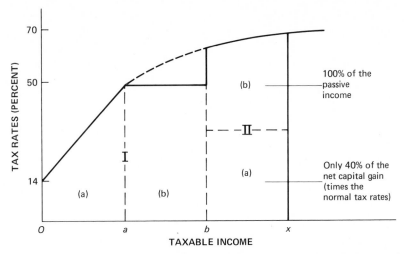

FIGURE **7-6**   Graphic Illustration of Noncorporate Long-Term Capital Gain Deduction

mal tax on the remaining (passive) income at the normal rates. Except for the obvious advantage associated with the 60 percent long-term capital gain deduction, the tax on distance *bx* is still computed exactly as explained earlier in this chapter.

The many other important and often complex details associated with capital gains taxation will be deferred to Part Six. Even without an examination of those details, however, it should be obvious that capital gains represent a major tax advantage to anyone fortunate enough to realize a substantial part of his or her income in that form. To quantify the overall importance of capital gains, review the message implicit in Figure 3-2 on page **3**/6. Briefly, for our wealthiest taxpayers, *the name of the tax game in the United States is capital gains.*

Income averaging

A third major aberration from our unitary tax rate structure is known as *income averaging.* Actually, two entirely different income averaging provisions exist, and both are available only to *individual* taxpayers. Furthermore, as indicated in the headnote to this chapter, income averaging may be elected only if the taxpayer foregoes the right to utilize the maximum tax provisions. Although the details of the two sets of income averaging rules differ greatly, in concept they are quite similar.

INCOME AVERAGING UNDER SEC. 402(e)   During their working years, many people participate in qualified pension and profit-sharing plans. In some instances, both the employer and the employee make frequent

contributions to the plan; in every instance, the amounts set aside are permitted to grow free of any income tax in the interim. In any event, when the time comes to withdraw the benefits, the individual typically is given a choice of how he or she wishes to receive the accumulated funds. Because the withdrawal of funds typically coincides with retirement, one option generally authorized is a lifetime annuity. In other instances, withdrawal may occur on the separation of an individual from a prior employment contract or at the time of death. In these cases, a lump-sum payment is quite often the appropriate settlement option.

Because quite large sums of money may have accumulated in a qualified pension or profit-sharing plan, and because the income tax is normally imposed with a progressive tax rate schedule, any lump-sum settlement would create an inordinately large income tax liability if there were no special treatment available for the previously untaxed benefits. Accordingly, the Code provides individual taxpayers with an option: They may elect to treat part of any lump-sum settlement as a capital gain and part as ordinary income. Alternatively, they may elect to treat the entire amount as ordinary income. Either way, however, the ordinary income portion is eligible for a special 10-year income averaging treatment.

Sec. 402(e) effectively breaks into ten equal parts any lump sum received from a qualified pension or profit-sharing plan. The taxpayer is then required to determine the income tax on one-tenth of the total as if that amount were the entire taxable income of a single individual for one year, ignoring the zero bracket amount. (The progressive tax rate applied to

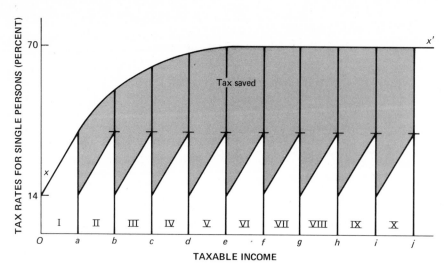

FIGURE **7-7**   Graphic Illustration of Income Averaging under Sec. 402(e)

this income begins at 14 percent on the first dollar of income.) Finally, the tax liability just determined is multiplied times 10, and the product is the optional income tax payable on the lump-sum settlement. Conceptually, this tax provision may be illustrated as in Figure 7-7. The distance *Oj* represents the total lump-sum settlement received. The distances *Oa, ab, bc,* and so on, are all equal to one-tenth of the total. Each area designated by a Roman numeral I through X represents, of course, the tax liability on one-tenth of the total settlement, using the tax rate schedule for a single person. The sum of these ten areas represents the aggregate tax liability, using the income averaging provision of Sec. 402(e). The total area under the curve *xx'* represents the hypothetical tax that would be paid on the entire distribution using

regular rates. Thus, the shaded area represents the tax saved by the averaging device.

In most cases, an individual receiving a lump-sum settlement will also have other taxable income in the year he or she receives the settlement. Accordingly, this income-averaged tax is really added to the person's other income tax determined in the normal way. Conceptually, this may be illustrated as in Figure 7-8. Obviously, this figure is nothing but a simplified combination of Figures 7-7 and 7-6. In a pure sense, Figure 7-8 is slightly misleading because taxpayers who are *not* single might use a different rate schedule for computing the tax on averaged income and the tax on other income. In spite of this theoretical flaw, the basic concept of the income-averaging rule provided in Sec. 402(e) is illustrated in Figure

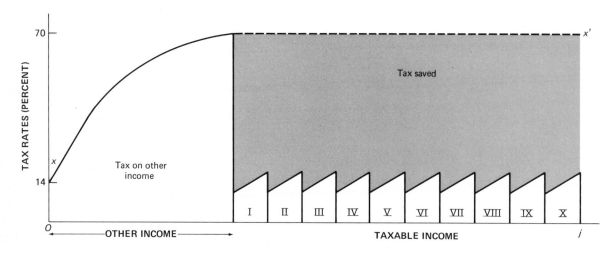

FIGURE **7-8**   Graphic Illustration of Total Tax Including Sec. 403(e) Income Averaging

7-8. Additional details of this provision are explained in Chapter 15.

INCOME AVERAGING UNDER SECS. 1301–1305   A second set of income-averaging rules may apply to any individual who simply has an unusually large taxable income in one tax year. This aberration from the rate schedules was placed in the Code in explicit recognition of the fact that unusually large incomes realized in a single year may well be subject to an unduly heavy income tax burden solely because of our progressive tax rate structure. In order to reduce the effect of the progressive rate schedule, an individual taxpayer may determine his or her tax using an optional calculation if certain other conditions are satisfied. The Code specifies these conditions and the necessary detailed calculations in Secs. 1301 through 1305.

Fundamentally, the rules are something like this:

1. Determine the taxpayer's *average* taxable income for the four prior years; this is called the *average-base-period income.*

2. Multiply that average base period income times 120 percent. This amount is called *nonaverageable income* and receives no special tax treatment.

3. Subtract the nonaverageable income computed in Step 2, above, from taxable income for the current year; this difference is called *averageable income.*

4. If averageable income is $3,000 or more, then an alternative income-averaging tax may be substituted for the normal tax calculation.

Figure 7-9 illustrates the basic concept of the averaging provision. To make this calculation, the taxpayer once again divides his or her total taxable income into two parts. Part I, represented by the distance Ob in Figure 7-9, is the nonaverageable income computed in Step 2, above, and the tax on this amount is computed in the normal manner. Part II, represented by the distance bB_5, is averageable income. Part II is then divided into five equal parts (bB, B_1B_2, and so on). The tax on one of these five parts is determined by adding that part to the nonaverageable income and computing the tax at the appropriate marginal rate. The tax on this one-fifth of averageable income is the amount shown in the area a_1 in Figure 7-9. That amount of tax (a_1) is then multiplied times five (a_1, a_2, a_3, a_4, and a_5), and the product is added to the tax determined on the Part I (nonaverageable) income in the normal way.

Because the entire calculation of income averaging under Secs. 1301–1305 takes place using the one rate schedule that would otherwise apply to the taxpayer anyway, Figure 7-9 does not suffer from the same theoretical flaw from which Figure 7-8 suffers. Other than that, the two calculations have many similarities. A further explanation of these income-averaging rules appears in Chapter 28.

The add-on minimum tax

A fourth major aberration from the otherwise unitary federal income tax rate schedule is known as the *minimum tax* or, sometimes, the *add-on minimum tax.* As opposed to the three other major exceptions considered in this chapter, the minimum tax is a pen-

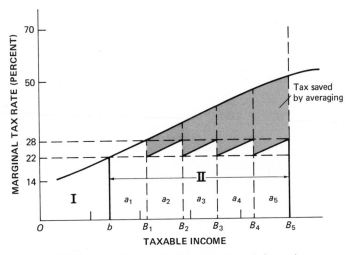

FIGURE **7-9**   Graphic Illustration of Income Averaging

alty tax. That is, the minimum tax is a penalty that must be *added to* the gross income tax determined in the normal way, if certain prescribed conditions are satisfied.

The conditions that trigger this penalty tax generally occur only if a taxpayer (individual, fiduciary, or corporation) has reduced an otherwise sizable gross tax liability simply by taking advantage of various tax preference provisions. The specified tax preference provisions are, in large measure, accelerated tax deductions placed in the Code in an attempt to stimulate investments in certain properties. The difference between accelerated and straight-line depreciation, the excess of the intangible drilling and development cost deductions over the income from oil and gas properties, and the excess of percentage depletion over the remaining basis (if any) of a mineral property are all examples of tax preferences that become the base for the minimum add-on penalty tax.

The amount of "minimum tax" may generally be determined as follows:

1. Determine the sum of all the tax preferences claimed by the taxpayer in the determination of taxable income.
2. Subtract from the sum determined in Step 1, above, the larger of (a) $10,000 or (b) one-half of the gross tax liability determined in the normal way.
3. Multiply the remainder (if any) in Step 2, above, by 15 percent.
4. The product of the multiplication in Step 3, above, is the total amount of the minimum add-on tax.

Additional details concerning this minimum tax may be found in Chapter 28.

The alternative minimum tax

In very rare circumstances, an *individual* (never a corporation or a fiduciary) taxpayer will not pay the income tax determined in the normal way. Instead, in these rare cases, he or she may have to pay an "alternative minimum tax," which is computed by a complex procedure. The alternative minimum tax is compared with the normal tax, and the larger amount is the tax liability for the year. This unusual aberration to the rate schedules occurs only if a taxpayer has an unduly small gross tax liability because of (1)

a large capital gain deduction and/or (2) a large amount of "excess itemized deductions." The detailed calculations are discussed in Chapter 28.

The taxation of nonresident aliens

The final aberration from the unitary tax rate schedules is the tax rate applied to nonresident alien taxpayers. As strange as it may seem, the United States theoretically taxes the income earned by *every* individual, *every* corporation, and *every* fiduciary, world wide! This income tax concept is known as a *global* tax. At first blush, the concept seems to suggest that the United States will tax the income of all citizens and aliens in exactly the same manner. As you might suspect, however, that would be a difficult feat indeed, since the United States government certainly does not have legal jurisdiction over most aliens.

In reality, the United States does attempt to tax the worldwide income of (a) all U.S. citizens (be they residents or nonresidents) and (b) all resident aliens, in exactly the same manner. Nonresident aliens, however, are subject to an income tax only on their income from U.S. sources. Furthermore, the tax rate imposed on such income is a flat 30 percent.

Conceptually, the income tax on a nonresident alien may be depicted as in Figure 7-10. The distance *Ox* represents the nonresident alien's U.S. source income only. Any income earned by a nonresident alien from a foreign source is not subject to a tax by the United States.

Additional details of foreign taxation are not included in this book; they are, however, covered in the second book in this series. Observe also that we have said nothing about the taxation of either foreign corporations or foreign fiduciaries. Such advanced topics in taxation are also deferred for study at a later time.

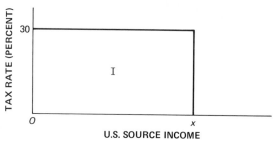

FIGURE **7-10**   Graphic Illustration of U.S. Taxation of Nonresident Alien

ADMINISTRATIVE CONSIDERATIONS

Before closing this conceptual overview of tax rates, we must consider briefly a couple of administrative considerations. The formula at the beginning of Chapter 5 suggests that every taxpayer must multiply the appropriate tax rate(s) times taxable income to determine gross tax liability. As a matter of fact, many individual taxpayers never make such a multiplication. Why?

Tax tables

As a matter of administrative convenience, the Internal Revenue Service has prepared a series of tax tables that must be used, under prescribed conditions, in lieu of the normal tax rate schedules. This procedure is prescribed solely because it simplifies taxpayer compliance for millions of persons. As everyone knows, it is easy to make an arithmetic error in any addition, subtraction, or multiplication problem. Consequently, the I.R.S. has deliberately minimized the number of arithmetic steps required to complete an individual tax return reporting a taxable income of $20,000 or less. (The comparable number is $40,000 for married persons filing a joint return.)

The tax tables set out the gross tax liability determined at the midpoint of the brackets (which are clearly indicated in the far left column). The several columns to the right of each bracket take into account the varying number of personal and dependent exemptions that the taxpayer may be entitled to claim. Accordingly, the only thing required of many taxpayers is finding the right number in a tax table. The number located is automatically the correct gross tax liability for the taxpayer, determined without performing a single multiplication.

The additional details concerning these tax tables are discussed in Chapter 9, along with a further explanation of tax table income, personal and dependent exemptions, and so on.

The FICA tax

Whenever a self-employed individual taxpayer completes his or her income tax return, he or she must also complete a Social Security (or FICA) tax return as part of the same procedure.

The Social Security tax is in addition to the income tax and is based on the amount of self-employment income realized by the taxpayer during the year and by a predetermined (and rapidly increasing) Social Security tax rate. (For 1980, the FICA tax rate of 8.1 percent is applied to a maximum of $25,900 in self-employment income.)

The only reason we are including even these few comments on the FICA tax in this chapter is that many people do not realize that the total tax on their income tax return may well include more than just the income tax. The inclusion of the FICA tax computation as part of the income tax return of a self-employed individual is strictly a matter of administrative convenience. A careful analysis of our federal income tax rates would require the clear separation of these two distinctly different taxes. Again, additional details concerning the Social Security tax are deferred to the book on advanced tax topics.

In summary, three general concepts concerning tax rates should be clearly understood. First, the U.S. income tax rates are generally progressive. Second, the precise degree of progressivity built into the rates varies from one class of taxpayers to another; that is, the prescribed tax rates for individuals, fiduciaries, and corporations have been differentiated deliberately. Third, subject to the several major aberrations described briefly in this chapter, a single set of tax rates applies to the entire taxable income reported by any one taxpayer in a given year. Among the major exceptions to the general rule just stated are the special tax provisions for:

1. A maximum tax on personal service income;
2. An alternative tax on certain corporate capital gains, and a special long-term capital gain deduction for noncorporate taxpayers;
3. Two income averaging options for individual taxpayers;
4. An add-on minimum tax for some taxpayers;
5. An alternative minimum tax for a few individual taxpayers; and
6. A flat (30 percent) tax rate for nonresident aliens.

WHAT'S LEFT OF THE UNITARY SYSTEM?

The preceding list of aberrations from the unitary system is by no means complete. We shall discuss others throughout this book. Even with this incomplete list, however, you may be asking: Is any source of income subject to the regular rates? The answer is yes, *but!*

Take, for example, the normal operating profit of a retail store operated as a sole proprietorship. The income here arises from the sale of inventory, which is not a capital asset. Thus, the capital-gain rules have no application. Of course, ordinary and necessary expenses are allowed as deductions, but the regular rates would apply to the net profit. But, wait! If the profits from the retail operation are large, the proprietor-taxpayer will transfer the business to a close corporation to limit the immediately applicable rate. The former proprietor is now the president of the corporation, and maximum tax on personal service income comes into play if the salary is high enough. Also, the president's employment contract will provide for the normal bundle of fringe benefits that result in a deduction for the corporate employer but no income to the employee. If after-tax profits of the business are invested in expansion, the value of the shares held by the owner increases. Gain realized on the subsequent sale of the stock is a capital gain, despite the fact that the increase arose as a result of profits on selling inventory. As you can see, the tax rate applicable to the inventory profits is now cloudy, to say the least.

Take another example. Income from interest and dividends on corporate securities is ordinary income. The maximum 70 percent rate applies to this income. If interest and dividend income is high, however, the taxpayer will likely transfer the assets producing some of that income to trusts for the benefit of parents, children, and grandchildren. The division of the income into smaller units in each trust lowers the applicable rates.

Despite all these exceptions, the U.S. income tax is essentially a unitary system, and one schedule of rates applies to the homogeneous taxable income of each taxpayer. The taxpayers affected most by this fact are individuals whose incomes are derived from salaries and wages and who own little, if any, income-producing property. That aptly describes most of our citizens.

PROBLEMS

1. Compare and contrast a unitary tax system with a schedular tax system.
2. Is the U.S. income tax system a schedular system or a unitary system—
   a. Technically?
   b. Practically?
   Explain.
3. What are the current highest marginal income tax rates for individual taxpayers in the United States? Where does most of the progressivity exist—at relatively lower or higher levels of taxable income?
4. What are the current lowest and highest marginal income tax rates for corporate taxpayers in the United States?
5. In what sense may a corporate entity be described as a tax shelter?
6. If a taxpayer is nearing the end of a year with an unusually large taxable income, to the extent that it is legally possible and administratively convenient, what should the taxpayer try to do about—
   a. Additional items of gross income?
   b. Additional deductions?
   Explain briefly.
7. In general, how do the maximum tax provisions modify our otherwise unitary tax rates?
8. In general, how do the capital-gain provisions modify our otherwise unitary tax rates for—
   a. Corporate taxpayers?
   b. Noncorporate taxpayers?

9. How do the income averaging provisions modify our otherwise unitary tax rates for individual taxpayers—
    a. In general?
    b. In the event of a lump-sum distribution from a qualified pension or profit-sharing plan?
10. Does the minimum (add-on) tax increase or decrease the normal income tax rates? Explain briefly.
11. In what fundamental way does the alternative minimum tax differ from the minimum (add-on) tax for individual taxpayers?
12. Must every taxpayer multiply the appropriate tax rate(s) times the taxable income to determine the gross tax liability for the year? Explain briefly.
13. Listed below are several sources of income realized by an individual. For each source, discuss the special provisions, if any, that might apply to the income. If no special provision applies, what could taxpayers do to reduce the rates on the income?
    a. Professional fees earned by a certified public accountant.
    b. Gains or profits from the sale of inventory items.
    c. Interest earned on corporate bonds.
    d. Rental income from an apartment house.
    e. Gain on the sale of corporate securities.
    f. Royalty income received on a book that was a best seller for six months.
    g. Bonus received by a college athlete upon signing a professional contract.
14. A citizen and resident of Great Britain has income from several countries, including the United States. If that person is not a resident of the United States, is the U.S. income subject to our tax? If so, what is the rate?
15. What general concepts or notions about taxation may be used to justify the income-averaging devices discussed in this chapter?

The Congressional preference for credits is partially due to the high visibility of credits. A subtraction directly from the tax on the face of Form 1040 gives the taxpayer a feeling that Congress has finally done something to reduce his taxes.

DR. EMIL SUNLEY,
The Brookings Institution

credits and prepayments: general concepts

The general tax formula given on page 5/1 for computing the net tax payable indicates that every taxpayer applies the proper tax rate to taxable income in order to arrive at the gross tax payable. The taxpayer then subtracts "credits and prepayments" to arrive at the net tax payable. Prepayments are amounts paid by the taxpayer before a tax return is filed, to be applied specifically against the taxpayer's gross tax liability and to be refunded to the extent they exceed the gross tax liability. Certain credits, such as the credit for excise taxes paid on motor fuels purchased for nonhighway use, are essentially prepayments and are treated as such in this chapter. Other credits are unrelated to amounts previously paid by the taxpayer. The latter are generally of greater significance in tax policy, and they will be discussed first. Most credits allowed are provided for in Secs. 31 through 45 of the Internal Revenue Code, as follows:

Sec. 31 Taxes withheld on wages.
Sec. 32 Tax withheld at source on nonresident aliens and foreign corporations and on tax-free covenant bonds.
Sec. 33 Taxes of foreign countries and possessions of the United States; possession tax credit.
Sec. 37 Credit for the elderly.
Sec. 38 Investment in certain depreciable property.
Sec. 39 Certain uses of gasoline, special fuels, and lubricating oil.
Sec. 40 Expenses of work incentive programs.
Sec. 41 Contributions to candidates for public office.
Sec. 42 General tax credit.

Sec. 43 Credit for certain earned income.
Sec. 44 Credit for purchase of new principal residence.
Sec. 44A Expenses for household and dependent care services necessary for gainful employment.
Sec. 44B Credit for employment of certain new employees.
Sec. 44C Residential energy credit.
Sec. 45 Overpayment of tax

In addition, Secs. 46 through 53 of the Code deal with computational aspects of credits, limitations on credits, and other details.

CREDITS VERSUS DEDUCTIONS

An important distinction between a credit or a prepayment and a deduction should be obvious—although credits and prepayments yield a dollar-for-dollar tax reduction, the tax decrease resulting from a one dollar deduction depends on the marginal tax rate being applied to net taxable income. To illustrate this important distinction, assume that an imaginary taxpayer's marginal (as well as average) tax rate is 20 percent and that his taxable income for the year is $10,000. Thus, the gross tax liability is $2,000 ($10,000 × 20%). Suppose that after computing taxable income and gross tax liability, as above, it is discovered that a $500 payment made by the taxpayer has been omitted from the computation. Suppose, too, that there is a legitimate question of whether the payment is properly to be considered a "deduction" or a "credit." The two tabulations below demonstrate the significant difference in impact on net tax payable resulting from this difference in classification.

	Payment treated as deduction	Payment treated as credit
Taxable income before considering this payment	$10,000	$10,000
Payment treated as deduction	(500)	—
Revised taxable income	$ 9,500	$10,000
Tax rate	× .20	× .20
Gross tax liability	$ 1,900	$ 2,000
Payment considered as a credit	—	(500)
Net tax payable	$ 1,900	$ 1,500

Observe that if the payment is a credit, the entire $500 reduces the net tax payable from $2,000 to $1,500. If the payment is assumed to be a deduction, however, the decrease in net tax payable is only $100—from $2,000 to $1,900. The important conclusion, stated earlier, is that the effect of a deduction on net tax payable depends wholly on the marginal tax rate. In the preceding example, if the taxpayer's marginal rate had been 70 percent, rather than 20 percent, a deduction of $500 would have resulted in a decrease of $350 in tax liability ($500 × 70%). It is apparent that the effect of a given deduction can have widely varying effects on the dollar amount of tax liability of taxpayers at different marginal rate levels. On the other hand, a tax credit will have the same dollar effect on the amount of net taxes payable, no matter what the taxpayer's rate level may be. The alert student can already sense that the alternative use of tax credits and deductions can easily be a tool for influencing the relative amount of taxes paid by taxpayers at different tax rate levels.

THE USE OF CREDITS PRIOR TO 1975

Economists and tax experts have long recognized the flexibility that credits provide in developing and modifying tax policy, but until 1975 their use had generally been limited to a small handful of specific applications designed either to encourage taxpayers to act in a desired manner or to provide greater equity in the tax structure. The most important pre-1975 credits that are still in use are the five provisions discussed below; they illustrate well the diverse purposes that credits may serve.

The investment credit

By far the most significant tax credit provision enacted prior to 1975, the investment credit (Code Sec. 38), was patterned by the Kennedy administration in 1962 after the tax laws of several European countries. That credit is computed by applying an arbitrary percentage to the "qualified investment" made in productive property by the taxpayer during the year. The purpose of the credit is to encourage investment by businesses, thereby increasing the rate of economic growth and helping to achieve the full employment of resources. But not all the investments made by business people increase the nation's productive capacity and provide employment for materials and labor. In some cases an investment may have little or no effect on the rate of economic activity. An investment in land is a good example; many security transactions similarly have little or no effect on productive activity. Thus, Congress was faced with the task of writing a law that would encourage only those investments having the maximum economic impact without granting a tax privilege to other investments. It solved this problem by granting the investment credit only for investments in qualified property. Qualified property includes primarily *new* tangible personal property subject to depreciation, with a limited credit for *used* depreciable personal property.

The basic rate for the investment credit is 10 percent. Only if the asset has a life of 7 years or more, however, does the entire cost qualify for the credit. Two-thirds of the cost qualifies if the life of the asset is from 5 to 7 years; only one-third qualifies if the life is at least 3 years but less than 5 years. There are various limitations, provisions for recapture, carrybacks and carryovers of unused credits, and other technical provisions that make the investment credit provisions very complex. In addition, this one credit has been terminated, reinstated, suspended, and reinstituted since 1962. Also, changes in the definition of "qualified investment" have been made almost yearly. In 1978 substantial changes were made in the law, and a number of "energy conservation" credits were added to Sec. 38. Because of the importance of the investment credit, it is examined in greater detail in Chapter 17.

Credit for the elderly

Another credit the basic principles of which are firmly established in our tax structure is the "credit for the elderly" (Code Sec. 37), which permits taxpayers who are 65 years of age or older to reduce their tax bill by an amount up to $375. The credit is 15 percent of the taxpayer's adjusted gross income up to $2,500. The credit begins to be phased out when the taxpayer's adjusted gross income reaches $7,500. The provision contains special rules for married couples and for those who receive social security benefits.

Prior to 1976 the credit for the elderly was 15 percent of the taxpayer's "retirement income" (dividends, taxable pensions, interest, royalties, and gross rents) up to $1,524. The original retirement income credit was an effort to at least partially equalize the tax effect on (1) "retirement income" subject to the income tax and (2) tax-free income from social security and railroad retirement benefits. The 1976 changes were intended to eliminate what was viewed as discrimination against those who are required to support themselves by working in their later years and also represented an attempt to simplify the rather complex computations required under the original law. This credit is discussed in greater detail in Chapter 15.

The foreign tax credit

Another credit, designed to alleviate the problem of double taxation, is the credit allowed for income taxes paid by a United States citizen or domestic corporation to a foreign government. Actually the taxpayer has a choice either to deduct a foreign income tax paid or to apply it as a credit against United States income tax. The foreign tax credit provision has been roundly debated in recent years, especially since attention has focused on the profits of oil producing companies and the income taxes paid on their overseas operations. There are special rules for computing the credit allowed on foreign income from oil and gas production. The foreign tax credit is not available to the extent that the taxpayer has excluded from gross income an amount of foreign income. Because the details of the foreign tax credit are complex, and because they affect relatively few taxpayers, they are not discussed further in this introductory text.

The work incentive program (WIN) credit

In an effort to foster training and employment for the hard-core unemployed who lack job skills, the Congress in 1971 passed a provision permitting the taxpayer to take a credit equal to 20 percent of the wages and certain other expenses incurred within the first 12 months of employment in on-the-job training or employment if he or she has been certified by the Secretary of Labor as being qualified under the program. The Revenue Act of 1978 brought the WIN credit into closer harmony with the "targeted jobs credit," discussed on pages **8**/5–**8**/6, for years beginning after 1978. That Act increased the credit to 50 percent of the amount paid to qualified individuals (up to $6,000 compensation for each individual) in the first year of employment, and 25 percent of the amount paid the employee (up to $6,000) in the second year of employment. Again, complex rules limit the amount deductible in any one year, provide for carrybacks and carryovers, and define in detail the types of employees and the nature of expenses incurred. The program allows a reduced credit for wages paid to qualified employees in nonbusiness activities; as a result, tax benefits have been made available through this credit not only to the unemployed but also to the wealthier taxpayer who is financially able to use such employees in nonbusiness jobs as domestic servants.

The credit for political contributions

Historically, the United States income tax laws have denied taxpayers the right to deduct contributions for any expenditures made for political purposes. In recent years, however, there has been a growing concern that many individual citizens have isolated themselves from political activities and a concomitant fear that the political processes have become subservient to those with large financial resources. Therefore, in 1971, Congress, in an attempt to broaden the base of citizen participation in political campaigns, enacted Sec. 40 of the Code, which permitted the taxpayer to obtain a tax benefit from political contributions.

At the present time, the individual taxpayer may take a credit equal to one-half of "contributions" made to political parties, a candidate for nomination or election to public office, or a candidate's organization.

The maximum credit is $50 for a single individual, $50 for a married person filing a separate return, and

$100 for a married couple filing jointly. (Prior to 1979 the taxpayer could elect instead of the credit, a deduction of the amount contributed, with limits.)

THE GROWTH OF CREDITS SINCE 1974

In addition to the provisions outlined above, a number of other minor credits have been used through the years. However, it was not until 1975 that Congress, in examining possible techniques to stimulate economic recovery, fully recognized that tax credits offer quick and effective tax relief that may help to achieve social and/or economic goals. The initiation of a host of credits in 1975 was a harbinger of things to come. Thus, an examination of several of the credits introduced by the 1975 Tax Reduction Act and subsequent acts may help to demonstrate the direction that future tax policy may be expected to take.

In 1974 and early 1975 consumer demand especially for durable goods and housing, had dropped precipitously. Unemployment had risen to its highest point since the depression of the 1930s, and the welfare rolls had increased to staggering levels. Skyrocketing inflation had added its toll, hitting low-income wage earners especially hard. Thus, the scene was set for the administration and Congress to reexamine federal monetary and fiscal policies in the hope that changes could be instituted to help get the economy on the road to recovery. One of the major results of this examination was the enactment of a series of tax-law innovations (many of them intended to be temporary) designed to reduce the income taxes of individuals, especially low-income taxpayers, and businesses and thus to stimulate consumer demand. Unfavorable economic conditions lingered on in 1976, with the result that the Tax Reform Act of 1976 continued or extended most of these innovations. The 1976 Act also contained a major new credit, the credit for child-care expenses, which replaced the former deduction for child care.

In early 1977 the nation was still plagued with high unemployment. Consequently, Congress passed a "new jobs credit" to encourage small businesses to employ additional workers. In 1978, still more credits were introduced, many of them designed to encourage taxpayers to make a wide variety of energy-saving investments, and additional energy-related credits were included in the Windfall Profit Tax Act of 1980.

The earned income credit

Perhaps the most significant and potentially far-reaching provision of the Tax Reduction Act of 1975 was the "earned income credit," containing many of the characteristics of a negative income tax. As initially enacted, this tax credit was available only for taxable years beginning in 1975; however, it was subsequently made permanent. Congress had several objectives in adding the credit, and they are reflected in the somewhat curious technical aspects of this provision (Sec. 43). In order to qualify for the earned income credit, a taxpayer is required to maintain in the United States a household that is the principal place of abode of the taxpayer and the taxpayer's dependent child. The credit is available to a married taxpayer and to certain unmarried taxpayers. If unmarried, the taxpayer must be qualified to file either as a "surviving spouse," or as a "head of household." (The requirements for filing as a head of household and as a surviving spouse are discussed in Chapter 9). If the taxpayer is a head of household, an unmarried child living with the taxpayer does not have to qualify as the taxpayer's dependent, although a married child *does* have to qualify as the taxpayer's dependent. The credit is based on "earned income," defined as salaries, wages, other employee compensation, and earnings from self-employment.

The gross credit is 10 percent of a taxpayer's first $5,000 of earned income, so that the maximum credit is $500. However, the gross credit is reduced by 12½ percent of that amount of the taxpayer's adjusted gross income (as defined in Chapter 9) or earned income, whichever is larger, that is in excess of $6,000. Thus, if the taxpayer has $10,000 or more of earned income or adjusted gross income, no credit would be allowed. To illustrate the computation, assume that a married taxpayer and spouse live in a home with their two dependent children. The taxpayer's adjusted gross income, solely from wages, totals $7,150, so there is no gross tax liability. Nevertheless, the taxpayer will file a tax return and receive a "refund" equal to the earned income credit. Theoretically, the earned income credit is $356.25, computed as follows:

Tentative credit, 10 percent of earned income
of $7,150 limited to $500 maximum $500.00
Less 12½ percent of adjusted gross income
in excess of $6,000 ($1,150 × 12.5%) ... 143.75
Credit (theoretically) $356.25

The actual amount of credit, however, must be determined from a table develped by the I.R.S. This table shows that if the amount subject to the credit is at least $7,100 but not over $7,105, the earned income credit is $359.

An employee who is eligible for the earned income credit may, by filling out a certificate, have his employer make "advance payment" of the credit to the employee. The amount to be advanced is determined under tables prescribed by the Internal Revenue Service. The employer offsets the advance against the employer's liability for the following taxes, in order: (1) income taxes withheld, (2) F.I.C.A. taxes withheld, and (3) the employer's share of F.I.C.A. taxes.

Obviously, the earned income credit is designed to benefit low-income taxpayers. It was passed with the specific intent of partially offsetting the rapidly growing impact of social security taxes. As noted previously, the real significance of this credit is that it provided, for the first time in this country, a form of "negative income tax." It differs from a true negative income tax in that the credit increases as the taxpayer's earned income increases (up to $5,000), and the taxpayer with no earned income would receive no credit. Most proposals for a negative income tax provide a larger "subsidy" as income decreases. However, one intent of the earned income credit is to encourage individuals to obtain employment. Presumably, Congress felt that the credit would effectively increase the wage rate for low-income taxpayers, thus providing added incentive to work.

Credit for child-care and dependent-care expenses

Prior to 1976, taxpayers were able to deduct as "itemized deductions" limited amounts paid by the taxpayer for the care of qualified individuals if the costs were incurred to enable the taxpayer to be gainfully employed. The 1976 Tax Reform Act eliminated the deduction and substituted instead a "credit for child-care expenses" (Sec. 44A). The credit is 20 percent of the employment-related expenses, including related "housekeeping costs," for the care of a qualified individual (generally the taxpayer's dependents under 15 years of age, the taxpayer's disabled spouse, or certain other disabled individuals for whom the taxpayer provides support). If there is one

qualified individual, the credit is limited to a maximum of $400 (20 percent of actual costs up to $2,000). If there are two or more qualified individuals, the credit is limited to $800 (20 percent of actual costs up to $4,000).

Conversion of the child-care deduction into a child-care credit was intended by Congress to simplify an unnecessarily complex deduction. (Few tax return preparers would regard the present rules as a simplification.) Second, and perhaps more important, under the previous provision only those taxpayers who "itemized" their deductions could benefit from the provision. Those taxpayers who took the "standard deduction" instead of itemizing deductions were denied any beneficial tax recognition of such expenditures. In general, the original deduction provision favored taxpayers in the higher marginal tax brackets, while the tax credit provides more help for taxpayers in lower brackets, not only because of the usual relative effects on tax liability of the two types of tax provisions but also because most low-income taxpayers do not itemize their deductions.

Since this important credit is closely related to the taxpayer's employment, it is examined in detail in Chapter 14, pages **14/1–14/3**.

Credit for purchasing a new residence

An interesting experiment that illustrates how the tax credit may be used in an attempt to achieve specific economic goals was the credit allowed in 1975 and 1976 for the purchase of a new home. Because the home construction industry had suffered a greater setback than any other major segment of the U.S. economy in the recession of 1974–75, Congress authorized individual taxpayers to claim an income tax credit simply by purchasing a new primary residence. In general, the tax credit was equal to 5 percent of the purchase price of a new home built during a specified period; however, the credit was limited to a maximum of $2,000. There were other highly technical provisions of the law.

The potential effects of this law were probably only partially realized because of misunderstanding and misinformation when the provision was first enacted. Its importance to tax policy stems from its isolation of a single industry. Relatively few tax breaks have been so selective in their intervention in the marketplace.

The new jobs credit (The "targeted jobs credit")

For 1977 and 1978, a "new jobs credit" (Code Sec. 44B) designed to encourage small businesses to hire new workers was allowed. The thrust of the new jobs credit was changed, and the detailed rules were substantially modified, by a provision known as the "targeted jobs credit" beginning in 1979. Under this provision, a credit may be elected by an employer on wages paid in a trade or business activity to new employees hired from certain "target groups" (generally handicapped individuals, youths from economically disadvantaged groups, persons receiving benefits under certain assistance programs, ex-convicts in certain programs, certain Vietnam veterans, and participants in certain cooperative educational programs). The targeted jobs credit is 50 percent of the first $6,000 of wages paid a qualified employee in the first 12 months of employment, and 25 percent of the first $6,000 of wages paid the employee in the second 12 months of employment. (However, the credit reduces the amount deductible for wages, so that the effective credit for an employer in the 70 percent bracket is only $900 per employee in the first year and $450 per employee in the second year.) The credit is subject to other limitations, and built into the law are complex provisions regarding carrybacks and carryovers of unused credits where the available credit exceeds the amount deductible in the year. This credit is discussed further in Chapter 16.

CREDITS RELATED TO ENERGY CONSERVATION

Even a person who doubted that the numerous credit provisions in the Tax Reduction Act of 1975 presaged a trend in federal tax legislation would likely be convinced by developments since that time, especially the host of new credits introduced by the Energy Tax Act of 1978. The credits in that Act, and additional proposals currently being considered by Congress, have the laudable goal of encouraging taxpayers to conserve energy (though their effectiveness remains to be proved). Some of the main provisions are reviewed briefly below.

Credits relating to taxpayer's residence

Under Code Sec. 44C, two major nonrefundable credits relating to energy conservation in connection with the taxpayer's principal residence were introduced. The first credit is allowed the taxpayer for expenditures made prior to January 1, 1986, for insulation, weather-stripping, and certain other energy-conserving components with a life of 3 years or more, provided construction of the residence was substantially completed before April 20, 1977. A detailed listing of qualified expenditures is included in the law.

The allowable credit is 15 percent of the first $2,000 (cumulative) of qualified expenditures, so that the maximum credit is $300. Any amount by which the potential credit exceeds the taxpayer's tax liability may be carried over to future years ending before 1988. No credit is allowed unless the amount of the credit is at least $10. The credit is allowed to homeowners, tenants, cooperative housing owners, and members of condominium management associations.

The second residential energy credit, applicable to expenditures for qualifying solar and wind energy equipment with a life of not less than 5 years, is far more generous. The credit is 30 percent of the first $2,000 and 20 percent of the next $8,000 of such cumulative expenditures. Thus, the maximum credit is $2,200. No credit is allowed unless the amount is at least $10. The credit is available for expenditures made before January 1, 1986, and any unused credit resulting because the available credit exceeds the taxpayer's tax liability can be carried forward through taxable years ending before January 1, 1988.

The Windfall Profit Tax Act of 1980 substantially modified the credit for renewable energy sources, increasing the credit to 40 percent of the first $10,000 spent on renewable energy-source property for a taxpayer's principal residence, for expenditures made *after* 1979. The 1980 act also added several new types of energy property, for example, equipment that generates electricity from solar, geothermal, or wind energy, and a solar roof panel installed as a roof.

Energy credits relating to business property

The Energy Tax Act of 1978, modified and enlarged by the Windfall Profit Tax Act of 1980, also added a host of credits related to expenditures for energy-saving devices used in the taxpayer's business. For example, business taxpayers may take a 10 percent nonrefundable credit (in addition to the regular investment credit) for expenditures made for specified energy-related property. The law contains a detailed listing of qualified assets, such as boilers using fuels other than oil or natural gas, equipment specifically designed to reduce the amount of energy consumed, recycling equipment, shale-oil equipment, and so on. In general, this credit is an extension of the regular investment credit, except that it may include assets that are considered structural components or in connection with lodging facilities—categories that do not qualify for the regular investment credit. The special investment credit applies to new equipment placed in service prior to January 1, 1983.

The same Section of the Energy Act of 1978 provides that equipment that uses solar energy or wind energy to heat or cool, to generate electricity, or to provide hot water in a structure is eligible for the 10 percent credit. The credit on such equipment is "refundable." No credit is allowed for "passive" solar or wind energy equipment.

There are complex rules for determining the order in which the regular investment credit and the special investment credits will be used.

Still another provision related to energy conservation specifies that if an employer purchases a new van with a useful life of at least 3 years and seating at least eight persons other than the driver, the employer is entitled to a 10 percent special investment credit on the cost of the van if at least 80 percent of its mileage is for transporting employees to and from work. The vehicle must have been acquired by the employer on or after November 9, 1978, and placed in service before January 1, 1986. All or part of the credit must be recaptured if the vehicle ceases to be used as a commuter vehicle.

Finally, the Energy Tax Act of 1978 made several items of energy-consuming equipment ineligible for the regular investment credit. For example, portable air conditioners and portable space heaters are no longer eligible. Boilers fueled by oil or natural gas also are generally ineligible for the credit.

The credits discussed in this chapter illustrate the wide variety of possibilities. Obviously, almost any type of expenditure could be encouraged or discouraged by the proper allowance or disallowance of credits. Because, as opposed to deductions, credits have a uniform effect on the tax liability of all taxpayers, and perhaps to some extent for the reason explained in the headnote to this chapter, we can reasonably expect an even greater increase in the use of credits in future legislation.

PREPAYMENTS

As noted earlier, there are several methods by which income taxes are deemed to be prepaid. The most common type of prepayment is the income tax withheld from salaries and wages of an employee. Other prepayments come from estimated payments, excess social security taxes, and nonhighway-use petroleum purchases.

Withholding from wages

Every employer is required to withhold from an employee's "wages" an amount of income tax based on the employee's marital status, number of exemptions claimed, and earnings and to remit the withholding to a depository of the federal government within specified times. Essentially, the withholding provision is designed to put the employee on a "pay-as-you-go" basis as far as his or her income tax is concerned. "Wages" include all remuneration for services performed by an employee for an employer, including the cash value of all remuneration paid in any medium other than cash. Each January the employer must give the employee two copies of Form W-2, showing the total amount of remuneration subject to income tax paid the employee during the year, the amount of income tax withheld, the amount of earnings subject to social security taxes, and the amount of social security tax withheld. The employee attaches one copy of this form to his or her income tax return sent to the Internal Revenue Service. The amount withheld for income taxes is, of course, a prepayment that is subtracted from the gross tax payable, after tax credits, to arrive at the net tax payable (or refundable).

Estimated tax payments

As we have already seen, the employee is placed on a pay-as-you-go basis by the employer's withholding of income taxes from the employee's earnings. But what about individuals who receive their income from sources other than wages? It would be unfair to require the wage earner to pay income tax throughout the year via withholding but to allow the self-employed person to defer payment until filing a tax return after the close of the year. To prevent this inequity, individual taxpayers may be required to file estimated tax returns and make "quarterly" payments of the estimated tax during the tax year. Individual taxpayers must file a "declaration" if they can reasonably expect their estimated tax (the amount by which the taxpayer's expected gross tax liability will exceed the various credits and withholdings) to be $100 or more, and

1. To have over $500 of gross income from sources other than wages subject to withholding, *or*
2. To have a gross income that exceeds $20,000. (There are special rules for married couples when both spouses have income.)

Note that even employees who have wages subject to withholding may be required to file an estimate. Obviously, many individuals are technically required to file an estimate but will owe very small amounts of taxes. In order to reduce the number of estimates filed, where little or no additional tax is due, the filing requirement is softened by the provision that no penalty is levied for failure to make a declaration. (Otherwise, many taxpayers might file an estimate in order to avoid a possible penalty even though they were reasonably certain that there would be no additional tax due.) Nevertheless, there is a penalty for failure to make timely payments of at least 80 percent of the gross tax liability for each quarter. There is no penalty, however, if any one of several tests is met—the simplest test being that an amount equal to one-fourth of the tax shown on the return for the preceding tax year be paid each quarter.

Simply stated, the penalty is an annual charge (at the rate of 6 percent through January 31, 1980, and 12 percent after January 31, 1980) on the difference between the amount paid in each quarter and 80 percent of the tax due each quarter, computed from the date due until the date paid. The penalty is treated as an addition to the tax. There are special rules for determining the due dates of estimates when the taxpayer first becomes required to file an estimate at some time during the tax year.

A corporation also is required to pay its estimated tax, if over $40, in installments during the year. The corporation's "estimated tax" is its expected income tax liability, less allowable credits.

Excess social security taxes

Each employer is required to withhold (and match) social security taxes from each employee's earnings each year, up to a specified amount. For 1980, the social security tax withheld is 6.13 percent of the first $25,900 paid an employee during the year. Thus, if an employee works for two employers during 1979, earning $20,000 from the first and $9,000 from the second, the first employer would withhold $1,260 and the second would withhold $551.70. However, any employee is subject to a maximum social security tax of $1,587.67 on a total of only $25,900 of wages paid during 1979. This means that the employee has overpaid the social security taxes by $224.03 through excess withholding by employers. On his or her income tax return for the year, the taxpayer treats the "excess social security tax withheld" as a prepayment in computing net tax payable (or refundable).

Excise tax paid on nonhighway use of petroleum products

When a consumer purchases gasoline or lubricating oil, the purchase price includes a federal excise tax imposed on users of highways to provide funds for construction and maintenance of roads. When the gasoline or oil is purchased for nonhighway uses, such as farming or operating a motorboat, the taxpayer must pay the tax on purchase but may file a refund claim for the amounts paid. In order to simplify the refund claim procedure, Sec. 39, allows the taxpayer to take a credit against his or her federal income tax for the amount of excise taxes paid on gasoline and oil bought for nonhighway use, thus providing a simple refund procedure. In essence, these amounts are treated as prepayments of income taxes.

Reporting credits and prepayments on the tax return

As you have seen, credits and prepayments may be grouped into three categories based on the nature of the tax benefits they yield:

1. Credits that provide a benefit only if there is a gross tax liability in the current year—for example, the credit for contributions to candidates for public office, the credit for the elderly, and the credit for child-care and dependent care expenses. There is no carryback or carryover of unused credits for these items.
2. Credits that provide a benefit for the current year if there is a tax liability, and to the extent they are not used in the current year, may be carried back or forward, as appropriate, to the other years. Exam-

Tax Compu- tation (See Instruc- tions on page 12)	32 Amount from line 31 (*adjusted gross income*)		**32**	
	33 If you do not itemize deductions, enter zero . . . . }		**33**	
	If you itemize, complete Schedule A (Form 1040) and enter the amount from Schedule A, line 41 . . . }			
	Caution: If you have unearned income and can be claimed as a dependent on your parent's return, check here ▶ ☐ and see page 12 of the Instructions. Also see page 12 of the Instructions if: • *You are married filing a separate return and your spouse itemizes deductions, OR* • *You file Form 4563, OR* • *You are a dual-status alien.*			
	34 Subtract line 33 from line 32. Use the amount on line 34 to find your tax from the Tax Tables, or to figure your tax on Schedule TC, Part I . . . . Use Schedule TC, Part I, and the Tax Rate Schedules ONLY if: • *Line 34 is more than $20,000 ($40,000 if you checked Filing Status Box 2 or 5), OR* • *You have more exemptions than are shown in the Tax Table for your filing status, OR* • *You use Schedule G or Form 4726 to figure your tax.* Otherwise, you MUST use the Tax Tables to find your tax.		**34**	
	35 Tax. Enter tax here and check if from ☐ Tax Tables or ☐ Schedule TC . .		**35**	193 00
	36 Additional taxes. (See page 12 of Instructions.) Enter here and check if from ☐ Form 4970, } ☐ Form 4972, ☐ Form 5544, ☐ Form 5405, or ☐ Section 72(m)(5) penalty tax . . }		**36**	
	37 Total. Add lines 35 and 36 . . . . ▶		**37**	193 00
Credits	38 Credit for contributions to candidates for public office . . .	**38**	7 00	
	39 Credit for the elderly (*attach Schedules R&RP*)	**39**		
	40 Credit for child and dependent care expenses (attach Form 2441) .	**40**		
	41 Investment credit (*attach Form 3468*)	**41**	32 00	
	42 Foreign tax credit (*attach Form 1116*)	**42**		
	43 Work incentive (WIN) credit (*attach Form 4874*)	**43**		
	44 Jobs credit (*attach Form 5884*)	**44**		
	45 Residential energy credits (*attach Form 5695*)	**45**	15 00	
	46 Total credits. Add lines 38 through 45		**46**	54 00
	47 Balance. Subtract line 46 from line 37 and enter difference (but not less than zero) . ▶		**47**	139 00
Other Taxes (Including Advance EIC Payments)	48 Self-employment tax (*attach Schedule SE*)		**48**	
	49a Minimum tax. Attach Form 4625 and check here ▶ ☐.		**49a**	
	49b Alternative minimum tax. Attach Form 6251 and check here ▶ ☐		**49b**	
	50 Tax from recomputing prior-year investment credit (*attach Form 4255*) . . .		**50**	
	51a Social security (FICA) tax on tip income not reported to employer (*attach Form 4137*) . .		**51a**	
	51b Uncollected employee FICA and RRTA tax on tips (*from Form W–2*)		**51b**	
	52 Tax on an IRA (*attach Form 5329*)		**52**	
	53 Advance earned income credit payments received (*from Form W–2*)		**53**	
	54 Total. Add lines 47 through 53 . . . . ▶		**54**	139 00
Payments Attach Forms W–2, W–2G, and W–2P to front.	55 Total Federal income tax withheld	**55**	200 00	
	56 1979 estimated tax payments and credit from 1978 return	**56**	120 00	
	57 Earned income credit. If line 32 is under $10,000, see page 2 of Instructions	**57**	275 00	
	58 Amount paid with Form 4868	**58**		
	59 Excess FICA and RRTA tax withheld (two or more employers)	**59**		
	60 Credit for Federal tax on special fuels and oils (*attach Form 4136 or 4136–T*)	**60**		
	61 Regulated Investment Company credit (*attach Form 2439*)	**61**		
	62 Total. Add lines 55 through 61 . . . . ▶		**62**	595 00
Refund or Balance Due	63 If line 62 is larger than line 54, enter amount **OVERPAID** . . . . ▶		**63**	456 00
	64 Amount of line 63 to be **REFUNDED TO YOU** . . . . ▶		**64**	
	65 Amount of line 63 to be credited on 1980 estimated tax . . . . . ▶	**65**		
	66 If line 54 is larger than line 62, enter BALANCE DUE. Attach check or money order for full amount payable to "Internal Revenue Service." Write your social security number on check or money order . . ▶ (Check ▶ ☐ if Form 2210 (2210F) is attached. See page 15 of Instructions.) ▶ $		**66**	

Please Sign Here

Under penalties of perjury, I declare that I have examined this return, including accompanying schedules and statements, and to the best of my knowledge and belief, it is true, correct, and complete. Declaration of preparer (other than taxpayer) is based on all information of which preparer has any knowledge.

▶ Your signature   Date   ▶ Spouse's signature (if filing jointly, BOTH must sign even if only one had income)

Paid Preparer's Information

Preparer's signature and date ▶	Check if self-em- ployed ▶ ☐	Preparer's social security no.
Firm's name (or yours, if self-employed) and address ▶	E.I. No. ▶	
	ZIP code ▶	

ples of credits of this type are the investment credit, the WIN credit, the targeted jobs credit, and the residential energy credit.

3. Credits that are "refundable," giving rise to a cash payment from the U.S. Treasury to the taxpayer in the current year to the extent the credits exceed the tax liability. Examples of refundable credits are the special investment credit on solar and wind energy equipment and the earned income credit. Of course, prepayments also are refundable even if the taxpayer has no tax liability for the year.

In addition, there is a rather complex "order" in which credits are to be taken. The technicalities of the interaction of credits is beyond the scope of this book. The arrangement of items on the tax returns, however, is designed to make it easier for the taxpayer to give proper effect to credits and prepayments in computing the net tax payable or the amount refundable. To illustrate, assume that Tom and Mary file a joint return. Tom earns a salary, while Mary operates a typing service. They have one child, age 7. Their adjusted gross income totals $7,800 for 1978, including Tom's salary of $7,500 and Mary's net income of $300. Their tax liability before any credits or prepayments is $193. Their credits for the year include:

1. Investment credit on a typewriter bought by Mary, $32.
2. Earned income credit computed $275.
3. Political contributions credit, $7 (one-half of $14 contributed).
4. Residential energy credit for insulation installed in home, $15 (15% of $100 spent).

During the year, Tom's employer withheld income tax of $200 from Tom's earnings. In addition, Mary had anticipated doing a big business in her typing service, so they had filed an estimated tax return and paid $120 of estimated tax for the year. The sections of the tax return that reflect these data are shown on page **8/9** for a 1978 form. Note in the illustration that the earned income credit is listed on line 57 as though it were a prepayment, even though the taxpayer may have no gross tax liability for the year. On the other hand, other credits provide a tax benefit only if there is a gross tax liability.

PROBLEMS

1. If, in fact, tax credits have taken on increased significance in our tax laws in recent years, what factors do you think account for this trend?

2. a. In 1978 a married couple filing a joint return could elect either to take a credit of one-half of "political contributions" (with a maximum credit of $50) or to deduct such contributions up to $200. In each of the following cases, indicate whether the taxpayers would elect to take the credit or the deduction, and compute the net effect on their tax liability.

   (1) Taxpayers' contributions total $60 and their marginal tax rate is 20 percent.

   (2) Taxpayers' contributions total $60 and their marginal tax rate is 60 percent.

   (3) Taxpayers' contributions total $180 and their marginal rate is 20 percent.

   (4) Taxpayers' contributions total $180 and their marginal rate is 60 percent.

   b. For years after 1978 the election to deduct political contributions was eliminated, and the limit on the credit was doubled. What group of married taxpayers was adversely affected by this move? What group was favorably affected?

3. Explain how the earned income credit described in this chapter resembles a "negative income tax."

4. Why is the taxpayer allowed a credit for the federal excise tax paid on nonhighway use of petroleum products?

5. Some tax scholars predict that tax credits are likely to grow in importance because the "visibility of credits" is appealing to politicians. What do you think the word "visibility" means in this context?

6. Explain how some tax credits can be viewed as direct subsidies to specific groups. In your discussion, give examples selected from the credits discussed in this chapter.

7. Why are some taxpayers required to file "declarations of estimated tax," whereas others are not?

8. As pointed out in the text, there is no penalty for not filing a declaration of estimated tax but there is a penalty for not paying the tax due under the estimated tax provisions. What do you think are the reasons for this apparent discrepancy?

9. Distinguish between a "credit" and a "prepayment" as used in this chapter.

10. Compare the apparent objectives of the Retirement Income Credit as it existed for several years with the objectives of the Credit for the Elderly in the Tax Reform Act of 1976.

11. One provision that has often been considered by Congress during deliberation of proposed tax legislation would allow taxpayers to take either a deduction of a specified amount or a credit of some other specified amount for each exemption. Assume that the choice was to be a credit of $250 or a deduction of $1,000 for each exemption. What option would be taken by a taxpayer with one exemption whose marginal tax rate is
    a. 20 percent?
    b. 50 percent?

12. What would be the effect of the proposed measure discussed in Problem 11, above, on the relative tax burdens of taxpayers with high income and those with lower incomes, compared with that of allowing only a deduction of $1,000 per exemption?

13. Marsha, single, expects to have adjusted gross income of $24,000, all of which is from a salary subject to withholding. Is Marsha required to file a declaration of estimated tax for the year? What is the penalty for not filing?

14. In each of the following independent cases, compute the "earned income credit" for 1980.
    a. Taxpayer and spouse file a joint return. They have no dependents. Their adjusted gross income consists of salaries of $6,800 and interest of $200. Gross tax liability is $320.
    b. Taxpayer and spouse file a joint return. They maintain a household for their dependent 14-year-old child. Their combined adjusted gross income is $6,400, all from wages. Gross tax liability is zero.
    c. Same facts as part b, except that their total adjusted gross income of $8,400 is made up of $7,800 wages and $600 of interest. Gross tax liability is $290.
    d. Same facts as part b, except that their adjusted gross income was $3,600 consisting solely of wages. Gross tax liability is zero.
    e. Same facts as part b, except that their adjusted gross income was $3,800, consisting solely of taxpayer's net profit from a small motor repair shop. Gross tax liability is zero.

15. In each case below, compute the taxpayers' credit for child-care expense.
    a. Taxpayers, married and filing a joint return, are both employed and qualify for the credit for child-care expenses. They pay a baby sitter $2,160 during the year to take care of their 4-year-old child while the taxpayers are at work. Their tax liability before credits is $920.
    b. Same facts as in part a, except that taxpayers have two children, ages 4 and 6, for whom they pay $2,160 in child-care expenses.

16. Pertinent facts about a married couple filing a joint return for 1979 are:
    a. Total salaries earned, $8,800. This is also the amount of adjusted gross income.

b. Exemptions claimed, 3 (husband, wife, and 4-year-old child).
c. Gross tax liability before credits, $338. (Assume that this amount is correct, regardless of the actual correct amount.)
d. Income tax withheld from earnings, $300.
e. During the year, taxpayers paid $600 for qualified child-care expenses.
f. During the year, they made political contributions of $80.
g. Also during the year they spent $300 to insulate their home constructed in 1965.

Compute the net amount of tax they still owe, or the amount of refund they have coming.

17. As you have seen in this chapter, a number of credits (for example the credit for child-care expenses) represent items that were in previous years treated as deductions rather than as credits. Explain why these items have been changed from deductions to credits.

in consequence of this perversion of the word Being, philosophers looking about for something to supply its place, laid their hands upon the word Entity, a peice of barbarous Latin, invented by the schoolmen to be used as an abstract name, in which class its grammatical form would seem to place it; but being seized by logicians in distress to stop a leak in their terminology, it has ever since been used as a concrete name.

JOHN STUART MILL
A System of Logic (1843)

(1) Person—The term "person" shall be constructed to mean and include an individual, a trust, estate, partnership, association, company and corporation.

Section 7701(a)(1)
Internal Revenue Code of 1954

PART

taxable entities

There is no doubt that the statute could tax salaries to those who earned them and provide that the tax could not be escaped by anticipatory arrangements and contracts however skillfully devised to prevent the salary when paid from vesting even for a second in the man who earned it.

JUSTICE HOLMES
Lucas v. *Earl,* 281 U.S. 111 (1930)

the individual taxpayer: basic rules

From the earliest days of the income tax in the United States, tax law has designated individuals, corporations, and fiduciaries (estates and trusts) as taxpayers. This chapter covers the basic rules for individuals; Chapter 10 deals with the income taxation of corporations; and Chapter 11 contains a brief discussion of the taxation of fiduciaries and some basic rules related to partnerships and Subchapter S corporations. Before turning to a detailed discussion of the taxation of individuals, some thought should be given to other entities that could be designated taxpayers.

The income tax could be levied on many different entites. Innumerable legal, economic, natural, and cultural entities exist in our society. A list of some of the more important ones will illustrate the diversity: natural persons or individuals; family units; business proprietorships; partnerships; corporations; groups of corporations with related owners; religious groups; eleemosynary organizations of all types; trusts; estates; government units; and social organizations of an infinite variety. Theoretically, any of these *could* serve as a taxable entity, and the entity's periodic income could be used as the base for an income tax; but some of them can almost automatically be excluded from consideration. To use cities or other local governmental units, for example, would create the problem of reallocating the tax imposed to the entity's citizens, though it would minimize the number of taxpayers. Taxation of churches, legitimate charities, and social organiza-

tions would serve to discourage these activities and to transfer the cost of many of their functions to governmental units. To avoid the centralization of all charitable functions within government, many citizens prefer to continue the indirect subsidy granted through tax exemptions.

The rationale for not levying a tax on business proprietorships and partnerships is more obtuse. Both are treated as separate entities for general accounting purposes, and obviously an income tax could be levied on them. Instead, for tax purposes, proprietorships and partnerships are mere "conduits"; their income, deductions, and credits pass through the entity to the individual proprietors and partners and are reported on the proprietors' and partners' individual returns.

Congress, in any event, has settled on individuals, corporations, and fiduciaries as the entities that must make their annual tithe to the federal government. Individuals, of course, eventually bear the economic burden of all taxes. In the final analysis, only individuals can consume goods and services, and the allocations from the private to the public sector resulting from taxation certainly affect the patterns of consumption of individuals in our society. While this is true, corporations and fiduciaries, as well as individuals, are subject to the income tax. As we shall see throughout the text, the choice of these taxable entities has not been without its problems. The reluctance of taxpayers to part with their funds and their ingenuity at developing schemes to avoid doing so have resulted in many complications in the law relating to the problem of just what entity must eventually pay the tax.

INDIVIDUAL TAXPAYER DEFINED

Section 1 of the Internal Revenue Code reads in part, " . . . there is hereby imposed on the taxable income of every individual . . . a tax. . . ." Note the selection of *every* individual and note that the term used is "individual," not "citizen" or some other term. Use of the term "every individual" raises several important questions. Are minors "individuals"? What about citizens of foreign countries who earn income in the United States as residents or nonresidents? How are United States citizens who are permanent residents of a foreign country taxed?

Age

The age of an individual is of no direct importance in determining the individual's standing as a taxpayer. The income tax is levied from the cradle to the grave, though the taxpayer's age may affect the amount paid in some instances. Generally, a legal minor cannot hold title to property directly. He or she can, however, hold title through a parent or other legal agent and thereby become liable for federal income tax. Thus if a proud grandparent makes a gift of cash to a newborn descendant, and that cash is placed in a savings account or otherwise invested to produce income, the newborn child becomes a taxpayer and a potential tax is due on the income.

Citizens and residents of the United States

Citizens of the United States are taxed on their worldwide incomes. A citizen who has established a permanent residence in a foreign country and never expects to return to the United States on a permanent basis remains a United States taxpayer until he or she officially renounces United States citizenship. Note that the foreign government may also levy a tax on that citizen's income, particularly on income derived from sources within the country of residence. A citizen's income may thus be taxed by two governments. In this situation, the United States tax law contains three major provisions aimed at reducing the impact of double taxation:

1. The foreign tax credit, briefly described in Chapter 8, may be applied against the U.S. tax.

2. A U. S. citizen who is a bona fide resident of a foreign country throughout a taxable year or is absent from the United States for a period of 510 days during 18 consecutive months and who has income earned abroad enjoys a reduction in the U. S. tax. Before 1979, citizens with foreign earned income who met the above criteria could exclude their foreign-earned income up to $25,000 in some cases. For 1979 and later, citizens working abroad may claim special deductions for excess living costs that arise because of their foreign residency. The excess living costs allowed are those related to the general cost of living in the foreign country, housing, schooling for dependents, and home leaves.

3. Our government has entered into tax treaties with many foreign countries aimed at eliminating double taxation.

The same income tax levied on United States citizens is also levied on all resident aliens. Regulations provide that "an alien actually present in the United States who is not a mere transient or sojourner is a resident of the United States for purposes of the income tax."[1] A visitor is a resident, even if he or she plans to return home, provided his or her length of stay here is indefinite.

GENERAL FORMULA TO DETERMINE THE INCOME TAX LIABILITY OF AN INDIVIDUAL TAXPAYER

An expanded version of the formula presented in Chapter 5 can be used to calculate the tax liability for an individual. While some key terms such as income, deductions, and credits were discussed at length in earlier chapters, the definition of other new terms in this formula is critical to an understanding of the income tax law as it relates to individuals.

With the exception of the multiplication of the tax rates times taxable income to obtain the gross tax, note that every arithmetic operation in this formula is a subtraction. The order of these subtractions is extremely important. The intermediate remainders—gross income and adjusted gross income—must be correctly calculated before several critical decisions may be made about the amount of tax due the government.

[1]Reg. Sec. 1.871-2(b)

Income broadly conceived
− Exclusions

= Gross income
− Deductions *for* adjusted gross income
    (A.G.I.)

= Adjusted gross income
− Deductions *from* A.G.I. [excess, if any,
    of itemized (personal) deductions over the
    zero bracket amount]
− Personal and dependent exemptions

= Taxable income
× Applicable tax rate(s)

= Gross Tax
− Tax credits and prepayments

    Net tax payable

Gross income

As discussed in Chapter 5, gross income is income broadly conceived after subtracting all allowed exclusions (Sec. 61). The correct definition of gross income is important because this amount determines which individual taxpayers are required to file a return. The precise amounts of gross income an individual must have before he or she is required to file a return are detailed later in this chapter.

To illustrate the importance of properly classifying exclusions and deductions, consider the following two situations: A wealthy widow has several million dollars in capital invested in tax-exempt municipal bonds. She realizes an income of $1,000,000 in 1978, all from the tax-exempt securities. Such interest is an exclusion and her gross income is zero. She is *not* required to file a return. A second widow depends on rental property for her livelihood. She received gross rents of $10,000 but incurred deductible expenses related to the rental property of $8,000. Her net income from the rental property is only $2,000, but her gross income is $10,000. She must file a return because the $10,000 of gross income exceeds the amount explained later. While logic might tell us that the widow with the million dollar income is a more likely candidate for reporting to the government, law clearly nominates the widow with the very small *net* income as the one who must make an accounting to the Internal Revenue Service.

Adjusted gross income

An important yet troublesome calculation in the tax formula for individuals is that of adjusted gross income (commonly abbreviated A.G.I.). Note from the formula on the left that the deductions allowed individuals are divided into two classes, deductions *FOR* A.G.I. and deductions *FROM* A.G.I. The proper classification of deductions is important because, for many taxpayers, the actual amount of the deductions *FROM* A.G.I. is based in part on A.G.I. In general, deductions *FOR* A.G.I. are deductions related to the individual's trade or business; deductions *FROM* A.G.I. are generally the allowed personal deductions (itemized deductions) in excess of the zero bracket amount. These generalizations, however, have only nominal value because of the numerous exceptions to them.

The term adjusted gross income is explicitly defined in the statute by Sec. 62, which is entitled "Adjusted Gross Income Defined." This Section is used for definitional purposes only. The determination of whether a given expenditure is deductible must be based on the sections discussed in Chapter 6. Section 62 is reproduced in its entirety below:

Sec. 62 Adjusted Gross Income Defined.
For purposes of this subtitle, the term "adjusted gross income" means, in the case of an individual, gross income minus the following deductions:
(1) Trade and business deductions.—The deductions allowed by this chapter (other than by part VII of this subchapter) which are attributable to a trade or business carried on by the taxpayer, if such trade or business does not consist of the performance of services by the taxpayer as an employee.
(2) Trade and business deductions of employees.—
  (A) Reimbursed expenses.—The deductions allowed by part VI (sec. 161 and following) which consist of expenses paid or incurred by the taxpayer, in connection with the performance by him of services as an employee, under a reimbursement or other expense allowance arrangement with his employer.
  (B) Expenses for travel away from home.—The deductions allowed by part VI (sec. 161 and following) which consist of expenses of travel, meals, and lodging while away from home, paid or incurred by the taxpayer in connection with the performance by him of services as an employee.
  (C) Transportation expenses.—The deductions allowed by part VI (sec. 161 and following) which consist of expenses of transportation paid or incurred by the taxpayer in connection with the performance by him of services as an employee.
  (D) Outside salesmen.—The deductions allowed by part VI (sec. 161 and following) which are attributable to a trade or business carried on by the taxpayer, if such trade or business consists of the performance of services by the taxpayer as an employee and if such trade or business is to solicit, away from the employer's place of business, business for the employer.

(3) Long-term capital gains.—The deduction allowed by section 1202.

(4) Losses from sale or exchange of property.—The deductions allowed by part VI (sec. 161 and following) as losses from the sale or exchange of property.

(5) Deductions attributable to rents and royalties.—The deductions allowed by part VI (sec. 131 and following), by section 212 (relating to expenses for production of income), and by section 611 (relating to depletion) which are attributable to property held for the production of rents or royalties.

(6) Certain deductions of life tenants and income beneficiaries of property.—In the case of a life tenant of property, or an income beneficiary of property held in trust, or an heir, legatee, or devisee of an estate, the deduction for depreciation allowed by section 167 and the deduction allowed by section 611.

(7) Pension, profit-sharing, annuity, and bond purchase plans of self-employed individuals.—In the case of an individual who is an employee within the meaning of section 401(c)(1), the deductions allowed by section 404 and section 405(c) to the extent attributable to contributions made on behalf of such individual.

(8) Moving expense deduction.—The deduction allowed by section 217.

(9) Pensions, etc., plans of electing small business corporations.—The deduction allowed by section 1379(b)(3).

(10) Retirement savings.—The deduction allowed by section 219 (relating to deduction for certain retirement savings) and the deduction allowed by section 220 (relating to retirement savings for certain married individuals).

(11) Certain portion of lump-sum distributions from pension plans taxed under section 402(e).—The deduction allowed by section 402(e)(3).

(12) Penalties forfeited because of premature withdrawal of funds from time savings accounts or deposits.—The deductions allowed by section 165 for losses incurred in any transaction entered into for profit, though not connected with a trade or business, to the extent that such losses include amounts forfeited to a bank, mutual savings bank, savings and loan association, building and loan association, cooperative bank or homestead association as a penalty for premature withdrawal of funds from a time savings account, certificate of deposit, or similar class of deposit.

(13) Alimony.—The deduction allowed by section 215.

(14) Deductions for certain expenses of living abroad.— The deduction allowed by section 913.

Nothing in this section shall permit the same item to be deducted more than once.

Thus, by omission, Sec. 62 also defines deductions *FROM* A.G.I., since any deduction not listed in Sec. 62 cannot be deducted from gross income to determine A.G.I. The content of Sec. 62 is paraphrased as follows:

1. All expenses that can be classified as
   a. Nonemployee trade or business expenses

(for example, all routine business expenses associated with the operation of a sole proprietorship).
   b. Expenses associated with the production of rents and royalties, whether or not the income-producing activity is a "trade or business."

2. Only certain expenses incurred as an *employee*, including
   a. All expenses of travel "away from home."
   b. All "transportation" expenses (which excludes both the cost of travel away from home and nondeductible—i.e., personal—commuting from home to work).
   c. Any other reimbursed business expenses, but only to the extent of the reimbursement.
   d. All expenses associated with activities conducted as an "outside salesman."

3. The long-term capital gain deduction (explained in Chapter 21).

4. Certain losses from the sale or exchange of trade, business, investment, or "nonbusiness" assets (explained in Chapters 21 and 22).

5. Moving expenses

6. Alimony

7. Some other miscellaneous deductions

While the above listing appears to be explicit and straightforward at first glance, it poses some difficult problems. As demonstrated in the following section, individual taxpayers gain a potential advantage when their deduction can be included in the *FOR* classification because such classification in many cases serves to increase deductions in the *FROM* classification. A correct application of the definition in Sec. 62 requires that all deductible items be divided into three categories: trade or business deductions, expenses incurred as an employee, and a limited number of other, specifically identified items.

The various tests applied to an activity to determine if that activity constitutes a trade or business were discussed in Chapter 6. On the list above, item 1(a) provides that expenses incurred in a trade or business are deductions for A.G.I. Note, however, the qualifying word "nonemployee." Business expenses of self-employed proprietors are deductions for A.G.I., but special restrictions apply to trade or business expenses incurred by an employee. Only those expenses listed under item 2 are deductions for A.G.I. for an employee. A brief example will help clarify this distinction. Assume the case of a C.P.A. who is a sole practitioner with a small office staff. The C.P.A. attends a seminar on recent tax developments and incurs the following expenses: registration fee, $105; air fare, $150; travel expenses away from home (meals, lodging, and incidentals), $90. As a sole proprietor, all these expenses are deductions for A.G.I. because they are trade or business expenses of an individual who is self-employed. As an alternative, assume the C.P.A. is an employee of a large firm, incurs the same costs, and is not reimbursed. The travel costs ($150 + $90, or $240) are deductions for A.G.I., but the registration fee ($105) is classified as a deduction from A.G.I. Finally, if the C.P.A.'s employer reimburses him or her for the registration fee, and the reimbursement is included in gross income, it becomes a deduction for A.G.I.

The rather illogical results of the preceding example bear an important message: To correctly classify deductions for and from A.G.I., one must know the rules set out in Sec. 62. Generalizations, reason, and logic will not suffice.

A confusing group of deductions are those related to transactions for profit. In the main, these are the deductions authorized by Sec. 212 for the production of income and the maintenance of income-producing property. The most common transactions in this category involve investments in securities and in unimproved land held for speculation. The distinction between an activity that constitutes a trade or business as opposed to a transaction for profit is often a very thin line. Does the ownership and rental of a single dwelling unit constitute a business? Is a college professor who writes one or two books engaged in the business of writing textbooks? Or, alternatively, are these activities properly classified as transactions for profit? Fortunately, we do not have to reach a decision in these examples for purposes of classifying deductions. Section 62 provides that all deductions related to the production of rents and royalties are deductions for A.G.I. (item 1(b) on the list). With this exception, however, other deductions under Sec. 212 related to transactions for profit are deductions from A.G.I. Examples include the amounts paid for subscriptions to investment services, fees paid to tax consultants, and similar expenses.

As explained briefly in Chapter 6, the law permits individuals to deduct the amounts spent for a few personal expenses. Medical costs, charitable contributions, interest, and taxes are the major ones. With the exceptions of moving expenses and alimony (items 5 and 6 on the above list), deductions of a personal nature when allowed are always deductions from A.G.I.

Deductions from A.G.I.

The deductions of individuals for various expenditures, after segregating and deducting those allowed *for* A.G.I., are allowed only to the extent they exceed the zero bracket amount. (Technically, the deduction for personal and dependent exemptions is a deduction *from* A.G.I., but the deduction for exemptions is allowed without regard to actual expenditures and presents none of the problems of classification discussed above.) For purposes of computing the gross tax liability of most individuals, the tax formula for individuals must be further expanded, as follows:

= Adjusted gross income
− Deductions *from* A.G.I. (excess, if any, of itemized deductions over the zero bracket amount)

= Tax table income
− Personal and dependent exemptions

= Taxable income

The intermediate remainder, tax table income, is used by most individuals to determine their gross tax from the tax tables. Tax table income is important for that purpose only, as we shall see after considering the zero bracket amount.

ZERO BRACKET AMOUNT   The terminology "zero bracket amount" was first introduced into the law in 1977 as part of Carter's tax simplification plan. Before 1977, the law provided for a "standard deduction." People who worked with the tax law prior to 1977 will undoubtedly continue, from time to time, to refer to the zero bracket amount as the standard deduction. Students should be aware of the fact that the two terms mean the same thing.

The zero bracket amounts are:

Single individuals	$2,300
Married individuals (and surviving spouses)	3,400
Married individuals filing separately	1,700

Refer to the rate schedules in Appendix A. On Schedule X, which applies to most single taxpayers, the initial bracket begins at $2,300, the zero bracket amount for single individuals. Similarly, the first bracket on Schedule Y (Married Filing Joint Returns) begins at $3,400. Finally, note that on Schedule Y (Married Filing Separate Returns) the first bracket begins at $1,700, which is one-half the amount allowed on a joint return. As you can see, this "automatic" deduction, the zero bracket amount, is incorporated directly into the rate schedules. As a result, only the itemized or personal deductions, if any, in excess of the zero bracket amount are deducted in the calculation of taxable income. If a single individual has itemized deductions of $2,000, the law provides for a minimum allowance of $2,300, the zero bracket amount, by levying a tax on taxable income in excess of $2,300. A single individual with itemized deductions of $3,000 deducts only $700 because, again, the rate schedule has a built-in automatic deduction of $2,300.

In certain situations, the law provides that taxpayers are not entitled to the zero bracket amount or are entitled to only part of it. The most common situation encountered has to do with a child of a taxpayer who has income and must file a return. As explained later relative to the gross income test for dependents, a child who is under 19 or who is a full-time student gets an exemption on his or her return and the parent also gets an exemption for the child provided the other tests for dependency are met. The law provides that when this double "exemption" occurs, the child is entitled to offset adjusted gross income by the zero bracket amount only to the extent of *earned* income, usually salary or wages. This disallowance of the zero bracket amount is necessary to prevent possible abuses by more affluent parents. If the dependent child were entitled to both the personal exemption *and* the zero bracket amount, the child could have income of $3,300 without paying a tax. This $3,300 is the sum of the $2,300 zero bracket amount plus the $1,000 exemption. A parent, for example, could give the child income-producing assets, such as cash in a savings account, corporate stocks, or bonds, and "shelter" the income from taxation. Assuming an 8 percent interest rate on a savings account, a gift of $41,250 could be made to each child, effectively avoiding the tax on a sizable amount of income from capital. The allowance of the zero bracket amount for only earned income in this situation gives rise to an "unused" zero bracket amount, which is an *addition* to A.G.I. to determine tax table income or taxable income.

To illustrate, assume that Jim, age 16 and a dependent of his parents, earns $900 from a part-time job and has interest income of $2,500 from a savings account. For simplicity, assume that Jim has no deductions for A.G.I. and no itemized deductions. Calculation of Jim's taxable income would be:

Gross income:		
Wages earned		$ 900
Interest income		2,500
Adjusted gross income		$3,400

Excess itemized deductions		-0-
Add: "Unused" zero bracket amount:		
Zero bracket amount for a single individual	$2,300	
Less: Earned income	900	1,400
Tax table income		$4,800
Less: One exemption deduction		1,000
Taxable income		$3,800

If the $1,400 is not added back, Jim's taxable income would be $2,400, the adjusted gross income less the $1,000 exemption, and Jim would have no tax liability because the tax is levied only on income in excess of the zero bracket amount. After adding back the "unused" zero bracket amount, the taxable income exceeds the zero bracket amount by $1,500 ($3,800 taxable income less $2,300), and that is the amount of the passive interest income of $2,500 less the $1,000 exemption deduction. This $1,500 is subject to the tax and cannot be offset by the zero bracket amount.

The necessity of adding back the unused zero bracket amount can also arise when married individuals file separate returns. If one spouse takes itemized deductions in excess of the zero bracket amount, the other spouse will have an unused zero bracket amount if his or her itemized deductions are less than $1,700. Finally, the unused zero bracket amount can arise in certain instances where nonresident aliens have U.S. source income and when taxpayers have exempt income from U.S. possessions.

Thus, the law provides that, without regard to the actual amounts spent by a taxpayer for personal living expenses, no tax is levied unless the taxpayer's A.G.I. exceeds the exemption deduction *plus* the zero bracket amount. Furthermore, if a taxpayer's *allowed* itemized or personal deductions exceed the zero bracket amount, such excess further reduces the tax base. The allowed itemized deductions include expenses incurred in transactions for profit under Sec. 212 and certain specific personal expenses such as medical expenses, contributions, interest, and taxes. These itemized deductions are considered in detail in Part Four.

The proper classification of an individual's deductions between those *for* A.G.I. and those *from* A.G.I. is critical if the maximum deduction *from* A.G.I. is to be obtained. Note first that the zero bracket amount is not related to the taxpayer's actual expenditures. Thus, if deductions are incorrectly classified as from A.G.I., the taxpayer may elect to take the larger itemized deductions, whereas a correct classification might permit some items to be deducted for A.G.I. and still permit the use of the zero bracket amount. To illustrate, assume that a bachelor has gross income of $9,000, all from wages, and allowable deductions of $2,400 consisting of $1,000 of employee transportation and travel plus $1,400 of personal interest, taxes, and contributions. If the deductions are all classified as from A.G.I., the taxpayer would elect to itemize, giving him a deduction of only $100 in excess of the zero bracket amount ($2,400 – $2,300). If the $1,000 spent for transportation and travel are correctly classified, however, the taxpayer's A.G.I. is $8,000 ($9,000 of gross income less $1,000 of deductions for A.G.I.). The taxpayer would still be entitled to the zero bracket amount of $2,300. The net effect is an increase in his total deductions to $3,300 ($1,000 for A.G.I. plus the $2,300 zero bracket amount) and a decrease in taxable income of $900.

The correct classification of deductions can also be important for taxpayers whose itemized deductions are clearly greater than the zero bracket amount. As explained in Part Four, medical expenses are generally deductible only if they exceed 3 percent of A.G.I. Thus, the correct classification of a deduction that lowers A.G.I. will automatically increase the medical deduction. The amount of A.G.I. affects in a similar manner other deductions and some credits.

TAX TABLE INCOME   In past years, taxpayers have often made mechanical errors in the calculation of their gross tax liability based on the rate schedules in Appendix A. To reduce these errors, the rules are now structured in a way that substantially increases the number of taxpayers who determine their gross tax liability from the tax tables reproduced in Appendix B. Unlike the rate schedules whose use requires both a multiplication and an addition, the tables only require the taxpayer to locate the correct income bracket and the correct column based on the number of exemptions allowed. The critical question is: Under what circumstances must a taxpayer determine his or her gross tax based on the tax rate tables? Use of the tables is not *optional,* and those taxpayers not required to use the tables calculate their gross tax based on the rate schedules.

The key to answering the preceding question is calculation of tax table income. Tax table income is:

Adjusted gross income
Less: Deduction *from* A.G.I.—excess, if any, of itemized deductions over the appropriate zero bracket amounts, *equals*
Tax table income

For many individuals, tax table income is the same as adjusted gross income because the zero bracket amount exceeds the amount of deductions *from* A.G.I. The following rules specify the individuals who must use the tax tables *for 1979* (the 1980 tables were not available when this was written):

Filing status	Tax table income is equal to or less than	Exemptions claimed are equal to or less than
Single individual	$20,000	3
Married individual filing jointly	40,000	9
Married individual filing separately	20,000	3
Head-of-household	20,000	8

When the tax tables are used, the resulting tax liability takes into account (1) the zero bracket amount and (2) the deduction for exemptions. Any "unused" zero bracket amount must be added back to arrive at tax table income.

Personal and dependent exemptions

Individuals are allowed a $1,000 deduction for each exemption provided by the law. For many years, this amount was only $600 until increased to $750 in 1975 and increased again to $1,000 in 1979. The specific question of how many exemptions the taxpayer may claim must now be answered. Personal exemptions fit into four categories:

1. An exemption for the taxpayer.
2. An exemption for the taxpayer's spouse.
3. Extra exemptions for the taxpayer or spouse who is blind and/or 65 years of age or over.
4. An exemption for each "dependent" of the taxpayer.

EXEMPTION FOR THE TAXPAYER   A basic exemption is *always* allowed the taxpayer, whether he or she is married or single, has a tax liability or not, and even though, in a few cases, the taxpayer may be claimed as a dependent of another taxpayer.

EXEMPTION FOR THE TAXPAYER'S SPOUSE   As explained later, a married couple will usually file a joint return. When a joint return is used, both spouses are considered to be "taxpayers," and each is entitled to an exemption of $1,000. Thus, there is always a minimum of $2,000 in personal exemptions on the joint return. If only one spouse files a return, that spouse may claim an exemption for the other spouse only if the latter has *no* gross income and is *not* claimed as a dependent of another taxpayer. Obviously, if spouses file separate returns, neither may take an exemption for the other.

"EXTRA" EXEMPTIONS   The taxpayer is entitled to an extra exemption of $1,000 beginning with the year he or she reaches the age of 65. (Technically, a taxpayer whose birthday falls on January 1 is considered to be 65 on the preceding December 31.) A similar extra exemption for age is allowed for the taxpayer's spouse who is 65 or over. If the taxpayer or spouse is blind at the end of the tax year, another extra exemption is allowed. Thus, exemptions for the taxpayer and spouse may total as much as $6,000—if, that is, both are 65 or older and both are blind.

The economic rationale behind extra exemptions for age and blindness is obvious: the blind and aged will presumably have higher living expenses and relatively low incomes. However, these provisions have been characterized as "makeshift welfare legislation" and have been criticized by many economists and tax experts, primarily on the basis that they are allowed to all the aged and all the blind without regard to need.[2]

EXEMPTIONS FOR DEPENDENTS   The rules governing exemption deductions for dependents are much more complex and difficult to interpret and apply than those relating to exemptions for the taxpayer and spouse. As a result, there have been many controversies on this point between taxpayers and the I.R.S., and numerous court decisions involving dependency exemptions have been reported. Although subject to many exceptions and special interpretations, there are five basic conditions or requirements that must be satisfied in order for the taxpayer to claim an exemption for a "dependent":

1. The dependent must *not* be a nonresident alien.

2. The dependent, if married, must not file a joint return with his or her spouse.

3. A specified "relationship" must exist between the taxpayer and the dependent.

4. The taxpayer must provide over one-half of the dependent's support for the year.

5. The dependent must have gross income of less than $1,000—the amount of an exemption for the year.

The first two requirements need no interpretation. The last three, however, require further explanation and elaboration.

The relationship test. The Internal Revenue Code generally provides that the dependent must be a *relative* of the taxpayer and delimits the necessary relationship as follows:

(1) A son or daughter of the taxpayer, or a descendant of either,
(2) A stepson or stepdaughter of the taxpayer,
(3) A brother, sister, stepbrother, or stepsister of the taxpayer,
(4) The father or mother of the taxpayer, or an ancestor of either,
(5) A stepfather or stepmother of the taxpayer,
(6) A son or daughter of a brother or sister of the taxpayer,
(7) A brother or sister of the father or mother of the taxpayer,
(8) A son-in-law, daughter-in-law, father-in-law, mother-in-law, brother-in-law, or sister-in-law of the taxpayer.[3]

When a joint return is filed, the relationship test is met if the person claimed as a dependent is a qualified relative of either spouse. Even after termination of a marriage, a relationship established by the marriage is continued for tax purposes. Finally, an adopted child is treated as a natural child for dependency purposes.

The law goes further, however, to make provision for the taxpayer to claim an exemption for an individual who *resides in* the taxpayer's home throughout a tax year, even though not a relative as specified above.

(9) An individual (other than an individual who at any time during the taxable year was the spouse, determined without regard to section 153, of the taxpayer) who, for the taxable year of the taxpayer, has as his principal place of abode the home of the taxpayer and is a member of the taxpayer's household. . . .[4]

This provision of the law permits dependency exemptions for persons, such as foster children not legally adopted, or foster parents, who do not meet the relationship test in (1) through (8). Under the

---

[2]For additional discussion of the special exemptions for the aged and blind, see Groves, *op. cit.,* pp 45–55; Wilbur J. Cohen, "Income and Tax Status of the Aged: Present Situation and Possible Modifications of Exising Policies," *1959 Compendium,* pp. 539–50; Eveline M. Burns, "Taxation of the Aged: Retirement Income Credit and the Like," *1959 Compendium,* pp. 552–53; and Joseph A. Pechman, *Federal Tax Policy* (Washington, D.C.: The Brookings Institution, 1966), pp. 85–86.

[3]Code Sec. 152(a)(1)–(8).
[4]Code Sec. 152(a)(9).

1969 Reform Act, foster children who meet the test of residence above are treated in all respects as though they were blood relatives of the taxpayer.

This provision does not apply if the relationship with the taxpayer is contrary to local law. For example, if state law prohibits common-law marriage, no exemption can be claimed for the taxpayer's consort. Children born into such an arrangement, however, can be dependents.

The support test. The taxpayer must provide over one-half the dollar value of the support of the dependent during the calendar year (or that part of the year that the dependent was alive). Support includes all expenditures for such items as food, clothing, shelter, medical care, education, and child care. A scholarship received by a student who is the taxpayer's child is not counted as part of the total support in determining whether the taxpayer provided more than half the student's support.

The major exception to the support test occurs when two or more persons furnish a dependent's support but no one taxpayer provides over half the support. In this event, any one of the taxpayers who provided over 10 percent of the dependent's support and who satisfies the relationship test may claim the exemption if every person who provides more than 10 percent of the dependent's support during the year, and who satisfies the relationship test, will sign a multiple support statement agreeing *not* to claim an exemption for the dependent. For example, if each of four brothers provides 25 percent of his father's support, any one of the four may claim the father as a dependent for the year provided the other three will sign a multiple support agreement.

If both divorced parents contribute support for their child or children, the parent who has custody for the major part of the calendar year is generally presumed to have provided more than 50 percent of the support. There are two exceptions to this presumption: (1) If the divorce decree provides, or if the parents enter into a written agreement not included in the divorce decree, that the parent not having custody shall be entitled to the exemption, the noncustodial parent will be entitled to the exemption for the child named in the decree or agreement provided the noncustodial parent actually provides at least $600 toward support of that child during the year. Note that $600 or more must be paid for each child under this exemption. (2) The second exception provides that the noncustodial parent is deemed to be entitled to the exemption deduction for each child for which he or she contributes at least $1,200 of support

unless the parent having custody can establish clearly that she or he provided more than half support.

The gross-income test. Section 151(e) provides that generally the dependent's gross income must be less than the amount of an exemption allowance for that year ($1,000 at present) in order for the taxpayer to claim an exemption for him or her. This rule does not apply to a taxpayer's child, or qualified foster child, who is either a full-time student *or* under age 19 at the close of the year. Generally, a "student" is defined as one who during each of any five months of the calendar year was in full-time attendance at an educational institution or took a full-time, on-farm training course during any five months of the year. The taxpayer's child who is either a student or under 19 and has sufficient gross income must, of course, file a tax return. On this return, the child may claim an exemption for himself or herself even though he or she also is claimed as a dependent by parents.

These exceptions to the gross-income test are designed to encourage students to earn an income, to encourage education or farm training, and to aid those with greatest financial need (where children must work to aid the family). These special provisions, however, like many others, may be criticized as rather inefficient devices to obtain worthy objectives. The basic criticism is that students who are the children of poor parents may have to earn more than half their expenses, but this deprives their parents of exemptions for them. Wealthier parents, on the other hand, whose children need earn far less, are thus assured of the dual exemptions.[5]

Computation of the tax liability

As explained above, most taxpayers will compute their tax table income and then determine their tax based on the tax tables in Appendix B. The tables in Appendix B are those applicable to 1979. Individuals who use the rate schedules must calculate their taxable income as illustrated earlier. Note that taxable income is tax table income less the exemption deduction. The rate schedules in Appendix A apply to 1979 and later years.

Once the gross tax liability is computed in the above manner, the credits and prepayments discussed in Chapter 8 are subtracted to determine the net tax or the amount of refund.

---

[5]An excellent criticism of these provisions may be found in C. Lowell Harriss, "Parent and Child—and Taxes: Some Problems in Dependency," *1959 Compendium*, pp. 531–35. A similar presentation may be found in Groves, *op. cit.*, pp. 39–43.

THE FAMILY AS TAXPAYER

The original selection of the individual as a basic taxpaying entity was virtually dictated by the property laws in this country. Excepting corporations for the moment, most property is owned by individuals, and the income from property benefits individuals. Similarly, only individuals are employed and earn income. Most personal income, however, is not used or consumed solely by the individual with the legal right to it. Instead, it goes into the family "coffers" and is used by the family. From 1913 to the present, Congress has made an effort to give consideration to the family situation in levying the tax.

When Congress wrote the first law, it had in mind as the taxpayer the usual case of a mature male adult, the head of a family and its principal wage earner. The original law provided for a basic family exemption that would leave "untouched" income sufficient to "rear and support" a family according to "a proper standard of living."[6] The exemption originally established was very high relative to the average family income of the period, and most personal income was therefore not subject to tax prior to World War II. At that time, however, Congress lowered the exemptions, ostensibly to finance the war but primarily in fact to control inflation. Exemptions were left at the lower levels after the war for the same purpose. As a result, the income tax was transformed from one that affected only 4 percent of the population in the boom year 1929 to one that affected 70 percent of the population in the middle 1950s.[7]

Between World War II and 1969, Congress resisted all efforts to increase exemptions. Beginning with the Tax Reform Acts of 1969 and 1971, as well as in later amendments, the exemptions were increased as was the standard deduction or zero bracket amount. These changes reaffirm the original policy of taxing the family as the basic taxable unit.

In the period immediately following World War II, changes in rates were made to reduce the tax on family units and to recognize the special circumstances of widows, widowers, and other unmarried individuals who maintain homes for relatives. In dealing with the problem of rates, Congress settled

on a "normal" progression of events for most citizens. First, single individuals with no direct family responsibilities use Rate Schedule X, which results in the highest tax.[8] Next comes marriage and a family where the husband and wife file jointly and generally enjoy the lowest rates on Schedule Y—Joint. In the event of the death of one spouse before the children are fully grown, the surviving spouse still enjoys low joint return rates for a two-year period. After the two-year period, the surviving spouse who still maintains a residence for his or her children becomes a head-of-household and enjoys approximately 50 percent of the benefits available from the joint return rates by using Schedule Z. Finally, after all family responsibilities are met, and assuming no remarriage, the taxpayer is again "single" and subject to the highest rates.

This simple scheme of things is, of course, subject to many exceptions. In addition, Congress did not hit upon the scheme and then enact the law as it now exists. As is often true, Congress rather wandered into the present framework over a period of years. Indeed, the first step, the joint return provisions, was passed to avoid a problem arising from state property laws.

Income splitting

Eight states have traditionally been community-property states—Arizona, California, Idaho, Louisiana, Nevada, New Mexico, Texas, and Washington. In a state with community-property laws, all income from personal services earned by either spouse is deemed to be earned in equal parts by both and is called community income. In addition, income from community property is community income. In several community-property states, even the income from separate property (property owned prior to the union or property received by gift or inheritance during the union) is treated as community income. Prior to 1948, the institution of community property permitted a couple to split their income between them and thus achieve a significant reduction in their federal income tax liability.

A brief illustration of the effects of income splitting is shown in Table 9-1. The illustration assumes that husband A resides in a noncommunity-property

---

[6]Everett M. Kassalow, "To Restore Balance and Equity in Family Income Taxation," *1959 Compendium,* p. 515, deals with the development of this doctrine.

[7]For detailed statistics on this shift, see L. H. Seltzer, "The Place of the Personal Exemptions in the Present-Day Income Tax," *1959 Compendium,* pp. 493–514.

[8]Actually, the rates on Schedule Y—Separate result in the highest tax. However, this is a historical accident.

TABLE **9-1**

THE ADVANTAGE OF INCOME SPLITTING

	Noncommunity property	Community property	
	Husband A	Husband B	Wife
Taxable income	$50,000	$25,000	$25,000
Tax	20,999	7,389	7,389
Total tax on B's income		$14,778	
Tax saving of B and wife ($20,999 − $14,778)		$ 6,221	

NOTE: While this illustration is based on rates in effect for 1979 (using basic rate schedule Y, separate returns, from Appendix A), the general result is the same because a similar progressive schedule was in effect prior to 1948.

state; husband B lives in a state with community-property laws, and there is only one rate schedule for individual taxpayers. Both families have a net taxable income of $50,000 provided entirely by the husband. Husband B and his wife would split the income, whereas husband A would carry the entire burden. The difference of $6,221 shown by the illustration is sizable.

Prior to World War II, the low tax rates, the high level of exemptions, and the relatively low level of family incomes combined to exempt most families from the tax. During the war and the years immediately afterward, higher rates and incomes and lower exemptions made income splitting important to many people. States without community-property laws began to make the inevitable change. By 1948, Oklahoma, Hawaii, Oregon, Nebraska, and Michigan had adopted community property, and it became evident to Congress that many others would follow suit unless Congress amended the law to remove the inequity.

The solution, added to the law in 1948, was a typical political one: The benefits of income splitting were extended to taxpayers in all states. Under the new rule, which is still in effect, a husband and wife may file a joint return and compute their tax as follows:

$$2\left[\frac{\text{Net taxable income of both}}{2} \times \begin{array}{l}\text{Rate per} \\ \text{Schedule Y—Separate}\end{array}\right]$$
$$= \text{Joint tax liability}$$

This computation gives the same result as filing separate returns with the net taxable income split equally between husband and wife. The joint tax liability can be obtained directly by using Rate Schedule Y—Joint.

The statute provides criteria that must be met before a taxpayer may elect to use the joint return. Two taxpayers may file a joint return if

1. They are married (not divorced or legally separated) on the last day of their taxable year, or they were married at the date of death of one spouse during the taxable year.

2. Neither spouse is a nonresident alien unless an irrevocable election is made to include the worldwide income of both husband and wife on the return.

Note that a joint return is permitted for the tax year within which one spouse dies, provided the survivor does not remarry before the end of the year.

In 1954 Congress recognized that the death of a spouse often causes economic hardship, especially if children are left in the home, and extended the benefits of income splitting by permitting the surviving spouse to use Schedule Y—Joint in the two years following the tax year in which the spouse dies, provided the surviving spouse has a dependent child or stepchild who lives with the taxpayer in the home. Of course, an exemption for the deceased spouse is not available on the return of the surviving spouse during those two years. The special status of surviving spouse is automatically terminated after the two-year period, by remarriage during the period, or by the loss of the dependency status of the child or stepchild.

For example, suppose that in 19x1 taxpayer's wife died, leaving in the home a 14-year-old child who qualifies as the survivor's dependent. In the year of death, taxpayer and the deceased spouse are entitled to file a joint return and claim three exemptions (one each for taxpayer, deceased spouse, and dependent child). If the child continues to live in taxpayer's home and to qualify as a dependent, the taxpayer will be entitled to use Schedule Y—Joint in 19x2 and 19x3 as well, but will be entitled to only two exemptions (one for the taxpayer and one for the dependent child) in those two years.

Head of household

An even earlier attempt to mitigate the tax effect on individuals who have family responsibilities was made by Congress in 1951. By extending the joint-return privilege to married taxpayers only, Congress ignored the case of widows and widowers as well as other individuals who have the responsibility for rearing children or maintaining a home for dependents. The increase in tax rates (above even the levels of World War II) occasioned by the Korean conflict and the attendant inflationary pressures magnified the conflict in Congress over income splitting. When Congress was asked to extend the benefits of income splitting to all family units, the compromise finally reached was the creation of Rate Schedule Z for taxpayers who meet the statutory tests for head of household. The new schedule gives the qualified taxpayers approximately 50 percent of the tax savings available from income splitting.

The major requirements for using the Head of Household rate schedule are

1. At the end of the tax year, the taxpayer cannot be classified as a married taxpayer or as a "surviving spouse." (However, as discussed later in this section, certain married persons living apart may be entitled to use the Head of Household rate schedule. In addition, in certain circumstances a taxpayer married to a nonresident alien may qualify.)

2. The taxpayer must maintain a home in which lives a relative, who is a dependent as defined in Sec. 152. However, if the relative is (a) a son or daughter, including a legally adopted child, or one of their descendants, (b) a stepchild, or (c) a foster child, the relative does not have to qualify as a dependent if he or she is unmarried. Any other relative must qualify as the taxpayer's dependent. Another exception exists in connection with the requirement that the relative must be a member of the taxpayer's home. If the relative is the taxpayer's parent, the parent need not live with the taxpayer.

3. The taxpayer must pay more than 50 percent of the cost of maintaining the home.

4. The taxpayer must be a citizen or resident alien.

As mentioned previously, the Head of Household rate table may also be used by a *married* person who meets certain special tests. These requirements are

1. The taxpayer must file a separate return.

2. Taxpayer must maintain a home that for the entire taxable year is the principal place of abode of a dependent child or stepchild for whom the taxpayer is entitled to a dependency exemption.

3. Taxpayer must furnish more than half the cost of maintaining the home.

4. Taxpayer's spouse must not live in the household at any time during the tax year.

This provision is apparently designed to provide a tax break for "abandoned" spouses, but is broad enough to include other married persons who simply choose to live apart but for some reason do not wish to file a joint return.

To illustrate application of the Head of Household requirement, let us return to the facts previously given in which taxpayer's spouse died in 19x1 leaving a dependent child who resides in the taxpayer's home. In 19x1 the taxpayer filed a joint return with the decedent, and in 19x2 and 19x3 taxpayer filed as a surviving spouse but was not entitled to an exemption for the deceased spouse. In 19x4 and later years, the taxpayer may use the Head of Household rate schedule if the child continues to reside in the household and taxpayer provides more than one-half the cost of maintaining the household. Even though the child may not qualify as taxpayer's dependent, taxpayer may still file as head of household unless the child is married.

The single individual

Married taxpayers enjoy the benefits of income splitting in all situations. The privilege is not affected by the level of income or by the number of family members. For this reason, some unmarried taxpayers claim that the joint-return rates are inequitable. In the upper middle and upper income brackets, only a minimal sacrifice is required to raise a family of the average size. Certainly it can be argued that a married man with no children who earns a salary of $50,000 a year is just as *able* to pay the income tax as a bachelor with the same income. One might argue that the bachelor's expenses are perhaps higher than the incremental amount spent by a married man as a result of being married.

The happily *unmarried* group finally got the ear of Congress in 1969, possibly because their numbers have increased in recent years but probably because of an organized lobby. For years after 1970, single individuals who are not heads of households may use Rate Schedule X. This schedule is basically the same as Rate Schedule Y—Separate except marginal rates are slightly lower in the middle income brackets. The decrease in the tax, while less than that from income splitting, can be significant.

It is interesting to observe that Rate Schedule X will, in a limited number of cases, introduce a new inequity. The new inequity will arise only when two persons are each earning a significant and approximately equal amount of taxable income and decide to marry. To illustrate, assume that two physicians married at a time when they were each earning a taxable income of $41,500. According to Rate Schedule X, their combined tax prior to their marriage would amount to $26,784 (2 × $13,392). After they were married, the tax on the same total income would amount to $32,098 (calculated from Rate Schedule Y—Joint). Thus, the new law penalizes this couple $5,314 per year for getting married. Whether or not that is sufficient penalty to cause many couples to live together without the benefit of a marriage ceremony remains to be seen.

A scheme that received some notoriety in the popular press illustrates the ingenuity of taxpayers and the extreme measures that some citizens will take to lower taxes. In late December, a married couple, both with substantial income, board a plane bound for a sunny Caribbean island and obtain a quick divorce under the lenient laws in that jurisdiction. Following a nice vacation, they return to their chilly homeland no longer man and wife. They then file as unmarried individuals, declare their incomes separately, and use the rates on Schedule X. Their combined tax is lower, as explained in the preceding paragraph, and the savings are enough to pay for the vacation. After filing, they remarry and live happily ever after. Not quite. The Internal Revenue Service has ruled[9] that divorces under these circumstances will be ignored as a sham having as their only purpose tax avoidance.

Married individuals filing separately

The law provides that married individuals may file separate returns. Only under most unusual circumstances will separate returns result in a lower tax, because Congress has taken great pains to close possible loopholes. Note that on separate returns the zero bracket amount is half the amount for joint returns. In a similar manner, most other possible advantages are eliminated by the statute. For the most part, married individuals filing separate returns

[9] *Rev. Rul.* 76-255, 1976-2 CB 40.

do so because of marital or financial disagreements that have not yet reached the point of divorce or legal separation. On a joint return, both spouses are jointly and severally liable for the *combined* tax, a legal obligation that one spouse may be unwilling to assume even if it results in a higher tax on his or her own income.

Sources of discontent

The compromise reached in Congress in the Reform Act of 1969, which lowered some marginal rates for single individuals, left many taxpayers discontent with the rate structures. Heads of household still think they should be taxed like other families, and single individuals still complain about the higher taxes they pay relative to married individuals with comparable incomes. What we have in the proliferation of rate schedules is an attempt to achieve horizontal equity using a base (income) that presumably assures vertical equity. But one fact is clear. We cannot have a separate schedule for every conceivable degree of family responsibility.

We must remember that the concept of a second rate schedule was a compromise to eliminate inequities between taxpayers in community-property states and those in other states. That Congress chose to solve that problem in that manner in 1948, we believe, is most unfortunate. The best solution to the problem lies in recognition of families as the basic taxable entities. Inequities because of family size and responsibility should be resolved through changes in basic exemptions or by tax credits.

COMPLIANCE CONSIDERATIONS

This final section on the basic rules for individual taxpayers treats some rules related to compliance. Given a knowledge of the zero bracket amount and the deduction for exemptions, we can now determine those individuals who must file a return. Then, the tax formula for individuals will be illustrated. Finally, there is an example illustrating completion of the simplest return form for individuals, Form 1040A.

Who must file

As mentioned earlier in this chapter, an individual whose *gross income* is below a specified amount is not required to file a return. Given the rules for exemptions and the zero bracket amount, it is obvious that certain taxpayers would never have a gross tax liability. The amounts listed below are for 1979 and later years:

	Gross income
Single, and under 65 years of age	$3,300
Single, and 65 years or older	4,300
Single, and claimed as a dependent on parent's return, and having taxable dividends, interest, or other unearned income	1,000
Qualified surviving spouse under 65	4,400
Qualified surviving spouse over 64	5,400
Married couple filing jointly, both under 65	5,400
Married couple filing jointly, one spouse over 64	6,400
Married couple filing jointly, both over 64	7,400

As explained above, a single individual who is a dependent of another and has unearned income (dividends, interest, etc.) must file a return if gross income exceeds $1,000. The law provides that the zero bracket amount can only be used to offset earned income.

Individuals whose gross incomes are below these amounts may, of course, elect to file a return to obtain a refund withheld from wages or to take advantage of the earned income credit. Remember, the test of who must file a return is based on *gross income,* not on adjusted gross income or taxable income.

The combination of the exemption deduction and the zero bracket amount sets an income "floor" for individuals that presumably represents a minimal subsistence level. The question of whether this "floor" is adequate and the equity of using deductions in this context are discussed in Chapter 12.

The individual's formula illustrated

To illustrate the general tax formula applicable to the individual taxpayer, consider the following income-tax-related items assumed for a given tax year:

Marital status: married (files jointly)
Number of exemptions: 4
(husband, wife, and two young children)
Income:

Salary	$10,000
Raffle prize	500
Employee travel allowance	1,800
Dividends (from domestic corporations)	50
Interest (from local bank)	100

Deductions:

Employee travel expenses	2,000
Charitable contributions	500
Interest paid	200
Real property taxes (on residence)	200

Prepayment:

Tax withheld from salary	490

Plugging the above data into the tax formula for individual taxpayers, we find that the net tax payable of this imaginary taxpayer is a negative $56; that is, the taxpayer is entitled to a refund of this amount. The solution is presented in Table 9-2. Note once again that the arithmetic in this formula is straightforward; the definitions and classifications prerequisite to the arithmetic are the complicating factors.

Return illustration—short form 1040A

The simplest return form available to the individual is Short Form 1040A. To use this form in 1977 and later years, the following conditions must be met:

1. The gross income of the taxpayer must be from the following sources only:
   a. Wages, salaries, etc., subject to withholding, but without limit as to the amount.
   b. Dividend income, but not in excess of $400.
   c. Interest income, but not in excess of $400.
2. The taxpayer may not report itemized deductions in excess of the zero bracket amount.

In addition to these restrictions, this form limits the credits that can be taken to include only the earned-income credit, the general tax credit, and the credit for political contributions. Taxpayers who have more than one employer can also secure a refund of F.I.C.A. taxes on Form 1040A if the amounts withheld exceed the maximum limit on this tax. Typically, this form is used by taxpayers in the middle and lower groups who use the tax tables. There is no limit on the amount of income that can be reported on Form 1040A, however, provided the income is from the sources listed above and provided the taxpayer does not have itemized deductions in excess of the zero bracket amount.

To illustrate the use of the form, assume the following facts:

Tom Jones, unmarried, age 30, and with good sight, has the following sources of income:

Wages subject to withholdings	$10,000
Dividends from taxable domestic corporations	350
Interest on savings accounts	200

TABLE **9-2**
USING THE INDIVIDUAL FORMULA

Income broadly conceived	$12,450	($10,000 + 500 + 1,800 + 50 + 100)
less		
↓		
Exclusions	(50)	(Dividends—up to $100/taxpayer per year)
↓		
equals		
↓		
Gross income	$12,400	
less		
↓		
Deductions for A.G.I.	(2,000)	(Employee travel "away from home")
equals		
↓		
A.G.I.	$10,400	
less		
↓		
Deductions from A.G.I.	-0-	(Excess over zero bracket amount)[a]
equals		
↓		
Tax Table Income	$10,400	
less		
↓		
Personal and Dependent Exemptions	(4,000)	($1,000 × 4)
equals		
↓		
Taxable Income	$6,400	
times		
Tax Rate	—	(Tax tables)[b]
↓		
equals		
↓		
Gross Tax	$434	
less		
↓		
Tax Credits and Prepayments	(490)	(Tax withheld from salary)
equals		
↓		
Net Tax Payable	($56)	(Refund due taxpayer)

[a] The zero bracket amount of $3,400 exceeds the actual itemized deductions.
[b] The tax tables for 1979 must be used based on the tax table income because that amount is less than $40,000 and the exemptions are less than 10.

Form **1040A**

Department of the Treasury—Internal Revenue Service
U.S. Individual Income Tax Return **1979**

Use IRS label. Other- wise, please print or type.	Your first name and initial (if joint return, also give spouse's name and initial)	Last name	Your social security number
	Tom J.	*Jones*	234 45 4567
	Present home address (Number and street, including apartment number, or rural route) *2101 Montrose Avenue*		Spouse's social security no.
	City, town or post office, State and ZIP code *Sometown, State 10201*	Your occupation ▶ *printer* Spouse's occupation ▶	

Presidential Election Campaign Fund ▶

Do you want $1 to go to this fund? . . . . [ ] Yes [////] [ ] No

If joint return, does your spouse want $1 to go to this fund? [ ] Yes [////] [ ] No

Note: Checking "Yes" will not increase your tax or reduce your refund.

Filing Status

Check Only One Box.

1 [✓] Single
2 [ ] Married filing joint return (even if only one had income)
3 [ ] Married filing separate return. Enter spouse's social security number above and full name here ▶
4 [ ] Head of household. (See page 8 of Instructions.) If qualifying person is your unmarried child, enter child's name ▶

For Privacy Act Notice, see page 14 of Instructions

Exemptions

Always check the box labeled Your- self. Check other boxes if they apply.

5a [✓] Yourself [ ] 65 or over [ ] Blind
b [ ] Spouse [ ] 65 or over [ ] Blind

Enter number of boxes checked on 5a and b ▶ | 1 |

c First names of your dependent children who lived with you ▶

Enter number of children listed ▶ | |

d Other dependents:		(3) Number of months lived in your home.	(4) Did dependent have income of $1,000 or more?	(5) Did you provide more than one-half of depend- ent's support?
(1) Name	(2) Relationship			

Enter number of other dependents ▶ | |

6 Total number of exemptions claimed . . . .

Add numbers entered in boxes above ▶ | 1 |

7	Wages, salaries, tips, etc. (Attach Forms W–2. If you do not have a W–2, see page 10 of Instructions)	**7**	10,000	00
8	Interest income (See pages 4 and 10 of Instructions)	**8**	200	00
9a	Dividends *350 00* (See pages 4 and 10 of Instructions) 9b Exclusion *100 00* Subtract line 9b from 9a	**9c**	250	00
10a	Unemployment compensation. Total amount received			
b	Taxable part, if any, from worksheet on page 11 of Instructions	**10b**		
11	Adjusted gross income (add lines 7, 8, 9c, and 10b). If under $10,000, see page 2 of In- structions on "Earned Income Credit"	**11**	10,450	00
12a	Credit for contributions to candidates for public office. (See page 11 of Instructions) . . . . **12a** *25 00* IF YOU WANT IRS TO FIGURE YOUR TAX, PLEASE STOP HERE AND SIGN BELOW.			
b	Total Federal income tax withheld (If line 7 is more than $22,900, see page 12 of Instructions) **12b** *1,450 00*			
c	Earned income credit (from page 2 of Instructions) **12c**			
13	Total (add lines 12a, b, and c)	**13**	1,475	00
14a	Tax on the amount on line 11. (See Instructions for line 14a on page 12; then find your tax in the Tax Tables on pages 15–26.) **14a** *1,266 00*			
b	Advance earned income credit payments received (from Form W–2) **14b**			
15	Total (add lines 14a and 14b).	**15**	1,266	00
16	If line 13 is larger than line 15, enter amount to be **REFUNDED TO YOU** . . . . ▶	**16**	209	00
17	If line 15 is larger than line 13, enter **BALANCE DUE.** Attach check or money order for full amount payable to "Internal Revenue Service." Write your social security number on check or money order . ▶	**17**		

Under penalties of perjury, I declare that I have examined this return, including accompanying schedules and statements, and to the best of my knowledge and belief it is true, correct, and complete. Declaration of preparer (other than taxpayer) is based on all information of which preparer has any knowledge.

▶ *Tom Jones*   *4-10-80* ▶
Your signature   Date   Spouse's signature (if filing jointly, BOTH must sign even if only one had income)

Paid Preparer's Information	Preparer's signature and date ▶		Check if self-em- ployed ▶ [ ]	Preparer's social security no.
	Firm's name (or yours, if self-employed) and address ▶		E.I. No. ▶	
			ZIP code ▶	

☆ U.S. GOVERNMENT PRINTING OFFICE: 1979—O-283-370 E. I. NO. 73-0667115

Form **1040A** (1979)

Please Attach Copy B of Forms W–2 Here

Attach Payment Here

Please Sign Here

Tom's itemized deductions are less than the zero bracket amount. He contributed $50 to the political campaign of a candidate for the presidential nomination. Tom's W-2 shows withholdings of $1,450 for 1979.

To prevent repetition, identification information is shown on the completed return. Note that Tom gets the $100 dividend exclusion. Further, Tom's gross tax was determined by reference to tax tables in Appendix B. The final result is a gross tax of $1,266, which is reduced by the prepayments and credits, resulting in a refund of $209.

PROBLEMS

1. Jim and Mary Barlow are married and have one daughter, Kristin, who is one year old. During the current year, Jim worked for Ace Corporation and earned $8,000; Mary sold cosmetics part-time and earned $1,000. Kris, an unusually beautiful one-year-old, modeled infants' clothing for the Best Department Store and earned $3,000. How many taxpayers are there in the Barlow family? As a minimum, how many tax returns must the Barlow family file? How do you account for the discrepancy between the number of taxpayers and the number of returns that must be filed? Would you advise Jim and Mary to file separate returns? Explain each answer.

2. Several years ago, David Nipon became disenchanted with U.S. politics and moved to France. He lives there on the Mediterranean Coast, taking his ease. Although he has not returned to the United States, he continues to draw income from extensive real estate holdings in Illinois and from various American securities. Nipon also has substantial wealth invested in companies located throughout Europe. As a resident of France, he is subject to the French income tax (although he continues to hold a U.S. passport). Is Nipon subject to the U.S. income tax? If so, does the U.S. tax cover his foreign-source income? If he is taxed by both countries, what provisions in the U.S. tax mitigate the effects of double taxation?

3. For each of the following independent situations, can John and Marsha file a joint return for 19x1? Explain your answers.
   a. John and Marsha married on December 20, 19x1, after a whirlwind courtship. On December 28, 19x1, following a violent argument. Marsha packed off home to mother, vowing never to return. No legal action was taken during 19x1.
   b. John and Marsha, after years of marriage, were legally separated on December 30, 19x1.
   c. John, while on temporary assignment in England for a large corporation, married Marsha, a citizen of Great Britain. They were still in London at the end of 19x1, but they returned to the United States in January 19x2. They made no election for 19x1 to include Marsha's worldwide income on a U.S. return.
   d. John died on January 2, 19x1, after years of happy marriage to Marsha.

4. In 1980 the federal income tax liability of a single person earning a $28,800 taxable income was $7,434. The tax liability on equivalent income earned by a married couple filing a joint return was approximately $5,849. Why does the $1,585 difference exist between these two tax liabilities? Is the difference justified? Explain.

5. Indicate in each of the following cases whether taxpayers may file a joint return. If they are not allowed to do so, indicate the reason.
   a. Jones, a widower, and his mother live in the same house. Jones has gross income of $8,000; mother has income of $6,000.

b. Kuehn, an American citizen, married Greta while he was stationed in Germany. Kuehn and his wife now live in New York. Greta is not yet an American citizen, but at the end of the tax year she was taking steps to become an American citizen.

c. Smith's wife died in the preceding tax year. Smith has not remarried. Smith's 3-year-old daughter lives with him.

d. Bellmon's wife died on January 2 of the current year. He has not remarried.

e. Ratliff and his wife were divorced on December 18 of the current tax year.

f. Whitlaw and his wife are both United States citizens. Whitlaw's wife's parents live in England, however, and both parents are seriously ill. The wife spent the entire tax year in England with her parents.

6. In the current year James Cochran had adjusted gross income of $46,000. His allowable itemized deductions totaled $3,500. (This does not include personal exemptions.) His wife, Mary, also was employed and had adjusted gross income of $6,500. Her allowable itemized deductions were $1,800. (This does not include exemptions.)

Compute the amount that the family unit saves in income taxes by filing a joint return rather than filing separately. (There are no dependents.) The exemption deduction is $1,000 for each taxpayer.

7. If you (a United States citizen) went to work in Australia for two years following graduation from college, would the wages you earn in Australia be subject to United States income taxation? What "special provisions" apply to such earnings?

8. The correct classification of the various subtractions is very important in the individual tax formula.

a. Why is the accurate calculation of gross income important?

b. Why is the accurate calculation of adjusted gross income important?

9. In each of the following independent cases, indicate whether the amount involved is (a) deductible *for* A.G.I., (b) deductible *from* A.G.I., or (c) not deductible at all.

a. Taxpayer paid $2,000 interest on her home mortgage.

b. Taxpayer gave $500 to his church.

c. Taxpayer paid $8 rent on a safety deposit box at the bank. In this box he kept the few shares of stock that he owned.

d. Taxpayer paid expenses of $1,200 applicable to rental property that he owned.

e. Taxpayer replaced roof on a home at a cost of $1,000.

f. Minor repairs to the taxpayer's home cost $85.

g. Taxpayer purchased a vacant lot for investment. During the year she paid $50 to have it mowed and cleaned.

h. Taxpayer, a nurse, is employed at the local hospital. She spent $105 for uniforms during the year.

i. Millsaps, a public school teacher, spent $40 for magazine subscriptions. The magazines were used in his classroom activities.

j. Herman, a department store "buyer," attended an out-of-town "market" at which he examined new merchandise. His total costs, including meals, lodging, and transportation were $308. He was not reimbursed by his employer.

k. Taxpayer is the proprietor of a profitable gift shop located in Chicago. In December she visited Florida to investigate the possibility of acquiring a franchise to operate a pizza parlor in Florida. She decided not to make the new investment.

l. Taxpayer paid $800 real estate taxes on his home.

m. Taxpayer paid $650 real estate taxes on property used in his trade.

n. Taxpayer, a carpenter working as an employee, spent $65 for small tools to be used on her job.

o. Taxpayer, an employee working for a public accounting firm, lives in a suburban community and commutes to the city to work. During the year commuting costs were $360.

p. Taxpayer operates an antique shop on the first floor of a house and lives on the second floor. Fire insurance for the entire house was $600 for the year (which does not include insurance on the antique inventory or personal furnishings). Floor space on each floor is approximately equal.

q. Taxpayer rents a home in which to live. His rental payments are $250 per month. In addition, his rental contract requires him to pay all real estate taxes on the home. During the current tax year these taxes totaled $750.

r. Taxpayer is a corporate executive. Because of his high pay, he receives no allowance or reimbursement of entertainment expenses even though his position requires him to entertain the corporation's customers. During the year he spent $2,200 on legitimate entertainment.

s. Taxpayer is an outside salesperson. Her expenses for transportation, meals, lodging, etc. in connection with her activities as an outside sales representative totaled $3,500.

t. Taxpayer is an employee. During the year he paid a "tax service" $15 for filling out his personal federal income tax return.

u. Taxpayer spent $90 for uniforms for use on his job. His employer reimbursed the taxpayer for $75 of this amount.

v. Taxpayer is a self-employed special duty nurse. He spent $120 for nursing uniforms.

w. Taxpayer is a teacher in the local school district and was required to obtain additional education to maintain her certificate. She spent six weeks away from home to take courses at State University. She incurred the following costs: (1) transportation to and from the university, $150; (2) meals, lodging, and incidentals while away from home, $800; (3) tuition, books, and fees, $175.

x. Taxpayer who owns and operates a truck on a contract basis paid $1,350 for state licenses for his truck.

10. Smith is a professor at a local university. In addition, he carries on a public accounting practice under the name "J. B. Smith, C.P.A." His records show the following items of income and expense for the current year.

Income:	Net amount received from University	$16,000
	(After deduction of $4,000 federal income taxes, $480 life insurance premiums, and $1,020 for teacher retirement program)	
	Interest from bank savings account	450
	Accounting fees	9,400
Expenses:	Membership dues in American Association of University Professors	$25
	Membership dues in American Institute of C.P.A.'s (in connection with accounting practice)	35
	Membership dues in State Society of C.P.A.'s	30
	Wages paid part-time helper in accounting practice	2,400
	Rent, utilities, supplies used in practice	2,000

Transportation around town in connection with accounting practice		220
Expenses of attending teachers' convention in another city:		
Transportation	$220	
Meals and lodging	80	
Registration fees	10	
Expenses of attending teachers' convention held in taxpayer's home town:		
Taxi fare	$ 4	
Meals	10	
Registration	12	
		26
Deductible amount of contributions, taxes, and interest paid		3,200
Payments of estimated tax		600

Smith is married and has four dependent children.
1. Compute Smith's gross income.
2. Compute his deductions *for* A.G.I.
3. Compute his A.G.I.
4. Compute his deductions *from* A.G.I. (excess over zero bracket amount).
5. Compute his tax table income.
6. Compute his gross tax. (Use current tax tables.)
7. Compute his net tax payable.

11. Listed below are statements and definitions. For each item, determine the precise term in the individual's tax formula applicable to that item.
    a. The tax base described in the Sixteenth Amendment.
    b. The amount of tax liability due with the return.
    c. The amount used to determine who must file a return.
    d. Amounts that, according to Congress, are not taxable income as described in the Sixteenth Amendment.
    e. The tax base provided by the Code.
    f. Amounts subtracted from the product of base times rate.
    g. The amount used to determine the medical deduction.
    h. Expenses related to the operation of a business.
    i. The amount excluded from taxation to provide a reasonable sustenance for every taxpayer plus the itemized deductions.
    j. The amount used to determine the amount of some itemized deductions.
    k. The product obtained by applying the rate to the base.
    l. Every increase in net worth.
    m. The amount obtained by subtracting the cost of an item from its sales price.
    n. Deductible travel expenses of an employee.
    o. Items that reduce the amount in (k) above on a dollar-for-dollar basis.

12. Answer the following questions. Use the italicized words in their precise meaning:
    a. Mrs. Jones, a 70-year-old widow, lives with her son and his family in Austin, Texas. During this year she received $4,350 of dividends on AT&T stock she owns. What is her *gross income*?
    b. Mrs. Smith is also a 70-year old widow who also resides with her son and his family in Austin, Texas. She received $4,350 from the rental of her

former residence. Expenses related to the rental property were $2,000 for the year. What is her *gross income*?

   c. Must either Mrs. Jones or Mrs. Smith file a federal income tax return?

13. The law contains a new term, tax table income. What is the significance of this amount? Explain the administrative purpose for creating tax table income.

14. Indicate which of the following expenditures by an individual would constitute (1) a deduction for A.G.I.; (2) a deduction from A.G.I.; or (3) a nondeductible, personal expense.

   a. Expenses associated with rental property.

   b. Expenses associated with investments in corporate securities (e.g., cost of broker's advice, of safety deposit box).

   c. Expenses associated with investments in state bonds.

   d. Travel expenses (away from home) incurred as an employee.

   e. Travel expenses incurred as a self-employed businessperson.

   f. Entertainment expenses incurred as an employee:

      1. If no reimbursement is made by the employer.

      2. If the reimbursement is less than the expense incurred.

   g. Entertainment expenses incurred as a self-employed businessperson.

15. Mary Burnes, unmarried and age 20, is a full-time student at State University. As a part-time employee, she earned $1,500 during the current year. She also received a $4,000 distribution from a trust created by her grandmother. All of the trust's income was from interest on corporate bonds. Mary's parents properly claimed a dependency exemption for Mary. Assume she had no deductions for adjusted gross income and that her itemized deductions were less than $2,300.

   a. Compute Mary's taxable income for the year. (She has no dependents.)

   b. Compute Mary's tax table income for the year.

   c. What is Mary's gross tax? What credits may Mary claim, assuming she consumed her entire income for personal use?

16. Your text specifies the conditions under which a taxpayer must use the tax tables. What are those conditions? Under what circumstances might a taxpayer who would otherwise be forced to use the tax tables elect to use the rate schedules?

17. Mary and John are married residents of New York and have two small children. They depend on John's salary of $50,000 per annum for their livelihood. In January 19x2, Mary learned that John was in hock to his bookie to the tune of $200,000 and that the bookie was getting impatient. New York is not a community property state. While Mary has no current income, her family is quite wealthy and she expects to inherit substantial amounts in the near future. What would you advise Mary about filing status for 19x1?

18. A review of Taxpayer C's financial records revealed the following data for 19x1:

Income items		*Expenditures*	
Salary	$12,000	Personal living costs	
Gross income from a		(rent, food, etc.)	$8,000
partnership (C's share		Expenses of partnership	
only)	4,000	(C's share only)	3,000
Dividend income[a]	300	Personal taxes, interest,	
Interest income (from		and contributions	3,550
local bank account)	200	Federal income tax	
		withheld from salary	2,200

[a] All stocks owned by husband in a common law state.

Assuming that Mr. C. is married and the father of two young sons, that neither he nor Mrs. C is 65 or over or blind, and that Mr. and Mrs. C file a joint tax return, calculate the Cs':

a. Income, in the broadest sense.
b. Exclusions.
c. Deductions for A.G.I.
d. Tax table income.
e. Taxable income.
f. Gross tax liability. (Use current tax rates.)
g. Net tax liability.

19. For each of the independent cases below, calculate the number of exemptions for the taxpayer, assuming the current tax year.

a. Lopez is 75, blind, and has A.G.I. of $7,200. His wife is 71. They file a joint return.
b. Mayfield is 54, unmarried. She supports her father, who is age 75 and blind, and her mother, who is 75 and has good vision.
c. Smith is 34. His wife is 31. They have a 5-year-old son and a daughter 3 years old. On January 18 of this year, Mrs. Smith gave birth to a son, who died on January 21.
d. Assume the same facts as in part c, except that the son born on January 18 was stillborn.
e. Porter is 53. He provides his father, who does not live with Porter, with $2,500 of living costs. During the year, the father had no income except from rental property. Gross rents totaled $1,200; rent-related expenses totaled $700. The father lived off the support of Porter and the net rentals.

20. In each of the independent cases below, calculate the *number* of exemptions for the taxpayer, assuming the current tax year.

a. Taxpayer, age 67, and wife, age 63, file a joint return.
b. Taxpayer, age 68, and wife, who became 65 on January 1 of the following year after the tax year, are both blind and file a joint return.
c. Taxpayer and husband, both 48, spent $1,600 toward living expenses of their son, who is 25 and in college. The son also earned $1,110 during the summer, received a scholarship of $400, and received $450 under the GI Bill. The son used all of these funds for his living costs.
d. Taxpayer, a woman, received a decree of divorce on January 8 and has not remarried. The divorce decree required the husband to pay $1,000 a year for the support of their child, who is 5 years old and lives with the mother. They have not discussed who is to claim an exemption for the child.
e. Assume the same facts as in part d, except that the divorced couple have agreed that the father is "to claim an exemption for the child." Taxpayer is the mother.
f. Taxpayer is 67 years old. He pays $350 per month to keep his mother, age 88, in a rest home. The mother also receives an "old-age pension" of $450 during the year and gross rental income of $1,200 (rental expenses consumed $300 of this). She uses all the available funds for routine living costs.
g. Taxpayer is 64; wife is 53. They provide over one-half the support for their 35-year-old son who became disenchanted with his occupation two years ago and since that time has been a full-time college student working on a degree in accounting. The son earned $1,100 during the year and also received a scholarship of $500. Both of these were used to help pay his living costs.

h. Smith and his wife have great compassion for orphaned children. Currently they have living in their household and are completely supporting five children, all of whom are in school. The five foster children have been living in Smith's home all year, but none of these has been adopted. None of the children has any income.

i. Williford and his wife have living in their home for the entire year a foster child for whom they provide major support. The foster child, age 15, has gross income of $1,200 for the year.

j. An unmarried taxpayer supports his 17-year-old brother, who does not live with the taxpayer. The brother earned $1,165 during the year.

21. For each of the following independent situations, determine the proper number of exemptions to be taken, assuming the current tax year.

a. Taxpayer, age 66, and spouse, age 62, file a joint return. Both have good vision. They have one son, age 22, who is a student at State University. The son earned $1,100 in a summer job and received a scholarship from State University for $1,000. During the year the son's total support cost $3,300, of which $1,200 was paid by the father.

b. Taxpayer and spouse, both under 65 and with good vision, file a joint return. They provided more than 50 percent of the support for two unmarried children, both under 19. However, one child earned $1,200 from part-time work. Taxpayer also provided most of the support for his blind mother, who is over 65. The mother received $750 in social security payments.

c. Taxpayer, unmarried, under 65 and with good vision, provides more than 50 percent of the support for his brother and sister-in-law who attend State University. The brother earned $1,200 in a part-time job. The sister-in-law had no income. The brother filed a separate return, claiming one exemption.

d. Taxpayer, unmarried, under 65 and with good vision, provides more than 50 percent of the support for his nephew and the nephew's wife, who attend State University. The nephew's wife had no income. The nephew earned $1,200 on a summer job. The nephew filed a separate return, claiming one exemption.

22. Determine the correct number of exemptions for each situation described below.

a. John Smith, a 66-year-old bachelor, maintains a home in which the 24-year-old son of a deceased friend has lived for the past 14 years. The young man is a full-time college student who earned $1,800 during the year. John can prove that he furnishes 65 percent of the support of the young man.

b. Jacques, a widower for four years, age 63, maintains a home that is the principal abode for himself, his married daughter Joan, and his grandchild Zed. Jacques's son-in-law is a wandering "bum." Jacques provides more than 50 percent of the support of all those who live with him. Joan and her husband file a joint return, but they do not claim Zed as their dependent because their joint earnings are only $4,800.

c. Alan Standard contributes more than half the support of both his mother and father, who live with him. Alan is 38 and single; his father is 66, his mother, 64. Alan's father earned $1,100 during the year and filed a separate return claiming himself as an exemption.

d. Jack and Jill (30 and 28, respectively) have two children. Andrea, their 5-year-old daughter, models clothes for a local department store. Because Andrea earned $1,200 during the year, she had to file a tax return. Their son Don, who is 2 years old, was born blind. For the past 3 years Jack and Jill have also been raising (without adopting) a 6-year-old boy, Ted, who was orphaned by an automobile accident. The total support expenditures for Ted amounted to $1,000 during the year. Of the $1,000, Jack and Jill paid $700 from their personal funds; the remainder was provided by a county welfare program.

23. Boyd, who is unmarried, maintains a home in which resides his 17-year-old first cousin. Boyd provides over one-half the support of the cousin. Because he is a high-school student, the cousin works only during the summer and on the weekends and earns a total of $1,200. May Boyd claim a dependency exemption for the cousin? What rate schedule can Boyd use?

24. During one year, Mrs. Eve Elderly lived in a small apartment, where she was supported by her three adult sons, Shem, Ham, and Japheth. Each son contributed one-third of his mother's financial support. Mrs. Elderly's only income was $1,101 in dividends, which she received on stocks she inherited from her late husband. Could any or all of the sons claim their mother as a dependent?

25. Jane, Mary, and Paul contribute to the support of their mother, age 71. The mother's total living costs for the year were $3,100, received from the following sources:

Jane	$ 800
Mary	1,400
Paul	300
Social Security	600

Who is entitled to claim the mother as a dependent? Explain.

26. In the following situations, can Mac use Rate Schedule Z (head of household) for the year involved?
   a. Mac maintains a home, and his unmarried grandson lives with him. The grandson is 23 years old and has a good job and therefore does not qualify as a dependent for Mac. (Mac is a widower.)
   b. Mac maintains a home for his two dependent children. Mac's wife died last year.
   c. Mac's parents live in an apartment at a resort center in Florida. They have no income, so Mac, who is a bachelor and lives and works in New York, supports them.
   d. Mac is a widower living in New York. His wife died 5 years ago. Mac pays all the living costs of his 18-year-old unmarried daughter, who has no income and lives in Miami Beach, Florida.

27. Indicate in each of the following independent cases whether the taxpayer may file a "surviving spouse" return.
   a. Taxpayer's husband died in the preceding tax year. Taxpayer maintains a home in which resides her unmarried 20-year-old daughter, a college student, who qualifies as taxpayer's dependent.
   b. Taxpayer's husband died in the preceding tax year. Taxpayer maintains a home in which resides her unmarried 20-year-old sister, a college student, who qualifies as taxpayer's dependent.
   c. Taxpayer's wife died during this tax year. Taxpayer maintains a home in which resides his unmarried 18-year-old daughter, who qualifies as taxpayer's dependent.
   d. Taxpayer's husband died during the preceding year. Taxpayer maintains a home in which resides her married 17-year-old daughter and the daughter's

18-year-old husband. Taxpayer supports both her daughter and son-in-law and properly claims both of them as her dependents.

   e. Taxpayer's wife died 4 years ago. Taxpayer has not remarried and maintains a home in which reside his two stepchildren, ages 7 and 8. Taxpayer properly claims both stepchildren as dependents.

28. Which rate schedule (X, Y—Joint, Y—Separate, or Z) *should* each of the following taxpayers use?

   a. Sue's husband died last year. She maintains a home in which live her married son and his wife. Both of them qualify as Sue's dependents.

   b. Mary's husband died last year. She maintains a home in which live her married son and his wife. Mary supports both of them, but the son and daughter-in-law file a joint return.

   c. Herman and Victoria were married on December 31 of the current tax year. Herman earned $18,000 during the year, and Victoria earned $7,200. Victoria is a resident alien. Victoria has income in several countries.

   d. Wilma's husband died 4 years ago. Wilma maintains a home in which reside her 6-year-old daughter, her 21-year-old son, and her 20-year-old daughter-in-law. The son and daughter-in-law file a joint return. Wilma provides all the support for everyone in the household.

   e. Jones, whose wife died earlier in the current tax year, has not remarried. He has no children or other dependents.

   f. Joe, a bachelor, maintains a home in which resides his nephew. The nephew is not a dependent.

   g. Thomas was divorced from his wife in November of the current tax year. Thomas's unmarried dependent daughter lives with him.

29. In May of 19x1, a 17-year-old cousin of Mrs. Jones came to live with the Jones family and stayed in the household until she graduated from high school in May 19x3. At that time, the cousin went away to college, but she still calls the Jones household "home." The Joneses provide full support of the cousin, who has had no income. May Mr. and Mrs. Jones claim a dependency exemption for the cousin in 19x1? 19x2? 19x3? Explain.

30. Robert and Mary were divorced on January 18, 19x1. The divorce decree awarded Mary custody of the couple's child but directed Robert to provide $100 per month of child support. No mention was made of which parent would be entitled to take the exemption. Robert actually made child-support payments totaling $680 during the year. Who is entitled to take the exemption for the child?

31. June and Tom were divorced two years ago. In the current year, Tom contributed $1,800 to June for the support of the couple's three children who were in June's custody. June provided the balance of their support. How many, if any, of the children may Tom claim as dependents?

SUPPLEMENTAL PROBLEMS

32. Professor Jones, a bachelor, earns a salary of $16,000. Because Mr. Jones lives in a rented apartment, his itemized deductions typically are less than the zero bracket amount. On July 1, 19x1, Professor Jones assumed duties (in addition to his university teaching appointment) as editor of a quarterly trade publication. As compensation, Professor Jones will be paid $3,000 annually by the association that publishes the quarterly journal. The first $3,000 payment will be made on June 30, 19x2.

In order to complete his new editorial duties, Professor Jones immediately hired an assistant to do typing and clerical work. The assistant earned $200 per month, which was paid from Professor Jones's personal funds. At the end of 19x1, therefore, Professor Jones had not received any payment for his services as editor although he had incurred and paid expenses of $1,200 in connection with these duties. In preparing his tax return for 19x1, Professor Jones asks you how he should report the $1,200 payment to his editorial assistant. If possible, Professor Jones desires to claim the usual $2,200 zero bracket amount. Using whatever materials are available in your school's library, determine if the $1,200 payment should be a deduction for or a deduction from the A.G.I. of Professor Jones.

33. Tom Turner is a widower whose wife died several years ago. Tom's only daughter is unmarried and attends State University. Tom provides her entire support. He still lives in the family residence and maintains his daughter's old room for her use. While the daughter was home for two days last Christmas, she was too busy to come home at any time during the current year. Using a tax service in your school's library, determine if Tom can file as a head of household.

RETURN PROBLEMS

1. John Harris is single and has no dependents. He lives with his parents at 714 Oak Street, Sometown, Texas 76201. (S.S. #458-10-6001) He is a part-time student at the local university and also worked for Wilton Packing Company. His W-2 form from the company shows a gross wage of $5,200 and income tax withheld of $454. In addition, he received $350 in gross dividends from stock of a taxable domestic corporation (the stock was a gift from his father several years ago). Given the above information, complete Form 1040A. Use the tax tables in Appendix B to compute the tax due (or refund).

2. Henry and Elaine Simpson, who reside at 2106 Avenue D, in Sometown, South Carolina 29204, are married and file a joint return. Henry (S.S. #491-20-8901) is a mechanic for United Textiles, Inc. Elaine (S.S. #493-21-2002) does not work but looks after their two small children, Ann and David, who are dependents. Henry's W-2 form from his employer shows the following: gross wages, $14,765; income tax withheld, $1,684. In addition, the Simpsons earned interest income of $210 on amounts deposited in a local savings association. Since they do not itemize and have no deductions for A.G.I., they use Form 1040A. They did contribute $200 for the election campaign of Senator Thurgood this year. Complete Form 1040A. Use the tax tables to compute the gross tax.

10

Whether the purpose be to gain an advantage under the law of the state of incorporation or to avoid or comply with the demands of creditors or to serve the creator's personal or undisclosed convenience, so long as that purpose is the equivalent of business activity or is followed by the carrying on of business by the corporation, the corporation remains a separate taxable entity.

Moline Properties, Inc. v. *Commissioner,* 319 U.S. 436 (1943)

the corporate taxpayer: basic rules

The individual is the ultimate taxpaying entity. As discussed in Chapter 3, we do not know, and have devised no method of determining, who finally bears the burden of any tax, especially the income tax. A fairly persuasive argument can be made that most, if not all, taxes levied on business units, including corporations, are passed on to the ultimate consumer of goods, the individual. Still, the income tax is levied on corporations, and their tax payments account for a sizable portion of total federal revenues.

As noted on page **4**/5, corporations had the dubious honor of being considered a taxable entity even prior to the first income tax law in 1913. This was due in part to the legal conception of the corporation. Under the law, corporations are distinct from the individuals and other entities who are the corporation's contractual owners. As such, a corporation may own property and may sue and be sued in its own name. This separate legal existence gives the corporate form its legal advantages of limited liability, transferability of shares, continuity of existence, and centralized management.

There are two polar and several intermediate alternatives to taxing the corporation as a separate entity. One polar possibility would be to allocate corporate income to the individual shareholders.

Obviously, this alternative would be administratively difficult for the publicly held corporation because of its constantly changing ownership. The other polar possibility would be to absolve the corporation from the tax and tax individual shareholders on property distributed to them by the corporation. But such a rule would create a major loophole, for every taxpayer would quickly transfer income-producing property to a corporate entity and take out of that corporation only enough to cover living expenses. Tax on the remainder would be deferred indefinitely. Faced with these alternatives, Congress chose to recognize the corporation as a basic taxpayer. The choice was also politically expedient, because the corporate income tax has consistently produced large amounts of revenue. Although there currently is some Congressional support for a partial solution to the corporate tax dilemma, the authors doubt that any corrective action is imminent.

THE CORPORATE TAX FORMULA

The formula used to determine the net tax payable of a corporation is the same as that first introduced on page **5**/1:

Income broadly conceived
− Exclusions
_____
= Gross income
− Deductions
_____
= Taxable income
× Applicable tax rate
_____
= Gross tax
− Tax credits and prepayments
_____
= Net tax payable

A comparison of this formula with that given for individuals on page **9/3** reveals only one major difference. For the individual taxpayer, allowed deductions must be divided between those *for* adjusted gross income and those *from* adjusted gross income because the amount of adjusted gross income is important in the determination of some deductions from adjusted gross income. For the corporation, no such distinction is necessary—the corporation has only "business" deductions and is not entitled to any of the deductions for personal expenses, the zero bracket amount, or the exemption deduction. With these exceptions, however, the general rules covering income and exclusions, deductions, and credits and prepayments (as discussed in Chapters 5, 6, and 8) apply to both individuals and corporations. The corporate tax rates are, however, quite different from the individual rates. Because of their nature, corporations are also allowed some deductions not allowed individuals. The most important of these deductions allowed corporations is related to the problem of double taxation.

Double taxation and the dividends-received deduction

Taxpayers who hold stock in corporations have complained since the beginning of the income tax that taxation of corporate dividends results in a *double* tax on corporate income. First, a tax is paid by the corporation, then a second tax is paid by the shareholders when the after-tax corporate income is distributed to them as a dividend or in liquidation. This double taxation, according to the argument, is an inequitable penalty on taxpayers doing business in the corporate form and presumably has several bad effects.

Double taxation, it is claimed, reduces the equity capital available to corporations and forces the corporations to rely heavily on debt equity. The contractual interest charges related to debt equities are tax deductions to the corporation. Interest is paid with *before-tax* dollars; dividends are paid with after-tax dollars. Heavy reliance on debt equities increases the risks in corporate operations because of the fixed interest charges and fixed maturities. The long-run result is alleged to be an unwillingness on the part of corporate management to undertake high risk ventures and a decrease in economic stability to the extent that corporations with high debt financing are forced to make capital adjustments because of insolvency. The bias in the tax law against equity financing results in a severe handicap to small, growing corporations, where risks are high and the supply of debt capital limited. Curtailing the economic activities of these small entrepreneurs may result in economic stagnation.

Double taxation of corporate income is presumed to work undue hardship also on small shareholders with low incomes. At present, the total tax paid on corporate earnings distributed as dividends to individuals in the top marginal bracket is about 82 percent—46 percent tax paid by the corporation and a tax of about 36 percent of the original corporate income paid by the individual when the remaining 54 percent is distributed (54 percent at 70 percent tax rate). Observe that this total of 82 percent is only 12 percentage points higher than the rate in the top bracket for individuals. The total tax to a shareholder in the lowest bracket is 54 percent (46 percent paid by the corporation and 14 percent of the remaining 54 percent paid by the individual); this is 40 percentage points higher than the 14 percent rate in the lowest bracket. The result is certainly not a progressive tax. The corporate tax falls proportionally on all shareholders—it reduces the earnings per share of a shareholder in the 14 percent bracket by the same amount as those of a shareholder in the 70 percent bracket. This penalty on the little person may reduce his or her willingness to invest in American industry, although it is doubtful that he or she ponders long over such an esoteric tax fact.

Those who complain about the double taxation of corporate income begin with the assumption that the tax falls on the corporation and is not shifted to suppliers and customers. As we discussed in Part One, however, the problem of tax incidence is complex, and no one is able to say with certainty just who bears the ultimate burden. Moreover, some empirical evidence exists that corporations are able to shift the tax. The rate of return on invested capital (using *after-tax* income) has remained fairly constant since the 1920s despite drastic changes in the tax rates on corporate income. This constant rate of return supposedly indicates a shift in the tax burden. Nevertheless, other empirical studies, using other data, have reached the opposite conclusion.[1] To the extent that the tax burden *is* shifted, there is no double taxation to the shareholders, except in their roles as consumers or as corporate employees.

The argument that double taxation penalizes the shareholder also ignores some important facts about the present securities market. The vast majority of shareholders acquired their shares in the marketplace, not by contributing to the capital of the corporation. And market values, to the extent that they are influenced by corporate income, are based not on *before-tax* income but on *after-tax* income. The prudent investor bases expectations of return on a continuation of the corporate tax and will pay a price for the shares consistent with the after-tax return. To eliminate or reduce the presumed double taxation would result in a huge windfall profit to the present shareholders as the market adjusted to increased expectations. On the other hand, present shareholders are penalized whenever corporate tax rates are increased unexpectedly and corporations are unable to shift the increased burden.

Finally, although the income-tax law has had a pronounced influence on the financial structure of corporations, the principal direction of its influence has not been toward greatly increased reliance on debt equities. Generally, since World War II, the portion of all new capital raised by corporations from debt equities has not varied significantly. In some years, when the market for new stock issues is soft, corporate management will turn to debt equities for new capital. The principal influence of the tax law has been to increase retention of corporate earnings, a financing policy that avoids the shareholders' recognition of ordinary income, which would be taxed at rates up to 70 percent. The earnings retained are reflected in increased market prices of shares, a source of income to the shareholder that is not taxed until the shares are disposed of and even then is usually taxed at reduced rates.

Despite the doubts just raised, the proposition that double taxation is inequitable has had strong advocates in Congress, and the law has contained various provisions to give "relief" to the shareholders. From 1913 through 1936, dividends were subject only to the surtax, not to the normal tax.[2] From 1936 to 1954, there were no relief provisions for individuals, but in 1954 two were added: an exclusion of a limited amount of dividend income and a credit against the tax equal to 4 percent of most of the dividends included in taxable income. These provisions were changed again in 1964. At present, there are two provisions in the law directly related to the problem of double taxation. One of these is the $100 *exclusion* allowed for dividends received by individuals from taxable domestic corporations (see Chapter 5). The second is the dividends-received *deduction* allowed corporations.

The problem of double taxation is particularly troublesome when the shareholder is a corporation. Without some special relief, a single corporate intermediary standing between the corporation earning the income and the individual taxpayers would have the effect of *triple* taxation: first, when the subsidiary corporation earns the income; next, when the income is distributed to the parent corporate shareholder; and, third, when the income is distributed as a dividend to individual stockholders. To relieve this inequity, a corporate shareholder is allowed a deduction equal to 85 percent of the dividends received from taxable domestic corporations. The deduction is 100 percent if the dividend is from small business investment companies (as specifically defined in the law). The dividend deduction is also 100 percent between members of an affiliated group of corporations as explained later in this chapter.

Other deductions for corporations only

The Internal Revenue Code contains a number of deductions for corporations (or provisions that have the effect of deductions) other than the dividends-received deduction. One such deduction relates to the corporation's organization expenses.

Under financial accounting practices, corporate organizational expenses are typically capitalized and carried on the corporate books as assets until the corporation ceases to exist. For tax purposes, the corporations may elect to defer such costs until liquidation or to amortize them over a 60-month period beginning with the month active business is begun. For this purpose, organization expenses are narrow-

---

[1] For a concise summary of the arguments on this point and for further references, see *The Federal Tax System,* Joint Economic Committee, 1964, pp. 54–55. See also Pechman and Okner, *Who Bears the Tax Burden?* Washington, D.C.: The Brookings Institution, 1974).

[2] Until the Reform Act of 1969, the tax rates for individuals contained both a normal tax and a surtax, though the distinction was not apparent in the rate schedules. The normal rate was a flat 3 percent, and everything else was a surtax.

ly defined as capital expenditures *directly* connected with the *creation* of the corporation. Though the amounts are usually small, most corporations elect the 60-month amortization to avoid the indefinite deferral of these costs.

While corporations do not incur many of the personal expenses incurred by individuals, e.g., medical expenses and alimony, they do make contributions to charitable organizations. Corporations are allowed to deduct contributions, but subject to a special limit of 5 percent of the corporation's income before the contribution deduction. What constitutes a deductible contribution and the application of this 5 percent limit are explained in Chapter 13.

Over the years, most special deductions allowed corporations have been added to the statute to encourage foreign trade. During the 1930s, our government's foreign policy was concerned with extending the political influence of the United States in China and the Western Hemisphere. As a result, special deductions were allowed companies engaged in trade in those two areas. Recognizing that these somewhat archaic policy goals should no longer be encouraged by reduced taxes, Congress provided for the elimination, or phase-out, of the special deductions for China Trade Corporations and Western Hemisphere Trade Corporations in the 1976 Tax Reform Act.

There remains, however, one fairly significant provision related to corporations engaged in foreign trade. Reacting to inordinately large negative balances in our international trade and payments accounts over several years, Congress added a provision for the Domestic International Sales Corporation (DISC) in 1971. The legislative plan was intended to work as follows: One or more United States producers or manufacturers would form a new corporation (DISC) and funnel export trade through it. Only one-half of the profits from the sale of products and commodities abroad would immediately be subject to U.S. taxation, provided the DISC reinvested its profits in export activities. The remaining one-half of the profits would be subject to U.S. taxation when the corporation used the resulting assets for any purposes other than foreign trade. The usual pattern was the formation of a DISC as a wholly owned subsidiary of a domestic corporation. Because of the sizable tax benefits available, the rules governing DISCs were rather complicated.

Since 1971, Congress has had second thoughts about what originally appeared to be a good way to stimulate foreign trade. In 1974, the DISC provisions

were changed to restrict the commodities covered. Then, in 1976, a more severe restriction was introduced that substantially reduces the amount of profit on which the tax may be deferred. While not dead, DISCs have been severely wounded, and their future importance in our national tax structure is uncertain.

CORPORATE TAX RATES

Unlike the basic rate schedules for individuals in Appendix A, the corporate rate structure has historically contained only one progression. For the decade preceding 1975, corporations were subject to a normal tax of 22 percent on all their taxable income and a surtax rate of 26 percent on all taxable income in excess of $25,000. In response to a growing concern over a shortage of investment capital in the next decade, Congress lowered the corporate tax rates for 1975 to:

20 percent on the first $25,000 of taxable income;

22 percent on the taxable income between $25,000 and $50,000; and

48 percent on all income in excess of $50,000.

Note that the rate on the first $25,000 of taxable income was lowered by 2 percent and the surtax exemption was increased from $25,000 to $50,000.

The Tax Act of 1978 made an even more substantial reduction in corporate rates effective for 1979 and later years. This reduction, as with the earlier reduction in 1975, was justified as a means of providing needed investment capital to corporations. The new rates have five progressive steps as follows:

If taxable income is			Tax is	
Over	But not over	Amount plus	% of	Excess over
-0-	$25,000	-0-	17	-0-
$25,000	50,000	$4,250	20	$25,000
$50,000	75,000	9,250	30	50,000
$75,000	100,000	16,750	40	75,000
$100,000	—	26,750	46	100,000

In all cases in which the taxable income is $100,000 or more, you can determine the tax by multiplying taxable income by 46 percent and subtracting $19,250.

To illustrate these rates, assume a corporation with taxable income of $110,000 for the calendar year ending December 31, 1979. The tax is:

Tax on first $100,000 from schedule	$26,750
Tax on excess over $100,000 ($10,000 × .46)	4,600
Total tax	$31,350

By the alternative method, since the taxable income is $100,000 or more, the tax is $31,350, or 46 percent of $110,000 ($50,600) less $19,250.

CONTROLLED GROUPS OF CORPORATIONS

Prior to 1970, a much used tax planning device was to divide a business or a group of businesses with common ownership into several separate corporations. For example, in a chain of retail outlets, each outlet would be organized as a separate corporation. Under this arrangement, each corporation enjoyed the lower rates on the first dollars of taxable income. For example, under the current rate schedule, each corporation would have $25,000 taxed at only 17 percent, $25,000 taxed at only 20 percent, and so on. Since 1969, this advantage has gradually been eliminated. At present, the taxable incomes of corporations that are members of a "controlled group" must be combined for purposes of applying the marginal rates below 46 percent.

A controlled group of corporations is defined in Sec. 1563 to include parent-subsidiary, brother-sister, and combined groups. The parent-subsidiary form includes any one or more chains of corporations connected with a common 80 percent corporate-parent ownership. Thus, for example, if Corporation C-1 owns 100 percent of Corporation C-2 and C-2 owns 80 percent of C-3, Corporations C-1, C-2, and C-3 would constitute a parent-subsidiary form of the controlled group and they would have to share a single surtax exemption.

A brother-sister group includes any two or more corporations (1) that are at least 80 percent owned by five or fewer persons (including individuals, estates, and trusts) and (2) in which those five or fewer persons own more than 50 percent of the value of all stock " . . . taking into account the stock ownership of each such person only to the extent such stock ownership is identical with respect to each such corporation" (Sec. 1563(a)(2)(B)). Obviously, reasonable people might well disagree as to the meaning of the quoted portion of the Code! In general, however, this subparagraph suggests that you must add together the common ownership in each set of com-

monly owned corporations to determine the "identical ownership" considering only the least common ownership percentage existing between the five or fewer common stockholders. To illustrate, consider the following ownership of a group of three corporations:

Individual stockholder	Percent of corporations owned			Identical ownership
	C-1	C-2	C-3	
1	40	30	20	20
2	40	40	20	20
3	20	30	60	20
Total ownership	100	100	100	
Identical ownership				60

This group of corporations (C-1, C-2, and C-3) would constitute a brother-sister form of the controlled group and would be required to share a single surtax exemption. If, however, we were to rearrange the ownership slightly, as follows,

Stockholder	Percent of corporations owned			Identical ownership
	C-1	C-2	C-3	
1	70	10	20	10
2	20	70	10	10
3	10	20	70	10
Total ownership	100	100	100	
Identical ownership				30

then, although the three common owners (1, 2, and 3) would still satisfy the 80 percent ownership test, the three corporations (C-1, C-2, and C-3) would *not* be considered a controlled group because the three owners do not satisfy the second (i.e., the 50 percent identical-ownership) test. Consequently, each of the three corporations could still claim its individual surtax exemption.

If a controlled group exists, the taxable incomes of group members are combined for purposes of applying the rates below 46 percent. Each $25,000 bracket subject to a tax rate lower than 46 percent must be allocated between the group members. The agreement between members of the group may specify the allocation of each $25,000 bracket separately, and the agreement may be changed each year to obtain maximum benefits.

Although we will ignore the definition of the combined group, and many other subtleties inherent in the statutory definition of a controlled group, we should note that the existence of a controlled group carries with it one small tax advantage. Dividends paid between corporate members of a controlled group (but not to individual stockholders) are granted a 100 percent dividends-received deduction rather than the 85 percent dividends-received deduction otherwise available on most domestic corporate dividends. This is a rather minor benefit, however, compared to the additional taxes that generally result when a controlled group exists.

In the treatment of multiple corporations, the tax law comes face to face with a real dilemma. Many of our large corporate enterprises do have an "existence" distinct from the existence of their contractual owners. Both common sense and administrative necessity indicate that these units should be subject to the tax as separate entities. On the other hand, most closely owned corporations are mere legal appendages to the business operations of an individual; they are formed, controlled, and terminated at the will of the individual owner. Such corporations are "artificial" beings; and the treatment of them as separate taxable entities is bound to create problems, for they are capable of manipulation purely for tax ends. The solution to the problem, it would seem, is a rule to distinguish the real from the artificial, permitting the taxation of the former as a separate entity and the treatment of the latter as a mere conduit for income that would be taxed to the individual owners. Admittedly, such a distinction would have to be made on arbitrary grounds. But in this situation, arbitrariness might be preferable to the surrealism of the present treatment of most corporations as separate taxable entities.

ILLUSTRATION OF THE CORPORATE FORMULA

An expanded statement of the corporate tax formula including the computation of the normal tax and surtax is presented in Table 10-1. The illustration is based on the following facts:

Revenues:

From sales of merchandise	$210,000
From (domestic) corporate dividends	10,000
From city bond obligations	5,000

Routine "expenses":

Cost of goods sold[3]	110,000
Wages and salaries	35,000
Other expenses	10,000
Prepayment of tax liability	11,000

THE CORPORATE TAX SHELTER

Each year, approximately 1.5 million corporate returns are filed, reporting net taxable income of about $100 billion. In a recent year, however, only 3,600 of these corporations accounted for more than two-thirds of the total income reported by corporations. In addition, there are about 14,000 publicly held corporations that come under the jurisdiction of the Securities and Exchange Commission, less than one percent of the corporations reporting for tax purposes. While a large number of corporations in existence may be partially accounted for by the financial and legal advantages of the corporate framework, it is safe to say that a vast majority of the smaller corporations exist solely because of our tax laws.

Benefits of incorporation

The basic tax benefit that can be obtained from the incorporation of a proprietorship, partnership, or other business entity is a substantial reduction in tax rates. The corporate rates are generally lower than those that apply to individuals. A contrast of marginal rates for corporations with those found on Schedule Y (joint) is shown in Figure 7-3 on page 7/4. The rate advantage that can be gained from the use of a corporation to conduct business operations is clear.

To illustrate the tax savings that can be obtained from incorporation, assume that two individuals, A and B, each operate a business that is their only source of income. A's business produces an income of $75,000 per year and B's business produces income of $200,000 per year. To keep the example simple, we will assume that both are married and file a joint return (with no dependent) and that neither A nor B has itemized deductions in excess of the zero bracket amount. If they operate their businesses as proprietorships, their gross tax liabilities are:[4]

---

[3] In accounting, the cost of goods sold is routinely treated as an expense. In tax, " . . . 'gross income' means total sales, *less the cost of goods sold.*" [Regs., 1.61–3(a)].

[4] These computations also ignore the possible tax reduction from the maximum tax on personal service income explained in Chapter 28.

TABLE **10-1**
USING THE CORPORATE FORMULA

Income Broadly Conceived	$115,000	[($210,000 − 110,000) + 10,000 + 5,000]
less		
↓		
Exclusions	(5,000)	(the interest on the city bond)
equals		
↓		
Gross Income	$110,000	(Again, observe that the cost of goods sold has already been "deducted" for tax purposes.)
less		
↓		
Routine Deductions	(45,000)	(35,000 + 10,000)
and		
Special Deductions	(8,500)	(85% × $10,000)
equals		
↓		
Corporate Taxable Income	$ 56,500	

times appropriate rate(s)
17% × $25,000 = $ 4,250
20% × $25,000 = 5,000
30% × $ 6,500 = 1,950
$11,200

equals		
↓		
Gross Tax	$ 11,200	
less		
↓		
Prepayments and Credits	(11,000)	
equals		
↓		
Net Tax Payable	$ 200	

	A	B
Net income from business after all deductions *for* A.G.I.	$75,000	$200,000
Exemption deduction	2,000	2,000
Taxable income	$73,000	$198,000
Gross tax liability from Schedule Y (Joint)	$26,698	$105,672

Now, assume that the businesses are incorporated and that A draws a salary of $30,000 and B a salary of $60,000. The corporations become separate entities and the salaries paid to A and B would be ordinary and necessary business deductions to the corporation even though A and B own all the stock of their respective corporations and control them absolutely. Of course, the salaries will be taxable income to A and B. After incorporation the total tax liability of each is:

	A	B
Tax on corporations:		
Net income of businesses	$75,000	$200,000
Less: Salary to officer-owners	30,000	60,000
Taxable income of corporation	$45,000	$140,000
Tax on corporation	$ 8,250	$ 45,150

Tax on individuals:		
Salary from corporation	$30,000	$ 60,000
Less: Exemption deduction	2,000	2,000
Taxable income	$28,000	$ 58,000
Gross tax from Schedule Y (Joint)	$ 5,585	$ 18,698
Combined tax on corporation and individual	$13,835	$ 63,848
Tax on income before incorporation	26,698	105,672
Tax savings	$12,865	$ 41,824

The amounts saved will vary depending on the salaries and other factors. Note, however, that the effect is that these savings are reinvested in the business and may earn a return of 10 percent or higher after taxes. Such savings over a period of years compounded at 10 percent become a very substantial sum.

In addition to lower rates, incorporation offers numerous other tax benefits. The owner-officers of the corporation become employees. As a result, the corporation can provide them with health and accident insurance, group-term life insurance, meals and lodging in some instances, pension and profit-sharing plans and various other "perks." Such payments made by the corporation on behalf of the owner-employees are legitimate business deductions of the corporation. The benefits, however, are excluded from the owner-employees' gross incomes, as explained in Chapter 5.

The stories that circulate in the press about the abuse of corporate benefits are unfortunately often true. Employment contracts between the corporate president (who also happens to own virtually all shares outstanding) and the corporation often provide for a "company" entertainment allowance (or even an airplane), and other similar items. These abuses will continue to plague us as long as the tax law views every corporation, even the "one-man" corporation, as a separate taxable entity.

Some disadvantages of incorporation

Incorporation of a business, like marriage, is an easy thing to get into but can be a very hard thing to get out of. Businesses can usually be incorporated, as explained on pages **26/2** and **26/3**, without incurring a taxable gain. But once established, the corporation becomes a taxable entity and we are then confronted with the problem of double taxation.

Our tax law generally treats distributions of a corporation's assets to its shareholders in two basic ways. First, if the distribution is connected with the liquidation of the corporate business, the law treats the shareholder as if he or she sold his or her shares to the corporation. Gain (or loss) is recognized, measure by the excess (deficit) of the fair market value of the assets received over the cost of the shareholder's stock. Gains recognized are capital gains subject to the favorable rates for capital gains explained in Chapter 7.

Second, the law treats distributions of assets that are not in liquidation as an ordinary dividend, up to the amount of the corporation's current or accumulated earnings and profits (E & P). The concept of E & P is similar to the notion of retained earnings in financial accounting. Most successful corporate businesses that have been in existence for any period of time have substantial amounts of E & P. As a result, most nonliquidating distributions result in ordinary dividends.

Note that both of the above alternatives result in double taxation. It is possible, of course, for the corporation to make *payments* to shareholders for services or other consideration the shareholder provides the corporation. Salary payments, interest on debt, and rental of assets are common examples of transfers to a shareholder in which the corporation obtains a deduction and double taxation is avoided. Such methods of passing property from the corporation to its shareholders are limited, however. For example, recall from Chapter 6 that the salary must be reasonable in amount, and "unreasonable" amounts paid to corporate officers are normally treated as a dividend paid by the corporation. Take the case of a president-owner who is in the 60 percent marginal rate for his personal income and whose corporation's taxable income exceeds $100,000. If $20,000 of salary is treated as a dividend, the following results: The corporation is disallowed a deduction of $20,000 and pays an additional tax of $9,200 ($20,000 × .46). The president includes the $20,000 in income and pays a tax of $11,940 ($20,000 less $100 exclusion times 60 percent). In short, we have a tax disaster.

The preceding illustration makes it clear that all advantages of the corporate rate shelter disappear when ordinary dividends are paid regularly. Tax experts have developed various schemes for effecting dividend-like distributions that are taxed as capital gains. But these schemes are all risky and there is still a double tax, although at the lower rates for capital gains. After-tax earnings of the incorporated business generally must be reinvested within the corporation. Furthermore, the earnings must be invested in active businesses, as opposed to passive investments, in order to avoid two tax "traps" that the law contains for close corporations. These two traps are the personal holding company tax and the accumulated earnings tax.

THE PERSONAL HOLDING COMPANY TAX   The first "trap" that a closely held corporation must avoid is the personal holding company tax (Secs. 541–547). A corporation will be classified as a personal holding company if both (1) five or fewer individuals own 50 percent or more of its stock *and* (2) more than 60 percent of its income is from passive investments, rather than active trades or businesses. Any corporation that meets both of these tests will be subject to a special tax equal to 70 percent of its undistributed personal holding company income.

The corporation that is caught in this trap will obviously end up paying as much or more tax than would the owner of the same assets held in noncorporate form. Thus, the effect of this tax is the creation of a penalty that makes the corporate tax shelter less viable for passive investment income. It does not, however, penalize a corporation engaged in the active conduct of a trade or business; neither will it reach the large, publicly owned investment corporation.

THE ACCUMULATED EARNINGS TAX   A second "trap" that can be as devastating as the personal holding company tax is the tax imposed on unreasonable accumulation of earnings in a corporation (Secs. 531–537). A profitable business conducted in the corporate form often has difficulty finding sound projects in which to invest its cash. Of course, the corporation can retain its earnings for legitimate needs such as planned expansion, additional working capital, and repayment of capital. In addition, the law allows every corporation to accumulate earnings up to $150,000. However, amounts accumulated in excess of $150,000 that are not for reasonable needs are subject to a special tax. The rate is 27½ percent for the first $100,000 unreasonably accumulated and 38½ percent for amounts above $100,000 that are unreasonably accumulated.

A corporation caught by this tax also could obviously end up paying a total rate greater than the maximum 70 percent applicable to individuals. Thus,

while incorporation of a business offers many tax benefits, the route leading to such benefits is hazardous, to say the least. Incorporation is a step that should be taken only after careful and thorough deliberations.

RETURN ILLUSTRATION—FORM 1120

The completion of the corporate return form is illustrated on pages **10**/10 and **10**/11. To avoid unnecessary detail, only page 1 of Form 1120, Schedule I, Schedule J, and Schedule M-1 are reproduced. The other schedules of Form 1120 are

Schedule A—Cost of Goods Sold
Schedule C—Dividends
Schedule E—Compensation of officers
Schedule F—Bad debts—reserve method
Schedule G—Depreciation
Schedule K—Record of estimated payments
Schedule L—Balance Sheet
Schedule M-2—Analysis of unappropriated retained earnings per books

Basically, lines 1 through 30 of page 1 are the same as an income statement, but show only income and deductions for tax purposes. Schedules A,C,E,F, and G support the amounts on page 1. The balance sheet on Schedule L is the balance sheet *per books*. Schedule M-1 reconciles the book income and the taxable income, and Schedule M-2 reconciles the retained earnings per books for the year. Schedule J is used for the tax computation.

To conserve space, the basic information for the computation of taxable income appears directly on page 1, lines 1 through 30. The dividend-received deduction is shown on Schedule I and amounts to $85,000 because all dividends were from taxable domestic corporations. Line 30, page 1, shows a taxable income of $151,000. The tax of $50,210 is computed on Schedule J and appears on line 11 of that schedule.

On Schedule M-1, the item needed to reconcile the income per books to the taxable income is the book income of $185,790 computed after the deduction for federal income taxes.

Form **1120**

Department of the Treasury
Internal Revenue Service

U.S. Corporation Income Tax Return

For calendar year 1979 or other taxable year beginning
.... , 1979, ending .... , 19......

19 79

Check if a—

A Consolidated return ☐
B Personal Holding Co. ☐
C Business Code No. (See Page 8 of instructions)

Use IRS label. Otherwise please print or type.	Name		
	Number and street		
	City or town, State, and ZIP code		

D Employer identification number (see instruction W)

E Date incorporated

F Enter total assets (see instruction X)
$

Gross Income

1 (a) Gross receipts or sales $.................. **(b)** Less returns and allowances $.................. Balance ▶	**1(c)**	2,500,000
2 Less: Cost of goods sold (Schedule A) and/or operations (attach schedule)	**2**	1,400,000
3 Gross profit	**3**	1,100,000
4 Dividends (Schedule C)	**4**	100,000
5 Interest on obligations of the United States and U.S. instrumentalities	**5**	
6 Other interest	**6**	
7 Gross rents	**7**	
8 Gross royalties	**8**	
9 (a) Capital gain net income (attach separate Schedule D)	**9(a)**	
(b) Net gain or (loss) from Form 4797, line 11, Part II (attach Form 4797)	**9(b)**	
10 Other income (see instructions—attach schedule)	**10**	
11 TOTAL income—Add lines 3 through 10	**11**	1,200,000

Deductions

12 Compensation of officers (Schedule E)	**12**	80,000
13 (a) Salaries and wages 130,000 **13(b)** Less WIN and jobs credit(s) .... Balance ▶	**13(c)**	130,000
14 Repairs (see instructions)	**14**	45,000
15 Bad debts (Schedule F if reserve method is used)	**15**	
16 Rents	**16**	55,000
17 Taxes	**17**	30,000
18 Interest	**18**	78,000
19 Contributions (not over 5% of line 30 adjusted per instructions—attach schedule)	**19**	
20 Amortization (attach schedule)	**20**	
21 Depreciation from Form 4562 (attach Form 4562) 426,000 , less depreciation claimed in Schedule A and elsewhere on return .... , Balance ▶	**21**	426,000
22 Depletion	**22**	120,000
23 Advertising	**23**	
24 Pension, profit-sharing, etc. plans (see instructions) (enter number of plans ▶ ....)	**24**	
25 Employee benefit programs (see instructions)	**25**	
26 Other deductions (attach schedule)	**26**	
27 TOTAL deductions—Add lines 12 through 26	**27**	964,000
28 Taxable income before net operating loss deduction and special deductions (subtract line 27 from line 11)	**28**	236,000
29 Less: (a) Net operating loss deduction (see instructions—attach schedule) **29(a)**		
(b) Special deductions (Schedule I) **29(b)** 85,000	**29**	85,000
30 Taxable income (subtract line 29 from line 28)	**30**	151,000

Tax

31 TOTAL TAX (Schedule J)	**31**	50,210
32 Credits: (a) Overpayment from 1978 allowed as a credit		
(b) 1979 estimated tax payments		
(c) Less refund of 1979 estimated tax applied for on Form 4466 ( )		
(d) Tax deposited: Form 7004.......... Form 7005 (attach)........ Total ▶		
(e) Credit from regulated investment companies (attach Form 2439)		
(f) Federal tax on special fuels and oils (attach Form 4136 or 4136–T)	**32**	
33 TAX DUE (subtract line 32 from line 31). See instruction G for depositary method of payment . (Check ▶ ☐ if Form 2220 is attached. See page 3 of instructions.) ▶ $..........	**33**	
34 OVERPAYMENT (subtract line 31 from line 32)	**34**	
35 Enter amount of line 34 you want: **Credited to 1980 estimated tax** ▶ Refunded ▶	**35**	

Please Sign Here

Under penalties of perjury, I declare that I have examined this return, including accompanying schedules and statements, and to the best of my knowledge and belief, it is true, correct, and complete. Declaration of preparer (other than taxpayer) is based on all information of which preparer has any knowledge.

▶ ....
Signature of officer .... Date

▶ ....
Title

Paid Preparer's Information

Preparer's signature and date ▶	Check if self-employed ▶ ☐	Preparer's social security no.
Firm's name (or yours, if self-employed) and address ▶	E.I. No. ▶	
	ZIP code ▶	

Schedule I — Special Deductions (See instructions for Schedule I)

1 (a) 85% of Schedule C, line 1	85,000
(b) 59.13% of Schedule C, line 2	
(c) 85% of Schedule C, line 3	
(d) 100% of Schedule C, line 4	85,000
2 Total—See instructions for limitation	
3 100% of Schedule C, line 8	
4 Deduction for dividends paid on certain preferred stock of public utilities (see instructions)	
5 Deduction for Western Hemisphere trade corporations (see instructions)	
6 Total special deductions—Add lines 2 through 5. Enter here and on line 29(b), page 1	85,000

Schedule J — Tax Computation

1 Taxable income (line 30, page 1)	151,000
2 (a) Are you a member of a controlled group? ☐ Yes ☒ No	
(b) If "Yes," see instructions and enter your portion of the $25,000 amount in each taxable income bracket:	
(i) $............... (ii) $............... (iii) $............... (iv) $...............	
3 Income tax (see instructions to figure the tax; enter this tax or alternative tax from Schedule D, whichever is less). Check if from Schedule D ▶ ☐	50,210
4 (a) Foreign tax credit (attach Form 1118)	
(b) Investment credit (attach Form 3468)	
(c) Work incentive (WIN) credit (attach Form 4874)	
(d) Jobs credit (attach Form 5884)	
5 Total of lines 4(a), (b), (c), and (d)	50,210
6 Subtract line 5 from line 3	50,210
7 Personal holding company tax (attach Schedule PH (Form 1120))	
8 Tax from recomputing prior-year investment credit (attach Form 4255)	
9 Tax from recomputing prior-year WIN credit (attach computation)	
10 Minimum tax on tax preference items (see instructions—attach Form 4626)	
11 Total tax—Add lines 6 through 10. Enter here and on line 31, page 1	50,210

Schedule M–1 — Reconciliation of Income Per Books With Income Per Return

1 Net income per books	185,790	7 Income recorded on books this year not included in this return (itemize)	
2 Federal income tax	50,210	(a) Tax-exempt interest $...............	
3 Excess of capital losses over capital gains			
4 Income subject to tax not recorded on books this year (itemize)...............			
		8 Deductions in this tax return not charged against book income this year (itemize)	
5 Expenses recorded on books this year not deducted in this return (itemize)		(a) Depreciation . . $...............	
(a) Depreciation . . . . $...............		(b) Depletion . . . $...............	
(b) Depletion . . . . . $...............			
		9 Total of lines 7 and 8	—0—
6 Total of lines 1 through 5	236,000	10 Income (line 28, page 1)—line 6 less 9	236,000

PROBLEMS

1. What justification may be given for levying a tax on the corporate entity?
2. a. As two extreme alternatives to our present entity structure, (1) we could exclude corporations from the list of entities recognized for tax purposes on the grounds that all corporate income ultimately belongs to individuals and that, until such time as that income is distributed by the corporation, it ought not to be subject to tax; or (2) we could tax all corporations exactly as we tax single taxpaying individuals and then exclude from individuals' income any amounts distributed (as dividends) by the corporations. What practical consequences would follow from each of these extreme alternatives? Explain.
   b. As another alternative to our present corporate income tax, we could *currently* allocate all corporate incomes to the (ultimate) individual stockholders, whether or not the corporation distributed any income. If we did this, we could then exclude corporations from any income tax. (In other words, we could treat corporations the way we treat partnerships for tax purposes.) What practical reasons preclude the general acceptance of this alternative?
   c. Finally, as another alternative to our present corporate income tax, we could recognize the corporation as a separate entity only to the extent that the corporation retained income. This could be accomplished very simply by allowing the corporation a deduction for dividends paid. (In essence, this is the way we treat trusts for tax purposes.) Why do you suppose that this alternative has never been accepted by Congress?
3. Many foreign countries levy very high taxes on corporate earnings that are not distributed to stockholders as dividends. Compare this to the United States treatment of corporate income and explain the probable effects of each alternative on the source of corporate funds.
4. In recent years, corporate tax rates have been reduced. The maximum rate is now 46 percent as opposed to 48 percent before 1979. Also, the amount subject to rates substantially lower than 46 percent has increased from $25,000 to $100,000. Explain the probable rationale used by Congress in making these reductions.
5. Following is a summary of income and expenses of the World Corporation during 19x1.

Income:

Sales of merchandise	$975,000
Interest from customers	2,300
Interest on investment in bonds of AT&T	4,000
Interest on bonds of State of New York	3,400
Life insurance received on death of treasurer of corporation	100,000
Refund of federal income taxes from previous year	12,000
Dividends received on investment in General Electric Co. stock	22,000

Expenses:

Cost of goods sold	$500,000
Salaries	122,000
Advertising, promotion, legal services	28,000
Depreciation of property	64,000
Taxes on real estate, payroll, etc.	32,000
Interest paid	4,000

Amortization of organization expenses	500
Office expenses, postage, computer service	80,000
Other business expenses	116,000

   a. What is the corporation's "gross income" for the year?
   b. What is the amount of "routine deductions"?
   c. What is the amount of "special deductions"?
   d. What is the amount of total tax liability?

6. ABC Corporation received the following items of income in the current year:

Revenue from sales of merchandise	$100,000
Dividends from domestic corporations	10,000
Interest from State of Kansas bonds	5,000

In addition, ABC Corporation incurred the following expenses:

| Cost of merchandise sold | $80,000 |
| Other operating expenses | 12,000 |

What is ABC Corporation's:
   a. Gross income?
   b. Exclusions?
   c. Deductions?
   d. Taxable income?

7. DEF Corporation received the following items of income in the current year:

| Revenue from sales of merchandise | $200,000 |
| Interest from State of Florida bonds | 50,000 |

DEF Corporation also incurred the following expenses:

| Cost of merchandise sold | $120,000 |
| Other operating expenses | 20,000 |

What is DEF Corporation's:
   a. Marginal tax rate?
   b. Average tax rate?
   c. "Real" or "effective" tax rate?

8. Individuals Able, Baker, and Cooke together own 100 percent of three corporations. Each corporation operates a separate "discount store" located in three different cities. Each store has annual income of $80,000.
   a. If each shareholder owns 33⅓ percent of each corporation's stock, compute the additional tax liability due for the current year compared with an arrangement in which Able, Baker, and Cooke each owned one of the corporations. Benefits from all brackets are allocated equally among the companies.
   b. Devise a scheme of ownership whereby Able, Baker, and Cooke may own the three corporations jointly and avoid treatment as a controlled group.
   c. Discuss why the three individuals would hesitate to adopt the pattern of ownership you devised in part b. For this purpose, assume that the stores have only been in existence for a brief period.

9. Charles Goodnight owns a successful men's clothing store, which he operates

as a proprietorship. Charles estimates that the net profits of the business for 1979 will be $110,000. He wonders if he can gain a tax advantage by incorporation. He has no other source of income, and he would need a salary of $40,000 from the corporation. Calculate the tax savings from incorporation if Charles is single, under 65 with no dependents, and has itemized deductions less than the zero bracket amount.

10. Jim Jacks is the majority shareholder of Jacks, Inc. On Jim's personal return, his marginal tax rate is 60 percent for 19x1. During 19x1, Jacks, Inc. paid Jim a salary of $120,000. After deducting this salary, the corporation's taxable income was $200,000. When examining the corporate return for 19x1, the agent of the I.R.S. proposes to disallow $40,000 of the salary because the salary is unreasonably high. Calculate the tax cost if the agent disallows the deduction.

SUPPLEMENTAL PROBLEMS

11. In 1977 Learning, Inc. reported a taxable income of $20,000; in addition the corporation earned $5,000 as interest on its investment in municipal bonds. The corporation also paid a dividend of $25,000. The corporation had no accumulated earnings and profits.
    a. On what amount of income must Learning, Inc. pay tax?
    b. On what amount of income must Learning's stockholders pay tax because of the dividends distributed?
    c. Based on your answers to parts a and b, what conclusions can you draw about the wisdom of a closely held corporation investing in tax-exempt securities?

12. Corporations A and B are the only members of a controlled group. In 1979, Corporation A has taxable income of $20,000 and B has taxable income of $110,000. Specify the allocations that the group should make between A and B for the four $25,000 brackets taxed below 46 percent.

13. New Corporation was formed in January 1979. It incurred organization costs of $5,000. The corporate officers anticipate that the corporation will have income well in excess of $100,000 per year. They have asked you if they should elect to amortize the organization costs or wait and deduct them 20 years hence when the corporation is liquidated. Compute the present value of the two tax alternatives.

RETURN PROBLEMS

1. Major Corporation, 1000 Broad Street, New York, N.Y. 10012 had the following trial balance for the current year relating to revenue and expenses:

	Dr.	Cr.
Sales revenue		$2,000,000
Dividends received (qualified corporations)		100,000
Interest on NYC short-term paper		90,000
Cost of goods sold	$ 950,000	
Compensation of officers	125,000	
Salaries and wages	300,000	
Repairs	5,000	
Rents	25,000	
Taxes	15,000	
Interest	45,000	
Depreciation per books	275,000	
Pension expense	126,000	
Book profit before taxes	324,000	
	$2,190,000	$2,190,000

For calculation of taxable income, the following additional information is provided: (1) Depreciation for taxes was $302,000; (2) pension expenses for taxes were $102,000.

Based on the above information, complete Form 1120 and Schedule J, Form 1120.

2. For the Major Corporation in Return Problem 1, prepare a reconciliation of book profit *after taxes* with the taxable income using Schedule M-1.

11

other entities:
basic rules

An organization will be taxed as a corporation if, taking all relevant characteristics into account, it more nearly resembles a corporation than some other entity.

JUDGE TANNENWALD,
Phillip G. Larson v. Commissioner, 66 TC 172 (1976)

The two preceding chapters explain the basic rules for determining the income tax liability of individuals and corporations, the two entities that account for the bulk of federal revenues from the income tax. Other accounting entities, nevertheless, play an important role in our tax scheme. While the entities discussed in this chapter have only marginal implications for the bulk of the nation's individual taxpayers, they may play a critical role in the tax plans of affluent taxpayers.

In this chapter, the tax-paying entity we shall consider first is the fiduciary. Then the tax rules related to partnerships will be discussed, with some information about how partnerships have been and are being used by those who seek to reduce their annual tax bills. Finally, we shall consider that peculiar tax entity, the Subchapter S corporation, which is partially partnership or proprietorship and partially corporation yet is treated as a separate entity for many purposes.

Before turning to the tax laws relative to these other entities, the role of the individual proprietor should be clarified. In financial accounting, a sole proprietorship is treated as a separate entity, and trade or business activities are separated from the proprietor's other financial activities when financial statements are prepared. Indeed, if the same individual is engaged in several, distinct businesses, accepted accounting practices would generally require a separate set of records and separate reports for each. Tax law, however, makes no distinction between an individual and the one or more business activities in which he or she is engaged as a proprietor. A medical doctor employed as a professor in a medical school, for example, may also operate a private practice in his or her specialty and concurrently be engaged in the business of farming or ranching. Despite these disparate activities, there exists only one taxable entity, the individual. The doctor would report his or her salary from the university on line 8, Form 1040, just like any other employee; his or her income from the medical practice on Schedule C of Form 1040; and the income or loss from farming-ranching activities on Schedule F of Form 1040. If prudent, the doctor will maintain separate records for each proprietorship. When filing a tax return, however, he or she must treat each proprietorship as a mere conduit through which items of income, deductions, and credits flow directly to the individual.

Other entities, which are not discussed in detail in this introductory text, are subject to their own tax rules. Special rules apply to foreign personal holding companies, foreign subsidiaries of domestic corporations, life insurance companies, banks, and savings and loan institutions. Any organization organized for a "nonprofit" purpose, whether a corporation, trust, or association, may be exempt from the tax law—for example, governmental units, churches, charities, clubs, and leagues. Generally, application must be filed to establish their tax-exempt status. While these organizations are exempt from the federal income tax, many of them are required to file an annual information return, which is used by the Internal Revenue Service to check on their ''nonprofit'' status. If tax-exempt organizations engage in certain prohibited transactions, they may be taxed on these transactions and/or their entire tax-exempt status may be revoked.

THE FIDUCIARY TAXPAYER

When the income-tax law was written in 1913, estates and trusts were treated merely as the agents for natural persons, the beneficiaries. The income tax was thus levied on the beneficiary of the trust, even though in some cases the agent (estate or trust) made the actual tax payment. This manner of taxing fiduciaries, however, ignored one important question: Who is taxed on the income of an *inter vivos* or testamentary trust when no natural person is currently designated as beneficiary—for example, when a grantor creates a trust for the benefit of individuals not yet born, with all income to accumulate until the occurrence of some subsequent event? The Revenue Act of 1916 eliminated this loophole and created a new taxable entity, the fiduciary. Before turning to discussion of the income taxation of estates and trusts, it will be instructive to examine the interrelationship between the federal estate and gift taxes and the income taxation of estates and trusts. Every student should understand clearly that the taxation of *income* earned by a trust or an estate has little or nothing to do with the estate or gift tax that may impinge when an estate or trust is first created.

Estate and gift taxes

Beginning in 1919, the federal government levied a tax on the *transfer of wealth* at death. Responsibility for payment of that tax usually falls on the executor appointed in the deceased taxpayer's will, or by a court-appointed administrator when the individual dies intestate (i.e., without a will). The initial imposition of a tax on death transfers created a problem: Given a modicum of faith on the part of the natural objects of his or her bounty, a taxpayer could evade the estate tax by giving away wealth before death. This rather obvious strategy prompted Congress to levy a tax on gifts of property. Originally passed in the early 1920s, the gift tax became a permanent feature of the federal tax structure in 1932.

The estate and gift taxes generally languished in the backwaters of federal tax policy from their enactment until passage of the 1976 Tax Reform Act. Prior to that change, the estate and gift taxes were treated as separate exactions. Progressive rate schedules applied to both taxes, but the rates for the gift tax in each bracket were 25 percent lower than the estate tax rates. This favorable disparity resulted in an obvious planning strategy. Wealth was disposed of by *inter vivos* gifts (gifts between living persons), and in many cases the gifts were made by creating trusts for the benefit of children, grandchildren, and other relatives. For elderly, wealthy individuals, these gifts in trust not only afforded the advantage of paying a lower wealth-transfer tax but often resulted in the income from the trust property being taxed at lower rates in the trust or to the beneficiaries. The only penalty was that the wealth-transfer tax had to be paid at the time of the gift rather than later when the donor died.

Another popular scheme was to create a trust with a life estate in the income from the trust's assets for the donor's children and grandchildren, with the remaining assets (or trust corpus) to pass in fee simple to great-grandchildren when they reached a specified age. By this device, the estate tax on the trust corpus was avoided on the death of the intervening generations because they owned only a right to income for as long as they lived.

The major change made in these transfer taxes by the 1976 Act was the ''unification'' of the tax base. As explained in Chapter 2, page **2**/4, total transfers at death and by gift after 1976 constitute the base to which the progressive rates in Appendix C must be applied. The estate tax, then, becomes equivalent to a final ''gift tax'' paid at the time of death. The new rules provide for a unified credit that has the effect of exempting wealth transfers of $175,625 or less. While a detailed explanation of the estate and gift tax rules is beyond the scope of this introduction to taxation, some knowledge of the basic framework of these laws is essential.

The beginning point for determination of the new unified transfer tax imposed at death is calculation of the decedent's taxable estate according to the following formula:

Gross estate—The fair market value of all property, wherever located, in which the decedent had an interest at death.
Less: (1) Funeral, administrative, and certain other expenses
(2) Debts owed by the decedent
(3) A marital deduction equal to the fair market value of property passing to the

decedent's surviving spouse. The marital deduction is limited to the larger of: one-half of the gross estate reduced by items (1) and (2) above, or $250,000. The $250,000 limit was introduced by the 1976 Act to permit the less affluent to avoid the transfer taxes where the property is left to the surviving spouse.

(4) Amounts bequeathed to charities

Equals: Taxable estate.

If a decedent has made no taxable gifts after 1976, the rates in Appendix C are applied to the taxable estate to determine his or her gross tax. The gross tax may be reduced by credits allowed for death taxes paid to states and for estate taxes paid on property included in the gross estate of a prior decedent within the last ten years. Finally, the gross tax is reduced by the unified credit.

If an individual makes gifts after 1976, the taxable gifts are computed by using the following formula:

Gross gifts for the calendar quarter or calendar year, depending on the amount of the gifts, measured by the fair market value of the gift property on the date of the gift

Less: (1) An exclusion of $3,000 per donee per year. This exclusion is intended to exclude from taxation nominal gifts, and no gift tax return need be filed unless gifts to one donee exceed $3,000 for the year.

(2) A marital deduction where the donee is the donor's spouse. The deduction is 50 percent of the gross gift to the spouse (but 100 percent of all gifts to a spouse up to $100,000 for the donor's lifetime may be deducted).

(3) Charitable gifts

Equals: Taxable gifts.

The rates in Appendix C are used to determine the gross tax. Because of the progressive rates, however, taxable gifts during the current period must be added to all prior taxable gifts (after 1976) to obtain the total base on which a tentative tax is computed. Taxes paid on prior gifts are then subtracted from the tentative tax, and the remainder is the current tax— usually at a higher marginal rate. The unified credit can then be applied against the gift tax. In most cases the credit should be used to offset the first transfer taxes levied to avoid or reduce payments to the government currently.

Upon the death of the donor who has made life-time taxable gifts, the calculation explained on page 2/4 is then made to determine the amount of the estate tax. The resulting total tax is approximately the same as that which would be levied in a situation where the decedent's entire wealth is transferred at death.

In addition to the unified rates, the unified credit, and the increased marital deductions, the 1976 Act closed some substantial loopholes and gave some taxpayers additional benefits:

1. Trust arrangements designed to avoid the estate tax on one or more generations by providing children and/or grandchildren with only life estates will have only limited usefulness in the future.

2. Death-bed gifts can no longer be used to reduce the gross estate. Under the old law, a person could, in contemplation of death, make a gift and pay the gift tax. Generally, these gifts would be ignored and included in the gross estate. However, the gift tax paid would reduce the estate. Under the 1976 Act, all gifts made within three years of death, *as well as* the gift taxes paid are now included in the gross estate.

3. Real estate used in farming and certain other closely held businesses can be valued using special methods designed to arrive at "current use" value as opposed to the "best use" value, which usually includes a speculative element. This provision will reduce the estate taxes of farmers where the farm is operated by a family member following the farmer's death.

The major objective of the reform of these taxes in the 1976 Act was the elimination of benefits accruing to *inter vivos* gifts. The goal was supposedly accomplished by the unified rates. However, a fairly comprehensive simulation involving *inter vivos* gifts of cash, corporate securities, and land, which are common properties used for gifts, showed that in most circumstances a greater amount of a family's wealth can still be passed to later generations through lifetime gifts than at death.[1] That study reveals that gifts during the donor's lifetime, provided they are made at least three years before death, are generally beneficial because the gift tax *paid* is in every event removed from the final tax base for wealth transfers. Gifts are especially advantageous where the donee's marginal income tax rate is lower

---

[1] Richard Byars, *Life-Time Gifts Versus Passage at Death: A Simulation,* an unpublished dissertation (North Texas State University, 1977).

than that of the donor, and where the property appreciates in value after the gift is made. Finally, the relative value of *inter vivos* gifts compared to transfers at death increases substantially as marginal tax rates applicable to wealth transfers increase.

Creation of fiduciary taxpayers

The structure of wealth-transfer taxes as just discussed accounts for the existence of many fiduciary taxpayers. The advent of death results in the estate tax and simultaneously creates a new income tax entity, the estate. Income of the decedent that arises before death must be reported on the final tax return of the decedent. If the decedent is married at death, a joint return can be filed, with the survivor including the income and deductions of the decedent until death and the income and deductions of the survivor for the remainder of the year. Income received or accruing to the decedent's property *after* death is reported on the income tax return of the estate, along with any applicable expenses. The decedent's estate will continue reporting the income and deductions related to the properties passed at death until the final distribution is made from the estate to the beneficiaries named in the will, or by operation of law where no will existed at the time of death. A final accounting to the probate court usually signals the end of the estate as a taxable entity.

Trusts are often created when property is distributed by an estate under the terms of a will. Termed testamentary trusts, these trusts are often provided for in the will of a decedent to pass property to minors and others whom the decedent does not think capable of the ownership and management of property. In other cases, the decedent merely wishes to relieve the beneficiaries of the problems of wise management of the property, leaving such chores in the hands of experienced trustees.

Wealthy taxpayers bent on decreasing their estate taxes often create trusts by *inter vivos* gifts, although the extent to which the transfer taxes motivated the creation of trusts is not clear.[2] No doubt many trusts are created by *inter vivos* gifts to assure the financial security of an elderly mother or father or to provide for the education of children and grandchildren. But even where the basic motivation is love or charity, the wise grantor of a trust will always consider the tax consequences of his or her proposed actions.

[2]For a discussion on this point, see Johnson and Vernon, "Income of Estates and Trusts," *1959 Compendium*, p. 1759. The conclusion there is that the use of trusts for tax avoidance may be greatly overestimated.

Basic income tax rules for estates and trusts

An estate or trust, once in existence, enjoys the mixed blessing of becoming an entity that may have to pay a tax on its income. The legal transfer of property from a decedent to his or her estate, or the transfer of property by a grantor to a trust, is not a taxable event for income tax purposes, although the transfers may be subject to the estate and gift tax. Similarly, a distribution of corpus from an estate or trust to its beneficiaries is not generally a taxable event (although there are important exceptions to this generalization). The income tax problems that arise when appreciated property, for example, is transferred to a trust by *inter vivos* gift and then later sold by the trust is beyond our scope here. That dramatic event, death, leaves no doubt concerning the bona fide existence of the resulting estate as a separate taxpayer. The creation of a trust by an *inter vivos* gift, however, can create problems concerning the "tax" existence of the trust.

EFFECTIVE GRANTOR TRUSTS   To illustrate the problem of whether an *inter vivos* gift in trust results in the creation of a new taxpayer, consider the following facts: A widow with substantial wealth has taxable income derived from dividends and interest amounting to $150,000 per annum. Her top marginal rate on this taxable income is 70 percent. Assume further that she has several grandchildren with virtually no taxable income. She intends to pass her wealth to them at death. For now, however, she is not willing to make outright gifts of her property to the grandchildren, even though such gifts would distribute the income among several taxpayers in lower brackets and substantially reduce the total tax burden. An ideal solution would be for her to create a trust for each grandchild, have each trust pay taxes at lower marginal rates, and yet retain the power to revoke the trusts and regain the property with the related income if she later needs it for her own use. With this arrangement she would have a nearly ideal tax situation, a lower total tax bill without giving up her claim on the property. This scheme, however, violates one of the basic doctrines in our tax law.

Stated simply, the question is: Can a person make an effective assignment of the income from property and have that income taxed to the assignee without relinquishing legal title to the property from which the income is derived? In a classic case, a father who owned corporate coupon bonds gave his son the right to clip the coupons as they matured, mail them in for payment, and retain the cash received. The son reported the interest income based on the somewhat fanciful argument that the coupons were "property" received by gift. The Supreme Court was not impressed with the argument and required that income be reported by the father.[3] The somewhat colorful legal analogy used is that a taxpayer cannot avoid picking the fruit (recognizing income) unless he is willing to give away the entire tree (the capital that produces the income).

To make an effective transfer of an income-producing property in trust, and thus shift the income from the grantor to the trust, the grantor cannot retain any of the following powers: to revoke the trust; to control the beneficial enjoyment of the trust's income or corpus; to administer the trust property in such a manner as to benefit the grantor; or to cause the income or corpus to revert to the grantor. Detailed application of these proscribed powers must be reserved for advanced study. However, one very important exception to the general idea that the grantor must divest himself of ownership and control of the trust deserves consideration. That exception is the "Clifford" trust, or short-term trust.[4] The grantor of a trust is not taxed on its income if he retains a reversionary interest in the trust corpus (or a power to revoke the trust) provided the reversion cannot occur until after a period of more than 10 years (or upon death of the beneficiary). Grantors can make effective use of these short-term trusts to provide for elderly dependents, for the college education of children and grandchildren, and for other similar objectives.

The rules just discussed serve as a good example of a bias that exists in much of our tax law. Given the doctrine that prohibits the assignment of *income* between taxpayers, a doctrine that is clearly essential with our progressive rate structure, the individual whose only source of income is earnings cannot use the trust device just explained to shift income to others. The "tree" of earned income is the taxpayer's body and mind; the "tree" of income that arises from property is that property. Rights to the income from the former tree cannot be assigned; income rights from the latter can be assigned if the property is also assigned. This inherent bias in our tax laws, which have traditionally favored income from property, becomes even more evident later when we consider the rules for capital gains in Part Six.

[3] *Helvering* v. *Horst,* 311 U.S. 112 (1940). Earlier, in *Lucas* v. *Earl,* 281 U.S. 111 (1930), the Supreme Court had held that a lawyer could not make an anticipatory assignment of future fees and shift the income to the assignee.
[4] The name is derived from *Helvering* v. *Clifford,* 309 U.S. 331 (1940), which dealt with a short-term trust.

COMPUTATIONAL RULES   Once created, estates and trusts are new taxpayers and are entitled to make the elections available under the law. They establish their own taxable year and elect the accounting methods to be used. Availability of new elections can have both good and bad results. For example, an estate may be a shareholder in a Subchapter S corporation if it so elects (see discussion below). However, if the decedent's will provides for the transfer of stock in a Subchapter S corporation to a testamentary trust, continued ownership by the trust will destroy the special election. The fact that the fiduciary is a new taxpayer can be an important consideration in establishing *inter vivos* trusts and in the timing of distributions from an estate to its beneficiaries.

Generally, estates and trusts compute their gross income, deductions, and credits under the same rules used by individuals. The general tax formula on page 5/1 is therefore applicable. The many exclusions, deductions, and credits that, by their nature, are intended for individuals only, are not available to fiduciaries. On the other hand, the law contains some special deductions applicable to fiduciaries only. Instead of the $1,000 exemption deduction, estates get an exemption of $600. Simple trusts, defined as those that are *required* to distribute all their income to beneficiaries currently, are allowed an exemption of $300. All other trusts get a $100 exemption. Of more importance is the deduction allowed for distributions of income to beneficiaries.

Under the simplest arrangement, estates and trusts are not taxpayers at all but mere conduits through which items of income and deductions flow to their beneficiaries. For example, consider the situation in which a wealthy man transfers $200,000 in cash to a trust, naming his mother as beneficiary. The trust instrument provides that all trust income as defined by the tax law, net of trust expenses, is to be paid out annually to his mother for her life, with the reversion of the corpus to him upon the mother's death. The purpose of this trust is to give the mother an income without also imposing on her the responsibility for investing the trust corpus and without the son first having to pay his own income tax on the income transferred to his mother. While the trust is a taxpayer, and must file a return, it will have no tax liability because it is allowed a deduction for the distribution of current income to the beneficiary. Under these circumstances, the tax burden for the trust's net income will fall on the mother because the distributions are income to her.

Most estates and trusts, however, do not distribute all income currently. Executors of estates may wish to retain some income until claims against the estate are settled. A trustee may be required to accumulate income until the beneficiaries reach a given age. The trust instrument may define income subject to current distribution in a manner different from the tax definitions, e.g., capital gains on sale of property may be allocated to trust corpus, not to income. Thus, for numerous reasons, the fiduciary may have undistributed income and be subject to the tax. The problems that arise when accumulated income is eventually distributed by the fiduciary are complex, and any attempt to generalize these rules for present purposes would be more dangerous than helpful.

As explained, an estate or trust that distributes income to its beneficiaries is not taxed on that income. Instead, the beneficiaries receiving the distributed income declare it on their individual returns. But what about the tax characteristics of the distributed income? Consider these facts: A complex trust realizes $3,000 of interest income on corporate bonds, $2,000 of interest on municipal bonds, and $5,000 of gain on capital assets. The trust pays various expenses of $1,000 and distributes the $9,000 remaining current income to its beneficiaries. Does the beneficiary enjoy the favorable classification for the municipal bond interest and the capital gain? Yes, the character of the income items is not changed but flows through the trust to the beneficiary. Thus, $2,000/$10,000, or 2/10, of the $9,000 distribution is excluded by the beneficiary, and 5/10 of the distribution is treated as a capital gain.

When a fiduciary has taxable income, it computes its tax using the rate schedule in Appendix E. This schedule has rates the same as those applicable to married individuals who file separately (but excluding the zero bracket amount). Whereas the tax is levied on the estate or trust, the executor or trustee has a legal obligation to file the return and pay the tax (though the fiduciary is normally not personally liable for the tax). The return is made on Form 1041.

PARTNERSHIPS

For tax purposes, "the term 'partnership' includes a syndicate, group, pool, joint venture, or other unincorporated organization through or by means of which any business, financial operation, or venture is carried on, and which is not, within the meaning of this title, a corporation or a trust or estate."[5] When two or more people join together to carry on a business or an investment activity for their joint profit, a partnership exists, unless the government can show that it is *de facto* a corporation or trust. While quite broad, this definition can be significant. A partnership is, for most purposes, viewed as an "aggregation" of individual proprietors joined together for mutual profit, and not as a separate entity, unlike a corporation. The partnership does not pay an income tax because it is treated as an "aggregation" of proprietors, not a separate entity.

Significance of the aggregate concept

As just noted, the major significance of the aggregate concept is that the partnership pays no tax. However, the aggregate concept also has other important ramifications. Consider two individuals who wish to join together in a venture to build an apartment complex. Taxpayer A will contribute the land for the project. The land has a current fair market value of $200,000, but A paid only $50,000 for the land several years ago. Taxpayer B will contribute $200,000 in cash, which will be used as seed money to borrow the $4 million needed to complete the project. A and B plan to operate the complex for a few years and then sell it. If A and B form Partnership AB, A can contribute the land without paying tax on the $150,000 appreciation under the general rule that a partner has no income or loss on the contribution of property to or the withdrawal of property from a partnership. This rule is consistent with the aggregate concept. Of equal importance, when Partnership AB later sells the apartment complex, assuming the value of the land has not changed, the partnership will have a gain on A's land of $150,000 and this gain will probably be taxed as a capital gain. In this situation, the partnership agreement would likely provide that all gain on the sale of the land will be allocated back to A, who contributed the land. Under the aggregate concept, the $150,000 gain flows through Partnership AB to A and retains its tax characteristics as a capital gain. This result assumes that the land was a capital asset in the hands of the partnership.

Take the same facts as above, but assume that Taxpayers A and B decide to carry on the venture in a corporation. Under a special rule discussed in Chapter 26, A would have no gain on the contribu-

---

[5] Section 761(a).

tion of the land, provided A and B controlled the new corporation formed for the venture. When the apartment complex is later sold by the corporation, however, a separate entity, the corporation recognizes the capital gain on the land, and if the proceeds from the sale are later distributed to A, A will have, in part at least, a dividend that is taxed as ordinary income unless the distribution is made in liquidation of the corporation.

This contrast between the aggregate concept and the separate entity concept is important for many other items of income and deductions. If a partnership invests in tax-exempt bonds, the interest flows through to the partners and retains its tax attribute as tax-exempt interest. A corporation, on the other hand, can exclude the tax-exempt interest from its own gross income, but a subsequent distribution of that income from the corporation to its shareholders will typically result in an ordinary taxable dividend.

Unfortunately, our tax law does not always consistently apply the aggregate concept to partnerships. For example, a newly formed partnership is a new "taxpayer" and must make all elections relative to its taxable year and accounting methods. In addition, a partner can sell his or her partnership interest and recognize a capital gain much as stockholders in a corporation sell their stock, although there are some important exceptions in which the partner's gain is treated partly as ordinary income. Finally, under certain circumstances a partner can have dealings with the partnership just like any stranger.

Some technical rules for partnerships

The general concepts discussed above should give the student an appreciation of how partnerships fit into our general tax scheme. The following is a brief introduction to some of the technical rules relating to selection of the partnership's taxable year, when a partner reports his share of partnership income, termination of a partnership, and the reporting requirements of the partnership.

TAXABLE YEAR   A partner reports his or her share of partnership income, deductions, etc., for the partnership year ending during the partner's taxable year. If Partner A files on a calendar year, and Partnership ABC has a taxable year ending on June 30, Partner A would include his or her share of the partnership items for the period July 1, 1978 through June 30, 1979 on the Form 1040 filed for the year ended December 31, 1979. Because of this rule, part-

ners on a calendar year typically like to have the partnership year end on January 31, thereby effectively deferring recognition of partnership income for eleven months. Anticipating this natural wish, the law provides that a new partnership must adopt the same taxable year as that of its principal partners. A principal partner is one who has a 5 percent or larger interest in partnership profits or capital. Because of this rule and the widespread use of the calendar year by individuals, most partnerships must also elect the calendar year. Where the principal partners have different taxable years, the partnership must elect the calendar year unless permission is obtained from the Commissioner to adopt some other year.

TERMINATION OF A PARTNERSHIP   Under the Uniform Partnership Act, a partnership terminates upon the withdrawal or death of a partner or the sale of a partnership interest. For tax purposes, a partnership is treated more like a separate entity and is terminated only on the occurrence of either of two events: (1) When it ceases to carry on *any* business or investment activity; (2) when 50 percent or more of the total interest in partnership capital and profits is sold within any 12-month period. Thus, for tax purposes, a partnership does not terminate on the death of a partner or upon the withdrawal of one or more partners, regardless of the percentage interest of the deceased or withdrawing partner.

REPORTING THE PARTNER'S DISTRIBUTIVE SHARES Conceptually, each item of income, each deduction, and each credit is distributed to the partners based on the provisions of the partnership agreement. For convenience, however, the partnership calculates its ordinary taxable income or loss. Included in this calculation are income items and deductions that are not subject to special treatment under the tax laws. Thus, ordinary taxable income in a trading venture would include the profits from sales of inventory and the ordinary trade or business deductions. Any tax item that is subject to special treatment—e.g., tax-exempt interest, capital gains and losses, charitable contributions, to name only three of a very long list of items receiving special treatment—are reported and distributed individually to the partners. A partner reports his or her share of (1) ordinary taxable income or loss and (2) each special item.

Each year, the partnership must file Form 1065. Ordinary taxable income (loss) is calculated on page 1 of that form. The special items are reported on Schedule K of Form 1065. The partnership provides each partner with Schedule K-1 (Form 1065), which shows the partner's distributive share of ordinary taxable income (loss) and of each special item. Partners use the information given them on Schedule K-1 to complete their individual returns. Note that the partners report their distributive shares of partnership items without regard to the actual cash or property distributed by the partnership.

Use of the partnership form

Because of the aggregate concept, the partnership form of organization is ideally suited for many business operations. Unlike most other entities, the legal formation of a partnership is very simple. When two or more parties join their capital and/or efforts with the intention of earning a profit, a partnership comes into existence. The mere act of joint enterprise is sufficient, even though the parties have no explicit oral or written agreement. In fact, the ease with which partnerships can be formed may result in undesired results. Consider, as an example, two individuals engaged separately in a business activity who claim double-declining depreciation of assets. If they join their operations, the partnership formed is a new entity for purposes of most tax elections, and the properties contributed to the partnership are therefore *used* property. The double-declining depreciation method will be lost because it is not available for used properties.

While no precise statistics are available, it is probably safe to say that most partnerships are used for small enterprises where two or three parties want to combine their talents and productive assets. Partnerships, for example, are common in the agricultural segment where one party furnishes land and a second party conducts the actual operations. At the other extreme, we find large syndicates, particularly in real estate, where limited partnerships with numerous partners are used as a vehicle to raise the capital needed for the venture. Finally, partnerships are common in oil and gas exploration where several parties join together to share high risks.

SUBCHAPTER S CORPORATIONS

In 1958, Congress provided for yet another tax entity, the Subchapter S corporation. The intent of Congress was to provide taxpayers with a vehicle they could use to obtain the financial benefits of a corporation (primarily limited liability for the shareholders) without bearing the cross of double taxation. The result is a tax hybrid—part corporation, part partnership—and a veritable jungle of complex tax rules. The Subchapter S corporation is like a corporation in that it can provide the usual fringe benefits to its owners who are employees, such as health insurance, group-term life insurance, and pension and profit-sharing plans. On this count, it is clearly superior to a proprietorship or partnership where the major employees are also the owners. The corporation obtains a deduction for the cost of the benefits, and their value is not included in the gross income of the employee-owners. This tax oddity is like a partnership in that its net taxable income or loss flows through to its shareholders and is reported by them on their individual returns. Thus, one or more taxpayers beginning a new venture (where losses may likely result) can obtain the benefit of deducting these losses immediately on their individual returns. The Subchapter S corporation is also useful in situations in which an ongoing business venture results in losses in some years and limited amounts of income in others. In short, given the proper circumstances, this vehicle gives the taxpayer the desired features of both a corporation and a partnership

Election of Subchapter S provisions

The Subchapter S provisions are elective and available only where the following conditions are met:

1. The corporation must be a domestic corporation with only one class of stock outstanding.
2. All stockholders must be individual citizens or residents, estates, or certain trusts.
3. There must be 15 or fewer stockholders.
4. The corporation must not be a member of an affiliated group.
5. Every stockholder must consent in writing to the original election.

Once made, the election applies to all subsequent years unless all shareholders agree to revoke the election. This power to revoke the election is essential to effective tax planning. For example, the election may be made for a new venture where losses are expected for a few years, then revoked after the operation has turned the corner and begins to produce substantial amounts of income. A Subchapter S corporation may also become disqualified and lose the benefits if a new shareholder dissents from the election or if a shareholder dies and his or her shares are placed in a trust. Disqualification also occurs if more than 80 percent of the corporation's gross receipts are from foreign sources or more than 20 percent of its gross receipts are from passive investments. This last rule prohibits the use of the provisions in most real estate operations because rents are treated as passive income.

Basic rules for operation

As stated above, a Subchapter S corporation is a hybrid in that its taxable income and losses flow through to its shareholders. It is not, however, taxed under the aggregate theory that applies to partnerships. The flow through is limited to only three major items:

1. The taxable income of the corporation is allocated to the shareholders according to the ratio of their stock holdings.
2. Capital gains flow through and are declared by shareholders on their returns. (Under certain conditions, the flow through of capital gains is limited.)
3. Net operating losses are currently deductible to the shareholders.

Relative to this last item, the amount deductible by each shareholder is limited to cost or basis in the stock plus any loans made by the shareholder to the corporation. This limitation, if ignored, can have disastrous results. Suppose a taxpayer invests $100,000 in the stock of a new corporation and receives 25 percent of the stock. A Subchapter S election is made because losses are anticipated in the start-up period. The corporation borrows substantial funds from a bank. In the first year of operations, there is a $400,000 operating loss, and in the second year a $300,000 loss. Note that the taxpayer gets 25 percent of the first year's loss, or $100,000, but cannot take advantage of any of the second year's loss because he or she has no remaining cost or basis.

A new corporation that makes the Subchapter S election is a new "taxpayer" and must make all elections relating to its taxable year and its accounting methods. If its shareholders report on the calendar year, it can end its year on January 31 and effectively defer for eleven months the reporting of income by its shareholders; there are no restrictions for a Subchapter S corporation like those applicable to partnerships. As in a partnership, however, shareholders in a Subchapter S corporation must report their share of the corporation's net income (or capital

gains) and pay taxes on these amounts without regard to the amount of cash or property actually distributed to them.

As noted earlier, a shareholder of a Subchapter S corporation may also be an employee of the corporation. As an employee, the shareholder's salary is treated as a salary from a regular corporation. The corporation must withhold income and F.I.C.A. taxes, and the shareholder-employee reports the salary as received (or accrued). The Subchapter S corporation's remaining income (computed after *all* salaries) is reported by the shareholders at the end of the corporation's taxable year.

Current distributions of assets from a Subchapter S corporation to its shareholders do not usually result in taxable income to the shareholders. The tax law treats the distribution as made from income that the shareholders report and pay taxes on as individuals. However, distributions can be ordinary dividends. Take the case of a corporation that operated profitably for several years before making the Subchapter S election. If a subsequent distribution of cash is made in excess of the corporate earnings after the election, that excess is treated as paid out of earnings and profits of the corporation. Such excess is an ordinary dividend.

Subchapter S corporations are *not* tax corporations "treated as partnerships," witness the dividend treatment of the above distribution. The generalization that Subchapter S corporations are treated as partnerships is a dangerous one. Indeed, the election affects only the flow-through of the items specified; for all other purposes the corporate tax rules apply. When the corporation is liquidated, for example, this transaction is treated by the shareholders as a sale or exchange of their shares and gain or loss is recognized. Like most beneficial tax provisions, the Subchapter S election should carry the label "User Beware."

COMPREHENSIVE ILLUSTRATION

Assume that Mr. and Mrs. Buz Ness are actively engaged in several business ventures and that they own a substantial number of corporate stocks. During the current year their activities encompassed no less than five ventures:

□ Buz Cleaners: a chain of drive-in laundry and dry cleaning establishments organized as a corporation. Mr. Ness receives a $20,000 annual salary from

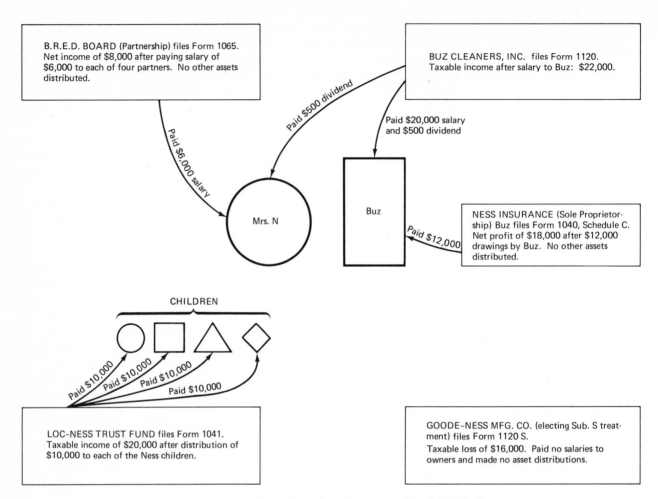

FIGURE **11-1**   Ness Family Business Interests and Cash Distributions

Buz Cleaners. After paying all of its expenses, including the owner-employee's salary, Buz Cleaners Incorporated reports a $22,000 taxable income. The corporation paid $1,000 in dividends to Mr. and Mrs. Ness, the sole owners of Buz Cleaners stock.

□ Goode-Ness Manufacturing Company: a new venture intended to produce commercial washing machines that will reduce waiting time by 50 percent. Goode-Ness is owned equally by James Goode and Buz Ness, who are not related. During the current year, Goode-Ness reported a taxable loss of $16,000. The firm is organized as a corporation but has elected Subchapter S treatment for tax purposes. Neither Mr. Goode nor Mr. Ness receives any salary from the firm, and no other assets were distributed by Goode-Ness during the year.

□ B.R.E.D. Board: a retail pastry shop organized as a partnership. Mrs. Ness owns a one-fourth inter-

est in the partnership assets and profits. As one of four partners she draws a $6,000 annual salary. After paying partners' salaries and all other operating expenses, B.R.E.D. Board reports a net income of $8,000. The entire $8,000 is reinvested in the business.

□ Loc-Ness Trust Fund: a collection of assets put into trust by Buz Ness's parents prior to their deaths several years ago. The trust agreement provides that the trustee can make distributions of trust income, at his discretion, to Mr. or Mrs. Ness or to any of their children. On the death of the last of Buz Ness's children the remaining assets are to be distributed to their heirs. During the current year, the trust earned a total income of $60,000. Of this, the trustee distributed $10,000 to each of the four Ness children. He retained $20,000 of the income within the trust fund.

◻ Ness Insurance: an insurance agency operated as a sole proprietorship. During this year, the agency earned an income of $30,000. Buz withdrew $1,000 a month from the agency for personal living expenses. The remaining $18,000 was reinvested in a new office building to house the insurance agency.

The Ness's five business ventures and the related cash flows between these ventures and the individual members of the Ness family can be diagrammed as in Figure 11-1. In terms of economic and physical realities, this arrangement obviously involves at least five distinct business operations and six people. In terms of taxable entities, however, there are one corporation (Buz Cleaners), one fiduciary (Loc-Ness), and six individuals (Mr. and Mrs. Ness and their four children). Two of the businesses (Goode-Ness and B.R.E.D. Board) must file information tax returns, but they are not liable for any tax as separate entities.

In terms of tax calculations, Mr. and Mrs. Ness probably will file one joint tax return on which they will report the following items of gross income:

From Buz Cleaners, Inc.:	
As salary	$20,000
As dividend	1,000
From Goode-Ness Manufacturing Co.:	
Half of the net operating loss	(8,000)
From Loc-Ness Trust Fund:	
Nothing	
From B.R.E.D. Board:	
As salary	6,000
As operating income (¼ interest)	2,000
From Ness Insurance Agency:	
As operating income	30,000
Total from all sources	$51,000

Observe that although the total cash received by Mr. and Mrs. Ness is only $39,000, they must report as gross income a total of $51,000 from their several business interests. Both Ness Insurance and B.R.E.D. Board contributed more to their gross income than to their cash flow; Goode-Ness Manufacturing Company, on the other hand, provided a tax deduction even though it did not require a cash contribution from either Mr. or Mrs. Ness.

On their joint tax return, Mr. and Mrs. Ness probably would be able to claim each of their four children as well as themselves as personal and dependent exemptions. Additionally, each of the children will have to file his or her own tax return and each will again claim himself or herself as a personal exemption there.

Buz Cleaners, Inc. would file a tax return and pay tax on an income of $22,000. Observe that Buz Cleaners gets a tax deduction for the salary it paid to its owner-employee, but that it does not get a deduction for the dividend it paid to Mr. and Mrs. Ness. Had Buz elected to do so, he may have been able to increase his salary to reduce or even eliminate any taxable income for Buz Cleaners, Inc. This action would, of course, have increased their personal tax liability accordingly.

Unlike Buz Cleaners, Loc-Ness Trust is treated as a separate taxable entity only to the extent that it retains its income. Thus, by paying out $10,000 to each of the four Ness children, Loc-Ness Trust reduced its taxable income from $60,000 to $20,000. Note, however, that the trust agreement is a little too good to be true. For income taxes, the arrangement can effectively spread the income between Mr. and Mrs. Ness and their children. The original grantors of the trust were Buz Ness's parents. Prior to 1976, this type of trust would pass the trust corpus to the great-grandchildren of the creators (or grantors) and successfully avoid the federal estate tax on the two intervening generations. Under new rules, upon the deaths of each succeeding generation that enjoys a life estate, which is a right to receive income for life, a wealth-transfer tax is levied on the trust corpus. The detailed rules governing the taxation of "generation-skipping" trusts are beyond our scope here. It is enough to appreciate that what was previously a good tax planning device has, in general, been eliminated.

This illustration shows how the various entities discussed in this part can be used to reduce the tax burden of a family. Income can be sheltered by the corporate rate schedule or by dividing it up among family members. Partnerships and Subchapter S corporations permit the flow through of losses and provide other benefits. We must end our discussion of this happy state of affairs on a note of caution. The various paths that lead to substantial savings are not wide, well-marked thoroughfares; they are more like jungle trails that only the foolish use without an expert guide. On the other hand, the many difficulties that must be overcome to assure a safe passage make the advanced study and the practice of taxation an exciting and rewarding vocation.

PROBLEMS

1. Contrast the tax treatment of corporations and partnerships in the United States. Why are these entities treated differently? In your answer, consider both historical accident and rational tax policy.

2. If Congress were suddenly to enact a change in our present tax laws that would treat sole proprietorships and partnerships as separate taxable entities, as they are treated in financial accounting, what would you expect to happen if
   a. These new taxable entities were subject to the same rates as unmarried individual taxpayers, like fiduciaries?
   b. These new taxable entities were subject to the same rates as are corporate taxpayers?
   c. Under either part a or b, would the concept of "controlled corporations" have to be extended to proprietorships and partnerships as well? Explain.

3. The Maturity Trust Fund is qualified as a "simple" trust, which is required to distribute all income currently. During 19x2 it had the following transactions:

Income received (all taxable)	$4,200
Expenses of administration and other expenses relating to income	1,000
Distributions of income taxable to beneficiaries	2,600

Compute the trust's federal income tax for the year.

4. Subchapter S corporations are often characterized as "tax corporations treated as partnerships." Is this true? If not, discuss some major differences between treatment of the two entities.

5. Herman Irish is married and has two small children who are dependent on him for support. For the current year, Herman expects to receive the following income:

Salary	$80,000
Dividends from taxable domestic corporations	6,000

The dividends will be paid on stock owned jointly by Herman and his wife, Betty. Herman expects the following deductions:

Unreimbursed travel and transportation related to his employment	$4,000
Itemized deductions	6,000
Exemption deductions for Herman, Betty, and two children	4,000

Herman's tax consultant has recommended that the stock owned by Herman and Betty be transferred to two trusts, one for each child. The trustees would be instructed to accumulate income and pay the accumulated income, as needed, for the college education of the children after they reach their majority. (This arrangement is a complex trust, and the annual exemption is $100 per trust.) The corpus of the trust, plus any accumulated income, would be paid to each child when he or she reaches the age of 30. The tax consultant also recommends that Herman and Betty retain enough stock to produce dividends of $200.

a. Compute Herman and Betty's tax liability for the current year, assuming they do *not* create the trusts.

b. Compute the combined liabilities of Herman and Betty and the two trusts, assuming the trusts are established on January 1 of the current year (ignore any federal gift taxes).

c. How much tax is saved by the trust arrangement?

6. Jack Warden, who files a joint return, is a successful banker who owns a small country bank. His income and deductions for recent years have been constant and, as a result, his taxable income has been about $103,200 for the past several years. In January 19x1, Jack decided to open a seed and fertilizer store in the rural town in which his bank is located. He found an experienced and dependable manager and initiated the new operation in January 19x1. The new venture was incorporated as the Community Seed and Fertilizer Company, Inc., of which Jack owns 100 percent of the stock. The operating results of the corporation were as follows:

	Gain (Loss)
19x1	($50,000)
19x2	(30,000)
19x3	5,000

a. Calculate the combined tax of the corporation and Warden for 19x1 through 19x3 (assuming that Warden's taxable income was $103,202 per year). Use the current year's tax rates. The corporate losses can be carried forward (but not back, since 19x1 was the first year of operation).

b. Calculate the total tax for Warden for 19x1 through 19x3, assuming that Warden made a proper election under Subchapter S for the years involved. Use the current year's tax rates. Warden's cost of his stock exceeds the losses.

7. a. Max and Ruth operate, as husband and wife, an interior decorating service in Texas. This year they had the following items of income and deductions:

Profits from the proprietorship	$80,000
Dividend income from taxable	
domestic corporations	2,800
Interest on savings	9,000
	$91,800

Max and Ruth have two children, aged 3 and 4, and are therefore entitled to four exemption deductions. Their itemized deductions were $3,500. Compute their gross tax liability for the current year, assuming the children are dependents and that the business is a proprietorship.

b. Devise a tax plan that will minimize the income tax of Max and Ruth. In your plan, assume that Max and Ruth have no particular need for interest income but that they would like to arrange for the maximum after-tax income in the corporation to provide for expected expansion. Both Max and Ruth expect that they will have to provide a college education for their children. (For simplicity, assume that Max and Ruth need a combined income of $30,000 before taxes from the decorating service for personal living expenses.)

8. James Hampton, a client of yours, owns a large city lot that cost him $15,000 several years ago. He has been leasing the lot, which has a fair market value of

$250,000, to a used car dealer. James has been approached by Henry Simon about building an office building on the property. Simon proposes to put $250,000 cash into the deal and then obtain a mortgage loan of $12 million to cover the building costs. James and Henry would operate the office building for five or six years and then sell it for a profit. List the advantages and disadvantages of using (a) a corporation, (b) a Subchapter S corporation, and (c) a partnership for the new venture.

9. Thomas and Lewis Thornton are brothers and partners in a hardware store, Thornton Bros. Hardware (a partnership). Both have substantial incomes from a trust established by their father. Their family lawyer has advised them that it might be wise to incorporate the hardware business. Upon inquiry, you find that the net profits from the store are erratic, with sizable losses occurring in one year out of three. Would you advise them to incorporate? If not, devise another plan that fits the circumstances.

10. Jim Jones recently completed the construction of an apartment house at a cost of $5 million. He borrowed the bulk of the money needed on a long-term mortgage. He also elected to depreciate the property using double-declining balance depreciation. His goal was to create tax losses to offset his ordinary income, a high five-digit salary as a corporate executive. Unfortunately, he succeeded too well—the tax losses on the apartment complex exceed his other income. He is thinking about forming a partnership with a friend to spread the losses. What tax problem will Jim encounter in the plan?

11. Tim Wortman died this year. His gross estate was valued at $2,450,000. He owed debts of $350,000, and the estate incurred administrative expenses of $50,000. There were no other estate deductions. During his life (and after 1976), Tim made taxable gifts totaling $550,000 and paid a gift tax of $127,300 on these gifts. Calculate the estate tax due the federal government, assuming the unified credit available is $47,000.

12. The statements below describe some major tax characteristics of one or more of the entities (other than individuals) discussed in this chapter—corporations, Subchapter S corporations, trusts, partnerships. For each statement, what is the appropriate entity or entities?
    a. A separate entity for all purposes under the tax law.
    b. An entity that serves only as a conduit for income and deductions.
    c. An entity that functions as a taxpayer only to the extent that its income is not distributed.
    d. An entity that serves as a rate shelter because it is subject to lower tax rates.
    e. An entity that serves as a rate shelter only because it increases the number of taxpayers.
    f. An entity that serves as a conduit only for taxable income and net operating losses.

SUPPLEMENTAL PROBLEMS

13. Mr. J. Vanderbuild VI invested $100,000 in High Risk, Inc., a new corporate business. In exchange for his investment, Vanderbuild received 20 percent of the outstanding stock of High Risk.
    a. Assume that during each of its first five years of operations High Risk Inc. reported a tax loss of $150,000 and that in the sixth year it went into bank-

ruptcy and notified all stockholders that they would receive nothing in return for their original investments.

1. If High Risk, Inc. is qualified as a Subchapter S corporation and Mr. J. Vanderbuild VI is in a 70 percent marginal tax bracket, what real economic loss did he sustain because of this investment?

2. If High Risk is not qualified for Subchapter S treatment, Vanderbuild will eventually report a capital loss of $100,000. Will Vanderbuild's real economic loss be greater or less under these conditions than it would be under those described in part a-1? Explain your answer as best you can at this point in the course.

3. As a library research project, determine what effect the qualification of High Risk's stock under Code Section 1244 would have on Vanderbuild's loss in part a-2.

b. Assuming that during each of its first five years of operations High Risk reported a taxable income of $150,000, that the corporation paid no dividends, and that Vanderbuild sold his interest in the corporation in the sixth year for $350,000:

1. If High Risk is qualified as a Subchapter S corporation and Vanderbuild is in a marginal tax bracket of 70 percent, what real economic gain did he experience because of this investment?

2. If High Risk does not qualify for Subchapter S treatment, what real economic gain did he experience because of this investment?

c. In view of your answers to parts a and b, under what fact conditions would you expect corporate directors to try to qualify their corporation for Subchapter S treatment? Explain.

d. In view of your answers to parts a and b, under what fact conditions would you expect corporate directors not to elect Subchapter S treatment? Explain.

e. Explain why both Subchapter S stocks and stocks qualified under Section 1244 may be good investments for high-income taxpayers even though the risks associated with those investments may be relatively high. (NOTE: To answer the Sec. 1244 question, you will have to do additional reading in your school library *or* read pages **23**/7–**23**/8 in this text.)

f. What can an investor lose by investing in a stock qualified under Section 1244 that he would not lose if the stock were not so qualified?

14. Ms. Susan Kemp is 65 years old and in very good health. Owing to the efforts of her energetic husband, now deceased, Ms. Kemp has about $5,000,000 invested in corporate stocks and bonds that produce an income of approximately $300,000 per year. She has only one child, a married son, who is quite wealthy in his own right, being the sole stockholder of a company that earns about $500,000 per year. However, the son has three children in their teens who have no current taxable income. Susan talked with her son and decided that her wealth should pass directly to her grandchildren. She has come to you for advice on the wisdom of several plans that have been recommended by others. Evaluate each plan and suggest alternatives.

a. One adviser told her that, because of the 1976 Act, she might as well wait and pass her property at death because the new law has equalized the tax treatment of *inter vivos* gifts and death transfers.

b. Another counselor suggested that she make a gift of the bulk of her securities in trust, keeping only enough to assure her sufficient income. As advised, one trust would be created with the trustee given the power to distribute income as needed for the welfare of the grandchildren. She was told to reserve the power to revoke the trust in the event the children did not "turn out well."

c. Yet another adviser suggested that she make a series of gifts every two years to a single trust for the benefit of the three grandchildren.

15. James Whitson owns 25 percent of the common stock of Prism, Inc., a calendar-year taxpayer. The corporation operated for several years before making a Subchapter S election for 19x1. In 19x1, the corporation had taxable income of $100,000 and made no distributions to its shareholders. Whitson properly reported $25,000 as his share of the corporate income on his individual return. In 19x2 Prism distributed the following amounts in cash to Whitson: March 1, $15,000; June 1, $20,000; October 1, $40,000. Corporate taxable income for 19x2 was $120,000.

a. Why might a profitable corporation such as Prism make a Subchapter S election?

b. How much income must Whitson report as a result of the distributions received in 19x2 and the corporation's taxable income?

Another example . . . took place within the lifetime of many of us; the revolution of the personal income tax. It has made impossible such displays of ostentatious magnificence as Hearst's Casa Grande in St. Simeon; it has stimulated the creation of foundations and nonprofit institutions; it has reduced the differences between the standards of living of various socioeconomic classes; it has brought about a clear-cut distinction between wages and take-home pay. And no amount of wishful thinking will ever bring us back to pre-income-tax days.

J. SAMUEL BOIS,
The Art of Awareness
Wm. C. Brown Company, 1966

The art of taxation consists in so plucking the goose as to obtain the largest amount of feathers with the least amount of hissing.

JEAN BAPTISE COLBERT, French Financial Minister under King Louis XIV (1638–1715)

PART

FOUR
the general welfare

The Committee Reports foreclose any reading of that provision which would permit this taxpayer to take the rental payments for his Florida apartment as "medical care" deductions.

JUSTICE HARLAN,
Commissioner v. *Bilder*, 369 U.S.499 (1962)

medical expenses and casualty losses

The income tax law of the United States is filled with special provisions and rules intended to promote the general welfare. Sometimes these special provisions mirror a consensus of public thought on the meaning of "general welfare"; in other cases they reflect Congress's perception of the general welfare; and in still other instances one is led to conclude that "general welfare" might be translated as meaning the well-being of a lobby group.

In Part Four we shall be examining some of the special provisions in the law. Most of the items discussed in this Part may be included in one of the classifications of personal deductions first encountered on page **6/12**. In Chapter 12 the tax treatment of certain items related to economic hardships of individuals will be reviewed. In Chapter 13, some deductions that may be viewed as subsidies (interest, taxes, and contributions) are analyzed. Chapter 14 surveys some of the controversial deductions related to earning income. Finally, in Chapter 15, attention is turned to the increasingly important tax problems of retirement plans. Obviously, no provisions of the tax law have more direct impact on the general welfare than the zero bracket amount and the deduction for personal exemptions, which were discussed in Chapter 9. Thus, in studying the specific deductions discussed in this Part, it is essential that you keep in mind their relationship to the more general deductions.

Personal expenditures that may be deducted are carefully spelled out in the tax law, and the most

important will be examined in the first three chapters of Part Four. One must conclude, however, that these items are less important for most taxpayers today than they were prior to 1977. From 1944 through 1976, the individual was permitted either to itemize the allowable personal expenditures or to take, instead, a "percentage standard deduction." Originally, the standard deduction was simply 10 percent of adjusted gross income, so that those with low income received very little benefit from the deduction. In 1964, a "minimum standard deduction" was introduced, which removed 1.5 million persons from the tax rolls. However, in 1969 it still left some 5.2 million taxpayers at or below the poverty level paying income taxes. The low income allowance in the Tax Reform Act of 1969 was designed to remove these 5.2 million returns from the tax rolls and to produce a reduction in taxes for another 7 million returns.[1] Subsequent changes increased the percentage standard deduction so that in 1976 the standard deduction was elected on 58.2 million individual returns (or 69 percent of the total filed), while itemized deductions were claimed on 26.0 million returns (or 31 percent).

As you have read, in 1977 the standard deduction was changed to a zero bracket income concept, but the basic idea remains the same. Since the 1980 tax

[1]Committee on Ways and Means, House of Representatives, 91st Congress, "Report accompanying H.R. 13270, A Bill to Reform the Income Tax Laws, with Separate and Supplemental Views" (House Report No. 91-413, Part I), August 2, 1969, p. 10.

rate schedules and the tax tables build in zero bracket income of $2,300 for a single person, $3,400 for a married couple filing jointly, and $1,700 for a married person filing separately, only those deductions from A.G.I. in excess of the zero bracket income (except for personal exemptions) are considered in the tax computations. Thus, the number of taxpayers itemizing deductions has decreased significantly since 1977.

Obviously, a significant decrease in the number of taxpayers itemizing their deductions greatly simplifies the work of the Internal Revenue Service. There is less chance for error, less temptation on the part of taxpayers to "cheat," and much less audit and verification work in examining returns. In addition, taxpayers have a lesser burden maintaining adequate records and preparing the tax return.

Nevertheless, the deductions discussed in Part Four are still important to millions of taxpayers. Let us begin our study of itemized personal deductions by examining the detailed rules that authorize deductions for medical expenses and casualty losses.

MEDICAL EXPENSES

General rule

The basic authority for deduction of medical expenses is Sec. 213, which reads in part as follows:

(a) Allowance of Deduction.—There shall be allowed as a deduction the following amounts, not compensated for by insurance or otherwise—
  (1) the amount by which the amount of the expense paid during the taxable year . . . for medical care of the taxpayer, his spouse, and dependents . . . exceeds 3 percent of the adjusted gross income, and
  (2) an amount (not in excess of $150) equal to one-half of the expenses paid during the taxable year for insurance which constitutes medical care for the taxpayer, his spouse, and dependents.

The problem of defining medical expenses

"Medical care" is further defined in Sec. 213(e)(1) as follows:

(1) The term "medical care" means amounts paid—
  (A) for the diagnosis, cure, mitigation treatment, or prevention of disease, or for the purpose of affecting any structure or function of the body,
  (B) for transportation primarily for and essential to medical care referred to in subparagraph (A), or
  (C) for insurance . . . covering medical care referred to in subparagraphs (A) and (B).

Thus, medical costs include unreimbursed amounts paid for medical and dental care, such as physicians' charges, hospital rooms, nursing care, laboratory charges, dentures, optical care, glasses, and similar costs. Amounts spent for drugs and medicines are included in medical costs only to the extent that they exceed 1 percent of A.G.I. Special treatment is given to amounts paid as premiums on health and hospitalization insurance policies, as discussed on the following page.

Expenses for items such as vitamins and toothpaste—that is, items intended to improve or preserve the general health—are generally not deductible. Vitamins prescribed or recommended by a physician, however, become deductible. The cost of birth control pills, as well as the cost of a vasectomy or a legal abortion, is deductible as a medical expense.

Although transportation costs "primarily for and essential to" medical care are considered medical costs, living expenses (such as meals and lodging on a trip essential to medical care) are not deductible. The taxpayer who uses his or her personal automobile for transportation to secure medical care may deduct either the actual expenses incurred or use the standard allowance of 8¢ per mile, plus parking fees and toll charges.

Capital expenditures related specifically to the illness of an individual may also be deductible. For example, the cost of a wheel chair would be deductible in full in the year purchased. However, capital expenditures that increase the value of property will not be allowed as a deduction to the extent of the increase in value of the property. To illustrate, the cost of an elevator installed in a home for the care of an invalid will be deductible only to the extent that its cost exceeds any increase it may cause in the value of the home.

The observant student will quickly recognize the familiar problem of distinguishing between expenses that are purely "personal" and those that are properly deductible. The problem has been particularly evident in cases in which pleasure activities are involved in the expenditure. For example, a physician may recommend that the taxpayer leave the cold weather of Michigan and go to the sunshine of

Arizona for the winter. Under the present rules, only the transportation costs involved would be in question. But, based on the simple facts given above, no hard and fast answer could be given to the question of whether even these costs are deductible. Presumably, if the change in climate is recommended for treatment of a specific or chronic ailment, the costs would be deductible. If the change were recommended for "general health" reasons, it would be disallowed.

Another common situation in which it is difficult to distinguish between a bona fide medical expense and simply a personal expenditure arises when a member of the family is placed in a nursing home or home for the aged. If the individual is placed in the institution because of his or her physical condition and the availability of medical care in the institution, all the costs incurred (including meals and lodging) would be considered medical costs. However, if the main reason for placing the individual in the institution is simply personal convenience or desire, only the costs actually spent for medical care would be deductible. Similarly, if an individual is hired to perform both nursing care and household work in the taxpayer's home, only that portion of the cost applicable to nursing care would be considered a medical cost. If an expense is allowed as the basis for a credit for child care under Section 44A, it cannot be treated as a medical expense.

Note that the medical-expense deduction is allowed only for amounts *paid* during the tax year. Thus, if the taxpayer incurs medical expenses in the current year, but does not make payment until next year, no deduction would be allowable until next year. However, if payment is made by credit card, the deduction must be taken in the year charged to the account. In general, no deduction can be taken for prepaid medical expenditures even though insurance premiums are deductible. A possible exception to this rule applies in the case of lump-sum payments to nursing homes and in the case of certain insurance premiums paid by a taxpayer before he reaches the age of 65 on an insurance policy covering medical care for the taxpayer, taxpayer's spouse, and dependents after the taxpayer reaches the age of 65.

Computing the deduction for medical expenses

The taxpayer may take a deduction only for medical expenses paid during the taxable year for himself or herself, a spouse, or a dependent[2]—and only to the extent that they are not reimbursed by insurance or otherwise. Special computations must be made to find the *amount* of expenses that will be deductible.

Half the premiums paid on insurance to cover medical expenses are deductible up to a maximum deduction of $150, regardless of the taxpayer's A.G.I. The remaining amount paid for medical insurance is included with other medical costs and is subject to the special "3 percent rule" discussed below. Amounts spent for medicines and drugs are considered "medical costs" only to the extent that they exceed 1 percent of A.G.I.; that excess, if any, is added to other medical costs. Then, 3 percent of A.G.I. is subtracted from total medical costs to arrive at the amount deductible. There is no maximum limit on the medical costs deductible during the year.

To illustrate the medical-expense deduction, let's assume that a taxpayer and spouse with an A.G.I. of $7,000 paid the following medical expenses during the tax year for themselves and dependents:

Hospital insurance premiums	$210
Medicines and drugs	203
Doctor bills	220
Dental care	70
Optical care	50
	$753

The taxpayers would be entitled to deduct $473, computed as shown in Table 12-1.

Reimbursement of medical expenses subsequent to year of deduction

When insurance or other reimbursement for medical expenses is received in a year after that in which the expenses were actually paid, the reimbursement is treated as income only to the extent that it represents repayment of expenditures that resulted in a tax benefit in a prior year. For example, suppose that last year a taxpayer had A.G.I. of $10,000, and had "excess deductions." The taxpayer paid medical costs (ignoring insurance premiums of $380, and so deducted medical expenses of $80 that year. This year the taxpayer receives insurance proceeds of

---

[2]It should be noted that for this purpose a person need satisfy only three of the usual five criteria applicable to the determination of dependency status. (See Chapter 11.) They are the "support," the "relationship," and the citizen or resident criteria.

TABLE **12-1**

COMPUTATION OF MEDICAL EXPENSE DEDUCTION

Hospitalization insurance premiums:		
Total, $210; one-half (up to $150) deductible—balance included with other medical costs.		$105
Medicines and drugs:		
Total spent	$203	
Less 1% of A.G.I.	70	
Amount considered as medical cost		$133
Other medical costs:		
Health and hospital insurance (see above)	$105	
Doctor bills	220	
Dental care	70	
Optical care	50	
Total		445
Total medical costs		$578
Less 3% of A.G.I.		210
Deductible medical expenses, other than insurance		368
Total medical-expense deduction		$473

$200 as reimbursement of part of the $380 spent last year. If the taxpayer had received the insurance payment last year, he or she would have had no medical-expense deduction. Thus, of the $200 received, $80 will be reported as gross income in this year because it represents repayment of an amount deducted last year; the other $120 will not be considered as gross income because it does not represent a tax benefit in prior years. Of course, if the taxpayer did not have "excess deductions" in the prior year, no part of the reimbursement would be considered income.

History and function of the medical deduction

Deductions for medical and dental expenses were first permitted in 1942. As stated by the Senate Finance Committee at that time, this provision was recommended "in consideration of the heavy tax burden that must be borne by individuals during the existing emergency and of the desirability of maintaining the present high level of public health and morale."[3]

The original legislation relating to medical expenses was proposed by the Treasury and was intended to give more equitable treatment to taxpayers with extraordinary expenses.[4] In the initial act of 1942, and until the 1954 law was passed, medical expenses in excess of 5 percent of A.G.I. were deductible. Beginning in 1954, those medical expenses in excess of 3 percent of A.G.I. were deductible. The 1954 Code also provided, however, that only those medicine and drug costs in excess of 1 percent of A.G.I. were to be considered medical expenses. Between 1951 and 1967, a taxpayer 65 years of age or older (or having a spouse 65 or older) was permitted to deduct all medical expenses, without regard to the percentage exclusion. And the 1964 act exempted the elderly from even the 1 percent exclusion on medicines and drugs. This favorable treatment for the elderly was eliminated in 1967, based, however, because of their new privileges under Medicare.

Much of the public discussion relating to the medical-expense deduction has stemmed from its rationale. The basic concept has been that only the extraordinary expenses should be deductible, since it is extraordinary expenses that reduce the taxpayer's disposable income and therefore his or her ability to pay taxes relative to other taxpayers with the same income. Obviously, however, what is considered "ordinary" and "extraordinary" is a matter of personal opinion. Apparently it was the belief of Congress, during the years 1942 through 1953, that "extraordinary" meant something in excess of 5 percent of A.G.I. Beginning in 1954, "extraordinary" meant something in excess of 3 percent of A.G.I. (or 4 percent, if we include the 1 percent exclusion of medicines and drugs). Also during the period 1951 through 1966, all medical expenses were "extraordinary" for the elderly.

Moreover, there also is a qualitative question. Some medical expenses are of a voluntary nature; for example, a luxury private suite cannot be equated to a bed in a 24-bed ward. The tax laws cannot clearly distinguish between the ordinary and necessary expenses and these semi-optional (personal) costs.

Special mention should be made of the treatment accorded premiums paid on medical insurance policies. Prior to 1967 these premiums were included among other medical costs and were subject to the 3 percent exclusion. This tax treatment tended to dis-

---

[3]Senate Report #1631, Senate Finance Committee, 77th Congress, 2nd Session (Washington, D.C.: U.S. Government Printing Office, 1942), p. 6.

[4]Statement of Randolph E. Paul, hearings before House Ways and Means Committee, "Revenue Revision of 1942," 77th Congress, 2nd Session (Washington, D.C.: U.S. Government Printing Office, 1942), pp. 1612–13.

criminate against those with adequate insurance because their costs tended to be more constant than those without insurance. It is conceivable that a taxpayer with insurance might never be entitled to any deduction, because his or her premiums were under the 3 percent floor each year. However, a taxpayer without insurance might pay the same total medical costs over a period of years as the one carrying insurance, but might be able to take substantial deductions because his or her costs were irregular and "bunched" into a few years. The present provision represented a compromise between those who argued that insurance premiums should be deducted in full, without regard to the floor, and those who argued that insurance premiums should be treated in the same manner as any other medical cost.

Many individuals feel that a prime concern of the community should be for the health and physical welfare of the individual and that the community has a responsibility for assuring that everyone receives adequate medical care. By making all medical costs deductible, the government would be furthering this goal by cutting the cost of medical care, while at the same time leaving the allocation of funds in the hands of individuals. Following this line of reasoning, it may be argued that the 3 percent floor on medical costs should be abolished.

CASUALTY AND THEFT LOSSES

The second type of deduction related to economic hardship of the taxpayer is the deduction for casualty or theft losses of the taxpayer's property. In this section we shall examine the general provisions controlling casualty and theft loss deductions and will explore some of the more commonly found detailed definitional and computational problems.

General provisions for deduction of casualty and theft losses

As you learned in Chapter 6 (page **6**/5) the general provisions of Section 165 permit the deduction of losses sustained during the year to the extent of any amount "not compensated for by insurance or otherwise" if the loss is incurred in a trade or business or in a transaction entered into for a profit. In addition, a deduction for losses of property not related to trade or business resulting from fire, storm, or shipwreck has been allowed since the original tax law of 1913. In 1916 the deduction was extended to include

losses from "other casualties, or from theft." Today, for individual taxpayers, Sec. 165(c)(3) provides for the deduction of unreimbursed losses

> . . .of property not connected with a trade or business, if such losses arise from fire, storm, shipwreck, or other casualty, or from theft. A loss described in this paragraph shall be allowed only to the extent that the amount of loss to such individual arising from each casualty, or from each theft, exceeds $100.

Generally, property held by a corporation is automatically deemed to be either used in trade or business or acquired as the result of a transaction entered into for a profit, so that for a corporation, losses on such property come under the general rule calling for recognition of losses.

The deduction for losses of nonbusiness property, like that for medical expenses, is intended to provide tax relief to taxpayers suffering unusual, involuntary losses large enough "to have a significant effect upon an individual's ability to pay Federal income taxes."[5]

Prior to 1964 the full amount of each casualty loss was deductible; since that year, the deduction for casualty and theft losses on property used in trade or business has continued to be deductible in full, but the deduction for such losses on nonbusiness property has been limited to the amount by which each loss exceeds $100. The $100 floor was initiated to permit a deduction only for those nonbusiness losses that are considered "extraordinary" or "unusual." There is still substantial criticism that the $100 floor is not sufficiently high to restrict deductions only to losses that seriously impair tax-paying ability, especially for higher income groups, and that a more equitable provision would permit only those losses in excess of some percentage of A.G.I.

Defining "casualty" and "theft"

Subsection 165(c) specifically includes "fire, storm, or shipwreck" in the definition of casualties, and it provides for the general inclusion of "other casualties." However, "other casualties" are not identified, and it is often difficult to determine if loss of property resulting from a particular event constitutes a casualty for tax purposes. In general the law requires a sudden, unexpected, or unusual event as

---

[5]House Report No. 749, House Ways and Means Committee, 88th Congress, 1st Session (Washington, D.C.: U.S. Government Printing Office, 1963), p. 52.

well as an external force before a given event can be considered a casualty. Thus losses caused by vandalism, car and boat accidents, earth slides, hurricanes, and sonic booms have been held deductible. No deduction is allowed for breakage of china, glassware, furniture, and similar items under normal conditions, and tax deductions have been disallowed for damage due to rust, corrosion, termites (although some courts have allowed deductions for termite damage), insects, disease, and other slow-acting destructive forces. Because of the imprecision of the general criteria pertinent to the determination of a deductible casualty loss, litigation of specific facts is commonplace.

The definition of a theft loss is somewhat clearer, but whether a theft has taken place is still a matter of factual determination. The term "theft" is deemed to include, but is not limited to, larceny, embezzlement, and robbery. No deduction is allowed for property the taxpayer simply lost or misplaced. The reasons for the stringent rules are apparent if you consider the multiple opportunities for tax evasion that would arise under more lenient rules.

A deduction is allowed for loss to the taxpayer's own property only; thus no deduction is allowed for damage caused by the taxpayer to the property or body of another. The regulations under Sec. 165 make it clear that a loss to the taxpayer's property may be deductible even though the taxpayer is at fault, but not if the loss is due to the willful act or willful negligence of the taxpayer.

Determining the basic amount of loss

The amount of loss for physical damage to the taxpayer's property is basically the decrease in value of the property resulting from the casualty (but the deduction cannot be in excess of the "adjusted basis" of the property). For example, if a taxpayer's property had a fair market value of $6,000 just before a casualty and a fair market value of $2,000 just after the casualty, the basic measure of loss sustained would be $4,000. In some cases, the cost of repairs to the property damaged is acceptable as evidence of the loss of value if (1) the repairs are necessary to restore the property to its condition immediately before the casualty, (2) the amount spent for such repairs is not excessive, (3) the repairs do not care for more than the damage suffered, and (4) the value of the property after the repairs does not exceed the value immediately before the casualty.

No provision is made for deduction of premiums paid for insurance against casualty losses (except, of course, under the general provisions concerning deductions related to trade, business, and income-producing activities). Tax scholars often charge that the nondeductibility of insurance premiums discriminates against the insured taxpayer, especially since any insurance proceeds received as a result of the loss reduce the amount otherwise deductible and actually result in gain to the extent that the proceeds exceed the adjusted basis of the property.

Determining the amount deductible

The amount of loss deductible from casualty or theft of the taxpayer's property depends on a number of factors: the decrease in value, whether the property is used in trade or business or for income production or is held for purely personal purposes, whether the property is completely destroyed or only partially destroyed, and the amount of insurance or other reimbursement.

PROPERTY COMPLETELY DESTROYED   If property used in trade or business or held for income production is completely destroyed, the adjusted basis of the property, less any amount of reimbursement, is deductible. (The nature and classification of the loss is discussed later in this chapter.) For example, a building with an adjusted basis of $20,000 and a fair market value of $15,000 that is used in the taxpayer's business, is completely destroyed by fire. The taxpayer collects insurance proceeds of $12,000 for the loss. The amount of deductible loss is $8,000.

On the other hand, if property held for purely personal use is completely destroyed, the amount deductible is the amount by which (1) the adjusted basis, or (2) the fair market value, whichever is smaller, reduced by insurance proceeds or other reimbursement, exceeds $100. For example, assume that a taxpayer's mountain cabin with a fair market value of $15,000 and an adjusted basis of $20,000 was completely destroyed by fire. The taxpayer received insurance proceeds of $12,000. The amount of deductible loss would be $2,900, computed as follows:

Lower of adjusted basis ($20,000,) or fair market value ($15,000)	$15,000
Less insurance proceeds	12,000
	3,000
Less $100 "floor"	100
Deductible Loss	$ 2,900

On the other hand, if the fair market value of the mountain cabin in the above case had been $26,000, with all other facts being the same, the deductible loss would have been $7,900 ($20,000 − $12,000 − $100).

PROPERTY PARTIALLY DESTROYED   Where property is only partially destroyed, the loss is computed in basically the same way for property used in business as for property held for purely personal use. The amount of loss is the adjusted basis of the property or its decrease in fair market value, whichever is smaller, reduced by insurance proceeds or other reimbursement. If the property is held for purely personal use, the loss is deductible only to the extent it exceeds the $100 floor. On the other hand, for property used in trade or business or held for income production, the $100 floor does not apply.

Two simple examples will illustrate the basic rules for computing the deductible amount of the casualty loss on nonbusiness property. Assume that the taxpayer owns a lakeside cabin that was damaged by fire. Its fair market value just prior to the fire was $8,000; after the fire it was appraised at $2,500. Insurance proceeds of $3,000 were received under a policy covering the fire. Assume in Case A that the adjusted basis (cost) of the cabin was $5,000 and in Case B that the basis was $9,000. The amount deductible in each case is computed as follows:

	Case A	Case B
Value before fire	$8,000	$8,000
Value after fire	2,500	2,500
Reduction in value	$5,500	$5,500
Basis of property	$5,000	$9,000
Loss before adjustments	$5,000	$5,500
Less insurance proceeds	3,000	3,000
	$2,000	$2,500
Less $100 floor	100	100
Deductible loss	$1,900	$2,400

As previously noted, if property used in trade or business is destroyed or damaged, the $100 floor does not apply. Thus, if the property in the preceding illustration had been used in a trade or business, the amount deductible in Case A would have been $2,000 and the amount deductible in Case B would have been $2,500.

If insurance proceeds or other reimbursement exceeds the basis of the property, the taxpayer will have a taxable gain (unless the gain is reinvested in replacement property, as discussed in Chapter 25.) For example, assume that the taxpayer owned jewelry costing $30,000 and that just before it was stolen it had a fair market value of $75,000. Insurance proceeds of $45,000 were received. Even though the taxpayer suffered a loss in terms of market value, a gain of $15,000 has resulted from this transaction.

Other considerations

A number of other factors arise that may complicate the proper tax treatment of casualty and theft losses. A few of the more common of these are briefly summarized in the following paragraphs.

Generally, a corporation's casualty and theft *losses* are combined with its *gains* from casualty and theft. If there is a net loss, the loss is treated as an ordinary deduction from gross income. For individual taxpayers, however, only a casualty or theft loss associated with property used in trade or business or with property used for the production of rents or royalties is treated as a deduction *for* adjusted gross income. Casualty and theft losses associated with other assets held for investment or income production by individuals, as well as property held for purely personal use, will generally be treated as itemized deductions *from* gross income. As will be pointed out in Chapter 22, casualty and theft *gains* (after recapture) and losses on all capital assets held for more than 12 months and on real and depreciable business property held more than 12 months are netted together. If there is a loss, it is deductible as an ordinary loss. On the other hand, any net gains from such events are treated as "Section 1231" transactions, which may have the effect of capital gains. These complications, however, must await further development in Part Six of this book.

Another complication arises in the case of married taxpayers. If the spouses file a joint return, they are subject to a single $100 floor for each casualty. If they file separate returns, however, each one is subject to the $100 floor for each casualty. Thus, if a thief in a single theft stole items belonging to both husband and wife, they would have a floor of $100 each for their personal casualty loss if they file separate returns. If they file a joint return, a single floor of $100 is imposed.

One final complication in measuring the amount of loss should be mentioned. In measuring the loss from casualty or theft related to business property, each single identifiable item damaged or destroyed is treated separately in measuring the decrease in value. For example, if a storm damages a building used in trade or business and also damages or destroys ornamental shrubs on the premises, the decrease in value of the building will be computed separately from the decrease in value of the shrubs. However, in the case of property not used in a trade or business, the real property and improvement must be considered an integral part of the property. Thus, if a storm damaged the building and shrubs on the premises, the decline in value would not be computed for each item, but a single figure for the total decline in overall value of the property would be determined.

A number of complications arise regarding the year in which a casualty or theft loss should be deducted. In general, a loss is allowed as a deduction only for the year in which the loss is sustained. A loss arising from theft, however, shall be treated as sustained in the year the theft is discovered, rather than in the year the actual theft took place. If there exists a claim for reimbursement and there is a reasonable prospect of recovery, no portion of the loss with respect to which reimbursement may be received is deductible until it can be determined with reasonable certainty whether reimbursement will be received. Any portion of the loss not covered by a claim for reimbursement will be deductible, however, in the year of the casualty occurred or the theft was discovered.

In some cases, if a loss results from a disaster in an area that the president of the United States subsequently declares to be a "disaster area" warranting federal assistance, the taxpayer may deduct the loss in the year the loss occurs or may elect to deduct the loss on the tax return for the year preceding the year in which the loss actually occurred.

If a taxpayer deducts a loss in one year and in a subsequent tax year receives reimbursement, he does not recompute the tax for the taxable year in which the deduction was taken, but includes the reimbursement in income in the year it is received, to the extent that the reimbursement represents recovery of an amount that gave rise to a tax benefit when the deduction was taken.

Another provision relating to insurance received in connection with casualties permits a taxpayer to exclude from gross income all or a portion of insurance proceeds received as reimbursement for living expenses during the period that the taxpayer must temporarily live in another residence while his or her home is being repaired. The exclusion is limited to the amount by which actual living expenses of the taxpayer's household exceed the living expenses it would normally have incurred during that period, and includes amounts spent for such items as rent, transportation, food, utilities, and so on.

Obviously, the tax laws are highly selective in determining which unusual and involuntary expenditures or losses are deductible, and many taxpayers may feel that other types of large, unusual, involuntary expenses that they incur are fully as deserving of a tax deduction as those discussed in this chapter. Unfortunately, equity in the tax laws is far from perfect.

PROBLEMS

For the following problems, ignore the "zero bracket income" effects on itemized deductions.

1. What common justification is given for permitting the deduction of both medical expenses and casualty losses?

2. What arguments may be used to support the provision that permits (within limits) one-half of amounts paid for health and hospitalization insurance premiums to be deducted without regard to the 3 percent floor? How does this argument apply to the tax treatment of insurance premiums for fire, theft, and other casualty insurance on non-income-producing assets (for example, a home)?

3. Define the terms "drugs" and "medical expenses" as used in federal income taxation. List several items that would be included and several that would be excluded in each category.

4. Under what circumstances, if any, would amounts paid by a taxpayer for costs of living in a retirement "nursing" home be deductible?

5. Two types of "floors" for determining the amount of involuntary costs (medical

expenses and casualty losses, for example) deemed to be extraordinary or unusual are discussed in this chapter. Compare the two, discussing their relative effects on taxpayers of different income levels.

6. What differences, if any, are found in measuring the deductible amount of a casualty loss on property held for personal use and property used in trade or business?

7. Under what circumstances, if any, may the taxpayer treat the amount of a repair bill as a measure of loss from a casualty?

8. To what extent, if any, does the quality of medical care or its luxuriousness determine the extent to which it is deductible? For example, are different rules applied in determining deductibility of a bed in a hospital ward compared with one in a luxurious private room in an exclusive hospital? For contact lenses versus ordinary glasses?

9. Compare the tax treatment of premiums on health and hospitalization insurance premiums and that of premiums for casualty insurance on the taxpayer's home or personal automobile.

10. What arguments can be given for removing the 3 percent floor on medical costs?

11. In 19x1, taxpayer's A.G.I. was $20,000. Her expenditures for allowable itemized deduction other than medical expenses in 19x1 were $3,200. In addition, her medical expenses that year, including medical insurance premiums of $408, totaled $920. She received no reimbursement for any part of these costs until 19x2, when she received a check for $360. What medical costs are deemed deductible in 19x1? What part, if any, of the insurance reimbursement should be reported as income in an amended tax return for 19x1? What part, if any, of the reimbursement should be included in 19x2 income?

12. Which of the following items are deductible as medicine or medical costs?
    a. Aspirin
    b. Vitamins prescribed by doctor
    c. Cost of dental plate
    d. Contact lenses
    e. Artificial limb
    f. Transportation to and from doctor's office
    g. Health food purchased by vegetarian
    h. Bill for having teeth "cleaned" by dentist
    i. Annual trip to Arizona to give the sinuses a rest
    j. A legal abortion
    k. A wheel chair
    l. Repairs to the wheel chair.
    m. Nonprescription antihistamines taken to combat allergies.

13. Erv Single took out a medical insurance policy at a cost of $44 per month. Fortunately for Erv, he was not sick once during 19x1 and therefore incurred no medical expenses. What is his medical-expense deduction for 19x1 if he earned a $10,000 A.G.I.?

14. Marcus and Tania reported A.G.I. of $20,000 in a year in which they incurred the following medical expenses:

Dentist's charges	$ 450
Physician's charges	900
Hospital costs	1,800
Drugs	180
Medical insurance premiums	700

The insurance company reimbursed Marcus and Tania for $1,700 of their hospital bill and $800 for their physician's charges. What is their medical-expense deduction for the year?

15. Compute the medical deduction in the following cases:

	Case A	Case B	Case C
Adjusted gross income	$12,000	$12,000	$12,000
Medicine	150	100	200
Medical costs (net of insurance claims)	500	200	200
Premiums on medical insurance	220	220	220

16. Ted Granger retired from Chicago to Miami, Florida, after 50 years of service with Bidwell Corporation. Each June Ted flies back to Chicago for an annual physical examination by Dr. Knowbetter, a heart specialist who treated Ted 10 years ago. This annual physical requires approximately one week to complete. Between trips to the physician's office, Ted visits family and friends. The trip costs him $500 for transportation, $300 for a hotel, $140 for food, $200 for medical expenses, and $100 for incidentals. Which of these costs, if any, might Ted deduct? Explain your answer.

17. John Beal, age 65, and wife, Miriam, age 39, filed a joint return for the current tax year showing an A.G.I. of $45,000. A son of Mrs. Beal by a former marriage is now a full-time university student and is fully dependent on the Beals. They also provide over 50 percent of the support of Mr. Beal's mother, who is 85 and bedridden. Grandmother Beal receives a $1,200-a-year payment from a trust fund. Medical expenses in excess of reimbursements were paid by John and Miriam in the amounts stated below:

	John	Miriam	Son	Mother
Hospital insurance premiums	$240	$—	$—	$—
Drugs	150	350	10	400
Medical expenses	200	300	100	300
Nurse				5,200

Show your computation for the medical-expense deduction that can be taken on Mr. and Mrs. Beal's joint tax return.

18. Last summer Korioth, a local professor, suffered severe pains in his neck. His local physician advised Korioth that he needed a most serious and delicate operation, which only a few surgeons in the United States were capable of performing. The recommended surgeon was at the Mayo Clinic in Rochester, Minnesota. Korioth flew to Minnesota for consultation with the surgeon. He spent $140 for transportation, $55 for hotel bills there, and $12 for food there. The surgeon recommended that the operation be performed as quickly as possible, which was two weeks later because the surgeon was leaving the country on vacation. He further advised Korioth that Korioth's wife should accompany him to Minnesota to be there during the surgery, to care for Korioth in a hotel for two weeks after surgery, and to return with him on his trip home. Korioth and his wife dutifully followed the doctor's instructions. The round-trip plane fare was $340 for the two of them. The hotel room cost a total of $600. This bill included $40 per day for the two of them during the period before surgery (2 days), $120 for Mrs. Korioth during the 4 days that Korioth was in the hospital, and $400 for the two of them for 10 days after his dismissal from the hospital.

Korioth's food costs outside the hospital were $150; Mrs. Korioth's food costs were $140. She spent $51 for taxi fares going to and from the hospital twice each day. Additionally, after Korioth's release, he spent $16 for taxi fares going to the hospital. What part of these costs are deductible?

19. Mary, a college student, has for several years been concerned about her "overbite" and its impact on her personal appearance. She visited a local orthodontist, who suggested that she have her teeth realigned and straightened. Total cost of the work is expected to be $3,000. During the current year, Mary paid $1,400 to the orthodontist. What amount, if any, is treated as medical expense this year? Explain.

20. Glenda had a legal abortion at a cost of $1,020. What part of this cost, if any, is a medical expense? Explain.

21. In each of the following cases, indicate the amount of "casualty loss" deductible and indicate how the loss would be handled on the income-tax return. Assume there are no other casualties or thefts.

   a. Taxpayer was vacationing in Miami. While taxpayer was swimming, a thief stole his wristwatch (cost, $220, with a fair market value of $180) and his billfold. The billfold contained $120 cash, which was not recovered. The billfold, itself, with a value of $5, cost $10. There was no insurance.

   b. Berry owned a lake cabin with an adjusted basis of $16,000. On January 18, the cabin had a fair value of $14,000. On the next day, a tornado completely demolished the cabin. It was not insured. The cabin was held solely for personal use.

   c. Corona owned a frame building with an adjusted basis of $20,000. In July of this year, the building caught fire and was partially destroyed. The value just before the fire was $21,000 and just after the fire $4,000. There was no insurance. The building was Corona's personal residence.

   d. Assume the same facts as in part c, above, except that insurance proceeds of $12,000 were received.

   e. Ishmael backed his car out of his garage into a neighbor's automobile. Ishmael's automobile suffered $600 damage. (Its basis was $3,500.) Damage suffered by the neighbor's automobile was $520, which Ishmael paid out of his own pocket since he carried no insurance of any kind.

   f. Jackson's home was burglarized. The thief took Mrs. Jackson's jewelry, which had a fair market value of $1,800. The jewelry had a basis of $1,200. He also took Jackson's watch, which had a fair value of $150 and a basis of $200. There was no insurance. Jackson and his wife filed a joint return.

   g. Assume the same facts as in part f, above, except that the Jacksons filed separate returns.

   h. Karl owns an automobile used half for business and half for pleasure. The automobile had cost $4,000 and Karl had taken depreciation of $600 on the business portion. In August of this year he had an accident. At that time the fair value of the auto was $2,200. Just after the accident the auto had a value of $1,500. Insurance proceeds of $620 were recovered.

   i. Long went hunting with his rifle, which had a basis of $160 and a fair market value of $150. Somehow, Long laid his rifle down in the woods and never was able to find it again. He had no insurance.

   j. In the current year Belcher was in an auto accident. As a result, he was sued by another individual in the accident and was required to pay "damages" of $16,000 to the other party.

22. Marcus owned a home. In his front yard he had a number of trees that he had set out some 15 years ago. This year a high wind demolished all the trees. A

man from the local "tree service" estimated the trees were worth $1,200, although Marcus had paid only $120 for them. Just before the wind, his home had an appraised value of $32,000 (cost, including trees, $20,200). Just after the wind, his home had an estimated value of $31,500. Marcus paid $160 to have the debris cleaned up. What is the amount of his casualty loss deduction?

23. A taxpayer was involved in a traffic accident and suffered substantial damage to his personal automobile (cost, $4,000) and to himself. Because the accident was the taxpayer's fault, he ended up paying $500 for damages to the other party's automobile, $800 for medical expenses of the other party, and $200 to avoid a lawsuit. In addition, he paid $150 in medical bills for himself. His automobile had an estimated value before the accident of $2,700; after the accident it was valued at $2,000. The taxpayer received a $595 reimbursement for damage to his own automobile; all other costs were paid from his personal funds. What is this taxpayer's deductible "casualty loss"?

SUPPLEMENTAL PROBLEMS

24. If a taxpayer were to build an indoor swimming pool at a cost of $194,660 "to prevent paralysis from . . . a spinal injury," what part of that cost do you think that taxpayer might deduct as a medical expense? After you have made a guess, read and prepare a short report on *Ferris* v. *Commissioner,* TC Memo 1977-186.

25. In the current year a single taxpayer's receipts were:

Salary (gross)	$10,000
Reimbursement from insurance company for medical costs incurred and paid by taxpayer in the preceding year. (Taxpayer did not have itemized deductions in excess of zero bracket income in the preceding year.)	$300

The taxpayer's disbursements included the following items in the current year:

Payments to doctors for medical care	$700
Premiums on health and hospital insurance policies that would reimburse taxpayer for a part of his medical bills.	960
Premiums on an insurance policy that would pay the taxpayer $50 per day for each day he is hospitalized, without regard to the actual cost incurred by the taxpayer.	180
Premium on "wage continuation plan" policy that contracts to pay the taxpayer 60 percent of his normal wages for each day he is hospitalized, beginning after a "waiting period" of 60 days.	240

What is the amount of the taxpayer's deduction for medical expenses in the current year?

26. Taxpayer lives in a three-story house. In 19x1, taxpayer suffered a severe heart attack. On the advice of his physician, he had an elevator installed in his home at a cost of $12,000. The elevator installation increased the value of the taxpayer's home by $12,000. After the elevator was installed and used several months, minor repairs and service to the elevator were required in 19x1. Cost of the

repairs and service, all paid in 19x1, was $210. What amount, if any, will the taxpayer be allowed to deduct as medical expense in 19x1?

27. In 19x1, taxpayer completed her 40th year of employment with National Company and retired. As a retirement award, the compnay paid for a 4-week worldwide tour for taxpayer and her spouse, beginning April 1, 19x1. While in Austrailia in the second week of April, taxpayer received a phone call from her neighbor telling her that a severe freeze had occurred and that the taxpayer's home had sustained broken water pipes. The taxpayer had not turned off the water because there had never been a freeze in that locality after approximately March 15. The total cost of repairing the water lines and damage to the floor in the taxpayer's home was $1,200. Is the taxpayer entitled to a deduction for a casualty loss? Explain your answer.

28. Taxpayer provided $600 per month during 19x1 toward the cost of maintaining his mother in the "Sunshine Nursing Home" for the aged. The Sunshine home was chosen in preference to several others considered primarily because it had a physician and nurse on duty at all times. Taxpayer's mother had a series of heart attacks in recent years, and although her situation was not critical and she was not confined to her bed, the taxpayer felt it necessary to have immediately available medical care for her. In addition to the $7,200 provided by taxpayer, the mother also received $3,600 from social security benefits and $2,000 from a fully taxable pension during 19x1.

What part, if any, of the $7,200 will the taxpayer be allowed to treat as medical expenses on his 19x1 tax return?

29. Taxpayer, a college professor in Indiana, left her home for a 3-week vacation in England on December 18, 19x1, as soon as she graded her final exam for the fall semester. When she returned in January 19x2, she discovered that her home had been burglarized. Two items were missing: a set of silver dinnerware that had cost $1,000 and had a fair value of $2,400, and a stereo sound system that had cost $1,000 and had a fair value of $500. In 19x2, she received insurance reimbursement totaling $800. A neighbor's home was burglarized on December 27, 19x1, and police speculate that the two burglaries occurred on the same night. How should the taxpayer treat these facts on her tax returns for 19x1 and 19x2?

30. Sam Schled suffered a kidney ailment that was incurable without a transplant from a member of his family. Sam's brother, Wayne, who lived in another state, volunteered to be a kidney donor. Wayne made a trip from his home to St. Louis, where Sam lived, for required tests in April of this year. The costs incurred on this trip, which were all paid by Wayne, were:

Transportation	$320
Hospital charges	800
Physician's charges	850

The tests were positive, and in July Wayne returned for the necessary surgery. Costs related to Wayne's trip and surgery were all paid by Sam. These costs were:

Transportation	$ 360
Hospital charges	8,080
Physician's charges	5,000

What part of the above costs are considered to be medical costs of Sam? of Wayne?

13

Taxes who benefit from special provisions commonly insist that these do not give them an advantage over the rest of the taxpaying public, but merely put them on a par with everyone else by recognizing that their situations are in fact somewhat different.

WALTER BLUM,
quoted in *Federal Tax Policy for Economic Growth and Stability* (1955)

taxes, contributions, and interest

The three largest itemized deductions through the years have been, in order of their importance, taxes, interest, and contributions. Table 13-1 shows that in 1976 these three deductions accounted for 82 percent of all itemized deductions on taxable returns. Because these items normally represent personal expenditures not related to the production of income, the granting of a tax deduction for each of them has frequently been criticized as an unjustified subsidy to a particular group in society. For example, the deductibility of the interest and property taxes incurred on an owner-occupied home has been said to constitute an inequitable subsidy to home owners because no comparable deductions are available to taxpayers who rent their dwelling.

In the following pages, some of the major controversies and problems concerning these three deductions are considered. Special emphasis is placed on the criticisms levied against them.

STATE AND LOCAL TAXES

Certain taxes paid to state and local governmental units are deductible even though they are not incurred in connection with a trade or business or other income-producing activity. Section 164(a) provides:

(a) General Rule.—Except as otherwise provided in this section, the following taxes shall be allowed as a

deduction for the taxable year within which paid or accrued:

(1) State and local, and foreign, real property taxes.
(2) State and local personal property taxes.
(3) State and local, and foreign, income, war profits, and excess profits taxes.
(4) State and local general sales taxes.

In addition, there shall be allowed as a deduction State and local, and foreign, taxes not described in the preceding sentence which are paid or accrued within the taxable year in carrying on a trade or business or an activity described in section 212 (relating to expenses for production of income).

To assist the taxpayer in determining a reasonable deduction for state sales taxes in the absence of an accurate record of expenditures, the I.R.S. has provided a series of tables (one for each state) that stipulate an acceptable sales-tax deduction. The tables, reproduced in Appendix D, are based on the amount of the taxpayer's adjusted gross income plus nontaxable receipts such as social security benefits, the capital gain deduction, dividend exclusion, and so forth, and the number of persons in the taxpayer's family. Taxpayers living in a city that imposes an additional sales tax can prorate an appropriate amount in addition to the amount stipulated for the state in the I.R.S. table to determine the total amount deductible. Finally, a deduction is allowed in addition to the amount shown in the tables for sales taxes paid on automobiles, boats, airplanes, materials to build a new home (under certain conditions), and mobile homes.

TABLE **13-1**

ITEMIZED DEDUCTIONS BY CLASSES—1976

Type	Amount (in billions)	Percentage of total
Medical expenses	$12.1	9.0%
Taxes	49.6	37.0
Contributions	16.8	12.6
Interest	43.4	32.4
Others	12.0	9.0
Total	$133.9	100.0%

SOURCE: *Preliminary Statistics of Income*, 1976.

Taxes have been specifically mentioned as a deduction in every federal income-tax law, including the 1861 act, although the 1865 act was the first to include specifically taxes not associated with income production. The 1865 law permitted the deduction of all national, state, county, and municipal taxes paid within the year. Similarly, the income-tax law of 1913 specifically allowed deductions for all "national, state, county, school, and municipal taxes paid during the year," including the federal income tax itself. Gradually, however, the number of deductible taxes has been reduced. The deduction for the federal income tax itself was eliminated in 1917; the federal excise tax deduction was ended in 1943; the deduction for many state and local taxes (on tobacco, alcoholic beverages, automobile licenses, drivers' licenses, and others) was removed in 1964;[1] and the deduction for state taxes on gasoline was eliminated for taxable years beginning after 1978.

In addition, the 1976 Tax Reform Act required that certain "construction period property taxes" and construction period interest be capitalized and amortized. (See pages **13**/11–**13**/12 for a discussion of this provision.)

Importance of the deduction for taxes

In spite of the elimination of many taxes from the list of those deductible, this item continues to be the largest on returns itemizing deductions. There has also been a rather consistent increase in the amount of taxes deducted, as shown in Table 13-2, as a result

of the very rapid growth of state and local property, sales, and income taxes. Table 13-1 shows that taxes are the most important itemized deduction, making up about 37.2 percent of the total in 1976.

Rationale for deducting taxes

Several arguments have been advanced to support the deduction of state and local taxes. Perhaps today the most important is that the deduction facilitates the smooth functioning of the federal system, providing a greater flexibility to local governmental units in their own taxing activities. In effect, the deduction represents a federal subsidy to state and local governments because it reduces the net cost of state and local taxes to those taxpayers who itemize deductions on their federal tax returns. Presumably, this permits, to a degree, local governmental units to increase taxes with less opposition from taxpayers. Furthermore, permitting state and local taxes to be deducted, since it tends to reduce intercity and interstate tax differentials, reduces the fear, common to many local governmental bodies, that higher tax rates will cause business and population to move to areas with lower tax rates.

Before the 1965 reduction of the maximum federal tax rate for individuals to 70 percent (from a previous high of 91 percent), it was often suggested that unless some provision was included in the federal tax structure for deduction of taxes paid to state

TABLE **13-2**

DEDUCTION FOR TAXES ON RETURNS
ITEMIZING DEDUCTIONS FROM A.G.I.

Year	Amount of taxes deducted (billions)
1954	$ 4.08
1956	5.83
1958	7.48
1960	10.53
1962	13.04
1964	14.07
1966	17.47
1968	24.36
1970	32.02
1972	36.17
1973	39.37
1975	44.11
1976	49.60

SOURCE: *Statistics of Income*, various years, and *Preliminary Statistics of Income*. 1976.

[1] Even though the specific provision authorizing the deduction of automobile licenses was repealed in 1964, the citizens of some states can still claim them as a deduction under Sec. 162(a)(2). That is, if the auto license fee is based on value (an *ad valorem* basis), it can be considered a property tax and, as such, is deductible.

and local governments, especially state and local income taxes, the marginal rate might be more than 100 percent. Although this extreme is not likely to occur, it does seem logical that a degree of coordination between taxing activities of the national and local governmental units is desirable, and the deduction for state and local taxes on the federal tax return gives some relief from multiple taxation and provides limited control of the total tax burden. (Incidentally, state income taxes usually allow a deduction for the federal income tax paid.)

Finally, some persons argue that the taxpayer should not be forced to pay "a tax on a tax." Essentially this concept considers taxes in much the same light as medical costs and casualty losses—unavoidable, involuntary payments that reduce the taxpayer's wherewithal to pay the federal income tax.

Arguments against the deduction for taxes

Most tax scholars favor the abolition of the deduction for taxes, with the exception, perhaps, of state and local income taxes. They refute most of the arguments supporting the deduction.

First, they point out that taxes paid state and local governmental units are actually for such services as police protection, schools, streets, and similar services, and are very much like payments for services from the private sector of the economy. This argument is sometimes deemed especially pertinent in the case of taxes earmarked for specific direct benefits or services. Most of these taxes (for example, auto licenses and drivers' licenses) have been made nondeductible in recent years. The logic may easily be extended to taxes not earmarked for specific purposes.

Most tax experts also point out that making state and local taxes deductible tends to reduce the progressivity that has been deliberately built into the tax structure. This is true because a deduction for state and local taxes generally results in a greater income-tax saving for those in higher income-tax brackets. Moreover, the deduction for state and local property taxes often discriminates between taxpayers with equal incomes and tax-paying ability. For example, it permits the homeowner to deduct taxes but allows no similar deduction to the tenant whose monthly rental just as surely includes an element for property taxes.

Even the most logical reason for permitting the deduction of state and local taxes—to make it easier for local governmental units to levy taxes—is subject to criticism. Not only is this a helter-skelter and inefficient means of providing a subsidy, but it provides assistance to the wrong communities. Presumably, there is greater need for federal aid in poorer communities, where both income and wealth (property) are relatively low. However, the aid provided by deduction of state and local taxes is of greatest benefit in communities whose taxpayers are in higher income-tax brackets and are wealthier.

Undoubtedly there will be increasing discussion in Congress, in spite of the political unpopularity of such a move, on abolishing the deduction for state and local taxes.

CONTRIBUTIONS

At the present time, both individual and corporate taxpayers may deduct contributions made to qualifying recipients. Most questions regarding contribution deductions involve either the determination of the eligibility of a particular gift to qualify for a deduction or the determination of the amount that may be deducted. Although many provisions applicable to contribution deductions are equally applicable to the individual and the corporate donor, enough differences do exist to justify their separate consideration.

Present provisions relating to contributions by individuals

Contributions made by individuals are deductible, within limits, if they are made to or "for the use of" one of the types of organization listed below:

(1) A State, a possession of the United States, or any political subdivision of any of the foregoing, or the United States or the District of Columbia, but only if the contribution or gift is made for exclusively public purposes.
(2) A corporation, trust, or community chest, fund, or foundation—
(A) created or organized in the United States or in any possession thereof, or under the law of the United States, any State, the District of Columbia, or any possession of the United States;
(B) organized and operated exclusively for religious, charitable, scientific, literary, or educational purposes or to foster national or international amateur

sports competition . . ., or for the prevention of cruelty to children or animals;

(C) no part of the net earnings of which inures to the benefit of any private shareholder or individual; and

(D) which is not disqualified for tax exemption under section 501(c)(3) by reason of attempting to influence legislation, and which does not participate in, or intervene in (including the publishing or distributing of statements), any political campaign on behalf of any candidate for public office.

A contribution or gift by a corporation to a trust, chest, fund, or foundation shall be deductible by reason of this paragraph only if it is to be used within the United States or any of its possessions exclusively for purposes specified in subparagraph (B).

(3) A post or organization of war veterans or an auxiliary unit or society of, or trust or foundation for, any such post or organization—

(A) organized in the United States or any of its possessions, and

(B) no part of the net earnings of which inures to the benefit of any private shareholder or individual.

(4) In the case of a contribution or gift by an individual, a domestic fraternal society, order, or association, operating under the lodge system, but only if such contribution or gift is to be used exclusively for religious, charitable, scientific, literary, or educational purposes, or for the prevention of cruelty to children or animals.

(5) A cemetery company owned and operated exclusively for the benefit of its members, or any corporation chartered solely for burial purposes as a cemetery corporation and not permitted by its charter to engage in any business not necessarily incident to that purpose, if such company or corporation is not operated for profit and no part of the net earnings of such company or corporation inures to the benefit of any private shareholder or individual.[2]

Note that in order to be deductible, charitable contributions must be made to a qualifying organization that fits into one of the classes listed in Code Sec. 170(c).

Measuring the amount contributed

To be deductible, a charitable contribution must be in money or property; the taxpayer cannot deduct the value of services donated to an organization. Contributions of tangible, personal property must be of "present interest"—that is, a taxpayer cannot get a deduction now for a transfer that will take place at his or her death if the property involved is tangible, personal property. In some instances it is difficult to

determine if a particular contribution consists of a property or a service; for example, the donation of blood has been held to be a service, not a property. Similarly, the law denies a taxpayer the value of "lost rents" as a deduction when the taxpayer permitted a charity to occupy rental property free of cost. A taxpayer who uses a personal automobile on behalf of a charitable organization is entitled to deduct only the out-of-pocket costs (gasoline, oil, etc.) or to deduct a flat amount of 8 cents per mile.

When the taxpayer contributes cash, there can be no question about the amount of the contribution. If the taxpayer contributes other property, the amount deemed to have been contributed depends on both the nature of the property and, in some cases, the nature of the donee organization.

ORDINARY INCOME PROPERTY   If property, the sale of which would have resulted in ordinary income, is contributed, the taxpayer may generally deduct only the fair market value of the property *less* the amount that would have been taxed as ordinary income had the property been sold. This means that in most cases the donor can deduct only the cost or adjusted basis of the property. This restriction is applied regardless of the nature of the donee organization. For example, if a businessperson contributes routine inventory items that cost $2,000 but had a normal retail sales price of $3,800, the amount of the contribution would usually be measured as $2,000. (The one major exception, for corporations only, to this rule is discussed on page **13**/7.)

Several other types of property, in addition to merchandise inventory, are included in this category:

1. Capital assets such as shares of stock, land, and art objects other than those described in 2, if held less than one year.

2. Art objects, literary works, etc., produced by the taxpayer. (See text page **20**/3 for a further discussion of this item.)

3. Property used in business or held for investment that would result in ordinary income (usually through depreciation recapture) if sold.

4. Inventories of consumable supplies that would be charged to expense when used in the business.

5. Letters and memoranda written by or to the taxpayer.

An application of the rule to a contribution of depreciable business property may be illustrated by a

[2]Code Sec. 170(c).

typical example. Suppose that in the current year a taxpayer contributes to the American Red Cross a truck used in business. The truck cost him $6,000 three years ago, and depreciation of $4,000 has been taken. The fair market value of the truck is $3,200. The taxpayer would be entitled to a charitable contribution deduction of $2,000:

Fair market value at date of gift	$3,200
Less amount that would be taxed as ordinary income under Sec. 1245 if the truck were sold at its fair market value.*	1,200
Amount of contribution	$2,000

*NOTE: Sec 1245 is explained in Chapter 22.

Prior to 1970 a taxpayer was entitled to deduct the fair market value of *any* noncash property contributed to a charity. As a result, it was possible to have a greater positive cash flow from making a contribution than from selling. For example, if a taxpayer in the 70 percent rate bracket in 1969 contributed to a qualified organization merchandise inventory that cost $1,000 but had a fair market value of $2,000, he or she would deduct $2,000 as a contribution, resulting in an income-tax saving of $1,400. Thus, the tax saving would exceed the cost of the item contributed by $400. Had the taxpayer sold the same inventory, the $1,000 ordinary income would have been subject to a $700 tax, thus leaving only $300 in excess of the cost after taxes.

CAPITAL-GAIN PROPERTY   If property, the sale of which would have resulted in long-term capital gain, is contributed to a qualified organization, the fair market value of the property is deemed to be the amount contributed with the following two exceptions:

1. Tangible *personal* property unrelated to the donee organization's exempt function (for example, an object of art that will be resold by the donee charity).
2. Any capital-gain property contributed to a nonoperating *private* foundation that does not meet certain technical requirements.

The property involved under this provision is "capital-gain" property held for more than one year. The most common capital assets would be shares of stock, land, buildings, and purchased works of art.

(See Chapter 20 for a further definition of capital-gain property.)

In the case of property that fits into the two exceptions above, the amount deemed to have been contributed is the property's fair market value *minus* 40 percent (60.9 percent for a corporate donor) of the amount of the property's appreciation over the taxpayer's basis in the property.

For example, if a taxpayer paid $1,000 for a painting four years ago and this year, when its fair market value was $4,000, contributed the painting to a university, the amount deductible would depend on the use made by the university of the property. If it were used in the university's art department or were hung in the art gallery, the amount deductible would be the fair market value of $4,000. On the other hand, if it were resold by the university for $4,000, the amount deductible would be $2,800: $4,000 fair market value *minus* 0.40 ($4,000 value less $1,000 basis).

The maximum amount deductible

The deduction for contributions by an individual can in no case exceed 50 percent of the taxpayer's adjusted gross income for the year. However, the limit in some cases may be less than 50 percent of adjusted gross income, depending on the nature of the property given and the type of donee to which the contribution is made.

CONTRIBUTIONS TO 50-PERCENT-LIMIT ORGANIZATIONS The deduction for total contributions made directly to "public charities" generally is limited to 50 percent of A.G.I. Public charities include church groups, educational institutions, institutions and organizations for medical care, governmental units or other organizations that get a substantial portion of their support from the public or from a governmental unit, and a relatively small number of "private foundations" that meet specific requirements.

The deduction for contributions to public charities of appreciated capital-gain properties is subject to a special limit of 30 percent of A.G.I. For example, assume that in the current year Mason, whose A.G.I. is $9,000, contributes a work of art (that cost him $2,000 ten years ago and had a fair market value of $8,000 at the date of gift) to the city art museum to be used as part of its permanent exhibition. The deduction for this contribution would be limited to 30 percent of A.G.I., or $2,700.

When applying the overall 50 percent limit, contributions of 30-percent-limit property are the last to be considered. For example, if a taxpayer with A.G.I. of $10,000 gives cash of $2,600 to public charities and an art work with a fair market value of $4,000 to the public museum, he can deduct only $5,000, or 50 percent of A.G.I. in this year. The deduction consists of the $2,600 cash contribution and $2,400 of the value of the art work. (The excess of capital-gain property contributed over the 50 percent limit can be carried forward to future years, as discussed later in this chapter.)

MAXIMUM CONTRIBUTIONS TO CERTAIN ORGANIZATIONS   The deduction for contributions to *private* foundations that do not meet specified requirements is limited to 20 percent of the taxpayer's A.G.I. The same limit also applies to contributions made *for the use of,* rather than *directly to,* public charities. If contributions are made to both public charities and private foundations, the contributions to public charities must be deducted first. These rules can be illustrated by two simple cases.

> CASE A Conrad has A.G.I. of $20,000. His only contributions were $5,500 cash to Harvard University and $6,000 cash to a private foundation. His deduction is limited to $9,500, consisting of the $5,500 given Harvard University and $4,000 of the contribution to the private foundation, which is limited to 20 percent of A.G.I.

> CASE B Assume the same facts as in Case A, except that Conrad's contribution to Harvard was $9,000. His deduction would be limited to $10,000 (50 percent of A.G.I.). The deduction would consist of $9,000 given to Harvard and $1,000 of the gift to the private foundation.

In cases in which the value of capital-gain properties contributed to public charities exceeds 30 percent of A.G.I. and contributions are also made to private foundations, the computation of the limit on the amount deductible for the private foundation contributions becomes more complex. Since this situation is rarely encountered, it is not discussed in this text.

TIME OF DEDUCTION   Under most circumstances an individual taxpayer is allowed to deduct contributions only in the year in which he or she actually transfers the cash or other property to the qualified recipient. Pledges of contributions are not deductible until paid. This restriction is equally applicable to accrual-basis taxpayers and to cash-basis taxpayers. Payments by credit card, however, are treated like cash payments in the year the credit slip is signed.

Any contributions to public charities in excess of 50 percent of the taxpayer's A.G.I. can be carried over to the following year and treated as having been paid in that year. If the sum of the carryover and the actual contributions made to public charities in the second year again exceeds 50 percent of the taxpayer's A.G.I., the excess may be carried over to the next following year. This procedure can be repeated for up to 5 years. If, because of the percentage limitation, a contribution cannot be fully deducted during the 5-year carryover period, any unused amount is simply lost as a deduction. In each year, the contributions actually paid during that year must be deducted before any of the contribution carryover can be applied. Contributions to private foundations, however, can never be used to determine a contribution carryover; there is a carryover only if contributions to public charities exceed 50 percent of A.G.I. (with the exception of carryovers of contributions of capital-gain property in excess of the 30 percent limit). Thus, in both Cases A and B, above, the taxpayer (Conrad) would lose some of the tax benefit associated with his contributions to a private charity. If excess contributions are carried over from more than one tax year, the carryovers are used in order of occurrence (a FIFO basis).

The calculation of the contribution carryover can be illustrated by the following tabulation, prepared for an individual with an A.G.I. of $10,000.

| | Amount contributed | | Maximum | |
	To public charities	To private foundations	deduction in current year	Contribution carryover
CASE A	$6,000	$ 0	$5,000	$1,000
CASE B	0	6,000	2,000	0
CASE C	5,500	800	5,000	500
CASE D	3,500	2,500	5,000	0

The relation between the contribution carryover and the contributions actually made during a year can also be illustrated in a simple tabulation. Assume that a taxpayer's only contributions were made in cash to public charities in the amounts shown in the tabulation below. Also, assume that the taxpayer had A.G.I. of $60,000 each year. This taxpayer must exhaust the 1980 contribution carryover by December 31, 1983, since it comes from the 1978 excess contributions.

Year	Amount contributed (all to public charities)	Amount deductible in current year	Contribution carryover
1975	$50,000	$30,000	$20,000
1976	40,000	30,000	30,000
1977	20,000	30,000	20,000
1978	32,000	30,000	22,000
1979	20,000	30,000	12,000
1980	20,000	30,000	2,000

Contributions of appreciated capital-gain property that are in excess of the 30 percent limitation may be carried over to future years and added to the capital-gain contributions of the future years, subject to a 5-year carryover.

Present provisions relating to contributions by corporations

Corporations also are permitted to deduct charitable contributions made to the same organizations previously listed for individual taxpayers. A special provision permits corporations using the *accrual* basis of accounting to deduct an accrued contribution as long as it is paid on or before the due date of the corporation's federal tax return. This exception is available only if the gift was authorized by the directors of the corporation prior to the close of the tax year.

Deductions for charitable contributions by a corporation are limited to 5 percent of taxable income computed before deductions for (1) the contributions themselves, (2) any net operating loss carryback to the taxable year, and (3) certain special deductions allowed corporations, the most important of which is the deduction for dividends received. Contributions in excess of the 5 percent limitation may be carried over for 5 consecutive years, and added to contributions made in the years to which they are carried, in the same manner as the carryover of contributions by individuals.

If a corporation contributes tangible, personal, "capital-gain" property unrelated to the donee organization's exempt function, or any capital-gain property to a nonoperating private foundation that does not meet certain technical requirements, the amount deemed to have been contributed is the market value of the property reduced by 60.9 percent of the amount of the property's appreciation over the taxpayer's basis in the property. (This compares to the 40-percent reduction for individuals.)

As previously noted, since 1969, the deduction for a contribution of "ordinary income" property has been limited to the fair market value of the property reduced by the amount that would have been reported as ordinary income if the property had been sold at its fair market value. Enactment of the 1969 provision effectively eliminated the abuses that led to its enactment and also resulted in reduced contributions of those types of property to charitable organizations. Charitable organizations that provide food, clothing, medical equipment, supplies, and so on, to the needy and disaster victims found that contributions of such items were reduced. As a result, in the Reform Act of 1976, Congress permitted corporations (other than Subchapter S corporations) a deduction for up to one-half the appreciation on certain types of ordinary income property contributed to a public charity (except governmental units) or to a private operating foundation. In order to qualify for this treatment, the donee must use the property in a use related to its exempt purpose and solely for the care of the ill, the needy, or infants. Certain other requirements must also be met. The amount of the deduction is generally the sum of (1) the taxpayer's basis in the property and (2) one-half the unrealized appreciation. In no event is a deduction to be allowed for an amount that exceeds twice the basis of the property, and no deduction is allowed for any part of the appreciation that would have been ordinary income (if the property had been sold) because of the application of various "recapture" provisions such as Sec. 1245.

Importance of the contributions deduction by individuals

Contributions are the third most important group of itemized deductions (following taxes and interest) made by individuals. As shown in Table 13-1, during 1976 deductions for contributions on individual returns totaled $16.8 billion, or 12.6 percent of the total of all itemized deductions on such returns.

It is normally assumed that persons subject to high tax rates are more influenced in their giving by tax considerations than those in lower brackets. Studies by the Internal Revenue Service have shown that contributions are relatively more important in the two highest brackets ($500,000 to $1,000,000, and over $1,000,000 A.G.I), but that a very substantial portion of contributions are made by taxpayers with incomes below $10,000. These studies also show a distinct difference in the pattern of giving by large and small contributors. Small income taxpayers tend to make most of their contributions to religious groups; large contributors give substantial support to educational institutions, hospitals, welfare agencies, and private foundations. Until 1970 wealthier taxpayers were able to use private foundations to achieve some personal financial or other objective, a problem discussed in more detail below.

The contribution deduction and social welfare

Deductions for contributions to philanthropic organizations were first allowed in 1917 because of the fear that high wartime tax rates would cause a decline in contributions. A deduction allowance for contributions is usually justified as an encouragement to a socially desirable activity. Presumably, contributions provide highly desirable activities with finances that are not adequately provided by other sources and would have to be provided by the state if they were not supplied by voluntary contributions. Many would describe the charitable deduction as simply a subsidy to charitable causes.

Many tax scholars question the effectiveness of the charitable deduction as an incentive for giving, pointing out that little is known about the actual value of gifts to philanthropies. For example, Professor Harry Kahn has presented evidence to indicate that the relation between contributions and income has been rather stable over the years, regardless of the contribution provisions of the income-tax laws in existence.[3] Various other studies have arrived at conflicting conclusions about the impact of deductibility on charitable giving.

A possible alternative to the contribution provision might be to eliminate the deduction, and, instead, allow the government to match contributions, at a given rate, by a refund of the contributor's tax directly to the philanthropy to which the taxpayer made the gift. This would overcome the almost impossible task the I.R.S. now has in auditing contribution deductions, because it would then deal with several thousand philanthropic organizations rather than millions of taxpayers. Also, this scheme would make it possible for Congress to delineate more clearly those activities it wishes to subsidize.

An important question is whether it is proper for the taxpayer, by making a deductible contribution, to force "the government in effect to make a partial matching grant for a purpose of his own choosing and

to an organization whose operations are not subject to government review or control. Sectarian, provincial, eccentric or frivolous uses of money may be aided along with the most worthy."[4] However, the lack of government control may be a positive advantage because it allows many educational, scientific, and cultural activities to maintain diversity and independence they would not have if Congress were to scrutinize each deduction. The appropriations process is not well suited to the nourishment of new and unpopular ideas, and the usual procedures for handling public funds to finance many activities of philanthropic organizations would be cumbersome and unsatisfactory.

Of course, freedom from control is not completely achieved under the present system of contribution deductions. Professor White observed this limitation of the present system in the following words:

> The policies and administration of recipient institutions can scarcely be expected to remain independent of the viewpoint of major suppliers of their funds. There are the limitations on the size of deductible contributions, probably rarely reached, and the Government itself sets eligibility requirements for recipient institutions. But . . . the Government's program is biased to expand the influence of the rich as compared to the moderate- and low-income giver.[5]

The problem of private foundations

Prior to 1970 there was significant public concern over the growth of "private foundations" and the use of these foundations as a means of avoiding taxes—that is, the use of privately held corporations as vehicles for reducing both income taxes and the federal estate tax. A common arrangement is to have the stock of a family corporation divided into voting and nonvoting classes. The former stock is retained by members of the family, while the nonvoting shares are given to a tax-free, nonprofit foundation established for "educational" or "religious" purposes. The basic benefit is twofold. First, the transfers of the nonvoting stock to the foundation create sizable income tax deductions. Second, the family, through ownership of the voting stock, continues to control the assets of the family corporation; but, since actual ownership of some of the family assets has been transferred to the foundation through the

[3]C. Harry Kahn, "Personal Deductions in the Individual Income Tax," *1959 Compendium*, pp. 392–95.

[4]Goode, *op. cit.*, p. 169.
[5]Melvin I. White, "Proper Income Tax Treatment of Deductions for Personal Expense," *1959 Compendium*, p. 371.

nonvoting stock, a large portion of the estate escapes the federal estate tax.

Charges have been made that some foundations engage in activities not contemplated in the laws granting them tax-free status, such as making loans to officers, engaging in politics, and similar activities. There has been increasing public concern over foundations, ostensibly set up for religious or educational purposes, whose actual activities largely involve using mass media, especially radio and television, to influence public opinion on political, economic, and social affairs. The I.R.S. has removed the tax-free status of several organizations and foundations in recent years because of their involvement in political activities.

As we have already seen, contributions to private foundations are limited to 20 percent of the donor's A.G.I. Contributions of capital-gain property by individuals to some private foundations are deductible to the extent of the fair market value reduced by 40 percent of the amount that would be taxed as capital gains if sold. Of vastly greater importance, however, are laws affecting the foundations themselves. The deductibility of any contribution to private foundations depends on the foundation's compliance with Treasury Department requirements. And, if a foundation is found to be no longer exempt, a steep penalty tax is imposed unless the foundation's assets are used for charitable purposes. Additionally, excise taxes are levied on certain types of transactions entered into by the foundation. These transactions are those by which the foundation seeks to achieve such aims as exerting political influence, provide operating capital for donor corporations, and other objectives not compatible with their tax-exempt status. The conditions that trigger special excise taxes are:

1. "Self-dealing," or certain specific transactions between "disqualified individuals." These transactions are essentially those that might be used to channel the foundation's funds into the hands of a donor or founder of the foundation.

2. Failure to distribute income.

3. Excess business holdings. (Generally, the foundation and disqualified persons must own no more than 20 percent of the voting stock of a corporation.)

4. Investments that jeopardize charitable purpose. (This provision is designed primarily to discourage speculative investments.)

5. Certain expenditures. These are expenditures

primarily to carry on propaganda, or otherwise to attempt to influence legislation, to attempt to influence the outcome of any public election, or for any purpose other than religious, charitable, scientific, literary, or for the prevention of cruelty to children or animals.

Obviously, all these rules are quite complex, but their intent is simply to make the foundation conform to its tax-exempt purposes.

INTEREST EXPENSE

Perhaps the most controversial itemized deduction is that for interest. Essentially, since the beginning of the modern income-tax law in 1913, nearly all interest expense has been deductible. Although it is almost unanimously agreed that interest incurred in trade or business, or in connection with the production of any other taxable income, should be treated in the same manner as other deductible expenses, there is far less agreement over the propriety of a deduction for interest paid on funds to finance the purchase of personal consumer goods and services.

The general provision authorizing the deduction of interest is contained in Sec. 163, which reads as follows:

(a) General Rule.—There shall be allowed as a deduction all interest paid or accrued within the taxable year on indebtedness.

This all-inclusive provision is somewhat modified and limited by several other sections disallowing certain types of interest. The most important disallowance prohibits the deduction of interest on funds borrowed to earn tax-exempt income and on those used to purchase a single-premium life insurance or endowment policy. Other limiting provisions require that the indebtedness be that of the taxpayer if a deduction is to be allowed. Another important restriction, to be discussed later in some detail, limits the amount of deductible "investment interest." Finally, certain "construction period" interest and taxes must be capitalized, as discussed later.

The Truth in Lending Act now requires that finance charges on a retail installment contract, bank credit card, and similar credit arrangements be disclosed as an annual percentage rate. All such charges are now deductible on the tax return. A carrying charge may also be deducted where the installment contract states the carrying charge separately but the interest charge cannot be ascertained. The deduction in this case is limited to an imputed interest equal to one-half of 1 percent (0.5 percent) of the unpaid monthly balance measured on the first day of each month of an account arising from the purchase of personal (nonreal) property or educational services. Obviously, this "standard" interest deduction is wholly inadequate for the typical consumer credit obtained today.

Controversies over the interest deduction

Presumably, the broad deductibility of interest results from the difficulty encountered in trying to distinguish clearly between borrowed funds used for income-producing activities and those used for personal activities. It is extremely difficult to trace the relationship between debts owed by the taxpayer and specific assets or services acquired. In many cases, funds borrowed ostensibly for business purposes are used for personal purchases, and funds acquired for consumption purposes are used in a business venture. In addition, prudent manipulation of the taxpayer's finances could ensure that borrowed funds would be used first in business and that equity capital would be used first for personal expenditures if interest on the former, but not the latter, were deductible.

Proponents of this deduction agree that interest expense represents a reduction of the taxpayer's economic income, regardless of why the expense was incurred, and thus should be deductible in order to give effect to this difference in wherewithal to pay tax. On the other hand, interest expense may be considered part of the purchase price of commodities or services acquired—a premium for obtaining the goods and services now rather than waiting until later. This element of price, so the argument goes, should be treated in the same manner as the other portions—that is, interest related to personal expenditures should be nondeductible.

The most difficult aspect of the interest deduction, and the most controversial one, relates to interest paid by the taxpayer on funds obtained to purchase a home or durable consumer goods. There is a definite inequity between the homeowner and the tenant, which can be easily seen by assuming that one taxpayer makes monthly rental payments of $200 on his residence, while a second taxpayer makes mortgage payments of $200 per month, including an

average of $100 per month in interest. The former taxpayer can take no deduction on his tax return, while the latter is entitled to deduct all of the interest paid; in addition, the homeowner also may deduct property taxes paid. Since the second taxpayer is not required to include in income the imputed rental value of his owner-occupied home, he or she obviously has a distinct tax advantage over the tenant, even though the two of them may have essentially the same economic income.

This inequity has been recognized throughout the history of the modern income tax. For example, in the debate over the initial act in 1913, it was pointed out that

> here is a man . . . who has purchased a home. He has given a mortgage upon it . . . and is paying . . . $1,000 in interest. Under this bill that would be deducted from his net income. But if his neighbor has rented a house, and instead of virtually paying what the first-named man does in the form of interest, he pays directly $1,000 rent. He gets no deduction whatever, and yet the situation of the two is to all intents and purposes precisely the same.[6]

Many tax scholars argue that the only real solution to this inequity is to require that the homeowner include in his or her taxable income the imputed rental value of his or her home. Then the interest paid on a home mortgage would be deductible as a cost of earning income. (This same rule would, apparently, have to be extended to other consumer durable goods.) The practical difficulties of this solution are obvious. Another suggested solution is to disallow the deduction for interest not specifically related to income, but it has already been pointed out that this, too, is not a practical solution because of the difficulty of distinguishing between interest on funds used for income production and that on funds obtained for personal use.

Some tax scholars suggest, as an alternative, that because of the difficulty in segregating personal interest from that relating to income production, all income from property might be pooled or lumped together and interest payments could be deductible up to the amount received from the income-producing property. The present law contains a provision that embodies the general concept of this proposal

---

[6]50 *Congressional Record* 3848 (1913) quoted in Samuel H. Hellenbrand, "Itemized Deductions for Personal Expenses and Standard Deductions in the Income Tax Law," *1959 Compendium*, p. 378.

but by no means goes to such extremes. Still, however, the limit on "excess investment interest" marks a move toward major restrictions on the interest deduction.

Excess investment interest

The rules that permitted deduction of all interest expense permitted taxpayers to voluntarily incur substantial interest expenses on funds borrowed to acquire or carry investment assets. Often these funds were used to purchase stocks that had growth potential but returned small dividends currently. This gave rise to an immediate deduction and permitted the taxpayer to report gain on sale of the appreciated securities as long-term capital gain. In order to curtail excessive abuse of this tax break, tax laws have limited the amount of interest deductible on funds borrowed after December 16, 1969, by noncorporate taxpayers to purchase investment property. The limitation for interest on indebtedness incurred after September 10, 1975, is the sum of (1) $10,000 ($5,000 if married and filing separately) and (2) net investment income for the year.

Investment income is defined as the income from interest, dividends, gross royalties, rents from "net leases," net short-term gains from the disposition of investment property, and amounts treated as ordinary income under depreciation recapture rules for real and personal property, where such property is held for investment. Expenses relating to investment properties are deducted from investment income to compute net investment income. These expenses include such items as taxes, amortizable bond premiums, and bad debts.

To illustrate the excess investment interest limitation, assume the following facts. A taxpayer this year paid interest of $45,000 on funds borrowed to purchase investment property. During the year she received investment income consisting of interest and dividends totaling $5,000 and incurred investment expenses of $2,000. Her investment interest deduction is limited to $13,000, computed as follows:

Basic amount deducted without restriction	$10,000
Excess of investment income over investment expenses ($5,000 − $2,000)	3,000
Amount of investment interest deducted this year	$13,000

The remaining $32,000 investment interest paid by the taxpayer is not deductible this year. However, any excess amount is carried forward and treated as interest paid or accrued in the succeeding tax year. Thus, there is, in effect, an unlimited carryover.

Increased limits exist when the taxpayer, the taxpayer's spouse, or the taxpayer's children own more than 50 percent of a partnership or corporation and the investment indebtedness was incurred in connection with the acquistion of the interest in the corporation or partnership.

Where investment interest is paid on indebtedness incurred on or after September 11, 1975 (known as "post-1975 interest.") as well as on indebtedness incurred before that date (known as "pre-1976 interest"), separate computations must be made for the excess investment interest for the two periods. The rules governing pre-1976 interest are not discussed in this book.

Capitalization of interest (and taxes) during construction period

Prior to 1976, amounts paid or accrued for interest, as well as for property taxes, attributable to the construction of real property were allowed as current deductions unless the taxpayer elected to capitalize those items as carrying costs (Sec. 266). As a result, taxpayers in high marginal income tax brackets, especially those involved in real estate "shelters," could avoid payment of income taxes on a substantial portion of their economic income by expensing such costs as they were paid or accrued.

However, interest and real estate taxes during the period beginning with the date on which the construction of a building or improvement begins and ending with the date on which the building or improvement is completed must be capitalized. The effective date of the law varies with the type of property involved, as follows.

Type of property	Provision effective for construction beginning on or after
Nonresidential real estate	January 1, 1976
Residential real estate	January 1, 1978
Low-income housing	January 1, 1982

The capitalized costs are then to be amortized over a specified period. The length of the ultimate 10-

year amortization period is to be phased in over a seven-year period. Interest and taxes paid or accrued in the first year that the provision is to apply will be amortized over a four-year period. The amortization period then increases by one year for each succeeding year until the amortization period becomes 10 years, so that costs paid or accrued in the second year after the provision becomes effective will be amortized over five years. Thus, the 10-year period is fully phased in for taxable years beginnning in 1982 in the case of nonresidential real estate, 1984 in the case of residential real estate, and 1988 in the case of low-income housing.

Interestingly, one reason advanced by the Joint Committee on Taxation for requiring capitalization of construction period interest and taxes was the following:

> The allowance of a deduction for construction period interest and taxes is contrary to the fundamental accounting principle of matching income and expense. . . .
>
> In the case of an individual who constructs a building and subsequently receives income in the form of rents from that building, the accounting concept of matching income against expenses *should require* [emphasis added] that the expenses incurred during the construction period be deducted against the income which is received over the life of the building . . .[7]

[7] *Ibid.*, p. 26.

TABLE 13-3
DEDUCTIONS FOR INTEREST ON RETURNS ITEMIZING DEDUCTIONS FROM A.G.I. (IN BILLIONS OF DOLLARS)

Year	Itemized interest deduction
1954	$ 3.20
1956	4.81
1958	6.27
1960	8.41
1962	10.27
1964	12.45
1966	14.97
1968	18.55
1970	23.93
1972	27.35
1973	31.94
1975	38.62
1976	43.47

SOURCE: *Statistics of Income,* various years, and *Preliminary Statistics of Income, 1976.*

There are more than a few accountants who might argue with this viewpoint.

Growth in the interest deduction

The extremely rapid growth in the itemized interest deduction on tax returns with A.G.I. is indicated in Table 13-3.

Although taxes, contributions, and interest are among the most controversial deductions for individuals, they certainly do not represent the totality of controversial items. In the next chapter we shall examine some items relating to income production.

PROBLEMS

For the following problems, ignore the "zero bracket income" floor under itemized deductions.

1. What reasons may be given to justify the deduction of taxes on non-income-producing property—for example, on the taxpayer's home?
2. Explain how the deduction for contributions may be considered a subsidy.
3. No interest deduction is allowed on loans made to carry an investment if the income from the investment is tax exempt, or on loans made to obtain a single-premium policy. Assume that this tax rule did not exist. Devise two schemes, one related to state or municipal bonds and one related to life-insurance contracts, that would result in a financial windfall from the assumed loophole.
4. It is often suggested by tax scholars that the rules governing various deductions related to the taxpayer's home (interest, taxes, insurance, and so on) could be

simplified and made more equitable if the taxpayer were required to include in gross income the "imputed rental value" of the home. Explain this argument. Point out the major problem involved.

5. Once a taxpayer has purchased a home, he or she will almost always have excess itemized deductions. Explain why this statement generally is accurate.

6. Explain the reasons for the limitation on the deduction for "investment interest."

7. "Construction period" interest and taxes must now be capitalized. What is the purpose of this provision? What difficulties do you see in its enforcement?

8. Which of the following taxes are deductible for federal income-tax purposes? (Assume all taxes were paid in the current year.)

    a. Gift tax.

    b. F.I.C.A. tax on business employees.

    c. State gasoline (excise) tax on gasoline used in family auto.

    d. Federal gasoline tax on gasoline used in family auto.

    e. State income tax.

    f. Property tax on family residence.

    g. State excise tax on cigarettes for personal consumption.

    h. State excise tax on liquor consumed while entertaining business clients.

    i. State excise tax on liquor for private consumption.

    j. Automobile license (your state) for family auto. (If you are an out-of-state student, solve this problem for the state in which your school is located.)

9. In each of the following independent cases, indicate the amount that the taxpayer may deduct as "taxes" on his or her federal income-tax return. Indicate whether any amount deductible is *for* A.G.I. or *from* A.G.I.

    a. In July of this year, Atkins inherited some property from a deceased aunt. He paid a state inheritance tax of $1,200 on the inheritance.

    b. During the year, Bartholomew purchased various bottles of alcoholic beverages for personal use. The amount he paid for these beverages included $118 federal excise taxes, $32 state excise tax, and $8 state retail sales taxes.

    c. During the year, Irma paid the following real estate taxes on her home: state, $69; county, $64; city, $345; school district, $360. In addition, the city made a special assessment for paving the street and installing a curb and gutter in front of her home, $280.

    d. Farmer had the following expenditures for taxes during the year 19x2: payment of 19x1 state income tax, $84; quarterly estimates of his 19x2 federal income tax, $4,600; final payment of net amount due on 19x1 federal income-tax return, $310.

    e. Goodman purchased real estate on May 1 of this year for $18,000. The estimated taxes for the year were prorated and the cash payment to the seller was reduced by $80, the estimated taxes through April 30. In December, Goodman paid the real estate taxes due for the year, $272.

    f. Homer operates a business. During the year he remitted to the federal government $19,000 of income taxes withheld from employees' earnings. He also remitted $9,000 in F.I.C.A. taxes, representing $4,500 deducted from employees' paychecks and Homer's matching contributions. Also he paid $170 federal unemployment compensation taxes and $920 state unemployment compensation taxes on his employees' earnings.

    g. Ironman operates a business. During the year he imported jewelry for resale in the business, paying an import tariff of $980. In addition he imported some furs for his wife's personal use, paying an import tariff of $230.

    h. Stella operates a retail gift shop. During 19x1, she paid $720 of "self-employment" taxes on her net earnings for the preceding year, 19x0. (Answer for year 19x1.)

10. In each of the following independent cases, indicate the amount that may be deducted as charitable contributions.

    a. Adamson has A.G.I. of $22,000. During the year he made the following cash contributions:

Boy Scouts	$3,000
Local church	6,000
Local university	4,200

    b. Bartholomew had A.G.I. of $16,500. During the year he made the following cash contributions:

Boy Scouts	$5,000
Democratic Party	2,000
Needy family in neighborhood	400
American Legion	200
London School of Economics (England)	800
Local hospital	1,000

    c. Converse owns 1,000 shares of X Corporation stock for which she paid $10,000 in 1962. During the current year she contributed 600 shares of this stock to the First Church of Centertown. On the date of the contribution the shares had a market price of $25 per share. Converse's A.G.I. this year was $25,000.

    d. Farley operates a retail furniture store. In July of this year he contributed to the local hospital a number of items of furniture (tables, chairs, and sofas) from his merchandise inventory. These items had cost him $3,800 but had a normal retail value of $7,400.

    e. Assume the same facts as in part d, except that Farley contributed the furniture to a private foundation.

    f. Inglewood is active in the Boy Scouts. During the past year he served as a scout master. At the end of the year he calculated that he had spent $80 for various scout activities such as fund-raising drives. In addition, he had driven his automobile an estimated 300 miles in connection with scout work. He also had lost 38 working hours from his job, with a loss in pay of $142.

11. What amount may the taxpayer deduct as "contributions" in each of the following cases?

    a. Jacques purchased five tickets from the Boy Scouts. These tickets were to a local benefit performance of the city symphony, with all proceeds going to the Scouts. Normal cost of these tickets would have been $2.50 each, but because they were for a benefit, the cost was $5 each. Jacques and his family attended the performance, using all five tickets.

    b. Assume the same facts as in part a, except that Jacques purchased the tickets as a purely charitable gesture with the intent of throwing them away—and he did so.

12. President Johnson and his predecessors in office obtained a sizable income-tax deduction for items contributed to their presidential libraries. Johnson's suc-

cessors in office, however, will obtain a much smaller income-tax deduction for the items they contribute to their presidential libraries.

    a. Explain the changes in the Tax Reform Act of 1969 that account for the differential treatment of the various presidents.

    b. State the best reason(s) that you can in support of the 1969 changes.

    c. State the best reason(s) that you can in opposition to the 1969 changes.

13. Alpha Corporation earned a $30,000 taxable income, excluding its contribution deduction, its dividends-received deduction, and any net operating loss carrybacks. What is the maximum deduction for charitable contributions that Alpha Corporation might claim in the current year?

14. a. In 19x1 a severe tornado struck Midtown. Martha, the sole proprietor of a retail drug store, answered the call for help by contributing medicines, drugs, bandages, and other items, to the local Red Cross to be used in treating the sick and wounded. The items cost Martha $800 and had a fair value of $1,400. What is the amount of Martha's "contribution"?

    b. Assume the same facts as in part a, except that the taxpayer was, instead of Martha, a corporation. What is the amount of the "contribution"?

15. In each of the following independent cases, indicate the amount that the taxpayer may deduct as interest on his or her federal income-tax return.

    a. Alexander paid interest of $2,100 on a loan secured to purchase bonds of the city of Midville on which he received interest of $2,800.

    b. On October 9, 19x1, Bunker purchased a refrigerator, which had a cash price of $350. He elected to use the installment-payment method and made a down payment of $70, agreeing to pay the balance of $480 plus carrying charges of $60 in 12 equal installments of $45 each. Payments were made promptly on November 9 and December 9. (Answer for 19x1.)

    c. In 19x2 Bunker (see part b) made all payments when due and the final payment was made on October 9. (Answer for 19x2.)

    d. Elmot made the following interest payments during the year: $60 on a loan obtained to buy his wife some jewelry on their 25th wedding anniversary; $670 on the mortgage on his home; $45 on a loan obtained at the bank by his dependent 23-year-old son (Elmot also paid the loan principal in order to protect the family name even though he had no legal liability for the note or interest); $48 to the life insurance company on the loan value of his life policy withdrawn to pay for his daughter's high school graduation present; and $92 on amounts owed on gambling debts.

    e. Goodwoman had a rather sizable income in 19x1, so she decided to make large contributions to various charities in order to get the tax deduction in 19x1. Unfortunately, her cash position was quite low, so she borrowed $30,000 for the purpose of making these contributions. In 19x2 her interest payments on these loans totaled $2,400. (Answer for 19x2.)

    f. Eileen is a majority stockholder in Town Corporation. In 19x1, Town suffered a financial reverse. In order to protect the corporation's good name, Eileen paid $6,000 of interest owed by the corporation to a local bank.

16. What amount may the taxpayer deduct as interest expense in each of the following cases?

    a. Dunham, a cash-basis taxpayer, discounted a $500 one-year note payable at the bank on June 1, receiving credit for the net proceeds of $460. He made monthly payments on the first day of each month beginning July 1.

    b. Fox and his sons formed a corporation two years ago. The corporation borrowed money from several banks, mainly on the strength of Fox's reputation. The business has suffered continual reverses, and during the current year Fox personally paid interest of $3,400 on the corporation's indebtedness to the banks.

17. In the current year, Lemon and his wife filed a joint return showing adjusted gross income of $80,000. Included in their tax information were the following items:

Interest paid on funds borrowed to purchase stocks and bonds, borrowed last year	$48,000
Investment income	12,000
Investment-related expenses	800
Interest paid on home mortgage	6,200
Interest on personal loans	3,500

Compute the Lemons' deduction for interest for the year.

18. Jill, a cash-basis taxpayer, borrowed $15,000 from a bank on September 1, 19x1. The loan, plus interest at a rate of 12 percent, is due on March 1, 19x2. On December 30, 19x1, Jill paid all the interest for the six-month period of the loan, $900, but no part of the principal.
    a. What amount of interest, if any, may Jill deduct in 19x1?
    b. What amount of interest, if any, may Jill deduct in 19x2?

19. Dr. and Mrs. Hardy, recent graduates of State University, moved to Middle City, where Dr. Hardy will attempt to establish a new dental practice. Because this young couple was financially strained, Mr. Hardy (Dr. Hardy's father) agreed to make all the *interest* payments on his son's new residence. Mr. Hardy did not own, directly or indirectly, the home in which his son lived. Could Mr. Hardy deduct the interest he paid for his son in this way? What alternative arrangement might have been more advantageous to the two Hardy families?

20. In 19x1, the Saver family decided to have a "garage sale" to dispose of unused clothing. To their surprise, the Savers found they had apparently discarded almost none of their old clothes through the years. They found dresses, pants, shirts, coats, and other items quickly outgrown by their children, relatively unused clothing of Ms. Saver, made obsolete by style changes, and many usable suits discarded by Mr. Saver because of the dress requirements of his job as attorney. Proceeds from the two-day sale were $180, but over half the clothes were unsold. As a matter of fact, the "price tags" on the unsold clothes totaled $210, which represented about 15 percent of the original cost. The Savers contributed the unsold items to the Salvation Army. Mr. Saver is obviously interested in the possibility of a tax deduction for the contribution. Advise him.

21. Giver contributed to two "funds" during the year, giving $100 to the City United Fund drive and $20 to the Office Remembrance Fund, where she is employed. The Remembrance Fund is used to buy flowers for employees who are ill, die, or get married. Also it is used to buy Christmas presents for custodial workers and for similar purposes. What part, if any, of these contributions will Giver be entitled to deduct on her tax return for the year?

22. Barry purchased a new home on March 1, 19x1. Included in his credits in the "closing statement" was "accrued taxes to date of sale" of $240 charged to the seller. On October 1, 19x1, Barry received his actual property tax statement for $1,680 for the year and he paid that amount on December 12, 19x1. What amount can Barry deduct for taxes in 19x1?

23. Last year Mary Smith, a self-employed C.P.A., established a "Keogh" retire-

ment plan to be administered by the trust department of her bank. She contributed $7,500 to the plan and properly deducted that amount in computing her federal income tax. Under the plan her contribution is invested in high-grade securities. The income from the investments is not taxable to the trust nor to Mary until she withdraws it from the trust. In order to make her "contribution" last year, Mary had to borrow the $7,500. In the current year Mary paid interest of $600 on the borrowed funds. May Mary deduct the $600 interest paid? Explain.

24. Esther Garcia was chairperson of the local United Fund drive this year. At the close of the current year's campaign Esther held a "victory dinner" at her home to which she invited all the leaders in the fund drive along with their spouses or guests. Total cost of the dinner was $247. Is this amount deductible by Esther as a contribution?

25. During 1980, Sammy Protho paid the following interest:

Interest on home mortgage	$3,600
Installment charge accounts	60
Interest on loan used to purchase tax-exempt bonds	300

In addition, $20,000 was borrowed from a bank on September 1, 1980, for financing a new business venture. Interest of $2,400 was deducted by the bank in advance, and the loan is being repaid in 12 equal monthly installments. Beginning October 1, 1980, Protho made all payments when due. What amount will Protho claim as interest expense in his itemized deductions?

SUPPLEMENTAL PROBLEMS

26. In 19x1, Jones had A.G.I. of $30,000. He made the following contributions during that year:
   a. Cash of $500 to his church.
   b. Shares of stock that cost him $10,000 in 1960 to Stanford University. Fair market value at date of gift was $12,000.
   c. A painting that cost him $3,000 in 1950 to a private foundation. Fair value at date of gift was $7,000. The private foundation immediately sold the painting.
      1. What amount may Jones deduct as contributions in 19x1?
      2. What amount, if any, will Jones carry forward to 19x2?

27. During 1980, a self-employed taxpayer paid the following taxes:

State inheritance tax	$2,600
Federal income tax	4,200
State income tax	2,000
Real estate taxes on land in England (held as an investment)	1,600
State sales taxes	500
Federal self-employment tax	1,280
State unincorporated business tax	200

What amount can the taxpayer deduct as itemized deduction for taxes in 1980?

28. The following data are given for Mayday Corporation for 1980:

Gross profit on sales	$2,000,000
Dividend income from nonaffiliated domestic corporations	5,000
Operating loss carryover from prior years	1,000
Operating expenses (exclusive of charitable contributions)	102,000
Charitable contributions	2,250

What is Mayday's taxable income?

Each group plays a powerful, persuasive or pitiful case. When power, persuasion, and pity are all rolled into one—and then circumstances combine to make tax relief appear as the only practical solution—who can blame Congress for occasionally succumbing?

WALTER HELLER,
1959 Compendium

expenses of earning income

As suggested in Chapter 6, the tax laws provide adequately for deduction of expenses incurred in carrying on a trade or business and those related to rental income. Similarly, expenses associated with profit-making transactions such as ownership of stocks and bonds are clearly deductible, although the latter may be treated either as itemized deductions from A.G.I. or as a reduction in sales price. Our concern in this chapter is primarily with expenses related to employment activities, a more difficult concept to master.

INCREMENTAL LIVING COSTS

Although equity suggests that the costs incurred in earning income should be deductible, any attempt to apply this principle rigidly and consistently to *all* costs associated with income-producing activities is most frustrating—and perhaps even impossible. The difficulty arises, as pointed out in Chapter 6, in determining precisely which costs relate to income production and which are merely personal consumption expenditures.

The credit for child-care expenses

Perhaps the most important group of expenses, in terms of the amounts involved and the potential social and economic effects, are incremental costs of those who work outside the home—both employees and self-employed persons. Many, if not most, taxpayers incur extra household expenses as a result of being employed, and almost all employed persons

must buy appropriate clothing, commute to work, and spend more for food because they are away from home during the day.

Additional household costs are particularly important when both the husband and wife are employed and it is necessary to pay someone to care for children or other dependents during working hours. Even when an employed couple find it necessary or desirable to hire domestic help for routine housekeeping—cleaning, preparing meals, laundering, etc.—while both are employed, the additional costs appear to be closely related to employment activities. When one considers whether such costs should be treated as deductible items on the tax return, however, serious problems of equity immediately become apparent.

To illustrate some of the difficulties involved, let's consider the case of two housewives. Suppose that one, for whatever reason, takes an outside job that pays her $9,000 per year. In turn, she pays a housekeeper $9,000. This housewife has no net cash inflow from her employment. The second wife chooses to remain at home and perform her own housework. She, too, has neither income nor housekeeping expenses and thus no net cash inflow. Let us assume that both taxpayers, as well as the household help employed by the first, work eight hours per day. If the first wife is required to include her earnings in income and is also permitted to deduct her housekeeping expenses, her decision to work outside the home has essentially no effect on her income-tax liability. If she is *not* permitted to deduct the expense of housekeeping, however, she has (assuming her husband has income in excess of their other deductions) an increase in taxable income of $9,000 even though she had no "net income from employment." The basic question, obviously, is whether the cost of household help is a consumption expenditure, a matter of preference, and therefore should not affect the tax liability, or is appropriately a reasonable and necessary cost of earning income.

A somewhat more debatable and complex problem arises when the relative value of services rendered and received varies. For example, suppose the employed taxpayer in the previous example works only four hours per day and earns income of $10,000 per year. She hires a maid who works eight hours per day for $6,000 per year. Various possibilities for determining the effects on the taxpayer's tax liability are apparent. They include permitting no tax effect or allowing the taxpayer to either deduct or take a credit on all or part of the expenditures. Although the tax laws have not permitted the deduction of "household expenses" in general, even by employed taxpayers, from 1954 through 1975 the law permitted some workers to deduct payments made to others for care of dependents where the payments were necessary in order that the taxpayer be gainfully employed. The Tax Reform Act of 1976 replaced the child-care deduction with a "credit for child-care expenses," as pointed out in Chapter 8. Because the credit is based on expenses related to employment activities, it is discussed in this chapter. The more important provisions of the current law are:

1. The credit is 20 percent of certain employment-related expenses, up to specified limitations, paid during the taxable year to enable the taxpayer to work either full-time or part-time as an employee or as a self-employed individual.

2. The credit is allowed on expenses for care of, or housekeeping related to, a member of the taxpayer's household who: (1) is a dependent under 15 years of age, (2) is a person physically or mentally incapable of self-care and for whom the taxpayer is entitled to claim a dependency exemption (or would be entitled to claim a dependency exemption except that the person had gross income of $1,000 or more), or (3) is the taxpayer's spouse who is physically or mentally incapable of self-care.

3. The credit is 20 percent of qualified expenses up to $2,000 for one qualifying individual or $4,000 for two or more qualifying individuals. Thus, the maximum credit is $400 where there is one qualifying individual or $800 where there are two or more qualifying individuals.

For dependents under age 15, qualified expenses can be for care outside the taxpayer's residence (although the taxpayer would still have to maintain a residence for the qualifying individual). Payments for food, clothing, and education do not qualify. However, if the care provided includes expenses that cannot be separated, the full amount paid will be considered for the qualifying individual's care. Thus, the full amount paid to a nursery school will be considered for the care of the child even though the school also furnishes a lunch. Educational expenses for a child in the first or higher grade level are not considered to be expenses for the child's care.

Although services outside the taxpayer's home are considered employment-related expenses for a dependent who has not reached his or her 15th birthday, expenses outside the taxpayer's household do not qualify if related to the taxpayer's incapacitated spouse or dependent.

4. Generally, the expenses that can be taken into account cannot exceed the earned income of the taxpayer. For single individuals, this rule means that earned income must at least equal the base for the credit. Special rules apply to married individuals. First, married couples must file joint returns. Second, the amount used as the base is the lesser of the husband's or wife's earned income. For purposes of this last test, where (1) one spouse is a full-time student (five months out of any calendar year) or (2) one spouse is incapable of self-care, some earned income is imputed to that spouse. If there is one qualifying individual in the household, the earned income imputed to the unemployed spouse is $166 per month (or $2,000 per year). If there are two or more qualifying individuals, the earned income imputed to the unemployed spouse is $333 monthly (or $4,000 per year). Imputing earned income to the unemployed spouse means that the full base is allowed if the earned income of the working spouse is equal to or greater than the base.

5. If a married taxpayer is legally separated from his or her spouse, the taxpayer is considered unmarried for purposes of this credit. The law contains a special rule for married individuals who are not legally separated but who live alone. These rules are similar to the abandoned spouse rule used for heads of household. A married individual is considered unmarried if he or she (1) maintains a household that is the principal place of abode for a qualifying individual for more than one-half of the tax year; (2) furnishes over 50 percent of the cost of maintaining the household for the taxable year; and if (3) the individ-

ual's spouse is not a member of the household during the last six months of the taxable year.

6. For divorced parents who have children under 15 or children incapable of self-care, a special rule applies. If both or either parent, without regard to which parent has custody, provides over 50 percent of the child's support for a taxable year, and if the child is in the custody of one or both parents for more than six months of such year, then the child shall be treated as a qualifying individual with respect to the parent who has custody for the longest period of time. This rule waives the strict dependency test under the circumstances outlined; that is, the taxpayer may have a "qualifying" child who is not that taxpayer's dependent.

7. Child-care costs qualify even though paid to a relative of the taxpayer (relative being defined in the same manner as for the dependency test) and even though the relative lives in the taxpayer's household, *provided* the relative is not a "dependent" of the taxpayer or the taxpayer's spouse and is not a child of the taxpayer who has not attained the age of 19 at the close of the taxable year in which the service was performed.

8. If payment for child care is made in a year subsequent to the year the service was rendered, the credit may be taken in the year of actual payment under certain circumstances.

The Senate Finance Committee Report on the Tax Reform Bill of 1976 made it clear that the primary purpose of the child-care credit is to permit working taxpayers to receive a tax benefit from necessary work-related expenses. The report pointed out that under the law in existence prior to 1976 the availability of the child-care deduction was severely restricted by its classification as an itemized deduction and by its complexity. (One has to be skeptical of the idea that the 1976 Act simplified the treatment of such costs.) Treating the child-care expenses as itemized deductions denied any beneficial tax recognition of such expenses to taxpayers who did not itemize deductions. This was especially typical of low-income taxpayers, who are in greatest need of a tax benefit from such payments. Although changing the deduction provision to a system of credits may provide greater relief for low-income groups, it can be argued that the law still discriminates in favor of those with higher incomes because those in lower income groups cannot afford to pay for such services as childcare or household work. These persons must perform the work themselves at night or on week-

ends, and their children may be left unattended. Undoubtedly, some discrimination does exist in favor of high-income persons employing baby sitters.

Although the amount deducted by taxpayers for child-care expenses in past years steadily increased ($1.33 billion on 1.67 million returns in 1975, the last year for which a deduction was allowed), the conversion to a credit promises to increase the tax benefits dramatically. In 1976, the first year of the credit, $458 million of credits were taken on 2.66 million returns. The Senate Finance Committee estimated that the 1976 change from a deduction to a credit would reduce budgeted receipts by $340 million in 1977 and by $483 million in 1981. The greatest importance of the child-care provision is not the amounts involved, however, but the fact that it established a major precedent that "unavoidable" work-related personal expenditures may be deductible or give rise to a credit. Similar treatment of other personal expenses, such as clothing, transportation to work, and even food consumed during working hours, may just as logically be justified on the basis of necessity, even though the law presently contains no provisions for such deductions.

Expenses related to employment in a foreign country

Another provision relating to incremental living costs is found in Sec. 913, effective for years beginning after 1978. This section is very complicated and permits, in certain instances, a U. S. citizen who is employed in a foreign country to deduct all or a part of the following items:

1. Cost-of-living differential (based on the excess of the cost of living in the foreign place over the general cost of living in the metropolitan area in the United States with the highest general cost of living.

2. Qualified housing costs (in excess of an amount computed under a complex formula).

3. Qualified schooling expenses (all or part of education expenses for taxpayer's children in elementary or secondary grades).

4. Qualified home-leave travel expenses (all or a part of the cost of not more than one round trip each 12-month period for the taxpayer, his or her spouse, and dependents, from the foreign country to the taxpayer's principal U. S. residence).

5. A hardship area deduction (a deduction, computed on a daily basis, at an annual rate of $5,000,

for days in which the taxpayer's home is in a "hardship" area).

The introduction of this complex deduction was coupled with elimination of the previously allowed exclusion for income earned abroad by U. S. citizens, and was at least partial recognition that living costs in foreign areas may be abnormal and place an economic hardship on the taxpayer. The deduction is limited to taxpayers who are bona fide residents of a foreign country, or who are abroad for at least 510 days out of a period of 18 consecutive months.

EDUCATION EXPENSES

In recent years much attention has been given the tax status of education expenses because of the substantial increase in educational costs at all levels. Various proposals have been made to grant special tax benefits to taxpayers incurring such costs, especially when related to higher education. These proposals have included recommendations that taxpayers with children in college either be permitted to deduct a part of the expenses involved or be granted a credit against the tax. It has also been suggested that taxpayers be allowed to capitalize the costs of their college education and to amortize these costs over their expected productive lives.[1]

At the present time, however, there are stringent limitations on the deduction of education expenses. The basic provisions relating to educational-expense deductions are explained in Regulation Sec. 1.162-5(a). A deduction may be taken for expenditures if the education—

(1) Maintains or improves skills required by the individual in his employment or other trade or business, or

(2) Meets the express requirements of the individual's employer, or the requirements of applicable law or regulations, imposed as a condition to the retention by the individual of an established employment relationship, status, or rate of compensation.

The intent of this regulation is to permit deductions only for education expenses incurred purely for business purposes. This has been interpreted to mean that the costs of acquiring the basic education necessary for the taxpayer's *entrance* into his or her

trade, business, or profession are *not* deductible, because they represent personal expenditures. After the taxpayer has attained the minimum educational requirements and is active in a job, however, he or she may deduct expenditures made to maintain or improve the skills of the job. Costs of education undertaken *primarily* to obtain a promotion, an increase in pay, or a new job are nondeductible. It is extremely difficult in many cases to determine why education costs are incurred by the taxpayer. As a result, there have been frequent changes in the regulations and many conflicting court decisions over the deductibility of education costs. In a recent decision the U.S. Tax Court allowed a teacher already certified to teach in Toronto, Canada, to deduct the costs of three education courses required for her certification to teach in New Jersey. In the decision, the court recognized the inconsistencies and noted that it had denied a deduction to a licensed New York attorney for bar review courses necessary to be licensed in California and that it had denied a deduction to a German lawyer who attended law school to get an American law degree. In another strange decision, the Tax Court recently permitted an unemployed high school principal who had resigned his position to deduct the expense of getting his Ph.D. in educational administration. It is not surprising that many tax advisors simply decide that if any doubt exists they should attempt to take a deduction for educational costs.

Expenses of transportation, travel (including meals and lodging while away from home overnight), and the reimbursed portion of other education-related expenses are deductible *for* A.G.I. Other deductible education-related expenses are deductible only *from* A.G.I. as itemized costs.

Many valid arguments support a liberalization of the policy on deduction of education costs. It may be argued that the costs of obtaining basic education contribute to future earning capacity and therefore are similar to capital outlays for machinery and equipment. If so, these costs should be capitalized when incurred and then amortized over the productive life of the taxpayer. It is also argued that regulations governing educational expense deductions do not provide adequate incentives or rewards for the ambitious taxpayer wishing to acquire higher skills and educational levels. William Vickery suggests that some provision for ultimate deduction of education costs, through amortization or otherwise, would encourage greater lending and borrowing for educational purposes, perhaps permitting tuition charges in

---

[1] For an interesting discussion of the treatment of education expenses, see Richard Goode, "Educational Expenditures and the Income Tax," in Selma J. Mushken, ed., *Economics of Higher Education,* Bulletin No. 5 (Washington, D.C.: U.S. Department of Health, Education, and Welfare, Office of Education, 1962), pp. 281–304.

some vocational and professional courses to be high enough to cover the full costs of such study.[2]

Although it is impossible to determine the marginal effect that the deductibility of education expenses would have on the number of individuals pursuing higher education, or on the intensity with which they would pursue their education, the argument that a highly educated populace is desirable for social, economic, and cultural reasons has encouraged considerable support for the liberalization of the present rules. This topic will continue to be a subject of popular debate, if for no other reason than the political appeal it has to the large number of voters who would be affected by such action.

As we saw in Chapter 8, Sec. 127 of the Revenue Code provides that amounts paid or expenses incurred by the employer for educational assistance to employees under a nondiscriminatory educational assistance program for years after 1978 and prior to 1984 will not be taxable to the employee. However, Sec. 127 specifically states that this provision does not affect the deduction of education expenses under Sec. 162.

COMMUTING AND TRANSPORTATION EXPENSES

A somewhat similar problem involves the tax treatment of the cost of commuting to the taxpayer's place of work. The Revenue Code prohibits the deduction of costs of commuting from one's residence to one's regular place of employment. If the taxpayer has more than one job, however, cost of going from the first job to the second one is deductible as a "transportation expense." Similarly, a taxpayer whose sole employment requires movement from one location to another during a single day (for example, a physician, a building contractor, or a plumber) may be entitled to a transportation deduction, excluding the cost of getting from home to the first work assignment and from the last assignment to home. Of course, any transportation cost incurred by the employee in connection with employment, while on the job, is deductible. The confusion surrounding travel to a temporary job site has been compounded by recent I.R.S. actions. In 1976 a Revenue Ruling was issued, to become effective on January 1,

1977, under which travel expenses between home and a temporary job site would not be deductible, regardless of the nature of the work, the distance traveled, the mode of transportation, or the degree of necessity. The ruling was postponed three times, and finally was suspended indefinitely.

The employee deducts actual transportation costs incurred if public transportation facilities are used. If the employee uses a personal automobile, he or she may deduct either the actual costs incurred or a standard mileage allowance of $18\frac{1}{2}$ cents per mile for the first 15,000 business miles driven during the year and 10 cents per mile for each mile in excess of 15,000.

In recent years there have been many court cases involving the transportation costs of a commuting employee who at the same time transports job-required tools or equipment. According to the I.R.S., the taxpayer is entitled to deduct only the difference between the cost of transportation actually used and the cost of the same mode of transportation without carrying the tools. In many cases, therefore, the deductible cost amounts to very little or nothing under this I.R.S. interpretation. This may appear to be grossly unfair to the worker who would ordinarily ride a bus to work, but because he is carrying tools must take an auto, thus increasing his transportation costs solely because of the tool problem.

TRAVEL AND ENTERTAINMENT COSTS

Two widely discussed and controversial deductions under the federal income-tax laws are for travel and entertainment expenses. During the past several years, there have been numerous changes in the regulations governing such costs. Most of the rule changes represent attempts to curtail the abuse of expense accounts and, at the same time, not make the accounting and reporting requirements unduly burdensome to the taxpayer. Regulations governing the procedures to be followed in accounting for these expenses have been especially subject to change. Because of the frequent revisions of rules, our concern must be, not with the detailed accounting requirements, but with the general problem of determining whether such costs are deductible.

Travel costs

The basic authority for deducting travel costs rests in Sec. 162(a)(2) of the Revenue Code, which provides for the deduction of all ordinary and necessary

[2] William Vickery, "A Proposal for Student Loans," in Selma J. Mushken, ed., pp. 268–80.

expenses paid or incurred during the year in carrying on a trade or business, including:

(2) traveling expenses (including amounts expended for meals and lodging other than amounts which are lavish or extravagant under the circumstances) while away from home in the pursuit of a trade or business. . . .

Although travel costs are deductible if they are incurred purely in connection with business "away from home," a fact question is often raised when the travel is for both business and personal purposes. For example, if the taxpayer, while on a business trip, takes time out for sightseeing or other pleasure activities, the question may arise whether all travel costs should be deductible as business expenses. The reverse situation also may be found; the taxpayer may take a pleasure trip and, while traveling, take time out for certain business activities. The question in this case is whether any part of the costs are deductible as business expenses.

The basic factors that must be considered in determining whether or not travel costs are deductible include the ordinary, necessary, and reasonable criteria discussed in Chapter 6. The rule followed is logical; if the trip is primarily for business purposes, incidental sightseeing or other pleasure activities will not change the character of the trip, and therefore expenses incurred—except those directly related to the personal pleasure activity—will be deductible. On the other hand, if the primary purpose of the trip is pleasure, incidental business activities will not change the nature of the trip, and only the expenses directly associated with the business activity will be deductible.

In many cases it is difficult, if not impossible, to determine the true intent of the taxpayer. The taxpayer may not know the real purpose of the trip. This is especially true of attendance at meetings or conventions of trade associations and professional organizations. Business conventions often are held in resort areas or other pleasant surroundings in order to encourage attendance by members. In some cases, the convention may be merely a sham, while in others a business convention may be invaluable to the participants.

In recent years many taxpayers have found it "necessary" to make "business" trips to foreign countries and have taken the opportunity to combine a personal vacation with the business trip.[3] If the tax-

payer travels on business, other than to attend conventions, seminars, etc., to foreign countries, special rules apply. If the travel does not exceed one week or if the portion of the taxpayer's time outside the U.S. that is not attributable to trade or business activity is less than 25 percent of the total time on such travel, all the transportation costs may be deductible. If more than one week is spent abroad and 25 percent or more of the time is spent on non-business activities, the transportation costs must be allocated on the basis of time spent, and the non-business portion is not deductible. Of course, all expenses attributable to nonbusiness activities are nondeductible, and if the primary purpose of the trip is nonbusiness, no part of the transportation costs is deductible. In recent years, much of the abuse of foreign travel has been in connection with conventions and "seminars." The Report of the Senate Finance Committee on the Tax Reform Bill of 1976 recognized this abuse:

The committee is concerned that the lack of specific requirements has resulted in a proliferation of foreign conventions, seminars, cruises, etc. which, in effect, amount to Government-subsidized vacations and serve little, if any, business purpose. The committee is aware that the promotional material often highlights the deductibility of the expenses incurred in attending a foreign convention or seminar and, in some cases, describes the meetings in such terms as a "tax-paid vacation" in a "glorious" location. In addition, the committee has been made aware that there are organizations that advertise that they will find a convention for the taxpayer to attend in any part of the world at any given time of the year.[4]

Thus, the 1976 Tax Reform Act included provisions designed to curtail this abuse. Limitations were imposed on deductions allowable for the expenses of taxpayers attending conventions, educational seminars, or similar meetings outside the United States or its possessions. Deductions are allowed for expenses incurred in attending not more than two foreign conventions per year. For these two conventions, the amount of the deduction for transportation expenses cannot exceed the cost of airfare based on coach or economy class. Transportation expenses are deductible in full only if more than one-half of the total days of the trip (excluding the days of transportation to and from the site of the convention) are devoted to business-related activities. In addition, deductions for subsistence expenses, such as meals, lodging,

---

[3]See, for example, Richard Joseph, "Your Friendly Internal Revenue Service Invites You to Live it up in Europe—Almost Free," *Esquire* (January, 1968), pp. 106–07, 130.

[4]Finance Committee, U.S. Senate, 94th Congress, 2nd Session, *op. cit.,* p. 102.

and other ordinary and necessary expenses paid or incurred while attending the convention are limited to the fixed amount of per diem allowed to U.S. government employees at the location where the convention is held. However, subsistence expenses are deductible only for those days when at least 6 hours of business activity are scheduled and the taxpayer attends at least two-thirds of the scheduled activity. If at least 3 hours are scheduled and the taxpayer attends at least two-thirds of the scheduled activity, one-half day's subsistence is allowed. The organization that sponsors the convention must provide a statement certifying amount of time that the taxpayer spent at seminars and other business-related functions in order for the taxpayer to take a deduction. One wonders if this requirement will not result in an unparalleled fabrication of bogus documentation.

The Carter administration, citing the complications of the present rules along with the high potential for converting a tax-deductible trip into a vacation, has recommended that no expenses for attending a convention or seminar outside the United States be deductible unless it is reasonable for the meeting to be held outside the United States because of the composition of the membership or the specific purposes of the organization.

Even though the various rules followed in determining if travel costs are deductible may be "logical," the application of the rules is often difficult, and the facts of each case must be studied carefully. Even then, skillful and rational people may disagree in their conclusions in a specific case.

Entertainment costs

Entertainment expenses—that is, expenses for food, liquor, theater tickets, sporting events, and similar activities—are often even more difficult to relate specifically to business purposes than are travel costs. Business entertainment costs are generally deductible; nonbusiness costs are treated as personal expenditures and are therefore not deductible. As a general rule, to be classified as a business-related activity, the entertainment must be of customers or others with whom the taxpayer has, or may be expected to have, a business relationship.

Most of the criticisms of "expense account" spending as a means of tax avoidance have dealt with entertainment costs. The reasons are obvious, as one single example will illustrate. Suppose the taxpayer enjoys the theater (or the night club, or any other particular form of entertainment). An individual with whom he has some business connection is coming to town, so the taxpayer purchases theater tickets for himself, his wife, and the visiting businessman. Is this expenditure really for business? What are the motives of making the expenditure? Was the attendance of the taxpayer's wife reasonable and necessary? As a result of this entertainment and the good will generated, the taxpayer may very well achieve important business objectives even though the two do not directly discuss business during the evening. The inherent problems are obvious.

The question of whether travel and entertainment costs are "ordinary," "necessary," and "reasonable" is largely a subjective one. For this reason, Sec. 274 of the Revenue Code contains unusually detailed rules for determining which costs should be allowed and which should not. Portions of this section are quoted below to indicate the nature of its restrictions:

[Sec. 274(a)] (1) In general.—No deduction otherwise allowable under this chapter shall be allowed for any item—

(A) Activity. With respect to an activity which is of a type generally considered to constitute entertainment, amusement, or recreation, unless the taxpayer establishes that the item was directly related to, or, in the case of an item directly preceding or following a substantial and bona fide business discussion (including business meetings at a convention or otherwise), that such item was associated with, the active conduct of the taxpayer's trade or business . . .

(B) Facility. With respect to a facility used in connection with an activity referred to in subparagraph (A).

. . .

[Sec. 274(a)] (2) Special rules. For purposes of applying paragraph (1)—

(A) Dues or fees to any social, athletic, or sporting club or organization shall be treated as items with respect to facilities.

(B) An activity described in section 212 shall be treated as a trade or business.

(C) In the case of a country club, paragraph (1) (B) shall apply unless the taxpayer establishes that the facility was used primarily for the furtherance of the taxpayer's trade or business and that the item was directly related to the active conduct of such trade or business

. . .

Sec. 274(b) Gifts.

(1) Limitation. No deduction shall be allowed under section 162 or section 212 for any expense for gifts made directly or indirectly to any individual to the extent that such expense, when added to prior expenses of the taxpayer for gifts made to such individual during the same taxable year, exceeds $25. . . .

. . .

[Sec. 274(d)] No deduction shall be allowed—

(1) under section 162 or 212 for any travel expense (including meals and lodging while away from home),

(2) for any item with respect to an activity which is of a type

generally considered to constitute entertainment, amusement, or recreation, or with respect to a facility used in connection with such an activity or

(3) for any expense for gifts,

unless the taxpayer substantiates by adequate records or by sufficient evidence corroborating his own statement (A) the amount of such expenses or other item, (B) the time and place of the travel, entertainment, amusement, recreation, or use of the facility, or the date and description of the gift, (C) the business purpose of the expense or other item and, (D) the business relationship to the taxpayer of persons entertained, using the facility, or receiving the gift.

The Carter administration's tax proposals have taken a rather stern view of "ordinary," "necessary," and "reasonable." The 1978 proposals included, in addition to the restrictions on foreign seminars, recommendations that deductions be totally disallowed for entertainment facilities such as yachts, hunting lodges, club dues, and entertainment activities such as the cost of tickets to theater and sports events. They also would have limited deductions for business meals to one-half the cost of such meals and would have disallowed the cost of first-class air fares to the extent they exceed coach fares for the same flight. All these restrictions were proposed on the basis of fairness and, implicitly, on the grounds that these items are not ordinary, necessary, and reasonable. For example, the Treasury Department's "Fact Sheet" on the proposal stated: "The additional personal comfort provided by first class accommodations is not necessary for the conduct of business. Both ends of the plane arrive at the same time."

Congress adopted only a minor portion of the proposals, however. Section 274 (b) (2) was modified, as shown above, so that after 1978 no tax deduction is allowed for maintaining such *entertainment facilities* as (1) a yacht, (2) a hunting lodge, (3) a swimming club, (4) a fishing camp or a tennis club. (Nevertheless, such costs as interest, property taxes, etc., on such facilities, which are otherwise authorized as tax deductions, will still be deductible.) On the other hand, tax deductions for "country clubs," athletic event tickets, theater tickets, and first-class air fare, continue as before the Carter proposals.

The applicable regulations are relatively precise in specifying the reporting and accounting requirements for such deductions. Because of the great amount of detail and because they are frequently changed, these reporting requirements are not examined here. Basically, however, the employee who "accounts to his employer" need not report business expenses or reimbursements on his own return if reimbursement equals expenditures. If reimbursement exceeds expenses, the employee must report the excess as income. If expenses exceed reimbursement and the employee claims a deduction for the excess, some of the details must be shown. An "accounting" includes either (1) a detailed record of expenses or (2) a reasonable per diem allowance and mileage allowance even though no detailed record is submitted by the employee. Per diem rates up to $44 per day or the maximum per diem rate authorized to be paid by the federal government in the locality in which the travel was performed and mileage allowances up to 18½ cents a mile are deemed to be "reasonable" by the I.R.S. Employees who do not account to employers must report details of expenses and reimbursements on their returns. Deductions for travel and entertainment expenses are a source of frequent conflict between the taxpayer and the I.R.S. personnel.

MOVING EXPENSES

Section 217 of the Revenue Code permits the taxpayer to deduct the expenses of moving either on beginning employment as a new employee or on changing job location in his or her present employment. The moving expense deduction is now available to both employees and self-employed persons. The major requirements for eligibility are:

1. The move must be to a new principal *job site* that is at least 35 miles farther from the old residence than was the old *job site;* or at least 35 miles from his former residence if he had no former principal place of work.

2. An *employee* must be a full-time employee at the new job location for at least 39 weeks during the 12-month period immediately following his arrival at his new job location. A *self-employed* person must perform services on a full-time basis in the new location for at least 78 weeks in the following 24-month period.

Death, involuntary separation, and another job transfer for the convenience of the employer remove the time limitations.

The deductible moving costs fit into two broad groups:

1. Direct costs, deductible without limit. There are two main elements of direct costs: (a) transporta-

tion of household goods and personal effects and (b) travel costs of the taxpayer and family en route from the former to the new residence. If the taxpayer uses a personal automobile in the move, he or she may deduct the actual out-of-pocket costs incurred (gasoline, oil, etc.) or use an allowance of 8 cents per mile.

2. Indirect costs, limited to a total deduction of $3,000. There are three main elements of indirect costs:

    a. Pre-move house-hunting costs at new location after new employment has been obtained.

    b. Temporary living costs for taxpayer and family at new principal job location (up to 30 days).

    c. Costs related to selling old residence, terminating old lease, and obtaining new residence or living quarters.

Furthermore, the amount deductible for house-hunting costs and temporary living quarters is limited to a total of $1,500.

Military personnel who must make service-connected moves are not required to meet either the 35-mile test or the 39-week test.

If the new place of employment is outside the United States, the period during which temporary living costs may be deducted is 90 days rather than 30 days. Similarly, the overall limit on indirect costs that may be deducted is $6,000 rather than $3,000, and the limit on the amount deductible for house-hunting costs and temporary living costs is $4,500 instead of $1,500.

OTHER AREAS OF CONFLICT

It should be obvious by now that one could prepare an almost unlimited list of expenditures that have some of the characteristics of both business and personal expense. We will mention only a few additional ones that have been of unusual public interest in recent years.

Prior to 1976, the taxpayer could deduct that portion of the costs (depreciation, utilities, insurance, etc.) of maintaining an office or other facility in his or her residence that was deemed applicable to trade or business, including his or her business as an employee. There were frequent changes in the detailed procedures for applying this general rule, especially in determining whether the business facil-

ity in the home is "necessary." In addition, there were frequent conflicts in determining the costs applicable to business when a portion of the house was used for both business and personal purposes. Similarly, there have been disputes over whether a taxpayer who needs to work at night on employment-related business, and who uses a portion of his or her house as an office for this purpose, should be entitled to a deduction if he or she has access to a regular office at his or her employer's place of business. To complicate matters, there were conflicting court decisions in many cases with similar facts.

In order to eliminate some of the conflicts and uncertainties and to reduce the instances in which taxpayers converted costs applicable to personal activities into tax deductions, the Congress in the Tax Reform Act of 1976 severely curtailed the deduction for costs of a home used as an office.

Section 280A of the Internal Revenue Code provides that a portion of the costs applicable to the taxpayer's home (other than expenses of taxes and interest) may be deductible only if that portion of the home is *exclusively* used on a *regular basis* as a principal place of business, or as a place for meeting with clients and customers in the normal course of the taxpayer's business. If the taxpayer is an employee, he or she must prove that the *exclusive* use of that portion of the home is for the convenience of the taxpayer's employer. (However, the "exclusive use" test does not apply to personal residences used for day-care services.)

It is obvious from reading the Congressional committee reports on the 1976 Act that Congress intended to virtually eliminate deductions for an employee's "office in the home" and to severely curtail deductions for trade or business activities carried on in the home. The impact on artists, writers, and similar professionals who frequently carry on their creative income-producing activities in their homes is quite severe. Many organizations of writers, professors, artists, and similar taxpayers complained bitterly, but to no avail, as Congress eliminated their long-cherished office-at-home deductions.

Section 280A places restrictions on still another group of deductions that may be viewed either as personal expenses of the taxpayer or as related to income production—expenses of maintenance, upkeep, and operation of the taxpayer's vacation home that is also rented during part of the year. A taxpayer who rents a vacation home for fewer than 15 days during the year does not treat the rent received as income and is allowed no deductions for expenses of the home (other than the usual deductions for interest and taxes). If the home is rented for 15 days or more, the taxpayer may have to make a complex computation of the amount of expenses deductible. The complexity of the rules merely illustrates the difficulty encountered in attempting to allow reasonable and necessary expenses of income-producing activities while at the same time preventing the deduction of purely personal costs.

Another common source of conflict is the attempt by taxpayers to deduct membership dues in such organizations as the Kiwanis Club or Rotary Club. Here the court cases have been conflicting, but as a general rule the taxpayer must be able to show a direct relationship between the club expenses and the taxpayer's business. Where the club is used for both business and personal purposes, an allocation of costs must be made. A deduction for membership in purely social clubs (as opposed to professional civic clubs such as the Rotary Club) would have to be justified as entertainment-facility expenses and would have to be used *primarily* for business purposes. Obviously, each case must be judged on its own facts, but it is also obvious that taxpayers may be tempted when filing their tax returns to decide that their memberships are primarily for business purposes. Generally, membership dues in purely professional organizations, such as the American Institute of C.P.A.'s, are deductible, as are dues in labor unions.

Fees paid to an employment agency for aid in securing employment and a few other (limited) expenses are deductible if the taxpayer is seeking employment in his or her present trade or business. The taxpayer seeking a new position generally cannot deduct the costs associated with job-hunting according to the I.R.S. In recent years, however, the I.R.S. has seemed to follow a policy that allows a deduction for job-hunting in the same field, but disallows all such costs related to jobs in a new "field." The courts have not agreed with these strict I.R.S. interpretations in every instance.

OTHER DEDUCTIONS

Although the deductions relating to income production, medical expenses, casualty losses, contributions, interest, and taxes make up the most important deductions for individuals, other than those deduc-

tions related to trade or business, two other deductions should be mentioned. They are for alimony payments and for costs of complying with tax laws.

Under present provisions, the taxpayer may deduct (for A.G.I.) amounts paid as "periodic" alimony (see page 5/17). The payments are, in turn, considered as income to the recipient. Alimony deductions have been supported on two grounds. First, they may be considered merely a means of dividing income between two taxpayers. Second, they may be considered in the nature of extraordinary, unavoidable expenses that have a significant effect on the taxpayer's ability to pay income taxes, very similar to casualty losses or medical expenses. The major controversy surrounding alimony payments in the tax structure is the distinction between periodic payments and nonperiodic payments (which are not deductible by the spouse making payment and are not taxable to the spouse receiving payment).

As you have previously read, the deduction for expenses associated with "the determination, collection, or refund of any tax" is permitted by Sec. 212, which relates to expenses for production of income. The amount deducted for this purpose each year as itemized deductions by individuals is relatively insignificant. It is impossible to measure the total deductions for expenses related to tax-return preparation, to refund claims, and to actions against proposed assessments because in many cases these expenses are included with business operating expenses by those engaged in a trade, business, or profession. Undoubtedly, the bulk of such deductions is taken by those with higher incomes, because low-income taxpayers cannot afford the high cost of contesting tax assessments or of carrying on court litigation.

ILLUSTRATIVE FORM 1040

Some of the principles of taxation you have learned up to now are applied in the tax forms for calendar year 1979 illustrated on the following pages. Although the forms and the tax tables used in determining the tax are based on 1979, the general principles are the same for any year. These forms reflect the following data for William Washington and his wife, Mary, who reside in Central City, Texas. William is employed as an accountant for a manufacturing company at a gross salary of $22,000 for the year, from which income tax of $3,200 was withheld. Mary, a salesperson, earned $11,000, from which $1,700 was withheld. In addition, they received interest of $700, and dividends of $320 on jointly owned stocks.

They have two children, George, age 4, and Marie, age 13, and paid $1,800 ($150 per month) to a baby sitter, Jane Doe, to take care of the 4-year-old while Mary worked.

The forms also reflect the following data:

1. Travel costs (unreimbursed) on out-of-town business trip by William:

Airline ticket	$250
Limousine	15
Taxis	5
Lodging	60
Meals	36

2. Use of personal auto in business in town, unreimbursed:

60 miles @ 18½¢

3. Dues paid by William:

Texas Society of C.P.A.'s	$35
Central City Chapter of C.P.A.'s	30

4. Subscriptions to professional publications by William, $60.

5. Medical expenses for family:

Health and hospital insurance	$620
Hospital bills (not reimbursed)	110
Doctor's bills (not reimbursed)	300
Dental care	340
Transportation (200 miles @ 8¢)	16
Medicines and drugs	168

6. Taxes paid:

Personal property	$ 45
Real estate	770
Sales taxes (from tables)	294

7. Contributions:

Cash:

First Church	$900
Boy Scouts	20
United Fund	100

Shares of stock in X Corporation, given to First Church on December 10, fair market value, $340. Cost $200 in 1966.

8. Interest:

On home mortgage	$2,040
On personal bank loans	108

9. Payments of estimated tax during the year, $500.

Form **1040** Department of the Treasury—Internal Revenue Service
U.S. Individual Income Tax Return **19 79**

For Privacy Act Notice, see page 3 of Instructions | For the year January 1–December 31, 1979, or other tax year beginning _____ 1979, ending _____ 19___

Use IRS label. Otherwise, please print or type.	Your first name and initial (if joint return, also give spouse's name and initial) **William + Mary**	Last name **Washington**	Your social security number **111 22 3333**
	Present home address (Number and street, including apartment number, or rural route) **1000 Main Street**		Spouse's social security no. **444 55 6666**
	City, town or post office, State and ZIP code **Central City, TX 00001**	Your occupation ▶ **Accountant** Spouse's occupation ▶ **Salesperson**	

Presidential Election Campaign Fund ▶

Do you want $1 to go to this fund? . . . . ☒ Yes ☐ No
If joint return, does your spouse want $1 to go to this fund? . . . ☒ Yes ☐ No

Note: Checking "Yes" will not increase your tax or reduce your refund.

Filing Status

Check only one box.

1 ☐ Single
2 ☒ Married filing joint return (even if only one had income)
3 ☐ Married filing separate return. Enter spouse's social security number above and full name here ▶ _____
4 ☐ Head of household. (See page 7 of Instructions.) If qualifying person is your unmarried child, enter child's name ▶ _____
5 ☐ Qualifying widow(er) with dependent child (Year spouse died ▶ 19___). (See page 7 of Instructions.)

Exemptions

Always check the box labeled Yourself. Check other boxes if they apply.

6a ☒ Yourself ☐ 65 or over ☐ Blind
 b ☒ Spouse ☐ 65 or over ☐ Blind
} Enter number of boxes checked on 6a and b ▶ **2**

 c First names of your dependent children who lived with you ▶ **George, Marie**
} Enter number of children listed ▶ **2**

d Other dependents: (1) Name	(2) Relationship	(3) Number of months lived in your home	(4) Did dependent have income of $1,000 or more?	(5) Did you provide more than one-half of dependent's support?

Enter number of other dependents ▶

Add numbers entered in boxes above ▶ **4**

7 Total number of exemptions claimed . . . .

Income

Please attach Copy B of your Forms W–2 here.

If you do not have a W–2, see page 5 of Instructions.

8	Wages, salaries, tips, etc.	8	33,000 00
9	Interest income (attach Schedule B if over $400)	9	700 00
10a	Dividends (attach Schedule B if over $400) **320 00**, 10b Exclusion **200 00**		
c	Subtract line 10b from line 10a	10c	120 00
11	State and local income tax refunds (does not apply unless refund is for year you itemized deductions—see page 10 of Instructions).	11	
12	Alimony received	12	
13	Business income or (loss) (attach Schedule C)	13	
14	Capital gain or (loss) (attach Schedule D)	14	
15	Taxable part of capital gain distributions not reported on Schedule D (see page 10 of Instructions)	15	
16	Supplemental gains or (losses) (attach Form 4797)	16	
17	Fully taxable pensions and annuities not reported on Schedule E	17	
18	Pensions, annuities, rents, royalties, partnerships, estates or trusts, etc. (attach Schedule E)	18	
19	Farm income or (loss) (attach Schedule F)	19	
20a	Unemployment compensation. Total amount received _____		
b	Taxable part, if any, from worksheet on page 10 of Instructions	20b	
21	Other income (state nature and source—see page 10 of Instructions) ▶ _____	21	
22	**Total income.** Add amounts in column for lines 8 through 21 . . . . ▶	22	33,820 00

Adjustments to Income

Please attach check or money order here.

23	Moving expense (attach Form 3903 or 3903F)	23		
24	Employee business expenses (attach Form 2106) . .	24	377 10	
25	Payments to an IRA (see page 11 of Instructions) . .	25		
26	Payments to a Keogh (H.R. 10) retirement plan . . .	26		
27	Interest penalty on early withdrawal of savings . . .	27		
28	Alimony paid (see page 11 of Instructions)	28		
29	Disability income exclusion (attach Form 2440) . . .	29		
30	**Total adjustments.** Add lines 23 through 29 . . . . ▶		30	377 10

Adjusted Gross Income

31 **Adjusted gross income.** Subtract line 30 from line 22. If this line is less than $10,000, see page 2 of Instructions. If you want IRS to figure your tax, see page 4 of Instructions . . . . ▶ | 31 | 33,442 90

Tax Compu-tation (See Instruc-tions on page 12)	32 Amount from line 31 *(adjusted gross income)*	32	33,442 90
	33 If you do not itemize deductions, enter zero . . . . } If you itemize, complete Schedule A (Form 1040) and enter the amount from Schedule A, line 41 . . . }	33	1724 71
	Caution: If you have unearned income and can be claimed as a dependent on your parent's return, check here ▶ ☐ and see page 12 of the Instructions. Also see page 12 of the Instructions if: • *You are married filing a separate return and your spouse itemizes deductions,* OR • *You file Form 4563,* OR • *You are a dual-status alien.*		
	34 Subtract line 33 from line 32. Use the amount on line 34 to find your tax from the Tax Tables, or to figure your tax on Schedule TC, Part I . . . . Use Schedule TC, Part I, and the Tax Rate Schedules ONLY if: • *Line 34 is more than $20,000 ($40,000 if you checked Filing Status Box 2 or 5),* OR • *You have more exemptions than are shown in the Tax Table for your filing status,* OR • *You use Schedule G or Form 4726 to figure your tax.* Otherwise, you MUST use the Tax Tables to find your tax.	34	31,718 19
	35 Tax. Enter tax here and check if from ☒ Tax Tables or ☐ Schedule TC	35	5505 00
	36 Additional taxes. (See page 12 of Instructions.) Enter here and check if from ☐ Form 4970, } ☐ Form 4972, ☐ Form 5544, ☐ Form 5405, or ☐ Section 72(m)(5) penalty tax . . }	36	
	37 **Total.** Add lines 35 and 36 . . . . ▶	37	5505 00
Credits	38 Credit for contributions to candidates for public office . . .	38			
	39 Credit for the elderly *(attach Schedules R&RP)*	39			
	40 Credit for child and dependent care expenses (*attach* Form 2441) .	40	360 00		
	41 Investment credit *(attach Form 3468)*	41			
	42 Foreign tax credit *(attach Form 1116)*	42			
	43 Work incentive (WIN) credit *(attach Form 4874)*	43			
	44 Jobs credit *(attach Form 5884)*	44			
	45 Residential energy credits *(attach Form 5695)*	45			
	46 **Total credits.** Add lines 38 through 45	46	360 00
	47 **Balance.** Subtract line 46 from line 37 and enter difference (but not less than zero) . ▶	47	5145 00
Other Taxes (Including Advance EIC Payments)	48 Self-employment tax *(attach Schedule SE)*	48	
	49a Minimum tax. Attach Form 4625 and check here ▶ ☐	49a	
	49b Alternative minimum tax. Attach Form 6251 and check here ▶ ☐	49b	
	50 Tax from recomputing prior-year investment credit *(attach Form 4255)*	50	
	51a Social security (FICA) tax on tip income not reported to employer *(attach Form 4137)* . .	51a	
	51b Uncollected employee FICA and RRTA tax on tips *(from Form W–2)*	51b	
	52 Tax on an IRA *(attach Form 5329)*	52	
	53 Advance earned income credit payments received *(from Form W–2)*	53	
	54 **Total.** Add lines 47 through 53 . . . . ▶	54	5145 00
Payments Attach Forms W–2, W–2G, and W–2P to front.	55 Total Federal income tax withheld	55	4900 00		
	56 1979 estimated tax payments and credit from 1978 return	56	500 00		
	57 Earned income credit. If line 32 is under $10,000, see page 2 of Instructions	57			
	58 Amount paid with Form 4868	58			
	59 Excess FICA and RRTA tax withheld (two or more employers)	59			
	60 Credit for Federal tax on special fuels and oils *(attach Form 4136 or 4136–T)*	60			
	61 Regulated Investment Company credit *(attach Form 2439)*	61			
	62 **Total.** Add lines 55 through 61 . . . . ▶	62	5400 00
Refund or Balance Due	63 If line 62 is larger than line 54, enter amount **OVERPAID** . . . . ▶	63	255 00
	64 Amount of line 63 to be **REFUNDED TO YOU** . . . . ▶	64	
	65 Amount of line 63 to be credited on 1980 estimated tax . . . . . ▶	65	255 00		
	66 If line 54 is larger than line 62, enter **BALANCE DUE.** Attach check or money order for full amount payable to "Internal Revenue Service." Write your social security number on check or money order . . ▶ (Check ▶ ☐ if Form 2210 (2210F) is attached. See page 15 of Instructions.) ▶ $	66	

Please Sign Here

Under penalties of perjury, I declare that I have examined this return, including accompanying schedules and statements, and to the best of my knowledge and belief, it is true, correct, and complete. Declaration of preparer (other than taxpayer) is based on all information of which preparer has any knowledge.

▶ Your signature _____ Date _____ | ▶ Spouse's signature (if filing jointly, BOTH must sign even if only one had income) _____

Paid Preparer's Information

Preparer's signature and date ▶	Check if self-em-ployed ▶ ☐	Preparer's social security no.
Firm's name (or yours, if self-employed) and address ▶	E.I. No. ▶	
	ZIP code ▶	

Schedules A&B—Itemized Deductions AND Interest and Dividend Income

(Form 1040)
Department of the Treasury
Internal Revenue Service

► Attach to Form 1040. ► See Instructions for Schedules A and B (Form 1040).

1979
08

Name(s) as shown on Form 1040

William + Mary Washington

Your social security number: 111 22 3333

Schedule A—Itemized Deductions (Schedule B is on back)

Medical and Dental Expenses (not paid or reimbursed by insurance or otherwise) (See page 16 of Instructions.)

1 One-half (but not more than $150) of insurance premiums you paid for medical care. (Be sure to include in line 10 below.) ►	150	00
2 Medicine and drugs	168	00
3 Enter 1% of Form 1040, line 31 . . .	334	43
4 Subtract line 3 from line 2. If line 3 is more than line 2, enter zero	-0-	
5 Balance of insurance premiums for medical care not entered on line 1	470	00
6 Other medical and dental expenses:		
a Doctors, dentists, nurses, etc. . . .	640	00
b Hospitals	110	00
c Other (itemize—include hearing aids, dentures, eyeglasses, transportation, etc.) ►		
Transportation (200 mi.)	16	00
7 Total (add lines 4 through 6c)	1236	00
8 Enter 3% of Form 1040, line 31 . . .	1003	29
9 Subtract line 8 from line 7. If line 8 is more than line 7, enter zero	232	71
10 Total medical and dental expenses (add lines 1 and 9). Enter here and on line 33 . ►	382	71

Taxes (See page 16 of Instructions.)

Note: Gasoline taxes are no longer deductible.

11 State and local income		
12 Real estate	770	00
13 General sales (see sales tax tables) . .	294	00
14 Personal property	45	00
15 Other (itemize) ►		
16 Total taxes (add lines 11 through 15). Enter here and on line 34 . . . . ►	1109	00

Interest Expense (See page 17 of Instructions.)

17 Home mortgage	2040	00
18 Credit and charge cards		
19 Other (itemize) ►		
Personal Bank Loans	108	00
20 Total interest expense (add lines 17 through 19). Enter here and on line 35 ►	2148	00

Contributions (See page 17 of Instructions.)

21 a Cash contributions for which you have receipts, cancelled checks, or other written evidence	1020	00
b Other cash contributions (show to whom you gave and how much you gave) ►		
22 Other than cash (see page 17 of instructions for required statement)	340	00
23 Carryover from prior years		
24 Total contributions (add lines 21a through 23). Enter here and on line 36 . ►	1360	00

Casualty or Theft Loss(es) (See page 18 of Instructions.)

25 Loss before insurance reimbursement .		
26 Insurance reimbursement		
27 Subtract line 26 from line 25. If line 26 is more than line 25, enter zero . . .		
28 Enter $100 or amount from line 27, whichever is smaller		
29 Total casualty or theft loss(es) (subtract line 28 from line 27). Enter here and on line 37 . ►		

Miscellaneous Deductions (See page 18 of Instructions.)

30 Union dues		
31 Other (itemize) ►		
Form 2106 attached	125	00
32 Total miscellaneous deductions (add lines 30 and 31). Enter here and on line 38 ►	125	00

Summary of Itemized Deductions (See page 18 of Instructions.)   **A**

33 Total medical and dental—from line 10 .	382	71
34 Total taxes—from line 16	1109	00
35 Total interest—from line 20	2148	00
36 Total contributions—from line 24 . . .	1360	00
37 Total casualty or theft loss(es)—from line 29 .		
38 Total miscellaneous—from line 32 . .	125	00
39 Add lines 33 through 38	5124	71
40 If you checked Form 1040, Filing Status box: 2 or 5, enter $3,400 . . . . 1 or 4, enter $2,300 . . . . 3, enter $1,700	3400	00
41 Subtract line 40 from line 39. Enter here and on Form 1040, line 33. (If line 40 is more than line 39, see the instructions for line 41 on page 18.) . . . . ►	1724	71

Name(s) as shown on Form 1040 (Do not enter name and social security number if shown on other side) | Your social security number

Part I   Interest Income

1 **If you received more than $400 in interest, complete Part I and Part III.** Please see page 9 of the instructions to find out what interest to report. Then answer the questions in Part III, below. If you received interest as a nominee for another, or you received **or** paid accrued interest on securities transferred between interest payment dates, please see page 18 of the instructions.

Name of payer	Amount	
First National Bank	700	00

2 **Total interest income.** Enter here and on Form 1040, line 9 . . . . | 700 | 00 |

Part III   Foreign Accounts and Foreign Trusts

If you are required to list interest in Part I or dividends in Part II, OR if you had a foreign account or were a grantor of or a transferor to a foreign trust, you must answer both questions in Part III. Please see page 19 of the instructions.

	Yes	No
A At any time during the tax year, did you have an interest in or a signature or other authority over a bank account, securities account, or other financial account in a foreign country (see page 19 of instructions)?		X
B Were you the grantor of, or transferor to, a foreign trust which existed during the current tax year, whether or not you have any beneficial interest in it? If "Yes," you may have to file Forms 3520, 3520–A, or 926.		X

Part II   Dividend Income

3 **If you received more than $400 in gross dividends (including capital gain distributions) and other distributions on stock, complete Part II and Part III.** Please see page 9 of the instructions. Write (H), (W), or (J), for stock held by husband, wife, or jointly. Then answer the questions in Part III, below. If you received dividends as a nominee for another, please see page 19 of the instructions.

Name of payer	Amount	
Central Mfg. Corp.	320	00

4 Total of line 3	320	00
5 Capital gain distributions. Enter here and on the appropriate line(s) on Schedule D. See Note below		
6 Nontaxable distributions		
7 Total (add lines 5 and 6)		
8 **Dividends before exclusion (subtract line 7 from line 4).** Enter here and on Form 1040, line 10a	320	00

B

Note: *If your capital gain distributions for the year do not include any gains before Nov. 1, 1978, and you do not need Schedule D to report any gains or losses, do not file that schedule. Instead, enter the taxable part of your capital gain distributions on Form 1040, line 15.*

Form 2106

Department of the Treasury
Internal Revenue Service

Employee Business Expenses

(Please use Form 3903 to figure moving expense deduction.)
▶ Attach to Form 1040.

1979

Your name: **William Washington**

Social security number: **111 22 3333**

Occupation in which expenses were incurred: **Accountant**

Employer's name:

Employer's address: **Central City, TX**

Instructions

Use this form to show your business expenses as an employee during 1979. Include amounts:

- You paid as an employee;
- You charged to your employer (such as by credit card);
- You received as an advance, allowance, or repayment.

Several publications, available free from IRS, give more information about business expenses:

Publication 463, *Travel, Entertainment, and Gift Expenses.*

Publication 529, *Miscellaneous Deductions.*

Publication 587, *Business Use of Your Home.*

Publication 508, *Educational Expenses.*

Part I.—You can deduct some business expenses even if you do not itemize your deductions on Schedule A (Form 1040). Examples are expenses for travel (except commuting to and from work), meals, or lodging. List these expenses in Part I and use them in figuring your adjusted gross income on Form 1040, line 31.

Line 2.—You can deduct meals and lodging costs if you were on a business trip away from your main place of work. Do not deduct the cost of meals you ate on one-day trips, when you did not need sleep or rest.

Line 3.—If you use your own car in your work, you can deduct the cost of the business use. Enter the cost here after figuring it in Parts IV, V, and VI. Base the cost on your actual expenses (such as gas, oil, repairs, depreciation) or on a mileage rate.

The mileage rate is 18½ cents a mile up to 15,000 miles. After that, or for all business mileage on a fully depreciated car, the rate is 10 cents a mile. (For depreciation, see **Publication 463.**)

Figure your mileage rate amount and add it to the business part of what you spent on the car for parking fees, tolls, interest, and State and local taxes (except gasoline tax).

Line 4.—If you were an outside salesperson with other business expenses, list them on line 4. Examples are selling expenses or expenses for stationery and stamps. An outside salesperson does all selling outside the employer's place of business. A driver-salesperson whose main duties are service and delivery, such as delivering bread or milk, is not an outside salesperson. (For outside salesperson, see **Publication 463.**)

Line 5.—Show other business expenses on line 5 if your employer repaid you for them. If you were repaid for part of them, show here the amount you were repaid. Show the rest in Part II.

Part II.—You can deduct other business expenses only if (a) your employer did not repay you, and (b) you itemize your deductions on Schedule A (Form 1040). Report these expenses here and under Miscellaneous Deductions on Schedule A. Examples are union or professional dues and expenses for tools and uniforms. (For details, see **Publication 529.**)

You can deduct expenses for business use of the part of your home that you exclusively and consistently use for your work. If you are not self-employed, your working at home must be for your employer's convenience. (For business use of home, see **Publication 587.**)

If you show education expenses in Part I or Part II, you must fill out Part III.

Part III.—You can deduct the cost of education that helps you keep or improve your skills for the job you have now. This includes education that your employer, the law, or regulations require you to get in order to keep your job or your salary. Do not deduct the cost of study that helps you meet the basic requirements for your job or helps you get a new job. (For education expenses, see **Publication 508.**)

Part V.—If you trade in a car you used in business for a new one you also used in business, fill out lines 1 through 15. If you paid cash for the new car or traded in a car not used in business, fill out only lines 10 through 15. Refigure the basis for depreciation each year in the future that your percentage of business use changes.

PART I.—Employee Business Expenses Deductible in Figuring Adjusted Gross Income on Form 1040, Line 31

1 Fares for airplane, boat, bus, taxicab, train, etc.	270 00
2 Meals and lodging	96 00
3 Car expenses (from Part IV, line 21)	11 10
4 Outside salesperson's expenses (see Part I instructions above) ▶	
5 Other (see Part I instructions above) ▶	
6 Add lines 1 through 5	377 10
7 Employer's payments for these expenses if not included on Form W–2	
8 Deductible business expenses (subtract line 7 from line 6). Enter here and include on Form 1040, line 24	377 10
9 Income from excess business expense payments (subtract line 6 from line 7). Enter here and include on Form 1040, line 21	

PART II.—Employee Business Expenses that are Deductible Only if You Itemize Deductions on Schedule A (Form 1040)

1 Business expenses not included above (list expense and amount) ▶ Membership dues: Texas Society of CPAs, $35.00; Central City CPAs, $30.00; Professional

2 Total. Deduct under Miscellaneous Deductions, Schedule A (Form 1040) Publication Subscriptions, $60.00 — **125.00**

PART III.—Information About Education Expenses Shown in Part I or Part II

1 Name of educational institution or activity ▶

2 Address ▶

3 Did you need this education to meet the basic requirements for your job? ☐ Yes ☐ No

4 Will this study program qualify you for a new job? ☐ Yes ☐ No

5 If your answer to question 3 or 4 is No, explain (1) why you are getting the education and (2) what the relationship was between the courses you took and your job. (If you need more space, attach a statement) ▶

6 List your main subjects, or describe your educational activity ▶

PART IV.—Car Expenses (Use either your actual expenses or the mileage rate)

	Car 1	Car 2	Car 3
A. Number of months you used car for business during 1979 . .	*12* months	_____ months	_____ months
B. Total mileage for months in line A	*12,800* miles	_____ miles	_____ miles
C. Business part of line B mileage	*60* miles	_____ miles	_____ miles

Actual Expenses (Include expenses for only the months shown in line A, above.)

	Car 1	Car 2	Car 3
1 Gasoline, oil, lubrication, etc.			
2 Repairs			
3 Tires, supplies, etc.			
4 Other: (a) Insurance			
(b) Taxes			
(c) Tags and licenses			
(d) Interest			
(e) Miscellaneous			
5 Total			
6 Business percentage of car use (divide line C by line B, above)	%	%	%
7 Business part of car expense (multiply line 5 by line 6) . . .			
8 Depreciation (from Part VI, column (h))			
9 Divide line 8 by 12 months			
10 Multiply line 9 by line A, above			
11 Total (add line 7 and line 10; then skip to line 19)			

Mileage Rate

12 Enter the smaller of (a) 15,000 miles or (b) the combined mileages from line C, above	*60* miles
13 Multiply line 12 by 18½¢ (10¢ if car is fully depreciated) and enter here	*$11.10*
14 Enter any combined mileage from line C that is over 15,000 miles	_____ miles
15 Multiply line 14 by 10¢ and enter here	
16 Total mileage expense (add lines 13 and 15)	*$11.10*
17 Business part of car interest and State and local taxes (except gasoline tax)	
18 Total (add lines 16 and 17)	

Summary:

19 Enter amount from line 11 or line 18, whichever you used	*$11.10*
20 Parking fees and tolls	
21 Total (add lines 19 and 20). Enter here and in Part I, line 3	*$11.10*

PART V.—Basis for Depreciation of Car Used in Business (See instructions on front)

Trade-in of Old Car:

1 (a) Total mileage at trade-in	_____ miles	
(b) Business mileage	_____ miles	
(c) Business percentage . . . . . (divide line (b) by line (a)) . . .	_____ %	
2 Purchase price or other basis		
3 Trade-in allowance		
4 Difference (subtract line 3 from line 2) .		

5 Multiply line 4 by percentage on line 1(c)	
6 Gain or (loss) on previous trade-in . .	
7 Balance of lines 5 and 6 (subtract gain or add (loss))	
8 Depreciation allowed or allowable . .	
9 Gain or (loss) on business part (Subtract line 7 from line 8 for gain; or line 8 from line 7 for (loss))	

New Car:

10 Purchase price or other basis	
11 Estimated salvage value	
12 Difference (subtract line 11 from line 10)	

13 Multiply line 12 by the percentage on line 6 of Part IV	
14 Enter gain or (loss) from line 9 . . .	
15 Basis for depreciation (Balance of lines 13 and 14: subtract gain or add (loss)) .	

PART VI.—Car Depreciation

Make and model of car (a)	Date acquired (b)	Basis (from line 15, Part V) (c)	Age of car when acquired (d)	Depreciation allowed in previous years (e)	Method of figuring depreciation (f)	Rate (%) or life (years) (g)	Depreciation this year (h)

| Form **2441**
Department of the Treasury
Internal Revenue Service | **Credit for Child and Dependent Care Expenses**
▶ Attach to Form 1040. ▶ See Instructions below. | **1979**
21 |

Name(s) as shown on Form 1040

William + Mary Washington

Your social security number 111 22 3333

1 See the definition for "qualifying person" in the instructions. Then read the instructions for line 1.

(d) During 1979, the person lived with you for:

(a) Name of qualifying person	(b) Date of birth	(c) Relationship	Months	Days
George Washington	1-10-74	Son	12	

2 Persons or organizations who cared for those listed on line 1. See the instructions for line 2.

(a) Name and address (If more space is needed, attach schedule)	(b) Social security number, if applicable	(c) Relationship, if any	(d) Period of care From Month—Day	To Month—Day	(e) Amount of 1979 expenses (include those not paid during the year)
Jane Doe			1-1	12-31	1,800 00

To Figure Your Credit, You MUST Complete ALL Lines That Apply

3 Add the amounts in column 2(e)	**3**	1,800 00
4 Enter $2,000 ($4,000 if you listed two or more names in line 1) or amount on line 3, whichever is less	**4**	1,800 00
5 Earned income (wages, salaries, tips, etc.). See the instructions for line 5. An entry MUST be made on this line.		
(a) If unmarried at end of 1979, enter your earned income	**5**	11,000 00
(b) If married at end of 1979, enter your earned income or your spouse's whichever is less		
6 Enter the amount on line 4 or line 5, whichever is less	**6**	1,800 00
7 Amount on line 6 paid during 1979. An entry MUST be made on this line	**7**	1,800 00
8 Child and dependent care expenses for 1978 paid in 1979. See instructions for line 8	**8**	-0-
9 Add amounts on lines 7 and 8	**9**	1,800 00
10 Multiply line 9 by 20 percent	**10**	360 00

11 Limitation:

a Enter tax from Form 1040, line 37	**11a**	
b Enter total of lines 38, 39, and 41 through 43 of Form 1040	**11b**	
c Subtract line 11b from line 11a (if line 11b is more than line 11a, enter zero)	**11c**	
12 Credit for child and dependent care expenses. Enter the smaller of line 10 or line 11c here and on Form 1040, line 40	**12**	

13 If payments listed on line 2 were made to an individual, complete the following:

	Yes	No
(a) If you paid $50 or more in a calendar quarter to an individual, were the services performed in your home?		X
(b) If "Yes," have you filed appropriate wage tax returns on wages for services in your home (see instructions for line 13)?		
(c) If answer to (b) is "Yes," enter your employer identification number ▶		

PROBLEMS

For the following problems, ignore the "zero bracket income" floor under itemized deductions.

1. Explain the basic problem in making tax rules to determine the deductibility of expenses related to income-producing activities as an employee.
2. What practical difficulties do you see in applying the rules governing deductibility of education expenses?
3. What rationale underlies the disallowance of commuting costs as a deductible expense related to earning income?
4. It has been suggested that as a gasoline-saving incentive taxpayers should be

allowed to deduct commuting costs when three or more individuals share a "car pool." Comment on this proposal.

5. Why is the cost of a uniform worn by a registered nurse normally deductible, whereas the cost of a suit of clothing worn by a C.P.A. on the job is not deductible?

6. The Tax Reform Act of 1976 made it virtually impossible for an employee to deduct any maintenance costs, operating expenses (other than taxes and interest), and depreciation on that portion of his or her home used as an office in connection with employment. Why, in your opinion, were these tough rules adopted?

7. How do you reconcile the apparent liberalization of tax laws relating to some expenses (such as the credit for child care and deduction for moving costs) with a simultaneous "tightening" of laws in other cases (such as curtailment of deductions relating to an office in the home and business travel)?

8. What groups of taxpayers benefited from the changes in the tax laws that converted the child-care deduction into a credit for child-care expenses?

9. The deduction for periodic alimony was converted from a deduction *from* A.G.I. to a deduction *for* A.G.I. in 1977. What, in your opinion, was the reason for this change in the law?

10. What is the purpose of the complex laws relating to deductions for expenses associated with the rental of vacation homes?

11. It is likely that some of the more exotic vacation spots within the United States and its possessions have become more popular as the sites for conventions and seminars after the 1976 Tax Reform Act. Explain.

12. In each of the following independent cases, determine the amount, if any, of the taxpayer's credit for "child-care" expenses. Assume that payment is made to enable taxpayer to be gainfully employed unless otherwise stated.

   a. Taxpayer is a widow employed as a corporate controller. She earns $88,000 during the current year. In order to be gainfully employed, she pays her cousin $60 per month to take care of her 6-year-old child in the cousin's home.

   b. Taxpayer is unmarried and supports her two younger brothers, ages 8 and 17. During the year she paid a baby sitter $80 per month to care for the 8-year-old.

   c. Sue is divorced. She earned $8,200 during the current year, but had to pay a housekeeper $200 per month to care for her two children, ages 4 and 5, while she worked. The housekeeper also cleaned the house and prepared all the meals. It is estimated that the housekeeper spends one-half of her time caring for the children and the other half doing housework.

   d. Margaret is unmarried. She has two dependent children, ages 8 and 14. Both children attend school, but she pays the 14 year old $380 during the year to take care of the younger child after school until 5:30 P.M. each day. Margaret earned $8,000 during the year.

   e. John is a bachelor and supports his aged parents. John pays a neighbor $300 per month during the year to take care of his parents, both of whom are bed-ridden, while John works.

   f. Macomb and his wife have five small children, ranging in age from 2 to 9. During the current year Macomb earned $7,400; his wife earned $8,200. They paid a baby sitter $200 per month during the year to care for the children while they both worked. They filed a joint return.

   g. Assume the same facts as in part f, above, except that they paid the sitter $410 per month for caring for the children.

h. Ann, a widow, was employed throughout the year, earning $10,200. She paid a baby sitter $70 per month throughout the year to care for her two children. The younger is 9, the other became 15 on August 1 of this year.

i. The taxpayer, a widow, works as an interior decorator and has income of $50,000. During the year she paid $400 per month for maid service including care of her two dependent children, ages 10 and 12. The amount allocated to child care was $1,500.

j. The taxpayer, a widow with A.G.I. of $12,000, paid her mother $100 per month during the year to care for her 5-year-old dependent child. The mother is not a dependent of the taxpayer.

k. John and Sue are married and file a joint return. John is a full-time college student but earned $1,000 from part-time jobs during 19x1. Sue is employed and earned $9,400 during the year. In order for Sue to work and John to attend classes, they paid a baby sitter $900 ($75 per month) to take care of their 2-year-old child.

l. Ray and Ellen are married and file a joint return. Ray is employed and earned $20,000 during 19x1. Ellen is not gainfully employed, but paid a college student $600 during the year to take care of her small child while Ellen did her shopping, attended meetings, and so on.

13. Indicate how much, if any, is deductible as educational expenses in each of the following independent cases. Briefly explain your answer, and indicate in each case whether the amount deductible is *for* A.G.I. or *from* A.G.I.

a. Haskins is a senior in college, majoring in accounting. His college expenses for the current year were:

Tuition	$1,200
Books and supplies	340
Room	540
Meals	1,680

b. Bernard was a practicing certified public accountant in the tax department of a national accounting firm. During July of this year Bernard decided that he should secure a law degree in order to further his career, so he resigned from the accounting firm and entered law school. His expenses relating to law school this year were $950.

c. Raymond works for an accounting firm. During this year he attended several professional development programs sponsored by the American Institute of Certified Public Accountants. These programs were two- or three-day seminars or workshops held in other cities (requiring overnight travel), dealing with areas of accounting in which Raymond is involved. His expenses in attending these programs totaled $800, and they were not reimbursed by his employer. The costs were: registration fees, $200; transportation, $400; lodging, $110; meals, $90.

d. Assume the same facts as in part c, above, except that Raymond is a self-employed accountant with his own public accounting practice.

e. Clifton is employed as a public school teacher. He possesses a B.A. degree, but the school board has stipulated that each teacher in the school system must return to college for additional course work at least each third summer. During this year Clifton returned to the state university. His costs were: tuition, $120; meals, $540; lodging, $285; transportation from his home town to the university and return, $23; and books, $40. Clifton is unmarried.

f. Myrtle is an elementary school art teacher. She has found that in recent years there has been a great increase in interest in ceramics, so this summer Myrtle returned to college to take some courses in ceramics. Her expenses were: tuition, $185; lodging, $200; food, $320; transportation, $18; and supplies, $65.

g. Professor Williams holds an M.A. degree. She is a nontenured assistant professor at a local college. The college administration has ruled that no one could be promoted to a rank higher than assistant professor unless she or he possesses the Ph.D. degree, so Williams returned to the university this fall to work on a doctorate. Her expenses for the four months were: tuition, $180; meals, $900; room, $400; supplies, $180; and transportation to university and return (one round trip), $16.

14. Determine the amount deductible by the taxpayer in the following cases. (Is the amount deductible, if any, a deduction *for* A.G.I. or a deduction *from* A.G.I.?)

a. Taxpayer, an employee, spent $1,000 for transportation during the year. Of this amount, $600 was allocated to the cost of going from home to the work sites and back, while $400 was spent on transportation between work sites during the workday.

b. Taxpayer, a self-employed plumber, incurred costs of $1,500 for transportation, which constituted the depreciation, gas, and oil, for a truck used in his business. He estimates that one-third of the miles were driven from his home to his shop and returning, while two-thirds were involved with on-the-job activities.

c. Taxpayer changed jobs in January of the taxable year. The new place of employment was 300 miles from the old one. Expenses of moving to a new home near the new job amounted to $500 and were not reimbursed. At year end, taxpayer was still employed on the new job.

d. Taxpayer, a physician, attended two professional conventions on the West Coast connected with his practice. The first convention was held on Monday, Tuesday, and Wednesday in Los Angeles. The second convention was held on Monday and Tuesday of the following week in San Francisco. Between the two conventions, the taxpayer stayed at Carmel for a short vacation. The costs were: air travel from his home to Los Angeles and from San Francisco to his home, $225; hotel and meals for three days in Los Angeles, $300; auto rental for trip from Los Angeles to Carmel and from Carmel to San Francisco, $180 (the doctor estimates that one-third of this cost represents the cost of pleasure trips while in Carmel); hotel and meals for two days in San Francisco, $205.

15. Assume that the first ten seats in a jet airliner flying from Los Angeles to New York City are filled with the following persons:

Seats 1 and 2: Mr. and Mrs. Farley Dickens, who are planning to attend a four-day insurance convention. Farley, an insurance salesman, is traveling at company expense; his wife (at two-thirds fare) is traveling at her own expense. While in New York, the insurance salespeople are kept in business sessions throughout each day; the spouses are entirely free to shop or do whatever they wish. The Dickenses plan to spend two additional days, following the convention, in personal sightseeing trips, attending the theater, and so on.

Seats 3 and 4: Mr. and Mrs. Chuck Hardsell, who are going to the same insurance convention. Like Farley, Chuck is traveling at company expense. Mrs. Hardsell's ticket also is being paid by Chuck's employer because he sold more insurance than any of the other agents in his district during the first six months of this year.

Seats 5 and 6: Mr. and Mrs. Samuel Johnson, who are moving to New York permanently so that Sarah may accept a new job with Dilly Corporation. The Johnsons sold their car before leaving California.

Seat 7: Ned Younger, a law student who is being interviewed by Ring, Rang, & Rung, a noted law firm. The firm will reimburse Ned for all his travel expenses regardless of his job decision.

Seat 8: Larry Outer, a college student who plans to interview at five firms for a possible position. Since Larry will soon graduate in the lower quarter of his class, none of the firms is willing to pay his transportation expenses for an interview trip. Larry, however, is convinced that a personal appearance will guarantee his getting a good job offer at a later date. (You may assume, in solving this problem, that he did get such an offer but that no one reimbursed him for his travel expenses.)

Seat 9: Ms. Jane Doe, a veteran stewardess for Tomorrow Airline. Jane is on her vacation and is flying without charge, on an employee's pass, to London via New York. Every airborne employee with more than ten years' service receives courtesy passes from connecting airlines to make worldwide travel "free" (except for meals, hotels, and other personal expenditures) for himself or herself and spouse (if married) or for himself or herself and parents (if single).

Seat 10: Mrs. Mary Doe, mother of Jane Doe. Mrs. Doe is accompanying her daughter without charge on the pass described above.

Which of these persons may deduct their travel expenses for federal income-tax purposes? Must any of these persons report receipt of taxable income because of this trip? Explain your answers.

16. In each of the following independent cases, indicate the amount, if any, that would be deductible by the taxpayer. If an appropriate answer depends on the circumstances, explain.

   a. Taxpayer is an importer of Italian shoes. In July of this year a group of Italian shoe manufacturers and commerce officials visited this country. Taxpayer invited them to be his guests for one evening. Cost of attending a Broadway show, cocktails, dinner, and after-dinner entertainment for the taxpayer and the seven guests totaled $840.

   b. Brown is a sales representative for a national machine manufacturer. In September of this year a convention of machine manufacturers was held in Brown's home town. Brown entertained six visiting manufacturers at a cost of $180.

17. Ronald Blue received his degree in accounting in June of this year. He took a job with a public accounting firm in a city 76 miles away from the university. He spent $350 to have his furniture moved to the new home. He and his wife drove their automobile to the new home. How much, if any, may they deduct as moving expense?

18. Arno Grey has lived in New Orleans for five years, working in an electrical manufacturing plant. In August of last year he moved to St. Louis to take a new job and was still employed there at the end of the year. A review of Grey's records revealed the following facts related to his move and new job.

   In June, Grey decided that he was tired of the hot weather in New Orleans, so he read the classified ads in the local newspaper and found a help-wanted ad by the St. Louis employer. He wrote the St. Louis Company and was told that all applicants must appear in person at the company's home office, but that the company could not pay his travel costs for an interview. Grey went to St. Louis in early July for the interview. Cost of the plane ticket was $180, and he paid $20 for limousine service to and from airports. He arrived in St. Louis on Sunday evening, spent the night, and visited the company on Monday morning. He was immediately hired and planned to return to New Orleans on Monday evening. However, the employer suggested that Grey should find a place to live. He therefore spent Tuesday and Wednesday looking at apartments and houses, spending $30 for taxi fares and telephone calls. Finding no suitable apartment, he purchased a house at a cost of $34,000. Grey's hotel room was $38 per night and he spent $21 each day for food (Monday, Tuesday, and Wednesday). He returned to New Orleans on Wednesday evening.

Grey owned a home in New Orleans, which he sold. He sold the house for $48,000 (it had cost him $19,000) but had to pay a real estate commission of $2,880 on the sale. Other selling costs included an abstract fee of $120 and legal fees of $105.

Grey shipped most of his furniture by truck, at a cost of $820, but he also rented a trailer and moved some himself. (Cost of trailer was $98.) He and his family drove by auto from New Orleans to St. Louis. Meals en route cost $52, and they spent one night in a motel (cost $45). He spent $84 for gasoline and $1.20 for oil on the trip. On arriving in St. Louis, Grey was shocked to find that the former owner of his house had not moved out, so Grey and his family took rooms in a hotel, where they had to live for 18 days. Their costs while living there totaled $900 for rooms and $808 for meals. In addition, Grey had to pay $96 to have his furniture stored, and another $157 to have it delivered when he got possession of his house. Determine Grey's moving expense deduction.

19. In each of the following independent cases, indicate whether the taxpayer will be entitled to deduct expenses (depreciation, utilities, insurance, etc.) applicable to an "office in the home."

   a. Pete is an accounting professor at a state university. In his home, one room has been converted into an "office" used by Pete solely for such tasks as grading papers, preparing exams, and reading journals.

   b. Joe is a law professor in a state university. In his home one room has been converted into an "office" used solely by Joe for grading papers and other class-related activities and also for writing and revising textbooks from which Joe receives substantial royalties.

   c. Marilyn, married, operates a part-time typing service in her home. In her bedroom, she has an "office" with desk, typewriter, file cabinet, etc. She uses the office approximately 15 hours per week in her typing service.

   d. Jane is a sales representative for several companies. She uses a room in her home solely as an office in which she takes orders, makes telephone calls, prepares reports, and so on.

SUPPLEMENTAL PROBLEMS

20. In August of this year, Hernandez quit his job in Tulsa, Oklahoma, and accepted a job with an oil company in Indonesia. The following costs were incurred by Hernandez:

Commission and closing costs incurred in selling his home in Tulsa	$ 3,200
Transportation for Hernandez and his wife to Indonesia	1,720
Cost of transporting personal effects from Tulsa to Indonesia	1,800
Temporary living costs for 45 days while seeking permanent living accommodations	4,050

The employer paid Hernandez $3,600, representing $860 for his transportation costs and $2,800 of the temporary living costs.

Determine the effects of all the items named above on Hernandez's taxable income.

21. In the current year, Mr. A. Big Shot, who operates an advertising agency, paid $1,600 for membership dues in a hunting lodge in Canada for the purpose of entertaining clients and prospective clients. In November Mr. Shot took three clients to the lodge for hunting. He paid their transportation costs, totaling $620; their meals for the three-day period at the lodge ($460 for the guests and $181 for Shot); their room costs ($900 for the guests and $300 for himself); $220 for a hunting guide; $210 for use of guns and ammunition; and $120 for miscellaneous items such as phone calls and drinks. What part of the expenditures named above will be deductible by Mr. Shot?

22. Tom Medirent, a physician, is employed in a hospital 40 hours per week. He also owns and manages six rental properties. He lives in a two-bedroom condominium and uses one bedroom exclusively as an office for bookkeeping and other tasks associated with the property management activities.
    a. Is the property management activity a "business"? Is the office a "principal place of business activity"?
    b. Can the costs (depreciation, utilities, taxes, interest) related to the office be deducted by the doctor?
    c. Can the transportation expenses incurred in driving from the office to the rental properties be deducted by the doctor as business expenses?

RETURN PROBLEM

23. Sam and Sally Simpson, both aged 40, have two children—Sloan, 8, and Sue, 14. Sue earned $820 by baby sitting during the year.

    Until July 1 of this year, Sam was employed in Big City by Acme Company but took a new job in Littletown, 140 miles from Big City, on that date. Sally took a job in Littletown after their move there. Data relating to the Simpsons' employment for the year are:

    Sam: Earnings from Acme Company, $10,000. Income tax withheld, $1,200; social security withheld, $613.

    Earnings from Baker Company in Littletown, $17,000. Income tax withheld, $2,800; social security withheld, $1,042.10.

    Sally: Earnings at Clamb Company, $4,000. Income tax withheld, $600; social security withheld, $245.20.

    Other income included:
    Interest on savings account at First Savings and Loan Association, $420.
    Dividends on jointly owned stock of Acme Corporation, $210.
    Information relating to expenditures for the year:
    1. Interest paid First State Bank on auto loan, $280.
    2. Taxes:
        a. Personal property, $44
        b. Real estate (on land inherited two years ago from Sam's father), $919.
        c. State and local sales tax as shown in the optional tax table, $310. In addition, during the year the Simpsons purchased a new auto on which there was a sales tax of $284.

    d. Cost of personal driver's licenses, $6.

    e. State income tax paid, $208.

3. Medical expenses (not reimbursed):

    a. Doctors' bills, $120.

    b. Dental care, $308.

    c. Optical care, $60.

    d. Medical insurance premiums, $424.

    e. Medicines and drugs, $210.

    f. Transportation, 120 miles in personal automobile.

4. Contributions:

    a. Cash contributions, paid by check, to church, $1,800.

    b. Cash contributions, no receipt or check, paid to church, $26.

    c. Cash contributions, paid by check, to Boy Scouts of America, $10.

    d. Cash contribution to Democratic Party, $20.

5. Casualty: During the year Mr. Simpson backed his automobile into a tree, causing damage to the car. Costs of repairing the damage totaled $280.

6. Business-related expenses:

    a. Mr. Simpson—travel to an employment-related convention (unreimbursed):

       Airfare, $160.

       Hotel (2 nights), $63.

       Meals, $38.

       Taxi, $10.

       Personal auto to airport and home—60 miles.

       Airport parking, $10.

    b. Mr. Simpson—union dues, $196.

    c. Ms. Simpson—cost of uniforms not suitable for off-duty wear, $64.

7. Child care: Payment to baby sitter and housekeeper to take care of children after school until Ms. Simpson's return from work in afternoon. Payment was $50 per month for 6 months (July through December), $300.

8. Payment for income tax return preparation, $45.

9. Moving costs to new job location (not reimbursed):

    a. Costs related to trip to find apartment:

       Auto—total miles driven, 300 miles.

       Hotel (one night), $40.

       Meals, $40.

    b. Payment to freight company for moving belongings, $600.

    c. Mileage for transportation of Simpson and family in personal automobile (140 miles).

Complete the Simpsons' tax return for the year. Use assumed data for address, social security number, and so on.

15

The treatment of pension and other employee benefit plans under the income tax laws is a vitally important aspect of the American tax structure. It affects, directly or indirectly, the great majority of taxpayers.

JOHN K. DYER, JR.,
1959 Compendium

retirement plans

United States tax policy has rather consistently provided preferential treatment for the aged. Several examples of this treatment have been noted in previous chapters; the extra exemption for a taxpayer or spouse aged 65 or over and the credit for the elderly are exemplary. In this chapter we shall examine an area of taxation filled with special rules resulting, at least in part, from the desire to encourage taxpayers and their employers to provide for financial security in old age through the use of public and private retirement plans.

RETIREMENT ANNUITIES

One of the simplest methods of providing for retirement income is the purchase of an annuity, a contract under which the annuitant makes payments (sometimes a lump sum) to an insurance company, which in turn agrees to make periodic payments to the annuitant beginning on a specified date. Payments under the annuity usually begin when the annuitant reaches a certain age and continue either for a specified period of time or throughout the lifetime of the annuitant.

Annuity contracts may be quite complex, especially for "joint and survivor" annuities covering two individuals and providing for differing benefits depending on the sequence of their deaths. Similarly, a contract may contain a "refund" feature that provides for a lump-sum payment to the beneficiary of the annuitant if he or she should die before recovering the cost. Some annuities provide for variable payments over the life of the contract. At this point,

however, we shall be concerned only with the basic concept of annuities and the techniques used for computing taxable income derived from simple annuity contracts. The same basic concept is used to determine taxable income from other types of retirement plans that are considerably more complex.

Assume that the taxpayer, a male, purchased in 19x1 an annuity contract for $27,000. Beginning in January 19x6, when he is 65, the taxpayer is to receive $200 each month during the remainder of his lifetime. The fundamental question is how the taxpayer should treat the $2,400 received each year.

From the inception of the income tax in 1913 to 1934, taxpayers were allowed to apply the first returns from an annuity to recovery of capital. No income was recognized until the returns exceeded the total premiums or cost of the annuity. This treatment of annuities had a major drawback in that it often created taxable income for the oldest taxpayers at a time when inflation had already reduced the adequacy of their annuity. Beginning in 1934, the 3 percent rule was placed in the law. Under this procedure, 3 percent of the total cost of the annuity was included in income each year. The portion of the annual return in excess of 3 percent of cost was treated as a return of capital. After total capital was recovered, however, the entire amount received was treated as income. The rule was unfavorable to taxpayers, because the 3 percent was actually higher than the interest paid by insurance companies at that time, and because it still taxed the oldest taxpayers at the most inopportune time.

Since 1954, consistent with the 3 percent rule, proceeds from an annuity are assumed to consist

TABLE **15-1**

EXPECTED RETURN MULTIPLES ON
ONE-LIFE ORDINARY LIFE ANNUITIES

Ages		
Male	Female	Multiples
61	66	17.5
62	67	16.9
63	68	16.2
64	69	15.6
65	70	15.0

partly of a return of investment and partly of interest income on the investment. The taxpayer is entitled to exclude the portion of the proceeds that represents return of investment. The portion excluded is the ratio that the investment in the contract bears to total expected return from the contract. In our example, the investment in the contract is obviously its cost, $27,000. The expected return must, however, be computed.

The I.R.S. provides actuarial tables to be used in computing the expected return under annuity contracts involving life expectancy. This table indicates a "multiple" to be applied to the annual payments received by taxpayers of various ages at the starting date of the annuity. A portion of the table pertaining to simple annuities is shown in Table 15-1.

This table shows that for a male, aged 65 at the annuity starting date, the appropriate multiple is 15.0. Thus, the total expected return under the contract is $36,000 ($2,400 × 15.0). The exclusion ratio is

$$\frac{\text{Investment in contract}}{\text{Total expected return}} = \frac{\$27,000}{\$36,000} = 75\%$$

Each year the taxpayer will exclude 75 percent of the $2,400 received, for an annual exclusion of $1,800. The remaining $600 is included in taxable income. Once the exclusion ratio is computed, it usually does not change, no matter how long the annuitant may live and receive benefits.

THE SOCIAL SECURITY PROGRAM

Undoubtedly the most important pension and retirement plan in the United States today is that provided under the Old Age, Survivors, and Disability Insurance Act (OASI) of the federal government, providing for old-age retirement benefits, disability benefits, benefits for survivors of the insured, and hospital insurance benefits. This program, generally referred to as "social security," becomes a more

important social and economic force each year as a larger portion of the citizenry becomes subject to its provisions, as both the number and percentage of the population actually receiving benefits increase, and as the payroll taxes levied to finance the plan increase. The tremendous growth in the social security program through 1978, the latest year for which data are available, is reflected in Table 15-2.

Tax status of contributions made

The social security program for employees is financed by charges levied equally against the employee and the employer, based on the employee's earnings during the year. Both the tax rates and the maximum amount of yearly earnings subject to the tax have increased over the years and are certain to increase still further in future years. The combined rate for old-age, survivors, disability insurance, and hospitalization insurance in 1980 is 6.13 percent. These rates are applied to the first $25,900 paid the employee during the year, and the employer and employee each contribute that amount. Thus, the total contribution in 1980 is 12.26 percent of the first $25,900 paid the employee during the year.

Self-employed persons are also included in the program. A self-employed person is required to contribute 9.1 percent of the first $25,900 earned during 1980.

The contribution of an employee or a self-employed person is not deductible in computing the federal income tax, but an employer may deduct social security taxes paid on the wages of an employee as an expense of conducting a trade or business. Social security taxes paid on wages of domestic servants and others rendering services of a purely personal nature are not deductible by the employer.

Tax status of benefits

All benefits received under the social security program are tax exempt under provision of an administrative decision made in 1941.[1] Exclusion of these benefits, especially the old-age retirement benefits, has often been criticized on the basis that the plan is essentially no different from other public and private pension plans, whose benefits *are* included in gross income to the extent that they exceed the recipients' own contributions. Since considerably less than half the benefits received at present by social security recipients can be attributed to their own contribu-

---

[1] IT 3447, 1941-1 C.B. 191. (See also Rev. Rul. 70-217, 1970-1 C.B. 12.)

TABLE **15-2**

FEDERAL RECEIPTS AND PAYMENTS OF BENEFITS FROM SOCIAL SECURITY AND

RAILROAD RETIREMENT PLANS

(IN MILLIONS OF DOLLARS)[a]

	1940	1950	1960	1969	1972	1976	1977	1978
Benefits paid								
Old-age retirement benefits	$100	$ 838	$ 8,790	$18,467	$28,756	$62,140[b]	$71,271	$78,524
Disability benefits	31	77	715	2,499	4,762	9,222	11,135	12,214
Survivorship benefits	7	321	2,517	6,777	9,932			
Total	$138	$1,226	$12,022	$27,743	$43,450	$71,362	$82,406	$90,738
Receipts	$725	$2,656	$10,818	$33,219	$43,200	$74,000	$86,200	$98,900

[a] Figures do not include the hospital insurance program nor the supplementary medical program. During 1972 receipts from these two programs totaled $8.8 billion and expenditures for benefits were $8.8 billion. During 1978 receipts were $27.6 billion and expenditures were $25.3 billion.
[b] Old-age retirement benefits and survivorship benefits are combined for 1976 and later years.
SOURCES: U.S. Bureau of the Census, *Statistical Abstracts of the United States,* various years (Washington, D.C.: U.S. Government Printing Office), and Joint Economic Committee, *The Federal Tax System: Facts and Problems,* 1964 (Washington, D.C.: U.S. Government Printing Office, 1964), p. 293.

tions to the program, preferential treatment may result for beneficiaries of the plans. Many attempts have been made in Congress to tax social security benefits in the same manner as similar benefits under other retirement plans.

Treatment of social security benefits in a manner comparable to the treatment of private plans would be difficult to implement. Proceeds from private retirement plans are treated in much the same way as proceeds from simple annuities. Such treatment requires an estimation of expected return under the contract. However, measurement of the expected benefits under social security is virtually impossible; benefit formulas can be changed at will by Congress and may fluctuate as amounts earned by the taxpayer from other sources change.

Applying the same tax rules to social security benefits as to other retirement plans might conflict with the social and economic objectives of the law. For example, poorly paid workers with many dependents contribute a substantially lower portion of their expected benefits than do higher paid workers with no dependents, and this disparity is increasing as the base subject to the tax increases. This benefit formula is intentional, making the plan provide benefits where they are most needed (even though the social security program is not technically supposed to be a "welfare" program). If the exclusion of benefits should be based on contributions made, the greatest tax benefit would be received by persons with the least need.

Passage of the "retirement income credit" provision in 1962 (changed to the Credit for the Elderly in 1976) greatly reduced the preferential treatment given social security recipients by removing from taxa-

tion a portion of income from other types of pension plans and by reducing the retirement income subject to the credit by the amount of social security benefits received. Undoubtedly, this special rule was enacted largely because of the widespread criticism levied against the preferential treatment given social security.

Payments made and benefits received under the Railroad Retirement Act are treated in the same manner as social security payments and benefits.

PRIVATE RETIREMENT PLANS

Perhaps no aspect of American economic life has had more far-reaching social implications than the tremendous growth in formal private retirement plans during the past thirty years. This growth through through 1975 is reflected in Table 15-3.

In a press release in November 1976, William J. Chadwick, Administrator of Pension and Welfare Benefit Programs, U.S. Department of Labor, reported that there were a total of 473,272 private pension plans but that two-thirds of those plans had 10 or fewer participants. Only 1 percent of the existing plans were reported to have more than 1,000 participants. However, Mr. Chadwick also reported that 90 percent of all participants are covered by a relatively few major plans. These statistics have probably changed little since 1976.

Reasons for growth

Many factors account for the growth of pension plans since 1940. Some of these factors reflect gener-

TABLE **15-3**

PRIVATE PENSION AND DEFERRED PROFIT-SHARING PLANS,[a] 1950–75

(ESTIMATED, IN MILLIONS)

Year	Coverage,[b] end of year	Employer contributions	Employee contributions	Number of beneficiaries, end of year	Amount of benefit[c] payments	Reserves, end of year (in billions)
1940	4.1	$ 180	$ 130	.2	$ 140	$ 2.4
1950	9.8	1,750	330	.5	370	11.7
1955	15.4	3,190	550	1.0	840	26.7
1960	21.2	4,470	770	1.8	1,710	49.9
1965	25.4	7,040	1,030	2.8	3,370	85.4
1968	28.2	9,380	1,260	3.8	5,030	115.3
1972	29.7	16,940	1,600	5.6	10,000	167.8
1975	30.3	27,560	2,290	7.1	14,810	212.6

[a] Includes pay-as-you-go, multiemployer, and union-administered plans, those of nonprofit organizations, and railroad plans supplementing the federal railroad retirement program. Insured plans are in general funded through trustees.
[b] Excludes annuitants.
[c] Includes refunds to employees and their survivors and lump sums paid under deferred profit-sharing plans.
SOURCE: Data for 1940 from Daniel M. Holland, ''Some Characteristics of Private Pension Plans,'' *1959 Compendium*, p. 1305. Data for 1950 and subsequent years from *Statistical Abstract of the United States*, various years.

al social and demographic changes in our society; others are the direct result of tax laws.

First, during and immediately following World War II, there were direct governmental controls over wages. As a result, workers became more interested in various ''fringe'' benefits, including pensions. Employers were eager to hold trained employees and looked on pensions and other fringe benefits as a relatively cheap method of doing so, especially because such costs were deductible in computing taxable income, which was subject to very high tax rates. In recent years, organized labor groups have placed far greater emphasis on fringe benefits, especially pension and profit-sharing arrangements. On the other hand, there has been a realization by business managers that favorable retirement plans may serve as a powerful incentive to workers, resulting in greater efficiency and a reduction in employee turnover.

The much-publicized increase in life expectancy, coupled with earlier retirement ages, has led not only to a much larger population in older age groups but also to a great increase in the average number of years spent in retirement—a time when some source of income is essential to replace the loss of wages. A growth in the general awareness and concern for economic security has been both a result and a cause of the widespread use of formal retirement plans. Another important factor has been the decline in the portion of the population engaged in agriculture and

the increase of those living in urban areas and requiring more complete and complex arrangements for financing the living costs of retirement.

Among the tax factors encouraging employee retirement plans is, as previously noted, the fact that the employer can deduct contributions to such plans. In addition, the Revenue Act of 1942, which allowed the employer to deduct contributions to a pension program only if the plan did not discriminate in favor of officers or other selected personnel, encouraged the broadening of coverage. On the employee side, the spread of pension plans has been encouraged by the provision that contributions to ''qualified'' pension plans are taxable to the employee, not when the contribution is made, but only when benefits are received from the plan. This allows the employee to defer (and often to reduce) his or her tax liability and at the same time benefit from a retirement program.

The 1974 Pension Reform Act

Unfortunately, many of the private pension and profit-sharing plans developed after World War II proved to exist almost solely on paper. A Congressional Committee investigation in 1974 disclosed that frequently pension plans were not adequately funded, that ''vesting'' schedules made it almost impossible for many participants ever to receive the full benefits they anticipated, and, in general, requirements of plans made it very difficult and costly for employees to change jobs. The result of this investigation was widespread public and congressional demand for reform of the entire private pension system, leading to passage of the Employee Retirement Income Security Act of 1974, popularly called either "ERISA" or "The 1974 Pension Reform Act."

This measure established detailed and complex rules governing such pension plan provisions as the maximum waiting period before an employee is covered, schedules for vesting of benefits from employee and employer contributions, financial reporting and disclosure of pension trust funds, and minimum funding requirements. It also set up a program for providing insurance for pension funds and developed many other rules designed to safeguard employee benefits and rights.

The full impact of the 1974 Pension Reform Act is still not clear six years later, but it has undoubtedly profoundly influenced the terms and conditions of most retirement plans. There is some evidence to suggest that the "tough" new rules are leading to curtailment or elimination of many employer-financed plans. Complex reporting requirements have been especially criticized. Many qualified employee retirement plans in existence when ERISA was enacted have been terminated. Before passage of ERISA, the number of new plans established each year had been rising steadily. One reason advanced for the decrease in new plans initiated and the increase in existing plans being terminated is, in part, the onerous reporting and disclosure requirements.

Types of retirement programs

Retirement plans usually take the form of pension plans, profit-sharing plans, or stock-purchase plans. Under pension plans, the employer normally makes periodic contributions to a trust or insurance company, which assumes the obligation of making benefit payments to employees as they fall due. Benefits are paid the employee after he or she has reached a specified age, completed a designated number of years of service, or met other conditions.

Pension plans are usually referred to as either "defined-benefit plans" or "defined-contribution plans." The former is a pension plan stating the benefits to be received by employees after retirement, or the method of determining benefits. Employer contributions to the plan are determined actuarially on the basis of benefits expected to become payable. Defined-contribution plans say nothing about what can be expected at retirement but

embody an agreement providing a formula for calculating the employer's contributions (such as output and percentage of compensation). In other words, some plans are benefit-oriented and others are contribution-oriented. Generally, however, some contribution by the employer is expected each year on behalf of the employees, regardless of profits.

Profit-sharing plans are similar to pension plans, except that the amount of the employer's contribution, and consequently the benefits payable to participants, is based on the employer's profits. The plan may specify that a constant percentage of each year's profits be contributed by the employer, (in essence, a "defined contribution" plan), or it may provide a more flexible approach, with the proportion of profits contributed each year determined at the end of the year.

The essence of stock-bonus plans is that payments are made in stock of the employing company. This is the least popular of the three types of programs. In recent years, however, a great deal of publicity has been given to employee stock ownership trust (ESOT) plans. Under an ESOT plan, the employer corporation may contribute its stock to a tax-exempt employees' trust, deducting the value of the stock. Under another form of ESOT, a trust is established that borrows money from a lending institution to purchase stock of the employer company. The loan, usually guaranteed by the employer corporation, is repaid by cash contributions made by the employer to the trust. ESOT plans have been allowed since 1954 but have not proved popular. Since 1975 employers have been permitted to increase their allowable investment credit to 11 percent (in some cases, 11½ percent) instead of the normal 10 percent if they establish ESOT plans and contribute the extra percentage point to a plan. There is little evidence that the additional investment credit has accelerated the use of ESOT plans.

The Revenue Act of 1978 added a new dimension to tax-sheltered retirement plans, the "simplified pension plan," involving employer contributions to individual retirement accounts for employees, discussed on page **15/11**.

Contributions to retirement plans are funded in trusts, group annuities, or individual annuity contracts. If the plan is "trusteed," a trust organization is created or designated to receive, handle, and manage contributions and to make benefit payments to employees in accordance with the terms of the plan. The income earned by the trust generally is not subject to the income tax. Sometimes group annuity plans are utilized. The employer pays to an insurance company the full premiums necessary to acquire annuity coverage on all employees. No trustee is necessary in this case. Or, finally, the employer may purchase an annuity contract or retirement income contract for each individual employee.

A few pension plans are not funded; i.e., there are no contributions to a fund during the working years of the employee. Instead, payments are made directly by the employer to the employee after retirement. There are no special tax problems in a pension plan of this sort; the payments are deductible by the employer when made and taxable to the employee when received.

Qualified plans versus nonqualified plans

Most of the controversy surrounding employee retirement programs involves the favorable treatment given "qualified plans." If a plan is qualified, employees are not taxed until they actually receive distributions from the fund, and income earned by the trust on the assets of the fund is not taxable to the trust. When payments are ultimately made to beneficiaries of the plan, they exclude from income that portion of the benefits representing their own already taxed contributions, if any, to the plan. Nevertheless, contributions to the plan are deductible by the employer when they are made.

On the other hand, contributions to nonqualified plans are deductible by the employer only if the employee's rights in the contributions become fully "vested" (nonforfeitable). Likewise, the employee must pay a tax on the employer's contributions to the plan at the time the contribution becomes vested. Thus, the qualified plan is ordinarily much more desirable from the tax standpoint.

Present tax requirements for qualified plans

The specific requirements for a qualified plan are spelled out in Sec. 401(a). The most important of these requirements are summarized briefly below.

1. It must be for the exclusive benefit of employees or their beneficiaries.

2. The sole purpose of the plan must be to offer the employees or their beneficiaries (a) a share of the profits, or (b) an income after retirement.

3. The contributions or benefits must not discriminate in favor of employees who are officers, shareholders, or highly paid employees. As a general

rule, the plan is held to be for the exclusive benefit of employees and not discriminatory if:

    a. Seventy percent or more of all employees participate in the plan, or

    b. Seventy percent or more of all employees are eligible and 80 percent of those eligible are in the plan, or

    c. The plan benefits employees qualifying under a classification set up by the employer that the I.R.S. does not find discriminatory.

4. The employee's accrued benefits resulting from the employer's contributions must vest under one of three different schedules. In each case at least 50 percent vesting must occur within 10 years of service, and 100 percent vesting after 15 years of service.

5. An employee must be permitted to participate in the plan on reaching age 25 and completing one year of service, unless there is 100 percent immediate vesting, in which case a three-year employment period can be required.

6. No maximum age for participation can be set except for "defined-benefit" plans. In that case, workers who start work when they are within five years of normal retirement age may be excluded.

7. The plan must be funded, and annual contributions of the employer must be adequate to cover current plan costs and to amortize past service liability arising from the employee's services before the plan was established within (normally) 30 years. (The funding requirements do not apply to profit-sharing or stock-bonus plans, however.)

Although the provisions listed above are the most important, there are numerous other rules, including restrictions on transactions between the trust and a plan fiduciary or certain other "disqualified" persons. Again, these rules are designed to safeguard and protect the participant's benefits.

A more detailed examination of the income-tax effects on the employer, the trust, and the employee will show the importance of meeting the tests for a qualified plan.

THE EMPLOYER   The employer may deduct contributions as they are made to qualified retirement programs. The maximum amount deductible depends on whether the plan is a pension, profit-sharing, or stock-bonus plan.

Deductions for contributions to qualified pension plans are limited to the normal cost of the plan plus payments for amortization of past service costs over a period of not less than 10 years. Alternative higher

TABLE **15-4**

Year	Compensation	15% of compen.	Amount contributed to trust	Deduction	Contribution carryover	Credit carryover
1976	$500,000	$75,000	$ 87,000	$ 75,000	$12,000	$ —
1977	500,000	75,000	70,000	75,000	7,000	—
1978	500,000	75,000	63,000	70,000	—	5,000
1979	600,000	90,000	60,000	60,000	—	35,000
1980	600,000	90,000	120,000	120,000	—	5,000

limits are based on the amount necessary for satisfying the minimum funding standard or the amount necessary to provide for all covered employees the remaining unfunded cost of their past and current service credits over the remaining future service of each employee. In addition, in 1980, contributions for any one individual under "defined contribution" plans cannot exceed the lesser of (1) $36,875 or (2) 25 percent of the individual employee's compensation. (Actually, the rules for determining the maximum amount deductible are much more complex than the simple statements above suggest.) In addition, there are limits on the benefits under defined benefit plans. For 1980, the limit is $110,625.

Contributions to qualified profit-sharing and stock-bonus plans likewise may be deducted currently, with a maximum deduction of 15 percent of the compensation earned by covered employees during the year. Contributions made in excess of the 15 percent limit may be carried over and added to contributions of succeeding years. If the contributions of a year are less than 15 percent of covered compensation for that year, a "credit carryover," which increases the 15 percent limit of future years, is allowed. The amount of carryover that can be used in a year is limited to 10 percent of the compensation in the year it is used. Thus, up to 25 percent of compensation might be deducted in a given year for contributions to profit-sharing or stock-bonus trusts (10 percent for contributions carried over and 15 percent of current year's contributions). The example in Table 15-4 illustrates the credit carryover and contribution carryover.

If the employer has set up a qualified combination pension, profit-sharing, and stock-bonus plan, the total deduction for contributions is usually limited to 25 percent of the compensation of covered employees during the year. Contributions in excess of this limit may be deducted in succeeding years provided the total deduction in the later year does not exceed 25 percent of the compensation of covered employees.

If contributions are made by the employer to plans that are not qualified, the contribution may be deducted if the employee's rights in the plan are nonforfeitable. If the employee's rights are not vested at the time the employer makes the contributions, a deduction can be taken at a later time when the rights become nonforfeitable, and at that time the amount that becomes vested will be reported as income by the employee.

THE EMPLOYEE   Contributions made by an employer in behalf of an employee to a qualified retirement plan are not included in the income of the employee at the time the contribution is made. Neither is income earned by the trust included in the employee's income for the year. Only when benefits are distributed to the employee will he or she have taxable income. Most employee contributions to a plan (if any) are treated as personal expenditures and are not deductible; in other words, generally the employee's payments are made with "after-tax" dollars.

If benefits from a qualified plan are received by the employee in the form of an annuity, the excluded portion is determined in the same manner as for an annuity purchased by the taxpayer (see page **15**/2). The employee's investment in the annuity is the amount paid into the plan by the employee and the employee's contributions represent a recoverable investment because they were made from after-tax income. The employer's contributions, on the other hand, were not previously taxed to the employee and therefore do not constitute recoverable investment. If the employee has made no after-tax contributions to the plan, all benefits received are included in gross income.

To illustrate, assume that Cecil Rust worked for the National Company from 1947 through 1979. During this period National Company made contributions totaling $20,000 to a qualified pension fund for Rust's benefit. Rust also contributed $20,000 to the fund. Since the fund was qualified, the contributions made by National were not taxable to Rust at the time they were made; but Rust's cost, which he is entitled to recover tax-free, is the $20,000 that he has contributed. When Rust began drawing benefits of $4,000 per year in 1980, he was 65 years old. Reference to the proper annuity table shows that the appropriate multiple is 15.0 (essentially meaning that Rust's life expectancy is 15 years). Thus, Rust would exclude from income each year the amount of $1,333:

$$\frac{\text{Cost } \$20,000}{\text{Expected return } \$60,000} \times \$4,000 = \$1,333.33$$
$$(\$4,000 \times 15)$$

The remaining $2,667 would be taxable to Rust. If Rust had made no contributions to the fund, the entire amount received would be taxable to him since he would have no "cost."

Two special situations give rise to different rules. If both employer and employee have contributed to the qualified plan, and if the amount to be received in the first three years exceeds the employee's contributions, the employee excludes from his or her income the full amount of each annuity payment received until the full contribution has been recovered; thereafter all future amounts are fully taxable unless they qualify for the special capital-gain rule.

For example, assume that an employee has contributed $8,000 toward the purchase of a qualified annuity, while his employer has contributed $32,000. The employee retired and began receiving retirement benefits of $400 per month on July 1, 19x1. Since the total amount received in the first three years ($14,400) exceeds his contributions of $8,000, the taxpayer will exclude the $2,400 received in 19x1, the $4,800 received in 19x2, and $800 of the amount received in 19x3. The remaining $4,000 received in 19x3 and all amounts received in following years will be fully taxable.

A more important and more controversial exception is made when the employee or beneficiary is paid a lump-sum distribution of the accumulated benefits under a qualified plan. Prior to 1970 the entire amount received in a lump-sum distribution was taxed, except for the employee's own contribution, as a long-term capital gain. The employee's contribution was, of course, a tax-free return of capital. For any distribution made after December 31, 1969, and through any tax year beginning prior to January 1,

1974, the portion of the distribution attributable to employer contributions made after 1969 was treated as ordinary income. The remainder of the distribution was either a return of capital or capital gain. Still another major change was made for lump-sum distributions received in a taxable year beginning after December 31, 1973.

The taxable portion of a lump sum distribution in a year beginning on or after January 1, 1974, is deemed to be the total amount of distribution less the amounts contributed to the plan by the employee, and less any unrealized appreciation of employer securities. The unrealized appreciation of employer securities will be taxed when the employee sells the securities. However, the cost basis of the employer securities contributed to the plan by the employer and distributed to the employee is included in the taxable portion of the distribution.

The taxable portion of the distribution is then allocated between ordinary income and capital gains on the ratio of the number of years the employee participated in the plan after 1973 and the number of years of participation prior to 1974, respectively. (The calculation is actually made in terms of calendar months. A part of a calendar year prior to 1974 is counted as 12 calendar months. A part of a calendar month after 1973 is counted as a whole calendar month.) A special 10-year averaging rule may be elected for the portion of the distribution taxed as ordinary income. Yet another election is provided by the 1976 Tax Reform Act to a taxpayer who has not treated any part of a post-1975 lump-sum distribution as capital gains. In this case the taxpayer may treat all the post-1975 distributions as if they were earned *after* 1973 (even though they may actually relate to earnings in 1973 or earlier years), so that the distributions will be taxed as ordinary income and will qualify for the 10-year income averaging.

Although the computations under the special income-averaging procedures applicable to the ordinary income portion of lump-sum distributions are complex, the basic process may be illustrated by assuming that in 1980 a taxpayer received a $100,000 lump-sum distribution, including a taxable portion of $60,000, under a qualified plan. Assume also that the taxpayer's other taxable income is $41,500 so that her tax bill before considering the distribution would be $13,392. Assume further that the taxpayer elected to treat pre-1974 participation as post-1973 participation, so that the entire $60,000 taxable amount is eligible for averaging. The tax computation is as follows:

(1) Total taxable distribution $60,000

(2) "Minimum distribution allowance" (One-half of the first $20,000 of the taxable amount. If the taxable amount is more than $20,000, the minimum allowance of $10,000 is reduced by 20% of the excess.) [$10,000 − .20($60,000 − $20,000)]   2,000

(3) Net $58,000

(4) Ten percent of the above (10-year average) $ 5,800

(5) Tax on taxable income equal to the amount determined in (4) plus $2,300, using rates for unmarried taxpayers*   996

(6) Total tax on distribution (10 × $996) $ 9,960

(7) Tax on other income (using appropriate table)   13,392

(8) Total tax for the year $23,352

*The rates for unmarried taxpayers must be used in this computation even if the taxpayer is married and filing a joint return.

The great advantage of this "ten-year forward averaging" can be seen by comparing the tax, $23,352, with the amount of tax that would have been paid if the entire $60,000 had been taxed as long-term gain. Again, assuming that the taxpayer's other taxable income was $41,500, the $60,000 of long-term capital gain would have resulted in a total income tax of $27,408. Thus the income-averaging device results in an income tax liability $4,056 less than would have been paid if the "favorable" pre-1970 rules still applied. As explained earlier, under current law the real option is even less desirable since only part of the $60,000 can be treated as long-term capital gain.

If the retirement plan is *non*qualified, the employee is required to report as income the employer's contribution when it is made if the employee's rights are vested at that time. If the employee's rights do not vest at the time the employer's contribution is made, but do become vested at a later date, the employee must report such contributions as income at the time of vesting.

If benefits from a nonqualified plan are paid to the employee as an annuity, the annuity proceeds are generally treated in the same way as annuity proceeds from a qualified plan. If the employee was required to report the employer's contribution as income when they were vested to the employee, however, the employee's "investment" in the contracts increased by the amount of employer's contributions previously included in the employee's income. The special rules applicable for cost recovery in the first 3 years of benefit payments applicable to an annuity under a qualified plan do not apply to

a nonqualified plan. The entire excess of a lump-sum distribution from a nonqualified plan over the employee's investment is treated in full as ordinary income in the year of distribution, and the special averaging rules do not apply.

THE TRUST   Income earned on the assets of a funded retirement plan is not taxable to the trust if the plan is qualified. A nonqualified employees' trust must pay a tax on its income in the same manner as any other taxable trust.

The importance of the tax-exempt status for the trust fund of a retirement plan cannot be overemphasized. The benefits of tax-free status can be dramatically illustrated by a simplified example. Assume that an employee works for 35 years for an employer with a pension plan and that the employer contributes $2,000 per year to the fund on behalf of the employee. Assume further that the average earnings of the pension plan are 6 percent before taxes, and that the trust would, if taxable, pay income taxes at a marginal rate of 50 percent. Thus, if the trust were taxable, its after-tax rate of earnings would be only 3 percent. Reference to a table showing the "amount of an annuity of $1 at end of each period" shows that a contribution of $2,000 per year for 35 years would accumulate to approximately $223,000 at the time of the employee's retirement if the rate of earnings is 6 percent. On the other hand, if the rate of earnings is only 3 percent, the contributions of $2,000 per year for 35 years will accumulate to approximately $121,000. If we further assume that the employee will draw benefits for 15 years after retirement, and using the same pretax earnings rate of 6 percent for the trust, the annual pension would be approximately $22,900 from a tax-exempt trust, while the annual pension from a taxable trust would be only about $10,000, considerably *less than half* that received from a tax-free trust.

Public retirement plans

In general, public retirement plans are treated the same as private pension plans, although a number of special rules do exist. There are also special rules for employees of tax-exempt organizations and public schools.

Self-employment retirement plans

For many years critics have complained that the tax laws permitting employees to benefit from retirement programs were unfair to those who are self-employed. After much controversy and conflict, Congress, in 1962, passed a law (P.L. 87-792) that permits self-employed persons to establish retirement plans for their own benefit and to deduct all or a part of the contributions made to such plans. These plans are popularly known as either "Keogh plans" or as H.R. 10 plans.

Several restrictions are placed on retirement plans for self-employed individuals. First, the self-employed persons (including partners) who get income entirely from investments cannot participate; they must perform personal services in the business. Second, and most important, the plan must provide comparable coverage for all full-time employees with three years or more of service with the employer. Third, in general, the employees included must have nonforfeitable rights in the plan. Fourth, distributions under the plan must be made to the self-employed person only after he or she becomes 59½, unless he or she is disabled. Benefits to an employee must start not later than age 70½ or at the time of retirement.

An "owner-employee," defined as a sole proprietor of a business or a partner who owns more than a 10 percent capital or profits interest in the partnership, may contribute up to 15 percent of earned income, with a limit of $7,500 per taxable year, and may deduct this amount. Other self-employed individuals who are not classified as owner-employee (for example, a partner who owns an interest of 10 percent or less) are subject to the same limitations on the amount they may *deduct*, but are not subject to the dollar limitation on their *contributions*.

To provide some benefit to those with low earned income, the law provides that a deductible contribution of up to $750 can be made without regard to the 15 percent limit, as long as the amount contributed does not exceed the individual's earned income.

Funds contributed to such plans may be put in a trust or custodial account (usually administered by a bank or savings and loan association), invested directly in individual annuity contracts issued by an insurance company, or invested in special retirement bonds issued by the federal government. Contributions for a taxable year must be made by the due date for filing the taxpayer's federal tax return for that year.

When distributions are made to self-employed persons, they are taxed in general in the same way as distributions from employee trusts. However, payments must not begin before the taxpayer reach-

es the age of 59½, unless he or she becomes permanently disabled, and to qualify for capital gains treatment and the 10-year averaging rules, a lump-sum payment must be made after the taxpayer reaches 59½ unless because of death it is made before that time. Special penalties are levied on premature distributions.

Taxation of shareholder-employees

The limits placed on deductions permitted an owner-employee for contributions to a retirement plan also apply to "shareholder-employees" of Subchapter S corporations (corporations electing to be taxed essentially as partnerships). As pointed out in Chapter 11, Subchapter S permits small businesses to incorporate for business purposes without being subject to corporate tax. A shareholder-employee who owns more than 5 percent of the shares of the Subchapter S corporation's stock must include in gross income the contributions made by the corporation under a qualified plan on his or her behalf to the extent that the contributions exceed the amount deductible by self-employed persons, as discussed above—currently 15 percent of his earned income or $7,500, whichever is less. Other employees, who are shareholders but own 5 percent or less of the stock in the Subchapter S corporation, are not subject to this rule.

Individual retirement accounts

Code Sec. 408 permits an individual who is not covered by a qualified private or governmental retirement plan to establish his or her own individual retirement plan and to deduct limited amounts of compensation (or earned income in the case of a self-employed person) for contributions to the plan. The deduction, for A.G.I., is limited to the lesser of $1,500 or 15 percent of the individual's compensation or earned income. Contributions must be made by the due date for filing the tax return for a year. The benefits of an I.R.A. have also been extended to certain nonworking spouses, in recognition of the fact that a spouse not working outside the home but performing valuable household work should have the privilege of a tax-sheltered retirement program. A working spouse who is not an active participant in a qualified pension plan may elect (in lieu of a traditional I.R.A.) to establish an account for the benefit of the nonworking spouse. The working spouse may establish an I.R.A. in joint names or, instead, may establish separate accounts for the two spouses.

1. If a joint account is opened, the maximum amount of deductible contribution is the lesser of 15 percent of compensation or $1,750.

2. If separate accounts are opened, the employed spouse must make equal contributions of $875 to each account to get the maximum deduction. If he or she makes unequal contributions to the two accounts, the amount deductible is two times the smallest contribution (not to exceed $875 for each account). Furthermore, the amount by which the largest contribution exceeds the amount contributed to the other spouse's account is subject to a 6 percent excise tax. (For example, if an employed spouse puts $700 in her account and $500 in her unemployed husband's account, the amount deductible will be $500 for each account. In addition, the $200 excess contribution to her own account is subject to a 6 percent excise tax.)

Under the law, the retirement funds can be invested in a custodial or trust account in a bank or savings association or similar organization, can be invested directly in an individual annuity contract issued by an insurance company, or can be invested in special retirement bonds issued by the federal government.

The retirement fund must not be withdrawn until the individual reaches age 59½ except in the case of death or disability, and the individual must start drawing it on reaching age 70½. Any distribution from an I.R.A. before the taxpayer reaches age 59½ is subject to a 10 percent penalty tax unless the taxpayer has been disabled. When the funds are received during retirement, the entire amount will be taxed as ordinary income.

One important, though incidental, use of I.R.A. accounts is the avoidance of the current taxation of lump-sum distributions where an employee leaves a covered employment and is required to withdraw his interest in the plan. The distribution will not be taxed if it is "rolled over" into an I.R.A. account. If the same employee later takes a job with a new employer he may be able to again "roll over" the earlier distribution into the qualified plan of the new employer if the plan so permits. If, between the two jobs, the employee is not covered by a qualified plan, he can begin his own I.R.A. account.

Since January 1, 1975, employers have been able to set up trusts with individual accounts for the exclusive benefit of employees and, where the trust meets all the requirements for I.R.A. trusts, for the parties to treat the employer's contributions to the trust as though the employer had paid the employee the amount contributed and the employee had in turn made a contribution to an I.R.A. account. The limit for such amounts has been the lesser of 15 percent of compensation or $1,500.

In an attempt to simplify some of the rules surrounding qualified retirement plans, the Revenue Act of 1978 greatly liberalized provisions permitting employers to deduct contributions to an employee's individual retirement account. The amount deductible by the employer is 15 percent of the employee's compensation, with a limit on the deduction of $7,500. The employee must include in gross income the employer's contributions to the I.R.A. but may deduct the amount of the employer's contribution up to 15 percent of compensation or $7,500, whichever is less. If the employer contributes less than the maximum amount permitted as a deduction by the employee under a regular I.R.A. plan (15 percent of compensation or $1,500, whichever is less), the employee may contribute and deduct the difference. If the amount contributed by the employer exceeds 15 percent of the compensation paid for the calendar year ending with or within the tax year, the excess can be carried over and deducted in succeeding years by the employer subject to the 15 percent limitation in those years.

A "simplified pension plan" has rather strict nondiscrimination provisions. Not only must the plan not discriminate in favor of officers, shareholders, self-employed individuals, or highly compensated individuals, but the employer contributions must be based on a written, specific allocation formula and bear a uniform relationship to the total compensation of each employee maintaining a simplified plan, and contributions must be made to the plan of each employee who has (a) attained age 25 and (b) performed services for the employer in at least three of the preceding five calendar years. In addition, there must not be prohibitions of withdrawals from the I.R.A. by the employee, the employee's rights to employer contributions must be 100 percent vested, and employer contributions must not be conditioned on the retention in the I.R.A. of any amount contributed by the employer.

If the employer makes contributions that are discriminatory on behalf of employees, the 15 percent up to $1,500 limit applies.

Approximately 2.5 million I.R.A.'s were created in 1977. In the aggregate, $2.5 billion dollars was set aside in these accounts. More than 80 percent of the funds were put into individual custodial or trust accounts.

Other deferred compensation plans

Although pension and profit-sharing plans are by far the most important devices for securing tax-sheltered deferred compensation and retirement income, both in terms of the number of taxpayers and the amounts involved, there are several other schemes for obtaining tax-sheltered deferred compensation.

One procedure commonly used by executives, athletes, entertainers, and other highly paid employees is a deferred pay arrangement similar to the following. The employer and employee enter into an employment contract for a fixed number of years that provides for a specified amount of current compensation and an additional amount of nonforfeitable deferred compensation. The deferred compensation is credited to a reserve account on the employer's books and is paid in a specified number of installments after the employee's retirement.

Revenue Ruling 60-31 describes in detail various types of arrangements, such as that above, that the I.R.S. considered, until very recently, to be eligible for tax deferral. In general, the employee could not have the right to receive the compensation immediately and the plan had to be unfunded. As long as these two requirements were met, the employee was not deemed to have "constructive receipt" and therefore no tax was payable until the money was received. The I.R.S. issued proposed regulations in 1978 that would have changed all these rules. In general, the proposed regulations would have ended the opportunity to defer any income to the future. However, Congress, in Sec. 132 of the Revenue Act of 1978, provided that "the taxable year of inclusion of gross income of any amount covered by a private deferred compensation plan shall be determined" under the rules in effect on February 1, 1978.

One benefit that has been almost eliminated, however, is a device formerly used to provide tax-deferred income to top executives—the qualified stock option plan under which shares of an employer's stock were sold to employees for less than market price, but because certain restrictions were attached the recognition of income was deferred until the time the restrictions were removed or the shares were sold. The 1969 Tax Reform Act substantially reduced the benefits under such plans, and the 1976 Tax Reform Act imposed additional restrictions that effectively abolish the use of stock option plans as tax-deferral devices.

The Revenue Act of 1978 added Code Sec. 457, which permits a generous deferral of compensation for certain taxpayers. It allows a state (including a political subdivision, agency or instrumentality thereof) or a tax-exempt rural electric cooperative to establish a nonqualified "salary reduction" deferred compensation plan under which, for years beginning after 1978, a participating employee may defer a portion of the employee's compensation until a later year. The amount that may be deferred in a given year is 33⅓ percent of the employee's "includible compensation," with a limit of $7,500 on the amount that may be deferred in a year. Because of the way in which "includible compensation" is defined, the percentage that may be deferred is essentially 25 percent of the employee's compensation before considering the deferral plan. The deferred amount must be deferred until a year not earlier than the year the employee is separated from the employer or is faced with an unforeseeable emergency (to be defined in regulations).

CONTROVERSIES OVER TAX TREATMENT OF RETIREMENT PLANS

Several aspects of the tax treatment of retirement plans have been severely criticized as being inequitable. Two of these major criticisms, the discrimination resulting from deferment of this one selected type of compensation and the favorable treatment given lump-sum payments of benefits, are sufficiently valid to warrant further examination. Although the Tax Reform Act of 1969 eliminated a part of the special capital-gains benefit, it did not wipe out preferential treatment. Neither did the 1974 Pension Reform Act eliminate this benefit; on the contrary, the 10-year averaging rules introduced by the Pension Reform Act and expanded by the Tax Reform Act of 1976 grant advantages to lump-sum distributions that far surpass benefits under the old capital gains treatment.

In general, the favorable tax treatment given deferred pension plans results in a loss in total tax revenue, even though technically taxes on employer contributions are not eliminated but are merely deferred for many years. The loss results because income is shifted from the taxpayer's earning years to retirement years—from relatively higher tax rates to relatively lower tax rates. In effect, the retirement program serves as an "averaging" device not available to other taxpayers. If tax revenues are lost as a result of preferential treatment given retirement plans, there may be a shift in the tax burden (at least relatively) from employees covered by such plans to those not covered. Employees not included in pension or other retirement income programs are often those who can least afford to bear the tax burden.

The employer's contributions to a retirement fund are inherently a part of the employee's total compensation. Were there no retirement funds, presumably the employers would pay the employees higher wages, which would be currently taxable. Critics conclude from this logic that the employer's contributions should be taxable to the employee when they are made to the fund. (Of course, if the employee's rights are not vested, this would be grossly inequitable.) The critics also argue that there will be increasing demands that a higher portion of remuneration be paid in the form of deferred payment plans, resulting in even greater shifting of the burden to those taxpayers who do not have an opportunity to avail themselves of special provisions of the tax law.

Prior to enactment in 1962 of the statute permitting self-employed individuals to participate in tax-sheltered plans, it was argued that they, too, were victims of discrimination. Although the 1962 Act extended coverage to many self-employed persons, there are some who argue that discrimination still exists because the rules governing such programs are too stringent. The increase of allowable contributions to 15 percent of earned income, with a maximum deduction of $7,500, by the 1974 Pension Reform Act has, at least temporarily, eliminated this complaint.

It is argued that special tax treatment of retirement plans not only discriminates between different types of income, but also discriminates between different types of savings, since there is no deferment allowed for other types of savings programs, although birth of the I.R.A. plan for those whose income is from "earned" sources but who are not covered by qualified employer-financed plans has dampened this criticism.

Furthermore, there may be no real advantage in deferring income until retirement if rapid inflation continues. With our progressive tax rate structure it is just possible that persons could be in higher marginal tax brackets after retirement than they were in their working years.

Economic and social controversies

Although the tax aspects of retirement programs are important, of far greater significance are some of their long-run social and economic effects. Since favorable tax treatment accorded qualified plans has been a major factor in their growth, it is appropriate that some attention be given the resulting economic and social implications. Among the questions that have been most intriguing are the effects on savings and investment and on the mobility of labor and capital.[2]

EFFECTS ON SAVINGS   Table 15-3 shows that at the end of 1976 the accumulated reserves of private retirement funds totaled $212.6 billion. Evidence is inadequate to show clearly the effect that these accumulated reserves have had on the total volume of personal savings, and there is probably no accurate way to determine whether retirement fund reserves represent, in whole, in part, or not at all, savings that would have been accumulated some other way in the absence of such plans.

Other sources make even higher estimates of the funds controlled by private pension plans. For example, the People's Business Commission, in a 1978 report, estimated that pension funds were worth more than $500 billion and were growing at the rate of $100 million a day, making them the largest single pool of private capital in the world.[3]

To the extent that taxpayers have in mind a definite amount of total savings, presumably the retirement fund would be considered merely a means of achieving these savings. On the other hand, if individuals have a given propensity to save a certain portion of their current cash income, the retirement fund probably represents, at least in part, additional savings. The degree of conscious rational consideration given to retirement funds by individuals in reaching decisions about the magnitude of their personal savings is a relatively unknown factor. It has been suggested that self-employment retirement funds, as well as deferred compensation contracts negotiated between an individual employee and the employer,

[2]For an interesting discussion of these questions, see the Joint Economic Committee, *op. cit.*, pp. 125–28.
[3]Rifkin, Jeremy and Randy Barber, *The North Will Rise Again: Pensions, Politics and Power in the 1980's*, (Washington: The People's Business Commission, 1978).

are important in the individual's decision on how much to save, whereas group retirement plans are less important. There seems to be little correlation between the percentage of wages contributed by employers to retirement plans and the relationship between personal savings and personal income.

On balance, it would seem that retirement funds do add substantially to the total volume of savings. Some economists express fear that continued increases in the number and size of retirement funds may result in too rapid a growth of savings, with the consequence that there will be an oversupply of investment funds and underconsumption that may cause severe economic imbalance. There is little worry about this problem today.

EFFECTS ON INVESTMENT   Proponents of tax laws designed to encourage retirement funds often base their arguments on the notion that these plans increase the supply of available funds for investment in industry. Statistical evidence showing an increase in the percentage and amount of retirement funds invested in corporate stock is offered to support this conclusion. Obviously, however, the mere investment of retirement funds in corporate stock does not necessarily indicate an inflow of capital into corporations but may represent the purchase of outstanding corporate shares, whose prices are pushed upward by the existence of large quantities of investment funds. At times there may be a special problem of "inflation" in market value of high-grade stocks; because of the legal, contractual, and financially prudent restrictions placed on the types of investments made by retirement funds, such stocks are in great demand, which limits the supply of these shares to other investors. An associated problem is that many funds acquire high-quality securities for long-term investment and then retire from the market, which results in a freezing of investment capital. Undoubtedly, however, the existence of retirement funds does tend to make it easier for an existing corporation to market new shares of stock.

Many financial experts argue that retirement funds exert a stabilizing influence in the economy because they are sensitive to short-run economic fluctuations. For example, in periods of high economic activity, retirement fund savings will rise, exerting a dampening influence by removing capital otherwise available for consumption expenditures. On the other hand, in recessionary periods savings of this type are decreased, leaving a greater percentage of personal income for consumption expenditures and thus exerting a countercyclical influence. It is

doubtful, however, whether the "automatic stabilizer" effect of retirement funds is really significant enough to be of major importance. One further comment on the effects of such large capital accumulation should be made. Many economists have expressed grave fears over the actual or potential economic power placed in the hands of a relatively few trustees and other administrators responsible for the management of trust funds.[4] The potential import of this problem is undoubtedly very great.

MOBILITY OF LABOR   Reduction of employee turnover is one of the major advantages sought by employers in establishing retirement plans. This also leads to one of the chief criticisms levied against such plans—the adverse effects on labor mobility.

Most employee plans provide that full vesting of the employee's rights will occur only after several years of participation in the plan. Thus, the employee who changes jobs after only a few years of coverage may lose all or part of his or her rights under the plan. Since it is impossible to transfer rights from one plan to another, labor mobility may be severely restricted. Unfortunately, the 1974 Pension Reform Act did not solve this problem even though it did require minimum vesting schedules that will in general provide improved vesting of benefits. In addition, mobility is increased because of the opportunity to avoid current taxation on a lump-sum distribution by placing it in an I.R.A. account. Obviously, under the existing law there is still a conflict between the social goals of providing pension income for retired persons and freedom of the individual to change jobs. This conflict is inherent in estimates that prior to the 1974 Act fewer than one-half the employees covered by a plan would ever receive benefits from it.

Some critics suggest that retirement plans also create a bias against the hiring of older employees. Qualified plans must not discriminate against workers on account of age, but the hiring of an older worker may necessitate higher employer contributions, causing some resistance to his or her employment.

Even in the case of individually negotiated plans,

---

[4]For example, see A. A. Berle, *Power Without Property* (New York: Harcourt Brace Jovanovich, 1959), p. 43 *et seq.,* one of the earliest books warning of this danger. Another interesting discussion of this problem is found in Rifkin and Barber, *op. cit.* They contend that pension funds own between 20 and 25 percent of the stock traded on the New York and American stock exchanges, and hold 40 percent of all corporate bonds. They decry the concentration of control over capital allocation and economic planning concentrated in the hands of a very few banks and insurance companies.

labor mobility is curtailed. Often key employees with deferred compensation contracts forgo higher current salaries to obtain the contract, especially where income-tax advantages are significant. A change in employment may result in the employee's giving up rights under the deferred payment contract or in unfavorable tax consequences. In addition, the high cost to a new employer of matching the employee's income given up under an old employment contract may be prohibitive.

THE CREDIT FOR THE ELDERLY

As pointed out in Chapter 8, one provision of the tax law designed to provide tax relief for some retired persons is the "credit for the elderly," which permits the taxpayer who is 65 or older to reduce his or her tax bill by an amount up to $375 for 1980 ($562.50 in the case of a married couple filing jointly if both are 65 or older). A modified credit for the elderly is also available to taxpayers under 65 who are retired under a "public retirement system plan"; however, our present concern is only with those 65 or older.

Although the credit for the elderly provision technically provides a "credit" (a direct reduction of the tax bill), its practical effect is that of an exclusion. The taxpayer computes gross tax in the usual way and reduces the gross tax by the "general credit" for exemptions. Then the taxpayer reduces the remaining tax by an amount equal to 15 percent of the amount subject to the credit. The base for the credit is what the statute calls an "initial amount," which is as follows: (1) $2,500 for a single person or for a married couple filing jointly where only one spouse is 65 or older; (2) $3,750 for a married couple filing jointly where both are 65 or older (only $1,875 on separate returns). The initial amount is reduced by the following items to arrive at the base for the credit: (1) social security retirement benefits; (2) railroad retirement benefits; (3) other income excluded from taxation except the exclusions under annuity rules, under qualified pension and profit-sharing plans, life insurance proceeds, compensation for personal injury or damages, and proceeds from health and accident insurance. In addition, the initial amount is reduced by one-half of the adjusted gross income on the return in excess of $7,500 for a single individual and $10,000 for married individuals ($5,000 if separate returns are filed).

To illustrate a simple computation of the credit for the elderly, assume an unmarried taxpayer, aged 68, has the following income during the year 1979.

Interest	1,310
Wages	7,800
Social security	400
Total received	$9,510

Since the social security benefits may be excluded, the taxpayer has adjusted gross income of $9,110. If he does not itemize deductions and if he claims two exemptions, his gross tax liability will be $881. From this tax liability, he will be able to deduct $194.25 retirement income credit, computed below.

Initial amount of income for credit computation		$2,500.00
Deduct: Social security benefits	$400.00	
Excess A.G.I.	805.00*	1,205.00
Balance subject to credit		$1,295.00
Tentative credit: 15% × $1,295		$194.25

* One-half of ($9,110 − $7,500) = $805.

Thus, the taxpayer will have a net tax payable of $686.75.

There are special rules for married persons 65 or over who file separate returns and have not lived with their spouses at any time during the tax year.

Prior to 1976, this credit existed in a different form as the "retirement income credit" and was applicable only to selected types of retirement income. The main purpose of the credit originally was to equalize the tax burden between those who received retirement income from social security and railroad retirement plans (both of which are tax free) and those who received retirement income from interest and other taxable income sources. In addition, the system imposed severe limits on the amounts of "earned income" that could be received without reducing the credit. The 1976 Tax Reform Act increased the coverage by making the credit applicable to gross income from any source and drastically increasing the amount of earnings that the retired person may receive without affecting the amount of the credit.

An illustration of Schedule R—Credit for the Elderly, using the assumed information in the preceding example, is shown on page **15/16**.

This concludes our discussion of special tax provisions enacted to promote the general welfare. In Part Five we shall examine some of the controversial provisions designed to stimulate full employment or to promote the national defense.

Schedules R & RP—Credit for the Elderly

(Form 1040)

Department of the Treasury
Internal Revenue Service

▶ See Instructions for Schedules R and RP.

▶ Attach to Form 1040.

1979

19

Name(s) as shown on Form 1040	Your social security number
John T. Jones	000 ¦ 11 ¦ 2222

Please Note: *IRS will figure your Credit for the Elderly and compute your tax. Please see "IRS Will Figure Your Tax and Some of Your Credits" on page 4 of the Form 1040 instructions and complete the applicable lines on Form 1040 and Schedule R or RP.*

Should You Use Schedule R or RP?

If you are:	And were:	Use Schedule:
Single	▶ 65 or over	R
	▶ under 65 and had income from a public retirement system	RP
Married, filing separate return [1]	▶ 65 or over (unless joining in the election to use Schedule RP with your spouse who is under 65 and had income from a public retirement system)	R
	▶ under 65 and had income from a public retirement system (unless your spouse is 65 or over and does not join in the election to use Schedule RP)	RP
Married, filing joint return	▶ both 65 or over	R
	▶ one 65 or over, and one under 65 with no income or income other than from a public retirement system	R
	▶ both under 65 and one or both had income from a public retirement system . .	RP
	▶ one 65 or over, and one under 65 with income from a public retirement system .	R or RP [2]

[1] You can take the credit on a separate return ONLY if you and **your spouse lived apart for the whole year.**
[2] Figure your credit on both schedules to see which gives **you more credit.**

Schedule R   Credit for the Elderly—For People 65 or Over

If you received nontaxable pensions (social security, etc.) of $1,875 or more, or your adjusted gross income (Form 1040, line 32) was $8,750 or more, you may not be able to take the credit for the elderly. Before you start to fill out the schedule, please see the table on page 24 of the instructions.

Filing Status and Age (check only one box)

- A ☐ Single, 65 or over
- B ☐ Married filing joint return, only one spouse 65 or over
- C ☐ Married filing joint return, both 65 or over
- D ☐ Married filing separate return, 65 or over, and did not live with spouse at any time in 1979

R

1 Enter: { $2,500 if you checked box A or B . . . . } { $3,750 if you checked box C . . . . } { $1,875 if you checked box D . . . . }	**1**	2,500	00

2 a Enter amounts you received as pensions or annuities under the Social Security Act or under the Railroad Retirement Acts (but not supplemental annuities), and certain other exclusions from gross income (see instructions). If none, enter zero . . . . **2a** | 400 | 00 |

b Enter amount from Form 1040, line 32	**2b**	9,110	00
c Enter: { $7,500 if you checked box A . . . } { $10,000 if you checked box B or C . } · { $5,000 if you checked box D . . }	**2c**	7,500	00
d Subtract line 2c from line 2b. If line 2c is more than line 2b, enter zero	**2d**	1,610	00

e Enter one-half (½) of line 2d . . . . **2e** | 805 | 00 |

3 Add lines 2a and 2e. (If line 3 is more than line 1, you cannot take the credit; do not complete this schedule. If line 3 is less than line 1, go on.)	**3**	1,205	00
4 Subtract line 3 from line 1	**4**	1,295	00
5 Multiply line 4 by 15% (.15)	**5**	194	25
6 Enter amount of tax from Form 1040, line 37. (If this amount is zero, you cannot take the credit; do not file this schedule.)	**6**	881	00
7 Enter the amount from line 5 or line 6, above, whichever is less. This is your **Credit for the Elderly.** Enter the same amount on Form 1040, line 39 . . . . ▶	**7**	194	25

PROBLEMS

1. What is an "annuity"? What unusual income-tax problems does a typical employee's retirement annuity present?

2. A taxpayer and his employer each contributed $25,000 to a retirement annuity, which paid the taxpayer $5,000 during each of his retirement years. The employer's contributions were *not* treated as taxable income of the employee at the time they were deposited in a tax-free employee trust fund. At retirement, the taxpayer's estimated life was 18 years. How much of his annual $5,000 retirement income must the employee report as taxable income?

3. How are retirement benefits received under the federal social security program taxed? Why are they not taxed like other employee annuities?

4. Why is the rapid growth in retirement plans receiving so much critical attention from scholars? What tax aspects of retirement plans are open to question? What nontax aspects of retirement plans are of major importance?

5. During the past 15 years, many employees have received an unusual benefit: They have been granted "full" retirement privileges under new employee annuity plans even though they have made contributions for a limited number of years (because of their advanced age at the time the annuities were instituted). These persons are subject to a "special" tax treatment. Demonstrate your comprehension of these "special circumstances" by determining the amount of taxable income received by the following taxpayer, in each of the years 19x1– 19x4. The taxpayer began receiving an employee annuity of $3,600 per year on January 1, 19x1, when his estimated remaining life was 15 years. Taxpayer had contributed only $8,000 to the annuity program at the time of his retirement. The remainder of the annuity premium was paid by his employer under a qualified plan.

6. If a taxpayer who owns a substantial retirement annuity has been fortunate enough to become wealthy during his lifetime, it is particularly important for him to be able to withdraw his annuity benefits in a qualified plan in a lump sum. Explain this statement.

7. What major controversies surround the tax status of the social security program?

8. Explain how (a) employer contributions, (b) trust income, and (c) annuity-type distributions are treated for tax purposes when there is a "qualified" plan.

9. Many political and economic writers deplore the concentration of economic power in the hands of a relatively few people who manage the assets of huge retirement funds. Explain how the tax laws have contributed to the growth of these funds.

10. The principal reason for original enactment of the Retirement Income Credit was to provide greater equity between taxpayers receiving social security and other tax-free retirement benefits and those whose income was primarily from "retirement income" sources. The 1976 Tax Reform Act extended the credit to all types of income of retired persons. What seems to be the reasoning behind this move? How does it compare with the original intent of the provision?

11. The Individual Retirement Account concept is intended to provide an opportunity for an employee not covered by qualified retirement plans in his or her employment to create a retirement fund with a tax incentive through permitting the taxpayer to deduct, within limits, his or her contributions to the fund.

    Are taxpayers who take advantage of this provision likely to be those in lower income levels or in higher income levels? Explain.

12. There is some evidence that in the first year of the I.R.A. (individual retirement account) plan, 1975, many self-employed individuals took advantage of this law even though they had previously shunned so-called "Keogh" of H.R. 10 plans. What reason(s) can you give for this?

13. Porkorny earned a salary of $30,000 from his employment by a public accounting firm during the current year. He is covered by a qualified employee annuity. In addition, he earned $700 as a consultant to a manufacturing corporation.
    a. Is Porkorny entitled to set up a Keogh plan covering his consulting income?
    b. If the answer to part a is yes, what amount may Porkorny contribute to the Keogh plan and deduct for 1980?

14. A. B. Cline retired from employment on December 31, 19x0. Beginning in January 19x1, Cline received monthly payments of $320 from his employer's qualified profit-sharing and pension plan. In recent years, the employer has made all contributions to the fund. Several years ago, however, the plan provided for optional contributions by the employee, and during that time Cline contributed $8,000 to the plan. At the date of retirement, Cline was 65 years old. Compute the amount Cline will include in income in 19x1.

15. Willford Manufacturing Company decided in 19x1 to establish a pension program for its employees. Mr. Willford, the president, was especially interested in this program, and the final proposed plan largely reflected his desires. The basic feature of the plan was a trust fund to which annual contributions would be made. Each employee with more than 5 years of service would be eligible to participate. A contribution equal to 5 percent of the employee's compensation would be made for each employee with earnings in excess of $25,000; contributions of 4 percent of compensation would be made for each employee with earnings in excess of $15,000 but less than $25,000; and contributions of 3 percent of compensation would be made for employees with earnings of $15,000 per year or less. Is this likely to be a "qualified" plan? Explain.

16. City Manufacturing Company has established a nonqualified pension trust. Contributions are made each year for each employee who has been employed by the company for more than one year. These contributions are forfeitable by the employee, however, if he or she leaves employment of the company at any time before 5 full years of employment. Howard McVey began work for the company in June 19x0. In 19x1, 19x2, 19x3, and 19x4 the company contributed $200 each year (in December) to the fund on behalf of McVey. On June 12, 19x5, McVey's rights in the plan became nonforfeitable.
    a. How much income, if any, did McVey report in 19x1, 19x2, 19x3, and 19x4?
    b. How much income, if any, did McVey report in 19x5?

17. Miss Able worked for her employer for 30 years. During that time she contributed $5,400 to a qualified retirement annuity program. She retired in June of 19x1 and began drawing monthly retirement checks of $200 per month, starting in August 19x2. During 19x2 she received checks totaling $1,000; in 19x3 she received $2,400; in 19x4 she received $2,400; and in 19x5 she received $2,400.
    How will Miss Able treat these receipts on her tax return each year?

18. Thomas Esquire is an attorney. He has only one employee, a secretary who has worked for him for 5 years. Esquire establishes a qualified retirement program for himself as an owner-employee and the secretary. In 19x1 he contributed $300 to the pension fund on behalf of the secretary and $1,800 to the fund for himself. May he deduct the contributions?

19. Joan owns 25 percent of the stock of Town Company, a Subchapter S corporation, and is president of the company. In the current year the corporation

contributed a total of $64,000 to a qualified employee trust. Of this amount $4,500 was contributed for the account of Joan.

   a. May the corporation deduct the $4,500 on its tax return?

   b. Is the $4,500 taxable to Joan?

20. John McGee is employed by a company that has no retirement plan. During the current year John earned a total salary of $8,000. He also had interest income of $210 and received dividends of $120.

   a. Would John be eligible to set up an I.R.A. account?

   b. What is the maximum amount of contribution that John could make and deduct this year if he is eligible?

   c. Where would John go to establish a plan? That is, where could he invest the money?

   d. When is the latest date for John to make his deposit for the current year?

21. William and Marcy are married and file a joint return. William, who is employed in a firm that has no retirement plan, earned $13,000. Marcy is unemployed. They have heard of I.R.A. accounts and come to you for advice. They would like to shelter the maximum amount possible. What is your advice to them?

22. Tom Executive began employment with Grosso Corporation on July 5, 1950, and retired from the company on June 30, 1980. He was covered by his employer's qualified retirement plan. During Tom's employment period, he contributed $18,000 to the plan and his employer contributed $62,000. On September 1, 1980, Tom withdrew his entire benefits in cash, $124,000, in a lump-sum distribution and invested the proceeds in a new business venture he started.

    Tom and his wife file a joint return. During 1980, he has other net taxable income of $60,000. Compute his tax liability for 1980, assuming he elects to use income averaging on the entire distribution.

23. Tom, 68, and Nelda, 66, file a joint return. During the year their income consisted of dividends from jointly owned stock, $900; interest, $1,000; social security benefits, $1,000; wages earned by Tom, $8,500. Compute their tentative credit for the elderly.

RETURN PROBLEM

Marie Antone, single, aged 65, retired from public school teaching on January 31, 19x1. On June 30, 19x1, she received her first monthly check for $350 under a lifetime annuity payable by the state teacher retirement system. During 19x1 she received seven of these monthly checks. During her teaching career Marie had contributed $10,000 to the teacher retirement annuity plan.

Also, beginning July 1, 19x1, Marie is paid $200 per month under an "ordinary life annuity" that she had purchased by making annual payments of $1,000 per year for 18 years. Under the plan she will be paid $200 per month for the remainder of her life. At the date of her first payment period, Marie was 65 years of age, and reference to an annuity table shows a "multiple" of 18.2 for a female aged 65.

Other income received by Marie in 19x1 was

Interest on savings accounts and corporate bonds	$3,200
Dividends on corporate common stock	1,700
Social security benefits	900
Salary for month of January 19x1 (income tax of $120 was withheld on this amount)	1,000

Marie's deductions include

Medical expenses (net deductible amount)	200
Taxes	600
Contributions	2,500
Miscellaneous	100

Complete the following tax schedules for Marie:

Schedule B (enter "various" for names of payers)
Schedule A (complete only the "Summary of Itemized Deductions" section)
Schedule R
Form 1040, pages 1 and 2. (Enter assumed data for address, etc.)

"I dislike all taxes," he asserts, adding particular dislike for using the tax laws "for other than revenue purposes."

Statement attributed to former Secretary of Treasury JOHN B. CONNALLY,
Wall Street Journal (March 22, 1971)

We must scrutinize our tax system carefully to insure that its provisions contribute to the broad goals of full employment, growth and equity.

President JOHN F. KENNEDY,
Economic Message to Congress (1962)

PART

FIVE

full employment and national defense

A word is not a crystal, transparent and unchanged; it is the skin of a living thought and may vary greatly in color and content according to the circumstances and the time in which it is used.

JUSTICE O. W. HOLMES,
Towne v. *Eisner*, 245 U.S. 418 (1918)

depreciation policy: a basic incentive

From the days of President Monroe, federal legislators and administrators have frequently used the goal of national defense to justify policies and new laws that would have profound effects on the nation's economy. In the conditions of today's world, which require our active participation in the international community and our economic competition with other ideologies, the national security demands a healthy, expanding economy and the full employment of all resources. The attainment of these objectives has thus become a national policy.

During the era of the New Deal, the Roosevelt administration vigorously pursued a policy aimed at increasing the level of employment of the nation's resources. The National Recovery Act, public works projects, and deficit spending were only a few of the methods tried in an effort to get the factories rolling and to increase the number of jobs. Though bitterly contested, this policy was formally adopted by Congress in the Employment Act of 1946, during Truman's Fair Deal. This act established the Council of Economic Advisers and assigned an important role to the federal government in economic affairs. The preamble to the act declares

It is the continuing policy and responsibility of the Federal Government to use all practicable means consistent with its needs and obligations and other essential considerations of national policy . . . to coordinate and utilize all its plans, functions, and resources for the purpose of creating and maintain-

ing . . . conditions under which there will be afforded useful employment opportunities . . . for those able, willing, and seeking to work, and to promote maximum employment, production, and purchasing power.

Since the passage of this act, the Korean conflict, the missile gap, and the Vietnam situation have established the interdependence of national defense and full employment. Recurring recessions in the United States, Europe, and Japan, combined with high, seemingly endemic inflation aggravated by the international cartel of oil producers, underscore the importance of strong economies and the interdependence of the industrialized, democratic states. Weak economies invite political unrest and threaten the delicate balance between relatively free democratic societies and political dictatorships.

Some of the most important provisions of the federal income-tax law affecting business are based on the goals of full employment and national defense; provisions enacted primarily to attain these goals constitute the subject matter of Part Five of this text. Since World War II, several tax provisions aimed at increasing investment in plant and equipment have been enacted in pursuit of the full-employment policy. Major changes in rules governing depreciation deductions were instituted in 1954, 1962, and 1971. An investment "credit" provision was adopted for the same reason in 1962. Rules governing the tax treatment of expenditures for research and development are also based partly on the desire to encourage these activities. These subjects are discussed in the present chapter and in Chapter 17. Special incentives for the development of natural resources are discussed in Chapter 18. That chapter also includes an overview of some major problems confronting the United States economy in the next decade and suggests tax policies that might help to solve the problems.

THE THEORETICAL BASIS FOR INVESTMENT INCENTIVES

The economic revolution of this century has been the widespread acceptance of the theory of income and employment expounded by John Maynard Keynes. A complete exposition of this theory is contained in his *General Theory of Employment, Interest, and Money,* published in 1935. In the four decades since its publication, this book has become a handbook for fiscal policy. Although space limitations preclude a complete review of Keynes's theory, a working knowledge of it is essential if one is to understand the role assigned to investment by our fiscal planners.

The theory is an attempt to define and relate the forces that determine the level of employment or income for an entire economy. Classical economic theory rests on the assumption that there will be full employment of labor and other resources when an economy is in equilibrium, a theoretical conclusion that did not appear to be supported by the facts. Keynes, therefore, was concerned with those situations where an economy is at a point of equilibrium but where plant capacity is not fully utilized and workers are idle.

In Keynes's system, the aggregate income (the level of employment) for a given period is equal to the aggregate consumption spending plus the aggregate investment spending. The portion of the income that is not consumed is, by definition, saved; therefore the aggregate investment for a given period of time must always be equal to the total savings. The usual expressions for these relations are as follows, where Y is income, I is investment, C is consumption, and S is savings:

$$Y = C + I \quad \text{and} \quad S = Y - C$$

Transposing the second equation, we get

$$Y = C + S$$

Therefore,

$$S = I$$

For a given period, if investment increases, income will increase until the savings out of this increased income are equal to investment. Conversely, if investment is decreased, income will decrease, and the decreased savings out of this decreased income will again equal investment.

Another important relationship in the theory is that between income and consumption. As the total income in an economy rises, the *percentage* of the income spent for consumption decreases. Where income is relatively low, a high percentage of income will be spent on consumption items; as income rises, the percentage spent on consumption (but not the absolute amount) will decrease. For example, with a total income of $400 billion, consumption might be $320 billion, or 80 percent of income; if income rises to $500 billion, consumption might rise to only $375 billion, or 75 percent of income. This relationship is due in part to the unequal distribution of income among the citizens. As income rises, those with very high incomes will receive even more income that cannot be consumed readily. There are also cultural inhibitions to consumption once income has passed the level required for "necessities." The relationship between income and consumption at a given level of income tends to be stable. A change in the percentage consumed can be effected only through a change in the distribution of income or through a change in the habits of consumption.

The relationship between income and consumption Keynes called the *propensity to consume.* Given the propensity to consume, a definite relationship, known as the *investment multiplier,* can be established between a change in investment and the resulting change in income. Let's assume a propensity to consume at 80 percent of income.[1] An increase of $1,000,000 in investment will increase income by several times $1,000,000 (hence the term "multiplier"). The new investment is income to those receiving it, and they will spend $800,000 (80 percent of the $1,000,000) on consumption. This $800,000 spent for consumption is income to those receiving it, and they, in turn, will spend $640,000 for con-

---

[1] This analysis of the multiplier is taken from Dudley Dillard, *The Economics of John Maynard Keynes* (Englewood Cliffs, N.J.: Prentice-Hall, Inc., 1948), Chapter 5, pp. 75–101. Beginning students will find this source useful for the precise arithmetic of the multiplier.

sumption. Given a time period long enough for the recurring income and consumption to work out to its ultimate effect, income will be increased by $5,000,000, five times the increase in investment. Out of this income $4,000,000 (80 percent) will be consumed and $1,000,000 saved, these savings being exactly equal to the new investment. In sum, given a propensity to consume 80 percent of income, the investment multiplier is five (income will increase by five times the increase in investment). As the propensity to consume decreases, the multiplier decreases. If only 50 percent of income is consumed, the multiplier is only two; under these conditions a great deal of investment is required to produce a substantial effect on income.

Except for the convulsions of 1973–75, the economy of the United States since 1954 has been fairly stable. There have been several sharp recessions and some periods of wasteful unemployment, but none of these fluctuations can compare with the Great Depression of the 1930s. National income throughout this period has been rising, and, with higher incomes, the portion spent for consumption has been falling. In short, an increasing rate of investment has been necessary to maintain, and particularly to increase, the level of employment and income.

A large part of the needed investment has been made by governmental units. National defense, space exploration, and other government programs account for a tremendous amount of investment spending. The rate of investment of this nature is determined by national and local governmental policy and by the demands of international politics. The effect of these governmental expenditures on the level of income varies, of course, with the method used to finance the expenditures. In the private sector, the rate of investment depends primarily on the rate of return expected by business, and, naturally, a sufficient return from an investment requires first a strong demand for the product. Thus, incentives for investment in the private sector originate in one of two ways. First, the tax law can be changed to increase aggregate demand and thereby induce new investments. The increases in the standard deduction in 1975 and 1977 (by then called the zero bracket amount), the increase in the exemption deduction in 1978, and the provisions for the earned income credit are examples of changes in the law aimed at increasing aggregate demand. A second alternative is to increase the *marginal efficiency of capital* by directly reducing the cost of capital through the various incentives discussed in this part.

The methods of capital recovery

A direct method of increasing the efficiency of a capital investment is to provide for a rapid recovery of capital, a point illustrated in detail below. The timing of the recovery of capital has been a constant problem for legislators, administrators and the courts. At present, the income-tax law provides four methods of cost recovery:[2]

1. Immediate deduction of the total cost when paid or incurred. This method is currently used for research and development (Chapter 17), for intangible development costs of natural resources (Chapter 18), and for other payments where the benefits received are intangible, such as in an advertising campaign. The usual result is a deduction of the expenditure prior to recognition of the income that arises from it.

2. Deferral of cost until property is sold or otherwise disposed of. Investments in land and securities are now treated in this manner, on the assumption that these properties do not waste away or necessarily depreciate in value over their lives. For years, railroads used this method, sometimes called the retirement method, for some properties. It results in no deduction for the use of property over its life but a sizable deduction on retirement if the property has in fact decreased in value.

3. A deduction based on a percentage of income from the property over its life. This method is now used to compute the deduction for depletion of most natural resources (Chapter 18).

4. "Timetable" deductions. With the exceptions mentioned above, the cost of property is deducted over a period of years, beginning at the date the property is placed in use, based on a more or less arbitrary timetable. This method of spreading cost is known as *depreciation*.

In this chapter we shall consider the various rules for "timetable" deductions, or depreciation. Because of the time value of money, which includes the payments by businesses of their income-tax bills, any provision that permits the immediate deduction of a capital investment is obviously superior to one that requires the recovery of capital over a period of years.

_____

[2] For a discussion of the different economic effects of these four methods, see Joel Dean, "Capital Wastage Allowances," *1959 Compendium*, pp. 813–26.

How accelerated capital recovery increases the return on capital investments

A prudent businessperson considering an investment in plant and equipment will ignore all *past* costs and expenses and look only at future *cash* transactions. In addition, the *timing* of future cash receipts and disbursements becomes extremely important; next year's expected cash receipts are not worth as much as today's cash receipts. Depreciation methods can have an important effect on the present value of future cash receipts.

To illustrate, let us imagine that a businessman is considering an investment in a new plant. He estimates that the new plant will produce a net cash return before taxes of $100,000 a year for 20 years, ignoring for now the effects of depreciation. His tax rate, we will assume, is 46 percent. Thus, his after-tax return will be $54,000 per year, still ignoring depreciation. He might begin with the following comparisons:

Outlay in cash now	$ 500,000
Expected cash return net of taxes (20 years at $54,000)	$1,080,000

A conclusion based on this simple analysis would be incorrect. The $500,000 cost is paid now, but the return is spread over 20 years. If we assume that the businessman uses 10 percent as an expected rate of return, the present value of the expected future returns would be only $459,756 ($54,000 annual net return after taxes times 8.514, the factor used to determine the present value of a series of twenty equal annual payments at 10 percent). If this amount, $459,756, is compared to the cost of the investment, $500,000, the investment appears to be unprofitable. This simple comparison is also deficient because it gives no effect to depreciation or amortization of cost of the investment.

Because of the time value of money, the sooner the tax law permits recovery of capital (by deducting it from gross income) the more likely a given investment will be attractive to the investor. Using the same facts as in the above illustration, assume that the tax law permitted an immediate deduction of $500,000 invested. Assume further that the taxpayer has enough income to use the entire deduction. If the taxpayer's marginal tax rate is 46 percent, the $500,000 deduction immediately produces a $230,000 decrease in tax payments and the net cost of the investment is only $270,000. When compared to the

present value of the expected returns from the investment of $459,756, there remains a handsome profit.

As a comparison, assume that the law required the depreciation of the $500,000 investment on a straight-line basis over a 20-year period. Calculation of the present value of the capital recovery would be:

Depreciation per year ($500,000/20 yrs.)	$ 25,000
Times tax rate	46%
Tax savings per year	$ 11,500
Present value of 20 annual payments of $11,500 each at 10%	$ 97,911

With this extended depreciation schedule, the net cost of the investment is $402,089; that is, the $500,000 paid out reduced by the $97,911 present value of the future depreciation. Given a present value of the expected return of $459,756, the investment might still be made, but its potential profitability is significantly reduced by the deferral of the deduction.

As a final illustration, let us now assume that this particular investment qualifies for depreciation or amortization over a 5-year period. In that event, tax savings will be $46,000 per year; that is, the $100,000 annual depreciation times the 46 percent tax rate. The present value of the savings, again using a 10 percent rate, is $174,377. This more rapid recovery reduces the net cost of the project to $325,623, and the prospects for the investment are enhanced significantly compared to the 20-year recovery period.

Since 1954, our depreciation policy has been based on the assumptions that the acceleration of deductions makes investments in depreciable plant more attractive to businesspeople, that this means more investments will be made, and that these investments will assure the full employment of resources.

EARLY HISTORY OF DEPRECIATION

When drafting the original income-tax law, Congress could not foresee the many problems that were to arise in administering it. As originally conceived, expenditures would be either revenue charges (current expense deductions) or capital charges (related to acquisition of property). Assets were divided on a common-sense basis between those properties that did not wear out or waste away and those that did. The cost of nondepreciable property could only be matched against the eventual sales price to determine gain or loss. For the other group of assets, the Revenue Act of 1913 provided "a reasonable allowance for depreciation by use, wear and tear of property, if any." Later acts used substantially identical language but included "obsolescence."[3]

The straight-line concept

Prior to passage of the first income-tax law, accountants had recognized the need for systematically spreading or allocating the cost of a wasting asset over the accounting periods benefited. At the turn of the century, accounting textbooks and manuals usually recommended the following procedure for determination of the periodic charge against revenue:

$$\frac{\text{Cost to be allocated}}{\text{Estimated life}} = \text{Depreciation}$$

An alternate expression is

$$\text{Cost to be allocated} \times \frac{1}{\text{Estimated life}} = \text{Depreciation}$$

(The fraction in the latter expression is the *rate* of depreciation.) This procedure provides for a constant charge for each period during which the asset is used. Prior to the influence of the tax law, however, most businesses did not use this systematic method but charged off varying amounts of depreciation from year to year. In good years, when income was high, a large amount of depreciation might be charged off, looking forward to the bad years when income would be insufficient to absorb depreciation.[4]

In the period from 1913 to 1933, the efforts of the Bureau of Internal Revenue were directed toward establishing *systematic* depreciation on a straight-line basis as outlined above. The Bureau allowed taxpayers maximum freedom in selecting the rate of depreciation, or estimated life. The attitude of the Bureau was summarized in the publication of Bulletin F in 1920: "It is considered impracticable to prescribe fixed, definite rates of depreciation which would be allowable for all property of a given class or

character. . . . The taxpayer should in all cases determine as accurately as possible according to his judgment and experience the rate at which his property depreciates."[5] Where the taxpayer used a rate systematically, the taxpayer's deductions were allowed unless the Bureau could produce clear and convincing evidence to show that the deduction was unreasonable. Needless to say, clear and convincing evidence was available only in extreme cases.

Prescribed rates

In 1933 the Roosevelt administration sought new sources of revenue to finance its ambitious programs. A subcommittee of the House Committee on Ways and Means proposed a reduction in the depreciation deductions of all taxpayers by one-fourth for a three-year period. As a more equitable solution, the Bureau proposed to decrease the deduction by exercising more control in three ways: (1) by requiring taxpayers to furnish detailed schedules of depreciation with their returns; (2) by shifting to the taxpayer the burden of proving the reasonableness of the rates used; and (3) by issuing a revision of Bulletin F that would specify "reasonable" rates of depreciation for numerous assets. The rates in Bulletin F would be used except in those cases where the taxpayer could prove that the specified rate was inappropriate.

With the adoption of these proposals, which remained unchanged until the early days of the Eisenhower administration in 1953, the depreciation deduction became a constant source of controversy between taxpayers and the Bureau. Taxpayers claimed that the lives in Bulletin F were unrealistically long, that the use of these long lives did not allow them to recover their investments rapidly enough, and that, as a result, investment in new plants and equipment was reduced. However, the Treasury Department remained firm, claiming that the rates in Bulletin F were based on empirical evidence and that, after all, the taxpayers could use shorter lives where individual circumstances warranted them (provided the taxpayer could prove that Bulletin F was inappropriate).

During the period from 1933 to 1953, the only relief measures from this restrictive depreciation policy were rapid amortization of emergency facilities and limited use of a modified "declining-balance method." During World War II and the Korean War,

---

[3] Eugene L. Grant and Paul T. Norton, Jr., *Depreciation* (New York: Ronald Press, 1955), p. 209. This book has a good discussion of the early history of depreciation.

[4] See Dorothy A. Litherland, "Fixed Asset Replacement a Half Century Ago," *The Accounting Review*, 26 (October, 1951), p. 475.

[5] Grant and Norton, *op. cit.*, p. 216.

taxpayers who constructed property necessary to the war effort could allocate the cost of the emergency property over a 60-month period, without reference to its actual life. The cost of property subject to emergency amortization had to be approved by the War (later Defense) Department. Emergency amortization could be applied also to grain storage facilities during a four-year period in the 1950s, the height of the grain glut. In 1946, the Bureau allowed, with its prior approval, the use of the declining-balance method with the rate limited to 150 percent of the straight-line depreciation. However, this method was seldom used because of the restrictions on the rate allowed.[6]

Most of the present law on depreciation has been written since President Eisenhower's inauguration in 1953. The major modifications during this time, which are still in effect, are acceptance of the accelerated methods, provision for additional first-year allowances, and the Class Life System to replace Bulletin F. In addition, in 1953 the I.R.S. issued a directive to the effect that estimated lives and rates used by taxpayers would not be challenged unless the I.R.S. could obtain "clear and convincing" evidence that the rates were unreasonable.[7] Of more importance, the years since 1953 have seen a widespread change in attitude toward depreciation. Legislators, taxpayers, and administrators now commonly accept the proposition that income-tax rules on depreciation can have a significant effect on the rate of investment in new plant and equipment and, therefore, an indirect effect on the level of employment.

THE PRESENT LAW

The general rule for depreciation, but not the accepted methods, has been virtually the same since 1913. Today, Sec. 167(a) of the Internal Revenue Code reads as follows:

> (a) General Rule.—There shall be allowed as a depreciation deduction a reasonable allowance for the exhaustion, wear and tear (including a reasonable allowance for obsolescence)—
> (1) of property used in the trade or business, or
> (2) of property held for the production of income.

Note that this general rule would apply both to tangible properties, such as buildings and equipment, and to intangible assets, such as patents, copyrights, and trademarks. Of course, no depreciation is allowed on property held for the personal use and enjoyment of the taxpayer, such as a personal residence or a pleasure automobile. Finally, the rule does not apply to properties that, by their nature, are not subject to wear and tear from use or to obsolescence of usefulness. Examples are corporate securities, land, and goodwill. While this general rule has a long history in the law, other subsections added to Sec. 167 have all been aimed at removing some restriction imposed under the general rule. The most important provision is the subsection dealing with allowable methods.

Depreciation methods

In 1954 Sec. 167(b) was added to the law. It reads as follows:

> (b) Use of Certain Methods and Rates.—For taxable years ending after December 31, 1953, the term "reasonable allowance" as used in subsection (a) shall include (but shall not be limited to) an allowance computed in accordance with regulations prescribed by the Secretary under any of the following methods:
> (1) the straight line method,
> (2) the declining balance method, using a rate not exceeding twice the rate which would have been used had the annual allowance been computed under the method described in paragraph (1),
> (3) the sum-of-the-years-digits method, and
> (4) any other consistent method productive of an annual allowance which, when added to all allowances for the period commencing with the taxpayer's use of the property and including the taxable year, does not, during the first two-thirds of the useful life of the property, exceed the total of such allowances which would have been used had such allowances been computed under the method described in paragraph (2).
> Nothing in this subsection shall be construed to limit or reduce an allowance otherwise allowable under subsection (a).

While this subsection specifies the use of the straight-line, declining-balance, and sum-of-the-years'-digits methods, it also provides for the use of "any other consistent method." The only restriction on the use of these other methods is that they must not produce a total allowance greater than the declining-balance method over the first two-thirds of the property's useful life. Congress has placed certain restrictions, to be discussed below, on the use of methods other than the straight-line method. Finally, the depreciable basis of property is the basis that would be used to determine gain on disposition.

---

[6]Joint Economic Committee, *The Federal Tax System: Facts and Problems, 1964* (Washington, D.C.: U.S. Government Printing Office, 1964), p. 94.
[7] *Ibid.*

TABLE **16-1**
AN EXAMPLE OF DECLINING-BALANCE DEPRECIATION

Year	Undepreciated balance	Rate (percent)	Depreciation deduction
1	$20,000	40	$ 8,000
2	12,000	40	4,800
3	7,200	40	2,880
4	4,320	—	2,160
5	2,160	—	2,160
		Total depreciation	$20,000

STRAIGHT-LINE METHOD   Under the straight-line method, the original cost of the property (including commissions, fees, and other incidental acquisition costs), less the salvage value, is allocated in equal amounts to each year of the property's estimated useful life. This method has been in general use since 1913 and corresponds to the accounting concept of straight-line depreciation. However, straight-line depreciation has been somewhat liberalized by the use of Class Lives (discussed in more detail later in this chapter) and by the provision of Sec. 167(f), which allows taxpayers to reduce or completely ignore salvage value in some cases.

For depreciable *personal* property acquired after October 10, 1962, with the exception of livestock, salvage value used may be reduced by an amount up to 10 percent of the basis (cost) of the property. The provision is elective and available only where the property has an estimated useful life of three years or more. Note that the rule applies only to personal property; real property, such as buildings, typically has *no* salvage value. Instead, salvage of depreciable real property very often results in expenditures greater than scrap value. The rule is intended to reduce the number of controversies over salvage value where salvage is an insignificant amount relative to cost. In many cases, salvage value may be ignored completely for the specified property. The rule applies to all depreciation methods.

DECLINING-BALANCE METHOD   Under the declining-balance method, a constant rate is applied to the undepreciated basis of the property. The maximum rate allowed is twice the straight-line rate, and most taxpayers who elect this method to accelerate their depreciation will choose the maximum rate. Double-declining balance is the method that gives the maximum deduction in the early years of an asset's life. The following example illustrates several problems connected with the use of this method.

A taxpayer acquires a new machine on January 2, 19x1, at a cost of $20,000. The estimated life is five years, and salvage value after five years is $1,500. The straight-line rate is 20 percent (1 ÷ 5 years), so the maximum rate permitted under declining balance is 40 percent. Depreciation allowed each year would be as shown in Table 16-1.

Two things should be noted in this example. First, since salvage value is less than 10 percent of the original cost, the calculation of depreciation ignores salvage value, and the total depreciation over the life of the property is $20,000. *But,* even if the taxpayer had not elected to ignore salvage value, or to the extent salvage had exceeded 10 percent of cost, the undepreciated basis would still *not* be reduced by salvage value. In the declining-balance method, the rate is always applied to cost before the reduction for salvage value. In situations where salvage value is used with this method, depreciation deducted in the later years may never reduce the undepreciated cost below salvage value.

The second point to note in our example is that the procedure of applying the 40-percent rate to the undepreciated balance is not used in years 4 and 5. If this rate procedure had been used, the depreciation in year 4 would have been only $1,728 and only approximately $1,041 in year 5. In this case, the entire cost of $20,000 would not have been spread over the five-year period. To overcome this inherent weakness in the declining-balance method, the law provides that taxpayers who use this method may elect to change at any time to the straight-line method. Thus, in year 4, the taxpayer in the example changes to the straight-line method and spreads the remaining $4,320 equally over years 4 and 5. The change from declining balance to straight line is made in the year when the straight-line rate exceeds the declining-balance rate. Thus, at the beginning of year 4, the asset has a remaining life of two years and the straight-line rate is ½ or 50 percent. The change

TABLE **16-2**

AN EXAMPLE OF SUM-OF-THE-YEARS'-DIGITS DEPRECIATION

Year	Depreciable basis	Rate	Depreciation deduction
1	$20,000	5/15	$ 6,667
2	20,000	4/15	5,333
3	20,000	3/15	4,000
4	20,000	2/15	2,667
5	20,000	1/15	1,333
15			
		Total depreciation	$20,000

to straight line can be made without the consent of the Commmissioner of Internal Revenue.

SUM-OF-THE-YEARS'-DIGITS METHOD The third method applies a declining rate to the depreciable cost, reduced by salvage value, if any. For the first year of the property's life, the rate, or fraction, is composed of a numerator equal to the estimated remaining life at the start of the year and a denominator equal to the sum of the numbers representing the successive years in the estimated life of the asset. For the second year, the numerator of the fraction is reduced by one, while the denominator remains unchanged. Applying this method to the facts in the preceding example, we get the depreciation shown in Table 16-2.

Salvage value, when applicable, must be subtracted from the cost basis to obtain the depreciable basis before applying the rate. The denominator, 15, is the sum of 5 + 4 + 3 + 2 + 1, an amount that can be obtained by using the formula for an arithmetic progression $\left(n \times \dfrac{n+1}{2} \right)$. The I.R.S. has constructed tables of rates that may be applied to the original basis minus prior depreciation (a declining basis) to obtain the sum-of-the-years'-digits depreciation. For example, the tables show a 33⅓-percent rate for assets with a remaining life of five years. With the sum-of-the-years'-digits method, there is no reason to change to the straight-line method in the later years; the entire depreciable basis is allocated to the five-year period because the sum of the five fractions is one.

A comparison of the two methods reveals that double-declining balance provides the larger deduction in the first year, $8,000 compared to $6,667. This fact, coupled with the comparative ease of computing the declining balance, has made it the more popular method.

RESTRICTIONS ON USE OF ACCELERATED METHODS Section 167(c) contains three restrictions on the use of the accelerated methods. These methods can be used only for properties that meet the following tests:

1. The property must have a useful life of three years or more.
2. The property must be tangible in nature; intangibles must be amortized on the straight-line basis. (Furthermore, as explained below, the most accelerated methods have been further restricted relative to certain real properties.)
3. The property must have been built or rebuilt by or for the taxpayer after 1953 or acquired *new* after 1953. Used tangible, personal property acquired after 1954 can be depreciated at 150-percent declining-balance method.

For several years in the late 1960s, the demand for new building construction ran well ahead of the capacity of the industry. This excess demand had two unwanted effects: First, construction costs rose rapidly, adding to the general inflation. Second, the available resources were being shifted from residential to commercial construction, with the result that fewer resources were available for renovation of slum properties and new residential construction. The shortage of low and lower-middle income housing is still acute. Thus, the Reform Act of 1969 included Subsection 167(j) by which Congress attempted to increase the flow of resources to residential construction by restricting the depreciation on commercial buildings.

Today the double-declining-balance and sum-of-the-years'-digits methods may be used only on non-realty and on new residential rental property. All other buildings and building components constructed after July 24, 1969, cannot be depreciated by these methods. Rather, the maximum allowance available for such new property will be determined by the 150-percent declining-balance method. *Used* residential real property is subject to a maximum schedule of 125 percent under the declining-balance method. However, the 125-percent rate can be applied only if the asset's remaining life is 20 years or more. For a building to qualify as residential property, at least 80 percent of the gross rents must come from dwelling units. This test must be met each year; if it is not, lower rates must be used *for that year.* A hotel or motel is not residential property if more than half of the establishment is used on a transient basis. All other *used* realty (''Section 1250 property'') acquired after July 24, 1969, which previously could be depreciated on the 150-percent declining-balance method, is now restricted to the straight-line method except for residential property.

The current rules can be summarized as shown in Table 16-3.

CHANGES IN DEPRECIATION METHOD   The law provides that taxpayers cannot change from one depreciation method to another without the consent of the Commissioner. There are two important exceptions to this general rule. First, as noted above, taxpayers can change from the declining-balance method to straight line. Second, taxpayers can also change from the sum-of-the-years'-digits to straight line for

properties subject to special recapture rules explained in Part Six of the text. In 1974, the I.R.S. announced that consent will be given on a liberal basis to other changes in method. The pronouncement specified the following changes: from straight-line to an accelerated method; from sum-of-the-years'-digits to declining-balance and vice versa; and from one declining-balance percentage to another percentage. The taxpayer who wishes to change must file an application with the Commissioner within the first 180 days of the year when the new method is to be used.

ACCOUNTING PROBLEMS   In the examples above, the property was acquired at the first of a taxable year, thereby eliminating a common complication. When property is bought or sold during a taxable year, only a fractional portion of the annual amount is deductible if asset records are maintained on an item-by-item basis. Normally, depreciation is computed to the nearest month. Where group or composite accounts are used, an averaging convention is usually adopted to handle acquisitions and retirements. One such convention is to compute depreciation based on the average between the beginning and ending balances. Another convention is to assume that all assets acquired within a given year were acquired at the midpoint of the year and thus one-half year of depreciation is taken on all acquisitions

TABLE **16-3**

ALLOWABLE METHODS OF DEPRECIATION

	Category of property				
	Tangible personal property		Intangible property	Real property [a]	
Method of depreciation	New	Used [b]	All	New	Used
Straight-line	×	×	×	×	×
Declining balance [c]					
200%	× [d]			× [e]	
150%	×	×		×	
Sum-of-the-years' digits	× [d]			× [e]	
Other	× [f(1)]			× [f(2)]	

[a] Special rules apply to residential rental property and for expenditures for rehabilitation of low-income housing, pollution-control facilities, on-the-job training or child care facilities, and rehabilitation of historic structures.
[b] For property acquired after 1953, accelerated depreciation is available without permission of the Secretary of the Treasury only if elected on first return where depreciation is allowable.
[c] The percentages for the declining balance methods are the maximums allowable. Any *lower* percentage of the straight-line rate is permissible.
[d] Life must be at least 3 years.
[e] For property acquired prior to July 25, 1969.
[f] Any other consistent method that does not result in cumulative depreciation over the first two-thirds of the life of the property in excess of what would have resulted from use of the declining balance method at (1) the rate of 200%, (2) the rate of 150%.

(called the "half-year convention"). Another half-year convention treats all assets placed in service in the last half of the preceding year and the first half of the current year as being placed in service on the first day of the current year. In no event may a convention be adopted that results in greater depreciation than the half-year convention.

Another common complication in calculating depreciation is a change in the estimated life of the asset. Rules provide that, at the end of any taxable year, the undepreciated cost of an asset (reduced by salvage value), will be depreciated over the estimated *remaining* life of the property. Estimated life is established when the property is originally acquired. This original estimate, however, should be changed whenever it becomes clear that the actual life of the property is more or less than the original estimate. In some cases, taxpayers have a written agreement with the I.R.S. concerning the estimated life of a property. Where such an agreement is in effect, changes in estimated life are prohibited.

To illustrate the effect of a change in estimated life, we can assume that a machine that cost $20,000 was originally estimated to last 20 years and that a $2,000 salvage has been used to calculate straight-line depreciation. After ten full years, prior depreciation deductions would amount to $9,000, or

$$\frac{\$20,000 - \$2,000}{20 \text{ years}} \times 10 \text{ years}$$

and the undepreciated cost would be $11,000 (i.e., $20,000 − $9,000). Assume, finally, that unusual wear and tear has reduced the remaining life to just five more years, with the same salvage value of $2,000. Depreciation the eleventh year would be $1,800 [or ($11,000 − $2,000) ÷ 5].

Similar procedures are followed when the accelerated methods are used. For the double-declining-balance method, the straight-line rate is computed based on the *new* estimate. The new rate is doubled and then applied to the undepreciated cost. With the sum-of-the-years'-digits method, change in life is effected very easily by using the decimal equivalent tables based on the remaining life of the property.

Amortization of intangibles

The general provisions of Sec. 167(a) apply to all properties, both tangible and intangible, that have a limited life, but intangibles can be amortized only on a straight-line basis. The life of some intangibles is limited by law (patents, 17 years; copyrights, the life of the author plus 50 years), and the legal life normally serves as a basis for amortization. The lives of some intangibles, such as trademarks and franchises, are sometimes limited by agreements. In still other situations, economic conditions may limit the life of an intangible. In any event, the period used for amortization of the costs should be the economic life of the asset to the taxpayer.

Most costs associated with lease arrangements must also be amortized on a straight-line basis. The cost to a lessee of acquiring a lease is amortized over the term of the lease. Where the lessee constructs depreciable property on leased real estate, the cost is amortized on a straight-line basis over the term of the lease unless the life of the depreciable property is *less* than the term of the lease. In the latter event, the depreciable property is subject to depreciation (as opposed to amortization), and the accelerated methods may be used.

Additional first-year depreciation

Congress further liberalized the deduction for depreciation in 1958 with the allowance of additional first-year depreciation. This new provision was aimed at stimulating the growth of small businesses, an ever popular cause in Congress. Limitations are so severe, in fact, that the provisions have significance only to very small businesses.

In the year of acquisition, an allowance equal to 20 percent of the cost of qualified property may be deducted *in addition* to depreciation deducted under the normal methods. The allowance is applicable only to the first $10,000 of cost to each taxpayer ($20,000 on a joint return). Thus, the additional first-year allowance cannot exceed $2,000 ($4,000 on a joint return). Where a taxpayer owns several businesses, the limit applies to the taxpayer, not to each business. A corporation, being one taxpayer, is also subject to the $10,000 limit. For years after 1975, the Tax Reform Act of 1976 also treats partnerships as a single taxpayer for this purpose. Thus, only $10,000 of qualified cost incurred by the partnership is passed through to the partners.

To qualify for the deduction, the property must be *tangible, personal* property that is acquired (new or used) after 1957 and has an estimated useful life of at least six years from the date of acquisition. Note that real estate and intangible assets do not qualify for the deduction. Nor does the allowance apply to property acquired from certain "related parties" as specified by statute.

The additional first-year allowance is calculated before computation of regular depreciation. To illustrate, assume that a single individual acquires qualified property at a cost of $25,000. If the taxpayer elects to do so, a first-year allowance of $2,000 is deducted, even if the acquisition is made on the last day of his taxable year. The remaining $23,000 is then subject to regular depreciation under the normal rules. If the cost of the qualified property were $8,000, the allowance would be $1,600 and the remaining $6,400 would be subject to regular depreciation.

THE CLASS LIFE SYSTEM

Since the adoption of the accelerated methods in 1954, there have been two important changes in depreciation policy and rules. In 1962, the Kennedy administration introduced a system referred to as Depreciation Guidelines. Under this system, Bulletin F, which gave estimated lives for thousands of specific properties, was replaced by a set of guideline lives for a limited number of very broad classes of assets. Under the Guidelines, a single life is used for "cement manufacture," "manufacturing-aerospace industry," "office furniture, fixtures, machines, and equipment," etc. The useful lives suggested by the Guidelines were "30 to 40 percent shorter than those suggested in Bulletin F and 15 percent shorter, on the average, than the useful lives actually being used at the time the new procedure was released."[8]

In early 1971, the Nixon administration introduced another innovation, titled the Asset Depreciation Range (ADR) System. This new system permitted a taxpayer to elect any estimated useful life that fell within the accepted range, which was 20 percent less to 20 percent greater than the Guideline lives. There is an element of "double-think" in this proposal, because the clear expectation was that most taxpayers would use the shortest life permitted in the range. The ADR System contained several other innovations intended primarily to reduce controversies between taxpayers and the Internal Revenue Service.

Following the announcement of ADR, some questions were raised about whether the administration had the power to initiate changes in procedures

such as those included in the ADR System. To clear the air, Congress adopted the new system in the Revenue Act of 1971, but with some modifications. Perhaps as a show of legislative independence, the procedures were given a new name, the Class Life System. In any event, the basic law itself now includes the major features of the Guidelines and the ADR System, but under the new name. The term "ADR System" is still commonly used.

In 1977 the Treasury Department issued Revenue Procedure 77-10, which changed the definitions for some classes of assets and established new class lives for several classes. Generally, the new class lives are longer than those previously allowed. A taxpayer who uses the lives specified in the Guidelines can avoid controversy with the I.R.S. However, taxpayers are entitled to use a life that represents the *economic* life of the property for each taxpayer. The "engineering" life is not relevant, and in many cases lives shorter than those in the Guidelines can be justified.

General rules for class life system

As instructed by Congress, the Treasury is to establish a limited number of broad industry classes of assets. In addition, there will be broad general classes of assets that apply to all industries, such as office fixtures and equipment, transportation equipment, and others. The Treasury is also to establish a single class life for all assets in each broad class and to revise these lives as conditions warrant. For a beginning point, Congress anticipated that the classes used and the class lives would be similar to those used under the Guidelines issued in 1962 and that additional classes and changes in lives would be made based on future studies.

Under the ADR System contrived by the administration, all assets would be covered except buildings and their structural components. However, Congress included buildings in the Class Life System with a special rule that lives for buildings that are shorter than the old Guideline lives could be used by taxpayers until new, more realistic lives (read as *shorter*) could be established for assets in these classes. The 20 percent range does not apply to buildings.

The Class Life System can be elected only for assets placed in service after 1970. To qualify, the asset must be used predominantly within the United States, which means it must be physically located in the United States for more than 50 percent of the

---

[8]Joint Economic Committee, *op. cit.*, p. 91.

time. The election is made annually and it covers all qualified assets placed in service by the taxpayer during the year. If used property accounts for more than 10 percent of the cost of property placed in service during a year, the taxpayer may elect the Class Life System for the new property and depreciate the used property under regular rules. He or she may also elect the new system for both new and used even when the used is more than 10 percent of the total.

The *benefit* of the election is that the taxpayer may use any estimated life within the acceptable range. Practically, this means he or she can use a life 20 percent less than that specified for the class. In addition, once the election is made, neither the taxpayer nor the I.R.S. can change the life used for the assets acquired that year. This inflexibility may or may not work to the taxpayer's advantage, depending primarily on the rate of technological change in the industry. One definite *disadvantage* of the system is the amount of detailed records that must be maintained in order to comply with the procedural requirements connected with the election.

Procedural requirements

Taxpayers may elect the Class Life System on an annual basis. For this reason, for years when the system is used, assets acquired must be grouped by their appropriate class in "vintage" accounts that show the year of acquisition. For example, as a minimum requirement, a taxpayer using the system must have an account for each class for each year.

Rules for the new system specify that the life chosen from the range for each class is treated as the estimated useful life for all purposes. Thus, if the life chosen is less than three years, accelerated depreciation cannot be used and salvage value of 10 percent of the asset's cost cannot be ignored. In addition, the estimated life is used to compute the investment credit, which is discussed in Chapter 17. In some cases, election of the shorter life under the Class Life System will decrease the amount of the investment credit.

If the Class Life System is elected, the taxpayer must use one of two permissible conventions for treatment of acquisitions during the year. First, the half-year convention, which assumes that all assets acquired during the year are placed in service on June 30, may be used. An alternative convention permits a full year of depreciation for all acquisitions placed in service before June 30 but allows no depreciation for assets placed in service after June 30. As

with the Class Life System generally, the taxpayer may elect the most favorable convention each year.

Election of the Class Life System does not affect the election of depreciation methods. Thus, any method can be used, subject to the general limitations on the use of accelerated methods and the restrictions on the use of accelerated methods for real estate imposed by the Reform Act of 1969.

The treatment of retirements of assets from a class life is also specified when the new system is used. All retirements are divided into two categories, ordinary and extraordinary. The rules define extraordinary retirements as those arising from casualties or from the cessation, termination, or disposition of a business, process, or facility. All retirements that are not extraordinary are ordinary. Thus sales and other dispositions in the ordinary course of a business will be ordinary retirements.

For ordinary retirements, no gain or loss is recognized. Any proceeds, such as sales price, are added to the depreciation reserve for that class. For extraordinary retirements, gain or loss is recognized, but subject to the general limitations on such recognition (see Part Seven of text). Recognized gains and losses are treated in the manner described in Part Six (capital, Sec. 1231, etc.). These rules may be disadvantageous to taxpayers in some instances. Most retirements will be ordinary, and this means that losses on such retirements otherwise allowed as ordinary deductions will not be allowed when the new system is used.

Percentage repair allowance

One objective of the new system is the reduction of disputes between the I.R.S. and taxpayers. For example, once the life from the acceptable range is selected, neither party may change it or question it. Another perennial source of conflict is over the distinction between capital expenditures and ordinary repairs. The new rules contain a unique provision to reduce these disputes when the system is used.

Taxpayers who elect the Class Life System may also elect to use new percentage repair-allowance rules. Under these rules, all additions, improvements, and repairs, with the exception of "excluded additions," are deductible currently up to the allowed percentage for the asset class in question. The Treasury has established "repair" percentages for classes in Rev. Proc. 77-10. To illustrate these rules, assume a taxpayer has a $200,000 investment in assets in a class, the amount of investment being measured by the unadjusted basis of the assets.

Assume further that the repair percentage allowed is 6 percent. The taxpayer may deduct actual expenditures up to $12,000 for repairs, additions, etc., provided there are no "excluded additions," and the I.R.S. cannot question the deduction. Amounts spent in excess of the allowed percentage are "property improvements" and must be accounted for in a separate vintage account. With careful planning, the expenditures can generally be timed to "fit" the prescribed percentage.

This repair-allowance rule effectively narrows the definition of capital expenditures for taxpayers who elect the new system. "Excluded additions" must always be treated as capital expenditures and accounted for in separate vintage accounts. "Excluded additions" are capital expenditures (under old rules) that *substantially* increase the productivity of a property over its productivity when first acquired, that modify a property for a substantially different use, or that are made to acquire a new identifiable property. A substantial increase in productivity is one that increases the capacity by more than 25 percent. This definition of "excluded additions" is much narrower than the definition of capital expenditures discussed in Chapter 6.

DEPRECIATION RULES AND TAX PLANNING

The addition of the accelerated methods to the tax law in 1954 either created, or enhanced the value of, certain tax shelters for affluent taxpayers with large amounts of ordinary income from salaries, professional fees, and other sources. A most popular shelter is real estate. A brief description of how the real estate shelter works will clarify the importance of accelerated depreciation to the plan.

Take the case of a physician who has $150,000 ordinary income from his medical practice each year. The doctor undertakes the development of an apartment complex. Prior to the Tax Reform Act of 1976, an election could be made under Sec. 266 to deduct interest, taxes, and other carrying charges during the construction period as well as "points" or "front-end" interest on the mortgage loan. The deductions created sizable losses even before the project produced any rental income. As explained in Chapters 6 and 13, these costs must now be capitalized and amortized. While these reforms reduced the tax attractiveness of a real estate venture, they by no means ended their usefulness in tax planning, as explained below.

Because of a high personal income, the doctor is in a position to obtain a large mortgage. When the property is placed in use, the doctor elects an accelerated method of depreciation. The high interest, combined with the accelerated depreciation, causes the property to show a sizable loss for tax purposes during the early years, even though the cash flow from the project may be positive (depending on the economic wisdom of the project). This loss is offset against the doctor's ordinary income with a most beneficial impact on the annual tax bill. At some point in the future, when the project begins to show a tax profit, the doctor may wish to dispose of this property and start again. Any disposition of the property, however, is likely to create a sizable amount of ordinary income in the year of disposition. Note that the time value of money is working for the taxpayer: The losses reduce taxes now even though an equivalent amount of taxes must be paid later. Finally, careful tax planning can reduce the ordinary income and increase the capital gains when the project is sold.

The changes made by the 1978 Act generally enhance the value of real estate shelters such as the one just described. First, the capital gain realized on the eventual sale of the apartment complex is taxed at lower rates under the new law. (See Part Six for details). Second, the capital gain from sale of the project does not reduce the doctor's ordinary income, which is subject to the 50 percent maximum tax on earned income, as explained in Chapter 29. Indeed, the 1978 Act generally increases the value of all tax plans that convert ordinary income into capital gains such as this real estate investment.

REPORTING DEPRECIATION DEDUCTIONS

The place and manner of reporting depreciation varies widely, depending on the type of taxable entity involved as well as the depreciation system used. For an individual in a trade or business as a proprietor, depreciation of the business assets are reported on Schedule C (Form 1040) at part C-3. For individuals with rental properties, depreciation is reported on Schedule E (Form 1040). For farmers, both individuals and corporations, Schedule F for Forms 1040 and 1120 provides a place for reporting depreciation. For nonfarm corporations, a part of Form 1120 is provided for depreciation. Often the space provided on the schedules and forms just mentioned is inadequate. The I.R.S. provides a special form with more space, Form 4562, which can be used by all taxpayers.

PROBLEMS

1. One critical variable in the calculation of depreciation is the "estimated life" of the depreciable asset. Assume, for purposes of this discussion, that the "actual" life of an asset could be scientifically determined to be *exactly* 10 years (that is, at the stroke of midnight, 10 years after manufacture, this particular asset would vanish into dust). Would the estimated life for the purchaser of that particular asset (assuming that he or she purchased it on the day the manufacturing process was completed) necessarily be 10 years? Explain.

2. The depreciation deduction for tax purposes often exceeds depreciation expense reported for financial accounting purposes. Cite three Code provisions that help to explain these differences. What reasons can be given in support of the different treatments for tax and accounting purposes?

3. On January 3 of the current year, Jed Clampitt purchased a new machine to be used on his farm. The Class Life System provides a life of 10 years for such farm machinery, and Jed agrees that 10 years is a reasonable life estimate. The machine cost Jed $28,000 and has an estimated salvage value of $3,000. Jed files a joint return on a calendar-year basis. Given these facts, and assuming no other purchases of depreciable machinery, what is the maximum depreciation deduction Clampitt can claim on this machine if he does not elect the Class Life System:
   a. For the current year?
   b. For next year? (Assume he claimed a maximum this year.)
   Support your answers with detailed calculations.

4. On which of the following properties could a taxpayer claim a depreciation deduction?
   a. Personal residence.
   b. A building used in business.
   c. The land on which the business building is located.
   d. A former residence, which the taxpayer now rents to another.
   e. A car used 25 percent of the time for personal reasons and 75 percent of the time for business purposes.
   f. A building leased from another taxpayer. (This building is used in a business.)
   g. A capital expenditure on a leased building. (For example, the addition of a new wing on an old, leased building.) On termination of the lease, the capital improvement would revert to the owner of the old building.

5. Explain what makes the accelerated depreciation methods advantageous to most taxpayers. Under what conditions might accelerated depreciation be a distinct disadvantage?

6. How do the class lives differ from those specified in Bulletin F? What purpose did the Treasury have for developing the class lives?

7. Four different methods by which we might account for the cost of an asset that will benefit more than one accounting period are listed below. Give an example of each that illustrates the use of this alternative in federal income taxation. If financial and tax accounting treat a particular item differently, explain a possible reason for the different treatments.
   a. Deduct entire cost when incurred.
   b. Deduct nothing until asset is disposed of; then calculate gain or loss.
   c. Select an estimated life and "write off" the cost of the asset in a consistent manner over that period of time.
   d. Select an arbitrary percentage of income produced by the property as a measure of the property "consumed" during that period.

8. On January 3, this year, McIntosh purchased some machinery for use in her incorporated laundry business. Cost of the machinery was $21,000, and its useful life is estimated as 10 years. Estimated salvage value at the end of its useful life is $4,000. McIntosh wishes to take the maximum depreciation possible as early in the asset's life as possible. What will be her maximum depreciation deduction in each of the next five years?

9. Thomas acquired a machine for use in his business. The asset was purchased on January 3, this year, at a cost of $24,000. Estimated life is six years, and estimated salvage is $900. Prepare a depreciation schedule for the six years of the asset's life, assuming that Thomas wishes to accelerate the depreciation as much as possible. Thomas is married and files a joint return with his wife, and this is the only asset purchased during the year.

10. Indicate whether each of the following statements is true or false.

   a. A taxpayer may switch from the double-declining method of depreciation to the straight-line method without approval of the I.R.S.

   b. A taxpayer may switch from the straight-line method of depreciation to the double-declining-balance method without prior approval of the I.R.S.

   c. All assets acquired after 1969 are subject to a maximum depreciation charge based on the 150-percent declining-balance method.

   d. A taxpayer may use the double-declining method in depreciating used residential property acquired in 1970.

   e. A taxpayer may use the double-declining method in depreciating new residential property acquired after 1970.

   f. A taxpayer may use the double-declining method in depreciating a new hotel built in 1970.

   g. A corporation may not take the special first-year depreciation charge.

   h. A taxpayer may apply the double-declining method in amortizing the cost of an intangible asset.

   i. Taxpayer acquired an asset for $40,000. Its estimated useful life is five years, and its estimated salvage value is $8,500. The maximum depreciable base of the property is $31,500, if taxpayer elects to use the straight-line method.

11. List the requirements that must be met before the double-declining-balance (or sum-of-the-years'-digits) method may be used:

   a. If the property was acquired before 1970.

   b. If the property was acquired after 1969.

12. What requirements must be met to qualify for the additional first-year depreciation? What are the limits on this allowance?

13. Taxpayer, a manufacturing corporation reporting on the calendar year basis, placed new equipment in service in 19x1 as follows:

Date	Equipment	Cost
June 15, 19x1	Lathes	$10,000
October 1, 19x1	Drill press	5,000

Taxpayer elected the ADR System that prescribes a single class with a life of five years. Taxpayer also elected to use the double-declining-balance method. It grouped these assets into a single vintage account. Compute taxpayer's depreciation for 19x1, assuming it uses the half-year convention. What are the principal disadvantages of electing the ADR System?

14. Mitchell Construction Corporation is engaged in road construction. In 19x1, the corporation received a large contract that will require the acquisition of approximately $500,000 in new equipment. The controller is considering the use of the

Class Life System. The new equipment of $500,000 is all in the same guideline class with a life of 10 years. The company is unable, in the controller's opinion, to justify a shorter life. The company will also acquire some miscellaneous properties, such as office equipment, but these items will have only a small cost compared to the construction equipment.

a. List the disadvantages of electing the Class Life System under the circumstances described.

b. If we assume the company wishes to make the purchase as late as possible during the year, what is the latest date the new equipment can be placed in service to get the full benefits of depreciation for the current year?

c. If the equipment is placed in service on June 29, 19x1, and we assume the company uses the double-declining balance method, compute the amount of additional depreciation the Class Life System will produce in the year of acquisition compared to an item-by-item accounting. Use all methods available to increase depreciation in the current year.

d. In January 19x3, the corporation sells for $39,000 equipment included in the $500,000 acquisition of 19x1. Explain how this disposition is treated under the Class Life System. Contrast this to the tax treatment if the corporation had *not* elected the Class Life System.

15. International Machines, Inc. is considering the investment of $1,000,000 in two alternative projects. In Project A, the cost of the investment can be recovered in five years using double-declining balance depreciation. In Project B, the cost must be amortized over 10 years on a straight-line basis. Both projects are expected to yield the same amount of net cash flow before depreciation, the present value of which is $940,000 using a 12-percent internal rate of return. The corporation's marginal rate is 46 percent. Compute the amount of the economic advantage arising from the rapid capital recovery of Project A as contrasted to Project B.

16. For the assets listed below, indicate the allowable method of depreciation that will result in the most rapid capital recovery, including additional first-year allowance. Assume the assets are used in a trade or business.

a. Copyright: Taxpayer can justify a 20-year life.

b. New office building: 30-year life

c. Building constructed on leased property by lessee: Life of building is 30 years, and the term of the lease is 20 years.

d. Same as part c, except the term of lease is 50 years.

e. Used factory building: 20-year life

f. New office furniture: 10-year life

g. Used adding machine: 5-year life

17. When a taxpayer uses the double-declining balance method, he or she must switch to the straight-line method at some point in the asset's life.

a. Why is this change of methods necessary?

b. In what year would the change be made if the estimated life is 6 years? 8 years? 20 years?

SUPPLEMENTAL PROBLEMS

18. Jim Coffee constructed an apartment complex under an FHA loan. Total cost of the project was $2,500,000. Some apartments were complete in January 19x1, and Jim began renting them as they were completed. In April about 40

percent of the completed apartments were rented. Also in April, Coffee received an attractive offer for the apartments, an offer that would mean a sizable gain for him. The offer was conditioned on the fact that the apartments would be "new" to the purchaser.

    a. Why is the condition "new" important in arriving at the sales price?

    b. Can the prospective purchaser treat the apartments as new for depreciation purposes?

19. The two basic methods of stimulating the economy are a decrease in taxes, which increases aggregate demand, and acceleration of capital recovery (or the investment credit), which increases the marginal efficiency of capital. Using materials in your library, determine, if possible, which approach is more effective as a short-run stimulant. In your research, consider the period beginning in 1960.

20. Taxpayer is an orthodontist with an annual net profit from the practice of $200,000. He has complained to you about his high tax bill and has asked your advice about how he might lower it. In talking with some colleagues, he discovered that a number of them had invested in office buildings during the 1960s. Advise him on a plan to save taxes.

21. James Realty Company is considering the renovation of two apartment houses. Each project will require an expenditure of $500,000. One project would qualify as low-income housing, and the renovation costs could be recovered over a five-year period. The cost of the other project could only be recovered over a 20-year period. Calculate the tax advantage of the low-income project over the other project, assuming that the company uses a 10 percent rate of return to evaluate projects and that its marginal tax rate is 46 percent. Also assume that the straight-line recovery will be used for both projects.

22. Recently, a national accounting firm issued a "white" paper that dealt in part with the rate of capital recovery in the United States compared to that in Great Britain, Germany, Japan, and our other major trading partners. With one minor exception, recovery was much more rapid in the other countries than allowed by U.S. tax laws.

    a. What conclusion do you suppose the firm reached?

    b. Relate your answer in part a to the international trading position of the United States and the impact of such a trading position on the value of Eurodollars.

Exchange between Rep. Joe Waggoner (D., La.) and Rep. Otis Pike (D., N. Y.)
Mr. Pike: And the special-purpose structure is a pigpen or a chicken coop; is that a fair statement?
Mr. Waggoner: The gentleman is streetwise in New York. I hope I am streetwise in hog and chicken country. Sometimes we jokingly refer to them as "chicken coops" and "pigpens."
Mr. Pike: When the gentleman is not jokingly referring to them, does he really call them "unitary hog-raising structures?"
Wall Street Journal (Dec. 7, 1978)

the investment credit and other incentives

The intention behind liberalized depreciation discussed in the preceding chapter is to encourage investment in buildings and equipment and thereby to assist in maintaining the full employment of resources. This acceleration of the depreciation deduction encourages investment solely because it reduces taxes in the years immediately following a capital investment, thus increasing the present value of the income-tax effect of capital recovery. In this chapter, other provisions of the law aimed at encouraging specific types of investment are examined. Some of the incentives discussed below (for example, the possibility of deducting research and development costs as incurred) are based on the same principle as liberalized depreciation—that is, on the acceleration of capital recovery.

When the reasoning applied to the acceleration of capital recovery is pushed to the limit, the result is the immediate deduction of the cost of an investment. Sometimes the entire cost of an investment may be deducted currently because it is impossible to determine how much of the cost is a current expense and how much represents the purchase price of an asset. For some investments, the future period benefited (the estimated useful life) is very indefinite. Advertising affords a good example of assets of this type, and advertising costs are univer-

sally charged to expense in the year they are paid or incurred. In other cases, an immediate deduction may be taken because Congress wishes to provide an investment incentive. Two such provisions are discussed in this chapter: research and development (R&D) costs and the cost of developing agricultural land. The 1969 Reform Act and subsequent acts added several new incentives with limited scope based on timing of capital recovery. The most important of these are for child-care facilities and pollution control.

Before discussing these other incentives in the law, which are based on the timing of capital recovery, we shall consider a wholly different kind of incentive for new investments, an incentive whereby the federal government effectively pays a portion of the cost of certain investments. This is the investment credit.

THE INVESTMENT CREDIT

The Kennedy administration added two important investment incentives to the tax law in 1962. One was the guidelines discussed in Chapter 16, which accelerated capital recovery by shortening estimated lives. The second is an idea borrowed from the tax laws of several European countries, a tax credit for qualified investment. Unlike accelerated capital recovery, the full impact of the investment credit is felt in the year of acquisition. The taxpayer is allowed to subtract the credit directly from gross tax liability just like other tax payments.

No provision in the history of our income-tax law can match the investment credit for its record in being added to and removed from the law. Following its original passage in 1962, the credit was "suspended" in the fall of 1966 only to be reinstated in March of 1967. The Reform Act of 1969 repealed the credit effective in 1969, but the Revenue Act of 1971 reenacted it with only a few modifications. In every case, the investment credit was suspended or repealed to combat inflation and then reinstated or reenacted to encourage investment. Congress and the Ford administration expressed their faith in the ability of the credit to stimulate investment by an increase in the rate of the credit in the Tax Reduction Act of 1975. Most recently, the Energy Tax Act of 1978 increased the credit allowed for investments that will conserve energy. Thus, while the credit has been an uncertain part of the tax landscape in the past, some evidence exists that, as of now, it is a fairly permanent provision.

Present law

The investment incentive added to the law in 1962 is a direct credit against the tax liability. The credit allowed each year is computed by applying an arbitrary percentage to the "qualified" investment made by the taxpayer during the year. This incentive is a *credit* subtracted from the gross tax to arrive at the net tax liability.

The credit allowed has no effect on the subsequent depreciation deduction. In its original form, the investment credit had to be subtracted from the taxpayer's adjusted basis in the property and therefore reduced subsequent depreciations. Because of administrative confusion, this rule was repealed in 1964, and now there is no reduction in basis or in depreciation. In effect, then, the taxpayer can shift a portion of the cost of a "qualified" investment to the federal government.

This investment credit is also new to the American experience because the incentive for investment is directed toward certain properties only; not all investments in assets to be used in a trade or business qualify. Finally, Congress was compelled to

place limits on the credit to avoid short-run inequities, and these limits necessitated a carryover rule to improve long-run equity.

RATES FOR THE CREDIT   Throughout its history before 1975, the rate for the investment credit has been 7 percent of the cost of qualified properties. The rate, as one would expect, was the result of a series of compromises between the administration, the House, and the Senate. Due to the depth of the recession experienced in late 1974, the rate was increased from 7 to 10 percent by the 1975 Reduction Act. The 10 percent rate was only a temporary measure until the 1978 Act made it permanent. In addition, the 1978 Act provides that "energy properties," a term defined below, will be entitled to an *additional* 10 percent if such properties are placed in service after October 1, 1978, and before December 31, 1982. The Windfall Profit Tax Act of 1980 further increased the credit on a few "energy properties" from 10 to 15 percent. The 1975 Reduction Act also extended the 10 percent rate to public utilities because of the severe needs for new investments in this area. Previously, public utility properties enjoyed only a 4 percent credit. Finally, present law permits corporations an additional 1 percent (and in some cases 1.5 percent) where the taxes saved are contributed by the corporation to employee stock ownership plans (ESOP). This additional credit for ESOP is also available through 1980. To summarize, the rate of the credit may be as low as 10 percent and as high as 26½ percent under the present schedule, which is:

10 percent for investments in "regular" qualified property (a permanent provision)
10 to 15 percent for "energy properties" acquired before 1982 (1985 for a few properties)
1 percent or 1½ percent for ESOP contributions through 1980

TABLE **17-1**
THE INVESTMENT CREDIT: SCHEDULE TO DETERMINE QUALIFIED INVESTMENT

If the estimated useful life is:	The percentage of cost included in qualified investment is:
Less than 3 years	0
3 years or more but less than 5 years	33⅓
5 years or more but less than 7 years	66⅔
7 years or more	100

The application of a single rate to all qualified properties would result in various inequities. Most of the assets used in some industries—the trucking industry, for example—have a relatively short life, whereas some industries—say, the steel industry—use assets with relatively long lives. If a single rate were used for all assets without regard to estimated life, industries whose primary investments are in assets with a short life would have a definite advantage. Frequent replacement would increase their investment credit. To reduce this inequity, the portion of the cost of a qualified *property* included in "qualified" *investment* depends on the estimated useful life of the property according to the schedule shown in Table 17-1. These percentages are applied to the cost of qualified property to determine the qualified investment; then the rate is applied to total qualified investment. The estimated useful life used for this purpose must in every case be the same as that adopted for depreciation.

An example should clarify the computation. Assume that the taxpayer purchased four assets that qualify for the credit during the taxable year:

	Cost	Estimated life (years)
Automobile	$ 5,000	2
Delivery truck	4,500	4
Office machine	6,000	6
Plant equipment	10,000	10
Total cost	$25,500	

Total *cost* of the qualified *property* is $25,500. The base for the credit, however, is qualified *investment*, computed as follows:

	Cost	Applicable percentage	Qualified investment
Automobile	$ 5,000	0	$ 0
Delivery truck	4,500	33⅓	1,500
Office machine	6,000	66⅔	4,000
Plant equipment	10,000	100	10,000
			$15,500

The tentative investment credit for the year, using the 10 percent rate, would be $1,550.

The credit may also be obtained by applying the percentages for the portion of the qualified cost to the 10 percent rate for the credit and then applying the resulting percentage to the total cost. This technique is illustrated below, using the facts for the above example and the 10 percent rate for the credit:

	Cost	Effective rate	Credit
Automobile	$ 5,000	0	$ 0
Delivery truck	4,500	3⅓% (⅓ of 10%)	150
Office machine	6,000	6⅔% (⅔ of 10%)	400
Plant equipment	10,000	10% (100% of 10%)	1,000
		Total credit	$1,550

Note that this approach will only work where the "regular" 10 percent rate applies.

The relationship of the amount of the credit to the estimated useful life of the property created a unique challenge for the lawmakers. What happens when a taxpayer declares the useful life of a property to be seven years, takes the full 10 percent credit, and then sells the property after only four years of use? If the taxpayer had originally estimated a life of only four years, the actual holding period, only 33⅓ percent of the asset's cost would have been included in qualified investment; the credit would have been only 3⅓ percent of the total cost, as opposed to the 10 percent claimed. The equitable solution, and the one adopted by Congress, is a repayment or recapture of the portion of the credit not earned from holding the asset. When property is disposed of by sale, exchange, gift, or involuntary conversion before the expiration of the estimated life used to compute the credit, the difference between the credit actually taken and the credit based on the actual holding period must be added back to the tax in the year of the disposition.

To illustrate, let us assume that the plant equipment in the preceding illustration (which cost $10,000 and had an estimated life of 10 years) is sold after six years. The credit taken at acquisition was $1,000; that is, 10 percent of the total cost. If the *actual* life had been used, the credit would have been only $667 (or $6,667 × 10 percent). The difference of $333 is recaptured in the year the asset is sold. That is, $333 must be added to the gross tax liability in the year of sale. Incidentally, no interest is charged by the government on this difference. Note, however, that the use of a longer life to increase the credit, even though it may be partially recaptured later, will reduce the depreciation deductions, resulting in a more undesirable effect than an interest charge.

QUALIFIED PROPERTY   The general purpose of the credit, as opposed to the energy tax credits explained later, is to encourage investment by businesses, thereby increasing the rate of economic growth and assuring the full employment of resources. But not all the investments made by businesses increase the nation's productive capacity and provide employment for materials and labor. In some cases, an investment may have little or no effect on the rate of economic activity. An investment in land is a good example; the transaction merely increases the liquidity of the seller (although other transactions that have substantial economic effect may follow the land transaction). Many security transactions have little or no effect on productive activity. Similarly, construction of a new office building in Manhattan by a steel company will not increase the capacity of that company to produce steel or directly improve the efficiency of its plant. To encourage such transactions that have only an indirect effect on our economic well-being would not further the basic policy of government. Thus, Congress was faced with the task of writing a law that would encourage investments having the maximum economic impact without granting a tax privilege to other kinds of investment. It solved the problem by granting the credit only to investments in *qualified* property. Qualified property is defined as follows:

1. Tangible, personal property subject to the depreciation deduction.
2. Tangible, real property subject to depreciation if used as an integral part of manufacturing, production, extraction, or furnishing of a utility service, or if constituting a research or storage facility for manufacturing, etc. With the exception of the rehabilitation cost of certain buildings, qualified property does not include the cost of a building or its structural components.
3. Elevators and escalators if built or acquired new after June 30, 1963.

The terms "real" and "personal" are used here in their legal sense. Real property is land and things permanently attached to land, while personal property includes movable tangible items as well as all intangible property rights. The principal assets excluded, as suggested above, are land, intangible assets (including securities), and buildings. The tangible, real property (item 2, above) is property directly connected with production but classed as realty or fixtures under state law. Examples are pipelines, blast furnaces, and electric transmission lines.

The above definition specifies the properties that qualify for the "regular" 10 percent credit (and the ESOP addition). Properties that qualify for the new 10 percent energy credit are defined later in this chapter.

Since the passage of the first investment credit in 1962, taxpayers have interpreted the definition of "qualified" in the broadest possible way. The I.R.S., as one would expect, has resisted these efforts by restricting the definition. Congress has often revised the statute, generally in favor of taxpayers. As a result, the general definition above must be applied in the light of numerous statutory provisions dealing with relatively narrow classes of assets. A listing of some of the more important of the detailed specific rules follows:

1. Livestock, except horses, qualify for the credit if used for work, breeding, or dairy purposes. Special rules apply where livestock have been disposed of and substantially identical livestock are acquired within a one-year period. Only the additional cost of the new herd (above the sales price of the old herd) is subject to the credit.
2. The credit is generally not available for furniture and other personal property used in the business of furnishing lodging facilities. Major exceptions to this rule are furnishings for hotels used predominately by transients and coin-operated vending, washing, and drying machines installed in lodging facilities.
3. Single-purpose structures used for livestock or horticulture qualify for the credit. Examples of single-purpose structures are dairy barns used for milking, hen housing used for layers, and greenhouses used to raise plants for resale. Congress included these structures as qualified properties in the 1978 Act to end a long controversy between the I.R.S. and taxpayers. The I.R.S. had used an "appearance" test, holding that these structures looked like buildings and should therefore be treated as buildings not subject to the credit.
4. Amounts spent after October 31, 1978 to rehabilitate buildings that have been in service for at least 20 years qualify for the credit. This rule, adopted by the 1978 Tax Act to encourage the use of older structures, extends to all work on older buildings provided the improvement has an estimated life of at least 5 years and provided not more than 25 percent of the structure's exterior walls are replaced. The credit, of course, is not available for properties held for personal use, such as a residence.
5. Some tangible personal property is ineligible

for the credit if it is deemed to be wasteful in terms of energy consumption. Portable air conditioners, portable space heaters, and certain boilers fueled by oil and gas fall in this category.

Special rules also apply to assets used outside the United States, to properties manufactured abroad, and to films and television tapes.

The "regular" credit applies primarily to property that is *new in use*. The maximum aggregate cost of used property that a taxpayer could treat as qualified property has historically been $50,000 per year. In 1975, the limit for used property was raised temporarily to $100,000, and this increased amount was made permanent in 1978. The $100,000 limit on used property applies to the total cost of qualified property, not the base of the tax. If a taxpayer pays $150,000 for a used property with a life of four years, $100,000 of the cost is taken into account but the qualified investment is only $33,333, the cost of the qualified property times $33\frac{1}{3}$ percent. If more than one used property is acquired in a given year and the cost of all used properties exceeds $100,000, the taxpayer may assign the $100,000 limit to those properties with the longest lives.

The investment credit is generally available only in the year when qualified property is placed in service. In some cases, however, credit may be taken as progress payments are made on long-term projects such as the construction of a nuclear power generator. For this purpose, a project is long term if it requires at least two years to complete. This measure is intended primarily to benefit public utilities.

LIMITATIONS AND CARRYOVER PROVISIONS The tentative (unadjusted) investment credit is subject to certain maximum limits; for example, it cannot reduce the gross tax liability below zero. Congress has also placed an additional maximum limitation on the investment credit in any one year. The limit is based on the taxpayer's gross tax after subtracting the foreign tax credit, credit for the elderly, and after making certain other adjustments. For 1978 and earlier years, the investment credit can offset the entire gross tax (after the above adjustments) up to $25,000 and 50 percent of the gross tax in excess of $25,000. A corporation, for example, with a gross tax of $70,000 for 1978 and no foreign tax credit or other adjustments, would be limited to an investment credit of $47,500 [$25,000 + 0.5 ($70,000 − $25,000)].

Note that this limit is based entirely on the gross tax; the amount of the tentative credit does not affect the computation.

The Tax Act of 1978 increases the above limit. After 1978, the credit still offsets the first $25,000 of gross tax, dollar for dollar. The percentage of gross tax in excess of $25,000 that determines the limit is 60 percent in 1979; 70 percent in 1980; 80 percent in 1981; and finally, 90 percent in 1982 and later years. A corporation with a gross tax of $70,000 would have a limit for 1980 of $56,500 [$25,000 + 0.70 ($70,000 − $25,000)] and for 1982 and later a limit of $65,500 [$25,000 + 0.90 ($70,000 − $25,000)]. (Railroads and public utilities are subject to special limitations.)

Because of the maximum limitation, Congress included a carryback and carryforward provision in the law. It would not be fair to encourage investment and subsequently deny the credit when operations for the year resulted in a loss (and therefore no tax). The portion of the credit not used because of the maximum limitation may be carried back to the three preceding years (beginning with the earliest year) and carried forward to the seven subsequent years. The carryback ordinarily results in a refund of taxes paid in previous years. If the tentative credit is so much larger than the maximum that it is not used up in the investment year *and* the three preceding years, the excess must be carried forward to the next seven years. Naturally, the investment credit for any year (including amounts carried forward from other years) cannot exceed the maximum limit in effect for that year. Where credits from two or more years are carried to the current year, the credits are used in chronological order.

The energy tax credit

The Energy Tax Act of 1978 contained two entirely different kinds of tax credits for taxpayers who invest in energy-saving contrivances. First, the new rules provide for credits on residential energy-saving devices. These credits that apply to the general public are explained in Chapter 8. Second, the law permits an additional investment credit for "energy properties" acquired for use in a business. While these latter provisions are needlessly complicated, the general framework of the "energy" investment credit is simple enough.

The taxpayer who invests in energy properties as defined below is entitled to a 10 percent credit based on the "qualified" cost of such property. The total cost of the property that qualifies for the credit depends on its estimated useful life (less than three years, 0; three and four years, 33⅓ percent; etc.). If the energy property meets the definition of qualified property for the "regular" investment credit, the 10 percent energy credit is *in addition to* the regular credit. Some energy properties, mainly those that are structural components of a building, will only qualify for the 10 percent energy credit.

"Energy properties" are items specified in the law as energy-saving devices that are acquired after October 1, 1978, and before January 1, 1982. The law contains no generic definition of energy properties but instead defines the term by a rather specific listing. A recitation of a few of the properties will give you some idea of what may be on the list: alternative energy properties such as boilers and burners designed to use an energy source other than oil or gas; solar and wind energy properties used to generate electricity or to heat or cool; equipment designed to recycle solid waste; equipment for producing or extracting oil from shale; and equipment used to produce natural gas from geopressural brine. To qualify, energy property must meet certain standards and tests for energy efficiency that will be subsequently set out by the federal government.

The Windfall Profit Tax Act of 1980 increased the energy credit for a few properties. Solar, wind, and geothermal properties are subject to a 15 percent credit, effective for the years 1980 through 1985. That act also expanded the definition of energy property and extended the effective dates for a few properties. Except for solar and wind energy, this 1980 provision will have a very limited impact.

The investment credit for energy properties is subject to limits different from those for the regular investment credit. For purposes of the limits, energy properties are divided into two groups: solar and wind energy properties and other energy properties. The credit for other energy properties, unlike the regular investment credit, offsets 100 percent of the gross tax. The credit for solar and wind energy property offsets 100 percent of the gross tax, and in addition, any credit in excess of the tax is "refundable." To illustrate, a corporation with a gross tax of $100,000 in 1980 has the following tentative credits for that year: regular investment credit, $82,000; investment credit from energy properties other than solar and wind energy properties, $24,000; investment credit from solar and wind energy properties, $15,000. First, the $82,000 regular credit is applied up to the limit of $77,500 [$25,000 + 0.70($100,000

− $25,000)]. The $4,500 excess ($82,000 − $77,500) is not allowed in 1980 but may be carried back (or forward) under the rules explained earlier. Next, the $24,000 credit for energy properties other than solar or wind energy properties is applied up to $22,500, the remaining gross tax ($100,000 less the $77,500 regular credit allowed). The remaining $1,500 ($24,000 less $22,500) is also carried back (or forward). The $15,000 credit for solar and wind energy properties exceeds the gross tax and is refundable.

Impact of the investment credit

When the credit was reenacted in 1971, the Treasury estimated that it would increase investment funds (that is, decrease tax revenues) by $1.5 billion in 1971, by about $3.6 billion in 1972, and slightly more in later years.[1] The increase in the rates in 1975 was estimated to result in about $3.5 billion additional investment funds for the years after 1976.[2] Of these amounts, approximately 80 percent goes to corporations. It is widely believed that these direct tax savings go directly into new investments.

One argument against the structure of the present investment credit is that the definition of qualified property is too narrow, particularly for some industries. For all industries combined, and considering corporations only, property qualifying for the investment credit was only 27.3 percent of total investment in a recent year.[3] In wholesale and retail establishments, only 10.8 percent of total investment qualified; in communications, 60 percent qualified, with other industries falling between these extremes. In 1975, the Ford administration supported a more liberalized credit that would drop the relationship to estimated lives and would remove the 50 percent limitation based on gross tax liability, permitting the credit to offset 100 percent of the liability. In the debates on the Tax Reform Act of 1976, Senator Edward Kennedy proposed an alternative to the present credit that would have given companies an additional credit of 5 percent (over and above the 10 percent credit) for incremental investments over the average investments made for the preceding three

[1] Senate Finance Committee, Report Accompanying H.R. 10947, 92nd Congress, 1st Session (Washington, D.C.: U.S. Government Printing Office, 1971), p. 17.

[2] H.R. 10612, 1st Session, 94th Congress (Washington, D.C.: U.S. Government Printing Office, 1975), p. 18.

[3] The amounts are taken from an address by Frederic W. Hickman, former Assistant Secretary of the Treasury for Tax Policy before the Taxation Division, AICPA, December 9, 1974.

years.[4] Numerous other proposed changes in the credit could also be cited; for example, the Carter proposals relative to inclusion of industrial buildings and increasing the maximum limit to 90 percent of the gross tax. This latter proposal was in fact adopted in the Tax Act of 1978.

Sometimes it seems that no one is really satisfied with the current rules. The many changes since the relatively recent enactment of the credit leads to the conclusion that the present discontent has existed since 1962. The problem is an old one in the formulation of tax policy. We have not as yet devised any reliable means of predicting the effects of a given tax provision on economic activity. The widespread discontent with the present investment credit almost certainly means that we can expect further changes in these rules soon.

RESEARCH AND DEVELOPMENT COSTS

Research and experimentation have been increasingly important to both American industry and the federal government since World War II. Every year, a substantial portion of the national effort is expended in laboratories to discover and develop new theories, processes, and products ranging from the essential to the frivolous. This comparatively recent emphasis on "R&D" is apparent in the growth of annual expenditures for this purpose. It is estimated that, prior to World War II, expenditures for research amounted to less than $1 billion per year, including the amounts spent by industry, government, and institutions. Such expenditures had increased to $5.4 billion in 1953 and to $10 billion in 1957. Industry alone accounted for $3.4 billion in 1953 and $7.2 billion in 1957.[5] Expenditures for R&D continued to grow throughout the 1960s and 1970s. A recent survey conducted by the National Science Foundation projects a growth rate of 3.5 percent per year for industrial R&D expenditures through 1985, when the amount (expressed in 1972 dollars) will reach $17.8 billion. [6] Expenditures by the federal government are also expected to increase through 1985 until the federal R&D budget reaches $19.3 billion (in 1972 dollars).

Rules prior to 1954

From the earliest days of the income tax, expenditures for R&D have received preferential treatment. Precedents were established when the amounts were immaterial, and the precedents were followed when the amounts became substantial because the I.R.S. did not believe that other rules were enforceable.

To be consistent with the tax treatment of other expenditures, the accounting for R&D would be along the following lines: The periodic cost of the laboratory (including the depreciation of the laboratory building and of other fixed capital used in the laboratory) would be allocated among the various research projects in progress during the period. The costs allocated to each project would be deferred until the project was completed. If, at the end of the work, the research proved useless, the costs allocated to it would be deductible as a loss. On the other hand, if the research proved successful, resulting in a new process or product, the cost of the project would be capitalized and depreciated or amortized over the periods benefited by the research.

Several difficulties arise when this ideal is applied to an actual case. First, no one may know whether a given project is worthless. Although research may produce no immediate benefits, it may lead to some new line of inquiry that is productive. At a minimum, if often tells the researcher what will *not* work. Second, it is often impossible to determine what the estimated life of an *idea* is. The product or process may be changed through further research or combined with other products to produce something altogether new. The results of old projects may live on indefinitely making some contribution, albeit small, to future research.[7]

Because of these practical difficulties, the first regulations dealing with R&D, which were issued in 1924, gave the taxpayer the option of either expensing these costs or capitalizing them and charging them off over the period selected by the taxpayer.[8] However, because of a 1926 decision of the Board of Tax Appeals (now the Tax Court), which held that the Bureau did not have the right to give taxpayers this option, the regulations were withdrawn. In the following years, other courts in numerous cases held that research expenditures connected with success-

[4] *Daily Executives' Report,* Bureau of National Affairs, June 9, 1976, p. J-3.

[5] National Science Foundation, *Review of Data on Research and Development* (Washington, D.C.: U.S. Government Printing Office), No. 14, August, 1959, p. 18.

[6] National Science Foundation, *1985 R&D Funding Projections* (Washington, D.C.: U.S. Government Printing Office).

[7] The decision by the FASB, which for all practical purposes adopted tax rules, is evidence that such an august body could not devise rules to solve these inherent difficulties.

[8] For a concise history of the treatment of R&D, see Charles R. Orem, Jr., "Research and Development Costs," *1959 Compendium,* pp. 1111–15.

ful projects resulting in new processes, formulas, or patents were capital expenditures. Despite these decisions, the I.R.S. generally allowed taxpayers to deduct R&D as incurred. In 1952, the Commissioner summarized the I.R.S. position before the Joint Committee on Internal Revenue as follows:

> Research and development expenses usually are a necessary part of most businesses. In the past, the expenses have consistently been charged to expense by the large majority of such taxpayers. The problem of allocating such expenditures to individual projects, so as to write off amounts applicable to failures, is most difficult and would require elaborate accounting procedures. Over a period of years the deduction of such items as expenditures are made does not appear to create a materially different tax result from the capitalization of all such items and the later allowance of deductions for abandoned or worthless projects and processes and the allowance of depreciation on successful ones.[9]

In this statement, the Commissioner went beyond the practical difficulties already mentioned to say that "over a period of years" the tax result is the same. This is true enough, if the time period is sufficiently long. Nevertheless, the income tax is an annual tax, and the advantages of deducting an item now that might otherwise be deducted over a number of years is obvious, assuming that income is adequate to absorb the deduction. If Congress follows even roughly the policy of equating governmental receipts and expenditures, the immediate deduction by industry of very large R&D expenditures means adjustments for the government. Other expenditures have to be reduced, or rates increased, or the tax base of other taxpayers increased to raise the lost revenue. In these circumstances, the tax burden is partly shifted from businesses with R&D expenditures to other taxpayers. Furthermore, the advantages of an immediate deduction of R&D are not uniform even among industrial concerns. Some industries—the drug industry is a classical example—are peculiarly dependent on R&D, and such industries enjoy a greater benefit from a policy of immediate write-off. In short, the immediate deduction of R&D *does* "create a materially different tax result."

The 1954 revision

The treatment of R&D expenditures was one subject considered by Congress in the major revision and reorganization of the Code in 1954. The Treasury Department recommended that taxpayers be allowed the option of treating R&D as a current expense or as a capital expenditure. This recommendation was probably based on the Commissioner's reluctance to undertake the treatment outlined earlier, which would be consistent with other parts of the law. One might have expected Congress to give some thought also to the larger question: Would the shift in the relative tax burden resulting from immediate deduction of R&D be justified by the benefits from such a provision? The record, however, reveals no serious consideration of this question. Congress and virtually all witnesses appearing at the hearings on the 1954 revision were content with a very loose argument containing the following elements: (1) A high rate of expenditure for R&D by American industry is desirable. (2) The immediate deduction of these costs will assure a high rate of expenditure. (3) Everything will come out the same in the long run. There was a complete absence of facts to support this argument, and no estimate was made of the tax revenue to be lost from the new rule. The only dissenting voice was a position statement from the American Federation of Labor read into the record of the hearings before the House Ways and Means Committee. But this statement was a weak dissent, merely arguing that R&D is a capital expenditure and should be treated as such.

Thus, with widespread support, Congress added Sec. 174 to the 1954 Code. Subsection (a) reads as follows:

> (a) Treatment as Expenses.—
> (1) In general.—A taxpayer may treat research or experimental expenditures which are paid or incurred by him during the taxable year in connection with his trade or business as expenses which are not chargeable to capital account. The expenditures so treated shall be allowed as a deduction.
> (2) When method may be adopted.—
> (A) Without consent.—A taxpayer may, without the consent of the Secretary, adopt the method provided in this subsection for his first taxable year—
> (i) which begins after December 31, 1953, and ends after August 16, 1954, and
> (ii) for which expenditures described in paragraph (1) are paid or incurred.

[9] *Ibid.*, p. 1112.

(B) With consent.—A taxpayer may, with the consent of the Secretary, adopt at any time the method provided in this subsection.

(3) Scope.—The method adopted under this subsection shall apply to all expenditures described in paragraph (1). The method adopted shall be adhered to in computing taxable income for the taxable year and for all subsection taxable years unless, with the approval of the Secretary, a change to a different method is authorized with respect to part or all of such expenditures.

Note that the section applies to "research and *experimentation*," not to "research and development." This phrase was used to indicate that the expenditures subject to the election are *laboratory* expenses. This includes, generally, costs incident to the development of an experimental or pilot model, a plant process, a product, a formula, an invention, or the improvement of existing property of the types just mentioned. The term does *not* include expenses of ordinary testing or inspection of materials, of efficiency or management studies, or of market or promotional surveys. The election in Sec. 174(a)(1) applies to expenses incurred directly by the taxpayer and to costs incurred indirectly for research and experimentation actually carried on by another individual or organization. The election to expense costs immediately also applies to costs that result in the issuance of a patent, including even the legal fees of making or perfecting a patent application.

The election allowed in Sec. 174(a)(1) may be adopted by a taxpayer without the consent of the Commissioner provided the election is made for the first taxable year in which the taxpayer incurs R&D expenses. Once made, the election is binding on all future years. Any change of method (except the original election to expense the costs) must be approved by the Commissioner.

This provision allows taxpayers to deduct as an expense many costs that might otherwise be capital items, but the treatment cannot be extended to cover the cost of acquiring capital assets used in research and experimentation. Thus, the acquisition costs of land, buildings, and equipment used in the research program must be capitalized. The periodic depreciation allowed on such assets, however, is an R&D expense and is included with all similar costs for purposes of the election.

Taxpayers who do not wish to expense R&D costs currently may treat them as deferred expenses and amortize them over future periods. The minimum period for amortization is 60 months, beginning with the month during which the taxpayer first realized benefits from the expenditures; longer periods may be used if desired. (The 60-month period for amortization of deferred R&D does not apply to the cost of capital assets used in R&D but only to the periodic depreciation assigned to successful projects and deferred under this election.) This election, once made, is binding on future years, and a change of method must be approved by the Commissioner. Where the taxpayer elects to defer R&D, and a patent is subsequently issued, the costs must be amortized over the life of the patent, normally 17 years.

No statistics are available on the exact amounts deducted each year under the provisions of Sec. 174. General information on the level of R&D expenditures suggests that the tax deduction is substantial relative to the net income of some business concerns. Whether the Sec. 174(a) election has resulted in an increase in the research activities in industry, and has thereby promoted the general welfare, remains an open question. Nevertheless, Congress and most taxpayers seem content with the present law, and most proposals for revision have been aimed at further liberalization of the rules.

INCENTIVES FOR SOME FARMERS, DISINCENTIVES FOR OTHERS

The agricultural segment of our economy poses a dilemma for tax policy. On one hand, we know that trace elements, humus, and natural plant nutrients are being depleted from the soil at an alarming pace in many areas. The erosion of topsoil also continues despite a fairly vigorous federal program that has been in existence for over four decades.

On the other hand, agricultural production has been high and there has been an oversupply of many basic commodities, particularly cereal grains. Hybrid strains of grains, processed fertilizers, chemical weed control, and labor-saving machines have made the American farmer the most efficient in the world. This efficiency on the farm is reflected in a decrease in the absolute number of farmers and a rapid decrease in farmers as a percentage of the total population. American consumers spend around 20 percent of their disposable income for food compared with from 40 to 60 percent in European countries and virtually 100 percent in some primitive economies.

The population "explosion" further complicates the equation. Will new technology enable the agricultural sector to keep pace with population growth without increases in food prices relative to other prices? Are some ecologists right when they predict that present misuse of the soil, combined with population growth, will result in a severe shortage of food? The policy makers in Washington have responded to the problem in two ways. They have written into the law some incentives that increase food production and, at the same time, have placed restrictions on deductions from agricultural activities that may reduce the flow of capital into the agricultural segment.

Incentives for farmers

Beginning with the Code revision in 1954, Congress has added to the law several sections aimed at encouraging good land use by farmers. Certain practices are encouraged by allowing the farmer to deduct immediately costs that would otherwise be added to capital accounts. Expenditures for the following purposes may be deducted in the year paid or incurred, subject to some rather severe maximum limits:

1. Soil and water conservation, including the cost of moving earth for leveling, grading and terracing, contour furrowing, construction of diversion channels, and similar projects (Sec. 175).
2. Fertilizer, lime, ground limestone, marl, or other materials to enrich, neutralize, or condition land (Sec. 180).
3. Clearing land, including eradication of tree stumps and brush, and the treatment and moving of earth (Sec. 182).

In every case, the taxpayer claiming a deduction for these expenditures must be engaged in the business of farming; for the first two deductions, the land must be used in farming. These requirements are intended to prevent the use of these provisions by speculators and developers to charge off costs that would otherwise be added to the basis of the land and be recovered at the point of sale. Recovery at point of sale would merely decrease the capital gain, while the immediate deduction might be offset in full against ordinary income.

The provisions governing soil and water conservation expenditures were added to the law in 1954.

The other two were enacted in the early 1960s. The hearings before the House Ways and Means Committee on soil and water conservation were combined with the hearings on R&D, and all witnesses appearing before the committee as well as all communications read into the record supported the measure. Arguments made for current deduction were similar to those made for the immediate deduction of R&D—with some special twists. Some witnesses noted the need to preserve our natural heritage, citing decreases in cultivable land due to wind and water erosion. Others cited as inequitable the fact that farmers who received government grants for conservation projects had to include the grant in income but could not deduct the costs until the land was eventually sold. (Capital expenditures would be added to the basis of the land.) Still other witnesses suggested that government subsidies for agricultural projects might eventually be reduced by encouraging investments by individual farmers. One candid witness recommended the provision because it would make the farmers honest; most farmers, according to this witness, were going to deduct these expenditures in any event.[10]

The taxpayer engaged in the business of farming may elect to treat all three types of expenditure as current deductions or as capital expenditures. Current deduction is an obvious choice, particularly for the large number of part-time farmers who are, by definition, engaged in the business of farming but who nevertheless have a speculative interest in land values. To these "gentlemen farmers," conservation, clearing, and soil improvement not only make sense agriculturally but increase the rate of appreciation in land values. And, of course, farming losses incurred by these part-time farmers may be deducted against income from other sources.

The facts just recited account for the rather strict limitations imposed by Congress on two of these incentives. The limitations are

1. *Soil and water conservation:* The deduction for any year is limited to 25 percent of the *gross income derived from farming.* Where these expenditures exceed 25 percent of gross income derived from farming, the amounts not deducted are carried over to later years (Sec. 175(b)).

---

[10]For testimony on this provision, see *Hearings on Internal Revenue Revision,* House Ways and Means Committee, 83rd Congress, 1st Session. Topic 21 (Washington, D.C.: U.S. Government Printing Office, 1953), p. 946.

2. *Clearing costs:* For any taxable year, the deduction is limited to the lesser of (a) $5,000 or (b) 25 percent of the *taxable* income derived from farming. This limit is more severe, being based on taxable income (Sec. 182(b)).

There is no limit on the deduction for fertilizer and the like.

Disincentives for farm losses

Like the real estate shelter described in Chapter 16, wealthy individuals, with their tax advisors, have dreamed up numerous ways to use agricultural operations as a tax shelter. All shelters related to farm operations have one thing in common: the taxpayer enters into some farming venture and elects the cash method. Usually the land needed is acquired with maximum leverage, and interest on the borrowed money creates substantial deductions. Money is spent for land development and these expenditures are wholly or partially deductible as general expenses or under the incentives discussed above. The results are substantial tax losses, which are used to offset the ordinary income of the taxpayer. In some later year, agricultural products are sold, or the land used in the venture is sold. As a minimum result, income is shifted to later years; in some schemes, the income is not only shifted but the final result is a long-term capital gain rather than ordinary income. The schemes range from short-term ventures involving raising laying hens or feeding lot cattle to long-range plans involving the creation of orchards and vineyards.

The 1969 Tax Reform Act contained several provisions designed to curtail some of these planning devices. The hobby rule, explained in Chapter 6, is one such provision. Other provisions, explained in Chapter 23, will result in the conversion of capital gains into ordinary income in situations where, for example, land development costs were deducted against ordinary income. That act specifically attacked the use of citrus groves as a means of creating current deductions by providing that all development costs must be capitalized for the first four years of the grove's life.

The Tax Reform Act of 1976 also contains several provisions designed to reduce the tax incentives for farming operations. Under Sec. 464, farming operations carried on by a syndicate must use the accrual method for feed, seed, fertilizer, and similar farm

supplies. A syndicate generally means a partnership where the sale of partnership participations is regulated by law or where a limited partnership may allocate more than 35 percent of the losses to limited partners. This provision is aimed at cattle-feeding operations and shelters involving chickens. Another provison of the Act, Sec. 465, limits the amount of losses deductible by individuals engaged in farming operations to the amount at risk, which is typically the cash contributed to the operation by the partner.

These reforms, however, only diminish somewhat the tax advantage of farm shelters. The high individual rates on ordinary income, combined with the general expectation that land values will increase, mean that many people will choose to invest in land and take current tax losses with the hope of later realizing capital gains.

OTHER INVESTMENT INCENTIVES

In the Tax Reform Act of 1969, Congress revived an old rule, emergency amortization, in an effort to stimulate capital investment and solve some pressing national problems. As explained in Chapter 16, emergency amortization, which was used in World War II and the Korean conflict, permits recovery of the capital over a 60-month period regardless of its actual estimated life. Since 1969, the special amortization rules have been applied to several social and/or economic problems. The list includes the following: cost of rehabilitating residential properties rented to families with low incomes; the cost of certified pollution control devices; the cost of certain railroad rolling stock; the cost of coal-mine safety devices; the cost of constructing child-care facilities; the cost of facilities to provide on-the-job training; and the cost of restoring certain historical sites. Most of these provisions have already come and gone, and the remainder, except for two, have only a brief remaining life. One exception is the five-year amortization for pollution control devices. To qualify for rapid amortization, the pollution controls must be "certified" by the state and federal agencies charged with enforcing the clean air and water standards and the controls must be added to a facility in operation on January 1, 1976. A second exception is rapid amortization of child-care facilities. This provision, scheduled to expire at the end of 1976, was given an additional 5-year life by the 1977 Tax Reduction and Simplification Act.

Form **3468**
Department of the Treasury
Internal Revenue Service

Computation of Investment Credit

▶ Attach to your tax return.

1979

22

Name   *TAXPAYER*

Identifying number as shown on page 1 of your tax return

Check the applicable box(es) below to elect the provisions of the specified code section(s):

A The corporation elects the basic or basic and matching ESOP percentage under section 48(n)(1) . . . . ☐

B I elect to increase my qualified investment to 100% for certain commuter highway vehicles under section 46(c)(6) . . . . . ☐

C I elect to increase my qualified investment under section 46(d) by all qualified progress expenditures made in the tax year and all subsequent years . . . . ☐

1 Use the format below to list your qualified investment in new or used property acquired or constructed and placed in service during the tax year. Also list (a) qualified progress expenditures made during the tax year and certain prior tax years and (b) qualified rehabilitation expenditures for the year. See the instructions for line 1(a) through 1(j).

If you are claiming 100% investment credit on certain ships, check this block ▶ ☐. See instruction K for details.

Note: Include your share of investment in property made by a partnership, estate, trust, small business corporation, or lessor.

Type of property		Line	(1) Life years	(2) Cost or basis (See instruction G)	(3) Applicable percentage	(4) Qualified investment (Column 2 x column 3)
New property		(a)	3 or more but less than 5	12,000	33⅓	4,000
		(b)	5 or more but less than 7		66⅔	
		(c)	7 or more	50,000	100	50,000
Commuter highway vehicle		(d)	3 or more		100	
Qualified progress expenditures	1974 through 1978	(e)	7 or more		20	
	1979	(f)	7 or more		100	
Used property (See instructions for dollar limits)		(g)	3 or more but less than 5		33⅓	
		(h)	5 or more but less than 7		66⅔	
		(i)	7 or more		100	
Commuter highway vehicle		(j)	3 or more		100	

2 Qualified investment—Add lines 1(a) through (j) (see instruction M for special limits) . . . . . . | 54,000

3 10% of line 2 . . . . | 5,400

4 7% (4% for public utility property) of certain property (see instruction Q) . . . . |

5 Corporations electing the basic or basic and matching ESOP percentage for contributions to ESOPs—Check election box A above (see instruction I and instruction for line 5)

    (a) Basic 1% credit—Enter 1% of line 2 . . . . |

    (b) Matching credit (not more than 0.5%)—Enter allowable percentage times adjusted line 2 (attach schedule) . . . . |

6 Patron's regular investment credit—Enter credit allocated from cooperative . . . . |

7 Total—Add lines 3 through 6 . . . . | 5,400

8 Carryover of unused credit(s) . . . . |

9 Carryback of unused credit(s) . . . . |

10 Tentative regular investment credit—Add lines 7, 8, and 9 . . . . | 5,400

Tax Liability Limitations

11 (a) Individuals—Enter amount from Form 1040, line 37, page 2 . . . . . . ⎫

    (b) Estates and trusts—Enter amount from Form 1041, line 27, page 1 . . . . . ⎬ . . . . | 9,700

    (c) Corporations—Enter amount from Schedule J (Form 1120), line 3, page 3 . . . ⎭

12 (a) Credit for the elderly (individuals only) . . . . |

    (b) Foreign tax credit . . . . |

    (c) Tax on lump-sum distribution from Form 4972 or Form 5544 . . . . |

    (d) Possessions corporation tax credit (corporations only) . . . . |

    (e) Section 72(m)(5) penalty tax (individuals only) . . . . |

13 Total—Add lines 12(a) through (e) . . . . | –0–

14 Subtract line 13 from line 11 . . . . | 9,700

15 (a) Enter smaller of line 14 or $25,000. See instruction M for special limits. (Married persons filing separately, controlled corporate groups, estates, and trusts, see instruction for line 15) . . . . . | 9,700

    (b) If line 14 is more than line 15(a) and you are a 1979 calendar year taxpayer, enter 60% of the excess (if your tax year ends in 1980, enter 70% of the excess). (Public utilities, railroads, and airlines, see instruction J.) . . . . |

16 Regular investment credit limitation—Add lines 15(a) and (b) . . . . | 9,700

(Continue computation on back.)

Form **3468** (1979)

17 Allowed regular investment credit—Enter smaller of line 10 or line 16 . . . . | *5,400*

   Note: *If line 10 exceeds line 16, the excess is an unused regular investment credit. See instruction F.*

18 Nonrefundable business energy investment credit limitation—Subtract line 17 from line 14 . . . . .

19 Enter nonrefundable business energy investment credit from line 8 of Schedule B (Form 3468) . . .

20 Allowed nonrefundable business energy investment credit—Enter smaller of line 18 or line 19 . . . .

   Note: *If line 19 exceeds line 18, the excess is an unused nonrefundable business energy investment credit. See instruction F.*

21 Total allowed regular investment credit and nonrefundable business energy investment credit—Add lines 17 and 20. Enter here and on Form 1040, line 41; Schedule J (Form 1120), line 4(b), page 3; or the appropriate line on other returns . . . . | *5,400*

| Schedule A | If any part of your investment in line 1 or 4 above was made by a partnership, estate, trust, small business corporation, or lessor, complete the following statement and identify property qualifying for the 7% or 10% investment credit. |

Name (Partnership, estate, trust, etc.)	Address	Property			Life years
		Progress expenditures	New	Used	
		$	$	$	

(If property is disposed of prior to the life years used in figuring the investment credit, see instruction E.)

It is always encouraging to see Congress address itself to grave national problems, but only an incorrigible optimist could believe that these incentives would solve these problems. Violations of mine safety rules are legion, large segments of our rail system are in shambles, and a single visit to a large city provides sufficient evidence of the conditions in our ghettos and the condition of the air. These problems, in fact, have reached such proportions that any solution other than massive government planning and control is, in our opinion, unlikely.

In 1977, Congress added a provision to reduce unemployment, the new jobs credit. The credit was based on an employer's increase in the base for the federal unemployment tax (FUTA). This general credit, applicable to all new jobs, was replaced for years after 1978, by the "targeted" job credit. Under this credit, an employer is entitled to a credit equal to 50 percent of the new employees' wages up to $6,000. The amount of the credit reduces the deduction for wages. The targeted job credit is available only for employees in seven specific groups, including, for example, individuals 18 to 25 years of age who are members of economically disadvantaged families, ex-felons who are members of economically disadvantaged families, and individuals who are receiving, prior to their employment, federal welfare payments. The objective is to make the credit available only for the chronically unemployed.

This targeted job credit can offset only 90 percent of the tax liability after all other credits. Amounts not allowed in the current year can be carried back three years and forward for seven years. Other applicable limits make it impossible for an employer to fire old employees and replace them with new ones who qualify for the credit.

This credit is currently scheduled for 1979 and 1980 only (though Conference Report indicates that it will also be available in 1981). One should not expect, of course, that this relatively minor incentive will solve the problem of the growing numbers of people who are marginally employable.

REPORTING THE INVESTMENT CREDIT

With the exception of the investment credit, the various incentives discussed in this chapter are treated as ordinary deductions on the routine forms and schedules. For example, research and development expenses of a corporation are reported as a deduction on Form 1120. Soil and water conservation expenses of an individual are reported on Schedule F, Form 1040.

The I.R.S. provides Form 3468, which is used by all taxpayers for the calculation of the investment credit. That form is reproduced on pages **17**/12 and **17**/13 illustrating the computation of the tentative credit for a taxpayer who acquired the following new properties in June, 1979:

Item	Cost	Estimated life
Delivery truck	$12,000	3
Production machinery	50,000	8

The tentative credit is $5,400. Limitations on the credit are computed at lines 11 through 16. Lines 17 through 21 on page 2 of Form 3468 are used when the taxpayer acquires property that qualifies for the energy credit. The energy credit is computed on Schedule B of Form 3468. A special form, Form 4255, is provided for the calculation of the recapture of the credit where property is disposed of prematurely.

PROBLEMS

1. What reasons underlie the special provisions for farmers discussed in this chapter?
2. a. During 19x1, Strom Corporation engaged in three R&D projects. Information on these projects, all of which were completed in 19x1, is presented below:

Project	Cost incurred	Outcome	Estimated years of contribution from project
1	$100,000	Successful	5
2	150,000	Unsuccessful	0
3	180,000	Successful	10

Compute the value to Strom Corporation of the immediate expensing of these three projects compared with treatment as deferred costs. Assume a 46-percent tax rate and an amortization period of 60 months, and use an interest rate of 10 percent.

b. What arguments, other than the investment incentive idea, may be used to justify the immediate expensing of R&D?

3. John Atwood, a successful attorney, earned a net profit of $80,000 from his practice in 19x1. John is also a "gentleman farmer," and the results of his farming operations for 19x1 were

Sales of livestock and commodities	$12,000
General operating expenses	14,000
Soil conservation expenditures	4,000
Fertilizer, soil improvements	3,000
Timber clearing costs	1,000

John had deductions from A.G.I. of $4,800 and deductions for exemptions of $3,000. Compute his taxable income.

4. John Howell, a corporate executive with a large salary, has decided to purchase a 500-acre farm. He intends to spend a considerable amount of money over the next few years on new fences, constructing ponds, leveling out erosion ditches, and planting high-yield permanent grasses. His aim is to run an efficient cattle operation eventually, but he expects to have sizable losses for several years.

   a. What election should he make relative to his accounting method? For other specific expenditures anticipated?

   b. Explain how Howell can make money on this scheme because of our tax laws even though he just breaks even economically.

   c. What can Howell do to avoid the "hobby loss" rules?

5. Jeb Jones is a self-employed contractor. Jeb is married and files a joint return. During 19x1, he purchased the following assets for use in his business:

Description	Cost	Guideline life
Patent	$15,000	Remaining legal life is 10 years.
Equipment (new)	12,000	5 years
Land	20,000	
Office building (used)	40,000	50 years
Office furniture (new)	5,000	10 years
Warehouse (new)	20,000	40 years
Truck (used)	3,000	2 years

   a. Which assets qualify for the 200-percent declining-balance depreciation?

   b. Which assets qualify for the 150-percent declining-balance method?

   c. Compute the tentative investment credit for 19x1. None of the properties qualifies for the energy credit.

6. During 19x1, John Hancock, an insurance agent, purchased the following assets:

Assets	Estimated life (years)	Cost
Calculator	10	$ 300
Typewriter	6	400
New residence	35	36,000
New automobile	4	4,000
Dictaphone (used)	2	200

The new residence included a large office attached to the garage. John intends to use this office exclusively for business purposes. One-sixth of the total cost of the new home can be allocated properly to this office. The car will be used 90 percent of the time for business purposes and 10 percent of the time for personal purposes.

a. What is John's investment credit for 19x1? (You may assume that his tax liability is larger than this tentative credit and that the energy credit is not applicable.)

b. Suppose that six years later (19x6) John is still using the same dictaphone purchased in 19x1. What effect, if any, will this fact have on John's tax liability for 19x1? For 19x6?

c. Suppose that after using the automobile purchased in 19x1 for 2½ years, John decides to trade it in for a new car to avoid costly repairs of this older model. What effect, if any, will John's decision to dispose of this car have on his 19x3 tax liability? Explain in detail.

d. Suppose that instead of trading the automobile (as suggested above), John sold his wife's older car and gave her the two-year-old model to use as a family car. He then purchased a new car for business purposes. Would this decision have any tax advantages over the trade-in suggested above? Explain.

7. In 19x3, Expanding Corporation (not a public utility) purchased enough qualified property to give it a tentative regular investment credit of $56,000. The corporation's tax liability before the investment credit for 19x3 was $27,000. Its tax liabilities for other years are: 19x0, zero (a loss was incurred in its first year of operations); 19x1, $2,000; 19x2, $12,000; 19x4, $18,000 (it had no investments in qualified property in 19x4).

a. What is the corporation's net tax liability for 19x3?

b. What can Expanding Corporation do with the "excess" investment credit in 19x3?

8. Exeter Company made the following asset acquisitions in 19x1:

Assets	Cost	Estimated life (years)
Automobiles	$ 20,000	3
Warehouse	140,000	25
Plant machines	80,000	10
Delivery equipment	42,000	7
Common stock of affiliate	100,000	—

a. Compute Exeter's tentative investment credit for 19x1. The energy credit is not available for these assets.

b. What is the allowable credit for 19x1 if Exeter's tax liability before the credit is only $20,000?

c. Assume that the credit disallowed in 19x1 is carried back and absorbed in the three preceding years. What is the effect on the corporation's tax liability for 19x3 if the automobiles are sold after two years of use?

9. Energy, Inc. is engaged in the business of extracting crude oil from oil shale. During the current year, the company acquired three substantial properties: (1) a new computer for use in accounting and other record keeping at a cost of $200,000, estimated to last eight years before obsolescence. (2) A large machine used to crush shale at a cost of $800,000, with an estimated life of five years. This machine is personal property. (3) A building used to house shale-processing machinery at a cost of $1.2 million, with an estimated life of 20 years. This building qualifies for the energy credit because of its use in shale oil extraction.

   Calculate the total tentative investment credit of Energy, Inc. for this year.

10. Stimson, Inc. has a gross tax (after the foreign tax credit) of $200,000 for 1979. It has the following tentative credits from property investments:

"Regular" investment credit property	$138,000
Energy properties other than solar and wind	
energy properties	76,000
Solar and wind energy property	45,000

    a. How do the above affect Stimson's tax liability for 1979?
    b. If any amounts are disallowed currently, explain their treatment.

11. In June of 19x1, Jenkins purchased an undeveloped farm for $80,000, paying cash of $23,000 and signing a note for the balance. During 19x1 he had the following expenditures relating to the farm:
    a. Erection of dirt dams for tanks. Total cost was $1,800. Of this amount, the U.S. government paid $500 under a water conservation program.
    b. Cost of setting out grass "sprigs" and planting grass seed, $680.
    c. Cost of removing undergrowth, leveling land, and filling ditches (on land to be used for pasture), $1,200.
    d. Cost of fertilizer for grass, $150.
    e. Construction of new fences on property, $450.
    f. Eradication of underbrush and scrub trees on area to be left for timber production, $300. Eradication was undertaken so that existing trees could grow.
    g. Costs of driving from home in city, where Jenkins practiced law, to farm for overseeing work and helping in work, $100, total 15 trips.
    h. Real estate taxes on property for period owned by Jenkins, $140.
    i. Interest paid on loan, $3,200.
    j. Cost of drilling well for water supply for cattle, $800.
    k. Equipment for water well, above, $250.
    l. Cost of cattle for breeding purposes, $4,000.
    Jenkins's only income from the property was from the sale of three calves for $240.
    a. Show the amount of each expenditure that Jenkins may deduct currently, assuming that he wishes to deduct the maximum.
    b. List the capital expenditures that qualify for the investment credit, assuming that all items have a life greater than three years.

12. In early January 1979, Z Corporation completed construction of a "certified" facility to control emissions of pollutants into a river contiguous to its plant. The plant has been in operation for several years. The facility cost $600,000 and has an estimated life of 20 years. Calculate the tax the corporation can save if it elects the special amortization rules. In your solution, assume that the corporation's marginal rate is 46 percent, that it uses 12 percent as the rate for evaluating decisions, and that the facility would be depreciated on the straight-line method if the special amortization were not available.

13. The properties in the list that follows are used in a variety of different business-es. Which of these eleven properties qualify for the investment credit? Assume that they all have lives in excess of three years.
    1. A railroad siding at a food processing plant used when raw materials are delivered to the plant and when finished products are shipped by rail.
    2. A horse acquired for racing purposes by a taxpayer engaged in the business of racing horses.
    3. A herd of registered Black Angus cattle acquired by a taxpayer just enter-ing the cattle business.
    4. The cost of paving a parking lot used by customers of a discount center.
    5. The cost of paving a driveway that leads to the loading dock of a manufac-turing plant.
    6. An automated dairy barn that has automated feed delivery and milking equipment, water connections for disposal of waste, refrigerated milk stor-age tanks, and many other labor-saving devices.
    7. A pipeline used to transmit natural gas owned by an oil company.
    8. A new computer acquired by a C.P.A. firm.
    9. A generating plant powered by natural gas.
    10. An office building adjacent to the generating plant.
    11. A general-purpose warehouse used to store finished goods (not fungible) and delivery equipment.

SUPPLEMENTAL PROBLEMS

14. World Airways paid $2,500,000 to Supersonic Transports, Inc. The payment was to defray a portion of Supersonic's costs of developing the prototype of a new plane that World Airways would like to use on intercontinental flights. The agreement covering the payment specified that the $2,500,000 could be deduct-ed from the purchase price of the new planes, if and when produced, provided World Airways purchased at least ten planes. Can World Airways deduct the $2,500,000 as R & D costs when paid to Supersonic? If not, how should the expenditure be treated? Is the payment income to Supersonic?

15. Ace Computer Service spent $400,000 in 19x1 developing computer "soft-ware," which it leases and sells to customers. Do these costs qualify as a deduction under Sec. 174?

16. One popular proposal for changing the investment credit eliminates the reduc-tion in qualified investment based on estimated life. List some industries that would benefit from this change. What would be the likely theoretical grounds for the change?

17. In late 1977 and early 1978, some American farmers made an attempt to organ-ize a general farm strike. One major goal was to force the government to sup-port grain prices at "parity" (an original base price adjusted for inflation).
    a. Explain why these farmers, usually considered rugged individualists, want-ed government invervention in the grain markets.
    b. What changes could be made in our tax laws to improve farm prices?
    c. Is the existence of excess cereal grains important to the United States rel-ative to foreign relations? Explain.

18. Research and development expenditures are treated as current expenses under the tax law (assuming the proper election). This rule applies to all taxpayers

including pharmaceuticals, communications, and other industries. Does the rule also apply to manufacturers of cosmetics? If so, prepare an argument that supports this evident tax subsidy for companies that manufacture perfumes, lipstick, eye shadow, and so forth.

RETURN PROBLEMS

1. In 1979, Long Corporation made the following purchases of new properties:

Property	Estimated life	Cost
Automobiles	3	$ 30,000
Office building	20	400,000
Production equipment	5	75,000
Steam furnace	20	100,000

Using Form 3468, compute the tentative credit for 1979, assuming the energy credit is not applicable.

2. Smith Corporation made the following purchases of fixed assets in 1979:

Type	Condition	Date of acquisition	Estimated life	Cost
Movable storage bins	used	June 20	10	$ 80,000
Delivery equipment	new	January 10	5	27,000
Machinery	used	September 30	3	70,000
Storage for fungible commodities*	new	February 2	10	120,000

* Used as an integral part of production.

Smith Corporation's gross tax before the credit was $32,000. Using Form 3468, compute the tentative and the allowable credit for 1979. The properties do not qualify for the energy credit.

18

In any case, the fundamental issues of proper policy appear to depend upon a series of empirical questions in which no more than a dent has been made. We have had decades of arguments, theoretical and ideological, about percentage depletion. It is not further "views of interested persons" that are needed, but the formulation of the relevant questions and a factual determination of the answers to these questions.

PETER O. STEINER,
1959 Compendium

incentives for
the extractive industries

Use of the income-tax law as a major instrument of fiscal policy is an experiment that was started in earnest after World War II, and the investment incentives discussed in the preceding chapters are thus relative newcomers to the tax scene. One provision of the law, however, has been justified ever since World War I on grounds similar to those used for the investment incentives. That provision, the depletion deduction for natural resources, is discussed in this chapter along with the tax treatment of several other expenditures that are unique to the extractive industries. Finally, at the end of this chapter, we shall consider briefly current economic conditions in the United States and make a general assessment of the effectiveness of the various investment incentives discussed in Part Five.

In Chapter 16 we suggested that the primary concern of the federal government in economic affairs is to encourage a high level of resource employment and thus to promote the general welfare. Frequently, however, administrations run into strong opposition in Congress to bills involving interference with the "free market economy." Many an administration has won its point by justifying its proposals as necessary for "national defense." In recent years economic measures have been enacted on the theory that a strong economy is necessary to withstand the onslaught of international communism.

Prior to World War II, before full employment became an accepted goal and before the era of internationalism in foreign policy, national defense policy was often aimed at maintaining a "Fortress America," a self-sufficient economy independent of imports and international trade; in short, it was a policy of isolationism. Advances in the "art" of warfare in World War I, which included the use of airplanes, tanks, and mechanized equipment generally, made petroleum and metals absolutely essential to any plan of national defense. Obviously, a policy of isolationism required rapid development of an adequate supply of these metals and minerals.

In the years following World War I, the lobbyists for the natural resource extraction industries, especially the petroleum industry, used this combination of isolationism and dependence of the military on mechanical contrivances to create some of the most unusual and controversial provisions in the tax law. One of these provisions is especially odd in that it permits a deduction, percentage depletion, that is determined by the gross income of the taxpayer, not by cost expenditures, which serve in every other instance as the basis for cost recovery. The result is a very substantial tax saving for a limited group of taxpayers.

The economics of the extractive industries are somewhat different from those of other industries. In the United States, natural resources are a part of the private domain. The enterprising prospector may become rich overnight by finding a deposit of minerals. Note, however, that there is a great deal of risk in the venture. Some prospectors spend their time and money in exploration and never make a discovery. For the lucky ones, the value of minerals or metals discovered may be disproportionately large compared to the costs incurred, and subsequent development and production may result in an extremely high income. The high income, in the absence of special relief provisions, would result in high taxes. Those who favor special relief for the extractive industries argue that high taxes coupled with high risk would discourage prospectors, with the result that there would be an inadequate supply of the minerals needed for an industrial economy.

CURRENT PROVISIONS

Under American property laws, the person who owns land in fee owns all mineral deposits on or under the land. Most land is owned in fee by farmers and ranchers or by investors who rent the land to others for agricultural or recreational purposes. A prospector who finds a mineral deposit does not normally purchase a fee interest in the land; he or she has no interest in the surface rights, only in the minerals. Usually, the right to develop the deposit and extract the minerals is obtained by leasing the mineral rights from the feeholder. Consideration for the lease is a royalty interest in the production from the deposit. Under the royalty arrangement, the feeholder (or other royalty owner) receives a percentage of the gross value of the minerals produced, or a specified amount for each unit produced (barrel, ton, etc.). In the petroleum industry, a lease bonus is also paid to the feeholder at the time the lease is made. The owner of the royalty interest does not pay any exploration, development, or production costs. He or she is, therefore, concerned mainly with the taxation of royalty income.

The prospector-developer-producer, hereinafter called the "operator" (though these functions may occasionally be performed by different persons), has several different types of costs—costs of finding the deposits (exploration), costs of getting the deposit ready for production (development), and costs of extracting the minerals from the earth (operation). Tax treatment of these costs must be considered before the provisions relating to depletion, which

was originally intended to be the recovery of capitalized costs, can be fully appreciated.

Exploration and development

Historically, generally accepted accounting principles for the extractive industries have been quite diverse. Financial Accounting Standards Board Standard 19, promulgated in the fall of 1977, established definite standards for treatment of exploration and development costs. The effective date for this pronouncement, however, was indefinitely postponed when the Securities and Exchange Commission announced in 1978 that companies under its jurisdiction could follow either Standard 19 or an alternative method of accounting. Furthermore, the SEC announced its intention to ultimately require oil and gas companies to use a value-based rather than a historical-cost-based accounting concept.

As used in the extractive industry, exploration costs are those incurred in finding mineral deposits. The techniques of exploration, and therefore the costs, vary widely depending on the type of mineral sought and may include anything from aerial surveys employing sophisticated measuring devices to holes dug in the earth with crude hand tools. Development costs are those incurred preparing the deposit for production. Development costs include such costs as removing the outer crust in strip mining and drilling the hole to the deposit in the oil and gas industry. (In the discussion that follows, the petroleum industry is treated separately because of the special provisions applicable to that industry only.)

MINING OPERATIONS   Accounting logic would seem to require capitalization of exploration costs and subsequent matching of these costs against revenues from the sale of minerals. Since 1951, however, the law has contained special elective provisions for these costs that have generally permitted the acceleration of their recovery. For many years, mine exploration costs could be deducted as incurred subject to a $400,000 limit for all years. A provision added in 1966 gave operators an alternative. They could elect to deduct all exploration costs currently and then include the deducted costs in gross income if and when the deposit became productive. As an alternative to recapturing the deduction by including it in gross income, the operator could forego depletion deductions on the deposit up to the amount of the deducted costs.

In 1969, the option of currently deducting costs up to the $400,000 limit without recapture was repealed, and since that date operators may elect to deduct all exploration costs currently. The deducted costs must be "recaptured" in one of two ways if the mine to which the expenditures relates becomes productive:

1. The operator may elect to include in gross income for the year an amount equal to the exploration costs applicable to all mines reaching the productive stage during that year. The amount recovered is, in turn, added to the depletable cost basis of the respective mines, or

2. If the election in (1) is not made, the operator must forego depletion on the mines involved until the amount of exploration cost deducted has been "recovered."

A new election of the recapture method can be made each year for all mines becoming productive that year. The change in 1969 also provides that the sale of a mineral deposit will result in ordinary income up to the amount of deducted exploration costs that have not been recaptured by including them in gross income or by reducing depletion deductions. (This conversion of capital gain into ordinary income by recapture of deductions is a general concept illustrated in Part Six.)

In every case, of course, the mine operator may elect to defer the deduction of exploration costs and treat them as part of the deposit's depletable cost to be recovered as the deposit is produced. Such deferral would be sensible only where the taxpayer could not offset the exploration costs against ordinary income. (Note again that these rules do not apply to oil and gas.)

Since 1951, mine operators also have been permitted to deduct development costs of a mine when the costs are incurred. Section 616(a) reads as follows:

(a) In General.—Except as provided in subsection (b) there shall be allowed as a deduction in computing taxable income all expenditures paid or incurred during the taxable year for the development of a mine or other natural deposit (other than an oil or gas well) if paid or incurred after the existence of ores or minerals in commercially marketable quantities has been disclosed. This section shall not apply to expenditures for the acquisition or improvement of property of a character which is subject to the allowance for depreciation provided in section 167, but allowances for depreciation shall be considered, for purposes of this section, as expenditures.

Development costs are those incurred after the existence of a commercial deposit is determined, including expenditures for mine shafts, tunnels, and stripping. Some development work may be done throughout the life of the mine. Development costs may be deducted, without limit, when incurred, even after the production stage has begun.

As in the case of exploration costs, the operator may elect to defer development costs and deduct them ratably as the mine produces. Deferred development costs, however, are not added to the depletable basis for purposes of determining cost depletion. Instead, the deferred costs are amortized against income from the deposit in addition to the deduction for depletion.

Production costs incurred after the mine is developed and normal operations begin are treated as current expenses. The amounts paid to the royalty interest (either a percentage or the unit rate) are treated as an allocation of the gross sales price of the minerals and are thus excluded from the operator's gross income.

PETROLEUM OPERATIONS   The elections available to mine operators concerning exploration and development costs constitute a typical congressional solution to an "inequity" in the law. Oil and gas operators have had the privilege since 1916 of expensing intangible development costs (IDC). Extension of a similar privilege to mine operators provided for equal treatment under the law without aggravating either group.

Intangible drilling and development costs include the intangible costs of drilling from the surface to the formation where a deposit may be present. Such costs as labor, taxes, supplies, power, contractual services, and rentals of equipment are included in the definition. Equipment that has a physical existence, such as casing and pipe, is not included in IDC. The petroleum industry is unique in that the usual methods of exploring for natural resources will not determine definitely the existence of a petroleum deposit. A hole must be drilled to the place where the prospector *thinks* the oil is located. Often the result is a dry hole. When oil is discovered, the major cost of finding and producing it, the cost of drilling the hole, has almost always been charged off as an expense. From 1916 through 1945, the privilege of expensing IDC was based on an administrative ruling; in 1945, a concurrent resolution in Congress assured the continuation of the privilege. Finally, the option was included in Sec. 263(e) of the 1954 Code.

While the treatment of development costs is now similar for all segments of the extractive industry, exploration costs incurred in the petroleum industry differ from those for other minerals. Exploration costs incurred in trying to locate oil or gas deposits are considered by the I.R.S. as capital in nature. Typically, the oil operator will undertake exploration on a large "prospect" of many thousand acres. If no "areas of interest" (smaller areas warranting detailed exploration work) are found, the costs of all work on the prospect are charged to expense. If any areas of interest are found, the costs of the general work on the prospect are allocated equally to each area of interest. In turn, if an area of interest is later abondoned, all the costs of the detailed exploration on the area, along with allocated prospect exploration costs, are charged to expense. On the other hand, if any acreage is leased as a result of the detailed survey, all costs applicable to the area, including any allocated costs of general exploration on the project, are capitalized and are allocated to each lease on the basis of the number of acres in each lease. Capitalized exploration costs become part of the depletable basis of the minerals.

Once a petroleum deposit is discovered and developed, all production costs are deductible when paid or incurred. Production costs would include the current depreciation allowance for production equipment.

Table 18-1 summarizes the treatment of different types of costs incurred by an oil and gas exploration and production company.

The petroleum industry, after enjoying several favorable tax provisions for years, has recently fallen on hard times in its relations with Congress. As explained below, the depletion allowance was reduced in 1975. The Tax Reform Act of 1976 also added a punitive provision relating to IDC. In past years, an operator could develop a property, deduct the IDC, and then later sell the deposit of oil or gas

TABLE **18-1**

TAX TREATMENT OF EXPENDITURES INCURRED TO FIND, ACQUIRE, DEVELOP, AND PRODUCE OIL AND GAS

Expenditure	Tax treatment
1. Geological and geophysical exploration: (a) On broad "prospects" [a]	1. (a) If no area of interest [b] is found, charge to expense. If area of interest is found, allocate costs equally to each area of interest, and defer costs.
(b) On "areas of interest"	(b) If no leases are taken, expense exploration costs applicable to area, including allocated costs from prospects. If leases are taken, allocate costs on a per-acre basis to all leases.
2. Lease acquisition costs (bonus, incidental acquisition costs, and any capitalized geological and geophysical costs)	2. Capitalize on acquisition. If lease is not productive, charge capitalized costs to expense when the lease is abandoned. If lease becomes productive, capitalized costs become part of depletable basis.
3. Lease rentals	3. Lease by lease and year by year election to capitalize or expense. If rents are capitalized, they become part of the depletable basis.
4. Intangible drilling and development costs	4. One-time election to expense or to capitalize all intangible drilling costs. If election is made to capitalize costs, a further election may be made to expense dry-hole costs.
5. Tangible equipment	5. Capitalize and depreciate.
6. Production costs	6. Expense as incurred.

[a] "Prospect" is a broad area selected by management as one on which coordinated exploration activities may be feasibly conducted. It may include, for example, 75,000 acres.
[b] An area of interest is a geological area that shows enough potential for containing hydrocarbons to warrant further detailed exploration. It might include, for example, 5,000 acres.

at a gain that was usually taxed at favorable capital gain rates. For 1976 and later years, however, the unrecovered IDC must be treated as ordinary income. To illustrate, assume an operator develops a property and deducts IDC of $300,000. Later, he sells the property and realizes a gain of $400,000. The amount of gain to be reported as ordinary income is the amount of IDC originally expensed, $300,000, reduced by the amount that total depletion on the property up to the date of sale would have been increased if the IDC had originally been capitalized instead of charged to expense. This calculation requires a recomputation of depletion for all prior years and is beyond the scope of this book.

Depletion

Depletion is generally thought to be a deduction for the exhaustion of natural resources whereby the taxpayer recovers his or her capital investment in the resources. Conceptually, the deduction for depletion is the same as that for depreciation, except that property subject to depletion is irreplaceable. Generally, capital invested in the property is recovered over the productive life of the property through depletion.

To be entitled to the deduction for depletion, the taxpayer must have an economic interest in the minerals in place. In the usual situation, both the lessor (landowner) and the lessee (operator) have such an economic interest. For the lessor, royalty payments representing his or her share of the value of production are subject to depletion. The lease bonus received by the lessor is also subject to depletion. Percentage depletion is not allowable on a bonus received for an oil or gas lease, however, although bonuses for other types of minerals or metals would be eligible for percentage depletion. As explained in detail later in this chapter, the Tax Reduction Act of 1975 made substantial changes in the statutory depletion rules for oil and gas. The lessee or operator typically has an economic interest in the minerals in place and is entitled to the depletion deduction. A person who merely enjoys an economic *advantage* from the production of the property, such as a contract miner, is not entitled to depletion.

There are two types of depletion for income-tax purposes: cost depletion and percentage depletion. For each tax year, the taxpayer entitled to depletion computes both cost and percentage depletion for each property and takes as a deduction the *larger* of the two amounts.

COST DEPLETION   Under cost depletion, the taxpayer's actual investment (depletable basis) in the natural resource is recovered ratably as the deposit is produced. The formula is as follows:

$$\frac{\text{Unrecovered depletable cost basis at end of year}}{\text{(before current year's depletion)}} $$

$$\frac{}{\begin{array}{c}\text{Estimated recoverable}\\\text{units remaining}\\\text{at start of year}\end{array}}$$

$$\times \begin{array}{c}\text{Number of units}\\\text{sold in tax year}\end{array} = \begin{array}{c}\text{Cost depletion}\\\text{for tax year}\end{array}$$

In some cases, residual value must be subtracted from depletable basis to determine the depletion per unit. The estimate of recoverable units in the deposit, which is usually based on geological or engineering studies, is revised periodically as the deposit is produced.

Cost depletion, like depreciation and other cost allocations, can never exceed the historical cost in the deposit. Thus, once the depletion deductions for the past years and the current year equal the original investment, there can be no further cost depletion on the property.

To illustrate the computation of cost depletion, assume that an oil operator paid a lease bonus of $50,000 to acquire oil rights in a property. There were no capitalized exploration costs, and all intangible development costs were expensed. Engineers estimate that the deposit contains 100,000 barrels of recoverable crude oil. During the first year of operations, 15,000 barrels were produced. Cost depletion for the year would be $7,500, computed as follows:

$$\frac{\$50,000}{100,000 \text{ bbls.}} \times 15,000 = \$7,500 \text{ cost depletion}$$

Note that the depletable basis does not include the cost of tangible equipment used on the lease. Depreciation on lease and well equipment is computed separately from the depletion deduction.

PERCENTAGE DEPLETION—GENERAL PROVISION Percentage depletion, which is also referred to as statutory depletion, is obtained by multiplying a percentage set by law times the "gross income from the property." The applicable percentages range from a high of 22 percent (for a number of metals and minerals) to a low of 5 percent (for sand and gravel). The limited and more complicated provisions for oil and gas are discussed separately below. The various percentages are summarized in the following list. (Section 613 contains a comprehensive listing.)

Depletable resource	Percentage rate
1. Sulfur and uranium and a series of minerals from deposits in U.S.	22
2. Gold, silver, oil shale, copper, and iron ore from deposits in U.S.	15
3. Asbestos, coal, sodium chloride, etc.	10
4. Shale and clay used for sewer pipes; or brick and clay, shale, and slate used for lightweight aggregates	7.5
5. Gravel, sand, and other items	5
6. Metals, other than those subject to 22% or 15% rate	14

The amount of percentage depletion is the applicable percentage applied to *gross income* from the property. Gross income from the property is the value of the metal or mineral when extracted, before any processing. Percentage depletion is limited, however, to 50 percent of the *net* income from the property excluding depletion. Net income from the property is computed by deducting (nondepletion) operating expense and taxes applicable to each property (including the general overhead of the operator). Any development costs that are incurred in the current year on a property and are expensed under the election must also be subtracted to arrive at net income for purposes of the 50-percent limit.

To illustrate the computation of percentage depletion, assume that a strip-mining operation in coal produced a gross income of $100,000 during a particular year. The lease provides for a 5-percent royalty to the lessor. Assume further that the operator has no depletable basis; that is, there are no lease bonus or other costs that have not already been recovered through depletion. Operating costs are $65,000. The percentage depletion would be determined as follows:

Gross proceeds from sale of coal	$100,000
Royalty interest paid to lessor	5,000
Gross income to lessee	$ 95,000
Operating expenses	65,000
Net income from the property	$ 30,000
Percentage depletion at 10% of gross income	$ 9,500

The 50-percent limit based on net income would not apply in this illustration because net income is $30,000 and the limit is, therefore, $15,000. If operating expenses had been $80,000, net income would have been only $15,000. Given these facts, the deductible depletion would be only $7,500, or 50 percent of the net income.

To a trained accountant, the rules for depletion of natural resources are strange indeed. First, a major "asset" related to the deposit, development costs, is expensed. Further, as the above example illustrates, depletion actually allowed *is not limited* to the taxpayer's cost basis. Where the taxpayer begins with a depletable basis because of exploration costs and/or a lease bonus, the depletable basis is reduced by the actual depletion deducted, the larger of cost or statutory depletion. When the depletable basis has been fully recovered, the taxpayer's cost depletion is, of course, zero. The taxpayer, however, is entitled to statutory depletion without reference to the original investment. This is a unique state of affairs, to say the least, and can only be understood in a political sense by a review of the legislative history of the depletion provisions. What that history boils down to is this: Congress settled on the current rules because all other alternatives were administratively or politically unacceptable.[1]

PERCENTAGE DEPLETION FOR OIL AND GAS   As originally passed by the House, the 1975 Tax Reduction Act completely eliminated percentage or statutory depletion for oil and gas. The Senate restored percentage depletion on a very limited scale, and the Senate's position prevailed in the Conference Committee.

Before the change in 1975, oil and gas producers and royalty owners were entitled to 22 percent depletion allowance, subject to the 50 percent limit based on net income from the property. These old rules still apply to certain "fixed price" contracts for natural gas. More important, the Senate preserved a more general allowance for "independent producers and royalty owners." For this purpose, an independent producer is one who does not control, directly or indirectly, retail outlets with total annual sales in excess of $5 million and who is not engaged, directly or indirectly, in a refining operation that has a "run" in excess of 50,000 barrels on any day of the year. A

[1] For a concise history of the provisions affecting the petroleum industry, see Stephen L. McDonald, *Federal Tax Treatment of Income from Oil and Gas* (Washington, D.C.: The Brookings Institution, 1963), pp. 11–16.

key word in the preceding definition is the word "indirectly." Thus, an independent operator is deemed to control or own indirectly the operations of corporations controlled by the operator or his or her spouse or children, of partnerships of which he or she is a member, and of trusts where he or she is beneficiary.

For qualified independents and royalty owners, the 22 percent depletion allowance is still available but limited to a maximum quantity of oil or gas produced. The quantity limitations are expressed in terms of average *daily* production. For 1980 and and future years, the average daily limit subject to depletion is 1,000 barrels of oil or 6 million cubic feet of natural gas.

To determine average daily oil production, the taxpayer divides total production of oil for the year by the number of days in the year. Taxpayers with interests in more than one property *must* allocate the daily allowance among all properties according to their share of the production from each. This latter rule is essential to avoid the use of the entire allowance on the properties that produce the greatest revenues. Where the taxpayer has an interest in a well that produces both oil and gas, the taxpayer *may elect* to allocate a portion of the allowance to the gas production.

In addition to the daily limitation on quantities, the rate applicable to the limited quantities is scheduled by law to decrease gradually from the present 22 percent. The decreased percentage rate begins in 1981 with a decline to 20 percent, and bottoms out at 15 percent for 1984 and later years. Some quick arithmetic will indicate that a royalty owner, for example, will get a fairly healthy statutory depletion allowance even after all the restrictions on the tax are in effect. A daily allowance of 1,000 barrels per day results in 365,000 barrels per year. If the oil is sold at the "new" price, say $20 per barrel, the total income for the year is $7,300,000 (365,000 barrels at $20), and the statutory depletion allowance will be $1,095,000 (15 percent of the income). Thus, although the new rules eliminate the depletion allowance for the giant integrated companies and substantially reduce depletion for all but the smallest independent producers, significant benefits still exist for the "little" person in the industry, especially for the royalty owners.

The above changes have no effect on the limitation based on 50 percent of net income from a property. However, a new limiting rule was imposed for years ending after 1974: The depletion allowance may not exceed 65 percent of the taxpayer's net tax-

able income from all sources computed before the deduction for depletion and the net operating loss deduction. This overall limit will avoid the situations in which statutory depletion might result in substantially reducing income from other sources. Where the 65-percent rule reduces the allowed deduction, there is a limited carryover rule.

In framing the new law, Congress took pains to avoid the multiplication of the number of taxpayers who may enjoy the maximum quantity limits. Thus, a controlled group of corporations (see Chapter 10) is treated as one taxpayer. Also the immediate family of the taxpayer (that is, spouse and children) is treated as one unit for purposes of the quantity limits. Finally, the transferee who receives a "proved" property in a sale or exchange after 1974 is denied any percentage depletion with respect to the transferred property.

The end of a long controversy

The changes made by the Tax Reduction Act of 1975 should bring to an end the long and heated controversy over depletion. Although the general framework is still there for natural resources other than oil and gas, denying the deduction to the large integrated oil companies has defused the issue. Historically, major oil companies have been the major beneficiaries of the rules explained in this chapter for two reasons. First, the percentage allowed for oil and gas has traditionally been the highest. The basic statutory rate was 27.5 percent for many years, until it was reduced to 22 percent by the Tax Reform Act of 1969. Second, the petroleum industry is unique in that its intangible development costs represent a disproportionately large part of the total costs when compared to those of other extractive industries. Thus, the oil companies could expense a large portion of production costs currently, yet still enjoy high depletion deductions (but note the recapture provisions on pages **18/4–18/5**).

The peculiar aspects of the changes made in 1975 and 1976 were their timing and the quiet acquiescence of the powerful oil lobby, which previously resisted change in "tooth-and-nail" fights. Given the drain on international payments caused by the pricing action of the OPEC, the usual arguments about the need for an America independent of foreign raw materials would seem to have been most effective— depletion for oil and gas has always been defended as a measure that encouraged exploration and development. Instead, Congress fixed an unwavering eye on the high profits of the integrated companies, which were earned despite, or because of, the higher international prices for crude oil, and general market uncertainties. Big oil, on the other hand, did not "stand in the trenches," as in the past, and the only logical explanation seems to be that they intend to adjust matters for their benefit by increasing the prices of their products. And, certainly, increased prices now can be laid at the feet of the international cartel of oil exporters. Nevertheless, in early 1980, Congress passed a special "windfall profit" tax designed to transfer to the public treasury a large portion of the benefit accruing to oil producers from oil and gas price increases. This new tax, which is not an income tax but an excise tax, will provide funds for developing alternative energy sources and for providing subsidies to some taxpayers.

The ironic result of amendments in recent years is that they leave virtually unmolested the people in the oil industry who least deserve any incentive, namely, the royalty owners. They are the passive parties in the process. Royalty owners risk no capital and reap a windfall profit usually not associated with business acumen, managerial skills, or any other praiseworthy attributes. They just happen to be there when it all happens.

INVESTMENT INCENTIVES AND ECONOMIC GROWTH

The theme throughout this Part is the use of the various incentives included in the law to assure full employment of our national resources. A healthy, growing economy in the United States is, of course, important for the general welfare of our citizens. Of equal importance, perhaps, is the need for stable economic growth in order to preserve the fragile existence of many other democratic societies throughout the world. Following World War II, our country became a bulwark of democratic principles. The United States, despite its considerable war effort, emerged from that holocaust as the only wealthy, powerful democratic state. As a result, the dollar became the Free World's monetary standard, and our ability to sustain an international armed presence, with advanced, expensive war technology, provided the security needed by many countries to pursue the goals of free societies. Now, after three decades, many economic seers question our ability to carry this burden indefinitely.

The current problem

The years 1977 and 1978 were generally considered good years for the U.S. economy in spite of "raging" inflation. There was some growth in G.N.P. in real terms. The rate of inflation for 1978 was approximately 10 percent, although the rate in 1979 was about 13 percent. For both years, unemployment rates were acceptable, and total employment was up substantially. The prognostications of the economic experts for 1980, however, are generally quite gloomy. A brief review of our national economic problems perhaps will give the reasons for the pessimism. First, the rate of inflation in the first quarter of 1980 was almost 20 percent. The growth in 1978 and 1979 was fueled by consecutive large federal deficits. These deficits raised the question of how long the economy could be propped up by deficit spending without resulting in intolerable inflation. The world money market has already passed judgment: The dollar declined in value sharply throughout the years 1977, 1978, and 1979 relative to other strong currencies—for example, the Deutsche mark and Swiss franc—a clear signal that international speculators anticipate future high inflation in the United States.

A second fact that can be read as a danger signal is the huge trade deficit of the United States in 1978 and 1979. These deficits are due in part to our continued reliance on OPEC oil, which has increased dramatically in price in recent years. But the problem is seriously aggravated by the unwillingness of some major trading partners, primarily West Germany and and Japan, to take actions necessary to increase the growth rates of their economies and to reduce their exports to and increase their imports from the United States. Despite pressure from our government, these trading partners have evidently placed the problem of controlling inflation ahead of the possibility of a major recession throughout the Free World.

As another problem, the OPEC nations could continue to raise oil prices at a rate that promises complete disruption of the economies of both industrialized and developing nations, an action that would place a further strain on our international trade account. They could be enticed into such action because of the declining worldwide value of the dollar. But, here, they are caught in a web of international finance that their previous increases in oil prices partially created. Any action on their part that weakens the dollar is counterproductive because the huge surpluses they have enjoyed in recent years are primarily invested in dollar assets.

The bleak picture just painted does contain some positive signs. First, the relative decline in the value of the dollar should improve our trade balance. American export products and commodities are relatively cheaper and the volume of exports should therefore increase. Second, the volume of petroleum imports stabilized during 1978 and 1979 due to slightly lower consumption and increased domestic production, especially in Alaska. Finally, in March 1980, the Carter administration took steps to balance the federal budget for fiscal 1981 and to control the growth of credit, moves that should help to curb runaway inflation. In addition, the administration proposed to further reduce oil consumption by levying an additional tax of 10 cents per gallon on gasoline. In fact, many petroleum experts who were pessimistic a few years ago have changed their dire predictions. Because of higher prices, discoveries of new reserves may be greater than anticipated.

Nevertheless, real danger signals cannot be dismissed out of hand. Faced with continued trade deficits, the administration and Congress could retaliate by adopting protectionist policies to reduce imports. Other countries might follow our lead, with a resulting sharp decline in world trade that could trigger a severe, extended recession in the United States, Japan, and Western Europe. This plausible scenario haunts the mind. Similar conditions existed in the early 1930s and were a major contributing factor in Hitler's rise to power. The entire world paid an incredible price for that mistake. One hopes that this time around, reason and international economic cooperation will prevail over national economic greed and chauvinism.

The need for private investment

The root of our current dilemma has been the recurring need for massive deficit spending by our government to maintain near full employment of our resources. Ideally, sustained investment by the private sector could assure stable growth. To date, we have little evidence to support the proposition that private investment will continue at adequate levels in a mature industrial economy *without* government intervention. We noted in Chapter 16, page **16**/3, that the tax law can affect the level of private investment in two ways. Indirectly, taxes can be increased (or decreased) and thereby change the aggregate demand for goods and services. Changes in the level

of aggregate demand in turn encourage (or discourage) private investment. Second, tax laws can directly affect the marginal efficiency of capital through provisions such as those discussed in this Part. While definitive, empirical research on the relative efficiency of these two approaches does not exist, one conclusion seems inescapable: The investment incentives currently in the law are not sufficient enticements to assure an adequate level of private investment.

Given this conclusion, the question becomes: Would additional tax incentives solve the problem? Some seem to think so and have proposed various changes to increase incentives. A review of these proposals will reveal possible future changes in the law.

1. Eliminate, or at least reduce, the double taxation of corporate dividends. Presumably, the tax dollars saved by corporations and investors would find their way back into new net investment. This scheme was proposed by the Ford administration in 1975 but was rejected by Congress. The Carter proposals have also rejected this approach. Its major weakness is its indirectness. How much time would lapse before the taxes saved would result in new investment, and how much of the savings would be diverted to uses that do not create new or improved productive capacity? In any event, the scheme directly affects the business sector primarily and would be hard to sell politically. The 1978 Act did, of course, reduce the burden on corporations somewhat by cutting corporate rates. The reduction of only 2 percent for larger corporations will hardly solve the problem of massive new investments.

2. Increase the dividends and interest exclusion for individuals. The provision passed in 1980 allowing single persons an exclusion of $200 and married couples an exclusion of $400 of either interest or dividends for years beginning after 1980 represented a break-through for this type of exclusion. This move is intended to stimulate savings.

3. Increase the credit for new investments or increase the rate of capital recovery or both. These incentives have been used effectively in the past by other industrial nations. Some evidence indicates, however, that this form of stimulation requires ever-increasing doses. As the rate of investment sags, a still larger credit is needed to encourage new investment or, alternatively, the recovery of capital must be further accelerated. With the exception of the energy credits discussed in Chapter 17 and acceler-

ated depreciation proposals discussed in Chapter 16, Congress and the administration have evidently abandoned this alternative temporarily.

4. Base capital recovery on replacement costs or on historical costs adjusted for price-level changes. This approach to the problem is appealing because it would reduce the tax burden on corporations needing capital for new investments—for example, railroads, utilities, and heavy industry. This possible solution suffers from one possibly incurable defect. Given the avarice of the normal American taxpayer confronting the government over the annual tax bill, the administration of such provisions would almost certainly result in endless disputes. In addition, the idea may be a bit too sophisticated, given the current Congressional atmosphere.

While these prospective future policies, as well as others not listed, may eventually play a role in obtaining the needed private investment, the short-run policy of the Carter administration was clear. Turning their back on major new direct investment incentives, they proposed to draw out the desired private capital by a sizable increase in aggregate demand. The several changes in the 1978 Act, described in Part Three, that reduce the taxes paid by individuals were passed as a result of that policy. Because of the high inflation rate, however, the emphasis on increase in aggregate demand was abandoned in early 1980.

Congress also initiated some changes in the 1978 Act that can be rationalized as investment incentives. The sizable decrease in the tax on capital gains explained in the following chapters was justified in part by our need for new investment.

The question remains: Will these changes be an adequate incentive for investment in the next few years? Indeed, there remains the basic question concerning the effectiveness of tax incentives for control of economic growth. Only one thing seems reasonably certain: The planners in Washington believe that tax laws can be effective tools of fiscal policy and will use them for that purpose in the future.

PROBLEMS

1. Recent changes in the depletion allowance for the oil and gas industry seem inconsistent with our energy crisis in that royalty owners and small producers are still entitled to percentage depletion while the large integrated companies get only cost depletion.
   a. Discuss these inconsistencies and give the probable reasons for them.
   b. Using classical economic assumptions, make an argument justifying the disallowance of percentage depletion for integrated companies. Do you think the argument is sound?
2. Oil and gas operators are permitted either to capitalize intangible drilling and development costs, or to charge such costs to expense as incurred. Which election do you think most companies make? Why?
3. Percentage depletion rates vary widely for different natural resources. In your opinion, how can these differences be explained?
4. The exclusion of independent "producers and royalty owners" permits all oil and gas producers who meet certain technical requirements to deduct percentage depletion on the first 1,000 barrels of average daily production. Severe computational problems are created by this provision for companies with many mineral properties. Why is this true?
5. Strangely enough, the percentage depletion previously enjoyed by oil and gas producers was severely limited in 1975, a time when the United States was faced with a critical energy shortage. Many interested parties argued that reduction or elimination of percentage depletion would greatly curtail oil and gas exploration, and that the depletion allowance should be increased rather than decreased. How do you explain this apparent paradox?
6. The rules that permit the immediate deduction of development costs for natural resources benefit the petroleum industry to a greater extent than companies

engaged in the extraction of other minerals. Why is this true? Is the immediate expensing of intangible development costs a strong incentive for new exploration? What new provision tends to reduce the effects of this incentive?

7. Listed below are various costs incurred by an oil operator in connection with exploration, development, and production of oil and gas. Indicate whether each item is a current deduction, a capital charge recovered through depreciation, or a capital charge recovered through depletion. If the taxpayer has an election relative to treatment of an item, give the election.

   a. Cost of pump used to lift oil to surface.
   b. Fee paid to geological consultant for analysis of exploration data on a lease. (Further exploration work is contemplated in the same area.)
   c. Cost of drilling a dry hole on a lease that has producing wells on it.
   d. Tanks used to store oil on lease.
   e. Fee paid to drilling contractor for drilling a producing well.
   f. Fee paid to have old well reworked with hope of increasing production.
   g. Geological survey costs incurred on a lease that later proves to be productive.
   h. Lease bonus paid to a farmer. (Later a well is drilled and oil is found.)

8. Big Mac Mining Company is engaged in the exploration for and the production of iron ore. During 19x1, Big Mac spent $350,000 on exploration at a new site in Minnesota and discovered a large deposit of low-grade iron ore. Mining of the ore is economically feasible only because the deposit is adjacent to water transportation and because Big Mac has developed an inexpensive process that increases the grade of the ore. In 19x2, Big Mac spent $500,000 in development costs to strip away the soil and rock surface covering the deposit. It also spent $2,000,000 for tangible mining equipment. Production began in 19x3. The gross value of the ore mined in 19x3 was $4,000,000. Of this gross value, $200,000 was paid to the land owners as royalties. Big Mac made no bonus payment for the base of the mineral rights. While Big Mac had gross receipts from the mine of $3,800,000, the net profit from the mining operation was $800,000 before depletion.

   a. How should Big Mac treat the exploration costs incurred in 19x1?
   b. How should it treat the development costs incurred in 19x2? The cost of the tangible mining equipment?
   c. Assuming that depreciation is recorded on the unit-of-production method and ignoring salvage, what would be the amount of depreciation for the year?
   d. How much depletion may the royalty owners deduct in 19x3?
   e. Compute the depletion deduction allowed Big Mac in 19x3.
   f. How would your answer in part d change if the net profit before depletion were $500,000?
   g. Compute the amount of amortization for Big Mac in 19x3.

9. Acme Oil company is a small independent producing company that has no retail outlets and no refining capacity. In the current year, Acme drilled three wells, each costing $250,000. Two wells were dry holes and the third contained a deposit sufficient for economic operation.

   a. How will Acme treat the $750,000 in development costs for tax purposes? (Include all alternatives.)
   b. Assume that Acme had a total of $400,000 capitalized depletable costs from the lease bonus and exploration costs on the third property, which was productive. Engineers estimated that the total oil in the deposit was 2,000,000 barrels. Given the annual figures below relative to annual production and profits, calculate (1) the depletion allowed and (2) the undepleted

cost for each of the next five years. In your answer, assume that the 22 percent rate applies to all years, that Acme's total production is within the quantity limits, and that the original estimate of reserves was not changed.

Year	Sales (in barrels)	Gross income	Net income (loss) (excluding depletion)
19x1	60,000	$1,200,000	$ (50,000)
19x2	60,000	1,200,000	50,000
19x3	120,000	2,400,000	650,000
19x4	120,000	2,400,000	1,100,000
19x5	200,000	4,000,000	3,500,000

10. In 1958, Ajax Mining Company acquired a coal deposit by outright purchase at a cost of $2,000,000. Between 1958 and this year, Ajax recorded cost depletion for book purposes of $1,250,000. Depletion deducted on its tax returns for that period amounted to $2,500,000. During the current year, Ajax sold the deposit for $1,400,000. Compute the gain or loss from the sale.

11. In 1979, Mr. Lucky Farmer leased his 640-acre farm to an oil company and received a lease bonus of $32,000. The company immediately drilled a gas well on the property and production was begun early in 1980. The well produced an average of 10,000,000 cubic feet per day. The gas was sold for $3.40 per 1,000 cubic feet, a total revenue of $12,444,000. Lucky received his one-eighth royalty in the above, which amounted to $1,555,500 (before any production taxes).

   a. How will Lucky treat for tax purposes the lease bonus received in 1979?
   b. Is Lucky entitled to statutory depletion on the $1,555,500 received in 1980? If so, how much depletion may he deduct?
   c. Assume the well was drilled by a large integrated oil company. What is the tax treatment of the bonus for the oil company?
   d. What rationale can be given for the varied treatment of the integrated oil company and Mr. Farmer relative to depletion? In your answer, consider the national energy crisis and the role of the two parties involved in coping with that crisis.

12. The following transactions took place between Independent Oil Company (operator) and Jeb Justrich (landowner) in 19x1, the current year.

Jan. 1, 19x1	Lease bonus paid to Jeb (Independent estimates 500,000 recoverable barrels)	$100,000
Dec. 15, 19x1	Royalty paid to Jeb by Independent	30,000

Other information concerning the Justrich lease:

Intangible drilling costs incurred by Independent	$170,000
Production costs incurred by Independent	20,000
Gross revenue from oil sales received by Independent (10,000 barrels were produced and sold)	240,000

NOTE: Independent Oil elects to expense all costs where an option is available. Assume that the 22 percent rate applies and that all production by both parties is less than the minimum quantity allowance.

   a. Compute Independent's cost depletion for 19x1.
   b. What is Independent's gross income subject to percentage depletion?
   c. Compute Independent's percentage depletion for 19x1.

d. Compute Independent's depletable basis for the oil property on January 1, 19x2.

13. Hendrix Mining, Inc. is engaged in strip mining coal on leased land. All depletable costs were recovered in prior years. In the current year, results of the mine operation were:

Gross sales of coal	$1,200,000
Less: Royalty payment	60,000
Net sales from operation	$1,140,000
Operating expenses	900,000
Net income before depletion	$ 240,000

a. How much depletion deduction is Hendrix allowed for this year?
b. What would your answer be to part a if Hendrix had incurred operating expenses of $1 million?

SUPPLEMENTAL PROBLEMS

14. The large integrated oil companies undoubtedly enjoy an oligopolistic position, particularly on the retail distribution of gasoline and fuel oils. Predict the long-run consequences on the retail prices of gasoline and fuel oils as a result of the repeal of statutory depletion for the large companies.

15. In early 1978, President Carter announced a new policy that placed a "floor" on the price of imported steel. The floor was based on the lowest production prices in the steel industry of the importing country.
   a. What was the purpose of establishing this floor?
   b. Suppose further trade barriers are imposed by our government against Japanese imports. What would you expect the Japanese government to do? If this became a widespread practice with all trading partners, speculate about the economic results.
   c. Within days after the "floor" price was announced, the steel industry announced increases in its prices affecting many products. What conclusions can you draw from this price increase relative to the efficiency of our steel industry? Relative to its management?

16. Before the dramatic increases in oil prices resulting from the OPEC cartel, the United States in most years enjoyed favorable trade balances. Exports of farm commodities played a major role in these favorable balances in many years.
   a. If the dollar continues to decline in value relative to other currencies, what should happen to the level of exports of farm commodities?
   b. What effects, if any, would your answer to part a of this problem have on the current complaints of farmers?

17. In 1980, Congress passed the Windfall Profit Tax Act. Under this law, a tax ranging up to 70 percent is levied on the excess of the selling price of oil or gas over a "base price." Thus, the tax is not an income tax but an excise tax. Using your school library or other sources, answer the following questions about the tax.
   a. What are the purposes of the act?
   b. What uses are to be made of the revenues generated?
   c. Is the tax likely to increase the supply of oil and gas?
   d. Many critics agree that the windfall profit tax law should have contained a provision permitting generous credits against the tax for amounts reinvest-

ed in the search for new oil and gas reserves. The bill did not contain this provision, however. Do you think such a provision would have been desirable? Why or why not?

e. Other critics suggest that the tax should have been levied on the increase in net income rather than, in effect, on the increase in gross receipts. Why, in your opinion, was this not done?

18. In 19x1, Ace Oil Company undertook an exploration project on 50,000 acres. A broad "reconnaissance" survey was carried out at a cost of $25,000. As a result of this preliminary exploration, two areas of interest that warranted further detailed exploration were found. Area 1 contained 3,000 acres, and Area 2 contained 5,000 acres. Detailed exploration work was carried out at costs of $22,000 on Area 1 and $20,000 on Area 2. The results on Area 1 were negative and no leases were taken. Two leases were taken in Area 2. Lease K-1 contained 500 acres and was acquired for a bonus of $30 per acre. Lease K-2 contained 600 acres and was obtained for a bonus of $50 per acre.

a. What amount of these expenditures would be charged to expense in 19x1?

b. What is the capitalized cost of each lease, K-1 and K-2?

That which flows from capital, like interest, rent and other items of income, is separate and distinct from the capital which produces it as gathered fruit is separate from the tree that bore it. While income may be transformed by accumulation into capital, like fruit, the seed of which produces another tree, the growth itself of neither capital nor the tree is income.

GODFREY N. NELSON,
"The Question of Taxing Capital Gains" (1940)

The root of the problem is that the capital gains concept itself is clear and consistent neither in practice nor in principle.

PETER MILLER,
"Capital Gains on Personal Efforts" (1954)

PART SIX
capital gains and losses

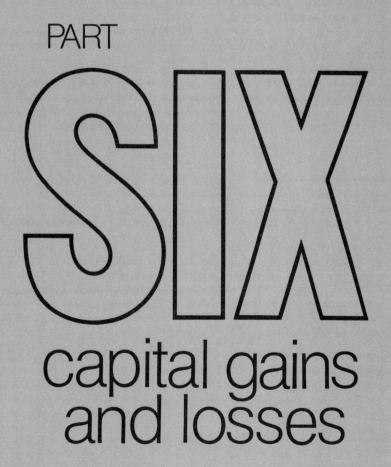

capital gain and loss: concept, history, and perspective

Although the United States purports to employ a unitary system of income taxation, since 1922 Congress has consistently extended special and advantageous tax treatment to those gains that could be classified as *capital gains*. In Part Six, we shall examine the evolution and current status of the capital gain and loss provisions. In Chapter 19, we explore briefly some alternative concepts of capital gain, the history of capital gains in the United States, and the arguments offered for and against the special treatment allowed. In Chapters 20 and 21, we discuss the more important features of the present formulation of the "pure" (statutory) capital gain and loss. In Chapters 22 and 23, we relate how this pure capital gain and loss formulation frequently has been modified to include gains and losses from the sale of noncapital assets and to exclude gains and losses from the sale of selected capital assets.

THE CAPITAL-GAIN CONCEPT

The American concepts of ordinary income and capital gain have evolved in large measure from the essential features of the economies prominent in the temperate zones of Europe during the eighteenth and nineteenth centuries.[1] In such economies, dependent

primarily upon agriculture, income appeared to be the value of an annual harvest, and capital was the land on which the annual harvest was nurtured to maturity. Under these conditions, both income and capital could be specifically identified, at least conceptually, as separate physical entities.

At the same time, the two concepts were further differentiated by the popularity of entailing estates. This legal practice enabled a landowner to limit the inheritance of his or her accumulated landed estate to a specified line of heirs. Each heir obtained only the right to occupy the land and to receive the income from any crops cultivated; he or she could not sell or bequeath the land itself (or any part of it) to any other person. Each heir was in the position of a life-tenant of specific property, which the courts would pass to a specified line of persons by rule of primogeniture. Under these conditions, it was most difficult for a life-tenant to realize much gain by sale of land because he or she could offer for sale only a life interest in that land—an asset that is particularly difficult to value since the life expectancy of any individual is not subject to precise prediction.

Because of the predominance of agriculture and the popularity of entailing estates, early concepts of income generally stressed the importance of the physical entity (or *res*), regularity of recurrence, and the role of intention. A crop could be easily identified, separated from the land, and sold, while leaving the land (or capital) untouched. In this setting,

[1] For an interesting development of this theme see Lawrence H. Seltzer, *The Nature and Tax Treatment of Capital Gains and Losses* (New York: National Bureau of Economic Research, Inc., 1951).

income could not be earned accidentally but was associated with the deliberate planting, cultivating, and harvesting of a crop. And, since crops tend to recur on an annual basis, regularity also was associated with income. George O. May, an accounting pioneer and an Englishman by birth, once noted this historical influence on English concepts of income taxation: " . . . the income tax in England was initiated when England was essentially a landholding, and agricultural, economy, when they thought in terms of annual income. In England they never talk of a landowner; it is a landholder, and they always talk in terms of annual income."[2]

The early American economy was not entirely comparable with this English setting. It, too, was initially an agricultural economy, but in America the growth of the frontier provided a major source of financial opportunity. Our country was long characterized by cheap, plentiful land, and land ownership carried limited social prestige. Pioneer families generally expressed little desire to retain land within a family by the entailing of an estate. Some of the first American fortunes were made from transactions in land, whereas stable incomes from rents and interest were relatively rare. Population was both growing and mobile. All these conditions were conducive to an increase in the market value of business enterprise and real estate, and entrepreneurs often realized substantial gains by selling their "basic" assets and reinvesting the proceeds in other ventures and in other locations. In short, the concept of capital prevalent in this country placed a greater emphasis on value and a lesser emphasis on things than the concept prevalent in England.

Judicial concept of a capital gain

In spite of the diversity between the early English and the early American economies, the first American courts to struggle with problems of income taxation and capital gain applied English common law and concluded that any gain realized on the sale of a capital investment was not income. In fact, little or no attention was given to the pecuniary measurement of capital investments. This legal concept prevailed in the case of *Gray* v. *Darlington,* in which Justice Field said:

> The mere fact that property has advanced in value between the date of its acquisition and sale does not authorize the imposition of the tax on the amount of

the advance. Mere advance in value in no sense constitutes the gains, profits, or income specified by the statute. It constitutes and can be treated merely as increase in capital.[3]

By 1918, however, the United States Supreme Court modified its earlier position and held that under the 1913 income-tax act the sale of an investment or capital asset resulted in a taxable gain or loss to the extent of the difference between the proceeds and the cost (or *adjusted basis*). The most widely quoted judicial statement of this revised position is found in *Eisner* v. *Macomber,* in which the Court, adopting the definition used in two earlier cases, said: "'Income may be defined as the gain derived from capital and from labor, or from both combined,' provided it be understood to include profit gained through a sale or conversion of capital assets. . . ."[4] As a consequence, between 1913 and 1922 the gain or loss thus determined was deemed subject to income taxation in precisely the same manner as were more ordinary forms of income. The Revenue Act of 1921, which became effective on January 1, 1922, provided the first special treatment for capital gain. *Some distinction between ordinary income and capital gain has been retained from 1921 to the present time.*

Because of the significant income-tax consequences that attach to a capital gain, it is appropriate to investigate further the essentials of the legal concept. Professor Seltzer once summarized these essentials in the following words:

> In both law and common speech, capital gains are generally regarded as the profits realized from increases in the market value of any assets that are not part of the owner's stock in trade or that he does not regularly offer for sale; and capital losses, as the losses realized from declines in the market value of such assets.[5]

Observe that this popular legal definition of a capital gain emphasizes the nature of the asset owner's trade or business or, more basically, the owner's intended use or disposition of a specific property. If the owner intends to hold a particular asset only until he can sell it at a price that will return a satisfactory profit,

---

[2]Tax Institute, Inc., *Capital Gains Taxation* (Lebanon, Pa.: Sowers Printing Co., 1946), p. 33.

[3]15 Wall. 63 (1872), p. 66.
[4]252 U.S. 189, p. 207 (1920). Quoted in the decision are words used earlier in *Stratton's Independence* v. *Howbert,* 231 U.S. 399 (1913) and *Doyle* v. *Mitchell Bros. Co.,* 247 U.S. 179, 185 (1918).
[5]Lawrence H. Seltzer, *The Nature and Tax Treatment of Capital Gains and Losses* (New York: National Bureau of Economic Research, 1961), p. 3.

then, according to the legal concept, any gain realized on sale or other disposition would constitute ordinary income. Alternatively, if the owner held the asset primarily for the production of recurring income or only as a long-range investment, with little or no intention of offering the basic asset for resale in the short run, even if the asset were to increase in value, the asset would constitute a capital asset and the gain realized on its sale would constitute a capital gain.

When applied to taxation, the legal definition of the capital gain creates the obvious difficulty of having a third party determine objectively the intentions of a taxpayer with regard to each asset owned. Moreover, it would be necessary to determine his or her intention at a particular moment in time, because an asset owner may alter his or her intentions over time. Thus an asset owner may discover that the sale of an item originally held solely for long-range investment purposes is now so valuable that it must be reclassified as held primarily for resale. And, of course, when the asset is actually sold and the gain is realized, the question arises of which date and which classification should prevail.

A second difficulty inherent in the conventional and legal definition of the capital gain is the requirement that the asset be offered *regularly* for sale before it is classified a noncapital asset. Are two, three, four, or five sales necessary (and over what time period) to categorize an item as one that is regularly offered for sale? Problems such as these force tax authorities to resort to common denominator tax classifications to expedite administration of a law that is less than perfect and that must be applied to a wide universe of slightly differing fact situations.[6]

It should be reemphasized that the legal concept of the capital gain depends on the relationship that exists between a taxpayer and each asset he or she owns. Even if one accepts the premise that a capital asset can be specifically identified, however, that fact does not necessarily lead to the conclusion that gains or losses on the disposition of such assets should be treated in any particular manner for tax purposes. If the pecuniary, or value, aspects of a transaction are the dominant feature, it can be forcibly argued that undue emphasis should not be placed upon the res, or thing, involved in that transaction.

On the other hand, if the res concept is deemed of primary importance, the value aspects may be subordinate.

The law generally retains a significant emphasis on the res concept. This is well illustrated in the case of trust law. The law ordinarily provides that the trustee clearly distinguish between the corpus and the income of the trust. Gains and losses realized on the sale or exchange of the corpus typically are recognized as part of the corpus and are not distributable to the income beneficiary. Similarly, depreciation deductions are used to reduce distributable income and to retain corpus. In short, the corpus of a trust is viewed as a distinct res, or thing, and changes in its value are not deemed to be income. For purposes of taxation, these gains are included in taxable income, but they are given special treatment. At this juncture, the important point is to understand that the law emphasizes the res concept so that capital gain and loss become distinguishable from other gain and loss.

Economic concept of a capital gain

In the classical economists' model of free enterprise, capital gain and loss are nonexistent. Such assumed parameters as perfect competition, perfect knowledge, conditions of certainty, and freedom of entry ensure the rapid and perfect adjustment of costs and prices throughout the market to eliminate pure economic profit. In the real world, of course, the assumed parameters do not exist. Economists concerned with divergences of the real world from the model sometimes define, often indirectly, the capital gain (or loss) as the gain attributable to one or more imperfect conditions.

WINDFALL GAINS AND LOSSES   Unanticipated gains and losses, especially if nonrecurring, are often described as "windfall" gains and losses and as such are distinguished from ordinary income. In practice, a recurrence criterion is somewhat easier to apply than is an unanticipated criterion, because the latter requires specific knowledge of expectations. Even such economically advanced countries as England have at times excluded from income taxation any windfall gains (determined primarily by a nonrecurrence criterion) on the grounds that these gains were not income. Theoretically, however, the unanticipated characteristic of such a gain is more important than its nonrecurrence.

In the classical economic model, the reallocation of scarce resources is attributable to the temporary

---

[6]Consider, for example, Code Sec. 1237, which provides that any gain from the sale of more than five lots or parcels of real estate from a single tract shall be considered ordinary income rather than capital gain. In this section, as elsewhere in the law, the arbitrary classifications involve numerous "qualifications."

existence of a pure economic profit (i.e., a greater-than-normal profit). Producers and suppliers allegedly migrate toward the pure-profit industry in the anticipation of making a greater-than-normal profit in the short run. In the longer run, of course, the reallocation process serves to drive down the price (and/or drive up the cost) until the pure profit has been eliminated. In this model, unanticipated gain and loss cannot serve to assist in the reallocation process except in an *ex post* way. That is, the first appearance of an unanticipated gain is what causes others to migrate to an industry. In this model, the unanticipated gain or loss is distinguished from the anticipated one and the former gain may, by default, be characterized as a capital gain or loss.

This concept of a capital gain leaves a great deal to be desired if applied to taxation. Observe that this concept, like the legal res concept, places a premium on a very personal factor; expectations are as difficult for courts and tax administrators to determine as are intentions. What is more, businesspersons normally have no specific expectation of gain on each and every asset they own. They believe, of course, that their operations as a whole will result in greater revenues than expenses, but they cannot identify with precision the gain anticipated on each asset. If such a measurement were possible, then part of the gain on the sale of ordinary inventory—that is, any excess of actual profit over anticipated profit—might be an economic capital gain. Finally, this concept of a capital gain—once more, like the res concept—presents a time specification that creates difficulties for tax assessment. If a taxpayer modifies expectations over time, which moment's expectation should control for tax purposes?

NONPRODUCTIVE GAIN AND LOSS   The branch of economics known as national income analysis produces yet another concept of the capital gain. Once again capital gain is distinguished from "national income," and once again the reason is conceptual. National income is conceived as a measure of the current economic productive activity of a country. Capital gain in this model is gain realized by the exchange of assets "produced" in another accounting period. If, for example, a person sells his or her personal residence at a gain, the "capital gain" is not reflected in the current year's national-income account because the home was constructed in another period. The value of newly discovered natural resources similarly are excluded from current national-income measures even if the property on which the resources are

discovered changes hands and the old owner realizes a significant gain on the sale. For national-income purposes, the income associated with the resources is reported in the period(s) of production, that is, when the resources are actually "tapped."

The economists' measures of national income are compiled, for reasons of convenience, largely on the basis of completed market transactions. It might appear, therefore, that this concept of income and capital gain would constitute a desirable basis for income taxation. But that conclusion is not justified, because the final measure of national income excludes a number of market transactions, including illegal activities and transfer payments as well as capital gains, and includes an imputed value for such selected nonmarket activities as owner-occupied dwellings and employee perquisites. Moreover, the arbitrary exclusion of "nonproductive" gain from income taxation would provide undue economic incentive to purely speculative transactions in existing assets and would place an economic disincentive on productive activities. The exclusion of illegal activities from income taxation would provide economic incentives for precisely those activities society desires to discourage. And both exclusions would create significant inequities between taxpayers that seem to be equally situated. Finally, the imputation of nonmarket transactions into a tax base is administratively cumbersome because of the subjectivity of the imputation process, particularly at the individual level. In short, neither the nonproductive-gain concept of the capital gain nor the national-income concept of income is useful for purposes of income taxation.

REAL INCOME AND CAPITAL GAIN   Many economists, particularly those concerned with consumption, stress the fact that monetary incomes cannot be equated to real incomes. These persons frequently contend that capital gain is simply the illusory gain created by changes in the price level. To illustrate, assume that a taxpayer purchased an asset 20 years ago for $10,000 and sold it this year for $15,000. If during the 20-year interval the general price level increased by 50 percent, then in terms of that taxpayer's command over the world's want-satisfying goods and services, the $5,000 "gain" realized on the sale is truly illusory. That is, today it would cost the full $15,000 to repurchase goods and services equivalent to those that could have been purchased for $10,000 20 years ago. Obviously, if a tax were imposed on the illusory gain, the taxpayer would be worse off after the sale because the after-tax proceeds would be insufficient to repurchase goods or services equivalent in value to those sold. In this sense, any tax imposed would constitute a tax on capital rather than a tax on income.

The problem is clear enough in principle, but those who use it as an objection to the taxation of capital gain generally fail to observe that the effects of a change in the price level are not restricted to a particular asset form. The retailer who discovers that the cost of replacing stock is increasing is faced with the identical problem: Paper profits exceed real income. The manufacturer with large investments in plant and equipment is in a comparable position: Charges for depreciation are inadequate for replacement, and therefore income is overstated and "overtaxed." Even the wage earner who receives a cost-of-living adjustment discovers that the larger paycheck is wholly illusory and that real after-tax income is decreased by a progressive tax system that fails to adjust for changes in the price level. If one is to argue against taxation of capital gain on the basis of changing price levels, it is necessary to argue that all gain (income) be similarly deflated (or inflated).

INTEREST RATES AND CAPITAL GAIN   Changes in the rate of interest cause problems in income measurement analogous to the questions raised by changes in the price level. Ordinarily, the fair market value of an interest-bearing obligation varies inversely with changes in the interest rate. If an investor purchases at par a $10,000 bond bearing 10-percent interest (assume for the sake of simplicity that the bond is a perpetuity—that is, that it has no due date), then the investor has guaranteed himself or herself a $1,000 annual return as long as the obligor remains solvent. If the "normal" interest rate (that is, the "price" of money) for investments of this type should fall from 10 percent to 5 percent, then this investor would discover that the market value of the bond had risen to approximately $20,000, since other investors could now obtain a $1,000 annual return only by investing that larger sum elsewhere. Those objecting to the taxation of capital gain contend that the gain on the sale of bonds under these circumstances ought not to be taxed, since the investor could not purchase an income stream equivalent to that held before sale if required to surrender any portion of the sale proceeds in the form of income taxes.

Once again the conceptual problem noted is a very real one, and there is a serious question of the wisdom of taxing such illusory gains (or of permitting

the deduction of such illusory losses). It must be understood, however, that once again the problem is not endemic to a limited form of investment. Although conventionally, the average businessperson, for accounting purposes, is not assumed to receive a specified rate of interest on a basic investment (including investment in inventory), the criticism leveled above is equally applicable to all investments and therefore to some parts of ordinary income.

An accounting concept of a capital gain

To the accountant, capital gain or loss is perhaps best described as that gain or loss that occurs only at irregular intervals and is attributable to imperfect knowledge and, hence, imperfect measurement of income in earlier periods. Oscar S. Nelson, a former Professor of Accounting at the University of Pennsylvania, expressed such an accounting concept in the following words:

> The question of the distinction between operating income and capital gains was raised at the recent meetings of the American Accounting Association. In theory there is no distinction, since both result from business effort, i.e., the employment of capital, labor and management by an enterprise with profit as the motive. Capital gains or losses are a manifestation of imperfect income measurement and result because of the requirement of modern business for periodic computation of net profit or loss. Capital gains or losses are composites of imperfect estimates of depreciation, imperfect allocations of costs, imperfect separation of capital and revenue expenditures, disregard of or imperfect adjustment for price level changes, etc.[7]

This accounting concept of capital gain is comparable to the economic concept in denying, in theory, the existence of a distinct thing that can be distinguished and meaningfully labeled as a capital gain. And, like the economist, the accountant observes certain phenomena that do not fit into the ideal model—the accountant recognizes the imperfections of the real world and seems to define capital gain and loss loosely as those income items that are attributable to real-world imperfections.

Except in acting as tax advisor, the accountant's concern with capital gain and loss is restricted to a

---

[7]Oscar S. Nelson, "Capital Gains from Price Level Increases," *The Accounting Review,* 26 (January, 1951), p. 31.

concern for presenting financial information fairly to third parties. Although the accountant considers it necessary to distinguish between routine income items and other "material amounts" of "nonrecurring" gains and losses, he or she sometimes may characterize such gains and losses as "capital" ones only because this terminology may have meaning to readers of financial statements. Thus, in presenting financial data, the accountant accepts the age-old notion that recurrence is a necessary condition of operating income and nonrecurrence a necessary condition of capital gain.

Beyond this, very little can be said to clarify the accounting concept of capital gain. And to admit that certain gain and loss occur because of imperfect knowledge and imperfect income measurement does nothing to provide a sound basis for deciding whether they ought to be excluded from income taxation, taxed at preferential rates, taxed at equal rates, or taxed at penalty rates. Since 1922, whether or not it has been justified, Congress has provided special and advantageous tax treatment for the peculiar transactions termed capital gains and losses. Even a brief examination of the changing provisions will reveal the complexity of the problem and the conceptual inadequacy of traditional solutions. Let us now look briefly at the history of these changing provisions from 1913 to the present.

HISTORY OF CAPITAL GAIN AND LOSS TAX PROVISIONS SINCE 1913

As we noted earlier, during the era of the Civil War income taxes, the American courts followed English precedent in finding that the excess of proceeds realized over cost on the sale of a capital investment were not income and therefore not subject to income taxation. On May 20, 1918, however, the Supreme Court reversed its earlier decision and declared that, at least for purposes of interpretation of the Corporate Excise Tax of 1909 (which effectively constituted a corporate income tax even before the passage of the Sixteenth Amendment), capital gain did constitute income. Some authorities suggest that this departure from the English precedent must be attributed in large measure to the great pressure for revenue exerted by World War I.[8] In any case, ever since 1918 the courts have consistently held that such

gains do constitute taxable income. The congressional tax treatment accorded such gains and losses, however, has varied considerably during the past half-century.[9]

The first period: 1913–22

The history of this tax treatment can be divided into six relatively distinct periods. During the first period—between 1913 and 1922—capital gains were taxed in precisely the same manner as were other forms of income. Section II(B) of the Revenue Act of 1913 defined net income as including "gains, profits, and income derived from . . . sales, or dealings in property, whether real or personal." Because no portion of any of the several revenue laws enacted prior to 1921 provided any special treatment for capital gains, the Treasury applied the full normal and surtax rates to them as part of total income.

Moreover, since the only loss deductions mentioned in the 1913 Act were losses "incurred in trade," the Treasury denied the taxpayer the right even to offset capital losses against capital gains. This deficiency in the original law was rectified in the Revenue Act of 1916, Sec. 5 of which provided for a deduction of nontrade or business losses from transactions entered into for profit; but it further provided that such losses could not exceed the profits arising therefrom. A 1918 provision modified the 1916 provision and permitted the complete deductibility of all losses, whether or not offset by gains of the same genus. Thus, within the first five years of income taxation following adoption of the Sixteenth Amendment, Congress disallowed capital losses completely, permitted their deduction to the extent of capital gains, and provided for their unlimited deduction from any kind of gain. These frequent modifications foreshadowed the continuing controversy over the correct or desirable tax treatment of certain forms of income.

The second period: 1922–33

The second period in the history of capital-gain taxation begins with the passage of the Revenue Act of 1921 (applicable to tax years beginning after December 31, 1921) and ends with the Act of 1934. During

---

[8] For example, see Godfrey N. Nelson, "Taxation of Capital Gains," *Taxes—The Tax Magazine,* 21 (June, 1943), p. 308.

[9] Anita Wells presented an excellent historical summary of the U.S. capital gain and loss provisions in "Legislative History of Treatment of Capital Gains Under the Federal Income Tax, 1913–1948," *National Tax Journal,* 2 (March, 1949), pp. 12–32. The authors readily acknowledge their debt to Ms. Wells for much of the historical material included in this chapter.

this period, Congress provided an optional alternative tax on selected "capital gains," which, of course, had to be defined with some precision. Congress chose to define capital assets and to provide that the gain or loss realized on sale of items so defined would be eligible for the special treatment.

The first capital-asset definition included both positive and negative elements—that is, for property to be classified as a capital asset it had to have been "acquired and held by the taxpayer for profit or investment for more than 2 years (whether or not connected with his trade or business)," and it could *not* be "property held for the personal use or consumption of the taxpayer or his family, or stock in trade of the taxpayer or other property of a kind which would properly be included in the inventory of the taxpayer if on hand at the close of the taxable year." This definition obviously followed the legal concept and placed primary emphasis on the relationship between the taxpayer and the asset at the time of purchase or disposition or both.

The advantage extended these long-term capital gains in 1922 was the *option* of paying a flat 12.5-percent tax on them, while continuing to pay the ordinary normal and surtax rates on all other income. As a practical matter, this meant that any taxpayer earning a taxable income in excess of $16,000 would find it advantageous to use the optional tax as fully as possible. The House Ways and Means Committee report on the 1921 tax bill suggests that the fundamental reason for this first alternative capital-gain tax rate was the popular belief that high surtax rates (up to 77 percent at that time) had previously deterred numerous taxpayers from selling their capital assets.

The 1924 Revenue Bill modified slightly the definition of a capital asset by removing the earlier provision that excluded from the definition of a capital asset any asset held for personal use. The Senate Finance Committee report explained this modification as a deliberate extension of the alternative rate to gains realized on the sale of a personal residence.

The 1924 act also revoked a capital-loss carryover provision that had been established in 1921 and limited the deductibility of capital loss to 12.5 percent of net capital loss. The base amount eligible for the alternative long-term capital-gain tax was also changed to a net basis (the excess of net long-term capital gain over net short-term capital loss). Other revisions, largely in the area of capital-loss deductions, were enacted by Congress in 1928, 1932, and 1933.

The third period: 1934–37

Between 1934 and 1937, the third and briefest of our six periods, the rationale of special capital-gain taxation was related to the problems created by a realization criterion. That is, when gains that accrue over several years are not recognized for tax purposes until they are realized in a completed transaction, the tax imposed by a progressive rate schedule often is inequitable. In an attempt to correct this inequity, Congress provided a capital-gain exclusion percentage that increased with the length of time the capital asset had been held prior to disposition. The percentage exclusions were as follows:

Holding period	Percentage exclusion
1 year or less	0%
1 to 2 years	20
2 to 5 years	40
5 to 10 years	60
More than 10 years	80

Since the exclusion was relatively high for assets held for more than 2 years, Congress further elected to discontinue the alternative (optional) capital-gain tax rate instituted in 1921—i.e., to make the portion of the capital gain that remained after deducting the exclusion subject to the normal and surtax rates applicable to ordinary income. This change was partially a response to charges that the alternative tax option benefited only persons in high income brackets.

The 1934 act again modified, very slightly, the definition of a capital gain; limited the capital-loss deduction to the sum of capital gains plus $2,000 of ordinary income; and disallowed losses incurred on transactions between certain related persons. Few other changes in capital gain and loss taxation were enacted until 1938.

The fourth period: 1938–49

By 1938 Congress was once again ready to revise capital-gain taxation significantly. Before enacting new legislation, however, it seriously considered eliminating entirely the taxation of capital gain and loss. Congress rejected this alternative on the grounds that

(1) capital gains represent taxpaying ability no less than equivalent income from other sources and repeal of the capital gains tax would increase the tax

burden on other income; (2) the great bulk of capital gains are realized in connection with transactions entered into for profit; and (3) complete exemption of capital gains from income taxes would permit tax avoidance through conversion of other types of income into capital gains.[10]

On the other hand, Congress apparently believed that an advantageous tax (relative to ordinary income-tax rates) was essential to encourage the realization of capital gain and thus to increase the mobility of capital in the economy.

The eventual 1938 solution was to divide capital gains and losses into three groups:[11] (1) long term (capital assets held more than 24 months), (2) medium term (capital assets held more than 18 months but less than 24 months), and (3) short term (capital assets held for less than 18 months). All short-term gains and losses were combined with ordinary income without benefit of exclusion; 33⅓ percent of the medium-term capital gains could be excluded from the income-tax base; and 50 percent of the long-term capital gains could be excluded. In addition, the alternative (flat-rate) capital-gain rate was reinstituted, this time at 30 percent of the net long-term gains (including both the long- and medium-term gains) after application of the appropriate percentage exclusion. Thus the 30-percent alternative tax, when combined with the percentage exclusion, made the effective maximum tax rate applicable to medium-term capital gains 20 percent and that applicable to long-term capital gains 15 percent.

The relatively short holding period required before capital-gain advantages accrued was explained as an additional incentive for realization of capital gain and, therefore, for increasing tax revenues. Additionally, the committee reports suggest that Congress believed the 24-month holding period adequately distinguished between "speculative gains" and true "investment profits."

In 1938, a major modification of the capital-asset definition was enacted, *excluding depreciable property used in the taxpayer's trade or business from the statutory definition of capital assets.* Reportedly, the change was made to benefit the taxpayer by permitting unlimited deductions for losses realized on the sale of machinery and/or buildings purchased during the inflationary period of the 1920s and sold during the depression years of the 1930s. By 1942, economic

conditions were reversed, and Congress enacted a unique section (Sec. 117(j) of the 1939 Code), which retained the definitional exclusion of depreciable trade or business assets from the capital-asset category but provided that if the gain exceeded the loss on the sale of these assets in a particular year, the gain should be treated as a capital gain. This provision is one of very few in the history of United States income taxation that, in effect, provided the taxpayer with the pleasure of both the cake and the eating.

In the early post-1938 period, short-term capital loss could be used only to offset short-term capital gain, any excess loss to be carried forward and offset against short-term capital gain of subsequent years. The provision for long-term capital loss was slightly more generous: If long-term capital loss exceeded long-term capital gain in a given year, the taxpayer was to pay the larger of (1) the ordinary tax rates on the excess of ordinary income over net long-term capital loss or (2) the normal and surtax rates on ordinary income less 30 percent of the net long-term capital loss.

In 1942, the short-term–long-term distinction was reduced to a simple six-month holding period. The Senate Finance Committee report justified the six-month period as a greater incentive to the realization of capital gain and thereby added revenue to the Treasury. The report further stated that the six-month holding period would be adequate to differentiate the purely speculative profit from the legitimate investment gain. Further modifications enacted in 1942 changed the capital-loss deduction provisions, the carryforward provisions, and the base for the alternative long-term capital-gain tax rate.

Finally, the 1942 provisions included an entirely new *deduction* equal to 50 percent of the excess of net long-term capital gain over net short-term capital loss. This deduction, which is the major capital-gain tax advantage today, made the substitution of a long-term capital gain for ordinary income advantageous to all taxpayers, including those persons in the lowest tax bracket. In addition, the retention of an alternative, maximum tax rate (until 1979) was particularly beneficial to taxpayers earning larger amounts of taxable income. These two tax advantages, coupled with the relatively high tax rates that were imposed on even moderate incomes by the time of World War II, were responsible for widespread efforts to convert ordinary income into long-term capital gain—a trend that will be considered in greater detail in Chapters 22 and 23.

[10] Anita Wells, *op. cit.,* p. 22.
[11] The descriptive titles used here are the authors', not those of the law.

The fifth period: 1950–69

It is not at all clear precisely where the fifth period in capital-gain history began, for Congress made no single major change in the definition of a capital asset, the holding period requirements, or the rationale for the special treatment between 1942 and 1969. Beginning with the Revenue Act of 1950, however, the focus in capital-gain legislation was clearly on closing loopholes observed in the law, and, in this sense, a fifth period was instituted.

The loophole closing was forced on Congress by widespread conversion of ordinary income into capital gain—which, of course, Congress itself encouraged by making the ordinary tax and surtax rates so high that the taxpayer was forced into this arbitrary method of reducing his tax bill. The 50-percent maximum surtax rate of 1921 became effective at taxable incomes in excess of $200,000, the 59-percent maximum of 1934 at $1,000,000, and the 75-percent maximum of 1938 at $5,000,000; but the 91-percent maximum of 1950 was applicable at only $200,000. This change to an extremely high surtax rate (91 percent) effective at a relatively low level of taxable income ($200,000), made the capital-gain provisions the primary loophole in the entire income-tax law, particularly for the taxpayer in the higher income strata.[12]

Congressional efforts did not provide any consistent philosophy for capital-gain taxation, and the importance of "political considerations" is apparent. In the 1950 law, for example, Congress condemned the use of a "collapsible corporation" as a vehicle for obtaining capital-gain treatment of personal-effort compensation, while the same law facilitated a similar phenomenon with the "restricted stock option" provisions. The 1950 act further denied the author, musician, or artist the right to capital-gain treatment on his or her work product, while it extended this right to the inventor. The "chameleon section," which provided that under certain circumstances gains on the sale of selected assets could be treated as capital gains while losses on the same assets (under other circumstances) could be treated as ordinary losses, was extended in 1951 to include livestock (if held for draft, breeding, or dairy purposes) and the sale of unharvested crops.

Although the Internal Revenue Code of 1954 re-numbered the 1939 Code sections, it did little to modify the substance of the prior law relative to capital gain and loss. The 1954 Code did include a typical array of capital-gain-related provisions, including new rules under which noncorporate owners of subdivided realty could claim capital-gain treatment, a section to end the practice of issuing noninterest-bearing obligations at substantial discounts so that the investor could claim capital gains upon retirement rather than interest income in the interim, and a section specifically making accounts and notes receivable obtained in the ordinary course of trade or business noncapital assets. Innumerable other relatively minor revisions in capital-gain taxation enacted between 1950 and 1969 could be cited, but none provided any real modification of the elementary capital-gain concept.

The sixth period: 1969–78

As we noted in Chapter 3, the capital gain and loss provisions were the single most important factor in explaining the large differences between the apparent average and the real effective marginal tax rates applicable to upper incomes of individual taxpayers prior to 1969. The extent to which persons in the higher income brackets were able to report their incomes as capital gains was revealed by Treasury Department data in both 1962 and 1964. Professor Martin David summarized some of the data for the

TABLE **19-1**

NET CAPITAL GAIN REPORTED ON INDIVIDUAL INCOME TAX RETURNS EXPRESSED AS A PERCENTAGE OF ADJUSTED GROSS INCOME, 1964

Adjusted gross income class	Percentage
Under $5,000	1.00
$5,000 under $10,000	0.51
$10,000 under $15,000	0.89
$15,000 under $20,000	2.02
$20,000 under $50,000	4.81
$50,000 under $100,000	9.94
$100,000 under $500,000	25.85
$500,000 under $1,000,000	51.34
$1,000,000 or more	54.70
All income classes	2.00

SOURCE: Martin David, *Alternative Approaches to Capital Gains Taxation* (Washington, D.C.: The Brookings Institution, 1968), Table 4-17, p. 86.

---

[12]The significance of the capital-gain provisions to high-income taxpayers is well illustrated in Pechman's graph reproduced in Chapter 3 of this text. See p. **3**/6.

latter year (see Table 19-1). The Treasury data further disclosed that most of the capital gains reported were derived from either the sale of securities or real estate.

Although these revelations were not truly new, Congress chose to act in 1969. Initially, the House sought to increase the long-term capital-asset holding period from six to twelve months. The Senate and the Conference Committees, however, voted to retain a six-month holding-period requirement. On the other hand, the majority of both Houses of Congress agreed to phase out the alternative tax by 1972, except for a $50,000 maximum for individual taxpayers, and to increase the alternative rate for corporate taxpayers. Congress further agreed to delete a few more assets from the definition of a capital asset, to place new restrictions on the deduction of long-term capital losses from ordinary income, and to require a greater portion of the gain realized on the sale of real property to be reported as ordinary income if the taxpayer had been depreciating the property using a rapid depreciation method. The relative advantage of capital gains was further reduced by the inclusion of the long-term capital-gain deduction within the tax base for the new minimum tax on tax preference items, instituted in 1969 and significantly expanded in 1976. Although the Tax Reform Act of 1976 did increase the amount of capital loss that could be offset against ordinary income, it also increased the holding period for long-term treatment from six months to one year. That same act also provided for even greater recapture of depreciation on residential real property that is depreciated on a rapid basis. And, possibly in the most significant change in years, the Tax Reform Act of 1976 provided for a carryover basis on inherited properties. Stated briefly, this meant that the income-tax potential, in a property that had increased in value, would be passed along from one generation to another.

The seventh period: 1979–?

After 10 years of steadily reducing the relative advantage of capital gains over ordinary income, Congress dramatically reversed this pattern in the Revenue Act of 1978. Most importantly, Congress (1) increased the long-term capital gain deduction for noncorporate taxpayers from 50 to 60 percent of the net capital gain and (2) removed the long-term capital gain deduction from the list of tax preference items that poisoned amounts of ordinary income that oth-

erwise were eligible for the maximum tax on personal service income. Although the details of these two changes may not be understood without further study, their significance can be grasped easily. In the extreme case, the combined effect of these two changes reduced the *maximum* effective tax rate on the net capital gains of individuals from approximately 50 to 28 percent! Obviously, a tax reduction of 22 percentage points should serve to rekindle efforts to once again convert ordinary income into capital gain.

In addition to the two major changes, the Revenue Act of 1978 also decreased the alternative capital-gains tax rate from 30 to 28 percent for corporate taxpayers and totally eliminated any alternative tax for noncorporate taxpayers. The 1978 Act also *retroactively* deferred the effective date of the carryover basis rules for inherited properties from December 31, 1976, to December 31, 1979. And the Windfall Profits Tax Act finally put an end to the carryover basis rules by retroactively repealing the rules that had been part of the 1976 Reform Act. Thus, by 1980, we are largely back to the rules of the 1950–69 period as far as capital gains are concerned.

Unfortunately, the most desirable tax treatment of a capital gain is not determined any more easily than is the concept of a capital gain. Once one accepts the notion that there is a transaction result deserving of special tax treatment, it becomes necessary to define the transaction result so that it may be recognized from among the many transactions subject to the income tax. Ideally, this definition would be subject to objective tests, render equitable results, and contribute to administrative simplicity. These are obviously conflicting objectives—however desirable they might be individually.

The frequency and severity of change in the capital gain and loss tax provisions implies that, at least for tax purposes, it is best to accept the notion that capital gain and loss are what the Code says they are—and nothing more pretentious. Concepts of capital gain differ in other disciplines; the greatest danger in making comparisons between these concepts lies in failing to realize that what constitutes a sound concept for one purpose is wholly inadequate for another purpose. A major disadvantage of the separation of ordinary income from capital gain for tax purposes is that this separation alone adds more complexity to our tax laws than any other single notion. Before we study those complex rules in detail, let us consider briefly the major arguments that have been made for and against them.

THE ISSUES: A BRIEF PERSPECTIVE

The fundamental issue in the area of capital-gain taxation is whether or not capital gain is sufficiently different from other, more ordinary, forms of income to be granted special treatment in the income-tax laws. At one end of the continuum are those who argue that capital gain by definition is not income and therefore ought not to be subject to income taxation at all. At the opposite end are those who argue that there simply are no meaningful differences between capital gain and ordinary income and both, therefore, ought to be treated equally for income-tax purposes. Between these extremes one discovers the many intermediate positions of those who hold that capital gain is sufficiently peculiar to justify some special tax treatment but insufficiently unlike other income to be excluded entirely from the income-tax base.

Professor Walter J. Blum, a noted income-tax authority, synthesized the many arguments in an article, "A Handy Summary of the Capital Gains Arguments."[13] In total, Professor Blum articulates twenty-five arguments favoring and eight arguments opposing the preferential tax treatment of capital gain. In spite of the imbalance in number of arguments, Blum's own conclusion is that "capital gains should be taxed as ordinary income."[14]

Arguments favoring preferential treatment

THE DEFINITIONAL ARGUMENT   The first point is that capital gain simply is not income by definition. To the extent that this argument stems from attributing capital gain to changes in the general price level or in the rate of interest, it was already discussed and will not be repeated here. Even disregarding these two special cases, however, the basic conceptual, or definitional, question remains: Is capital gain income?

Some authorities, like Professor Blum, argue that the answer is not pertinent to tax questions. For example, in an exchange of ideas on this point Blum wrote:

There is thus little to be learned by asking whether capital gains are "income." The pertinent question for tax policy is whether income for tax purposes should be defined to include capital gains. This challenge requires that we delineate the aims of using income as a tax base, and that we examine the equity and economic effects of including or excluding capital gains in the light of those goals.[15]

To this, Henry C. Wallich, the professor disagreeing with Blum in this exchange, responded: "I must strongly disagree with Blum about his efforts to downgrade the question whether capital gains are income. This is indeed the crux of the matter, in terms of theory, behavior, and, if I may be forgiven, of politics."[16]

On balance, we believe Professor Blum's case is the stronger of the two—that is, that tax policy should be built upon its own models, separate and distinct from the models of economics, law, public administration, or accounting. Hence, the inclusion or exclusion of capital gain in the income definition is a matter for Congress to decide. It is our opinion that taxation is a separate discipline, which, admittedly, draws heavily on economics, law, public administration, and accounting but which should not be confused with them in objective, concept, definition, theory, or practice.

THE MOBILITY OF CAPITAL   The taxation of capital gain, runs a second argument, seriously inhibits the mobility of capital. This idea has been frequently cited in justification of the tax-favored treatment capital gain has received in the United States since 1922. In its most elementary form, the argument states simply that any tax on the gain realized on the sale of a capital asset—for example, the sale of a security—increases the cost of selling, while there is no comparable cost to retaining the investment in question. Hence, other things being equal, capital asset owners will favor retention of their value-appreciated capital assets over their sale. Often these asset owners are described as being "locked in" their investment. It is argued that ultimately this sale-inhibiting factor produces an undesirable allocation of economic resources and, in particular, an inadequate supply of capital for new enterprise.

On an *a priori* basis, the reasoning appears valid enough. Unfortunately, there has been pitifully little

[13] Walter J. Blum, "A Handy Summary of the Capital Gains Arguments," *Taxes, The Tax Magazine,* 35 (April, 1957), pp. 247–66.
[14] *Ibid.,* p. 248.

[15] Walter J. Blum, "Taxation of Capital Gains in the Light of Recent Economic Developments—Some Observations," *National Tax Journal,* 18 (December, 1965), p. 430.
[16] Henry C. Wallich, "Rejoinder," *National Tax Journal,* 18 (December, 1965), p. 437.

empirical investigation to substantiate or to quantify the importance of this tax factor in actual operation. As Professor Wallich observed, "The behavior of stock market investors is largely unexplored, and what we know is not always in obvious accord with what appears to be rationality."[17]

Even if it could be established that the presence of the capital-gain tax does inhibit the sale of securities, that fact alone cannot be equated with the conclusion that the income tax on these gains ought to be reduced or repealed. For example, it would be possible, theoretically, to nullify the bias in favor of retaining appreciated capital assets by taxing unrealized as well as realized capital gains at the end of each year. Admittedly, at the present time this solution seems to be unsatisfactory on grounds of the administrative difficulties of valuation. It has been suggested, alternatively, however, that we retain the present realization concept but tax as income any unrealized capital gain when the asset is given away or when it is passed to another as part of a decedent's estate. This modification of the present position would reduce the benefit of retention over selling to the (uncertain) difference between the present value of a tax paid now and the tax that would be due at gift or death. At the same time, it retains most of the administrative advantages of the realization criterion.

Considering the alternatives, Professor Blum's conclusion is sound:

Still, the resulting immobility is not to be overdramatized. It is highly improbable that the locking-in tendency of the tax would cause any substantial amount of investment to remain in dying or stagnant industries or dry up the sources of equity capital for dynamic and promising ones. The intelligent investor is unlikely to be lured by the tax into remaining with a sinking enterprise, for he understands that a partial after-tax gain is always better than a loss.[18]

THE INEQUITY OF THE REALIZATION CRITERION   Since capital gains often accrue to an asset over several years, taxing them at progressive rates in the year of realization produces an inordinately high tax. As

noted earlier, this third reason constituted the primary rationale for the tax-favored treatment of capital gain during the third period in the history of U.S. capital gain—1934–37. Obviously, this argument was negated by the mere six-month holding period requirement for "long-term" capital-gain advantages that existed between 1942 and 1976.

When the fact condition postulated in this argument exists, the tax result certainly can be inequitable. However, this phenomenon is *not* restricted to the capital gain—it is equally applicable to income of any variety. Certainly our accounting experience substantiates the conclusion that the measurement of income for any period as short as a year is at best hazardous. The answer to this objection lies in a sound and comprehensive income-averaging law. The income-averaging law enacted in 1964 and liberalized in 1969, while much less than a perfect solution, is a vast improvement over its predecessor. Some authorities argue that if unrealized capital gain were taxed at gift or death, then an all-inclusive averaging provision would be the only other special tax benefit really necessary to solve the capital-gain dilemma.

A PLANNED REFUGE   In a country with a highly progressive and comprehensive personal income tax, capital gain constitutes the only conceivable remaining method of amassing a fortune—a necessary possibility in a free-enterprise economy. Although not widely *cited* as a major reason for preferential capital-gain taxation, this proposition may have more effective influence with the political bodies that enact our tax laws than any other single argument offered. Conceivably, this proposition may be given even greater weight than all others combined. Professor Seltzer states this argument clearly:

Many congressmen and other persons . . . do not want an airtight tax system. They want to preserve the opportunity for a man to make a financial home-run, a touchdown, a killing. The preferential tax treatment of capital gains has the virtue, in their minds, of offering just such an opportunity.[19]

This argument must have tremendous appeal to anyone born in a free country. Yet it cannot be made the answer to the more fundamental question inevitable with progressive income taxation—that is, just

[17] *Ibid.,* p. 437. But see Martin S. Feldstein, "Personal Taxation and Portfolio Composition: An Econometric Analysis," *Econometrica,* Vol. 44, July, 1976, p. 4; M. S. Feldstein and Shlomo Yitzhaki, "The Effect of the Capital Gains Tax on the Selling and Switching of Common Stock," *Journal of Public Economics,* February, 1978; and Charles Holt and J. Shelton, "The Lock-In Effect of the Capital Gains Tax," *National Tax Journal,* December, 1962.

[18] Walter J. Blum, "A Handy Summary of the Capital Gains Arguments," *Taxes, The Tax Magazine,* 35 (April, 1957), pp. 257–58.

[19] Lawrence H. Seltzer, "Capital Gains and the Income Tax," *American Economic Review,* 40 (May, 1950), p. 378.

how progressive (and to what rate) ought the progressive rate structure be? The authors would argue that our present tax rates are indeed unduly progressive to an unreasonably high surtax rate applicable at relatively modest income levels. Except for the 50-percent maximum tax on *personal service* income, which was instituted by the Tax Reform Act of 1969 and expanded by the 1976 Reform Act, the 70-percent top rate is applicable to all noncorporate taxable incomes in excess of $215,400 under the most favorable circumstance (the married taxpayer, filing jointly). A few years ago it was even worse: a 91-percent top rate applied to all taxable income other than capital gain. Could not the American dream of rags to riches better be restored by lowering the entire rate structure, especially at the higher income levels, than by giving preferential treatment only to that gain that can be twisted into a relatively narrow statutory definition called a long-term capital gain?

While discussing this same issue, Professor Blum goes on to observe:

> There is yet another danger in this *realpolitik* approach to taxation. Those who get the advantage of sufficiently important special preferences lose interest in facing up to the problem of improving the tax system as a whole. The very persons who might furnish the energy and intelligence for sound reform are thus transformed into active bystanders or opponents of constructive change.[20]

WORLD TRADE DEMANDS IT Numerous writers have suggested that the United States is one of very few countries imposing a tax on capital gain. Some of these writers go on to suggest that if we are to compete in world trade markets we cannot tax capital gains either. Like many statements, this one is at best a half-truth. First, and most important, the definition of a capital gain is significantly narrower in many countries than it is in the United States. Thus, for example, until 1965 the United Kingdom imposed no tax on capital gain—however, tax-free gain was restricted to "casual profits," a concept *much* narrower than the capital-gain concept in U.S. tax law.

Second, some of the countries that do not impose the income tax on capital gains do exact a capital or other tax on capital assets, which compensates for the exclusion of the gain on the sale of these assets from the income tax. Germany's capital tax is an example.

The developing nations, which are adopting income taxation with increasing frequency, do have a tendency to exclude capital gain from income taxation because of the ubiquitous problems in taxing it. This tendency has an unsatisfactory economic consequence in that it provides an incentive for the wealthier members of those societies to invest in foreign exchange, diamonds, real estate, and other "riskless" assets rather than in the productive industries so essential to economic development.

These, then, are the major arguments made in support of a special tax treatment for capital gain. What arguments are made on the other side?

Arguments opposing preferential treatment

INCOME: A FUNGIBLE COMMODITY Implicit in a unitary system of income taxation is the premise that every dollar of economic gain is equal to every other dollar of economic gain. Theoretically, at least, a dollar of capital gain can be used in the same manner as any other dollar of income. Given this premise, any provision that treats certain dollars of gain in a preferential manner is unwarranted unless a major advantage is gained. There are, of course, advantages now associated with capital-gain taxation, but critics argue that they could be achieved more directly by (1) an all-inclusive income-averaging provision; (2) modification in the realization criterion (treating transfers by death and/or gift as appropriate moments for the imposition of an income tax); and (3), most importantly, drastic reductions in the tax-rate structure, especially at the upper income levels. These modifications would, respectively, (1) avoid the injustice of progressive tax rates applied to gains accumulated over several years but realized in a single year; (2) minimize the economic disincentive associated with realizing capital gain (rather than retaining it in unrealized form); and (3) make possible the accumulation of a personal fortune even in a country with a relatively high personal income tax.

ADMINISTRATIVE SIMPLICITY The capital-gain provisions constitute the largest single complication of our present tax structure. Many do not deem the social benefit of this complexity sufficient to compensate for the social cost associated with it. Obviously, an adequate evaluation of this argument would require both a measurement technique and a detailed listing of all advantages and disadvantages associated with the capital-gain tax. Even without such an evalua-

[20]Walter J. Blum, "A Handy Summary of the Capital Gains Arguments," *Taxes, The Tax Magazine,* 35 (April, 1957), pp. 260–61.

tion, however, few persons deny the tremendous complexity associated with the capital-gain provisions or that the demise of these provisions not only would simplify the existing law but would ease the administration of it by putting an end to the seemingly endless search by tax advisors for new methods of converting ordinary income into capital gain. These efforts are often of sufficient complexity to require major attention by both the Revenue Service and the courts.

CONFLICT WITH OTHER OBJECTIVES   Capital-gain provisions currently do serious damage to our tax objective of wealth redistribution and our tax canon of horizontal equity. The severity of the effect of capital-gain taxation on wealth redistribution is directly related to the amount of income the high-income earner can realize in the form of a statutory capital gain that can be taxed at the alternative rate. It is also directly related to the difference between the marginal tax rate applicable to the taxpayer's ordinary income and the rate applicable to net capital gain. Obviously, a great diversity of opinion exists as to how much wealth ought to be redistributed through income taxation. To those persons who would minimize this objective, the argument carries little weight.

The impact of the alternative tax on the canon of horizontal equity is easily demonstrated. Table 19-2 compares the income tax results since 1913 for a taxpayer earning (only) a $50,000 ordinary income with those for a taxpayer earning (only) a $50,000 net capital gain. This illustration assumes in each case a married, citizen, taxpayer having a net income, after personal exemptions and the zero bracket amount, of $50,000. One taxpayer's income is wholly ''ordi-

nary''; the other's entirely net capital gain. The years selected for this table demonstrate some of the major changes in the tax law; yet the comparison is much less than perfect because of changes in both rates and capital asset definitions through the years. A more comprehensive demonstration of the impact of capital gain taxation is explicit in Figure 3-2 and implicit in Figure 3-3.

WASTE OF HUMAN RESOURCES   No one could dispute the fact that the capital-gain provisions have had a pervasive influence on tax planning. One writer suggested that ''businessmen devote as much thought and effort to converting ordinary income into capital gains as they devote to actually increasing their earnings.''[21] Another writer has suggested that these conversion efforts are today's equivalent of yesterday's alchemy—the ancient science that attempted the conversion of base metals into gold.[22] Although one might reasonably deplore this economically nonproductive use of scarce talent, one cannot blame either the tax advisor or the businessman for utilizing the provisions to their best advantage as long as they remain within the law. Ultimately, Congress must be held responsible for any waste of resources in this manner because only Congress can legislate to correct the shortcomings of the present provisions.

In summary, the capital-gain problem is a very real one in income taxation. There are sound arguments on both sides of the special treatment question.[23] On balance, the greatest damage done by such

TABLE **19-2**

CAPITAL-GAIN EFFECTS ON HORIZONTAL EQUITY

Year	Tax on taxpayer earning a $50,000 ordinary income		Tax on taxpayer earning a $50,000 net long-term capital gain		Total tax paid by both taxpayers	
	Dollars	Percentage of total tax paid	Dollars	Percentage of total tax paid	Dollars	Percentage
1913	1,715	50	1,715	50	3,340	100
1919	18,635	50	18,635	50	37,270	100
1922	9,590	61	6,250	39	15,840	100
1934	12,300	71	4,920	29	17,220	100
1938	9,700	56	7,500	44	17,200	100
1950	26,820	79	7,230	21	34,050	100
1980	16,444	80	4,169	20	20,613	100

[21]James J. Mahon, Jr., "Converting Future Income Into Current Capital Gains," *Journal of Accountancy,* 102 (July, 1956), p. 78.
[22]Maurice H. Rich, "Getting Maximum Benefits Out of Code Section 117," *Taxes, The Tax Magazine,* 30 (July, 1952), p. 587.
[23]The most definitive, recent examination of the capital-gain issue was written by Martin David in 1968. His work, titled *Alternative Approaches to Capital Gain Taxation,* was published by the Brookings Institution. A prior benchmark was written by Lawrence H. Seltzer, a professor of economics at Wayne State University, and published by the National Bureau of Economic Research. His work, titled *The Nature and Tax Treatment of Capital Gains and Losses,* exceeds 550 pages in length. Other less thorough, but most informative, publications include a 1951 U.S. Treasury Department tax study, *Federal Income Tax Treatment of Capital Gains and Losses,* and a 1946 symposium, published under the aegis of the Tax Institute of America, titled *Capital Gains Taxation.*
    The periodical literature of the past two decades is replete with individuals' efforts to shed some little light on the capital-gain controversy. A few of the more scholarly (in our view) of these efforts are referenced directly or by footnote throughout these chapters. Finally, the tax student ought to appreciate the wealth of tax information contained in the hearings and reports of the various governmental committees and agencies. Relative to capital-gain taxation, especially noteworthy among these is the three-volume *Tax Revision Compendium* submitted to the House Ways and Means Committee late in 1959, particularly Volume 2, pp. 1193–1299. For a more recent statement, see, for example, the *President's 1963 Tax Message,* Hearings Before the Committee on Ways and Means, Part 1, pp. 367–87; or *Tax Reform Studies and Proposals: U.S. Treasury Department,* Joint Publication of Committee on Ways and Means and Committee on Finance, February 5, 1969, Part 1, esp. pp. 79–95.

special provisions is the damage to interpersonal equity. Just why the person who dabbles in timber, securities, or livestock ought to be provided substantial tax benefits over the one who dabbles in automobiles, hardware, or groceries is indeed difficult to determine. Professor Haig stated this objection well when he wrote:

> But what is to be said for the fairness of an income tax that levies its toll on the pay envelope of the wage-earner, the monthly check of the salaried man, the annual profit of the merchant and manufacturer, and the interest coupon of the widow, but that, at the same time, exempts the winnings of the successful stock-gambler and the unearned increment of the fortunate speculator in vacant land?[24]

If the extension of the capital-gain provisions is the consequence of unduly high surtax rates, especially on the upper income groups, and of the consequent political pressures that inevitably follow from these high surtax rates, then the provisions are not justified. Instead we ought to concentrate our attention directly on the problem of unreasonable surtax rates rather than on the opportunities for avoiding them.

[24]Robert M. Haig, "Taxation of Capital Gains," *The Wall Street Journal*, 67 (March 25, 1937), p. 4.

PROBLEMS

1. Does there appear to be any clear-cut trend or pattern in income-tax history to develop a rational philosophy toward tax treatment of capital gain? Explain with reference to the historical periods suggested in the chapter.
2. Courts and tax commentators have for years compared capital to a tree and income to the fruit of that tree. That is, income is viewed as something that can be separated from capital, leaving the productive base "unscathed." Discuss the possible weaknesses of this simile.
3. Assume that 10 years ago a high-school teacher earned an annual salary of $12,000 and that today his or her annual salary had risen to $18,000. If we can establish that the general price level increased 50 percent in the interim, what increase in real income did the teacher have, in terms of the (original) "base" salary, in the 10-year interval? What portion of the $6,000 increase would be treated as a capital gain for tax purposes?
4. Match each period in the alphabetic listing below with the basic provision applicable to capital gains during that period from the numbered list that follows.

a. 1861–72	b. 1913–22	c. 1922–33	d. 1934–37
e. 1938–49	f. 1950–69	g. 1969–78	h. 1979–present

(1) Special treatment was determined in large measure by the number of years an asset had been held prior to disposition.
(2) Capital-gain provisions were extended and contracted on an *ad hoc* basis, with primary attention given to closing unintended loopholes.
(3) Capital gains were taxed exactly as other forms of income.
(4) The only advantage of the capital gain was a flat, alternative tax beneficial only to the wealthier taxpayers.
(5) Capital gains were wholly excluded from taxable income.
(6) Capital-gain provisions were extended and contracted on an *ad hoc* basis, with primary attention given to economic conditions of the times.
(7) Capital-gain privileges for higher level income persons were reduced through a limitation on the amount of capital gain eligible for the alternative tax and a reduction in the value of long-term loss deductions.
(8) After several years of reducing the relative advantage of capital gains, Congress suddenly reversed the trend.

5. Many of the less economically developed nations of the world have begun to institute an income tax during the past 20 years. Generally, these countries exclude "capital gain" from the income tax base. What good reasons might they have for such an exclusion? What undesirable consequence, in terms of economic development, could follow from this exclusion?

6. Based on your own intuition, how would you describe a "capital gain"? (In responding to this question, *ignore* this textbook and base your answer on any general notions you might have gathered from your other studies thus far in college.) As a part of your class discussion, be prepared to explain why basic differences in concepts exist.

7. Some authorities have proposed the elimination of all taxes on capital gains. They argue that such a change would eliminate many complexities from the law. Do you agree? Why or why not?

8. Briefly summarize the arguments for and against special treatment of capital gain.

9. An investor is frequently said to be "locked in" an investment by the operation of the tax law. What is meant by this phrase? Explain what two extreme alternative tax measures could be enacted to put an end to this phenomenon. What good reasons can be given in opposition to each of these extreme alternatives?

10. In 1938 Congress changed the tax law to exclude most plant and equipment—in accounting terminology, fixed assets—from the capital asset definition.
    a. Why did Congress make this change in 1938?
    b. What problems did this create just four years later?
    c. How did Congress solve the second problem in 1942?

11. Assume that your grandfather purchased a property in 1900 and that your mother inherited that property from him in 1945. Further assume that your mother died in 1977 and left the property to you and that you sold it today for $1,001,000. How much taxable income (capital gain) do you believe that you should have to report on the sale of this property if:

    Your grandfather paid $1,000 for it in 1900;

    It had a fair market value of $500,000 in 1945 when your mother received title to it; and

    It had a fair market value of $991,000 when you took title in 1977?

    Explain your answer briefly. (NOTE: This question does not ask you to answer based on what the law provides; rather, it asks you to determine how you personally feel about one very important issue in capital gains taxation today.)

12. In 1960 Betty paid $10,000 for property A and Bob earned $10,000 for his services. In 1980 Betty sold property A for $20,000 and Bob was paid $20,000 for his services. If the consumer price index (CPI) increased from 100 in 1960 to 200 in 1980:
    a. How much real income has Betty realized on property A in 1980?
    b. How much of an increase in real wages has Bob realized after 20 years' work?
    c. Do you believe that Betty should pay an income tax on the sale of the property in 1980? Explain briefly. (NOTE: This question asks for personal opinion; not the answer per the Code.)
    d. On what amount of income do you believe Bob should pay an income tax in 1980? Explain briefly. (NOTE: State your personal opinion.)
    e. Based on our current tax law (the Internal Revenue Code of 1954, as amended), will either Betty or Bob automatically get a tax break? If so, which one—Betty or Bob? What will this "tax break" be called?

13. Country N imposes no tax on capital gains; Country O treats capital gains just like ordinary income; Country P taxes capital gains as income, but at prefer-

ential rates. If (1) the tax rates on ordinary income are substantial but identical in Countries N, O, and P, and (2) the definition of capital assets is identical in Countries N. O, and P:

   a. Would you expect to find a difference in the investments commonly made by the taxpayers in each of the three countries? Explain briefly.

   b. Which country would be the most industrial (other things being equal)?

SUPPLEMENTAL PROBLEMS

14. As an alternative to present practices, gains and losses on capital assets might be recognized annually based on changes in value of specific assets. What are the advantages and disadvantages of this recognition scheme?

15. The difference between original cost and current value of assets not subject to physical wear and tear may be due to general price-level changes, to changes in the value of the specific asset, or to both. How might these two effects be isolated? Assuming that some practical method exists for isolating the effects of specific and general price changes, should the tax treatment of the two types of gain or loss be different?

16. Capital-gain provisions are concerned with gains and losses on properties—economic capital. Recently, some economists have proposed that the concept of capital itself might be inadequate because it ignores the economic value of the skills and abilities of individuals. Devise a concept of "human capital gains" comparable to the present capital-gains concept. Should such gains receive favored treatment also? Explain.

17. A substantial portion of the capital gains realized each year is realized from the sale of shares in corporations. Why have the values of corporate shares generally increased since World War II? What part, if any, have our tax laws played in the trend? How? Compare the gains on corporate shares with the idea of the fruit and the tree. Are they the same?

18. What practical difficulties would you encounter if, as a politician, you advocated a concurrent end to capital-gain privileges and a significant reduction in the high surtax rates applied to large incomes? What facts could you summon in support of such a proposition? Do you think that such arguments would be politically "popular"? Why would the low-income taxpayer not be impressed with such arguments? Why would the high-income taxpayer not support such a campaign?

19. When Nelson Rockefeller died, he left an estate of approximately $66 million. That estate, however, represented only a small part of his wealth. A greater amount—estimated at $250 to $500 million—automatically passed to others via trusts that had been created by his father and grandfather.

   a. Why do you suppose Rockefeller's father and grandfather left Nelson only a life estate in the larger amounts?

   b. Since the capital-gain provisions apply equally to all taxpayers, how can some individuals claim that they are unduly favorable to persons like Nelson Rockefeller?

20. Approximately 55 percent of all outstanding corporate stock in the United States is owned by 1 percent of the population. That same 1 percent owns 60 percent of all outstanding bonds and 90 percent of all trust assets. Of what significance are these facts to the taxation of capital gains?

The term "capital assets" includes all classes of property not specifically excluded by section 1221.

Reg. Sec. 1.1221-1 (a)

capital gain and loss today: the pure case

The general student of business need understand only the general outline of the capital gain and loss provisions of the Code to appreciate the importance of these provisions in the conduct of everyday business affairs. The competent tax practitioner, however, must understand an almost infinite array of technicalities that surround all business transactions, capital as well as noncapital, if he or she is to advise businesspeople correctly on the tax aspects of daily events. In this chapter you will be introduced to the seemingly endless tax sophistications that the latter must be familiar with. Perhaps at the outset you would find it comforting to know that Albert Einstein found it necessary to use a tax consultant; he found the Code "too difficult for a mathematician . . . it takes a philosopher."[1]

Even a cursory appreciation of the pure (statutory) capital gain and loss provisions requires an investigation into at least five separate and distinct questions. They are: (1) Precisely which transactions result in a capital gain or loss for tax purposes? (2) How does a taxpayer determine the amount of such a gain or loss? (3) What is the difference between short- and long-term capital gain and loss? (4) What special tax treatment is given to net capital gains? (5) What is the tax consequence of incurring greater capital losses than capital gains in a given tax year? In answering the last two of these five questions, it is

further necessary to isolate those fact cases in which the taxpayer is a corporation from those in which the taxpayer is an individual or a fiduciary. This chapter answers the first three questions in the sequence listed. Chapter 21 then answers the last two questions, first for the noncorporate taxpayers and then for the corporate taxpayers.

Before you begin the next four chapters, you would be well advised to recognize the fact that the rules that determine the correct taxation of capital gains and losses constitute one of the more complex areas of our income tax structure. Because capital gain is once again "the name of the tax game" in the United States, we believe it is justifiable to require an unusual effort, even in an introductory text.

Taxpayers are confronted with the problems in this chapter, and the three that follow, only when they have a disposition by sale or exchange of some property, whether tangible or intangible, real or personal. Every disposition of property, except by gift, bequest, or devise, creates three problems. First, there is the problem of measuring the gain or loss from the disposition. The measurement rules are generally covered in this Part. Second, the taxpayer must determine whether a *realized* gain or loss must be recognized in the year of disposition. Is the gain or loss included in the computation of taxable base for the current year? (Recognition problems were introduced on pages **5/4** and **5/8**; some additional recognition rules are discussed in this Part. However, the major exceptions to the general realization rules

---

[1] As reported by Senator Magnuson, *Congressional Record,* May 12, 1966, p. 9903.

are treated in Part Seven.) Third, exactly what is the correct tax treatment of a *realized* and *recognized* gain or loss? This chapter and the three that follow are primarily concerned with this third problem.

CAPITAL GAIN AND LOSS DEFINED

The Internal Revenue Code does not define capital gains and losses *per se;* rather, it defines a capital asset and then states that a capital gain or loss is simply the gain or loss from the sale or exchange of a capital asset. It should be observed further that the Code defines capital asset negatively—that is, it states that *all property except that specifically exempted by the Code is a capital asset.* The complete statutory definition of a *pure* capital asset is as follows:

Sec. 1221. Capital Asset Defined.
For purposes of this subtitle, the term "capital asset" means property held by the taxpayer (whether or not connected with his trade or business), but does not include—
(1) stock in trade of the taxpayer or other property of a kind which would properly be included in the inventory of the taxpayer if on hand at the close of the taxable year, or property held by the taxpayer primarily for sale to customers in the ordinary course of his trade or business;
(2) property, used in his trade or business, of a character which is subject to the allowance for depreciation provided in section 167, or real property used in his trade or business;
(3) a copyright, a literary, musical, or artistic composition, a letter or memorandum, or similar property, held by—
(A) a taxpayer whose personal efforts created such property,
(B) in the case of a letter, memorandum, or similar property, a taxpayer for whom such property was prepared or produced, or
(C) a taxpayer in whose hands the basis of such property is determined, for the purpose of determining gain from a sale or exchange, in whole or in part by reference to the basis of such property in the hands of a taxpayer described in subparagraph (A) or (B);
(4) accounts or notes receivable acquired in the ordinary course of trade or business for services rendered or from the sale of property described in paragraph (1); or
(5) an obligation of the United States or any of its possessions, or of a State, or any political subdivision thereof, or of the District of Columbia, issued on or after March 1, 1941, on a discount basis and payable without interest at a fixed maturity date not exceeding one year from the date of issue; or
(6) a publication of the United States Government (including the Congressional Record) which is received from the United States Government or any agency thereof,

other than by purchase at the price at which it is offered for sale to the public, and which is held by—
(A) a taxpayer who so received such publication, or
(B) a taxpayer in whose hands the basis of such publication is determined, for purposes of determining gain from a sale or exchange, in whole or in part by reference to the basis of such publication in the hands of a taxpayer described in subparagraph (A).

Numerous interesting questions become apparent on even the most superficial examination of this definition. Such phrases as "stock in trade," "primarily for sale," and "trade or business" contain enough ambiguities to guarantee ample controversy between taxpayers and the government. For example, suppose a taxpayer inherited some jewelry that he or she had no intention of keeping and, in fact, promptly disposed of through another party. Would those jewels be "property held by the taxpayer primarily for sale to customers"? If so, the gain on their sale would be ordinary income; if not, the gain would be capital gain.[2]

An interesting corollary issue is the definition of a taxpayer's "trade or business." Many challenging tax problems arise because of this phrase. For instance, can a taxpayer have more than one trade or business concurrently?[3] Assume that a salaried employee also owns, and rents to another, a single dwelling unit. Does this rental activity constitute a second and separate trade or business for the taxpayer? If it does, the dwelling becomes depreciable property used in the trade or business and, therefore, is not a capital asset. If the rental activity is not a trade or business, then the property is a capital asset.[4]

Perhaps the most illogical part of the capital-asset definition is the exclusion [in Sec. 1221 (2)] of depreciable and real property used in the trade or business. If asked to give an example of a capital asset, most business-oriented persons uninitiated in federal taxation would be quick to respond with such examples as plant, equipment, and business realty. Yet these items are clearly eliminated from the capital-asset definition in the Code. Recall from page **19/8** that in the Depression years of the late 1930s, Congress decided that the limitation on the deduction of capital losses was unduly restricting the sale of plant

---

[2] For a decision of the First Circuit Court of Appeals on this fact case, see *R. Foster Reynolds* v. *Commissioner,* 155 F 2d 620 (1946).
[3] Apparently so. See John H. Saunders, *Trade or Business—Its Meaning Under the Internal Revenue Code,* 12th Annual Institute on Federal Taxes, University of Southern California, 1960, p. 693.
[4] See *Hazard,* 7 TC 372 (1946).

and equipment purchased in the roaring twenties. Hence, Congress enacted this definitional exclusion, which effectively transformed the losses on the sale of such assets into ordinary losses and therefore into losses not subject to capital-loss limitations. At the same time, of course, the definitional exclusions also transformed the gains into ordinary gains, which are taxed in a less advantageous way. By 1942 this factor was so important, since tax liability was becoming sizable on such gains, and pressures for change had so built up, that Congress modified the Code (Sec. 1231).[5] The modification allows certain gains to be *treated* as capital gains (when the gains exceed the losses on the sales and exchanges of certain properties during a given tax period) although by definition several of the assets included are still *not* capital assets. To complicate matters further, this definitional riddle has been modified again so that today some portion or all of the gain that could be treated as capital gain under Sec. 1231 must now be treated as ordinary income because of Secs. 1245, 1250, or related sections, which deal with the recapture of depreciation charges for tax purposes. (These and other matters are discussed in Chapter 22 and are mentioned here only so you will be forewarned.)

The exclusion in Sec. 1221(3) is an interesting example of a conceptual problem inherent in capital gain taxation. The only way that most persons can earn a living is by "selling" a service that involves a physical or mental process or both. For example, a person might dig a ditch, diagnose an illness and prescribe a medication, or repair an automobile. A few persons, however, create a property that when sold provides an income. For example, artists create art objects; authors and composers create copyrighted works; and inventors create patentable ideas. If all property were a capital asset, then persons whose efforts resulted in a property would reap the benefits of the capital gains tax, whereas all other persons would be subject to the less-favorable ordinary tax rates. To preclude this result, Sec. 1221(3) was inserted into the Code. Observe, however, that the present statute does not exclude patents, and that the exclusion extends only to the individual whose efforts created the property and to those who assume the creator's tax basis. (The basis concept is clarified later in this chapter.)

The exclusion contained in Sec. 1221(3)(B) was added to the Code in 1969 to put an end to the large

tax deductions previously available to former presidents of the United States. Under prior law, whenever an ex-president contributed his papers and other memorabilia to a specially created library named in his honor, a major charitable deduction was created. After lengthy debate, Congress decided that Lyndon Johnson was to be the last of the presidents to be so privileged. As explained on page **13**/4, the present law states that the measure of a charitable deduction of property depends on the classification of that property. "Ordinary income property" creates a deduction equal only to the taxpayer's basis in the property. Since a president's basis in his papers is generally zero, and since Sec. 1221(3)(B) makes such properties "ordinary income properties," future presidents will no longer be able to get major personal tax benefits from their public service. The attempt by Richard Nixon to claim a charitable contribution deduction for the alleged donation of his vice-presidential papers before the effective date of this change in the tax law was widely reported in the daily press.

One final observation relative to the definition of capital assets ought to demonstrate the care that must be exercised in dealing with this portion of the Code. Suppose a local accountant sells his entire practice to another accountant for a fixed sum, payable immediately. Is all or any part of the sales proceeds to be allocated to the sale of a capital asset? More specifically, if the proceeds exceed the fair market value of the tangible assets and uncollected receivables, does the excess represent the sale of goodwill, and, if so, is this intangible asset a capital asset? As a general rule it is; however, a slight difference in facts may modify this conclusion. If, for example, the covenant of sale includes an agreement not to compete, the excess may be ordinary income. Careful tax planning by an expert is absolutely essential to guarantee the tax rights of both the purchaser and seller in these and other similar arrangements.[6]

For tax purposes, the most numerically important group of capital assets is stocks and bonds. Except when held for resale by dealers, these assets generally are capital assets, and therefore the gain or loss on their sale or exchange is a capital gain or loss. Personal assets such as residences, family automobiles, and pleasure boats are also common forms of capital asset. Observe that a single asset may be both capital and noncapital—for example, a car that is used 50 percent of the time in a trade or business and

---

[5] Originally Sec. 117(j) of the 1939 Code. Review p. **19**/8.

[6] As an illustration of this conclusion, read the decision in *Dairy Service*, TC Memo 1966–113.

50 percent of the time for family driving is treated for tax purposes as two assets, one capital, the other not.

To determine that a particular gain or loss is a capital gain or loss, however, is not always the most important tax fact. Even though the loss on the sale of a personal residence may correctly be categorized as a capital loss, the most significant tax factor in this instance is that this loss is never deductible. The reason for this result stems from a fundamental rule suggested on page **6**/1; that is, *nothing is deductible unless authorized by the Code or regulations*. As noted on page **6**/5, losses on purely personal property are deductible *only* if they arise from a casualty or theft. Hence the loss realized on the *sale* of a personal residence would not be deductible even though a gain on that same residence would be taxed like any routine capital gain. In other instances nonrecognition of gains and losses stems from other special statutory provisions.

GAINS AND LOSSES REALIZED BUT NOT RECOGNIZED

Primary among these are the sections that, under specified circumstances, provide that the gain or loss *realized* on a particular transaction may not be *recognized* for tax purposes in the year it is first realized. Even though these sections are not restricted to capital gain and loss transactions, they are often of importance to them. Because the nonrecognition sections are discussed in much greater detail in Part Seven of this text, the following discussion will be relatively brief.

Four important nonrecognition provisions are contained in Sec. 1031 (the exchange of property held for productive use or investment); Sec. 1033 (the possible gain on the involuntary conversion of a taxpayer's property); Sec. 1034 (the sale or exchange of a personal residence); and Sec. 1091 (the loss on the sale of securities—commonly dubbed "wash sales"). The rationale of three of these sections was explained briefly on page **5**/7 in connection with the wherewithal-to-pay tenet. The fourth section (Sec. 1091) is a "loophole closer," without which taxpayers would be able to sell securities solely to obtain a tax deduction and, at the same time, retain their real economic position by an immediate repurchase of the securities sold. The effect of Sec. 1091 is to deny a taxpayer an *immediate* loss deduction for any security sold if within thirty days before or after that sale he or she purchases substantially identical securities. The loss denied is then added to the "new" basis of the securities purchased so that the tax consequence on final disposition will give recognition to the loss deduction denied earlier.

Whatever the reasons for the various provisions, the important conclusion for our present purposes is that *if* certain conditions prevail, a gain or loss realized from a consummated transaction may *not* be immediately recognized for tax purposes. Suppose, for example, that a taxpayer exchanges his GMC stock, which has a fair market value of $100,000 but which cost him $70,000 several years ago, for shares of an equivalent fair market value in the Ford Motor Company. Because there is no provision in the Code that modifies the general rule in this case, the $30,000 gain realized in this transaction (the exchange) must be recognized for tax purposes. On the other hand, suppose that the same taxpayer also exchanged a warehouse having a fair market value of $100,000 (but having an adjusted tax basis of only $70,000) for a $100,000 vacant lot. Section 1031 would require the taxpayer to defer recognition of this $30,000 gain, even though the gain was realized in the same sense that it was in the GMC-Ford exchange.

CAPITAL GAIN AND LOSS MEASURED

Briefly, the amount of a capital gain or loss is the difference between the "amount realized" and the "adjusted basis" of the capital asset that has been sold or exchanged. The phrases "amount realized" and "adjusted basis" obviously are technical terms that need to be studied with care.

Amount realized

The Code Sec. 1001 definition of "amount realized" is as follows:

(b) Amount Realized.—The amount realized from the sale or other disposition of property shall be the sum of any money received plus the fair market value of the property (other than money) received. In determining the amount realized—
(1) there shall not be taken into account any amount received as reimbursement for real property taxes which are treated under section 164(d) as imposed on the purchaser, and
(2) there shall be taken into account amounts representing real property taxes which are treated under section 164(d) as imposed on the taxpayer if such taxes are to be paid by the purchaser.

(For our purposes, subparagraphs (1) and (2) add little to the general definition, but they demonstrate a basic quality of the Code—extensive cross-referencing—that is often frustrating to the tax student.) In addition, the student of taxation must be aware that case law, that law decided by judges, often constitutes an important adjunct to understanding the statutory law. In determining the amount realized, the courts have held that the assumption of a seller's mortgage by a buyer constitutes a positive element in the calculation of amount realized just as much as do money and fair market value of property received.[7] For example, suppose the buyer of a home gave the seller $10,000 cash and a second-hand car with a fair market value of $1,500, and that the buyer assumed the seller's mortgage on the home in the amount of $48,000. The amount realized by this seller would be $59,500 ($10,000 + $1,500 + $48,000).

One of the most *administratively* difficult aspects of this definition is establishing the fair market value of property received, and the practical importance and complexity of establishing such valuations in the real world should not be underestimated. The phrase "fair market value" assumes a willing buyer and a willing seller acting with full knowledge and without obligation in an arm's-length transaction. The value is, therefore, ultimately a question of fact that frequently must be determined by a court. Fortunately for the student, fair market values are almost always explicitly stated in the textbook and thus a major problem in actual tax administration has been circumvented.

Adjusted basis

"Adjusted basis" is much more difficult to define than "amount realized." The applicable Code section is deceptively brief:

Sec. 1011. Adjusted Basis for Determining Gain or Loss.
(a) General Rules.—The adjusted basis for determining the gain or loss from the sale or other disposition of property, whenever acquired, shall be the basis [determined under section 1012 or other applicable sections of this subchapter and subchapters C (relating to corporate distributions and adjustments), K (relating to partners and partnerships), and P (relating to capital gains and losses)], adjusted as provided in section 1016.

The necessarily elementary discussion of adjusted basis that follows will proceed by considering, in

[7]See *Crane* v. *Commissioner,* 331 U.S. 1 (1935).

turn, purchased property, inherited property, and property acquired by gift, because the method of acquisition is often a critical factor in determining the adjusted basis of a particular property. (The cost basis of property acquired in a nontaxable or partially taxable exchange can be sufficiently difficult to determine that it is not discussed here but is deferred to Part Seven for separate consideration.)

PROPERTY ACQUIRED BY PURCHASE The determination of the tax basis of purchased property generally coincides closely with the determination of "book value" in accounting. That is, under most circumstances, the adjusted basis is the sum of the historical cost of the original property and the cost of any capital improvements made to that property subsequent to acquisition, less the depreciation claimed (for tax purposes) on the same property and improvements since acquisition. To illustrate, assume that a building was purchased in 1960 for $100,000 and that an addition costing $25,000 was constructed in 1965. If depreciation charges on the building and the addition total $50,000 through last year, then the adjusted basis for tax purposes on January 1 of this year (and the book value for accounting purposes) would be $75,000 ($100,000 + $25,000 − $50,000).

Obviously, in implementing this kind of basis definition, the tax accountant shares many of the financial accountant's problems. For example, in determining historical cost at acquisition, the following problems are typical: separating a single purchase price into costs of component assets (for which the financial accountant and the tax accountant resort to a common solution: allocation of purchase price on the basis of relative fair market values of the component assets); determining fair market values of noncash acquisitions; and allocating overhead and other indirect costs to assets constructed by the taxpayer for his or her own use. Another common problem, although greater for tax than for financial accounting, is the strong pressure to charge to expense (and hence to obtain an immediate tax deduction) what is actually a capital expenditure that should be charged to an asset account. As one might expect, controversy in this area of income taxation is commonplace.

One major tax modification to the definition of basis for purchased property should be noted, even though it is of decreasing significance. Since income was not subject to taxation in the United States in the four decades immediately preceding 1913, property that was purchased prior to that date *and that had increased in value by March 1, 1913,* takes a "substituted basis" for tax purposes. The rule, stated in Sec. 1053, is that for tax purposes property acquired prior to March 1, 1913, will take as its basis on that date the higher of its cost or its fair market value. Notice that this gives the taxpayer a "heads-I-win, tails-you-lose" position. If market values decreased between the date of purchase and March 1, 1913, the taxpayer retains his or her higher cost basis in the determination of gain or loss—that is, the taxpayer pays tax on a smaller gain. On the other hand, if market values increased between the purchase date and March 1, 1913, the taxpayer may use the higher fair market value as basis and thereby again minimize the taxable gain.

PROPERTY ACQUIRED BY INHERITANCE   As noted in Chapter 19, the Tax Reform Act of 1976 initially made what promised to be sweeping changes to the rules that determine the basis of property received from a decedent. Those changes originally were effective for any property received from a decedent dying after December 31, 1976. When President Carter signed the Windfall Profits Tax Act, however, those changes were permanently scuttled.

Accordingly, the basis of property received from a decedent generally is the fair market value of the property on the date of the decedent's death. An exception to this general rule applies if the executor or executrix of the estate elects the alternate valuation date; in that event, the basis is the fair market value six months after the decedent's death. To illustrate these rules, assume that Tom Tucket purchased stock A for $10,000 on February 5, 1970, and stock B for $20,000 on September 5, 1974. If Tom died on October 16, 1980, when the fair market values of both stock A and stock B were $15,000, any beneficiary of Tom's estate who received those shares would take as his or her basis the $15,000 fair market value on Tom's death, assuming that Tom's executor or executrix made no election to value properties on the alternate valuation date. This means, of course, that the $5,000 unrealized or "paper" *gain* implicit in stock A would forever go unrecognized for income tax purposes, and the $5,000 unrealized or "paper" *loss* implicit in stock B would also forever go unrecognized for income tax purposes.

If an executor or executrix elects the alternate valuation date *and* also distributes some property prior to that date, then—for the property distributed before the valuation date—the basis shall be the fair market value of the property on the date it was distributed.

PROPERTY ACQUIRED BY GIFT   A third common method by which an individual taxpayer acquires property is by gift. January 1, 1921, marked a major change in the rules of determining the basis of property received by gift. A taxpayer's basis for property acquired by gift and disposed of after December 31, 1920, is generally the donor's adjusted basis. A major exception to the general rule just stated controls if the fair market value of the property given is less than the donor's basis on the date of the gift. In that event, the donee's basis for loss (only) becomes the fair market value on the date of the gift. This means, of course, that a donee may have two different tax bases for properties, that is, one basis for gain and another for loss.

To understand the idea behind the law, we need only observe the possibilities for tax avoidance in the absence of such wording. If the law provided simply that in all cases the donee would take the donor's cost basis (as it did prior to 1921), then a donor in a low tax bracket could give a property with a substantial "paper loss" to a family member, friend, or acquaintance in a higher tax bracket, and the two individuals combined could achieve a significantly greater tax benefit from the one economic or paper loss than the donor alone could have received. On the other hand, suppose the law provided simply that the donee had to take the *lesser* of the fair market value of the property on the date of the gift or the donor's cost basis. In that case, if the donor's cost basis was higher than fair market value at date of gift, and if the donee eventually sold the property for more than that cost basis, an unrealistically large gain (in a consolidated sense) would have to be reported. Hence the law is written as it is—trying concurrently to close a loophole and yet not to create an unduly harsh tax result.

The provisions that relate to gift taxes further complicate the rules used to determine the cost basis of property acquired by gift. For gifts acquired after September 2, 1958, and before January 1, 1977, if the donor pays a federal gift tax on the transfer of the property, the donee can increase his or her basis by the total amount of the gift tax as long as the sum of the two (donor's cost and gift tax) does not exceed the fair market value on the date of the gift. If the sum of these two amounts does exceed the fair market value, then the donee's basis will be the fair market value on the date of the gift. Note that as long as the donor's cost exceeds the fair market value on the date of the gift, none of the gift tax paid can ever be added to the donee's basis, even if the property is eventually sold for more than the donor's cost. To illustrate the basis rules applicable to gifts made before January 1, 1977, consider the following three examples:

Example 1: Taxpayer A purchased a stock for $15,000. On the date of the gift, the stock had a fair market value of $20,000. Gift taxes of $1,000 were paid. In this case, the donee's basis for gain and loss will be $16,000 ($15,000 cost plus $1,000 in gift taxes).

Example 2: Taxpayer B purchased a stock for $15,000. On the date of the gift, the stock had a fair market value of $10,000. Gift taxes of $1,000 were paid. In this case, the donee's basis for gain is $15,000; the donee's basis for loss, $10,-000. If the stock is sold by the donee for any amount greater than $10,000 and less than $15,-000, he or she will report neither gain nor loss.

Example 3: Taxpayer C purchased a stock for $15,000. On the date of the gift, the stock had a fair market value of $15,500. Gift taxes of $1,000 were paid. In this case, the donee's basis for gain and for loss is $15,500 (the sum of the donor's basis plus the gift tax paid, but not in excess of the fair market value of the property on the date of the gift).

The Tax Reform Act of 1976 changed the rules for property acquired by gift after December 31, 1976, insofar as the step-up in basis for gift taxes is concerned. The 1976 Act provides that the gift tax to be added to appreciated property shall be calculated as follows:

$$\text{Addition to basis} = \text{Gift tax paid} \times \frac{\text{Net appreciation in gift property}}{\text{Total value of gift property}}$$

The "net appreciation" is equal to the excess of the gift's fair market value over the donor's basis on the date of the gift.

To illustrate the step-up in basis for gift taxes paid on gifts made after December 31, 1976, consider the following three examples:

Example 1: Taxpayer X purchased securities for a cost of $20,000 in 1970. In 1978 he gave these securities to a donee when their fair market value was $50,000. Total gift tax paid on the transfer was $10,000. The donee's basis for gain and loss is $26,000 (the donor's cost plus three-fifths of the $10,000 in gift taxes paid). Under the rules in effect prior to January 1, 1977, the donee's basis would have been $30,000 ($20,000 cost plus $10,000 in taxes).

Example 2: Taxpayer Y purchased securities for a cost of $20,000 in 1970. In 1978 he gave these securities to a donee when their fair market value was $15,000. Total gift tax paid on the transfer was $1,000. The donee's basis for gain is $20,000; the basis for loss is $15,000. No portion of the gift tax can ever be added to the donee's basis, since the fair market value on the date of the gift was less than the donor's cost.

Example 3: Taxpayer Z purchased securities for a cost of $48,000 in 1970. In 1978 he gave these securities to a donee when their fair market value was $50,000. Total gift tax paid on the transfer was $10,000. The donee's basis for gain and loss is $48,400 (the donor's cost plus two-fiftieths of the $10,000 in gift taxes paid). Under the rules in effect for gifts prior to January 1, 1977, the donee's basis for gain and loss would have been $50,000 (the $48,000 cost plus $2,000 in gift taxes).

TRANSFERS SHORTLY BEFORE DEATH   What happens if a donor taxpayer dies shortly after giving property to another? Will the recipient determine the basis according to the gift rules or according to the inherited property rules? The answer, as a general rule, for gifts made prior to January 1, 1977, was that if the donor's death followed within three years or less of the date of the gift *and* if the donee had not disposed of the property by the date of the donor's death, then the transfer would be assumed to be a *transfer in contemplation of death,* and the donee would determine the basis by the rules applicable to inherited property. That presumption was subject to rebuttal. If the donee had disposed of the property in an arm's-length transaction prior to the donor's death, then the gift rules still applied.

For gifts made after December 31, 1976, and within three years of the donor's death, the value of the gift plus the value of any gift tax paid will automatically be included in the donor's estate for purposes of determining the gross estate and, therefore, the estate tax payable. There is no longer a mere presumption, and it no longer makes any difference what the donee may have done with the gift in the meantime. All taxable gifts made in that three-year period, plus the gift tax, will be included in the donor's estate. Although the reason for this change may not be obvious, suffice it to observe that the old rule provided an unintended loophole for persons with large amounts of accumulated property. The stricter new rule eliminates the old loophole and effectively does away with any major tax reasons for death-bed giving.

SUMMARY   In summary, the amount of a capital gain or loss is the difference between the amount realized on the sale or exchange of a capital asset and the adjusted basis of that capital asset on the date it is sold or exchanged.

The amount realized is

  □ Money received, *plus*
  □ Fair market value of other property received, *plus*
  □ Amount of debt transferred from the seller to the buyer.

The adjusted basis of property *acquired by purchase* generally is

  □ Cost of the property surrendered, *plus*
  □ Cost of capital improvements to that property, *less*
  □ Depreciation claimed on the property.

The adjusted basis of property acquired by inheritance or by gift is determined according to special rules.

SHORT- OR LONG-TERM CAPITAL GAIN AND LOSS

The tax consequences of a capital gain or loss are significantly affected by its categorization as short or long term. How, then, is this distinction determined? The answer to that question is contained in Sec. 1222:

Sec. 1222. Other Terms Relating to Capital Gains and Losses.
For purposes of this subtitle—
(1) Short-term capital gain.—The term "short-term capital gain" means gain from the sale or exchange of a capital asset held for not more than 1 year, if and to the extent such gain is taken into account in computing gross income.
(2) Short-term capital loss.—The term "short-term capital loss" means loss from the sale or exchange of a capital asset held for not more than 1 year, if and to the extent that such loss is taken into account in computing taxable income.
(3) Long-term capital gain.—The term "long-term capital gain" means gain from the sale or exchange of a capital asset held for more than 1 year, if and to the extent such gain is taken into account in computing gross income.
(4) Long-term capital loss.—The term "long-term capital loss" means loss from the sale or exchange of a capital asset held for more than 1 year, if and to the extent that such loss is taken into account in computing taxable income.

Obviously, the distinction between the short- and long-term categorization depends simply on the period of time the seller has owned the capital asset. As a general proposition, no tax benefit attaches to a *net* short-term capital gain, whereas substantial tax benefits attach to a *net* long-term capital gain. As indicated in the preceding chapter, just why a short holding period should be an appropriate method of separating the tax-gifted from the tax-deprived capital gain has never been abundantly clear. An examination of appropriate congressional records yields only the suggestion that this distinction is sufficient to separate an "investment" gain from a purely "speculative" profit.

Although the theoretical rationale of the holding period requirement may be elusive, the application of the requirement to specific factual circumstances is not particularly difficult. As usual, there are some administrative rules that ought to be noted, since they can have considerable importance in practical applications. For example, exactly how long is one year? A stock purchased on March 10, 19x1, will be assumed to have been owned for exactly one year on March 10, 19x2. To be categorized as a long-term capital gain, a capital asset must be held for *more than* one year; hence a stock purchased on March 10, 19x1, cannot be sold before March 11, 19x2, if the gain (or loss) on its sale is to be categorized as long term.

Relative to securities transactions, the purchase and sale dates, which are referred to as the "trade" or "execution" dates in the financial press, are the critical dates in determining how long a security has been held. The trade dates must be carefully distinguished from order dates, settlement dates, and other special dates that may determine the year in which a particular transaction is to be reported for income-tax purposes. Generally, the year of reporting follows routine accounting conventions: Cash-basis taxpayers use settlement dates and accrual-basis taxpayers use execution (that is, "trade") dates. An important exception to the usual rule exists in the case of *loss* sales by cash-basis taxpayers. In this instance, a loss must be recognized for tax purposes in the year the sale is executed, even though settlement takes place in the next year. Note, however, that the usual rule applies for gains. Hence a cash-basis taxpayer generally must place sell orders several days prior to the year end if he or she wishes to record a gain for tax purposes in a year about to end. The New York Stock Exchange generally follows a five-business-day delivery rule. Therefore, in some years, cash-basis taxpayers desiring to establish *gains* have to execute their orders no later than December 23 if they wish to report the gain on their current year's income-tax return.

To illustrate the rules just explained, assume that a cash-basis calendar-year taxpayer ordered his or her broker to purchase 100 shares of ABC common stock at the market price on March 26, 19x1. Further assume that this purchase order was actually executed on the exchange the following day and that the investor paid the brokerage firm the $2,400 purchase price, including a $75 brokerage fee, on April 8, 19x1. If this investor ordered the broker to sell these same shares at the market on December 28, 19x1, and the broker executed the sale on that date for $2,875 less another $75 brokerage fee, the investor would report a short-term capital gain on the sale of $400 (that is, $2,800 − $2,400), but this gain would not be reported until he or she filed a *19x2* tax return. The gain would be short term because a capital asset purchased on March 27, 19x1 was sold on December 28, 19x1, and was thus held for less than one year. The gain, however, would not be included with 19x1 transactions because (1) the taxpayer reported on a cash basis; (2) the transaction resulted in a gain; *and* (3) the settlement date occurred in 19x2. If any one of these three factors had not been true, the transaction would have been reported with the taxpayer's other 19x1 transactions. For example, if the transac-

tion had resulted in a loss, or if the taxpayer had reported on an accrual basis, then the transaction would have been included on the 19x1 tax return.

The date on which a taxpayer can start to count his or her holding period obviously is as important as the date on which it ends. We shall refer to the former date as the "date basis" of property. Like the adjusted ("cost") basis, the date basis is dependent in large measure on the method of acquisition.

The rule for *purchased* property is that the date basis is the day on which the property is actually purchased, that is, the date title passes. A major exception to this rule applies to property acquired in a barter, or trade, transaction. In that event, the date basis of the newly acquired property *may* be the date the property surrendered in the trade was acquired if the transaction is considered a nontaxable exchange. (Since a discussion of the cost basis of property acquired in a nontaxable exchange was deferred to Part Seven for separate consideration, so also is any further consideration of its date basis.)

The date basis of a capital asset acquired from a decedent is immaterial. The Code provides that all gains and losses on the sale or exchange of inherited capital assets are *long-term* gains or losses.

In one sense, the date-basis rules applicable to property acquired by *gift* parallel the cost-basis rules for the same property. That is, if in the calculation of gain or loss the donee takes the donor's cost as his or her cost basis, then the donee's date basis is the date the *donor* acquired the property. If the donee takes as the basis the fair market value on the date of the gift (because this value is lower than the donor's cost basis and because the property is eventually sold for less than this amount), then the date basis is the date of the gift.

Although much more could be said about the rules used to determine the holding period of capital assets, these rules would do little to expand our appreciation of the basic problem: the tax treatment of capital gains and losses. To appreciate that aspect of the problem we must turn next to the statutory requirements relative to short-term and long-term transactions.

COMBINING SHORT- AND LONG-TERM GAIN AND LOSS

In order to determine the important tax results, it is necessary to consolidate all short-term capital gains and losses and to consolidate long-term capital gains and losses and thus to determine the *net* short-term capital gain or loss and the *net* long-term capital gain or loss for a given tax period. For example, suppose that in a given year a taxpayer had three transactions that could be categorized correctly as short-term capital transactions: one resulting in a $600 gain, a second resulting in a $100 loss, and a third resulting in a $200 loss. This taxpayer would have a net short-term capital gain of $300 ($600 − $100 − $200). Suppose that instead of the $200 loss assumed above, the third transaction had resulted in a loss of $1,000; then the taxpayer would have had a net short-term capital loss of $500 ($600 − $100 − $1,000). In the same manner, the taxpayer must combine all long-term capital gains and losses to determine net long-term capital gain or loss.

Finally, it is possible for the taxpayer to combine net short-term and net long-term capital gains and losses into a single net capital gain or loss, an amount that the Code refers to as "capital gain net income."[8] This final combination, however, is meaningful only in certain select cases. (If it always were meaningful, of course, there would be no reason to distinguish between short- and long-term capital transactions in the first place.) Before trying to understand the tax treatment applicable to each of the potential "cases," you should understand clearly the range of possibilities that can obtain. The thirteen possibilities can be presented concisely in the form of the simple matrix shown in Figure 20-1.

The necessity of entering all three symbols in cell (1) of the matrix can be better understood if we let quantity *a* equal the net long-term capital gain and quantity *b* equal the net short-term capital loss. Obviously, then, the relation between the quantities *a* and *b* can be any one of three:

> *a* may be greater than *b*
> *a* may be equal to *b*
> *a* may be less than *b*

If $a > b$, the result is a net gain (+); if $a = b$, the result is neither gain nor capital loss (0); if $a < b$, the result is a net loss (−).

---

[8] Unfortunately for everyone, in the name of simplification Congress coined some truly nonsensical phrases. The everyday English interpretation of the phrase "net capital gain" (or *NCG*) would seem to demand the definition: $LTCG + STCG − LTCL − STCL = NCG$. Believe it or not, after the 1976 Reform Act, the Code defines "net capital gain" as $NLTCG − NSTCL$! (See Sec. 1222(11).) Under prior law, that same arithmetic difference was known as "net Section 1201 gain." Under the present Code, what common sense and good English would describe as "net capital gain" is now technically known as "capital gain net income." (See Sec. 1222(9).)

NET LONG-TERM CAPITAL POSITION

NET SHORT-TERM CAPITAL POSITION		Gain	Zero	Loss
	Loss	− 0 (1) +	−	−
	Zero	+	0	−
	Gain	+	+	− 0 (2) +

FIGURE **20-1**   Net Capital Possibilities

The reason for entering three symbols in cell (2) of the matrix is much the same. The net long-term capital loss in the vertical column can exceed, equal, or be exceeded by the net short-term capital gain in the horizontal row yielding, respectively, a combined minus, zero, or plus.

This process of combining capital gains and losses can be illustrated in another manner, which may be easier to understand. Think of capital gains and losses as small, round cells showing the appropriate plus or minus sign. Further, think of short-term gains and losses as, say, black cells and long-term gains and losses as, say, gray cells. Now imagine that these cells can be combined in the chemical apparatus illustrated in Figure 20-2.

Up to this point, all we have done is net the short-term capital gains and losses on the one side and the long-term ones on the other. When we try to understand how the two net quantities are then treated for tax purposes, however, complications arise because at least three distinct alternatives exist:

1. Some part or all of a net gain (in Code parlance, "capital gain net income") may get special tax treatment in the form of either a long-term capital-gain deduction or an alternative long-term capital-gain tax.

2. Some part or all of a net gain (again, in Code parlance, "capital gain net income") may be treated in the same manner as an equivalent amount of ordinary income.

3. If the result is a net loss, the taxpayer may be entitled to deduct part or all of the loss.

In order to understand the eventual tax treatment

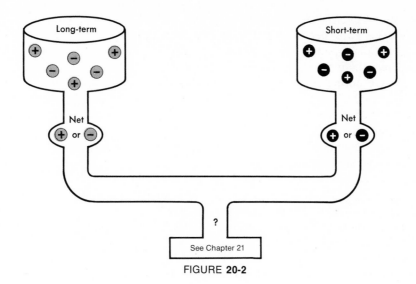

FIGURE **20-2**

given capital gains and losses, the student must study carefully the rules applicable to the long-term capital-gain deduction, the alternative long-term capital-gain tax rate, and the treatment of net capital losses. Unfortunately, these rules vary for corporate and noncorporate taxpayers. They will be examined in detail in Chapter 21. At this point, we can summarize our knowledge about pure capital gains and losses. Based on the Code provisions presented thus far, we should be able to

1. Examine most transactions and correctly categorize the result as either an ordinary gain or loss or a capital gain or loss.

2. Determine the amount of the capital gain or loss.

3. Classify the quantified capital gains and losses into their short- and long-term components.

PROBLEMS

(NOTE: If no year is stated, assume that the transaction took place in the current year.)

1. Harry Fox operates a retail hardware store and owns the property listed below. Indicate whether each property is, for federal tax purposes, a capital asset or a noncapital asset in Fox's hands.

   a. A sailboat used solely for pleasure.
   b. The building that houses his retail store.
   c. A warehouse in which he stores his hardware.
   d. The hardware items in the store.
   e. The hardware items in the warehouse.
   f. His personal residence.
   g. His automobile, used 25 percent of the time for business, 75 percent for pleasure.
   h. One hundred shares of Alpha Corporation stock.
   i. A valuable painting, inherited from a favorite aunt.

2. The *Washington Dispatch,* a Delaware corporation, sold the following assets during the current year:

   a. A letter it received a year earlier from a well-known politician.
   b. A letter from a former U.S. president to a New York attorney, which the

Washington Dispatch purchased (from the attorney) in conjunction with a story it published this year.

c. A set of 25 photographs, taken by a staff photographer, which graphically depict the terror associated with a recent skyjacking.

d. Above normal sales (say, 100,000 extra copies) of a special edition of the *Dispatch*.

e. A set of classified government documents given to the *Dispatch* by an anonymous person.

f. All the common stock of a subsidiary corporation that publishes another newspaper in another city.

g. A three-year-old printing press deemed obsolete.

h. Illinois State bonds, which the *Dispatch* treasurer purchased as a temporary investment for excess corporate cash.

Which of the sales by the *Washington Dispatch* corporation involved capital assets?

3. Helen and Maria, two University of Hartford students, have almost covered the walls of their apartment with oil paintings. Helen's favorite painting is not a capital asset; Maria's favorite is a capital asset. Explain how this could be true.

4. In the six cases that follow, a donee has received property as a gift and subsequently disposed of it through sale. For each case, compute the donee's gain on the subsequent sale if

a. The gifts were made in 1976.

b. The gifts were made in 1977 or a later year.

Case	Donor's adjusted basis	Fair market value at date of gift	Gift tax paid	Amount realized
1	$10,000	$20,000	$1,000	$21,000
2	10,000	15,000	1,000	15,000
3	10,000	15,000	1,000	9,000
4	10,000	8,000	500	11,000
5	10,000	8,000	500	7,500
6	10,000	8,000	500	9,000

5. Taxpayer Y sold a building to Taxpayer Z. Z paid Y $10,000 cash and assumed the $52,000 mortgage on the property. In addition, Z agreed to pay property taxes of $320 accrued to the date of the sale. What is the amount realized by Y? What is Z's adjusted basis at the time of purchase?

6. On August 10, Linn Berg, an airline pilot, sold 100 shares of Trimotor Aircraft Corporation stock (a listed security) for $1,000. What gross amount of capital gain or loss should Linn report for the current year if:

a. He purchased the shares on February 15 for $800?

b. He received the shares as a gift from his Uncle Jim on July 2 when their fair market value was $900? Assume that Jim purchased the shares for $300 on December 4, 1962, and that he paid a gift tax of $60 on this transfer.

c. All facts as in part b, except that Jim purchased the shares for $1,020 rather than for $300?

d. He inherited the shares from his father, Charles, who died July 8, 1979? Charles had purchased the shares for $300 on December 4, 1962. The fair market value of the shares on July 8, 1979 was $1,200. The executrix of Charles's estate elected to value all assets in the estate six months after Charles's death. On December 31, 1979, the shares had a fair market value of $900. On January 8, 1980, the shares had a fair market value of $880. The shares were distributed by the executrix to Linn on June 21, 1980, when they had a fair market value of $1,100.

7. Reread each of the situations in Problem 6, above, and determine whether the transaction resulted in a short- or a long-term capital gain or loss.

8. Assume that on February 14 a donee sold, under the alternative conditions detailed below, an investment property she had received as a gift on January 8. Assume further that the donor had purchased the property on October 26, 1974. State the amount and class (short-term/long-term) of capital gain or loss realized.

	Donor's adjusted basis	Gift tax paid by donor	Value on date of gift	Amount realized on sale
a.	$11,000	$ 600	$12,000	$13,000
b.	11,000	1,200	12,000	13,000
c.	11,000	500	10,000	9,000
d.	11,000	500	10,000	12,000
e.	11,000	1,500	10,000	10,500

9. Determine the amount and the short- or long-term classification of each of the following capital-asset transactions.
    a. On December 1, taxpayer sold ABC shares for $1,000. The shares had been purchased for $800 on January 30.
    b. On October 7, taxpayer sold DEF shares for $2,500. The shares were acquired from taxpayer's deceased grandmother's estate. Grandmother died on November 5, 1978. Grandmother had purchased shares on February 10, 1960, for $500; they had a fair market value of $1,500 on November 5, 1978. The shares were distributed to taxpayer on October 2, 1980, when they had a fair market value of $1,800. Value on December 31, 1979, was $2,000.
    c. On July 28, taxpayer sold GHI shares for $10,000. Shares were acquired by gift from Aunt Mary, who purchased them for $5,000 on January 24, 1954. Mary gave GHI shares to taxpayer on February 14, 1977, when their value was $12,000. Mary paid gift tax of $600 on the transfer.

10. Taxpayer, a surgeon, realized the following gains and losses during the current year:
    Personal car sold at $1,600 loss.
    Business car sold at $200 gain.
    Personal home sold at $2,000 loss.
    Rental property sold at $3,000 gain.
    Purchased oil painting, from personal art collection, sold at $100 gain.
    Bronze statue, cast by taxpayer in spare-time hobby, sold at $20 loss.
    Bronze statue, cast by taxpayer in spare-time hobby, stolen from uninsured private collection; cost, $180.
    a. Which of the above gains and losses can be classified as capital gains and losses? Explain any troublesome classifications.
    b. Which of the above gains and losses would not be recognized for tax purposes in the current year?

11. On June 26, the Investment Committee of GCM Corporation instructed its treasurer to invest excess corporate cash in various common stocks. The treasurer

immediately called the firm's broker, who completed all the investment transactions that same day. On July 2, the GCM treasurer drew a check on company accounts to pay for these purchases. Because GCM again needed the cash, the same investments were sold by a broker for GCM on December 28. Settlement was completed on January 5 (next year). Assuming that GCM Corporation is an accrual-basis taxpayer that files its income-tax returns on a calendar-year basis, answer the following questions:

a. Will the gains and/or losses realized on these security transactions be short or long term?

b. Will the gains and/or losses realized on these security transactions be reported by GCM as part of its tax return for the current or the following year?

c. If all facts were as stated above except that GCM were a partnership rather than a corporation, would your answers to part a or b differ? Explain.

d. If all facts were as originally stated above except that GCM Corporation reported on a cash basis rather than on an accrual basis, would your answers to part a or b differ? Explain.

12. Taxpayer Y, a dealer in appliances, sold the following properties during the year. In every case the property was sold *at a loss*. Which of the losses is recognized for tax purposes? Is the loss a capital loss or an ordinary loss?

a. Automobile used by wife for personal transportation.

b. Farm land inherited from father but held for investment.

c. Vacant lot used in trade or business.

d. Corporate securities purchased from business funds.

e. Diamond ring purchased by wife for personal use.

13. Jim inherited four properties from his Aunt Zelda, who died on September 30. The executrix of Zelda's estate valued all properties on the date of death for estate tax purposes. Using the information below, determine Jim's tax basis in each property.

Property	Date purchased by Zelda	Cost to Zelda	FMV on Sept. 30
Stock A	8/62	$10,000	$20,000
Bond B	6/22/68	20,000	10,000
Land	9/1/75	30,000	50,000
Oil painting	11/14/78	2,000	2,500

14. Which of the following assets, owned by Mary and Don Persons, is a pure capital asset per Sec. 1221?

a. Half of the duplex in which taxpayers live.

b. Other half of duplex, which taxpayers rent to a couple of students. (Assume this is the Persons' only rental property and that they are not, therefore, deemed to be in the trade or business of renting property.)

c. A valuable oil painting purchased by Mary to hang in their living room. Artist is Mary's great-aunt.

d. A valuable letter written to Mary and Don on their wedding, signed by their uncle, the president of the United States.

e. Land on which their duplex is built.

f. The Persons' car used solely for personal transportation.

15. Determine the adjusted basis of the three assets detailed below.

a. A building purchased for $100,000 16 years ago. Taxpayer paid $20,000 down and signed an $80,000 12-percent note payable. To date only $35,000 in principal has been paid on this $80,000 note. After acquiring the building, taxpayer incurred $10,000 in repairs (which were expensed) and made $25,000 worth of capital improvements. Taxpayer has claimed depreciation of $50,000 on the building since acquisition.

b. Taxpayer received a gift of 100 shares of ABC stock from his girlfriend. She purchased the stock in 1975 for $500. On the date of the gift, the shares were worth $1,000. A gift tax of $10 was paid.

c. Taxpayer received stock 2 years ago as a gift from her grandmother. On the date of the gift, the stock was valued at $10,000; no gift tax was paid. Grandmother had purchased the stock in 1929 for $500. Grandmother died this year when the stock was valued at $11,000. Taxpayer, who was executrix of her grandmother's estate, did not elect the alternate valuation date. Six months after her grandmother's death, the same shares were valued at $12,000.

SUPPLEMENTAL PROBLEMS

16. Older, wealthy taxpayers who own capital assets that have appreciated substantially in value often contend that they are "locked-in" to their investments by the high rate of tax on capital gains.

    a. Explain what these taxpayers mean when they say they are "locked-in."

    b. Did the changes included in the Tax Reform Act of 1976 increase or decrease the locked-in effect as that law was *originally* enacted?

    c. If Congress were to leave the gift provisions as they currently read but modify the rules applicable to property held at death and to treat death as a realization event (thus triggering all previously unrealized gains and losses for inclusion with the decedent's final tax return), what would you expect wealthy taxpayers to do? Would the change you anticipate be "good" or "bad" for the economy? Explain briefly.

    d. How might other tax provisions relating to gifts be modified to minimize any problems you saw implicit in the suggestion in part c?

    e. If both death transfers and gift transfers were treated as a realization event, what social or economic ill might be exacerbated? Explain briefly, as best you can.

. . .section 1201 (a) imposes an alternative tax in lieu of the tax imposed by sections 11 and 511, but only if such alternative tax is less than the tax imposed by sections 11 and 511.

Reg. Sec. 1.1201-1(a)(1)

capital gain and loss today: the pure case — concluded

After all of a taxpayer's capital gains and losses for a particular year have been correctly identified, quantified, and classified as long or short term, the taxpayer must run a complex maze to determine the correct and most beneficial tax treatment available. The four most pertinent Code provisions are Sec. 1201, which permits corporate taxpayers to apply a special tax rate to some portion or all of the capital gains realized; Sec. 1202, which allows noncorporate taxpayers the right to claim a deduction based on some part or all of the capital gains realized; and Secs. 1211 and 1212, which prescribe the tax treatment of net capital losses. The specific provisions differ significantly for corporate and noncorporate taxpayers. Therefore, in this chapter, we shall separate our discussion into two parts: The first portion deals with the rules applicable to capital gains and losses realized by individual and fiduciary taxpayers, and the second deals with corporate capital gains and losses.

NONCORPORATE TAXPAYERS

The noncorporate taxpayer generally prefers a net long-term capital gain to an equal amount of ordinary income because of a fundamental tax advantage that accrues to only the former kind of income. That advantage is the long-term capital-gain deduction. It is advantageous to all taxpayers having some taxable income because it automatically creates an otherwise unavailable tax deduction and thereby reduces both taxable income and the tax payable. Although net long-term capital gains are generally advantageous taxwise, net capital losses are generally not as beneficial as equal amounts of ordinary losses. Let us begin by examining the advantageous rules first.

The long-term capital-gain deduction defined

The statutory authority for the long-term capital-gain deduction is found in Sec. 1202, which reads in part as follows:

> Sec. 1202. Deduction for Capital Gains.
> If for any taxable year, a taxpayer other than a corporation has a net capital gain, 60 percent of the amount of the net capital gain shall be a deduction from gross income.

And Sec. 1222(11) defines a net capital gain as "the excess of the net long-term capital gain for the taxable year over the net short-term capital loss for such year." This definition can be stated concisely in a simple formula:

$$LTCG \text{ deduction} = 60\% \, (NLTCG - NSTCL)$$

where $NLTCG$ = net long-term capital gain and $NSTCL$ = net short-term capital loss. The larger the $NLTCG$ and the smaller the $NSTCL$, the greater the long-term capital-gain deduction. This conclusion is demonstrated in Table 21-1.

TABLE **21-1**
THE LONG-TERM CAPITAL-GAIN DEDUCTION

Net long-term gain (loss)	Net short-term gain (loss)	Capital gain net income	Net capital gain	Amount of LTCG deduction
$ 8,000	$ 0	$ 8,000	$8,000	$4,800
8,000	(2,000)	6,000	6,000	3,600
8,000	(10,000)	(2,000)	0	0
8,000	5,000	13,000	8,000	4,800
0	5,000	5,000	0	0
(5,000)	8,000	3,000	0	0
(5,000)	(8,000)	(13,000)	0	0

Several aspects of the table deserve emphasis. First, notice that the first two columns are *net* quantities; it is immaterial how many individual long- and short-term gains and losses are incurred to arrive at these net quantities. Second, note that, in common-sense English, the "net capital position" is *not* the base for determining the long-term capital-gain deduction. Unfortunately, however, the Code uses the phrase "net capital gain" to mean "*NLTCG − NSTCL.*" In Codese, the net capital position is called "capital gain net income." Third, observe that whenever a *net* short-term capital gain is reported (even if that net quantity includes several individual short-term capital losses), a zero is substituted for *NSTCL* in the formula suggested earlier. Fourth, notice that no long-term capital-gain deduction can be gained from an excess of net short-term gains over net long-term losses, but that net long-term capital losses are offset against net short-term capital gains.

To repeat an earlier observation, the long-term capital-gain deduction provides a potential benefit to every taxpayer who has taxable income sufficiently large to make him or her subject to even the lowest income-tax rate. That is, regardless of the marginal bracket at which he or she pays tax, and regardless of the ability to itemize deductions, the taxpayer who is fortunate enough to record net long-term capital gains in excess of net short-term capital losses will automatically be entitled to a tax deduction equal to 60 percent of that excess.

To illustrate the long-term capital gain deduction, assume that a single taxpayer had a $12,000 ordinary tax table income and a $5,000 long-term capital gain. This taxpayer would compute his or her tax liability as follows:

Ordinary tax table income		$12,000
Long-term capital gain	$5,000	
Less LTCG deduction	(3,000)	
Taxable portion of capital gain		2,000
Total tax table income		$14,000

This taxpayers's gross tax liability, determined in the normal way and assuming one exemption, would be $2,079.

Observe that the highest marginal tax rate applicable to noncorporate taxpayers is currently 70 percent. Thus, the effect of the long-term capital gain deduction is, for all practical purposes, to place a *maximum* 28 percent tax rate on the excess of net long-term capital gains over net short-term capital losses.

The discussion of tax benefits just concluded has been confined to the situations that were depicted in the first column of the capital-gain–loss matrix presented in the last chapter—that is, where there were greater net long-term capital gains than net short-term capital losses. To complete our discussion of capital gain and loss taxation for noncorporate taxpayers, we must comment on the situations, depicted in the second and third columns of the matrix, in which there are either (1) net short-term capital gains or (2) net capital losses, whether short or long term.

Net short-term capital gains can be dealt with in summary fashion. They are first combined with net long-term capital losses (if any), and the excess of any such gains is included in the determination of ordinary income without tax benefit. If the net long-term capital losses should exceed the net short-term capital gains, the net capital loss would be subject to the limitations explained below. If there are both net short-term capital gains and net long-term capital gains, the former gains are simply combined with ordinary income, while the latter gains are eligible for the special 60 percent deduction.

Tax consequence of net capital loss

Tax detriment, as well as tax benefit, can result from transactions involving capital assets. First, many capital losses simply are not deductible for tax purposes. As explained earlier, the capital loss sustained on the sale of a personal residence or personal automobile is *not* deductible, even though the gains on the sale of the identical assets would be taxable. This rather peculiar situation results from two basic Code provisions noted in Chapter 6: (1) that all income, regardless of source, shall be subject to the income tax unless it is specifically excluded by another Code section and (2) that no deduction is allowed unless specifically provided by the Code. And the Code authorizes neither exclusion of the gain on the sale of personal capital assets nor deduction of the loss on the sale or exchange of personal capital assets. Because casualty losses are deductible under Sec. 165(c), however, the destruction (total or partial) by fire, flood, or wind of a personal residence or personal automobile *could* result in a tax deduction, while the routine loss on the sale or exchange of that asset could not achieve the same tax status. The precise treatment of deductible casualty losses is discussed in Chapter 23. At this juncture it is necessary only to realize that many capital losses simply are not tax deductible.

A second possible tax detriment in transactions involving capital assets occurs because even those capital losses that are deductible are subject to maximum limitations. As a general proposition, in any given year *net capital losses* are deductible (if deductible at all) only to the *lesser* of (1) $3,000 or (2) taxable income determined without subtracting personal exemptions. (The maximum for married taxpayers filing separate returns is $1,500.) Notice that the rule just stated is concerned with *net* capital losses; in other words, capital losses can be offset against capital gains without limit.

A third and final tax detriment in transactions involving capital assets occurs when net *long-term* capital losses are offset against ordinary income. For all such losses incurred after December 31, 1969, the losses must be offset on a $2-for-$1 basis. That is, it requires $2,000 of a net long-term capital loss to create a $1,000 deduction from ordinary income. This 50-percent dilution is applicable only to net long-term losses; short-term losses are applied on a dollar-for-dollar basis. This provision, instituted in the Tax Reform Act of 1969, was intended to bring the tax treatment of net long-term capital losses in line with the treatment of net long-term capital gains (which were taxed at only one-half their value). The parity of gain and loss treatment was not continued in the Revenue Act of 1978, however, because that law did *not* change the 2-for-1 loss provision when it increased the LTCG deduction from 50 to 60 percent.

If the deductible net capital loss in any particular year exceeds the maximum, for all noncorporate taxpayers the excess is carried forward to subsequent tax years until exhausted. In each of the subsequent years the capital loss retains its short- and long-term character as established in the year it was realized. (This was not true for individuals prior to 1964; it still is not true for corporations, as we will see in the final pages of this chapter.) The taxpayer with both net short-term and net long-term capital losses in any given year must deduct short-term capital losses first.

To illustrate the rules applicable to net long-term capital losses, assume that in 19x1 a taxpayer had a $20,000 ordinary taxable income and that, in addition, he recognized a deductible net long-term capital loss of $5,800 and a net short-term capital loss of $500. This taxpayer would offset the maximum net capital loss of $3,000 against his ordinary income (the $500 short-term loss and $2,500 long-term loss) but it would cost him $5,000 of his $5,800 net long-term capital loss to do so. He could carry forward only the remaining $800 net long-term capital loss into 19x2. His net taxable income would be calculated as follows:

Ordinary taxable income	$20,000
Less: $3,000 maximum net capital-loss determined as follows:	
Net short-term capital loss first (on dollar-for-dollar basis)	(500)
Net long-term capital loss next (on two-for-one basis) $800 carried to 19x2	(2,500)
Net taxable income for 19x1	$17,000

If this taxpayer had no further capital transactions in 19x2, the $800 long-term loss carried forward would yield only a $400 deduction from his ordinary income. Long-term capital losses realized prior to January 1, 1970, retain their full dollar-for-dollar offsetting value, even though they may be applied to a post-1969 year through a carryforward.

It should be noted that the taxpayer is not given an option in deciding to offset his net capital losses against ordinary income in a particular year; he or she must do so if possible. If this were not stipulated, a taxpayer, under some circumstances, might be tempted to defer deducting losses until he or she could use them dollar-for-dollar. As a practical matter, of course, this means that a little year-end tax planning can often pay sizable dividends.

TABLE **21-2**

INDIVIDUAL NET CAPITAL LOSSES AND THE CAPITAL LOSS CARRYFORWARD

Year	Assumed capital gains and losses excluding carryforward		Capital losses to be carried forward to subsequent year	Explanation of loss carryforward
19x1	NLT	($2,000) [a]	($2,000)	Carried forward
	NST	(3,000)	0	$3,000 deducted from ordinary
	Net capital	($5,000)		income (maximum)
19x2	NLT	($4,000)	($6,000)	19x1 ($2,000) + 19x2 ($4,000)
	NST	($4,000)	(1,000)	$3,000 deducted from ordinary
	Net capital	($8,000)		income (maximum); $1,000 carried forward
19x3	NLT	$7,000	0	Offset all LT carryforward + $1,000 short-term loss of current year
	NST	(4,000)	($1,000)	$3,000 (maximum) deducted from ordinary income; ($1,000) from 19x2 carried forward [b]
	Capital gain net income	$3,000		
19x4	NLT	$1,000	0	
	NST	$1,000	0	Offset by ST carryforward
	Net capital	$2,000		

[a]Parentheses denote capital loss; absence of parentheses indicates capital gain.
[b]Observe that the $6,000 long-term carryforward is used to offset the current year's $7,000 long-term capital gain before applying any of the current year's short-term capital loss against the current year's long-term capital gain. If the opposite procedure were required, then no carryforwards would have been left.

Table 21-2 demonstrates the proper handling of net capital losses and the determination of the capital loss carryforward. This tabulation assumes a taxpayer with taxable income, excluding capital transactions and personal exemptions, of more than $3,000. (In other words, the maximum capital loss offset against ordinary income is assumed to be available each year.)

The rules that determine the tax treatment of long- and short-term capital gains and losses for noncorporate taxpayers can now be illustrated, as in Figure 21-1, with an extension of the chemical-beaker apparatus of Figure 20-2 (p. **20**/11). On initial examination, both the student and the instructor may be inclined to dismiss Figure 21-1 as too confusing. Our experience, however, has been that this one illustration is more readily digested than the hundreds of words required to replace it. In working with this illustration, note, for example, that all gray positives and negatives first combine into a single net quantity. Similarly, all black positives and negatives also combine into another single net quantity. These two net quantities, however, will combine into another single net quantity *only if they are of opposite signs*. That is, net long-term gains will always combine with net short-term losses to form a single net gain or loss. Also, net long-term losses will always combine with net short-term gains to form a net loss or gain. If the grays and the blacks are of the same sign, positive or negative, they will never combine. If they are both net positives, the one (the long-term gains) gets special treatment, whereas the other (the short-term gains) gets the same treatment as more ordinary income. If both nets are negative, the short-term negatives go through the system first; additionally, the long-term negatives may be diluted by 50 percent if and when they are used to offset ordinary income.

Tax planning

In addition to making it easier to learn the basic rules, we have found that the use of Figure 21-1 also helps to identify major tax-planning opportunities. Consider the fact that this system of beakers "dumps" or "flushes" only once each year, at midnight on the last day of the taxpayer's taxable year. Therefore, the taxpayer is often in a position to modify the final result in a most advantageous way shortly before the year ends. To illustrate just a couple of opportunities, consider a year in which a taxpayer

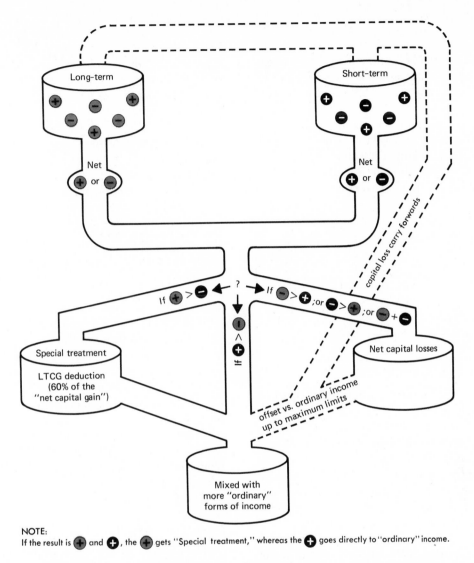

NOTE:
If the result is ⊕ and ➕, the ⊕ gets "Special treatment," whereas the ➕ goes directly to "ordinary" income.

FIGURE **21-1**   Tax Treatment of Capital Gains and Losses: Individual Taxpayer

has recognized no long-term capital gains or losses but in which she has already realized (and must recognize) a $10,000 net short-term capital gain. In terms of our chemical apparatus, we can picture a system that is about ready to "flush" as follows:

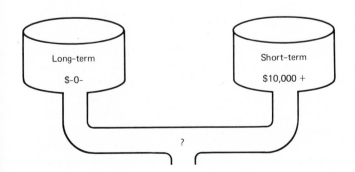

If this taxpayer does nothing further, we know that, at the end of the year, the $10,000 net short-term capital gain will proceed through the system and end up being taxed as ordinary income. This would be a perfect time, therefore, for this taxpayer to realize and recognize a $10,000 long-term capital loss (assuming that the taxpayer already holds capital assets with such a "paper loss" in her portfolio, that would otherwise not be sold at this time). In this manner, a $10,000 long-term capital loss can be used to offset an equivalent of $10,000 in ordinary income on a 1-for-1 basis! If that same capital loss were deferred and not so effectively used, it might have to offset an otherwise tax-favored long-term capital gain in another year, or it might be parceled out as capital loss deductions against ordinary income over several years on a 2-for-1 basis and thus be of much less monetary value. Of course, the taxpayer making such a disposition could not, for 30 days, repurchase shares identical to those just sold at a loss or she would run afoul of the wash sale provisions. (See page **20**/4.)

As a second illustration of possible year-end tax planning, consider the situation of a taxpayer who has already recognized both a $10,000 long-term capital gain and a $10,000 short-term capital loss. The illustrative beakers for this taxpayer would appear as follows:

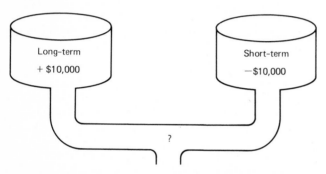

If this taxpayer does nothing further before the end of the year, we know that the short-term capital loss will completely devour the tax-favored long-term capital gain. Therefore, this would be a good time to introduce a $10,000 short-term capital gain into the system if at all possible. To do so would cause the previously realized short-term capital loss to combine with the newly induced short-term capital gain and thereby allow the long-term capital gain to pass untouched through the system and to be taxed in the most favorable manner. Obviously, the final result does involve an increase in the tax, but remember that a taxpayer can seldom, if ever, do better than to realize gains in the form of a net long-term capital gain (which exceeds net short-term capital losses). Incidentally, in this instance, the taxpayer could *immediately* repurchase the shares just sold if he or she desired to return to the former portfolio position; the wash sale rules apply only to losses. The only cost in doing this would be the broker's fee.

CORPORATE CAPITAL GAIN AND LOSS

Thus far in Chapter 21 we have discussed the current status of the capital gain and loss in the pure (statutory) case as applicable to the *individual taxpayer* only. Now let us examine the provisions applicable to the corporate taxpayer.

To return briefly to Chapter 20, remember that both corporations and individuals define capital assets in the same way; both determine the amount of the gain or loss in the same manner; and both distinguish between the short- and long-term capital gains and losses in the same way. The tax treatment given those gains and losses differs significantly, however, depending upon whether the taxpayer is an individual or a corporation. One of these differences is quite easy to state: *There simply is no long-term capital-gain deduction for the corporate taxpayer.*

The alternative tax defined

Corporate net capital gain is eligible for a 28-percent alternative tax. Because the corporate income-tax rate is a five-step progression (i.e., 17 percent on the first $25,000 of taxable income; 20 percent on the second $25,000; 30 percent on the third $25,000; 40 percent on the fourth $25,000; and 46 percent on all remaining corporate taxable income), and because the corporate taxpayer is never entitled to a long-term capital-gain deduction, application of the alternative tax is usually a simple matter. As a general proposition, it would be correct to state that a corporation earning less than $50,000 (taxable income) would not compute the alternative tax, because it would obviously yield a larger total tax liability. On the other hand, the corporation earning more than $50,000 (ordinary taxable income) generally will compute the alternative tax because the applicable rate is higher than the 28-percent alternative tax. For corporations with taxable incomes just slightly in excess of $50,000 *including the net capital gain,* both computations must be made to determine the method that yields the lesser tax. This is true because the alternative tax, if applied at all, must be applied to the entire excess of net long-term capital gain over net short-term capital loss—not to just that portion of it that causes taxable income to exceed $50,000.

Tax consequence of net capital loss

The third and final major difference between personal and corporate capital gain and loss taxation is found in the treatment of a net capital loss. When a corporation incurs a net capital loss it cannot offset any of the net capital loss against its ordinary income, but it is given a special capital-loss carryback-carryforward privilege. In addition, all corporate net capital losses are carried back and forward as short-term capital losses; they do *not* retain their short- or long-term character as they now do for the individual taxpayer. Finally, capital losses of the corporation can under no circumstances be carried forward for more than five years. If the corporation has been unable to generate sufficient capital gains to offset capital-loss carryforwards by the end of the five-year carryforward period, then the capital losses are lost forever for tax purposes. If a corporation has capital losses in two or more successive years, the losses are offset in the order in which they were incurred; in other words, they are applied on a first-in, first-out basis.

To illustrate the corporate capital-loss carryback provisions, let us assume the following facts about an imaginary corporate taxpayer:

Year	Ordinary income	Net short-term capital gain (or loss)	Net long-term capital gain (or loss)
19x1	$150,000	$10,000	$20,000
19x2	150,000	0	20,000
19x3	150,000	40,000	50,000
19x4	160,000	0	(80,000)
19x5	170,000	10,000	(100,000)

After realizing the $80,000 net long-term capital loss in 19x4, the corporation would file for a partial refund of the taxes paid on the capital gains recognized in the three prior years. In making the refund calculations, the $80,000 net capital loss for 19x4 is treated as if it had been a short-term capital loss. The refund, therefore, would be determined as follows:

		Refund
19x1	First $30,000	
	Short-term (46% × $10,000)*	$4,600
	Long-term (28% × $20,000)	5,600
19x2	Next $20,000	
	Short-term	0
	Long-term (28% × $20,000)	5,600
19x3	Last $30,000	
	Short-term (46% × $30,000)	13,800
Refund claimed in 19x4		$29,600

* The calculations in this illustration are based on current corporate tax rates.

Because this corporation incurred a second large capital loss in 19x5, it would have another carryback. The 19x5 carryback of $90,000 would be applied as follows. (Observe that the short-term capital gain of 19x5 is offset against the long-term capital loss before beginning the carryback procedure.)

		Refund
19x2	Previously reduced to zero by the 19x4 carryback	$ 0
19x3	First $60,000	
	Short-term (46% × remaining $10,000)	4,600
	Long-term (28% × $50,000)	14,000
19x4	None available since that too was a net capital-loss year	0
Refund claimed in 19x5		$18,600

In this case, since the corporation was able to use only $60,000 of its $90,000 capital loss through carrybacks, it would carry forward the remaining net capital loss of $30,000 and apply it against the capital gain net income recognized during the next five years. If only $20,000 in capital gain net income were recognized during those years, the remaining $10,000 would expire without tax benefit on December 31, 19x0.

The rules that determine the proper tax treatment of long- and short-term capital gains and losses for corporate taxpayers can now be illustrated with the chemical-beaker apparatus, as in Figure 21-2. A careful comparison of Figures 21-1 and 21-2 will pay handsome dividends for the serious student interested in understanding the complex rules applicable to capital gain and loss taxation.

Unfortunately for the average citizen and tax student alike, the *pure case* of the capital gain and capital loss has been so frequently contaminated that even an elementary understanding of the capital gain and loss complex requires far more knowledge than that contained in the last two chapters. Therefore, in the two following chapters, we shall consider some of the major divergences from the pure case. Before we proceed to examine the special rules, however, let us briefly consider the ways in which taxpayers report capital gains and losses.

REPORTING CAPITAL GAINS AND LOSSES

If an individual taxpayer has any recognizable capital gains or losses for the tax year, he or she must file Schedule D, Form 1040. An example of the 1979 form appears as Figure 21-3. Ignoring the numbers that we have entered on that form for the moment, observe that the 1979 form is divided into five "parts," two parts appearing on the front of the first page. Part I is used to report only short-term capital transactions and, as such, serves much the same purpose as the short-term beaker in our chemical-appa-

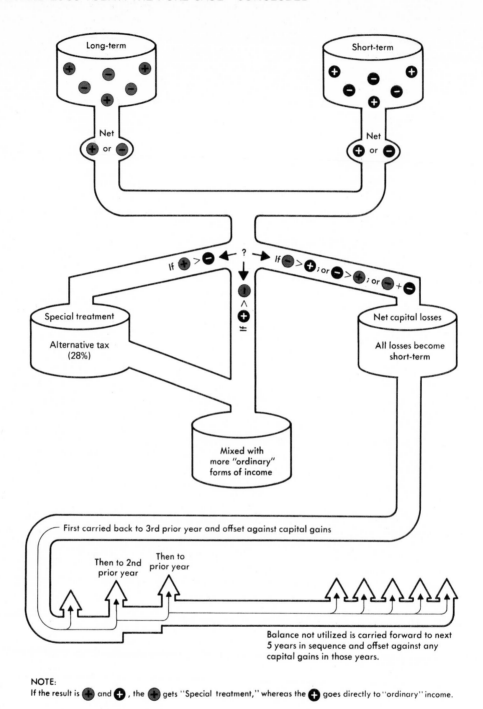

NOTE:
If the result is ⊕ and ⊕ , the ⊕ gets "Special treatment," whereas the ⊕ goes directly to "ordinary" income.

FIGURE **21-2**   Tax Treatment of Capital Gains and Losses:
Corporate Taxpayer

FIGURE 21-3

SCHEDULE D
(Form 1040)

Department of the Treasury
Internal Revenue Service

Capital Gains and Losses (Examples of property to be reported on this Schedule are gains and losses on stocks, bonds, and similar investments, and gains (but not losses) on personal assets such as a home or jewelry.)
▶ Attach to Form 1040. ▶ See Instructions for Schedule D (Form 1040.)

19 79
12

Name(s) as shown on Form 1040

Your social security number

Caution: Columns f and g are not the same as last year. Most other lines have also been changed.

Part I   Short-term Capital Gains and Losses—Assets Held One Year or Less   **D**

a. Kind of property and description (Example, 100 shares 7% preferred of "Z" Co.)	b. Date acquired (Mo., day, yr.)	c. Date sold (Mo., day, yr.)	d. Gross sales price less expense of sale	e. Cost or other basis, as adjusted (see instructions page 20)	f. LOSS if column (e) is more than (d) subtract (d) from (e)	g. GAIN if column (d) is more than (e) subtract (e) from (d)
1 1,000 shares ABC	3-10-79	9-4-79	$40,000	$30,000		$10,000 —

2 Enter your share of net short-term gain or (loss) from transactions entered into by partnerships and fiduciaries after 10/31/78 . . . . **2**   —0—

3 Add lines 1 and 2 in column f and column g . . . . **3**   10,000 —

4 Combine line 3, column f and line 3, column g and enter the net gain or (loss) . . . . **4**   10,000 —

5 Short-term capital loss carryover from years beginning after 1969 . . . . **5** (—0—)

Note: If there is an entry on this line and line 7 or 19, see instructions for lines 7 and 19.

6 Net gain or (loss), combine lines 4 and 5 . . . . **6**   10,000 —

7 Enter your share of net short-term gain or (loss) from transactions entered into by parterships and fiduciaries before 11/1/78 . . . . **7**   —0—

8 Net short-term gain or (loss), combine lines 6 and 7 . . . . **8**   10,000 —

Part II   Long-term Capital Gains and Losses—Assets Held More Than One Year

9 100 shares XYZ	10-12-72	8-14-79	$14,000	$9,000		5,000 —
Personal residence.	6-10-69	5-8-79	52,000	40,000		12,000 —

10 Enter your share of net long-term gain or (loss) from transactions entered into by partnerships and fiduciaries after 10/31/78 . . . . **10**   —0—

11 Add lines 9 and 10 in column f and column g . . . . **11**   17,000 —

12 Combine line 11, column f and line 11, column g and enter the net gain or (loss) . . . . **12**   17,000 —

13 Capital gain distributions from transactions entered into after 10/31/78 . . . . **13**   —0—

14 Enter gain, if applicable, from Form 4797, line 6(a)(1) from transactions entered into after 10/31/78 . **14**   —0—

15 Enter your share of net long-term gain from transactions entered into by small business corporations (Subchapter S) after 10/31/78 . . . . **15**   —0—

16 Combine lines 12 through 15 . . . . **16**   17,000 —

17 Long-term capital loss carryover from years beginning after 1969 . . . . **17** (2,000)

Note: If there is an entry on this line and line 7 or 19, see instructions for lines 7 and 19.

18 Net gain or (loss), combine lines 16 and 17 . . . . **18**   15,000 —

19 Enter your share of capital gain distributions and net long-term gain or (loss) from transactions entered into by partnerships, fiduciaries, small business corporations, real estate investment trusts, and regulated investment companies before 11/1/78 . . . . **19**   —0—

20 Net long-term gain or (loss), combine lines 18 and 19 . . . . **20**   15,000 —

Note: If you have capital loss carryovers from years beginning before 1970, do not complete Parts III or V. See Form 4798 instead.

Part III   Summary of Parts I and II

21 Combine lines 8 and 20, and enter the net gain or (loss) here . . . . | 21 | 25,000 | —

    Note: *Do not complete line 22 if lines 20 and 21 show a gain, and there is a net gain on line 7 or 19. Instead, complete Part IV.*

22 If line 21 shows a gain—
    a Enter 60% of line 20 or 60% of line 21, whichever is smaller. Enter zero if there is a loss or no entry on line 20 * . . . . | 22a | 9,000 | —

    b Subtract line 22a from line 21. Enter here and on Form 1040, line 14 . . . . | 22b | 16,000 | —

23 If line 21 shows a loss—
    a Enter one of the following amounts:
        (i)   If line 8 is zero or a net gain, enter 50% of line **21,**
        (ii)   If line 20 is zero or a net gain, enter line 21; or,
        (iii)   If line 8 and line 20 are net losses, enter amount on line 8 added to **50% of** the amount on line 20 . . . . | 23a |
    b Enter here and enter as a loss on Form 1040, line 14, the smallest of:
        (i)   The amount on line 23a,
        (ii) $3,000 ($1,500 if married and filing a separate return); or,
        (iii)   Taxable income, as adjusted . . . . | 23b |
    Note: *If the loss on line 23a is more than the loss shown on line 23b, complete Part V to determine post-1969 capital loss carryovers from 1979 to 1980.*

Part IV   Computation of Capital Gain Deduction for Sales or Exchanges Before 11/1/78

24 Enter the smaller of line 20 or line 21 (or Form 4798, lines 8 and 9) . . . . | 24 |
25 If line 18 (or Form 4798, line 5) is a gain, combine lines 6 and 18 (or Form 4798, lines 1 and 5), and enter here. If this line or line 18 (or Form 4798, line 5) shows a loss or zero, skip to line 29 and enter zero on line 27 . . . . | 25 |
26 Enter smaller of line 18 (or Form 4798, line 5) or line 25 . . . . | 26 |
27 Enter smaller of line 24 or line 26 . . . . | 27 |
28 Enter 60% of amount on line 27 . . . . | 28 |
29 Subtract line 27 from line 24 . . . . | 29 |
30 Enter 50% of amount on line 29 . . . . | 30 |
31 Add line 28 and line 30. This is your capital gain deduction * . . . . | 31 |

32 Subtract line 31 from line 21 (or Form 4798, line 9). Enter here and on Form 1040, line 14 . . . . | 32 |

Part V   Computation of Post-1969 Capital Loss Carryovers from 1979 to 1980
      (Complete this part if the loss on line 23a is more than the loss shown on line 23b)

Section A.—Short-term Capital Loss Carryover

33 Enter loss shown on line 8; if none, enter zero and skip lines 34 through 38—then go to line 39 . . . | 33 |
34 Enter gain shown on line 20. If that line is blank or shows a loss, enter zero . . . . | 34 |
35 Reduce any loss on line 33 to the extent of any gain on line 34 . . . . | 35 |
36 Enter amount shown on line 23b . . . . | 36 |
37 Enter smaller of line 35 or line 36 . . . . | 37 |

38 Subtract line 37 from line 35 . . . . | 38 |
    Note: *The amount on line 38 is the part of your short-term capital loss carryover from 1979 to 1980 that is from years beginning after 1969.*

Section B.—Long-term Capital Loss Carryover

39 Subtract line 37 from line 36 (**Note:** *If you skipped lines 34 through 38, enter amount from line 23b*) . | 39 |
40 Enter loss from line 20; if none, enter zero and skip lines 41 through 44 . . . . | 40 |
41 Enter gain shown on line 8. If that line is blank or shows a loss, enter zero . . . . | 41 |
42 Reduce any loss on line 40 to the extent of any gain on line 41 . . . . | 42 |
43 Multiply amount on line 39 by 2 . . . . | 43 |

44 Subtract line 43 from line 42 . . . . | 44 |
    Note: *The amount on line 44 is the part of your long-term capital loss carryover from 1979 to 1980 that is from years beginning after 1969.*

* If the amount you enter on this line is other than zero, you may be liable for the alternative minimum tax. See Form 6251.

FIGURE 21-4

SCHEDULE D
(Form 1120)
Department of the Treasury
Internal Revenue Service

Capital Gains and Losses

▶ Attach to your income tax return.

1979

Name

Employer identification number

Part I Short-term Capital Gains and Losses—Assets Held ONE YEAR or Less

a. Kind of property and description (Example, 100 shares of "Z" Co.)	b. Date acquired (mo., day, yr.)	c. Date sold (mo., day, yr.)	d. Gross sales price less expense of sale	e. Cost or other basis	f. Gain or (loss) (d less e)
1					

2 Unused capital loss carryover (attach computation) . . . .

3 Net short-term capital gain or (loss) . . . .

Part II Long-term Capital Gains and Losses—Assets Held More Than ONE YEAR

4 Enter section 1231 gain from Form 4797, line 6(a)(1) . . . .

5					

6 Net long-term capital gain or (loss) . . . .

Part III Summary of Schedule D Gains and Losses

7 Enter excess of net short-term capital gain (line 3) over net long-term capital loss (line 6) . . . .

8 Net capital gain. Enter excess of net long-term capital gain (line 6) over net short-term capital loss (line 3) . .

9 Total of lines 7 and 8. Enter here and on Form 1120, line 9(a), page 1 . . . .

Part IV Alternative Tax Computation

10 Taxable income (Form 1120, line 30, page 1) . . . .

11 Net capital gain from line 8 . . . .
Note: *If Part I or Part II above includes transactions entered into by conduits (partnerships, etc.) before January 1, 1979, see instructions for line 12. If no such transactions are included, enter the amount from line 11 on line 12.*

12 Enter the net capital gain from all transactions entered into after December 31, 1978, but not more than the amount entered on line 11 (see instructions) . . . .

13 Subtract line 12 from line 11 . . . .

14 Subtract line 11 from line 10 . . . .

15 Partial tax. Compute the tax on line 14 in accordance with the instructions for Form 1120, Schedule J . . .

16 28% of line 12 . . . .

17 30% of line 13 . . . .

18 Alternative tax—total of lines 15 through 17. If applicable, enter here and on Form 1120, line 3, Schedule J, and check box for Schedule D . . . .

ratus simulator. Part II does the same thing for long-term capital transactions. Part III is the "directing" mechanism that, in effect, routes the various components and possible combinations of net capital gains and losses to their proper container (that is, to special treatment, ordinary income, and/or net capital loss, in our apparatus). Observe also that the instructions on line 22 serve to give the taxpayer the benefit of the long-term capital-gain deduction. Part IV, of Schedule D in effect allows the taxpayer to deduct up to $3,000 of net capital loss from ordinary income. Part V is a record of any capital loss carryforwards.

In order to discover the various rules for tax basis, holding period, and so on, you would have to read the "Instructions for Schedule D" that accompany this form. We have not reproduced those instructions here. Observe, however, that the rules become operative whenever the taxpayer enters the amounts in the various columns of this form. Thus, column e of Part I should reflect the cost basis (which differs, as we have seen, with the method of acquisition). The time lapse between columns b and c determines the correct holding period and, therefore, the correct classification as a short- or long-term component.

The amounts entered on Schedule D in Figure 21-3 are based on the following assumed transactions for a married couple filing a joint return:

1. Sale of ABC stock at a $10,000 short-term capital gain;
2. Sale of XYZ stock at a $5,000 long-term capital gain;
3. Sale of a personal residence at a $12,000 long-term capital gain (assuming the taxpayer elects not to purchase another residence); and

4. A $2,000 long-term capital loss carryforward from last year.

In this example, line 22b instructs the taxpayer to carry $16,000 to line 14 of Form 1040. The effect of that instruction is, of course, to cause the following to be taxed as ordinary income:

1. All the $10,000 net short-term capital gain, but only
2. Forty percent of the $15,000 net long-term capital gain.

The corporate taxpayer must file Schedule D, Form 1120, if it has any recognizable capital gains or losses for the tax year. An example of the 1979 form appears as Figure 21-4. The corporate Schedule D reflects the fact that the applicable rules are simpler for corporations than they are for individuals; in fact, the entire form is printed on only one side of one page. Just as with individual taxpayers, Part I is used to summarize net short-term capital gains and losses and Part II summarizes net long-term capital gains and losses. On the corporate form, however, Part III is a simple three-line summary, which instructs the corporation to enter any net capital gain on page 1, line 9a of the basic Form 1120. If nothing further is done, the corporation automatically pays the ordinary tax rate on its capital gains. Part IV provides the only tax relief available to the corporation reporting an excess of net long-term capital gain over net short-term capital loss. That is, by completing Part IV the corporation will pay the 28 percent alternative tax on its "net capital gain." Because Schedule D, Form 1120, is largely self-explanatory, we have not entered any illustrative amounts in Figure 21-4. Incidentally, corporations claim their refund for net capital losses by filing a separate form, Form 1139.

PROBLEMS

(NOTE: If no year is stated, assume that the transaction took place in the current tax year.)

1. Arnold Roger sold the following securities:

Security	Date acquired	Date sold	Cost	Sales price
ABC	9/21 two years ago	10/4	$2,000	$1,800
DEF	10/29 last year	3/10	6,000	6,600
GHI	1/15 last year	8/16	1,700	1,400
JKL	1/20 last year	3/10	3,000	4,500
MNO	5/8 last year	12/31	5,000	4,700
PQR	5/8 last year	12/31	5,000	5,300

Assuming that Mr. Roger is a cash-basis taxpayer and that the above transactions constitute all of his "Schedule D" transactions for this year, calculate:
  a. His net short-term capital gain or loss.
  b. His net long-term capital gain or loss.
  c. His long-term capital-gain deduction.
  d. His capital-loss carryforward to next year.

2. This year, four unrelated corporate taxpayers (A through D) will recognize the taxable incomes indicated in the table below:

	Taxpayer			
Income components	A	B	C	D
Ordinary taxable income	$21,200	$40,200	$73,200	$173,200
Net short-term gain (loss)	(5,000)	6,000	(8,000)	30,000
Net long-term gain (loss)	11,000	10,000	20,000	60,000

  a. Determine *by inspection only* which of these taxpayers should
    1. Use no special capital-gain tax treatment;
    2. Use the 28-percent alternative tax.
  b. Which of the above determinations was difficult to make "by inspection only"? Why? Explain briefly.

3. Corporations are not allowed a long-term capital-gain deduction. The corporate alternative for capital-gain treatment is to compute the tax on net taxable income including the net capital gain or to pay a 28 percent alternative tax on the net capital gain plus the ordinary tax on the rest. Does this tend to provide greater tax breaks for some corporations than for others? Explain.

4. Assume that Harold Vine, a married taxpayer who files a joint return, had the following components of taxable income this year:

Salary	$53,200
Interest, rents, etc.	30,000
Net short-term capital gain	10,000
Net long-term capital gain	75,000
Excess deductions from A.G.I. (including exemptions)	(20,000)

  a. What is Vine's taxable income for the year?
  b. What is his "net capital gain"?
  c. Calculate Vine's minimum income-tax liability. Use the current tax rates.

5. This year the Zeta Corporation realized a $320,000 ordinary taxable income and an $80,000 excess of net long-term capital gains over net short-term capital losses. What is Zeta Corporation's minimum gross tax liability? Use current tax rates.

6. Adam Smith, who earned a $23,200 taxable income from ordinary sources in each of the years 19x1 through 19x3, also realized the following capital gains and losses:

Year	Net short term*	Net long term*
19x1	$ 0	($7,000)
19x2	(3,600)	(3,200)
19x3	4,000	0

* Excluding any losses carried forward

a. Assuming that Smith is married and files a joint return, complete the following table by entering the amount of capital loss that he should carry forward in each case.

	Short term	Long term
From 19x1 to 19x2	————	————
From 19x2 to 19x3	————	————
From 19x3 to 19x4	————	————

b. By what amount is Smith's ordinary taxable income in 19x2 reduced because of the capital loss?

7. During years 1 through 4, the Tandy Corporation realized the following ordinary incomes and capital gains and losses:

Year	Ordinary income	Net long-term capital gain (or loss)*	Net short-term capital gain (or loss)*
1	$ 60,000	$ 20,000	$ 5,000
2	80,000	10,000	20,000
3	100,000	15,000	0
4	120,000	(35,000)	10,000

*Excluding any losses carried back or forward

a. Explain the correct tax treatment of the $35,000 net long-term capital loss incurred by Tandy Corporation in year 4.
b. Compute the amount of the tax refund due Tandy Corporation in year 4. Use the current tax rates.

8. Sandra Beckett, a single individual, had the following components of taxable income this year:

Salary	$38,200
Dividends from domestic corporations (after $100 exclusion)	30,000
Net short-term capital loss	(10,000)
Net long-term capital gain	80,000
Excess itemized deductions (including exemptions)	(10,000)

Determine Ms. Beckett's minimum gross tax liability for this year.

9. The Easy Corporation realized the following capital gains and losses this year:

Short-term capital losses totaling	$15,800
Short-term capital gains totaling	3,200
Long-term capital losses totaling	10,500
Long-term capital gains totaling	29,400

Assuming that the corporation had no capital-loss carryforwards from prior years and that ordinary (operating) taxable income for the year was $130,000, indicate which of the following statements are true and which are false. Explain why any false statements are not true.

a. The $10,500 of long-term capital losses should be treated as short-term losses since the taxpayer is a corporation.

b. The only option available to Easy Corporation is the option to pay the regular corporate tax on the $130,000 ordinary income and a 28-percent alternative tax on $6,300 rather than the regular corporate tax on a total taxable income of $136,300.

c. Easy Corporation may elect either to pay the 28-percent alternative tax or to claim a 60 percent long-term capital-gain deduction based on the $6,300 excess of net long-term capital gains over net short-term capital losses.

d. The $26,300 in capital losses ($15,800 short term and $10,500 long term) should be carried back and offset against Easy Corporation's capital gains in the three prior years.

10. Taxpayers Alpha and Beta realized the capital gains and losses detailed below. Assume that neither taxpayer had any capital-loss carryforwards from prior years.

	Alpha	Beta
Short-term capital gain	$20,000	$60,000
Long-term capital gain	90,000	80,000
Short-term capital loss	30,000	40,000
Long-term capital loss	20,000	20,000

a: If Alpha and Beta are noncorporate taxpayers, answer each of the following questions:

1. What is the amount each taxpayer will claim as a long-term capital-gain deduction in the current year?
2. What is the maximum amount each taxpayer could elect to tax at the 28-percent alternative rate this year?
3. What amount of capital gain must each taxpayer include with ordinary income *without any special tax benefit?*

b. If Alpha and Beta are corporate taxpayers, answer each of the same questions (1–3, above).

11. Dan, who will graduate from your university in December of this year with a B.B.A. degree, will earn a total salary of $3,400 during the current year. His new job, which begins January 1 next year, will pay him a salary of $13,500. Throughout his college career Dan has managed to save and invest relatively modest sums of money. At the present time (assume that you are near the end of the current year), Dan owns two stocks, as follows:

Stock	Date purchased	Cost	Current value
ABC	February 8, last year	$1,200	$2,200
DEF	September 1, this year	3,500	2,500

Dan is most discouraged by his last purchase and therefore is about to sell both of his stocks and invest the $4,700 in a badly needed new car and a few pieces of essential furniture, including a good stereo.

Because you are completing a course in taxation, Dan asked you if there were any tax aspects that he should consider before selling the shares in the next few days. Because you understand the rules of capital gain and loss taxation, you tell Dan that it would be wiser for him to sell only his ABC shares prior to December 31 and the DEF shares early next year. To prove your point, *calculate the total tax saving that Dan will realize if he follows your advice and explain, as best you can, what accounts for the tax savings.*

In making your calculations you may assume that Dan is single and claims only himself as an exemption; that Dan will not itemize deductions in either the current or the next following year; that the market price of DEF will not change materially before early next year; and that Dan had no other capital asset transactions in either year.

12. Near the end of the year Neal Downs reviewed his completed capital transactions and discovered that thus far he had realized a net short-term capital gain of $800 and a net long-term capital gain of $2,100. He further reviewed his portfolio of stocks and discovered that his unrealized or "paper" gains and losses included a total of $1,800 in additional short-term gains; $2,100 in short-term losses; $3,200 in long-term losses; and $10,800 in long-term gains. Neal also is aware that he will have ordinary taxable income of approximately $45,-000 this year.

    a. Assuming that Neal's ordinary income is not likely to change drastically in the next few years, what would you recommend that he consider by way of year-end tax planning relative to his capital asset position? Explain your recommendations.

    b. Assuming that Neal is about to retire and therefore anticipates a substantial reduction in his ordinary taxable income in future years, what would you recommend that he consider by way of year-end tax planning relative to his capital asset position? Explain your recommendations.

    c. Assuming that Neal will begin to receive a much larger ordinary income in future years, because of a large inheritance, what would you recommend that he consider by way of year-end tax planning relative to his capital asset position? Explain your recommendations.

    d. How would each of your answers have differed in a through c, above, if Neal had already realized a $2,100 net long-term capital *loss* (instead of gain, as originally stated)? Assume all other facts as before.

13. Determine Kathy Little's minimum federal income tax liability assuming that she (1) is single; (2) earned a $40,200 ordinary *taxable* income; and (3) realized a $70,000 net capital gain.

14. Determine Tawdry Corporation's minimum federal income tax liability assuming that it earned a $40,200 ordinary taxable income and realized a $70,000 net capital gain.

15. Dan D., a single taxpayer, realized the following capital gains and losses this year:

    LTCG, $2,000; LTCL, $3,200; STCG, $6,500; STCL, $8,000

    Dan also had a long-term capital loss carryforward of $2,000 from last year. Dan's ordinary taxable income is $30,000.

    a. What is Dan's taxable income for the current year?
    b. What capital loss carryforward (if any) does Dan have for next year?

16. Jack E., a single taxpayer, realized the following capital gains and losses this year:

    LTCG, $10,000; STCL, $9,000

    What effect will these two transactions have on Jack's adjusted gross income for the year?

SUPPLEMENTAL PROBLEMS

17. In addition to all the facts stated in Problem 1, above, assume that Mr. Roger had an ordinary income of $10,000, a net short-term capital loss of $1,700, and a net long-term capital loss of $3,400 in the prior year.
    a. What is Mr. Roger's net short-term capital gain or loss in these revised circumstances?
    b. What is his revised net long-term capital gain or loss?
    c. Complete a Schedule D, Form 1040, for Arnold Roger.
18. What was the primary reason that Congress had for enacting several major changes in the area of capital gains in the Revenue Act of 1978?
19. Adams Corporation purchased 1,000 shares of Eve common stock for $88,500 on July 8 last year. On December 15 of last year, the Adams Treasurer ordered the broker to sell *short* 1,000 shares of Eve. Adams's broker completed the short sale the same day. On January 10 of this year, Adams's Treasurer delivered the 1,000 shares of Eve purchased on July 8 last year, to "cover" the short sale made on December 15. Assume that Eve was selling at $97 per share on December 15 and at $83 per share on January 10. (An ordinary short sale involves the sale of something the seller does not currently own; he makes the sale hoping that the item sold will fall in price so that, at some future date, he may buy the same item and "cover" his prior short sale and thus reap a profit. In the meantime, of course, the broker on behalf of the seller has to borrow the item sold from another taxpayer so that the sales transaction may be completed. The fact situation detailed here is referred to as a short sale "against the box" because the seller already owned a number of shares equal to those sold short.) To appreciate both the economic and tax significance of what Adams Corporation was doing, find answers in a tax service to the following questions:
    a. Ignoring any interest charged for the shares borrowed, what amount of gain or loss did Adams Corporation realize from its temporary ownership of Eve Corporation common stock?
    b. In which year, this year or last year, will the transaction be reported, assuming that Adams is a calendar-year taxpayer?
    c. Will the transaction in Eve stock be classified as short or long term?
    d. If Adams Corporation had sold short 2,000 shares of Eve common on December 15 (rather than 1,000 shares, as originally stated) and if Adams had closed the short sale on January 10 by delivering the 1,000 shares purchased on July 8 and additionally delivering another 1,000 shares purchased on January 10, what amount of gain or loss would it recognize? Would this gain or loss be short or long term?
20. This year both Corporation X and Corporation Y realized a $100,000 net capital loss. Both corporations filed for a tax refund based on a $100,000 capital loss carryback. Corporation X received a refund check of $48,000; Corporation Y received only $30,000. Assuming that there was no administrative error, explain the difference. (Also assume that neither corporation has any capital loss carryforward remaining at the end of the year, after receipt of the refund check.)

Mr. Gross: ... Why ask the farmers to hold their breeding stock for 12 months, whereas in any other matter it is a 6 months' proposition; why should there be a differential?
Mr. Mills: Of course there should not be a differential between the farmer and anyone else in the treatment afforded tax-wise; the gentleman is right about that. But I had understood that the livestock people were very well satisfied with this provision.
Congressional Record (1951)

capital gain and loss today: modifications to the pure case

Chapters 20 and 21 were titled *Capital Gain and Loss: The Pure Case* because we assumed, for pedagogical purposes, that the only capital gains and losses are those realized on the sale or exchange of a capital asset as defined in Sec. 1221. As a matter of fact, the Code contains numerous other sections that modify that definition. In some instances, the modifying sections serve to exclude a definitionally "pure" capital asset from capital gain and loss treatment. At other times, they serve to provide capital-gain treatment for assets that do not satisfy the puristic definition.

Part IV of Subchapter P (the subchapter of the Code concerned with capital gain and loss) contains many of the special rules to be applied in particular fact circumstances. The following list of the sections contained in Part IV suggests the breadth of these special rules:

Sec. 1231. Property used in the trade or business and involuntary conversions.
Sec. 1232. Bonds and other evidence of indebtedness.
Sec. 1233. Gains and losses from short sales.
Sec. 1234. Options to buy or sell.
Sec. 1235. Sale or exchange of patents.
Sec. 1236. Dealers in securities.
Sec. 1237. Real property subdivided for sale.
Sec. 1238. Amortization in excess of depreciation.
Sec. 1239. Gain from sale of depreciable property between certain related taxpayers.

Sec. 1241. Cancellation of lease or distributor's agreement.
Sec. 1242. Losses on small business investment company stock.
Sec. 1243. Loss of small business investment company.
Sec. 1244. Losses on small business stock.
Sec. 1245. Gain from dispositions of certain depreciable property.
Sec. 1246. Gain on foreign investment company stock.
Sec. 1247. Election by foreign investment companies to distribute income currently.
Sec. 1248. Gain from certain sales or exchanges of stock in certain foreign corporations.
Sec. 1249. Gain from certain sales or exchanges of patents, etc., to foreign corporations.
Sec. 1250. Gain from disposition of certain depreciable realty.
Sec. 1251. Gain from disposition of property used in farming where farm losses offset nonfarm income.
Sec. 1252. Gain from disposition of farm land.
Sec. 1253. Transfers of franchises, trademarks, and trade names.
Sec. 1254. Gain from disposition of interest in oil or gas property.

The objective of this chapter is to explain three of the more important modifications to the pure case of capital gain and loss taxation. Sections 1231, 1245, and 1250 will receive our major attention because of their pervasive influence in business decisions. Collectively, these three sections deal with depreciable and real properties used in trade or business—those "chameleon assets" that are not capital assets by Code definition, but gains from the disposition of which may or may not be eligible for capital-gain treatment.

DEPRECIABLE AND REAL PROPERTIES USED IN TRADE OR BUSINESS

Although excluded by the Code from the definition of a capital asset, depreciable and real properties used in trade or business effectively *may* result in a capital gain when sold or exchanged. The conditions that must be satisfied for this result to obtain are delineated in Code Sec. 1231.

Section 1231

The study of Sec. 1231 must be made with care. Three distinct complications are apt to confuse: First, the group of transactions that collectively constitute the whole of Sec. 1231 are at best described as mysterious; second, the import of Sec. 1231 cannot be determined until a tax period has closed and the net position of all Sec. 1231 transactions is known with certainty; and third, the apparent consequences of Sec. 1231 are often overridden by other sections that deal with the "recapture" of ordinary deductions. In the following pages, we shall discuss these three complications, in the order stated, in some detail.

Section 1231 encompasses two major classes of transactions:

1. Gains and losses from the sale or exchange of property used in the trade or business, *but gains are included only to the extent not subject to such "recapture" sections as 1245 and 1250;* and

2. Gains and losses from the involuntary conversion of both (A) property used in a trade or business and (B) capital assets held for more than one year, *but only if the gains from such involuntary conversions, which are casualties, exceed the losses from casualties.*

To make matters even more complex, Sec. 1231(b) defines property used in a trade or business to include

1. Real and depreciable properties used in a trade or business if held for more than one year;

2. Timber, coal, and domestic iron ore (with respect to which Sec. 631 applies);

3. Livestock—but
   a. if cattle and horses held for draft, breeding, dairy, or sporting purposes, only if held for more than 24 months;
   b. if other livestock (i.e., other than cattle or horses) held for draft, breeding, dairy, or sporting purposes, only if held for more than 12 months;
   c. never to include poultry; and

4. Unharvested crops, but only if the crop and the land are sold, exchanged, or involuntarily converted at the same time and to the same person.

The reason for treating such a diverse collection of assets in a unique manner wholly escapes logic. The only good explanation of the above definition is a historical one. As noted on page **19**/8, Sec. 1231 originated in the turmoil between the Great Depression and World War II. Initially it was intended to provide taxpayers with the rare opportunity of treating only the net gains on the sale of real and depreciable properties used in a trade or business as if they were capital gains and of treating net losses on the sale or exchange of those same properties as if they were ordinary (or noncapital) losses. This, of course, was the best of both possible tax worlds and it is not surprising, therefore, that special interest groups sought to be included within the purview of this provision. As suggested by the headnote to this chapter—a quote of a conversation between two Congressmen—logic often gave way to whatever satisfied those special interest groups.

In addition to the diverse collection of assets included within the definition of "property used in a trade or business," observe that Sec. 1231 becomes applicable for different kinds of assets under different conditions: It applies to *sales and exchanges* of properties used in a trade or business and to the *involuntary conversion* of a still larger set of assets. In the latter category, pure capital assets held for over one year as well as property used in a trade or business are combined in a unique manner. Recognized gains and losses from involuntary conversions due to condemnations or the threat thereof are included in the Sec. 1231 category in every event. If the involuntary conversion is a casualty, however, gains and losses are first brought together to determine whether the gains from casualties exceed casualty losses. If a net gain results, the casualty gains and losses are included in the Sec. 1231 melting pot. If a loss results, all gains and losses from casualties are treated as ordinary gains and losses.

TABLE **22-1**

SECTION 1231 AND RELATED CASUALTY LOSS PROVISIONS

Kind of property involved in the casualty or theft	Holding period		
	Equal to or less than one year	More than one year	
		If casualty and theft losses exceed gains	If casualty and theft gains exceed losses
Real or depreciable property used in a trade or business	Ordinary deduction *for* A.G.I.	Ordinary deduction *for* A.G.I.	Sec. 1231
Income-producing capital asset (e.g., a single rental unit not deemed to be a "trade or business")	Ordinary deduction *from* A.G.I. unless associated with production of rents or royalties, then *for* A.G.I.	Ordinary deduction *from* A.G.I. unless associated with production of rents or royalties, then *for* A.G.I.	Sec. 1231
Non-income-producing capital asset (e.g., the family automobile)	Ordinary deduction *from* A.G.I.	Ordinary deduction *from* A.G.I.	Sec. 1231
Inventory	Ordinary deduction *for* A.G.I.	Ordinary deduction *for* A.G.I.	Ordinary income

NOTE: For corporate taxpayers there is no for-from A.G.I. distinction; therefore, the Sec. 1231 classification of corporate casualty loss deductions is simply a matter of ordinary versus Sec. 1231 treatment. Additionally, corporate assets generally are presumed to be either inventory or trade-business related.

Observe that Sec. 1231 does not provide statutory authority for the deduction of losses incurred in an involuntary conversion. That authority stems from Sec. 165. Section 1231 simply tells the taxpayer how to treat certain gains and losses; that is, it tells the taxpayer whether to treat a select group of transactions as ordinary transactions or as transactions involving long-term capital assets. The proper tax treatment of casualty losses can be summarized usefully as in Table 22-1.

The concept of a gain associated with a casualty or theft loss may seem strange. The answer to the apparent conundrum is, of course, that the casualty or theft may trigger a retribution payment, most frequently in the form of an insurance claim, that is greater than the adjusted basis of the property that was destroyed or stolen. Thus, there has been a realization of gain even though there was no voluntary sale or exchange. If the retribution payment is less than the adjusted basis of the property destroyed or stolen, the amount deductible as a casualty loss depends in part on the classification of the property involved. The general rules needed to quantify casualty and theft losses are as follows:

1. For total destruction of business or investment property, the deduction equals the adjusted basis of the property destroyed less any insurance, salvage value, or other proceeds on disposition.

2. For partial destruction of business or investment property, the deduction equals the *lesser* of

   a. the difference between the fair market value of the property before and after the casualty, less insurance, salvage, or other proceeds; *or*

   b. the adjusted basis of the property destroyed less insurance, salvage, or other proceeds.

3. For the total or partial destruction of personal-use property, the same rules apply as in 2, above, less $100 per casualty.

To illustrate the application of Sec. 1231, assume that in a given year a sole proprietor incurred two unusual gains and losses: first, a gain of $10,000 on the sale of a store building purchased twenty years earlier and depreciated on a straight-line basis; and second, a loss of $3,800 on an 18-month-old family automobile demolished in a collision. Both of these events would appear to fall within the purview of Sec. 1231. However, because the taxpayer incurred a net loss on casualty events, the $3,700 (i.e., $3,800 less $100 since the automobile destroyed was personal-use property and no insurance was collected) deductible casualty loss would be treated as a direct deduction from adjusted gross income and not be combined with the taxpayer's sole Sec. 1231 gain— the $10,000 attributable to the store building.

If we were to modify the facts in the preceding paragraph and attribute the $10,000 gain on the building to the difference between the insurance collected after the store was destroyed by fire and the adjusted basis of the building, the net of the two casualty events would be a gain, and both the automobile loss and the building-fire gain would become part of Sec. 1231. The eventual disposition of the two transactions would then depend, in turn, on the net balance of the taxpayer's Sec. 1231 transactions for the year.

If the aggregate of all Sec. 1231 transactions is a net gain, each of the transactions included therein is treated for tax purposes as if it involved the sale or exchange of a capital asset held for more than one year. On the other hand, if the aggregate of all Sec. 1231 transactions for a year is a net loss, each of the transactions included therein is treated for tax purposes as if it involved a noncapital asset.

To illustrate this final result, let us return to our sole proprietor and assume that he sustained three unusual events in the current year: the $3,800 loss in the auto collision; the $10,000 gain from the destruction of the store by fire; and the sale of the land on which the store building had stood at a $5,000 gain. As explained earlier, if the net of the two casualty events is a gain, both casualty transactions will become part of the Sec. 1231 melting pot. Since the only additional Sec. 1231 transaction in this example also involves a gain, the net Sec. 1231 position is also a net gain and, therefore, all three of these transactions will be treated as if they had involved capital assets held for more than one year. In terms of the pure definition contained in Sec. 1221, only the family automobile is a capital asset. The store building and the land are excluded from the pure definition by Sec. 1221(2). The building and the land are effectively reinstated to capital asset status by operation of Sec. 1231.

As a final illustration, assume that in a particular year a corporate taxpayer incurred a $20,000 loss on the sale of a warehouse and a $5,000 loss on the theft of a pure capital asset. In these circumstances, the $5,000 deductible theft loss would not become part of Sec. 1231, because the net of the corporation's casualty and theft transactions for the year resulted in a loss. As indicated in Table 22-1, that $5,000 loss would become an ordinary deduction for the corporation. The $20,000 loss on the sale of the warehouse

would automatically become part of the corporation's Sec. 1231 transactions. Since we assumed that that was the corporation's only Sec. 1231 transaction, and since that involved a loss, that loss also would be treated as an ordinary loss. Obviously, the net effect in this instance is the conversion of a $5,000 pure capital loss into an ordinary loss by operation of Sec. 1231.

The primary importance of Sec. 1231 should now be obvious: As a general proposition it permits taxpayers to deduct losses on the sale or exchange of properties used in the trade or business, as well as casualty losses of these or of capital assets, without the restrictions imposed by the dollar limitations on the deductibility of net capital losses. On the other hand, it permits the taxpayer to tax as long-term capital gains the gains on the sale of properties used in the trade or business as long as these gains exceed the losses from the transactions described in Sec. 1231(a).

In concert with other Code provisions, Sec. 1231 eventually came to be a basic method for tax minimization. After the 1954 Code permitted businesses to speed up depreciation (effected by the sum-of-the-years-digits and the double-declining-balance methods), it was not unusual for property used in the trade or business to be depreciated at an unrealistically rapid pace and then sold at a substantial gain. The large depreciation deductions obviously reduced taxable income—and therefore the ordinary income-tax liability—by substantial amounts, while the gain realized on the sale of the asset could often be treated as a tax-favored capital gain. In short, it was possible to convert ordinary income into capital gain through the combined use of rapid depreciation deductions and Sec. 1231 gains.

In the most blatant cases, taxpayers could repeat this conversion more than once with a single property! They did it by selling a depreciated property to a very closely related taxpayer. For example, a husband could sell to his wife, or an individual stockholder could sell to a controlled corporation, and (because of Sec. 1231) the seller would pay only a capital gains tax on the gain realized. The related purchaser, however, would have a new and higher cost basis in the asset purchased, which would once more give rise to a large depreciation deduction to be offset against ordinary income.

Corrective legislation came in two steps. First, in 1939 Congress readily passed Sec. 1239, which provides that any gain realized on the sale of a depreciable property to a related taxpayer must be reported as ordinary income. That, however, did not stop the parlay of ordinary income into capital gain when bona fide sales were made to third parties. That stopped when Congress was persuaded in 1962 to enact Sec. 1245, which now significantly modifies the effect of Sec. 1231 for many assets.

Section 1245

The effect of Sec. 1245 is to provide that any gain recognized on the disposition of depreciable property other than buildings and building components shall be ordinary income to the extent that depreciation has been claimed on the asset since December 31, 1961, Sec. 1231 notwithstanding. The technical definition of Sec. 1245 property is almost identical to the definition of property that qualifies for the investment credit (p. **17**/3). If the gain on the sale or other disposition is greater than the depreciation claimed since December 31, 1961, then the remainder of the gain gets Sec. 1231 treatment. If the gain is equal to or less than the post-1961 depreciation, the entire gain is ordinary income.

These rules of Sec. 1245 can be illustrated readily on a simple graph (Figure 22-1). Let distance OA represent the cost of a depreciable business property purchased at date t_0 and the curve represent the adjusted basis of this asset between t_0 and the date of sale (t_1). (The linear function suggests that a straight-line depreciation method is being used.) If the asset is sold at t_1 for any amount less than that represented by distance OC, the resulting loss is a "Sec. 1231 loss." If the asset is sold at t_1 for any amount greater than OC but less than OB (which is called the "recomputed basis"), then the resulting gain is wholly ordinary income by operation of Sec. 1245. If this

asset is sold at t_1 for an amount greater than OB, then the portion of the gain equal to distance BC would be "recaptured" as ordinary income by operation of Sec. 1245, whereas the remainder of the gain (that in excess of OB) would still be "Section 1231 gain."

With the passage of time, the obvious result of Sec. 1245 will be the negation, for all practical purposes, of the tax results achieved under Sec. 1231, at least as far as depreciable property other than buildings and building components is concerned. Suppose, for example, that early this year a taxpayer sold some depreciable equipment used in business for the preceding ten years. Further suppose that this equipment had originally cost the taxpayer $10,000, that it had been depreciated $1,000 per year in each of the intervening ten years, and that it is sold for $3,000. Under these circumstances, the entire gain of $3,000 must be recognized as ordinary income under Sec. 1245, since the gain ($3,000 sale price less zero basis) is less than the post-1961 depreciation ($10,000). If the property had been sold for more than it originally cost—a highly unlikely prospect!—then $10,000 of the gain would be ordinary income, and any remaining gain would be treated as Sec. 1231 income—getting ordinary or capital treatment, as appropriate for that year, considering *all* Sec. 1231 transactions collectively.

Before examining the second major provision concerned with the recapture of depreciation, it would be well to reemphasize that *Section 1245 applies to gains from the disposition of depreciable nonrealty* (as well as certain real estate) *regardless of the depreciation method used and regardless of the number of years the asset has been held prior to*

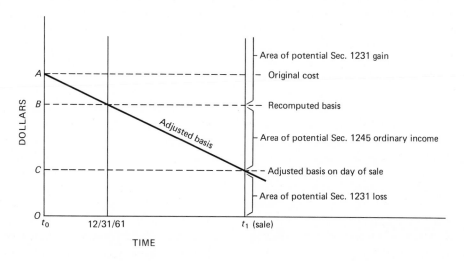

FIGURE **22-1** Sections 1231 and 1245: Combined Rules

disposition. Additionally, Sec. 1245 tends to override most other provisions of the Code. To illustrate this last point, consider a situation in which a taxpayer realized a $5,000 gain because the insurance proceeds exceeded the adjusted basis of business equipment destroyed by fire. If the taxpayer elected to recognize the gain (that is, did not elect to apply the nonrecognition provision contained in Sec. 1033), he or she might reasonably wonder if the entire gain could be mixed with other casualty transactions, and thus possibly end up with Sec. 1231 gains, or if only that portion of the gain not subject to recapture of depreciation under Sec. 1245 could even be eligible for the casualty treatment. The taxpayer would discover that, unfortunately, Sec. 1245 takes precedence and only the gain in excess of the Sec. 1245 gain could even be considered along with his or her remaining casualty transactions.

Section 1250

In 1964 Congress extended the basic idea of recapturing depreciation to buildings, building components, and leaseholds by enacting Code Sec. 1250. However, unlike the earlier provision applicable to most depreciable personalty (a legal term for nonrealty), *Sec. 1250 provides for the recapture of depreciation as ordinary income only if a rapid depreciation method has been used* by the taxpayer. If that were the end of the story, it would be easy to proceed to illustrate the way those rules work out in a typical situation. Unfortunately, however, Congress modified the rules in 1969 and in 1976. On each occasion the new rules were not made retroactive; consequently, a single building purchased before 1964 and sold after 1975 can actually be subject to four different sets of rules simultaneously! In trying to determine the amount of the gain that should be treated as ordinary income by operation of Sec. 1250, rather than as Sec. 1231 income, the taxpayer must begin with the most recent set of rules and work backward until either the entire gain realized has been exhausted—that is, the entire gain has been disposed of according to one of the sets of rules imposed by Sec. 1250 since 1964—or until all of the recapture rules have been satisfied and some gain remains (in which case the remainder becomes Sec. 1231 gain). Although it is tempting to go into the details of these provisions—to demonstrate how ridiculous the tax law can actually become, if for no other reason—we have elected instead to include in this introductory text only the rules applicable to

nonresidential buildings acquired after December 31, 1969, and to residential buildings after December 31, 1975. Individuals interested in the other possibilities will simply have to consult a current tax service for additional details. Alternatively, they can try to follow the instructions of Form 4797.

The rules of Sec. 1250 as applied to buildings, building components, and leaseholds, other than residential housing, acquired after December 31, 1969, and as to residential housing acquired after December 31, 1975, can be illustrated readily on a simple graph (Figure 22-2). It must be emphasized that Figure 22-2 cannot be used for residential housing acquired before 1976 *or* for other buildings acquired prior to 1970. As we move further and further away from those dates, however, Figure 22-2 will become illustrative of the interaction between Sec. 1250 and Sec. 1231 for most depreciable buildings.

In Figure 22-2, distance *OC* represents the initial cost of a depreciable building. The linear curve represents the adjusted basis of the building based on straight-line depreciation; the nonlinear curve represents the actual adjusted basis of the building based on the rapid depreciation method elected. The vertical difference between the two curves at any time represents the cumulative *excess depreciation* claimed. Thus at t_1, the date of sale, the excess depreciation would be represented by the distance *AB*. If the building were sold at t_1 for anything less than its adjusted basis, represented by the distance *OA*, the resulting loss would be a Sec. 1231 loss. If the building were sold at t_1 for something more than that represented by the distance *OA* but for less than that represented by the distance *OB*, the entire gain would be ordinary income by operation of Sec. 1250. Finally, if the building were sold at t_1 for something more than that represented by the distance *OB*, part of the gain—that represented by the distance *AB*— would be ordinary income via Sec. 1250 and the remainder would be classified as Sec. 1231 gain.

As a detailed investigation of Figure 22-2 would prove, the effect of Sec. 1250 on the sale or exchange of a building or building component is not as all-encompassing as the effect of Sec. 1245 on the sale or exchange of other depreciable property used in a trade or business. The smaller impact is attributable to the fact that Sec. 1250 will not apply at all unless a rapid depreciation method has been utilized and, even if such a method has been used, the longer the asset is held the smaller the amount of excess depreciation, since at some point in the life of any asset, the straight-line depreciation exceeds the rapid

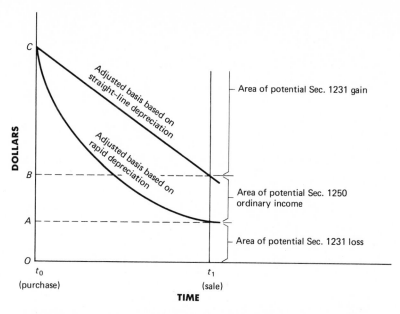

FIGURE **22-2**   Sections 1250 and 1231: Combined Rules for Nonresidential Buildings Purchased After December 31, 1969, and for Residential Buildings Purchased After December 31, 1975

depreciation and the cumulative excess is slowly reduced. *Note also that Sec. 1250 applies only to the gain attributable to the building; the gain on the sale of the land is always Sec. 1231 income.* Thus, the allocation of the sales price between the land and the building can be very important.

The tax student ought, then, to understand the interaction of the capital gain and loss provisions and Secs. 1231, 1245, and 1250. We can say, in summary, that depreciable properties used in the trade or business are excluded from capital gain and loss treatment by the definition of a capital asset in Sec. 1221. Nevertheless, part or all of the gain on the sale of these same properties can, under certain circumstances, be treated as long-term capital gain by operation of Sec. 1231. The amount of the gain eligible for Sec. 1231 treatment has been significantly reduced in the recent past by the depreciation-recapture provisions contained in Sec. 1245 and 1250. The effect of these provisions is illustrated in the tax-octopus of Figure 22-3. (With laws as complex as these, is it any wonder that Albert Einstein found a tax consultant necessary?)

The concept of recaptured depreciation, as embodied in Secs. 1245 and 1250, was extended in the Tax Reform Act of 1969 to include the potential recapture of farm losses in circumstances where farm losses have been used to offset nonfarm income

(in Sec. 1251) and to the gain from the disposition of farm land (in Sec. 1252). These provisions will be considered briefly in Chapter 23.

Tax planning

Once again, both the student and the instructor may be inclined to dismiss Figure 22-3 as too confusing. We urge you not to do so. Our experience is that a little work with this figure will confirm the old adage that one picture is worth a thousand words. Once Figure 22-3 is mastered, tax-planning opportunities become almost obvious. Think of the tax-octopus as a giant road map and each transaction as a vehicle moving along that map. By examining the transaction carefully, determine if that "vehicle" must exit at the first, second, third, fourth, fifth, or sixth "off ramp." In other words, if the transaction results in a gain or loss that you know is not recognized for tax purposes (for example, a $5,000 loss realized on the sale of a personal residence), mentally enter that amount in the first box on the far left side of page **22/** 8. If the transaction results in a $10,000 gain on the sale of an inventory asset, mentally move that amount down the second exit to the ordinary income residual. A pure capital gain would, of course, move down the last exit to one of the capital gain beakers. Finally, understand that this system "dumps" or

FIGURE 22-3 Interplay of Capital Gains and Secs. 1231, 1245, and 1250

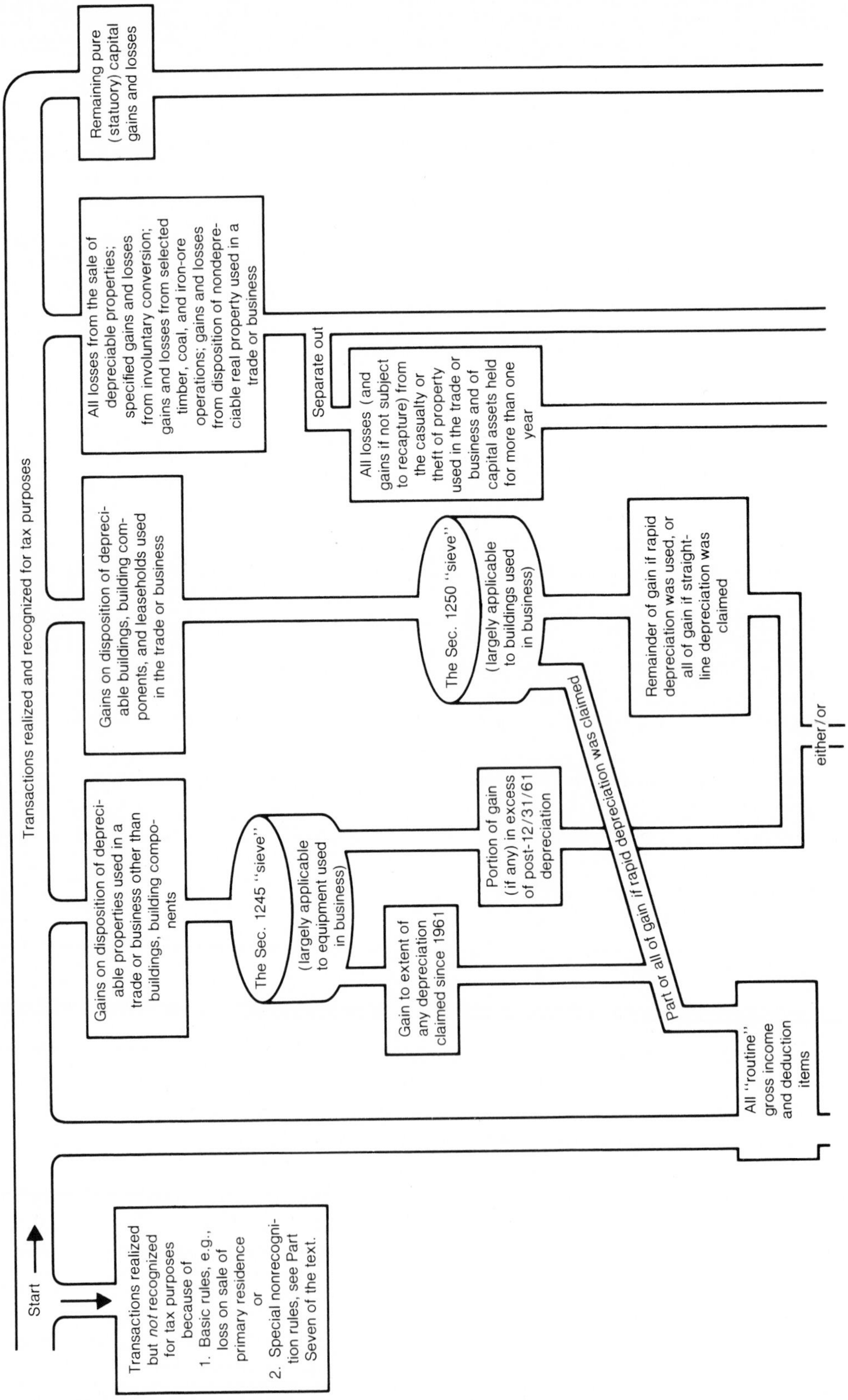

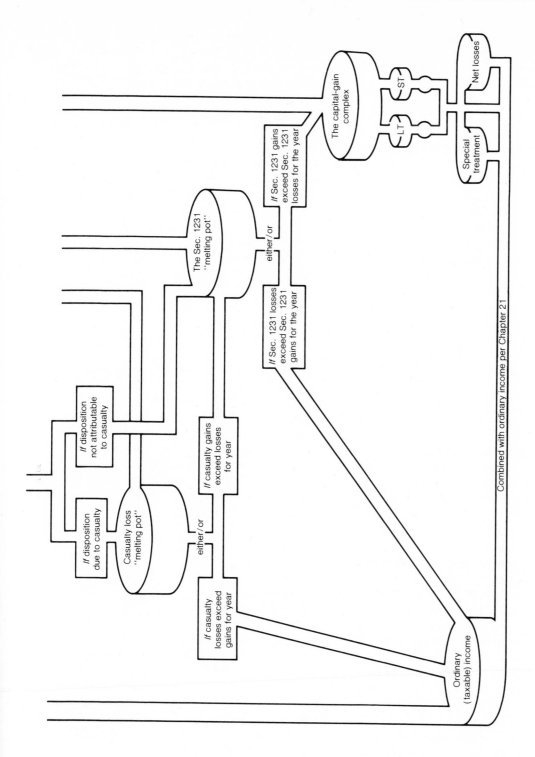

"flushes" once each year, at midnight on the last day of the taxable year. Until that dumping occurs, certain amounts will be temporarily retained at critical points in the tax-octopus:

1. The casualty-loss "melting pot."
2. The Sec. 1231 "melting pot."
3. The long-term capital-gain beaker.
4. The short-term capital-gain beaker.

Furthermore, when dumping does occur, it happens in the order just indicated. That is, the net casualty determination must be made first; the Sec. 1231 determination, second; and only then can the capital gains and losses combine as suggested in Chapter 21.

With this as background, imagine the situation in which a taxpayer has already realized a Sec. 1231 loss of $50,000. If that taxpayer also has the opportunity to make a year-end disposition of land used in business at a $50,000 gain, would you recommend that the taxpayer hurry and complete the sale this year or defer it for a few days, until the new year? If you understand Figure 22-3 you can answer immediately: Under normal circumstances, the taxpayer should defer the sale, which will result in the Sec. 1231 gain being recognized in the next year. To do so will allow the taxpayer to claim the entire Sec. 1231 loss previously realized as an ordinary deduction this year and to tax the $50,000 gain as a long-term capital gain next year. If you have understood the material presented earlier in the text, you will readily appreciate that a $50,000 ordinary loss combined with a $50,000 net long-term capital gain is of significantly more value to most taxpayers than a simple netting of those two equal amounts.

Similar tax-planning opportunities may also be encountered with casualty gains and losses. The gain realized through a casualty-associated disposition can often be deferred by exercising an option available in the nonrecognition provisions of the Code. Thus, if a taxpayer has realized both casualty gains and losses during a particular tax year, it is often to his or her benefit to recognize the losses immediately, as ordinary losses, and to defer the recognition of gains by exercising the option available in Sec. 1033. Because the details of that section are deferred to Part Seven, we shall not illustrate the opportunity further at this point. Even without the detail, however, Figure 22-3 helps to explain why tax savings are likely in that situation.

As a final illustration of tax planning implicit in Figure 22-3, consider the importance of the allocation of sales price in the disposition of real estate used in a trade or business. Suppose that a taxpayer has an opportunity to sell a motel for $1,500,000. Would it make any difference how the sales contract allocated that amount between equipment (beds, television sets, chairs, etc.), the building, and the land? To make answering the question easy, assume that the adjusted basis of the equipment is $100,000; the building, $500,000; and the land, $400,000. Obviously, therefore, the net gain on the sale will amount to $500,000 (that is, $1,500,000 realized less $1,000,000 adjusted basis). Next, using Figure 22-3, determine the tax result implicit in each of two dispositions, as follows:

Contract No.	Allocation of sales price			
	Equipment	Building	Land	Total
1	$500,000	$700,000	$300,000	$1,500,000
2	100,000	600,000	800,000	1,500,000

The first contract would, of course, produce $400,000 ordinary income (via Sec. 1245) from the sale of the equipment; $200,000, probably ordinary income via Sec. 1250, from the sale of the building (actually this determination would depend on the method of depreciation used, the holding period, etc.); and a $100,000 Sec. 1231 loss (probably ordinary loss) from the sale of the land. If the taxpayer were so unfortunate as to have the loss on the sale of the land offset some other realized Sec. 1231 gain "holding" in the melting pot, the first contract could actually have the effect of reporting $600,000 in ordinary income and $100,000 in capital loss, much to the detriment of the taxpayer.

The second contract would produce no gain or loss on the equipment; probably a $100,000 ordinary income (via Sec. 1250) on the sale of the building; and a $400,000 Sec. 1231 gain on the sale of the land. It is highly probable that the Sec. 1231 gain would end up being treated like long-term capital gain, much to the pleasure of the selling taxpayer.

Incidentally, observe that the best interests of the seller are, in general, exactly the opposite of those of the buyer. In our prior example, a buyer would strongly prefer contract 1 because he or she would want most of the purchase price allocated to the equipment and building so that future depreciation deductions could be maximized. Because of the adverse interests in such contracts, the I.R.S. and the courts frequently accept any allocations of sales price agreed to by the buyer and seller. In many instances, therefore, if both the buyer and the seller are wholly aware of the tax implications of their sales agreement, they will refuse to stipulate any allocation in the contract. This allows each taxpayer to "go his own way" and hope for the best in any disputes with the Internal Revenue Service. If only one party understands the tax implications of the contract, he or she generally will arrange the allocations in a way most favorable to his or her position. The other party is often surprised when, at a later date, the I.R.S. will not allow a more desirable reallocation of the amounts. Once again, we believe that a good understanding of Figure 22-3 goes a long way in explaining this important conclusion.

REPORTING SEC. 1231 TRANSACTIONS

Any taxpayer disposing of real or depreciable property used in a trade or business must file Form 4797 with his or her tax return. That form, which is reproduced as Figure 22-4, is identical for individual and corporate taxpayers. As you might expect, the instructions for completing Form 4797 are as difficult to understand as the rules we have just studied. Before getting involved in a more detailed example, let us examine the general format of Figure 22-4. Observe that Part I is divided into two sections: Section A is used to report involuntary conversions that

are casualties or thefts, Section B to report most other sales or exchanges of Sec. 1231 property. Part III, on the back of the form, is used to separate ordinary income from Sec. 1231 gain, based on the recapture rules. Thus, line 18 summarizes ordinary income arising because of Sec. 1245; line 19, because of Sec. 1250; etc. The summary of Part III gains, at the bottom of the second page, carries the total ordinary income and/or Sec. 1231 gain back to the front of the form. Part II, the residual portion of this form, summarizes the ordinary gain or loss based on the various possible combinations of the amounts already entered. It is only with the most inordinate expenditure of time that a person can determine the rule being implemented by each line of the form. Because that kind of knowledge pays absolutely no dividend, we shall ignore it and only examine how the disposition of one asset might be reported on a Form 4797.

To illustrate the use of Form 4797, suppose that a corporate taxpayer acquired a factory building on January 2, 1973, for $200,000 and that it depreciated the building for tax purposes on a 150-percent declining-balance method, using an estimated life of 40 years. If this calendar-year corporate taxpayer sold the factory building on December 31, 1979, for $170,000, it would report a $16,949 gain. The data pertinent to the calculation of the way this gain should be treated for tax purposes can be summarized as follows:

Year	Depreciation claimed	Accumulated depreciation	Adjusted basis 12-31-xx	Straight-line depreciation	Cumulative "excess" depreciation
1973	$7,500	$ 7,500	$192,500	$5,000	$ 2,500
1974	7,219	14,719	185,281	5,000	4,719
1975	6,948	21,667	178,333	5,000	6,667
1976	6,687	28,354	171,646	5,000	8,354
1977	6,437	34,791	165,209	5,000	9,791
1978	6,195	40,986	159,014	5,000	10,986
1979	5,963	46,949	153,051	5,000	11,949

The total gain is, of course, the difference between the $170,000 amount realized and the $153,051 adjusted basis, or $16,949. Of this total gain, $11,949 (the lesser of the gain realized or the cumulative *excess* depreciation) must be recognized as ordinary income by operation of Sec. 1250. The remaining $5,000 of gain can be reported as Sec. 1231 gain. These conclusions are a specific example of the general concept implicit in Figure 22-2. They would be

reported by the corporate taxpayer as indicated on Figure 22-4.

One final comment on the reporting of casualty losses seems appropriate. Individual taxpayers can often avoid the completion of Form 4797 by filing Form 4684 if they have only a casualty or theft of a personal (i.e., a nondepreciable) property. The latter form, reproduced without an illustration and without instructions, appears as Figure 22-5.

FIGURE 22-4

Form **4797**

Department of the Treasury
Internal Revenue Service

Supplemental Schedule of Gains and Losses

(Includes Gains and Losses From Sales or Exchanges of Assets
Used in a Trade or Business and Involuntary Conversions)
To be filed with Form 1040, 1041, 1065, 1120, etc.—See Separate Instructions

1979

Name(s) as shown on return

Identifying number as shown on page 1
of your tax return

Part I — Sales or Exchanges of Property Used in Trade or Business, and Involuntary Conversions (Section 1231)

Caution: *If you sold property on which you claimed the investment credit, you may be
liable for recapture of that credit. See Form 4255 for additional information.*

SECTION A.—Involuntary Conversions Due to Casualty and Theft (See Instruction F)

a. Kind of property (if necessary, attach additional descriptive details not shown below)	b. Date acquired (mo., day, yr.)	c. Date sold (mo., day, yr.)	d. Gross sales price less expense of sale	e. Depreciation allowed (or allowable) since acquisition	f. Cost or other basis, and cost of subsequent improvements (if not purchased, attach explanation)	g. Gain or loss (d plus e less f)
1						

2 Gain, if any, from line 25, Part III on back of this form attributable to casualty and theft . . . . _____

3 Combine the amounts on lines 1 and 2. Enter here, and on the appropriate line as follows . . . . _____

  (a) For all except partnership returns:
    (1) If line 3 is zero or a gain, enter that amount in line 4, column g.
    (2) If line 3 is a loss, enter the loss on line 7.
  (b) For partnership returns: Enter the amount shown on line 3 above, on Schedule K (Form 1065), line 7.

SECTION B.—Sales or Exchanges of Property Used in Trade or Business and Certain Involuntary Conversions
        (Not Reportable in Section A) (See Instruction F)

a. Kind of property	b. Date acquired	c. Date sold	d. Gross sales price less expense of sale	e. Depreciation allowed	f. Cost or other basis	g. Gain or loss
4						

5 Gain, if any, from line 25, Part III on back of this form attributable to other than casualty and theft $5,000

6 Combine the amounts on lines 4 and 5. Enter here, and on the appropriate line as follows $5,000

  (a) For all except partnership returns:
    (1) If line 6 is a gain, enter the gain as a long-term capital gain on Schedule D (Form 1040, 1120, etc.) that is being filed. See instruction F.
    (2) If line 6 is zero or a loss, enter that amount on line 8.
  (b) For partnership returns: Enter the amount shown on line 6 above, on Schedule K (Form 1065), line 8.

Part II — Ordinary Gains and Losses

a. Kind of property (if necessary, attach additional descriptive details not shown below)	b. Date acquired (mo., day, yr.)	c. Date sold (mo., day, yr.)	d. Gross sales price less expense of sale	e. Depreciation allowed (or allowable) since acquisition	f. Cost or other basis, cost of subsequent improvements (if not purchased, attach explanation)	g. Gain or loss (d plus e less f)
7 Amount, if any, from line 3(a)(2)						_____
8 Amount, if any, from line 6(a)(2)						
9 Gain, if any, from line 24, Part III on back of this form						$11,949
10 Other ordinary gains and losses:						

11 Combine amounts on lines 7 through 10. Enter here, and on the appropriate line as follows $11,949

  (a) For all except individual returns: Enter the gain or (loss) shown on line 11, on the line provided for on the return (Form 1120, etc.) being filed. See instruction G for specific line reference.

  (b) For individual returns:
    (1) If the gain or (loss) on line 11, includes losses that are to be treated as an itemized deduction on Schedule A (Form 1040) (see instruction G), enter the total of the loss(es) here. Include that amount on Schedule A (Form 1040), line 29 and identify as "loss from Form 4797, line 11(b)(1)" . . . .
    (2) Redetermine the gain or (loss) on line 11, excluding the loss (if any) entered on line 11(b)(1). Enter here and on Form 1040, line 16 . . . .

Form **4797** (1979)

Part III   **Gain From Disposition of Property Under Sections 1245, 1250, 1251, 1252, 1254, 1255—Assets Held More Than One Year (See Separate Instructions)**

Note: *For livestock, see section 1231(b)(3) or instruction A for a longer holding period.*

Skip lines 20 and 21 if there are no dispositions of farm property or farmland, or if this form is filed by a partnership.

12 Description of sections 1245, 1250, 1251, 1252, 1254, and 1255 property:

	Date acquired (mo., day, yr.)	Date sold (mo., day, yr.)
(A) *Factory Building*	1-2-73	12-31-79
(B)		
(C)		
(D)		

Relate lines 12(A) through 12(D) to these columns ▶▶▶	Property (A)	Property (B)	Property (C)	Property (D)
13 Gross sales price less expense of sale	$170,000			
14 Cost or other basis	200,000			
15 Depreciation (or depletion) allowed (or allowable)	46,949			
16 Adjusted basis, subtract line 15 from line 14	153,051			
17 Total gain, subtract line 16 from line 13	16,949			
18 If section 1245 property:				
(a) Depreciation allowed (or allowable) after applicable date (see instructions)				
(b) Enter smaller of line 17 or 18(a)				
19 If section 1250 property:				
(a) Additional depreciation after 12/31/75 (see instructions)	3,596			
(b) Applicable percentage times the smaller of line 17 or line 19(a) (see instruction H.4)	3,596			
(c) Subtract line 19(a) from line 17. (If line 17 is not more than line 19(a), skip lines 19(d) through 19(h). Enter the amount from line 19(b) on line 19(i))	13,353			
(d) Additional depreciation after 12/31/69 and before 1/1/76	8,353			
(e) Applicable percentage times the smaller of line 19(c) or 19(d) (see instruction H.4)	8,353			
(f) Subtract line 19(d) from line 19(c). (If line 19(c) is not more than line 19(d), skip lines 19(g) and 19(h). Combine the amounts on lines 19(b) and 19(e) on line 19(i))	5,000			
(g) Additional depreciation after 12/31/63 and before 1/1/70	-0-			
(h) Applicable percentage times the smaller of line 19(f) or 19(g) (see instruction H.4)	-0-			
(i) Add lines 19(b), 19(e), and 19(h)	11,949			
20 If section 1251 property:				
(a) If farmland, enter soil, water, and land clearing expenses for current year and the four preceding years				
(b) If farm property other than land, subtract line 18(b) from line 17; if farmland, enter smaller of line 17 or 20(a) (see instruction H.5)				
(c) Excess deductions account (see instruction H.5)				
(d) Enter smaller of line 20(b) or 20(c)				
21 If section 1252 property:				
(a) Soil, water, and land clearing expenses made after 12/31/69				
(b) Amount from line 20(d), if none enter a zero				
(c) Subtract line 21(b) from line 21(a). (If line 21(b) is more than line 21(a), enter zero.)				
(d) Line 21(c) times applicable percentage (see instruction H.5)				
(e) Subtract line 21(b) from line 17				
(f) Enter smaller of line 21(d) or 21(e)				
22 If section 1254 or 1255 property:				
(a) Intangible drilling and development costs deducted after 12/31/75 or ordinary income under section 1255 (see instruction H.6)				
(b) Enter smaller of line 17 or 22(a)				

Summary of Part III Gains (Complete Property columns (A) through (D) through line 22(b) before going to line 23)

23 Total gains for all properties (add columns (A) through (D), line 17) $16,949

24 Add columns (A) through (D), lines 18(b), 19(i), 20(d), 21(f), and 22(b). Enter here and on Part II, line 9   11,949

25 Subtract line 24 from line 23. Enter the portion attributable to casualty and theft on Part I, line 2; enter the portion attributable to other than casualty and theft on Part I, line 5 $5,000

FIGURE 22-5

Form **4684**
Department of the Treasury
Internal Revenue Service

Casualties and Thefts

▶ See instructions on back.
▶ Attach to Form 1040.

1979

Name(s) as shown on Form 1040 | Social Security Number

Part I — Casualty or Theft

	Item or article	Item or article	Item or article	Item or article
1 Kind of property				
2 Cost or basis				
3 Insurance or other reimbursement				
4 Gain from casualty or theft. If line 3 is more than line 2, enter difference here and on line 15 or 20 below. Also, skip lines 5 through 14 . . . . *If line 2 is more than line 3, enter zero on line 4 and complete lines 5 through 14.*				
5 Fair market value of property before casualty or theft				
6 Fair market value of property after casualty or theft				
7 Subtract line 6 from line 5				
8 Enter smaller of line 2 or line 7 . . . . . . **Note:** *If the loss was to property used in a trade or business or for income-producing purposes and totally destroyed by a casualty or lost from theft, enter on line 8, in each column, the amount from line 2.*				
9 Subtract line 3 from line 8				

10 Casualty or theft loss. Add amounts on line 9 . . . . _____

11 Enter part of line 9 that is from trade, business, or income producing property here and on line 15 or 20 below . _____

12 Subtract line 11 from line 10 . . . . _____

13 Enter the amount from line 12 or $100, whichever is smaller . . . . _____

14 Subtract line 13 from line 12. Enter here and on line 15 or 20 below . . . . _____

Part II — Summary of Gains and Losses

(A) Identify casualty or theft	(B) Losses from casualties or thefts		(C) Gains from casualties or thefts includible in income
	(i) Trade, business, rental or royalty property	(ii) Other property	
Casualty or Theft of Property Held One Year or Less			
15			
16 Totals. Add amounts on line 15 for each column			

17 Combine line 16, columns (B)(i) and (C). Enter here and on Form 4797, Part II, line 10, column g **(Note:** *if Form 4797 is not required for other transactions, enter amount on Form 1040, line 16—identify as "4684")* .

18 Enter amount from line 16, column (B)(ii) here and on Schedule A (Form 1040), line 29—identify as "4684" .

Casualty or Theft of Property Held More Than One Year			
19 Any casualty or theft gains from Form 4797, Part III, line 25			
20			

21 Total losses. Add amounts on line 20, columns (B)(i) and (B)(ii) . .

22 Total gains. Add lines 19 and 20, column (C) . . . . _____

23 Add line 21, columns (B)(i) and (B)(ii) . . . . _____

24 If the loss on line 23 is more than the gain on line 22 . . . .

    a. Combine line 21, column (B)(i) and line 22. Enter here and on Form 4797, Part II, line 10, column g **(Note:** *if Form 4797 is not required for other transactions, enter amount on Form 1040, line 16—identify as "4684")* . . . . _____

    b. Enter amount from line 21, column (B)(ii) here and on Schedule A (Form 1040), line 29—identify as "4684" . . . . _____

25 If the loss on line 23 is equal to or smaller than the gain on line 22, enter the difference here and on Form 4797, Part I, line 4, column g—identify as "Gain from Form 4684, Part II, line 25" . . . . _____

Form **4684** (1979)

PROBLEMS

(NOTE: If no year is stated, assume that the transaction took place in the current tax year.)

1. On January 10, Ed Burns sold some of his business equipment. He had purchased this equipment for $3,750 seven years ago and had claimed straight-line depreciation of $500 per year since acquisition. The tax consequences of this sale depend on the selling price of the equipment. Indicate, for each of the selling prices listed below, whether the result would be taxable as ordinary income under Sec. 1245 or a Sec. 1231 gain or loss.

   a. $1,400   b. $2,600   c. $3,800   d. $5,000

2. "The probability of a taxpayer's being able to recognize a capital gain on the sale of depreciable personal property (nonrealty) used in a trade or business has diminished to the point where, today, it is practically zero." True or false? Explain.

3. On January 8, Tom Lock sold a light-construction warehouse that he had used in his business since building it eight years ago. The warehouse had cost Tom $40,000; he had depreciated it on a 150-percent declining-balance method. The estimated life of the building was 20 years (thus a 7.5-percent depreciation rate was used by Tom).

   a. If Tom sold the warehouse for $22,500, what amount of his gain is ordinary income (Sec. 1250), and what amount is Sec. 1231 income?

   b. If Tom had claimed straight-line depreciation on this warehouse, what amount of his gain would have been ordinary income?

4. Classify each of the following gains and losses as to whether it (1) has no tax consequence, (2) is ordinary income (or loss), (3) capital gain (or loss), or (4) a Sec. 1231 item. In each case, indicate the correct dollar amount that would be so classified. Treat each item individually; for example, in part c, assume it is the taxpayer's only casualty loss for the year.

   a. Sold personal oil painting at a $500 gain. (Taxpayer was not the artist or an art dealer.)

   b. Sold pleasure sailboat at a $500 loss.

   c. Collision damage to family car repaired at cost of $350. The car was two years old.

   d. Sold business car at a $300 gain. Depreciation claimed since 1961 was $3,000.

   e. Sold business building at a $4,000 gain. Building had been used for previous 15 years. Straight-line depreciation had been claimed.

   f. Wind damage to rent property (assume the rent property does *not* constitute a trade or business) restored at cost of $6,000. Property had been owned for six years; insurance reimbursed $4,000. Adjusted basis at time of damage is $5,000.

5. Six years ago Hawk Dovens purchased asset A for $12,000 for use in his business. He depreciated this asset at the rate of $1,500 per year. What amount and kind of gain or loss should Dovens report on the sale of this asset in early January of this year if

   a. He sold it for $7,000 and asset A was a Sec. 1245 property?

   b. He sold it for $7,000 and asset A was a Sec. 1250 property?

   c. He sold it for $11,000 and asset A was a Sec. 1245 property?

   d. He sold it for $11,000 and asset A was a Sec. 1250 property?

6. Baldwell, a calendar-year taxpayer, operates a small manufacturing plant as a sole proprietor. He files a joint return with his wife. Both are under 65 and have good vision. They have no dependents. During the year Baldwell disposed of the following property:

Jan. 3 Sold the family automobile for $2,000; acquired on January 16 two years ago for $4,500.

Jan. 28 Sold a machine for $4,500; acquired five years earlier for $10,000. It had an estimated life of 10 years. Baldwell elected the 200-percent declining-balance method of depreciation and deducted the following:

Year 1	$2,000
Year 2	1,600
Year 3	1,280
Year 4	1,024
Year 5	819

Apr. 3 Sold 100 shares of ABC, Inc., for $4,000; purchased 16 months ago for $3,400.

July 16 Sold a truck for $2,800; purchased two years ago for $8,000. Truck had an estimated life of four years. Under the 200-percent declining-balance method of depreciation, the following depreciation was deducted:

Year 1	$4,000
Year 2	2,000

Nov. 5 Sold storage building for $9,000; acquired four years earlier for $12,000. Its estimated life was 10 years. Using the 150-percent-declining-balance method of depreciation, the following depreciation was deducted:

Year 1	$1,800
Year 2	1,530
Year 3	1,300
Year 4	1,106

Sold the lot on which the building was located for $12,750; cost of lot was $6,500.

All property sold was used in Baldwell's business except for the automobile and the ABC shares. In addition, Baldwell had net business income of $22,000 and deductions for adjusted gross income of $2,160. Assume that no depreciation is allowed in year of sale because of an accounting convention Baldwell adopted. Compute Baldwell's gross tax liability for the current year. Pay attention to the organization of your answer; label all amounts.

7. In years 1, 2, and 3, a taxpayer incurred the gains and losses shown at the top of page 22/17.
   a. If the taxpayer in this problem were a corporation:
      1. What amount of taxable income should it report in year 1?
      2. Would its capital-loss carryback be short- or long-term capital loss?
      3. What amount would be eligible for the alternative long-term capital gains tax in year 2?
      4. What would be its gross liability for federal income taxes in year 3? (Compute the lowest possible tax; use current rates.)

Item of income or loss	Year 1	Year 2	Year 3
Routine *taxable* income, *excluding* all transactions detailed below	$10,200	$28,200	$37,200
Capital asset transactions:			
Net short-term gain (or loss)[a]	800	200	1,000
Net long-term gain (or loss)[a]	(3,000)	4,600	3,000
Recapture of depreciation, under Secs. 1245 and/or 1250	1,000	1,100	3,000
Net gain (or loss) subject to Sec. 1231	(2,000)	3,000	2,000

[a] *Excluding* both capital-loss carryforwards and Sec. 1231 transactions, detailed below.

  b. If the taxpayer in this problem were an individual:
    1. What would his or her taxable income be for year 1?
    2. Would his or her capital-loss carryforward to year 2 be short- or long-term loss?
    3. The long-term capital-gain deduction would amount to how much in year 2? (Assume year 2 is the current year.)

8. Listed below are various assets, their uses and owners. In each case, indicate whether the asset is Sec. 1245 property, Sec. 1250 property, or neither.
  a. Family automobile.
  b. Machine used in a trade or business.
  c. Family home.
  d. Warehouse of manufacturing concern.
  e. Electric transmission lines of a utility.
  f. Apartment house.

9. Anders Industry, a corporate enterprise, realized the following items of taxable income or loss during the current year:
    Ordinary operating income, $46,300.
    Casualty loss on real property due to windstorm, $5,500.
    Excess of insurance proceeds over basis of building destroyed in a plant fire, $8,900 (straight-line depreciation had been claimed on the building prior to its destruction).
    Amount embezzled by petty cashier, $1,400.
    Gain on sale of security held for 90 days, $3,700.
    Gain on sale of land used in business, $10,200 (held 10 years).
    Gain on sale of building $3,400 (post-1969 excess depreciation amounted to $4,100).
  a. What is Anders Industry's taxable income for the year?
  b. What is Anders Industry's gross tax liability for the year?

10. Harry Stark, a college student, purchased a new automobile two years ago for $3,600. Harry used this car 60 percent of the time in his business as an encyclopedia salesman and 40 percent of the time for personal use. He claimed $600 depreciation on the car for tax purposes in years 1 and 2 before selling the car for $2,000 early this year. Harry contends that he has a $400 loss on the sale

(i.e., $2,000 realized less $2,400 adjusted basis) and that 60 percent of this $400 loss should be deductible for tax purposes. Explain the correct tax treatment of the sale.

11. On July 4 this year, while the Kerns were enjoying a family picnic, someone forcibly broke into Jerry Kern's home and stole a valuable painting. This painting had been purchased at an art auction in 1880 by Jerry's grandfather for $100. Jerry's father had inherited the painting from his father in 1938 when it was valued for estate tax purposes at $800. Jerry received the painting from his father as a Christmas gift in 1968. Before giving it as a Christmas gift Jerry's father had had the painting cleaned by a competent art dealer who estimated its value at $1,500. Nothing had happened to the painting between 1968 and July 4, this year, and therefore the Kerns believe that it was worth at least $1,500. What is the amount of Jerry Kern's tax deduction for this theft loss?

12. Why are the Internal Revenue Service and the courts inclined to accept without questions the allocation of purchase price, as between several assets, which is agreed to by a buyer and a seller in an arm's-length transaction?

13. Assume these facts:

	Taxpayers		
	A	B	C
Taxable income excluding all transactions below	$43,200	$43,200	$43,200
Short-term capital gains	3,000	4,000	10,000
Short-term capital losses	(7,000)		
Long-term capital gains	30,000	3,000	22,000
Long-term capital losses		(13,000)	
Sec. 1245 and 1250 income	5,000		10,000
Sec. 1231 gains	2,000	5,000	3,000
Sec. 1231 losses	(12,000)		(5,000)
Casualty gains			14,000
Casualty losses		(1,000)	(4,000)

a. If the taxpayers in this question were married individuals, filing a joint return, determine
  1. The taxable income of each taxpayer.
  2. The amount of the long-term capital-gain deduction, if any.
  3. The amount and "type" (short- or long-term) of capital-loss carryforward, if any. (Use current year's rules.)

b. If the taxpayers in this question were corporations, determine
  1. The taxable income of each taxpayer.
  2. The amount and "type" (short- or long-term) of capital-loss carryback, if any.
  3. Which taxpayer(s), if any, should elect the 28-percent alternative tax in the current year.

14. The courts of the United States do not agree on whether or not an individual taxpayer who rents only one piece of real property is engaged in a "trade or business." (The Tax Court says he or she is; see *Hazard,* 7 TC 372. The Second Circuit Court of Appeals says he or she is not; see *Grier* v. *U.S.,* 218 F.2d 603.) If a taxpayer sells his or her only rental property at a profit, will it make any difference which of the court opinions the taxpayer assumes is controlling if that property has been depreciated on
  a. A straight-line method?
  b. A rapid depreciation method?
     Explain briefly.

15. To determine the final import of property transactions on a taxpayer's taxable income, one must first classify the property gains and losses in one of several ways and then correctly combine those amounts. Assume that all classifications given for cases 1–4 are correct. Demonstrate your knowledge of how the several amounts would combine to form taxable income in each case.
Solve this problem for a noncorporate taxpayer.

	Case 1	Case 2	Case 3	Case 4
Property transactions:				
Net LT gain (loss)	$10,000	$ 5,000	($ 4,000)	($ 2,000)
Net ST gain (loss)	(2,000)	1,000	1,000	(2,000)
Net Sec. 1231 gain (loss)	(3,000)	3,000	3,000	(2,000)
Net casualty gain (loss)	1,000	(4,000)	3,000	(2,000)
All other (net) ordinary gain (loss)	30,000	40,000	50,000	60,000
Taxable income	$	$	$	$

16. Solve Problem 15 for a corporate taxpayer.

17. The tax treatment of property transactions depends on their proper classification in one of the following five categories:
    A—Ordinary gain or loss
    B—Sec. 1231 gain or loss
    C—Casualty gain or loss (really a subset of Sec. 1231)
    D—Long-term capital gain or loss
    E—Short-term capital gain or loss

By using the identifying letter indicated above, classify each of the following independent transactions in the way it should be treated *initially*.
a. Gain from sale of raised livestock held for three years for breeding purposes.
b. Fire loss on inventory held four months.
c. Gain from sale of antique auto held for 10 months by dealer in "classic cars."
d. Gain on sale of pleasure boat owned for 14 months.
e. Loss on sale of customers' receivables held for 14 months. (Assume an accrual-basis taxpayer.)
f. Loss on condemnation of taxpayer's business parking lot.

18. Assume that a taxpayer had realized an ordinary taxable income of $30,000 exclusive of each property transaction described below. Determine the taxpayer's correct taxable income for the year, *including* the property transactions, in each of the five independent cases if:
a. The taxpayer is an individual.
b. The taxpayer is a corporation.

Case I:
Gain on sale of investment in stock, held 2 years — $4,000
Gain on sale of speculative land, held 2 months — 2,200
Case II:
Gain on sale of business machinery ($6,000 depreciation claimed in years since 1961) — $3,800
Loss from fire damage to roof of business building (building owned for 6 years) — 2,700

Case III:

Loss on sale of investment securities, owned 7 months	$9,600
Gain on sale of land used in business for 10 years	12,400

Case IV:

Gain on sale of investment securities, owned 7 months	$9,600
Loss on sale of land used in business for 10 years	12,400

Case V:

Gain on sale of business building, owned 8 years (excess depreciation after 1969, $15,000)	$8,000
Gain on sale of land on which above building was located	16,000

In your solution, assume that the taxable year is the current year.

19. Joe Schmoo purchased a small apartment house as an investment 4 years ago. Joe paid $50,000 for the land and $200,000 for the apartment house. For the next 4 years, Joe claimed 150 percent declining-balance depreciation on this property, as follows: year 1, $7,500; year 2, $7,219; year 3, $6,948; and year 4, $6,687. Straight-line depreciation would have been $5,000 per year. If Joe were to sell this property, the tax consequences of the sale would depend to a great extent on both the selling price and the allocation of that price between land and buildings. Indicate, for each of the four alternative sales prices below, the amount that must be treated as ordinary income (per Sec. 1250) and the amount to be treated as Sec. 1231 gain or loss.

a. Sales price, $230,000: $50,000 allocated to the land.
b. Sales price, $230,000: $40,000 allocated to the land.
c. Sales price, $230,000: $70,000 allocated to the land.
d. Sales price, $280,000: $70,000 allocated to the land.

20. Beverly Levine sold some of her business equipment this year. She had purchased this equipment for $100,000 6 years ago and has claimed straight-line depreciation of $60,000 since acquisition. The tax consequences of Beverly's sale depend on the selling price of the equipment. Indicate, for each of the four alternative sales prices below, the amount to be treated as ordinary income (per Sec. 1245) and the amount to be treated as Sec. 1231 gain or loss.

a. $3,000
b. $5,500
c. $10,000
d. $12,000

SUPPLEMENTAL PROBLEMS

21. Able and Baker invested $50,000 in ABL and BAK, respectively. ABL and BAK were small, new corporate business ventures. Initially both Able and Baker were confident that their corporations would become successful business enterprises and that their modest investments would eventually be worth thousands of times their initial value. Reality returned when, two years after they made these investments, each corporation went into bankruptcy and announced that there would be no return whatever on any capital investments. The ABL management had taken the time to qualify its stock under Sec. 1244; BAK management failed to take this precaution because failure seemed unlikely just two years earlier. Fortunately, both Able and Baker are men of independent means who report annual incomes of anywhere between $250,000 and

$500,000. Assume that in the year ABL and BAK went bankrupt, Able and Baker each earned an ordinary taxable income of $250,000 and an additional long-term capital gain of $50,000 exclusive of their loss in ABL and BAK, respectively.

   a. What real economic loss did Able experience because of his investment in ABL?

   b. What real economic loss did Baker experience because of his investment in BAK?

   c. Explain any difference between your answers to parts a and b.

22. Grand Corporation experienced two serious casualty losses this year. In May, Plant A burned to the ground; in September, Plant B was totally destroyed by a hurricane. Grand's adjusted basis in Plant A was $550,000; fire insurance proceeds amounted to only $350,000. Plant B was a much older operation, and therefore it had an adjusted basis of only $80,000 at the time it was destroyed. Because Plant B was still in good repair, however, Grand's management had insured the plant for $250,000. By the end of the year, the management of Grand Corporation had settled with the insurance company on the Plant A claim and was about to settle with another insurance company on the Plant B disaster when the controller suggested that any settlement on the latter be deferred until next year. Explain the apparent tax reason that could have prompted the controller to make this suggestion and try to determine whether or not his tax plan would be likely to succeed. Demonstrate his apparent objective with calculations based on the assumptions that Grand Corporation is an accrual-basis taxpayer that realized a $400,000 ordinary taxable income and a $60,000 excess of net long-term capital gain over net short-term capital loss this year. (The amounts given in the preceding sentence exclude both of the casualty events.)

23. In 1970 Al Alred incorporated his automotive repair business as AA Motors, Inc. Because of failing health, Al decided to sell his business to Andy Algreen, AA's best mechanic. Andy told Al that it was immaterial to him whether he purchased (1) Al's stock in AA Motors, Inc. or (2) the individual assets that AA Motors owned, that is, the customer lists, accounts receivable, tools and equipment, building, and so on. At the time of the sale, Al owned 100 percent of the outstanding shares of AA Motors, Inc.

   a. If Andy purchases the shares of stock, who will be the selling taxpayer— Al or AA Motors, Inc.?

   b. If Andy purchases the individual assets, who will be the selling taxpayer— Al or AA Motors, Inc.?

   c. If Andy purchases the AA stock, will the seller report ordinary income, capital gain, or both?

   d. If Andy purchases the individual assets, will the seller report ordinary income, capital gain, or both?

   e. If Andy purchases the AA stock, what will the basis of the various assets be?

   f. If Andy purchases the individual assets, what will the basis of the various assets be?

24. Will it make any difference taxwise to the selling taxpayer whether part of the sales price involved in the sale of a business is allocated to a "covenant not to compete" rather than to "goodwill"? Explain.

25. Will it make any difference taxwise to the purchasing taxpayer whether part of the purchase price involved in the purchase of a business is allocated to a "covenant not to compete" rather than to "goodwill"? Explain.

26. Chapter 22 includes a discussion of three of the more important statutory exceptions to the pure capital asset definition of Sec. 1221. The courts have added yet other judicial exceptions not explained in this text. Perhaps the benchmark case is *Corn Products Refining Company* v. *Commissioner*, 350 U.S. 46 (1955). A recent restatement of this same judicial doctrine is found in *W. W. Windle Company*, 65 TC 694 (1976). Locate these two judicial decisions in your school library (you may have to go to the law library, and you may need some help in finding the correct volumes), read them, and then summarize very briefly the judicial modifications to Sec. 1221 as detailed in the two cases.

Tax law is littered with cases manifesting the constant struggle to capture the preferred treatment accorded capital gains and losses in contrast to ordinary income and loss transactions.

JUDGE FINNEGAN,
Chandler v. *United States*, 226 F2d, 403 (CCA-7, 1955)

capital gain and loss today: modifications to the pure case— concluded

The statutory definition of a capital asset in Sec. 1221 has been modified with regard to many assets in addition to depreciable and real properties used in a trade or business. Unfortunately for the student, even the lengthy but orderly list of special rules included in Subchapter P, reprinted on page **22/1**, is incomplete. Other scattered Code sections make still further modifications to the capital gain and loss complex. A partial list of those sections includes:

Sec. 165 (g).	Worthless securities.
Sec. 166 (d).	Nonbusiness bad debts.
Sec. 166 (f).	Reserve for certain guaranteed debt obligations.
Sec. 302.	Distributions in redemption of stock.
Sec. 303.	Distributions in redemption of stock to pay death taxes.
Sec. 304.	Redemption through use of related corporations.
Sec. 306.	Dispositions of certain stock.
Sec. 331.	Gain or loss to shareholders in corporate liquidations.
Sec. 341.	Collapsible corporations.
Sec. 631.	Gain or loss in the case of timber, coal, or domestic iron ore.

The person interested in becoming a tax expert will have to study far beyond the confines of this text because, even in this final chapter on the modifications to the pure case, we cannot consider each rule.

Although the only unifying principle common to this diverse array of Code provisions is the fact that they all modify the general rules otherwise applicable to capital gains and losses, some of the provisions can be subgrouped in a meaningful way. For example, several of the provisions are primarily intended to close tax loopholes that would otherwise exist.[1] Others provide standard guidelines intended to minimize administrative disputes between the taxpayer and the I.R.S. And yet others are meant to provide economic incentives for select situations that Congress deemed especially deserving. In this chapter we shall consider a few exemplary sections in each of these subsets.

LOOPHOLE-CLOSING SECTIONS

The largest subset of statutory modifications to the usual rules probably is the collection of sections generally enacted to interdict any unintended tax benefits. Historically, these provisions frequently represent a final chapter in one branch of the ongoing saga in humanity's search for lower taxes. The story often begins with an isolated discovery: That is, an

---

[1] As the word "loophole" is used here, it refers to a beneficial tax result not intended by Congress.

isolated taxpayer (or tax advisor) discovers a unique combination of facts and tax rules that lead to an unexpected tax windfall. The idea spreads—or is "rediscovered" by others—until the I.R.S. initiates administrative action intended to curb what it views as an abuse of the law. Typically the I.R.S. is challenged by one or more taxpayers, and our judicial system is called upon to settle the dispute. Judicial solutions to conflicting interpretations of tax statutes are almost always very slow and frequently unsatisfactory to all parties. A court can only address the precise situation presented to it; slightly different circumstances may call for, or at least may receive, different answers. Consequently, major differences of opinion are often best settled by remedial legislation.

The recapture provisions

A good example of the evolutionary process just described can be found in the Code sections that provide for the recapture of depreciation. As explained earlier, prior to the enactment of Secs. 1245 and 1250, taxpayers were able to convert large amounts of ordinary income into capital gain via the parlay of large (ordinary) depreciation deductions followed by profitable dispositions under Sec. 1231 (usually capital gain). Once the current depreciation recapture sections became operative, the only remaining major benefit of rapid depreciation is that derived from the present value of money.

The idea of "recapturing," from what otherwise would be capital gain, some part or all of any previous deductions against ordinary income, was extended in Secs. 1251 and 1252 to certain gains on the disposition of farm properties. As explained on page **17/11**, wealthy taxpayers who are gentlemen farmers have for years converted ordinary income into capital gains through farming activity, particularly ranches and citrus groves. In the past, the costs of developing farming properties could be deducted currently, usually creating an operating loss that could be offset against ordinary income from other sources. The agricultural business would elect the cash basis, and all costs would be deducted currently. Ranchers would raise herds over several years. Others developed citrus groves that produced no income at all until the trees reached maturity. Usually the expenditures that produced the losses increased the value of Sec. 1231 property used in the farming business, such as breeding herds, citrus groves, and land. At disposition of the improved

property, a sizable gain could be recognized as a Sec. 1231 gain, and thereby would usually receive capital-gain treatment.

The 1969 Tax Reform Act expanded the recapture rules in three ways in an effort to close the "farm loss" loophole:

1. *Purchased* livestock held for breeding, draft, or dairy purposes are now subject to the recapture rules of Sec. 1245 to the extent of depreciation deducted after December 31, 1969.

2. Under Sec. 1251, gain from the sale of farm properties will result in ordinary income to the extent of the "excess-deduction account." The farm properties included are depreciable personal property and land (including unharvested crops) held for over six months, and livestock held for over two years. Buildings are not included. The excess-deduction account is generally an accumulation of net farm losses incurred after 1969 and before 1976. Losses are included in the excess-deduction account only to the extent that they exceed $25,000 per year, and only when the taxpayer has an adjusted gross income from nonfarming activities of $50,000 or more. The excess-deduction account is reduced by the amount of gain recaptured. Furthermore, the Tax Reform Act of 1976 terminated all additions after December 31, 1975.

3. Under Sec. 1252, land-development expenditures that are deductible against ordinary income may be recaptured on sale of the land. Deductions claimed after 1969 for expenditures on soil and water conservation and for land-clearing costs are subject to partial recapture unless the land is held for more than 10 years. The percentage of such expenditures recaptured as ordinary income on disposition of the property at a gain is shown in the schedule below:

Holding period	Percentage recaptured
5 years or less	100 %
6 years	80
7 years	60
8 years	40
9 years	20
10 years	0

The percentage is applied to either the deductible expenditures or the actual gain, whichever is less.

These recapture provisions clearly overlap. Furthermore, the preceding explanation has of necessity been grossly oversimplified. The regulations clear up

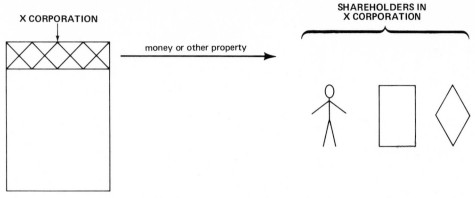

FIGURE **23-1**   The Dividend Concept

some of the procedural questions, but others must await final regulations, subsequent I.R.S. pronouncements, or eventual litigation.

The most recent extension of the recapture notion is contained in Sec. 1254, which was added by the Tax Reform Act of 1976. It is conceptually similar to Sec. 1250 in that it provides for the recapture of only what might be termed *excess* depletion. For any oil or gas property disposed of after December 31, 1975, the taxpayer must recapture as ordinary income the difference between the intangible drilling costs actually charged to expense after 1975 and the amount that would have been expensed had the taxpayer originally capitalized these costs and amortized them over the useful life of the well.

The anti-corporate-manipulation provisions

As we have observed on several prior occasions, the corporate entity is frequently an essential ingredient in tax planning. The closely held corporation is particularly susceptible to favorable manipulation, because it lacks the implicit diverse interests commonly found in large numbers of stockholders. Consequently Congress has been forced to enact several complicated Code sections to modify rules that would otherwise yield unreasonably favorable tax results. Several of these prohibiting sections involve the distinction between capital and ordinary gains and losses.

SECTION 302   Any time a corporation distributes corporate assets to its shareholders in their role as shareholders, the distribution is likely to be labeled a dividend and taxed accordingly. Technically, the conclusion just stated is generally correct to the extent that the distributing corporation has either current or accumulated earnings and profits.[2] The fundamental elements of a dividend can be easily portrayed as in Figure 23-1. To understand the illustration, assume that the size of the rectangle represents the value of the net assets owned by the corporate entity. Thus, an ordinary dividend necessarily reduces the size of the rectangle—i.e., it results in a diminution of the corporation's asset—in a "one-sided" transaction. Observe that the shareholders (individual, corporate, or fiduciary, as depicted by the stickperson, the rectangle, and the diamond, respectively) give nothing to the distributing corporation in exchange for the assets received. We know from prior chapters that such dividend distributions usually create ordinary income for the recipient shareholder.

In a closely held corporation, the shareholders could readily agree to give up some stock in the distributing corporation if it would benefit them to do so. In financial parlance, this would convert the "dividend" into a "stock redemption." The essential elements of a stock redemption are obvious in Figure 23-2. But what is the tax impact of a stock redemption?

Generally, we know that a taxpayer must recognize as gross income the difference between any value received and any basis surrendered in a transaction. We know further that the character of that gross income is generally determined by the nature of the property surrendered. Applying these general rules to the stock-redemption transaction suggests

---

[2] This rule is found in Secs. 301(c) and 316. Nowhere in the Code, however, is there a definition of "earnings and profits." Although the two are close relatives, the retained earnings concept of accounting is not wholly comparable.

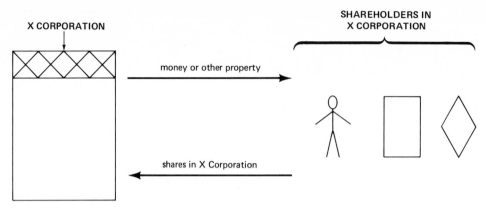

FIGURE **23-2**   The Stock Redemption Concept

that the shareholder should recognize capital gain or loss. Even momentary reflection on the possibilities this creates for the closely held corporation are euphoric. If not constrained in some way, closely held corporations could convert what otherwise would be an ordinary dividend into a capital loss! That is, each shareholder could surrender a pro-rata share of ownership interest sufficient to cause the basis surrendered to be greater than the value received and thereby recognize a capital loss for tax purposes at no real economic cost.

As you might suspect, this is just too good to be true. Section 302 provides a relatively complex set of rules to determine whether a stock redemption should be treated as ordinary income or as capital gain. The result, in the situation described above, would be ordinary income. Hence, another exception to the general capital gain and loss complex has been created by necessity. The general tax rules will apply only if a stock redemption is "substantially disproportionate" or results in the complete "termination of a shareholder's interest" (Secs. 302(b)(2) and 302(b)(3), respectively). As tempting as it is to delve into the definition of the critical terms just suggested, we must leave the study of those interesting words and phrases to other, more advanced volumes on income taxation.

SECTION 331   Before moving on, however, we must briefly consider one other very closely related Code section. Section 331(a)(2) states that amounts "distributed in partial liquidation of a corporation (as defined in Sec. 346) shall be treated as in part or full payment in exchange for the stock." These words suggest that we might relabel anything that resembles a stock-redemption transaction as a partial liqui-

dation and thereby safely reach the promised land of capital gains after all! In other words, how can anyone possibly distinguish between a stock redemption and a partial liquidation? Both transactions have in common (1) the distribution of assets by the corporation and (2) the surrender of some of their shares by the stockholders!

In this instance, the tax obstacle can be found in the definitional provision, Sec. 346. That definition reserves the term partial liquidation for significant corporate contractions. Unless the assets distributed previously constituted a properly aged, active trade or business *and* unless the distributing corporation continues to conduct a properly aged, active trade or business after the distribution, the transaction generally will *not* qualify as a partial liquidation. In that event the transaction must still stand the tests suggested for stock redemptions before the taxpayer is free to report a capital gain.

SECTION 304   Another variant of essentially the same tax scheme involved the use of two or more closely held corporations. This plan took the legal form of an apparent sale. To illustrate the basic idea, suppose that taxpayer A owned either (1) 100 percent of Corporations X and Y or (2) 100 percent of X, which, in turn, owned 100 percent of Y.[3] How should A report, for tax purposes, the sale to Y Corporation of some portion of his or her shares in X Corporation? The essential elements of this arrangement can be depicted as in Figure 23-3.

---

[3] The first ownership arrangement is commonly known as a brother-sister group; the second as a parent-subsidiary group. Although the difference has some legal significance, the economic reality of the arrangement is obvious.

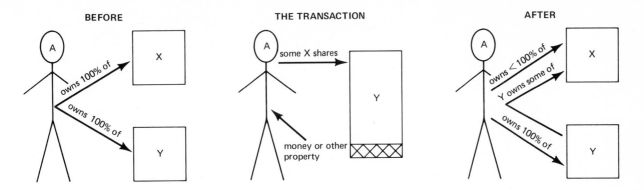

FIGURE **23-3**   Redemption Through Related Corporation

Both before and after the transaction, taxpayer A *effectively,* although not "legally," owns all of both corporations. Afterward, Y legally is the owner of some shares in X. The important fact, however, is that taxpayer A has more money (or other property) after the transaction and this money came from Y Corporation. Should the transaction be treated as the sale of a capital asset, as it appears on the surface to be, or should it be treated as a dividend?

Without Sec. 304, the tax result would be a capital gain or loss. As you probably suspect, Sec. 304 is the loophole-closing provision that converts the entire amount received by A into an ordinary dividend if the "seller" owns (directly or indirectly) 50 percent or more of the two corporations involved in this transaction. Indirect ownership is imputed to A using the constructive ownership rules found in Sec. 318(a).

These are but a few of the many sections put into the Code to stop the manipulations of corporate transactions that would otherwise yield capital-gain benefits to an undeserving shareholder. The preferred stock bailout (Sec. 306) and the collapsible corporation (Sec. 341) provisions involve even more complex plans and, therefore, more complex rules to preclude similar results.

ADMINISTRATIVE CONVENIENCE SECTIONS

Some of the apparently complicating provisions in the capital gain and loss complex are intended to simplify rather than to complicate procedures. We would include in this category such provisions as Secs. 1236 and 1237 and Subsection 165(g). In order to understand the first two of these three provisions, it may be necessary to refresh your memory concerning the statutorily pure definition of a capital asset contained in Sec. 1221(1). There, you may recall, the Code says that all assets are capital assets except those held "primarily for sale to customers." But how are we to make the determination of whether or not certain assets are held primarily for resale?

Section 1236

If it were not for Sec. 1236, a securities dealer might find it impossible to make a normal capital investment in a corporate stock or security. Because the security dealer's ordinary inventory consists of stocks and bonds, he or she must find some way to segregate personal investments from inventory assets. Otherwise the dealer might be tempted to report only those transactions that involved securities held for more than one year *and* produced gains as sales of capital assets. All other transactions would be treated as inventory sales; that is, as ordinary gains and losses. The Internal Revenue Service would, of course, be subject to exactly the opposite temptation. That is, the I.R.S. agent would argue that only the long-term losses involved capital assets; all other sales would appear to involve ordinary inventory assets.

Section 1236 solves this potential dispute before it can begin. It simply provides a 30-day period following acquisition during which a securities dealer must clearly identify purchases made for investment purposes. If such an early identification is not made, then the dealer must report any gain or loss as an ordinary one.

Section 1237

A problem very similar to that of the dealer in securities is often encountered by the land developer. It frequently is difficult to distinguish between land held by the developer as a genuine personal investment and land held as a part of ordinary inventory. Section 1237 is intended to distinguish between the two by providing certain arbitrary tests that must be reported on the disposition of real property subdivided for sale.

In general, Sec. 1237 provides that an individual taxpayer who is *not* a real estate dealer can report a capital gain on the sale of subdivided real estate only if

1. The tract sold, or any part thereof, had not *previously* been held by the taxpayer as one primarily for resale;

2. In the year sold, the seller does not hold any other tract, or part thereof, as one primarily for resale;

3. The taxpayer directly or indirectly made no "substantial improvements" to increase the value of the lots sold during period of ownership; and

4. The land was owned for five years prior to sale, unless it was inherited.

Furthermore, even if all the above conditions are satisfied, only the gains on the sale of the first five lots from such a tract are entirely capital gain. Profits from the sale of the sixth and subsequent lots produce ordinary income equal to 5 percent of the selling price (unless a period of five years or longer has lapsed with no sales); only the remainder is capital gain. Selling expenses can, however, be offset against the ordinary income portion, rather than the capital gain, once the sixth and subsequent sales are made.

Although the enactment of Sec. 1237 does serve to simplify a tax conclusion in a few circumstances, it is at best a quixotic solution to a much larger problem. Anyone interested in the continuing problem should study the several decisions in *Malat* v. *Riddell*. There one taxpayer had to fight his case all the way to the Supreme Court only to discover that the word "primarily" means "of first importance" or "principally."[4] The continuation of very similar cases in the post-*Malat* era suggests that even this startling discovery by our Supreme Court has not ended the controversy.

[4]383 U.S. 569 (1966).

Subsection 165(g)

An entirely different kind of problem has been resolved by Subsection 165(g). Only the most meticulous study of Subchapter P of the Code would reveal the critical importance of a few words contained in Sec. 1222. It is there that the term capital gain (or loss) is defined as the gain (or loss) "*from the sale or exchange* of a capital asset." Given this choice of words, what happens taxwise when a taxpayer experiences a loss because a security has become wholly worthless? Obviously, if it is truly worth nothing, the taxpayer can neither sell it nor exchange it for anything else of value. Will this fact deny the taxpayer the right to deduct any loss? Much to their surprise, many years ago several taxpayers found this to be the conclusion of both the I.R.S. and the courts. Subsequently, taxpayers were usually able to find someone who would give them a dollar or two for what was, in reality, worth nothing.

In order to correct this obvious misinterpretation of the law, Congress passed the predecessor of Subsection 165(g) to create an artificial sale or exchange in the event of worthlessness. It reads as follows:

> If any security which is a capital asset becomes worthless during the taxable year, the loss resulting therefrom shall, for purposes of this subtitle, be treated as the loss from the sale or exchange, on the last day of the taxable year, of a capital asset.

Observe that this subsection does more than create the artificial sale or exchange; it also determines the end of the holding period. Unfortunately, however, it cannot, and does not, solve the problem of determining when a security finally becomes "worthless." Therefore, taxpayers and I.R.S. agents continue to disagree with some frequency over the exact year in which a taxpayer should claim a loss deduction on worthless securities.

ECONOMIC INCENTIVE SECTIONS

Still other complications to the capital gain and loss complex must be attributed to a congressional desire to intervene in the marketplace of supply and demand. Other things being equal, the demand for any property can generally be increased if (1) the income from that property can be reclassified as capital gain, rather than as ordinary income; or (2) any loss realized in relation to the property can be reclassified as an ordinary loss, rather than as a capital loss.

Section 631

In consort with Sec. 1231, Sec. 631 provides that the gain or loss derived from certain timber, coal, and domestic iron ore operations may be treated as if it were derived from the sale or exchange of a capital asset held for more than one year. Presumably, the special treatment for timber is justified by the fact that the gain, which accrued over several years (during the growth of the timber), would otherwise be subject to a disproportionately heavy tax if the entire amount had to be recognized in the single year of realization. Another unusual aspect associated with the lumber industry is the fact that the taxpayer may, under specified conditions, treat the mere cutting of timber as the equivalent of a sale or exchange. In addition, investments in timber may be depleted for tax purposes. These special provisions have favored investments in timber, including evergreen trees to be sold as Christmas trees if allowed to grow for more than six years.

If a taxpayer not involved in a mining operation has owned an economic interest in a coal mine or a domestic iron ore deposit for more than one year, that taxpayer may be eligible to report any gain on a disposition under a royalty contract as a Sec. 1231 gain. As noted in Chapter 18, however, the taxpayer may have to recapture any previously deducted exploration expenditures before being eligible for this potential capital-gain treatment. Because these sections affect relatively few taxpayers, we shall not investigate any details of these special provisions in this text.

Section 1244

Small corporations often find it very difficult to raise sufficient capital to underwrite the costs commonly associated with new ventures. Congress has enacted several laws intended to assist those firms. Two of the tax provisions that help to reduce the risk of an investment in a small new corporation are the Subchapter S provisions and Sec. 1244. As we noted earlier, the general tax effect of making a Subchapter S election is to convert an otherwise separate taxable entity (the corporation) into a mere tax conduit for its owners. This election is especially useful to the new firm experiencing net operating losses in its first few years of operation. The election allows high-marginal bracket investors to offset those "corporate" operating losses against their individual incomes from other sources. This opportunity causes many investors to assume risks they might otherwise be unwilling to

consider. An investor in a 70-percent marginal tax bracket, for example, can make a $200,000 capital investment, with a real economic risk equivalent to only $60,000, if he or she can be assured that any loss sustained can be recognized for tax purposes as an ordinary loss. The Subchapter S election guarantees that tax result to the extent of the investor's pro rata share of the new corporation's net operating losses.

Section 1244 expands on the same fundamental economic incentive by providing an investor with the right to claim an *ordinary* loss deduction for up to $50,000 per year ($100,000 for married taxpayers filing a joint return) from any loss on the sale or exchange of stock in a "small business corporation." The Code goes on, of course, to define small business corporations in detail. In general, that term can readily be made to apply to the common stock of any corporation with less than $1 million in equity capital. In order to qualify, however, the corporation must adopt a plan to offer not more than $1 million as stock that qualifies under Sec. 1244. Thus, by combining the Subchapter S election with Sec. 1244 stock, the venture capital corporation is often able to market securities that otherwise would have a very limited reception. Observe that if the new corporation becomes a financially successful enterprise, the investor will have been allowed to convert ordinary loss deductions (via the early years, Subchapter S losses) into long-term capital gain (on the subsequent sale of the shares at a market price that reflects the financial success of the entity). In the interim, the investor was partially insured against further downside market values for the stock by Sec. 1244 protection.

Incidentally, the advantages of Sec. 1244 are not restricted to the disinterested investor. For example, we have personal knowledge of one case in which a successful dentist decided to sell his practice and begin a new career as a (fishing) charter-boat captain. Because of the high liability risk in the new venture, the man incorporated his business. The new business was a financial disaster and, within a few years, the owner returned to the practice of dentistry. Unfortunately, however, he had not obtained competent tax advice and, therefore, his large loss was wholly realized in the form of a long-term capital loss on the disposition of the stock in his corporation. As such, he could only carry that capital loss forward and offset it against ordinary income at the rate of $1,000 per year (it would have been $3,000 in years after 1977), on a 2-for-1 basis! Consider how much better off this taxpayer would have been with a large net operating-loss deduction that he could have carried back and offset against the ordinary income previously reported during the years of his first dental practice! That would have been the result, of course, had he understood the tax rules contained in Subchapter S and Sec. 1244.

Section 1253

By reclassifying a usually profitable ordinary asset as a noncapital asset, Congress can, of course, create an economic *disincentive*. The gain typically realized on the transfer of a franchise or a trade name was effectively removed from capital-gain treatment by the enactment of Sec. 1253 in 1969. That section reads in part as follows:

> (a) General Rule.—A transfer of a franchise, trademark, or trade name shall not be treated as a sale or exchange of a capital asset if the transferor retains any significant power, right, or continuing interest with respect to the subject matter of the franchise, trademark, or trade name.

It is hoped that this recent transformation of what previously had been capital gain into ordinary income may dampen the almost uncontrolled growth of the franchising business. Concurrently it may reduce the monotony of the traditional building that houses franchised restaurants, ice-cream parlors, automotive brake and transmission shops, and even tax-return preparation businesses. Although the growth of these businesses is not harmful, the frequency of financial disaster associated with these operations suggests the need for some restraint. In all too many instances, it seems that the only person who benefits from the franchise is the party selling "the deal."

OTHER MISCELLANEOUS MODIFICATIONS

Although this discussion of some modifications to the "pure case" of capital gain and loss can by no means be considered complete, a few of the modifications not discussed thus far seem to be of sufficient importance, for one reason or another, to justify brief comment here.

Section 166(d)

Section 166 authorizes the deduction of bad debts in the computation of taxable income. Subsections (a)

through (c) are concerned with business bad debts; subsection 166(d) reads as follows:

> (1) General rule.—In the case of a taxpayer other than a corporation—
>   (A) subsections (a) and (c) shall not apply to any nonbusiness debt; and
>   (B) where any nonbusiness debt becomes worthless within the taxable year, the loss resulting therefrom shall be considered a loss from the sale or exchange, during the taxable year, of a capital asset held for not more than one year.
> (2) Nonbusiness debt defined.—For purposes of paragraph (1), the term "nonbusiness debt" means a debt other than—
>   (A) a debt created or acquired (as the case may be) in connection with a trade or business of the taxpayer; or
>   (B) a debt the loss from the worthlessness of which is incurred in the taxpayer's trade or business.

At least three aspects of this subsection are important. First, note that subparagraph (1)(B) makes a deduction possible by *considering* a bad debt *as* a loss from a "sale or exchange." Second, observe that this provision authorizes what, in its absence, would not be deductible because of its personal character. Recall that a personal capital loss, such as that incurred on the sale of a family car or residence, is not generally deductible in the computation of taxable income. Third, note that the Code specifies that nonbusiness bad debts must be treated as short-term capital losses, regardless of the time period they were owing to the taxpayer prior to worthlessness.

This provision allows a taxpayer to deduct as a short-term capital loss an amount loaned to a personal friend many years ago if the taxpayer can prove both the debt's existence and the fact that it is now worthless. The most surprising part of this subsection's interpretation, however, usually involves the closely held corporation. It is not unusual for the owner of a small, incorporated business to loan "the business" additional funds from personal assets to pay employees, utility bills, rent, and other general corporate creditors. Unfortunately, it is also not unusual for these small corporations to become worthless (i.e., to become bankrupt). In that event, taxwise, how should the loans made by the stockholder to his or her own corporation be treated? That is, are they "business" or "nonbusiness" bad debts?

Paragraph 166(d)(2) defines a nonbusiness debt as one *not* "created or acquired . . . in connection with a trade or business of the taxpayer." Most small business owners believe that they made those loans in connection with *their* trade or business. The I.R.S. agent will usually contend, however, that the trade or business belongs to the corporation, not to the individual who may own and operate that entity. Consequently, the personal loans are generally found to be nonbusiness debts and their worthlessness is treated as a short-term capital loss, not as an ordinary loss deduction. The courts have generally sustained the I.R.S. position, unless the taxpayer can prove that he or she (individually) is in the business of making loans, of creating venture corporations for resale, or operates some other unique business that commonly requires the personal debt obligation. In the vast majority of the litigated cases, taxpayers have lost their attempts to claim the ordinary deduction.

Section 303

The modifications of the "pure case" found in Sec. 303 are of a different variety. As explained earlier in this chapter, a corporation's redemption of stock from its shareholders in the absence of complete or partial liquidation of the corporation may be treated either as a sale of stock by the shareholder or as a dividend. Many redemptions in closely held corporations are treated as dividend distributions and are taxed to the recipient as ordinary income.

Section 303 extends the capital-gain treatment to the proceeds when stocks are redeemed to pay death taxes, as long as the conditions of Sec. 303 are satisfied. Among these conditions are the following:

1. The stock being redeemed must have been included in the decedent's gross estate for federal estate-tax purposes.
2. The redemption must take place after a stockholder's death and within a time period (which may be up to 10 years) specified by the Code.
3. The value of the decedent's ownership in the corporation(s) concerned must have been more than 50 percent of the value of the adjusted gross estate.
4. The gain given this special capital-gain treatment cannot exceed the amount by which the redeemed shareholder's interest in the estate has been reduced by death taxes and funeral and administrative expenses.

The importance of this Code provision to taxpayers is that it permits a limited amount of what might otherwise be ordinary income to be recognized as capital gain. Because of the long-term capital-gain deduction, this can be of benefit to some taxpayers.

IN SUMMARY

The Code sections related to capital gain and loss constitute a major exception to the generally accepted methods of income measurement and taxation as practiced in the United States today. Two aspects of these sections are of primary importance: First, the existence of a flat 28 percent alternative tax constitutes an important exception to the application of the normally progressive tax-rates of corporate taxpayers; second, the presence of the 60 percent long-term capital-gain deduction creates for the noncorporate taxpayer a substantial tax benefit to the items of income that can be categorized as net capital gains. Collectively, these two features of capital-gain taxation constitute a major motivating force in tax planning that is an integral part of the business-decision-making process.

As suggested in the last four chapters, moreover, innumerable subtleties—some obvious, some not so obvious—must be applied to nearly every conceivable fact situation to determine (1) if the result of any particular business transaction is or is not eligible for special capital-gain treatment and (2) if it is, what that treatment shall be.

PROBLEMS

1. Barton Spring and Dayton Fall each organized a new corporate business venture in year 1. Both men invested $100,000 cash in their wholly owned corporation, and both corporations experienced $20,000 operating losses in years 1, 2, and 3. Barton qualified his corporation under Subchapter S, whereas Dayton elected to have his corporation taxed in the normal way. In year 4 each man sold his corporation's stock for $40,000. Because of the Subchapter S election, Barton offset his corporation's annual $20,000 loss against his income from other sources, at the "cost" of reducing his basis in the corporate stock. Day-

ton, on the other hand, got no current deductions for the losses experienced by his corporation in years 1 through 3, but neither did he have to reduce the basis of his stock. Therefore, on the sale of their corporate stock in year 4, Barton recognized no additional gain or loss, whereas Dayton recognized a $60,000 long-term capital loss.

   a. Assuming that each man is independently wealthy and that each typically reports a substantial ordinary income as well as capital gain, which man made the better choice? Explain.

   b. Would it have been beneficial for either taxpayer to qualify the stock under Sec. 1244? Explain briefly.

2. Ed Dreamer spent his spare time writing novels, while his neighbor, Tom Fixit, spent his time tinkering with mechanical devices. Each man earned a normal taxable income of $20,200. However, each man "hit it big" this year when Ed sold the copyright on his first really good novel for $50,000 and Tom sold the patent on his first really good invention for $50,000. Calculate each man's tax liability for this year, assuming that each files a joint return with his wife and that each had no income or deductions other than their usual $20,200 taxable (i.e., after all deductions and exemptions) income and the extra $50,000 for the year.

3. Jan Drew made several stops on her way to the bank where she planned to make a deposit of $500 cash. Unfortunately, somewhere along the way Jan left the cash unattended and, when she retraced her steps, she simply could not locate the money. She concluded that someone had stolen the $500.

   a. Assuming that Jan is the cashier for Bout Corporation, would Bout claim a tax deduction for the loss? Explain, and cite your statutory authority for a deduction, if any.

   b. Assuming that Jan was depositing her own personal cash, could she claim a tax deduction for the loss? Explain, and cite your statutory authority for a deduction, if any.

4. While a student at Ohio University 10 years ago, you loaned $300 cash to Barry Doubtful. This year you learned that Barry died penniless from an overdose of drugs. Taxwise, how should you report your $300 bad debt loss in the current year?

5. Philomena Leahy owned 38 percent of the outstanding stock of Leaky Corporation; her husband, Jack, owned another 10 percent; and her son, Joey, owned 5 percent. Philomena also owned 60 percent of Sneaky Corporation. On April 1, Philomena sold 500 shares of her Leaky stock to Sneaky Corporation for $25,000. Philomena's tax basis in the shares sold was $5,000. Assuming that Philomena had owned the Leaky shares for 12 years prior to this sale, what amount and kind of income should she report this year because of the sale?

6. On March 3 of this year, Walter Caringounce, a real estate dealer, sold a 12-acre tract of land for $120,000. Although Walter had purchased the property for $40,000 as an investment six years ago, he did make minor improvements to the land during the past 18 months and he actively advertised the property for sale for a year before "closing the deal" this year.

   Walter's wife, Mary, is a licensed stock broker. On March 3, of this year, Mary sold 1,200 shares of Rocks common stock for $120,000. Mary had purchased the shares for $40,000 six years ago; at the time of the purchase she clearly identified them as a personal investment. During the 18 months prior to sale, Mary watched the market on Rocks stock very closely and she also helped prepare her firm's brochure that described Rocks stock as an excellent buy.

   a. How should Walter report his $80,000 gain this year?

b. How should Mary report her $80,000 gain this year?

c. Are the tax laws equitable between Walter and Mary? Explain briefly.

7. Laura Engles owns 100 percent of Missouri Corporation, which in turn owns 100 percent of Ozark Corporation. On April 1, Laura sold 5,000 shares of Missouri common (which had a tax basis of $50,000) to Ozark Corporation for $150,000. (Assume that both Missouri and Ozark Corporations had substantial amounts of earnings and profits.)

   a. What apparent tax advantage is Laura trying to obtain? Explain briefly.

   b. Do you think that this tax plan will work? (If not, cite any Code section that you think might interdict the intended results.)

8. Jerry Tight frequently loans his personal money to business acquaintances at the maximum legal rate of interest. Two years ago he loaned $5,000 to his brother, Jeff. This year Jeff was forced to declare bankruptcy and Jerry had to write off the $5,000 loan he made two years earlier. How should Jerry treat this $5,000 bad debt for federal income tax purposes? Explain briefly.

9. "Big" Fish owns all outstanding stock of three corporations, namely, Little Corporation, Pond Corporation, and Dud Corporation. The first two corporations (Little and Pond) have been highly successful financial ventures. Dud, however, was a financial failure. During this year, Mr. Fish engaged in the three transactions detailed below. In each separate transaction, determine the amount and kind of income that Mr. Fish must report for federal income tax purposes.

   a. Transaction 1: On November 19, Mr. Fish sold 50 of his 500 shares of common stock in Little Corporation to Pond Corporation for $500,000 cash. His adjusted basis in the 50 shares sold was $10,000. The date basis of these shares was April 1, 1960.

   b. Transaction 2: On December 1, Mr. Fish sold all his stock in Dud Corporation to Evan Moore Stupid for $1,000 cash. His basis in the Dud shares sold was $45,000. The shares had a date basis of July 1, 1975. The Dud stock was fully qualified as Sec. 1244 stock.

   c. Transaction 3: On December 31, Mr. Fish was notified that Dud Corporation had been declared bankrupt and that no assets were available to distribute to any creditors. Accordingly, Mr. Fish knew that the $10,000 that he had loaned to Dud Corporation on September 1, 1978, would never be repaid.

SUPPLEMENTAL PROBLEMS

10. Jones and Smith each own 2,500 of the 5,000 outstanding shares of JS Corporation stock. Each man has a tax basis of $10 per share of stock that he owns. For years the two owners have allowed JS Corporation to accumulate most of the corporate profits for expansion of the business. In the current year, however, the owners see no further need for additional accumulation with JS.

   a. If the JS Corporation declares a dividend of $60,000, how will Jones and Smith report the $30,000 that they each receive?

   b. If Jones and Smith were each to surrender back to JS Corporation 500 of the 2,500 shares of stock they each own, thereby technically creating a "stock redemption" rather than a simple "dividend," how would Jones and Smith report the $30,000 that they each received?

   c. Suppose that Jones was looking forward to an early retirement, whereas

Smith anticipated a long future with JS Corporation. Under these circumstances the two men may agree to distribute the entire $60,000 to Jones in exchange for 1,000 of his 2,500 shares of stock. How will Jones report the $60,000 he receives?

d. If, at the time of incorporating their business, both Jones and Smith loaned JS Corporation $50,000 in long-term debt in addition to the capital investment they made, how would each man report the receipt of $30,000 in the current year if the corporate records clearly supported the contention that the distribution of cash was made as a reduction of this long-term debt?

e. What does this problem suggest about the form of the capital structure of any new corporation?

11. Indicate the effect for income tax purposes of each of the following independent transactions on the stockholders of Berger Corporation. The corporation owns assets that have an adjusted basis of $50,000,000 and only one class of stock and bond outstanding, which is closely held. Liabilities total $20,000,000.

a. The corporation distributes a parcel of land to its shareholders. Cost of the land to the corporation was $200,000, and fair market value at the time of distribution was $450,000. No stock is surrendered by shareholders.

b. The corporation distributes capital assets with a basis of $300,000 and fair market value of $400,000. Each shareholder surrenders 10 percent of his shares in Berger. The distribution does not constitute an important "corporation contraction."

c. The corporation distributes assets with a basis of $10,000,000 and a fair market value of $15,000,000 in exchange for 25 percent of the corporate stock. Assume that this is considered a partial liquidation.

12. The recapture rules for farm losses ignore several important aspects of the problem. Discuss the conditions under which the "farm-loss loophole" is still good tax planning for a wealthy individual, despite the new rules.

13. In addition to a sizable income from outside business activities, Mr. Big earns a $275,000 annual salary as the president of the Hi-Jinx Corporation. Because of his high marginal tax rate, Big chose to "invest" $100,000 in a livestock venture every year for the past three years. The details of this venture were handled through a brokerage house, and therefore Big was never required to visit the scene of his farming activities. The $100,000 annual investment did not produce any income until this year, when Big asked the brokerage firm to sell the older half of his growing herd. This sale yielded Mr. Big cash receipts of $400,000.

a. How would Mr. Big report the receipt of the $400,000 on his tax return?

b. Would Mr. Big be in danger of having his livestock operation declared a hobby and thus lose all his related tax deductions? Explain.

14. On November 14 of the current year, the authorities suspended all trading in Equity Funny Corporation stocks. Radcliff had purchased 1,000 shares of Equity Funny on February 13, last year, for $32,500. The closing quotation for these shares on November 13 this year was $5 per share. The trading suspension was still in effect on December 31, so Radcliff could not sell his 1,000 shares although he desperately wanted to do so. What amount of capital loss can Radcliff deduct in the current year as far as his Equity Funny stock is concerned? Explain briefly.

15. An investor in an oil and gas drilling venture is frequently able to deduct as much as 80 percent of the investment in the first year because of the tax treatment of intangible drilling and development costs. Although this rule was *not* changed by the Tax Reform Act of 1976, the relative advantage of this opportunity was significantly reduced by other provisions of that Act. Explain briefly.

16. Ted Engles, who is independently wealthy and earns a large income each year, also owns 3,000 shares of Onnex Corporation stock. Ted's basis in these shares is $30,000; their current fair market value is $330,000. Ted fears that the value of Onnex common may drop significantly in the near future, and therefore he would like to sell about one-half of the shares. He does not, however, want to pay a big capital gains tax immediately. Suppose that Ted were to sell half of his Onnex shares to his wife, Laura, for $165,000 in an installment sale calling for payment of $35,000 for each of the next five years. Suppose also that Laura almost immediately resold those same shares to an independent third party for $165,000 cash.

  a. What apparent tax advantage is Ted trying to obtain? Explain briefly.

  b. What are the tax consequences to Laura when she sells all the shares she recently purchased? Explain briefly.

  c. Do you think that this tax plan will work? (If not, cite any Code section that you think might interdict the intended results.)

The administrative requirement of collection results in an exception to generally accepted accounting principles. As a practical matter, the timing of the tax should occur when the taxpayer can most readily pay and the I.R.S. can most readily collect.

SHELDON S. COHEN,
"Accounting for Taxes, Financial and Regulatory Purposes—Are Variances Necessary?" (1966)

The basic position of the committee on federal taxation of the American Institute of Certified Public Accountants has long been and continues to be that there should be greater conformity between the rules of tax accounting and generally accepted accounting principles.

DONALD T. BURNS,
quoted in the Bureau of National Affairs' *Daily Reporter System* (1966)

PART

SEVEN

the wherewithal-to-pay concept

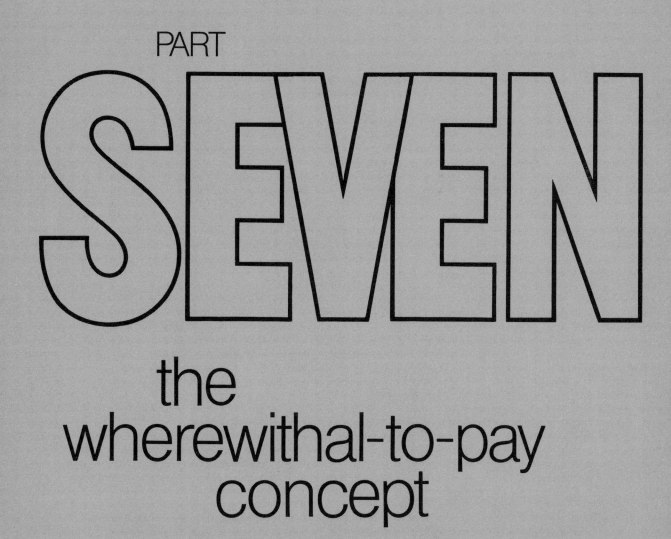

24

This concept renders realization devoid of any special meaning; realization is made merely a synonym for *recognition.* According to this concept, all amounts appearing in financial statements are necessarily deemed to be realized by virtue of their appearance there.

ROBERT T. SPROUSE,
"Observations Concerning the Realization Concept" (1965)

the realization criterion

The words realization, recognition, and transaction are found scattered throughout the literature of law, economics, and accounting. In the introductory literature, especially, these words are typically used without specific definition. Authors of this literature seem to presume that the reader can apply a generally accepted definition to each word and thereby reach a reasonably accurate conclusion about the thought the author is trying to convey. In order to understand the significance of these words to income taxation, a more detailed analysis of each word is required.

Part Seven of this text attempts to demonstrate that a wherewithal-to-pay concept is at least as important to understanding the income tax as the realization concept, which is much more frequently cited. In other words, the authors believe that Congress, the I.R.S., and the judiciary rely as often upon a wherewithal-to-pay concept as on a realization concept in settling specific income-measurement problems for tax purposes.

The present chapter is largely conceptual in nature, deriving the definitions and general rules important to understanding a wherewithal-to-pay concept. Chapter 25 is a discussion of the "common nontaxable exchanges," and Chapter 26 is an introduction to a few of the nontaxable transactions that are commonplace between corporations and their shareholders. Collectively these two groups of transactions represent the most important exceptions to the general rule that requires that income be recognized for tax purposes as soon as it has been realized. A major reason for these exceptions is the fact

that the taxpayers involved often have less funds with which to pay a tax than they have in realized income.

FUNDAMENTAL CONCEPTS

The income-generating cycle begins with an idea and ends with consumption. Intermediate steps may be numerous and complex or few and simple; the process may be concluded in a brief time span or it may extend over many years. The more numerous, complex, and time consuming the intermediate steps, the greater are the problems of income measurement.

As noted in Chapter 5, the income concept common to taxation is more like the accounting concept than like the economic concept. That is, for both tax and accounting purposes, income under most circumstances must be "realized" before it will be "recognized." But what does it mean to say that income is "realized"?

The realization criterion in accounting

The verb "realize" has several possible meanings. Perhaps the three most common are: (1) to make real; (2) to convert into cash (money); and (3) to understand clearly.[1] Obviously the second of these three meanings is the one pertinent to this discus-

---

[1] *The Random House Dictionary of the English Language,* unabridged edition (New York: Random House, 1973); lists eight different meanings, p. 1196.

sion. When the realization concept is first introduced into a freshman or sophomore accounting course, the text—and often the instructor—hastens to illustrate the concept with a little story that usually goes something like this: "On August 10 Mr. Jones purchased 100 shares of ABC common stock for $600. On December 31 these shares had a fair market value of $700. What is Mr. Jones' income for the year from this investment?" The student is expected, of course, to reply that Mr. Jones has no income because his "$100 gain" has not yet been "realized."

Applying the second definition to the problem about Mr. Jones, a student would be correct in assuming that until the shares are sold for cash (or money), no income is "realized." An accountant would probably not be as demanding as this definition. That is, the accountant likely would be willing to admit that income is realized as soon as the shares are converted into another property that has a high degree of *liquidity* and *measurability*. A *Dictionary for Accountants* defines "realize" in this way:

> To convert into cash or a receivable (through sale) or services (through use); to exchange for property which at the time of its receipt may be classified as, or immediately converted into, a current asset.[2]

This broader interpretation of the realization criterion is consistent with the position taken by American Accounting Association committees in 1957 and 1964. The 1957 committee statement suggests that "the essential meaning of realization is that a change in an asset or liability has become sufficiently definite and objective to warrant recognition in the account."[3] The 1964 committee added: "It is difficult to be precise about what is the current prevailing practice, but it appears that presently accepted tests for realization require receipt of a current (or liquid) asset capable of objective measurement in a market transaction for services rendered."[4]

The last pronouncement of the American Institute of Certified Public Accountants on the matter of realization comes reasonably close to the tax position. In its Statement No. 4, the Accounting Princi-

ples Board assigned the concept of realization the position of a pervasive measurement principle and then described it as follows:

> Revenue is generally recognized when both of the following conditions are met: (1) the earning process is complete or virtually complete, and (2) an exchange has taken place.[5]

This statement seems to differ from those offered earlier through a reduction in the emphasis placed on the liquidity of the asset received and an increase in the emphasis on the completion of the earning process.

Although much more could be written about the realization concept in accounting, the most important facts are already apparent. At least until 1970, accountants generally held that income (revenue) was not realized until a transaction had been consummated and a measurable, liquid asset received. The latter requirement was consistent with the accountants' objectivity principle; for external financial reporting purposes, the accountant generally remains interested in minimizing the need to establish fair market values in the absence of an arm's-length transaction.

The realization criterion in income taxation

The realization concept in income taxation is similar but not identical to the accounting concept just reviewed. Most of the differences between them are best explained by practical constraints—that is, by the accountants' legal liability for accurate statements, on the one hand, and by the objectives and administrative considerations common to income taxation, on the other.

The realization criterion of income taxation is an interesting blend of statutory, administrative, and judicial law. In Code Sec. 61, which contains the general definition of gross income, the word realization does not appear. The Code provides only, as noted earlier, that "gross income means all income from whatever source *derived*."[6] The Treasury Department's interpretation of this statute does introduce the realization concept. It reads as follows:

[2] Eric L. Kohler, *A Dictionary for Accountants* (2nd ed.) (Englewood Cliffs, N.J.:Prentice-Hall, 1957), p.407.
[3] American Accounting Association, *Accounting and Reporting Standards for Corporate Financial Statements* (Menasha, Wisc.: George Banta Co., Inc., 1957), p. 3.
[4] 1964 Concepts and Standards Research Study Committee. "The Realization Concept," *The Accounting Review* (April, 1965), p. 314.

[5] Accounting Principles Board, Statement No. 4, *Basic Concepts and Accounting Principles Underlying Financial Statements of Business Enterprise* (New York: American Insititue of Certified Public Accountants, Inc., 1970), p. 59.
[6] Code Sec. 61(a) (emphasis added).

(a) General definition. Gross income means all income from whatever source derived, unless excluded by law. Gross income includes income *realized* in any form, whether in money, property, or services. Income may be *realized,* therefore, in the form of services, meals, accommodations, stock, or other property, as well as in cash.[7]

Observe that this administrative interpretation of the Code suggests that realization requires the receipt of some new service, property, or property right but does not specify anything relative to either the liquidity or the measurability of that item. This very broad interpretation of realization is a practical necessity. In its absence, taxpayers would seek out obscure ways of avoiding income taxation by earning their income through barter transactions of infinite variety. Interestingly, Code Sec. 1001, which is titled "Determination of Amount of and Recognition of Gain or Loss," refers to "Amount *realized.*"

The realization criterion has received judicial support from the very beginning. The most celebrated statement is contained in a 1920 decision, in which the Supreme Court said

> Here we have the essential matter: *not* a gain *accruing* to capital, not a *growth* or *increment* of value *in* the investment; but a gain, a profit, something of exchangeable value *proceeding from* the property, *served from* the capital however invested or employed, and *coming in,* being *"derived,"* that is, *received* or *drawn by* the recipient (the taxpayer) for his *separate* use, benefit and disposal;—*that* is income derived from property. Nothing else answers the description.[8]

The words of the Court, like those of the Regulation, seem to require a transaction, or some significant event, in addition to appreciation. These authorities make it amply clear that a mere appreciation in value, without realization, will not be taxed as income. The important question remains, however: Exactly what is required before income is said to be "realized"?

For purposes of income taxation, assume that the singular requirement pertinent to the realization concept is the consummation of an "external transaction." The fact that nothing more is required is amply demonstrated in the case of *United States* v. *Davis.* In that case the Supreme Court found that a husband who transferred an appreciated property to his wife "in full settlement and satisfaction of any and all claims and rights against the husband"[9] realized gain equal to the difference between the fair market value of the rights received and the adjusted basis of the property transferred. Since the "rights received" were unique and certainly not liquid or easily measured—that is, they could be "purchased" only by this one man—the Court had to find that the value of the rights could be presumed to be equal to the (estimated) value of the property surrendered in order to measure gain. In brief, in income taxation, the realization concept does not require the receipt of a measurable, liquid asset.

Interestingly, the wife in the *Davis* case apparently did not realize taxable income by surrendering her rights against her ex-husband for a property. One possible reason for the different treatment of these two taxpayers is that her settlement can be viewed as a restitution. That is, her receipt of the property can be viewed as simply restoring her to the financial position she had prior to her release of rights. In a sense, this treatment is comparable to that given a taxpayer who receives money or other property to compensate him or her for the loss of a body member or body function or the award of damages relating to personal or family rights. In these cases, the taxpayer-recipient will generally not be treated as having received any taxable income; rather, the payment will be viewed essentially as restoring the taxpayer to his or her former position without gain. Legal damages awarded for lost profits and treble damages (that is, punitive damages) are considered taxable income.

Transaction defined

As illustrated by the *Davis* decision, the word "transaction" must be defined broadly and positively for income-tax purposes. In addition, the transaction concept must be separated clearly from the realization concept. Whenever these two concepts are not clearly distinguished, it is all too commonplace to find circular definitions, such as that (1) income will be recognized in the books of account only if it has been realized; (2) the realization of income (revenue) requires a transaction with specified characteristics; and (3) a transaction is any event or condition that gives rise to an accounting entry.

[7]Treasury Regulation Sec. 1.61-1(a) (emphasis added).
[8]*Eisner* v. *Macomber,* 252 U.S. 189 (1920), p. 207.

[9]370 U.S. 65 (1962), p. 67.

As an alternative to such circular definitions, we can define a *transaction* as *any significant change in the form or the substance of any property or property right. Internal transactions* are those involving only one entity; *external transactions* are those that necessarily involve more than one entity.

As stated earlier, the realization of taxable income generally requires the consummation of an external transaction. This transaction could be a sale, an exchange, an abandonment, or almost any other modification in a property or a property right. The transfer of raw materials into goods in process and eventually into finished inventory will not give rise to taxable income as long as the transfer does not extend beyond a single taxable entity. Such a transfer would constitute an "internal transaction" because it represents a significant change in the form of property. As such, it would be the occasion for an entry in the accounting records even though it would not be sufficient to trigger the realization of taxable income.

The discovery of oil in land owned by a taxpayer would not give rise to taxable income because it did not either create a new property or property right or change the form of an existing one. Rather, the discovery simply made the land-owning taxpayer aware of a new dimension of the property rights that he or she had owned all along. The discovery of buried treasure trove, on the other hand, would give rise to taxable income because of the existence of possible adverse interests in such property by another entity and because of the fact that treasure trove is not deemed to be part of the basic collection of rights that collectively constitute land ownership.

An interesting exception to the general rule we have just stated occurs when a taxpayer mortgages a property that he or she already owns. The placing of a mortgage against an appreciated property certainly could be classified as a significant change in that property owner's rights. For example, suppose that a taxpayer borrowed $10,000 against a property with an adjusted basis of $2,000 and a fair market value of $14,000. In an important sense this taxpayer has realized at least part of his or her appreciation gain. Yet, the borrowing transaction, even when executed between external parties, either does not constitute realization or, alternatively, does not give rise to income because there is no net increase in the taxpayer's net worth. That is, when the taxpayer borrows, liabilities increase by the same amount as assets, and therefore the taxpayer is deemed to have no taxable income. This exception to the usual rule

that gain must be realized on the consummation of an external transaction is, in turn, subject to at least two notable exceptions. First, if a taxpayer transfers property with a related debt in excess of its adjusted basis in a transaction that would otherwise permit the temporary deferral of gain, the gain must be realized. Second, if an individual embezzles assets, he or she is treated as having realized an equivalent amount of income notwithstanding the fact that he or she, at least technically, owes a debt equal in amount to that taken illegally.

Another interesting aspect of the realization-transaction criterion of income taxation can be observed in the transfer of property between business entities. It is important here to recall that entities recognized for tax purposes are not identical to entities recognized for accounting purposes. The transfer of, say, a building from a personal account to a sole proprietorship would most likely give rise to an accounting entry and possibly even to accounting income. It would not, however, give rise to taxable income because the sole proprietorship is not viewed *for tax purposes* as an entity distinct from the individual owner. On the other hand, the transfer of the same building from the taxpayer to his or her wholly owned corporation *could* give rise to taxable income, as well as to an accounting entry, because the corporation is deemed to be a separate taxable entity.

The word "could," in the preceding sentence, is of particular importance. Realization, as defined here, is a necessary but not a sufficient condition for recognition of taxable income.

Recognition

The adjective "recognized," when used to modify income, means simply that the income item is to be admitted or acknowledged for the purpose at hand. Thus, for example, income recognized for accounting purposes is simply income that will be included in the appropriate financial statement(s) prepared for that accounting period. Similarly, income recognized for tax purposes is simply income that must be included in the tax base reported for a given time period.

For financial accounting purposes, it frequently is argued that income should be recognized (under specified fact circumstances) prior to realization.[10] In

[10]For example, see Charles T. Horngren, "How Should We Interpret the Realization Concept?" *The Accounting Review,* XL (April, 1965), pp. 323-33.

general, these arguments are made to bring accounting income closer to the concept of economic income. The fact circumstances typically cited as justifying a pre-realization recognition of income in financial statements are those involving a minimum of judgment in establishing fair market value. Thus, for example, if oil has been extracted and refined by a United States producer but has not been sold or exchanged, a strong case can be made for the "early" recognition of this income because the price of domestic oil is relatively stable and easily determined. Accountants hold widely varying opinions about (1) the degree of price predictability and (2) the state of completion that must be required before unrealized income should be recognized in financial statements. The accountant will only rarely argue that income recognition should be delayed until sometime after realization. In those few cases where this is done, the accountant usually does so because of an inability to estimate accurately some material post-realization expense. For example, if collection and foreclosure costs are estimated to be material in amount, and if they are not subject to reasonably accurate estimation, then the accountant may argue for a cash-collection basis of revenue recognition rather than a realization basis.

For tax purposes, income generally must be recognized in the same accounting period that it is realized. There are, however, a number of exceptions to this general rule. For tax purposes income recognition almost never precedes realization, but it quite often follows realization. This significant difference in income-measurement techniques between accounting and taxation can be explained by the tax tenet called "wherewithal to pay." The tenet suggests, as noted on page 5/7, that under many circumstances "the income tax shall impinge at whatever time the taxpayer has the funds with which to pay the tax." In numerous situations, wherewithal to pay seems to outrank in importance more sophisticated refinements of income measurement that would cause income to be recognized at a time other than when the funds are readily available. Perhaps the outstanding example is the taxation of certain unearned revenues at the time of receipt.

In summary, the realization criterion of income taxation is like the accounting criterion in its insistence upon a transaction. Unlike its accounting counterpart, however, the income-tax criterion does *not* always depend on the receipt of a measurable, liquid asset. Furthermore, and also in contrast with accounting, income recognition almost never precedes realization for tax purposes but is often postponed until long after realization.

NONTAXABLE TRANSACTIONS

Income that has been realized by a taxpayer may (1) be recognized immediately, (2) be permanently excluded from gross income by definition or by act of Congress, or (3) have recognition partially or wholly deferred temporarily by Code provision. The third type of transaction is often referred to as a "nontaxable transaction." In other words, the phrase "nontaxable transaction" is often a misnomer; *as often as not, a nontaxable transaction is at least partially taxable.*

Let us review briefly what was said earlier about taxability. All realized income is deemed taxable unless the taxpayer can point to a specific authority for excluding the income item from the tax base. The list of permanent exclusions is relatively brief. It includes gifts; inheritances; insurance proceeds paid on the death of the insured (unless the recipient has a purchased interest in the policy); interest paid on state and local government bonds; "sick pay" (under specified circumstances); scholarships and fellowships (also under specified conditions); property settlements in lieu of alimony; on-premise food and lodging (conditions specified); the value of group life (to $50,000 face), health, and accident insurance premiums (paid by the employer for the employees); social security and railroad retirement benefits; and a few other miscellaneous items. The most important definitional exclusion is the "return-of-capital" concept, which is aptly demonstrated by the calculation of taxable gain on the sale of a security. A more complex illustration of the return-of-capital concept is embodied in the calculation of taxable gain on the receipt of a purchased annuity payment (illustrated on pages 15/7–15/8).

In addition, many routine transactions in which income is realized are not considered of immediate tax consequence because of the accounting method selected for reporting purposes by the taxpayer. For example, if a taxpayer can properly elect to report income on a cash basis, the only revenue transaction that assumes importance for all *routine* business transactions is the collection of cash. Note, however, that even a cash-basis taxpayer must resort to other rules to determine the tax consequences of any nonroutine transaction in which he or she may be involved. It is in the latter group of transactions that the "nontaxable transactions" become especially important.

The general rule

As a general rule, it is most accurate to presume that income must be recognized for tax purposes at the time it is realized unless a taxpayer can find good authority for a contrary treatment. As we have said, three levels of contrary authority are pertinent:

1. The realized income may constitute one of the income items permanently excluded from the income-tax base.
2. The realized income may derive from a routine business transaction that is being reported to the government for tax purposes on some alternative but acceptable accounting method.
3. The Code may provide for the deferral of recognition of gain realized for this specific kind of property or for this particular form of disposition.

In general the rationale for the last two groups of exceptions, above, is that the income tax should be deferred until such time as the taxpayer has the funds with which to pay the tax.

Exception by accounting method

The installment sales method of accounting (like the cash method) represents a typical option available whereby a taxpayer may elect to defer the recognition of realized income until such time as he or she has the wherewithal to pay the income tax. The detailed requirements pertinent to the installment sales method of accounting are contained in Sec. 453. Suffice it to note here that the requirements differ slightly for "dealer" and for "nondealer" installment sales; they also differ slightly for sales of personal property and for sales of realty. Perhaps the two most important nondealer installment-sale restrictions are contained in Sec. 453(b). One of these provides that this option cannot be elected if the taxpayer receives more than 30 percent of the selling price in the year of the sale; the other requires that the sale price be greater than $1,000 if the sale is of personal property.

Assuming that all the conditions are satisfied and that the taxpayer elects this accounting option, he or she reports as taxable income in any year only a fraction of the cash collections received from the

installment sale. The appropriate fraction is called the "gross profit ratio." This is the ratio of the gross profit realized on the sale to the "total contract price."[11] Total contract price means the amount of cash the seller will eventually receive under the sale contract, excluding interest.

To illustrate the effect of electing the installment sale option, assume the following facts. In 19x1 Mr. Ben, not an art dealer, made a casual sale of a painting for $2,000. He had purchased this painting for his personal enjoyment five years earlier, at which time he paid $1,200. The 19x1 sale contract called for five annual payments of $400, plus 6 percent interest on the unpaid balance; the first payment was due on delivery of the painting. Mr. Ben receives payment as follows:

November 10, 19x1: $400
November 10, 19x2: $496
November 10, 19x3: $472
November 10, 19x4: $448
November 10, 19x5: $424

Assuming that Mr. Ben, ordinarily a cash-basis taxpayer, elects to report the gain on the sale of his painting on an installment basis, we can summarize the tax consequences of the transaction as shown in Table 24-1.

TABLE **24-1**
INSTALLMENT BASIS REPORTING

Year	Cash collected	Ordinary taxable income reported (interest)[a]	Long-term capital gain reported[b]
19x1	$400	$ 0	$160
19x2	496	96	160
19x3	472	72	160
19x4	448	48	160
19x5	424	24	160

[a] Reported on a cash basis.
[b] The gross profit ratio on this sale was 40 percent—that is ($2,000 − $1,200) ÷ $2,000. Hence, 40 percent of every noninterest dollar collected after the sale must be reported as taxable income in the year of receipt.

This example is important for at least two reasons. First, it demonstrates the possibility that a taxpayer may defer recognition of taxable income until such time as he or she has the wherewithal to pay simply by electing an appropriate accounting method. Had this option not been available, Mr. Ben

---

[11] Reg. Sec. 1.453-1(b) (1): "Gross profit, in the case of a sale of real estate by a person other than a dealer and a casual sale of personal property, is reduced by commissions and other selling expenses." In other words, in these cases, gross profit is usually equal to the gain realized.

would have had to recognize the entire $800 long-term capital gain in the year it was realized (19x1), even though he was a cash-basis taxpayer for routine business purposes. Second, the sale contract illustrated above makes an explicit provision for interest on the unpaid debt. Since June, 1963, an installment sale contract that does not provide for interest at the rate of 6 percent or more per annum will automatically be presumed to include an implicit interest of 7 percent per annum. The reason for this presumption is apparent from the illustration. Until 1963 a seller was able to convert ordinary (interest) income into a tax-favored long-term capital gain by increasing a contract price and reducing (or eliminating) interest. Although this conversion of ordinary income into capital gain is now limited, the cash-collection basis of accounting for the interest still makes it possible to defer recognition of the interest portion of the sale until the taxpayer has the funds with which to pay the tax. Furthermore, the difference between the low (6 percent) statutory rate and the current market rate of interest leaves room for substantial conversion of ordinary income in many installment contracts.

Special rules are provided in the Code for early dispositions of installment sale obligations and for foreclosures on installment sale contracts. The student interested in these and other possible complications is urged to consult a current and authoritative tax service for details.

Exceptions for specific transactions

Accounting methods are of general applicability to all qualifying transactions without regard for the nature of the property involved. Infrequently, however, the Code specifies a special method of reporting income from sales of selected forms of property or from properties disposed of in a certain manner. These unusual or irregular provisions are often best understood in light of a wherewithal-to-pay concept. More of these special cases are discussed in Chapter 25, but we shall review one of them (Sec. 1031) here to conclude this introduction to the fundamental idea.

THE EXCHANGE OF PRODUCTIVE USE OR INVESTMENT PROPERTIES

The student who has already studied elementary and intermediate accounting is likely to have encountered Sec. 1031, although he or she probably did not

recognize it as such. This tax phenomenon is typically discussed in the elementary accounting literature in conjunction with the problem of valuing assets at cost where a new asset is acquired in a barter (or at least partially a barter) transaction. For example, if a businessperson acquires a new delivery truck with a list price of $8,000 by trading in an old truck and paying $5,500, what is the *cost* of the new truck? Assuming that the cost of the old truck was $4,500, depreciation accumulated to date of sale was $3,000, and estimated fair market value at date of sale was $2,000, most elementary accounting texts would suggest either $8,000 (the list price of the new truck) or, better yet, $7,500 (the $5,500 cash payment plus the $2,000 estimated fair market value of the old truck). Accounting texts usually suggest, as a poor third alternative, a "tax method" whereby the new truck would be recorded at $7,000 (the sum of the $5,500 cash payment and the $1,500 book value of the old truck). The effect of this tax method is, of course, to avoid the recognition of any gain or loss on the exchange by "plugging" the cost of the new truck in the accounting entry. Actually, the Code says nothing about accounting for such an acquisition for financial accounting purposes; it says, simply, that for tax purposes (including the determination of subsequent tax depreciation deductions and calculations of gain or loss on resale), the *tax basis* of the new truck will be determined by this third (tax) method.

The criticism frequently directed by accountants against this Code provision is often based on the critic's failure to observe that the concept developed for tax purposes was never intended to have pertinence to financial accounting or to other concepts developed for wholly different purposes. For tax purposes, there are at least three good reasons for the failure to recognize taxable income in this situation. First, the tax method avoids the administrative disputes that frequently accompany arbitrary determinations of fair market value. Second, the tax method rejects arbitrary "list price" valuations, which, if accepted, often allow the taxpayer golden opportunities for tax avoidance.[12] Third, the tax method postpones the liability for any income tax that might attach to the exchange until such time as the taxpayer has the wherewithal to pay the tax.

---

[12] A major *potential* loophole was reduced significantly by the enactment of Sec. 1245. As explained on page **22/4**, the big advantage of a high list price would have been to get large deductions for depreciation (which reduce ordinary income) at the cost of realizing a tax-favored long-term capital gain on disposition of the asset (via operation of Sec. 1231).

Statutory requirements

The exchange of delivery trucks, as explained above, is only illustrative of the effect of Sec. 1031. A more comprehensive view of this Code section must begin with an examination of pertinent portions of the statutory provision:

(a) Nonrecognition of Gain or Loss from Exchanges Solely in Kind.—No gain or loss shall be recognized if property held for productive use in trade or business or for investment (not including stock in trade or other property held primarily for sale, nor stocks, bonds, notes, choses in action, certificates of trust or beneficial interest, or other securities or evidences of indebtedness or interest) is exchanged solely for property of a like kind to be held either for productive use in trade or business or for investment.[13]

Several aspects of Sec. 1031(a) cannot be over-emphasized. First, observe that this section is mandatory, but it is applied only to *direct exchanges.* That is, a taxpayer who *exchanges* one qualifying property for another has no option to recognize gain or loss if he or she wants to do so. Furthermore, if a taxpayer sells property and subsequently uses the proceeds of the sale to purchase similar or even identical property, such a transaction is *not* within the confines of Sec. 1031(a).

Second, note that not every property held for trade, business, or investment purposes qualifies for Sec. 1031(a) treatment. Gains realized on the exchange of inventories (or other property held primarily for resale), stocks, bonds, and receivables are specifically *excluded* from any special treatment. The specific exclusion of inventory and receivables is for obvious reasons; if this were not provided, the practical consequence of a high income tax would be to force businesspeople into many barter transactions for routine operations. The reason for the exclusion of stocks and bonds from possible nontaxable exchange privileges is less apparent; perhaps Congress decided that more than adequate tax benefits had been made available for these gains in the provisions for long-term capital gains. Specifically, the availability of the long-term capital-gain deduction and the alternative tax may have been considered adequate to protect the taxpayer from unduly harsh taxation of these gains. In addition, most traded securities present a minimal problem of valuation, and, because of the ease of divisibility of this investment, wherewithal to pay can be less critical.

Third, observe that the exchange must involve "property of a like kind" before the gain or loss realized is not recognized by operation of Sec. 1031. The general "like kind" requirement is explained in the Treasury Regulations as follows:

As used in section 1031(a), the words "like kind" have reference to the nature or character of the property and not to its grade or quality. One kind or class of property may not, under that section, be exchanged for property of a different kind or class. The fact that any real estate involved is improved or unimproved is not material, for that fact relates only to the grade or quality of the property and not to its kind or class. Unproductive real estate held by one other than a dealer for future use or future realization of the increment in value is held for investment and not primarily for sale.[14]

It is apparent from this regulation and from related judicial decisions that realty cannot be exchanged for personalty and still qualify for nonrecognition of gain under Sec. 1031. Beyond that general statement, however, it is difficult to be sure about the precise limits of the "like kind" requirement. Suffice it to note that the courts have been reasonably liberal in their interpretation of this provision. Incidentally, the Tax Reform Act of 1969 added Sec. 1031(e), which explicitly removes livestock of different sexes from like-kind property. This exclusion was intended to reduce a taxpayer's opportunity to convert ordinary income into capital gain through livestock breeding and feeding operations.

The role of "boot"

It is unusual to find two taxpayers who are anxious to enter into an exchange of like-kind property and whose properties just happen to be equal in value. Disparity in values, however, need not preclude the possibility of entering into a "tax-free" exchange. As with the exchange of delivery trucks, an additional "side payment" of cash constitutes the usual adjustment mechanism for the difference in the fair market values of the two properties. Giving "boot" (which is defined as the cash or other nonlike-kind property involved in the exchange) may or may not result in the recognition of gain; receiving boot literally guarantees the recognition of some gain.

Giving boot causes the recognition of gain only in the event that the boot given constitutes property

---

[13]Code Sec. 1031 (a).

[14]Reg. Sec. 1.1031 (a)-1(b).

that (1) cannot be part of a nontaxable exchange—for example, an item of inventory, a stock, bond, or a property of nonlike kind—and (2) has a fair market value greater than its tax basis. To illustrate this possibility, let's return to the earlier example of the delivery trucks and assume that the taxpayer who traded the old truck gave the other party to the exchange a stock with a fair market value of $5,500 (rather than paying $5,500 cash). In that event, the difference between the taxpayer's basis in the stock and its fair market value would have to be recognized as taxable gain (or loss) at the time of the exchange. That is, if the taxpayer had paid $2,000 for the stock, he or she would have to recognize a $3,500 gain at the time it was transferred to the truck dealer (even though he or she had no real wherewithal to pay).

Receiving boot necessitates the recognition of taxable gain equal to the lesser of the gain realized or the boot received. This provision is, however, consistent with the wherewithal-to-pay concept. Since the boot received represents "surplus" tax-paying ability, it determines the amount of gain that must be recognized, subject, of course, to the fact that a taxpayer *never* need recognize more gain than he or she realized on the exchange. This conclusion can be demonstrated simply in the following tabulation for a taxpayer who receives boot in an exchange of like-kind properties:

	Boot received	Gain realized	Gain recognized
Case A	$500	$1,000	$500
Case B	500	200	200

The exchange of a mortgaged property ordinarily is treated as an exchange involving boot. That is, the taxpayer who is relieved of the mortgage (which may be accomplished by the other party's either assuming the mortgage or taking the property subject to the mortgage) is treated as having received cash in an amount equal to the face of the mortgage. Obviously, the assumption that release from a mortgage constitutes tax-paying ability equal to the receipt of a comparable amount of cash is subject to challenge in many circumstances. This conclusion is virtually necessary, however, to close what could otherwise be a major loophole in the nontaxable-exchange provisions. To illustrate the potential loophole, assume that taxpayer A owned outright a piece of investment property that cost $1,000 but had a fair market value of $5,000. If A could find a satisfactory property of like kind that he or she preferred to own, A might

first mortgage the present property and acquire, say, $3,000 cash. Then, having mortgaged the old property, A would proceed to enter into a nontaxable exchange and acquire a new property. If the transfer of the mortgage to the former owner of the new property were not considered to be boot, taxpayer A would be able to avoid taxes even though he or she obviously had at least $3,000 in wherewithal to pay. In short, even though treating the transfer of a mortgage as equivalent to receiving cash of an equal amount may sometimes necessitate the recognition of taxable income where no tax-paying ability exists, the alternative assumption could lead to an equally unsatisfactory conclusion, at least as far as the I.R.S. is concerned.

If both properties involved in a nontaxable exchange are mortgaged properties, then only the difference between the face amounts of the two mortgages is treated as boot. That is, the taxpayer who is relieved of the larger mortgage will be assumed to have received boot equal to the difference between the mortgage transferred to the other party and the mortgage assumed.

Finally, it should be noted that Sec. 1031 may cause a realized loss to remain unrecognized. If a taxpayer exchanges a productive use or investment property with an inherent or "paper" loss for another property of like kind, the loss realized on the exchange cannot be recognized for tax purposes. If the taxpayer desires to recognize such a tax loss, it is necessary that he or she first sell the old property and then use the sales proceeds to purchase the second property in a separate transaction. On the other hand, losses will be recognized on any boot property included in an otherwise nontaxable exchange. That is, if a taxpayer who owned a bond with a basis of $1,300 and a fair market value of $1,000 decided to exchange that bond and an old delivery truck for a new delivery truck, the $300 loss realized on the exchange of the bond would be recognized because a bond cannot generally be part of a "common nontaxable exchange."

Basis adjustment

The realized gain or loss that may be deferred in an exchange of like-kind properties is ordinarily a temporary deferment. Recoupment of the gain or loss under normal circumstances is guaranteed by the reduction of basis in the property received. The basis of property acquired in a nontaxable exchange may be calculated in one of two ways:

Method I:

Basis of old property (property given up in the exchange)
+ Boot given
+ Gain recognized
− Boot received
− Loss recognized
= Basis of new property (like-kind property received)

Method II:

Fair market value of property received (like-kind property only)
+ Loss *not* recognized on the exchange
− Gain *not* recognized on the exchange
= Basis of new property (like-kind property only)

The successful application of these formulas to specific fact situations requires a fair degree of imagination and understanding. Consequently, at the outset, it is recommended that you attempt to solve every application using both formulas. If the results agree, the calculations are probably correct; if the results disagree, the facts should be investigated for alternative interpretations under the circumstances. To assist you, a comprehensive illustration of the nontaxable-exchange provision applicable to like-kind properties is included in the following section.

Before proceeding to that illustration, however, one additional note on basis seems pertinent. As explained on page **20/9**, it is sometimes necessary for a taxpayer to determine a "date basis" as well as a "cost basis" for selected properties. This is especially important for transactions involving capital assets or properties that potentially may be included in the Sec. 1231 melting pot. Properties that acquire a *substituted basis*—that is, properties that take as a basis some amount other than cost, by operation of one of the nontaxable exchange provisions—are typically considered to be a mere extension of the original property for purposes of determining the holding period. As a consequence, the holding period of the two assets is assumed to "tack"; that is, it includes the period of time the "old" asset was held as well as the period of time the "new" asset was held prior to disposition. For example, assume that a taxpayer owned a particular capital asset for two years, after which time he or she exchanged the asset for a like-kind asset in a nontaxable exchange. Then, two months later, this taxpayer decided to dispose of the new asset in a taxable transaction. Would the capital gain or loss be classified as long or short term? The correct answer generally is long term; the taxpayer's holding period is presumed to run from the date he or she acquired the original asset, *not* from the date of the exchange. (An early disposition may, however, be viewed as evidence that the taxpayer did not intend to hold the new property as "productive use" or as "investment" property and thus disqualify the exchange for Sec. 1031 treatment.)

Comprehensive illustration

Assume that taxpayer R (a rancher) exchanged some ranch land for an apartment complex (land and buildings) and some bonds, which had been owned by taxpayer D (a dentist). Facts pertinent to the exchange are shown in Table 24-2.

The important tax questions that attach to this exchange may be summarized as follows:

1. What taxable income, if any, must R recognize on the exchange?
2. What taxable income, if any, must D recognize on the exchange?
3. What is the basis of (a) the apartment house, (b) the land, and (c) the bonds in R's hands after the exchange has been completed?
4. What is the basis of the ranch land in D's hands after the exchange has been completed?

TABLE **24-2**
DATA ON A NONTAXABLE EXCHANGE

Facts relative to the ranch land		Facts relative to the land, apartment house, and bonds	
FMV of land	$230,000	FMV of the apartment complex	$160,000
Tax basis (in R's hands)	50,000	Tax basis (in D's hands)	100,000
Mortgage on property		FMV of bonds	40,000
(to be assumed by D)	30,000	Tax basis (in D's hands)	50,000

To determine the answers to these questions, several calculations must be made. The first calculation should determine the gain realized. Let us begin with taxpayer R:

$230,000 Amount realized ($160,000 FMV of apartment complex + $40,000 FMV of bonds + $30,000 mortgage transferred to D)
− 50,000 Basis given up (R's basis in ranch land)
= $180,000 Gain realized

Of the $180,000 gain realized, how much gain must R recognize? Remember that in an exchange of like-kind productive use or investment property, a taxpayer who receives boot must recognize gain equal to the lesser of (1) the gain realized or (2) the boot received. In this instance, R received $70,000 in boot: $40,000 (FMV) in bonds and $30,000 by transfer of a mortgage. Hence, R must recognize $70,000 in taxable income; $110,000 of the realized gain remains untaxed (or unrecognized at the present time) by operation of Sec. 1031.

Determining the basis of the apartment complex and the bonds in R's hands, after the exchange, is not so simple. Because any nonlike-kind property is not within the protection of Sec. 1031, it becomes fully taxable and takes as a basis its cost (or fair market value) at the date of the exchange. Therefore, we can begin by stating that the bonds must have a basis in R's hands of $40,000. In other words, the receipt of any property that cannot be part of the nontaxable exchange is automatically given a basis equivalent to what it would have received in any routine business transaction. The basis of the apartment complex is best determined by substituting pertinent data in the formula suggested earlier:

$50,000 R's basis in ranch land given up
+   0 Boot given
+ 70,000 Gain recognized
− 70,000 Boot received: $40,000 bonds and $30,000 mortgage transferred
−   0 Loss recognized
= $50,000 Basis of apartment complex in R's hands

Using the alternative formula, we can confirm the above calculation:

$160,000 FMV of apartment complex
+   0 Loss not recognized on the exchange
− 110,000 Gain not recognized on the exchange: $180,000 realized − $70,000 recognized
= $50,000 Basis of apartment complex in R's hands

Because the apartment complex includes both land (a nondepreciable asset) and buildings (a depreciable asset), it is further necessary to divide the $50,000 basis between the two assets. This is done on a relative fair market value apportionment. That is, if we assume the land is estimated to be worth $32,000 and the buildings $128,000, then $\frac{1}{5}$ ($32,000/$160,000) of the $50,000 basis, or $10,000, must be allocated to land. The remaining $\frac{4}{5}$, or $40,000, must be allocated to the buildings.

The tax questions applicable to taxpayer D can be answered in a similar manner. First, determine the amount of gain realized by D as follows:

$230,000 Amount realized (FMV of ranch land)
− 180,000 Basis given up ($100,000 basis in apartment complex + $50,000 basis in bonds + $30,000 in mortgage assumed)
= $50,000 Gain realized *(net)*

Observe that the $50,000 gain realized is composed of two parts: a $60,000 gain realized on the apartment complex ($160,000 fair market value less $100,000 in basis) and a $10,000 loss realized on the bonds ($40,000 fair market value less $50,000 basis). Because the bonds cannot be part of a nontaxable exchange, the $10,000 loss is recognized. Since D did not receive any boot, he need not recognize any gain; hence, his $60,000 realized gain on the apartment complex remains unrecognized at this time.

D's basis in the ranch land may be computed as follows:

$150,000 D's old basis in the apartment and bonds ($100,000 + $50,000)
+ 30,000 Boot given (mortgage assumed)
+   0 Gain recognized
−   0 Boot received
− 10,000 Loss recognized
= $170,000 Basis of ranch land in D's hands

Using the alternative formula, we can again confirm this calculation:

$230,000 FMV of ranch land
+ 0 Loss not recognized on the exchange
− 60,000 Gain not recognized on the exchange
= $170,000 Basis of ranch land in D's hands

Note that in the first calculation the bonds were included with the basis of the property given, not with the boot given. They cannot be included in both places without double counting. They are included in the property basis because a later line in the formula takes recognition of the fact that a loss was recognized on this portion of the exchange. In other words, the bonds could have been included with "boot given" (rather than with basis of old property); however, if that had been done the bonds would have to be entered at their after-loss recognition value ($40,000), and *no* further entry under loss recognized would be appropriate since the $10,000 recognized loss is implicitly included with the $40,000 valuation of the bonds.

It should be emphasized that Sec. 1031 harbors significant opportunities for tax-saving ideas. Cor- porations, businesspeople, and taxpayers of substantial means often find it advantageous to exchange productive use and investment properties rather than to dispose of them in some other manner because of the tax consequences that attach to each disposition. By minimizing the tax cost of the transaction, the taxpayer can maximize the capital value that remains "at work" producing further income. Under some circumstances, of course, the taxpayer may prefer to recognize the entire gain on a disposition in order to get a stepped-up basis on the property received. This is especially true of depreciable properties that are to be put to use by a taxpayer in a high tax bracket.

These provisions, relating to the tax treatment of gain that may be realized on the exchange of productive use or investment property, are simply illustrative of several statutory modifications to the realization concept. They should serve to illustrate that realization is a necessary but not a sufficient condition to the recognition of income for tax purposes. They should also serve to illustrate how Congress tries, in certain circumstances, to postpone the recognition of income until the taxpayer is most able to pay an income tax. Several further illustrations of this important conclusion will be considered in Chapters 25 and 26.

PROBLEMS

1. Which of the following events would increase a taxpayer's "taxable income"? Explain each answer.
   a. Finding a $100 bill on the sidewalk.
   b. "Scalping" four 50-yard-line seats at a big football game for $100 each. The tickets cost $6.00 each. (Scalping tickets is illegal in the state in which they were sold and the game played.)
   c. Having a $100 debt forgiven by a business creditor. (The creditor hoped, in this manner, to encourage you to do more business with him in the future.)
   d. Embezzling $100 from your employer's check-cashing fund.
   e. Having a $100 personal debt gratuitously forgiven by your brother.
   f. Selling a fishing boat for $100. (The boat originally cost you $200.)
2. Distinguish between "realized" income and "recognized" income for tax purposes.
3. What is the major difference between "realized" income for tax purposes and "realized" income in financial accounting?
4. Accountants sometimes argue that tax rules should be changed to agree with generally accepted accounting principles.
   a. Suggest some of the ways that taxpayers could avoid the tax if the realization test for tax purposes were the same as for financial accounting.
   b. Suggest some effects on taxpayers if the tax law followed generally accepted accounting principles for income recognition.

5. Several years ago, John Marsh, a calendar-year taxpayer, purchased a tract of land at a cost of $100,000. The unimproved realty was held as an investment. The land appreciated in value, and on December 29, 19x1, John sold it for $400,000. The purchaser paid John $100,000 in cash on December 29, 19x1, and, in accordance with the sales contract, a second installment of $300,000, plus interest for the two months' period, was paid on February 27, 19x2. How will John's income be taxed, assuming he makes the elections necessary to defer the tax as long as possible?

6. Howitz Appliance Corporation uses the installment method of reporting income. Howitz had sales and gross profits on installment sales of home appliances as follows in 19x1, 19x2, and 19x3:

Year	Installment sales	Gross profit
19x1	$240,000	$ 84,000
19x2	250,000	90,000
19x3	300,000	100,000

During 19x3, collections on installment sales by year of sale were as follows (interest charged is *excluded* from these collections):

Year	Amount collected in 19x3
19x1	$ 50,000
19x2	105,000
19x3	120,000

How much gross profit must Howitz report in 19x3?

7. Corporation P, a manufacturing corporation, owns 100 percent of the outstanding stock of Corporation S, a sales corporation. P and S file a consolidated tax return. During the current year, P sold S widgets at a cost of $100,000; these widgets had cost P $80,000 to manufacture. P also sold widgets to nonrelated purchasers. Total sales to nonrelated purchasers for the year were $200,000; cost of these sales to P was $160,000.
   a. How much income did P realize?
   b. How much income did S realize?
   c. How much income would P and S report for the year on their consolidated tax return?
   d. Explain the tax treatment of any difference between your answer to part c and the sum of your answers to parts a and b.

8. Explain briefly the reasons for the existence of Sec. 1031 relating to the nonrecognition of gain or loss on the exchange of assets held for productive use.

9. Dusty Rhodes, a road contractor, owned a light airplane used in his business. This plane had an adjusted basis of $8,000 when he exchanged it for a smaller plane with a fair market value of $10,000. Dusty *received* $3,000 cash when he made this trade. Straight-line depreciation claimed on the old plane since acquisition totaled $10,000.
   a. How much gain was *realized* on this exchange?
   b. What minimum gain must be *recognized* on this exchange?
   c. Is the recognized gain a capital gain, ordinary income, or part of Sec. 1231? Explain.
   d. What is Dusty's tax basis in the new plane?

10. Assume the following facts apply to a like-kind exchange of productive use or investment property and complete the schedule.

Adjusted basis of property surrendered	Cash given (or received)	FMV of property received	Recognized gain (or loss)	Basis of new property
a. $19,000	$5,000	$30,000	$———	$———
b. 8,000	(4,000)	20,000	———	———
c. 17,000	0	25,000	———	———
d. 17,000	0	15,000	———	———

11. Tora Corporation owned a machine, used in its business, that had cost $6,000 and on which depreciation of $2,200 had been taken up to January 2 this year. On that date Tora exchanged the old machine for a new one to serve the same purpose. Using these facts, in each of the following cases compute (1) the *recognized* gain or loss on the exchange and (2) the tax basis of the new machine.

   a. Value of new asset, $4,000; no boot given or received.
   b. Value of new asset, $3,000; boot *received*, $400.
   c. Value of new asset, $3,000; boot *given*, $300.
   d. Value of new asset, $4,000; boot *received*, $300.
   e. Value of new asset, $4,000; boot *given*, $300.
   f. Value of new asset, $3,700; boot *received*, $300.

12. On October 10, 1946, Rancher Alpha purchased 500 acres of land on the Colorado River for $40,000. He used this land to graze cattle until this year, when, on November 1, he traded the ranch for a small complex of land and buildings that had just been completed in Nearby City. This complex was intended to constitute a neighborhood "shopping center." At the time of the trade, the estimated fair market value of the ranch was $250,000; that of the shopping center, $300,000. To equate the exchange, Rancher Alpha gave the builder 1,000 shares of Tractor stock, which had cost him $20,000 in 1965; they were worth $50,000 at the time of the exchange.

   Builder Beta, the contractor who constructed the shopping center complex, works independently with a small group of men. He makes his living by building homes and office buildings and selling them to interested parties. His construction cost in this particular complex was $270,000; he started construction on February 4 of last year.

   a. Relative to Rancher Alpha:
      1. What amount of gain (or loss) did he *realize* on the exchange of the ranch and Tractor shares for the shopping center?
      2. What minimal amount of gain (or loss) must he *recognize* on this same exchange?
      3. What is the tax basis in the shopping center after the exchange has been completed, assuming he elects to pay a minimum tax now?
      4. What is his "*date* basis" in the shopping center?
      5. Is the shopping center a capital asset in Rancher Alpha's hands after the exchange? Explain.
      6. Can you foresee any reason why Rancher Alpha may prefer to make this a taxable (rather than a nontaxable) event? Explain.
   b. Relative to Builder Beta:
      1. What amount of gain (or loss) did he *realize* on the exchange of the shopping center for the ranch and Tractor stock?
      2. What amount of gain (or loss) must he *recognize* on the exchange?

3. What is his tax basis in the ranch after the exchange has been completed?

4. What is his tax basis in the Tractor shares after exchange?

5. What is his "*date* basis" in the ranch and the shares?

6. Is the ranch a capital asset to Beta? Explain.

7. Are the Tractor shares a capital asset to Beta? Explain.

13. Sam Jones has operated a dairy farm on the outskirts of a large city for a number of years. He owns 200 acres of land for which he originally paid $150 per acre. The land is situated adjacent to a railway tract, and a freeway through the area (but not on Sam's place) was recently completed. The Boyce Corporation has approached Sam about buying his place to use as the site for a large manufacturing plant. They offered Sam $1,000 per acre. Sam intends to continue in the dairy business but does not want to sell his land because he will get less than its value after paying the tax. Devise a plan that will allow Boyce to obtain Sam's land and leave Sam without diminution of the value of his investment in land.

14. Bracket Corporation's Board voted to close Plant 12 located in a congested area of New Jersey and to open the same operation in a semi-rural setting somewhere in the southwestern part of the United States. After making this decision, Bracket sent its Secretary and Treasurer on a search for the new plant site. Eventually the two corporate officers selected an ideal 80-acre tract that was for sale for $75,000. Instead of arranging an outright purchase of the new site, the men contracted with a New York broker, who agreed to acquire the 80 acres and to exchange it plus $5,000 cash for Bracket's old Plant 12. The parties agreed that the approximate fair market value of Plant 12 was $84,000: $52,000 for the building and $32,000 for the land. Bracket's adjusted basis in the old building was $24,000; in the old land, $30,000. The broker was actually able to acquire the new 80-acre tract for $72,000.

a. What amount of taxable gain must Bracket Corporation report in the year it completed this exchange?

b. What kind of gain—ordinary income, capital gain, or Section 1231 gain—does Bracket Corporation report because of this transaction?

c. What is Bracket's tax basis in the (new) 80-acre tract?

d. Why might Bracket Corporation have preferred to purchase the new site directly from the owner had it included a building as well as land? Explain.

e. What amount of taxable income must the New York broker report because of his role in this exchange?

f. Would the broker's income be ordinary income or capital gain? Why?

15. For each of the independent situations below, determine (1) the amount of gain or loss realized; (2) the amount of gain or loss recognized; and (3) the tax basis of the new land. Assume that during the current year the taxpayer exchanged one parcel of farm land for another; further assume that the taxpayer had held the original land for six years and that it had an adjusted tax basis of $50,000 at the time of the exchange.

a. Taxpayer received only the "new" land, which had a fair market value of $60,000.

b. Taxpayer received the "new" land, with a fair market value of $60,000, and $15,000 cash.

c. Taxpayer gave the other party to the exchange $5,000 cash, in addition to the land, and received in return land worth $45,000.

d. Taxpayer received only the "new" land, which had a fair market value of $60,000, and the other party to the exchange assumed taxpayer's mortgage on "old" land in the amount of $20,000.

e. Taxpayer took the "new" land and assumed a mortgage against that land in the amount of $10,000. The other party to the exchange also assumed taxpayer's mortgage on "old" land in the amount of $6,000. "New" land has estimated value of $60,000.

16. On July 22, this year, taxpayer exchanged 170 shares of Otis common stock for 300 shares of Lifter. Taxpayer's basis in the Otis shares was $850; Lifter shares were selling for $7 per share on the day of the exchange. Neither corporation was involved in any kind of reorganization.
    a. What gain or loss must taxpayer recognize in this year?
    b. What is taxpayer's basis in the 300 shares of Lifter stock?

17. On June 7, this year, Bud exchanged his 1966 Dodge for a 1973 Honda. Bud paid $895 for his car seven years ago and used it solely for personal transportation all these years. The Honda had a fair market value of $350 at the time of the exchange. What amount of gain or loss did Bud realize this year? What amount of gain or loss will he recognize this year? What is his tax basis in the Honda?

18. Hanna, a professional artist, exchanged two of her recent oil paintings for a Salinas original, which she intends to hold as an investment. Although Hanna's direct costs (canvas, oil paint, etc.) in the two paintings was only $40, they were considered quite valuable because she is rapidly becoming a well-known artist. She often charges $50 per hour on commission work, and these two paintings took approximately 60 hours of her time. Hanna estimates the current value of the Salinas original to be $3,000. Must Hanna recognize any gain or loss this year because of this exchange? If so, how much? Explain briefly.

19. Items a–h are eight suggested property exchanges. Which of the eight would *not* wholly qualify as a (tax-free) like-kind exchange? Explain any of the exchanges that would partially qualify. Assume that none of the property is an inventory item.
    a. Gold jewelry for Dodge van. (Both for personal use.)
    b. Ranch land for fully equipped restaurant (land, building, equipment).
    c. Stallion for a gelding. (Both used in business.)
    d. Sailboat for a racehorse. (Both held as investment properties.)
    e. Corporate stock for corporate bond.
    f. Personal residence for a rental property.
    g. Business truck for gold bullion. (Gold held for investment.)
    h. Apartment house for bulldozer. (Apartment is investment; bulldozer is productive-use property.)

20. UAS Corporation exchanged land it owned near Tempe, Arizona, for other land near Provo, Utah. UAS's basis in the Arizona land was $800,000; it had a $750,000 mortgage outstanding against this property. The other party to the exchange, YUB Corporation, assumed the $750,000 mortgage. In order to complete the exchange, UAS Corporation paid YUB Corporation $300,000 cash (boot). The Utah land was valued at $850,000 and was clear of debt; the Arizona land was valued at $1,300,000. Assuming that both properties were held by UAS Corporation as an investment, what taxable gain, if any, must UAS recognize?

21. Bill Bass, a commercial fisherman, owned a 25-foot boat, which he used in his business. Bill traded this boat for a new 22-foot boat, which had a fair market value of $20,000. The old boat had originally cost $36,000 and had an adjusted basis of $16,000 on the date the trade was completed. As part of the deal, Bill received $6,000 cash.
    a. What amount of gain did Bill realize because of this trade?

b. What amount of gain must Bill recognize because of this trade?

c. What is Bill's tax basis in his new 22-foot boat?

22. Pearl Diver, a commercial deep-sea diver, owned a 25-foot boat, which she used in her business. Pearl traded this boat for a new 32-foot boat, which had a fair market value of $40,000. The old boat had originally cost $36,000 and had an adjusted basis of $16,000 on the date the trade was completed. As part of the exchange, Pearl gave the seller of the new boat her personal dinner ring (which contained a beautiful, black pearl that Pearl had found while diving several years earlier). The dinner ring had a cost basis of $500; it had an estimated fair market value of $17,500 on the date the trade was completed.

a. Taking all the facts stated at their face value, what is the apparent fair market value of Pearl's old (25-foot) boat on the date of this trade? (Assume, in answering this question, that the trade proposed is an arm's-length deal that is entirely fair to both parties.)

b. What amount of gain did Pearl realize because of this trade?

c. What amount of gain must Pearl recognize because of this trade?

d. What is Pearl's tax basis in her new 32-foot boat?

23. Pamela Pearch owned a miniature boat made of 18-karat gold. She purchased this boat as an investment in gold for $12,000. When the price of gold began to fall, Pamela decided to exchange the miniature boat of gold for a sterling silver vase and $1,000 cash. On the date of the exchange, the miniature boat had an estimated fair market value of only $10,000; the sterling silver vase had an estimated fair market value of $9,000. Pamela kept the sterling silver vase solely as an investment; she never removed it (at any time) from her lock box in a bank where she kept all her other investments.

a. What amount of gain (or loss) did Pamela realize because of this trade?

b. What amount of gain (or loss) must Pamela recognize because of this trade?

c. What is Pamela's tax basis in the new sterling silver vase?

24. An investor sold 1,000 shares of IBM stock for $80,000. This investor had paid $20,000 for these shares 20 years earlier. The sale contract calls for a current year payment of $23,000. The $57,000 balance plus 12 percent interest is to be paid one year later. What minimum amount of gross income must this investor report this year? What kind of gain is this?

25. An investor sold undeveloped land for $40,000. This land had cost the investor $15,000 eight years ago. The sale contract called for a down payment of $16,000 with the $24,000 balance to be paid, with 12 percent interest, in three equal annual installments. What minimum amount of gross income must this investor report this year? What kind of gain is this?

SUPPLEMENTAL PROBLEMS

26. Art Stahls, a cash basis taxpayer, began his career as a professional writer in 19x1. He spent most of his first year writing a short but exciting novel, which he attempted to sell to a publisher during November and December. Although several publishers expressed an interest in this novel, only one made Art a firm offer of $3,000 for the manuscript. In March 19x2, he received a second offer, which gave him the option of receiving $5,000 ($3,000 immediately and $2,000 in November, 19x3) or a 15-percent royalty based on actual sales. Art accepted the fixed-price option and received both payments as agreed.

Year	Economics	Accounting	Taxation
19x1			
19x2			
19x3			
Total			

a. Draw up a table like the one above to indicate, as best you can, how each discipline—economics, accounting, and tax law—would likely "recognize" Art's income for the years 19x1-x3.

b. Explain the reasons that account for the differneces in the annual incomes recognized by each discipline, as detailed above.

c. In what year (or years) did Mr. Stahls "realize" his $5,000 income?

d. What changes in the schedule you have made for item a would be appropriate had Mr. Stahls elected the 15 percent royalty rather than the fixed fee? (Explain possible reasons for such changes.)

27. Capital Construction Corporation frequently undertakes contracts that require anywhere from 6 months to 3 years to complete. Relative to its long-term contracts, what accounting method options are available to Capital? Generally, would it be to Capital's advantage to pay the tax as it receives partial payments or to wait and pay the tax at the completion of the entire contract? Explain.

28. In April Lucky was notified that he had won a preliminary round of a sweepstakes contest and that his $2 (cost) ticket had already won $8,000. By winning the preliminary round, he became eligble for the Grand Prize. Before the final selection was made, Lucky gave his winning ticket to his two children, making clear that they could have as a gift any amounts paid on the ticket. Eventually, Lucky's ticket was selected as the sweepstakes winner and the children were paid the $75,00 Grand Prize.

a. When was the $75,000 income realized? How much, if any, of the $75,000 that the children received was a gift and thus not subject to the income tax?

b. What amount of income, if any, must Lucky report?

c. What amount of income, if any, must Lucky's children report?

d. Would the taxable income be ordinary income or capital gain?

29. Ms. Reynard owned acreage on the outskirts of Modest City, California, which she decided to sell. Her basis in this property was only $50,000, although the property had an estimated fair market value of $150,000. After trying to sell the property for three or four months, Ms. Reynard was approached by a realtor who suggested that she exchange her acreage (property A) for another property (B), which was also valued at approximately $150,000. The realtor made this suggestion because he had good reason to believe that he could quickly sell property B for Ms. Reynard and thus earn a substantial commission. Ms. Reynard proceeded to make the exchange, and two weeks later the realtor completed the sale of property B for $160,000 of which the buyer paid $25,000 down.

Ms. Reynard reported the exchange of property A for property B as a Sec. 1031 (nontaxable) exchange and the sale of property B as an installment sale (under the provisions of Sec. 453). Is this a correct tax accounting for the facts indicated? If not, how should these events be reported, and what are the tax consequences of the alternative reporting? Support your conclusion with a citation to a case that involved facts similar to those recounted above.

30. On December 12 of last year, the Board of Schmart Shops, Inc. voted to sell its 500 shares of Inland Steel for $35,000. These 500 shares had been purchased 14 months earlier at a cost of $42,000. On its tax return for last year, Schmart

Shops deducted the $7,000 long-term capital loss on the 500 Inland Steel shares from a $10,000 short-term capital gain it had recognized on another investment sold earlier in the year. On January 8, this year, the Board reviewed its earlier action and, believing the market for Inland Steel was going to increase, voted to purchase 600 shares of Inland Steel at the market price of $71 per share.

a. Was the tax treatment of the Inland Steel investment correctly reported for last year by Schmart Shops, Inc.? Explain.

b. What is Schmart Shops' tax basis in the 600 shares of Inland Steel it acquired on January 8? Explain briefly.

c. If the Board had invested in U. S. Steel, rather than Inland Steel, on January 8, would your answer to part a have been different? Explain.

31. Because she was about to leave on a 36-month overseas assignment, Sarah Levitine decided to exchange her former residence for a new duplex that would make a good investment property. Sarah had paid $42,000 for the home four years earlier; the estimated fair market value of the home (and of the new duplex that she traded it for) was $48,000 at the time of the exchange. Will this exchange qualify for nonrecognition treatment under Section 1031? Explain. How might a slight change in Levitine's actions have changed the tax result in a favorable way? (Again, explain.)

32. Early in 1976, the Bicentennial year, a 26-year-old New Jersey resident, Eric C. Leek, won a state lottery that will pay him $1,776 a week for as long as he lives. If Eric lives a normal life (that is, if he lives as long as a normal life-expectancy table would predict—approximately 76 years), he will collect in excess of $4.5 million from this lottery. Incidentally, the lottery contract provides that his heirs are guaranteed a minimum of $1,847,040 if Eric dies before he has received that amount.

a. According to the general principles of income taxation suggested in this text, what amount of gross income would Eric Leek have had to report in 1976 because of his winning the New Jersey lottery? Explain briefly.

b. Locate Rev. Rul. 62-74 in your library and determine how the I.R.S. taxed a more modest prize payable over a shorter time period. Write a brief summary of that Revenue Ruling.

c. Do you think it likely that the I.R.S. would apply the conclusion of Rev. Rul. 62-74 to the facts of Eric Leek (a true story!)? Why or why not? Explain briefly.

33. Which of the following eight transactions a–h constitute a realization event that ordinarily will trigger the recognition of gain by a cash basis taxpayer? To understand the question better, assume that the property involved is the taxpayer's private residence with a fair market value of $100,000 and a tax basis of $60,000.

a. Sold for $100,000 cash.

b. Sold for $40,000 cash and $60,000 promissory notes.

c. Exchanged for speculative land worth $100,000.

d. Mortgaged home for $75,000 cash. (Invested cash in stock market.)

e. Gave home to daughter and her husband.

f. Left home to church (a charitable organization) by will, at death.

g. Converted personal residence to a rental property.

h. Exchanged for corporate stocks valued at $100,000.

34. a. On page **24**/4 we define a transaction as "any significant change in the form or the substance of a property or property right." Review each of the eight events detailed in Problem 33 and explain briefly what change in property or property rights is involved.

b. On page **24**/4 we go on to suggest that all transactions can be classified as either internal or external. Again review the eight events detailed in Problem 33 and determine which, if any, are properly classified as internal transactions.

c. On page **24**/4 we suggest that as a general rule an external transaction is sufficient to trigger the realization and recognition of gain for tax purposes (barring application of some special statutory provision to the contrary). Review each of the eight events detailed in Problem 33 and determine the three exceptions to the general rule proposed. (Except for these three exceptions, we believe the rule holds. If you think of other exceptions, please let us know!)

Congress has found it desirable to provide a large number of special rules having to do with the timing of income and deductions which, for the most part, make no specific reference to "the method of accounting on the basis of which the taxpayer regularly computes his income in keeping his books."

LESLIE MILLS,
1959 Compendium

recognition postponed:
the common nontaxable exchanges

Subchapter O, Part III, of the Internal Revenue Code contains sections that may be referred to collectively as the "common nontaxable exchanges." They are

Sec. 1031. Exchange of property held for productive use or investment.
Sec. 1032. Exchange of stock for property.
Sec. 1033. Involuntary conversions.
Sec. 1034. Sale or exchange of residence.
Sec. 1035. Certain exchanges of insurance policies.
Sec. 1036. Stock for stock of same corporation.
Sec. 1037. Certain exchanges of United States obligations.
Sec. 1038. Certain reacquisitions of real property.
Sec. 1039. Certain sales of low-income housing projects.
Sec. 1040. Use of certain appreciated carryover basis property to satisfy pecuniary bequest.

In every instance, the important consequence of the section is to establish unequivocally that a specified transaction, which might otherwise trigger the realization and recognition of a taxable gain or a deductible loss, is to be treated as a wholly or partially nontaxable event. Sections 1031, 1033, and 1034 are particularly good illustrations of the wherewithal-to-pay concept. In this chapter, Secs. 1033 and 1034 will be given primary attention; a discussion of Sec. 1031 is not reconsidered here because it was included as an illustration in the preceding chapter. The seven remaining sections of Part III, Subchapter O, will be discussed in a summary fashion only.

In addition to this orderly collection of special rules that may defer the recognition of realized taxa-

ble income (or loss), the Code contains other sections that reach a similar result but are scattered throughout the Code. Three such sections (1091, 267, and 172) will be examined briefly in this chapter to illustrate how the wherewithal-to-pay concept has also been used to deny the recognition of a realized *loss* for tax purposes.

INVOLUNTARY CONVERSION

Gains realized by a taxpayer because of an involuntary conversion of one or more assets generally are not recognized for tax purposes if the taxpayer replaces the property and elects the deferred treatment. This option to defer the recognition of a realized gain is contained in Sec. 1033.

Statutory requirements

Section 1033 in its entirety is a relatively long and complex provision. It includes seven subsections, which deal with such special cases as "property sold pursuant to reclamation laws" [Sec. 1033(c)] and "livestock destroyed by disease" [Sec. 1033(d)]. In actual practice, therefore, it is important for the taxpayer and his or her tax advisor to double-check the Code for special cases whenever they are dealing with an actual involuntary conversion. For purposes of general education, only selected portions of this section need be studied. The following portions are most important:

(a) General Rule.—If property (as a result of its destruction in whole or in part, theft, seizure, or requisition or condemnation or threat or imminence thereof) is compulsorily or involuntarily converted.—

(1) Conversion into similar property.—Into property similar or related in service or use to the property so converted, no gain shall be recognized.

(2) Conversion into money.—Into money or into property not similar or related in service or use to the converted property, the gain (if any) shall be recognized except to the extent hereinafter provided in this paragraph:

(A) Nonrecognition of gain.—If the taxpayer during the period specified in subparagraph (B), for the purpose of replacing the property so converted, purchases other property similar or related in service or use to the property so converted, or purchases stock in the acquisition of control of a corporation owning such other property, at the election of the taxpayer the gain shall be recognized only to the extent that the amount realized upon such conversion (regardless of whether such amount is received in one or more taxable years) exceeds the cost of such other property or such stock. Such election shall be made at such time and in such manner as the Secretary or his delegate may by regulations prescribe. For purposes of this paragraph—

(i) no property or stock acquired before the disposition of the converted property shall be considered to have been acquired for the purpose of replacing such converted property unless held by the taxpayer on the date of such disposition; and

(ii) the taxpayer shall be considered to have purchased property or stock only if, but for the provisions of subsection (c) of this section, the unadjusted basis of such property or stock would be its cost within the meaning of section 1012.[1]

In common language, the recognition of a gain realized on the involuntary conversion of a taxpayer's property generally can be deferred by operation of Sec. 1033 if the taxpayer converts directly or indirectly (within prescribed time periods) into another property that is "similar or related in service or use" to the property involuntarily converted. If the taxpayer invests less in this replacement property than he or she realized on the involuntary conversion, the excess funds retained will be considered as

representing a wherewithal to pay, and the taxpayer will be taxed accordingly. If the proceeds received in the involuntary conversion are less than the taxpayer's basis in the property destroyed, the realized loss will be recognized for tax purposes, provided the property is not held for personal use and the conversion is not a casualty. One especially interesting aspect of this provision is that it permits the taxpayer to acquire "similar or related" property indirectly by acquiring an 80-percent voting interest in a corporation that owns such property. In the routine involuntary conversion, the taxpayer receives an indemnification payment from an insurance company (or a government unit that is condemning the property) and then reinvests this payment in comparable property.

"Similar or related in service or use"

One of the more perplexing phrases in Sec. 1033 is that which requires the replacement property to be "similar or related in service or use" to the property involuntarily converted. Although this requirement may appear to be equivalent to the like-kind requirement of Sec. 1031, the two have been interpreted quite differently. The criterion of "similar or related in service or use" for most involuntary conversions has been interpreted by the I.R.S. and the courts to mean *functionally* related. That is, a delivery truck would have to be replaced with another delivery truck, an apartment complex would have to be replaced with another apartment complex, and so on. In the case of *McCaffrey* v. *Commissioner,* the court found that replacement of a rented parking lot with a rented warehouse was not within the meaning of this phrase.[2] The courts have permitted the replacement of used property with new property as long as the two were functionally related.

Subsection 1033(f) provides a special exception to the "similar or related in service or use" test for condemned *real* property held for productive use in a trade or business or for investment purposes. That special exception says that "property of a like kind . . . shall be treated as property similar or related in service or use to the property so converted." In other words, Subsection 1033(f) effectively substitutes the like-kind test of Sec. 1031 for the similar-or-related-in-service-or-use test of Sec. 1033 in the case

[1] Code Sec. 1033(a).

[2] 275 F.2d 27 (1960).

of condemned real property after 1957. Just why the more liberal rules of Sec. 1031 should be applicable to only real property condemnations is not at all clear; perhaps it speaks to the strength of the real estate lobby in Washington.

Time requirements

If the taxpayer replaces involuntarily converted property indirectly—that is, if the taxpayer goes from property to cash to similar property—it is ncesssary to acquire the replacement property within prescribed time periods if the taxpayer wishes to defer the recognition of gain. These requirements are stipulated in Sec. 1033(a)(2)(B) as follows:

> (B) Period within which property must be replaced.—The period referred to in subparagraph (A) shall be the period beginning with the date of the disposition of the converted property, or the earliest date of the threat or imminence of requisition or condemnation of the converted property, whichever is the earlier, and ending—
> (i) two years after the close of the first taxable year in which any part of the gain upon the conversion is realized, or
> (ii) subject to such terms and conditions as may be specified by the Secretary or his delegate, at the close of such later date as the Secretary or his delegate may designate on application by the taxpayer. Such application shall be made at such time and in such manner as the Secretary or his delegate may by regulations prescribe.

In other words, the taxpayer must make the replacement sometime during a period beginning with the earlier of (1) the date of disposition of the converted property or (2) "the date of the beginning of the threat or imminence of requisition or condemnation,"[3] and ending (a) two years after the close of the taxable year in which any part of the gain was first realized or (b) at a later date if such an agreement has been reached between the taxpayer and the I.R.S. A special rule applies to the involuntary conversion of real property used in a trade or business or held for investment. For condemned real property (only) after October 3, 1976, the replacement period is three years, not the two-year period applicable to all other properties. Generally, the I.R.S. is lenient in granting extensions beyond the periods allowed by the law, especially where taxpayers can show that

they have made a bona fide effort to acquire replacement property.

The few practical problems that arise in relation to timely replacements of involuntarily converted property typically arise in conjunction with condemnation proceedings. It is sometimes difficult to know exactly what event should be deemed the first threat or imminence of requisition or condemnation. Rumors may precede actual condemnation action by a governmental body by several years. Obviously, if a taxpayer makes a direct replacement with similar property, time requirements cannot be a problem.

An illustration

The following assumed facts will illustrate the most important aspects of Code Sec. 1033. Taxpayer F's warehouse was completely destroyed by fire on the morning of March 1, 19x1. This warehouse had a basis in F's hands of $200,000; it had been insured for its estimated fair market value of $250,000. On October 1, 19x1, the insurance company settled the claim by paying taxpayer F $240,000. Although taxpayer F has realized a $40,000 gain on this involuntary conversion in 19x1, it will not be necessary to recognize that gain if (1) sometime before December 31, 19x3, he or she replaces the destroyed warehouse with another warehouse costing $240,000 or more or (2) during the same time period he or she acquires for $240,000 or more an 80-percent voting control of a corporation that owns such a warehouse.

If taxpayer F replaces the warehouse with another costing less than $240,000, some part or all of the realized gain must be recognized. The following tabulation suggests the importance of the wherewithal-to-pay concept in determining the amount of gain to be recognized in this situation:

Insurance proceeds	Gain realized	Amount reinvested	Gain recognized
$240,000	$40,000	$210,000	$30,000
240,000	40,000	150,000	40,000
240,000	40,000	260,000	0

In short, the recognized gain will always be the lesser of the gain realized or the portion of the insurance proceeds not reinvested in replacement property.

If we modify the above illustration and assume that the insurance company paid taxpayer F only $170,000 (because of a coinsurance clause or some other requirement), it is immaterial whether the tax-

[3]Reg. Sec. 1.1033(a)-2(c)(3).

payer replaces the property or not. Under any assumption, he or she would recognize the $30,000 loss realized.

Basis adjustment

If a taxpayer properly elects to defer the recognition of a gain realized on an involuntary conversion, the replacement property will take a substituted basis. Because boot ordinarily is not a problem in the involuntary conversion cases, the basis of the replacement property is most readily computed using the following formula:

$$\begin{pmatrix} \text{Cost of} \\ \text{replacement} \\ \text{property} \end{pmatrix} - \begin{pmatrix} \text{Gain not recognized} \\ \text{on the involuntary} \\ \text{conversion} \end{pmatrix}$$
$$= \begin{pmatrix} \text{Substituted basis} \\ \text{of replacement} \\ \text{property} \end{pmatrix}$$

This formula is essentially equivalent to the Method II formula on page 24/10, excluding the possibility of nonrecognition of losses. As is apparent in the basis adjustment process, the intention of Sec. 1033 is to permit only a temporary deferment of gain.

Replacing a principal residence

Section 1034 provides a mandatory, special rule that defers any gain a taxpayer realizes on the sale or exchange of his or her principal residence. As usual in tax matters, certain conditions must be satisfied before this special rule will be applicable.

STATUTORY REQUIREMENTS   Once again this Code section is a relatively long and complex provision. The most important and common restricting conditions, however, are stated in Subsection 1034(a), which reads as follows:

> (a) Nonrecognition of Gain.—If property (in this section called "old residence") used by the taxpayer as his principal residence is sold by him, and, within a period beginning 18 months before the date of such sale and ending 18 months after such date, property (in this section called "new residence") is purchased and used by the taxpayer as his principal residence, gain (if any) from such sale shall be recognized only to the extent that the taxpayer's adjusted sales price (as defined in subsection (b)) of the old residence exceeds the taxpayer's cost of purchasing the new residence.

The remaining subsections deal with many special cases including the tenant-stockholder in a cooperative housing corporation (1034(f)); members of the armed forces (1034(h)); and condemnation of homes (1034(i)). Thus, a tax advisor must always determine if any special rule might apply to a particular situation. The general rules, however, are adequately covered in Subsection 1034(a).

The important consequence of that subsection is that it provides that under specified circumstances a (pure) capital gain that has been realized need not be recognized for tax purposes in the year it is first realized. The important conditions for this result to obtain include occupancy of the old residence as a principal residence prior to sale; acquisition of a new principal residence within 18 months (generally) from the date of sale of the old residence; and an investment in the new residence in an amount equal to or greater than the "adjusted sales price" of the old residence.

These general rules, as broadly stated above, are replete with exceptions and definitional distinctions not apparent to the uninitiated. For example, a taxpayer who owns more than one home can receive the special treatment only on the home that constitutes his or her "principal residence." If a taxpayer begins to construct a new home within 18 months before or after the sale of the old one, he or she has 2 years (rather than 18 months) before he or she must occupy the new residence. (But this special exception does not apply if the taxpayer buys a home that a contractor had already started to build as a speculative venture.) The period of time a taxpayer has to acquire a new home is extended to four years if either the taxpayer is a U. S. citizen working overseas or the taxpayer serves on extended active duty with the United States military services in the interim. The term "principal residence" includes condominiums and cooperative apartments as well as mobile homes and houseboats. Finally, the meanings of "adjusted sales price" and "selling expenses" are specifically detailed in the Code and the related Regulations.

AN ILLUSTRATION   Although the special exceptions and restricted definitions noted above can be most important in particular fact cases, a thorough understanding of each of these is not necessary for an appreciation of the general application of Sec. 1034. The important general concept can be demonstrated simply as in Figure 25-1.

Suppose that a taxpayer purchased a home 10 years ago for $28,000 and sold this same home this

FIGURE **25-1**   Diagram of Section 1034

Sales Price (Old Home)
− Selling Expenses[a]

= Amount Realized   *less* Adjusted Basis (Old Home)   *equals*   Gain Realized
− Fixing-up Expenses[b]   *less*

= Adjusted Sales Price   *less* Cost of New Home   *equals*   Gain Recognized[c]
                              ↓
                    less ──────────────────────────→   Gain Not Recognized
                                                          equals
                                                          Tax Cost Basis (New Home)

[a] Perhaps the most important "selling expense" is the broker's commission. See Reg. Sec. 1.1034-1(b) (4).
[b] "Fixing-up expenses" are defined rather narrowly in Reg. Sec. 1.1034-1(b) (6). The phrase refers to expenses incurred to help sell a property and includes such things as painting and papering a home. To qualify, however, these expenses must be incurred and paid within specified time periods. See a tax service for further details.
[c] Only if > 0; also, "gain recognized" can never be > "gain realized."

year for $44,500 cash. Were it not for Sec. 1034, the taxpayer would have to recognize a taxable gain of $13,500. Because of Sec. 1034, however, he or she may not have to recognize part or all the gain *if* a new home is purchased within 18 months. Let's assume, in fact, that the taxpayer paid a $3,000 realtor's commission on the sale of the old home; that fixing-up expenses of $1,500 were incurred preparing the old home for sale; and $50,000 was invested in a new home five months later. Given these additional facts, and substituting pertinent data in the diagram, we can conclude that this taxpayer need recognize none of the gain this year and that the tax basis of the new home is $36,500. The calculation is shown in Figure 25-2.

The relation of Sec. 1034 to the wherewithal-to-pay concept is demonstrated even more vividly if we assume, in the above example, that the taxpayer invested only $38,500 in the new home. In that event, this taxpayer would be forced to recognize a gain of

$1,500 ($40,000 adjusted sales price less $38,500 cost of new home). In a very important sense, this $1,500 of recognized taxable income is equal to this person's wherewithal to pay. The calculation process takes account of the fact that the taxpayer had expenses of sale and that he or she purchased another home. Even after considering all of these facts, however, this taxpayer had $1,500 "left over," which therefore must be recognized as taxable income.

Notice also that the effect of Sec. 1034 (alone) does *not* permanently excuse the taxpayer from paying income taxes on this realized gain. The technique used to *defer* the gain temporarily is the basis adjustment. Although the taxpayer in the original example paid $50,000 for the new home, the tax basis in the new property is reduced by the amount of gain *not* recognized on the sale of the old home. Thus, if and when the taxpayer finally decides to sell the "new" home, and if at that time the taxpayer does not elect

FIGURE **25-2**   Applying Section 1034

$44,500   Sales Price (Old Home)
− 3,000   Selling Expenses

= $41,500   Amount Realized   *less* $28,000 Adjusted Basis (Old Home) *equals* $13,500 Gain Realized
− 1,500   Fixing-up Expenses   *less*

= $40,000   Adjusted Sales Price   *less* $50,000 Cost of New Home *equals*   0 Gain Recognized
                                          ↓
                                                                            equals
                    less ──────────────────────────→ $13,500 Gain Not Recognized

                                                          equals

                                                          $36,500 Tax Basis of New Home

to purchase another residence that costs at least as much as the adjusted sales price of the home sold, then the taxpayer must recognize the gain previously deferred. To illustrate, assume all facts as originally stated and further assume that two years later this taxpayer sold the new home for $51,000 without incurring any additional brokerage fees or fixing-up expenses. If the taxpayer decides to reside in a rented apartment for the next few years, then he or she will have to recognize at that time a $14,500 gain on the sale of the home. Effectively this recognized gain would consist of the $13,500 gain deferred on the original sale and the additional $1,000 gain attributable to the last home ($51,000 sales price less $50,000 cost). Because the taxpayer elected not to reinvest in a new home he or she supposedly has the wherewithal to pay taxes on the entire gain at the later date.

SPECIAL RULE FOR OLDER TAXPAYERS   Section 121 provides an *exclusion* for part or all of the gain realized on the sale of a residence by a taxpayer 55 years of age or older. Although this special provision is really an exception to the wherewithal-to-pay concept of this chapter, it must be part of any discussion relative to the gain from the sale of a personal residence.

If a taxpayer is 55 years of age or older at the time his or her residence is sold; if that sale (or exchange) was made after July 26, 1978; and if the taxpayer at the time of the sale has resided in the house for at least five of the eight years prior to sale, then up to $100,000 of the gain realized may be permanently excluded. To illustrate, let's assume that a 56-year-old taxpayer sold the home in Figure 25-2 and that he or she qualified for and elected to apply Sec. 121 privileges. In that event, the entire $13,500 gain realized could be permanently excluded from income even if the taxpayer did not purchase another home. This is, however, a once-in-a-lifetime election. And if the realized gain exceeds $100,000, only that amount can be excluded from gross income.

REPORTING CONSIDERATIONS   Because the rules that determine the proper tax treatment of the gain realized on the sale or exchange of a home are reasonably complicated, and because sales of residences are commonplace, the I.R.S. has prepared a special form to help the taxpayer report properly. The 1979 Form 2119 is illustrated in Figure 25-3. We have entered on that form the assumed facts of Figure 25-2. The results are, of course, the same as

those previously determined without the help of the form. If the taxpayer in Figure 25-3 were 55 or older and wanted to claim the once-in-a-lifetime exclusion, under Sec. 121, lines 15 through 20 of this form would also have to be completed.

The special $100,000 exclusion for older taxpayers is intended to help avoid the taxation of the only savings available for retirement for many lower income taxpayers. The often illusory (monetary) gain realized on the sale of a home owned for many years may thus be triply protected: by the "rollover" provisions of Sec. 1034; by the exclusion of Sec. 121; and by the capital gain deduction of Sec. 1202.

A COMPARISON

The observant student will have noted many similarities between the Code provisions for the deferral of gain on the sale of a residence (Sec. 1034), the deferral of gain on the exchange of productive use or investment properties (Sec. 1031), and the deferral of gain on an involuntary conversion (Sec. 1033). The most important similarity is that in each instance the gain that may be recognized is determined in large measure by the taxpayer's wherewithal to pay following a given transaction or series of transactions. Table 25-1 depicts the major similarities and differences between these Code sections.

OTHER COMMON NONTAXABLE EXCHANGES

We have now discussed three of the common nontaxable exchanges, which are of general interest to most taxpayers; the other provisions contained in Part III of Subchapter O are of limited interest.

Section 1032 provides that a corporate taxpayer need not recognize any taxable gain when it receives money or other property in exchange for its own stock. Since 1954 this conclusion has been equally valid if the shares issued are treasury shares or original issue. Prior to 1954 a corporation had to recognize gain or loss on treasury share transactions as if they were stock in another corporation.

By operation of Sec. 1036, a stockholder need not recognize any taxable gain on the exchange of stock for essentially identical stock of the same corporation. Thus a taxpayer may avoid any recognition of gain realized on the exchange of common shares for

FIGURE 25-3

Sale or Exchange of Personal Residence

Form 2119

Department of the Treasury
Internal Revenue Service

▶ See instructions on back.
▶ Attach to Form 1040.

1979

Note: Do not include expenses that are deductible as moving expenses on Form 3903.

Name(s) as shown on Form 1040

Your social security number

		Yes	No
1(a) Date former residence sold ▶ 10-4-80			
(b) Have you ever postponed any gain on the sale or exchange of a personal residence?			X
(c) Have you ever claimed a credit for purchase or construction of a new principal residence? (If "Yes," see Form 5405.)			X

(d) If you were on active duty in the U.S. Armed Forces or outside of the U.S. after the date of sale of former residence, enter dates. From _____ to _____

(e) If married at time of sale, was the residence owned by: ☐ you, ☐ your spouse, ☐ both of you.

(f) Social security number of spouse at time of sale, if different from number on Form 1040 ▶

2(a) Date new residence was bought ▶ 12-18-79

(b) If new residence was constructed by you, date construction began ▶

(c) Date you occupied new residence ▶ 12-19-79

	Yes	No
(d) If you answered "Yes" to 1(c), did anyone live in your new replacement residence before you did?		

		Yes	No
(e) Were both the old and new properties used as your principal residence?		X	
(f) Were any rooms in either residence rented out or used for business at any time? (If "Yes," see note in line 8 and attach computation.)			X
(g) If you were married, do you and your spouse have the same proportionate ownership interest in your new residence as you had in your old residence? (If "No," see the Consent below.)		X	

3 (a) Were you 55 or over on date of sale? Was your spouse 55 or over on date of sale?

(b) If you answered "Yes" to 3(a), did you own and use the property sold as your principal residence for a total of at least 3 years (except for short temporary absences) of the 5-year period before the sale? (If you are 65 or over, see instruction C.)

(c) If you answered "Yes" to 3(b), do you elect to exclude gain on the sale from your gross income? (If "Yes," check Yes box and fill in lines 15–20 below.)

Computation of Gain and Adjusted Sales Price

4 Selling price of residence. (Do not include selling price of personal property items.)	4	$44,500
5 Commissions and other expenses of sale	5	3,000
6 Amount realized (subtract line 5 from line 4)	6	41,500
7 Basis of residence sold	7	28,000
8 Gain on sale (subtract line 7 from line 6). If line 7 is more than line 6 there is no gain. Do not complete the rest of form. A loss on the sale of a personal residence is not deductible	8	13,500

Note: Do not include in line 8 the amount attributable to rented rooms or other business purposes; instead, report separately on Form 4797.

9 Fixing-up expenses	9	1,500
10 Adjusted sales price (subtract line 9 from line 6)	10	40,000

Computation of Gain to be Reported and Adjusted Basis of New Residence
(Complete lines 11 through 14 if you did not check "Yes" to question 3(c).)

11 Cost of new residence	11	50,000
12 Gain taxable this year (line 10 less line 11, but not more than line 8). If line 11 is more than line 10, enter zero. Enter on Schedule D (Form 1040), line 1 or 9, column g	12	-0-
13 Gain on which tax is to be postponed (subtract line 12 from line 8)	13	13,500
14 Adjusted basis of new residence (subtract line 13 from line 11)	14	36,500

Exclusion, Gain to be Reported, and Adjusted Basis of New Residence
(For use of taxpayers 55 years of age or over who checked "Yes" in 3(c) above.)

15 Exclusion: Enter the smaller of line 8 or $100,000 ($50,000, if married filing separately)	15	
16 Part of gain included (subtract line 15 from line 8)	16	
17 Cost of new residence. If a new personal residence was not bought, enter "None," and do not complete the rest of form. Enter the amount from line 16 on Schedule D (Form 1040), line 9, column g	17	
18 Gain taxable this year. (Subtract the sum of lines 15 and 17 from line 10.) This amount may not be more than line 16. If line 17 plus line 15 is more than line 10, enter zero. Enter here and on Schedule D (Form 1040), line 9, column g	18	
19 Gain on which tax is to be postponed (subtract line 18 from line 16)	19	
20 Adjusted basis of new residence (subtract line 19 from line 17)	20	

Consent of You and Your Spouse to Apply Separate Gain on Sale of Old Residence to Basis of New Residence
(Applies only if you and your same spouse use both residences as your principal residence. See instruction D.)

The undersigned taxpayers, you and your spouse, consent to have the basis of the joint or separate interest in the new residence reduced by the amount of the joint or separate gain on the sale of the old residence which is not taxable only because of the filing of this Consent.

Your signature ▶ _____ Date ▶ _____

Spouse's signature ▶ _____ Date ▶ _____

		Your part	Spouse's part
21 Adjusted sales price of old residence (from line 10)	21		
22 Cost of new residence (from line 11 or 17)	22		

TABLE **25-1**

COMPARISON OF SECTIONS 1031, 1033, and 1034

Comparison	Sec. 1031: Exchange of productive-use or investment property	Sec. 1033: Involuntary conversions	Sec. 1034: Sale of a residence
1. Gain recognized, if any, is the lesser of the gain realized or . . .	Boot received	Proceeds not reinvested in similar property	Proceeds not reinvested in another residence
2. Indirect as well as direct conversion permitted?	No	Yes	Yes
3. Time allowed for replacement?	None; must be a direct exchange	Generally 2 years after end of year gain was first realized	18 months if existing home is acquired; 2 years if new home is constructed
4. Is provision mandatory or elective?	Mandatory	Elective	Mandatory with gains
5. Can loss be recognized if realized?	No; but basis carryover is permitted	Yes, always	Never: home is a purely personal asset

common shares in the same corporation or preferred shares for preferred shares in the same corporation. One important conclusion of this provision is that gains that might be considered realized by the declaration of a stock split will not be recognized for tax purposes.

Section 1035 provides for nonrecognition of gain or loss realized on the exchange of certain life insurance policies. The nontaxable exchanges possible under this provision include those of contracts of life insurance for other contracts of life insurance, for endowment insurance, or for an annuity contract; endowment insurance for other endowment insurance, as long as payments under the new contract will begin no later than they would have under the old contract; endowment insurance for an annuity contract; and annuity contracts for other annuity contracts.

Section 1037 permits the tax-free exchange of certain United States obligations. Special rules apply to the exchange of United States obligations issued at a discount.

Section 1039 was added by the Tax Reform Act of 1969 as an incentive to increase investments in a particular type of housing. This section authorizes the nonrecognition of gain realized on the sale of a low-income housing unit to its tenants or occupants, or to a nonprofit organization formed solely for the benefit of such persons. Before nonrecognition privileges will be granted, the sale must be approved by the Secretary of Housing and Urban Development. The seller has one year after the end of the year in which the sale was made to reinvest in another qualified housing project. Failure to reinvest in a qualified project within the prescribed time period, or failure to reinvest the entire proceeds of the sale, will cause the recognition of all or part of the gain realized. Also, following the usual rules, the cost basis of the new property is its cost less any gain not recognized on the related sale. The holding periods of the two properties generally tack. However, if the investment in the new property exceeds the amount realized on the sale of the old property, the additional investment is treated as a separate property with a new holding period for purposes of recapture of depreciation under Sec. 1250.

The newest of the common nontaxable exchanges, Sec. 1040, allows an executor to satisfy a pecuniary bequest with an appreciated carryover basis property without triggering the recognition of gain in the estate. This special treatment does not apply, however, to any gain occurring after the property is valued for estate purposes and before the date it is distributed.

Anyone interested in the many specific details applicable to Sections 1032, 1035, 1036, 1037, 1038, 1039, or 1040 should consult a current and authoritative tax service. Only the highlights of these provisions have been noted here.

LOSSES AND WHEREWITHAL TO PAY

The wherewithal-to-pay concept seems to have pertinence also to the nonrecognition of losses in certain circumstances. As briefly explained on page **20/4**, the loss realized on a "wash sale" will not be recognized for tax purposes even though it would be recognized for accounting purposes. If a taxpayer elects to repurchase (within thirty days before or after a sale) securities "substantially identical" to those just sold at a loss, it is generally apparent that the taxpayer has not suffered a real economic loss. That is, his or her early repurchase of substantially identical securities would suggest that this taxpayer was quite willing to retain a basic investment in a particular security and that the apparent reason for selling the security was solely to realize a loss that might reduce reported taxable income. Under these circumstances the Code provides in Sec. 1091 that the realized loss will not be recognized. This treatment can be justified *because* the taxpayer did not suffer an actual reduction in wherewithal to pay by going through the formalities of a sale and almost immediate repurchase of identical securities. If the taxpayer is willing to switch the investment to shares of another firm in the same industry, then he or she can recognize the loss, since these shares will not be considered to be "substantially identical" to those sold.

For essentially the same reasons, Sec. 267 denies a taxpayer the right to deduct a loss realized on the sale of property to a "related taxpayer." Among the relationships specified are family members and corporations in which the seller owns an interest of 50 percent or more. In the interest of equity, the related purchaser can add any disallowed loss to the tax basis of the acquired property, but only for purposes of determining gain.

A third possible illustration of the importance of wherewithal to pay and the recognition of losses is implicit in the statutory provisions for a net operating loss. Although the details of these provisions, Sec. 172, are as complex as any in the Code, the essential feature can be grasped quickly. If a taxpayer has greater deductions than recognizable gross income in any year, he or she ordinarily is granted a "net

operating loss deduction," which is first carried back three years and used to redetermine taxable income in that earlier year. If the loss carryback deduction is greater than adjusted taxable income in that year, the taxpayer proceeds to recalculate tax liability for the second preceding year. In other words, a taxpayer who incurs a net operating loss in 19x4 will *first* carry the loss back to recalculate taxable income in 19x1. If some loss remains after reducing that year's taxable income to zero, he or she will then carry the remaining loss back to recalculate taxable income in 19x2; if additional loss remains, the taxpayer proceeds to redetermine taxable income for 19x3. Based upon these redeterminations of taxable income, the taxpayer may be entitled to a refund of part or all of the income tax paid in the three preceding years. If the net operating loss is greater than the *adjusted* taxable income for the three preceding years combined, the taxpayer may proceed to carry the remaining loss forward for as long as the next seven years. If, at that time, additional loss remains, it is permanently lost as a deduction by the taxpayer.

Thanks to the Tax Reform Act of 1976, a taxpayer may now elect to ignore the carry*back* aspects of a net operating loss and carry *forward* (only) any net operating loss incurred after December 31, 1975. In other words, a taxpayer need *not* carry a net operating loss back to any prior year if it would be preferable to carry that same loss forward to the next seven years, for years after 1975. The relative value of a carryback and/or a carryforward is, of course, directly dependent upon the marginal tax rate of the taxpayer in the various years. In many cases a new taxpayer earns relatively modest amounts of taxable income in the first few years of doing business. Consequently, these are frequently low marginal tax-rate years. If in, say, the fourth or fifth year of business a corporation were to report a loss, it might well elect to forgo the immediate refund based on low marginal tax rates for a future deduction that could be offset against anticipated larger incomes to be taxed at progressively higher tax rates in future years.

The relation between the wherewithal-to-pay concept and net operating losses is best demonstrated by the adjustments that must be made to "negative taxable income" before it is converted into a "net operating loss deduction." In general, the taxpayer must "add back" to negative taxable income those deductions that are ordinarily allowed but do not require the disposition of any funds. Thus, for example, an individual taxpayer may have to add back personal exemption deductions and the long-term capital-gain deduction before he or she could begin to carry back a net operating loss.

To illustrate an overly simplified net operating loss (NOL) calculation for an individual taxpayer, assume that a single person reported the following items of gross income and deduction:

Revenue (sole proprietorship, Schedule C, Form 1040)		$ 70,000
Less operating expenses of sole proprietorship		(120,000)
Net business loss		($50,000)
Net capital gain	$40,000	
Less long-term capital gain deduction	(24,000)	16,000
Adjusted gross income		($34,000)
Less personal exemption deduction		(1,000)
Taxable income (negative amount)		($35,000)

Although this taxpayer has a $35,000 negative taxable income, he or she would not have a net operating loss deduction of that amount. As noted earlier, this taxpayer would have to add back the $24,000 long-term capital gain deduction and the $1,000 personal exemption deduction in determining his or her NOL deduction. In other words, in this example the NOL carryback would be only $10,000. The amounts to be added back may include several items not illustrated

here; in addition, some of the add-backs illustrated here may be further affected by their "business" or "nonbusiness" character if the taxpayer had other items of income and deduction. Anyone interested in the details of the NOL deduction should consult a current tax reference work.

The obvious effect of adding back deductions is to equate the loss recognized more closely with the real dollar loss sustained. In short, the taxpayer's wherewithal to pay is deemed to be greater than the unadjusted negative income would suggest. The carryback provisions associated with the net operating loss provide another interesting aspect of wherewithal to pay: The potential refund of three previous years' taxes may help a taxpayer by providing him or her with additional cash when he or she most needs it.

In summary, the Code contains numerous provisions that have the effect of determining taxable income as much on the basis of taxpayer's wherewithal to pay as on the basis of gains or losses realized during a given year. The accountant in particular should understand that numerous good reasons exist in support of these nonrecognition provisions for tax purposes. Realization may indeed be a more important concept than wherewithal to pay for the determination of income for financial reporting purposes. That conclusion does not, however, necessitate the same conclusion for the recognition of *taxable* income.

PROBLEMS

1. Assume the following facts apply to an involuntary conversion of business property, and complete the schedule.

	Adjusted basis of property destroyed	Insurance proceeds	Amount expended for immediate replacement of property	Recognized gain (or loss)	Basis of new property
a.	$26,000	$16,000	$24,000	$——	$——
b.	17,000	21,000	20,000	——	——
c.	20,000	25,000	27,000	——	——

2. Investo Corporation purchased several acres of land in 1936 for $400. This year that land was taken by the state government to be used for highway right of way, and the taxpayer was awarded $21,000 for the land. Investo first received notification of the prospective conversion on January 4 and received full payment for the land on November 30. In each of the following cases, compute

(1) the recognized gain or loss on the conversion under Sec. 1033 and (2) the tax basis of the replacement property in those cases where the property was replaced.

    a. The land was not replaced.

    b. New land was purchased on June 1 for $16,000.

    c. New land was purchased on December 1 for $22,000.

    d. New land was purchased on December 1 for $10,200.

    e. New land was purchased on December 1 of the next following year for $24,000.

    f. New land was purchased on June 10 of the second following year for $30,000.

3. Categorize each of the following as (1) a like-kind exchange, (2) a replacement of similar property, or (3) neither.

    a. Inventory of a trade or business is exchanged for an automobile to be used in a trade or business.

    b. Land and a building used in a trade or business are exchanged for unimproved land that will be held for investment.

    c. Common stock held by an individual is traded for land that will be held as an investment.

    d. Manufacturing machinery used to produce metal tanks is destroyed by fire; proceeds are used to acquire machines used to produce combat boots.

    e. An office building held as rental property is condemned by the city for a new park. Proceeds are used to acquire farm land, which is rented immediately following acquisition.

    f. A dump truck used by a dirt contractor is exchanged for a family car.

    g. Machinery used to produce farm equipment is exchanged for office furniture that will be placed in rental property.

    h. Unimproved land is exchanged for machinery to be used in a trade or business.

    i. Four bulls are exchanged for 12 heifers by a rancher.

4. In 1960 Tom Fahr purchased an $18,000 frame house for his family. Eventually this house became too small for Tom and his growing family, so in April of this year, he sold the frame house for $32,000. The broker's fee on the sale was $1,900; Tom incurred $600 in fixing-up expenses prior to completing the sale. On June 1 the Fahr family moved into their new brick house. What gross income must the Fahrs report this year because of the sale of their frame house if

    a. The new residence cost them $40,000?

    b. The new residence cost them $30,000?

    c. The new residence cost them $26,000?

What is the tax basis for the Fahrs' brick house in each of the above situations?

5. A taxpayer purchased a residence in 1950 for $10,000. This year he sold the home for $21,000. In order to sell the house he incurred and paid "fixing-up" costs of $300 in the month before sale. Also, he paid a real estate agent a commission of $1,260. Seven months after the sale of the old residence, the taxpayer purchased a new mobile home for $26,000. (It is a primary residence.)

    a. What is the amount of gain recognized by the taxpayer under Sec. 1034?

    b. What would be the tax basis of the new home under Sec. 1034?

6. Assume the same facts as those in Problem 5, above, except that the new mobile home cost $15,400.

    a. Under Sec. 1034 what would be the recognized gain on the sale?

    b. What would be the tax basis of the new mobile home?

7. This year Mr. Elder (age 64) sold his residence for $140,000. He and Mrs. Elder had lived in this home since 1940. They originally paid $18,000 for the home, but they immediately remodeled it at a cost of $3,000. Since then only routine upkeep was required. The Elders paid a realtor $8,400 commission for selling the house; they also incurred fixing-up expenses of $500 one month prior to the sale. One month after selling their home, the Elders purchased a small cottage on a nearby lake for $48,000. They intend to make this lake cottage their home whenever they are not traveling.
   a. What minimum amount of gain must the Elders include on their tax return this year because of the sale of their old home?
   b. Would this be a capital gain or ordinary income?
   c. If Mr. Elder had been 54, rather than 64, when he sold this home, what minimum amount of gain would he have been required to report as taxable income?
8. Discuss briefly the rationale behind
   a. The "wash sale" provisions.
   b. Net operating loss provisions.
9. Jetstream Airlines, a Delaware corporation, reported the following taxable income during years 1 through 5:

Year	Taxable income
1	$ 82,500
2	23,000
3	190,000
4	230,000
5	(250,000)

The large loss in year 5 was attributable to a general strike that lasted for over four months and increased labor costs after settlement by 14 percent. Explain, in general, how Jetstream will handle this net operating loss.
10. Taxpayer, age 57, sold her former home for $132,500. Broker's commission on this sale was $8,000. Fixing-up expenses totaled $350. Taxpayer's basis in her old home was $24,000. What is the minimum amount taxpayer must reinvest in a new home if she is to avoid any recognition of taxable gain this year (assuming she makes the election to exclude as much of her gain as possible)?
11. On March 19, 1956, Red inherited a home from his mother. His mother's basis in this home was $40,000; it was valued at $50,000 for estate tax purposes. Red immediately occupied the home as his own primary residence.
   On May 15, 1964, Red sold this home for $60,000. Broker's commission on the sale was $3,600. Two weeks prior to making this sale, Red purchased a new primary residence for $55,000.
   On July 24, 1971, Red's residence was condemned by the State Highway Commission. Red received a condemnation award of $60,000. On November 22, 1971, Red purchased his next primary residence for $56,000 and elected to pay the minimum possible tax for 1971.
   On February 14, 1975, Red gave his primary residence to his daughter as a wedding gift. On the day of the gift the home was valued at $60,000. Red paid a gift tax of $1,500 before leaving for a round-the-world cruise.
   On December 15 of this year, Red's daughter sold the home, which she had occupied as her primary residence since February 15, 1975, for $65,000. Because she sold the home herself, there was no commission on this sale. She elected to move into a rented apartment and has no intention of returning to home ownership in the near future. What gain or loss must Red's daughter recognize on the sale she made this year?

12. State whether each of the following statements is true or false. If false, explain why.

   a. The "like-kind" requirement of Sec. 1031 is generally interpreted more narrowly than the "similar or related in service or use" requirement of Sec. 1033.

   b. Any item of inventory must be considered as boot in an exchange that otherwise qualifies under Sec. 1031.

   c. An exchange of realty for personalty may sometimes qualify as a "like-kind" exchange under Sec. 1031.

   d. Loss may not be recognized following an involuntary conversion if the taxpayer reinvests all proceeds in similar property within the time period specified in Sec. 1033.

   e. Giving boot in a like-kind exchange will not necessitate the recognition of gain by the taxpayer giving the boot.

13. On April 18 Tom's Cleaners, Inc., had one of its delivery vans completely destroyed in an auto accident. The van had an adjusted basis of $3,200 at the time of the accident. Straight-line depreciation of $4,000 had been claimed on the van before the accident. Insurance proceeds of $5,000 were received on May 1. On April 20, Tom's Cleaners, Inc., purchased a new delivery van for $8,000.

   a. What amount of gain did Tom's Cleaners, Inc., realize because of the accident?

   b. What *minimum* amount of gain must Tom's Cleaners, Inc., recognize because of the accident?

   c. If Tom's Cleaners, Inc., recognizes only the minimum amount of gain, what is the tax basis in the van purchased on April 20?

   d. What *maximum* amount of gain may Tom's Cleaners, Inc., recognize because of the accident? What kind of gain is this?

   e. If Tom's Cleaners, Inc., recognizes the maximum amount of gain, what is its tax basis in the van purchased on April 20?

14. Taxpayer purchased a primary residence in 1965 for $18,000. She sold that same residence for $38,000 this year. In order to sell the home, however, taxpayer incurred and paid fixing-up expenses of $400 and a real estate commission of $2,280. Three months after this sale, but within the current year, taxpayer purchased a new home for $35,500. Taxpayer is 40 years old.

   a. What amount of gain did taxpayer realize because of the home sale?

   b. What *minimum* amount of gain must taxpayer recognize because of the home sale?

   c. If taxpayer recognizes only the minimum amount of gain, what is the tax basis of the new home?

15. Plush resides in his palatial home in Austin, Texas. During the year, Plush sold his Lake Travis cottage for $40,000. Plush has occupied this cottage for 4 to 6 weeks each year since building it for $28,000 4 years ago. Plush paid fixing-up expenses of $200 and a real estate commission of $2,400 to sell the cottage. Two months later Plush purchased a mobile land cruiser for $42,000, which he intends to use as his "vacation home."

   a. What amount of gain did Plush realize because of the sale of his Lake Travis cottage?

   b. What *minimum* amount of gain must Plush recognize because of the sale of his Lake Travis cottage?

   c. If Plush recognizes only the minimum amount of gain, what is the tax basis of his new mobile land cruiser?

16. Embryo, Inc., suffered a net operating loss of $10,000 in 19x4. The loss was

attributable to circumstances that management does not expect to recur. Embryo, Inc., has reported taxable income since its inception in 19x1 as follows:

Year	Taxable income
19x1	$ 5,000
19x2	30,000
19x3	90,000
19x4	(10,000)

Management projects Embryo's taxable income to be $150,000 in 19x5. Using current corporate tax rates in all years (19x1 through 19x5), explain the potential value of the 19x4 corporate net operating loss by completing the following blanks: Management has a choice; it may elect to receive a refund of $_____immediately or hope for a deduction worth as much as $_____next year.

SUPPLEMENTAL PROBLEMS

17. In 1950 Mr. and Mrs. Sword purchased for $12,000 an old, rundown home located on a twelve-acre tract of land on the outskirts of Small City, U.S.A. Of the $12,000 cost, $2,000 was allocable to the old home. The Swords invested $10,000 in remodeling this old home and used the acreage for lawn and a large garden. By this year the growing city had completely surrounded the Sword property, and a builder-developer offered them a new home (estimated fair market value was $55,000) and $25,000 cash for the old property. The Swords accepted this offer and moved into their new home late this year.

In order to determine their gain on this sale as well as their basis in the new home, the Swords requested formal appraisals of their old property from two knowledgeable realtors. Each of the realtors estimated the value of the old property at $80,000. However, one estimated the value of the old home at $25,000, and the value of the acreage at $55,000; the other realtor estimated the value of the old home at $40,000 and the acreage at $40,000.

At the time of this sale-exchange, Mr. and Mrs. Sword were 53 and 54 years of age, respectively. They intended to reside in their new home until Mr. Sword reached retirement age (62), at which time they planned to sell the new home and move into an apartment. Assuming that the Swords are free to elect either of the two appraisals as accurate, which figures would you recommend that they accept? Explain your answer with calculations that assume that the Swords actually do retire in 1984 and that they then sell their "new" home for $66,000 without paying a commission.

18. Mr. and Mrs. Saver in 1953 purchased a home from Mrs. Saver's father's estate for $15,000. At the time of purchasing this home they intended to rent it until their retirement at age 65, at which time they would move into the home and occupy it as their principal residence. In the meantime, they continued to live in a rented home in another city. By the time of their retirement this year, the Savers decided that they would prefer to live in a warmer climate and they decided to sell the rented home to obtain the capital necesssary to purchase their retirement home. Between 1953 and the present, depreciation totaling $10,000 had been claimed on the rented home; nevertheless, the fair market value of the home has increased to $30,000. Although the Savers have decided to live in a warmer climate, they are in no hurry to move to that locale if they can see good reason for postponing such a move. As their tax advisor, what

would you recommend this couple do to minimize the tax consequences of selling their rented home and purchasing their retirement residence?

19. In each of the following independent transactions, (1) state the amount of gain or loss the taxpayer must recognize this year; (2) if gain or loss must be recognized, indicate whether that gain or loss is an element of ordinary income, Sec. 1231 gain or loss, or a capital gain or loss; and (3) determine the tax basis of the newly acquired property.

   a. Tractor used in taxpayer's business was totally wrecked on May 16. Insurance proceeds were $7,400. Adjusted basis of tractor at time of the accident was $5,900 ($2,500 straight-line depreciation had been claimed in prior years). Taxpayer invested $8,300 in new tractor 11 days after the accident.

   b. Taxpayer's warehouse was destroyed by fire on September 4. Insurance proceeds amounted to $34,000. Taxpayer's adjusted basis in warehouse was $40,000; $10,000 straight-line depreciation had been claimed in 5 prior years. New warehouse, purchased within 30 days of the fire, cost $39,000.

   c. Taxpayer exchanged 1,000 acres of Arizona ranch land for a duplex in Tempe. Taxpayer had inherited the land from her father's estate in 1971 when the land was valued at $30 an acre. The duplex had an estimated value of $46,000. Taxpayer, recently divorced, planned to live in half the duplex and to rent the other half. What amount of gain or loss, if any, must taxpayer recognize in this year because of this exchange? What is taxpayer's basis in the half of the duplex in which she lives? In the half that she rents?

20. In 1960, Ted Saldin built a new primary residence for $40,000 in Kansas City. Because he feared that a neighbor would build another home closer than he desired, Ted also bought the one vacant lot between his new residence and a neighboring home for $8,000. In 1970, Ted was transferred to New York. He sold the Kansas City home and acquired another in Greenwich, Connecticut. Ted did not, however, sell the vacant lot. Rather, he kept it as both an investment and a possible retirement site. By 1978, Ted decided that he would not retire in Kansas City and began to think about retiring somewhere in Florida. Because Ted is in a high tax bracket, he is reluctant to sell the lot, which has appreciated to about $28,000 in value. Nevertheless, he has no good reason to retain ownership.

   a. Suggest a tax saving plan that will achieve Ted's objectives.

   b. What precautions do you suggest that Ted take to be certain that the plan succeeds.

21. Relative to the facts described in Problem 20, if Ted had sold the extra lot along with his Kansas City home in 1970, could he have deferred the gain realized on the sale of the lot as part of his residence (Sec. 1034), assuming that he reinvested the total proceeds in the new home in Greenwich? Would it make any difference if Ted had sold the Kansas City residence to one purchaser and the lot to another, six weeks later? What if the additional land had been 10 acres rather than a mere lot? Twenty acres? Obviously, this is a research question. Use your school library to locate answers to the several questions.

22. Nontaxable exchanges generally share the requirement that any acquired property take a carryover (or substituted) tax basis. If a property has increased substantially in value since it was originally acquired, taxpayers frequently assume that it is preferable to arrange a nontaxable transaction (rather than a taxable one) because this allows them to defer the tax liability. Assuming money has a present value, deferral of a tax obligation seems desirable. Describe briefly three circumstances that would augur for immediate recognition of a potentially deferable gain.

There are, however, a variety of transactions in which the taxpayer's gain or loss goes unrecognized under the Internal Revenue Code, either because it is regarded as inchoate or "unrealized" or because non-recognition is thought to be good economic policy; and many of these "non-recognition transactions" involve corporate stock or securities.

BORIS I. BITTKER and JAMES S. EUSTICE,
Federal Income Taxation of Corporations and Shareholders (1966)

recognition postponed: corporate-shareholder transactions

Recognition of a gain or loss that technically has been realized is frequently postponed in a second group of transactions—those between a corporation and its shareholders. The Code provisions establishing the tax treatment of these transactions are contained largely within Subchapter C but, unlike the common nontaxable exchanges discussed in the preceding chapter, are not collected neatly in a single subdivision. We shall consider in this chapter, not all the nonrecognition provisions applicable to corporate-shareholder transactions, but a few sections selected both because they illustrate well the importance of wherewithal to pay and because they are of almost universal interest in any economically developed nation. Those discussed here are

Sec. 305. Distribution of stock and stock rights.
Sec. 311. Taxability of corporation on distribution.
Sec. 337. Gain or loss on sales or exchanges in connection with certain liquidations.
Sec. 351. Transfer to corporation controlled by transferor.
Sec. 354. Exchanges of stock and securities in certain reorganizations.
Sec. 361. Nonrecognition of gain or loss to corporations.
Sec. 368. Definitions relating to corporate reorganizations.

It must be clearly understood that the discussion in this chapter will only scratch the surface of the complex sections listed above. No portion of the Internal Revenue Code is more complex than Subchapter C. Students who are interested in learning more about the fascinating tax problems of corporate-shareholder relations are urged to read an authoritative text devoted solely to these provisions.[1]

One reason for the unusual complexity of these provisions is the fact that corporate-shareholder transactions typically present nonroutine tax problems for both parties to the transaction. In most of the other nonrecognition transactions mentioned thus far, the transaction was routine for at least one of the parties involved. For example, the payment of an insurance claim by an insurance company is a routine transaction and presents "unusual tax problems" only for the recipient of the payment; similarly, the sale of a residence ordinarily creates special tax problems only for the seller. If one party is a dealer in the assets exchanged, an exchange of productive use or investment property for property of a like kind also creates interesting tax problems only for the nondealer.

A second reason for the unusual complexity in corporate-shareholder transactions is the fact that distributions by a corporation to its shareholders may be treated as (1) dividends, which are taxed as ordinary income; (2) partial liquidations or stock redemptions, which may be taxed either as ordinary income, as capital gains, or as part gain and part

---

[1]In particular, we recommend Boris I. Bittker and James S. Eustice, *Federal Income Taxation of Corporations and Shareholders,* 4th ed. (Boston: Warren, Gorham, & Lamont, Inc., 1979).

return of capital; or (3) complete liquidations, which typically involve a return of capital as well as capital gain or loss.

A final complexity is added to corporate-shareholder transactions because the shareholder may be an individual, another corporation, or a fiduciary. Even though each of these separate taxable entities is subject to the same income-tax provisions generally, enough differences in specific tax provisions do exist to make an already complex tax problem even more difficult.

TAX ASPECTS OF FORMING A CORPORATION

Among the transactions common to the formation of a corporate entity are those involving an exchange of cash, other property, or services for stock or securities in the corporate entity. The exchange of cash for stock or securities presents few tax problems to either party. As noted in Chapter 25, Sec. 1032 provides that the corporation need not recognize gain when it issues its own stock or securities for money or other property; the stockholder who pays cash for corporate stock has, in most circumstances, simply purchased another asset and established a cost basis in the shares acquired. In short, the cash-for-stock transaction generally does not create taxable gain (or loss) for either party.

At the other extreme, the exchange of personal services for stock in a corporation necessarily causes the realization and recognition of taxable income for the taxpayer who renders the service and receives the shares. Neither the Code nor the regulations provide an exception to the general rules of income recognition in this situation; therefore, taxable income equal to the fair market value of the shares transferred must be recognized. The most difficult practical problem in this transaction generally is obtaining agreement on fair market value; the smaller, more risky, and more closely held the corporation, the greater the difficulty in establishing value. If, at approximately the same time, other taxpayers have paid cash or transferred property with readily determinable values for substantially identical shares, the value of the shares exchanged for services may be imputed from these other exchanges. Without such transactions, however, the determination of value is a most difficult practical problem.

Tax problems also are created by the exchange of noncash property for corporate stock or securities.

The critical question in that transaction is whether the gain or loss realized on the exchange should be recognized for tax purposes. For example, if a taxpayer exchanges a building with a basis of $50,000 for corporate shares valued at $75,000, must the taxpayer recognize the $25,000 income realized? Under ordinary circumstances, the taxpayer would have to, for corporate stocks are treated as boot in an otherwise nontaxable exchange, and (except for Sec. 351, which is discussed below) no other provision would seem to justify the failure to recognize this gain.

Section 351(a)

Prior to 1921, the transaction described in the preceding paragraph would have been treated as a taxable event. In that year, however, Congress decided that an exception should be made in certain circumstances in order to facilitate business readjustments. Today the "certain circumstances" that would preclude the recognition of gain realized by the transfer of noncash property to a corporation in exchange for that corporation's stock are specified in Sec. 351(a), which reads, in part, as follows:

> (a) General Rule.—No gain or loss shall be recognized if property is transferred to a corporation by one or more persons solely in exchange for stock or securities in such corporation and immediately after the exchange such person or persons are in control (as defined in section 368 (c)) of the corporation. For purposes of this section, stock or securities issued for services shall not be considered as issued in return for property.

Incidentally, Sec. 368(c) defines control as ownership of "at least 80 percent of the total combined voting power of all classes of stock entitled to vote and at least 80 percent of the total number of shares of all other classes of stock of the corporation." Section 351(a) has, in its turn, created a number of new problems and has required considerable interpretation.[2]

---

[2]To illustrate just a few of the possible problems of interpretation that might arise under this Code provision, consider the following questions. Can shares issued for cash be included with those transferred for property in determining whether or not control has been obtained? Is there any limit to the number of persons constituting the group having control? If several taxpayers are transferring property concurrently and as part of a single plan, what time span will be allowed to complete these transfers and still satisfy the "immediately after the exchange" requirement? If momentary control is achieved, but the taxpayers quickly dispose of some of their interest so that the 80-percent control requirement is no longer satisfied, could the exchange remain unrecognized anyway? As noted earlier, these and similar questions constitute a fascinating aspect of the corporation-shareholder transaction arena.

Section 351(b)

The primary reason for not recognizing the gain realized by the transfer of property to a controlled corporation in exchange for its stock or securities is undoubtedly a desire to facilitate business readjustments. In the absence of such a provision, the tax cost of forming a corporation might be prohibitive. Certainly the best economic interests of a nation are served whenever businesspeople are not unduly hampered by tax considerations in selecting and effecting the form of business organization most appropriate to their needs and circumstances.

The importance of wherewithal to pay is, however, also of major interest. This consideration was noted in the case of *Portland Oil Co.* v. *Commissioner,* when the Court said

> It is the purpose of §112(b)(5) [Sec. 351 in the 1954 Code] to save the taxpayer from an immediate recognition of a gain, or to intermit the claim of a loss, in certain transactions where gain or loss may have accrued in a constitutional sense, but where in a popular and economic sense there has been a mere change in the form of ownership and *the taxpayer has not really 'cashed in' on the theoretical gain.* . . . [3]

The same conclusion is further demonstrated by the requirements of Sec. 351(b). That subsection provides that the receipt (by the shareholder) of any property other than stock or securities shall be treated essentially like boot in the nontaxable exchange. It reads as follows:

> (b) Receipt of Property.—If subsection (a) would apply to an exchange but for the fact that there is received, in addition to the stock or securities permitted to be received under subsection (a), other property or money, then
> (1) gain (if any) to such recipient shall be recognized, but not in excess of—
>   (A) the amount of money received, plus
>   (B) the fair market value of such other property received; and
> (2) no loss to such recipient shall be recognized.[4]

Thus, if the shareholder receives anything other than the controlled corporation's stock or securities, he or she is considered to have the wherewithal to pay to the extent of the other property received.

Basis adjustment

The nonrecognition of gain in a transfer of property to a controlled corporation is like most other temporary nonrecognition provisions in that it demands an adjustment in the basis of the property received. If no gain is recognized on the exchange, the transferor simply takes as his or her basis in the stocks or securities whatever basis he or she had in the property transferred to the controlled corporation. In those rare instances where gain must be recognized because the shareholder received other property, the determination of basis in the shares follows the usual nontaxable exchange pattern. In this case, the basis of the stocks or securities would be determined as follows:

> Basis of property transferred to the controlled corporation
> − Cash or FMV of other property received from the corporation
> + Gain recognized on the exchange
> = Basis of shares or securities received

This conclusion and a provision for relative fair market value allocations if more than one class of share or security is received are contained in Sec. 358.

The corporation's basis in the property it receives is also determined, in most circumstances, by the shareholder's former basis in the property. If the shareholder was forced to recognize gain (because he or she received property other than stocks or securities), the corporation also may increase its basis in the property received by the amount of gain the shareholder recognized.

CORPORATE-SHAREHOLDER TRANSACTIONS SUBSEQUENT TO ORGANIZATION

The tax problems associated with corporate-shareholder transactions become, if anything, more complex after the organizational period. The possible range of these transactions is infinite. Among the more important post-organization transactions are those in which the corporation distributes assets to the shareholders. These may include routine cash dividends, common stock dividends, preferred stock dividends, property dividends, partial liquidations, divisive reorganizations, nondivisive reorganiza-

---

[3]109 F.2d 479 (1940) at p. 488 (emphasis added).
[4]Code Sec. 351(b).

tions, and complete liquidations. A complete liquidation may be permanent, or it may be followed momentarily by a subsequent organization that makes the procedure tantamount to reorganization. The tax consequences and complexity of each of the suggested transactions are enormous. In this chapter we can only note some of the more important transactions that defer the recognition of a realized gain or loss.

Property dividends

Except in the event of a partial or complete liquidation, the vast majority of asset distributions by corporations to their shareholders are made in the form of cash. When cash is distributed by the corporation to stockholders in their role as stockholders (rather than as, say, employees or creditors), the only question that ordinarily arises is whether the distribution constitutes a taxable dividend or a return of capital. As explained on page 23/3, that determination is dependent on the presence or absence of corporate "earnings and profits." To the extent that the corporation has either current earnings and profits *or* earnings and profits accumulated since 1913, the cash distributions are dividends and are taxed accordingly.[5]

Distributions of corporate assets other than cash present additional problems. One of the problems involves recognition—that is, should the corporation making the distribution be required to recognize any gain or loss on the property distributed to its shareholders? Prior to 1954, this was an open question, and the I.R.S. sometimes argued that this event was sufficient to cause the recognition of taxable income. The 1954 Code included a new provision, Sec. 311(a)(2), which specifically precludes the recognition of gain or loss by the corporation on such a transaction. Section 311(a) reads as follows:

> (a) General Rule.—Except as provided in subsection (b),
> (c), and (d) of this section and section 453(d), no gain
> or loss shall be recognized to a corporation on the
> distribution, with respect to its stock of—
> (1) its stock (or rights to acquire its stock), or
> (2) property.

Subsections (b), (c), and (d) are special provisions dealing with distribution of LIFO (last-in, first-out)

inventory, property with a liability in excess of basis, and appreciated property used to redeem stock, respectively. Section 453(d) establishes another special rule if the asset distributed is an installment obligation. Except for these special cases, it is now clear that the corporation normally will not recognize any gain or loss when it distributes noncash property to its shareholders in their role as shareholders. If it distributes such property to a shareholder in his or her role as an employee, the corporation would be forced to recognize the gain or loss, and the stockholder-employee would report the fair market value as ordinary income (wages and salary).

A second question that arises when a corporation distributes noncash property to its stockholders concerns the tax treatment of that distribution by the recipient. If the recipient shareholder is an individual or a fiduciary taxpayer, he or she generally recognizes dividends equal to the fair market value of the property received (assuming the corporation's earnings and profits—current or post-1913—are equal to or greater than that value). If, however, the recipient shareholder is another corporate entity, Sec. 301(b)(1)(B) provides for another possible nonrecognition situation: The recipient corporation recognizes as dividend income the *lesser* of (1) the fair market value of the property received or (2) the adjusted basis of the property in the hands of the distributing corporation. The recipient corporation also takes as its basis in the property received the amount of dividend income it recognized, per the above calculation. The reason for this nonrecognition rule is *not* primarily a concern for wherewithal to pay; rather, it is a potential "loophole closer." If the corporation that received the property were permitted to recognize the fair market value without limit, it could in the proper circumstances convert low-tax income into high-tax deductions. That is, since the recipient corporation would be entitled to an 85-percent (or even a 100-percent) dividends-received deduction, it could afford to recognize a sizable quantity of dividend income at little or no tax cost and then proceed to depreciate a highly stepped-up basis and achieve a substantial reduction in ordinary taxable income.

Stock dividends

Corporations frequently distribute their own shares to stockholders in what has become known as a "stock dividend." In several ways, this is a most unfortunate phrase to describe what has taken place; witness the fact that the corporation is not distributing a corporate asset (the corporation's own shares

---

[5]As explained earlier, individual and fiduciary taxpayers are ordinarily granted an annual exclusion of $100 for dividends received; corporate stockholders typically are allowed a deduction equal to 85 percent of the dividends received from other domestic corporations.

can never constitute an asset to that entity), which is requisite to any true "dividend." As long as the distribution of stock is pro rata among all shareholders, the shareholders effectively have received nothing. Admittedly they have received additional pieces of paper, but collectively their ownership rights after the stock dividend are exactly equal to the rights they possessed prior to the dividend. If the distribution of stock is not pro rata, however, a significant change in ownership rights may be achieved.

Prior to the Tax Reform Act of 1969, stock dividends generally were not taxable as long as they were made *in the same class of stock* unless either (1) any shareholder of that class had an option to receive cash or other property or (2) the stock dividend was in discharge of a preference dividend for the current or the preceding year. By carefully delineating the rights of various classes of stock, corporate managements were able effectively to accommodate the desires of some shareholders to receive cash and of others to accumulate their income rights for greater capital gain. Alternatively, by carefully timing disproportionate stock redemptions, dividends could effectively be paid at the cost of a capital gain tax. To discourage this managerial intrigue, Congress in 1969 amended Sec. 305 to make taxable a number of previously untaxable stock dividends. Under the present law, it is sometimes difficult to discern whether a particular distribution should be treated as a taxable or a nontaxable event. To complicate matters further, certain distributions made prior to January 1, 1991, are exempted from the 1969 changes. Unfortunately, the revised Sec. 305 is too complex to justify a thorough discussion in an introductory text. Suffice it to observe that if a stock dividend changes the proportionate interest of one or more groups of shareholders, the result very likely will be a taxable transaction today. Because of the uncertain limits of some portions of the 1969 amendments to Sec. 305, further litigation in this area seems probable.

Ignoring the more difficult question of determining whether a particular stock dividend is a taxable or a nontaxable event, we quickly can summarize the result once the prior issue has been resolved. If a stock dividend is a taxable distribution, the shareholder recognizes ordinary (dividend) income equal to the fair market value of the shares received. The new shares take this value as their tax basis, and the date of the distribution becomes the beginning of the holding period for the newly acquired shares.

Upon receipt of a nontaxable stock dividend, the taxpayer must allocate his or her cost basis among the new, larger number of shares. If the shares received are identical to the shares already owned, the taxpayer simply divides the old basis by the new, larger number of shares to determine the adjusted basis per share. If the shares received are not identical to the shares owned, the taxpayer must allocate the original basis on the relative fair market value of each class of stock he or she now possesses. To illustrate, assume that taxpayer C owned 100 shares of ABC common, purchased for $2,200 several years earlier. If C received an additional ten shares of ABC common as a nontaxable stock dividend, C's basis would be readjusted from $22 per share ($2,200/100) to $20 per share ($2,200/110). The date basis of the ten dividend shares would be the same as that of the original 100 shares. If, therefore, taxpayer C sold the ten dividend shares two days after receiving them, he or she would recognize a long-term capital gain or loss equal to the difference between the amount realized and the $20 basis per share surrendered in the transaction. (This assumes, of course, that the shares were a capital asset in taxpayer C's hands.)

If these ten shares had been received in a *taxable* stock dividend, no allocations would have been made, and the taxpayer would have recorded as dividend income their fair market value on the date distributed. Any future gain or loss on the sale two days later would have been short-term capital gain or loss.

If taxpayer C had received ten shares of preferred stock, rather than ten shares of common stock, as a *nontaxable* stock dividend, C would have allocated the old $2,200 basis between the two classes of stock based on their relative fair market values. If we assume that on the date the dividend was distributed the ten preferred shares had a fair market value of $600 and the 100 common shares a fair market value of $2,400, then the basis of the ten preferred shares would be $440 [$2,200 × ($600/$3,000)] and the basis of the 100 common shares would be $1,760 [$2,200 × ($2,400/$3,000)]. Although the date basis would still "tack," the taxpayer may have to recognize *ordinary* income on disposition of the preferred shares. The reason for this conclusion is not evident, and an adequate investigation of the problem leads one into Sec. 306 and the subject of preferred stock bail-outs. Since time and space constraints prohibit such an investigation, suffice it here to note that because the receipt of a stock dividend may not necessitate the recognition of income, and because the sale of corporate shares ordinarily results in capital gain rather than ordinary income, the distribution of a preferred stock dividend could—in the absence of Sec. 306—

be abused to disguise a dividend payment (ordinary income) as a stock redemption (capital gain). In short, retained profits could be "bailed out" as capital gains rather than as ordinary dividend income.

Stock rights

The distribution of stock rights, rather than actual shares, presents tax problems very similar to those of the stock dividend. The general rules can be summarized briefly. First, the taxability of the stock right is determined in the same manner as the taxability of the stock dividend. Second, if the distribution is nontaxable, the recipient must allocate basis only if on the date of distribution the fair market value of the rights is equal to or greater than 15 percent of the fair market value of the shares; if the rights have a value of less than 15 percent of the shares, allocation is optional for each recipient taxpayer. Third, if the taxpayer sells the rights, the date basis is presumed to "tack"—that is, the date basis of the rights is the same as the date basis of the old shares. If, however, the taxpayer exercises the rights and acquires new shares, the new shares take a new date basis on the date they were purchased. The determination of a cost basis (and, therefore, of the gain or loss on the sale of the rights or of newly acquired shares) depends on whether or not the taxpayer voluntarily or involuntarily allocated part of the basis of the old shares to the rights.

To illustrate, let's assume that taxpayer F acquired 100 shares of DEF common on May 1, 19x1, for $1,600. On June 10, 19x4, she received 100 stock rights, which permitted her to buy additional shares at a bargain price. The agreement provided that one new share could be purchased for five rights and $20. If we assume that DEF common at that time was selling at approximately $30 per share, the rights obviously would be selling at approximately $2 per right. Since the value of the 100 rights ($200) is less than 15 percent of the value of the 100 shares ($3,000), taxpayer F would not be required to allocate any basis to the rights. If she elected to allocate, she would do so on a fair market value basis—that is, she could elect to allocate $100 [$1,600 × ($200/$3,200)] to the rights. If she does make this election, the basis in the 100 shares is, of course, reduced from $1,600 to $1,500. After receiving this stock right, taxpayer F has two intelligent options: She might elect to sell the rights, or she might exercise them if she desires to acquire an additional interest in DEF. If she sells the rights for $200, she must recognize

long-term capital gain equal to the difference between the $200 realized and the basis of the rights ($0 or $100, the latter amount if she elects to allocate basis). If she exercises the rights and acquires twenty new shares for her 100 rights and $400, the twenty new shares take a new date basis (the date they were acquired) and a new cost basis of $400 or $500 (the latter amount if taxpayer F elected to allocate). Taxpayer F also has one unintelligent option—to let the option lapse. If she does so, no loss will be recognized.

In summary, the receipt of a stock dividend or a stock right in the distributing corporation's own shares may or may not trigger the recognition of a gain or loss that might be considered realized. If the taxpayer receives a property other than stock or rights in the distributing corporation, or if the relative rights of various owners are modified by the distribution, the shareholder is deemed to have the wherewithal to pay a tax, and income, usually in the form of a dividend, must be recognized. The distributing corporation typically does not recognize gain or loss when it distributes property to its shareholders in their role as shareholders.

Reorganizations

Corporate reorganizations may be divided into two broad groups: divisive and nondivisive. A divisive reorganization separates one corporate entity into two or more entities. A nondivisive reorganization usually combines two or more corporate entities into one. In each instance the "old" entity may remain or disappear after the reorganization. In the divisive reorganization, for example, existing corporation A may be divided into corporations A and B or into new corporations B and C. In the nondivisive reorganization, existing corporations A and B may be "merged" into continuing corporation B, or existing corporations A and B may be "consolidated" into new corporation C.

Regardless of such details, reorganizations necessitate numerous transactions. A reorganization, for example, may involve the transfer of properties between corporate entities as well as the exchange of corporate stocks and securities by shareholders. Since any transaction may be deemed adequate to cause the realization of taxable income or loss, the question of recognition becomes paramount. As noted earlier, the reorganization provisions are inordinately complex and cannot be discussed even in a summary fashion. Consequently, we are forced at this juncture to paint only the broadest of pictures and to warn constantly that no attempt should be made to ''utilize'' this picture in any factual situation.

In general, Sec. 354 provides that ''no gain or loss shall be recognized if stock or securities in a corporation that is a party to a reorganization are, in pursuance of the plan of reorganization, exchanged solely for stock or securities in such corporation or in another corporation a party to the reorganization.''[6] Obviously, the importance of this section is that it sometimes permits a taxpayer to exchange stocks and securities in different corporate entities and to avoid the recognition of any gain or loss realized by this exchange transaction. The critical requirement, of course, is that the exchanged shares be in corporations that are *parties to a reorganization*. Whether or not a corporation is a party to a reorganization is determined by Sec. 368.

Section 368 is exclusively a definitional provision. Paragraph (1) of Subsection 368(a) describes six transactions deemed to constitute a reorganization for tax purposes. Reorganizations not falling within one of these prescribed transactions are ordinarily subject to no special tax treatment. It is, therefore, of utmost importance in most corporate reorganizations to determine well in advance whether or not a proposed transaction will fit within a Sec. 368 definition. Even the most sophisticated tax advisor will typically insist on an advance ruling from the I.R.S. on a given set of fact circumstances before deeming it safe to proceed with a proposed corporate change.[7] In some instances, of course, the parties may desire recognition of losses, or they may desire recognition of gains to obtain a stepped-up basis in the assets received. In many other instances, the parties could not proceed with the reorganization if it were to be a taxable transaction.

Section 361, like Sec. 354, depends on the definitional distinctions of Sec. 368 to determine its importance. In general, Sec. 361 permits one corporate party to a reorganization to exchange its property for stock or securities in another corporate party to the reorganization and to avoid the recognition of gain realized by this exchange.

In many respects, the importance of wherewithal to pay in the corporate reorganization is exhibited in

Secs. 356, 357, 358, and 362. Stated very crudely, the first two of these provisions determine the consequences of receiving boot (including the transfer of a liability) in a corporate reorganization. The other two provisions require a basis adjustment intended to guarantee that a nonrecognized gain or loss will be recognized for tax purposes at a later date. Although innumerable special rules apply in each of many situations, the general conclusion is the same as that derived in the preceding chapter. Realized gain must be recognized in most situations to the extent of the lesser of boot received or gain realized. Any gain *not* recognized will reduce the basis of the ''new'' property from its cost or fair market value to a lower figure. Unrealized loss, on the other hand, may increase basis above cost.

In short, the theory behind the nonrecognition of gain in a corporate reorganization is comparable to that of other nontaxable exchanges: The taxpayer is deemed to have only a new ''form'' for an old investment. In a popular sense, this taxpayer has no funds with which to pay an income tax, and so no tax is assessed until he or she disposes of the new property in a taxable transaction. At that time, it is presumed, the deferred gain will be recouped. If the taxpayer does acquire, as part of the reorganization, a limited amount of property that cannot be treated as a mere continuation of the old investment, gain must, to that extent, be recognized immediately; the remainder of the realized gain may go unrecognized.

Even this very brief introduction to the corporate reorganization tax provisions should suggest their major impact on American business. The closely held corporation is often used as a temporary tax-rate shelter by individuals. By merging the closely held corporate entity, with large amounts of accumulated earnings and profits, into a conglomerate entity, the owner of the closely held firm can effectively ''cash in'' on previously sheltered corporate earnings with no immediate tax cost. That is, the taxpayer can exchange the shares in his or her closely held corporation for shares in the merger-minded conglomerate giant without the imposition of an income tax if the transaction can be arranged as a qualifying corporate reorganization. In this manner, a business owner can free himself or herself of the day-to-day responsibilities of corporate management and obtain the economic diversification (and supposedly the minimization of risk) represented by the stock in the acquiring corporation. In many cases, the former owner of the acquired corporation is given a choice between receiving low-dividend, high

---

[6] Code Sec. 354(a).

[7] An advance ruling is an administrative procedure by which a taxpayer may be able to get a generally binding agreement with the I.R.S. on the tax consequences of a proposed transaction. This ruling is not binding on other parties in similar circumstances.

growth potential stocks; high-dividend, low-growth stocks; or some combination of the two. In this way, he or she can try to ensure that his or her retirement years include both a sufficient income flow and a strong capital base to make life as comfortable as possible. If an income tax had been imposed before the taxpayer could make such a change, the capital base and, therefore, the income flow would have been materially reduced. Finally, with the step-up in basis of inherited property, what started out as a temporary deferral of the income tax often becomes a permanent exclusion from the income tax when the shares pass through an estate.

Although the almost rampant merger movement of the decade 1962–72 was largely halted by the stock market decline in 1973 and 1974, the momentum provided by the nontaxable reorganization provisions suggests that the movement may reoccur if and when the market value of the acquiring corporations' shares adequately recovers. We can only hope that the new conglomerate giants will emerge and grow with more caution than many of their predecessors. The failure to investigate fully, and the failure to provide knowledgeable management in diverse industries, all too often resulted in economic chaos rather than the comfortable retirement liquidity sought by the stockholder of the acquired corporation.

Complete liquidation

Corporate reorganizations often mean the termination of one or more corporate entities, but the liquidation in such a case may be considered a subproblem of the corporate reorganization. A slightly different tax problem must be solved when a corporate entity simply decides to dissolve itself and to distribute its remaining assets to its shareholders. As noted earlier, a corporation ordinarily does not recognize gain or loss when it distributes corporate property to its shareholders in their role as shareholders. On the other hand, it ordinarily must recognize gain (or loss) when it sells or otherwise disposes of property to an unrelated third party. Until Congress enacted Sec. 337, these two tax rules created a dilemma for the owners of a corporation about to liquidate.

Before 1954, the corporation that disposed of its property prior to dissolution had to pay the corporate income tax on any gain realized. Then, when the after-tax proceeds were distributed to the stockhold-

ers in liquidation, they further had to recognize a capital gain (usually long-term) on the difference between the amount received and the basis of their shares. On the other hand, if the corporation distributed all the corporation's property to the shareholders and the shareholders then sold the assets to the unrelated third parties, the corporate income tax on the gain could be wholly eliminated with only a minimal increase in the shareholders' capital-gain tax. That is, when the shareholders received the corporate property in complete liquidation of their interest, they would recognize as a capital gain (usually long-term) the difference between the fair market value of the property received and the basis in the shares surrendered. This would increase the shareholders' basis in the property received to its fair market value, so that when the property was sold to the third parties no further gain would have to be recognized. Because of the significant tax advantage of this alternative, corporations owning assets with values greatly in excess of their basis simply could not afford to consummate a liquidation sale prior to distribution. Shareholders, on the other hand, were not often in a position to find as good a buyer for corporate assets as corporate management could find. Thus, as a practical matter, prior to 1954 the corporate officers would literally bring the final sale to consummation prior to distribution, but they would take care to provide that technically the property had first been distributed to the shareholders.

This situation presented a difficult problem in tax administration. The I.R.S. is reluctant to allow a substantial tax opportunity to go unchallenged when the sole reason for the result is what appears to be an inconsequential difference in the form of a transaction. That is, if the substance of the transaction would seem to yield a different tax conclusion, the I.R.S. is prone to argue that the courts should ignore the form and adjudicate the issue on its merit (substance). Sometimes the courts will agree with the I.R.S.; at other times they seem to agree with the taxpayer, saying that it is up to the Congress to correct inadequate statutory provisions. The difficulty of knowing how any court will rule in a given fact case is a common litigation hazard for both the I.R.S. and the taxpayer.

Section 337 was included as part of the 1954 Code to solve this particular tax problem. In general, it provides that the *corporation's* gain or loss on the sale or exchange of property may go (permanently) unrecognized if (1) the corporation adopts a plan of complete liquidation and (2) it proceeds to dispose of all its assets within a period of twelve months from the date it adopted such a plan. Obviously, the net result of such a provision is to permit the same tax consequence as would have prevailed if property had been distributed to the shareholders in complete liquidation and subsequently sold by the shareholders. This section also has the usual list of exceptions and special cases. For example, it will not apply to collapsible corporations, it may (or may not) apply to sales of inventory or installment sales obligations, and it may be "outranked" by such provisions as Secs. 1245 and 1250 (see Chapter 21). Finally, a complete liquidation followed immediately by reincorporation may be treated as a mere reorganization.

This very brief exposure to the myriad problems of realization and recognition in corporate-shareholder transactions should have given the student interested in a tax career some insight into a most important part of the tax advisor's challenge. Hopefully, it also served to reemphasize a basic tenet that explains many differences between tax accounting and financial accounting: The mere realization of a gain or loss may not be deemed to constitute the type of event that should trigger the recognition of taxable income, especially in those instances where the taxpayer is left after the transaction with little or no wherewithal with which to pay a tax. The failure to recognize taxable income immediately, however, may not constitute a permanent avoidance of the deferred gain—an adjustment in the tax basis of the property received is often adequate to provide for a later recapture of the deferred income.

PROBLEMS

1. Discuss the problems that arise from applying the general rules to determine the tax consequences of a particular transaction in each of the following fact situations. How has each problem been "resolved"?
    a. Henry Dee had operated a corner grocery store as a sole proprietorship for several years. Because the store had grown to reasonable size, Henry decided to incorporate his business as Henry's Groceries, Inc. To accomplish this, Henry transferred all business assets to the new corporation in exchange for all 1,000 shares of the corporation's voting stock. (Consider both Mr. Dee's tax problems and those of Henry's Groceries, Inc.; discuss questions of "basis" as well as problems in "recognition of gain or loss.")
    b. After operating and expanding this grocery business for another 10 years, Henry "merged" his corporation with Giant Corporation, a national chain of food stores. Giant gave Henry the three options detailed below. (Discuss the tax consequences of each option.)
        1. A cash purchase of all operating assets for $300,000.
        2. An exchange of 500 shares of Giant voting stock for all the operating assets of Henry's Groceries, Inc.
        3. A statutory merger of Henry's Groceries, Inc., into Giant Corporation by an exchange of 400 shares of Giant for all 1,000 shares of Henry's (after which Henry's Groceries, Inc. would be liquidated).
    c. Assume that Henry accepted option 3, above, and that five years later Giant Corporation was consolidated with ten other firms engaged in various businesses into a new corporation, Conglomerage American. Thus, Henry Dee ended up holding a small interest in a new and highly diversified corporate entity. Do the tax consequences of this series of transactions square with the idea that Henry has experienced only an insignificant change in the "form" of his investment? Do they square with a wherewithal-to-pay concept? Explain.
2. Susan purchased 100 shares of DEF common on February 12, 19x1, for $4,800. On October 1, 19x4, she received twenty additional shares of DEF common as a nontaxable stock dividend.

    a. What is Susan's cost basis *per share* after receipt of the stock dividend?

    b. What is Susan's "date basis" in each of the twenty "dividend shares"?

    c. Suppose that instead of twenty additional shares of DEF common, Susan had received twenty shares of GHI common (which had been held by DEF corporation as an investment).

        1. Would Susan report the receipt of the twenty shares of GHI as ordinary income (dividend), as capital gain, or as a nontaxable distribution?

        2. Assume that DEF had paid $50 per share for the GHI stock two years prior to distributing it, and that at the time of distribution it had a fair market value of $60 per share. Would DEF have to recognize the $10-per-share gain inherent in the GHI stock at the time it distributes the stock to its shareholders?

3. John Doe purchased 100 shares of ABC common on October 30, 19x3, for $680. On March 1, 19x4, John received 100 stock rights. The provision of the rights agreement authorized John to purchase one new share of ABC common for $5 and four rights. Immediately following issuance of these rights, ABC common is selling ex-rights at $8 per share; the rights are selling for $0.50 each.

    a. Does John have to report taxable income in 19x4 because he received this right to purchase additional shares of stock?

    b. What is John's cost basis for his 100 stock rights, assuming the distribution was nontaxable?

    c. Assuming that John elects to allocate basis of the rights and that he exercises his option and purchases the shares:

        1. What is his cost basis for each newly acquired share?

        2. What is his "date basis" in each of the new shares?

        3. What is his cost basis in each of his old shares?

4. James Madison and Henry Clay formed a corporation on July 1 of this year. Madison transferred to the corporation the assets of his existing hardware business, which had a basis of $8,000, while Clay transferred assets that had a basis of $18,000. Each individual received 200 shares of stock in the new corporation; each share had a fair market value of $80 per share. In addition, Madison's wife was issued one share of stock on the investment of $80 in cash. Discuss the tax consequences of this transaction, including the basis of shares received and the basis of the corporation in the property.

5. State briefly the underlying rationale for the "nontaxability" of certain corporate reorganizations.

6. Taxpayer owns 100 shares of XYZ common stock, which she acquired several years ago. Her basis is $40 per share. On May 5 of the current year, when the stock was $60 and the rights $1, she received 100 nontaxable rights from the corporation. For each ten rights and a payment of $50, the stockholder may acquire an additional share of XYZ common.

    a. If the taxpayer sells the rights on November 15 of the same year for $1.50 each, what is her gain or loss, and how is it taxed: (1) if she elects to allocate basis? (2) if she does not allocate?

    b. If the taxpayer exercises her rights on November 15 and sells the ten shares acquired thereby on December 3 of the same year for $68 per share, what is her gain or loss, and how is it taxed: (1) if she allocates the basis? (2) if she does not allocate the basis?

7. On July 1 of the current year, Arvid Corporation merged into Berrium Incorporated in a transaction that qualified under Code Sections 354 and 368(a). As a result of this corporate merger, Homer exchanged 2,000 shares of Arvid stock

for 500 new shares of Berrium and $1,219 cash. Homer's basis in the 1,000 shares of Arvid was $8,237; the fair market value of the 500 Berrium shares was $34,977 on the day they were received.

    a. What income did Homer realize on this exchange?

    b. How much of this realized income must Homer recognize this year?

    c. What is Homer's tax basis in the 500 shares of Berrium?

8. Kyle, Dan, and Bob decided to pool some assets in a new corporate business to be known as KDB Company. Kyle agreed to contribute $4,000 cash plus equipment with a fair market value of $26,000 and a tax basis of $15,000. Dan agreed to contribute land with a fair market value of $30,000 and a tax basis of $40,000. Bob agreed to contribute $20,000 cash and a good deal of work, which all parties agreed was worth $10,000. In exchange, each of the three received 1,000 shares of KDB stock.

    a. If all the contributions are made under a single plan so that the transaction qualifies under Sec. 351(a):

        1. How much taxable income or loss will each man recognize in the year because KDB incorporated?

        2. What is the tax basis of the 1,000 shares of KDB each man owns?

        3. What is the tax basis of the equipment and land owned by KDB Company?

        4. Why might Dan strongly prefer to arrange the incorporating transaction in a way that would not qualify it under Sec. 351(a)?

        5. Why might Kyle strongly prefer to keep the transaction as it is currently arranged?

    b. If the incorporation plans were revised so that initially Dan were to contribute $30,000 cash and subsequently, in a wholly separate transaction, KDB Company were to purchase the land from Dan at a cost of $30,000, why might both Kyle and Dan be satisfied?

    c. Under either plan (a or b, above), each of the owners has contributed $30,000 in cash, equivalent property, and/or services to KDB Company in exchange for 1,000 shares of stock. Nevertheless, in one important sense Kyle has not contributed his fair share. Explain.

9. Twenty years ago Bob and Ray jointly invested in an 80-acre tract of vacant land at a cost of $8,000. Today that land is ready to be developed into a first-class residential area. Conservative estimates place the value of the land at $88,000. Bob and Ray are considering the possibility of joining with two builder-developers in a corporate business that would actually develop this land. What good tax reasons might Bob and Ray have to prefer a taxable transfer of their land to the new corporation rather than a nontaxable transfer under Section 351(a)? Explain.

10. On March 20 of this year, Ida exchanged all of her shares of common stock in Ida Marie Cosmetics for 350,000 shares of Wellblest Corporation and $100,000 cash. Ida, the original stockholder of Ida Marie Cosmetics, had an adjusted basis of only $75,000 in the shares she gave up. Wellblest shares were selling for $8 on the day of the exchange.

    a. What amount of gain did Ida realize on this exchange?

    b. What amount of gain must Ida recognize this year if the exchange does *not* qualify as a reorganization under Sec. 368?

    c. What amount of gain must Ida recognize this year if the exchange does qualify as a reorganization under Sec. 368?

    d. What kind of income—ordinary or capital—is Ida's gain?

e. If Ida's exchange qualifies as a reorganization and she does not dispose of her Wellblest shares prior to her death, who will finally pay the income tax on the taxable gain deferred at the time of this exchange? Explain briefly.

SUPPLEMENTAL PROBLEMS

11. Should corporate financial accounting be of any significance in the determination of tax consequences of a given transaction? Explain your answer, giving some consideration to the following quotation from *Bazley* v. *Commissioner* (331 U.S. 740):

> No doubt there was a recapitalization of the Bazley Corporation in the sense that the symbols that represented its capital were changed, so that the fiscal basis of its operations would appear very differently on its books. But the form of a transaction as reflected by correct corporate accounting opens questions as to the proper application of a taxing statute; it does not close them. Corporate accounting may represent that correspondence between change in the form of capital structure and essential identity in fact which is the essence of a transaction relieved from taxation as a reorganization.

12. Imagine that you are doing tax planning for a very wealthy individual with interests in several different industries. List some of the ways in which the reorganization provisions might be used to reduce his tax burden. Consider both divisive and nondivisive reorganizations.

13. As the owners of closely held corporate businesses approach retirement, they often are willing to merge their corporations with other corporate organizations. In the recent past, conglomerates—that is, large publicly held organizations engaged in a wide diversity of enterprises—have been particularly successful in negotiating these exchanges. What good reasons do the sellers have for preferring (1) an exchange and (2) an exchange with a conglomerate to other methods of disposing of their businesses? Explain as best you can.

14. Two sets of preferences are common to the negotiations involved in the acquisition-disposition of a closely held corporate business:

> First, the purchaser of the business typically will prefer to make the acquisition in a taxable transaction rather than in some form of a nontaxable exchange. On the other hand, the seller of a business will generally prefer a nontaxable exchange to a taxable disposition.

> Second, when the parties agree upon a taxable transaction, the buyer often will prefer to acquire assets directly rather than indirectly (through the acquisition of a controlling interest in the voting stock of the selling corporation). On the other hand, the seller often will prefer to dispose of his business assets indirectly through the disposition of his stock rather than directly through the sale of the assets per se.

a. Discuss tax factors that contribute to these buyer and seller preferences.
b. Suggest some possible fact situations that might call for a reversal of the "normal" roles. That is, what facts might cause a seller to prefer the taxable disposition and the buyer the nontaxable one?
c. How has the enactment of Sec. 337 helped to reduce the strength of the seller's preference in the second case noted above?

d. As a research project, explain how the enactment of Sec. 334(b)(2) helped to reduce the strength of the buyer's preference in the first case noted above.

15. All of the outstanding stock of Eva Corporation is owned by Ms. Eva Maddox, corporate president and chairperson of the board. Eva Corporation has been very successful and has accumulated over $10 million in earnings and profits. Ms. Maddox has just determined to build herself a personal residence on some oceanfront property near San Diego that is owned by Eva Corporation. The corporation wisely bought this land as an investment 15 years ago. Because Ms. Maddox controls everything the corporation does, she can easily arrange a transfer of the land from Eva Corporation to herself in any one of several ways. Assuming that the corporation has a tax basis of $100,000 in the land, and that the land has a current fair market value of $225,000, determine the tax consequences of each of the four transactions suggested below, both to the Eva Corporation and to Ms. Maddox as an individual taxpayer.

   a. Eva Corporation distributes the land as a property dividend.
   b. Eva Corporation distributes the land to Ms. Maddox in lieu of her normal cash bonus paid at the end of each year.
   c. Eva Corporation sells the land to Ms. Maddox for $225,000 cash.
   d. Eva Corporation sells the land to Ms. Maddox for $100,000 cash.

16. All of the outstanding stock of Whon Corporation is owned by Don Whon, corporate president and chairman of the board. Whon Corporation would like to build a new retail store on some land that Mr. Whon foolishly bought as an investment 15 years ago. Because Mr. Whon controls everything the corporation does, he can easily arrange a transfer of the land to Whon Corporation in any one of several ways. Assuming that Mr. Whon's tax basis in this land is $225,000, and that it is currently worth only $100,000, determine the tax consequences of each of the four transactions suggested below, both to the Whon Corporation and to Mr. Whon as an individual taxpayer.

   a. Don simply transfers the land (as an additional contribution to capital) to the corporation. The corporation may or may not issue additional shares at the time of the transfer.
   b. Don transfers title to the land in exchange for the corporation's cancellation of a note that he (Don) gave years ago when the corporation loaned him $100,000 cash.
   c. Don sells the land to the corporation for $100,000 cash.
   d. Don sells the land to the corporation for $250,000 cash.

17. Compare and contrast the very similar facts described in Problems 15 and 16. Then explain, as best you can, why an Internal Revenue agent would be likely to take generally inconsistent positions in any disputes that he or she may have with Ms. Maddox and Mr. Whon.

The politics of taxation in the U.S. has been a war between the redistributors and the growthpeople. (Redistributors think that America will go to hell in a limousine unless we do things to stop the rich from getting richer while the poor get poorer. Growthpeople think that America will go to hell on foot unless we do things to increase the reward for thrift and initiative.)

Redistributors win most of the big battles, like progressive income tax rates, high rates on corporations and taxes on property. Growthpeople win most (but not all) of the skirmishes, like rapid depreciation, tax exempt interest and investment credit.

(Another team, the Simplifiers, occasionally gets into a fight with one of the big two. The Simplifiers get creamed every time.)

The big picture of tax politics, today, is a standoff. We have some redistribution of income by way of taxes, but not much. We have some growth incentives, but the U.S. growth rate is not much. This sounds like good old American compromise, and, by the ghost of Henry Clay, it should be a happy ending. It's not.

. . .

Instead of constructive synthesis, we have compromised by selecting the worst from each side. We have managed to snatch defeat from the jaws of victory.

GERARD M. BRANNON
Statement to the Senate Committee on Finance (1977)

PART

EIGHT

taxation:
a dynamic process

the compliance process

Clutching a bundle of odd receipts, canceled checks and a couple of penciled lists, the taxpayer plods timidly in to do battle with the tax agent. Bureaucrats make him nervous. He recalls vague stories about criminal tax prosecutions.

SENATOR MAGNUSON,
Congressional Record (1966)

Until now, our discussions have proceeded on the assumption that taxation is a static body of written law. The questions raised have been concerned with the *what* and the *why* of the various statutory provisions. For most introductory purposes this assumption is acceptable, since the first order of business must be to gain familiarity with the words of the Code. Nevertheless, such an assumption about the tax law is unrealistic and may even be harmful. If the law *exists* in any significant meaning of that term, its existence must be in the relationships between government, persons, and property. We must not think of the tax law as simply words in a Code, for it is a composite of the legislative actions of Congress, the administrative actions of the I.R.S., the filing of returns, the payment of taxes, and the litigation of disputes. We can understand the law only when we give up the attempt to separate its content from the very human *process* of taxation; content has real significance only when viewed from the perspective of the taxing process.

In Chapter 4, we explained how Congress creates new tax laws and how the administration interprets the Congressional acts in regulations and rulings. That chapter also includes a discussion of how courts make law by settling disputes between the government and taxpayers. You should review that material before you begin a study of the tax process in this Part.

Part Eight is a three-chapter introduction to this dynamic process of taxation. Chapter 27 reviews some details of taxpayer compliance and describes how disputes over tax questions are resolved. Chapter 28 explains some recent history in a long struggle for tax reform. And Chapter 29 describes in broad outline the ever-popular American game called tax planning.

TAXPAYER COMPLIANCE AND ADMINISTRATIVE REVIEW

The federal income tax is a self-assessed tax. Every taxpayer has the responsibility for calculation of his or her tax, completion and submission of a return form, and payment of the tax. Once a return is filed, the I.R.S. has the responsibility of reviewing and auditing returns. The purpose of this administrative review is to make sure that the tax is computed properly and that the correct tax is paid.

Responsibilities of taxpayers

As stated above, the basic responsibilities of taxpayers are computation of their tax, completion and submission of the proper return form, and payment of the tax. The first of these duties is the really complicated part—witness the preceding twenty-six chapters. Completion of returns, filing, and payment are more procedural questions. These duties, nevertheless, are important, and failure to comply with procedural requirements can result in financial penalties.

INDIVIDUALS   All individuals must make their tax computations on either Form 1040A or Form 1040. In many situations, one or more schedules accompanying Form 1040 must be filed, depending on the sources of the taxpayer's income and the nature of his or her deductions.

Annual returns of individuals are due on the fifteenth day of the fourth month following the end of the taxable year. For calendar-year taxpayers, this means April 15. When the due date of any return (or other prescribed act) falls on a Saturday, Sunday, or legal holiday, the due date is the following day.[1] Also, a return is timely filed by mail if it is postmarked on the due date. The taxpayer may obtain an automatic extension of 60 days by filing Form 4868 on or before the due date of the return and paying at least 90 percent of the tax due with the extension. Further extensions for reasonable cause can be obtained by filing Form 2688; however, these extensions should be filed in time for approval by the I.R.S.

FIDUCIARIES   Returns of fiduciaries are filed on Form 1041. Returns are due on the fifteenth day of the fourth month after the close of the taxable year. Fiduciaries are not required to pay the tax in advance so the entire amount is due with the return. Estates may elect to pay their taxes in four equal installments—one with the return, and one before the end of each of the three succeeding three-month periods.

CORPORATIONS   Corporations report their incomes on Form 1120. Their returns are due on the fifteenth day of the *third* month after year end (March 15 for a calendar-year corporation). Corporations may obtain an ''automatic'' extension of time for filing their returns by filing a tentative return or by filing Form 7004. The automatic extension is for a ninety-day period.

Corporations are also on a pay-as-you-go basis and must declare their estimated tax and pay the tax on a quarterly basis during the taxable year. The corporate tax not paid in advance may be paid in two equal installments. The first installment is due on the

due date of the return (fifteenth day of third month); the final installment is due three months later (fifteenth day of sixth month).

Penalties and interest

The Internal Revenue Code includes a number of penalties intended to encourage taxpayers to file a timely and accurate return and to pay their tax. The more important penalties are

1. *Failure to file annual returns.*   If the taxpayer fails to file a timely return, 5 percent of the net tax liability is added for each month or part of month the return is delayed. The maximum added is 25 percent. This penalty is not imposed if the taxpayer's failure is due to a reasonable cause.

2. *Failure to pay tax.*   If the taxpayer fails to pay his or her tax on time, interest is added to the tax, currently at 12 percent per annum. The interest runs from the due date of the return without considering extensions of time for filing. Because of high interest rates in recent years, some taxpayers have filed and declared their income but not paid their tax, thereby enjoying an automatic (though uncertain) loan. The Reform Act of 1969 added an additional $\frac{1}{2}$ of 1 percent per month (or fractional part of a month) as a penalty. Note that the additional $\frac{1}{2}$ of 1 percent is a penalty, not interest, and is therefore not deductible on subsequent returns. The penalty is not imposed if the taxpayer can show that the payment deficiency was due to a reasonable cause and was not willful neglect.

3. *Deficiencies in tax paid.*   If the tax computation is incorrect and the tax payment is less than the tax owed, a penalty of 5 percent of the understatement is added to the tax where the deficiency is due to negligence. If the deficiency is due to willful negligence or fraud, a penalty of 50 percent of the deficiency is added to the tax. When the fraud penalty is imposed, the penalty for failure to file and the 5-percent penalty for negligence are not imposed.

4. *Criminal penalties.*   The willful failure to pay the tax, to make a return, to keep adequate records, or to evade or defeat the tax, and willful making and subscribing to a false return are criminal acts, misdemeanors or felonies. Fines up to $10,000 and imprisonment of up to five years are the punishment for these criminal acts.

The criminal penalties are imposed only after the taxpayer is found guilty in criminal proceedings. The other penalties, however, are imposed by the I.R.S.

[1]Reg. 1.6012-1(a)(7).

The assessment of penalties by the I.R.S. is subject to administrative and judicial review, which will be explained later in this chapter.

As noted in item 2 above, the current rate of interest on underpayments is 12 percent. This rate became effective on February 1, 1980. For the two preceding years, the rate had been only 6 percent. Traditionally, the rate assessed by the government has been low relative to actual market rates. Section 6621 was added to the I.R.S. Code in January 1975 to discourage taxpayers from procrastinating in paying their taxes because of the attractiveness of low interest charges. It provides that the I.R.S. will review the prime rates in the market each September and adjust its rate to within the nearest full percent of the prime rate. The new rate will be announced on October 15 and become effective on February 1 of the following year. The current 12 percent rate thus reflects the high rates prevailing in October 1979. This rate will remain in effect until February 1982, even if the market rate is either higher or lower for most of the two-year period.

Role of the tax expert

The preceding list of responsibilities of taxpayers leads to an obvious conclusion: Many taxpayers are unable to fulfill their duties personally. Rules governing unusual or complex transactions are often beyond the scope of the average citizen's knowledge. Many taxpayers seem unable to comprehend the instructions on the return forms. And certainly a taxpayer with a high income will do everything possible to reduce tax liability. For all these reasons, there exists, predictably, a group of specialists or experts willing to assist a taxpayer for a fee.

The number of tax experts offering their services to the public probably exceeds 200,000. Unfortunately, no comprehensive system of regulation exists to assure that persons engaged in tax practice meet reasonable standards of competence. In the past, the only effective regulation of tax practice has come from the Treasury Department. The department issues Treasury cards to practitioners, which entitle them to represent taxpayers before the I.R.S. Licensed lawyers and certified public accountants can practice before the I.R.S. without a Treasury card, and only a few individuals have taken the exams and obtained a Treasury card. In general, the groups in our society best qualified to give taxpayers advice on tax matters are licensed attorneys and accountants. Yet they are in the minority when it comes to the number of "tax experts" advising tax-

payers. This fact raises a serious question: What training and qualifications do the unlicensed "experts" have?

Beyond a doubt, many people who present themselves to the public as tax practitioners have little or no expertise in tax matters. State laws are silent on who may engage in tax practice. And, while practitioners holding Treasury cards must observe the provisions of Treasury Circular 230, those practitioners without Treasury cards have no similar restrictions on their activities. They are free to advertise, to represent themselves as "experts," and to make any sort of arrangement regarding fees. It is all too common for a practitioner to rent a vacant building during tax season, engage in extensive advertising, charge a fee based on the "refund" obtained, and then close shop before the I.R.S. has an opportunity to review the returns filed. As an advertising gimmick, some practitioners "guarantee" their returns, promising to pay deficiencies assessed on the returns they prepare. Normally such a guarantee is worthless. Some practitioners with Treasury cards are not above doubt either, and many others look on the practice as just another business, paying maximum attention to efficient return preparation and minimum attention to equitable administration of the law.[2]

The Tax Reform Act of 1976 gives the Treasury some needed powers to ensure that all individuals involved in the preparation of tax returns for remuneration observe some nominal rules of conduct. These new rules will have little impact on attorneys and licensed accountants, because most of the actions proscribed by the new law are rules of conduct that most knowledgeable practitioners have previously observed. The new rules make it a misdemeanor subject to a $1,000 fine and/or imprisonment up to one year for the unauthorized disclosure of information obtained during the preparation of a return. The practitioner can, however, and often must, disclose information to I.R.S. agents and to related taxpayers under certain conditions. The rules also assess civil penalties ranging from $5 up to $500 for each wrongful act related to the preparation of returns. Acts that result in a penalty are: (1) failure to sign a return as preparer or failure to provide the preparer's identification number; (2) failure to retain a copy of returns filed for a three-year period; (3) failure to provide the I.R.S. certain information

---

[2]For a good description of how one national tax service operates, see "Storefront Tax Service Earns a Good Return," *Business Week* (March 25, 1967), pp. 196–202.

about employees who prepare returns; (4) failure of the preparer to provide the taxpayer with a copy of his or her return; (5) understatement of the tax liability due to negligent or intentional disregard for the tax laws; (6) endorsement or negotiation of any check issued to the taxpayer. Observe that these new penalties do not give the Treasury powers to improve the technical qualifications of return preparers. The criminal and civil penalties only increase the risks for the unscrupulous or uninformed preparer.

The tax law is indeed complex. Many taxpayers will need professional assistance in fulfilling their responsibilities and, incidentally, in minimizing their tax liability. In view of the preceding facts, however, the taxpayer should be cautious when seeking "expert" assistance. Those who publicly claim the status of experts necessarily may be the least qualified because those with at least the minimal qualifications may be forbidden by their professions to claim any such status. Recently, some state bar associations have allowed lawyers specializing in tax matters to identify themselves in advertisements. In addition, the American Institute of Certified Public Accountants made a change in 1978 in the code of ethics that permits limited advertising by CPAs. Under the new rules, members can advertise, including the firm name and members, services offered, fees charged, and general information about qualifications. The new rule prohibits self-laudatory statements, invidious comparisons with other professionals, and testimonials or endorsements. While a CPA cannot list the "24 reasons" why he or she should file your return, members can get their names before the public. Despite this limited advertising by lawyers and accountants, it remains true that those "experts" who make public pronouncements about their expertise are generally the least qualified to give taxpayers assistance.

Review by the Internal Revenue Service

Taxpayers file their returns at an I.R.S. regional service center. The United States is divided into seven "regions," and there is a service center in each region. These centers utilize the latest data-processing equipment in handling returns. The United States is also divided into 58 "districts." In recent years, the mechanical processing of returns has been shifted from district offices to the service centers. Personnel in the district offices, however, still perform most of the important review work.

AUDITING PROCEDURES   All returns received by the I.R.S. are checked for mechanical accuracy, which includes the following:

1. Arithmetic, including computation of tax.
2. Transfer of amounts from supporting schedules to return.
3. Matching information returns filed with the income reported on the return. For example, the employer submits a copy of each employee's Form W-2 (withholding) to the I.R.S. The I.R.S. also receives a veritable mountain of Forms 1099 showing the amounts of interest paid to taxpayers by financial institutions, the dividends paid to shareholders by corporations, and certain other payments. In 1977 the I.R.S. expanded its efforts to match the information contained on Forms 1099, 1087, and W-2 to individual returns. This action resulted from public and Congressional pressures after disclosure of the fact that only 175 million of the 435 million information returns filed in 1975 were ever "matched" against returns by the I.R.S. computers. Even though Congress mandated a *full* matching program in 1962, we are still a long way from achieving that objective.

The service centers, using automated equipment, do most of this mechanical work. If a mechanical error that results in an understatement of tax is discovered, a bill for the deficiency is sent to the taxpayer. If an error has resulted in an overpayment, the excess payment is credited to the taxpayer or refunded.

In addition to the mechanical processing just described, the computers are programmed to select certain returns for further examination. Using multiple discriminate analysis, the program selects those returns that, upon audit, are most likely to yield additional taxes. In addition, certain returns are automatically tagged for examination based on arbitrary criteria such as large refunds and reported income in excess of a certain amount. Finally, the computer makes a random selection of returns for examination. These returns are used in the "compliance program," where the error rate on the sample selected is used to infer statistically the error rate on all returns. The number of returns selected for examination varies from year to year based mainly on the personnel available to conduct audits.

The returns selected for audit by the service centers are forwarded to the appropriate district office. There, the returns are eventually assigned to revenue

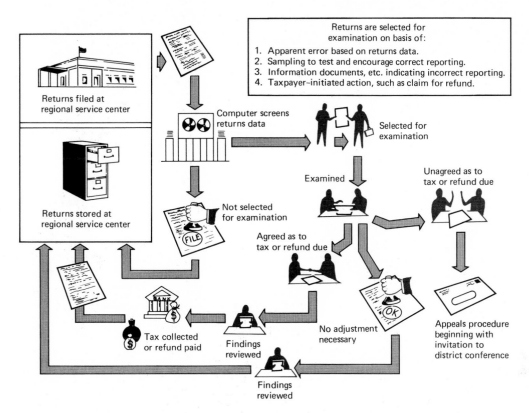

Returns are selected for examination on basis of:
1. Apparent error based on returns data.
2. Sampling to test and encourage correct reporting.
3. Information documents, etc. indicating incorrect reporting.
4. Taxpayer-initiated action, such as claim for refund.

Returns filed at regional service center

Returns stored at regional service center

Computer screens returns data

Selected for examination

Not selected for examination

Examined

Unagreed as to tax or refund due

Agreed as to tax or refund due

No adjustment necessary

Appeals procedure beginning with invitation to district conference

Tax collected or refund paid

Findings reviewed

Findings reviewed

FIGURE 27-1   Income-Tax Audit Procedure of the Internal Revenue Service

agents for audit. This examination may be an "office audit" or a "field audit." For the office audit, the taxpayer is notified of the items under examination and is requested to bring to the district office the necessary records and supporting documents. For taxpayers with extensive records, the agents go to the taxpayer's place of business to perform a field audit.

Upon completion of the agent's examination, the agent normally confers with the taxpayer about his or her findings. In some cases, the agent communicates the findings to the taxpayer by letter. The smart taxpayer will have expert help during these conversations if any material amounts are involved. Technically, only practitioners with Treasury cards, lawyers, and accountants can represent taxpayers; most agents, however, are willing to work with the "preparer" or advisor to the taxpayer even if the person does not have a Treasury card or is not a lawyer or a certified public accountant.

This contact between taxpayers and the examining agents can have any one of three results:

1. The agent may find that the return as filed is correct. In this event, the findings of the agent are reviewed by the audit division and, if the reviewer agrees with the findings, the audit is finished.

2. The agent may propose adjustments, which normally increase the tax, and the taxpayer may agree. The agent then makes an assessment of the deficiency on Form 870. After review of the findings by the review staff, the taxpayer signs Form 870 and pays the deficiency. The payment normally closes the return, which means that no subsequent adjustments are made to the tax for that year. In a few cases the adjustments may result in a refund to the taxpayer.

3. The agent may propose adjustments resulting in a deficiency, and the taxpayer may disagree. When no agreement is reached between the agent and the taxpayer, the taxpayer may obtain either a conference in the Appeals office, or move directly to obtain judicial review. These alternatives are explained later. The auditing process in the I.R.S. is depicted in Figure 27-1.

Taxpayers experiencing their first tax return examination often become apprehensive when they are notified of the impending audit. Some undoubtedly have visions of a merciless inquisition that finally wrings out the last possible tax dollar. Taxpayers with this mistaken notion are sometimes surprised to find that the agents are reasonable persons who are trying to administer fairly a complex law. Only taxpayers guilty of fraud or gross negligence have anything to fear. This does not mean, of course, that the taxpayer will necessarily win his or her case. One serious criticism of the tax process at the audit level is the lack of training and expertise of many agents. This criticism is more frequently valid for personnel in the I.R.S. who conduct office audits. Because of lower pay and a somewhat limited opportunity for rapid advancement, the better graduates from strong accounting and law programs in colleges and universities very often opt for careers in public practice or in industry. Given a national shortage of individuals with training and expertise in the tax law, the I.R.S. has been forced to hire some individuals with doubtful qualifications. We believe that beginning salaries for agents should be increased and that promotion policies in the I.R.S. should place great emphasis on merit. These changes would place the I.R.S. in a better position to compete for the limited talent available.

The initial review by the I.R.S. just described has a major weakness. Taxpayers and their expert advisors receive assessments for additional taxes and/or penalties that are automatically produced by the computer in the service centers. In many cases, the assessment or penalty is incorrect. For example, legitimate deductions reported at the wrong place on the tax forms may be automatically disallowed. As another example, a penalty for late filing may be assessed even though a covering letter clearly shows that such delay was not willful. To set things right, practitioners often find themselves in an extended correspondence with the computer itself. That is, any new information provided merely results in another printout containing the same error. The problem arises because of a shortage of qualified personnel at the service centers. In any event, it can be a frustrating experience, and practitioners have adopted various techniques to solve the problem. We know of one taxpayer who prepared a large rubber stamp with the words "For Human Processing Only." He claims that this message, in red ink, superimposed on letters to the service centers is effective.

APPEALS CONFERENCES When the taxpayer refuses to agree to the agent's proposed adjustments, the agent prepares a complete report of the findings, which is submitted to the review staff in the district office. After review (and changes, if required), the report on the examination is mailed to the taxpayer. The covering letter, called the "30-day letter," notifies the taxpayer of the proposed deficiency and normally gives the taxpayer a 30-day period in which to decide on a course of action. Three avenues are open to the taxpayer at this point:

1. Taxpayer may accept the examiner's findings, sign Form 870, and close the case.

2. Taxpayer may request a conference with the Appeals office. The conferees in this office are organized under the Regional Director of Appeals, and they have broad powers to settle disputes with taxpayers as explained below.

3. Taxpayer may ignore the 30-day letter and wait for the formal deficiency notice, called the "90-day letter." On receipt of the 90-day letter, the taxpayer must either pay the deficiency or take the case to the courts.

The Appeals conference. The right of appeal to the Appeals office is automatic upon receipt of the 30-day letter. Where the amount of the deficiency is more than $2,500, the taxpayer must file a written protest before the conference. No specific form for the protest is dictated; however, the protest must include certain elements:

1. A statement that the taxpayer wishes to appeal the assessment to either the district conference or the appellate conference.

2. The taxpayer's name and address.

3. The date and symbols of the 30-day letter and the finding being protested.

4. The tax year or years involved.

5. An itemized schedule of unagreed adjustments.

6. A statement supporting facts in contested factual issues.

7. Arguments and authorities upon which the protest is based.

8. A declaration, signed by the taxpayer, that he or she believes, under penalty of perjury, that facts stated are "true, correct, and complete."

It is generally agreed that the protest should include all issues that the taxpayer intends to raise during the conference. While no rule prohibits the taxpayer from raising new issues, surprise moves during the conference are rarely effective.

The conference is informal. There are no formal rules for procedure. If the taxpayer is being represented by an accountant or lawyer, which is the common practice, the taxpayer's agent must present a power of attorney. The points of departure are typically the revenue agent's report (RAR) and the taxpayer's protest, if one is filed. The factual and/or legal points at issue are then discussed.

Before October 1978, administrative review by the I. R. S. consisted of a two-level conference procedure. First, taxpayers had the right to a conference in the district office. This level was known as the "informal" conference, and historically the conferees from the district staff had only limited powers to settle disputes. If agreement could not be reached at the informal conference, the taxpayer next took the dispute to a "formal" conference with the regional appellate staff. These conferees traditionally could settle disputes based on the "hazards of litigation." This term refers to an assessment of the probability that the government might lose the dispute in judicial proceedings. Instead of settling disagreements on a yes-no basis, the appellate conferees had the power to bargain for a compromise settlement. Because of this power, which the district conferees did not have, most disputes were settled at the formal conference, especially those involving large amounts.

The recent change eliminates the duplication of effort by essentially eliminating the district or informal conference. There is now only an administrative review office, the Appeals office. The conferees here have broad powers of settlement, including the power to compromise an issue based on the hazards of litigation. The settlement authority, however, depends upon whether the case is " non-docketed" or "docketed."

Non-docketed cases are those that reach the Appeals office before the statutory notice of deficiency (90-day letter) is issued. For non-docketed cases, the Appeals office has exclusive jurisdiction. New facts can be presented by depositions and by the testimony of witnesses. While the rules of evidence applicable to court proceedings are not followed, the taxpayer's case is strengthened if the new facts presented would be admissible in court. The conferees are required to consider the hazards of litigation without regard to the amount involved. The purpose of the Appeals office is to keep disputes out of the courts. If the law is uncertain, the appellate conferees welcome offers to compromise the issues and will themselves make such offers. However, offers of 20 percent or less will generally be ignored because the conferees are instructed not to accept offers that have only nuisance value. After the conference, agreements reached, if any, are reviewed by

the head of the Appeals office at the regional office. If, upon review, the settlement is not acceptable, the taxpayer is generally given an opportunity to hold a conference with the reviewer. If agreement is reached, Form 870-AD is completed and the case, for all practical purposes, is closed. If no agreement is reached, the 90-day letter is then issued.

Docketed cases are those where the 90-day letter has already been issued and the taxpayer has filed a petition in the Tax Court. Each petition filed is given a docket number and the case formally becomes the responsibility of the regional counsel and is assigned to an attorney who represents the Justice Department but works at the regional office of the I.R.S. In the period after a case is docketed but before a date for trial is set, settlement authority is effectively shared by the Appeals office and the regional counsel, although the latter has final jurisdiction formally. Thus, the docketed case is referred to the Appeals office, and an effort is made to reach a compromise. This is generally true even though the same dispute may have already been handled in an appeals conference. At this point, maximum pressure is on both the government and the taxpayer to reach a settlement since neither typically wants to incur the bother and costs of court proceedings.

Taxpayers who permit their disputes to reach the docketed status are very often gambling that the regional counsel will take a more cautious stance relative to the hazards of litigation than that taken by the Appeals office. After all, some attorney in the regional counsel office must consider the actual trial. On the other hand, any offer previously made by the appellate division before the case is docketed is no longer in effect. The taxpayer may find that regional counsel has a more optimistic outlook and be forced to accept a reduced offer, to capitulate entirely, or to go to trial.

After a case is set for trial, settlement authority rests solely with the regional counsel. From this point on, the licensed accountant can play only an advisory role. Direct negotiations with government counsel by an accountant would certainly be construed as the practice of law.

Calculating the odds. While the preceding discussion refers to the taxpayer as the active participant, wise taxpayers usually seek professional help for appeals conferences. Indeed, most practitioners will advise their clients not to attend the proceedings unless they are knowledgeable in tax matters. Representation at the conferences by skilled professionals costs money. As a result, the betting odds favor the taxpayer with a relatively large amount in dispute, because of three factors. First, the *absolute* amount that can be gained from the conferences is greater. Second, the cost of professional representation will increase as the amount in dispute increases, but less than proportionally. Third, the fees paid for professional help are income tax deductions, and the after-tax cost of these services declines relatively as the taxpayer's marginal tax rate increases.

Some simple arithmetic will illustrate the point. Take the situation of two taxpayers, A and B, who are considering the wisdom of hiring a professional to represent them at an appellate conference. Relevant facts are:

	A	B
Amount of tax in dispute	$6,000	$100,000
Accountant's fee for preparing protest and handling conference	2,000	10,000
Marginal tax rate	25%	60%
After-tax cost of professional service	$1,500	$ 4,000
Estimated probability of winning	50%	50%

Taxpayer A is faced with a $1,500 net cost to gain $3,000 (50 percent of $6,000), an even-money bet. B, on the other hand, is betting $4,000 to gain $50,000, odds of almost 12 to 1.

Calculation of the odds is made more difficult because your chances of being audited and finally assessed additional taxes and penalties may depend in part on where you live. Some I.R.S. statistics show, for example, that a New Yorker has one chance in 39 of being audited, whereas a resident of New Mexico has only one chance in 78. District conferences in New York settled on 30 percent of the additional assessments, while those in Baltimore obtained 74 percent.[3] The process is thus somewhat chancy and is clearly biased toward the more affluent. The process of judicial review discussed next has the same attributes.

JUDICIAL REVIEW

Before turning to judicial consideration of tax conflicts, we should note that the tax process has many procedures built into it to protect the rights of taxpayers, although the system is biased in favor of the more affluent. First, the law is enacted by elected

[3] *Wall Street Journal,* Tax Reports, p. 1, April 14, 1976.

officials. Before enactment, individual taxpayers and special interest groups are given an opportunity to express their opinions of the proposals at the congressional committee hearings. After enactment, the administration must set out its interpretation of the law in regulations. Proposed regulations are circulated to interested parties before final adoption. The I.R.S. makes numerous rulings that help taxpayers assess the impact of the income tax on their financial affairs. This part of the process is explained in Chapter 4. After the taxpayer files a return, proposed adjustments to the tax calculation are considered carefully in conferences with agents and conferees. Finally, the conflict is considered by the Appeals office, whose primary function is settlement of conflicts.

This lengthy process can hardly be termed arbitrary. The government cannot be said to "run roughshod" over the taxpayer. Indeed, a fairer criticism of the process might be that it is too cumbersome, that too much time and effort are spent on safeguarding property rights. In any event, taxpayers who cannot reach an agreement with the I.R.S. may take their cases to the courts. Through appeals, each taxpayer may insist on the protection of his or her rights until a decision has been rendered by the Supreme Court.

Three avenues for judicial review are open to taxpayers. The taxpayer may have his or her case heard first by the Tax Court of the United States, or he or she may go first to a U.S. district court or to the Court of Claims. Since the popular alternative is the Tax Court, we will consider it first.

The Tax Court route

Taxpayers who do not reach an agreement with the appellate division receive the 90-day letter, which is the formal deficiency notice. The letter gives the taxpayer a 90-day period within which to file a petition with the Tax Court. If a petition is not filed, the I.R.S. will assess the additional tax and, if the taxpayer fails to pay, will take legal steps to force payment.

If a petition is filed, the conflict will be heard by the Tax Court (called the Board of Tax Appeals prior to 1943). This court is specially organized to hear tax cases and is completely independent of the I.R.S. Judges are appointed to the Tax Court for a 15-year term by the president. Although the Tax Court has its headquarters in Washington, D.C., sessions are held in all major cities at various times, and the taxpayer may request a hearing in his or her general area.

The Tax Court is a trial court, at which taxpayers may represent themselves or be represented by counsel. Generally, only attorneys are admitted to practice in the Tax Court, although some C.P.A.'s have been granted this right by examination. At the hearing, depositions of witnesses and oral and written arguments of the parties are presented to the Court. There is no jury. The Court arrives at its decision and writes up its findings in an opinion. This opinion is presented to the parties. (The more important, or "regular," decisions of the Tax Court are printed and distributed by the government, and are cited T.C.[4] For decisions prior to 1943, the citation is B.T.A.)

The 1969 Reform Act permitted the Tax Court to set up a small claims division to handle disputes where the amount in contest does not exceed $1,500 plus any amounts conceded by the parties. Hearings are not before judges but before commissioners appointed by the Chief Judge of the Tax Court. In the small claims division, formal rules of evidence need not be followed; the Tax Court can prescribe rules of evidence it feels to be appropriate. The findings of the commissioner are not reported in formal written opinions, and the opinions cannot be used as precedent in other cases. Finally, the decisions in small claims cases cannot be appealed to a higher court—the decision is final for both parties.

Throughout the review process, the taxpayer must take the initiative. He or she must ask for the conferences with the I.R.S. and for the hearing before the Tax Court. In all conferences and hearings, the determination of the I.R.S. is presumed to be correct. The taxpayer generally must carry the burden of proving that the proposed adjustments are incorrect. The decision of the Tax Court, however, may be disputed by either party. If the decision goes against the government, the Justice Department may appeal. Taxpayers also have the right of appeal. (Decisions in the small claims division cannot be appealed by either party.)

Appeals from decisions of the Tax Court are made to the U.S. Court of Appeals. There are ten Courts of Appeals in the country. Here, again, oral and written arguments are presented by the parties, and a decision is reached by the judges of the court. (Court of Appeals decisions are cited F.2nd.) The final appeal is, of course, to the U.S. Supreme Court (cited U.S. or S.Ct.). Either party to the dispute may

ask the Court to consider the case by asking for a writ of *certiorari*. The Supreme Court normally will only hear cases when the Courts of Appeals have reached different conclusions on the same issue or where, in the Court's opinion, the constitutionality of a tax law is questionable.

Throughout the lengthy process of administrative and judicial review, the taxpayer is *not* assessed for the deficiency until the review process is complete if the Tax Court route is selected. The taxpayer pays the tax according to *his* or *her* computation; additional assessments are made only at the end of the review process. The taxpayer is required, however, to pay interest on any eventual deficiencies. Interest runs from the due date of the return.

The district court route

For reasons too sophisticated to explain here, taxpayers may wish to avoid the hearing before the Tax Court. To do so, the taxpayer merely pays the proposed deficiency at any point in the process before the petition to the Tax Court. He or she may then file a claim for refund of the deficiency paid.

The claim for refund sets in motion the administrative review procedures previously discussed. Thus, the claim is considered by the district office. If the claim is denied, as it normally will be, a 30-day letter is sent, which may lead to a district conference and/or an appellate division conference. If no agreement is reached in these conferences, the refund claim is denied by the I.R.S. When a claim for refund is denied, the taxpayer has a statutory right to sue the government for the tax illegally (in the eyes of the taxpayer) assessed and collected.

Most suits to force a refund are brought in U.S. district courts (cited F.Supp.). In this court, the taxpayer must be represented by an attorney. A jury of peers may be used to determine the facts. The judge of a district court, however, decides the law. Once a decision is reached in this court, either party may ask for an appeal to the appropriate circuit court of appeals. The decision of this court may, in turn, be appealed to the Supreme Court.

The taxpayer may also take the suit for the refund to the U.S. Court of Claims in Washington, D.C. Decisions of this court are appealed directly to the Supreme Court.

The procedures for administrative and judicial review of conflicts are briefly summarized in Figure 27-2. This diagram, from an I.R.S. publication, has been changed to show the combination of the district and appellate conferences into a single conference in

---

[4]A complete citation consists of the volume number, the reporter series, and a page (or case) number. For example, 47 T.C. 212 references volume 47 of the Tax Court reporter, p. 212.

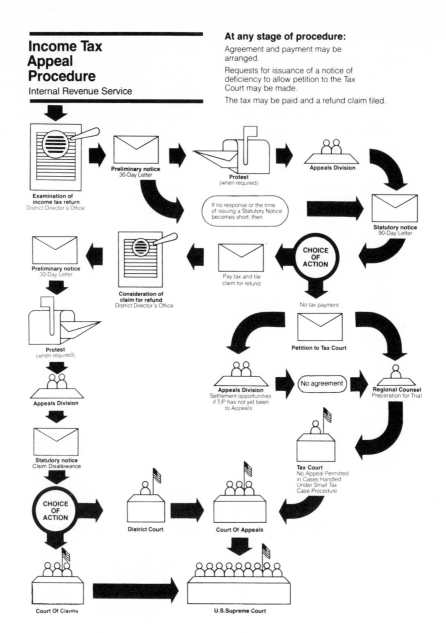

FIGURE **27-2**   Income-Tax Appeal Procedure of the Internal Revenue Service

the Appeals office. Note that agreement may be reached at any step in the process. Even after the petition is filed with the Tax Court, or suit filed in a district court, court conferences between the government and the taxpayer are frequent, and agreement may be reached at any time.

How the I.R.S. plays the judicial game

The person not yet initiated into the subtleties of the compliance process would logically assume that once a court has reached a decision and the loser

does not appeal that decision, then that decision can be safely relied on by other taxpayers. For example, if a taxpayer wins a fight with the I.R.S. in the Tax Court and the I.R.S. does not appeal the Tax Court decision, then other taxpayers with the same factual situation should be able to rely on the court's opinion. Unfortunately, while logical, the compliance game is played using more complicated rules.

When the I.R.S. loses in the Tax Court, it may follow one of four possible alternative procedures. First, it can appeal the decision as discussed earlier. This appeal, of course, is a clear signal that the

I.R.S. does not agree with the Tax Court's conclusions. Second, the General Counsel for the I.R.S. may announce an "acquiescence," which lets everyone know that the I.R.S. will follow the decision in other situations with the same facts. Third, the I.R.S. may announce a "non-acquiescence," a clear signal that it will not follow the decision, even though it may not choose to appeal it. Finally, it may remain silent, in which case we do not know what it will do in similar situations.

For decisions reached by district courts and by the Court of Claims, the I.R.S. has two courses of action, either an appeal to the appropriate court or silence. Silence, however, cannot be interpreted as acquiescence. As with the Tax Court decisions, silence may signify agreement or disagreement. Taxpayers and their advisors may rely on a decision of a district court or the Court of Claims, but this does not mean that the I.R.S. will not attempt to enforce a rule of law contrary to the decision.

What happens if the I.R.S. has appealed a Tax Court or district court decision and has lost again? Logically, this should be the end of the matter. But, again, logic goes for naught. The I.R.S., it is true, must follow decisions of the Circuit Courts of Appeals, but *only* in that particular circuit. Often, the government will apply a contrary rule in the jurisdiction of other Circuit Courts. The government's intention is to obtain a conflicting ruling in another circuit. Given a conflict of opinion between Circuit Courts of Appeal, the case *may* then be heard before the Supreme Court and the question finally resolved.

The process just described seems, at first glance, grossly unfair and wasteful. However, we must remember the extraordinary measures taxpayers take to reduce their taxes and the enormous stakes involved in the annual contest, and remember also that the I.R.S. is charged with the role of protecting the revenues by enforcing the laws passed by Congress. That the government occasionally persists beyond reason to enforce the law based upon *its* interpretation is a natural result of the process.

Congress is currently considering a change in our court system that could reduce the number of conflicts with the attendant uncertainty. The change being considered would create a new Court of Tax Appeals. This new court would hear all appeals of tax cases from the Tax Court and from the District Courts. The result would be consistent treatment at the appeals level as opposed to conflicting opinions between the several circuits. The judges on the proposed court would be lawyers who have specialized

in the tax law. Given the numerous uncertainties that exist in the practice of taxation at present, any change that reduces uncertainty should be given serious consideration.

Despite the several criticisms of the compliance process noted in this chapter, the overall process is a relatively fair one, in which citizens are safeguarded against arbitrary administration and confiscation. Maintenance of a fair, equitable process is essential if the income tax law is to play the vital role assigned to it in our political and economic system. We must nevertheless note in passing that it is a complicated process involving many people, including many with a sizable vested interest in the process as it now exists. As a result, tax reforms—changes in the process—are not easily made, as we will see in the following chapter.

SOME STATISTICS ON THE TAX PROCESS

The process described above is a complicated one. To help the student place the various steps in proper perspective, it might be helpful to review some statistics on how well the taxpayer does in the process relative to the government. The statistics are restricted to the administrative and judicial review.[5] How the taxpayer fares in the legislative process cannot be reduced to neat numbers.

In 1978 approximately 137 million returns were filed, including about 87 million individual income tax returns and 2.4 million corporate income tax returns. Of this total, about 2.2 percent (1.9 million) of the individual returns and about 6.1 percent (147,000) of the corporate returns were examined. The I.R.S. assessed additional taxes and penalties of $6.3 billion on the returns examined. Individual and fiduciary income tax returns accounted for $1.8 billion, and corporate returns accounted for $3.3 billion. The remainder, of course, came from other taxes.

The vast majority of disputes are settled at the audit level. In 1978, of the 2.3 million returns audited, which resulted in additional assessments and penalties of $6.3 billion, more than 2.1 million were settled at the audit level. The conference procedures resulted in the settlement of an additional 54,715 cases; administrative review procedures settled

---

[5] *Annual Report of the Commissioner of the Internal Revenue Service* (Washington, D.C.: U.S. Government Printing Office, 1978).

about 97 percent of the cases referred, with only 3 percent going to trial. In summary, most disputes are settled in the administrative review procedures, and in a typical year taxpayers eventually pay about 50 percent of original assessments for additional taxes and penalties. This percent varies significantly, however, at different levels of income. Unfortunately, the settlement ratio is disproportionately high at the low end of the income scale. This could be due to poor representation on behalf of the low-income taxpayer; a realization that it does not "pay" to dispute small amounts of tax; an unreasonable attitude of agents in small cases; or any of several other factors. At any event, the fact bears further investigation.

The taxpayers' record in the courts is not quite as good as in the administrative review based on the number of cases won. The record for opinions rendered in 1978, the last year available, are as follows:

	Percent won by taxpayer	Percent lost by taxpayer	Percent partially won by taxpayer
Tax Court of the U.S.	11	51	38
U.S. District Courts	26	63	11
U.S. Court of Claims	26	64	11

These percents may be misleading, however, because they do not reveal the amounts involved, a statistic that is not available.

The number of litigated decisions is very small relative to disputes settled in the administrative review procedures. On the other hand, over 13,000 cases related to the federal tax laws are filed annually in the Tax Court alone. That amounts to a sizable body of "new" law and underscores the point that taxation is a human process, never static, but always in a state of flux.

PROBLEMS

1. a. What are the three courts in which legal action may be begun in income-tax matters?
   b. Which of these courts may include a jury trial?
   c. To which court are the majority of tax disputes taken?
   d. What is the appeal route from each court?
2. What do the following references mean? Make your answers complete.
   a. 48 T.C. 896
   b. 262 U.S. 430
   c. 118 F.Supp. 102
   d. 280 F.2nd 300
3. What alternatives are available to a taxpayer on receipt of the 30-day letter? The 90-day letter?
4. Assume that a calendar-year taxpayer fails to file a return until December 30. Outline the statutory (as opposed to criminal) penalties that might be imposed by the I.R.S., assuming:
   a. The failure was willful (but not fraudulent).
   b. The failure was fraudulent.
5. The text describes the different levels of administrative and judicial review. What requirements must a tax practitioner meet in order to represent taxpayers at the different levels?
6. Below are statements about the tax process. State whether each is true or false. If false, explain why.
   a. The statutory notice of a tax deficiency is issued following the completion of the audit process.
   b. A taxpayer cannot obtain court action on a tax case until he or she has exhausted all procedures for relief within the I.R.S.
   c. Taxpayers have an undisputed right to a hearing before the Supreme Court after proper actions have been brought at the appropriate lower courts.

d. Most tax disputes between the I.R.S. and taxpayers are settled at the informal conference level.

e. Taxpayers must have a formal protest prepared before they are entitled to a hearing at the appeals conference.

f. Most taxpayers elect to carry their disputes to federal district courts, if they decide to go to court.

g. In tax matters, our system of justice is even-handed, affording equal opportunities in our society.

7. Robert McFee filed his income tax return, due April 15, on May 12. He had not requested an extension of time for filing. The delay was attributable to the fact that McFee, an accountant, was simply too busy filing returns for other people. An analysis of his return showed that he had made quarterly estimated payments of $8,400, whereas the actual tax liability for the year is $9,200. Describe the penalties and other action that McFee faces.

8. Assume the same fact as in Problem 7, except that the quarterly payments totaled $9,200, whereas McFee's actual tax liability for the year was $8,400. Describe the penalties and other action that McFee faces.

9. a. In a previous year, the taxpayer reported gross income of $6,000. On this income he paid a tax of $320. In reviewing his records during the current year he discovered a "remittance advice" for $120 that he had received in the previous tax year. Further investigation revealed that he had failed to report this $120 of taxable income on his tax return for that year. What is your advice to him? What types of liabilities will he have if he follows your advice?

b. A friend of the taxpayer in part a suggests to the taxpayer that he should "just forget that $120. They [the I.R.S.] never audit returns with income as low as yours." Reply to this, including in your answer a review of the procedures by which returns are selected for audit.

10. On his tax return for the year 19x1, Omar claimed a dependency exemption for his mother. His return was audited, and an agent disallowed the dependency exemption. Omar received a "30-day letter" notifying him of a proposed additional tax liability of $182. Omar is very perturbed over this assessment and comes to you as a tax expert, saying "I'll take it to court. I'm just not going to pay this $182."

a. What procedure do you suggest that Omar follow?

b. What procedure would be necessary to literally "take it to court"?

11. A majority of cases involving tax questions are decided by the Tax Court of the United States. List some reasons that probably explain this fact.

12. a. Explain the difference between a "non-docketed" and a "docketed" case.

b. Why might a taxpayer refuse an offer of compromise from the appellate conferee and file a petition with the Tax Court, even when he or she does not anticipate actual litigation?

c. Who has settlement jurisdiction for non-docketed cases? For docketed cases? For cases scheduled for trial?

13. List three factors that cause the compliance process to be biased in favor of wealthier taxpayers.

14. a. When can a taxpayer unquestionably rely on a Tax Court case, given the same facts?

b. To the contrary, what signal or signals does the I.R.S. give taxpayers that indicate that a Tax Court decision will not be followed?

15. John Price recently received a letter from the I.R.S. stating that John's return for a recent year is being examined. John, an engineer, prepared the return

himself. The letter asks John to bring his records for the year under examination when he appears for the office audit. John is convinced that he has made some terrible mistake in the computation of his tax. He is worried. What can you tell him that will ease his mind?

16. Consider the material in Chapter 4 and in this chapter. Make a list of the sources of tax law that you could possibly consult to find an answer to a tax question. In your answer, consider only primary sources, not secondary sources such as your textbook and other commentaries.

SUPPLEMENTAL PROBLEMS

17. The Alpha Company is engaged in the business of manufacturing hot and cold patches for automobile tires. The company began business as a partnership in 1936 and has just incorporated under Sec. 351. In years past, the company has been moderately successful, due in a large part to its patented "hot patch." The advent of the tubeless tire has adversely affected their sales, however, and the company is extremely short of working capital and in need of financing. The owners of Alpha Company have been approached by a Mr. Vez, a business promoter and financial consultant, who has recently acquired all the stock of Omega Company, a Cleveland-based corporation engaged in the manufacture of rubber floor mats for automobiles. Omega was a closely held family corporation that was sold when the founder and patriarchal head of the family died. Omega is also in need of working capital because it has invested most of its profits in acquiring special-order rubber fabrication machinery. Mr. Vez has proposed that Alpha buy Omega and thus obtain much-needed diversification. As a part of the deal, Vez proposes to arrange the requisite financing for both companies.

After due consideration, Alpha's board of directors have authorized and caused to be issued $4,500,000 in 20-year 7-percent level monthly payment registered bonds secured by Alpha's cash flow and by a $6,800,000 secured negotiable note of Air & Earth Investment Company, payable to Alpha. (This note was given to Alpha when it sold to and then leased back all its operating equipment from Air & Earth.) The bonds are to be purchased by Vez from Alpha for less than their face value (hereinafter referred to as discount) in exchange for the following: (1) All the capital stock of Omega Corporation (having a value of $1,750,000); (2) $1,375,000 in cash (borrowed by Vez from bank); and (3) Mr. Vez's five-year 5-percent negotiable note in the face amount of $250,000. Bonds of Alpha having a par value of $2,750,000 will be pledged by Mr. Vez to a bank for a five-year loan of $1,750,000. As described in (2), $1,375,000 of the loan proceeds will be delivered to Alpha by Vez. The remaining $1,750,000 in bonds will be delivered by Vez to the family owners of Omega to secure the payment by Vez of the purchase price of the stock of Omega.

a. What are the federal income tax consequences to Alpha?

b. What are the federal income tax consequences to Mr. Vez?

18. During his lifetime, Sam Jones has amassed a great deal of wealth, consisting of property, stocks, and cash. A number of years ago, Sam came to you with an idea about setting up a trust to take care of his brothers and sisters in the event of his death. A plan was worked out to his satisfaction.

When Sam died several years ago, all the properties except the stock were sold and all the cash was divided among two brothers, two sisters, three daughters, and assorted grandchildren.

The stock, which constituted the controlling interest in Jones Van Lines, Inc. and J.&L. Management Co., Inc., was to be held in a trust. Income from the stock would go to the two sisters, ages 63 and 68, and the two brothers, 60 and 64, for the remainder of their lives.

Each beneficiary received a certain sum per month. Any excess amount not paid would accumulate as part of the corpus. With the death of the last brother or sister, the trust would terminate and equal shares would be distributed to Ralph, Waldo, and Emmett, three of Sam's grandchildren.

The two companies' earnings and dividends for 19x1–x3 were as follows:

	Jones Earnings	Dividends	*J. & L.* Earnings	Dividends
19x1	$764,890.06	$37,550	$66,482.57	$11,675
19x2	687,934.50	29,500	65,994.60	11,550
19x3	701,650.35	32,400	66,891.66	12,045

In early 19x4, Ralph, Waldo, and Emmett came to you for help. Because you are the family's tax advisor and consultant, they ask you for advice. With the two companies' stock tied up in the trust, they cannot run the businesses with the flexibility they would like.

Although they will eventually receive the stock, they would like to have it now so that they might run the businesses as they would like.

a. Can the three men gain possession of the stock immediately?

b. If they can obtain the stock, will any tax advantage be available to them?

RETURN PROBLEM

Howard and Linda Crowsley live at 802 Main Street, Sometown, State 72102. They have three children: Anthony, 8; Robert, 6; and Susan, 6 months. Howard is a patrolman for the City of Sometown. His W-2 Form for 1979 gives the following information:

Soc. Sec. No.	Gross wages	Income tax withheld	FICA withheld
459-73-2710	$7,009.96	1,159,96	410.08

In order to keep his job as patrolman, the City of Sometown required Howard to attend an eight-week (five-day week) training course at the Regional Police Officers' Academy in Big Town, located 75 miles north of Sometown. The City of Sometown paid his tuition of $550 for the course. Other expenses paid by Howard, other than his commuting costs to and from the school each day, were: gun and holster, $125, police officer's equipment, $59. He also spent $2.00 a day for his lunch while in Big Town. The uniforms, which were required by the city, cost $65 in 1979. Howard is required to provide a CB in his personal auto and telephone service in his home so that he may be reached at any time in case of an emergency. The CB radio cost $240 in 1979 and had an estimated life of three years. (Use straight-line depreciation.) Howard estimates the telephone in his home is used one-fourth of the time for business. His phone bill was $120 during 1979.

In January, 1977, Howard and Linda had established a dry cleaning service,

Sometown Cleaners, 200 Main Street. When Howard took the patrolman's job in January, 1979, Linda continued the operation by employing additional help. Their depreciation schedule indicated the following through December 31, 1978:

Date acquired	Item	Cost	Estimated life	Method[a]	Depreciation through 12/31/78
1/1/77	Land	$ 2,000			
1/1/77	Building	18,000	15 yr	SL	$2,400.00
1/1/77	Used presses	875	5 yr	150DB	446.25
1/1/77	Used boiler	1,750	5 yr	150DB	892.50
1/1/77	Used delivery truck	2,400	3 yr	150DB	1,800.00

[a] SL = straight line. 150DB = 150% declining balance.

In 1977 the Crowsleys did not take bonus depreciation but did take the investment credit. (In your solution, assume no salvage value.)

During 1979, they had the following additional income and expense items relative to the cleaning business:

Gross receipts	$6,301
Expenses:	
Naphtha	228
Plastic bags	110
Hangers	158
Press pads	235
Advertising	85
Utilities	261
Presser's salary	1,200
Taxes on building	85
Insurance on building	75
Employer's shares FICA	57
Interest on equipment loan	85
Gas and oil for truck	240
Contribution to United Way	30

After their third baby was born in 1979, the Crowsleys found it necessary on July 1 to sell the cleaning operation. They received a total of $24,000, which was allocated as follows:

Land	$ 4,000
Building	16,000
Used presses	700
Used boiler	1,500
Delivery truck	1,800

During the six months that Linda operated the cleaners, she paid her mother $100 a month to look after the children in her home. Her mother is not a dependent, and FICA taxes were paid on the mother's wages.

Other expenses that Howard and Linda paid during 1979 were:

Hospitalization insurance	$ 225
Medicine and drugs	112
Doctors and dentists (not reimbursed)	505
Eyeglasses	38
Trips to doctors' offices, 700 mi	

Taxes on home	600
Miles driven on personal business during 1979—7,000 mi	
Interest on home	1,250
Interest on auto loan	420
Finance charges on credit accounts	140
Church contributions	35
Income tax preparation	75
Tax on automobile	27

On December 10, 1979, they ran short of cash and had to sell 20 shares of RCA stock they had purchased for $2,000 on July 7, 1979. The sales price was $1,800, but a commission of $108 was deducted on the sale.

Prepare a joint return for the Crowsleys for 1979.

the reform process

In the preceding chapter, we saw that the compliance process is rather complex. Like most processes involving many people, the process tends to resist change. This tendency to inertia is due in part to the reluctance with which people approach changes in their behavior patterns. In the case of the tax law, this understandable human tendency is strengthened by the network of vested interests that segments of the population have in the law as it stands at any point in time. People who earn a substantial portion of their income from trading in corporate stocks, land, and other capital assets like the rules for capital gains. The business community generally enjoys the broad interpretation of "ordinary and necessary" for travel and entertainment expenses. It would be a peculiar world indeed if proposals to change these rules, which could result in higher taxes for the people involved, were not resisted vigorously.

Yet another, and perhaps more important, reason exists for the resistance to change in the taxing process. Once a tax law is passed and remains in effect for several years, financial transactions are modified to "fit" the law. Our ways of "doing business" change to accommodate the law. Our financial transactions in turn affect the distribution of the nation's wealth, the level of employment of the nation's resources, and other facets of our daily existence. In short, the taxing process is a major thread in our socioeconomic fabric. To propose a change in that process is to propose a change in that fabric. No one can guarantee what the end result will be when he or she begins to think about changing the "apparently stable world."

For all these reasons, use of the word "reform" relative to our tax laws is usually inappropriate, as the headnote suggests. To reform means literally "to form again." Yet, when we study the changes made in the federal income-tax law, we find that the changes typically are either alterations or extensions of some concept already in the law or a very tentative trial of some new concept. The usual "reform" is not a repeal of some old rule and a bold adventure with some new rule. Instead we find changes that are akin to tactical military probes to observe the foe's reaction. In the taxing process, the maneuvers are made cautiously, and the political, social, and economic reactions carefully noted. Perhaps one should not quarrel with this type of reform. Considering the complexity of the problem of predicting the results of sweeping reforms, the wiser course may be that currently followed. A more adventuresome approach might lead to chaos.

Given the several reasons for inertia in the process, what countervailing forces cause the seemingly continuous, if only gradual, changes in the law? Three general causes for change are apparent. Within the process itself, there are some built-in safeguards against complete stagnation. Tax specialists, in and out of government, continually study the law and its effect and recommend changes. Their objectives cover the entire spectrum from relieving gross inequities to securing special benefits for a select few. The development of the rules for income averaging, discussed later in this chapter, is a good illustration of a gradual change in the law intended to relieve inequities. The extension of the benefits of Sec. 1231 discussed in Chapter 22 is a good example of gradual changes that benefit small groups of taxpayers.

On rare occasions, Congress undertakes a reform

of the tax law due to massive public discontent. The Tax Reform Act of 1969 was a response to a wave of articles in the popular press and books that enjoyed unusual notoriety. The picture painted in these articles and books was one of a tax system that amounted to a federal subsidy for the very rich at the expense of the remaining citizenry. Often, the authors implied that if the rich only paid their fair share, there would be enough additional revenue to support needed social programs.

While much of what appeared in the popular press before and during the 1968 election bordered on "yellow" journalism, Congress did feel compelled to act. It is interesting to note that the Nixon administration played only a nominal role in the passage of the Tax Reform Act of 1969; Congress apparently reacted to public sentiment.

Many changes in our tax laws over the last two decades came about because of economic conditions. In the early 1960s, tax rates were lowered and the investment credit was added to increase the growth rate of the economy. The Tax Reduction Act of 1975 was a response to the recession of that period.

The Tax Reform Act of 1976 is somewhat unique from a historical perspective. While it is true that the general public remains discontented, the news media evidently did not find such discontent especially newsworthy during 1975 and 1976. The Ford administration did offer Congress some encouragement, particularly in late 1975, although Congress chose to ignore their proposals. The 1976 Act is perhaps best described as a congressional convulsion brought on by numerous nagging problems related to the tax law. Congress had been aware of the problems for years, of course, but did not seem able to arouse itself sufficiently to act. One can only hypothesize that the need for certain reforms created enough tension to overcome the congressional tendency to inertia. We must also remember that politicians are still in a post-Watergate trauma and one should expect some erratic behavior from them. Two examples, unified rates for the estate and gift tax and syndicated tax shelters, may help the reader understand how cumulative problems, taken together, resulted in the reforms passed in 1976.

Prior to 1977, the tax rates applicable to gifts were lower than those applicable to transfers at death. The result was a widely used planning device to avoid death taxes: *inter vivos* gifts. Beginning as early as 1947, an advisory group to the Treasury recommended a unification of the two taxes. In 1969, the American Law Institute and the American Bar Association instituted a special project, which made a thorough study of the problem of unification.[1] These proposals fell on deaf ears until 1976, despite the efforts of many competent, respected tax practitioners and scholars. Yet, in 1976, Congress acted, and the question is: Why then?

A problem that legislators always had to face when considering estate and gift tax reform was the question of step-up in basis of inherited property for income tax purposes (see Chapter 20). Alternatives to the "fair market rule at death" were bullets few in Congress wished to bite. Early in the presidential primaries of 1975–76, however, some candidate came up with a proposal to save the family farm from the tax collector.[2] As the campaign progressed, the political leaning of the farm belt was in serious doubt and the theme became quite popular. Saving the family farm was soon expanded into a broader program for reform that would exempt more estates entirely from the death levy, a proposal that every hopeful candidate had to endorse. Thus, in a most peculiar way, the opinions of a sizable portion of the electorate were placed on record.

With a proposal that had been on the shelf for years, Congress changed the estate and gift tax laws. The extent of the reforms, it seems safe to say, was much broader than most had anticipated, and one plausible explanation is that Congress wanted to get this old problem out of the way, along with many others. Another explanation might be that many did not really understand what had been proposed. The fact that the carryover basis rules were retroactively rescinded in 1980 supports the latter explanation.

A second major change of the 1976 Tax Reform Act was aimed at "tax shelters." In the 1960s, various promoters happened upon a tax device that gave potential investors the best of all possible tax worlds: current ordinary deductions, deferral of income, and, in some cases, treatment of the investor's eventual gain as a capital gain. The legal organization used was a limited partnership, and the property invested in ranged from chickens to real estate. The typical scheme worked as follows: The promoter would organize a limited partnership and assume the

[1] For a thorough study of unification of the two taxes as well as other proposals eventually adopted in part in 1976, see Gersham Goldstein, *Readings in Death and Gift Tax Reform* (Mineola, N.Y.: The Foundation Press, 1971).

[2] After some research, we believe that this notion was first put before the public by Senator Birch Bayh in the fall of 1975.

role of general partner early in the year. The promoter would, of course, incur legal and accounting costs of organizing and promoting the venture. Toward the end of the year, when taxpayers with high incomes needed deductions, they would be offered participation in the venture as limited partners. Even if the investors bought shares of the deal in December, they could enjoy a deduction for their share of the "losses" for the entire year. Usually the venture was organized to produce "losses" for several years. In some cases, due to the rules relating to nonrecourse debt in a limited partnership, the investors were entitled to a deduction for losses in excess of their total capital investment. In every case, income from the venture was deferred for at least one year, and for certain types of properties the profit eventually recognized was a capital gain.

In short, investors were enticed into participation because of the desirable tax effects, not because of the economic soundness of the investment, and, incidentally, the promoters were usually the only ones who made a "killing." A tax law that encouraged this kind of reckless speculation was not, Congress concluded, a good tax law. Why Congress waited until 1976 to take action is another question. It did not act in 1976 to curtail the syndicates *before* promoters had bilked investors; most investors had learned their lessons the hard way by investing in unsound projects before 1976. Instead, it appears that the problem of syndicates was but one of many problems that, taken together, were enough to overcome inertia. In any event, the new law should curtail the use of syndicates and force investors to consider the soundness of the project as opposed to its tax benefits.

As a historical aside, but one that underscores the problems faced by Congress relative to tax reforms, investments in real estate are not covered by the harsher rules relative to syndicates. Thus, real estate syndicates are not subject to the "at risk" limits that effectively limit the deduction of losses by partners to their capital invested in the venture. This exception is ironic because the scheme described above, where nonrecourse debt is used, is used predominantly in real estate. The reason for all this is quite simple. By the time the 1976 Act reached the floor of the Senate, enough time had elapsed to allow the real estate lobby to exert its maximum force. The exception was inserted quietly by a Senate floor amendment and then survived the Conference Committee after a rather perfunctory debate.

The Revenue Act of 1978 can only be described as a reactionary political bill. The administration, initially pledged to a continuation of tax reform à la 1969 and 1976, quietly surrendered when President Carter reluctantly signed the bill on November 6, 1978. That Act included very few changes that anyone would describe as significant tax reform. Instead, the new law reflected a growing political concern for a perceived rejection by the masses of unduly high taxes, derived largely from the California voters' approval of Proposition 13. In spite of the rather obvious and unique problems of real property taxation in California, many politicians were certain that this vote was but the tip of an iceberg of taxpayer sentiment. Consequently, many politicians were pledged to reduce taxes, but nobody could agree on just which taxes to cut. To the surprise of almost everyone, a proposal originally introduced by the late Representative Steiger of Wisconsin was the big winner. As a result of the Steiger Amendment, capital gains taxes, for the first time in many years, were significantly reduced, especially for the high-marginal-bracket taxpayer. And the thousand and one lesser changes in the 1978 Act guaranteed that every voter could be told that he or she had been a winner in the new bill. In spite of this big buildup, the Congressional elections of 1978 demonstrated relatively little voter interest in matters of taxation. To the extent taxes were an issue, there clearly was no consensus of opinion at the polls. What these most recent events imply for the future is certainly unclear, at least to us.

In summary, the forces that result in tax reform are the quiet, yet constant, pressures brought upon Congress by tax specialists, the discontent of the general public, and the need to solve some evident economic or social problem. We do not suggest that every change in the law can be neatly attributed to one force. To the contrary, the several forces generally work together to produce change. A perfect example was the Tax Reduction Act of 1975, which was primarily concerned with the business recession. It nevertheless gave Congress an opportunity to repeal statutory depletion for large oil companies, in response to a feeling among the public that oil companies were making inordinately high profits. It is the interaction of the different forces that makes it so difficult to predict just how and when Congress will react to a problem. Indeed, after the zealous, unanticipated efforts that resulted in the Tax Reform Act of 1976, and after the largely reactionary politics of the 1978 Revenue Act, most "Congress watchers" have sensibly adopted an attitude of wait and see.

In this chapter, three important reform provisions are explained: the minimum tax on preferences, the maximum tax on personal service income, and income averaging. Each is a case study in tax reform, and the history of each provision reflects the varied forces that cause reform as well as the way Congress usually responds to those forces.

THE MINIMUM TAX ON PREFERENCES

As noted in the preceding discussion, Congress is generally reluctant to repeal major provisions of the law that favor certain segments of our society. Indeed, basic reforms such as the unified rates for estates and gifts are relatively rare. Noting this tendency, the tax specialists in the Treasury and on the staff of the Joint Committee on Taxation apparently decided in the late 1960s that a tactic other than direct repeal was needed to increase the tax burden of taxpayers in the upper income brackets. The tactic adopted was a new concept—a tax on preferences or loopholes. According to one source, the original idea to levy a tax on loopholes is credited to Joseph A. Pechman, a well-known tax scholar of the Brookings Institution.[3] One of the last acts of the Treasury Department under the Johnson administration was to devise a tax-reform proposal that included such a tax. Although the Johnson administration never officially sent the proposal to Congress, the Ways and Means Committee used it as a starting point for its deliberations on the Tax Reform Act of 1969.[4]

The basic idea of the 1979 version of a minimum tax is to sum up the net income of a taxpayer that escapes taxation because of special provisions—called tax preferences—and use this sum as the gross base for an additional tax at a proportionate rate. The sum of the preferences (the gross base) is reduced by an exemption plus a portion of the gross income tax liability to obtain the tax base.

The 1978 Revenue Act introduced a second alternative minimum tax. In the next section of this chapter, we shall first discuss and illustrate the original add-on minimum tax on tax preferences; thereafter, we shall discuss and illustrate the new minimum alternative tax. The former is called an add-on tax

because it must be paid *in addition to the regular income tax* determined in the normal way. The latter is an alternative tax because it must be paid *in lieu of the regular income tax*, determined in the normal way, if that alternative is larger than the regular tax. As anyone who has suffered through twenty-seven chapters of this text knows, the income tax determined even in the normal way can hardly be described as routine!

Tax preferences

The beginning point for computing the minimum tax is the sum of the taxpayer's tax preferences. Of the provisions in the law that reduce the effective tax rate, the following are now defined as preferences subject to the tax.[5]

1. Excess of intangible drilling cost deductions over any income from oil and gas properties. (Incidentally, the cost of drilling dry holes does *not* reduce the amount of income from oil and gas production for purposes of computing this tax preference item.)
2. Excess of accelerated depreciation on Sec. 1250 property over the straight-line depreciation.
3. Excess of the special 60-month amortization of certain items over straight-line depreciation. The major items in this group are certified pollution control devices (see p. **17**/11).
4. Excess of percentage depletion over the property's adjusted basis (before depletion) at the end of the year.
5. Bargain element in qualified stock options. (As noted in Chapter 15, this preference for corporate executives was effectively eliminated by the Tax Reform Act of 1976, except for previously outstanding options.)
6. The excess of accelerated depreciation over straight-line depreciation on Sec. 1245 property leased to another. (This preference is aimed at tax shelters involving leveraged leases of tangible personal property. It is *not* a tax preference for corporate taxpayers, other than Subchapter S corporations.)

All preference items listed above are combined to form the gross tax base for the add-on minimum tax.

[3]"Returns Roll in for Tax Reform," *Business Week,* February 8, 1969, p. 34.

[4]*Ibid.,* p. 32.

[5]The general rules given here apply only to individuals and most corporations; special rules apply to fiduciaries, tax-option corporations, and certain financial institutions. In addition, there are special preference items for a few industries, for example, the timber industry. See Secs. 56 and 57.

One very important preference is conspicuously absent from this list: interest on tax-exempt bonds of state and local governments. The House version of the bill in 1969 included this as a preference, but when the measure reached the Senate the Capitol was inundated by a tide of governors, mayors, and other local government officials. Their complaint was a real one: To include such interest as a preference would raise rates of their bonds and further compound the precarious financial condition of these units. Congress yielded to the pressure.

A second important preference that is conspicuously absent is the long-term capital-gain deduction. That item was a tax preference prior to 1979. The 1978 Revenue Act, however, permanently removed it from the list of tax preferences for individual taxpayers when it introduced the new alternative minimum tax. For corporate taxpayers, however, an amount equal to 39.13 percent of the net capital gain reported for the year does remain a tax preference item.

Illustration of minimum tax computation

The add-on minimum tax, by its nature, cannot be computed until the regular tax calculation is complete. Given the information on a completed return, the calculation of the preference tax is relatively simple.[6] To illustrate the computation, assume that the return of an *individual* taxpayer contains the following:

Net capital gain (total amount)	$150,000
Percentage depletion deduction (basis of property before the deduction was $15,000)	32,000
Declining-balance depreciation on real estate (depreciation on the straight-line method would have been $35,000)	60,000
Regular tax (after all credits)	54,500

The minimum tax would be:

Preferences:	
Excess percentage depletion ($32,000 less basis of $15,000)	$17,000
Excess depreciation on real estate ($60,000 less $35,000 straight-line)	25,000
Total preferences (gross base)	$42,000

Less: Larger of $10,000 or one-half of regular tax of $54,500	27,250
Base for tax	$14,750
Rate	× .15
Preference tax (rounded)	$2,213

The add-on minimum tax on tax preferences for this taxpayer would be $2,213. The total income tax liability for the same taxpayer would be $56,713; i.e., $54,500 determined in the normal way plus the $2,213 minimum tax.

The alternative minimum tax

As explained above, the new minimum alternative tax is a substitute for the normal income tax.[7] The base for this alternative minimum tax is the excess of the sum of three items, namely—

1. Taxable income computed in the normal way (with possible adjustments for net operating losses);
2. The long-term capital gain deduction; and
3. Excess itemized deductions—

over a $20,000 exemption. Thus, the alternative tax base will always be zero (and we can forget it) unless the sum of the three items listed above exceeds $20,000. When they do exceed $20,000, however, you must then compute the income tax in both the normal way and in this alternative way and pay the larger of the two.

The tax rate applied to the alternative minimum tax base is graduated as follows: First $40,000 at 10 percent; next $40,000 at 20 percent; and any amount in excess of $80,000 at 25 percent. Perhaps the most difficult aspect of the alternative minimum tax is the definition of excess itemized deductions. To review that definition, study the illustration that follows.

Illustration of alternative minimum tax computation

To illustrate the calculation of the alternative minimum tax, let us assume that an imaginary individual taxpayer reported the following:

Adjusted gross income	$82,000
Medical expense deduction	3,000
Casualty loss deduction	15,000
Deduction for state and local taxes	12,000
Total itemized deductions	46,000

---

[6]Special rules beyond the scope of this text apply where the return shows a net operating loss or an excess of deductions over income. See Sec 56(b).

[7]See Sec. 55 for additional details.

Based on these assumptions, we can determine the excess itemized deduction (if any), as follows:

Total itemized deductions		$46,000
Less: deductions for		
Medical expenses	$ 3,000	
Casualty losses	15,000	
State and local taxes	12,000	30,000
Equals remaining itemized deductions		$16,000
Less an "adjusted A.G.I.," computed as follows:		
Adjusted gross income	$82,000	
Less: deductions for		
Medical expenses	$ 3,000	
Casualty losses	15,000	
State and local taxes	12,000	
Sum of above	30,000	
Remaining A.G.I.	$52,000	
Multiplied by 60 percent	× .60	
This product is the "adjusted A.G.I."		31,200
Remainder, if any, is the amount known as "Excess Itemized Deductions"		$-0-

If this same imaginary taxpayer also reported:

Net capital gain (gross amount)	$150,000
Taxable income (computed in the normal way)	54,000
Regular tax (after all credits)	15,000

we can then compute the alternative minimum tax. That calculation would be made as follows:

Taxable income (computed in normal way)		$ 54,000
+ Long-term capital gain deduction (60% × $150,000)		90,000
+ Excess itemized deductions		-0-
= Total		$144,000
Exemption (always $20,000)		20,000
= Base for alternative minimum tax		$124,000
Alternative tax determined as follows:		
First $40,000 at 10 percent	$ 4,000	
Second $40,000 at 20 percent	8,000	
Remaining $44,000 at 25 percent	11,000	
Alternative minimum tax		$ 23,000

Because this taxpayer's alternative minimum tax ($23,000) is greater than the regular income tax determined in the normal way ($15,000), he or she would have to pay the alternative amount, namely, $23,000.

In general, the new minimum alternative tax will be payable only if a taxpayer has a relatively large net capital gain and little or no taxable income (and, therefore, a relatively small income tax determined in the "normal" manner). In political terms, the new minimum alternative tax was the price extracted from the proponents of the major reductions for capital gains in the 1978 Act. Those who opposed the changes introduced by Representative Steiger wanted to be assured that persons with large amounts of long-term capital gains paid some minimally respectable amount of income tax. They apparently were not convinced that the extant add-on minimum tax was adequate, and, therefore, they insisted on this new alternative. Whether or not the new tax is an adequate safeguard, worth its cost in terms of the additional complication introduced, remains to be seen.

THE MAXIMUM TAX ON PERSONAL SERVICE INCOME

Chapters 11 and 19 contain a discussion of a bias in the tax law favoring income from property. Taxpayers can shelter property income in numerous ways, the capital gain rules being the most common. On the other hand, taxpayers find it difficult, and often impossible, to shelter income from salaries and compensation for personal services. Farm losses, stock options, and deferred compensation plans are some of the shelters developed to shield earned income from the maximum 70 percent rate.

An important innovation in the Tax Reform Act of 1969 is the provision that places a maximum marginal rate of 50 percent applicable to *personal service* income. This idea, like the minimum tax on preferences, was part of the reform proposals developed in the last year of the Johnson administration and used by the Ways and Means Committee as a starting point in 1969. Justification for the new maximum rate on personal service income was succinctly stated as follows by the Ways and Means Committee:

> The 50-percent limit on the tax rate applicable to earned income was adopted not as a tax relief measure but to reduce the pressure for the use of tax loopholes.[8]

Given the 50-percent maximum rate, the new provision will have the maximum impact on executives, professionals, athletes, artists, and others whose income is high enough to worry about tax shelters.

[8]H. R. 13270, 1st Session, 91st Congress, p. 208.

Note that restoration of equity between earned and unearned (property) income was not a stated objective. Although the original net effect was to reduce substantially the differential between the effective rate paid on salaries and other compensation for services and that on long-term capital gains, the changes to capital-gains taxation in the 1978 act re-created a significant differential: At present it is 22 percent (or 50 percent less 28 percent).

Personal service taxable income

The 50 percent maximum rate applies only to *personal service taxable income,* a new concept computed by use of the following formula:

$$\frac{\text{Personal service net income}}{\text{Adjusted gross income}} \times \begin{array}{c} \text{Net taxable} \\ \text{income} \end{array}$$

$$\textit{less} \text{ Tax preferences} = \begin{array}{c} \text{Personal service} \\ \text{taxable income} \end{array}$$

The general term *personal service income* includes wages, salaries, and other forms of compensation for personal services. Where an individual is engaged in a trade or business and *both* capital and personal services are a material income-producing factor, the portion of the income subject to the maximum rate is a reasonable allowance for compensation.

The Tax Reform Act of 1976 enlarged the definition of personal service income to include deferred compensations, pension payments, and payments under annuities that represent deferred compensation for years after 1976. However, lump-sum distributions from pension and profit-sharing plans are not personal service income. (Note that lump-sum distributions enjoy either a partial capital-gain treatment or the 10-year averaging rules explained in Chapter 15.) *Personal service net income* is the gross income from wages, salaries, and other forms of compensation for personal services *less* deductions *for* adjusted gross income that are allocable to this income. To obtain *personal service taxable income,* the net taxable income must be apportioned between the earned and the "unearned" income. In addition, personal service taxable income must be reduced by the "tax preferences."

The formula for the computation of personal service taxable income has two objectives. First, it serves to allocate the deductions from adjusted gross income between personal service and unearned net income. Second, it serves to reduce the personal service taxable income by the "economic" income that already gets beneficial tax treatment due to other special provisions, that is, by the tax preferences as defined for purposes of the add-on minimum tax (only).

Illustration of the maximum tax

To illustrate the application of the maximum rate on personal service income, assume that James Hall, who is single, has the following items of income this year:

Personal service net income (salary less deductions for A.G.I.)	$120,000
Adjusted gross income	150,000
Net taxable income	140,000
Tax preferences (as defined above)	25,000

Hall's personal service taxable income is

$$\left(\frac{\$120,000}{\$150,000} \times \$140,000\right) - \$25,000 = \$87,000$$

Assuming that Hall is single, we can compute his tax as follows:

Tax on first $41,500 (i.e., the portion of income that would normally be taxed at a marginal rate of 50 percent or less)		$13,392
Limits of tax on personal service taxable income at 50 percent (($87,000 − $41,500) × 0.50)		22,750
Tax on other income (at highest marginal rate applicable):		
Tax on taxable income of $140,000	$77,887	
Less: Tax on $87,000 personal service taxable income	41,213	36,674
Total tax		$72,816

Without this special provision, Hall's tax would have been $77,887, or $5,071 more than the tax under the new provisions.

The concept underlying the above calculation is illustrated graphically by Figure 28-1. In this figure (a) equals the portion of taxable income taxed at a marginal rate of less than 50 percent by virtue of the normal rate progression, (b) equals the portion of taxable income defined as personal service taxable income, and (c) equals total taxable income—both personal service and other.

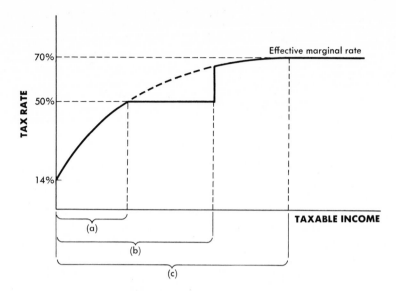

FIGURE **28-1**   Graphic Illustration of Calculation of
Maximum Tax on Earned Income

Notice that the calculation proceeds in such a way as to ensure that unearned income is deemed to be the second tier of taxable income and is therefore taxed at the highest possible marginal rates. In other words, the tax on the portion of income represented by the distance (c) minus (b) is determined by calculating the tax on a taxable income of (c) dollars and then subtracting the tax on a taxable income of (b) dollars, both calculated without the benefit of the new maximum marginal tax on personal service income.

INCOME AVERAGING

You may recall that all revenue laws were first organized into the Internal Revenue Code in 1939. Prior to the enactment of that Code in 1939, Congress took a fairly comprehensive look at the overall impact of the income tax. One inequity noted was that caused by the combination of progressive tax rates and the bunching of income recognition in a single year. This bunching effect is one of the principal arguments used to support the preferential treatment of long-term capital gains. Congress recognized in 1939 that, in some cases, realization of compensation for personal services may also be bunched. For example, a lawyer may work on one case for several years and yet receive the bulk of the fee in a single taxable year.

The original income-averaging rule provided that when personal services were provided over a period of at least 36 months, the compensation for such services could be taxed as though received pro rata over a maximum of the last 36 months. To elect this averaging, at least 80 percent of the compensation had to have been accrued or received in a single taxable year. "Back pay" was also subject to these averaging rules. From this meager beginning developed the comprehensive averaging provisions contained in the present law.

The intermediate steps from 1939 to 1969 provide a good example of how continuous scrutiny of the law gradually reformed it over a 30-year period. In 1942 the income derived from artistic works and inventions was made eligible for the provisions. The work period was reduced to only 24 months and, for inventions, the averaging period was increased from three years (36 months) to five years (60 months). The Internal Revenue Code of 1954 further liberalized the provision by setting out rules governing the definition of an employment or work. Then, in 1964, a general provision was adopted covering all sources of income with an averaging period of five years. All earlier rules were repealed at that time. This first general averaging convention contained special rules for capital-gain net income and excluded from income averaging wagers and income from gifts and bequests. Finally, the Tax Reform Act of 1969 increased the amount of income that could be spread back (or averaged) and removed the strictures on capital gains, wagering income, and income from gifts and bequests.[9] The current provision is a comprehensive averaging rule that by and large removes the inequities that can result when the income in a single tax year is abnormally high relative to the preceding four years. Observe that it still provides no relief when the income of a single taxpayer is abnormally low relative to the preceding four years.

That this provision now exists is not due to public clamor and a flood of mail to Congress. It exists because people interested in the tax law have pressed relentlessly for more equitable treatment for all taxpayers. Once introduced and accepted as an appropriate vehicle for tax policy, other provisions are regularly changed as a result of continual pressure by the "kitchen" bureau and other lobby interests concerned with the law. Note that the other provisions discussed in this chapter have undergone a similar evolution since their enactment in 1969. The tax on preferences was first weakened by the changes in 1971, which permitted a reduction in the base for regular taxes not previously offset against preferences; then significantly strengthened by the changes in 1976; and further modified by the 1978 changes. The maximum tax on personal service income was also changed in 1976 so that it is now more compatible with Congress's stated policy. In a similar manner, the basic statutory law evolved with only occasionally an entirely new idea or policy.

Limitation on the tax from the averaging rules

The averaging rules are contained in Secs. 1301 through 1305. The key provision is Sec. 1301, "Limitation on Tax":

> If an eligible individual has averageable income for the computation year, and if the amount of such income exceeds $3,000, then the tax imposed by section 1 for the computation year which is attributable to the averageable income shall be 5 times the increase in tax under such section which would result from adding 20 percent of such income to 120 percent of the average base period income.

One cannot argue with the conciseness of this draftsmanship, but all can agree that the language leaves something to be desired by way of clarity.

To unravel the syntax, each term used must first be defined. First, only certain *individuals* qualify for

averaging; eligibility is discussed in a later section. The computation year is the year in which "above average" income is received; that is, the year when the averaging rules are applied. Averageable income is the taxable income of the computation year in excess of 120 percent of the average base-period income. The average base-period income is the total taxable income for the four preceding taxable years divided by four.

Note that the averaging rules apply only where the averageable income exceeds $3,000. Small fluctuations in income do not result in serious inequities. Second, income subject to the averaging rules (averageable income) is only income in excess of 120 percent of the base-period income (average taxable income for the last four years). This rule also excludes small fluctuations in income from averaging.

The objective of the limitation is to tax the averageable income as though it were received ratably over the four base-period years and the computation year. To illustrate the key terms in the above rules, assume that a taxpayer who files a joint return had the following amounts of taxable income for the indicated years:[10]

Year 1	$12,000
Year 2	10,000
Year 3	9,000
Year 4	17,000
Year 5	50,000

The average income for the base period is the sum of the taxable income for years 1 through 4 of $48,000 ($12,000 + $10,000 + $9,000 + $17,000) divided by 4, or $12,000. Next we must determine 120 percent of the average base period income, which is $14,400 ($12,000 × 120 percent) in this illustration. "Averageable income" is the excess of taxable income in the current year (or computation year) over 120 percent of the average base period income; in this case $35,600 ($50,000 − $14,400).

The intent of the law is to tax the averageable income as though received over a five-year period, using whatever marginal rates would be applicable beginning wherever the nonaverageable income

---

[9]Certain trust accumulation distributions and premature distributions under some pension plans are the only sources of income not subject to averaging.

[10]As a practical matter, the amount of taxable income may have to be adjusted for years prior to 1977 and the introduction of the zero bracket amount. Whether or not the adjustments are equitable is a matter of current debate. Legislation has been introduced (but not enacted) that would delete the adjustments currently required. See Schedule G, Form 1040, pages **28**/14–**28**/15 for the current law.

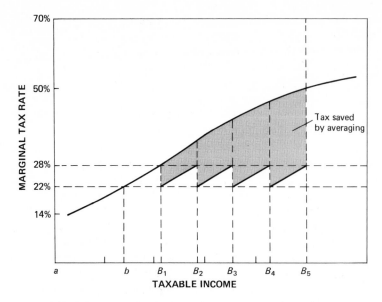

FIGURE **28-2**   Graphic Illustration of Income Averaging

ends. Figure 28-2 should aid in understanding these rules. The distance *ab* on the horizontal axis represents the nonaverageable income of $14,400, which is 120 percent of the base-period average. Normal rates apply to this portion of income; that is, if the taxpayer filed a joint return, that tax is $1,929. The distance *aB₁* is nonaverageable income plus one-fifth of the averageable income, here $14,400 plus $35,600 ÷ 5 or a total of $21,520. The tax rates that apply to one-fifth of the averageable income are the rates for the distance *bB₁*. This can be determined by applying the tax rates to the distance *aB₁* and subtracting the tax on the distance *ab:*

Nonaverageable income (*ab*)	$14,400
+ ⅕ averageable income (*bB₁*)	7,120
= Distance *aB₁*	$21,520
Tax on above (married taxpayer)	$ 3,643
− Tax on nonaverageable income (*ab*)	1,929
= Tax on ⅕ averageable income (*bB₁*)	$ 1,714

The rates applicable to one-fifth of the averageable income (*bB₁*) can be used for the remaining averageable income: that is, *B₁B₂*, *B₂B₃*, *B₃B₄*, etc. Thus, the tax on the averageable income is $1,714 × 5, or $8,570. The total tax using income averaging is computed as follows:

Tax on $14,400 of nonaverageable income (distance *ab*)	$ 1,929

+ Five times the tax on ⅕ the averageable income (*bB₁*)	8,570
= Total gross tax liability	$10,499

In Figure 28-2, the tax saved is represented by the shaded area from *B₁* to *B₄*, the rates that would have applied to the $50,000 of taxable income but for the averaging rules.

Without the averaging provisions, the taxpayer would have paid the normal rates on a $50,000 taxable income, or a gross tax of $14,778. Based on these facts, the averaging rules reduced the tax by $4,279 ($14,778 less $10,499). If the taxpayer's income remains constant at $50,000, the amount of averageable income will decrease and the benefits will correspondingly decrease over the next few years. Given a constant income, averageable income will eventually be less than $3,000, and no further benefits will accrue from these rules.

Eligible individuals

Only individuals qualify for the averaging rules. Corporations have only limited progression in their rates, and income bunching does not result in the same inequity as in the case of individuals. To qualify, an individual must first be a resident or a citizen throughout the computation year. In addition, the individual must have been a citizen or resident throughout the base period.

Generally, the taxpayer must provide at least 50

percent of his or her support in each of the years in the base period. Students and others who are just beginning work cannot take advantage of these rules unless they supported themselves throughout the base period. There are three exceptions to this rule:

1. If the taxpayer is at least 25 years of age during the computation year and has not been a full-time student for at least four tax years after age 21, he or she may average income. This provision extends the benefits of income averaging to taxpayers who have experienced prolonged unemployment.

2. If the taxpayer's income in the computation year is attributable to work performed substantially in two or more of the base-period years, he or she may also average income. This provision is included for artists, inventors, and others who depend on others for support until they produce a valuable property.

3. A married individual who files a joint return with his or her spouse may use the averaging rules if the spouse who provided his or her own support in the base period accounts for 75 percent or more of the combined adjusted gross income in the computation year.

The objective of the self-support rule is to prohibit taxpayers from enjoying unintended benefits from averaging. Incidentally, income from a scholarship cannot be counted as self-support income by a college student.

REPORTING

Special forms are provided by the I.R.S. for use in reporting the computation of the tax on preferences, the maximum tax on personal service income, and income averaging. The minimum tax on preferences is reported on Form 4625, which is applicable to all taxpayers. That form follows generally the calculation of the tax on preferences as illustrated in this chapter. The maximum tax on personal service income is reported on Form 4726, and it also generally follows the illustrations in the chapter. Blank forms only are illustrated here.

Income averaging is reported on Schedule G of Form 1040. This schedule applies to more taxpayers than the tax on preferences or the maximum tax on personal service income. In addition, the computations on Schedule G are somewhat different procedurally from those explained in the text. For these

reasons, a completed illustration of Schedule G seems appropriate.

Take the same facts as those set out earlier in this chapter; that is, a married taxpayer filing a joint return has the following amounts of base period income:

Year 1 = 1975	$12,000
2 = 1976	10,000
3 = 1977	9,000
4 = 1978	17,000
5 = 1979	50,000

A 1979 Schedule G is shown on pages **28**/14–**28**/15. The computation on Schedule G is the same as that in the text with some minor exceptions. Lines 4, 8, and 10 deal with adjustments beyond the scope of this text. Lines 2 and 5 adjust old numbers to the current definition of taxable income. At line 13, the nonaverageable income is obtained by taking 30 percent of total base-period income, a procedure that gives the same result as that obtained by dividing the total by 4 and then multiplying by 120 percent. At line 24, the tax on one-fifth of the averageable income is multiplied by only 4; however, the tax on line 20 is the tax on the nonaverageable income plus the tax on one-fifth of the averageable income. The final tax is, of course, the same under both calculations.

CONCLUSION

The taxing process is a dynamic one. The tax law is not a known or knowable set of rules that, once learned, serve for a period of time. Instead, the process is forever changing both the people involved and their actions. And as the process changes, so does the amount of funds transferred from the private to the public sector. But like all human processes, the taxing process has a great deal of built-in inertia. This tendency toward stability is due in part to the natural urge of people to resist change. Added to this is the considerable vested interest of many segments of the population in the law at any point in time. A final force that reduces change is our inability to predict the consequences of the changes proposed.

Here we have a seeming paradox—a process in a state of flux that tends to be inert. We submit that all our institutions are similarly schizophrenic and the fact that the taxing process is the same is no cause for alarm. Changes occur because there always are some who do not like the status quo; they

Form **4625**
Department of the Treasury
Internal Revenue Service

Computation of Minimum Tax—Individuals

▶ See instructions on back.
▶ Attach to Form 1040.

1979

25

Name(s) as shown on Form 1040	Your social security number

File this form if the total of tax preference items (line 2) is more than $10,000 ($5,000 if you are married filing separately) even though you owe no minimum tax, **OR** if you have any minimum tax liability deferred from an earlier tax year until this year. If this is a short-period return, see instructions for line 8.

1 Tax preference items:
   (Note: Adjusted itemized deductions and capital gains are now tax preference items for the alternative minimum tax. See Form 6251.)

   (a) Accelerated depreciation on real property—
       (1) Low-income rental housing under section 167(k) or amortization of certified historic structures under section 191   **1a(1)**
       (2) Other real property   **1a(2)**
   (b) Accelerated depreciation on personal property subject to a lease   **1b**
   (c) Amortization of certified pollution control facilities   **1c**
   (d) Amortization of railroad rolling stock   **1d**
   (e) Amortization of on-the-job training facilities   **1e**
   (f) Amortization of child care facilities   **1f**
   (g) Reserves for losses on bad debts of financial institutions   **1g**
   (h) Stock options   **1h**
   (i) Depletion   **1i**
   (j) Intangible drilling costs   **1j**

2 Total tax preference items. Add lines 1(a) through 1(j)   **2**
3 Amount from Form 1040, line 47*   **3**
4 Tax from recomputing prior-year investment credit   **4**
5 Tax from recomputing prior-year Work Incentive (WIN) credit   **5**
6 Tax on premature redemption of Individual Retirement Bond(s)   **6**

7 Add lines 3 through 6   **7**
8 Enter the larger of: (a) one-half of the amount on line 7, or (b) $10,000 ($5,000 if you are married filing separately)   **8**

9 Subtract line 8 from line 2 (If line 8 is more than line 2, enter zero)   **9**

10 Multiply amount on line 9 by 15%   **10**
11 Enter any 1979 net operating loss carryover to 1980 (attach statement showing computation)   **11**

12 Multiply amount on line 11 by 15%   **12**
13 Deferred minimum tax. Enter the amount from line 10 or line 12, whichever is smaller   **13**

14 Minimum tax. Subtract line 13 from line 10   **14**
15 Enter minimum tax deferred from earlier year(s) until this year (attach statement showing computation)   **15**

16 Total minimum tax. Add lines 14 and 15   **16**
17 Excess tax credits. See instructions for line 17 before completing this section. If Form 1040, line 47, is more than zero, this section will not apply; skip lines 17(a) through 18 and enter the amount from line 16 on line 19.
   (a) Credit for the elderly   **17a**
   (b) Credit for political contributions   **17b**
   (c) Credit for child care expenses   **17c**
   (d) Residential energy credits   **17d**

18 Add lines 17(a) through 17(d)   **18**

19 Subtract line 18 from line 16. Enter here and on Form 1040, line 49a   **19**

*Do not include any tax from Form 4970, Form 4972, Form 5544, or any penalty tax under sec. 72(m)(5).

Form **4726**
Department of the Treasury
Internal Revenue Service

Maximum Tax on Personal Service Income

▶ See instructions on back.
▶ Attach to Form 1040 (or Form 1041).

1979
26

Name(s) as shown on Form 1040 (or Form 1041)	Identifying number

Do not complete this form if—(a) Taxable income or personal service taxable income is:

$41,500 or less, and on Form 1040, you checked box 1,

$60,000 or less, and on Form 1040, you checked box 2 or box 5,

$44,700 or less, and on Form 1040, you checked box 4,

$28,300 or less, and this is an Estate or Trust return (Form 1041);

(b) You elected income averaging; or

(c) On Form 1040, you checked box 3.

Personal Service Income			Deductions Against Personal Service Income		

1 Total personal service income . . . . | **1** | | | **2** Total deductions against personal service income . . . . | **2** |

3 Personal service net income—Subtract total of line 2 from total of line 1 . . . . | **3** |

4 Enter your adjusted gross income . . . . | **4** |

5 Divide the amount on line 3 by the amount on line 4. Enter result as a percentage. If more than 100%, enter 100%. Round to nearest 4 numbers . . . . | **5** |

6 Enter your taxable income . . . . | **6** |

7 Multiply the amount on line 6 by the percentage on line 5 . . . . | **7** |

8 Enter the total of your 1979 tax preference items . . . . | **8** |

9 Personal service taxable income. Subtract line 8 from line 7 . . . . | **9** |

10 If: on Form 1040, you checked box 1, enter $41,500 . . . .
on Form 1040, you checked box 2 or box 5, enter $60,000 . . . .
on Form 1040, you checked box 4, enter $44,700 . . . .
you are filing Form 1041, enter $28,300 . . . . | **10** |

11 Subtract line 10 from line 9. If line 10 is more than line 9, do not complete rest of form . . . . | **11** |

12 Enter 50% of line 11 . . . . | **12** |

13 Tax on amount on line 6* . . . . | **13** |

14 Tax on amount on line 9* . . . . | **14** |

15 Subtract line 14 from line 13 . . . . | **15** |

16 If the amount on line 10 is: $41,500, enter $13,392 . . . .
$60,000, enter $19,678 . . . .
$44,700, enter $13,961 . . . .
$28,300, enter $9,839 . . . . . . | **16** |

17 Add lines 12, 15, and 16. This is your maximum tax . . . . | **17** |

*Use Tax Rate Schedules from Form 1040 or Form 1041 instructions.

283–175–2

Form **4726** (1979)

SCHEDULE G (Form 1040)

Department of the Treasury
Internal Revenue Service

Income Averaging

▶ See instructions on pages 2 and 3.
▶ Attach to Form 1040.

1979

18

Name(s) as shown on Form 1040

Your social security number

Base Period Income and Adjustments	(a) 1st preceding base period year 1978		(b) 2d preceding base period year 1977		(c) 3rd preceding base period year 1976		(d) 4th preceding base period year 1975	
1 Enter amount from: Form 1040 (1977 and 1978)—line 34 Form 1040A (1977 and 1978)—line 10 . .								
2 Multiply $750 by the total number of exemptions claimed in 1977 and 1978								
3 Taxable income (subtract line 2 from line 1) If less than zero, enter zero (see instructions) .								
4 Income earned outside of the United States or within U.S. possessions and excluded under sections 911 and 931								
5 On your 1979 Form 1040, if you checked box {2 or 5 enter $3,200} {1 or 4 enter $2,200} {3 enter $1,600 . .} {in columns (c) and (d)}								
6 Base period income (add lines 3, 4 and 5) .	17,000		9,000		10,000		12,000	

Computation of Averageable Income

7 Taxable income for 1979 from Schedule TC (Form 1040), Part I, line 3 . . .	7	50,000	
8 Certain amounts received by owner-employees subject to a penalty under section 72(m)(5)	8		
9 Subtract line 8 from line 7	9	50,000	
10 Excess community income	10		
11 Adjusted taxable income (subtract line 10 from line 9). If less than zero, enter zero	11	50,000	
12 Add columns (a) through (d), line 6, and enter here	12	48,000	
13 Enter 30% of line 12	13	14,400	
14 Averageable income (subtract line 13 from line 11)	14	35,600	

If line 14 is $3,000 or less, do not complete the rest of the form. You do not qualify for income averaging.

G

Computation of Tax

15 Amount from line 13	15	14,400	
16 20% of line 14	16	7,120	
17 Total (add lines 15 and 16)	17	21,520	
18 Excess community income from line 10	18		
19 Total (add lines 17 and 18)	19	21,520	
20 Tax on amount on line 19 (see caution below)	20	3,643	
21 Tax on amount on line 17 (see caution below)	21	3,643	
22 Tax on amount on line 15 (see caution below)	22	1,929	
23 Subtract line 22 from line 21	23	1,714	
24 Multiply the amount on line 23 by 4	24	6,856	
Note: If no entry was made on line 8 above, skip lines 25 through 27 and go to line 28.			
25 Tax on amount on line 7 (see caution below)	25		
26 Tax on amount on line 9 (see caution below)	26		
27 Subtract line 26 from line 25	27		
28 Tax (add lines 20, 24, and 27). Enter here and on Schedule TC (Form 1040), Part I, line 4 and check Schedule G box	28	10,499	

Caution: Use Tax Rate Schedule X, Y or Z from the Form 1040 instructions to figure your tax on lines 20, 21, 22, 25 and 26. Do not use the tax tables.

Computation of Taxable Income for 1975 if You Used the Tax Tables

		1975	
1 Enter amount from: Form 1040 (1975), line 15 } Form 1040A (1975), line 12 }	**1**		
2 a Enter 16% of line 1: but not more than $2,300 if you were single (or a head of household) . . . . . } but not more than $1,300 if you were married filing separately . . . . }	**2a**		
b Enter: $1,900 if you were married filing jointly (or a qualifying widow(er)) } $1,600 if you were single (or a head of household) . . . . . } . . . . . $950 if you were married filing separately . . . . }	**2b**		
c Standard deduction. Enter the amount from line 2a or 2b, whichever is more. (If you were married and filed separately and your spouse used the percentage standard deduction (line 2a), then you must also use it.)	**2c**		
3 Subtract line 2c from line 1	**3**		
4 Multiply $750 by the total number of exemptions claimed	**4**		
5 Taxable income (subtract line 4 from line 3). Enter here and on page 1, line 3, column (d)	**5**		

want change for all sorts of reasons. In taxation, the people who most frequently seek change are the tax specialists, the lobbyists, and legislators-on-a-crusade. Occasionally the people who presumably mold public opinion, who move the inert mass of public attention, settle on taxation for a brief time and have a decided impact on Congress. Between these two forces for change, the old is often altered and occasionally discarded. And thus it goes.

The reforms of 1969 were followed by additional changes in 1971 and 1975. The Tax Reform Act of 1976 was even more comprehensive than the major changes in 1969. Under the Carter administration, we have "enjoyed" the 1977 Tax Reduction and Simplification Act, the Revenue Act of 1978, and the Windfall Profits Tax Act. The tax law is on the move, with no end in sight. In the next chapter, we shall look at what lies ahead for the tax practitioner faced with the problem of planning clients' affairs to minimize taxes.

PROBLEMS

1. In calendar year 19x1, Sam Eisner, who is unmarried and does not qualify as the head of a household, had the following status:

Personal service net income (salary less deductions for A.G.I.)	$150,000
Adjusted gross income	200,000
Net taxable income	182,200
Tax preferences	21,650

What would his tax liability be if there were no maximum tax provisions? What is his tax using those provisions?

2. A taxpayer has a gross tax liability of $22,500 (after all credits). Given the following additional facts, compute the taxpayer's "minimum tax on preferences," assuming no gross tax credit carryforward.

Long-term capital-gain deduction	$41,000
Percentage depletion taken	34,000
Basis of property on which depletion was taken	0

3. In computing the personal service taxable income (the amount to which the maximum rate of 50 percent applies), net taxable income is allocated between the earned and unearned portions. What is the purpose of this allocation?

4. The list of tax preferences subject to the minimum tax does not include either interest on state and local government bonds or long-term capital gains (for individual taxpayers).

   a. Why are these "preferences" not included?

   b. What would be the effect of including these items as preferences?

5. List the reasons for placing a maximum tax on personal service income.

6. Sam Nichol is married and files a joint return. His return for the current year includes the following:

Net capital gains	$60,000
Accelerated depreciation on an apartment complex*	80,000
Gross tax (after credits)†	35,000

   * Straight-line depreciation would have been $55,000.
   † Based on rate schedules in Appendix B.

Compute Sam's minimum tax on preferences.

7. The final step in the computation of the maximum tax on personal service income is to compute the tax on total net taxable income, compute the regular tax on the personal service taxable income, and subtract to determine the difference. Explain the necessity of this complicated procedure.

8. John Umber is single. He attended night school for six years to obtain a law degree. His parents are not wealthy, and therefore John made his own way, working as a machinist in a local plant. His taxable income for the years 19x1–x4 was as follows: 19x1, $5,400; 19x2, $5,800; 19x3, $6,200; 19x4, $7,400. He graduated with honors in January, 19x5, and took a position with a prominent local law firm. His taxable income for 19x5 was $14,240.

   a. Compute his gross tax liability for 19x5; use 1979 tax rates and ignore any changes in the definition of taxable income during the base period years.

   b. Compute his gross tax liability for 19x6, assuming his net taxable income for that year was $17,292.

   c. Compute his gross tax liability for 19x7, assuming his taxable income is still $17,292.

9. Ms. Longterm recognized only two items of gross income in 1979, namely:

Salary $16,000
Net capital gain   100,000

Assuming that Ms. Longterm is a single woman who does *not* itemize deductions and who is entitled to no tax credits, determine

   a. Her income tax calculated in the "normal" way.

   b. Her alternative minimum income tax.

10. Klammer, Monroney, and Nelson are three citizens of Detroit. Each is single and has the following items of income and expense for 19x1.

	Klammer	Monroney	Nelson
Salary	$200,000		
Business profit		$200,000	
Interest on state bonds			$120,000
Long-term capital gains			80,000
Deductions from A.G.I. (including exemptions)	12,000	12,000	12,000

    a. Compute the income-tax liability of each person for the year.

    b. Comment on the horizontal equity involved.

11. Assume that I.B. Free reports the following for the current year:

Regular income tax liability (after all credits)	$30,000
Taxable income	83,000
Long-term capital gain deduction	40,000
Declining-balance depreciation of real estate (straight-line depreciation would have been $10,000)	15,000
Interest on City of Atlanta bonds	10,000
Percentage depletion deduction (basis of property before this deduction was $25,000)	65,000

    a. Compute I.B.'s "minimum (add-on) tax on tax preferences," assuming no gross tax credit carryforward.

    b. Compute I.B.'s "alternative minimum tax," assuming no excess itemized deductions.

    c. What amount of income tax must I.B. Free actually pay this year?

12. N.O. Flunky, a head of household, has the following items of income this year:

Personal service net income (salary less deductions for A.G.I.)	$150,000
Adjusted gross income	200,000
Net taxable income	160,000
Tax preference items	60,000

    a. What is N.O.'s personal service taxable income?

    b. What is N.O.'s income tax liability?

SUPPLEMENTAL PROBLEMS

13. Tom Watts graduated from college in June of 19x1. While in college, his total support was provided by his parents. He had no income for the four years of college. After a summer in Europe, Tom returned to the U.S. in September and accepted a position with a brokerage house. In October he met and married Jane Volts. Jane had worked and supported herself as a model for the last five years. At the end of 19x1, Tom had an adjusted gross income of $6,000, all earned after his return from Europe. Jane's adjusted gross income for 19x1 was $12,000, the highest income that she had experienced in the modeling business. Can Tom and Jane file a joint return and use income averaging? Consult an outside reference, if necessary, to solve this problem.

14. In 1975 Congress repealed the statutory depletion allowance for integrated oil companies. In 1976, it provided for recapture of I.D.C. deductions upon the sale of an oil or gas property and also included I.D.C. deductions as a preference item for individuals. How can these changes be justified given the energy

crisis? Did Congress have the same goals for all three changes? Explain.

15. When President Carter first took office he appeared to support (1) an end to all special treatment for capital gains; (2) an end to the maximum tax on personal service income; and (3) a reduction in the highest marginal tax rates for individual taxpayers from 70 to 50 percent. Less than one year later he had given up on all three proposals.

a. What good reasons are there to support the three proposals as part of a package deal?

b. Does this turn of recent events support or discredit Professor Brannon's observations, detailed in the long headnote to Part Eight? (See page immediately preceding page **27/1**.) Explain briefly.

16. Professor Stanley S. Surrey, a former Assistant Secretary of the Treasury for Tax Policy and a noted tax authority, published an article in which he criticizes the federal "tax expenditures budget." By this term Surrey refers to some $55 to $60 billion per year (about 25 percent of the regular cash budget) that the government excuses from income taxation by way of "tax incentives" or "subsidies."

a. Give an educated guess as to which five tax provisions constitute the largest entries, in terms of dollar amounts, in Surrey's tax expenditure budget.

b. Why might Surrey and other tax critics prefer to rearrange these items as direct monetary subsidies to specific industries, firms, or individuals, rather than permit them to continue as special provisions in the Internal Revenue Code?

RETURN PROBLEMS

1. For the years 19x1 through 19x4, James Whitson worked as a part-time accountant for an individual practitioner while he attended State University. He began work after completing his junior year as an accounting major and then continued his education until he received the degree of Master of Science in Taxation. Upon graduation in June 19x4, he took a job with an accounting firm that specialized in taxation. Because of his education in taxation, his pay was increased substantially during 19x5. He had, due to his part-time experience in return preparation, a sound background in return procedures, and as a result his new employer in 19x5 was able to use him on research and planning problems. He provided his entire support for years 19x1 through 19x4. His taxable income for the years involved was

19x1	$ 5,400*
19x2	6,200*
19x3	6,400*
19x4	8,800*
19x5	16,200

*In other words, enter these amounts as "base period income," on a 1979 Schedule G (Form 1040) and ignore lines 1 through 5.

Assuming that James is unmarried on December 31, 19x5, complete Schedule G, Form 1040 for the calculation of his gross tax for 19x5, using 1979 tax rates.

2. As a continuation of Return Problem 1, James progressed rapidly in his new job and had a taxable income of $18,700 for 19x6.
Complete Schedule G, again assuming that James is not married.

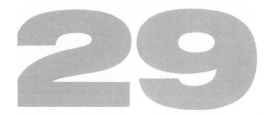

Close the loopholes and you will not get a bunch of contented taxpayers; you will get a lot of dropouts from the rat race, and the whole economy will go to hell from sheer despair.

LARRY MARTZ,
New York (1969)

the tax planning process

A final tax liability is a function of three variables: the law, the facts, and an administrative (and sometimes judicial) process. Most of this book is an explication of the law; a few pages describe the administrative and judicial processes that operationalize the written rules or law. Except for a few problem assignments, we have given little attention to the critical role of facts. In this final chapter, we shall demonstrate how important the facts are to the determination of any tax liability.

Observe also that facts are the one variable that almost everyone can do something about. If you are not satisfied with either the law or the administrative and judicial processes, there is relatively little that you can do (unless, of course, you are a veritable mogul in American society).[1] The facts, however, are generally amenable to modification. If you are wise enough to understand when and how to modify them, you may very well reduce your tax liability significantly. The most highly qualified professional tax experts, described briefly on page **27/3**, earn most of their lucrative fees by giving advice on alternative ways of arranging facts! In other words, most professional tax planning is little more than the prearrangement of facts in the most tax-favored way.

AVOIDANCE VERSUS EVASION

Successful tax planning, or tax *avoidance,* must be clearly distinguished from tax *evasion.* In tax jargon,

the latter term refers to the *illegal* reduction of a tax liability, whereas the former term encompasses only *legal* means of achieving that same objective. For example, if a taxpayer were to claim as a fact on his federal income tax return that he had ten dependent children when he actually had only two such dependents, that misrepresentation of fact would constitute a simple form of tax evasion and the guilty taxpayer would be subject to both criminal and monetary penalties. Backdating an important tax document would constitute an equally obvious form of tax evasion. Deceit, concealment, and misrepresentation are common elements in most illegal tax plans.

On the other hand, careful planning and full disclosure are common elements in tax avoidance. If, for example, a taxpayer can significantly reduce income tax liability by operating a business as a corporation rather than as a sole proprietorship, there is, obviously, nothing illegal about making such a change in the facts. Perhaps the most celebrated statement made in defense of tax planning came from the pen of Judge Learned Hand. In a dissenting opinion, in *Commissioner* v. *Newman,* he once said:

> Over and over again courts have said that there is nothing sinister in so arranging one's affairs as to keep taxes as low as possible. Everybody does so, rich or poor, and all do right, for nobody owes any public duty to pay more than the law demands: taxes are enforced exactions, not voluntary contributions. To demand more in the name of morals is mere cant.[2]

---

[1] In other words, only a very few people have enough money and clout to get a tax law changed by Congress. The administrative and judicial processes are similarly resistant to personal intervention.

[2] 159 F. 2d 848 (CCA-2, 1947).

Although this quotation is from a dissenting opinion and, therefore, of no value as legal precedent, it is widely quoted in support of tax planning. Other judges have said essentially the same thing in majority opinions, but their choice of words is less striking.

Unfortunately, the line between avoidance and evasion is not always as clear as the earlier examples would appear to suggest. Some tax plans so distort the apparent "truth" that they approach the status of evasion. In this chapter, we are not primarily concerned with making fine-line distinctions. Nevertheless, we would encourage our readers to develop a natural instinct to be suspicious of anything that sounds too good to be true in tax planning. As suggested in the following discussion, many apparently viable tax plans have already been curbed by statutory, judicial, or administrative action.

THE CRITICAL VARIABLES

There are alternative ways to approach tax planning systematically. One possibility is to return to the general formula used to determine the income-tax liability of any taxable entity, as introduced on page 5/1, and to modify it slightly, as follows:

Line No.		Item
1		Income broadly conceived
2	−	Exclusions
3	=	Gross income
4	−	Deductions
5	=	Taxable income
6	×	Applicable tax rate(s)
7	=	Gross tax payable
8	−	Tax credits and prepayments
9	=	Net tax payable

Because the ultimate objective of income-tax planning is the minimization of the bottom line—that is, the minimization of the net tax payable—the rules of simple arithmetic suggest that tax planning must necessarily involve the maximization of tax credits, the minimization of the applicable tax rate(s), and the maximization of deductions and exclusions. In other words, the items on all even-numbered lines in the above formula constitute the critical variables in tax planning. In the next few pages, we shall consider some fundamental tax-planning ideas implicit in the provisions already introduced in earlier chapters. In

some instances, we shall then consider other provisions that have been enacted to preclude the apparent tax plan from being successful. Finally, after considering the more isolated examples, we shall examine a typical tax-planning situation to see what an ordinary businessperson might do to reduce taxes.

Maximizing exclusions

Simple illustrations of maximizing exclusions can be readily constructed. Let us begin with the case of taxpayer Lucky. Assume that Lucky is married and files a joint return in which he reports a $215,400 ordinary taxable income and pays a tax of $117,504 each year. If we assume that $106,000 of Lucky's annual income comes from interest on bank deposits or commercial loans, we can quickly see how some elementary tax planning could reduce taxes. If Lucky were to switch his investments from bank deposits or commercial loans to state government bonds, the interest could be excluded from taxable income, and Lucky's net tax payable would decrease from $117,504 per year to $47,544 (that is, to the tax for a married couple reporting $109,400 taxable income). This plan would save Lucky $69,960 per year in taxes. That fact alone does not, however, support a conclusion that a switch of investments, from bank deposits to state government bonds, is necessarily wise.

In order to determine the wisdom of proposing such a tax plan for Lucky, we must examine the after-tax rate of return on the investment. In order to keep the arithmetic as simple as possible, let us assume that Lucky is earning a 10.6 percent rate of return on his original investment in bank deposits or commercial loans. To receive a $106,000 annual interest income, Lucky must have $1 million invested. If the interest rate on state government bonds was only 6 percent, Lucky's annual interest income would drop from $106,000 per year to $60,000 per year, other things being equal. However, the sum of the tax savings of $69,960 plus the $60,000 annual interest exceeds the original return by $23,960 per year. Thus, with the assumed interest rates of 10.6 and 6 percent, and with Lucky's marginal tax bracket, this tax plan is indeed a favorable plan. Further study of this example will quickly explain why tax-exempt securities are especially favorable investments to taxpayers in the highest marginal tax brackets while the same securities are of little or no interest to taxpayers in the lower marginal tax brackets. The after-tax rate of return on tax-exempt securities correlates directly with the taxpayer's marginal tax bracket.

A much more modest tax plan could motivate another couple to switch a small investment from a rent property to a corporate stock or a C.D. (certificate of deposit) in order to take advantage of the $400 annual exclusion. The principle at work is, of course, the same: Maximize exclusions. Both plans would be wholly beyond reproach by either the I.R.S. or the courts. Only a change in the law could modify their effectiveness.

Another tax plan might be based on those exclusions that can be thought of as "wage and salary supplements." To illustrate those opportunities briefly, let us consider the case of taxpayer Black. Suppose that Black has operated a small-town mortuary as a sole proprietorship for many years. He has always purchased life, health, and accident insurance from his own after-tax funds; he has always provided his own meals and lodging from the same source; and he has never had any "death benefits." What is to keep Black from forming a corporation (in which he and his family own the entire equity interest) and then transferring all (or most) of his assets to the new corporation, which would then "hire" Black as its principal employee? Couldn't the new corporation provide its employees (including Black) with certain "supplemental benefits" and get a tax deduction for the cost of the (group-term) life insurance premiums, the health and accident insurance premiums, the casualty insurance, utilities, and upkeep on the home? If Black can exclude the receipt of those benefits from his own gross income (under the conditions stipulated in the statutory authorities noted earlier), and if Black's corporation can deduct the cost of those benefits in the calculation of its own taxable income, won't Black have implemented a successful tax plan that involves both the maximization of exclusions (for himself) and the maximization of deductions (via his new corporate entity)?

Under the proper circumstances the Internal Revenue Service would have a difficult, if not impossible, task in challenging such a tax plan. Although many aspects of this proposal could be subject to attack, if the taxpayer were sufficiently careful in his attention to detail—i.e., if Black's tax advisor very carefully planned, executed, and documented each step in this proposal—there is no fundamental reason that the plan could not succeed. The myriad of detail necessary to reach that happy result must remain outside the confines of this introductory text. However, even momentary reflection on the basic idea should be instructive.

Maximizing deductions

To illustrate how tax planning can be achieved through the maximization of deductions, consider another simplified example. Suppose that Ms. Ionna Stoor is a very successful, single businesswoman with an annual taxable income of $108,300. In addition, Ms. Stoor is the sole stockholder of the Stoor Corporation, which operates a large brewery. If Ms. Stoor were suddenly to inherit a large block of stock in other corporations, which paid her $100,200 in dividends per year, she would discover that Uncle Sam took most of her additional income by way of income taxes. Her annual taxable income would have increased from $108,300 to $208,300 (assuming that she could exclude $200 of the new dividend), and her annual tax liability would have increased from $55,697 to $125,697. In other words, after paying income taxes, Ms. Stoor would have only $30,200 of her $100,200 annual dividend income to reinvest in other property.

With a little tax planning, Ms. Stoor might well transfer her newly inherited stocks to her wholly owned corporation, the Stoor Corporation. As a corporation, the latter taxpayer would be entitled to an 85 percent dividends-received deduction. Thus, if the Stoor Corporation were to receive an additional $100,000 in dividends each year, it could deduct $85,000 of that amount and increase its taxable income by only $15,000. The corporation's federal income tax on $15,000 would amount to $6,900 (assuming a 46 percent marginal corporate tax rate). Thus, by putting the title to the stocks in a corporate entity, and thereby maximizing deductions, Ms. Stoor would have reduced the income tax on the $100,200 in annual dividends from $70,000 to $6,900; at the same time she would have increased her reinvestment potential from $30,200 to $93,300 per year!

The preceding example is a dramatic illustration of how taxes can be saved by maximizing deductions. There are many other, sometimes equally convoluted, possibilities based on the same basic principle. Under the heading of maximizing exclusions, we briefly considered the possibility of an imaginary taxpayer, Black (the operator of a small-town mortuary), decreasing his tax liability through the use of such corporate fringe benefits as life, health, and accident insurance; meals and lodging; and certain death benefits. We pointed out in that earlier discussion the fact that Black benefited because he did not have to report as gross income the value he received in the form of group-term life, health, and accident insurance, meals and lodging, and death benefits, because of the exclusion provisions of the Code. Note, however, that the real tax benefits implicit in those examples depend not only on the fact that they can be excluded from the calculation of Black's personal taxable income, but also on the fact that the cost of those same benefits can be deducted as ordinary and necessary business expenses by Black's wholly owned corporation, which pays the bills. In summary, therefore, the tax savings implicit in those examples really stems from the maximization of both exclusions and deductions. Through the use of a corporate entity, Black is able to convert what would otherwise largely have been nondeductible personal expenditures into tax-deductible expenses without creating any taxable income for himself (because of the statutory exclusion provisions). A third critical variable in tax planning is the applicable tax rate.

Minimizing the tax rate

As noted on page **3/5**, the marginal tax rate is to business affairs what the law of gravity is to physics. Just as water seeks its lowest level (due to the laws of gravity), so also taxable income seeks its lowest marginal tax rate. The tax planning objective is achieved, of course, when the marginal tax rate is minimized. The application of this principle can once again be readily illustrated through a simple example.

Suppose that Mr. and Mrs. Isadore Safe, a highly successful locksmith and his wife, report an annual taxable income of $109,400. If Mrs. Safe were suddenly to inherit $100,000 cash from her recently deceased uncle, Willis More, she might be tempted to put the inheritance into a bank savings account and to save the interest to help finance the education of her three small children. If Mrs. Safe were to receive 10 percent interest on her savings account, she would discover that the additional $10,000 in interest each year caused an increase of $6,400 in the annual income tax liability payable by her and Mr. Safe. In other words, only $3,600 would be left after taxes to apply toward the children's education fund. With a little tax planning, Mrs. Safe might put the $100,000 that she inherited "in trust" for a period of at least 10 years and 1 day, and instruct the trustee

to distribute the $10,000 annual interest equally to her three minor children.[3] Each of the Safe children would now receive $3,333 per year (for 10 years) in interest. If we assume that the children received no other income, they would each pay an income tax of $356.[4] In this way the aggregate tax liability on the $10,000 of interest each year would have been reduced from $6,400 to $1,068, and the amount left to accumulate in the children's education fund would have increased from $3,600 to $8,932 per year.

The tax savings implicit in this simple example is attributable to the combined effect of minimizing the tax rate and maximizing deductions. Mr. and Mrs. Isadore Safe were in a 64 percent marginal tax bracket; their minor children were in a 14 to 18 percent marginal tax brackets. Thus, by transferring the $10,000 annual interest income from their higher marginal tax bracket to the children's lower marginal tax brackets, a substantial tax savings was possible. The aggregate tax saving was further increased by the fact that the children were able to be claimed as dependents by their parents and at the same time claim a personal exemption on their own tax returns. In this way, the family as a whole was able to maximize deductions for personal and dependent exemptions from $5,000 (5 × $1,000) to $8,000 (8 × $1,000). This example demonstrates clearly how useful trusts can be to tax plans that depend on the minimization of tax rates.

Corporate entities are another useful vehicle in minimizing tax rates. If one individual owns the entire equity interest in a corporation, that corporation is, obviously, a mere alter ego of the sole stockholder. Nevertheless the I.R.S. and the courts will recognize the existence of a separate (corporate) taxpayer as long as it has a legitimate business purpose. As explained on pages **10/5–10**/6, however, since December 31, 1974, multiple corporate entities owned by the same few owners may be treated as a single taxpayer.

The corporate tax rate for even one corporation is, nevertheless, a good tax-rate shelter for many individuals. To draw this important conclusion, we need recall only that the current corporate tax rate is 17 percent on the first $25,000 of taxable income; 20

---

[3]If the trust were created for any period shorter than 10 years and 1 day, the income would still be taxed to Mr. and Mrs. Safe, regardless of the distribution of income made by the trustee. See discussion in Chapter 11.
[4]The $356 net tax liability is based on a taxable income determined without a zero bracket amount. Subsection 141(e) of the Code, added by the Revenue Act of 1971, denies the zero bracket amount to any taxpayer who is claimed as the dependent of another taxpayer except to the extent that he or she has earned income.

percent on the next $25,000; 30 percent on the third $25,000; 40 percent on the fourth $25,000; and 46 percent thereafter. Recall also that the tax rates applicable to single individuals exceed 17 percent for all taxable incomes in excess of $4,400 (for married persons the pertinent amount is $7,600). This fact goes a long way in explaining why approximately 1.8 million corporate returns are filed each year. Collectively those returns report a net taxable income of about $120 billion. In one recent year, however, only 4,000 corporations (with assets in excess of $50 million) reported over two-thirds of that $113 billion. Many of the remaining 1,796,000 corporations were used as tax-rate shelters.

Maximizing credits

Relative to the three other variables already discussed, the opportunity to save taxes through the maximization of credits is limited. Nevertheless, there are things a taxpayer can do to help maximize the value of available credits. For example, a taxpayer intending to purchase an asset that qualifies for the investment credit can make that purchase (and place the asset in service) near the end of one tax year, rather than waiting until early the next year. Other things being equal, because of the time value of money, the taxpayer will have acted wisely for tax purposes.

Once an asset is acquired, a taxpayer might also extend his or her otherwise unbiased estimate of that asset's useful life to obtain a larger investment credit. Remember, only assets estimated to last 7 years or longer are eligible for the full credit. Obviously, this last choice is sometimes a mixed blessing; the longer life generally reduces the annual depreciation deduction and, to that extent, there may be a trade-off between the investment tax credit and maximizing deductions. A taxpayer who makes an early disposition of an investment-credit property may have to recapture some portion (or all) of the credit previously claimed. Nevertheless, because no interest or penalty attaches to the amount recaptured, the decision to estimate the life of a property on the long side sometimes pays dividends. Observe also that if a taxpayer underestimates the life of an investment-credit-eligible property, there is no mechanism that would permit the taxpayer to claim a belated investment credit for the extra years the asset was actually used.

Finally, observe that a taxpayer can often avoid any recapture of the investment credit by briefly deferring an intended disposition. In other words, by waiting until a new year to make a planned asset disposition, a taxpayer may be able to avoid the need to recapture this credit.

ANOTHER VIEW OF THE OPPORTUNITIES

An alternative way of viewing tax-planning opportunities is to observe that our income tax is constrained by time, entity, and accounting method. We could, therefore, go back and review each illustration and reclassify the tax savings as being attributable to time, entity, or accounting-method manipulation rather than as maximizing deductions, minimizing the rate, etc. However, our objective here is not to derive the best possible classification system for tax planning. It is, rather, to emphasize fundamental ways in which one should examine routine facts to aid in the determination of the tax-preferred alternative. Consequently, we shall proceed to very briefly examine a few additional planning ideas in this new way.

The time constraint

Observe that our income tax rates "start over" with each new tax year. Because very few taxpayers have a constant level of taxable income in each year, there tend to be high-tax years and low-tax years. As explained in the introduction to Chapter 8, the "tax value" of a deduction is directly dependent on the marginal tax bracket of the party reporting it. Obviously, therefore, taxpayers tend to recognize losses and other deductions in high-tax years and to defer the recognition of taxable income to low-tax years. To the extent that a taxpayer can control tax timing, he or she should do so only after giving full consideration to the time value of money. Sometimes the financial cost of deferral is greater than the tax benefit.

The time constraint may also be important in working with closely held corporations. Very often a taxpayer can gain an advantage by the careful selection of a corporate fiscal year. He or she might, for example, have the corporate year end on January 31. By paying a year-end bonus to the owner-operator in late January, the corporation could almost immediately realize the tax value of the additional deduction, while the recipient owner-employee would not have to report that bonus on his or her personal tax return until the second-following April 15th, i.e.,

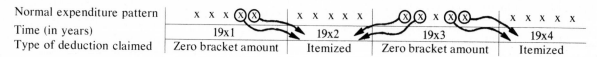

Normal expenditure pattern	x x x (X)(X)	x x x x x	(X)(X) x (X)(X)	x x x x x
Time (in years)	19x1	19x2	19x3	19x4
Type of deduction claimed	Zero bracket amount	Itemized	Zero bracket amount	Itemized

some 14½ months later. This illustration obviously makes use of the time, the entity, *and* the accounting-method constraints. We can sometimes embellish this plan yet a little more through additional accounting method considerations. For example, we might arrange to have the corporation report on an accrual basis and the owner-operator on a cash basis; in that way we can sometimes gain the immediate benefit of an extra tax deduction without having to make an immediate expenditure of corporate funds. In the case of closely held corporations, however, Sec. 267 severely limits the benefits that could otherwise be obtained from such accounting legerdemain.

The accounting-method constraint

Each taxable entity is generally free to select its own accounting method. Sometimes even a single entity may utilize more than one accounting method if it has more than one trade or business. By selecting accounting methods carefully, a taxpayer is often able to save many tax dollars. The rush of American corporations to the LIFO (last-in, first-out) inventory costing method in 1973–74 is a vivid case in point. Because of the rapid inflation experienced during those years, the cost of goods sold determined under the LIFO method was considerably larger than it would have been under any other method for most businesses. Accordingly, the switch was commonly made largely to save taxes because of the lower incomes that were thereby reported.

In the case of an individual taxpayer, the exact definitional distinction between accounting methods and certain tax options is sometimes blurred. To illustrate this opportunity, consider the case of the wage earner whose itemized deductions are nearly always equal to the zero bracket amount. That taxpayer is likely to conclude that there is no tax planning that can help. Actually such a taxpayer does have one limited chance at playing the tax game too. Because he or she can make a new election between taking the zero bracket amount and itemizing deductions each year and can report taxable income on a cash basis of accounting, he or she can benefit by carefully timing expenditures and keeping good records. The basic idea involves itemizing deductions every other year. In years when deductions will not

exceed the zero bracket amount, the taxpayer should defer all tax-deductible expenditures to the maximum extent possible. For example, in those years the taxpayer should

1. Make minimal charitable contributions;
2. Defer interest payments;
3. Stall on doctor and dentist bills; and
4. Avoid making property tax payments.

In years when deductions will exceed the zero bracket amount, the taxpayer should do just the opposite. This tax plan can be illustrated easily, as in the diagram at the top of the page. In this way, the taxpayer's aggregate deductions will be greater and tax liability smaller, over several years.

Many other examples of successful tax planning could be included here. Those examples would add little, if any, to the fundamentals already introduced. Therefore, rather than belabor isolated examples, let us turn next to some limitations that often constrain otherwise viable tax plans.

SOME LIMITATIONS

Tax planning is not always as simple as it has been made to appear in the examples of this chapter. The Internal Revenue Service, Congress, and the courts are constantly putting limitations on some of the more grandiose ideas intended to save taxes. Although we cannot stop to explore this fascinating subject in depth, we might examine briefly two statutory limitations to some of the more obvious tax-saving opportunities. To do this, let us return to a slightly modified version of the facts in the example of Ms. Ionna Stoor.

Again assume that Ms. Ionna Stoor is a very successful, single businesswoman with an annual taxable income of $108,300 who inherits a large block of stocks that pays her an additional $100,200 in dividends each year. This time, however, assume that Ms. Stoor does *not* already own the outstanding stock of a viable manufacturing corporation. Having inherited this stock, and knowing about the corporate dividends-received deduction, Ms. Stoor might be tempted to create a new corporate entity and to transfer to it her interest in the newly inherited shares. She would be hoping, of course, to reduce her tax on the $100,000 in dividends from $70,000 (if received by her directly) to $2,550 (if received by her newly created corporation). The corporate tax would equal 17 percent of $15,000 (i.e., a $100,000 dividend less an $85,000 dividends-received deduction). Such a plan could not be successful.

The personal holding company tax

Unfortunately, this time our apparently grand tax plan is indeed too good to be true. Realizing the existence of the possibility just described, Congress long ago enacted the personal holding company tax (Secs. 541–547). Under the proposed tax plan, Ms. Stoor's new corporation would constitute a personal holding company and be subject to a separate tax (in addition to the $2,550 income tax) of $68,215 (i.e., 70 percent of $100,000 less $2,550). The many details of Code Secs. 541–547 must remain beyond the scope of this elementary text. We need observe only that the personal holding company tax generally applies only to corporations: (1) whose stock is closely held (more than 50 percent of its stock is owned by or for any five or fewer individuals); and (2) whose income is largely from passive sources (more technically, "at least 60 percent of its adjusted ordinary gross income . . . for the taxable year is personal holding company income." Sec. 542(a)(1)). The definitional nuances implicit in any interpretation of the Code section just quoted are among the more complex to be found in our tax laws. Nevertheless, even the beginner can readily understand why the idea just suggested for Ms. Stoor cannot succeed as proposed.

If, however, Ms. Stoor could transfer these shares into a corporation that also was engaged in the conduct of an *active* trade or business, as originally proposed, and if the extra dividends (along with any other personal holding company income) did not exceed 60 percent of that corporation's "adjusted ordinary gross income," then the annual tax savings explained above could actually be realized. In other words, the basic idea suggested is viable, but only if done with proper regard for the possible limitations imposed by Secs. 541–547.

The accumulated earnings tax

A second possible hindrance to the achievement of the intended tax savings suggested in this example could arise from problems with Secs 531–537. Those sections of the Code impose another tax, called an accumulated earnings tax, on any corporation that accumulates its earnings "beyond the reasonable needs of the business."[5] The purpose of this penalty tax is to force corporations either to use any accumulation of retained earnings in reasonable business needs or to distribute those same amounts to its stockholders. In the case of Ms. Stoor's corporation, the fact that the newly expanded brewery would be receiving relatively large amounts of dividend income each year (assumed to be $100,000 annually) would mean that the Stoor Corporation would be a prime candidate for this tax even if it could escape the personal holding company tax. Unless the corporation could use the accumulated earnings for reasonable business needs, it would have to either pay the penalty tax or distribute the excess corporate funds as a dividend to Ms. Stoor.[6] The latter alternative is not satisfactory from her standpoint, because it would result in the dividends being taxed at 70 percent after all. Consequently, the desirable tax result *is* possible, but only if Ms. Stoor can avoid *both* the personal holding company tax and the accumulated earnings tax.

Again we will not stop to discuss the many complexities associated with the accumulated earnings tax. We need observe only that reasonable people frequently disagree over the reasonableness of earnings accumulated in American corporations, especially in closely held corporations. Thus, it is commonplace to find I.R.S. agents and taxpayers in disagreement over the proper application of this tax provision to specific corporate circumstances. The question that must be answered is, ultimately, a question of *fact* (not a question of law) that can be finally resolved only by the decision of a court if the agent and the taxpayer cannot reach an earlier settlement. The value of a tax expert's assistance in the bargaining process that takes place should be obvious.

A SPECIFIC EXAMPLE OF TAX PLANNING

Suppose that Mr. and Mrs. Grub have for years operated the family restaurant as a sole proprietorship. The restaurant, which is very popular, pro-

---

[5] Section 535(c)(2) provides a minimum accumulation of $150,000 without the imposition of this tax. However, the accumulation of earnings beyond this *de minimis* amount can be retained without penalty only for "reasonable business needs."

[6] The rate of this penalty tax is 27½ percent of the first $100,000 of unreasonably accumulated earnings and 38½ percent of any additional amounts so accumulated.

duces an annual operating income of about $43,200. In addition, the Grubs own (inherited) stocks that produce about $1,200 in dividends each year. Finally, Mrs. Grub owns 50 percent of a new venture that, because of its highly risky nature, was incorporated. As expected, the new business venture reported a $20,000 taxable loss this year; the owners hope it can begin to make a profit within three years.

If the Grubs are unaware of their tax opportunities, they would probably report a taxable income of $42,000 and pay an income tax of $11,086 this year. Calculation of those amounts can be detailed as follows, assuming the Grubs do not itemize deductions:

Income from sole proprietorship		$43,200
Dividends	$1,200	
Less dividend exclusion (jointly owned)	400	800
Adjusted gross income		$44,000
Less personal exemptions		2,000
Taxable income		$42,000
Gross tax liability (joint return)		$11,086

Let us further assume that the Grubs require $20,000 for personal consumption expenditures each year and that they reinvest any excess funds in their family restaurant. This means, of course, that in the current year they would have $13,314 available for reinvestment. That is,

Gross income received		$44,400
Less:		
Personal consumption expenditures	$20,000	
Income tax	11,086	31,086
Available for reinvestment		$13,314

If the Grubs understood our tax laws a little better, they might very possibly:

1. Transfer their restaurant assets to a newly created, family-owned corporation;

2. Transfer most of their inherited stocks to the same corporation (keeping only enough to pay them $400 in dividends each year);

3. Arrange to have themselves paid a salary (from their own corporation) of $22,000 for their work in the restaurant; and

4. Elect to have the new business venture, in which Mrs. Grub invested, make the Subchapter S election.

As revised, there are now two separate taxable entities whose taxable incomes and tax liabilities can be computed as follows:

Grubs Corporation	
Operating income	$43,200
+ Dividends received	800
− Salary paid owners	(22,000)
− Dividends received deduction	(680)
Taxable income	$21,320
Tax liability	$ 3,624

Mr. and Mrs. Grub	
Salary received	$22,000
+ Dividends received	400
− Dividend exclusion	(400)
− Subchapter S loss	(10,000)
− Personal exemptions	(2,000)
Taxable Income	$10,000
Gross Tax liability	$ 1,062

Accordingly, the total "family" tax liability for the year would be $4,686 and they would have $19,714 available for reinvestment in their business. The latter amount would be determined as follows:

Grubs Corporation	
Income earned	$44,000
− Salary paid owners	(22,000)
− Income tax paid	(3,624)
Available for reinvestment	$18,376

Mr. and Mrs. Grub	
Income earned	$ 22,400
− Personal consumption	(20,000)
− Income tax paid	(1,062)
Available for reinvestment	$ 1,338

The treatment of the $10,000 loss deduction from the new business venture deserves further comment. As explained earlier, Subchapter S corporations are treated as quasi conduits for tax purposes, much like partnerships. Consequently, as a 50 percent owner in this venture, Mrs. Grub is entitled to deduct 50 percent of the $20,000 loss incurred by the corporation. If the new corporation does not elect Subchapter S treatment, the net operating loss would remain with the corporate entity. Ordinarily, a net operating loss is carried back and treated as an additional deduction against any taxable income reported by the same entity three years earlier. Because our illustration assumed a *new* venture, the corporation would have no prior years to which it could carry back its current loss. If Mrs. Grub does not elect Subchapter S treatment, the loss can only be carried forward and offset against future taxable income (if any is ever earned). Whether or not the Subchapter S election is "wise" from a tax standpoint depends on (1) the comparative marginal tax bracket of the entities that can claim the deduction and (2) the time value of money.

In summary, the Grub family would save about 50 percent of their tax bill by doing some elementary tax planning. Because of this, they could increase their reinvestment in their income-producing activity by about 50 percent. Other things being equal, this should increase their income in the future. Admittedly the story is again less than 100 percent complete. For example, the Grubs' extra funds are now "tied up" in a corporate entity; the basis of their stock in the venture corporation is lower; they would have incurred extra record-keeping costs with the new corporation; and their social security and business franchise taxes may be slightly higher. Even with these added costs, however, the illustration demonstrates that tax planning can pay dividends even in a small business and without resort to any remotely questionable practices.

TAX PLANNING FOR SMALLER BUSINESSES IN GENERAL

As we have demonstrated, successful tax plans may take a wide variety of forms. One major, integrated set of tax plans common to smaller businesses prior to 1970 involved the use of multiple corporate entities to gain maximum advantage of the corporate rate shelter. The essential elements of this scheme can be readily depicted as in Figure 29-1. The size of the income stream produced directly and indirectly by taxpayer O/O (an owner/operator) can be depicted by the size of the arrow on the left side of Figure 29-1. This income typically was protected from our high individual income-tax rates by the creation of multiple corporate entities. In one sense, then, the corporations served as a fence to block the income from flowing directly and immediately to taxpayer O/O. Because of the corporate surtax exemption, the number of corporations necessitated by good tax planning was determined by dividing the size of the income stream by $25,000. Thus, if the taxpayer's personal efforts plus property ownership produced an annual income of approximately $100,000, four corporations would have been used. An annual income of $300,000 would have required 12 corporations.

The owner/operator would extract from the corporations only enough income to satisfy personal

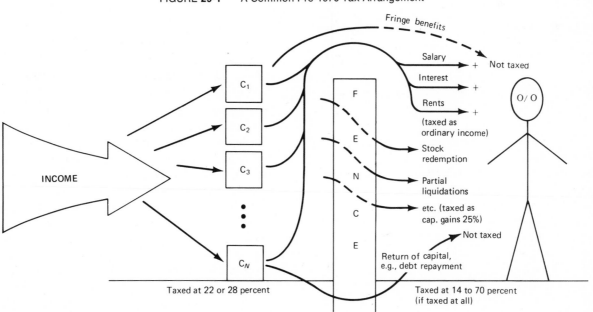

FIGURE **29-1**   A Common Pre-1970 Tax Arrangement

consumption function requirements. He or she would further be certain to extract income only in a form that would, at worst, be deductible to the corporation and taxable to him or her as ordinary income. Thus, salary, interest (on debt), and rents (on property owned by taxpayer O/O, but leased to and used by his or her corporations) were common vehicles used to extract whatever income O/O deemed necessary for personal comfort. Obviously, to the extent available, taxpayer O/O developed an even stronger appetite for items whose cost could be immediately deducted by corporations and never taxed to the taxpayer as an individual. The problems commonly encountered in the "fringe benefits" area are illustrative. That is, the common phenomena of the company car, the vacation/convention, the private jet, the entertainment overload, and the executive dining room (if not the executive mansion), all owe much of their existence to our tax provisions. In general, the costs of those fringe benefits have been deductible by the employer corporation, while they could be excluded from the gross income of the benefactor/recipient.[7]

Many of the tax disputes of the past two decades, and many of the complex rules noted earlier in this text, derived naturally from this setting. For example, one of the tax problems of the past involved the need to distinguish clearly between corporate debt and equity. Taxpayers, such as O/O in Figure 29-1, commonly created their closely held corporations with minimum equity and maximum debt. They would prefer to record a $100,000 investment in say, C_5 (i.e., corporation no. 5) as $80,000 long-term debt and $20,000 common stock, rather than as $20,000 debt and $80,000 equity, because

1. The existence of the debt gave rise to an immediately deductible corporate interest payment (whereas dividends of an equivalent amount could not have been deducted).

2. The existence of the debt could sometimes be used to justify the accumulation of earnings (to pay off the debt at a later date) and thus to avoid the penalty tax associated with any "unreasonable" accumulations of earnings.

3. The payment of the face of the debt would result only in a return of capital to the owner—an event delightfully free of any tax consequences.

[7]For further development of this basic theme, see Ray M. Sommerfeld, *Tax Factors in Business Decisions*, revised edition (Homewood, Ill.: Richard D. Irwin, Inc., 1978), Chapter 7.

The owner-operator who needed still more cash than that obtainable through debt repayment, salaries, interest, and rents commonly tried to obtain it as a tax-favored capital gain. Thus, the tax problems associated with stock redemptions and partial liquidations, discussed briefly in Chapter 23, were born.

In summary, a common pre-1970 tax picture found the owner-operator sheltering much of "his or her" income at tax rates of from 22 to 28 percent (a 6 percent penalty tax was added to the then 22 percent normal corporate tax rate that was, before 1970, applied to the first $25,000 of taxable income reported by multiple corporate entities) by retaining most of the income in multiple corporate entities. The owner-operator would extract from the corporations as much money as possible by way of tax-free fringe benefits and payments involving a return of capital. Beyond that, the owner typically would satisfy personal consumption needs by salary, interest, and rent payments. Larger, sporadic needs were often better served by stock redemptions and partial liquidations. Retirement generally involved a tax-free reorganization, such as a merger.

Important changes in the 1969 Tax Reform Act

The Tax Reform Act of 1969 included several new provisions intended to modify the tax scene just described. Most importantly, that act concurrently introduced (1) the phase-out of the multiple corporate surtax exemption and (2) the maximum tax on personal service income. In addition, the same act effectively increased the tax rate applicable to the net capital gains reported by the more affluent taxpayers from 25 to nearly 50 percent. After January 1, 1975, when the surtax exemption phase-out was complete, the result of these changes was to tax almost any income left in many corporations (on the left side of Figure 29-1) at 48 percent, while income extracted for the owner-operator in the form of personal service income would be taxed immediately, but at no more than a 50 percent marginal rate.

If that were the end of the saga, we could safely predict that all owner-operated corporations would by now have increased salaries paid to owners in a dramatic way. After all, most owner-operators would prefer the unrestricted use of personal funds rather than the use of restricted corporate money, if the differential in the tax rate were only 2 percentage points. Early evidence suggests that this process was well under way shortly after 1972. One bit of evidence is apparent in the following tabulation:

Year	Number of taxpayers electing maximum tax option	Estimated tax saved (in millions)
1971	9,185	$ 26
1972	88,085	271
1973	115,998	326
1974	148,579	495
1975	185,810	662
1976	231,877	896

No data are available for years after 1976. Nevertheless, this information from the annual I.R.S. reports suggests that a new trend is well under way. The upward movement in personal service income is further confirmed by a comparison from the same source:

Adjusted gross income class	Number of taxpayers in	
	1975	1976
Under $100,000	90,269	110,313
$100,000 to $200,000	79,672	100,085
$200,000 to $500,000	14,308	19,506
$500,000 to $1,000,000	1,236	1,583
Over $1,000,000	325	390

While inflation may account for some of this trend, we doubt that inflation is the full explanation. Rather, we suspect that tax planning has played a major role.

Complicating factors

There are many reasons why owner-operators were slow to modify their behavior and take advantage of the new tax rules. The high degree of interdependence between the new and old laws and their sheer complexity was in no small measure accountable for the delayed reaction. In many ways, the post-1969 tax plan for the same group of "small businesses" required an entirely new game plan, at least until the Revenue Act of 1978. Old habits were hard to break, especially when they had served a person very well in the past, and the 1969–76 changes in the law called for an entirely new approach.

PERSONAL TAX RATES   To understand one important element in the 1969–78 tax era, we must review at least two aberrations in the tax-rate schedule for individual taxpayers. In reality, our marginal tax rates do not move progressively higher from 14 to 70 percent, as illustrated in Figure 3-1. Instead, they more realistically progress in an irregular fashion as shown in Figure 29-2. Observe that to determine the federal income-tax liability of a large personal income in a post-1978 year, we very often must first separate that income into three categories:

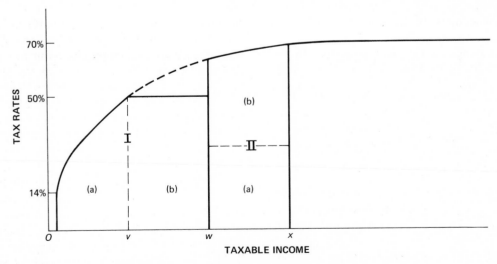

FIGURE **29-2**   Conceptual View of Marginal Income Tax Rates for Individual Taxpayers

Tier I is "personal service" taxable income;

Tier II(b) is *neither* personal service taxable income nor net capital gain; and

Tier II(a) is 40 percent of the net capital gains (i.e., *NLTCG − NSTCL*).

The tax rates normally begin at 14 percent and continue upward in a routine way *only* until the 50 percent marginal rate. At that point, to the extent that the taxpayer has additional amounts of *personal service taxable income*, our marginal rates become flat. Thus, the tax liability on Tier I is the sum of the areas labeled I(a) and I(b) in Figure 29-2. This is, of course, the same idea as that introduced in Figure 28-1.

Our tax rates return to "normal" as far as Tier II income is concerned. Because of the aberration introduced by Tier I(b), however, the determination of the "normal" tax liability on Tier II is somewhat unusual. In effect, we "back into" the tax on this portion of income, represented by area II in Figure 29-2, by determining the tax in a "normal" way on an income equal to distance *Ox* and subtract from that the tax determined in a normal way on an income equal to distance *Ow*. The difference between these two amounts is, of course, the tax on distance *wx*, determined in a normal way, beginning at the *w* point in the rate scale.

On Tier II(a) income—that is, net capital gains—the tax liability is also determined in the "normal" way, but only after deducting the 60 percent long-term capital-gain deduction. That is, because of the long-term capital-gain deduction, a dollar's worth of net capital gain amounts to only 40 cents worth of taxable income.

THE PUSH-FORWARD EFFECT   One reason why owner-operators did not find the maximum tax on personal service income to be as desirable as they may have anticipated can be attributed to the "push-forward" effect. By these words we refer simply to the fact that the introduction of substantially larger salaries necessarily "pushes" the taxpayer's Tier II income into significantly higher tax brackets. The increased tax on this Tier II income was sometimes sufficiently large to discourage the declaration of the larger salary. Conceptually this effect can be readily illustrated as in Figure 29-3.

To continue this illustration, let us assume that distance *Oa* = $60,000; *Ob* = $90,000; and *ab* = $30,000. Let us further assume that $60,000 represents the salary paid an owner-operator and that the

$30,000 represents the interest and rents paid that same person. Using the current tax rate scales, we would find the tax on that $90,000 taxable income to be $36,098. What would happen if we increased this taxpayer's salary by $49,400 (to $109,400 per year)? If one considered *only* the tax on personal service income, one would conclude that this taxpayer's income-tax liability would increase by $24,700 (that is, 50 percent of $49,400, assuming that the taxpayer is married and files a joint return). In fact, however, his or her income-tax liability would increase by $30,646. The extra $5,946 in tax is attributable to the tax on the Tier II income that has been pushed into the higher marginal tax brackets by the introduction of the increased salary. Thus, one might say that the true marginal tax cost of the extra salary is really not 50 percent, but 62 percent (i.e., $30,646 ÷ $49,400).

THE SLIDE-BACK EFFECT   A second reason why owner-operators did not find the maximum tax on earned income to be as desirable as they may have anticipated can be attributed to the "slide-back" effect. By these words we refer to the additional tax on what otherwise would have been personal service income but became unearned income because of a definitional nuance. On page **28**/7, we noted that personal service taxable income equals adjusted earned net income *less certain tax preferences*. In prior years, tax advisors frequently helped owner-operators shelter their incomes in ways that produced substantial tax preferences. Because of this, many taxpayers had to give up much of the benefit that would otherwise have accrued to increased salaries. In effect, certain tax preferences convert the last dollars of Tier I income into the first dollars of Tier II income, and the extra tax on that amount can be referred to as the slide-back effect. Conceptually this effect can be illustrated as in Figure 29-4. If the taxpayer's taxable income from salaries was equal to distance *Ob,* and passive income equal to distance *bc,* the introduction of certain tax-preference items equal to distance *ab* would increase this taxpayer's net tax payable by the tinted area in Figure 29-4. This tax "penalty" can be referred to as the slide-back effect.

Until January 1, 1979, the long-term capital gain deduction was included as a tax preference item for individual taxpayers. Consequently, a net capital gain was often of relatively limited interest to an individual taxpayer with a large personal service income. Because the Revenue Act of 1978 both (1)

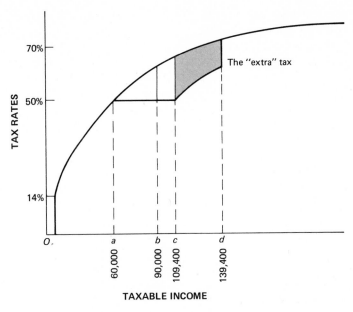

FIGURE **29-3**   The Push-Forward Effect

increased the long-term capital gain deduction from 50 to 60 percent and (2) removed the capital gain deduction from the list of tax preferences that poisoned what otherwise would have been personal service income, capital gains have once again returned to their position of preeminence in tax planning. It is still too early to tell just how important this change will be as far as the trend toward increasing salaries is concerned. It is a safe bet to assume, however, that tax advisors are once again giving a lot of thought to converting ordinary income into capital gain.

THE ENLARGED SURTAX EXEMPTION   A third reason why owner-operators found the maximum tax on personal service income to be less desirable then they originally anticipated can be attributed to the modification of the corporate surtax exemption in 1975. Before 1975, the first $25,000 in corporate taxable income was taxed at 22 percent; additional

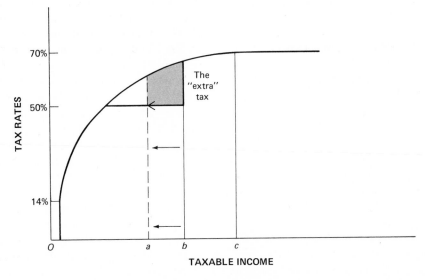

FIGURE **29-4**   The Slide-Back Effect

amounts at 48 percent. Ever since the Tax Reduction Act of 1975, Congress has steadily reduced the effective marginal tax rates on corporate taxable income. These lower tax rates on corporate taxable incomes have, of course, encouraged owner-managers to retain larger amounts within the corporate entity. For many of the smaller firms, this has been sufficient reason for not increasing the owner's salary.

Because of the complicating factors just described, one might conclude that the changes introduced by the Tax Acts of 1969, 1976, and 1978 will not have much of an effect on tax planning for the owner-operator after all. We suspect that that conclusion is not valid. Instead, we see a number of likely changes being made gradually.

Anticipated changes

If we think about the push-forward effect for a moment, it will become obvious that a taxpayer can minimize this tax result if willing to divest himself or herself of the property that produced the passive income. In many cases the taxpayers should be willing to do that. At least to the extent that this taxable income derives from interest on debts held by his or her corporation (in lieu of additional equity shares) and from property leased to the corporation by the owner, the solution is easy. The taxpayer can convert the debt to equity and transfer title to the rental property to the corporation as a tax-free contribution to capital. Alternatively, the taxpayer might be wiser to transfer the title to both the corporate debt and the rented property to a trust created for the benefit of children, grandchildren, and parents.

In many cases, taxpayers will find it beneficial to create trusts with a limited life that provide for return of the corpus to the taxpayer at the end of the term. As explained in Chapter 11, the short-term or "Clifford" trust shifts the income if the trust is for a term of more than 10 years, or for the life of the beneficiary. These trusts are ideal in cases in which the beneficiaries are aging parents, children, or grandchildren of the taxpayer who may need financial help for a limited period. Either of these actions would get the Tier II income out of the owner-operator's taxable income (but keep it "within the family") and thus allow him or her to side-step the push-forward effect.

Tax planning to avoid or minimize the slide-back effect necessitates a change in investment strategies. If a taxpayer decides to use the maximum tax on personal service income as a major tax-planning opportunity, he or she will have to reevaluate all tax shelters that produce tax-preference items. Thus, for example, instead of investing in oil-drilling ventures, the taxpayer utilizing the maximum tax on earned income is more likely to turn to the state and municipal bond markets for tax-sheltered investments. Not only do these bonds provide tax-free interest, they also produce no tax preference, according to the Code! Capital gains are also desirable because they too create no tax preferences for the individual taxpayer, at least as far as the minimum tax rules are concerned.

In summary, we anticipate that some owner-managers will continue to increase their salaries significantly in the future but that, as they do this, they will also make concurrent modifications in the composition of their income stream and in the character of their tax-sheltered investments. This requires a major rethinking by tax advisors as well as taxpayers. Much of what they very carefully constructed in the past must now be substantially restructured if taxpayers are to minimize their tax liability in the future. Based on history, however, we are firmly convinced that these changes will continue over the next decade or two.

The reasonable salary issue

If we are correct in our predictions to this point, it is equally certain that the I.R.S. will raise the question of unreasonable salaries with greater frequency and renewed vigor in the future. As explained in Chapter 6, a wage or salary can be deducted by a corporation only if it is "reasonable in amount." And a wage or salary can be reported as personal service income only if it is a reasonable compensation for services rendered. But who really knows what is "reasonable"? The donning of black robes does little to help one answer such esoteric questions. The essence of the issue was grasped clearly many years ago by a judge in Nebraska. There the court said, " . . . an attempt to give a specific meaning to the word 'reasonable' is trying to count what is not number and measure what is not space."[8]

Actually, at least in the case of the owner-operator, the problem is even more complicated than is suggested by the reasonableness criterion. Because the owner-operator is clearly in command of his or her employer-corporation, the labels attached to self-serving disbursements are often selected with tax considerations in mind. What, for example, is to

---

[8] *Altshuler* v. *Coburn,* 38 Nebr. 881, 47 N. W. 836 (1894).

keep the owner-operator from calling a dividend salary? If the owner-operator is both the sole stockholder and the chief corporate officer-employee, both distributions would create additional taxable income for the recipient but only the salary would provide the distributing corporations with an equivalent tax deduction. Because of the need to overcome such obvious temptations, some courts have added their own requirements to those stipulated in the Code. Perhaps the high water mark for the I.R.S., relative to the reasonable salary issue, is found in *Charles McCandless Tile Service* v. *U.S.*[9] There the Court of Claims concluded that even though the amount paid the owner-operator was, in fact, a reasonable salary, part of the payment represented a dividend! The primary reason for the court's conclusion was apparently based on the poor dividend history of the distributing corporation. Although most closely held corporations have an equally poor dividend record, subsequent courts have not wholly accepted the automatic dividend rule implicit in *McCandless*. Nevertheless, this decision and others like it represent a constant hazard to the owner of the closely held corporate business who is interested in using the maximum tax to a significant degree. For that person, dividends are doubly painful: First, their payment yields no corporate deduction and, second, their receipt adds to Tier II income. As usual, however, there may be an intermediate solution to even this apparent tax dilemma.

The stockholder in a closely held corporation might cause the corporation to distribute a nonvoting preferred stock dividend. The receipt of such stock would probably be nontaxable, although the stock would carry a Sec. 306 taint. That is, it might pro-

[9]191 Ct. Cl. 108 (1970).

duce ordinary income if sold. Instead of selling such stock, however, the owner could give the shares to his or her children, grandchildren, or parents who are in lower tax brackets. For those persons, Tier II income represents no special tax penalty. By paying a reasonable annual cash dividend to these nonvoting, family-member shareholders, the corporation may be able to distribute larger salaries to the owner-operator without fear of the automatic dividend conclusion. And at some distant future date, the nonvoting shareholders just may be able to dispose of their preferred shares at capital-gains rates after all.

Multiple corporations reborn?

Although large salaries remain a real possibility for many of the owner-operators of American businesses, the significant reduction in corporate tax rates introduced in 1978, along with the major reduction in the tax on net capital gains, may mean an entirely different tax game plan for many other taxpayers. These latest changes in our tax laws once again make (1) multiple corporations and (2) the retention of corporate earnings desirable tax objectives. The new challenge lies in avoiding classification as a controlled group of corporations.

The potential value of splitting a corporate taxable income of $200,000 between two corporate entities—rather than reporting all of it in one entity—is clearly demonstrated in Figure 29-5. A more general appreciation of the potential tax saving possibilities can be extracted from Table 29-1. Observe that there is, of course, no tax benefit whatsoever in multiple corporations as long as the amount of taxable income retained within the corporation(s) does not exceed $25,000. As soon as the retained income exceeds that amount, however, some tax benefit is inevitable. The

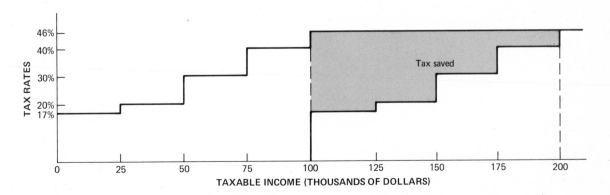

FIGURE **29-5**   Tax Advantage of (Two) Multiple Corporations after 1978

TABLE **29-1**

TAX SAVINGS POSSIBLE WITH MULTIPLE CORPORATIONS

No. of corporations	Corporate taxable income retained			
	$25,000	$100,000	$300,000	$500,000
2 vs. 1	$ 0	$8,250 (31%)	$19,250 (16%)	$19,250 (9%)
3 vs. 1	0	9,000 (34%)	38,500 (32%)	38,500 (18%)
4 vs. 1	0	9,750 (36%)	51,750 (44%)	57,750 (27%)
5 vs. 1	0	9,750 (36%)	57,500 (48%)	77,000 (37%)

larger the retained corporate taxable income, in general, the greater the number of corporations desired. For example, if the retained corporate taxable income is $300,000 each year, splitting that taxable income among five corporations (rather than allowing all of it to be earned by one corporation) would yield a tax saving of $57,500, or 48 percent of the total corporate tax liability! An annuity of $57,500 per year for 30 years, earning 6 percent after taxes, is worth approximately $4.5 million! Obviously, therefore, the owners of the smaller American businesses once again have a very real incentive to (1) create multiple corporations and (2) retain more income within those corporations. This incentive just may cause some owner-operators to reduce their salaries for years after 1978. The reasons to retain income were further accentuated with the repeal of the carryover basis rules as part of the windfall profits tax bill early in 1980. By retaining income within multiple family corporations, and by passing ownership of those corporations from one generation to another only at the death of the prior owner, vast amounts of taxable income can be sheltered from the relatively high U.S. personal income tax rates.

The question remains: Are multiple corporations even possible after the 1969 tax law changes? The answer is yes, at a price. A detailed analysis of the definitional nuances associated with a controlled group of corporations must remain largely beyond the confines of this text solely because of the time and space required to explain them adequately. We can, however, look at one possible family ownership arrangement that could become increasingly typical in the years ahead. Figure 29-6 demonstrates how one parent and two *adult* children could own 100 percent of five separate corporations and still avoid classification as a controlled group of corporations.

As explained on page **10**/5, a controlled group of corporations is defined by two tests: an 80 percent test *plus* a 50 percent test. The former test requires that five or fewer persons own 80 percent of the stock of the several corporations being tested. In

Figure 29-6, three persons own 100 percent of the five corporations (A through E); hence, the 80 percent test is satisfied.[10] The 50 percent test, however, is *not* satisfied, at least as the law is now written. That test requires that five or fewer persons own *more than* 50 percent of the stock of two or more corporations, "taking into account the stock ownership of each such person only to the extent such stock ownership is identical with respect to each such corporation" (Sec. 1563(a)(2)(B)). In Figure 29-6, this "identical ownership" is *exactly* 50 percent; it never *exceeds* 50 percent for any group of two or more corporations. Consequently, none of these five corporations is deemed to be a member of a controlled group.

This means, of course, that the family unit P (parent), C-1 (adult child no. 1), and C-2 (adult child no. 2) could amass an estate that is at least $4.5 million greater simply because of the multiple corporations. That will be the result as long as each of the five corporations retains an annual taxable income of $60,000 or more for 30 years, and these tax savings can be reinvested at a 6 percent after-tax rate of return. None of those conditions is at all unrealistic for literally thousands of American family-owned corporate businesses. Note, however, that if the family in Figure 29-6 were to change its ownership ratios, however slightly, the results would be dramatically less satisfactory. If, for example, the parent (P) were to insist on a 51 percent ownership in B and D corporations (and reduce the adult child's share to 49 percent), then corporations A, B, and D would form a controlled group, and most of the tax savings (and the "extra" estate of $4.5 million) would disappear.

Whether or not this is sufficient tax incentive to restructure the ownership of thousands of American family-owned corporations remains to be seen. It

---

[10] Actually, this conclusion is currently at issue. The Tax Court contends that neither the 80 percent test nor the 50 percent test is satisfied in the example of Figure 29-6. Four circuit courts of appeal, the I.R.S., and the regulations hold, however, that the 80 percent test is satisfied.

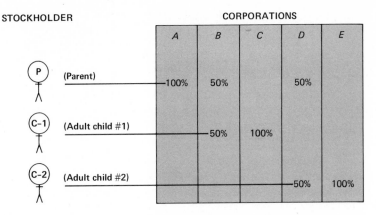

STOCKHOLDER

CORPORATIONS

FIGURE **29-6**   Example of Ownership Arrangement Required in Family to Avoid Controlled
Corporation Status

seems reasonable to assume, however, that such changes are entirely possible—even likely—as taxpayers and tax advisors come to appreciate the financial importance of the newest tax rules.

SUMMARY

It is hoped that the discussion just completed demonstrates the constantly increasing complexity in tax planning. Each year it is truer than it was the year before that everything depends on everything. The maximum tax on personal service income and multiple corporations can be quite beneficial, but only if certain conditions are satisfied. Taxpayers will learn to use these special provisions to their best advantage, but they will also learn that doing so may require several changes in old habits and procedures. The I.R.S. will resist new plans, and their resistance will cause still further modifications. Like the ever-flowing river, the process of taxation will forever continue to modify human behavior, while human behavior will modify the process itself.

PROBLEMS

1. For the past several years Ellen Fox, a single individual has earned the following items of income:

Salary	$35,000
Dividends, interest, rents	20,000*
Net capital gain	10,000

*After $200 dividend exclusion.

Ellen's deductions from adjusted gross income, in excess of the zero bracket amount and including her personal exemption deduction, amount to $8,000.
   a. If Ellen's income remains as it has been in the past several years, what will be her gross income-tax liability for this year?
   b. If Ellen's salary were suddenly to increase to $75,000 this year, what would her gross income tax liability be for this year?
   c. What is the marginal rate of tax Ellen would pay on the extra $40,000 in salary this year?
   d. If your answer to part c, above, is more than 50 percent, explain briefly why the maximum tax on personal service income does not "protect" this increment from tax rates in excess of 50 percent.

2. Milt Stein reported the following items of gross income this year:

Salary	$60,000
Interest	10,000
Net capital gain	80,000

If Milt's deductions from adjusted gross income (in excess of the zero bracket amount) are $5,000 (including his exemption deductions) and if Milt files as a head of household, determine his gross tax liability for this year. Would any portion of Milt's salary be taxed at more than 50 percent? Explain.

3. Many specific business transactions, as well as business operations more generally, are modified significantly by our federal income-tax provisions. Demonstrate your understanding of this statement by answering the following questions:

   a. Detail three specific business transactions that would be susceptible to modification for tax reasons and explain the way in which you think the tax provision would affect the transaction.

   b. Cite two recent, major changes in the United States tax laws, and explain how these changes have (or will) modify American business behavior.

4. For years the Italians did not impose a real property tax on buildings "under construction." Discuss the effects of this rule.

5. For years the French had a tax based on the number of windows a building had. Discuss the effects of using this tax base.

6. Esther White, M.D., owned several pieces of rental property and also shares of stock in numerous corporations. A friend advised her that in order to save income taxes she should transfer some of the assets to a corporation. The doctor accepted this advice and transferred numerous properties to a newly formed corporation. The doctor gave one-third of the shares to her son, one-third to her daughter, and retained one-third in her own name. During the first year of operations, the following income statement was prepared for the corporation.

Interest on bonds	$24,000
Dividends on stocks owned	20,000
Net rental income from properties	40,000
Total	$84,000
Deductible operating expenses	4,000
Net income	$80,000

In order to minimize taxes on the doctor and her children, no dividends were paid.

   a. Compute the federal tax liability of the corporation.

   b. What advice can you give the doctor?

7. Mr. and Mrs. Busy own and operate several business ventures in Boulder, Colorado. Although several of their businesses are profitable, the Busys do not distribute any cash from any of them. They prefer to accumulate all business profits within each business and reinvest them for, hopefully, still larger profits in the future. The Busys actually live on a $60,000 cash distribution that they receive annually from the Busy Trust Fund, which was created by Mr. Busy's grandfather. During the current year, the Busys' businesses reported the following taxable incomes. (Losses are indicated by parentheses.)

Busy Book Store (a sole proprietorship)	$ 5,000
Western Manufacturing Corporation (which is 100 percent owned by Mr. and Mrs. Busy)	(25,000)
Rocky Mountain Crater Corporation (a Subchapter S corporation 80 percent owned by Mr. and Mrs. Busy)	10,000

Mesa Wholesale Drugs (a partnership in which Mr. Busy has
a one-half interest)   20,000

Assuming that the above information constitutes all of Mr. and Mrs. Busy's
business and income data for this year, and assuming that the amounts indicated represent the total income or loss for the entire business venture (not just
the Busys' share):

a. What amount of gross income must Mr. and Mrs. Busy report on their joint
tax return?
b. Which of these business ventures are taxable entities?
c. Which of these businesses need file only information tax returns?
d. What happens to the $25,000 loss incurred by Western Manufacturing
Corporation?
e. Considering only this one year, should the Busys have elected Subchapter
S treatment for Western Manufacturing Corporation? Explain.

8. Mr. I. M. Rich earned the following income during 19x1:

Operating income from sole proprietorship (Drag Cleaners)	$56,000
Dividends from various domestic corporate stocks (These stocks were jointly owned by Mr. and Mrs. Rich.)	20,400
Interest on state bonds (tax exempt)	10,000
Total income for 19x1	$86,400

Assuming that Mr. Rich is married, has one dependent child, is 45 and of good
vision, does not itemize deductions, and files a joint return with his wife (who
is 43 and also of good vision), what is Rich's:

a. Taxable income?
b. Gross tax liability for 19x1? (Use current rates.)
c. Amount available for reinvestment in the Drag Cleaners if the Riches spent
$21,000 for personal consumption in 19x1?

Could the Riches do anything to reduce their income tax to provide themselves
with additional capital for reinvestment in the Drag Cleaners chain? Specifically, could they gain any tax advantages by incorporating the business? Answer
the above question by answering the questions below:

d. If the Riches do incorporate the business venture, should they transfer the
state bonds to the new corporation? Explain.
e. If they do incorporate, should they transfer all of the dividend-producing
investments to the corporation? If not, how much (minimum) should they
retain in their own names? Why?

Regardless of how you answered any of the questions above, *assume* that the
Riches actually do form a corporation and transfer all of their operating assets
(those that comprise the chain of cleaners) and most of the corporate investments to this new corporation. The income result (assuming the same operating
results as were reported in 19x1) would look something like this:

Corporation		*Personal*	
Operating income	$56,000	Operating income (all corp.)	$ 0
Less salary paid to Mr. Rich	16,000	Salary from corporation	16,000
Operating income after salary	40,000	Dividends (remainder was transferred to	
Dividends received	20,000	corporation)	400
Total income	$60,000	Tax-exempt interest on state government bonds	10,000
		Total income	$26,400

(NOTE: The combined income, before income taxes, is exactly the same now as it was prior to incorporation in 19x1.) Recalculate the tax liability for 19x1, assuming the above distribution of income and assets.

a. Corporation's taxable income.

b. Corporation's tax liability. (Use current rates.)

c. Personal taxable income (assume all facts as before in dependents, joint return, etc.).

d. Personal tax liability. (Use current rates.)

e. Total taxes paid (combined personal and corporate).

f. Amount available for reinvestment in Drag Cleaners (assuming, again, that the Riches spent $21,000 for personal consumption items).

g. Explain any future taxes that might diminish the desirability of the "tax plan" outlined above for Mr. and Mrs. Rich.

SUPPLEMENTAL PROBLEMS

9. Saunkefin and Ungeld Mariscus, husband and wife, are very wealthy. Like most wealthy people, they have discovered several tax loopholes applicable to them. Saunkefin and Ungeld, who enjoy spending their money on themselves, have four children to whom they would like to give money. Realizing that using a trust can save them money, Saunkefin and Ungeld establish forty trusts for their four children. Admitting that they are doing it for tax-avoidance reasons, Saunkefin and Ungeld carefully set up the trusts in proper legal form so that they look like separate trusts even though the beneficiaries are the same four children (ten trusts for each child). Saunkefin and Ungeld give various amounts of cash to each trust and also loan money to these trusts. Each trust also has a separate bank account and files a separate tax return. Each trust also has a separate set of books. Legally, everything is in perfect order and a total appearance of forty separate trusts is firmly established.

Saunkefin and Ungeld's oldest son asks you, a tax authority, if these trusts can be taxed as four separate trusts instead of forty separate trusts. He also wants to know if there is really a great tax savings from creating forty trusts.

a. Are there four primary trusts or are there forty trusts?

b. Is there really a savings from creating forty trusts?

10. Tom Wealthy, a bachelor playboy, inherited a large estate that increased his annual taxable income from approximately $108,300 to $208,300 per year. Most of his additional income was attributable to dividends. After a year of this new wealth, Tom discovered that the federal income tax took approximately $70,000 of his additional annual income. To reduce this high tax, he considered two alternatives: First, he considered marrying; second, he considered creating a new corporation and transferring all of the stocks into this corporation so that it would become eligible for the corporate dividends-received deduction.

a. How much would Tom save each year in taxes by marrying a woman who had no income?

b. What will prevent Tom's second plan from succeeding?

c. What might Tom do to achieve a less spectacular result than his second plan which would still provide a significant tax saving?

11. Lib Corporation is equally owned by two stockholders, Mr. Aye and Ms. Zee.

Mr. Aye is a man with little accumulated wealth. His taxable income has never exceeded $10,000 in the past 15 years. Ms. Zee, on the other hand, is independently wealthy; her taxable income has never been less than $100,000 during the past 15 years. As corporate officers and members of the Lib Corporation Board of Directors, Aye and Zee often argue for different corporate management policies.

Match the eight alternative corporate policies, below, with the board member (Aye or Zee) most likely to support each. If both Aye and Zee might support a given corporate management policy, list that policy after the name of only the one who would benefit most (taxwise) from it. If both might oppose a given policy, list that policy after the name of only the one who would be harmed least by it.

(1) Subchapter S status if Lib Corporation incurs operating losses.

(2) Subchapter S status if Lib Corporation reports an operating income and distributes much of that income to its owners.

(3) Relatively large salaries for corporate officers, payable in cash.

(4) Relatively large salaries for corporate officers, payable in Lib Corporation stock.

(5) Generous dividend payments by Lib Corporation.

(6) Maximum retention of corporate profits for reinvestment within Lib.

(7) "Tax-free" employee fringe benefits such as company-provided meals and lodging; group term life insurance (to $50,000); health and accident insurance; liberal travel (convention) policies; etc.

(8) Reorganizing Lib Corporation and operating it as a partnership if Lib regularly reports substantial operating losses.

12. Ted owns numerous properties, including several different business ventures. Ted needs approximately $60,000 annually to live in the style to which he has become accustomed. Anything in excess of $60,000 (cash) he prefers to reinvest in various income-producing properties. At present, Ted's major properties can be described as follows:

Property	Approximate annual income
Business venture A	$50,000 ordinary (active) income
Investment B	$50,000 capital gain only
Investment C	$30,000 tax-exempt interest
Business venture D	$40,000 ordinary (passive) income
Investment E	$60,000 dividends (domestic corporations)
Business venture F	$50,000 ordinary (active) income

Assuming that none of the business ventures involves any unusual risk or other nontax problems, answer the following questions:

a. Which of the properties do you recommend that Ted keep outside a corporate entity? Explain briefly.

b. If Ted were to incorporate either business venture D or investment E in a separate corporation, he would incur an unnecessary tax risk. Explain.

c. Would it benefit Ted to create one or more corporations to hold title to any of these properties? Explain briefly.

13. The tax savings calculated in Table 29-1 assume that the retained taxable income generated by multiple corporations is equally distributed among the several corporations.

a. Demonstrate your comprehension of the tax advantage implicit in multiple corporations by making the detailed computation necessary to arrive at the $57,500 tax saving shown on line 4, column 3, of Table 29-1.

b. Demonstrate your comprehension of the critical assumption (explicitly stated in the first sentence of this question) by determining the tax savings implicit in an *unequal* distribution of a $300,000 retained taxable income in five corporations.

   c. How is Sec. 482 related to the problem of multiple corporations? Explain briefly.

14. Footnote 10, page **29**/16, states that a precise interpretation of the 80 percent test (for controlled corporations) is in judicial conflict.

   a. Go to your tax library and locate the citations to the major cases that represent this conflict.

   b. Explain the alternative judicial interpretations briefly.

appendix
A

1979 Tax Rate Schedules

If you cannot use one of the Tax Tables, figure your tax on the amount on Schedule TC, Part I, line 3, by using the appropriate Tax Rate Schedule on this page. Enter the tax on Schedule TC, Part I, line 4.

Note: *Your new zero bracket amount has been built into these Tax Rate Schedules.*

SCHEDULE X—Single Taxpayers

Use this schedule if you checked **Filing Status Box 1 on Form 1040—**

If the amount on Schedule TC, Part I, line 3, is: Enter on Schedule TC, Part I, line 4:

Not over $2,300........ —0—

Over—	But not over—		of the amount over—
$2,300	$3,400	14%	$2,300
$3,400	$4,400	$154+16%	$3,400
$4,400	$6,500	$314+18%	$4,400
$6,500	$8,500	$692+19%	$6,500
$8,500	$10,800	$1,072+21%	$8,500
$10,800	$12,900	$1,555+24%	$10,800
$12,900	$15,000	$2,059+26%	$12,900
$15,000	$18,200	$2,605+30%	$15,000
$18,200	$23,500	$3,565+34%	$18,200
$23,500	$28,800	$5,367+39%	$23,500
$28,800	$34,100	$7,434+44%	$28,800
$34,100	$41,500	$9,766+49%	$34,100
$41,500	$55,300	$13,392+55%	$41,500
$55,300	$81,800	$20,982+63%	$55,300
$81,800	$108,300	$37,677+68%	$81,800
$108,300	....	$55,697+70%	$108,300

SCHEDULE Y—Married Taxpayers and Qualifying Widows and Widowers

Married Filing Joint Returns and Qualifying Widows and Widowers

Use this schedule if you checked **Filing Status Box 2 or 5 on Form 1040—**

If the amount on Schedule TC, Part I, line 3, is: Enter on Schedule TC, Part I, line 4:

Not over $3,400........ —0—

Over—	But not over—		of the amount over—
$3,400	$5,500	14%	$3,400
$5,500	$7,600	$294+16%	$5,500
$7,600	$11,900	$630+18%	$7,600
$11,900	$16,000	$1,404+21%	$11,900
$16,000	$20,200	$2,265+24%	$16,000
$20,200	$24,600	$3,273+28%	$20,200
$24,600	$29,900	$4,505+32%	$24,600
$29,900	$35,200	$6,201+37%	$29,900
$35,200	$45,800	$8,162+43%	$35,200
$45,800	$60,000	$12,720+49%	$45,800
$60,000	$85,600	$19,678+54%	$60,000
$85,600	$109,400	$33,502+59%	$85,600
$109,400	$162,400	$47,544+64%	$109,400
$162,400	$215,400	$81,464+68%	$162,400
$215,400	....	$117,504+70%	$215,400

Married Filing Separate Returns

Use this schedule if you checked **Filing Status Box 3 on Form 1040—**

If the amount on Schedule TC, Part I, line 3, is: Enter on Schedule TC, Part I, line 4:

Not over $1,700........ —0—

Over—	But not over—		of the amount over—
$1,700	$2,750	14%	$1,700
$2,750	$3,800	$147.00+16%	$2,750
$3,800	$5,950	$315.00+18%	$3,800
$5,950	$8,000	$702.00+21%	$5,950
$8,000	$10,100	$1,132.50+24%	$8,000
$10,100	$12,300	$1,636.50+28%	$10,100
$12,300	$14,950	$2,252.50+32%	$12,300
$14,950	$17,600	$3,100.50+37%	$14,950
$17,600	$22,900	$4,081.00+43%	$17,600
$22,900	$30,000	$6,360.00+49%	$22,900
$30,000	$42,800	$9,839.00+54%	$30,000
$42,800	$54,700	$16,751.00+59%	$42,800
$54,700	$81,200	$23,772.00+64%	$54,700
$81,200	$107,700	$40,732.00+68%	$81,200
$107,700	....	$58,752.00+70%	$107,700

SCHEDULE Z—Heads of Household (including certain married persons who live apart (and abandoned spouses)—see page 7 of the Instructions)

Use this schedule if you checked **Filing Status Box 4 on Form 1040—**

If the amount on Schedule TC, Part I, line 3, is: Enter on Schedule TC, Part I, line 4:

Not over $2,300........ —0—

Over—	But not over—		of the amount over—
$2,300	$4,400	14%	$2,300
$4,400	$6,500	$294+16%	$4,400
$6,500	$8,700	$630+18%	$6,500
$8,700	$11,800	$1,026+22%	$8,700
$11,800	$15,000	$1,708+24%	$11,800
$15,000	$18,200	$2,476+26%	$15,000
$18,200	$23,500	$3,308+31%	$18,200
$23,500	$28,800	$4,951+36%	$23,500
$28,800	$34,100	$6,859+42%	$28,800
$34,100	$44,700	$9,085+46%	$34,100
$44,700	$60,600	$13,961+54%	$44,700
$60,600	$81,800	$22,547+59%	$60,600
$81,800	$108,300	$35,055+63%	$81,800
$108,300	$161,300	$51,750+68%	$108,300
$161,300	....	$87,790+70%	$161,300

appendix
B

1979 Tax Table A—SINGLE (Filing Status Box 1)

(For single persons with income of $20,000 or less on Form 1040, line 34, who claim 3 or fewer exemptions)

To find your tax: Read down the income column until you find your income as shown on Form 1040, line 34. Read across to the column headed by the total number of exemptions claimed on Form 1040, line 7. The amount shown where the two lines meet is your tax. Enter on Form 1040, line 35. The $2,300 zero bracket amount and your deduction for exemptions have been taken into account in figuring the tax shown in this table. **Do not take a separate deduction for them.**

Caution: *If you can be claimed as a dependent on your parent's return* **AND** *you have unearned income (interest, dividends, etc.) of $1,000 or more* **AND** *your earned income is less than $2,300, you must first use Schedule TC (Form 1040), Part II.*

If Form 1040, line 34, is— Over	But not over	1	2	3
If $3,300 or less your tax is 0				
3,300	3,350	4	0	0
3,350	3,400	11	0	0
3,400	3,450	18	0	0
3,450	3,500	25	0	0
3,500	3,550	32	0	0
3,550	3,600	39	0	0
3,600	3,650	46	0	0
3,650	3,700	53	0	0
3,700	3,750	60	0	0
3,750	3,800	67	0	0
3,800	3,850	74	0	0
3,850	3,900	81	0	0
3,900	3,950	88	0	0
3,950	4,000	95	0	0
4,000	4,050	102	0	0
4,050	4,100	109	0	0
4,100	4,150	116	0	0
4,150	4,200	123	0	0
4,200	4,250	130	0	0
4,250	4,300	137	0	0
4,300	4,350	144	4	0
4,350	4,400	151	11	0
4,400	4,450	158	18	0
4,450	4,500	166	25	0
4,500	4,550	174	32	0
4,550	4,600	182	39	0
4,600	4,650	190	46	0
4,650	4,700	198	53	0
4,700	4,750	206	60	0
4,750	4,800	214	67	0
4,800	4,850	222	74	0
4,850	4,900	230	81	0
4,900	4,950	238	88	0
4,950	5,000	246	95	0
5,000	5,050	254	102	0
5,050	5,100	262	109	0
5,100	5,150	270	116	0
5,150	5,200	278	123	0
5,200	5,250	286	130	0
5,250	5,300	294	137	0
5,300	5,350	302	144	4
5,350	5,400	310	151	11
5,400	5,450	319	158	18
5,450	5,500	328	166	25
5,500	5,550	337	174	32
5,550	5,600	346	182	39
5,600	5,650	355	190	46
5,650	5,700	364	198	53
5,700	5,750	373	206	60
5,750	5,800	382	214	67
5,800	5,850	391	222	74
5,850	5,900	400	230	81

Continued next column

If Form 1040, line 34, is— Over	But not over	1	2	3
5,900	5,950	409	238	88
5,950	6,000	418	246	95
6,000	6,050	427	254	102
6,050	6,100	436	262	109
6,100	6,150	445	270	116
6,150	6,200	454	278	123
6,200	6,250	463	286	130
6,250	6,300	472	294	137
6,300	6,350	481	302	144
6,350	6,400	490	310	151
6,400	6,450	499	319	158
6,450	6,500	508	328	166
6,500	6,550	517	337	174
6,550	6,600	526	346	182
6,600	6,650	535	355	190
6,650	6,700	544	364	198
6,700	6,750	553	373	206
6,750	6,800	562	382	214
6,800	6,850	571	391	222
6,850	6,900	580	400	230
6,900	6,950	589	409	238
6,950	7,000	598	418	246
7,000	7,050	607	427	254
7,050	7,100	616	436	262
7,100	7,150	625	445	270
7,150	7,200	634	454	278
7,200	7,250	643	463	286
7,250	7,300	652	472	294
7,300	7,350	661	481	302
7,350	7,400	670	490	310
7,400	7,450	679	499	319
7,450	7,500	688	508	328
7,500	7,550	697	517	337
7,550	7,600	706	526	346
7,600	7,650	716	535	355
7,650	7,700	725	544	364
7,700	7,750	735	553	373
7,750	7,800	744	562	382
7,800	7,850	754	571	391
7,850	7,900	763	580	400
7,900	7,950	773	589	409
7,950	8,000	782	598	418
8,000	8,050	792	607	427
8,050	8,100	801	616	436
8,100	8,150	811	625	445
8,150	8,200	820	634	454
8,200	8,250	830	643	463
8,250	8,300	839	652	472
8,300	8,350	849	661	481
8,350	8,400	858	670	490
8,400	8,450	868	679	499
8,450	8,500	877	688	508

Continued next column

If Form 1040, line 34, is— Over	But not over	1	2	3
8,500	8,550	887	697	517
8,550	8,600	896	706	526
8,600	8,650	906	716	535
8,650	8,700	915	725	544
8,700	8,750	925	735	553
8,750	8,800	934	744	562
8,800	8,850	944	754	571
8,850	8,900	953	763	580
8,900	8,950	963	773	589
8,950	9,000	972	782	598
9,000	9,050	982	792	607
9,050	9,100	991	801	616
9,100	9,150	1,001	811	625
9,150	9,200	1,010	820	634
9,200	9,250	1,020	830	643
9,250	9,300	1,029	839	652
9,300	9,350	1,039	849	661
9,350	9,400	1,048	858	670
9,400	9,450	1,058	868	679
9,450	9,500	1,067	877	688
9,500	9,550	1,077	887	697
9,550	9,600	1,088	896	706
9,600	9,650	1,098	906	716
9,650	9,700	1,109	915	725
9,700	9,750	1,119	925	735
9,750	9,800	1,130	934	744
9,800	9,850	1,140	944	754
9,850	9,900	1,151	953	763
9,900	9,950	1,161	963	773
9,950	10,000	1,172	972	782
10,000	10,050	1,182	982	792
10,050	10,100	1,193	991	801
10,100	10,150	1,203	1,001	811
10,150	10,200	1,214	1,010	820
10,200	10,250	1,224	1,020	830
10,250	10,300	1,235	1,029	839
10,300	10,350	1,245	1,039	849
10,350	10,400	1,256	1,048	858
10,400	10,450	1,266	1,058	868
10,450	10,500	1,277	1,067	877
10,500	10,550	1,287	1,077	887
10,550	10,600	1,298	1,088	896
10,600	10,650	1,308	1,098	906
10,650	10,700	1,319	1,109	915
10,700	10,750	1,329	1,119	925
10,750	10,800	1,340	1,130	934
10,800	10,850	1,350	1,140	944
10,850	10,900	1,361	1,151	953
10,900	10,950	1,371	1,161	963
10,950	11,000	1,382	1,172	972
11,000	11,050	1,392	1,182	982
11,050	11,100	1,403	1,193	991

Continued on next page

1979 Tax Table A—SINGLE (Filing Status Box 1) (Continued)

(If your income or exemptions are not covered, use Schedule TC (Form 1040), Part I to figure your tax)

If Form 1040, line 34, is— Over	But not over	And the total number of exemptions claimed on line 7 is— 1	2	3
		Your tax is—		
11,100	11,150	1,413	1,203	1,001
11,150	11,200	1,424	1,214	1,010
11,200	11,250	1,434	1,224	1,020
11,250	11,300	1,445	1,235	1,029
11,300	11,350	1,455	1,245	1,039
11,350	11,400	1,466	1,256	1,048
11,400	11,450	1,476	1,266	1,058
11,450	11,500	1,487	1,277	1,067
11,500	11,550	1,497	1,287	1,077
11,550	11,600	1,508	1,298	1,088
11,600	11,650	1,518	1,308	1,098
11,650	11,700	1,529	1,319	1,109
11,700	11,750	1,539	1,329	1,119
11,750	11,800	1,550	1,340	1,130
11,800	11,850	1,561	1,350	1,140
11,850	11,900	1,573	1,361	1,151
11,900	11,950	1,585	1,371	1,161
11,950	12,000	1,597	1,382	1,172
12,000	12,050	1,609	1,392	1,182
12,050	12,100	1,621	1,403	1,193
12,100	12,150	1,633	1,413	1,203
12,150	12,200	1,645	1,424	1,214
12,200	12,250	1,657	1,434	1,224
12,250	12,300	1,669	1,445	1,235
12,300	12,350	1,681	1,455	1,245
12,350	12,400	1,693	1,466	1,256
12,400	12,450	1,705	1,476	1,266
12,450	12,500	1,717	1,487	1,277
12,500	12,550	1,729	1,497	1,287
12,550	12,600	1,741	1,508	1,298
12,600	12,650	1,753	1,518	1,308
12,650	12,700	1,765	1,529	1,319
12,700	12,750	1,777	1,539	1,329
12,750	12,800	1,789	1,550	1,340
12,800	12,850	1,801	1,561	1,350
12,850	12,900	1,813	1,573	1,361
12,900	12,950	1,825	1,585	1,371
12,950	13,000	1,837	1,597	1,382
13,000	13,050	1,849	1,609	1,392
13,050	13,100	1,861	1,621	1,403
13,100	13,150	1,873	1,633	1,413
13,150	13,200	1,885	1,645	1,424
13,200	13,250	1,897	1,657	1,434
13,250	13,300	1,909	1,669	1,445
13,300	13,350	1,921	1,681	1,455
13,350	13,400	1,933	1,693	1,466
13,400	13,450	1,945	1,705	1,476
13,450	13,500	1,957	1,717	1,487
13,500	13,550	1,969	1,729	1,497
13,550	13,600	1,981	1,741	1,508
13,600	13,650	1,993	1,753	1,518
13,650	13,700	2,005	1,765	1,529
13,700	13,750	2,017	1,777	1,539
13,750	13,800	2,029	1,789	1,550
13,800	13,850	2,041	1,801	1,561
13,850	13,900	2,053	1,813	1,573
13,900	13,950	2,066	1,825	1,585
13,950	14,000	2,079	1,837	1,597
14,000	14,050	2,092	1,849	1,609
14,050	14,100	2,105	1,861	1,621

Continued next column

If Form 1040, line 34, is— Over	But not over	And the total number of exemptions claimed on line 7 is— 1	2	3
		Your tax is—		
14,100	14,150	2,118	1,873	1,633
14,150	14,200	2,131	1,885	1,645
14,200	14,250	2,144	1,897	1,657
14,250	14,300	2,157	1,909	1,669
14,300	14,350	2,170	1,921	1,681
14,350	14,400	2,183	1,933	1,693
14,400	14,450	2,196	1,945	1,705
14,450	14,500	2,209	1,957	1,717
14,500	14,550	2,222	1,969	1,729
14,550	14,600	2,235	1,981	1,741
14,600	14,650	2,248	1,993	1,753
14,650	14,700	2,261	2,005	1,765
14,700	14,750	2,274	2,017	1,777
14,750	14,800	2,287	2,029	1,789
14,800	14,850	2,300	2,041	1,801
14,850	14,900	2,313	2,053	1,813
14,900	14,950	2,326	2,066	1,825
14,950	15,000	2,339	2,079	1,837
15,000	15,050	2,352	2,092	1,849
15,050	15,100	2,365	2,105	1,861
15,100	15,150	2,378	2,118	1,873
15,150	15,200	2,391	2,131	1,885
15,200	15,250	2,404	2,144	1,897
15,250	15,300	2,417	2,157	1,909
15,300	15,350	2,430	2,170	1,921
15,350	15,400	2,443	2,183	1,933
15,400	15,450	2,456	2,196	1,945
15,450	15,500	2,469	2,209	1,957
15,500	15,550	2,482	2,222	1,969
15,550	15,600	2,495	2,235	1,981
15,600	15,650	2,508	2,248	1,993
15,650	15,700	2,521	2,261	2,005
15,700	15,750	2,534	2,274	2,017
15,750	15,800	2,547	2,287	2,029
15,800	15,850	2,560	2,300	2,041
15,850	15,900	2,573	2,313	2,053
15,900	15,950	2,586	2,326	2,066
15,950	16,000	2,599	2,339	2,079
16,000	16,050	2,613	2,352	2,092
16,050	16,100	2,628	2,365	2,105
16,100	16,150	2,643	2,378	2,118
16,150	16,200	2,658	2,391	2,131
16,200	16,250	2,673	2,404	2,144
16,250	16,300	2,688	2,417	2,157
16,300	16,350	2,703	2,430	2,170
16,350	16,400	2,718	2,443	2,183
16,400	16,450	2,733	2,456	2,196
16,450	16,500	2,748	2,469	2,209
16,500	16,550	2,763	2,482	2,222
16,550	16,600	2,778	2,495	2,235
16,600	16,650	2,793	2,508	2,248
16,650	16,700	2,808	2,521	2,261
16,700	16,750	2,823	2,534	2,274
16,750	16,800	2,838	2,547	2,287
16,800	16,850	2,853	2,560	2,300
16,850	16,900	2,868	2,573	2,313
16,900	16,950	2,883	2,586	2,326
16,950	17,000	2,898	2,599	2,339
17,000	17,050	2,913	2,613	2,352
17,050	17,100	2,928	2,628	2,365

Continued next column

If Form 1040, line 34, is— Over	But not over	And the total number of exemptions claimed on line 7 is— 1	2	3
		Your tax is—		
17,100	17,150	2,943	2,643	2,378
17,150	17,200	2,958	2,658	2,391
17,200	17,250	2,973	2,673	2,404
17,250	17,300	2,988	2,688	2,417
17,300	17,350	3,003	2,703	2,430
17,350	17,400	3,018	2,718	2,443
17,400	17,450	3,033	2,733	2,456
17,450	17,500	3,048	2,748	2,469
17,500	17,550	3,063	2,763	2,482
17,550	17,600	3,078	2,778	2,495
17,600	17,650	3,093	2,793	2,508
17,650	17,700	3,108	2,808	2,521
17,700	17,750	3,123	2,823	2,534
17,750	17,800	3,138	2,838	2,547
17,800	17,850	3,153	2,853	2,560
17,850	17,900	3,168	2,868	2,573
17,900	17,950	3,183	2,883	2,586
17,950	18,000	3,198	2,898	2,599
18,000	18,050	3,213	2,913	2,613
18,050	18,100	3,228	2,928	2,628
18,100	18,150	3,243	2,943	2,643
18,150	18,200	3,258	2,958	2,658
18,200	18,250	3,273	2,973	2,673
18,250	18,300	3,288	2,988	2,688
18,300	18,350	3,303	3,003	2,703
18,350	18,400	3,318	3,018	2,718
18,400	18,450	3,333	3,033	2,733
18,450	18,500	3,348	3,048	2,748
18,500	18,550	3,363	3,063	2,763
18,550	18,600	3,378	3,078	2,778
18,600	18,650	3,393	3,093	2,793
18,650	18,700	3,408	3,108	2,808
18,700	18,750	3,423	3,123	2,823
18,750	18,800	3,438	3,138	2,838
18,800	18,850	3,453	3,153	2,853
18,850	18,900	3,468	3,168	2,868
18,900	18,950	3,483	3,183	2,883
18,950	19,000	3,498	3,198	2,898
19,000	19,050	3,513	3,213	2,913
19,050	19,100	3,528	3,228	2,928
19,100	19,150	3,543	3,243	2,943
19,150	19,200	3,558	3,258	2,958
19,200	19,250	3,574	3,273	2,973
19,250	19,300	3,591	3,288	2,988
19,300	19,350	3,608	3,303	3,003
19,350	19,400	3,625	3,318	3,018
19,400	19,450	3,642	3,333	3,033
19,450	19,500	3,659	3,348	3,048
19,500	19,550	3,676	3,363	3,063
19,550	19,600	3,693	3,378	3,078
19,600	19,650	3,710	3,393	3,093
19,650	19,700	3,727	3,408	3,108
19,700	19,750	3,744	3,423	3,123
19,750	19,800	3,761	3,438	3,138
19,800	19,850	3,778	3,453	3,153
19,850	19,900	3,795	3,468	3,168
19,900	19,950	3,812	3,483	3,183
19,950	20,000	3,829	3,498	3,198

1979 Tax Table B—MARRIED FILING JOINT RETURN (Filing Status Box 2) and QUALIFYING WIDOW(ER)S (Filing Status Box 5)

(For married persons filing joint returns or qualifying widow(er)s with income of $40,000 or less on Form 1040, line 34, who claim 9 or fewer exemptions)

To find your tax: Read down the income column until you find your income as shown on Form 1040, line 34. Read across to the column headed by the total number of exemptions claimed on Form 1040, line 7. The amount shown where the two lines meet is your tax. Enter on Form 1040, line 35. The $3,400 zero bracket amount and your deduction for exemptions have been taken into account in figuring the tax shown in this table. **Do not take a separate deduction for them.**

If $5,400 or less your tax is 0

Over	But not over	2	3	4	5	6	7	8	9
5,400	5,450	4	0	0	0	0	0	0	0
5,450	5,500	11	0	0	0	0	0	0	0
5,500	5,550	18	0	0	0	0	0	0	0
5,550	5,600	25	0	0	0	0	0	0	0
5,600	5,650	32	0	0	0	0	0	0	0
5,650	5,700	39	0	0	0	0	0	0	0
5,700	5,750	46	0	0	0	0	0	0	0
5,750	5,800	53	0	0	0	0	0	0	0
5,800	5,850	60	0	0	0	0	0	0	0
5,850	5,900	67	0	0	0	0	0	0	0
5,900	5,950	74	0	0	0	0	0	0	0
5,950	6,000	81	0	0	0	0	0	0	0
6,000	6,050	88	0	0	0	0	0	0	0
6,050	6,100	95	0	0	0	0	0	0	0
6,100	6,150	102	0	0	0	0	0	0	0
6,150	6,200	109	0	0	0	0	0	0	0
6,200	6,250	116	0	0	0	0	0	0	0
6,250	6,300	123	0	0	0	0	0	0	0
6,300	6,350	130	0	0	0	0	0	0	0
6,350	6,400	137	0	0	0	0	0	0	0
6,400	6,450	144	4	0	0	0	0	0	0
6,450	6,500	151	11	0	0	0	0	0	0
6,500	6,550	158	18	0	0	0	0	0	0
6,550	6,600	165	25	0	0	0	0	0	0
6,600	6,650	172	32	0	0	0	0	0	0
6,650	6,700	179	39	0	0	0	0	0	0
6,700	6,750	186	46	0	0	0	0	0	0
6,750	6,800	193	53	0	0	0	0	0	0
6,800	6,850	200	60	0	0	0	0	0	0
6,850	6,900	207	67	0	0	0	0	0	0
6,900	6,950	214	74	0	0	0	0	0	0
6,950	7,000	221	81	0	0	0	0	0	0
7,000	7,050	228	88	0	0	0	0	0	0
7,050	7,100	235	95	0	0	0	0	0	0
7,100	7,150	242	102	0	0	0	0	0	0
7,150	7,200	249	109	0	0	0	0	0	0
7,200	7,250	256	116	0	0	0	0	0	0
7,250	7,300	263	123	0	0	0	0	0	0
7,300	7,350	270	130	0	0	0	0	0	0
7,350	7,400	277	137	0	0	0	0	0	0
7,400	7,450	284	144	4	0	0	0	0	0
7,450	7,500	291	151	11	0	0	0	0	0
7,500	7,550	298	158	18	0	0	0	0	0
7,550	7,600	306	165	25	0	0	0	0	0
7,600	7,650	314	172	32	0	0	0	0	0
7,650	7,700	322	179	39	0	0	0	0	0
7,700	7,750	330	186	46	0	0	0	0	0
7,750	7,800	338	193	53	0	0	0	0	0
7,800	7,850	346	200	60	0	0	0	0	0
7,850	7,900	354	207	67	0	0	0	0	0
7,900	7,950	362	214	74	0	0	0	0	0
7,950	8,000	370	221	81	0	0	0	0	0
8,000	8,050	378	228	88	0	0	0	0	0
8,050	8,100	386	235	95	0	0	0	0	0
8,100	8,150	394	242	102	0	0	0	0	0
8,150	8,200	402	249	109	0	0	0	0	0

Continued next column

Over	But not over	2	3	4	5	6	7	8	9
8,200	8,250	410	256	116	0	0	0	0	0
8,250	8,300	418	263	123	0	0	0	0	0
8,300	8,350	426	270	130	0	0	0	0	0
8,350	8,400	434	277	137	0	0	0	0	0
8,400	8,450	442	284	144	4	0	0	0	0
8,450	8,500	450	291	151	11	0	0	0	0
8,500	8,550	458	298	158	18	0	0	0	0
8,550	8,600	466	306	165	25	0	0	0	0
8,600	8,650	474	314	172	32	0	0	0	0
8,650	8,700	482	322	179	39	0	0	0	0
8,700	8,750	490	330	186	46	0	0	0	0
8,750	8,800	498	338	193	53	0	0	0	0
8,800	8,850	506	346	200	60	0	0	0	0
8,850	8,900	514	354	207	67	0	0	0	0
8,900	8,950	522	362	214	74	0	0	0	0
8,950	9,000	530	370	221	81	0	0	0	0
9,000	9,050	538	378	228	88	0	0	0	0
9,050	9,100	546	386	235	95	0	0	0	0
9,100	9,150	554	394	242	102	0	0	0	0
9,150	9,200	562	402	249	109	0	0	0	0
9,200	9,250	570	410	256	116	0	0	0	0
9,250	9,300	578	418	263	123	0	0	0	0
9,300	9,350	586	426	270	130	0	0	0	0
9,350	9,400	594	434	277	137	0	0	0	0
9,400	9,450	602	442	284	144	4	0	0	0
9,450	9,500	610	450	291	151	11	0	0	0
9,500	9,550	618	458	298	158	18	0	0	0
9,550	9,600	626	466	306	165	25	0	0	0
9,600	9,650	635	474	314	172	32	0	0	0
9,650	9,700	644	482	322	179	39	0	0	0
9,700	9,750	653	490	330	186	46	0	0	0
9,750	9,800	662	498	338	193	53	0	0	0
9,800	9,850	671	506	346	200	60	0	0	0
9,850	9,900	680	514	354	207	67	0	0	0
9,900	9,950	689	522	362	214	74	0	0	0
9,950	10,000	698	530	370	221	81	0	0	0
10,000	10,050	707	538	378	228	88	0	0	0
10,050	10,100	716	546	386	235	95	0	0	0
10,100	10,150	725	554	394	242	102	0	0	0
10,150	10,200	734	562	402	249	109	0	0	0
10,200	10,250	743	570	410	256	116	0	0	0
10,250	10,300	752	578	418	263	123	0	0	0
10,300	10,350	761	586	426	270	130	0	0	0
10,350	10,400	770	594	434	277	137	0	0	0
10,400	10,450	779	602	442	284	144	4	0	0
10,450	10,500	788	610	450	291	151	11	0	0
10,500	10,550	797	618	458	298	158	18	0	0
10,550	10,600	806	626	466	306	165	25	0	0
10,600	10,650	815	635	474	314	172	32	0	0
10,650	10,700	824	644	482	322	179	39	0	0
10,700	10,750	833	653	490	330	186	46	0	0
10,750	10,800	842	662	498	338	193	53	0	0
10,800	10,850	851	671	506	346	200	60	0	0
10,850	10,900	860	680	514	354	207	67	0	0
10,900	10,950	869	689	522	362	214	74	0	0
10,950	11,000	878	698	530	370	221	81	0	0
11,000	11,050	887	707	538	378	228	88	0	0
11,050	11,100	896	716	546	386	235	95	0	0
11,100	11,150	905	725	554	394	242	102	0	0
11,150	11,200	914	734	562	402	249	109	0	0

Continued on next page

1979 Tax Table B—MARRIED FILING JOINT RETURN (Filing Status Box 2) and QUALIFYING WIDOW(ER)S (Filing Status Box 5)

(Continued)

(If your income or exemptions are not covered, use Schedule TC (Form 1040), Part I to figure your tax)

Over	But not over	2	3	4	5	6	7	8	9
11,200	11,250	923	743	570	410	256	116	0	0
11,250	11,300	932	752	578	418	263	123	0	0
11,300	11,350	941	761	586	426	270	130	0	0
11,350	11,400	950	770	594	434	277	137	0	0
11,400	11,450	959	779	602	442	284	144	4	0
11,450	11,500	968	788	610	450	291	151	11	0
11,500	11,550	977	797	618	458	298	158	18	0
11,550	11,600	986	806	626	466	306	165	25	0
11,600	11,650	995	815	635	474	314	172	32	0
11,650	11,700	1,004	824	644	482	322	179	39	0
11,700	11,750	1,013	833	653	490	330	186	46	0
11,750	11,800	1,022	842	662	498	338	193	53	0
11,800	11,850	1,031	851	671	506	346	200	60	0
11,850	11,900	1,040	860	680	514	354	207	67	0
11,900	11,950	1,049	869	689	522	362	214	74	0
11,950	12,000	1,058	878	698	530	370	221	81	0
12,000	12,050	1,067	887	707	538	378	228	88	0
12,050	12,100	1,076	896	716	546	386	235	95	0
12,100	12,150	1,085	905	725	554	394	242	102	0
12,150	12,200	1,094	914	734	562	402	249	109	0
12,200	12,250	1,103	923	743	570	410	256	116	0
12,250	12,300	1,112	932	752	578	418	263	123	0
12,300	12,350	1,121	941	761	586	426	270	130	0
12,350	12,400	1,130	950	770	594	434	277	137	0
12,400	12,450	1,139	959	779	602	442	284	144	4
12,450	12,500	1,148	968	788	610	450	291	151	11
12,500	12,550	1,157	977	797	618	458	298	158	18
12,550	12,600	1,166	986	806	626	466	306	165	25
12,600	12,650	1,175	995	815	635	474	314	172	32
12,650	12,700	1,184	1,004	824	644	482	322	179	39
12,700	12,750	1,193	1,013	833	653	490	330	186	46
12,750	12,800	1,202	1,022	842	662	498	338	193	53
12,800	12,850	1,211	1,031	851	671	506	346	200	60
12,850	12,900	1,220	1,040	860	680	514	354	207	67
12,900	12,950	1,229	1,049	869	689	522	362	214	74
12,950	13,000	1,238	1,058	878	698	530	370	221	81
13,000	13,050	1,247	1,067	887	707	538	378	228	88
13,050	13,100	1,256	1,076	896	716	546	386	235	95
13,100	13,150	1,265	1,085	905	725	554	394	242	102
13,150	13,200	1,274	1,094	914	734	562	402	249	109
13,200	13,250	1,283	1,103	923	743	570	410	256	116
13,250	13,300	1,292	1,112	932	752	578	418	263	123
13,300	13,350	1,301	1,121	941	761	586	426	270	130
13,350	13,400	1,310	1,130	950	770	594	434	277	137
13,400	13,450	1,319	1,139	959	779	602	442	284	144
13,450	13,500	1,328	1,148	968	788	610	450	291	151
13,500	13,550	1,337	1,157	977	797	618	458	298	158
13,550	13,600	1,346	1,166	986	806	626	466	306	165
13,600	13,650	1,355	1,175	995	815	635	474	314	172
13,650	13,700	1,364	1,184	1,004	824	644	482	322	179
13,700	13,750	1,373	1,193	1,013	833	653	490	330	186
13,750	13,800	1,382	1,202	1,022	842	662	498	338	193
13,800	13,850	1,391	1,211	1,031	851	671	506	346	200
13,850	13,900	1,400	1,220	1,040	860	680	514	354	207
13,900	13,950	1,409	1,229	1,049	869	689	522	362	214
13,950	14,000	1,420	1,238	1,058	878	698	530	370	221
14,000	14,050	1,430	1,247	1,067	887	707	538	378	228
14,050	14,100	1,441	1,256	1,076	896	716	546	386	235
14,100	14,150	1,451	1,265	1,085	905	725	554	394	242
14,150	14,200	1,462	1,274	1,094	914	734	562	402	249
14,200	14,250	1,472	1,283	1,103	923	743	570	410	256
14,250	14,300	1,483	1,292	1,112	932	752	578	418	263
14,300	14,350	1,493	1,301	1,121	941	761	586	426	270
14,350	14,400	1,504	1,310	1,130	950	770	594	434	277
14,400	14,450	1,514	1,319	1,139	959	779	602	442	284
14,450	14,500	1,525	1,328	1,148	968	788	610	450	291
14,500	14,550	1,535	1,337	1,157	977	797	618	458	298
14,550	14,600	1,546	1,346	1,166	986	806	626	466	306
14,600	14,650	1,556	1,355	1,175	995	815	635	474	314
14,650	14,700	1,567	1,364	1,184	1,004	824	644	482	322
14,700	14,750	1,577	1,373	1,193	1,013	833	653	490	330
14,750	14,800	1,588	1,382	1,202	1,022	842	662	498	338
14,800	14,850	1,598	1,391	1,211	1,031	851	671	506	346
14,850	14,900	1,609	1,400	1,220	1,040	860	680	514	354
14,900	14,950	1,619	1,409	1,229	1,049	869	689	522	362
14,950	15,000	1,630	1,420	1,238	1,058	878	698	530	370
15,000	15,050	1,640	1,430	1,247	1,067	887	707	538	378
15,050	15,100	1,651	1,441	1,256	1,076	896	716	546	386
15,100	15,150	1,661	1,451	1,265	1,085	905	725	554	394
15,150	15,200	1,672	1,462	1,274	1,094	914	734	562	402
15,200	15,250	1,682	1,472	1,283	1,103	923	743	570	410
15,250	15,300	1,693	1,483	1,292	1,112	932	752	578	418
15,300	15,350	1,703	1,493	1,301	1,121	941	761	586	426
15,350	15,400	1,714	1,504	1,310	1,130	950	770	594	434
15,400	15,450	1,724	1,514	1,319	1,139	959	779	602	442
15,450	15,500	1,735	1,525	1,328	1,148	968	788	610	450
15,500	15,550	1,745	1,535	1,337	1,157	977	797	618	458
15,550	15,600	1,756	1,546	1,346	1,166	986	806	626	466
15,600	15,650	1,766	1,556	1,355	1,175	995	815	635	474
15,650	15,700	1,777	1,567	1,364	1,184	1,004	824	644	482
15,700	15,750	1,787	1,577	1,373	1,193	1,013	833	653	490
15,750	15,800	1,798	1,588	1,382	1,202	1,022	842	662	498
15,800	15,850	1,808	1,598	1,391	1,211	1,031	851	671	506
15,850	15,900	1,819	1,609	1,400	1,220	1,040	860	680	514
15,900	15,950	1,829	1,619	1,409	1,229	1,049	869	689	522
15,950	16,000	1,840	1,630	1,420	1,238	1,058	878	698	530
16,000	16,050	1,850	1,640	1,430	1,247	1,067	887	707	538
16,050	16,100	1,861	1,651	1,441	1,256	1,076	896	716	546
16,100	16,150	1,871	1,661	1,451	1,265	1,085	905	725	554
16,150	16,200	1,882	1,672	1,462	1,274	1,094	914	734	562
16,200	16,250	1,892	1,682	1,472	1,283	1,103	923	743	570
16,250	16,300	1,903	1,693	1,483	1,292	1,112	932	752	578
16,300	16,350	1,913	1,703	1,493	1,301	1,121	941	761	586
16,350	16,400	1,924	1,714	1,504	1,310	1,130	950	770	594
16,400	16,450	1,934	1,724	1,514	1,319	1,139	959	779	602
16,450	16,500	1,945	1,735	1,525	1,328	1,148	968	788	610
16,500	16,550	1,955	1,745	1,535	1,337	1,157	977	797	618
16,550	16,600	1,966	1,756	1,546	1,346	1,166	986	806	626
16,600	16,650	1,976	1,766	1,556	1,355	1,175	995	815	635
16,650	16,700	1,987	1,777	1,567	1,364	1,184	1,004	824	644
16,700	16,750	1,997	1,787	1,577	1,373	1,193	1,013	833	653
16,750	16,800	2,008	1,798	1,588	1,382	1,202	1,022	842	662
16,800	16,850	2,018	1,808	1,598	1,391	1,211	1,031	851	671
16,850	16,900	2,029	1,819	1,609	1,400	1,220	1,040	860	680
16,900	16,950	2,039	1,829	1,619	1,409	1,229	1,049	869	689
16,950	17,000	2,050	1,840	1,630	1,420	1,238	1,058	878	698
17,000	17,050	2,060	1,850	1,640	1,430	1,247	1,067	887	707
17,050	17,100	2,071	1,861	1,651	1,441	1,256	1,076	896	716
17,100	17,150	2,081	1,871	1,661	1,451	1,265	1,085	905	725
17,150	17,200	2,092	1,882	1,672	1,462	1,274	1,094	914	734
17,200	17,250	2,102	1,892	1,682	1,472	1,283	1,103	923	743
17,250	17,300	2,113	1,903	1,693	1,483	1,292	1,112	932	752
17,300	17,350	2,123	1,913	1,703	1,493	1,301	1,121	941	761
17,350	17,400	2,134	1,924	1,714	1,504	1,310	1,130	950	770
17,400	17,450	2,144	1,934	1,724	1,514	1,319	1,139	959	779
17,450	17,500	2,155	1,945	1,735	1,525	1,328	1,148	968	788
17,500	17,550	2,165	1,955	1,745	1,535	1,337	1,157	977	797
17,550	17,600	2,176	1,966	1,756	1,546	1,346	1,166	986	806
17,600	17,650	2,186	1,976	1,766	1,556	1,355	1,175	995	815
17,650	17,700	2,197	1,987	1,777	1,567	1,364	1,184	1,004	824
17,700	17,750	2,207	1,997	1,787	1,577	1,373	1,193	1,013	833
17,750	17,800	2,218	2,008	1,798	1,588	1,382	1,202	1,022	842
17,800	17,850	2,228	2,018	1,808	1,598	1,391	1,211	1,031	851
17,850	17,900	2,239	2,029	1,819	1,609	1,400	1,220	1,040	860
17,900	17,950	2,249	2,039	1,829	1,619	1,409	1,229	1,049	869
17,950	18,000	2,260	2,050	1,840	1,630	1,420	1,238	1,058	878
18,000	18,050	2,271	2,060	1,850	1,640	1,430	1,247	1,067	887
18,050	18,100	2,283	2,071	1,861	1,651	1,441	1,256	1,076	896
18,100	18,150	2,295	2,081	1,871	1,661	1,451	1,265	1,085	905
18,150	18,200	2,307	2,092	1,882	1,672	1,462	1,274	1,094	914
18,200	18,250	2,319	2,102	1,892	1,682	1,472	1,283	1,103	923
18,250	18,300	2,331	2,113	1,903	1,693	1,483	1,292	1,112	932
18,300	18,350	2,343	2,123	1,913	1,703	1,493	1,301	1,121	941
18,350	18,400	2,355	2,134	1,924	1,714	1,504	1,310	1,130	950

Continued next column

Continued on next page

1979 Tax Table B—MARRIED FILING JOINT RETURN (Filing Status Box 2) and QUALIFYING WIDOW(ER)S (Filing Status Box 5)

(Continued)

(If your income or exemptions are not covered, use Schedule TC (Form 1040), Part I to figure your tax)

If Form 1040, line 34, is—		And the total number of exemptions claimed on line 7 is—							
Over	But not over	2	3	4	5	6	7	8	9
		Your tax is—							
18,400	18,450	2,367	2,144	1,934	1,724	1,514	1,319	1,139	959
18,450	18,500	2,379	2,155	1,945	1,735	1,525	1,328	1,148	968
18,500	18,550	2,391	2,165	1,955	1,745	1,535	1,337	1,157	977
18,550	18,600	2,403	2,176	1,966	1,756	1,546	1,346	1,166	986
18,600	18,650	2,415	2,186	1,976	1,766	1,556	1,355	1,175	995
18,650	18,700	2,427	2,197	1,987	1,777	1,567	1,364	1,184	1,004
18,700	18,750	2,439	2,207	1,997	1,787	1,577	1,373	1,193	1,013
18,750	18,800	2,451	2,218	2,008	1,798	1,588	1,382	1,202	1,022
18,800	18,850	2,463	2,228	2,018	1,808	1,598	1,391	1,211	1,031
18,850	18,900	2,475	2,239	2,029	1,819	1,609	1,400	1,220	1,040
18,900	18,950	2,487	2,249	2,039	1,829	1,619	1,409	1,229	1,049
18,950	19,000	2,499	2,260	2,050	1,840	1,630	1,420	1,238	1,058
19,000	19,050	2,511	2,271	2,060	1,850	1,640	1,430	1,247	1,067
19,050	19,100	2,523	2,283	2,071	1,861	1,651	1,441	1,256	1,076
19,100	19,150	2,535	2,295	2,081	1,871	1,661	1,451	1,265	1,085
19,150	19,200	2,547	2,307	2,092	1,882	1,672	1,462	1,274	1,094
19,200	19,250	2,559	2,319	2,102	1,892	1,682	1,472	1,283	1,103
19,250	19,300	2,571	2,331	2,113	1,903	1,693	1,483	1,292	1,112
19,300	19,350	2,583	2,343	2,123	1,913	1,703	1,493	1,301	1,121
19,350	19,400	2,595	2,355	2,134	1,924	1,714	1,504	1,310	1,130
19,400	19,450	2,607	2,367	2,144	1,934	1,724	1,514	1,319	1,139
19,450	19,500	2,619	2,379	2,155	1,945	1,735	1,525	1,328	1,148
19,500	19,550	2,631	2,391	2,165	1,955	1,745	1,535	1,337	1,157
19,550	19,600	2,643	2,403	2,176	1,966	1,756	1,546	1,346	1,166
19,600	19,650	2,655	2,415	2,186	1,976	1,766	1,556	1,355	1,175
19,650	19,700	2,667	2,427	2,197	1,987	1,777	1,567	1,364	1,184
19,700	19,750	2,679	2,439	2,207	1,997	1,787	1,577	1,373	1,193
19,750	19,800	2,691	2,451	2,218	2,008	1,798	1,588	1,382	1,202
19,800	19,850	2,703	2,463	2,228	2,018	1,808	1,598	1,391	1,211
19,850	19,900	2,715	2,475	2,239	2,029	1,819	1,609	1,400	1,220
19,900	19,950	2,727	2,487	2,249	2,039	1,829	1,619	1,409	1,229
19,950	20,000	2,739	2,499	2,260	2,050	1,840	1,630	1,420	1,238
20,000	20,050	2,751	2,511	2,271	2,060	1,850	1,640	1,430	1,247
20,050	20,100	2,763	2,523	2,283	2,071	1,861	1,651	1,441	1,256
20,100	20,150	2,775	2,535	2,295	2,081	1,871	1,661	1,451	1,265
20,150	20,200	2,787	2,547	2,307	2,092	1,882	1,672	1,462	1,274
20,200	20,250	2,799	2,559	2,319	2,102	1,892	1,682	1,472	1,283
20,250	20,300	2,811	2,571	2,331	2,113	1,903	1,693	1,483	1,292
20,300	20,350	2,823	2,583	2,343	2,123	1,913	1,703	1,493	1,301
20,350	20,400	2,835	2,595	2,355	2,134	1,924	1,714	1,504	1,310
20,400	20,450	2,847	2,607	2,367	2,144	1,934	1,724	1,514	1,319
20,450	20,500	2,859	2,619	2,379	2,155	1,945	1,735	1,525	1,328
20,500	20,550	2,871	2,631	2,391	2,165	1,955	1,745	1,535	1,337
20,550	20,600	2,883	2,643	2,403	2,176	1,966	1,756	1,546	1,346
20,600	20,650	2,895	2,655	2,415	2,186	1,976	1,766	1,556	1,355
20,650	20,700	2,907	2,667	2,427	2,197	1,987	1,777	1,567	1,364
20,700	20,750	2,919	2,679	2,439	2,207	1,997	1,787	1,577	1,373
20,750	20,800	2,931	2,691	2,451	2,218	2,008	1,798	1,588	1,382
20,800	20,850	2,943	2,703	2,463	2,228	2,018	1,808	1,598	1,391
20,850	20,900	2,955	2,715	2,475	2,239	2,029	1,819	1,609	1,400
20,900	20,950	2,967	2,727	2,487	2,249	2,039	1,829	1,619	1,409
20,950	21,000	2,979	2,739	2,499	2,260	2,050	1,840	1,630	1,420
21,000	21,050	2,991	2,751	2,511	2,271	2,060	1,850	1,640	1,430
21,050	21,100	3,003	2,763	2,523	2,283	2,071	1,861	1,651	1,441
21,100	21,150	3,015	2,775	2,535	2,295	2,081	1,871	1,661	1,451
21,150	21,200	3,027	2,787	2,547	2,307	2,092	1,882	1,672	1,462
21,200	21,250	3,039	2,799	2,559	2,319	2,102	1,892	1,682	1,472
21,250	21,300	3,051	2,811	2,571	2,331	2,113	1,903	1,693	1,483
21,300	21,350	3,063	2,823	2,583	2,343	2,123	1,913	1,703	1,493
21,350	21,400	3,075	2,835	2,595	2,355	2,134	1,924	1,714	1,504
21,400	21,450	3,087	2,847	2,607	2,367	2,144	1,934	1,724	1,514
21,450	21,500	3,099	2,859	2,619	2,379	2,155	1,945	1,735	1,525
21,500	21,550	3,111	2,871	2,631	2,391	2,165	1,955	1,745	1,535
21,550	21,600	3,123	2,883	2,643	2,403	2,176	1,966	1,756	1,546
21,600	21,650	3,135	2,895	2,655	2,415	2,186	1,976	1,766	1,556
21,650	21,700	3,147	2,907	2,667	2,427	2,197	1,987	1,777	1,567
21,700	21,750	3,159	2,919	2,679	2,439	2,207	1,997	1,787	1,577
21,750	21,800	3,171	2,931	2,691	2,451	2,218	2,008	1,798	1,588
21,800	21,850	3,183	2,943	2,703	2,463	2,228	2,018	1,808	1,598
21,850	21,900	3,195	2,955	2,715	2,475	2,239	2,029	1,819	1,609
21,900	21,950	3,207	2,967	2,727	2,487	2,249	2,039	1,829	1,619
21,950	22,000	3,219	2,979	2,739	2,499	2,260	2,050	1,840	1,630

Continued next column

If Form 1040, line 34, is—		And the total number of exemptions claimed on line 7 is—							
Over	But not over	2	3	4	5	6	7	8	9
		Your tax is—							
22,000	22,050	3,231	2,991	2,751	2,511	2,271	2,060	1,850	1,640
22,050	22,100	3,243	3,003	2,763	2,523	2,283	2,071	1,861	1,651
22,100	22,150	3,255	3,015	2,775	2,535	2,295	2,081	1,871	1,661
22,150	22,200	3,267	3,027	2,787	2,547	2,307	2,092	1,882	1,672
22,200	22,250	3,280	3,039	2,799	2,559	2,319	2,102	1,892	1,682
22,250	22,300	3,294	3,051	2,811	2,571	2,331	2,113	1,903	1,693
22,300	22,350	3,308	3,063	2,823	2,583	2,343	2,123	1,913	1,703
22,350	22,400	3,322	3,075	2,835	2,595	2,355	2,134	1,924	1,714
22,400	22,450	3,336	3,087	2,847	2,607	2,367	2,144	1,934	1,724
22,450	22,500	3,350	3,099	2,859	2,619	2,379	2,155	1,945	1,735
22,500	22,550	3,364	3,111	2,871	2,631	2,391	2,165	1,955	1,745
22,550	22,600	3,378	3,123	2,883	2,643	2,403	2,176	1,966	1,756
22,600	22,650	3,392	3,135	2,895	2,655	2,415	2,186	1,976	1,766
22,650	22,700	3,406	3,147	2,907	2,667	2,427	2,197	1,987	1,777
22,700	22,750	3,420	3,159	2,919	2,679	2,439	2,207	1,997	1,787
22,750	22,800	3,434	3,171	2,931	2,691	2,451	2,218	2,008	1,798
22,800	22,850	3,448	3,183	2,943	2,703	2,463	2,228	2,018	1,808
22,850	22,900	3,462	3,195	2,955	2,715	2,475	2,239	2,029	1,819
22,900	22,950	3,476	3,207	2,967	2,727	2,487	2,249	2,039	1,829
22,950	23,000	3,490	3,219	2,979	2,739	2,499	2,260	2,050	1,840
23,000	23,050	3,504	3,231	2,991	2,751	2,511	2,271	2,060	1,850
23,050	23,100	3,518	3,243	3,003	2,763	2,523	2,283	2,071	1,861
23,100	23,150	3,532	3,255	3,015	2,775	2,535	2,295	2,081	1,871
23,150	23,200	3,546	3,267	3,027	2,787	2,547	2,307	2,092	1,882
23,200	23,250	3,560	3,280	3,039	2,799	2,559	2,319	2,102	1,892
23,250	23,300	3,574	3,294	3,051	2,811	2,571	2,331	2,113	1,903
23,300	23,350	3,588	3,308	3,063	2,823	2,583	2,343	2,123	1,913
23,350	23,400	3,602	3,322	3,075	2,835	2,595	2,355	2,134	1,924
23,400	23,450	3,616	3,336	3,087	2,847	2,607	2,367	2,144	1,934
23,450	23,500	3,630	3,350	3,099	2,859	2,619	2,379	2,155	1,945
23,500	23,550	3,644	3,364	3,111	2,871	2,631	2,391	2,165	1,955
23,550	23,600	3,658	3,378	3,123	2,883	2,643	2,403	2,176	1,966
23,600	23,650	3,672	3,392	3,135	2,895	2,655	2,415	2,186	1,976
23,650	23,700	3,686	3,406	3,147	2,907	2,667	2,427	2,197	1,987
23,700	23,750	3,700	3,420	3,159	2,919	2,679	2,439	2,207	1,997
23,750	23,800	3,714	3,434	3,171	2,931	2,691	2,451	2,218	2,008
23,800	23,850	3,728	3,448	3,183	2,943	2,703	2,463	2,228	2,018
23,850	23,900	3,742	3,462	3,195	2,955	2,715	2,475	2,239	2,029
23,900	23,950	3,756	3,476	3,207	2,967	2,727	2,487	2,249	2,039
23,950	24,000	3,770	3,490	3,219	2,979	2,739	2,499	2,260	2,050
24,000	24,050	3,784	3,504	3,231	2,991	2,751	2,511	2,271	2,060
24,050	24,100	3,798	3,518	3,243	3,003	2,763	2,523	2,283	2,071
24,100	24,150	3,812	3,532	3,255	3,015	2,775	2,535	2,295	2,081
24,150	24,200	3,826	3,546	3,267	3,027	2,787	2,547	2,307	2,092
24,200	24,250	3,840	3,560	3,280	3,039	2,799	2,559	2,319	2,102
24,250	24,300	3,854	3,574	3,294	3,051	2,811	2,571	2,331	2,113
24,300	24,350	3,868	3,588	3,308	3,063	2,823	2,583	2,343	2,123
24,350	24,400	3,882	3,602	3,322	3,075	2,835	2,595	2,355	2,134
24,400	24,450	3,896	3,616	3,336	3,087	2,847	2,607	2,367	2,144
24,450	24,500	3,910	3,630	3,350	3,099	2,859	2,619	2,379	2,155
24,500	24,550	3,924	3,644	3,364	3,111	2,871	2,631	2,391	2,165
24,550	24,600	3,938	3,658	3,378	3,123	2,883	2,643	2,403	2,176
24,600	24,650	3,952	3,672	3,392	3,135	2,895	2,655	2,415	2,186
24,650	24,700	3,966	3,686	3,406	3,147	2,907	2,667	2,427	2,197
24,700	24,750	3,980	3,700	3,420	3,159	2,919	2,679	2,439	2,207
24,750	24,800	3,994	3,714	3,434	3,171	2,931	2,691	2,451	2,218
24,800	24,850	4,008	3,728	3,448	3,183	2,943	2,703	2,463	2,228
24,850	24,900	4,022	3,742	3,462	3,195	2,955	2,715	2,475	2,239
24,900	24,950	4,036	3,756	3,476	3,207	2,967	2,727	2,487	2,249
24,950	25,000	4,050	3,770	3,490	3,219	2,979	2,739	2,499	2,260
25,000	25,050	4,064	3,784	3,504	3,231	2,991	2,751	2,511	2,271
25,050	25,100	4,078	3,798	3,518	3,243	3,003	2,763	2,523	2,283
25,100	25,150	4,092	3,812	3,532	3,255	3,015	2,775	2,535	2,295
25,150	25,200	4,106	3,826	3,546	3,267	3,027	2,787	2,547	2,307
25,200	25,250	4,120	3,840	3,560	3,280	3,039	2,799	2,559	2,319
25,250	25,300	4,134	3,854	3,574	3,294	3,051	2,811	2,571	2,331
25,300	25,350	4,148	3,868	3,588	3,308	3,063	2,823	2,583	2,343
25,350	25,400	4,162	3,882	3,602	3,322	3,075	2,835	2,595	2,355
25,400	25,450	4,176	3,896	3,616	3,336	3,087	2,847	2,607	2,367
25,450	25,500	4,190	3,910	3,630	3,350	3,099	2,859	2,619	2,379
25,500	25,550	4,204	3,924	3,644	3,364	3,111	2,871	2,631	2,391
25,550	25,600	4,218	3,938	3,658	3,378	3,123	2,883	2,643	2,403

Continued on next page

1979 Tax Table B—MARRIED FILING JOINT RETURN (Filing Status Box 2) and QUALIFYING WIDOW(ER)S (Filing Status Box 5)

(Continued)

(If your income or exemptions are not covered, use Schedule TC (Form 1040), Part I to figure your tax)

If Form 1040, line 34, is—		And the total number of exemptions claimed on line 7 is—							
Over	But not over	2	3	4	5	6	7	8	9
		Your tax is—							
25,600	25,650	4,232	3,952	3,672	3,392	3,135	2,895	2,655	2,415
25,650	25,700	4,246	3,966	3,686	3,406	3,147	2,907	2,667	2,427
25,700	25,750	4,260	3,980	3,700	3,420	3,159	2,919	2,679	2,439
25,750	25,800	4,274	3,994	3,714	3,434	3,171	2,931	2,691	2,451
25,800	25,850	4,288	4,008	3,728	3,448	3,183	2,943	2,703	2,463
25,850	25,900	4,302	4,022	3,742	3,462	3,195	2,955	2,715	2,475
25,900	25,950	4,316	4,036	3,756	3,476	3,207	2,967	2,727	2,487
25,950	26,000	4,330	4,050	3,770	3,490	3,219	2,979	2,739	2,499
26,000	26,050	4,344	4,064	3,784	3,504	3,231	2,991	2,751	2,511
26,050	26,100	4,358	4,078	3,798	3,518	3,243	3,003	2,763	2,523
26,100	26,150	4,372	4,092	3,812	3,532	3,255	3,015	2,775	2,535
26,150	26,200	4,386	4,106	3,826	3,546	3,267	3,027	2,787	2,547
26,200	26,250	4,400	4,120	3,840	3,560	3,280	3,039	2,799	2,559
26,250	26,300	4,414	4,134	3,854	3,574	3,294	3,051	2,811	2,571
26,300	26,350	4,428	4,148	3,868	3,588	3,308	3,063	2,823	2,583
26,350	26,400	4,442	4,162	3,882	3,602	3,322	3,075	2,835	2,595
26,400	26,450	4,456	4,176	3,896	3,616	3,336	3,087	2,847	2,607
26,450	26,500	4,470	4,190	3,910	3,630	3,350	3,099	2,859	2,619
26,500	26,550	4,484	4,204	3,924	3,644	3,364	3,111	2,871	2,631
26,550	26,600	4,498	4,218	3,938	3,658	3,378	3,123	2,883	2,643
26,600	26,650	4,513	4,232	3,952	3,672	3,392	3,135	2,895	2,655
26,650	26,700	4,529	4,246	3,966	3,686	3,406	3,147	2,907	2,667
26,700	26,750	4,545	4,260	3,980	3,700	3,420	3,159	2,919	2,679
26,750	26,800	4,561	4,274	3,994	3,714	3,434	3,171	2,931	2,691
26,800	26,850	4,577	4,288	4,008	3,728	3,448	3,183	2,943	2,703
26,850	26,900	4,593	4,302	4,022	3,742	3,462	3,195	2,955	2,715
26,900	26,950	4,609	4,316	4,036	3,756	3,476	3,207	2,967	2,727
26,950	27,000	4,625	4,330	4,050	3,770	3,490	3,219	2,979	2,739
27,000	27,050	4,641	4,344	4,064	3,784	3,504	3,231	2,991	2,751
27,050	27,100	4,657	4,358	4,078	3,798	3,518	3,243	3,003	2,763
27,100	27,150	4,673	4,372	4,092	3,812	3,532	3,255	3,015	2,775
27,150	27,200	4,689	4,386	4,106	3,826	3,546	3,267	3,027	2,787
27,200	27,250	4,705	4,400	4,120	3,840	3,560	3,280	3,039	2,799
27,250	27,300	4,721	4,414	4,134	3,854	3,574	3,294	3,051	2,811
27,300	27,350	4,737	4,428	4,148	3,868	3,588	3,308	3,063	2,823
27,350	27,400	4,753	4,442	4,162	3,882	3,602	3,322	3,075	2,835
27,400	27,450	4,769	4,456	4,176	3,896	3,616	3,336	3,087	2,847
27,450	27,500	4,785	4,470	4,190	3,910	3,630	3,350	3,099	2,859
27,500	27,550	4,801	4,484	4,204	3,924	3,644	3,364	3,111	2,871
27,550	27,600	4,817	4,498	4,218	3,938	3,658	3,378	3,123	2,883
27,600	27,650	4,833	4,513	4,232	3,952	3,672	3,392	3,135	2,895
27,650	27,700	4,849	4,529	4,246	3,966	3,686	3,406	3,147	2,907
27,700	27,750	4,865	4,545	4,260	3,980	3,700	3,420	3,159	2,919
27,750	27,800	4,881	4,561	4,274	3,994	3,714	3,434	3,171	2,931
27,800	27,850	4,897	4,577	4,288	4,008	3,728	3,448	3,183	2,943
27,850	27,900	4,913	4,593	4,302	4,022	3,742	3,462	3,195	2,955
27,900	27,950	4,929	4,609	4,316	4,036	3,756	3,476	3,207	2,967
27,950	28,000	4,945	4,625	4,330	4,050	3,770	3,490	3,219	2,979
28,000	28,050	4,961	4,641	4,344	4,064	3,784	3,504	3,231	2,991
28,050	28,100	4,977	4,657	4,358	4,078	3,798	3,518	3,243	3,003
28,100	28,150	4,993	4,673	4,372	4,092	3,812	3,532	3,255	3,015
28,150	28,200	5,009	4,689	4,386	4,106	3,826	3,546	3,267	3,027
28,200	28,250	5,025	4,705	4,400	4,120	3,840	3,560	3,280	3,039
28,250	28,300	5,041	4,721	4,414	4,134	3,854	3,574	3,294	3,051
28,300	28,350	5,057	4,737	4,428	4,148	3,868	3,588	3,308	3,063
28,350	28,400	5,073	4,753	4,442	4,162	3,882	3,602	3,322	3,075
28,400	28,450	5,089	4,769	4,456	4,176	3,896	3,616	3,336	3,087
28,450	28,500	5,105	4,785	4,470	4,190	3,910	3,630	3,350	3,099
28,500	28,550	5,121	4,801	4,484	4,204	3,924	3,644	3,364	3,111
28,550	28,600	5,137	4,817	4,498	4,218	3,938	3,658	3,378	3,123
28,600	28,650	5,153	4,833	4,513	4,232	3,952	3,672	3,392	3,135
28,650	28,700	5,169	4,849	4,529	4,246	3,966	3,686	3,406	3,147
28,700	28,750	5,185	4,865	4,545	4,260	3,980	3,700	3,420	3,159
28,750	28,800	5,201	4,881	4,561	4,274	3,994	3,714	3,434	3,171
28,800	28,850	5,217	4,897	4,577	4,288	4,008	3,728	3,448	3,183
28,850	28,900	5,233	4,913	4,593	4,302	4,022	3,742	3,462	3,195
28,900	28,950	5,249	4,929	4,609	4,316	4,036	3,756	3,476	3,207
28,950	29,000	5,265	4,945	4,625	4,330	4,050	3,770	3,490	3,219
29,000	29,050	5,281	4,961	4,641	4,344	4,064	3,784	3,504	3,231
29,050	29,100	5,297	4,977	4,657	4,358	4,078	3,798	3,518	3,243
29,100	29,150	5,313	4,993	4,673	4,372	4,092	3,812	3,532	3,255
29,150	29,200	5,329	5,009	4,689	4,386	4,106	3,826	3,546	3,267

Continued next column

If Form 1040, line 34, is—		And the total number of exemptions claimed on line 7 is—							
Over	But not over	2	3	4	5	6	7	8	9
		Your tax is—							
29,200	29,250	5,345	5,025	4,705	4,400	4,120	3,840	3,560	3,280
29,250	29,300	5,361	5,041	4,721	4,414	4,134	3,854	3,574	3,294
29,300	29,350	5,377	5,057	4,737	4,428	4,148	3,868	3,588	3,308
29,350	29,400	5,393	5,073	4,753	4,442	4,162	3,882	3,602	3,322
29,400	29,450	5,409	5,089	4,769	4,456	4,176	3,896	3,616	3,336
29,450	29,500	5,425	5,105	4,785	4,470	4,190	3,910	3,630	3,350
29,500	29,550	5,441	5,121	4,801	4,484	4,204	3,924	3,644	3,364
29,550	29,600	5,457	5,137	4,817	4,498	4,218	3,938	3,658	3,378
29,600	29,650	5,473	5,153	4,833	4,513	4,232	3,952	3,672	3,392
29,650	29,700	5,489	5,169	4,849	4,529	4,246	3,966	3,686	3,406
29,700	29,750	5,505	5,185	4,865	4,545	4,260	3,980	3,700	3,420
29,750	29,800	5,521	5,201	4,881	4,561	4,274	3,994	3,714	3,434
29,800	29,850	5,537	5,217	4,897	4,577	4,288	4,008	3,728	3,448
29,850	29,900	5,553	5,233	4,913	4,593	4,302	4,022	3,742	3,462
29,900	29,950	5,569	5,249	4,929	4,609	4,316	4,036	3,756	3,476
29,950	30,000	5,585	5,265	4,945	4,625	4,330	4,050	3,770	3,490
30,000	30,050	5,601	5,281	4,961	4,641	4,344	4,064	3,784	3,504
30,050	30,100	5,617	5,297	4,977	4,657	4,358	4,078	3,798	3,518
30,100	30,150	5,633	5,313	4,993	4,673	4,372	4,092	3,812	3,532
30,150	30,200	5,649	5,329	5,009	4,689	4,386	4,106	3,826	3,546
30,200	30,250	5,665	5,345	5,025	4,705	4,400	4,120	3,840	3,560
30,250	30,300	5,681	5,361	5,041	4,721	4,414	4,134	3,854	3,574
30,300	30,350	5,697	5,377	5,057	4,737	4,428	4,148	3,868	3,588
30,350	30,400	5,713	5,393	5,073	4,753	4,442	4,162	3,882	3,602
30,400	30,450	5,729	5,409	5,089	4,769	4,456	4,176	3,896	3,616
30,450	30,500	5,745	5,425	5,105	4,785	4,470	4,190	3,910	3,630
30,500	30,550	5,761	5,441	5,121	4,801	4,484	4,204	3,924	3,644
30,550	30,600	5,777	5,457	5,137	4,817	4,498	4,218	3,938	3,658
30,600	30,650	5,793	5,473	5,153	4,833	4,513	4,232	3,952	3,672
30,650	30,700	5,809	5,489	5,169	4,849	4,529	4,246	3,966	3,686
30,700	30,750	5,825	5,505	5,185	4,865	4,545	4,260	3,980	3,700
30,750	30,800	5,841	5,521	5,201	4,881	4,561	4,274	3,994	3,714
30,800	30,850	5,857	5,537	5,217	4,897	4,577	4,288	4,008	3,728
30,850	30,900	5,873	5,553	5,233	4,913	4,593	4,302	4,022	3,742
30,900	30,950	5,889	5,569	5,249	4,929	4,609	4,316	4,036	3,756
30,950	31,000	5,905	5,585	5,265	4,945	4,625	4,330	4,050	3,770
31,000	31,050	5,921	5,601	5,281	4,961	4,641	4,344	4,064	3,784
31,050	31,100	5,937	5,617	5,297	4,977	4,657	4,358	4,078	3,798
31,100	31,150	5,953	5,633	5,313	4,993	4,673	4,372	4,092	3,812
31,150	31,200	5,969	5,649	5,329	5,009	4,689	4,386	4,106	3,826
31,200	31,250	5,985	5,665	5,345	5,025	4,705	4,400	4,120	3,840
31,250	31,300	6,001	5,681	5,361	5,041	4,721	4,414	4,134	3,854
31,300	31,350	6,017	5,697	5,377	5,057	4,737	4,428	4,148	3,868
31,350	31,400	6,033	5,713	5,393	5,073	4,753	4,442	4,162	3,882
31,400	31,450	6,049	5,729	5,409	5,089	4,769	4,456	4,176	3,896
31,450	31,500	6,065	5,745	5,425	5,105	4,785	4,470	4,190	3,910
31,500	31,550	6,081	5,761	5,441	5,121	4,801	4,484	4,204	3,924
31,550	31,600	6,097	5,777	5,457	5,137	4,817	4,498	4,218	3,938
31,600	31,650	6,113	5,793	5,473	5,153	4,833	4,513	4,232	3,952
31,650	31,700	6,129	5,809	5,489	5,169	4,849	4,529	4,246	3,966
31,700	31,750	6,145	5,825	5,505	5,185	4,865	4,545	4,260	3,980
31,750	31,800	6,161	5,841	5,521	5,201	4,881	4,561	4,274	3,994
31,800	31,850	6,177	5,857	5,537	5,217	4,897	4,577	4,288	4,008
31,850	31,900	6,193	5,873	5,553	5,233	4,913	4,593	4,302	4,022
31,900	31,950	6,210	5,889	5,569	5,249	4,929	4,609	4,316	4,036
31,950	32,000	6,229	5,905	5,585	5,265	4,945	4,625	4,330	4,050
32,000	32,050	6,247	5,921	5,601	5,281	4,961	4,641	4,344	4,064
32,050	32,100	6,266	5,937	5,617	5,297	4,977	4,657	4,358	4,078
32,100	32,150	6,284	5,953	5,633	5,313	4,993	4,673	4,372	4,092
32,150	32,200	6,303	5,969	5,649	5,329	5,009	4,689	4,386	4,106
32,200	32,250	6,321	5,985	5,665	5,345	5,025	4,705	4,400	4,120
32,250	32,300	6,340	6,001	5,681	5,361	5,041	4,721	4,414	4,134
32,300	32,350	6,358	6,017	5,697	5,377	5,057	4,737	4,428	4,148
32,350	32,400	6,377	6,033	5,713	5,393	5,073	4,753	4,442	4,162
32,400	32,450	6,395	6,049	5,729	5,409	5,089	4,769	4,456	4,176
32,450	32,500	6,414	6,065	5,745	5,425	5,105	4,785	4,470	4,190
32,500	32,550	6,432	6,081	5,761	5,441	5,121	4,801	4,484	4,204
32,550	32,600	6,451	6,097	5,777	5,457	5,137	4,817	4,498	4,218
32,600	32,650	6,469	6,113	5,793	5,473	5,153	4,833	4,513	4,232
32,650	32,700	6,488	6,129	5,809	5,489	5,169	4,849	4,529	4,246
32,700	32,750	6,506	6,145	5,825	5,505	5,185	4,865	4,545	4,260
32,750	32,800	6,525	6,161	5,841	5,521	5,201	4,881	4,561	4,274

Continued on next page

1979 Tax Table B—MARRIED FILING JOINT RETURN (Filing Status Box 2) and QUALIFYING WIDOW(ER)S (Filing Status Box 5)

(Continued)

(If your income or exemptions are not covered, use Schedule TC (Form 1040), Part I to figure your tax)

If Form 1040, line 34, is—		And the total number of exemptions claimed on line 7 is—							
Over	But not over	2	3	4	5	6	7	8	9
		Your tax is—							
32,800	32,850	6,543	6,177	5,857	5,537	5,217	4,897	4,577	4,288
32,850	32,900	6,562	6,193	5,873	5,553	5,233	4,913	4,593	4,302
32,900	32,950	6,580	6,210	5,889	5,569	5,249	4,929	4,609	4,316
32,950	33,000	6,599	6,229	5,905	5,585	5,265	4,945	4,625	4,330
33,000	33,050	6,617	6,247	5,921	5,601	5,281	4,961	4,641	4,344
33,050	33,100	6,636	6,266	5,937	5,617	5,297	4,977	4,657	4,358
33,100	33,150	6,654	6,284	5,953	5,633	5,313	4,993	4,673	4,372
33,150	33,200	6,673	6,303	5,969	5,649	5,329	5,009	4,689	4,386
33,200	33,250	6,691	6,321	5,985	5,665	5,345	5,025	4,705	4,400
33,250	33,300	6,710	6,340	6,001	5,681	5,361	5,041	4,721	4,414
33,300	33,350	6,728	6,358	6,017	5,697	5,377	5,057	4,737	4,428
33,350	33,400	6,747	6,377	6,033	5,713	5,393	5,073	4,753	4,442
33,400	33,450	6,765	6,395	6,049	5,729	5,409	5,089	4,769	4,456
33,450	33,500	6,784	6,414	6,065	5,745	5,425	5,105	4,785	4,470
33,500	33,550	6,802	6,432	6,081	5,761	5,441	5,121	4,801	4,484
33,550	33,600	6,821	6,451	6,097	5,777	5,457	5,137	4,817	4,498
33,600	33,650	6,839	6,469	6,113	5,793	5,473	5,153	4,833	4,513
33,650	33,700	6,858	6,488	6,129	5,809	5,489	5,169	4,849	4,529
33,700	33,750	6,876	6,506	6,145	5,825	5,505	5,185	4,865	4,545
33,750	33,800	6,895	6,525	6,161	5,841	5,521	5,201	4,881	4,561
33,800	33,850	6,913	6,543	6,177	5,857	5,537	5,217	4,897	4,577
33,850	33,900	6,932	6,562	6,193	5,873	5,553	5,233	4,913	4,593
33,900	33,950	6,950	6,580	6,210	5,889	5,569	5,249	4,929	4,609
33,950	34,000	6,969	6,599	6,229	5,905	5,585	5,265	4,945	4,625
34,000	34,050	6,987	6,617	6,247	5,921	5,601	5,281	4,961	4,641
34,050	34,100	7,006	6,636	6,266	5,937	5,617	5,297	4,977	4,657
34,100	34,150	7,024	6,654	6,284	5,953	5,633	5,313	4,993	4,673
34,150	34,200	7,043	6,673	6,303	5,969	5,649	5,329	5,009	4,689
34,200	34,250	7,061	6,691	6,321	5,985	5,665	5,345	5,025	4,705
34,250	34,300	7,080	6,710	6,340	6,001	5,681	5,361	5,041	4,721
34,300	34,350	7,098	6,728	6,358	6,017	5,697	5,377	5,057	4,737
34,350	34,400	7,117	6,747	6,377	6,033	5,713	5,393	5,073	4,753
34,400	34,450	7,135	6,765	6,395	6,049	5,729	5,409	5,089	4,769
34,450	34,500	7,154	6,784	6,414	6,065	5,745	5,425	5,105	4,785
34,500	34,550	7,172	6,802	6,432	6,081	5,761	5,441	5,121	4,801
34,550	34,600	7,191	6,821	6,451	6,097	5,777	5,457	5,137	4,817
34,600	34,650	7,209	6,839	6,469	6,113	5,793	5,473	5,153	4,833
34,650	34,700	7,228	6,858	6,488	6,129	5,809	5,489	5,169	4,849
34,700	34,750	7,246	6,876	6,506	6,145	5,825	5,505	5,185	4,865
34,750	34,800	7,265	6,895	6,525	6,161	5,841	5,521	5,201	4,881
34,800	34,850	7,283	6,913	6,543	6,177	5,857	5,537	5,217	4,897
34,850	34,900	7,302	6,932	6,562	6,193	5,873	5,553	5,233	4,913
34,900	34,950	7,320	6,950	6,580	6,210	5,889	5,569	5,249	4,929
34,950	35,000	7,339	6,969	6,599	6,229	5,905	5,585	5,265	4,945
35,000	35,050	7,357	6,987	6,617	6,247	5,921	5,601	5,281	4,961
35,050	35,100	7,376	7,006	6,636	6,266	5,937	5,617	5,297	4,977
35,100	35,150	7,394	7,024	6,654	6,284	5,953	5,633	5,313	4,993
35,150	35,200	7,413	7,043	6,673	6,303	5,969	5,649	5,329	5,009
35,200	35,250	7,431	7,061	6,691	6,321	5,985	5,665	5,345	5,025
35,250	35,300	7,450	7,080	6,710	6,340	6,001	5,681	5,361	5,041
35,300	35,350	7,468	7,098	6,728	6,358	6,017	5,697	5,377	5,057
35,350	35,400	7,487	7,117	6,747	6,377	6,033	5,713	5,393	5,073
35,400	35,450	7,505	7,135	6,765	6,395	6,049	5,729	5,409	5,089
35,450	35,500	7,524	7,154	6,784	6,414	6,065	5,745	5,425	5,105
35,500	35,550	7,542	7,172	6,802	6,432	6,081	5,761	5,441	5,121
35,550	35,600	7,561	7,191	6,821	6,451	6,097	5,777	5,457	5,137
35,600	35,650	7,579	7,209	6,839	6,469	6,113	5,793	5,473	5,153
35,650	35,700	7,598	7,228	6,858	6,488	6,129	5,809	5,489	5,169
35,700	35,750	7,616	7,246	6,876	6,506	6,145	5,825	5,505	5,185
35,750	35,800	7,635	7,265	6,895	6,525	6,161	5,841	5,521	5,201
35,800	35,850	7,653	7,283	6,913	6,543	6,177	5,857	5,537	5,217
35,850	35,900	7,672	7,302	6,932	6,562	6,193	5,873	5,553	5,233
35,900	35,950	7,690	7,320	6,950	6,580	6,210	5,889	5,569	5,249
35,950	36,000	7,709	7,339	6,969	6,599	6,229	5,905	5,585	5,265
36,000	36,050	7,727	7,357	6,987	6,617	6,247	5,921	5,601	5,281
36,050	36,100	7,746	7,376	7,006	6,636	6,266	5,937	5,617	5,297
36,100	36,150	7,764	7,394	7,024	6,654	6,284	5,953	5,633	5,313
36,150	36,200	7,783	7,413	7,043	6,673	6,303	5,969	5,649	5,329
36,200	36,250	7,801	7,431	7,061	6,691	6,321	5,985	5,665	5,345
36,250	36,300	7,820	7,450	7,080	6,710	6,340	6,001	5,681	5,361
36,300	36,350	7,838	7,468	7,098	6,728	6,358	6,017	5,697	5,377
36,350	36,400	7,857	7,487	7,117	6,747	6,377	6,033	5,713	5,393

Continued next column

If Form 1040, line 34, is—		And the total number of exemptions claimed on line 7 is—							
Over	But not over	2	3	4	5	6	7	8	9
		Your tax is—							
36,400	36,450	7,875	7,505	7,135	6,765	6,395	6,049	5,729	5,409
36,450	36,500	7,894	7,524	7,154	6,784	6,414	6,065	5,745	5,425
36,500	36,550	7,912	7,542	7,172	6,802	6,432	6,081	5,761	5,441
36,550	36,600	7,931	7,561	7,191	6,821	6,451	6,097	5,777	5,457
36,600	36,650	7,949	7,579	7,209	6,839	6,469	6,113	5,793	5,473
36,650	36,700	7,968	7,598	7,228	6,858	6,488	6,129	5,809	5,489
36,700	36,750	7,986	7,616	7,246	6,876	6,506	6,145	5,825	5,505
36,750	36,800	8,005	7,635	7,265	6,895	6,525	6,161	5,841	5,521
36,800	36,850	8,023	7,653	7,283	6,913	6,543	6,177	5,857	5,537
36,850	36,900	8,042	7,672	7,302	6,932	6,562	6,193	5,873	5,553
36,900	36,950	8,060	7,690	7,320	6,950	6,580	6,210	5,889	5,569
36,950	37,000	8,079	7,709	7,339	6,969	6,599	6,229	5,905	5,585
37,000	37,050	8,097	7,727	7,357	6,987	6,617	6,247	5,921	5,601
37,050	37,100	8,116	7,746	7,376	7,006	6,636	6,266	5,937	5,617
37,100	37,150	8,134	7,764	7,394	7,024	6,654	6,284	5,953	5,633
37,150	37,200	8,153	7,783	7,413	7,043	6,673	6,303	5,969	5,649
37,200	37,250	8,173	7,801	7,431	7,061	6,691	6,321	5,985	5,665
37,250	37,300	8,194	7,820	7,450	7,080	6,710	6,340	6,001	5,681
37,300	37,350	8,216	7,838	7,468	7,098	6,728	6,358	6,017	5,697
37,350	37,400	8,237	7,857	7,487	7,117	6,747	6,377	6,033	5,713
37,400	37,450	8,259	7,875	7,505	7,135	6,765	6,395	6,049	5,729
37,450	37,500	8,280	7,894	7,524	7,154	6,784	6,414	6,065	5,745
37,500	37,550	8,302	7,912	7,542	7,172	6,802	6,432	6,081	5,761
37,550	37,600	8,323	7,931	7,561	7,191	6,821	6,451	6,097	5,777
37,600	37,650	8,345	7,949	7,579	7,209	6,839	6,469	6,113	5,793
37,650	37,700	8,366	7,968	7,598	7,228	6,858	6,488	6,129	5,809
37,700	37,750	8,388	7,986	7,616	7,246	6,876	6,506	6,145	5,825
37,750	37,800	8,409	8,005	7,635	7,265	6,895	6,525	6,161	5,841
37,800	37,850	8,431	8,023	7,653	7,283	6,913	6,543	6,177	5,857
37,850	37,900	8,452	8,042	7,672	7,302	6,932	6,562	6,193	5,873
37,900	37,950	8,474	8,060	7,690	7,320	6,950	6,580	6,210	5,889
37,950	38,000	8,495	8,079	7,709	7,339	6,969	6,599	6,229	5,905
38,000	38,050	8,517	8,097	7,727	7,357	6,987	6,617	6,247	5,921
38,050	38,100	8,538	8,116	7,746	7,376	7,006	6,636	6,266	5,937
38,100	38,150	8,560	8,134	7,764	7,394	7,024	6,654	6,284	5,953
38,150	38,200	8,581	8,153	7,783	7,413	7,043	6,673	6,303	5,969
38,200	38,250	8,603	8,173	7,801	7,431	7,061	6,691	6,321	5,985
38,250	38,300	8,624	8,194	7,820	7,450	7,080	6,710	6,340	6,001
38,300	38,350	8,646	8,216	7,838	7,468	7,098	6,728	6,358	6,017
38,350	38,400	8,667	8,237	7,857	7,487	7,117	6,747	6,377	6,033
38,400	38,450	8,689	8,259	7,875	7,505	7,135	6,765	6,395	6,049
38,450	38,500	8,710	8,280	7,894	7,524	7,154	6,784	6,414	6,065
38,500	38,550	8,732	8,302	7,912	7,542	7,172	6,802	6,432	6,081
38,550	38,600	8,753	8,323	7,931	7,561	7,191	6,821	6,451	6,097
38,600	38,650	8,775	8,345	7,949	7,579	7,209	6,839	6,469	6,113
38,650	38,700	8,796	8,366	7,968	7,598	7,228	6,858	6,488	6,129
38,700	38,750	8,818	8,388	7,986	7,616	7,246	6,876	6,506	6,145
38,750	38,800	8,839	8,409	8,005	7,635	7,265	6,895	6,525	6,161
38,800	38,850	8,861	8,431	8,023	7,653	7,283	6,913	6,543	6,177
38,850	38,900	8,882	8,452	8,042	7,672	7,302	6,932	6,562	6,193
38,900	38,950	8,904	8,474	8,060	7,690	7,320	6,950	6,580	6,210
38,950	39,000	8,925	8,495	8,079	7,709	7,339	6,969	6,599	6,229
39,000	39,050	8,947	8,517	8,097	7,727	7,357	6,987	6,617	6,247
39,050	39,100	8,968	8,538	8,116	7,746	7,376	7,006	6,636	6,266
39,100	39,150	8,990	8,560	8,134	7,764	7,394	7,024	6,654	6,284
39,150	39,200	9,011	8,581	8,153	7,783	7,413	7,043	6,673	6,303
39,200	39,250	9,033	8,603	8,173	7,801	7,431	7,061	6,691	6,321
39,250	39,300	9,054	8,624	8,194	7,820	7,450	7,080	6,710	6,340
39,300	39,350	9,076	8,646	8,216	7,838	7,468	7,098	6,728	6,358
39,350	39,400	9,097	8,667	8,237	7,857	7,487	7,117	6,747	6,377
39,400	39,450	9,119	8,689	8,259	7,875	7,505	7,135	6,765	6,395
39,450	39,500	9,140	8,710	8,280	7,894	7,524	7,154	6,784	6,414
39,500	39,550	9,162	8,732	8,302	7,912	7,542	7,172	6,802	6,432
39,550	39,600	9,183	8,753	8,323	7,931	7,561	7,191	6,821	6,451
39,600	39,650	9,205	8,775	8,345	7,949	7,579	7,209	6,839	6,469
39,650	39,700	9,226	8,796	8,366	7,968	7,598	7,228	6,858	6,488
39,700	39,750	9,248	8,818	8,388	7,986	7,616	7,246	6,876	6,506
39,750	39,800	9,269	8,839	8,409	8,005	7,635	7,265	6,895	6,525
39,800	39,850	9,291	8,861	8,431	8,023	7,653	7,283	6,913	6,543
39,850	39,900	9,312	8,882	8,452	8,042	7,672	7,302	6,932	6,562
39,900	39,950	9,334	8,904	8,474	8,060	7,690	7,320	6,950	6,580
39,950	40,000	9,355	8,925	8,495	8,079	7,709	7,339	6,969	6,599

1979 Tax Table C—MARRIED FILING SEPARATE RETURN (Filing Status Box 3)

(For married persons filing separate returns with income of $20,000 or less on Form 1040, line 34, who claim 3 or fewer exemptions)

To find your tax: Read down the income column until you find your income as shown on Form 1040, line 34. Read across to the column headed by the total number of exemptions claimed on Form 1040, line 7. The amount shown where the two lines meet is your tax. Enter on Form 1040, line 35. The $1,700 zero bracket amount and your deduction for exemptions have been taken into account in figuring the tax shown in this table. **Do not take a separate deduction for them.**

Caution: *If your spouse itemizes deductions and your itemized deductions are less than $1,700 (or if you can be claimed as a dependent on your parent's return AND you have unearned income (interest, dividends, etc.) of $1,000 or more AND your earned income is less than $1,700), you must first use Schedule TC (Form 1040), Part II.*

If Form 1040, line 34, is— Over	But not over	1	2	3	If Form 1040, line 34, is— Over	But not over	1	2	3	If Form 1040, line 34, is— Over	But not over	1	2	3
		Your tax is—					Your tax is—					Your tax is—		
If $2,700 or less your tax is 0					5,200	5,250	392	223	74	8,000	8,050	928	718	536
2,700	2,725	2	0	0	5,250	5,300	401	231	81	8,050	8,100	938	728	545
2,725	2,750	5	0	0	5,300	5,350	410	239	88	8,100	8,150	949	739	554
2,750	2,775	9	0	0	5,350	5,400	419	247	95	8,150	8,200	959	749	563
2,775	2,800	12	0	0	5,400	5,450	428	255	102	8,200	8,250	970	760	572
2,800	2,825	16	0	0	5,450	5,500	437	263	109	8,250	8,300	980	770	581
2,825	2,850	19	0	0	5,500	5,550	446	271	116	8,300	8,350	991	781	590
2,850	2,875	23	0	0	5,550	5,600	455	279	123	8,350	8,400	1,001	791	599
2,875	2,900	26	0	0	5,600	5,650	464	287	130	8,400	8,450	1,012	802	608
2,900	2,925	30	0	0	5,650	5,700	473	295	137	8,450	8,500	1,022	812	617
2,925	2,950	33	0	0	5,700	5,750	482	303	144	8,500	8,550	1,033	823	626
2,950	2,975	37	0	0	5,750	5,800	491	311	151	8,550	8,600	1,043	833	635
2,975	3,000	40	0	0	5,800	5,850	500	320	159	8,600	8,650	1,054	844	644
3,000	3,050	46	0	0	5,850	5,900	509	329	167	8,650	8,700	1,064	854	653
3,050	3,100	53	0	0	5,900	5,950	518	338	175	8,700	8,750	1,075	865	662
3,100	3,150	60	0	0	5,950	6,000	527	347	183	8,750	8,800	1,085	875	671
3,150	3,200	67	0	0	6,000	6,050	536	356	191	8,800	8,850	1,096	886	680
3,200	3,250	74	0	0	6,050	6,100	545	365	199	8,850	8,900	1,106	896	689
3,250	3,300	81	0	0	6,100	6,150	554	374	207	8,900	8,950	1,117	907	698
3,300	3,350	88	0	0	6,150	6,200	563	383	215	8,950	9,000	1,127	917	707
3,350	3,400	95	0	0	6,200	6,250	572	392	223	9,000	9,050	1,139	928	718
3,400	3,450	102	0	0	6,250	6,300	581	401	231	9,050	9,100	1,151	938	728
3,450	3,500	109	0	0	6,300	6,350	590	410	239	9,100	9,150	1,163	949	739
3,500	3,550	116	0	0	6,350	6,400	599	419	247	9,150	9,200	1,175	959	749
3,550	3,600	123	0	0	6,400	6,450	608	428	255	9,200	9,250	1,187	970	760
3,600	3,650	130	0	0	6,450	6,500	617	437	263	9,250	9,300	1,199	980	770
3,650	3,700	137	0	0	6,500	6,550	626	446	271	9,300	9,350	1,211	991	781
3,700	3,750	144	4	0	6,550	6,600	635	455	279	9,350	9,400	1,223	1,001	791
3,750	3,800	151	11	0	6,600	6,650	644	464	287	9,400	9,450	1,235	1,012	802
3,800	3,850	159	18	0	6,650	6,700	653	473	295	9,450	9,500	1,247	1,022	812
3,850	3,900	167	25	0	6,700	6,750	662	482	303	9,500	9,550	1,259	1,033	823
3,900	3,950	175	32	0	6,750	6,800	671	491	311	9,550	9,600	1,271	1,043	833
3,950	4,000	183	39	0	6,800	6,850	680	500	320	9,600	9,650	1,283	1,054	844
4,000	4,050	191	46	0	6,850	6,900	689	509	329	9,650	9,700	1,295	1,064	854
4,050	4,100	199	53	0	6,900	6,950	698	518	338	9,700	9,750	1,307	1,075	865
4,100	4,150	207	60	0	6,950	7,000	707	527	347	9,750	9,800	1,319	1,085	875
4,150	4,200	215	67	0	7,000	7,050	718	536	356	9,800	9,850	1,331	1,096	886
4,200	4,250	223	74	0	7,050	7,100	728	545	365	9,850	9,900	1,343	1,106	896
4,250	4,300	231	81	0	7,100	7,150	739	554	374	9,900	9,950	1,355	1,117	907
4,300	4,350	239	88	0	7,150	7,200	749	563	383	9,950	10,000	1,367	1,127	917
4,350	4,400	247	95	0	7,200	7,250	760	572	392	10,000	10,050	1,379	1,139	928
4,400	4,450	255	102	0	7,250	7,300	770	581	401	10,050	10,100	1,391	1,151	938
4,450	4,500	263	109	0	7,300	7,350	781	590	410	10,100	10,150	1,403	1,163	949
4,500	4,550	271	116	0	7,350	7,400	791	599	419	10,150	10,200	1,415	1,175	959
4,550	4,600	279	123	0	7,400	7,450	802	608	428	10,200	10,250	1,427	1,187	970
4,600	4,650	287	130	0	7,450	7,500	812	617	437	10,250	10,300	1,439	1,199	980
4,650	4,700	295	137	0	7,500	7,550	823	626	446	10,300	10,350	1,451	1,211	991
4,700	4,750	303	144	4	7,550	7,600	833	635	455	10,350	10,400	1,463	1,223	1,001
4,750	4,800	311	151	11	7,600	7,650	844	644	464	10,400	10,450	1,475	1,235	1,012
4,800	4,850	320	159	18	7,650	7,700	854	653	473	10,450	10,500	1,487	1,247	1,022
4,850	4,900	329	167	25	7,700	7,750	865	662	482	10,500	10,550	1,499	1,259	1,033
4,900	4,950	338	175	32	7,750	7,800	875	671	491	10,550	10,600	1,511	1,271	1,043
4,950	5,000	347	183	39	7,800	7,850	886	680	500	10,600	10,650	1,523	1,283	1,054
5,000	5,050	356	191	46	7,850	7,900	896	689	509	10,650	10,700	1,535	1,295	1,064
5,050	5,100	365	199	53	7,900	7,950	907	698	518	10,700	10,750	1,547	1,307	1,075
5,100	5,150	374	207	60	7,950	8,000	917	707	527	10,750	10,800	1,559	1,319	1,085
5,150	5,200	383	215	67										

Continued next column   Continued next column   Continued on next page

1979 Tax Table C—MARRIED FILING SEPARATE RETURN (Filing Status Box 3)

(Continued) (If your income or exemptions are not covered, use Schedule TC (Form 1040) Part I to figure your tax)

If Form 1040, line 34, is—		And the total number of exemptions claimed on line 7 is—			If Form 1040, line 34, is—		And the total number of exemptions claimed on line 7 is—			If Form 1040, line 34, is—		And the total number of exemptions claimed on line 7 is—		
Over	But not over	1	2	3	Over	But not over	1	2	3	Over	But not over	1	2	3
		Your tax is—					Your tax is—					Your tax is—		
10,800	10,850	1,571	1,331	1,096	13,800	13,850	2,421	2,120	1,840	16,800	16,850	3,424	3,061	2,741
10,850	10,900	1,583	1,343	1,106	13,850	13,900	2,437	2,134	1,854	16,850	16,900	3,443	3,077	2,757
10,900	10,950	1,595	1,355	1,117	13,900	13,950	2,453	2,148	1,868	16,900	16,950	3,461	3,093	2,773
10,950	11,000	1,607	1,367	1,127	13,950	14,000	2,469	2,162	1,882	16,950	17,000	3,480	3,110	2,789
11,000	11,050	1,619	1,379	1,139	14,000	14,050	2,485	2,176	1,896	17,000	17,050	3,498	3,128	2,805
11,050	11,100	1,631	1,391	1,151	14,050	14,100	2,501	2,190	1,910	17,050	17,100	3,517	3,147	2,821
11,100	11,150	1,644	1,403	1,163	14,100	14,150	2,517	2,204	1,924	17,100	17,150	3,535	3,165	2,837
11,150	11,200	1,658	1,415	1,175	14,150	14,200	2,533	2,218	1,938	17,150	17,200	3,554	3,184	2,853
11,200	11,250	1,672	1,427	1,187	14,200	14,250	2,549	2,232	1,952	17,200	17,250	3,572	3,202	2,869
11,250	11,300	1,686	1,439	1,199	14,250	14,300	2,565	2,246	1,966	17,250	17,300	3,591	3,221	2,885
11,300	11,350	1,700	1,451	1,211	14,300	14,350	2,581	2,261	1,980	17,300	17,350	3,609	3,239	2,901
11,350	11,400	1,714	1,463	1,223	14,350	14,400	2,597	2,277	1,994	17,350	17,400	3,628	3,258	2,917
11,400	11,450	1,728	1,475	1,235	14,400	14,450	2,613	2,293	2,008	17,400	17,450	3,646	3,276	2,933
11,450	11,500	1,742	1,487	1,247	14,450	14,500	2,629	2,309	2,022	17,450	17,500	3,665	3,295	2,949
11,500	11,550	1,756	1,499	1,259	14,500	14,550	2,645	2,325	2,036	17,500	17,550	3,683	3,313	2,965
11,550	11,600	1,770	1,511	1,271	14,550	14,600	2,661	2,341	2,050	17,550	17,600	3,702	3,332	2,981
11,600	11,650	1,784	1,523	1,283	14,600	14,650	2,677	2,357	2,064	17,600	17,650	3,720	3,350	2,997
11,650	11,700	1,798	1,535	1,295	14,650	14,700	2,693	2,373	2,078	17,650	17,700	3,739	3,369	3,013
11,700	11,750	1,812	1,547	1,307	14,700	14,750	2,709	2,389	2,092	17,700	17,750	3,757	3,387	3,029
11,750	11,800	1,826	1,559	1,319	14,750	14,800	2,725	2,405	2,106	17,750	17,800	3,776	3,406	3,045
11,800	11,850	1,840	1,571	1,331	14,800	14,850	2,741	2,421	2,120	17,800	17,850	3,794	3,424	3,061
11,850	11,900	1,854	1,583	1,343	14,850	14,900	2,757	2,437	2,134	17,850	17,900	3,813	3,443	3,077
11,900	11,950	1,868	1,595	1,355	14,900	14,950	2,773	2,453	2,148	17,900	17,950	3,831	3,461	3,093
11,950	12,000	1,882	1,607	1,367	14,950	15,000	2,789	2,469	2,162	17,950	18,000	3,850	3,480	3,110
12,000	12,050	1,896	1,619	1,379	15,000	15,050	2,805	2,485	2,176	18,000	18,050	3,868	3,498	3,128
12,050	12,100	1,910	1,631	1,391	15,050	15,100	2,821	2,501	2,190	18,050	18,100	3,887	3,517	3,147
12,100	12,150	1,924	1,644	1,403	15,100	15,150	2,837	2,517	2,204	18,100	18,150	3,905	3,535	3,165
12,150	12,200	1,938	1,658	1,415	15,150	15,200	2,853	2,533	2,218	18,150	18,200	3,924	3,554	3,184
12,200	12,250	1,952	1,672	1,427	15,200	15,250	2,869	2,549	2,232	18,200	18,250	3,942	3,572	3,202
12,250	12,300	1,966	1,686	1,439	15,250	15,300	2,885	2,565	2,246	18,250	18,300	3,961	3,591	3,221
12,300	12,350	1,980	1,700	1,451	15,300	15,350	2,901	2,581	2,261	18,300	18,350	3,979	3,609	3,239
12,350	12,400	1,994	1,714	1,463	15,350	15,400	2,917	2,597	2,277	18,350	18,400	3,998	3,628	3,258
12,400	12,450	2,008	1,728	1,475	15,400	15,450	2,933	2,613	2,293	18,400	18,450	4,016	3,646	3,276
12,450	12,500	2,022	1,742	1,487	15,450	15,500	2,949	2,629	2,309	18,450	18,500	4,035	3,665	3,295
12,500	12,550	2,036	1,756	1,499	15,500	15,550	2,965	2,645	2,325	18,500	18,550	4,053	3,683	3,313
12,550	12,600	2,050	1,770	1,511	15,550	15,600	2,981	2,661	2,341	18,550	18,600	4,072	3,702	3,332
12,600	12,650	2,064	1,784	1,523	15,600	15,650	2,997	2,677	2,357	18,600	18,650	4,092	3,720	3,350
12,650	12,700	2,078	1,798	1,535	15,650	15,700	3,013	2,693	2,373	18,650	18,700	4,113	3,739	3,369
12,700	12,750	2,092	1,812	1,547	15,700	15,750	3,029	2,709	2,389	18,700	18,750	4,135	3,757	3,387
12,750	12,800	2,106	1,826	1,559	15,750	15,800	3,045	2,725	2,405	18,750	18,800	4,156	3,776	3,406
12,800	12,850	2,120	1,840	1,571	15,800	15,850	3,061	2,741	2,421	18,800	18,850	4,178	3,794	3,424
12,850	12,900	2,134	1,854	1,583	15,850	15,900	3,077	2,757	2,437	18,850	18,900	4,199	3,813	3,443
12,900	12,950	2,148	1,868	1,595	15,900	15,950	3,093	2,773	2,453	18,900	18,950	4,221	3,831	3,461
12,950	13,000	2,162	1,882	1,607	15,950	16,000	3,110	2,789	2,469	18,950	19,000	4,242	3,850	3,480
13,000	13,050	2,176	1,896	1,619	16,000	16,050	3,128	2,805	2,485	19,000	19,050	4,264	3,868	3,498
13,050	13,100	2,190	1,910	1,631	16,050	16,100	3,147	2,821	2,501	19,050	19,100	4,285	3,887	3,517
13,100	13,150	2,204	1,924	1,644	16,100	16,150	3,165	2,837	2,517	19,100	19,150	4,307	3,905	3,535
13,150	13,200	2,218	1,938	1,658	16,150	16,200	3,184	2,853	2,533	19,150	19,200	4,328	3,924	3,554
13,200	13,250	2,232	1,952	1,672	16,200	16,250	3,202	2,869	2,549	19,200	19,250	4,350	3,942	3,572
13,250	13,300	2,246	1,966	1,686	16,250	16,300	3,221	2,885	2,565	19,250	19,300	4,371	3,961	3,591
13,300	13,350	2,261	1,980	1,700	16,300	16,350	3,239	2,901	2,581	19,300	19,350	4,393	3,979	3,609
13,350	13,400	2,277	1,994	1,714	16,350	16,400	3,258	2,917	2,597	19,350	19,400	4,414	3,998	3,628
13,400	13,450	2,293	2,008	1,728	16,400	16,450	3,276	2,933	2,613	19,400	19,450	4,436	4,016	3,646
13,450	13,500	2,309	2,022	1,742	16,450	16,500	3,295	2,949	2,629	19,450	19,500	4,457	4,035	3,665
13,500	13,550	2,325	2,036	1,756	16,500	16,550	3,313	2,965	2,645	19,500	19,550	4,479	4,053	3,683
13,550	13,600	2,341	2,050	1,770	16,550	16,600	3,332	2,981	2,661	19,550	19,600	4,500	4,072	3,702
13,600	13,650	2,357	2,064	1,784	16,600	16,650	3,350	2,997	2,677	19,600	19,650	4,522	4,092	3,720
13,650	13,700	2,373	2,078	1,798	16,650	16,700	3,369	3,013	2,693	19,650	19,700	4,543	4,113	3,739
13,700	13,750	2,389	2,092	1,812	16,700	16,750	3,387	3,029	2,709	19,700	19,750	4,565	4,135	3,757
13,750	13,800	2,405	2,106	1,826	16,750	16,800	3,406	3,045	2,725	19,750	19,800	4,586	4,156	3,776
										19,800	19,850	4,608	4,178	3,794
										19,850	19,900	4,629	4,199	3,813
										19,900	19,950	4,651	4,221	3,831
										19,950	20,000	4,672	4,242	3,850

Continued next column   Continued next column

1979 Tax Table D—HEAD OF HOUSEHOLD (Filing Status Box 4)

(For unmarried (including certain married persons who live apart and abandoned spouses) or legally separated persons who qualify as heads of household with income of $20,000 or less on Form 1040, line 34, who claim 8 or fewer exemptions)

To find your tax: Read down the income column until you find your income as shown on Form 1040, line 34. Read across to the column headed by the total number of exemptions claimed on Form 1040, line 7. The amount shown where the two lines meet is your tax. Enter on Form 1040, line 35. The $2,300 zero bracket amount and your deduction for exemptions have been taken into account in figuring the tax shown in this table. **Do not take a separate deduction for them.**

If Form 1040, line 34, is— Over	But not over	And the total number of exemptions claimed on line 7 is— 1	2	3	4	5	6	7	8
		Your tax is—							
If $3,300 or less your tax is 0									
3,300	3,350	4	0	0	0	0	0	0	0
3,350	3,400	11	0	0	0	0	0	0	0
3,400	3,450	18	0	0	0	0	0	0	0
3,450	3,500	25	0	0	0	0	0	0	0
3,500	3,550	32	0	0	0	0	0	0	0
3,550	3,600	39	0	0	0	0	0	0	0
3,600	3,650	46	0	0	0	0	0	0	0
3,650	3,700	53	0	0	0	0	0	0	0
3,700	3,750	60	0	0	0	0	0	0	0
3,750	3,800	67	0	0	0	0	0	0	0
3,800	3,850	74	0	0	0	0	0	0	0
3,850	3,900	81	0	0	0	0	0	0	0
3,900	3,950	88	0	0	0	0	0	0	0
3,950	4,000	95	0	0	0	0	0	0	0
4,000	4,050	102	0	0	0	0	0	0	0
4,050	4,100	109	0	0	0	0	0	0	0
4,100	4,150	116	0	0	0	0	0	0	0
4,150	4,200	123	0	0	0	0	0	0	0
4,200	4,250	130	0	0	0	0	0	0	0
4,250	4,300	137	0	0	0	0	0	0	0
4,300	4,350	144	4	0	0	0	0	0	0
4,350	4,400	151	11	0	0	0	0	0	0
4,400	4,450	158	18	0	0	0	0	0	0
4,450	4,500	165	25	0	0	0	0	0	0
4,500	4,550	172	32	0	0	0	0	0	0
4,550	4,600	179	39	0	0	0	0	0	0
4,600	4,650	186	46	0	0	0	0	0	0
4,650	4,700	193	53	0	0	0	0	0	0
4,700	4,750	200	60	0	0	0	0	0	0
4,750	4,800	207	67	0	0	0	0	0	0
4,800	4,850	214	74	0	0	0	0	0	0
4,850	4,900	221	81	0	0	0	0	0	0
4,900	4,950	228	88	0	0	0	0	0	0
4,950	5,000	235	95	0	0	0	0	0	0
5,000	5,050	242	102	0	0	0	0	0	0
5,050	5,100	249	109	0	0	0	0	0	0
5,100	5,150	256	116	0	0	0	0	0	0
5,150	5,200	263	123	0	0	0	0	0	0
5,200	5,250	270	130	0	0	0	0	0	0
5,250	5,300	277	137	0	0	0	0	0	0
5,300	5,350	284	144	4	0	0	0	0	0
5,350	5,400	291	151	11	0	0	0	0	0
5,400	5,450	298	158	18	0	0	0	0	0
5,450	5,500	306	165	25	0	0	0	0	0
5,500	5,550	314	172	32	0	0	0	0	0
5,550	5,600	322	179	39	0	0	0	0	0
5,600	5,650	330	186	46	0	0	0	0	0
5,650	5,700	338	193	53	0	0	0	0	0
5,700	5,750	346	200	60	0	0	0	0	0
5,750	5,800	354	207	67	0	0	0	0	0
5,800	5,850	362	214	74	0	0	0	0	0
5,850	5,900	370	221	81	0	0	0	0	0

Continued next column

If Form 1040, line 34, is— Over	But not over	And the total number of exemptions claimed on line 7 is— 1	2	3	4	5	6	7	8
		Your tax is—							
5,900	5,950	378	228	88	0	0	0	0	0
5,950	6,000	386	235	95	0	0	0	0	0
6,000	6,050	394	242	102	0	0	0	0	0
6,050	6,100	402	249	109	0	0	0	0	0
6,100	6,150	410	256	116	0	0	0	0	0
6,150	6,200	418	263	123	0	0	0	0	0
6,200	6,250	426	270	130	0	0	0	0	0
6,250	6,300	434	277	137	0	0	0	0	0
6,300	6,350	442	284	144	4	0	0	0	0
6,350	6,400	450	291	151	11	0	0	0	0
6,400	6,450	458	298	158	18	0	0	0	0
6,450	6,500	466	306	165	25	0	0	0	0
6,500	6,550	474	314	172	32	0	0	0	0
6,550	6,600	482	322	179	39	0	0	0	0
6,600	6,650	490	330	186	46	0	0	0	0
6,650	6,700	498	338	193	53	0	0	0	0
6,700	6,750	506	346	200	60	0	0	0	0
6,750	6,800	514	354	207	67	0	0	0	0
6,800	6,850	522	362	214	74	0	0	0	0
6,850	6,900	530	370	221	81	0	0	0	0
6,900	6,950	538	378	228	88	0	0	0	0
6,950	7,000	546	386	235	95	0	0	0	0
7,000	7,050	554	394	242	102	0	0	0	0
7,050	7,100	562	402	249	109	0	0	0	0
7,100	7,150	570	410	256	116	0	0	0	0
7,150	7,200	578	418	263	123	0	0	0	0
7,200	7,250	586	426	270	130	0	0	0	0
7,250	7,300	594	434	277	137	0	0	0	0
7,300	7,350	602	442	284	144	4	0	0	0
7,350	7,400	610	450	291	151	11	0	0	0
7,400	7,450	618	458	298	158	18	0	0	0
7,450	7,500	626	466	306	165	25	0	0	0
7,500	7,550	635	474	314	172	32	0	0	0
7,550	7,600	644	482	322	179	39	0	0	0
7,600	7,650	653	490	330	186	46	0	0	0
7,650	7,700	662	498	338	193	53	0	0	0
7,700	7,750	671	506	346	200	60	0	0	0
7,750	7,800	680	514	354	207	67	0	0	0
7,800	7,850	689	522	362	214	74	0	0	0
7,850	7,900	698	530	370	221	81	0	0	0
7,900	7,950	707	538	378	228	88	0	0	0
7,950	8,000	716	546	386	235	95	0	0	0
8,000	8,050	725	554	394	242	102	0	0	0
8,050	8,100	734	562	402	249	109	0	0	0
8,100	8,150	743	570	410	256	116	0	0	0
8,150	8,200	752	578	418	263	123	0	0	0
8,200	8,250	761	586	426	270	130	0	0	0
8,250	8,300	770	594	434	277	137	0	0	0
8,300	8,350	779	602	442	284	144	4	0	0
8,350	8,400	788	610	450	291	151	11	0	0
8,400	8,450	797	618	458	298	158	18	0	0
8,450	8,500	806	626	466	306	165	25	0	0

Continued on next page

1979 Tax Table D—HEAD OF HOUSEHOLD (Filing Status Box 4)

(Continued)   (If your income or exemptions are not covered, use Schedule TC (Form 1040), Part I to figure your tax)

If Form 1040, line 34, is— Over	But not over	1	2	3	4	5	6	7	8	If Form 1040, line 34, is— Over	But not over	1	2	3	4	5	6	7	8
		Your tax is—										Your tax is—							
8,500	8,550	815	635	474	314	172	32	0	0	11,500	11,550	1,428	1,208	995	815	635	474	314	172
8,550	8,600	824	644	482	322	179	39	0	0	11,550	11,600	1,439	1,219	1,004	824	644	482	322	179
8,600	8,650	833	653	490	330	186	46	0	0	11,600	11,650	1,450	1,230	1,013	833	653	490	330	186
8,650	8,700	842	662	498	338	193	53	0	0	11,650	11,700	1,461	1,241	1,022	842	662	498	338	193
8,700	8,750	851	671	506	346	200	60	0	0	11,700	11,750	1,472	1,252	1,032	851	671	506	346	200
8,750	8,800	860	680	514	354	207	67	0	0	11,750	11,800	1,483	1,263	1,043	860	680	514	354	207
8,800	8,850	869	689	522	362	214	74	0	0	11,800	11,850	1,494	1,274	1,054	869	689	522	362	214
8,850	8,900	878	698	530	370	221	81	0	0	11,850	11,900	1,505	1,285	1,065	878	698	530	370	221
8,900	8,950	887	707	538	378	228	88	0	0	11,900	11,950	1,516	1,296	1,076	887	707	538	378	228
8,950	9,000	896	716	546	386	235	95	0	0	11,950	12,000	1,527	1,307	1,087	896	716	546	386	235
9,000	9,050	905	725	554	394	242	102	0	0	12,000	12,050	1,538	1,318	1,098	905	725	554	394	242
9,050	9,100	914	734	562	402	249	109	0	0	12,050	12,100	1,549	1,329	1,109	914	734	562	402	249
9,100	9,150	923	743	570	410	256	116	0	0	12,100	12,150	1,560	1,340	1,120	923	743	570	410	256
9,150	9,200	932	752	578	418	263	123	0	0	12,150	12,200	1,571	1,351	1,131	932	752	578	418	263
9,200	9,250	941	761	586	426	270	130	0	0	12,200	12,250	1,582	1,362	1,142	941	761	586	426	270
9,250	9,300	950	770	594	434	277	137	0	0	12,250	12,300	1,593	1,373	1,153	950	770	594	434	277
9,300	9,350	959	779	602	442	284	144	4	0	12,300	12,350	1,604	1,384	1,164	959	779	602	442	284
9,350	9,400	968	788	610	450	291	151	11	0	12,350	12,400	1,615	1,395	1,175	968	788	610	450	291
9,400	9,450	977	797	618	458	298	158	18	0	12,400	12,450	1,626	1,406	1,186	977	797	618	458	298
9,450	9,500	986	806	626	466	306	165	25	0	12,450	12,500	1,637	1,417	1,197	986	806	626	466	306
9,500	9,550	995	815	635	474	314	172	32	0	12,500	12,550	1,648	1,428	1,208	995	815	635	474	314
9,550	9,600	1,004	824	644	482	322	179	39	0	12,550	12,600	1,659	1,439	1,219	1,004	824	644	482	322
9,600	9,650	1,013	833	653	490	330	186	46	0	12,600	12,650	1,670	1,450	1,230	1,013	833	653	490	330
9,650	9,700	1,022	842	662	498	338	193	53	0	12,650	12,700	1,681	1,461	1,241	1,022	842	662	498	338
9,700	9,750	1,032	851	671	506	346	200	60	0	12,700	12,750	1,692	1,472	1,252	1,032	851	671	506	346
9,750	9,800	1,043	860	680	514	354	207	67	0	12,750	12,800	1,703	1,483	1,263	1,043	860	680	514	354
9,800	9,850	1,054	869	689	522	362	214	74	0	12,800	12,850	1,714	1,494	1,274	1,054	869	689	522	362
9,850	9,900	1,065	878	698	530	370	221	81	0	12,850	12,900	1,726	1,505	1,285	1,065	878	698	530	370
9,900	9,950	1,076	887	707	538	378	228	88	0	12,900	12,950	1,738	1,516	1,296	1,076	887	707	538	378
9,950	10,000	1,087	896	716	546	386	235	95	0	12,950	13,000	1,750	1,527	1,307	1,087	896	716	546	386
10,000	10,050	1,098	905	725	554	394	242	102	0	13,000	13,050	1,762	1,538	1,318	1,098	905	725	554	394
10,050	10,100	1,109	914	734	562	402	249	109	0	13,050	13,100	1,774	1,549	1,329	1,109	914	734	562	402
10,100	10,150	1,120	923	743	570	410	256	116	0	13,100	13,150	1,786	1,560	1,340	1,120	923	743	570	410
10,150	10,200	1,131	932	752	578	418	263	123	0	13,150	13,200	1,798	1,571	1,351	1,131	932	752	578	418
10,200	10,250	1,142	941	761	586	426	270	130	0	13,200	13,250	1,810	1,582	1,362	1,142	941	761	586	426
10,250	10,300	1,153	950	770	594	434	277	137	0	13,250	13,300	1,822	1,593	1,373	1,153	950	770	594	434
10,300	10,350	1,164	959	779	602	442	284	144	4	13,300	13,350	1,834	1,604	1,384	1,164	959	779	602	442
10,350	10,400	1,175	968	788	610	450	291	151	11	13,350	13,400	1,846	1,615	1,395	1,175	968	788	610	450
10,400	10,450	1,186	977	797	618	458	298	158	18	13,400	13,450	1,858	1,626	1,406	1,186	977	797	618	458
10,450	10,500	1,197	986	806	626	466	306	165	25	13,450	13,500	1,870	1,637	1,417	1,197	986	806	626	466
10,500	10,550	1,208	995	815	635	474	314	172	32	13,500	13,550	1,882	1,648	1,428	1,208	995	815	635	474
10,550	10,600	1,219	1,004	824	644	482	322	179	39	13,550	13,600	1,894	1,659	1,439	1,219	1,004	824	644	482
10,600	10,650	1,230	1,013	833	653	490	330	186	46	13,600	13,650	1,906	1,670	1,450	1,230	1,013	833	653	490
10,650	10,700	1,241	1,022	842	662	498	338	193	53	13,650	13,700	1,918	1,681	1,461	1,241	1,022	842	662	498
10,700	10,750	1,252	1,032	851	671	506	346	200	60	13,700	13,750	1,930	1,692	1,472	1,252	1,032	851	671	506
10,750	10,800	1,263	1,043	860	680	514	354	207	67	13,750	13,800	1,942	1,703	1,483	1,263	1,043	860	680	514
10,800	10,850	1,274	1,054	869	689	522	362	214	74	13,800	13,850	1,954	1,714	1,494	1,274	1,054	869	689	522
10,850	10,900	1,285	1,065	878	698	530	370	221	81	13,850	13,900	1,966	1,726	1,505	1,285	1,065	878	698	530
10,900	10,950	1,296	1,076	887	707	538	378	228	88	13,900	13,950	1,978	1,738	1,516	1,296	1,076	887	707	538
10,950	11,000	1,307	1,087	896	716	546	386	235	95	13,950	14,000	1,990	1,750	1,527	1,307	1,087	896	716	546
11,000	11,050	1,318	1,098	905	725	554	394	242	102	14,000	14,050	2,002	1,762	1,538	1,318	1,098	905	725	554
11,050	11,100	1,329	1,109	914	734	562	402	249	109	14,050	14,100	2,014	1,774	1,549	1,329	1,109	914	734	562
11,100	11,150	1,340	1,120	923	743	570	410	256	116	14,100	14,150	2,026	1,786	1,560	1,340	1,120	923	743	570
11,150	11,200	1,351	1,131	932	752	578	418	263	123	14,150	14,200	2,038	1,798	1,571	1,351	1,131	932	752	578
11,200	11,250	1,362	1,142	941	761	586	426	270	130	14,200	14,250	2,050	1,810	1,582	1,362	1,142	941	761	586
11,250	11,300	1,373	1,153	950	770	594	434	277	137	14,250	14,300	2,062	1,822	1,593	1,373	1,153	950	770	594
11,300	11,350	1,384	1,164	959	779	602	442	284	144	14,300	14,350	2,074	1,834	1,604	1,384	1,164	959	779	602
11,350	11,400	1,395	1,175	968	788	610	450	291	151	14,350	14,400	2,086	1,846	1,615	1,395	1,175	968	788	610
11,400	11,450	1,406	1,186	977	797	618	458	298	158	14,400	14,450	2,098	1,858	1,626	1,406	1,186	977	797	618
11,450	11,500	1,417	1,197	986	806	626	466	306	165	14,450	14,500	2,110	1,870	1,637	1,417	1,197	986	806	626

Continued next column   Continued on next page

1979 Tax Table D—HEAD OF HOUSEHOLD (Filing Status Box 4)

(Continued) (If your income or exemptions are not covered, use Schedule TC (Form 1040), Part I to figure your tax)

If Form 1040, line 34 is Over	But not over	And the total number of exemptions claimed on line 7 is— 1	2	3	4	5	6	7	8
		Your tax is—							
14,500	14,550	2,122	1,882	1,648	1,428	1,208	995	815	635
14,550	14,600	2,134	1,894	1,659	1,439	1,219	1,004	824	644
14,600	14,650	2,146	1,906	1,670	1,450	1,230	1,013	833	653
14,650	14,700	2,158	1,918	1,681	1,461	1,241	1,022	842	662
14,700	14,750	2,170	1,930	1,692	1,472	1,252	1,032	851	671
14,750	14,800	2,182	1,942	1,703	1,483	1,263	1,043	860	680
14,800	14,850	2,194	1,954	1,714	1,494	1,274	1,054	869	689
14,850	14,900	2,206	1,966	1,726	1,505	1,285	1,065	878	698
14,900	14,950	2,218	1,978	1,738	1,516	1,296	1,076	887	707
14,950	15,000	2,230	1,990	1,750	1,527	1,307	1,087	896	716
15,000	15,050	2,242	2,002	1,762	1,538	1,318	1,098	905	725
15,050	15,100	2,254	2,014	1,774	1,549	1,329	1,109	914	734
15,100	15,150	2,266	2,026	1,786	1,560	1,340	1,120	923	743
15,150	15,200	2,278	2,038	1,798	1,571	1,351	1,131	932	752
15,200	15,250	2,290	2,050	1,810	1,582	1,362	1,142	941	761
15,250	15,300	2,302	2,062	1,822	1,593	1,373	1,153	950	770
15,300	15,350	2,314	2,074	1,834	1,604	1,384	1,164	959	779
15,350	15,400	2,326	2,086	1,846	1,615	1,395	1,175	968	788
15,400	15,450	2,338	2,098	1,858	1,626	1,406	1,186	977	797
15,450	15,500	2,350	2,110	1,870	1,637	1,417	1,197	986	806
15,500	15,550	2,362	2,122	1,882	1,648	1,428	1,208	995	815
15,550	15,600	2,374	2,134	1,894	1,659	1,439	1,219	1,004	824
15,600	15,650	2,386	2,146	1,906	1,670	1,450	1,230	1,013	833
15,650	15,700	2,398	2,158	1,918	1,681	1,461	1,241	1,022	842
15,700	15,750	2,410	2,170	1,930	1,692	1,472	1,252	1,032	851
15,750	15,800	2,422	2,182	1,942	1,703	1,483	1,263	1,043	860
15,800	15,850	2,434	2,194	1,954	1,714	1,494	1,274	1,054	869
15,850	15,900	2,446	2,206	1,966	1,726	1,505	1,285	1,065	878
15,900	15,950	2,458	2,218	1,978	1,738	1,516	1,296	1,076	887
15,950	16,000	2,470	2,230	1,990	1,750	1,527	1,307	1,087	896
16,000	16,050	2,483	2,242	2,002	1,762	1,538	1,318	1,098	905
16,050	16,100	2,496	2,254	2,014	1,774	1,549	1,329	1,109	914
16,100	16,150	2,509	2,266	2,026	1,786	1,560	1,340	1,120	923
16,150	16,200	2,522	2,278	2,038	1,798	1,571	1,351	1,131	932
16,200	16,250	2,535	2,290	2,050	1,810	1,582	1,362	1,142	941
16,250	16,300	2,548	2,302	2,062	1,822	1,593	1,373	1,153	950
16,300	16,350	2,561	2,314	2,074	1,834	1,604	1,384	1,164	959
16,350	16,400	2,574	2,326	2,086	1,846	1,615	1,395	1,175	968
16,400	16,450	2,587	2,338	2,098	1,858	1,626	1,406	1,186	977
16,450	16,500	2,600	2,350	2,110	1,870	1,637	1,417	1,197	986
16,500	16,550	2,613	2,362	2,122	1,882	1,648	1,428	1,208	995
16,550	16,600	2,626	2,374	2,134	1,894	1,659	1,439	1,219	1,004
16,600	16,650	2,639	2,386	2,146	1,906	1,670	1,450	1,230	1,013
16,650	16,700	2,652	2,398	2,158	1,918	1,681	1,461	1,241	1,022
16,700	16,750	2,665	2,410	2,170	1,930	1,692	1,472	1,252	1,032
16,750	16,800	2,678	2,422	2,182	1,942	1,703	1,483	1,263	1,043
16,800	16,850	2,691	2,434	2,194	1,954	1,714	1,494	1,274	1,054
16,850	16,900	2,704	2,446	2,206	1,966	1,726	1,505	1,285	1,065
16,900	16,950	2,717	2,458	2,218	1,978	1,738	1,516	1,296	1,076
16,950	17,000	2,730	2,470	2,230	1,990	1,750	1,527	1,307	1,087
17,000	17,050	2,743	2,483	2,242	2,002	1,762	1,538	1,318	1,098
17,050	17,100	2,756	2,496	2,254	2,014	1,774	1,549	1,329	1,109
17,100	17,150	2,769	2,509	2,266	2,026	1,786	1,560	1,340	1,120
17,150	17,200	2,782	2,522	2,278	2,038	1,798	1,571	1,351	1,131
17,200	17,250	2,795	2,535	2,290	2,050	1,810	1,582	1,362	1,142
17,250	17,300	2,808	2,548	2,302	2,062	1,822	1,593	1,373	1,153

If Form 1040, line 34 is Over	But not over	And the total number of exemptions claimed on line 7 is— 1	2	3	4	5	6	7	8
		Your tax is—							
17,300	17,350	2,821	2,561	2,314	2,074	1,834	1,604	1,384	1,164
17,350	17,400	2,834	2,574	2,326	2,086	1,846	1,615	1,395	1,175
17,400	17,450	2,847	2,587	2,338	2,098	1,858	1,626	1,406	1,186
17,450	17,500	2,860	2,600	2,350	2,110	1,870	1,637	1,417	1,197
17,500	17,550	2,873	2,613	2,362	2,122	1,882	1,648	1,428	1,208
17,550	17,600	2,886	2,626	2,374	2,134	1,894	1,659	1,439	1,219
17,600	17,650	2,899	2,639	2,386	2,146	1,906	1,670	1,450	1,230
17,650	17,700	2,912	2,652	2,398	2,158	1,918	1,681	1,461	1,241
17,700	17,750	2,925	2,665	2,410	2,170	1,930	1,692	1,472	1,252
17,750	17,800	2,938	2,678	2,422	2,182	1,942	1,703	1,483	1,263
17,800	17,850	2,951	2,691	2,434	2,194	1,954	1,714	1,494	1,274
17,850	17,900	2,964	2,704	2,446	2,206	1,966	1,726	1,505	1,285
17,900	17,950	2,977	2,717	2,458	2,218	1,978	1,738	1,516	1,296
17,950	18,000	2,990	2,730	2,470	2,230	1,990	1,750	1,527	1,307
18,000	18,050	3,003	2,743	2,483	2,242	2,002	1,762	1,538	1,318
18,050	18,100	3,016	2,756	2,496	2,254	2,014	1,774	1,549	1,329
18,100	18,150	3,029	2,769	2,509	2,266	2,026	1,786	1,560	1,340
18,150	18,200	3,042	2,782	2,522	2,278	2,038	1,798	1,571	1,351
18,200	18,250	3,055	2,795	2,535	2,290	2,050	1,810	1,582	1,362
18,250	18,300	3,068	2,808	2,548	2,302	2,062	1,822	1,593	1,373
18,300	18,350	3,081	2,821	2,561	2,314	2,074	1,834	1,604	1,384
18,350	18,400	3,094	2,834	2,574	2,326	2,086	1,846	1,615	1,395
18,400	18,450	3,107	2,847	2,587	2,338	2,098	1,858	1,626	1,406
18,450	18,500	3,120	2,860	2,600	2,350	2,110	1,870	1,637	1,417
18,500	18,550	3,133	2,873	2,613	2,362	2,122	1,882	1,648	1,428
18,550	18,600	3,146	2,886	2,626	2,374	2,134	1,894	1,659	1,439
18,600	18,650	3,159	2,899	2,639	2,386	2,146	1,906	1,670	1,450
18,650	18,700	3,172	2,912	2,652	2,398	2,158	1,918	1,681	1,461
18,700	18,750	3,185	2,925	2,665	2,410	2,170	1,930	1,692	1,472
18,750	18,800	3,198	2,938	2,678	2,422	2,182	1,942	1,703	1,483
18,800	18,850	3,211	2,951	2,691	2,434	2,194	1,954	1,714	1,494
18,850	18,900	3,224	2,964	2,704	2,446	2,206	1,966	1,726	1,505
18,900	18,950	3,237	2,977	2,717	2,458	2,218	1,978	1,738	1,516
18,950	19,000	3,250	2,990	2,730	2,470	2,230	1,990	1,750	1,527
19,000	19,050	3,263	3,003	2,743	2,483	2,242	2,002	1,762	1,538
19,050	19,100	3,276	3,016	2,756	2,496	2,254	2,014	1,774	1,549
19,100	19,150	3,289	3,029	2,769	2,509	2,266	2,026	1,786	1,560
19,150	19,200	3,302	3,042	2,782	2,522	2,278	2,038	1,798	1,571
19,200	19,250	3,316	3,055	2,795	2,535	2,290	2,050	1,810	1,582
19,250	19,300	3,331	3,068	2,808	2,548	2,302	2,062	1,822	1,593
19,300	19,350	3,347	3,081	2,821	2,561	2,314	2,074	1,834	1,604
19,350	19,400	3,362	3,094	2,834	2,574	2,326	2,086	1,846	1,615
19,400	19,450	3,378	3,107	2,847	2,587	2,338	2,098	1,858	1,626
19,450	19,500	3,393	3,120	2,860	2,600	2,350	2,110	1,870	1,637
19,500	19,550	3,409	3,133	2,873	2,613	2,362	2,122	1,882	1,648
19,550	19,600	3,424	3,146	2,886	2,626	2,374	2,134	1,894	1,659
19,600	19,650	3,440	3,159	2,899	2,639	2,386	2,146	1,906	1,670
19,650	19,700	3,455	3,172	2,912	2,652	2,398	2,158	1,918	1,681
19,700	19,750	3,471	3,185	2,925	2,665	2,410	2,170	1,930	1,692
19,750	19,800	3,486	3,198	2,938	2,678	2,422	2,182	1,942	1,703
19,800	19,850	3,502	3,211	2,951	2,691	2,434	2,194	1,954	1,714
19,850	19,900	3,517	3,224	2,964	2,704	2,446	2,206	1,966	1,726
19,900	19,950	3,533	3,237	2,977	2,717	2,458	2,218	1,978	1,738
19,950	20,000	3,548	3,250	2,990	2,730	2,470	2,230	1,990	1,750

Continued next column

appendix C

Unified Estate and Gift Tax Rates

(Applicable after December 31, 1976)

(A) Taxable transfer equal to or more than	(B) Taxable transfer less than	(C) Tax on amount in column (A)	(D) Rate of tax on excess over amount in column (A)
			Percent
$ 0	$ 10,000	$ —	18
10,000	20,000	1,800	20
20,000	40,000	3,800	22
40,000	60,000	8,200	24
60,000	80,000	13,000	26
80,000	100,000	18,200	28
100,000	150,000	23,800	30
150,000	250,000	38,800	32
250,000	500,000	70,800	34
500,000	750,000	155,800	37
750,000	1,000,000	248,300	39
1,000,000	1,250,000	345,800	41
1,250,000	1,500,000	448,300	43
1,500,000	2,000,000	555,800	45
2,000,000	2,500,000	780,800	49
2,500,000	3,000,000	1,025,800	53
3,000,000	3,500,000	1,290,800	57
3,500,000	4,000,000	1,575,800	61
4,000,000	4,500,000	1,880,800	65
4,500,000	5,000,000	2,205,800	69
5,000,000		2,550,800	70

appendix
D

1979 Optional State Sales Tax Tables

Your itemized deduction for general sales tax paid can be estimated from these tables plus any qualifying sales taxes paid on the items listed on page 16.

To use the tables:

Step 1—Figure your total available income.[1]

Step 2—Count the number of exemptions for you and your family. Do not count exemptions claimed for being 65 or over or blind as part of your family size.

Step 3 A—If your total available income is not over $40,000, find the income line for your State on the tables and read across to find the amount of sales tax for your family size.

Step 3 B—If your income is over $40,000 but not over $100,000, find the deduction listed on the income line "$38,001–$40,000" for your family size and State. For each $5,000 (or part of $5,000) of income over $40,000, increase the deduction by the amount listed for the line "$40,001–$100,000."

Step 3 C—If your income is over $100,000, your sales tax deduction is limited to the deduction for income of $100,000. To figure your sales tax deduction, use Step 3 B but don't go over $100,000.

On Schedule A, line 13, enter the larger of the sales tax estimate from this table or the amount your records show that you paid.

Income [1]	Alabama [2] Family size 1	2	3	4	5	Over 5	Arizona [3] Family size 1	2	3	4	5	Over 5	Arkansas Family size 1	2	3	4	5	Over 5	California [4] Family size 1&2	3&4	5	Over 5
$1–$8,000	93	115	122	131	142	160	107	133	140	149	159	178	78	97	102	109	116	132	125	147	155	164
$8,001–$10,000	109	132	142	153	165	185	125	152	163	174	185	206	91	111	118	127	135	152	147	173	183	193
$10,001–$12,000	124	147	161	173	187	208	141	169	184	196	209	232	103	123	134	143	153	170	167	198	208	219
$12,001–$14,000	138	161	178	191	206	228	156	184	204	217	232	255	115	134	148	158	169	187	186	220	232	243
$14,001–$16,000	152	174	194	209	225	248	171	199	222	237	253	277	125	145	161	173	184	202	204	242	255	266
$16,001–$18,000	164	186	210	226	242	266	185	213	240	256	273	298	135	154	174	186	198	217	222	263	276	288
$18,001–$20,000	176	197	225	242	259	284	198	225	257	274	292	317	145	163	186	199	212	231	238	282	297	309
$20,001–$22,000	188	208	239	257	275	301	210	237	273	291	310	336	154	172	198	212	225	245	254	301	317	330
$22,001–$24,000	199	218	253	271	290	317	222	249	288	308	328	354	163	181	209	224	238	258	270	320	336	349
$24,001–$26,000	210	228	266	285	305	332	234	261	303	324	345	372	172	189	220	235	250	270	285	338	355	368
$26,001–$28,000	221	238	279	299	320	347	245	272	318	339	362	389	180	197	230	246	262	282	299	355	373	386
$28,001–$30,000	231	247	291	313	334	362	256	283	332	354	378	405	188	204	240	257	273	294	313	372	391	404
$30,001–$32,000	241	256	303	326	347	376	267	293	346	369	393	421	196	211	250	268	284	305	327	389	408	422
$32,001–$34,000	251	265	315	338	360	390	278	303	359	384	408	437	204	218	260	278	295	316	341	405	425	439
$34,001–$36,000	261	274	327	350	373	403	288	313	372	398	423	452	211	225	270	288	306	326	354	421	441	455
$36,001–$38,000	271	282	338	362	386	416	298	322	385	411	438	466	218	232	279	298	316	336	367	436	457	471
$38,001–$40,000	280	290	349	374	399	429	308	331	398	424	452	480	225	239	288	308	326	346	380	451	473	487
$40,001–$100,000 (See Step 3B)	14	15	17	19	20	21	15	17	20	21	23	24	11	12	14	15	16	17	19	23	24	24

Income [1]	Colorado [3] Family size 1	2	3	4	5	Over 5	Connecticut Family size 1&2	3,4&5	Over 5	Dist. of Columbia Family size 1	2	3	4	5	Over 5	Florida Family size 1&2	3	4	5	Over 5	Georgia [2] Family size 1	2	3	4	5	Over 5	Hawaii Family size 1&2	3	4	5	Over 5
$1–$8,000	74	93	97	104	112	126	112	121	127	74	90	102	102	107	116	72	83	83	88	93	82	103	110	116	125	141	158	180	183	190	204
$8,001–$10,000	87	106	113	121	130	145	134	147	153	86	104	118	119	126	135	86	98	98	105	110	95	117	127	135	145	161	181	206	209	219	235
$10,001–$12,000	98	117	128	137	146	163	154	172	178	97	117	134	136	143	152	99	113	114	121	127	107	130	143	152	163	180	201	228	234	245	263
$12,001–$14,000	109	128	141	151	161	179	174	195	202	108	128	148	152	160	168	111	127	129	136	142	118	141	157	167	179	198	220	249	256	269	288
$14,001–$16,000	119	138	154	165	176	193	193	218	225	118	139	161	167	175	184	123	140	144	151	157	129	152	171	182	195	214	238	268	277	292	312
$16,001–$18,000	129	147	166	177	189	207	211	240	248	127	149	173	181	190	198	134	153	158	165	171	139	162	184	196	210	229	254	286	297	313	335
$18,001–$20,000	138	156	177	189	202	221	228	261	270	136	159	185	195	205	212	145	165	172	179	185	149	171	196	209	224	244	270	303	315	333	356
$20,001–$22,000	147	164	188	201	214	233	245	282	291	144	168	197	208	219	225	156	177	185	192	199	158	180	208	222	237	258	285	319	333	352	377
$22,001–$24,000	155	172	199	212	226	245	261	302	312	152	177	208	221	232	238	166	189	198	205	212	167	189	219	234	250	271	299	335	350	371	397
$24,001–$26,000	163	180	209	223	237	257	277	322	332	160	186	219	234	245	250	176	200	211	217	224	176	198	230	246	262	283	313	350	366	389	416
$26,001–$28,000	171	187	219	234	248	268	293	342	352	168	194	229	246	258	262	186	211	224	229	236	184	206	240	258	274	295	326	364	382	406	434
$28,001–$30,000	179	194	229	244	259	279	308	361	372	175	202	239	258	270	274	196	222	236	241	248	192	213	250	269	286	307	339	378	397	423	451
$30,001–$32,000	187	201	238	254	269	290	323	380	391	182	210	249	270	282	285	205	232	248	253	260	200	220	260	280	297	319	351	391	412	439	468
$32,001–$34,000	195	208	247	264	279	300	338	398	410	189	218	259	281	294	296	214	242	260	265	272	208	227	270	290	308	330	363	404	426	454	485
$34,001–$36,000	202	214	256	273	289	310	353	416	429	196	225	268	292	305	307	223	252	272	276	283	215	234	279	300	319	341	375	416	440	469	501
$36,001–$38,000	209	220	265	282	299	320	367	434	448	203	232	277	303	316	318	232	262	283	287	294	222	241	288	310	330	352	386	428	454	484	517
$38,001–$40,000	215	226	273	291	308	329	381	452	466	209	239	286	314	327	328	241	272	294	298	305	229	247	297	320	340	362	397	440	467	499	533
$40,001–$100,000 (See Step 3B)	11	11	14	15	15	16	19	23	23	10	12	14	16	16	16	12	14	15	15	15	11	12	15	16	17	18	20	22	23	25	27

Income [1]	Idaho Family size 1	2	3	4	5	Over 5	Illinois [5] Family size 1	2	3	4	5	Over 5	Indiana Family size 1&2	3&4	5	Over 5	Iowa Family size 1&2	3,4&5	Over 5	Kansas [2] Family size 1	2	3	4	5	Over 5
$1–$8,000	68	84	89	97	106	120	119	151	161	173	187	214	93	110	118	124	71	79	85	75	94	100	107	113	129
$8,001–$10,000	80	96	104	113	123	138	139	171	187	201	216	243	109	130	138	145	83	93	100	88	108	116	124	132	149
$10,001–$12,000	91	107	118	128	138	155	157	189	210	225	242	270	124	148	157	165	95	107	114	99	120	131	141	149	167
$12,001–$14,000	101	117	131	142	153	170	174	206	232	249	267	294	138	165	175	183	106	120	127	110	131	145	156	165	183
$14,001–$16,000	111	127	143	155	166	184	190	222	252	270	290	316	151	181	191	200	116	132	139	120	142	159	170	181	199
$16,001–$18,000	120	136	155	167	179	197	206	236	271	291	311	337	164	196	207	216	126	143	151	130	152	171	183	195	213
$18,001–$20,000	129	144	166	179	192	210	220	250	289	310	332	357	176	211	222	232	135	154	162	139	161	183	196	209	227
$20,001–$22,000	137	152	176	190	204	222	234	263	307	329	352	376	187	225	237	247	144	165	173	148	170	195	209	222	240
$22,001–$24,000	145	160	186	201	215	234	248	275	324	347	371	394	198	238	251	261	153	176	183	156	178	206	221	235	253
$24,001–$26,000	153	168	196	212	226	245	261	287	340	364	389	411	209	251	265	275	162	186	193	164	186	217	232	247	265
$26,001–$28,000	161	175	206	222	237	256	273	299	356	381	406	428	220	264	278	289	170	196	203	172	194	228	243	259	277
$28,001–$30,000	169	182	215	232	247	267	285	310	371	397	423	444	230	277	291	302	178	206	213	180	202	238	254	271	288
$30,001–$32,000	176	189	224	242	257	277	297	321	386	413	440	459	240	289	304	315	186	215	222	188	209	248	265	282	299
$32,001–$34,000	183	196	233	251	267	287	309	331	400	429	456	474	250	301	316	327	194	224	231	195	216	258	275	293	310
$34,001–$36,000	190	202	242	260	276	297	320	341	414	444	472	489	259	313	328	339	201	233	240	202	223	267	285	304	320
$36,001–$38,000	197	208	251	269	285	306	331	351	428	458	487	503	268	324	340	351	208	242	249	209	230	276	295	315	330
$38,001–$40,000	203	214	259	278	294	315	342	360	441	472	502	517	277	335	352	363	215	251	258	216	236	285	304	325	340
$40,001–$100,000 (See Step 3B)	10	11	13	14	15	16	17	18	22	24	25	26	14	17	18	18	11	13	13	11	12	14	15	16	17

Income [1]	Kentucky Family size 1&2	3&4	5	Over 5	Louisiana [6] Family size 1&2	3&4	5	Over 5	Maine [7] Family size 1&2	3&4	5	Over 5	Maryland Family size 1&2	3	4	5	Over 5	Massachusetts [8] Family size 1 & 2	Over 2	Michigan Family size 1&2	3&4	5	Over 5	Minnesota [9] Family size 1&2	Over 2
$1–$8,000	100	113	119	125	60	67	70	73	89	100	103	109	88	102	102	107	113	58	63	88	102	108	113	55	58
$8,001–$10,000	118	134	141	147	71	80	84	88	106	120	124	130	105	121	121	128	134	69	76	103	121	127	133	66	70
$10,001–$12,000	135	154	162	169	82	92	97	101	121	139	144	150	121	139	139	147	154	79	89	118	138	145	151	76	82
$12,001–$14,000	151	173	181	189	92	104	109	113	135	157	163	169	136	156	158	166	173	89	101	131	154	161	168	86	93
$14,001–$16,000	166	191	200	208	101	115	121	125	149	175	181	188	150	172	175	183	191	98	113	144	169	177	184	95	104
$16,001–$18,000	180	209	218	226	110	126	132	137	162	192	198	205	163	187	192	200	208	107	124	156	184	192	199	104	114
$18,001–$20,000	194	226	235	243	119	136	143	148	175	208	215	222	176	202	209	216	224	116	135	168	198	207	214	112	124
$20,001–$22,000	208	242	252	260	128	146	153	159	187	224	231	239	189	216	225	232	240	124	146	180	211	221	228	120	134
$22,001–$24,000	221	258	268	276	136	156	163	169	199	239	247	255	202	230	241	247	255	132	157	191	224	234	241	128	144
$24,001–$26,000	233	273	284	292	144	166	173	179	211	254	263	271	214	243	256	262	270	140	168	202	237	247	254	136	153
$26,001–$28,000	245	288	299	308	152	175	183	189	222	269	278	286	226	256	271	277	285	148	178	212	249	260	267	143	162
$28,001–$30,000	257	303	314	323	160	184	193	199	233	283	293	301	237	269	286	291	299	155	188	222	261	272	280	150	171
$30,001–$32,000	269	317	328	338	168	193	202	209	244	297	308	316	248	281	300	305	313	162	198	232	273	284	292	157	180
$32,001–$34,000	281	331	342	352	175	202	211	218	255	311	322	330	259	293	314	319	327	169	208	242	284	296	304	164	189
$34,001–$36,000	292	345	356	366	182	211	220	227	265	325	336	344	270	305	328	332	340	176	217	252	295	308	316	171	197
$36,001–$38,000	303	359	370	380	189	219	229	236	275	338	350	358	281	317	342	345	353	183	227	261	306	319	327	178	206
$38,001–$40,000	313	372	384	393	196	227	238	245	285	351	364	371	291	329	356	358	366	190	236	270	317	330	338	185	214
$40,001–$100,000 (See Step 3B)	16	19	19	20	10	11	12	12	14	18	18	19	15	16	18	18	18	10	12	14	16	17	17	9	11

[1] Total of amount on Form 1040, line 31, and nontaxable receipts such as social security, veterans', railroad retirement benefits, workmen's compensation, untaxed portion of long-term capital gains or unemployment compensation, dividends exclusion, disability income exclusion, and public assistance payments.

[2] Local sales taxes are not included. Add an amount based on the ratio between the local and State sales tax rates considering the number of months the taxes have been in effect.

[3] Local sales taxes are not included. Add the amount paid.

[4] The 1¼ percent local sales tax is included. If the ½ of 1 percent sales tax is paid all year (Alameda, Contra Costa, San Francisco, and Santa Clara counties) add 8 percent to the table amount.

[5] Local sales taxes are included.

[6] If your local sales tax applies to food for home consumption contact your local IRS office for the correct deduction. Otherwise see footnote 2.

[7] Sales tax paid on purchase of electricity of 750 KWH or more per month, can be added to the table amounts.

[8] Sales tax paid on the purchase of any single item of clothing for $175 or more can be added to the table amounts.

[9] Sales tax paid on purchases of natural gas or electricity can be added to the table amounts. For local sales tax see footnote 2.

1979 Optional State Sales Tax Tables—Cont.

Your itemized deduction for general sales tax paid can be estimated from these tables plus any qualifying sales taxes paid on the items listed on page 16. To use the tables:

Step 1—Figure your total available income.[1]

Step 2—Count the number of exemptions claimed for you and your family. Do not count exemptions claimed for being 65 or over or blind as part of your family size.

Step 3 A—If your total available income is not over $40,000, find the income line for your State on the tables and read across to find the amount of sales tax for your family size.

Step 3 B—If your income is over $40,000 but not over $100,000, find the deduction listed on the income line "$38,001–40,000" for your family size and State. For each $5,000 (or part of $5,000) of income over $40,000, increase the deduction by the amount listed for the line "$40,001–$100,000."

Step 3 C—If your income is over $100,000, your sales tax deduction is limited to the deduction for income of $100,000. To figure your sales tax deduction, use Step 3 B but don't go over $100,000.

On Schedule A, line 13, enter the larger of the sales tax estimate from this table or the amount your records show that you paid.

Income[1]	Mississippi						Missouri[2]						Nebraska[2]						Nevada[3]				
Family size	1	2	3	4	5	Over 5	1	2	3	4	5	Over 5	1	2	3	4	5	Over 5	1 & 2	3	4	5	Over 5
$1–$8,000	142	174	185	195	206	230	82	102	107	114	122	138	79	98	103	111	119	135	72	84	87	94	103
$8,001–$10,000	166	199	215	227	241	266	95	116	124	132	142	158	92	111	120	129	138	154	84	99	103	110	120
$10,001–$12,000	187	222	243	256	272	299	108	128	140	149	160	177	104	123	135	145	155	172	96	113	118	125	136
$12,001–$14,000	207	243	268	283	301	330	119	140	154	165	176	194	115	134	149	160	171	189	107	126	132	140	151
$14,001–$16,000	226	262	293	309	329	358	130	151	168	179	191	210	125	145	162	174	185	204	117	138	145	153	165
$16,001–$18,000	244	281	316	333	355	385	140	161	181	193	206	225	135	154	174	187	199	218	127	150	158	166	178
$18,001–$20,000	262	298	337	357	380	411	150	170	193	206	220	239	145	163	186	199	213	232	136	161	170	179	191
$20,001–$22,000	278	314	358	379	404	435	160	179	205	219	233	253	154	172	198	211	226	245	145	172	182	191	203
$22,001–$24,000	294	330	379	400	427	459	169	188	216	231	246	266	163	180	209	223	238	257	154	183	193	202	215
$24,001–$26,000	310	345	398	421	450	481	178	196	227	243	258	279	171	188	219	234	250	269	162	193	204	213	226
$26,001–$28,000	325	360	417	441	471	503	187	204	238	254	270	291	179	196	229	245	261	281	170	203	215	224	237
$28,001–$30,000	339	374	436	461	492	524	195	212	248	265	282	303	187	203	239	256	272	292	178	213	226	235	248
$30,001–$32,000	353	388	454	480	513	545	203	219	258	276	293	314	195	210	249	266	283	303	186	222	236	245	259
$32,001–$34,000	367	401	471	499	533	565	211	226	268	287	304	325	203	217	258	276	293	314	194	231	246	255	269
$34,001–$36,000	380	414	488	517	552	585	219	233	278	297	315	336	210	224	267	286	303	324	202	240	256	265	279
$36,001–$38,000	393	427	505	535	571	604	226	240	287	307	325	346	217	230	276	295	313	334	209	249	266	275	289
$38,001–$40,000	406	439	521	552	590	622	233	246	296	316	335	356	224	235	285	304	323	343	216	257	275	284	298
$40,001–$100,000 (See Step 3B)	20	22	26	28	30	31	12	12	15	16	17	18	11	12	14	15	16	17	11	13	14	14	15

Income[1]	New Jersey		New Mexico[2]						New York[4]				North Carolina[5]						North Dakota				Ohio[2]				Oklahoma[2]					
Family size	1 & 2	Over 2	1	2	3	4	5	Over 5	1&2	3&4	5	Over 5	1	2	3	4	5	Over 5	1&2	3&4	5	Over 5	1&2	3&4	5	Over 5	1	2	3	4	5	Over 5
$1–$8,000	73	79	117	144	152	158	167	185	86	99	103	108	92	114	121	130	139	159	58	64	68	71	67	75	78	81	52	63	68	71	76	85
$8,001–$10,000	87	95	136	165	177	185	195	214	103	118	123	128	108	131	141	151	162	183	69	77	81	84	80	90	94	97	61	72	78	82	88	99
$10,001–$12,000	100	111	153	184	199	209	221	241	118	136	141	147	123	146	159	171	182	204	79	89	93	97	92	104	109	113	69	80	88	93	99	111
$12,001–$14,000	112	126	169	201	220	231	244	266	132	152	159	165	137	159	176	189	202	224	89	100	105	109	104	118	123	127	76	88	97	103	110	122
$14,001–$16,000	124	141	184	217	239	252	267	290	146	168	176	182	150	172	192	206	220	243	98	111	116	120	115	131	136	141	83	95	106	113	120	132
$16,001–$18,000	135	155	198	232	258	272	288	312	159	183	192	198	162	184	207	222	237	261	107	122	127	131	126	144	149	155	90	101	114	122	129	142
$18,001–$20,000	146	169	211	246	275	292	308	333	172	198	208	214	174	195	222	237	253	277	115	132	137	141	136	157	162	168	97	107	122	130	138	151
$20,001–$22,000	156	182	224	259	292	310	328	353	184	212	223	229	185	206	236	252	268	293	123	142	147	151	146	169	174	181	103	113	129	138	147	160
$22,001–$24,000	166	195	236	272	308	328	347	373	196	226	238	244	196	216	249	266	283	308	131	152	157	161	156	181	186	193	109	119	136	146	155	168
$24,001–$26,000	176	208	248	284	324	345	365	392	208	240	252	258	207	226	262	280	298	323	139	161	166	170	166	192	198	205	115	125	143	154	163	176
$26,001–$28,000	186	221	260	296	339	362	382	410	219	253	266	272	217	236	275	293	312	337	146	170	175	179	175	203	209	217	121	130	149	162	171	184
$28,001–$30,000	195	233	271	307	354	378	399	428	230	266	280	286	227	245	287	306	325	351	153	179	184	188	184	214	220	228	126	135	155	169	179	192
$30,001–$32,000	204	245	282	318	368	394	416	445	241	278	293	299	237	254	299	319	338	364	160	188	193	197	193	225	231	239	131	140	161	176	186	200
$32,001–$34,000	213	257	293	329	381	409	432	462	252	290	306	312	247	263	310	331	351	377	167	197	202	206	202	236	242	250	136	145	167	183	193	207
$34,001–$36,000	222	269	303	340	395	424	448	478	262	302	319	325	257	271	321	343	364	390	173	206	210	214	210	247	253	261	141	149	173	189	200	214
$36,001–$38,000	231	281	313	350	408	439	464	494	272	314	332	337	266	279	332	355	376	402	180	214	218	222	218	257	263	272	146	153	179	195	207	221
$38,001–$40,000	240	292	322	360	421	453	479	510	282	326	345	349	275	287	343	366	388	414	186	222	226	230	226	267	273	283	151	157	185	201	214	228
$40,001–$100,000 (See Step 3B)	12	15	16	18	21	23	24	26	14	16	17	17	14	14	17	18	19	21	9	11	11	12	11	13	14	14	8	8	9	10	11	11

Income[1]	Pennsylvania		Rhode Island		South Carolina						South Dakota[6]						Tennessee[2]						Texas[2]			
Family size	1&2	Over 2	1&2	Over 2	1	2	3	4	5	Over 5	1	2	3	4	5	Over 5	1	2	3	4	5	Over 5	1&2	3&4	5	Over 5
$1–$8,000	73	78	88	94	105	129	136	145	157	176	111	136	142	150	159	179	114	137	146	155	167	192	67	77	82	87
$8,001–$10,000	88	95	104	113	123	147	158	169	181	202	129	156	165	175	186	207	133	157	170	181	194	220	79	92	98	104
$10,001–$12,000	102	111	120	131	139	163	178	190	203	225	146	173	187	198	210	232	151	175	191	204	219	245	91	106	113	119
$12,001–$14,000	115	126	134	148	154	178	197	209	224	247	162	190	207	219	233	256	167	191	212	225	241	269	102	120	127	134
$14,001–$16,000	128	141	148	164	168	192	215	228	243	267	177	205	226	239	254	278	183	207	231	246	263	291	113	133	141	148
$16,001–$18,000	141	156	161	180	182	205	231	245	261	286	191	219	244	258	275	299	198	221	249	265	283	311	123	146	154	162
$18,001–$20,000	153	170	174	196	195	217	247	262	279	304	204	232	261	277	294	319	212	235	266	283	302	331	133	158	167	175
$20,001–$22,000	164	183	187	211	207	228	262	278	295	321	217	245	278	294	313	338	226	248	283	301	321	349	142	170	179	188
$22,001–$24,000	175	196	199	225	219	239	277	293	311	338	230	258	294	311	331	357	239	260	299	318	339	367	151	181	191	200
$24,001–$26,000	186	209	210	239	230	250	291	308	327	354	242	270	309	328	348	375	252	272	314	334	356	384	160	192	203	212
$26,001–$28,000	197	222	221	253	241	260	305	322	342	369	254	281	324	344	365	392	264	284	329	350	372	401	169	203	214	224
$28,001–$30,000	208	235	232	267	252	270	318	336	356	384	265	292	338	359	382	409	276	296	344	365	388	417	177	214	225	235
$30,001–$32,000	219	248	243	281	263	280	331	350	370	398	276	303	352	374	398	425	288	307	358	380	404	432	185	225	236	246
$32,001–$34,000	230	261	254	294	273	289	344	363	384	412	287	313	366	389	413	441	300	317	372	395	419	447	193	235	247	257
$34,001–$36,000	240	273	265	307	283	298	356	376	397	425	298	323	380	403	428	456	311	327	385	409	434	462	201	245	257	268
$36,001–$38,000	250	285	276	320	293	307	368	389	410	438	308	333	393	417	443	471	322	337	398	423	449	476	209	255	267	279
$38,001–$40,000	260	297	286	333	302	315	380	401	422	451	318	342	406	431	458	485	333	347	411	436	463	490	217	265	277	289
$40,001–$100,000 (See Step 3B)	13	15	14	17	15	16	19	20	21	23	16	17	20	22	23	24	17	17	21	22	23	25	11	13	14	14

Income[1]	Utah[7]						Vermont						Virginia[3]						Washington[8]				West Virginia						Wisconsin				Wyoming[2]					
Family size	1	2	3	4	5	Over 5	1	2	3	4	5	Over 5	1	2	3	4	5	Over 5	1&2	3&4	5	Over 5	1	2	3	4	5	Over 5	1&2	3&4	5	Over 5	1	2	3	4	5	Over 5
$1–$8,000	120	143	152	161	172	195	35	41	46	46	49	53	88	111	117	127	137	156	98	112	114	119	72	85	91	96	103	116	89	100	104	110	81	98	104	109	117	132
$8,001–$10,000	140	164	177	188	200	225	41	48	55	55	58	63	104	127	137	148	159	179	116	134	137	143	85	98	106	112	121	134	105	119	124	130	95	112	121	127	136	152
$10,001–$12,000	159	183	200	213	226	252	47	55	63	64	67	72	118	141	155	166	179	200	133	155	159	166	97	110	121	128	137	152	120	137	142	149	107	125	136	144	153	170
$12,001–$14,000	176	201	222	236	251	277	53	61	70	72	76	80	131	154	171	184	197	220	149	174	180	187	108	121	134	142	152	168	134	153	159	166	119	136	151	159	169	187
$14,001–$16,000	193	217	242	258	274	300	58	67	77	80	84	88	143	167	187	201	215	238	164	193	200	207	119	132	147	156	167	183	147	169	176	183	130	147	164	173	184	202
$16,001–$18,000	209	232	261	278	295	323	63	72	84	88	92	96	155	178	202	216	231	255	179	211	219	227	129	141	159	169	181	197	159	184	191	199	140	157	176	187	198	217
$18,001–$20,000	224	247	279	298	316	344	68	77	91	96	100	104	166	189	216	231	247	271	193	229	238	246	139	150	171	182	194	210	171	198	206	214	150	167	188	200	212	231
$20,001–$22,000	238	261	297	317	336	364	73	82	98	103	107	111	177	199	230	245	262	286	207	246	256	265	149	159	182	194	206	223	183	212	221	229	159	176	200	213	225	244
$22,001–$24,000	252	274	314	335	355	383	77	87	104	110	114	118	188	209	243	259	276	301	220	263	274	283	158	168	193	205	218	236	194	225	235	243	168	185	211	225	237	257
$24,001–$26,000	266	287	330	353	374	402	81	92	110	117	121	125	198	219	256	273	290	315	233	279	292	300	167	176	204	216	230	248	205	238	249	257	177	193	222	236	249	269
$26,001–$28,000	279	299	346	370	392	420	85	97	116	124	128	132	208	228	268	286	304	329	245	295	309	317	176	184	214	227	242	260	216	251	262	270	186	201	232	247	261	281
$28,001–$30,000	292	311	362	387	409	437	89	102	122	131	135	138	218	237	280	298	317	342	257	310	326	334	185	192	224	238	253	271	226	264	275	283	194	209	242	258	273	293
$30,001–$32,000	304	322	377	403	426	454	93	106	128	138	142	144	227	246	292	310	330	355	269	325	342	351	193	199	234	249	264	282	236	276	288	296	202	216	252	269	284	304
$32,001–$34,000	316	333	392	419	443	470	97	110	134	145	148	150	236	254	303	322	342	368	281	340	358	367	201	206	243	259	275	293	246	288	301	309	210	223	261	280	294	315
$34,001–$36,000	328	344	406	434	459	486	101	114	140	151	154	156	245	262	314	334	354	380	293	355	374	383	209	213	252	269	285	304	256	300	313	321	218	230	270	290	304	326
$36,001–$38,000	340	355	420	449	475	502	105	118	145	157	160	162	254	270	325	345	366	391	304	370	390	399	217	220	261	279	295	314	266	311	325	333	226	237	279	300	314	336
$38,001–$40,000	351	365	434	464	490	517	109	122	150	163	166	168	263	277	336	356	378	402	315	384	405	414	224	227	270	288	305	324	275	322	337	345	233	244	288	310	324	346
$40,001–$100,000 (See Step 3B)	18	18	22	23	25	26	5	6	8	8	8	8	13	14	17	18	19	20	16	19	20	21	11	11	14	14	15	16	14	16	17	17	12	12	14	16	16	17

[1] Total of amount on Form 1040, line 31, and nontaxable receipts such as social security, veterans', railroad retirement benefits, workmen's compensation, untaxed portion of long-term capital gains or unemployment compensation, dividends exclusion, disability income exclusion, and public assistance payments.

[2] Local sales taxes are not included. Add an amount based on the ratio between the local and State sales tax rates considering the number of months the taxes have been in effect.

[3] Local sales taxes are included.

[4] **Local sales taxes are not included. If paid all year add 26 percent of the table amount for each 1 percent of local sales tax rate. Otherwise use a** proportionate amount. For New York City use 107 percent of the table amount to include personal services taxed.

[5] Local sales taxes are included. Taxpayers not paying local sales tax should use 75 percent of the amount allowed.

[6] Local sales taxes are not included. Add the amount paid.

[7] Local ¾ percent sales taxes are included. Add 5 percent of table amount if the ¼ percent county sales tax for transportation is paid all year. Otherwise add a proportionate amount (see footnote 2).

[8] Local ½ percent sales taxes are included. If the 3/10's of 1 percent sales tax for public transportation is paid all year add 6 percent to the table amount. Otherwise add a proportionate amount (see footnote 2).

appendix
E

Income Tax Rates Applicable to
Fiduciaries

"If taxable income is:	The tax is:
Not over $1,050	14% of taxable income.
Over $1,050 but not over $2,100	$147, plus 16% of excess over $1,050.
Over $2,100 but not over $4,250	$315, plus 18% of excess over $2,100.
Over $4,250 but not over $6,300	$702, plus 21% of excess over $4,250.
Over $6,300 but not over $8,400	$1,132.50, plus 24% of excess over $6,300.
Over $8,400 but not over $10,600	$1,636.50, plus 28% of excess over $8,400.
Over $10,600 but not over $13,250	$2,252.50, plus 32% of excess over $10,600.
Over $13,250 but not over $15,900	$3,100.50, plus 37% of excess over $13,250.
Over $15,900 but not over $21,200	$4,081, plus 43% of excess over $15,900.
Over $21,200 but not over $28,300	$6,360, plus 49% of excess over $21,200.
Over $28,300 but not over $41,100	$9,839, plus 54% of excess over $28,300.
Over $41,100 but not over $53,000	$16,751, plus 59% of excess over $41,100.
Over $53,000 but not over $79,500	$23,772, plus 64% of excess over $53,000.
Over $79,500 but not over $106,000	$40,732, plus 68% of excess over $79,500.
Over $106,000	$58,752, plus 70% of excess over $106,000.".

index

Note: Page numbers in italics refer to tables or figures.

A 0
B 1
C 2
D 3
E 4
F 5
G 6
H 7
I 8
J 9